NEW SOCIETY

NEW SOCIETY

Sixth Edition

Robert J. Brym
University of Toronto

NELSON / EDUCATION

NELSON / EDUCATION

New Society, Sixth Edition
by Robert J. Brym

**Vice President and
Editorial Director:**
Evelyn Veitch

Editor-in-Chief:
Anne Williams

Executive Editor:
Laura Macleod

Executive Marketing Manager:
David Tonen

Developmental Editor:
Liisa Kelly

Photo Researcher:
Nicola Winstanley

Permissions Coordinator:
Natalie Russell

**Senior Content Production
Manager:**
Natalia Denesiuk Harris

Copy Editor:
Lisa Berland

Proofreader:
Dawn Hunter

Indexer:
Andrew Little

Production Coordinator:
Ferial Suleman

Design Director:
Ken Phipps

Managing Designer:
Franca Amore

Interior Design Modifications:
Olena Sullivan

Cover Design:
Ryan Wilson

Cover Image:
B&Y Photography Inc./First Light

Compositor:
Knowledgeworks Global Limited

Printer:
RRDonnelley

**Library and Archives Canada
Cataloguing in Publication Data**

Brym, Robert J., 1951–

New society / Robert J. Brym. —
6th ed.

Previous eds. under title: New
society: sociology for the 21st
century.

Includes bibliographical references
and index.
ISBN 978-0-17-650183-9

1. Sociology—Textbooks.
I. Title.

HM586.B79 2010   301
C2009-905921-5

ISBN-13: 978-0-17-650183-9
ISBN-10: 0-17-650183-5

For my students. — RB

PREFACE

The job of figuring out what to do with our lives and how to act in the world is more difficult than ever. Sociology helps by analyzing the pressing social issues of the day, showing how those issues affect all of us, and setting out options for dealing with them. Moreover, as you will learn in the following pages, sociology views social issues from a unique disciplinary perspective. All in all, it is a controversial and exciting business. Social problems are typically complex. The options for action often involve different benefits and disadvantages for different groups. Sociologists usually see things differently from other social and natural scientists. Not surprisingly, therefore, sociology, like any vibrant academic discipline, involves a lot of heated debate.

Unfortunately, most introductory sociology textbooks don't give much of a feel for the excitement of the discipline. They usually resemble encyclopedias full of definitions and presumably undeniable facts. They make sociological knowledge resemble the tablets some people say were brought down by Moses from Mount Sinai: abstract principles carved in stone, eternal truths that most people agree with but that tell us little about the way life is actually lived.

In preparing this book, I tried to overcome this deficiency in two ways. First, when I recruited authors to write chapters, I asked them to focus on social issues that are likely to be of real, everyday concern to Canadian undergraduates. Second, I asked the authors to highlight the controversies in the field, not the clichés. There is no sense keeping secret what any good scientist knows: advances in knowledge usually result from intellectual conflict, not consensus.

WHAT'S NEW IN THE SIXTH EDITION

In preparing the sixth edition of *New Society*, I benefited from the recommendations that emerged from Nelson's excellent user survey. Major changes include the following:

- The sixth edition of *New Society* has been thoroughly updated to reflect the results of the latest census of Canada and the most recent sociological research findings in the various fields covered in the text.
- Two chapters have been replaced outright to better reflect the interests of users and the state of the discipline:
  - Chapter 9, Development and Underdevelopment
  - Chapter 14, Deviance and Crime
  We welcome new authors Tony Winson and Julian Tanner.
- Two chapters have undergone major revisions:
  - Chapter 5, The Mass Media
  - Chapter 17, Health and Aging
- The design has been revised to increase visual appeal, with new part- and chapter-opening designs and the inclusion of new photos in every chapter.
- All of the ancillaries (see p. IX) have been thoroughly revised.

ORGANIZATION OF THE TEXT

Chapter 1 (Introducing Sociology) sets the tone for the rest of the book and stands alone in Part 1. Instead of sermonizing on the question "What is sociology?" as most other textbooks do, I ask "Why sociology?"—that is, why does an undergraduate in this particular time and place need to know what sociology has to offer? My chief aim in Chapter 1 is to show how sociological thinking can clarify and perhaps help resolve the real-life social issues that confront all of us here and now.

The remainder of the book is divided into five parts. Part 2 could be subtitled "Becoming Human." In Chapter 2 (Culture), I make a case for the view that ours is an increasingly fragmented and globalized postmodern culture that increases our freedom to fashion identities that suit our individual tastes. I also show that, paradoxically, our increased cultural freedom develops within definite limits beyond which it is more and more difficult to move. In Chapter 3 (Socialization), William

Shaffir and Michael Rosenberg thoroughly discuss the interactive mechanisms through which we learn beliefs, symbols, values, and self-identities throughout the life cycle and in various institutions. Rhonda L. Lenton then devotes Chapter 4 (Gender and Sexuality) to an indepth analysis of what might seem to be the most intimate and biologically determined aspects of our identity—our gender and sexuality—and demonstrates that in fact they have deep roots in culture and society. In Chapter 5 (The Mass Media), Graham Knight and Josh Greenberg analyze the impact of one of the most pervasive and influential social institutions today. In sum, the analyses of Part 2 will give the reader a solid appreciation of how we become part of society and how society becomes part of us through the transmission of culture from generation to generation.

Part 3 is about how people become and remain unequal. Harvey Krahn shows in Chapter 6 (Social Stratification) that despite recent assertions of the demise of social classes, stratification persists and continues to structure our life-chances in profound ways. In Chapter 7 (Gender Inequality: Economic and Political Aspects), Monica Boyd convincingly demonstrates that gender is an equally important basis of social inequality, both in the economic and the political sphere. Vic Satzewich devotes Chapter 8 (Race and Ethnic Relations) to highlighting the deficiencies of biological and purely cultural approaches to understanding the bases of ethnic and racial inequality. Finally, in Chapter 9 (Development and Underdevelopment), Anthony Winson incisively criticizes modernization and other theories of economic underdevelopment and global inequality, offering a compelling argument for the analytical benefits of a modified dependency approach to the problem. The reader will complete Part 3 with a firm understanding that people are highly differentiated and differentially rewarded, depending on their social location.

Part 4 shifts the reader's attention to some of society's fundamental institutions. A virtue of Bonnie Fox's analysis in Chapter 10 (Families) is that she usefully draws on a broad historical and anthropological literature to supplement her sociological overview, providing a clear sense of how families have developed and where they may be headed. Sandy Welsh devotes Chapter 11 (Work and Occupations) to tracing the development and future shape of work. In Chapter 12 (Education), Scott Davies dissects our educational system, demonstrating that, paradoxically, it is as much a cause of the persistence of inequality as it is an avenue for upward mobility. And in Chapter 13 (Religion), Reginald W. Bibby assesses the social origins, consequences, and future of religion, relying heavily on his own fundamentally important survey research to argue his case.

Change and conflict are the subjects of Part 5. Here the reader is introduced to the main forces of turbulence in our society. In Chapter 14 (Deviance and Crime), Julian Tanner elegantly analyzes one form of social conflict: deviant and criminal behaviour. He undermines several common misconceptions in the process. John Hannigan's analysis in Chapter 15 (Population and Urbanization) is a novel and revealing look at how human populations have developed in cities from preindustrial to postmodern times. He then devotes Chapter 16 (Sociology and the Environment) to one of the most pressing issues of the day—the environment—and analyzes such problems as the scope and social roots of the environmental movement and the process by which environmental issues are socially constructed. In Chapter 17 (Health and Aging), Neena L. Chappell and Margaret J. Penning expertly discuss the aging of the Canadian population and attendant health issues. In Chapter 18 (Politics and Social Movements), I survey the evolution of politics and social movements, showing how various forms of conflict emerge, change our lives, and become institutionalized. Finally, Globalization is the title of Chapter 19, by Josée Johnston. She shows that culturally, politically, and economically, the world is becoming a single place and its inhabitants are developing a global consciousness. This does not imply that we are becoming one big happy family. To the contrary, conflict has persisted and even intensified in the early twenty-first century.

In Part 6, Chapter 20 (Research Methods) masterfully and concisely outlines how sociologists do their work. Neil Guppy's clarity, research experience, and balanced approach add much-needed lustre to a subject that first-year students often find dull. Guppy leaves the reader with the firm sense that, for all the intellectual liveliness and controversy displayed in this book, sociology can be and is disciplined by the judicious use of logic and evidence.

As a bonus feature, John Lie, Steven Rytina, and I prepared Online Chapter 21 (Networks, Groups, Bureaucracies, and Societies) that draws the connection between microlevel interactions and macrolevel social forces and institutions. We recommend that the chapter be assigned after Chapter 3 (Socialization). This chapter may be accessed at www.newsociety6e. nelson.com.

FEATURES OF THIS TEXT

While the content and organization of this text have been carefully rendered, you will also find updated visual and pedagogical features in *New Society*, Sixth Edition.

NEW PART AND CHAPTER OPENERS

A fresh new look for part and chapter openers uses vivid colours and arresting photos to engage students with sociological concepts.

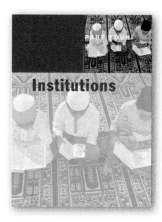

Additionally, a point-form chapter overview—"*In this chapter, you will learn …*"—prepares those students to think critically and to absorb the material.

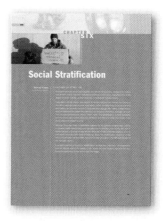

BOXES

Key subjects are explored further using boxes that break up the content of each chapter. Many of these discuss real-life examples drawn from current news-papers, journals, and academic papers, while others expand on a concept recently introduced. The effect is to provide visual interest and help readers to connect what they're learning to the outside world.

FIGURES AND TABLES

Current census data and other up-to-date research is easily compared when presented in one of 48 tables and 84 figures integrated throughout the book to enhance student learning. Fourteen of these figures are completely new, and *New Society*, Sixth Edition, also includes two new maps.

END-OF-CHAPTER RESOURCES

Each chapter concludes with a set of end-of-chapter resources to help students review and apply their knowledge. A **summary** of numbered key points helps students to see the "bigger picture"—to interact with concepts, not just facts—while a set of **Questions to Consider** encourages each one to think critically about the material and to apply what they've learned against their own values, ideas, and experiences. A **glossary** of key terms with definitions is also included, alongside a list of **Suggested Readings** that encourages students to research independently. Finally, readers can make use of Nelson's additional study tools through a list of **online resources**.

ANCILLARIES FOR INSTRUCTORS

INSTRUCTOR'S RESOURCE CD

(ISBN 978-0-17-647849-0) All testing and presentation software is now available in one place: the *New*

Society Instructor's Resource CD. This resource contains the NETA Instructor's Manual, NETA Test Bank and Computerized NETA Test Bank in ExamView®, the PowerPoint® slides, and the Instructor's Guide for Think Outside the Book: Nelson Videos for Introductory Sociology.

NETA Products

Nelson Education Testing Advantage

Engagement * Assessment * Success
The **Nelson Education Teaching Advantage program** is designed to ensure that instructors and students have access to research-based resources that enable the success of Canadian students and educators.

ENGAGEMENT: NETA GUIDE TO CLASSROOM ENGAGEMENT The *Guide to Classroom Engagement for* New Society, *Sixth Edition*, includes a range of activities that give instructors a practical, user-friendly way to incorporate interactive learning activities in both large and small classrooms. The *Guide* is focused on four core principles: student-centred learning, deep learning, active learning, and creating positive classroom environments. All of these principles are based on decades of research into what helps students learn best and are designed to foster classroom engagement.

Each NETA *Guide* includes a section outlining the research underlying these principles, which will help you create engaging classrooms. The *Guide* was written by Dr. Roger Fisher and created in partnership with an interdisciplinary board of scholars of teaching and learning. All NETA *Guide* authors have been trained in the principles underlying the program.

EDITORIAL ADVISORY BOARD

NORMAN ALTHOUSE, HASKAYNE SCHOOL OF BUSINESS, UNIVERSITY OF CALGARY

SCOTT FOLLOWS, MANNING SCHOOL OF BUSINESS ADMINISTRATION, ACADIA UNIVERSITY

GLEN LOPPNOW, DEPARTMENT OF CHEMISTRY, UNIVERSITY OF ALBERTA

TANYA NOEL, DEPARTMENT OF BIOLOGY, YORK UNIVERSITY

GARY POOLE, DIRECTOR, CENTRE FOR TEACHING AND
    ACADEMIC GROWTH AND SCHOOL OF POPULATION AND
    PUBLIC HEALTH, UNIVERSITY OF BRITISH COLUMBIA

DAN PRATT, DEPARTMENT OF EDUCATIONAL STUDIES,
    UNIVERSITY OF BRITISH COLUMBIA

BRENDA CHANT-SMITH, DEPARTMENT OF PSYCHOLOGY, TRENT
    UNIVERSITY

ASSESSMENT: NETA TEST BANK

In most post-secondary courses, a large percentage of student assessment is based on multiple-choice testing. Many instructors use multiple-choice reluctantly, believing that it is a methodology best used for testing what a student *remembers* rather than what she or he has *learned*.

Nelson Education Ltd. understands that a good quality multiple-choice test bank can provide the means to measure ***higher-level thinking*** skills as well as recall. Recognizing the importance of multiple-choice testing in today's classroom, we have created the Nelson Education Teaching Advantage program (NETA) to ensure the value of our high quality test banks.

The testing component of our NETA program was created in partnership with David DiBattista, a 3M National Teaching Fellow, professor of psychology at Brock University, and researcher in the area of multiple-choice testing. NETA for testbanks ensures that subject-matter experts who author test banks have had training in two areas: avoiding common errors in test construction, and developing multiple-choice test questions that "get beyond remembering" to assess higher-level thinking.

All NETA test banks include David DiBattista's guide for instructors, "Multiple Choice Tests: Getting Beyond Remembering." This guide has been designed to assist you in using Nelson test banks to achieve your desired outcomes in your course. See the Instructor's Resource CD button "NETA Guidelines" for this valuable resource.

Computerized NETA Test Bank in ExamView®:

Create, deliver, and customize tests (both print and online) in minutes with this easy-to-use assessment and tutorial system. *ExamView* offers both a *Quick Test Wizard* and an *Online Test Wizard* that guide you step-by-step through the process of creating tests. The test appears on screen exactly as it will print or display online. Using *ExamView's* complete word-processing capabilities, you can enter an unlimited number of new questions or edit existing questions. ExamView is offered in both PC and Mac platforms.

PowerPoint® Slides:

More than 400 full-colour slides offer a detailed summary of each chapter of the book, along with supplementary graphs, tables, and diagrams to illustrate key points. The slides can be easily output from a computer in several formats. The PowerPoint® Viewer that is packaged with the slides enables them to be (1) viewed on a computer or (2) projected from a computer to a viewing screen in the classroom. If you have the entire Microsoft PowerPoint® package, the slides can also be (3) printed out as full-colour transparencies for use with an overhead projector, or (4) printed out as black-and-white handouts for students.

Instructor's Guide for Think Outside the Book: Nelson Videos for Introductory Sociology:

This guide includes a synopsis of each video, questions for critical analysis, and references to Nelson's innovative and imaginative introductory sociology titles.

THINK OUTSIDE THE BOOK: NELSON VIDEOS FOR SOCIOLOGY

Be part of something exciting! Nelson is proud to present our Think Outside the Book: Nelson Videos for Introductory Sociology. This five-volume series, which includes video segments that are each 5 to 27 minutes long, was created to stimulate discussion in your classroom. Many selections are excerpted from national and international award-winning films.

Videos were selected by leading sociologist Robert Brym. His keen eye for finding relevant, powerful, and engaging selections allows students to "think outside the book" and brings sociology concepts to life. A video guide for instructors (available on the Instructor's Resource CD) will include a synopsis of each video, questions for critical analysis, and references to Nelson's innovative and imaginative introductory sociology titles. Visit www.thinkoutsidethebook.nelson.com or ask your Nelson representative for more details.

JOININ™ ON TURNINGPOINT®

Transform your lecture into an interactive student experience with JoinIn. Combined with your choice of keypad systems, JoinIn turns your Microsoft® PowerPoint® application into audience response software. With a click on a handheld device, students can respond to multiple-choice questions, short polls, interactive exercises, and peer-review questions. You can also take attendance, check student comprehension of concepts, collect student demographics to better assess student needs, and even administer quizzes. In addition, there are interactive text-specific slide sets that you can modify and merge with any of your own PowerPoint® lecture slides. This tool is available to qualified adopters at http://turningtechnologies.com/groupresponsesystemsupport/downloads.cfm.

NEW SOCIETY ON THE WEB

http://www.newsociety6e.nelson.com/instructor

Downloadable versions of the Instructor's Manual, PowerPoint® presentations, and Instructor's Guide for Think Outside the Book: Nelson Videos for Introductory Sociology, plus an image bank of photos from the text and Robert J. Brym's online lectures, can be accessed from the password-protected instructor's page of the companion website.

INFOTRAC® COLLEGE EDITION

Ignite discussions or augment your lectures with the latest developments in sociology and societal change. Create your own course reader by selecting articles or by using the search keywords provided at the end of each chapter. InfoTrac College Edition (available as a free option with this text) gives you and your students four months of free access to an easy-to-use online database of reliable, full-length articles (not abstracts) from hundreds of top academic journals and popular sources. Among the journals available 24 hours a day, 7 days a week are the *Canadian Review of Sociology and Anthropology*, the *Canadian Journal of Sociology*, *Canadian Ethnic Studies*, *Public Policy*, the *American Journal of Sociology*, *Social Forces*, *Social Research*, and *Sociology*. Contact your Nelson representative for more information. InfoTrac College Edition is available only to North American college and university students. Journals are subject to change.

ANCILLARIES FOR STUDENTS

STUDENT STUDY GUIDE

(ISBN 0176478574). This concise guide, available online, helps students to check their progress with sample quizzes. Critical-thinking questions encourage them to use their imaginations to develop a richer sociological perspective.

NEW SOCIETY ON THE WEB

http://www.newsociety6e.nelson.com

The *New Society* website contains much more than the standard features you have come to expect from Nelson Web ancillaries. In addition to chapter-by-chapter links to secondary sources, online quizzes, and other self-testing material, it boasts exciting original features, including interactive exercises, online research projects, video exercises, and a focus on Canada in a global context. Also, visit the online lecture hall to hear lectures delivered in audio by a range of prominent sociologists, including Robert Brym. These features, and others, make the *New Society* website unique and useful to Canadian instructors and students. It allows students to do sociology and better understand their place in the world.

INFOTRAC COLLEGE EDITION

http://www.infotrac-college.com

This website offers access to more than 20 million articles from nearly 6000 sources—a valuable resource when you do online research. See the description above for more details.

ACKNOWLEDGMENTS

The sixth edition of *New Society* still bears the imprint of Heather McWhinney, Dan Brooks, Megan Mueller, Semareh Al-Hillal, Brad Lambertus, and Camille Isaacs. They shepherded the book through its first editions, helping to make *New Society* distinctive and highly successful.

For the past year I was privileged to work closely with publishing professionals of the highest calibre, all of whom contributed heavily to the successful completion of the sixth edition. In particular, Laura Macleod worked diligently and with good humour on this complex project, always mindful of the need to balance the diverse needs of instructors, students, and authors. Liisa Kelly's energetic and meticulous approach to the project was evident from beginning to end. Visually and linguistically, this book owes much to her exemplary skill as developmental editor. I would also like to thank Nicola Winstanley (photo researcher), Natalia Denesiuk Harris (content production manager), David Tonen (marketing manager), Lisa Berland (copy editor), Dawn Hunter (proofreader), and Natalie Russell (permissions coordinator).

New Society could not have become what it is without the authors of each chapter. They are among the very best sociologists in Canada. I believe that, although concentrating on the exposition of their own subfields, they have conveyed to the novice a real sense of the excitement and promise of sociology. I am deeply indebted to them, as tens of thousands of introductory sociology students and their instructors inevitably have been and will be.

Finally, I would like to thank the following reviewers, whose insightful comments helped shape this edition:

Guy Letts, Georgian College
Lorna Doerkson, University of Saskatchewan
Peter Landstreet, York University
Kate Krug, Cape Breton University
Morgan Holmes, Wilfrid Laurier University

R.J.B.
Toronto

CONTRIBUTORS

REGINALD W. BIBBY, UNIVERSITY OF LETHBRIDGE

MONICA BOYD, UNIVERSITY OF TORONTO

ROBERT J. BRYM, UNIVERSITY OF TORONTO

NEENA L. CHAPPELL, UNIVERSITY OF VICTORIA

SCOTT DAVIES, MCMASTER UNIVERSITY

BONNIE FOX, UNIVERSITY OF TORONTO

JOSH GREENBERG, CARLETON UNIVERSITY

NEIL GUPPY, UNIVERSITY OF BRITISH COLUMBIA

JOHN HANNIGAN, UNIVERSITY OF TORONTO

JOSÉE JOHNSTON, UNIVERSITY OF TORONTO

GRAHAM KNIGHT, MCMASTER UNIVERSITY

HARVEY KRAHN, UNIVERSITY OF ALBERTA

RHONDA L. LENTON, YORK UNIVERSITY

JOHN LIE, UNIVERSITY OF CALIFORNIA AT BERKELEY

MARGARET J. PENNING, UNIVERSITY OF VICTORIA

MICHAEL ROSENBERG, DAWSON COLLEGE

STEVEN RYTINA, MCGILL UNIVERSITY

VIC SATZEWICH, MCMASTER UNIVERSITY

WILLIAM SHAFFIR, MCMASTER UNIVERSITY

JULIAN TANNER, UNIVERSITY OF TORONTO

SANDY WELSH, UNIVERSITY OF TORONTO

ANTHONY WINSON, UNIVERSITY OF GUELPH

BRIEF CONTENTS

PART ONE INTRODUCTION

2 CHAPTER ONE **INTRODUCING SOCIOLOGY**
ROBERT J. BRYM

PART TWO CULTURE

28 CHAPTER TWO **CULTURE**
ROBERT J. BRYM

48 CHAPTER THREE **SOCIALIZATION**
WILLIAM SHAFFIR, MICHAEL ROSENBERG

73 CHAPTER FOUR **GENDER AND SEXUALITY**
RHONDA L. LENTON

97 CHAPTER FIVE **THE MASS MEDIA**
JOSH GREENBERG, GRAHAM KNIGHT

PART THREE INEQUALITY

122 CHAPTER SIX **SOCIAL STRATIFICATION**
HARVEY KRAHN

154 CHAPTER SEVEN **GENDER INEQUALITY: ECONOMIC AND POLITICAL ASPECTS**
MONICA BOYD

179 CHAPTER EIGHT **RACE AND ETHNIC RELATIONS**
VIC SATZEWICH

206 CHAPTER NINE **DEVELOPMENT AND UNDERDEVELOPMENT**
ANTHONY WINSON

PART FOUR INSTITUTIONS

226 CHAPTER TEN **FAMILIES**
BONNIE FOX

253 CHAPTER ELEVEN **WORK AND OCCUPATIONS**
SANDY WELSH

284 CHAPTER TWELVE **EDUCATION**
SCOTT DAVIES

309 CHAPTER THIRTEEN **RELIGION**
REGINALD W. BIBBY

PART FIVE CHANGE AND CONFLICT

336 CHAPTER FOURTEEN **DEVIANCE AND CRIME**
JULIAN TANNER

362 CHAPTER FIFTEEN **POPULATION AND URBANIZATION**
JOHN HANNIGAN

387 CHAPTER SIXTEEN **SOCIOLOGY AND THE ENVIRONMENT**
JOHN HANNIGAN

409 CHAPTER SEVENTEEN **HEALTH AND AGING**
NEENA L. CHAPPELL, MARGARET J. PENNING

429 CHAPTER EIGHTEEN **POLITICS AND SOCIAL MOVEMENTS**
ROBERT J. BRYM

451 CHAPTER NINETEEN **GLOBALIZATION**
JOSÉE JOHNSTON

PART SIX METHODS

478 CHAPTER TWENTY **RESEARCH METHODS**
NEIL GUPPY

505 **REFERENCES**

547 **INDEX**

21-1 ONLINE CHAPTER TWENTY-ONE **NETWORKS, GROUPS, BUREAUCRACIES, AND SOCIETIES***
ROBERT J. BRYM, JOHN LIE, STEVEN RYTINA

*AVAILABLE ONLINE ONLY AT WWW.NEWSOCIETY6E.NELSON.COM.

CONTENTS

PART ONE INTRODUCTION

CHAPTER ONE

2 INTRODUCING SOCIOLOGY ROBERT J. BRYM

3   INTRODUCTION
3   Why I Decided *Not* to Study Sociology
4   A Change of Mind
4   The Goals of This Chapter
5   THE SOCIOLOGICAL PERSPECTIVE
6   The Sociological Explanation of Suicide
6   Suicide in Canada Today
8   From Personal Troubles to Social Structures
9   The Sociological Imagination
10 Origins of the Sociological Imagination
11 SOCIOLOGICAL THEORIES
11 The Origins of Sociology
14 Theory, Research, and Values
14 Functionalism
15 Conflict Theory
16 Symbolic Interactionism
17 Feminist Theory
18 THEIR REVOLUTION AND OURS
18 The Industrial Revolution
20 Postindustrialism and Globalization:
    Opportunities and Pitfalls
22 Why Sociology?
24 SUMMARY
24 QUESTIONS TO CONSIDER
24 GLOSSARY
26 SUGGESTED READING
26 NOTES
26 WEB RESOURCES

PART TWO CULTURE

CHAPTER TWO

28 CULTURE ROBERT J. BRYM

29 INTRODUCTION
29 Culture as Problem Solving
30 The Origins of Culture
31 Culture from the Margins
32 The Two Faces of Culture
33 CULTURE AS FREEDOM
33 Cultural Diversification and Globalization
36 The Rights Revolution
38 Postmodernism
41 CULTURE AS CONSTRAINT AND AS DANGER
41 Rationalization
43 Consumerism
44 From Counterculture to Subculture
45 SUMMARY
46 QUESTIONS TO CONSIDER
46 GLOSSARY
47 SUGGESTED READING
47 NOTES
47 WEB RESOURCES

CHAPTER THREE

48 SOCIALIZATION WILLIAM SHAFFIR, MICHAEL ROSENBERG

49 WHAT IS SOCIALIZATION?
50 Nature and Nurture
52 The Self and Socialization
52 TWO EARLY THEORISTS
52 Charles Horton Cooley
53 George Herbert Mead
55 Willis's Application and Extension of Mead's Theory

56   Gender Socialization
58   SOCIALIZATION THROUGH THE LIFE COURSE
58   Adolescence and Youth
59   Adult Socialization
61   Socialization among Seniors
61   AGENTS OF SOCIALIZATION
62   Families
63   Schools
64   Peer Groups
65   Media and Technology
66   Other Socializing Agents
67   IDENTITY AND SOCIAL CHANGE
68   Resocialization
70   SUMMARY
71   QUESTIONS TO CONSIDER
71   GLOSSARY
72   SUGGESTED READING
72   WEB RESOURCES

CHAPTER FOUR

73   GENDER AND SEXUALITY RHONDA L. LENTON

74   INTRODUCTION
74   Gender, Sex, and the Case of David/Brenda
75   DEFINING MALE AND FEMALE: SEX AND GENDER
78   SEXUALITY
78   SEXUAL ATTITUDES AND BEHAVIOUR
83   DOES SEX DETERMINE DESTINY?
83   Essentialism
87   Social Constructionism
88   CONSTRUCTING GENDER THROUGH SOCIALIZATION
88   Primary Socialization
89   Secondary Socialization
89   The Mass Media
89   GENDER SOCIALIZATION AND SEXUALITY
90   BODY IMAGE AND EATING DISORDERS
91   MALE VIOLENCE AGAINST WOMEN
91   Sexual Assault
93   Sexual Harassment
93   LOOKING AHEAD: TOWARD A NEW SEXUAL ETHIC
93   Sexual Pluralism
94   SUMMARY

94   QUESTIONS TO CONSIDER
95   GLOSSARY
95   SUGGESTED READING
95   NOTES
96   WEB RESOURCES

CHAPTER FIVE

97   THE MASS MEDIA JOSH GREENBERG, GRAHAM KNIGHT

98   INTRODUCTION
98   The Technological Perspective
99   The Critical Perspective
100 POLITICAL ECONOMY OF THE MEDIA
101 Newspapers: Concentration, Monopoly, and Advertising
103 Television: Economy, Culture, and Identity
105 REPRESENTATION AND IDEOLOGY: THE MEANING OF THE MESSAGE
105 News and Ideology
109 MEDIA EFFECTS AND AUDIENCES
109 Media Violence
111 Audience Research: Interpretation and Media Use
111 THE INTERNET: COMPUTER-MEDIATED COMMUNICATION
113 The Digital Divide: CMC and Social Inequality
115 Virtual Community: The Internet's Impact
117 SUMMARY
117 QUESTIONS TO CONSIDER
118 GLOSSARY
118 SUGGESTED READING
119 WEB RESOURCES

PART THREE INEQUALITY

CHAPTER SIX

122 SOCIAL STRATIFICATION HARVEY KRAHN

123 INTRODUCTION
124 STRATIFICATION: A CORNERSTONE OF SOCIOLOGY
125 SOCIAL HIERARCHIES IN STRATIFIED SOCIETIES
125 Ascribed and Achieved Status
126 Open and Closed Stratification Systems
127 Class and Structure
128 EXPLANATIONS OF SOCIAL STRATIFICATION
128 Karl Marx: Capitalism, Exploitation, and Class Conflict
130 Max Weber: Class and Other Dimensions of Inequality
131 Davis and Moore: A Functional Theory of Stratification
132 Gerhard Lenski: Technology and Stratification Systems
133 Erik Olin Wright: A Neo-Marxist Approach
133 Frank Parkin: A Neo-Weberian Approach
135 Explanation of Social Stratification: Summing Up
136 OCCUPATIONS, SOCIAL CLASS, AND INEQUALITY IN CANADA
136 Occupational Shifts over Time
138 Occupational Mobility and Status Attainment
139 The Distribution of Wealth
140 Income Distribution
142 The Poor
147 Material Inequality in Canada: Summing Up

148 Consequences of Material Inequality
149 RESPONDING TO INEQUALITY
150 SUMMARY
151 QUESTIONS TO CONSIDER
151 GLOSSARY
152 SUGGESTED READING
153 WEB RESOURCES

CHAPTER SEVEN

154 **GENDER INEQUALITY: ECONOMIC AND POLITICAL ASPECTS** MONICA BOYD

155 INTRODUCTION
155 UNDERSTANDING GENDER INEQUALITY
155 Gender Inequality Defined
157 Explaining Gender Inequality
158 Exercising Power
158 Separate Spheres
160 SITES OF WORK
160 Female Labour-Force Participation
161 Domestic Labour
162 LABOUR-FORCE INEQUALITIES
162 Occupational Segregation and Sex Typing
164 Power at Work
164 Gender and Skill
165 Nonstandard Work
166 Earnings
166 Explanations of Women's Lower Pay
167 Birthplace and Colour Matter
169 Women's Groups: Organizing for Change
170 GENDER IN POLITICS
170 Voting Rights
171 Participating in the World of Politics
172 Explaining the Political Participation of Women
173 Representation by Women, Representation for Women
174 ELIMINATING GENDER INEQUALITY
174 Models of Change
174 Public Policy and Gender Inequality in the Labour Force
175 Correcting the Balance: Women in Politics
176 SUMMARY
177 QUESTIONS TO CONSIDER
177 GLOSSARY
178 SUGGESTED READING
178 WEB RESOURCES

CHAPTER EIGHT

179 **RACE AND ETHNIC RELATIONS** VIC SATZEWICH

180 INTRODUCTION
181 ETHNICITY AND RACE: THE SOCIAL CONSTRUCTION OF DIFFERENCE
181 Ethnicity and Race
186 Theories of Race and Ethnic Relations
189 ABORIGINAL PEOPLES
190 Explanations of Aboriginal Conditions
192 Class and Gender Diversity
193 QUEBEC: NATIONALISM AND IDENTITY
193 The Social Basis of Québécois Nationalism

195 Who Is Québécois?
196 IMMIGRATION: STATE FORMATION AND ECONOMIC DEVELOPMENT
197 Factors That Shape Canadian Immigration
199 Contemporary Immigration Categories
200 ETHNIC INEQUALITY AND THE CANADIAN LABOUR MARKET
200 John Porter and the Vertical Mosaic
200 The Declining Significance of the Vertical Mosaic
203 SUMMARY
204 QUESTIONS TO CONSIDER
204 GLOSSARY
204 SUGGESTED READING
205 WEB RESOURCES

CHAPTER NINE

206 **DEVELOPMENT AND UNDERDEVELOPMENT** ANTHONY WINSON

207 MY MOTHER'S PET THEORY
207 WHAT IS DEVELOPMENT?
208 The Relevance of Development and Global Inequalities: Social Justice and Security
209 EARLY THEORIES OF DEVELOPMENT
209 Development in Stages
209 Development as a State of Mind
210 DEVELOPMENT AS DEPENDENCY
210 From Contact to Conquest
210 The Slave Trade
211 The Structural Roots of Underdevelopment
212 Countries versus Classes as Causes of Underdevelopment
212 Not All Countries Are Alike: Class Alliances and State Control
213 Beyond Dependency: Agrarian Class Structure and Underdevelopment
214 GEOGRAPHY AND BIOLOGICAL RESOURCES
214 Criticisms of Diamond's Thesis
214 THE NEOLIBERAL ERA: DEBT, STRUCTURAL ADJUSTMENT, AND UPHEAVAL IN THE SOUTH
214 The Rise of Neoliberalism
215 Neoliberalism and SAPs as Solutions to Poverty
219 STATE VIOLENCE, WAR, AND THE PRODUCTION OF POVERTY
220 RESISTANCE TO THE NEOLIBERAL NEW WORLD ORDER
220 Government Resistance
221 Popular Resistance
223 SUMMARY
223 QUESTIONS TO CONSIDER
223 GLOSSARY
224 SUGGESTED READING
224 NOTE
224 WEB RESOURCES

PART FOUR INSTITUTIONS

CHAPTER TEN

226 **FAMILIES** BONNIE FOX

227 INTRODUCTION
227 EXPLORING THE FAMILIAR: FAMILIES IN WESTERN
     SOCIETY TODAY
227 Dilemmas of Contemporary Family Life
229 Myths about Family
229 The Myth of the Natural Family
230 Conceptualizing and Defining Family
231 A LOOK AT OTHER FAMILY PATTERNS
231 Foraging Societies: The Communal Household
233 Preindustrial Agricultural Societies: Household Economies
234 THE ORIGINS OF CONTEMPORARY FAMILY PATTERNS IN
     WESTERN SOCIETIES
234 The Middle Class
235 The Working Class
236 SOCIAL RELATIONS IN FAMILIES TODAY
236 Main Features
241 Sexuality and Families
242 Gender and Families
243 Marriage and Divorce
244 Housework and Motherwork
245 Becoming Parents
246 Divorce and Its Aftermath
247 Policies to Support Families
249 CONCLUSION
250 SUMMARY
250 QUESTIONS TO CONSIDER
251 GLOSSARY
251 SUGGESTED READING
251 NOTE
252 WEB RESOURCES

CHAPTER ELEVEN

253 **WORK AND OCCUPATIONS** SANDY WELSH

254 AN INTRODUCTION TO WORK IN CANADA
254 Working in Retail
254 The First and Second Industrial Revolutions

257 WORK IN THE SERVICE ECONOMY
258 Good Jobs or Bad Jobs?
259 Nonstandard Jobs
261 Why the Rise of Nonstandard Work?
262 Are Nonstandard Jobs Bad Jobs?
263 Work Hours and Work Arrangements
265 LABOUR-MARKET SEGMENTATION
266 Job Ghettos and Disadvantaged Groups
268 Professions
269 Unions
269 TECHNOLOGY
270 BUREAUCRACIES AND WORK ORGANIZATIONS
272 Managerial Strategies for Organizing Work
274 "WILL I LIKE MY JOB?" JOB SATISFACTION
     AND ALIENATION
275 What Determines Job Satisfaction?
276 Alienation
279 Finding Work
281 THE FUTURE OF WORK
282 SUMMARY
282 QUESTIONS TO CONSIDER
282 GLOSSARY
283 SUGGESTED READING
283 WEB RESOURCES

CHAPTER TWELVE

284 **EDUCATION** SCOTT DAVIES

285 INTRODUCTION
285 HOW SCHOOLS CONNECT TO SOCIETY: CLASSICAL
     AND CONTEMPORARY APPROACHES
286 SELECTION
287 Changing School Structure
289 Inequality Among Students
292 SOCIALIZATION
294 Changing Forms of Moral Education
295 Creating Identities? Gender and Race
297 The Limits of School Socialization
299 SOCIAL ORGANIZATION
299 Theories of School Organization
300 School Authority: From Tradition to
     Rationality to Markets?
306 CONCLUSION
306 SUMMARY
307 QUESTIONS TO CONSIDER
307 GLOSSARY
307 SUGGESTED READING
308 WEB RESOURCES

CHAPTER THIRTEEN

309 **RELIGION** REGINALD W. BIBBY

310 INTRODUCTION
311 SOCIOLOGY AND RELIGION
311 THEORETICAL TRADITIONS
311 Marx and Conflict
312 Durkheim and Collectivity
314 Weber and Ideas
314 THE NATURE OF RELIGION
315 Personal Religiosity

316 Collective Religiosity
321 THE SOURCES OF RELIGION
322 Individual-Centred Explanations
323 Structure-Centred Explanations
325 THE CONSEQUENCES OF RELIGION
326 Personal Consequences
327 Interpersonal Consequences
328 Societal Consequences
330 THE FUTURE OF RELIGION
332 SUMMARY
333 QUESTIONS TO CONSIDER
333 GLOSSARY
334 SUGGESTED READING
334 WEB RESOURCES

PART FIVE CHANGE AND CONFLICT

CHAPTER FOURTEEN

336 **DEVIANCE AND CRIME** JULIAN TANNER

337 INTRODUCTION
337 CONCEPTIONS OF CRIME AND DEVIANCE
337 Crime and Deviance as Norm-Violating Behaviour
340 Crime and Deviance as Labels and Social Constructs
342 CRIME IN THE NEWS
342 COUNTING CRIME AND DEVIANCE: NUMBERS AND
       MEANING
342 Official Statistics
343 Regional Variations in Crime Rates
344 Homicide Rates
346 Other Data Sources: Self-Report Surveys
       and Direct Observation
347 CORRELATES OF CRIME
348 THEORIES OF CRIME AND DEVIANCE
348 Strain Theory
350 Social Learning Theories: Edwin Sutherland and
       Differential Association
350 Control Theory
351 Routine Activities Theory
351 TYPES OF CRIME AND DEVIANCE
351 Gender and Crime
353 Youth, Crime, and Deviance
356 RESPONDING TO CRIME AND DEVIANCE
356 Incarceration
358 Intervention
358 Preventing Crime
359 SUMMARY
360 QUESTIONS TO CONSIDER
360 GLOSSARY
361 SUGGESTED READING
361 WEB RESOURCES

CHAPTER FIFTEEN

362 **POPULATION AND URBANIZATION** JOHN HANNIGAN

363 INTRODUCTION
364 EARLY CITIES

365 POPULATION ISSUES AND URBAN GROWTH
365 The Demographic Transition
367 The Industrial City
367 The Development of an Urban-Industrial Economy in
       Canada
369 Researching the Industrial City: The Chicago School
370 Ecology of the Industrial City
372 Urbanization of the Developing World
373 THE CORPORATE CITY
374 The Corporate Suburb
376 THE POSTMODERN CITY
377 The Edge City
378 The Multiethnic City
379 The Dual City
383 SUMMARY
384 QUESTIONS TO CONSIDER
385 GLOSSARY
385 SUGGESTED READING
386 WEB RESOURCES

CHAPTER SIXTEEN

387 **SOCIOLOGY AND THE ENVIRONMENT** JOHN HANNIGAN

388 INTRODUCTION
388 TOWARD ENVIRONMENTAL SOCIOLOGY
389 ENVIRONMENTAL VALUE CONFLICT
391 ENVIRONMENTAL ATTITUDES, CONCERNS,
       AND BEHAVIOURS
394 THE ENVIRONMENTAL MOVEMENT
394 Social Base and Composition
395 Environmental Mobilization
397 Ideological Divisions
399 POLITICAL ECONOMY OF THE ENVIRONMENT
401 RISK AND RISK ASSESSMENT
402 Organizational Basis of Risk
402 Community Perception of Risk
404 Social Distribution of Risk
405 SOCIAL CONSTRUCTION OF ENVIRONMENTAL
       PROBLEMS
406 SUMMARY
406 QUESTIONS TO CONSIDER
407 GLOSSARY

408 SUGGESTED READING
408 WEB RESOURCES

CHAPTER SEVENTEEN

409 **HEALTH AND AGING** NEENA L. CHAPPELL, MARGARET J. PENNING

410 CHALLENGING COMMONSENSE BELIEFS ABOUT HEALTH AND AGING
411 INDIVIDUAL AND POPULATION AGING
414 DIVERSITY IN AGING
414 Socioeconomic and Class Differences
414 Gender
414 Ethnicity and Race
415 Apocalyptic Demography
416 HEALTH AND OLD AGE
417 Inequality, Health, and Aging
420 Explaining Social Inequalities in Health
421 Intersecting Inequalities and Health over the Life Course
422 HEALTH CARE
422 Self-Care and Informal Care
423 Formal Medical and Home Care
424 Health-Care System Change and Reform
425 Globalization and Profit Making
426 SUMMARY
427 QUESTIONS TO CONSIDER
427 GLOSSARY
428 SUGGESTED READING
428 WEB RESOURCES

CHAPTER EIGHTEEN

429 **POLITICS AND SOCIAL MOVEMENTS** ROBERT J. BRYM

430 INTRODUCTION
432 POWER FROM ABOVE: NORMAL POLITICS
433 Pluralist Theory
433 Elite Theory
436 Power-Balance Theory
438 State-Centred Theory
440 POWER FROM BELOW: POLITICS BEYOND THE RULES
440 Relative-Deprivation Theory
440 Resource Mobilization Theory
442 Framing Discontent
442 Refrain: Back to 1968
443 THE HISTORY AND FUTURE OF SOCIAL MOVEMENTS
443 I. The Rich Countries
446 II. The Other 85 Percent
448 SUMMARY
449 QUESTIONS TO CONSIDER
449 GLOSSARY
450 SUGGESTED READING
450 NOTES
450 WEB RESOURCES

CHAPTER NINETEEN

451 **GLOBALIZATION** JOSÉE JOHNSTON

452 INTRODUCTION
452 The Burger and Fries Go Global
453 Globalization or "Globaloney"?
453 Defining Globalization
454 The Global and the Ethical
455 Top-down versus Bottom-up Globalization
456 CAPITALISTS GO GLOBAL
456 The Rise of Financial Capital
457 Overcapacity and Centralization
458 Growth of the Corporate Giants
458 Critics of Corporate Power
459 ARE STATES RELEVANT IN THE GLOBAL WORLD?
460 The Three Sisters
461 A U.S. Empire?
461 Global Inequality and the "Fourth World"
462 THE GLOBAL CONSUMER
463 A Global Glut
463 Culture as Commodity?
463 Cultural Imperialism?
464 Global Brand Backlash
465 Consumer Alternatives: Fair Trade
465 Ecological Consequences of Consumerism
466 GLOBAL WORKERS
467 Wage Labour and Wage Inequality
469 Searching for Cheap Labour: "The Race to the Bottom"
470 GLOBAL ECOLOGY
470 Global Food
473 SUMMARY
474 QUESTIONS TO CONSIDER
474 GLOSSARY
475 SUGGESTED READING
475 WEB RESOURCES

PART SIX METHODS

CHAPTER TWENTY

478 **RESEARCH METHODS** NEIL GUPPY

479 INTRODUCTION
479 PERSPECTIVE

480 Science as a Social Practice
480 Minimizing Bias in Social Science
481 Scientific versus Nonscientific Thinking
482 Natural versus Social Science
483 METHODS OF SOCIAL RESEARCH
483 Explanation
485 Understanding
486 TECHNIQUES OF SOCIAL RESEARCH
486 Experiments
489 Survey Research
493 Observational Studies
496 Other Methods of Research
498 THE ANALYSIS OF NUMERICAL DATA
500 THE FUTURE OF SOCIAL RESEARCH
502 SUMMARY
502 QUESTIONS TO CONSIDER

503 GLOSSARY
503 SUGGESTED READING
504 NOTES
504 WEB RESOURCES

505 REFERENCES

547 INDEX

ONLINE CHAPTER TWENTY-ONE

21-1 NETWORKS, GROUPS, BUREACRACIES, AND SOCIETIES* ROBERT J. BRYM, JOHN LIE, STEVEN RYTINA
*AVAILABLE ONLINE ONLY AT
WWW.NEWSOCIETY6E.NELSON.COM.

PART ONE

Introduction

SOURCE: jdurham/Morguefile

Introducing Sociology

Robert J. Brym
UNIVERSITY OF TORONTO

In this chapter you will learn that

- The causes of human behaviour lie partly in the patterns of social relations that surround and penetrate people.

- Sociologists examine the connection between personal troubles and social relations.

- Sociological research is often motivated by the desire to improve the social world. At the same time, sociologists adopt scientific methods to test their ideas.

- Sociology originated at the time of the Industrial Revolution. The founders of sociology diagnosed the massive social transformations of their day. They also suggested ways of overcoming the social problems created by the Industrial Revolution.

- Today's Postindustrial Revolution similarly challenges us. The chief value of sociology is that it can help clarify the scope, direction, and significance of social change. Sociology can also suggest ways of managing change.

INTRODUCTION

WHY I DECIDED *NOT* TO STUDY SOCIOLOGY

When I started university at the age of 18, I was bewildered by the wide variety of courses I could choose from. Having now taught sociology for 30 years, and having met a few thousand undergraduates, I am quite sure most students today feel as I did then.

One source of confusion for me was uncertainty about why I was in university in the first place. Like you, I knew higher education could improve my chance of finding good work. But, like most students, I also had a sense that higher education is supposed to provide something more than just the training necessary to embark on a career that is interesting and pays well. Several high school teachers and guidance counsellors had told me that university was also supposed to "broaden my horizons" and teach me to "think critically." I wasn't entirely sure what they meant, but they made it sound interesting enough to make me want to know more. Thus, I decided in my first year to take mainly "practical" courses that might prepare me for a law degree (economics, political science, and psychology). I also enrolled in a couple of other courses to indulge my "intellectual" side (philosophy, drama).

One thing I knew for sure: I didn't want to study sociology. Sociology, I came to believe, was thin soup with uncertain ingredients. When I asked a second-year student what sociology is, he told me it deals mainly with why people are unequal—why some are rich and others poor, some powerful and others weak. Coming as I did from a poor immigrant family in the Maritimes, an economically depressed region, it

Life is finite, and if we want to make the most of it, we must figure out how best to live. Sociology offers a useful perspective for understanding our current predicament and seeing possible ways of dealing with it.

appeared that sociology could teach me something about my own life. But it also seemed a lot like what I imagined economics and political science to be about. What, then, was unique about sociology? My growing sense that sociology had nothing special to offer was confirmed when another second-year student told me that sociologists try to describe the ideal society and figure out how to make the world a better place. That description appealed to my youthful sense of the world's injustice. However, it also sounded a lot like philosophy. A third-year student explained that sociology analyzes how and why people assume different roles in their lives. She made sociology appear similar to drama. Finally, one student reported that in her sociology class she was learning why people commit suicide, homicide, and other deviant acts. That seemed like abnormal psychology to me. I concluded that sociology had no distinct flavour all its own. Accordingly, I decided to forgo it for tastier courses.

A CHANGE OF MIND

Despite the opinion I'd formed, I found myself taking no fewer than four sociology courses a year after starting university. That revolution in my life was due, in part, to the pull of an extraordinary professor I happened to meet just before I began my second year. He set me thinking in an altogether new way about what I could and should do with my life. He exploded some of my deepest beliefs. He started me thinking sociologically.

Specifically, he first put Yorick's dilemma to me. Yorick is a character—sort of—in *Hamlet*. Toward the end of the play, Hamlet finds two gravediggers at work. They unearth the remains of the former court jester, Yorick, who used to amuse Hamlet and carry him around on his back when Hamlet was a child. Holding high his old friend's skull, Hamlet reflects on what we must all come to. Even the remains of Alexander the Great, he says, turn to dust.

This incident implies Yorick's dilemma and, indeed, the dilemma of all thinking people. Life is finite. If we want to make the most of it, we must figure out how best to live. That is no easy task. It requires study, reflection, and the selection of values and goals. Ideally, higher education is supposed to supply students with just that opportunity. Finally, I was beginning to understand what I could expect from university apart from job training.

The professor I met also convinced me that sociology in particular could open up a new and superior way of comprehending my world. Specifically, he

said, it could clarify my place in society, how I might best manoeuvre through it, and even, perhaps, how I might contribute to improving it, however modestly. Before beginning my study of sociology, I had always taken for granted that things happen in the world— and to me—because physical and emotional forces cause them. Famine, I thought, is caused by drought, war by territorial greed, economic success by hard work, marriage by love, suicide by bottomless depression, rape by depraved lust. But now, this professor repeatedly threw evidence in my face that contradicted my easy formulas. If drought causes famine, why have so many famines occurred in perfectly normal weather conditions or involved some groups hoarding or destroying food so others would starve? If hard work causes prosperity, why are so many hard workers poor? If love causes marriage, why are so many families sites of violence against women and children? And so the questions multiplied.

As if it were not enough that the professor's sociological evidence upset many of my assumptions about the way the world worked, he also challenged me to understand sociology's unique way of explaining social life. He defined **sociology** as the systematic study of human behaviour in social context. He explained that *social* causes are distinct from physical and emotional causes. Understanding social causes can help clarify otherwise inexplicable features of famine, marriage, and so forth. In public school, my teachers had taught me that people are free to do what they want with their lives. However, my new professor taught me that the organization of the social world opens some opportunities and closes others, thus constraining our freedom and helping to make us what we are. By examining the operation of these powerful social forces, he said, sociology can help us to know ourselves, our capabilities and limitations. I was hooked. And so, of course, I hope you will be too.

THE GOALS OF THIS CHAPTER

In this chapter I aim to achieve three goals:

1. I first illustrate the power of sociology to dispel foggy assumptions and help us see the operation of the social world more clearly. To that end, I examine a phenomenon that at first glance appears to be solely the outcome of breakdowns in individual functioning: suicide. You will see that, in fact, *social relations* among people powerfully influence suicide rates. This exercise introduces you to what is unique about the sociological perspective.

2. I show that, from its origins, sociological research has been motivated by a desire to improve the social world. Thus, sociology is not just a dry, academic exercise but a means of charting a better course for society. At the same time, however, sociologists adopt scientific methods to test their ideas, thus increasing the validity of the results. I illustrate these points by briefly analyzing the work of the founders of the discipline.

3. I suggest that sociology can help you come to grips with your century, just as it helped the founders of sociology deal with theirs. Today we are witnessing massive and disorienting social changes. Entire countries are breaking up. Women are demanding equality with men in all spheres of life. New religions are emerging and old ones reviving. People's wants are increasingly governed by the mass media. Computers are radically altering the way people work and entertain themselves. There are proportionately fewer good jobs to go around. Environmental ruin threatens us all. As was the case a hundred years ago, sociologists today try to understand social phenomena and suggest credible ways of improving their societies. By promising to make sociology relevant to you, this chapter should be viewed as an open invitation to participate in sociology's challenge.

But first things first. Before showing how sociology can help us comprehend and better our world, let us briefly examine the problem of suicide. That will help to illustrate how the sociological perspective can clarify and sometimes overturn commonsense beliefs.

THE SOCIOLOGICAL PERSPECTIVE

By analyzing suicide sociologically, you can put to a tough test my claim that sociology gives you a unique, surprising, and enlightening perspective on social events. After all, suicide appears to be the supremely antisocial and non-social act. It is condemned by nearly everyone in society. It is typically committed in private, far from the public's intrusive glare. It is rare. In recent years, there have been about 13 suicides annually for every 100 000 people in Canada (Statistics Canada, 2004). Canada's suicide rate places us 36th among the 74 countries that publish suicide statistics; see Figure 1.1. And when you think about why people commit such acts, you are likely to focus on their individual states of mind rather than on the state of society. In other words, what usually interests us are the aspects of specific individuals' lives that caused them to become depressed or angry enough to do something as awful as killing themselves. We usually do not think about the patterns of social relations that might encourage such actions in general. If sociology

FIGURE 1.1   SUICIDE RATES, SELECTED COUNTRIES

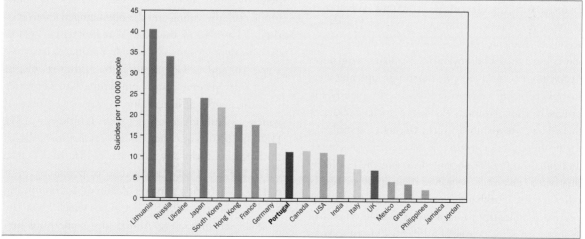

The world's highest suicide rates are found in some countries of the former Soviet Union (Belarus, Kazakhstan Latvia, Lithuania, Russia, Ukraine) and Hungary. The world's lowest suicide rates (zero or close to zero) are found in two clusters, one in certain Caribbean island states (Antigua and Barbuda, Haiti, Jamaica, Saint Kitts and Nevis), the other in parts of the Arab world (Egypt, Syria, Jordan, Palestine).

SOURCE: World Health Organization, 2008, "Suicide Rates per 100,000 by Country, Year and Sex (Table), Most Recent Year Available as of 2008." On the World Wide Web at http://www.who.int/mental_health/prevention/suicide_rates/en/index.html (23 November 2008).

Reprinted from www.who.int/mental_health/prevention/suicide_rates/en/index.html with permission from the World Health Organization.

can reveal the hidden social causes of such an apparently antisocial and non-social phenomenon, there must be something to it!

THE SOCIOLOGICAL EXPLANATION OF SUICIDE

At the end of the nineteenth century, French sociologist Émile Durkheim (1951 [1897]), one of the pioneers of the discipline, demonstrated that suicide is more than just an individual act of desperation resulting from psychological disorder, as was commonly believed at the time. Suicide rates, he showed, are strongly influenced by social forces.

Durkheim made his case by examining the association between rates of suicide and rates of psychological disorder for different groups. The idea that psychological disorder causes suicide is supported, he reasoned, only if suicide rates tend to be high where rates of psychological disorder are high, and low where rates of psychological disorder are low. But his analysis of European government statistics, hospital records, and other sources revealed nothing of the kind. He discovered there were slightly more women than men in insane asylums. Yet there were four male suicides for every female suicide. Jews had the highest rate of psychological disorder among the major religious groups in France. However, they also had the lowest suicide rate. Psychological disorders occurred most frequently when a person reached maturity. Suicide rates, though, increased steadily with age.

Clearly, suicide rates and rates of psychological disorder did not vary proportionately. What then accounts for variations in suicide rates? Durkheim argued that suicide rates vary because of differences in the degree of **social solidarity** in different groups. According to Durkheim, the more a group's members share beliefs and values, and the more frequently and intensely they interact, the more social solidarity there is in the group. In turn, the more social solidarity there is in a group, the more firmly anchored individuals are to the social world, and the less likely they are to take their own lives if adversity strikes. In other words, Durkheim expected groups with a high degree of solidarity to have lower suicide rates than groups with a low degree of solidarity did—at least up to a certain point (see Figure 1.2).

To support his argument, Durkheim showed that married adults are half as likely as unmarried adults are to commit suicide. That is because marriage usually creates social ties and a sort of moral cement that bind the individual to society. Similarly, he argued

FIGURE 1.2   DURKHEIM'S THEORY OF SUICIDE

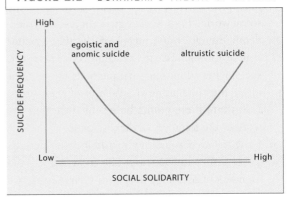

Durkheim argued that as the level of social solidarity increases, the suicide rate declines. Then, beyond a certain point, it starts to rise. Hence the U-shaped curve in this graph. Durkheim called suicides that occur in high-solidarity settings altruistic. Altruism means devotion to the interests of others. **Altruistic suicide** occurs when norms tightly govern behaviour, so individual actions are often in the group interest. For example, when soldiers knowingly give up their lives to protect members of their unit, they commit altruistic suicide out of a deep sense of comradeship. In contrast, suicide that occurs in low-solidarity settings is egoistic or anomic, said Durkheim. **Egoistic suicide** results from a lack of integration of the individual into society because of weak social ties to others. *Anomie* means "without order." **Anomic suicide** occurs when norms governing behaviour are vaguely defined. For example, in Durkheim's view, when people live in a society that lacks a widely shared code of morality, the rate of anomic suicide is likely to be high.

that women are less likely to commit suicide than men are. Why? Women are generally more involved in the intimate social relations of family life. Jews, Durkheim wrote, are less likely to commit suicide than Christians are. The reason? Centuries of persecution have turned them into a group that is more defensive and tightly knit. And seniors are more prone than the young and the middle-aged are to take their own lives in the face of misfortune. That is because they are most likely to live alone, to have lost a spouse, and to lack a job and a wide network of friends. In general, Durkheim wrote, "suicide varies with the degree of integration of the social groups of which the individual forms a part" (Durkheim, 1951 [1897]: 209). Note that his generalization tells us nothing about why any particular individual may take his or her life. That is a question for psychology. But it does tell us that a person's likelihood of committing suicide decreases with the degree to which he or she is anchored in society. And it says something surprising and uniquely sociological about how and why the suicide rate varies from group to group.

SUICIDE IN CANADA TODAY

Durkheim's theory is not just a historical curiosity. It sheds light on the factors that account for variations in

FIGURE 1.3   SUICIDE BY AGE AND SEX, 2004

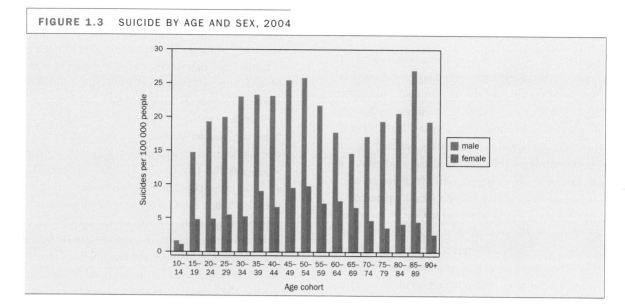

SOURCES: Statistics Canada, 2008, CANSIM, "Deaths, by Cause, Chapter XX: External Causes of Morbidity And Mortality (V01 to Y89), Age Group and Sex, Canada, Annual (number) (table)"; "Estimates of Population (2001 Census and Administrative Data), by Age Group and Sex. Canada, Provinces, Territories, Health Regions (June 2005 boundaries) and Peer Groups, Annually (Number)." On the World Wide Web at http://dc1.chass.utoronto.ca.myaccess.library.utoronto.ca/cgi-bin/cansimdim (3 January 2008).

suicide rates here and now. Consider Figure 1.3, which shows suicide rates by age and sex in Canada for 2004. Comparing rates for men and women, we immediately see that, as in Durkheim's France, men are about four times more likely than women are to commit suicide. However, looking at differences between age groups, we see a striking difference between Durkheim's France and contemporary Canada. When Durkheim wrote, youth suicide was extremely rare and suicide among working-age people was uncommon. In Canada today, suicide among people between the ages of 15 and 64 is much more common, having increased substantially since the 1960s. Suicide rates do *not* increase steadily with age in Canada today. True, the suicide rate is highest among people over the age of 84. However, it is higher for people between the ages of 20 and 59 than it is for people between the ages of 60 and 84. Moreover, the rate of suicide for people between the ages of 15 and 19, practically zero in Durkheim's France, stands at nearly 10 per 100 000 in Canada today.

Although the rate of suicide among youth was negligible in Durkheim's France, his theory of social solidarity helps us to understand why it has risen so quickly in Canada. In brief, shared moral principles and strong social ties have eroded since the early 1960s for Canada's youth. Consider the following facts:

• Church, synagogue, mosque, and temple attendance is down, particularly for young people.

Thus, more than half of Canadians attended religious services weekly in the 1960s. Today the figure is less than one-third, and it is only one-sixth for people born after 1960.

• Unemployment is up, again especially for youth. Thus, the unemployment rate was around 3 percent for most of the 1960s. It rose steadily to around 10 percent for most of the 1990s and stood at 8.6 percent in June 2009. Moreover, the unemployment rate is more than twice as high for Canadians under the age of 20 as it is for older Canadians.

• The rate of divorce has increased sixfold since the early 1960s. Out-of-marriage births are also much more common than they used to be. As a result, children are more often brought up in single-parent families than in the past. This suggests that they enjoy less frequent and intimate social interaction with parents and less adult supervision.

In sum, the figures cited above suggest that the level of social solidarity is now lower than it was just a few decades ago for young people. Less firmly rooted in society, and less likely to share moral standards, young people in Canada today are more likely than they were 50 years ago to take their own lives if they happen to find themselves in the midst of a personal crisis.

FROM PERSONAL TROUBLES TO SOCIAL STRUCTURES

You have known for a long time that you live in a society. Yet until now, you may not have fully appreciated that society also lives in you. That is, patterns of social relations affect your innermost thoughts and feelings, influence your actions, and thus help shape who you are. As we have seen, one such pattern of social relations is the level of social solidarity characteristic of the various groups to which you belong.

Sociologists call relatively stable patterns of social relations **social structures.** One of the sociologist's main tasks is to identify and explain the connection between people's personal troubles and the social structures in which people are embedded. This work is harder than it may at first seem. In everyday life, we usually see things mainly from our own point of view. Our experiences appear unique to each of us. If we think about them at all, social structures may appear remote and impersonal. To see how social structures operate inside us, we require sociological training.

An important step in broadening our sociological awareness involves recognizing that three levels of social structure surround and penetrate us. Think of these structures as concentric circles radiating out from you:

1. **Microstructures** are patterns of intimate social relations. They are formed during face-to-face interaction. Families, friendship circles, and work associations are all examples of microstructures.

   Understanding the operation of microstructures can be useful. Let us say you are looking for a job. You might think you would do best to ask as many close friends and relatives as possible for leads and contacts. Sociological research shows, however, that people you know well are likely to know many of the same people. After asking a couple of close connections for help landing a job, you would therefore do best to ask more remote acquaintances for leads and contacts. People to whom you are weakly connected (and who are weakly connected among themselves) are more likely to know different groups of people. Therefore, they will give you more information about job possibilities and ensure that word about your job search spreads farther. You are more likely to find a job faster if you understand "the strength of weak ties" in microstructural settings (Granovetter, 1973).

2. **Macrostructures** are patterns of social relations that lie outside and above your circle of intimates and acquaintances. Macrostructures include class relations and **patriarchy,** the traditional system of economic and political inequality between women and men in most societies.

   Understanding the operation of macrostructures can also be useful. Consider, for example, one aspect of patriarchy. Most married women who work full-time in the paid labour force do more housework, child care, and eldercare than their husbands do. Governments and businesses support this arrangement insofar as they give little assistance to families in the form of nurseries, after-school programs for children, senior homes, and so forth. Yet the unequal division of work in the household is a major source of dissatisfaction with marriage, especially in families that cannot afford to buy these services privately. Thus, sociological research shows that when spouses share domestic responsibilities equally, they are happier with their marriages and less likely to divorce (Hochschild with Machung, 1989). When a marriage is in danger of dissolving, it is common for partners to blame themselves and each other for their troubles. However, it should now be clear that forces other than incompatible personalities often put stresses on families. Understanding how the macrostructure of patriarchy crops up in everyday life, and doing something to change that structure, can thus help people lead happier lives.

3. The third level of society that surrounds and permeates us comprises **global structures.** International organizations, patterns of worldwide travel and communication, and the economic relations between countries are examples of global structures. Global structures are increasingly important as inexpensive travel and communication allow all parts of the world to become interconnected culturally, economically, and politically.

   Understanding the operation of global structures can be useful, too. For instance, many people are concerned about the world's poor. They donate money to charities to help with famine and disaster relief. Some people also approve of the Canadian government giving foreign aid to poor countries. However, many of these same people do not appreciate that charity and foreign aid alone do not seem able to end world poverty. That is because charity and foreign aid have been unable to overcome the structure of social relations among countries that have created, and now sustain, global inequality.

Let us linger on this point for a moment. As we will see in Chapter 9, Development and Underdevelopment, Britain, France, and other imperial powers locked some countries into poverty when they colonized them between the seventeenth and nineteenth centuries. In the twentieth century, the poor (or "developing") countries borrowed money from these same rich countries and Western banks to pay for airports, roads, harbours, sanitation systems, basic health care, and so forth. Today, poor countries pay far more to rich countries and Western banks in interest on those loans than they receive in aid and charity. In 2002, foreign aid to the world's developing countries was only one-seventh the amount that the developing countries paid to Western banks in loan interest (United Nations, 2004: 201). It thus seems that relying exclusively on foreign aid and charity can do little to help solve the problem of world poverty. Understanding how the global structure of international relations created and helps maintain global inequality suggests new policy priorities for helping the world's poor. One such priority might involve campaigning for the cancellation of foreign debt in compensation for past injustices. Some Canadian and British government officials have been promoting this policy for the past few years.

As these examples illustrate, personal problems are connected to social structures at the micro-, macro-, and global levels. Whether the personal problem involves finding a job, keeping a marriage intact, or figuring out a way to act justly to end world poverty, social-structural considerations broaden our understanding of the problem and suggest appropriate courses of action.

THE SOCIOLOGICAL IMAGINATION

Half a century ago, the great American sociologist C. Wright Mills (1959) called the ability to see the connection between personal troubles and social structures the **sociological imagination.** He emphasized the difficulty of developing this quality of mind. His language is sexist by today's standards, but his argument is as true and inspiring today as it was in the 1950s:

When a society becomes industrialized, a peasant becomes a worker; a feudal lord is liquidated or becomes a businessman. When classes rise or fall, a man is employed or unemployed; when the rate of investment goes up or down, a man takes new heart or goes broke. When war happens, an insurance salesman becomes a rocket launcher; a store clerk, a radar man; a wife lives alone; a child grows up without a father. Neither the life of an individual nor the history of a society can be understood without understanding both.

Yet men do not usually define the troubles they endure in terms of historical change. . . . The well-being they enjoy, they do not usually impute to the big ups and downs of the society in which they live. Seldom aware of the intricate connection between the patterns of their own lives and the course of world history, ordinary men do not usually know what this connection means for the kind of men they are becoming and for the kind of history-making in which they might take part. They do not possess the quality of mind essential to grasp the interplay of men and society, of biography and history, of self and world. They cannot cope with their personal troubles in such a way as to control the structural transformations that usually lie behind them.

What they need . . . is a quality of mind that will help them to [see] . . . what is going on in the world and . . . what may be happening within themselves. It is this quality . . . that . . . may be called the sociological imagination. (Mills, 1959: 3–4)

The sociological imagination is a recent addition to the human repertoire. It is only about two centuries old. True, in ancient and medieval times, some philosophers wrote about society. However, their thinking was not sociological. They believed God and nature controlled society. They spent much of their time sketching blueprints for the ideal society and urging people to follow those blueprints. And they relied on speculation rather than on evidence to reach conclusions about how society works.

The sociological imagination was born when three modern revolutions pushed people to think about society in an entirely new way. First, the **Scientific Revolution** began about 1550. It encouraged the view that sound conclusions about the workings of society must be based on solid evidence, not just speculation. Second, the **Democratic Revolution** began about 1750. It suggested that people are responsible for organizing society and that human intervention can therefore solve social problems. Third, the **Industrial Revolution** began about 1780. It created a host of new and serious social problems that attracted the attention of many social thinkers. Let us briefly consider these three sources of the sociological imagination.

ORIGINS OF THE SOCIOLOGICAL IMAGINATION

The Scientific Revolution

It is said that a group of medieval monks once wanted to know how many angels could dance on the head of a pin. They consulted ancient books in Hebrew, Greek, and Latin. They thought long and hard. They employed all their intellectual skills to debate the issue. They did not, however, resolve the dispute. That is because they never considered inspecting the head of a pin and counting. Any such suggestion would have been considered heresy. We, in contrast, would call it the beginning of a scientific approach to the subject.

People often link the Scientific Revolution to specific ideas, such as Copernicus's theory that Earth revolves around the sun and Newton's laws of motion. However, science is less a collection of ideas than a method of inquiry. For instance, in 1609, Galileo pointed his newly invented telescope at the heavens, made some careful observations, and showed that his observations fit Copernicus's theory. This is the core of the scientific method: using evidence to make a case for a particular point of view. By the mid-1600s, some philosophers, such as Descartes in France and Hobbes in England, were calling for a science of society. When sociology emerged as a distinct discipline in the nineteenth century, commitment to the scientific method was one firm pillar of the sociological imagination.

The Democratic Revolution

The second pillar of the sociological imagination is the realization that people control society and can change it. Four hundred years ago, most Europeans thought otherwise. For them, God ordained the social order. Consider the English engraving reproduced in Figure 1.4. It shows how most educated Europeans pictured the universe in Shakespeare's time. Note the cloud at the top of the circle. The Hebrew name of God is inscribed on it. God's hand extends from the cloud. It holds a chain, which is attached to a woman representing Nature. Nature also holds a chain in her hand. It is connected to "the ape of Nature," representing humankind. The symbolism is clear: God and his intermediary, Nature, control human action. Note also that the engraving arranges everything in a linked hierarchy. The hierarchy includes the mineral, vegetable, and animal kingdoms; the elements; heavenly objects; angels; and so forth. Each level of the hierarchy corresponds to and controls some aspect of the level below it. For example, people believed Archangels regulate the movements of the planet Mercury and the movements of Mercury affect human commerce. Similarly, in the medieval view, God ordained a hierarchy of people. The richest people were seen as the closest to God and therefore deserving of great privilege. Supposedly, kings and queens ruled because God wanted them to (Tillyard, 1943).

The American Revolution (1775–83) and the French Revolution (1789–99) helped to undermine these ideas. These democratic political upheavals showed that society could experience massive change in a short period. They proved that people could replace unsatisfactory rulers. And they suggested that *people* control society. The implications for social thought were profound, for if it was possible to change society by human intervention, then a science of society could play a big role. The new science could help people figure out ways of overcoming various social problems, improving the welfare of all citizens, and finding the most effective way to reach given goals. Much of the justification for sociology as a science arose out of the democratic revolutions that shook Europe and North America.

The Industrial Revolution

The third pillar of the sociological imagination was the Industrial Revolution. It began in England about 1780. Because of the growth of industry, masses of people moved from countryside to city, worked agonizingly long hours in crowded and dangerous mines and factories, lost faith in their religions, confronted faceless bureaucracies, and reacted to the filth and poverty of their existence by means of strikes, crime, revolution, and war. Scholars had never seen a sociological laboratory like this. The Scientific Revolution suggested that a science of society is possible. The Democratic

FIGURE 1.4   THE ELIZABETHAN WORLDVIEW

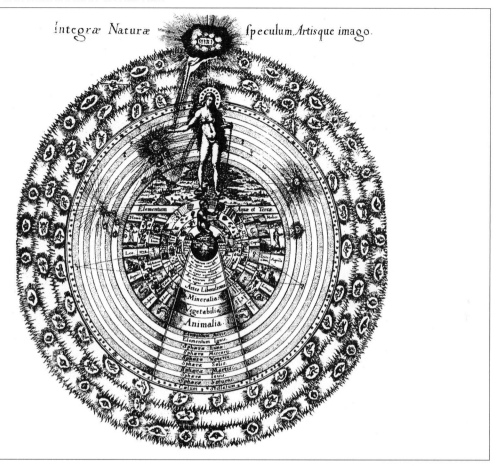

SOURCE: From Robert Fludd's *Utriusque Cosmi Historia* (1617–19). Photograph courtesy of Houghton Library, Harvard College Library.

Revolution suggested that people *can* intervene to improve society. The Industrial Revolution now presented social thinkers with a host of pressing social problems crying out for a solution. They responded by giving birth to the sociological imagination.

SOCIOLOGICAL THEORIES

THE ORIGINS OF SOCIOLOGY

The term *sociology* was coined by the French social thinker Auguste Comte in 1838 (Thompson, 1975). Comte tried to place the study of society on scientific foundations. He wanted to understand the social world as it is, not as he or anyone else imagined it should be. This was a highly original approach to the study of society. In ancient and medieval times, philosophers from diverse civilizations had sketched blueprints for the ideal society. We see evidence of

this in the work of Confucius in China, Ibn Khaldun in Tunisia, and Plato and Aristotle in Greece, to name only a few of the best-known figures. But Comte was swept up in the scientific revolution of his time. He was inspired by the astronomers and physicists of the modern era—Copernicus in Poland, Galileo in Italy, Newton in England. He wanted to test the validity of his ideas through careful observation of the real world rather than assuming that "God" or "human nature" determined the shape of society (see Box 1.1, p. 12).

Despite Comte's breakthrough, there was a tension in his work, for although he was eager to adopt the scientific method in his study of society, he was a conservative thinker, motivated by strong opposition to rapid change in French society. His was a time not only of scientific but also of political and social revolution. Comte witnessed the democratic forces unleashed by the French Revolution, the early industrialization of society, and the rapid growth of

BOX 1.1   **SCIENTIFIC VERSUS COMMONSENSE KNOWLEDGE**

To better understand how scientific and non-scientific knowledge differ, consider the following statements, each of which represents a commonly accepted basis for knowing that something is "true" in our everyday lives:

1. "The proper place for women is in the home. That's the way it's always been." This statement represents knowledge based on tradition. Although some traditional knowledge is valid (sugar will rot your teeth), some is not (masturbation will not blind you). Science is required to sort out valid from invalid knowledge.

2. "Apparently, weak magnets can be used to heal many illnesses. I read all about it in the newspaper." This statement represents knowledge based on authority. We often think something is true because we read it in an authoritative source or hear it from an expert. But authoritative sources and experts can be wrong. For example, nineteenth-century Western physicians commonly "bled" their patients with leeches to draw "poisons" from their bodies, often doing more harm than good. As this example suggests, scientists should always question authority to arrive at more valid knowledge.

3. "The car that caused the accident was dark brown. I was driving my bike last night when I saw the car accident." This statement represents knowledge based on casual observation. However, we are usually pretty careless observers. That is why good lawyers can often trip up eyewitnesses in courtrooms; eyewitnesses are rarely certain about what they saw. In general, uncertainty can be reduced by observing in a conscious and deliberate manner and by recording observations. That is just what scientists do.

4. "If you work hard, you can get ahead. I know because several of my parents' friends started off poor but are now comfortably middle class." This statement represents knowledge based on overgeneralization. For instance, if you know a few people who started off poor, worked hard, and became rich, you may think any poor person can become rich if he or she works hard enough. You may not know about the more numerous poor people who work hard and remain poor. Scientists, however, sample cases that are representative of entire populations. This enables them to avoid overgeneralization. They also avoid overgeneralization by repeating research. This ensures that research findings are not idiosyncratic.

5. "I'm right because I can't think of any contrary cases." This statement represents knowledge based on selective observation. Sometimes we ignore evidence that challenges our firmly held beliefs. Thus, you may know people who work hard but remain poor. To maintain your belief that hard work results in wealth, you will have to ignore those cases. The scientific requirement that evidence be drawn from representative samples of the population minimizes bias arising from selective observation.

6. "Mr. Smith is poor even though he works hard but that's because he has a disability. People with disabilities are the only exception to the rule that if you work hard you can get ahead." This statement represents knowledge based on qualification. Qualifications or "exceptions to the rule" are often made in everyday life—and they are in science too. The difference is that in everyday life qualifications are easily accepted as valid, whereas in scientific inquiry, they are typically treated as hypotheses that must be tested as rigorously as the original hypothesis.

7. "The Toronto Blue Jays won 50 percent of their baseball games last month but 80 percent of the games they played on Thursdays. Because it happened so often before, I bet they'll win next Thursday." This statement represents knowledge based on illogical reasoning. In everyday life, we may expect the recurrence of events without reasonable cause, ignoring the fact that rare sequences of events often occur just by chance. For example, it is possible to flip a coin 10 times and have it come up heads each time. On average, this will happen once every 1024 times you flip a coin 10 times. In the absence of any apparent reason for this happening, it is merely coincidental. It is illogical to believe otherwise. Scientists refrain from such illogical reasoning. They also use statistical techniques to distinguish between events that are probably due to chance and those that are not.

8. "I just can't be wrong." This statement represents knowledge based on ego-defence. Even scientists may be passionately committed to the conclusions they reach in their research because they have invested much time and energy in them. It is other scientists—more accurately, the whole institution of science, with its commitment to publishing research results and critically scrutinizing findings—that strictly limits ego-defence in scientific understanding.

9. "The matter is settled once and for all." This statement represents knowledge based on the premature closure of inquiry. This involves deciding that all the relevant evidence has been gathered on a particular subject. Science, however, is committed to the idea that all theories

(continued)

are only temporarily true. Matters are never settled.

10. "There must be supernatural forces at work here." This statement represents knowledge based on mystification. When we can find no rational explanation for a phenomenon, we may attribute it to forces that cannot be observed or fully understood. Although such forces may exist, scientists remain skeptical. They are committed to discovering real, observable causes of real, observable effects.

SOURCE: From *The Practice of Social Research,* by Earl Babbie. ©1992 Wadsworth, a part of Cengage Learning, Inc. Reprinted by permission. www.cengage.com/permissions

cities. What he saw shocked and angered him because rapid social change was destroying many of the things he valued, especially respect for authority. He therefore urged slow change and the preservation of much that was traditional in social life. Thus, at its very origin, sociological research was motivated by adherence to scientific methods of research *and* a vision of the ideal society.

The same sort of tension is evident in the work of the most important early figures in the history of sociology: Karl Marx, Émile Durkheim, and Max Weber. These three men lived in the period from 1820 to 1920. They witnessed various phases of Europe's wrenching transition to industrial capitalism, and they wanted to understand and explain it. Like Comte, they were all committed to the scientific method of research. However, they also wanted to chart a better course for their societies. The ideas they developed are therefore not just diagnostic tools from which we can still learn much but also, like many sociological ideas, prescriptions for combating social ills.

Before delving into social research, a sociologist must first develop hypotheses—testable claims about the social world. Testing hypotheses by means of research helps determine the validity of theories.
SOURCE: © iStockphoto.com/Winston Davidian.

THEORY, RESEARCH, AND VALUES

To clarify the tension in sociology between analysis and ideal, diagnosis and prescription, we can usefully distinguish three terms: theory, research, and values.

Sociological ideas are generally stated in the form of theories. A **theory** is a tentative explanation of some aspect of social life that states how and why certain facts are related. For example, in his theory of suicide, Durkheim showed how facts about suicide rates are related to facts about social solidarity. This enabled him to explain suicide as a function of social solidarity. In this broad definition, even a hunch qualifies as a theory if it suggests how and why certain facts are related.

After theories are formulated, the sociologist can conduct research. **Research** is the process of carefully observing social reality to assess the validity of a theory. It is because research can call the validity of a theory into question that theories are said to be only "tentative" explanations. The research process is discussed in detail in Chapter 20, Research Methods.

Before sociologists can formulate a theory, however, they must decide which problems are important enough to study and how the parts of society fit together. If they are going to recommend ways of improving the operation of some aspect of society, they must even have an opinion about what the ideal society ought to look like. As we will soon see, these issues are shaped in large measure by sociologists' values. **Values** are ideas about what is right and wrong, good and bad. Inevitably, values help sociologists formulate and favour certain theories over others (Edel, 1965; Kuhn, 1970). So sociological theories may be modified and even rejected because of research, but they are often motivated by sociologists' values.

Durkheim, Marx, and Weber initiated three of the major theoretical traditions in sociology: functionalism, conflict theory, and symbolic interactionism. A fourth approach, feminism, has arisen in recent decades to correct some of the deficiencies of the three long-established traditions. It will become clear as you read this book that there are many more sociological theories than just these four. However, because these four traditions have been especially influential in the development of sociology, you will find it useful to read a thumbnail sketch of each one here at the beginning.[1]

FUNCTIONALISM

Durkheim's theory of suicide is an early example of what sociologists now call **functionalism.** Functionalist theories incorporate four features:

1. They stress that human behaviour is governed by relatively stable patterns of social relations, or social structures. For example, Durkheim emphasized how suicide rates are influenced by patterns of social solidarity. Usually the social structures analyzed by functionalists are macrostructures.
2. Functionalism underlines how social structures maintain or undermine social stability. Typically, Durkheim analyzed how the growth of industries and cities in nineteenth-century Europe lowered the level of social solidarity and contributed to social instability. One aspect of instability, said Durkheim, is a higher suicide rate. Another is frequent strikes by workers.
3. Functionalist theories emphasize that social structures are based mainly on shared values. Thus, when Durkheim wrote about social solidarity, he sometimes meant the frequency and intensity of social interaction, but more often he thought of social solidarity as a sort of moral cement that binds people together.
4. Functionalism suggests that re-establishing equilibrium can best solve most social problems. Thus, Durkheim said that social stability could be restored in late-nineteenth-century Europe by creating new associations of employers and workers that would lower workers' expectations about what they could expect out of life. If, said Durkheim, more people could agree on wanting less, social solidarity would rise and there would be fewer strikes, fewer suicides, and so on. Functionalism, then, was a conservative response to widespread social unrest in nineteenth-century France. (A more radical response would have been to argue that if people are expressing discontent because they are getting less out of life than they expect, discontent can be lowered by figuring out ways for them to get more out of life.)

Although functionalist thinking influenced North American sociology at the end of the nineteenth century, it was only during the continent's greatest economic crisis ever, the Great Depression of 1929–39, that functionalism took deep root here (Russett, 1966). With 30 percent of the paid labour force unemployed and labour unrest reaching unprecedented levels, it is not surprising that sociologists with a conservative frame of mind were attracted to a theory that focused on how social equilibrium could be restored. Functionalist theory remained popular in North America for 30 years. It experienced a minor revival in the early 1990s but never regained the dominance it enjoyed from the 1930s to the early 1960s.

Sociologist Talcott Parsons was the foremost proponent of functionalism. He is best known for identifying how various institutions must work to ensure the smooth operation of society as a whole. For instance, when the family successfully raises new generations, the military successfully defends society against external threats, schools are able to teach students the skills and values they need to function as productive adults, and religions create a shared moral code among people, then, said Parsons, society is well integrated and in equilibrium (Parsons, 1951).

Parsons was criticized for exaggerating the degree to which members of society share common values and social institutions contribute to social harmony. This led North America's other leading functionalist, Robert Merton, to propose that social structures may have different consequences for different groups of people. Merton noted that some of those consequences might be disruptive or **dysfunctional** (Merton, 1968 [1949]). Moreover, said Merton, although some functions are **manifest** (visible and intended), others are **latent** (invisible and unintended). For instance, a manifest function of schools is to transmit skills from one generation to the next. A latent function of schools is to encourage the development of a separate youth culture that often conflicts with parents' values (Coleman, 1961; Hersch, 1998).

CONFLICT THEORY

The second major theoretical tradition in sociology emphasizes the centrality of conflict in social life. **Conflict theory** incorporates these four features:

1. It generally focuses on large, macrolevel structures, such as relations between or among classes.
2. Conflict theory shows how major patterns of inequality in society produce social stability in some circumstances and social change in others.

3. Conflict theory stresses how members of privileged groups try to maintain their advantages while subordinate groups struggle to increase theirs. From this point of view, social conditions at a given time are the expression of an ongoing power struggle between privileged and subordinate groups.
4. Conflict theory typically leads to the suggestion that eliminating privilege will lower the level of conflict and increase the sum total of human welfare.

The conflict paradigm originated in the work of Karl Marx. A generation before Durkheim, Marx observed the destitution and discontent produced by the Industrial Revolution and proposed a sweeping argument about the way societies develop (Marx, 1904 [1859]; Marx and Engels, 1972 [1848]). Marx's theory was radically different from Durkheim's. Class conflict lies at the centre of his ideas.

Marx argued that owners of industry are eager to improve the way work is organized and to adopt new tools, machines, and production methods. These innovations allow them to produce more efficiently, earn higher profits, and drive inefficient competitors out of business. However, the drive for profits causes capitalists to concentrate workers in larger and larger establishments, keep wages as low as possible, and invest as little as possible in improving working conditions. Thus, said Marx, in factory and in mine, a large and growing class of poor workers comes to oppose a small and shrinking class of wealthy owners.

Marx felt that workers would ultimately become aware of belonging to the same exploited class. Their sense of "class consciousness," he wrote, would encourage the growth of trade unions and labour parties. These organizations would eventually seek to put an end to private ownership of property, replacing it with a system in which everyone shared property and wealth. This was the "communist" society envisaged by Marx—a society in which there is no private property and everyone shares property and wealth.

Weber

Although some of Marx's ideas have been usefully adapted to the study of contemporary society, his predictions about the inevitable collapse of capitalism have been questioned. Max Weber, a German sociologist who wrote his major works a generation after Marx, was among the first to find flaws in Marx's

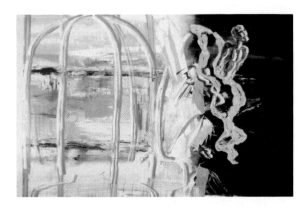

Max Weber wrote that the modern era is a bureaucratically organized "iron cage." Sociology promises to teach us both the dimensions of that cage and the possibilities for release.
SOURCE: Carol Wainio, *Untitled* (1985). Acrylic on canvas, 33″ × 350″. Photograph courtesy of the S.L. Simpson Gallery, Toronto. Courtesy Carol Wainio.

argument (Weber, 1946). Weber noted the rapid growth of the "service" sector of the economy with its many non-manual workers and professionals. He argued that many members of these occupational groups stabilize society because they enjoy higher status and income than do manual workers employed in the manufacturing sector. In addition, Weber showed that class conflict is not the only driving force of history. In his view, politics and religion are also important sources of historical change (see the following section). Other writers pointed out that Marx did not understand how investing in technology would make it possible for workers to toil fewer hours under less oppressive conditions. Nor did he foresee that higher wages, better working conditions, and welfare state benefits would pacify manual workers. Thus, we see that many of the particulars of Marx's theory were called into question by Weber and other sociologists. Nonetheless, Marx's insights about the fundamental importance of conflict in social life were influential—and still are today.

SYMBOLIC INTERACTIONISM

Above we noted that Weber criticized Marx's interpretation of the development of capitalism. Among other things, Weber argued that early capitalist development was caused not just by favourable *economic* circumstances. In addition, he said, certain *religious* beliefs facilitated robust capitalist growth. In particular, sixteenth- and seventeenth-century Protestants believed their religious doubts could be reduced, and a state of grace ensured, if they worked diligently and lived modestly. Weber called this belief the **Protestant**

ethic. He believed it had an unintended effect: People who adhered to the Protestant ethic saved and invested more than others. Thus, according to Weber, capitalism developed most robustly where the Protestant ethic took hold. He concluded that capitalism did not develop because of the operation of economic forces alone, as Marx argued. Instead, it depended partly on the religious meaning individuals attached to their work (Weber, 1958 [1904–05]).

In much of his research, Weber emphasized the importance of empathetically understanding people's motives and the meanings they attach to things to gain a clear sense of the significance of their actions. He called this aspect of his approach to sociological research the method of *Verstehen* (pronounced Fer-SHTAY-en, meaning "understanding" in German).

The idea that subjective meanings must be analyzed in any complete sociological analysis was only one of Weber's contributions to early sociological theory. Weber was also an important conflict theorist, as you will learn in later chapters. At present, however, it is enough to note that his emphasis on subjective meanings found rich soil in North America, for here was an idea that resonated deeply with the individualism of North American culture. A century ago, it was widely believed that individual talent and initiative could achieve just about anything on this continent of opportunity. Small wonder, then, that much of early North American sociology focused on the individual or, more precisely, on the connection between the individual and the larger society. For example, George Herbert Mead at the University of Chicago was the driving force behind the study of how individual identity is formed in the course of interaction with other people. We discuss his contribution in Chapter 3, Socialization. Here we note only that the work of Mead and his colleagues gave birth to symbolic interactionism, a distinctively North American theoretical tradition that continues to be a major force today.

Functionalists and conflict theorists assume that people's group memberships—whether they are young or old, male or female, rich or poor—determine their behaviour. This can sometimes make people seem like balls on a pool table: They get knocked around and cannot determine their destinations. We know from our everyday experience, however, that people are not like that. You often make choices, sometimes difficult ones. You sometimes change your mind. Moreover, two people with similar social characteristics may react differently to similar social circumstances because they may interpret those circumstances differently.

Recognizing these issues, some sociologists focus on the subjective side of social life. They work in the symbolic interactionist tradition. **Symbolic interactionism** incorporates these four features:

1. It focuses on face-to-face communication or interaction in microlevel social settings. This distinguishes it from both the functionalist and the conflict paradigms.
2. Symbolic interactionism emphasizes that an adequate explanation of social behaviour requires understanding the subjective meanings people attach to their social circumstances.
3. Symbolic interactionism stresses that people help to create their social circumstances and do not merely react to them.[2]
4. By underscoring the subjective meanings people create in small social settings, symbolic interactionists validate unpopular and unofficial viewpoints, thus increasing our understanding and tolerance of people who may be different from us.

To understand symbolic interactionism better, let us return briefly to the problem of suicide. If a police officer discovers a dead person at the wheel of a car that has run into a tree, it may be difficult to establish with certainty whether the death was an accident or a suicide. Interviewing friends and relatives to discover the driver's state of mind just before the crash may help to rule out the possibility of suicide. But, as this example illustrates, understanding the intention or motive of the actor is critical to understanding the meaning of a social action and explaining it. Suicide, then, is not just an objective social fact but also an inferred, and therefore subjective, social fact. A state of mind must be interpreted, usually by a coroner, before the dead body becomes a suicide statistic (Douglas, 1967).

For surviving family and friends, suicide is always painful and sometimes embarrassing. Insurance policies often deny payments to beneficiaries in the case of suicide. As a result, coroners are inclined to classify deaths as accidental whenever such an interpretation is plausible. Being human, they want to minimize the family's pain after such a horrible event. Sociologists believe that, for this reason, official suicide rates are about one-third lower than actual suicide rates.

The study of the subjective side of social life reveals many such inconsistencies, helping us to go beyond the official picture, deepening our understanding of how society works, and supplementing the insights gained from macrolevel analysis. Moreover, by stressing the importance and validity of subjective meanings, symbolic interactionists also increase respect for and tolerance of minority and deviant viewpoints.

FEMINIST THEORY

Few women figured prominently in the early history of sociology, largely because the strict demands placed on women by the nineteenth-century household and the lack of opportunity outside the household prevented most of them from obtaining a higher education and finding work that could support sociological research. Not surprisingly, therefore, the women who did make their mark on the discipline in its early years had unusual social backgrounds. These exceptional people introduced into the discipline gender issues that were largely ignored by Marx, Durkheim, and Weber. Appreciation for the sociological contribution of these pioneer women has grown in recent years as concern with gender issues has come to form a substantial part of the modern sociological enterprise.

Harriet Martineau is often called the first woman sociologist. Born in England at the beginning of the nineteenth century to a prosperous family, she never married and was able to support herself comfortably from her journalistic writings. Martineau translated Comte into English. She undertook critical studies of slavery and factory laws. She also wrote about gender inequality and was a leading advocate of voting rights and higher education for women, as well as gender equality in the family. As such, Martineau was one of the first feminists (Yates, 1985).

Despite its auspicious beginnings, feminist thinking had little impact on sociology until the mid-1960s, when the rise of the modern women's movement drew attention to the many remaining inequalities between women and men. Since then, feminist theory has had such a big influence on sociology it may now fairly be regarded as sociology's fourth major tradition. There are several variants of modern feminism (see Chapter 7, Gender Inequality: Economic and Political Aspects). However, the various strands of **feminist theory** share the following four features:

1. Feminist theory focuses on various aspects of patriarchy, the system of male domination in society. Patriarchy, feminists contend, is at least as important as class inequality in determining a person's opportunities in life, and perhaps more so.

2. The feminist paradigm holds that male domination and female subordination are determined not by biological necessity but by structures of power and social convention. From their point of view, women are subordinate to men only because men enjoy more legal, economic, political, and cultural rights.

3. The feminist paradigm examines the operation of patriarchy in both micro and macro settings.

4. The feminist paradigm contends that existing patterns of gender inequality can and should be changed for the benefit of all members of society. The main sources of gender inequality include differences in the way boys and girls are brought up, barriers to equal opportunity in education, paid work, and politics, and the unequal division of domestic responsibilities between women and men.

The theoretical traditions outlined above are summarized in Table 1.1. As you will see in the following pages, sociologists in Canada and elsewhere have applied them to all branches of the discipline (see Box 1.2). They have elaborated and refined each of them. Some sociologists work exclusively within one tradition. Others conduct research that borrows from more than one tradition. But all sociologists are deeply indebted to the founders of the discipline.

THEIR REVOLUTION AND OURS

In the nineteenth century, the founders of the discipline devoted their lives to solving the great sociological puzzle of their time: the causes and consequences of the Industrial Revolution. But the ideas that stirred them did not spring fully grown from their minds. Rather, their social experiences helped to shape their ideas. There is an important lesson to be learned here. In general, sociological ideas are influenced by the social settings in which they emerge.

This lesson immediately suggests two important questions. First, what are the great sociological puzzles of *our* time? Second, how are today's sociologists responding to the challenges presented by the social settings in which *they* live? We devote the rest of the book to answering these questions in depth. In the remainder of this chapter, we offer an outline of what you can expect to learn. To provide a context for this outline, we first say a few words about how the Industrial Revolution of the nineteenth century was transformed into the Postindustrial Revolution of our day.

THE INDUSTRIAL REVOLUTION

The Industrial Revolution involved the application of science and technology to industrial processes, the

---

TABLE 1.1   THE MAIN THEORETICAL TRADITIONS IN SOCIOLOGY

PARADIGM	MAIN LEVEL OF ANALYSIS	MAIN FOCUS	MAIN QUESTION	IMAGE OF IDEAL SOCIETY
Functionalism	Macro	Values	How do the institutions of society contribute to social stability?	A state of equilibrium
Conflict theory	Macro	Class inequality	How do privileged groups seek to maintain their advantages and subordinate groups seek to increase theirs, often causing social change in the process?	The elimination of privilege, especially class privilege
Symbolic interactionism	Micro	Meaning	How do individuals communicate so as to make their social settings meaningful?	Respect for the validity of minority views
Feminism	Micro and macro	Patriarchy	Which social structures and interaction processes maintain male dominance and female subordination?	The elimination of gender inequality

BOX 1.2 THE FOUR PARADIGMS IN CANADA

Each of the four major sociological paradigms has influenced research in Canada. This is evident from the following portraits of some of Canada's leading sociologists.

S. D. Clark (1910–2003) received his Ph.D. from the University of Toronto. He became the first chair of the Department of Sociology at that institution. Born in Lloydminster, Alberta, he is especially well known for his studies of Canadian social development as a process of disorganization and reorganization on a series of economic frontiers (Clark, 1968). The influence of functionalism on his work is apparent in his emphasis on the way society re-establishes equilibrium after experiencing disruptions caused by economic change.

SOURCE: Photo courtesy of Ed Clark.

John Porter (1921–79) was Canada's premier sociologist in the 1960s and 1970s. Born in Vancouver, he received his Ph.D. from the London School of Economics. He spent his academic career at Carleton University in Ottawa. There he served as chair of the Department of Sociology and Anthropology, dean of Arts and Science, and vice-president. His major work, *The Vertical Mosaic* (1965), is a study of class and power in Canada. Firmly rooted in the conflict paradigm, it influenced a generation of Canadian sociologists in their studies on social inequality, elite groups, French–English relations, and Canadian–American relations.

SOURCE: Reprinted with permission from Carleton University Archives.

Erving Goffman (1922–82) was born in Mannville, Alberta. He studied sociology and anthropology as an undergraduate at the University of Toronto and completed his Ph.D. at the University of Chicago. He pursued his academic career at the University of California, Berkeley, and the University of Pennsylvania. Goffman developed an international reputation for his "dramaturgical" approach to symbolic interactionism. This approach highlights the way people present themselves to others, managing their identities to create desired impressions on their "audience," in much the same way as actors do on stage (Goffman, 1959).

SOURCE: Courtesy the American Sociological Association.

Margrit Eichler (1942–) was born in Berlin, Germany. She did her Ph.D. at Duke University in the United States before beginning her academic career in Canada. She served as chair of the Department of Sociology at the Ontario Institute for Studies in Education and head of the Women's Studies Programme at the University of Toronto. She is internationally known for her work on feminist methodology (Eichler, 1987). Her work on family policy in Canada has influenced students, professional sociologists, and policymakers for more than two decades (Eichler, 1988).

SOURCE: Photo © Don Payne. Courtesy Margrit Eichler.

creation of factories, and the formation of a large class of "blue-collar" workers. Within about a century, it had taken root throughout Western Europe, North America, and Japan. A century after that, industry had begun implanting itself in most of the rest of the world.

As noted in our discussion of Marx, the industrial working class protested long workdays, low pay, and dangerous working conditions. Workers went on strike, formed unions, and joined political parties. Their protests forced governments to tax citizens to provide at least minimal protection against ill health, unemployment, and poverty. Working-class protests also forced employers to limit the length of the work-week to 40 hours, improve working conditions, and raise wages. Employers were still able to increase their profits, however, by making the organization of work more efficient and introducing new technologies.

Collecting taxes, administering social services, and investing heavily in technological change required the growth of government and business offices, hospitals, schools, universities, and research laboratories. Thus, alongside the old manufacturing sector of the economy, the new "service" sector was born. Its employees came to be known as "white-collar" workers. Highly trained professionals stood at the peak of the service sector. Secretaries and clerks were positioned near its base. By 1980, more than half of all people working in Canada's paid labour force were in non-manual occupations (Ornstein, 1983: 252). Sociologists call this most recent transformation of human society the **Postindustrial Revolution.** Specifically, the Postindustrial Revolution refers to the technology-driven shift from manufacturing to service industries and the consequences of that shift for virtually all human activities (Bell, 1976; Toffler, 1990).

Especially since the early 1980s, the Postindustrial Revolution has been sped up by **globalization**—the process by which formerly separate economies, states, and cultures become tied together and people become increasingly aware of their growing interdependence (Giddens, 1990: 64; Guillén, 2001). In recent decades, rapid increases in the volume of international trade, travel, and communication have broken down the isolation and independence of most countries and people. Also contributing to globalization is the growth of many institutions that bind corporations, companies, and cultures together. These processes have caused people to depend more than ever on people in other countries for products, services, ideas, and even a sense of identity.

The causes and consequences of postindustrialism and globalization form the great sociological puzzles of our time. Much of this book is devoted to analyzing postindustrialism, globalization, and their effects. In concluding this chapter, a review of some of the sociological issues raised by the Postindustrial Revolution and globalization is therefore in order.

POSTINDUSTRIALISM AND GLOBALIZATION: OPPORTUNITIES AND PITFALLS

Toward the end of the twentieth century, many observers were wildly optimistic about the benefits that postindustrialism and globalization were supposedly going to bring to humanity. One commentator proclaimed "the end of history," by which he meant that liberal capitalism had become the unrivalled socioeconomic system in the world and its dominance was bound to usher in a long era of peace, freedom, and prosperity, leaving no corner of the world untouched (Fukuyama, 1992). Similarly, in a special issue of the *New York Times Magazine* devoted to technology, one staff writer gushed:

> Individuals are acquiring more control over their lives, their minds and their bodies, even their genes, thanks to the transformations in medicine, communications, transportation and industry. At the same time, these technologies are providing social benefits and undoing some of the damage of the past. Technology helps to conserve natural resources and diminish pollution. . . . The Information Revolution, besides enabling us to visit Mars at will, is fostering peaceful cooperation on Earth by decentralizing power. Political tyrants and demagogic warmongers are losing control now that their subjects have tools to communicate directly with one another. People are using the tools to do their jobs without leaving their families. They're forming new communities in cyberspace and forming new bonds with their neighbors in real space. Technology has the potential to increase individual freedom and strengthen community. (Tierney, 1997: 46–7)

This and similar outpourings of optimism were written before the stock-market crash of 2000, the terrorist attacks of September 11, 2001, the second invasion of Iraq by the United States in 2003, and heightened fears about the consequences of climate change that surrounded the 2005 hurricane season. But even before these devastating shocks changed the minds of all but the most starry-eyed observers, sociologists were more realistic about the prospects of humanity. On the whole, they agreed that postindustrialism and globalization promise many exciting opportunities to enhance the quality of life and increase human freedom. But they also saw many social-structural barriers to the realization of that promise.

The unresolved social issues that confront us in the era of postindustrialism and globalization fall under three headings. Each issue is addressed in later chapters:

1. *Autonomy versus constraint.* One of the major themes that emerges from *New Society* is that many people are freer to construct their own identities than ever before. Almost everyone used to retain their religious, ethnic, racial, and sexual identities for a lifetime, even if they were not particularly comfortable with them. In the era of postindustrialism and globalization, however, various social developments and technological advances, ranging from international migration to the World Wide Web to greater acceptance of sexual diversity, free people from traditional constraints. The theme of increasing personal autonomy is taken up in Chapter 2, Culture; Chapter 3, Socialization; Chapter 4, Gender and Sexuality; Chapter 5, The Mass Media; and Chapter 13, Religion.

   Some chapters, however, point out that we experience increased freedom only within certain limits. For example, we can choose a far wider variety of consumer products than ever before. But consumerism itself increasingly seems a compulsory way of life (Chapter 2, Culture). Moreover, it is a way of life that threatens the natural environment (Chapter 16, Sociology and the Environment). Meanwhile, new technologies, such as surveillance cameras, cause us to modify our behaviour and act in more conformist ways (Chapter 14, Deviance and Crime). As these examples show, the autonomy promised by postindustrialism is only half the story. The other half is that postindustrialism places new constraints on us.

2. *Prosperity versus inequality.* The second major theme that emerges from *New Society* is that postindustrialism opens up new economic, political, and educational opportunities. It makes work less onerous for many people. It raises the average standard of living. It enables women in particular to make rapid strides in all institutional spheres.

Again, however, we must face the less rosy aspects of postindustrialism. Tremendous economic and political inequality persists between women and men (Chapter 7, Gender Inequality: Economic and Political Aspects). So does inequality between Aboriginal and other Canadians (Chapter 8, Race and Ethnic Relations). Inequality between rich and poor in Canada has not decreased (Chapter 6, Social Stratification). It is maintained partly by the educational system (Chapter 12, Education). Inequality between rich and poor nations has increased sharply (Chapter 9, Development and Underdevelopment). There are more good jobs at the top of the occupational structure but many more bad jobs at the bottom (Chapter 11, Work and Occupations). The quality of the Canadian health-care system is threatened at precisely the moment when our population is rapidly aging and most in need of health care (Chapter 17, Health and Aging). And although elections are regularly held throughout much of the world, it is an illusion to think that democracy has conquered the planet (Chapter 18, Politics and Social Movements). Thus, economic and political inequality persist despite growing prosperity and opportunity.

3. *Diversity versus uniformity.* The third major theme that emerges from *New Society* is that postindustrial society is more tolerant of diversity than any previous form of society. Immigration policies no longer stipulate racial, ethnic, or religious criteria for entry into the country. As a result, our cities are more socially heterogeneous than ever before (Chapter 15, Population and Urbanization). The traditional nuclear family made up of mother, father, and children has given way to a wide variety of new family forms. Dozens of radio stations, hundreds of TV channels, thousands of newspapers and magazines, hundreds of thousands of CD titles, millions of books, and tens of millions of websites are now available to us.

   Yet despite growing social diversity, there is a strong push to conformity in many spheres of life. For example, most of our diverse cultural consumption is governed by the tastes and the profit motive of vast media conglomerates, most of them American-owned (Chapter 5, The Mass Media). Powerful interests are trying to shore up the traditional nuclear family despite its inappropriateness for many people in postindustrial society (Chapter 10, Families). The globalization of economic, political, and cultural affairs may be threatening the survival of distinct national cultures (Chapter 19, Globalization). The push to uniformity thus counters the trend toward growing social diversity.

WHY SOCIOLOGY?

The renowned English sociologist Anthony Giddens wrote that we live in an era "suspended between extraordinary opportunity . . . and global catastrophe" (Giddens, 1982: 166). Because of the collapse of the USSR in 1991 and the work of international terrorists, nuclear, chemical, and biological catastrophes are more likely now than they were just a few years ago. A whole range of environmental issues, profound inequalities in the wealth of nations and of classes, racial and ethnic violence, and unsolved problems in the relations

between women and men continue to stare us in the face and profoundly affect the quality of our daily life.

Despair and apathy is one possible response to these complex issues. But it is not a response that humans have often favoured. If it were our nature to give up hope, we would still be sitting around half-naked in the mud outside a cave.

People are more inclined to look for ways of improving their lives, and this period of human history is full of opportunities to do so. We have, for example, advanced to the point where for the first time we have the means to feed and educate everyone in the world. Similarly, it now seems possible to erode some of the inequalities that have always been with us and have always been the major source of human conflict. Students of sociology pursue careers that further such goals (see Box 1.3).

BOX 1.3   CAREERS IN SOCIOLOGY

Students often ask, "Can I get a good job with a sociology degree?" "Exactly what kind of work could I do with a major in sociology?" "Aren't all the good jobs these days in technical areas and the natural sciences?" To answer these questions—and to help you decide whether a sociology or other social science major makes sense for you—consider the following data on the employment of Canadians with degrees in sociology and related fields.

A study based on 1988 data found that a higher percentage of Canadian sociology graduates were employed full-time than were graduates in the other social sciences (Guppy and Hedley, 1993). A study based mainly on 1996 data (Allen, 1999) showed that, in Canada

· the unemployment rate among social science graduates was lower than among graduates in math, physics, engineering, agriculture, and biology
· between 1991 and 1996, there were more new jobs for people with social science degrees than for people with degrees in other fields
· although women earned less than men in all fields in 1996, the discrepancy between men's and women's income was smallest among social science graduates

On the basis of these findings it seems that sociology degrees promise more employment security for both men and women, and less income discrimination against women, than other degrees. It also seems that the postindustrial economy requires more new employees with a social science background than new employees with a background in some technical and scientific fields.

Tens of thousands of Canadians have sociology B.A.s. A sociology B.A. improves your understanding of the diverse social conditions affecting men and women, people with different sexual orientations, and people from different countries, regions, classes, races, and ethnic groups. Therefore, people with a B.A. in sociology tend to be attracted to jobs requiring good people skills and jobs involved with managing and promoting social change (see Table 1.2). Often, people with a B.A. in sociology go on to graduate school and obtain professional degrees in other fields, including law, urban planning, industrial relations, social work, and public policy. You will therefore find many people with sociology B.A.s working as lawyers, urban planners, city managers, and health-care and education administrators.

Most people with a graduate degree in sociology teach and conduct research in universities, with research being a more important component of the job in larger and more prestigious institutions. But many sociologists do not teach. Instead, they conduct research and give policy advice in a wide range of settings outside the system of higher education. In many federal government agencies, for example, sociologists are employed as researchers and policy consultants. Sociologists also conduct research and policy analysis in trade unions, non-governmental organizations, and professional and public interest associations. In the private sector, you can find sociologists practising their craft in firms specializing in public opinion polling, management consulting, market research, standardized testing, and "evaluation research," which assesses the impact of particular policies and programs before or after they go into effect. *(continued)*

BOX 1.3   *(continued)*

One way of seeing the benefits of a sociological education is to compile a list of some of the famous practical idealists who studied sociology in university. That list includes several former heads of state, among them President Fernando Cardoso of Brazil, President Tomas Masaryk of Czechoslovakia, Prime Minister Edward Seaga of Jamaica, and President Ronald Reagan of the United States. The current first lady of the United States, Michelle Obama, also has a sociology degree. The former vice-president of the Liberal Party of Canada and former president and vice-chancellor of York University in Toronto, Lorna Marsden, is a sociologist. Anthony Giddens, former director of the London School of Economics and adviser to former British Prime Minister Tony Blair, also holds a sociology doctorate. So do Martin Goldfarb,

chairman, president, and CEO of Goldfarb Consultants International; and Donna Dasko, senior vice-president of Environics, two of Canada's leading public opinion firms with offices and affiliates around the world. Alex Himelfarb, former clerk of the Privy Council, former secretary to the Cabinet in Ottawa, and now the Canadian ambassador to Italy, holds a sociology Ph.D. too. British Columbia native Steve Nash of the Phoenix Suns is widely considered the best team player in professional basketball today. His agent claims he is "the most color-blind person I've ever known" (Robbins, 2005). Arguably, Nash's sociology degree contributes to his team-building ability and his performance on the court by helping him to better understand the importance of groups and diverse social conditions in shaping human behaviour.

TABLE 1.2 JOBS COMMONLY HELD BY CANADIANS WITH DEGREES IN SOCIOLOGY

Government

community affairs officer
urban/regional planner
legislative aide
affirmative action/employment equity worker
foreign service officer
human rights officer
personnel coordinator

Research

social research specialist
consumer researcher
data analyst
market researcher
survey researcher
census officer/analyst
demographer/population analyst
system analyst

Community Affairs

occupational/career counsellor
homeless/housing worker
public health/hospital administrator
child development technician
public administration assistant
social assistance advocate
resident planning aide
group home worker
rehabilitation program worker
rural health outreach worker
housing coordinator
fundraising director/assistant
caseworker/aide
community organizer
youth outreach worker

Corrections

corrections officer
criminology assistant
police officer
rehabilitation counsellor
criminal investigator
juvenile court worker
parole officer

Teaching

college/university placement worker
public health educator
teacher
admissions counsellor

Business

market analyst
project manager
sales representative
real estate agent
journalist
public relations officer
actuary
insurance agent
human resources manager
production manager
labour relations officer
administrative assistant
quality control manager
merchandiser/purchaser
computer analyst
data entry manager
publishing officer
advertising officer
sales manager

SOURCE: Guppy and Hedley (1993). Reprinted with permission from the Canadian Sociological Association.

Although sociology offers no easy solutions as to how the goal of improving society may be accomplished, it does promise a useful way of understanding our current predicament and seeing possible ways of dealing with it, of leading us a little farther away from the mud outside the cave. You sampled sociology's ability to tie personal troubles to social-structural issues when we discussed suicide. You reviewed the major theoretical perspectives that enable sociologists to connect the personal with the social-structural. When I outlined the half-fulfilled promises of postindustrialism and globalization, you saw sociology's ability to provide an understanding of where we are and where we can head.

I frankly admit that the questions raised in this book are tough to answer. Sharp controversy surrounds them all. However, I am sure that if you try to grapple with them, you will enhance your understanding of your society's, and your own, possibilities. In brief, sociology can help you figure out where you fit in to society and how you can make society fit you. That, fundamentally, is sociology's goal.

SUMMARY

1. Durkheim showed that even apparently non-social and antisocial actions are influenced by social structures. Specifically, he showed how levels of social solidarity affect suicide rates.

2. Because of the rise in youth suicide, the pattern of suicide rates in Canada today is not exactly the same as in Durkheim's France. Nevertheless, Durkheim's theory explains the contemporary Canadian pattern well.

3. Sociologists analyze the connection between personal troubles and social structures.

4. Sociologists analyze the influence of three levels of social structure on human action: microstructures, macrostructures, and global structures.

5. Values suggest which sociological research questions are worth asking and how the parts of society fit together. Values underlie sociological theories. A theory is a tentative explanation of some aspect of social life. It states how and why specific facts are connected. Research is the process of carefully observing social reality to assess the validity of a theory.

6. There are four major theoretical traditions in sociology. Functionalism analyzes how social order is supported by macrostructures. Conflict theory analyzes how social inequality is maintained and challenged. Symbolic interactionism analyzes how meaning is created when people communicate in microlevel settings. Feminism focuses on the social sources of patriarchy in both macro and micro settings.

7. The rise of sociology was stimulated by the Scientific, Industrial, and Democratic Revolutions.

8. The Postindustrial Revolution is the technology-driven shift from manufacturing to service industries and the consequences of that shift for virtually all human activities. Globalization is the process by which formerly separate economies, states, and cultures become tied together and people become increasingly aware of their growing interdependence.

9. The causes and consequences of postindustrialism and globalization form the great sociological puzzle of our time. The tension between autonomy and constraint, prosperity and inequality, and diversity and uniformity are among the chief interests of sociology today.

QUESTIONS TO CONSIDER

1. Do you think the promise of autonomy, prosperity, and diversity will be realized in the twenty-first century? Why or why not?

2. In this chapter you learned how variations in the level of social solidarity affect the suicide rate. How do you think variations in social solidarity might affect other areas of social life, such as criminal behaviour and political protest?

3. Is a science of society possible? If you agree that such a science is possible, what are its advantages over common sense? What are its limitations?

GLOSSARY

Altruistic suicide occurs in settings that exhibit high levels of social solidarity, according to Durkheim. Altruistic suicide results from norms very tightly governing behaviour.

Anomic suicide occurs in settings that exhibit low levels of social solidarity, according to Durkheim. Anomic suicide results from vaguely defined norms governing behaviour.

Conflict theory generally focuses on large, macrolevel structures, such as the relations between or among classes. It shows how major patterns of inequality in society produce social stability in some circumstances and social change in others. It stresses how members of privileged groups try to maintain their advantages while subordinate groups struggle to increase theirs. And it typically leads to the suggestion that eliminating privilege will lower the level of conflict and increase the sum total of human welfare.

The **Democratic Revolution** began about 1750. It suggested that people are responsible for organizing society and that human intervention can therefore solve social problems.

Dysfunctional consequences are effects of social structures that create social instability.

Egoistic suicide results from a lack of integration of the individual into society because of weak social ties to others.

Ethnomethodology is the study of how people make sense of what others do and say in terms of norms that exist independently of individual social actors.

Feminist theory claims that patriarchy is at least as important as class inequality in determining a person's opportunities in life. It holds that male domination and female subordination are determined not by biological necessity but by structures of power and social convention. It examines the operation of patriarchy in both micro and macro settings. And it contends that existing patterns of gender inequality can and should be changed for the benefit of all members of society.

Functionalist theory stresses that human behaviour is governed by relatively stable social structures. It underlines how social structures maintain or undermine social stability. It emphasizes that social structures are based mainly on shared values or preferences. And it suggests that re-establishing equilibrium can best solve most social problems.

Global structures are patterns of social relations that lie outside and above the national level. They include international organizations, patterns of worldwide travel and communication, and the economic relations between and among countries.

Globalization is the process by which formerly separate economies, states, and cultures are becoming tied together and people are becoming increasingly aware of their growing interdependence.

The **Industrial Revolution** refers to the rapid economic transformation that began in Britain in the 1780s. It involved the large-scale application of science and technology to industrial processes, the creation of factories, and the formation of a working class.

Latent functions are invisible and unintended effects of social structures.

Macrostructures are overarching patterns of social relations that lie outside and above one's circle of intimates and acquaintances. Macrostructures include classes, bureaucracies, and power systems, such as patriarchy.

Manifest functions are visible and intended effects of social structures.

Microstructures are the patterns of relatively intimate social relations formed during face-to-face interaction. Families, friendship circles, and work associations are all microstructures.

Patriarchy is the traditional system of economic and political inequality between women and men.

The **Postindustrial Revolution** refers to the technology-driven shift from manufacturing to service industries and the consequences of that shift for virtually all human activities.

The **Protestant ethic** is the Protestant belief originating in the sixteenth and seventeenth centuries that religious doubts can be reduced, and a state of grace ensured, if people work diligently and live ascetically. According to Weber, the Protestant ethic had the unintended effect of increasing savings and investment and thus stimulating capitalist growth.

Research is the process of systematically observing reality to assess the validity of a theory.

The **Scientific Revolution** began about 1550. It encouraged the view that sound conclusions about the workings of society must be based on solid evidence, not just speculation.

Social solidarity refers to (1) the degree to which group members share beliefs and values and (2) the intensity and frequency of their interaction.

Social structures are relatively stable patterns of social relations.

The **sociological imagination** is the quality of mind that enables a person to see the connection between personal troubles and social structures.

Sociology is the systematic study of human behaviour in social context.

Symbolic interactionism focuses on face-to-face communication, or interaction in microlevel social settings. It emphasizes that an adequate explanation of social behaviour requires understanding the subjective meanings people attach to their social circumstances. It stresses that people help to create their social circumstances and do not merely react to them. And by underscoring the subjective meanings people create in small social settings, symbolic interactionism validates unpopular and non-official viewpoints. This increases our understanding and tolerance of people who may be different from us.

A **theory** is a tentative explanation of some aspect of social life that states how and why certain facts are related.

Values are ideas about what is right and wrong.

SUGGESTED READING

Brym, Robert J. (2009). *Sociology as a Life or Death Issue.* Toronto: Nelson. A guide to the sociological craft for beginners, emphasizing how sociology can help people live longer and better lives. Focuses on the sociological analysis of "natural" disasters, suicide, and hip-hop.

The *Canadian Journal of Sociology* will give you a taste of the practice of sociology in Canada. Go to http://ejournals.library.ualberta.ca/index.php/CJS/index for book reviews and online articles. Visit the website of the Canadian Sociological Association at http://www.csaa.ca for sociological news and conferences.

Stephens, W. Richard, Jr. (1998). *Careers in Sociology.* New York: Allyn & Bacon. In this book, 18 sociology graduates talk about the diverse and fascinating careers they have pursued. It is available online at http://www.abacon.com/socsite/careers.html.

NOTES

1. You will find more detailed discussion of these theories throughout the book. For example, on functionalism, see Chapters 12 and 13. On conflict theory, see Chapters 6, 10, 13, and 18. On symbolic interactionism, see Chapters 3 and 14. On feminism, see Chapters 4, 7, 10, and 18.

2. By emphasizing how social reality is constructed during interaction, symbolic interactionists downplay the importance of norms and understandings that precede any given interaction. **Ethnomethodology** tries to correct this shortcoming. Ethnomethodologists study how people make sense of what others do and say but stress that norms exist independently of individual social actors. Indeed, in the ethnomethodological view, everyday interactions could not take place without pre-existing shared norms. Say you pass an acquaintance on the street, who offers a friendly "How are you?" If you proceed to outline in detail your financial situation, your love life, interesting developments at work, and so forth, the acquaintance will quickly become annoyed. Most people expect "How are you?" to be answered with an equally brief reply. Violate the norm, and communication quickly breaks down (Garfinkel, 1967).

WEB RESOURCES

Companion Website for This Book

http://www.newsociety6e.nelson.com
Begin by clicking on the Student Resources section of the website. Next, select the chapter you are studying from the pull-down menu. From the Student Resources page, you have easy access to InfoTrac College Edition® and other resources, such as the Glossary, Test Yourself questions, and additional readings. The website also has many useful tips to aid you in your study of sociology.

InfoTrac College Edition Search Terms

Visit http://www.infotrac-college.com for access to more than 20 million articles from nearly 6000 sources when doing your online research.

PART TWO

Culture

CHAPTER TWO

Culture

Robert J. Brym
UNIVERSITY OF TORONTO

In this chapter you will learn that

- Culture is the sum of ideas, practices, and material objects that people create to adapt to, and thrive in, their environments.

- Humans have been able to thrive in their environments because of their unique ability to think abstractly, cooperate with one another, and make tools.

- We can see the contours of culture most sharply if we are neither too deeply immersed in it nor too much removed from it.

- As societies become more complex, culture becomes more diversified and consensus declines in many areas of life. This increases human freedom.

- As societies become more complex, the limits within which freedom may increase become more rigid. This constrains human freedom.

- Although culture is created to solve human problems, it sometimes has negative consequences that create new problems.

INTRODUCTION

CULTURE AS PROBLEM SOLVING

Canadian hockey legend Wayne Gretzky refused to get his hair cut while playing on the road because the last time he did, his team lost. He always put his equipment on in the same order: left shin pad, left stocking, right shin pad, right stocking, pants, left skate, right skate, shoulder pads, left elbow pad, right elbow pad, and finally, jersey—with only the right side tucked into his pants. During warm-up, he would always shoot his first puck far to the right of the goal. When he went back to the dressing room, he would drink a Diet Coke, a glass of ice water, a Gatorade, and another Diet Coke—and always in that order ("Mad About Hockey," 2002). He believed these routines brought him luck.

Like soldiers going off to battle, university students about to write final exams, and other people in

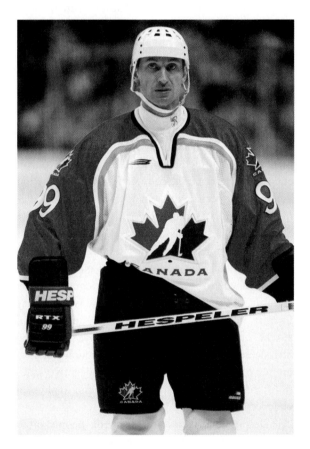

Hockey legend Wayne Gretzky would tuck only the right side of his jersey into his pants. This superstitious practice helped to put his mind at ease before and during play. It is an example of how people create culture to cope with anxiety and other concrete problems they face.

SOURCE: © The Canadian Press (F. Scott Grant).

high-stress situations, athletes invent routines to help them stop worrying and focus on the job at hand. Some wear a lucky piece of jewellery or item of clothing. Others say special words or a quick prayer. Still others cross themselves. And then there are those who engage in more elaborate rituals. For example, sociologists Cheryl and Daniel Albas of the University of Manitoba interviewed 300 university students about their superstitious practices before final exams. One student felt she would do well only if she ate a sausage and two eggs sunny-side up on the morning of each exam. The sausage had to be arranged vertically on the left side of her plate and the eggs placed to the right of the sausage so they formed the "100" percent she was aiming for (Albas and Albas, 1989). Of course, the ritual had more direct influence on her cholesterol level than on her grade. But indirectly it may have had the desired effect. To the degree it helped to relieve her anxiety and relax her, she may have done better in exams.

When some people say *culture*, they refer to opera, ballet, art, and fine literature. For sociologists, however, this definition is too narrow. Sociologists define **culture** broadly as all the socially transmitted ideas, practices, and material objects that people create to deal with real-life problems. For example, when Gretzky developed his dressing habits and the university student invented the ritual of preparing for exams by eating a sausage and eggs arranged just so, they were creating culture in the sociological sense. These practices helped Gretzky and the student deal with the real-life problem of high anxiety. Similarly, tools help people solve the problem of how to plant crops and build houses. Religion helps people face the problem of death and how to give meaning to life. Tools and religion are also elements of culture because they, too, help people solve real-life problems.

Note, however, that religion, technology, and many other elements of culture differ from the superstitions of athletes and undergraduates in one important respect. Superstitions are often unique to the individuals who create them. In contrast, religion and technology are widely shared. They are even passed on from one generation to the next. How does cultural sharing take place? By means of human interaction, communication, and learning. In other words, culture becomes shared when it is socially transmitted. A **society** involves people interacting socially and sharing culture, usually in a defined geographical area.[1] Culture, then, is the sum of the *socially transmitted* ideas, practices, and material objects that enable people to adapt to, and thrive in, their environments.

THE ORIGINS OF CULTURE

You can appreciate the importance of culture for human survival by considering the predicament of early humans about 100 000 years ago. They lived in harsh natural environments. They had poor physical endowments, being slower runners and weaker fighters than many other animals. Yet, despite these disadvantages, they survived. More than that—they prospered and came to dominate nature. This was possible largely because they were the smartest creatures around. Their sophisticated brains enabled them to create cultural survival kits of enormous complexity and flexibility. These cultural survival kits contained three main tools. Each tool was a uniquely human talent. Each gave rise to a different element of culture.

The first tool in the human cultural survival kit was **abstraction,** the capacity to create ideas or ways of thinking. **Symbols,** for example, are one important type of idea. They are things that carry particular meanings. Languages, mathematical notations, and signs are all sets of symbols. Symbols allow us to classify experience and generalize from it. For example, we recognize that we can sit on many objects but that only some of those objects have four legs, a back, and space for one person. We distinguish the latter from other objects by giving them a name: "chairs." By the time a baby reaches the end of her first year, she has heard that word repeatedly and understands that it refers to a certain class of objects. True, a few chimpanzees have been taught how to make some signs with their hands. In this way, they have learned a few dozen words and how to string together some simple phrases. But even these extraordinarily intelligent animals cannot learn any rules of grammar, teach other chimps what they know, or advance much beyond the vocabulary of a human toddler (Pinker, 1994). Abstraction at anything beyond the most rudimentary level is a uniquely human capacity. The ability to abstract enables humans to learn and transmit knowledge in a way no other animal can.

Cooperation is the second main tool in the human cultural survival kit. It is the capacity to create a complex social life by establishing **norms.** Norms are standards of behaviour or generally accepted ways of doing things. When we raise children and build schools, we are cooperating to reproduce and advance the human race. When we create communities and industries, we are cooperating by pooling resources and encouraging people to acquire specialized skills, thus enabling them to accomplish things no person could possibly do alone. An enormous variety of social arrangements and institutions, ranging from health-care systems to forms of religious worship to political parties, demonstrate the advanced human capacity to cooperate and adhere to norms. Of course, there is also plenty of war, crime, and revolution in the world. However, even when people engage in conflict, they must cooperate and respect norms or fail to achieve their survival aims. The bank robber who is left stranded by his getaway man will be caught; the navy captain whose sailors mutiny will lose the battle.

Production is the third main tool in the human cultural survival kit. It involves devising and using tools and techniques that improve our ability to take what we want from nature. Such tools and techniques are known as **material culture.** Of course, all animals take from nature in order to subsist, and an ape may sometimes use a rock to break another object or use a stick to keep its balance in a fast-flowing stream. But only humans are sufficiently intelligent and dexterous to *make* tools and use them to produce everything from food to computers. Understood in this sense, production is a uniquely human activity.

Table 2.1 illustrates each of the basic human capacities and their cultural offshoots in the field of medicine. As in medicine, so in all fields of human endeavour: abstraction, cooperation, and production give rise to specific kinds of ideas, norms, and elements of material culture.

In concluding this discussion of the origins of culture, we must note that people are usually rewarded when they follow cultural guidelines and punished when they do not. Taken together, these rewards and punishments, aimed at ensuring conformity, are known as **sanctions** or the system of **social control.** Rewards (or positive sanctions) include everything from praise and encouragement to money and power. Punishments (or negative sanctions) range from avoidance and contempt to physical violence and arrest.

Despite efforts to control them, people often reject elements of existing culture and create new elements of culture. Reasons for this are discussed in Chapter 14 (Deviance and Crime) and Chapter 18 (Politics and Social Movements). Here, it is enough to say that, just as social control is needed to ensure stable patterns of interaction, so resistance to social control is

TABLE 2.1 THE BUILDING BLOCKS OF CULTURE

THE HUMAN CAPACITY FOR . . .	ABSTRACTION	COOPERATION	PRODUCTION
Gives rise to these elements of culture . . .	Ideas	Norms and values	Material culture
In medicine, for example...	*Theories* are developed about how a certain drug might cure a disease	*Experiments* are conducted to test whether the drug works as expected	*Treatments* are developed on the basis of the experimental results

SOURCE: Adapted from Robert Bierstedt, *The Social Order* (New York: McGraw-Hill, 1963).

needed to ensure cultural innovation and social renewal. Stable but vibrant societies are able to find a balance between social control and cultural innovation.

CULTURE FROM THE MARGINS

Martians can never hope to grasp the tacit knowledge of real human beings. On the other hand, they sometimes see things real human beings fail to notice.

— Michael Ignatieff (2000: x)

I was once introduced to an interesting woman at a party and began a conversation with her that started agreeably. Within ten minutes, however, I found myself on the other side of the room, my back pressed hard against the wall, trying to figure out how I could politely end our interaction. I wasn't immediately aware of the reason for my discomfort. Only after I told the woman that I had to make an important phone call and had left the room did I realize the source of the problem: She had invaded my culturally defined comfort zone. Research shows the average North American prefers to stand 75 to 90 centimetres (30 to 36 inches) away from strangers or acquaintances when they are engaged in face-to-face interaction (Hall, 1959: 158–80). But this woman had recently arrived from her home in a part of the Middle East where the culturally defined comfort zone is generally smaller. She stood only about 50 centimetres (20 inches) from me as we spoke. Without thinking, I retreated half a step. Without thinking, she advanced half a step. And soon we had waltzed across the faculty club lounge, completely unaware of what we were doing, until I had no further room to retreat and had to concoct a means of escape.

As this example shows, culture, despite its central importance in human life, is often invisible to people who are immersed in it. That is, people tend to take their own culture for granted; it usually seems so sensible and natural they rarely think about it. I was unable to understand how my culture was affecting me while I was in its grip. I understood its effect only when I removed myself from the faculty club lounge, the immediate context of its operation, and thought hard about how it was making me behave.

Taking public transportation often forces us to abandon our culturally defined personal space. However, this abandonment of personal space is itself a cultural norm.
SOURCE: Andrew Benyei, *Commuters*.

If people often take their own culture for granted, they are often startled when confronted by cultures other than their own. That is, the ideas, norms, and techniques of other cultures frequently seem odd, irrational, and even inferior. Judging another culture exclusively by the standards of our own is called **ethnocentrism.** Ethnocentrism impairs the sociological understanding of culture as much as taking our own culture for granted does.

The negative effect of ethnocentrism on sociological understanding may be illustrated by a practice that seems bizarre to many Westerners: cow worship among Hindu peasants in India. Hindu peasants refuse to slaughter cattle and eat beef because, for them, the cow is a religious symbol of life. Pin-up calendars throughout rural India portray beautiful women with the bodies of fat white cows, milk jetting out of each teat. Cows are permitted to wander the streets, defecate on the sidewalks, and stop to chew their cud in busy intersections and on railroad tracks, causing traffic to come to a halt. In Madras, the police maintain fields where stray cows that have fallen ill can graze and be nursed back to health. The government even runs old age homes for cows, where dry and decrepit cattle are kept free of charge. All this seems inscrutable to most Westerners, for it takes place amid poverty and hunger that could presumably be alleviated if only the peasants would slaughter their "useless" cattle for food instead of squandering scarce resources on feeding and protecting them.

The trouble is, ethnocentrism misleads many Western observers (Harris, 1974: 3–32). Cow worship, it turns out, is an economically rational practice in rural India. For one thing, Indian peasants can't afford tractors, so cows are needed to give birth to oxen, which are in high demand for plowing. For another, the cows produce hundreds of millions of kilograms of recoverable manure, about half of which is used as fertilizer and half as cooking fuel. With oil, coal, and wood in short supply, and with the peasants unable to afford chemical fertilizers, cow dung is, well, a godsend. What is more, cows in India don't cost much to maintain since they eat mostly food that isn't fit for human consumption. And they represent an important source of protein and a livelihood for members of low-ranking castes, who have the right to dispose of the bodies of dead cattle. These "untouchables" eat beef and form the work force of India's large leather-craft industry. Thus, the protection of

cows by means of cow worship is in fact a perfectly sensible and highly efficient economic practice. It only seems irrational when judged by the standards of Western agribusiness.

We can draw much the same lesson from the case of cow worship in India as from my hurried exit from the faculty club lounge. Culture is most clearly visible from the margins, as it were. We see its contours most sharply if we are neither too deeply immersed in it (as I was during the faculty club conversation) nor too much removed from it (as most Western observers are when they analyze cow worship in India). Said differently, if you refrain from taking your own culture for granted and judging other cultures by the standards of your own, you will have taken important first steps toward developing a sociological understanding of culture.

THE TWO FACES OF CULTURE

Having defined culture, discussed its origins, and located the ideal vantage point for analyzing it, we can now turn to the chapter's main theme. You will now see that although some aspects of culture make us freer, others constrain and even endanger us.

When we develop new ideas, practices, and artifacts, we give ourselves more choices and often come closer to realizing our full human potential. For example, you will see in the following text that we are now freer than ever to draw on all cultures in all their variety. This allows us to fashion our identities to suit our individual tastes. The story is much the same whether we consider ethnic identities, religious beliefs, political affiliations, or sexual orientations. We now become who we are less because traditional authority imposes a set of cultural definitions on us, and more because we are able to choose who we want to be.

However, cultural freedom develops within definite limits. Beyond those limits it is more and more difficult to move. In particular, our lives are increasingly governed by the twin forces of rationalization and consumerism:

- **Rationalization** is the application of the most efficient means to achieve given goals and the unintended, negative consequences of doing so. Modern bureaucracies exemplify the rationalization process (Weber, 1946 [1922]). The factory, the government office, the military, the system of higher education, and the institutions of science

Rationalization constrains freedom.
© iStockphoto.com/Alex Gumerov.

all seek to apply the most efficient means to achieving given goals (see Box 2.1, p. 34). Yet bureaucracies are composed of unelected officials. Consequently, they concentrate power and threaten democracy. Moreover, bureaucracies discourage officeholders from considering what the goals of their organization ought to be. Bureaucrats are asked only to determine the best way of achieving the goals defined by their superiors. Officeholders thus lose their spontaneity and their inventiveness. Like other aspects of the rationalization process, the growth of bureaucracy thus constrains our freedom.

- **Consumerism** is a lifestyle that involves defining ourselves in terms of the goods we purchase. Some sociologists argue that consumerism impoverishes the self and society by drawing resources and attention away from pressing social issues and encouraging environmentally dangerous levels of consumption. From this point of view, culture, which started out as a means of solving real-life problems, has become the biggest real-life problem of all (Postman, 1992).

Let us begin our examination of the two faces of culture by first considering the ways in which culture makes us freer.

CULTURE AS FREEDOM

CULTURAL DIVERSIFICATION AND GLOBALIZATION

In the 1950s, the Christmas pageant was a fixture of every elementary school in the country. Today, some Canadian public schools have abolished Christmas pageants. Others have put Christmas on par with the Hindu Diwali, the Jewish Chanukah, and the seasonal festivals of other ethnic and religious groups. In some schools, an ethnically and religiously neutral "winter solstice" forms the basis of celebration in mid- to late December. The reason for this change is plain: According to the most recent census, 23 percent of Canadians do not identify with Christianity (Statistics Canada, 2005). Moreover, many Christians recognize that the use of public institutions to promote their religion is an imposition that creates discomfort for many minority students and denies the value of

In the last quarter of the nineteenth century, it was already clear that turning scientific principles into technological innovations was going to require not just genius but substantial resources, especially money and organization. The first "invention factory" was established by Thomas Edison at Menlo Park, New Jersey, in the late 1870s. Historian of science Robert Pool notes:

> The most important factor in Edison's success—outside of his genius for invention—was the organization he had set up to assist him. By 1878, Edison had assembled at Menlo Park a staff of thirty scientists, metalworkers, glassblowers, draftsmen, and others working under his close direction and supervision. With such support, Edison boasted that he could turn out "a minor invention every ten days and a big thing every six months or so." (1997: 22)

The phonograph and the electric light bulb were two such "big things." Both were inspired by Edison. Both, however, were also expensive team efforts, motivated by vast commercial possibilities. (Edison founded General Electric, one of the most profitable companies in the world and one of the most valuable based on market capitalization.)

By the middle of the twentieth century, the great bulk of technological innovation was organized along industrial lines. Entire armies of experts and vast sums of capital were required to run the new invention factories. Only governments and, increasingly, giant multinational corporations could afford to sustain the research effort of the second half of the twentieth century. In the course of the century, the number of research scientists in the industrialized countries increased a hundredfold. In the United States between 1960 and 2000, research and development spending tripled after taking inflation into account, and the proportion spent by corporations increased from one-third to two-thirds of the total (Hobsbawm, 1994: 522–57; U.S. Department of Commerce, 1998: 609).

In light of these developments, it should come as no surprise that military and profit-making considerations now govern the direction of most research and development. A reporter once asked the infamous bank robber Willy Sutton why he robbed banks. Sutton answered: "Because that's where the money is." This

is by no means the only motivation prompting scientists and engineers to research particular topics. Especially in theoretical (as opposed to applied) research and especially in universities (as opposed to the research institutes of governments and private industry), the direction of inquiry is strongly influenced by personal interests, individual creativity, and the state of a field's intellectual development. It would, however, be naïve to think that practicality doesn't also enter into the scientist's calculation of what he or she ought to study. Even in a more innocent era, Sir Isaac Newton studied astronomy partly because the explorers and mariners of his day needed better navigational cues, just as Michael Faraday was partly motivated to discover the relationship between electricity and magnetism by his society's search for new forms of power (Bronowski, 1965: 7–8). The connection between practicality and research is even more evident today, when many researchers—even many of those who do theoretically driven research in universities—are pulled in particular directions by large research grants, well-paying jobs, access to expensive state-of-the-art equipment, and the possibility of winning patents and achieving commercial success. For example, many of the leading molecular biologists have established genetic engineering companies, serve on their boards of directors, or receive research funding from them. In not a few cases, these companies have been bought out by major pharmaceutical and agrochemical corporations who see their vast profit potential (Rural Advancement Foundation International, 1999; Rifkin, 1998: 56).

Economic lures, increasingly provided by the military and big corporations, have generated moral and political qualms among some researchers. Some scientists and engineers wonder whether research on particular topics achieves optimum benefits for humanity, and some are even troubled by the possibility that some types of research may be harmful to humankind. A growing number of researchers, however, if they are at all preoccupied by these issues, recognize that to do cutting-edge research they must still any residual misgivings, hop on the bandwagon, and adhere to military and industrial requirements and priorities. That, after all, is where the money is.

non-Christian cultures. Therefore, particularly in big-city schools, where students who are members of minority groups are sometimes in the numerical majority, cultural uniformity has given way to cultural diversity.

Canada used to be composed almost exclusively of northern Europeans and an Aboriginal minority. By eliminating overt racism in its immigration policies in

the 1960s, Canada began to diversify culturally. In the 1970s, the Canadian government continued the trend by adopting a policy of multiculturalism, which funds the maintenance of cultural diversity (Fleras and Elliott, 2002).

Canada's growing cultural diversification is well illustrated in Figure 2.1. For immigrants who arrived in

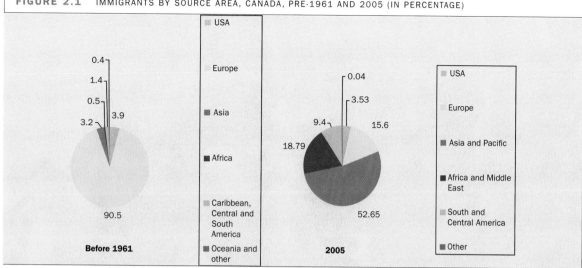

FIGURE 2.1   IMMIGRANTS BY SOURCE AREA, CANADA, PRE-1961 AND 2005 (IN PERCENTAGE)

SOURCE: Citizenship and Immigration Canada, 2006, "Annual Report to Parliament on Immigration, 2006." On the World Wide Web at http://www.cic.gc.ca/english/pub/annual-report2006/section1.html (13 April 2007).

Canada before 1961, about 95 percent of immigrants came from Europe and the United States. In 2005, about 80 percent of immigrants came from *outside* Europe and the United States. As a result of the inflow of immigrants from non-traditional sources—especially China, India, Pakistan, and the Philippines—16.2 percent of the population was non-white in 2006 (excluding Aboriginal Canadians). In Montreal, Edmonton, Calgary, and Winnipeg, the figure was about 25 percent. In Vancouver, it was nearly 40 percent, while in Toronto non-whites made up about 45 percent of the population (Brym, 2009).

Some critics argue that our immigration and multiculturalist policies weaken Canada's social fabric. Specifically, multiculturalism supposedly encourages immigrants to cling to their past rather than shrug off their old self-conceptions and create a distinctive *Canadian* identity (Bissoondath, 2002). This viewpoint has two problems. First, it is by no means certain that we lack a distinctive Canadian identity. In fact, as noted below, a defining element of our distinctive Canadian identity is precisely our deep respect for diversity. Second, contrary to the claims of the critics of multiculturalism, survey research shows that support for multiculturalism is *not* correlated with traditional attitudes (such as religiosity) that keep people rooted in the past. Support for multiculturalism *is* correlated with various modern trends, such as support for equality between women and men (Adams, 1997: 173).

From this point of view, Canada's multiculturalist policies are simply the latest stage in a long process of cultural evolution. In general, cultures tend to become more diverse or heterogeneous as societies become more complex, with important consequences for everyday life. Thus, in preliterate or tribal societies, cultural beliefs and practices are virtually the same for all group members. For example, many tribal societies organize puberty ceremonies to mark the end of childhood and the beginning of adulthood, fertility dances to pray for good crops and healthy babies, and other rites. These rituals involve elaborate body painting, carefully orchestrated chants and movements, and so forth. They are conducted in public. No variation from prescribed practice is allowed. Culture is homogeneous (Durkheim, 1976 [1915]).

In contrast, preindustrial Western Europe and North America were rocked by artistic, religious, scientific, and political forces that fragmented culture. The Renaissance, the Protestant Reformation, the Scientific Revolution, the French and American Revolutions—between the fourteenth and eighteenth centuries, all these movements involved people questioning old ways of seeing and doing things. Science placed skepticism about established authority at the very heart of its method. Political revolution proved there was nothing ordained about who should rule and how they should do so. Religious dissent ensured that the Catholic Church would no longer be the supreme interpreter of God's will in the eyes of all

Multiculturalism on the move.
SOURCE: © Mike Randolph/Masterfile.

Christians. Authority and truth became divided as never before.

Cultural fragmentation picked up steam during industrialization, as the variety of occupational roles grew and new political and intellectual movements crystallized. Its pace is quickening again today in the postindustrial era under the impact of a variety of globalizing forces.

The roots of globalization are many (see Chapter 19). International trade and investment are expanding. Members of different ethnic and racial groups are migrating and coming into sustained contact with one another. A growing number of people from these diverse groups date, court, and marry across religious, ethnic, and racial lines. Influential "transnational" organizations have been created, such as the International Monetary Fund, the European Union, Greenpeace, and Amnesty International. Inexpensive international travel and communication make contacts between people from diverse cultures routine. The mass media make Vin Diesel and *The Office* nearly as well known in Warsaw as in Winnipeg, and MTV brings rock music to the world

via MTV Latino, MTV Brazil, MTV Europe, MTV Asia, MTV Japan, MTV Mandarin, MTV India, and MTV Canada (Hanke, 1998). Globalization, in short, destroys political, economic, and cultural isolation, bringing people together in what Canadian communications guru Marshall McLuhan (1964) called a "global village." As a result of globalization, people are less obliged to accept the culture into which they are born and freer to combine elements of culture from a wide variety of historical periods and geographical settings. Globalization is a Mumbai schoolboy listening to Bob Marley on his MP3 player as he rushes to slip into his Levis, wolfs down a bowl of Kellogg's Basmati Flakes, and says goodbye to his parents in Hindi because he's late for his English-language school (see Box 2.2).

THE RIGHTS REVOLUTION

Underlying cultural diversification is the **rights revolution,** the process by which socially excluded groups have struggled to win equal rights under the law and in practice. After the outburst of nationalism,

BOX 2.2   THE GLOBALIZATION OF ENGLISH

The spread of English is a key marker of the extent of globalization. In 1600, English was the mother tongue of between 4 million and 7 million people. Not even all people in England spoke it. Today, 750 million to 1 billion people speak English worldwide, more than half as a second language. With the exception of the many varieties of Chinese, English is the most widespread language on Earth, and it is by far the most important. More than half the world's technical and scientific periodicals are written in English. English is the official language of the Olympics, of the Miss Universe contest, of navigation in the air and on the seas, and of the World Council of Churches.

English is dominant because Britain and the United States have been the world's most powerful and influential countries—economically, militarily, and culturally—for more than two centuries. (Someone once defined language as a dialect backed up by an army.) In recent decades, the global spread of capitalism, the popularity of Hollywood movies and American TV shows, and widespread access to instant communication via telephone and the Internet have increased the reach of the English language. There are now more speakers of excellent English in India than in the United Kingdom, and when a construction company jointly owned by German, French, and Italian interests undertakes a building project in Spain, the language of business is English (McCrum, Cran, and MacNeil, 1992).

Even in Japan, where relatively few people speak the language, English words are commonly used and Japanese words that are badly translated into English often become popular. The result is what is commonly known as "Japlish." Sometimes the results are unintelligible to a native English speaker. "Push to my nose! I might be changing to you?" says the catchy sign in a T-shirt store in Tokyo's Ueno district. Certain computer terms are more comprehensible to a native English speaker. For example, when you learn to open a computer file's *ai-kon* (icon) you are told to *daburu-kurikku* (double-click) the *mausu* (mouse; Kristof, 1997).

In view of the extensive use of English in Japan, *The Japanese Times,* one of Tokyo's four English daily newspapers, ran a story a few years ago noting the pressures of globalization and suggesting it might be time for Japan to switch to English. However, it met with an official backlash. To limit the Anglicization of Japanese, the Ministry of Health and Welfare banned excessive use of English in its documents a couple of years ago. The Ministry of Education is now replacing many English words in official documents—such words as *sukeemu* (scheme), *eensenchibu* (incentive), *deribatibu* (derivative), and *identyityi* (identity). Whether official pronouncements will have much effect on the way English and Japlish are used in advertising and on the streets is, however, another question entirely. As one Japanese newspaper pointed out, given the popularity of English words, it's doubtful there will be much *foro-uppu* (follow-up).

For Japanese teenagers, English and Japlish are certainly considered the very height of fashion. "Japlish words are easy to pronounce. And English sounds very cool," says 11-year-old Mai Asai (quoted in Delmos, 2002). A 15-year-old girl, wearing her trademark *roozu sokusu* (loose socks), might greet a friend sporting new sunglasses with a spirited *chekaraccho* (Check it out, Joe). If she likes the shades, she might say they're *cho beri gu* (ultra-good) and invite her friend *deniru* (to go to a Denny's restaurant) or *hageru* (to go to a Häagen-Dazs ice cream outlet). Of course, the girl might also *disu* (diss, or show disrespect toward) her friend. She might come right out and inform him that the new shades look *cho beri ba* (ultra-bad) or *cho beri bu* (ultra-blue, depressing, or ultra-ugly). If so, the situation that develops could be a little *denjarasu* (dangerous). Terms of affection, such as *wonchu* (I want you), might not be exchanged. The boy might decide that he has made a *misu* (mistake) and that the girl is too *hi mentay* (high maintenance) to justify pursuing. The budding relationship might go nowhere. Nonetheless, we can be pretty sure that Japanese teenagers' use of English slang will intensify under the pressures of globalization.

Less humorously, the rise of English (as well as the influence of French, Spanish, and the languages of a few other colonizing nations) is eliminating several thousand languages around the world. These endangered languages are spoken by the tribes of Papua New Guinea; the native peoples of the Americas; the national and tribal minorities of Asia, Africa, and Oceania; and marginalized European peoples, such as the Irish and the Basques. An estimated 5000 to 6000 languages spoken in the world today will be reduced to 1000 to 3000 in a century. Much of the culture of a people—its prayers, humour, conversational styles, technical vocabulary, myths, and so on—is expressed through language. Therefore, the loss of language amounts to the disappearance of tradition and perhaps even identity. These are often replaced by the traditions and identity of the colonial power, with television playing an important role in the transformation (Woodbury, 2003).

racism, and genocidal behaviour among the combatants in World War II, the United Nations proclaimed the Universal Declaration of Human Rights in 1948. Its preamble reads in part,

> Whereas recognition of the inherent dignity and of the equal and inalienable rights of all members of the human family is the foundation of freedom, justice and peace in the world. . . . Now, therefore The General Assembly proclaims this Universal Declaration of Human Rights as a common standard of achievement for all peoples and all nations, to the end that every individual and every organ of society, keeping this Declaration constantly in mind, shall strive by teaching and education to promote respect for these rights and freedoms and by progressive measures, national and international, to secure their universal and effective recognition and observance. (United Nations, 1998)

Fanned by such sentiment, the rights revolution was in full swing by the 1960s. Today, women's rights, Aboriginal rights, gay and lesbian rights, the rights of people with special needs, constitutional rights, and language rights are a key part of our political discourse. As a result of the rights revolution, democracy has been widened and deepened (see Chapter 18, Politics and Social Movements). The rights revolution is by no means finished—many categories of people are still discriminated against socially, politically, and economically—but in much of the world all categories of people now participate more fully than ever before in the life of their societies (Ignatieff, 2000).

The rights revolution raises some difficult issues. For example, groups that have suffered extraordinarily high levels of discrimination historically, such as Aboriginal Canadians, Jewish Canadians, Chinese Canadians, and Japanese Canadians, have demanded reparations in the form of money, symbolic gestures, and, in the case of Aboriginal Canadians, land and political autonomy.[2] Much controversy surrounds the extent of the obligation of current citizens to compensate past injustices.

Another problem raised by the rights revolution concerns how we can achieve an acceptable balance between the right to be equal and the right to be different. For example, most residents of Quebec expect all Quebeckers to be able to compete on an equal footing for jobs, regardless of whether they are of French, English, or other origin. This is the right to equality. But Quebeckers of French origin have also exercised their right to be different. They have, for instance, passed laws restricting the use of English on public signs. These laws are controversial. Some English Quebeckers accept them as legitimate; others do not. Controversy therefore persists regarding the balance between the right to equality and the right to be different.

These problems notwithstanding, the rights revolution is here to stay and it affects our culture profoundly. Specifically, the rights revolution fragments Canadian culture by legitimizing the grievances of groups that were formerly excluded from full social participation and renewing pride in their identity and heritage. Our history books, our literature, our music, our use of languages, our very sense of what it means to be Canadian have diversified culturally. White male heterosexual property owners of British origin are still disproportionately influential in Canada, but our culture is no longer dominated by them in the way that it was just four or five decades ago.

POSTMODERNISM

In part because of the rights revolution, so much cultural fragmentation and reconfiguration has taken place in the last few decades that some sociologists think a new term is needed to characterize the culture of our times: **postmodernism.**

Postmodern culture has three main features:

1. It involves *an eclectic mixing of elements from different times and places.* That is, in the postmodern era it is easier to create individualized belief systems and practices by blending facets of different cultures and historical periods. Consider religion. Surveys conducted by Reginald Bibby of the University of Lethbridge show that Canadians often supplement Judeo-Christian beliefs and practices with less conventional ideas about astrology, psychic powers, communication with the dead, and so forth (Bibby, 1987). People who attend church regularly are just as likely to hold such unconventional beliefs as non-attenders. But despite the widespread acceptance of unconventional beliefs, the overwhelming majority of Canadians still turn to established religions for **rites of passage,** or cultural ceremonies that mark the transition from one stage of life to another (e.g., baptisms, confirmations, weddings) or from life to death (funerals). Individuals thus choose their own mix of unconventional and conventional beliefs and practices. They draw on

religions much like consumers shop in a mall; as Bibby says, they practise religion à la carte. Meanwhile, the churches in Canada have diversified their menus to appeal to the spiritual, leisure, and social needs of religious consumers and retain their loyalties in the competitive market for congregants and parishioners. The mix-and-match approach we see when it comes to religion is evident in virtually all spheres of culture.

2. Postmodernism also involves *the erosion of authority*. Half a century ago, Canadians were more likely than they are today to defer to authority in the family, schools, politics, medicine, and religion. In fact, Canadians were often characterized as an especially deferential people,

more respectful of authority than their individualistic, revolutionary, violent, and entrepreneurial cousins in the United States. In the second half of the twentieth century, however, Canadians grew skeptical about authority in many institutions, especially political institutions—even more skeptical than Americans in many respects (Brym with Fox, 1989; Nevitte, 1996; see Figure 2.2 and Box 2.3, p. 40). For example, voting and other forms of conventional politics are less popular than they used to be, while nonconventional political action is more popular. In 2000, 30 percent of Canadians said they had participated in nonconventional political actions (joining a boycott, taking part in an unlawful demonstration, joining an unofficial strike, or occupying a building or a factory). That was up from 24 percent in 1980. Meanwhile, just 59.1 percent of eligible voters cast a ballot in the 2008 federal election, down from 69.0 percent in 1980 (see Figure 2.3).

3. Finally, postmodernism is characterized by *the decline of consensus around core values*. Half a century ago, people's values remained quite stable over the course of their adult lives and many values were widely accepted. Today, value shifts are more rapid and consensus has broken down on many issues. For instance, half a century ago, the great majority of adults remained loyal to one political party from one election to the next. Today, people are more likely to vote for different parties in succeeding elections (Clarke, Jenson, LeDuc, and Pammett, 1996: 139–46).

FIGURE 2.2 PERCENTAGE OF PEOPLE WITH "A GREAT DEAL OF CONFIDENCE" IN PARLIAMENT/ CONGRESS, CANADA/UNITED STATES, 1981–2000

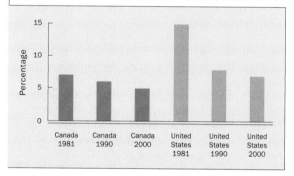

SOURCE: World Values Survey (2000). Reprinted with permission from the Inter-university Consortium for Political and Social Research.

FIGURE 2.3 PERCENTAGE OF ADULTS VOTING IN FEDERAL ELECTIONS AND PARTICIPATING IN NONCONVENTIONAL POLITICAL ACTION, SELECTED YEARS

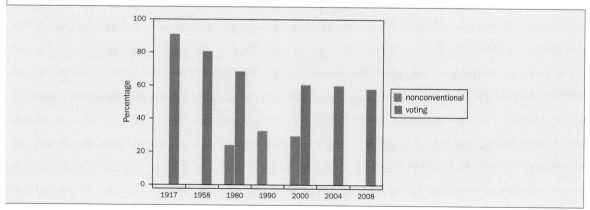

SOURCES: Elections Canada (2008); "Voter Turnout" (2004); World Values Survey (2000). Reprinted with permission.

Until the mid-1960s, the image of Canadians among most sociologists was that of a stodgy people: peaceful, conservative, respectful of authority, and therefore quite unlike our American cousins.

According to conventional wisdom, the United States was born in open rebellion against the British motherland. Its Western frontier was lawless. Vast opportunities for striking it rich bred a spirit of individualism. Thus, American culture became an anti-authoritarian culture.

Canada developed differently according to the conventional view. It became an independent country not through a revolutionary upheaval but in a gradual, evolutionary manner. The Northwest Mounted Police and two highly hierarchical churches (Roman Catholic and Anglican) established themselves on the Western frontier before the era of mass settlement, allowing for the creation of an orderly society rather than a "wild West." Beginning with the Hudson's Bay Company, large corporations quickly came to dominate the Canadian economy, hampering individualism and the entrepreneurial spirit. Thus, Canadian culture became a culture of deference to authority. That, at least, was the common view until the 1960s (Lipset, 1963).

Although the contrast between deferential Canadian culture and anti-authoritarian American culture may have had some validity 40 or 50 years ago, it is an inaccurate characterization today (Adams, 1997: 62–95). As we have seen, the questioning of authority spread throughout the Western world beginning in the 1960s. Nowhere, however, did it spread as quickly and thoroughly as in Canada. Canadians used to express more confidence in big business than Americans did, but surveys now show the opposite. Canadians used to be more religious than Americans, but that is no longer the case. Fewer Canadians (in percentage terms) say they believe in God and fewer attend weekly religious services. Confidence in government has eroded more quickly in Canada than in the United States. Americans are more patriotic than Canadians, according more respect to the state. Finally, Americans are more likely than Canadians to regard the traditional nuclear family as the ideal family form and to think of deviations from tradition—same-sex couples, single-parent families, cohabitation without marriage—as the source of a whole range of social problems. Thus, whether sociologists examine attitudes toward the family, the state, government, religion, or big business, they now find that Americans are more deferential to traditional institutional authority than Canadians are.

Because Canadians are less deferential to traditional institutional authority than Americans are, some commentators say that Canadians lack a distinct culture. For example, American patriotism sparks awareness of great national accomplishments in art, war, sports, science, and, indeed, all fields of human endeavour. Anthems, rituals, myths, and celebrations recognize these accomplishments and give Americans a keen sense of who they are and how they differ from non-Americans. Not surprisingly, therefore, a larger percentage of Americans than of Canadians think of themselves in unhyphenated terms—as "Americans" plain and simple rather than, say, Italian-Americans. In Canada, a larger percentage of the population thinks of itself in hyphenated terms; compared with the Americans, our identity is qualified, even tentative.

Does this mean that Canadians lack a distinct national culture? Hardly. It means that although American culture is characterized by a relatively high degree of deference to dominant institutions, Canadian culture is characterized by a relatively high degree of tolerance and respect for diversity. We are more likely than Americans to favour gender equality, accept gay and lesbian relationships, encourage bilingualism and multiculturalism, and accept the right of Aboriginals to political autonomy. Characteristically, a large international survey by a condom manufacturer found that Americans have sex more often than Canadians but Canadians are most likely to say that the pleasure of their partner is very important. As public opinion pollster Michael Adams writes,

> Twenty-five years of public-opinion polling in Canada has taught me a seemingly paradoxical truth. Canadians feel strongly about their weak attachments to Canada, its political institutions and their fellow citizens. In other words, they feel strongly about the right to live in a society that allows its citizens to be detached from ideology and critical of organizations, and not to feel obliged to be jingoistic or sentimentally patriotic. Canadians lack of nationalism is, in many ways, a distinguishing feature of the country. (1997: 171)

In short, Canadian culture is distinctive, and its chief distinction may be that it qualifies us as the first thoroughly postmodern society.

The decline of consensus can also be illustrated by considering the fate of Big Historical Projects. For most of the past 200 years, consensus throughout the world was built around Big Historical Projects. Various social movements convinced people they could take history into their own hands and create a glorious future just by signing up. German Nazism was a Big Historical Project. Its followers expected the Reich to enjoy 1000 years of power. Communism was an even bigger Big Historical Project, mobilizing hundreds of millions of people for a future that promised to end inequality and injustice for all time. However, the biggest and most successful Big Historical Project was not so much a social movement as a powerful idea—the belief that progress is inevitable, that life will always improve, mainly because of the spread of democracy and scientific innovation.

The twentieth century was unkind to Big Historical Projects. Russian communism lasted 74 years, German Nazism a mere 12. And the idea of progress fell on hard times as 100 million soldiers and civilians died in wars; the forward march of democracy took wrong turns into fascism, communism, and regimes based on religious fanaticism; and pollution from urbanization and industrialization threatened the planet. In the postmodern era, more and more people recognize that apparent progress, including scientific advances, often has negative consequences (Scott, 1998; see Figure 2.4).

The aspects of postmodernism listed previously—the eclectic mixing of cultural elements from different times and places, the erosion of authority, and the decline of consensus around core values—have many parents, teachers, politicians, religious leaders, and not a few university professors worried. How can we make binding decisions? How can we govern? How can we teach children and adolescents the difference between right and wrong? How can we transmit accepted literary tastes and artistic standards from one generation to the next? These are the kinds of issues that plague people in positions of authority today. Although their concerns are legitimate, many of them seem not to have considered the other side of the coin: The postmodern condition, as described above, empowers ordinary people and makes them more responsible for their own fate. It renders them more tolerant and appreciative of ethnic, racial, religious, and sexual groups other than their own—no small matter in a world torn by group conflict. The postmodern attitude encourages a healthy skepticism about rosy and naive scientific and political promises. And it frees people to adopt religious, ethnic, and other identities they are comfortable with, as opposed to identities imposed on them by others.

Thus, the news about postmodern culture is not all bad. However, as you will now see, it's not all good either.

CULTURE AS CONSTRAINT AND AS DANGER

We noted previously that culture has two faces. One we labelled "freedom," the other "constraint." Diversity, globalization, and postmodernism are all aspects of the new freedoms that culture allows us today. We now turn to an examination of two contemporary aspects of culture that act as constraining forces on our lives: rationalization and consumerism.

RATIONALIZATION

In fourteenth-century Europe, an upsurge in demand for textiles caused loom owners to look for ways to increase productivity. To that end, they imposed longer hours on loom workers and installed the first public clocks. The clocks, known as *Werkglocken* ("work clocks") in German, signalled the beginning of the workday, the timing of meals, and quitting time.

Workers were accustomed to enjoying many holidays and a flexible and vague work schedule regulated only approximately by the seasons and the rising and setting of the sun. The regimentation imposed by the work clocks made life harder. So the workers staged uprisings to silence the clocks. But to no avail. City

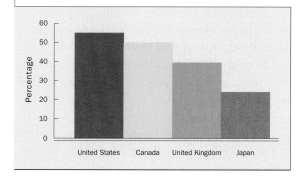

FIGURE 2.4 PERCENTAGE WHO BELIEVE SCIENTIFIC ADVANCES WILL HELP HUMANITY, 2000

SOURCE: World Values Survey (2000). Reprinted with permission from the Inter-university Consortium for Political and Social Research.

officials sided with the employers and imposed fines for ignoring the *Werkglocken*. Harsher penalties, including death, were imposed on anyone trying to use the clocks' bells to signal a revolt (Thompson, 1967).

Now, more than 600 years later, many people in the world's rich countries—especially big-city couples who are employed full-time in the paid labour force and have preteen children—are, in effect, slaves of the *Werkglocke*. Life often seems an endless round of waking up at 6:30 a.m., getting everyone washed and dressed, preparing the kids' lunches, getting them out the door in time for the school bus or the car pool, driving to work through rush-hour traffic, facing the speed-up at work that resulted from the recent downsizing, driving back home through rush-hour traffic, preparing dinner, taking the kids to their soccer game, returning home to clean up the dishes and help with homework, getting the kids washed, brushed, and into bed, and (if you haven't brought some office work home) grabbing an hour of TV before collapsing, exhausted, for six-and-a-half hours before the story repeats itself. Life is less hectic for residents of small cities and towns, unmarried people, couples without small children, retirees, and the unemployed. But the lives of most people are so packed with activities that time must be carefully regulated, each moment precisely parcelled out so we may tick off item after item from an ever-growing list of tasks that need to be completed on schedule (Schor, 1992). In 2000, 14 percent of Canadians in the paid labour force worked for pay 50 or more hours a week, up from 11 percent in 1976. In 1999, the figure was 38 percent among senior managers, the most overworked job category. Among transport and equipment operators, the second most overworked job category, the figure was 27 percent. Among teachers and professors, the sixth most overworked job category, the figure was 18 percent (Lowe, 2001: 8, 9).

After more than 600 years of conditioning, it is unusual for people to rebel against the clock in the town square anymore. In fact, we now wear a watch on our wrist without giving it a second thought, as it were. This signifies that we have accepted and internalized the regime of the work clock. Allowing clocks to regulate our activities precisely seems the most natural thing in the world—which is a pretty good sign that the internalized *Werkglocke* is, in fact, a product of culture.

Is the precise regulation of time rational? It certainly is rational as a means of ensuring efficiency, that is, maximizing how much work you get done in a day. But is it rational as an end in itself? For many people, it is not. The precise regulation of time has gotten out of hand. Life has simply become too hectic for many people to enjoy fully. In this sense, rationality of means has led to irrationality of ends.

For American sociologist George Ritzer, the McDonald's fast-food restaurant epitomizes the rationalization process. Ritzer speaks of the "McDonaldization" of the world, by which he means that the organizational principles of the fast-food restaurant are coming to dominate everywhere (Ritzer, 1993, 1996).

At McDonald's, a set list of carefully weighed food portions with identical ingredients are cooked according to a uniform and precisely timed process. But, says Ritzer, the application of assembly-line procedures to meal preparation is dehumanizing for both employees and customers. Thus, the work is done by mainly nonunionized, uniformed, teenage workers who receive minimum wage. To boost sales, they are required to smile as they recite fixed scripts ("Would you like some fries or a drink with your burger?"). Nearly half of all McDonald's employees are so dissatisfied with their work they quit after a year or less. To deal with this problem, McDonald's is field-testing self-service kiosks in which an automated machine cooks and bags French fries while a vertical grill takes patties from the freezer and grills them to your liking (Carpenter, 2003). Meanwhile, customers are expected to spend as little time as possible eating the food—hence the drive-through window, chairs designed to be comfortable for only about 20 minutes, and small express outlets in subways and department stores where customers eat standing up or on the run. In short, McDonald's executives have carefully thought through every aspect of your lunch. With the goal of making profits, they have rationalized food preparation, making it as inexpensive and as fast as possible.

Taking McDonaldization to a new extreme, one restaurant in Japan has even installed a punch-clock for its customers. The restaurant offers all you can eat for 35 yen per minute. As a result, "the diners rush in, punch the clock, load their trays from the buffet table, and concentrate intensely on efficient chewing and swallowing, trying not to waste time talking to their companions before rushing back to punch out. This version of fast food is so popular that, as the restaurant prepares to open at lunchtime, Tokyo residents *wait in line*" (Gleick, 2000: 244; emphasis in the original). Meanwhile, in New York and Los Angeles, some upscale restaurants have got in on the act. An increasingly large number of business clients are so pressed for time they feel the need to pack in *two* half-hour lunches with successive guests. The restaurants oblige, making the resetting of tables "resemble the pit-stop activity at the Indianapolis 500" (Gleick, 2000: 155).

As the examples of the *Werkglocke* and fast food show, rationalization enables us to do just about everything more efficiently, but at a steep cost. In fact, because it is so widespread, rationalization is one of the most constraining aspects of culture today. In Weber's view, it makes life in the modern world akin to living inside an "iron cage."

The second constraining aspect of culture that we will examine is consumerism, the tendency to define our selves in terms of the goods we purchase.

CONSUMERISM

A few years ago, the Gap hired Hollywood talent to create a slick and highly effective series of TV ads for khaki pants. According to the promotional material for the ad campaign, the purpose of the ads was to "reinvent khakis," that is, to stimulate demand for the pants. In *Khakis rock*, "skateboarders and in-line skaters dance, glide, and fly to music by the Crystal Method." In *Khakis groove*, "hip-hop dancers throw radical moves to the funky beat of Bill Mason." In *Khakis swing*, "two couples break away from a crowd to demonstrate swing techniques to the vintage sounds of Louis Prima" (Gap.com, 1999).

About 55 seconds of each ad featured the dancers. During the last 5 seconds, the words "GAP khakis" appeared on the screen. The GAP followed a similar approach in another ad campaign a couple years later. Inspired by the 1957 musical, *West Side Story*, the 30-second spots replaced the play's warring street gangs, the Jets and the Sharks, with fashion factions of their own, the Khakis and the Jeans. Again, most of the ad was devoted to the riveting dance number. The pants were mentioned for only a few seconds at the end.

As the imbalance between stylish come-on and mere information suggests, the people who created the ads understood that it was really the appeal of the dancers that would sell the pants. They knew that to stimulate demand for their product, they had to associate the khakis with desirable properties, such as youth, good health, coolness, popularity, beauty, and sex. As an advertising executive said in the 1940s: "It's not the steak we sell. It's the sizzle."

Because advertising stimulates sales, business has a tendency to spend more on advertising over time. Because advertising is widespread, most people unquestioningly accept it as part of their lives. In fact, many people have *become* ads. Thus, when your father was a child and quickly threw on a shirt, allowing a label to hang out, your grandmother might admonish him to "tuck in that label." Today, in contrast, many people proudly display consumer labels as marks of status and identity. Advertisers teach us to associate the words "Gucci" and "Nike" with different kinds of people, and when people display these labels on their clothes they are telling us something about the kind of people they are and whom they associate with. Advertising becomes us.

Recent innovations in advertising take full advantage of our tendency to define ourselves in terms of the goods we purchase. For example, when channel surfing and the use of personal video recorders spread, advertisers realized they had a problem on their hands. Viewers started skipping TV ads that cost millions of dollars and untold hours of creative effort to produce. As a result, advertisers had to think up new ways of drawing products to the attention of consumers. One idea they hit on was paying to place their products in TV shows and movies. They realized that when Brad Pitt or some other big star drinks a can of Coke or lights up a Marlboro, members of the audience tend to associate the product with the star. Wanting to be like the star, they are increasingly likely to buy the product. In the slick 2003 movie, *The Italian Job*, starring Mark Wahlberg and Charlize Theron, a small fleet of high-performance Morris Minis plays a key role in the big heist. As expected, sales of the Morris Mini skyrocketed soon after the film was released. The product became part of who we are or who we want to be.

Since the 1980s, there has been an explosion of advertising directed at children. Here, advertisers recognized, was a vast untapped market; children could be used to nag their parents to buy more products. The manipulation of children by advertisers soon became a sort of quasi-science. One advertising expert said there are seven basic types of nagging tactics that can be unleashed by effective child-directed advertising:

> A *pleading* nag is one accompanied by repetitions of words like "please" or "mom, mom, mom." A *persistent* nag involves constant requests for the coveted product and may include the phrase "I'm gonna ask just one more time." *Forceful* nags are extremely pushy and may include subtle threats, like "Well, then, I'll go and ask Dad." *Demonstrative* nags are the

most high-risk, often characterized by full-blown tantrums in public places, breath-holding, tears, a refusal to leave the store. *Sugar-coated* nags promise affection in return for a purchase and may rely on seemingly heartfelt declarations like "You're the best dad in the world." *Threatening* nags are youthful forms of blackmail, vows of eternal hatred and of running away if something isn't bought. *Pity* nags claim the child will be heartbroken, teased, or socially stunted if the parent refuses to buy a certain product. (Schlosser, 2002: 44)

Note that getting children to nag their parents to buy more products is only one aim of child-directed advertising. In addition, advertisers recognize that ads directed at children can be used to develop brand loyalty that will, in the ideal case, last a lifetime. A few years ago executives at one large brewery must have been delighted to read the results of a consumer survey that found that the most popular ads among American children were a Taco Bell commercial featuring a talking Chihuahua and an ad for Budweiser beer.

The rationalization process enables us to produce more efficiently, to have more of just about everything than our parents did. But it is consumerism, the tendency to define ourselves in terms of the goods we purchase, that ensures the goods will be bought. Of course, people living in the world's rich countries have lots of choice. We can select from dozens of styles of running shoes, cars, and all the rest. We can also choose to buy items that help to define us as members of a particular **subculture,** adherents of a set of distinctive values, norms, and practices within a larger culture. But, regardless of individual tastes and inclinations, nearly all of us have one thing in common: We tend to be good consumers. We are motivated by advertising, which is based on the accurate insight that people will likely be considered social outcasts if they fail to conform to stylish trends. By creating those trends, advertisers push us to buy. That is why North Americans' "shop-till-you-drop" lifestyle prompted French sociologist Jean Baudrillard to remark pointedly that even what is best in North America is compulsory (Baudrillard, 1988 [1986]).

FROM COUNTERCULTURE TO SUBCULTURE

In concluding my discussion of culture as a constraining force, I want to note that consumerism is remarkably effective at taming countercultures.

Countercultures are subversive subcultures. They oppose dominant values and seek to replace them. The hippies of the 1960s formed a counterculture and so do environmentalists today.

Countercultures rarely pose a serious threat to social stability. Most often, the system of social control, of rewards and punishments, keeps countercultures at bay. In our society, consumerism acts as a social control mechanism that normally prevents countercultures from disrupting the social order. It does that by transforming deviations from mainstream culture into means of making money and by enticing rebels to become entrepreneurs (Frank and Weiland, 1997). Two examples from popular music help illustrate the point:

- Ozzy Osbourne was an important figure in the counterculture that grew up around heavy metal music beginning in the late 1960s. He and his band, Black Sabbath, inspired Metallica, Kiss, Judas Priest, Marilyn Manson, and others to play loud, nihilistic music, reject conventional morality, embrace death and violence, and spark youthful rebellion and parental panic. In 1982, Osbourne bit the head off a bat during a performance and urinated on the Alamo. He was given rabies shots for the former and arrested for the latter. Around the same time, Tipper Gore, wife of the future presidential candidate, formed the Parents' Music Resource Center to fight against violence and sex in the lyrics of popular music. Osbourne was one of the committee's principal targets. The "Prince of Darkness," as he was often called, was about as rebellious a figure as one could imagine in 1982.

  Flash forward 20 years. Osbourne, at 53, had the sixth most popular show on North American television among 18- to 34-year-olds, just behind *Survivor* in the ratings, from 2002 to 2005. MTV placed a dozen cameras throughout his Beverly Hills mansion, and every Tuesday night viewers got to see everything going on in the Osbourne household for half an hour. According to *USA Today*, Osbourne is "a lot like anyone's adorable dad. Shuffles a bit. Forgets things. Worries about the garbage. Snores on the couch while the TV blares. Walks the dog" (Gunderson, Keveney, and Oldenburg, 2002: 1A). CNN's Greta Van Susteren said she finds the Osbournes "charming," and Rosie O'Donnell said to Ozzy's wife, Sharon, "What I love most about [your show] is not only the relationship you have with Ozzy—and you obviously adore each other—but the honesty with which you relate to your children. The love is so evident between all of you. It's heartwarming" (Gunderson, Keveney, and Oldenburg, 2002: 2A). Sharon and Ozzy Osbourne were invited to dinner at the White House in 2002, and in the same year, former Republican Vice President Dan Quayle (who in 1992 criticized the TV character Murphy Brown for deciding to have a baby out of wedlock) admitted "there are some very good lessons being transmitted" by the Osbournes (Beck, 2002). *The Osbournes*, it turns out, was a comfort to many people. The show seemed to prove that heavy metal's frightening rejection of mainstream culture in the 1970s and 1980s was just a passing phase and that the traditional nuclear family remains intact. Ozzy Osbourne was thus transformed from the embodiment of rebellion against society to a family man, a small industry, and a conservative media icon.

- The development of hip-hop also illustrates the commercialization and taming of rebellion (Brym, 2001). Originating in the squalor of inner-city American ghettoes in the 1970s, hip-hop gave rise to a highly politicized counterculture. Early hip-hop artists glorified the mean streets of the inner city and held the police, the mass media, and other pillars of white society in utter contempt, blaming them for arbitrary arrests, the political suppression of black activists, and the spreading of lies about African Americans. However, by the time *Public Enemy* became a hit in the late 1980s, MTV had aired its first regular program devoted to the genre

Diddy marketing "rebellion."
SOURCE: © Reuters/Corbis.

and much of hip-hop's audience comprised white, middle-class youth. Hip-hop artists were quick to see the potential of commercialization. Soon Wu-Tang Clan had its own line of clothes, Versace was marketing clothing influenced by ghetto styles, and Puff Daddy (who later had a makeover as P. Diddy and now as Diddy) was reminding his audience: "N—— get money, that's simply the plan" (from his CD, *Forever*). No less than heavy metal and punk, most of hip-hop's radicalism gave way to the lures of commerce.

The stories of heavy metal and hip-hop are testimony to the capacity of consumerism to change countercultures into mere subcultures, thus constraining dissent and rebellion. They are compelling illustrations of culture's second face.

SUMMARY

1. Humans have been able to adapt to their environments because they are able to create culture. In particular, the ability to create symbols, cooperate, and make tools has enabled humans to thrive.

2. Culture can be invisible if we are too deeply immersed in it. The cultures of others can seem inscrutable if we view them exclusively from the perspective of our own culture. Therefore, the best vantage point for analyzing culture is on the margins—neither too deeply immersed in it nor too much removed from it.

3. Culture becomes more diversified and consensus declines in many areas of life as societies become more complex. This increases human freedom, giving people more choice in their ethnic, religious, sexual, and other identities.

4. So much cultural diversification and reconfiguration has taken place that some sociologists characterize the culture of our times as postmodern. Postmodernism involves an eclectic mixing of cultural elements from different times and places, the erosion of authority, and the decline of consensus around core values.

5. Underlying cultural diversification is the rights revolution, the process by which socially excluded groups have struggled to win equal rights under the law and in practice.

6. Although the diversification of culture increases human freedom, the growth of complex societies also establishes definite limits within which diversification may occur. This is illustrated by the process of rationalization (the optimization of means to achieve given ends) and the growth of consumerism (which involves defining one's self in terms of the goods one purchases).

QUESTIONS TO CONSIDER

1. We imbibe culture but also create it. What elements of culture have you created? Under what conditions were you prompted to do so? Was your cultural contribution strictly personal or was it shared with others? Why?

2. Do you think of yourself in a fundamentally different way from the way your parents (or other close relatives or friends at least 20 years older than you) thought of themselves when they were your age? Are your attitudes toward authority different? Interview your parents, relatives, or friends to find out. Pay particular attention to the way in which the forces of globalization have altered ethnic, racial, and religious self-conceptions and how your attitudes to authority differ from those of your elders.

3. One of the main themes of this chapter is that rationality of means sometimes results in irrationality of ends. Select a sphere of culture (religion, education, the mass media, etc.) and illustrate the point.

GLOSSARY

Abstraction is the human capacity to create complex symbols, including languages, mathematical notations, and signs, in order to classify experience and generalize from it.

Consumerism involves defining ourselves in terms of the goods we purchase.

Cooperation is the human capacity to create a complex social life by establishing norms.

Countercultures are subversive subcultures. They oppose dominant values and seek to replace them.

Culture is the sum of socially transmitted practices, languages, symbols, beliefs, values, ideologies, and material objects that people create to deal with real-life problems. Cultures enable people to adapt to, and thrive in, their environments.

Ethnocentrism is the tendency to judge other cultures exclusively by the standards of our own.

Material culture comprises the tools and techniques that improve our ability to take what we want from nature.

Norms are standards of behaviour or generally accepted ways of doing things.

Postmodernism is characterized by an eclectic mixing of cultural elements, the erosion of authority, and the decline of consensus around core values.

Production is the human capacity to make and use tools. It improves our ability to take what we want from nature.

Rationalization is Max Weber's term for the systematic application of standardized means to predetermined ends.

The **rights revolution** is the process by which excluded groups have obtained equal rights under the law and in practice.

A **rite of passage** is a cultural ceremony that marks the transition from one stage of life to another or from life to death.

Sanctions are rewards and punishments intended to ensure conformity to cultural guidelines.

The system of **social control** is the means by which members of society ensure people conform to cultural guidelines.

A **society** involves people interacting socially and sharing culture, usually in a defined geographical area.

A **subculture** is a distinctive set of values, norms, and practices within a larger culture.

A **symbol** is anything that carries a particular meaning, including the components of language, mathematical notations, and signs. Symbols allow us to classify experience and generalize from it.

SUGGESTED READING

Adams, Michael. (1997). *Sex in the Snow: Canadian Social Values at the End of the Millennium.* Toronto: Penguin. Adams is a sociologist and one of Canada's leading public opinion pollsters. Here he identifies and analyzes the core values of Canadian culture, highlighting differences by generation, gender, and country (Canada versus the United States).

Klein, Naomi. (2000). *No Logo: Taking Aim at the Brand Bullies.* Toronto: Vintage Canada. This is the definitive work on the negative effects of marketing on our culture.

Schlosser, Eric. (2002). *Fast Food Nation: The Dark Side of the All-American Meal.* New York: Perennial. You may never eat another fast-food meal after reading this insightful exposé, but you will learn much about the major forces shaping our culture.

Spillman, Lyn, ed. (2002). *Cultural Sociology.* Oxford, UK: Blackwell. This book comprehensively analyzes major issues in the sociological study of culture.

NOTES

1. New forms of society on the Internet ("virtual communities") show that physical proximity is not always a necessary part of the definition.

2. Many children of Aboriginal Canadians were put into residential schools in the twentieth century, and many of them were physically and sexually abused by the ministers, priests, and nuns who ran these schools. Many Aboriginal Canadians also claim that much land was taken from them illegally. Some 21 000 Japanese Canadians living within 160 kilometres of the Pacific Coast, three-quarters of them Canadian citizens, were forcibly moved to prisoner-of-war, internment, and work camps in 1942. They lost most of their property. Descendants of many Chinese Canadians were forced to pay an exorbitant "head tax" in the late nineteenth and early twentieth centuries, the purpose of which was to encourage them to leave the country. The Nazis enslaved and slaughtered millions of European Jews in World War II and stole their property. Survivors, a considerable number of them residing in Canada, later sought and received reparations from the German and Swiss governments.

WEB RESOURCES

Companion Website for This Book

http://www.newsociety6e.nelson.com

Begin by clicking on the Student Resources section of the website. Next, select the chapter you are studying from the pull-down menu. From the Student Resources page, you have easy access to InfoTrac College Edition® and other resources, such as the Glossary, Test Yourself questions, and additional readings. The website also has many useful tips to aid you in your study of sociology.

InfoTrac College Edition Search Terms

Visit http://www.infotrac-college.com for access to more than 20 million articles from nearly 6000 sources when doing your online research.

SOURCE: © nfsphoto/Shutterstock

CHAPTER THREE

Socialization

William Shaffir
McMASTER UNIVERSITY

Michael Rosenberg
DAWSON COLLEGE

In this chapter you will learn that

- Socialization refers to the processes that allow people to become members of society, develop a sense of self, and learn to participate in social relationships with others.

- Socialization takes place at all stages of the life cycle and in a variety of settings: families, schools, peer groups, the mass media, and occupational groups.

- Among the major contributors to socialization theory are Charles Cooley (who argued that individuals develop a sense of self as they interact with others), George Herbert Mead (who focused on the way we actively create a sense of self by taking the roles of others), and Paul Willis (who demonstrated that young people creatively participate in generating and maintaining their sense of self, both in accordance with and sometimes in opposition to their social context).

- Socialization continues into adulthood. As people work, marry, divorce, raise children, and retire, they enter new relationships with others, learn new behaviour, and adopt new roles.

- Sometimes our self-concept undergoes abrupt change as we learn new role identities and negotiate a new self-image. Such "resocialization" occurs when we replace our way of life with a radically different one. It is most evident in jails, psychiatric hospitals, and boot camps, and in religious and political conversions.

WHAT IS SOCIALIZATION?

Anyone who has been a parent is probably all too familiar with the "terrible twos," the stage many two-year-olds pass through and that childhood development experts call the "negativism" stage. During negativism a child will often be contrary and obstinate, refusing to cooperate even in simple tasks and saying "no" to everything and everyone. What's worse, the child may often willfully break norms, or generally accepted ways of doing things, in the household—sometimes also breaking valued objects, dishes, and almost anything else that comes to hand. Negativism can be a difficult stage to live through for both the parents and the child. Yet, childhood socialization experts insist, it is an essential stage in developing a sense of self and becoming an autonomous human being.

An anecdote will illustrate what is meant by negativism. One of the authors of this chapter used to have a large houseplant in his living room of which he and his wife were very fond. When their first child was still young, they made it clear that he was not to touch the plant. "Plants are beautiful things that we must cherish, nourish, and allow to grow," they explained. Still, there was always a gleam in their son's eyes when he looked at the plant, and they were careful never to leave him alone when he was near it.

One day, when he was about one-and-a-half, the child walked into the living room where his father was reading, approached the plant, observed it for several seconds and then muttered "No" to himself. He then looked at his father with a big smile on his face. His father, smiling back at him, said, "That's right. No." The boy left, but came back a few minutes later and repeated his actions, once again reminding himself

The terrible twos.
SOURCE: © Shanta Giddens/Shutterstock.

with a smile, "No." His father, not yet sensing disaster, smiled back. The boy left, but a few minutes later returned yet again, walking up close to the plant, looking at it, and saying "No" with a big smile. But this time he grabbed the largest leaf of the plant as he spoke and, crushing it, repeated "No" yet again. The plant was given to neighbours the next day.

The truth is, of course, that young children are constantly being told "No" by the adults around them: "Don't touch that!" "Don't eat this!" "Don't go there!" If children always listened to what their parents said, they would never be able to do anything. Negativism is the way a child learns what really can or cannot be done. It is a way of testing the limits to find out which of the many no's they hear are serious and which are only a preference. It is also a form of rebellion whereby the child sets limits for the parents as well. Parents also have to learn how far they can go in restricting and controlling the child. Children are not robots who just follow instructions; they need to develop as autonomous, competent, and self-directed actors if they are to be full-fledged members of a family—and of society. The social process whereby they undergo such development through interacting with the people around them is known as **socialization.**

To be socialized means to learn how to act and interact appropriately with others, to become a competent and effective member of society. Yet, paradoxically, sociologists assert that to be socialized is also to develop a **self**, a sense of individual identity that allows us to understand ourselves and differentiate ourselves from others. Each of these processes depends on and implies the other: To have a self, we must interact with others; to interact competently, we must reflect on and understand ourselves in relation to those others. That is why understanding socialization requires us to examine both people's sense of belonging and their sense of autonomy, both how people are constrained by norms and values (shared ideas about what is right and wrong) and how people are autonomous agents able to make decisions for themselves. Freedom and constraint, we will see, are not opposites but interconnected features of everyone's ordinary, everyday life.

The approach taken in this chapter is that socialization is an active process, one in which those being socialized participate and to which they contribute. It is also an interactive process in which those who are socializing, like the parents in the example above, are themselves undergoing a learning process. Of course, we may learn from others without their knowledge; we learn from role models, from stories about heroes or villains, from the example of our parents and friends, and just by observing the people around us. But the most important learning, the crucial learning that transforms us into cultural beings, proceeds through interaction with others who are important to us and—usually—to whom we are important. Socialization, then, is a lifelong process of social interaction during which the individual acquires a self-identity and skills needed for living in society.

The crucial learning process that occurs in childhood and makes us members of society is called **primary socialization.** Because primary socialization is so important to becoming who and what we are, it is the focus of the first part of this chapter. But because humans are creative, adaptable beings, learning and change continue throughout our lives. Learning to be a student, a husband or wife, or a parent; learning a job and how to carry it out effectively; making new friends and undertaking new commitments—all these involve socialization. This kind of learning is called **secondary socialization** because it occurs after people have already undergone primary socialization. It is traditionally seen as occurring following the first few years of life when the individual is able to communicate symbolically, has developed a sense of self, and can well imagine himself or herself in someone else's position. However, it is not secondary in importance. We live in a world of constant and dramatic change, and secondary socialization is an ongoing feature of our lives. As we shall see, Mead (1934) observed that the achievement of this ability requires that we are able to develop a mental conception of what we think people think of us.

As Chapter 2 showed, culture provides us with the tools to solve the problems of survival. Symbols, norms, values, and everyday practices are examples of such tools. Their use allows us to master nature and build orderly societies; they must, however, be learned. Indeed, insofar as human beings are cultural beings, these tools must become a part of us—internalized through socialization. In a very real sense, then, it is socialization that makes social interaction, social organization, and social order possible.

Think of all the things we do every day involving other people. When we walk along a busy sidewalk, for example, we are able to pass many pedestrians heading toward us without colliding with any of them. This is possible because of the norms that regulate sidewalk behaviour without our being aware of them. Most of the time each of us will move to the right to avoid colliding with someone walking toward us. We don't even have to think about it; we simply move

to the right. If we move to our right when walking toward others and they move to their right (which is our left) when walking toward us, then we will not collide (Wolff, 1973). Such norms as these make social life orderly and allow us to deal with and interact with hundreds of anonymous strangers daily. It is not only norms that regulate behaviour, however. There are also many conventions, rituals, rules, and laws that direct our behaviour both with people whom we know well, such as co-workers, and with strangers.

How do we know to act on such norms, conventions, or rules? How do we know to move to the right to avoid colliding with a fellow pedestrian? We know through socialization. There is nothing "natural" about moving to the right to avoid a collision. In some societies, people move to the left; in others they don't particularly mind bumping into others. In our society we have learned to move to the right by watching others, and by seeing how others react when, on occasion, we have moved to the left by mistake. In this respect, norms constrain us; they channel and guide our behaviour in everyday life. Consider the alternative: Imagine what it would be like to have to decide separately as we walked along a sidewalk which way we should move to avoid colliding with each person we were walking toward. Norms make smooth and orderly interaction possible, freeing us from the need to plan every step we take and communicate in detail with everyone we meet about all the possible ways we could interact.

Because the process of becoming socialized occurs in a cultural context, the content of socialization differs greatly from one society to another. People in a particular society learn the norms, values, and lifestyles specific to their social environment. At the same time, however, within every society individuals differ in significant ways from one another. Such individual differences, too, are to some extent the product of socialization. Each person is influenced by distinctive or overlapping subcultures of family and friends, by class and gender. A subculture is a group within the larger culture that has distinctive values, norms, and practices. Our unique personal histories permit us not only to share in the larger society but also to participate in a specific part of it. The socialization process helps to explain both similarities and differences among people in a particular society.

NATURE AND NURTURE

Does that mean that everything we do and know is a product of socialization? Don't we have **instincts,** such as an instinct for survival or a maternal instinct? What about natural differences among people? Aren't there people with charismatic personalities, who have more of an impact on others than ordinary people do? Aren't some brighter than others, some more aggressive than others, some more compliant than others? Aren't there people who simply won't get out of the way when you walk toward them?

Although natural differences obviously exist among people, such differences explain very little about social behaviour or how a society is organized. It is doubtful, for instance, that human beings have either an instinct for survival or a maternal instinct. There are countless examples of people who clearly give little thought to their own survival or who have proven to be indifferent or abusive parents. Still, we can't deny that some human behaviour is the outcome of biological factors, and the debate over whether it is nature (biological inheritance) or nurture (the social environment) that is more important in shaping our beliefs and behaviour is an old one. Most sociologists who participate in this debate emphasize the importance of society and of socialization, suggesting that someone who is aggressive in our society might well have become gentle—or at least less aggressive—had that person been born in some other society or raised in some other set of circumstances.

Sociologists are also suspicious of explanations that emphasize biological inheritance because such explanations often shift from an initial focus on individual differences to an emphasis on group differences. In this way, they often lead to racist or sexist explanations or views (Gould, 1996). An example is the longstanding debate over intelligence: Is our intelligence the outcome of hereditary and genetic factors, or is it a product of social variables, such as class and family structure? Phrased that way, the debate is about the sources of individual differences. True to many sociologists' concerns, however, this debate has shifted from a question about individual differences to one focused on the supposed connection between race and IQ test scores (Herrnstein and Murray, 1994).

It is becoming more and more apparent today that the old debate on nature versus nurture sets up a false opposition. It is clear that nature and nurture are both complementary and inseparable. The human brain provides the physiological apparatus required for interpreting experiences, but unless children have the opportunity to learn, reason, and solve problems in early life, the brain itself may not fully

Most socialization takes place informally, with the participants unaware that they are being socialized. These little girls are unconsciously learning gender roles by playing dress-up.
SOURCE: Photo courtesy of Nurit Bodemann and Shira Brym.

develop (Begley, 1995). Attempts at determining the relative importance of nature and nurture in human development are much like trying to establish whether width or height is more significant in determining area.

We are not born human. We become human through the process of social interaction. Indeed, strong evidence exists that human beings have a biologically grounded need for social interaction and intimate relations with others. Evidence suggests that human infants have both a biological and an emotional need to cling to and interact with a warm, sheltering figure. Verbal communication may not be part of this contact, but some form of communication is—whether smiles, laughs, or touch. Without this contact, socialization is impaired, the individual is but a shell of a human being, and irreversible damage may be done to the person's sense of self.

Convincing evidence comes from studies of children raised in isolation by their families. The case of Anna is the best-known instance of the long-term social isolation of an infant. Anna was an illegitimate child hidden away in a room until she was nearly six years old. Her mother gave her only enough care to keep her alive. When she was discovered, her clothing and bedding were filthy, she was emaciated, and she was unable to walk, talk, feed herself, or respond to others. As she was cared for and began to interact with others, Anna made slow yet steady progress, but years of social isolation left her with permanent disabilities. By the age of eight, Anna's mental and social development was still less than that of a two-year-old.

Not until she was ten did she show the first signs of using language (Davis, 1947).

The importance of social contact in the development of human infants was also demonstrated when one research compared infants raised in an orphanage with those raised in a women's prison nursery (Spitz, 1945). The infants in the prison nursery interacted with their own mothers for the first year of their lives, whereas infants raised in the orphanage were attended only by nurses and spent their days lying on their backs, seeing and hearing very few people, and lacking social stimulation. Although in the beginning the orphan children were as healthy as those in the nursery, after two years the development of some of children in the orphanage was retarded, and all were psychologically and socially underdeveloped for their age. More shockingly, by age four a third of them had died! No such problems were observed among the prison nursery infants.

These examples show that socialization is essential both to the physical well-being and to the social competence of an infant. Even when, as in the case of Anna, infants survive lack of interaction and caring in early childhood, they are incapable of becoming fully competent, active members of society. This is not just a matter of "intelligence." Rather, the children have not had the opportunity to develop a self; they have no sense of social identity in terms of which they understand themselves and others around them. We can view the self as the point of reference for planning and orientation, for sorting and assessing life's situations in terms of their relative importance. As noted earlier, the self refers to our awareness of ideas and attitudes about our own personal and social identity. It is through interaction that such a sense of self emerges, and the development of the self is a crucial part of socialization.

THE SELF AND SOCIALIZATION

Where does our sense of self come from? Sociologists and psychologists alike have sought to answer that question. They have examined how individuals develop and modify a sense of who they are—their sense of self—and found that self-image greatly depends on social interaction. For instance, the newborn does not differentiate itself from its mother (Piaget, 1950). Such differentiation occurs gradually as the newborn learns to see its mother as a separate person. Through interaction the infant acquires the ability to see himself or herself reflected in the eyes of

others and to sense his or her own identity. It is precisely this ability that children who have been reared in isolation lack.

Though sociologists typically focus on the development of the social self, it is important to recognize the connections between the physical and the social selves. Research demonstrates the importance of the body for constructing self and identity. One sociologist recently examined women's experiences following weight-loss surgery, reporting on how it influenced their sense of embodiment and self during the transition from presurgery to postsurgery. Her study confirms that non-normative bodies can profoundly influence a person's self and identity. The women in the surgical group maintained that they were "new" people, both in terms of body and self. Although the women did not feel they were fundamentally different since their surgery, "they thought the surgery removed the layers of fat to reveal the 'real' body and its corresponding 'real' self" (Joanisse, 2005). This study illustrates that the self is not fixed. A person can modify the self, when necessary radically altering it in response to interactions with others.

Socialization, then, involves not only learning about others but also developing a sense of self. To understand the process of self-growth, we will examine the theories of two early scholars—Charles Horton Cooley (1864–1929) and George Herbert Mead (1863–1931). We will then see how their ideas were used and modified by a more recent sociologist, Paul Willis.

TWO EARLY THEORISTS

CHARLES HORTON COOLEY

In the early 1900s, few sociologists or psychologists paid much attention to the role of interaction in socialization. In this respect, Cooley's work was groundbreaking. Cooley (1902) introduced the idea of the **looking-glass self,** suggesting that the gestures and reactions of others are a mirror or "looking glass" in which we see ourselves. Just as we look in a mirror to see a reflection of our physical body, we look to others to see a reflection of our psychological and social self. Cooley's emphasis was less on the actual responses of others than on our imagination, or interpretation, of those responses. And just as we may be pleased or displeased with what we see when we look at ourselves in a mirror, depending on our expectations about ourselves physically, so too are our conceptions about ourselves socially—our feelings about who and what we are—organized around our evaluation of how we believe ourselves to be judged by others.

This means that without the social mirror, there can be no sense of self. For Cooley, self-image emerges as a product of involvement in groups and communication with others. The first images of the self are received from **significant others**—those people, such as parents, who are of central importance to the individual in the development of the self. Later, other images both complement and supplant those first images, especially as the child's interaction network expands. Particularly important in this regard is the role played by the **primary group,** the small group (especially the family) that is characterized by intimate, face-to-face association and cooperation. Through repeated processes of imagination and identification, the self-concept is built and organized. In this way, Cooley suggested, the structure and content of the self are derived from society, which is represented by the groups and significant others surrounding the individual.

GEORGE HERBERT MEAD

Mead followed Cooley's lead, concentrating his analysis on the importance of the interplay between society and the individual. His major contribution was a theory of the relationship among mind, self, and society that became the foundation of symbolic interactionism (see Chapter 1) and influenced many sociologists who use a wide variety of other perspectives.

Unlike Cooley, Mead did not assume that socialization consists largely of learning to conform to the rest of society. Rather, he saw socialization as an active process in which individuals play a crucial role in their own development.

Key to that process, Mead (1934) suggested, is the ability to communicate, especially to make use of symbolic communication. Symbols are gestures, objects, or sounds that stand for something else and whose meaning depends on shared understandings. A dove, for example, is a bird, but when we see a picture of a dove on a poster, we know that it is supposed to represent—or be a symbol of—peace. Like other animals, human infants first communicate through nonverbal gestures. Unlike animal communication, however, even at this rudimentary level, most human communication is symbolic, as infants and the others around them develop shared understandings about

George Herbert Mead (1863–1931) was the driving force behind the study of how individual identity is formed in the course of interaction with other people. The work of Mead and his colleagues gave birth to symbolic interactionism, a distinctively North American theoretical tradition that continues to be a major force in sociology today.
SOURCE: Granger Collection.

the meaning of the gestures. This process lays the foundation for the development of language, which makes possible the replacement of gestures with ideas. The use of symbols enables the child to think of itself in relation to others and is at the core of all stages of the socialization process.

Suppose that you are not sure how another person understands the meaning of an action, an object, or a word. Because you share a language, you can ask the other person what he or she means and determine whether your understanding and the other person's are the same. Of course, that is not always possible or desirable. If you are attending a job interview, you would not wear a pair of dirty jeans and then ask the interviewer whether he or she considers your clothing to be appropriate. Instead you would try to anticipate in advance how others will see and react to you. You will "take the role of the other," that is, attempt to determine or appreciate someone else's perspective in a particular situation.

What is true for us only sometimes is always true for infants. Infants do not know how others understand

and react to the world and especially to the infants themselves. **Taking the role of the other,** then, is an essential skill children must develop to be effective members of society. Children are not born with the ability to understand other people. As Mead showed, children, through their interaction with others, develop an ability to take the role of the other. This ability is central to children's understanding of others and to the internalization of the values, attitudes, and beliefs of the society in which they live. Mead, though, went even further. He suggested that it is through taking the role of the other that children also develop a sense of self. That is, conformity and individuality are interconnected; mind, self, and society are the product of interaction.

Three Stages in Taking the Role of the Other

The ability to take the role of the other, Mead suggested, is acquired in three stages. First is the **imitative stage.** Children two years old and under do not interact effectively with others because they cannot take the role of the other. They lack the verbal and other skills needed to communicate effectively. Much of their behaviour is imitative make-believe. At this stage of development, children have no real conception of themselves as separate social beings or understanding of what it is like to be a mother, father, or doctor. When they play, they may act out the behaviour associated with these roles, but what they are doing is not true role-playing, only imitation.

The second developmental stage described by Mead is the **play stage** in which children begin to adopt the roles of significant others—a parent, a sports celebrity, a storybook hero—and their play shifts from imitative to imaginative. Through play they learn to imagine how people will respond without actually having to act out the situation. Though language, children can now manipulate the various roles without physical action. At this stage, the role need not be firmly rooted in reality but can be defined according to the children's own wishes or their desire to please significant others. Children do not yet see role-playing as a social necessity—they merely play at the social roles of life.

Still, children at the play stage have difficulty coordinating their actions with others. Look at a group of four- or five-year-olds playing a game like soccer, for example. Typically, such children will pay no attention to the team they are supposed to be part of, caring only that they get to the ball and have the opportunity to kick it. They have no concept of playing a particular position. Almost all of them will be wherever the ball is. Often they shove and push others to get at the ball—including those who are supposed to be their own teammates. The idea that there are rules, positions to be played, and actions to take in cooperation with others is difficult for children at this stage to grasp.

The third and final stage in the development of the self is the **game stage.** In this stage children have developed a generalized impression of the behaviour people expect as well as awareness of their own importance to the group and vice-versa. Mead used the metaphor of a game to describe the complex behaviour that is required at this stage. In an organized game, such as baseball, a player must continually adjust behaviour to the needs of the team as a whole and to the specific situations that arise in the game. If the batter is running to first base, the outfielder does not throw the ball to the second baseman because she likes him better than the first baseman. Instead, her actions are oriented to the general rules and practices that make up the game. At this point, Mead held, children are responding to what he called the **generalized other,** a conception of how people in general—not someone specific in particular—will respond in a situation. This generalized other is internalized. It comprises the values, attitudes, and beliefs that the individual understands to be a part of the society and in terms of which the individual assumes others will react. In effect, taking the role of the generalized other means that we respond to our idea of the organized group or community of which we are a part.

Suppose you are among a group of strangers when you do something embarrassing, such as tripping and falling. Chances are you will feel embarrassed even though you know none of the people around you. You may look to see how they are reacting to what you have done or you may studiously avoid looking at anyone else, but in either case your response is not really to the particular people present but to your own idea of how people in general will respond to what you have done. You have, in effect, internalized the attitudes, values, and beliefs that are a part of the society in which you live. Internalization means that the attitudes, values, and beliefs that were at one time imposed on you by others, such as parents, come to be a part of you; you are the one who reacts with shame when you do something embarrassing.

Socialization in this sense is an active process because it proceeds through interaction with others.

Our ability to communicate allows us not only to interact with others but also to communicate with ourselves. As we observe the conduct and reactions of other people, learning their expectations and point of view, we anticipate how *we* should react in a particular situation and then plan, rehearse, modify, and perfect our own behaviour. We may debate alternative courses of action, impress ourselves with our own wit, or cringe in remembered embarrassment at some ancient gaffe. In these and many other ways, we engage in what Mead called an internal conversation, and it is through such internal conversations that we come to develop an integrated sense of self. To the degree that we experience the generalized other as a unity, our sense of self, too, will be unitary.

The "Me" and the "I"

In a way, then, we are not only subjects—thinking, knowing, and feeling beings—but also objects to ourselves—social and cultural beings whom we can evaluate, respond to, have feelings about, and try to modify. Because we first imagine ourselves from the perspectives of other people, Mead suggested that we are first aware of ourselves as social objects. He called this objective element of the self the **me**. Accompanying the me is the subjective or active part of the self, which Mead called the **I**. It is this subjective component of the self that allows us to react to and assess ourselves, to engage in what Mead described as an "internal conversation." Have you ever done something and then asked yourself, "Why did I do that?" Asking such a question implies that we can question ourselves, wonder at our motives, analyze our feelings, and respond to ourselves as we would respond to someone else. But who is it we are responding to? Mead's answer is that all social experience involves an interaction of the I and the me, with the I initiating action and the me reflectively taking the role of the other. In other words, the self is both spontaneous (the I) and conformist (the me), both active (the I) and reflective (the me), both experiencing (the I) and experienced (the me). Throughout our life, our sense of self continues to develop, Mead suggested, because our experiences involve a continuing conversation between the me and the I. Changing contexts and contacts produce new opportunities for learning. But Mead also believed that our decisions and choices about action affect others. In other words, human beings shape their own circumstances and lives, and those of the people around them.

Mead's discussion of childhood socialization remained rather general. Yet, precisely because we are creative participants in the socialization process, we do not all respond in the same way to the same circumstances; that is, we do not all share a "generalized other." The generalized other is not society; it is not even a set of rules, norms, or guidelines imposed by society. Rather, the generalized other is our particular set of ideas about how others will respond (or should respond) to what we do. That means that not everyone is socialized in the same way. The self we develop is not purely the result of our own intentions, preferences, and interactions. There are constraints, such as class, ethnic, religious, and geographic differences, that have a profound impact on how a person is socialized, on his or her sense of self and self-worth, and on that person's understanding of others. We are not free to become whomever or whatever we want to be.

WILLIS'S APPLICATION AND EXTENSION OF MEAD'S THEORY

The recognition that socialization implies both conformity and creativity and that the individual must both deal with constraints and take advantage of opportunities underlies the work of British sociologist Paul Willis. Willis uses a theoretical approach similar to that of Mead but extends it by looking at youths rather than at children and, more importantly, by recognizing the institutional and social contexts within which the self is forged, maintained, and transformed.

Typically, sociologists have assumed that the most fundamental forms of socialization occur in childhood and that after children start school, most socialization consists of little more than learning institutional roles. Willis (1990) disagreed with this assumption, arguing instead that teens and young adults are still engaged in a process of developing their identity and sense of self.

As children we may take the role of the other, but as young people we tend to be more concerned with our own identity and with announcing ourselves to others. What becomes evident when we look at youths, rather than at children, is the significance of social location, that is, class, race, ethnicity, gender, and the other institutional and social collectivities of which people may be members. Membership makes a difference, if only in the kind of symbolic resources available to people to express themselves and to have an impact on how others see them. Commercialization also makes a difference, as cultural industries try to profit from the desire of young people to have fun, express themselves, and be up-to-date. Understanding socialization, Willis asserts, requires that we recognize "the materiality of context as well as the symbolism of self" (1990). As Willis explains, "Memberships of race, class, gender, age and region are not only learned, they are lived and experimented with. This is so even if only by pushing up against the oppressive limits of established order and power" (1990: 12).

Willis's argument is that we are all creative individuals trying to transform the world in ways that allow us to express and control our selves. Take the e-mail usernames that young people adopt. An e-mail user name can be boring and to the point—like the usernames of most professors. The addresses invented by students, conversely, tend to be communicative in their own right. They provide students with the opportunity to name themselves in a way that tells others something distinctive about them. We do not believe our students are in any sense unusual, despite having such usernames as I_hate_being, partyguy109, malaprohibita_oyvey, mymyopicview, crazygirl378, filthylummox, and the like. As stuffy adults, the authors of this chapter would never think of employing such evocative usernames, but the people who chose them were expressing something they consider important about themselves and saying (sometimes ironically), "This is who I am." The username has a meaning that goes beyond a simple identifier. Even if we don't get it, we understand that the name means something and we may be curious what that meaning is. The username is a creative way of generating interest; it attempts to control how others respond to the user. In fact, the Internet as a whole is an explosion of opportunities for creativity. People can design their own websites; communicate with others at any time by using chat programs, e-mail, and blogs; share art work, photos, music, poems, and stories; write fan fiction; contribute to online journals; and play games. In all these ways they communicate creatively, indicating to others by symbolic means what matters to them and who they really are.

In stressing the link among creativity, identity, and social context, Willis does not mean to imply that all young people are "artists" but that they take advantage of every opportunity to make the everyday world around them meaningful, as we see in the example of e-mail usernames. Another example centres on the way young people use musical taste as a means of signifying identity. The teenage daughter of one of this chapter's authors recently announced that she "could never date someone with different musical

taste from mine." Music, in this case, is seen less as a means of entertainment than as a sign of group membership. Music can also serve as a set of markers indicating change and development. Reflection on changing musical taste, from pop to rock to jazz, for example, can indicate to the individual that he or she has "grown up" and is no longer a teeny-bopper, an immature adolescent, or a rebellious teen (Jackson and Rosenberg, 2004).

Like Mead, Willis reminds us that the human being is a creative and strategic social actor, rather than a social dope or the pawn of vast, impersonal forces. Still, Willis acknowledges, social categories do make a difference. Socialization is not a unitary process. Different categories of people will participate in socialization in different ways. One of the most important of those differences is gender. In many societies it makes an enormous difference whether a person is socialized male or female, a difference that determines the course of life.

GENDER SOCIALIZATION

What about our own society? What does it mean to be male or female here and now? How are we socialized to be male or female? Are gender definitions changing? Are socialization processes with respect to gender changing as well? Let us examine these questions in detail.

Gender socialization is the "process through which individuals learn to become feminine and masculine according to expectations current in their society" (Mackie, 1991: 75). As discussed in detail in Chapter 4, gender identity is learned. Still, gender appears as so much a natural part of everyday life that we typically take it for granted. We assume that people are either male or female and we quickly learn how each sex is expected to behave. Sometimes, though, we find ourselves in situations where someone's behaviour deviates from expectations. In such a situation, we are unsure how to relate to that person. Although gender identity, or identification of oneself as male or female, ordinarily emerges early in life and remains unchanged, the experiences of transvestites and transsexuals suggest that moderate to radical changes are possible (Williams, 2002).

To the extent that a culture defines male and female roles as distinctly different, parents raise boys and girls so that they *will* be different. Moreover, boys and girls grow up *wanting* to be different, believing that gender role differences are normal and necessary.

Patterns of gender role socialization reveal that, from the first days of life, an infant is not simply a child but a boy or a girl. Infant boys are usually addressed differently from infant girls, the blankets in which they are covered are usually different colours, and the rooms in which they sleep are usually decorated to show their gender. One of the first things that a child learns is whether he or she is a "he" or a "she." From an early age, children show marked gender-specific preferences for certain toys and activities (Davies, 1990). These preferences are reinforced in later years. For example, among preteens femininity is constructed partly by means of shopping. Specialty stores and specialized departments in large department stories define (and, every season, redefine) certain clothing, hair styling products, cosmetics, and accessories as appropriate and fashionable for girls. In this way, the meaning of becoming a woman is tied to various aspects of consumer culture (Russell and Tyler, 2002).

Parents are usually the first source of children's gender learning, and indications are that parents hold and communicate different expectations for males and females. An early study compared two groups of first-time parents: those who had daughters and those who had sons (Rubin, Provenzano, and Luria, 1974). Within 24 hours of their child's birth, the parents of daughters tended to describe their child as soft, fine-featured, and delicate, while parents of sons tended to describe their child as firm, strong, well coordinated, hardy, and alert. Similarly, a study of children's assigned household tasks found a clear gender division of labour (Cohen, 2004): Boys were expected to mow the lawn, shovel snow, take out the garbage, and do yard work, while the girls were expected to clean house, wash dishes, cook, and babysit younger children. Although couples today enter parenthood with a stronger commitment to sharing household responsibilities than couples did in the past, most nevertheless develop a gendered division of labour (Fox, 1998, 2001).

The mass media, too, present idealized images and stereotypes of appropriate masculine and feminine characteristics (Goffman, 1979). To the degree that females were portrayed in a narrow and biased way by the media for years, the impact of gender-role stereotypes negatively affected how children perceived themselves (Adams and Bettis, 2003; Massoni, 2004). Oversimplified gender-role stereotypes affected children's self-concept and interaction with peers and adults (Kortenhaus and Demarest, 1993). More recently, researchers examined 83 leading children's books in terms of the gender of the main

character, illustrations, and title (Gooden and Gooden, 2001). They found that although gender stereotyping has decreased since the 1970s, it is still prevalent.

Stereotyping contributes to the streaming of males and females into traditional "male" and "female" jobs. More often than not, teachers and guidance counsellors unwittingly encourage boys and girls to pursue occupational goals that are perceived as appropriate to their gender. This becomes a self-fulfilling prophecy: Girls develop a self-image consistent with others' perceptions of them. Thus, one study of 150 Canadian teenagers found a tendency for girls to make traditionally feminine occupational choices and to express less confidence than boys that they would realize their occupational goals (Baker, 1985). About three-quarters of the girls planned to hold paying jobs as adults. However, they tended to see the responsibility for the household and for child care as primarily theirs and to assume that paid work must fit in with these other duties. This expectation about the future fits with the actual division of household tasks (Barber and Allen, 1992; Blau and Ferber, 1992; South and Spitze, 1994). Although more and more women are choosing careers that are not traditionally feminine, women still do not have the range of choice that is available to men. Even today there are many careers that most of the public does not see as "appropriate" for women (Brooks, Jarman, and Blackburn, 2003).

The study of gender shows us that children and adults are socialized to respond to their social world by developing certain potentials and inhibiting others. It is less their innate differences than it is differences in the socialization of males and females that affect the assumption of "masculine" and "feminine" characteristics (Buysse and Sheridan Embser-Herbert, 2004).

The prevailing importance of gender socialization, especially as men and women cross gender lines in work and leisure and participate more fully in previously gender-segregated activities, is examined in a recent study of how traditional gender roles are reproduced in modern wedding showers (Montemurro, 2005). Showers are ideal areas of social life in which to investigate shifts in gender socialization because they involve well-defined gender "scripts" and rituals that tend to celebrate heterosexuality. Based on in-depth interviews with 51 young women, along with participant observation conducted at five bridal showers, the author concludes that men's presence at wedding showers does not reflect gender convergence or alterations in traditional marriage roles: "Rather, the fact that the co-ed shower was a supplement, that women still had traditional bridal showers, and that jokes were often made that reinforced traditional notions of husband and wife roles during the gift opening at co-ed showers all suggest a lack of change" (Montemurro, 2005: 33). Hence, the author concludes that bridal and co-ed showers perpetuate traditional gender roles in marriage.

SOCIALIZATION THROUGH THE LIFE COURSE

Childhood socialization is referred to as primary socialization because it lays a foundation that influences our self-concept and involvement in social life for as long as we live. But socialization continues throughout life, as we now show.

ADOLESCENCE AND YOUTH

As Willis noted, during adolescence and youth, dramatic transformations of identity, **status,** and social relationships tend to occur. (Although in everyday speech *status* means "prestige," in sociology it refers to the culturally and socially defined position a person occupies in an interaction.) We enter adolescence as children and are somehow transformed by the end of that period into young adults.

Adolescence, the period between childhood and adulthood, is a crucial period of life in which people undergo new experiences, deal with new demands and responsibilities, and strive to develop an identity that is distinctively their own. Even more than in childhood, socialization during adolescence requires that we find a balance between autonomy and conformity, between freedom and constraint. Unlike children, however, most adolescents are acutely aware of the demands being placed on them by others and of the demands they place on themselves. This makes adolescence a difficult time of life, not only for adolescents but also for parents, friends, and teachers.

Because adolescence is such a difficult time for many people, we generally associate it with emotional and social turmoil. Young people experience conflict with their parents and other adults as they attempt to develop their own identity, act on their own preferences, and form their own relationships. Though much of the social turmoil at this stage is often attributed to physiological changes linked to the onset of puberty, a more sociological way of thinking focuses on inconsistencies in the socialization process.

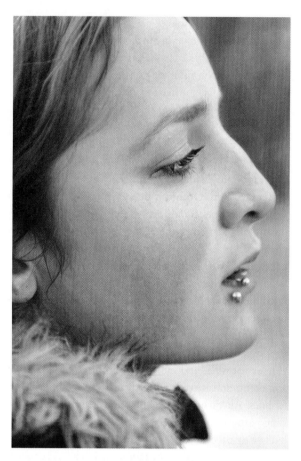

It is during adolescence that the most dramatic transformations of identity, status, and social relationships tend to occur.
SOURCE: © Benis Arapovic/Shutterstock.

Adolescents, for example, are repeatedly told by adults to "grow up" but are treated as if they are still children. Sexuality is a case in point. Adolescents receive messages of encouragement from the mass media and restraint from parents. Although adolescents associate adulthood with freedom, they get the confusing message from adults that in order to "act like an adult" they must not decide for themselves but rather do exactly what adults tell them to do.

This would not be such a problem if most adolescents did not live at home under the authority of adults. But that has not always been so. In premodern societies, adolescence did not exist as a separate and prolonged stage of life. Young people would often marry by the age of 16 or 17, sometimes even younger. If they did live at home, they had large responsibilities of their own and ways to demonstrate competence and maturity.

Adolescence as a distinct period of life is a product of industrialization and the extension of education that it introduced. Mass education and compulsory school attendance altered the role of the family and helped give rise to adolescence. Because young people were required to remain in school, they were not expected to assume economic responsibility as soon as they reached sexual maturity. Instead they continued to live at home. Burgess and Richardson (1984) traced the distinctiveness of adolescence to the modern high school, where students became educated in skills and knowledge that the family was not equipped to impart. Paradoxically, although high school may provide skills that eventually allow the adolescent to become independent of the family, it does so in a context where students have little autonomy.

Although many families subscribe to the ideal of democracy, the reality is otherwise (Solomon, Warin, Lewis, and Langford, 2002). Parents and teenagers often claim that openness is the route to intimacy and democracy, but in practice young people experience rules imposed by parents who are often unwilling to compromise. Parents, seeking to preserve their own identity, exercise control and seek to monitor the adolescent's behaviour. This is a source of resentment among adolescents who realize that reciprocity in communication is often lacking in parent–teenager relationships. As parents demand more and more information, the relationship moves further away from friendship.

We should not exaggerate adults' impact on adolescents. Although, on average, the family exerts more of an influence than peer groups do regarding such fundamental matters as religious orientation, political preferences, and career aspirations, occasions also arise when young people are less influenced by their families or teachers than by their peers, and this peer influence promotes youthful autonomy. It is not that adults give young people freedom but that the conflicting and confusing messages they receive from adults, peers, the media, and their own experience require them to make up their own minds. For those who are unable to reconcile the demands of the new and the old, adolescence may be a time of considerable confusion and turmoil (Hogan and Astone, 1986). Yet for all the turbulence and rebellion generally associated with adolescence, evidence suggests that most teenagers have good experiences of adolescence and believe they have positive relationships with their parents (Coleman and Hendry, 1990).

Why is this so? Adolescents may experience adolescence positively because much of it is exciting and fun. Friendships, for example, take on a different character in adolescence than in childhood. They often become very intense, and people come to feel very close to their friends, developing attachments that often last a lifetime. Many new interests arise in music, art, and fashion that are used by adolescents as symbols of group membership and indicators of personal taste and status. This allows for the development of passionate commitments and a sense of satisfaction and achievement when, for example, a favourite musical group has a number one song on the charts. Then, of course, there is the excitement of dating, the thrill of romance and sex, and the intense involvement in all of the accompanying activities, such as gossiping with friends, showing off a boyfriend or girlfriend, and going places together.

Finally, adolescence is also a period of **anticipatory socialization,** "the process by which aspirants to a particular social role begin to discern what it will be like to function in that position" (Stebbins, 1990: 99). Through interaction with people who act out various roles, and by observing how roles are portrayed in the mass media, adolescents learn to incorporate the perspectives and expectations of the larger society and imagine what it would be like to enact the roles to which they aspire (Stryker, 1980: 63).

Our ability to anticipate others' behaviour, or how to conduct ourselves in situations that are unfamiliar, rests on our familiarity with norms and expectations characterizing particular settings and situations. As students of social behaviour have observed, it isn't at all unusual for us to begin socializing ourselves before we start playing new roles. Sociologists identify anticipatory socialization as a process of preparing oneself for acquiring new norms and behaviour. In effect, the individual "rehearses" for future positions, social relationships, and even occupations. Thus, for example, students intending to enter the legal profession try imagining how this experience, in its many aspects, will affect their next few years; and successful applicants for immigration to Canada try anticipating how this experience will influence the organization of family life, gender relations, occupational choice, and the like. Again, many young people experience this kind of anticipatory socialization as fun. Ahead of them, though, lies an uncertain future and the responsibilities of adulthood.

ADULT SOCIALIZATION

Adult socialization is the process by which adults take on new statuses and acquire new and different social identities. Adults frequently find themselves in new situations at work or in private life, meeting new people and taking on new responsibilities. To participate effectively in their society, adults must continue to undergo socialization (Clausen, 1986; Hogan and Astone, 1986).

Adult socialization differs from adolescent socialization in several important respects (Brim, 1968). Whereas adolescents seek to achieve autonomy, adults generally have control over the content and direction of their socialization. Although adolescents often have little choice but to participate in various activities, adults usually engage in socializing activities voluntarily, such as enrolling in evening courses or joining a church. Because adults can often choose roles of their own free will, they can better understand and articulate their motives for new undertakings.

When we assume new statuses as adults, we need to become familiar with the expectations associated with them, learning how the statuses are best performed. Frequently such learning occurs over a considerable period as individuals interact with others in a similar situation.

The status of university student is a case in point. New students discover an institutional and social scene unlike any they have encountered and whose demands and requirements are initially unclear. In high school, young people have little autonomy and are continually being told what to do. In university, they find themselves in a very different milieu. University students vary widely in age, are in a better position to follow their interests, and are usually expected by their professors to be autonomous, mature adults.

Research by University of Manitoba sociologists Cheryl and Dan Albas focuses on how university students learn to perform a seemingly natural activity: studying. Based on data derived from their own observations, interviews, and logs obtained from students in their classes, the researchers demonstrate that students must learn to approach, accomplish, and maintain their study practices. As they assert: "While they build on the stock of knowledge required in high school, they also find themselves subjected to a potentially conflicting set of definitions which predate their presence, but characterize the university subculture" (Albas and Albas, 1994: 288).

Concentrating their analysis on the drama surrounding exam preparation, Albas and Albas (1994) distinguished three types of students:

1. The diligently planning, high-achieving "Aces" recognize the importance of keeping their nose to the grindstone, are never satisfied with a grade lower than A, and plan their schedule to allow for adequate exam preparation.
2. The procrastinating, low-achieving "Bombers" make use of "wise nostrums, self-lulling mantras, and numerous convenient distractions, all of which are directed toward delaying serious study until the very last moment when guilt and fright force them into it" (Albas and Albas, 1994: 281).
3. The "Moderates" form the largest category of students. They are most likely to have to juggle multiple roles (student, parent, spouse, caregiver, and so forth) so they have to ration their time and energy among roles.

These three categories, according to the Albases, are roles that students learn to play. In the process of learning them, they become aware of the significance of demonstrating competence or coolness in their everyday experiences in the university setting. Moreover, once students are categorized or categorize themselves as Aces, Moderates, or Bombers, their identity plays an important role in structuring action. For example, students who view themselves as Aces and discover their grades are faltering typically study more or consult with the professor. In contrast, Bombers conclude they have little to lose by weak performance. "Give me a C and let me be free" is their motto. The Albases observe that students who share similar identities tend to be attracted to one another. They find that studying is easier if they interact with others like themselves.

Marriage constitutes one of the most important changes in anyone's life and is therefore perhaps the most important example of adult socialization. Although many of the traditional role expectations of marriage are no longer accepted uncritically, most people still choose to get married. In contrast to an earlier period when tradition largely determined the choices new couples would make, newlyweds and live-in partners now chart their own course. This independence is highly valued by most people, but it can lead to stress and strain in relationships with friends, family, and partners. There are no courses on how to adapt to married life. Most socialization consists of a couple learning, through trial and error, how to get along with others (such as in-laws) as a couple and how to get along with each other.

A significant decision during adulthood is whether to become parents. Becoming a parent also involves acquiring new skills and statuses. Although the statuses are conferred automatically, the roles and expectations accompanying them must be learned. As parents inevitably discover, relationships with children require active negotiation and adjustment. Moreover, children grow and change. This means that adults cannot simply adjust to their new role as parents and then relax. They must continuously adapt and accommodate to changing circumstances. No wonder many parents try to take control in rigid ways; they are simply trying to achieve some measure of stability in their lives and that of their family.

Socialization during adulthood also may involve the development of a career. As many postsecondary graduates discover, the difficulty of meeting this challenge successfully is increased by an economy in which employment prospects are uncertain. A set of "R words" serve as signposts of the changes taking place in the workplace—restructuring, reorganization, rationalizing, and re-engineering—that strike fear in the hearts of employees and postsecondary students (Lawson, 1996). As well, the type of employment offered to graduates is in flux. Many positions are now contractual, making employment less secure and stable (see Chapter 11). People can now expect to undergo career changes, with accompanying retraining, several times in their lives.

SOCIALIZATION AMONG SENIORS

Some of the most difficult changes in adult attitudes and behaviour occur in the later years of life (Erikson, 1982). It is during this period that the individual is most directly confronted by lowered prestige, decreased physical ability, and the prospect of chronic illness and death. Our society extends little dignity to aging. Although medical advances have prolonged lives, they have given little esteem to older people. The mass media present seniors in stereotypical terms. Consequently, many of us see old age as a period of increasing helplessness and dependence. Most of what we see is that achieving the status of "senior" is often accompanied by the loss of useful roles and valued statuses, such as those of worker and spouse.

Although many people spend a good part of their working life looking forward to retirement from the paid labour force, the realities of retirement may create identity problems for the retiree. Although most Canadians retire at age 65, they have made little preparation for retired life. Cut off from work at an arbitrary age, retirees are forced to assume what has been called a "roleless status" (Hooyman and Kiyak, 1993; Shanas, Townsend, Wedderburn, Friis, Milhøj,

and Stehouwer, 1972). The transition from work to retirement typically carries negative consequences:

> If the older worker incorporates the negative societal stereotypes, a gradual shift in self-image will occur. . . . When the negative appraisal summarized in "We see you as a bumbling fool" becomes internalized to "I am a bumbling fool," a downward spiral is set in motion that is difficult to break. (Hendricks and Hendricks, 1986: 332)

Many older people, particularly women, must also face the loss of a spouse. Widowhood, like retirement, is a roleless status for which society offers little preparation and little guidance. Few defined norms govern when "normal" functioning should be resumed or how this should come about. This period also involves stress as the widow seeks to accommodate a new status, a new identity, and a new set of problems.

Finally, socialization in old age also involves facing death and dying. Western society attempts to deny death and to remove all reference to it in everyday life (Ariès, 1981). We are taught not to talk about death, particularly to the dying. Relatives often attempt to keep the dying person from knowing his or her condition, and dying people sometimes keep their own prognosis secret (Atchley, 1994; Glaser and Strauss, 1967; Leming and Dickinson, 1990). As one sociologist comments, "The status of a dying person is, like retirement and widowhood, a status almost devoid of roles" (Shepard, 1993: 153).

AGENTS OF SOCIALIZATION

Whatever stage of the life course we may be in, socialization, as we have continually stressed, is a *social* process in which we interact with others, are changed by others, and in turn may have an impact on them. Who are these others? They can be almost anyone, but as we have already noted certain categories of people are especially likely to influence us, such as family members or peers. They serve as **agents of socialization**—individuals, groups, and institutions that impart, and from which we acquire, the range of information required to interact effectively and participate in society. In addition to parents and peers are social institutions, such as schools and the mass media, which have a significant impact on us and socialize us. We cannot interact with such institutions directly, although we do interact with people, such as classmates, with whom we participate in these institutions.

Since they provide a context within which we come to take on new ideas and, sometimes, new roles, institutions too can serve as agents of socialization.

You may note that some agents of socialization, such as the family and the school, receive a mandate from society to "train" the next generation of members. In contrast, the peer group and the mass media do much of their "teaching" less formally or directly. Nonetheless, they can profoundly influence how individuals perceive and respond to the people and the world around them.

FAMILIES

For young children in most societies, the family is virtually their entire world for the first few years of life. Parents are in a powerful position to influence their child. After all, the newborn is helpless, and his or her survival, physical and emotional, depends on the parents, who are the source of all rewards: security, love, affection, food, and approval. Through close interaction with parents and a small number of other people, the child learns to think and speak; internalizes norms, beliefs, and values; forms basic attitudes; develops a capacity for intimate and personal relationships; and begins to develop a self-image (Handel, 1990). Later experiences may lead to a modification of what is learned in the family, but it is not unusual for people to bring into adult life habits and expectations that characterized their childhood. Often, young people who rebelled against their parents' way of life and values as adolescents adopt the very same way of life and values when they become parents.

We discussed socialization into gender roles earlier. Although various institutions, including schools, the mass media, the church, and sports, may contribute substantially to the child's socialization into feminine and masculine norms and activities, the family's role is critical (Fox, 2001). Parents may not deliberately teach boys to be aggressive or girls to be submissive and dependent (Lytton and Romney, 1991), but in the family gender-typing prevails. This is evident in how children play, which toys are chosen for them, and how household chores are assigned. It is also in the family that children observe and model their parents' gender roles (Stockard and Johnson, 1992; Weitzman, 1979).

Family life also teaches about affection, anger management, financial responsibilities, and respect for others (Benokraitis, 1997). Such socialization

occurs informally, often offering a tentative model of marriage and parenthood.

In some ways, the family is well suited to the task of socialization. It is a small group in which all members can have constant face-to-face contact with one another. As a result, children's progress can be closely observed and adjustments made as necessary. Also, parents are usually well motivated. They have a strong emotional tie to their children, and the most meaningful and effective kind of social interaction for the purpose of socialization is that it is fused with emotion.

However, the family is not always an effective or efficient agent of socialization. Parents may be negative role models too. For instance, highly career-oriented parents may be surprised when their son opts to drop out of university to enjoy life, rejecting a way of life that requires enormous sacrifices be made for career success. Some parents have little understanding of parenting. They may be unprepared for it emotionally and their dedication and commitment to the task may be offset by competing considerations (see Figure 3.1). Some parents neglect, abuse, or even abandon their children. As well, much evidence indicates that parents may reproduce in their children the negative modelling they experienced in their own upbringing.

At the same time, however, families bestow statuses on us—such as class statuses—that may significantly affect our lives and sense of self. Class status will very likely place constraints on the opportunities

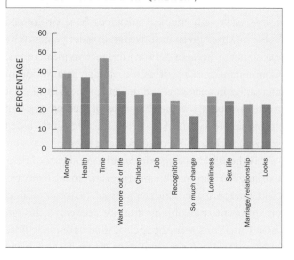

FIGURE 3.1   TOP 12 CONCERNS OF CANADIANS (PERCENTAGE CONCERNED "A GREAT DEAL" OR "QUITE A BIT")

SOURCE: Adapted from Reginald W. Bibby, *The Boomer Factor* (Toronto: Bastian Books, 2006), p. 115. Used with the permission of the author.

that we are afforded. Research suggests that middle-class parents tend to rear their children differently from working-class parents (Kohn, Naoi, Schooler, and Slomczynski, 1990). Middle-class families are likely to instill such values as achievement and independent thinking in their children, encouraging their curiosity and initiative. Working-class and poor families, by contrast, stress obedience and authority, punishing their children's transgressions by withholding privileges.

Kohn and his colleagues (1990) explained their findings by looking at the different work situations of the two groups. Whereas middle-class parents often work at jobs that reward autonomy and creativity, the jobs of working-class parents often involve the repetitive performance of tasks under close supervision. Parents, they concluded, socialize their children in ways that reflect their experiences of autonomy and conformity on the job. However, such differences in socialization patterns have narrowed as families of different social class backgrounds have tuned to similar media sources, including books, television talk shows, and magazines, for advice on rearing children (Luster, Rhoades, and Haas, 1989).

The impact parents have on their children's educational aspirations and occupational success has occupied an important place in the sociological literature. Here again, research suggests that class differences exist in parents' attitudes toward education, which have a significant effect on their children's educational aspirations. For example, in line with conflict theorists' claims that socialization reproduces the class structure in successive generations, Ballantine (1997) has shown that children in poor and low-income families are socialized to believe that aspiring to lofty ambitions and acquiring an education may be unrealistic in light of existing economic conditions in the family. Middle- and upper-income families emphasize and instill ideas of social success in their children. A culture of professionalism drives the attitudes of middle-class parents toward education. In contrast, working-class people see their chances of upward mobility as slim. For that reason, they resist the advice of the educational establishment (Lareau, 1987).

Three macrosocial changes over the past century have strained the institution of the family (Skolnick, 1991). First, the shift from an industrial to an information and service economy drew women into the labour force and set the stage for both a feminist revival and an adolescent rebellion. Second, demographic change shortened the active parenting stage and extended old age and living alone as expected

parts of the life course. Third, people are increasingly preoccupied with the quality of intimate relationships, which has contributed to rising divorce rates. Other social changes have also contributed to the reversal of past family trends, including increasing age at marriage, lower rates of marriage, increasing rates of cohabitation outside of marriage, and more single-parent households with "latch-key" children who return home from school before their parents return home from work (Baker, 1989).

Finally, we should mention the ever-increasing diversity of forms taken by the family. It is becoming less and less reasonable to use such terms as the "middle-class" family or the "working-class" family as we did above. Families come in all shapes and sizes and the socialization of children and young people in the family can be very different from one household to the next. Will the child of two gay men be brought up in the same way as a child living in a blended family with half-brothers and half-sisters? How relevant is it that in both cases the parents are middle-class?

Dependence on parents shifts as the child interacts with other adults and peers. The latter also offer approval and emotional support, and they may offer alternative views of reality. This sets up additional challenges in the socialization process, as we will now see.

SCHOOLS

Traditionally, schools have been seen as settings within which social learning is just as important as learning such skills as reading, writing, and arithmetic. One of the authors of this chapter used to drive past a high school that had carved out in large letters above its main entrance the phrase "To Build Character." Building character is what most teachers, school administrators, and parents expect the school system to do. Parents send their children to school to be socialized, and schools are deliberately organized to achieve that goal.

School is also usually the first setting in which children are supervised by adults who are not relatives or friends of the family. Moving from an environment of personal and intimate relationships to one that is impersonal is difficult for many children and something of a shock to almost all of them. Whereas parents may praise their children regardless of the talent they display, teachers typically seek to evaluate all students by a common set of standards. As a place where children are taught indirectly to be less emotionally dependent, the school serves as a model of much of the adult world. Although some interpersonal relationships may be based on love and affection, others are impersonal and defined by society with little regard for the particular individuals who enter them. Of all the functions of the school, adjusting children to its social order—which offers a preview of what will be expected of them as they negotiate their way among the institutions of adult society—may be the most important (Bodine, 2003; Devine, 2002; Raby, 2005).

Building character takes time. Accompanying the formal curriculum of the school is a "hidden curriculum"—the informal teaching that helps ensure students' integration into society (Richer, 1988). Students are exposed to, and rewarded for, the acquisition and display of such desired qualities as discipline, conformity, respect for authority, and cooperation. Gender socialization messages, for example, are imparted by teachers who may ask girls to perform "feminine" tasks, such as cleaning the board or tidying a shelf, while delegating more "masculine" tasks to boys, such as rearranging desks or carrying sports or audiovisual equipment (Best, 1983; Thorne, 1993). In research on the effects of the teacher's gender, the student's gender, and the classroom subject, researchers found that both elementary and high-school classroom interactions are related to teachers' and students' genders (Duffy, Warren, and Walsh, 2001–2002; Hopf and Hatzichristou, 1999). Specifically, female math teachers, male literature or language teachers, and female literature or language teachers directed more interactions toward male than female students. Such interactions may help to shape emerging self-concepts among male and female students.

PEER GROUPS

Although the family is the most important socializing agent in the early years, peers often begin to influence even young children. Children eventually disengage from the family as their cast of significant others begin to shift to those of similar age and interests. A **peer group** comprises individuals who are usually of the same age and enjoy approximately equal status. The earliest peer contacts often occur under the watchful eye of parents or adults, such as teachers in a nursery school or daycare centre, who are supervising the children's activities. In time, however, the influence of the peer group may totally supersede, and even conflict with, parents and familial expectations.

In childhood, peer groups are formed largely by the accident of association. Members of the same peer group are not necessarily friends. For instance, all children in a given classroom may constitute a peer group, but they are not necessarily all friends. Later in life, however, we *choose* peer groups on the basis of such criteria as common interests and activities and similar income level or occupation.

Significantly, the peer group is the only agent of socialization in childhood and youth that is not controlled mainly by adults (Corsaro, 1992). Although parents typically play the initial leading roles in the inculcation of basic values, peers seem to have the greatest influence in lifestyle issues, such as appearance, social activities, and dating (Sebald, 1992). Research indicates that, especially during adolescence, peers can strongly shape the individual's aspirations and behaviour with respect to both acceptable and criminal behaviour (Giordano, Cernkovich, and DeMaris, 1986). Certainly, the peer group contributes to socialization by enabling children to engage in experiences that may not be provided in the family. Here they can interact in give-and-take relationships—relationships involving conflict, competition, and cooperation—that are not always possible at home. In this manner, children are provided with opportunities for self-direction and self-expression (Adler and Adler, 1998). Peer groups allow young people to examine feelings, beliefs, and ideas that are unacceptable to the family. Friends share a vision of the world. They discuss sexual and emotional relationships and developments within their school and friendship circle.

Often, peer group socialization is not very subtle. Peers may pressure one another to conform to a

The student's values are strongly influenced by his or her peer group, which consists of people of similar age and status, regardless of whether they are friends.
SOURCE: © Stockbyte Platinum/Alamy.

standard deemed appropriate by the group. Little deviation may be tolerated from group norms concerning speech, attitudes, and dress. Adolescents, preoccupied with gaining autonomy from their parents, and anxious about gaining acceptance from others like themselves, may find such pressures difficult to resist (Thorne, 1993). In fact, by the teenage years, the peer group may demand behaviour that conflicts sharply with the norms and values of the parental generation. In this regard, it is understandable that parents often express concern about their children's friends, particularly during the teenage years.

If peer groups often reject the norms and values of their parents, from where does the group get its norms and values? Chances are, from the mass media. Peer groups are fascinated by the media and look to media heroes as symbols of identity. Taste in music, movies, television shows, and fashion express not only common preferences but also a common style that sets the group apart, both from parents and from other sets of peers (Hebdige, 1979). In fact, a "generation gap" may characterize relations between the peer group and parents, and the peer group can rival parental influence. For example, the structure and dynamics of the peer group may help us better understand peer abuse—the abuse of children by children. Relentless teasing by peers can result in brutal beatings and even murder (for instance, the 1997 case of 14-year-old Reena Virk of Victoria) and various other milder forms of social bullying.

Peer groups influence us at every stage of life, but it is during adolescence that they take on particular significance. As we have seen, adolescence is often a time of physical and emotional turmoil, but also of social turbulence as individuals develop new interests, new friendships, and a new identity. Given the dramatic and sometimes traumatic changes going on within and around them, adolescents often turn to peers for support since adults often have difficulty empathizing with adolescent concerns and are often likely to respond with anxiety of their own.

We often use the term *peer pressure* to emphasize the influence peers have on adolescents, but research by Cynthia Lightfoot (1997) suggests that the impact of peers is more complex than the concept of peer pressure implies. Lightfoot did research on risk-taking among adolescents and found that the impact of peers is less a case of pressure and more a matter of example. As one of her research subjects commented, "the idea of peer pressure is a lot of bunk . . . You go somewhere and everyone else is doing it and you'd think . . . they

seem to be having a good time—now why wouldn't I do this?" (Lightfoot, 1997: 36).

More generally, Lightfoot found that adolescent risk can have multiple effects during adolescent development. It may help to generate a sense of individuality and self through opposition to others or established authority; negativism has the same effect on infants. It may create a bond among people who act together and share the thrill, sense of accomplishment, or feeling of relief that comes from engaging in reckless behaviour. It may generate a sense of pride or raise one's status with peers. Or it may just be fun to do. Telling someone not to do something because it is dangerous or reckless will not be effective, Lightfoot suggests, if the perceived benefits of the action are only possible because it is dangerous or reckless.

MEDIA AND TECHNOLOGY

Sociologists agree that the mass media are powerful socializing influences but it is difficult to measure their effects. Most forms of mass media, such as television, radio, newspapers, videos, magazines, movies, CDs, DVDs, and books, are impersonal; information is transmitted in just one direction. This creates an audience conditioned to passively receive what is sometimes called mass culture, consisting of whatever news, messages, programs, or events are brought to them. About 20 years ago, a new mass medium was introduced. Allowing information to be communicated to a global audience, the World Wide Web gives children relatively unfettered access to pornography and groups propagating racial strife and violence. Music videos and films, also available on the Internet, contain controversial content that alarms some people concerned about their impact on youth.

Television has attracted considerable critical attention in light of its portrayal of violence, both on the news and in TV dramas. Some analysts argue that pervasive violence on television fosters violent behaviour on the part of some viewers while at the same time making the majority of people more indifferent to, and thus more accepting of, a violent society. The killings at Columbine High School in Colorado and W.R. Myers High School in Alberta—and the suspected linkage between the two—are examples of incidents sometimes blamed at least in part on television violence (Garbarino, 1999). The American Academy of Pediatrics holds that television viewing can affect the mental, social, and physical health of young people. In studies by the American Medical

Association, the American Psychiatric Association, and other agencies, violence in movies and television is linked to violent behaviour in young people.

Sociological research on violence in the mass media and the real world suggests a weaker connection between the two. As you will read in Chapter 5, the consensus is that violence in the mass media may push some people who may already be predisposed to aggression to engage in more violent acts. But it is doubtful that most viewers are similarly incited.

In contrast to television violence, which is passively experienced, video and computer games promote acting out violent scenarios. The player not only watches violence but also initiates it and is then rewarded for using it effectively. An example is *Grand Theft Auto: Vice City*, one of the best-selling video games at the time of this writing, described by one reviewer as "a lush and wild adrenaline-fuelled, shoot-'em-up role-playing game that is surely the most ambitious piece of interactive entertainment ever made" (Fussel, 2003: D16). The player can kill police officers by blowing up their cars, commit drive-by shootings, blow people's heads off with a sniper rifle and watch blood spew from their necks, distribute pornography, and traffic cocaine for organized crime.

Critics of the game have sounded an alarm because it rewards players for criminal behaviour. Whether the game influences anyone to actually commit a crime, the critics suggest, misses the point. Violent video games increase aggressive thoughts and behaviour, thus increasing the likelihood that children will get into fights in school. Such games, critics say, increasingly desensitize successive generations to violence.

Apart from the issue of violence, there is no denying that the mass media have a profound impact on the public. By selecting and emphasizing certain topics, stressing particular views and interpretations, and concentrating on specific themes, the media create, manage, and control impressions of what is important and real. The Web and video games have enabled outside influences to help shape the direction of socialization, frequently in opposition to values and beliefs conveyed in the family. By displaying role models that the young imitate, the media may inadvertently perpetuate stereotypes. For example, some parents work against the transmission of gender stereotypes to their children but video games often characterize women as subservient to men in the family and the workplace. As well, media influences are not always apparent, as when they teach individuals to become obedient consumers, for example.

OTHER SOCIALIZING AGENTS

The family, school, peer group, and mass media are the main socializing agents, but other agents of socialization are important too. Religious institutions, for example, may deeply affect the moral outlook of young people even in highly secular societies, such as Canada's. Athletic teams may teach young people to compete, cooperate with others, follow rules, and make friends. Youth groups may be instrumental in teaching young people about group rules and expectations about conformity, and even about deviance. In such complex societies as ours, conflict among the agencies of socialization is virtually inevitable. Moreover, conflict may also occur within a single socializing agency. For instance, soccer coaches may extol the virtues of cooperation but also insist on and emphasize the importance of winning at all costs.

Some socialization takes place in so-called people-processing institutions, "whose primary goal is the shaping, reshaping, removing, overhauling, retooling, reassembling, and recording the physical, psychological, legal, and moral aspects of human subjects" (Goffman, 1961; Kitsuse, 1970: 163). Such institutions carefully direct their charges to behave, think, and feel as prescribed by the institutions.

A classic illustration of socialization in a people-processing institution is a study of the socialization of the blind (Scott, 1969). Rather than identifying the attitudes and behaviour patterns of blind people as inevitable and natural, the sociologist who conducted the study maintained that they are learned. Thus, new students in schools for the blind are typically admonished by others, including medical and welfare specialists, friends, and family, to "face the facts." Even students who were previously treated as sighted people experiencing difficulty seeing are now redefined as blind people with residual vision. Consequently, "many of the basic techniques that were originally devised for people who are completely blind may be taught to the [legally] blind person who has [some] vision. Such persons may be expected to learn Braille, even though special lenses would enable them to read ordinary or enlarged ink print. . . . They may also be trained for jobs that were originally devised for totally blind persons, even though their remaining vision would enable them to continue doing the jobs they have always done" (Scott, 1969: 74). In this manner, people with vision impairments come under strong pressure to define themselves as blind and as requiring extensive social services: "The visually impaired person's readiness for the offered service is measured by his willingness to admit to himself the fact of his blindness and to show that he is resigned to the alleged permanence of his condition" (Scott, 1969: 74).

Other sociologists have investigated socialization into the world of the deaf. The claim that the deaf must be socialized may appear strange. A person does not, after all, learn to be deaf. Children who are deaf do, however, learn the behaviours and attitudes associated with being deaf, not so much at home as in institutions devoted to their education. Specifically, in schools for the deaf, the hearing world typically serves as the yardstick for what is considered normative. Thus, chewing gum may be forbidden because the sound of smacking lips, which children who are deaf cannot hear, may offend people who can hear: "The message is always the same: hearing people must not be offended or intruded upon by the noises of the deaf" (Evans and Falk, 1986: 157). It is in this sense that people who are deaf learn how to act like normative people who are deaf in institutions devoted to their education.

IDENTITY AND SOCIAL CHANGE

Are we free to become whomever we want, however we want? Of course not. Socialization is an active process in which we transform our identity as we take on new roles, but we do not always do so in conditions of our own choosing. It is important to remember that the social circumstances of life powerfully influence identity. Premodern societies formed relatively cohesive communities in which most people could find solidarity and meaning in primary groups, such as the family. Although primary groups limit the range of personal experience, they confer a strong sense of identity and purpose. Modernity expanded the range of personal choice and permitted a greater

diversity of beliefs. Still, although modernization has emancipated people from the tyranny of tradition, it leaves people without the comfort and security of heritage and roots. Modern societies, in general, offer more autonomy but less sense of purpose and fewer enduring social ties than past societies. Not surprisingly, many people have difficulty establishing a stable and coherent sense of who they are in modern and postmodern societies.

The result is that some people shuttle from one identity to another, changing their lifestyle in search of an elusive "true self." They may join various social groups in search of purpose and belonging, and even experiment with various religions in the hope of finding a system of beliefs that "fits" them (Wuthnow, 1998). In sociological terms, the difficulty in developing a stable and coherent identity is rooted in the individual's social surroundings. The problem of answering the question "Who am I?" reflects not only a personal crisis but also the complexity and instability of modern and postmodern societies (Berger, 1970).

Understanding the connection between personal development and social conditions calls for a malleable view of human development, one in which there is the constant possibility of change—even radical change. In fact, as many of us are only too aware, we have not only changed but we also know others who have experienced substantial transformations, either forcibly or voluntarily. Some changes are minor or inconsequential, such as developing a new taste in clothes or dieting for a brief period. But there are also more profound life-altering experiences over which we may exercise relatively little control. A life-threatening illness, imprisonment, and severe depression that requires institutionalization are examples. In each instance, people must learn to adapt to fundamental alterations in daily routines. Although these changes may be temporary, they nevertheless strongly influence the individual's identity (Box 3.1).

BOX 3.1   THE CLOAK OF COMPETENCE

Medical students during clerkship believe they are expected to act as if they are in the know, not in ways that might put their developing competence into question. The pressure to be seen as competent by faculty, fellow students, hospital personnel, and patients narrows the range of alternative roles

students can assume. Students recognize their low status in the hospital hierarchy and on hospital rotations. They realize that the extent of their medical knowledge can easily be called into question by fellow students, tutors, interns, residents, and faculty. To reduce the possibility of embarrassment and

(continued)

BOX 3.1   *(continued)*

humiliation, which, at this stage in their medical career, is easily their fate, students attempt to reduce the unpredictability of their situation by mani-pulating an impression of themselves as enthusiastic, interested, and eager to learn. At the same time, students seize opportunities which allow them to impress others, particularly faculty and fellow students, with their growing competence and confidence.

A strategy shared by students to manage an appearance of competence is to limit their initiatives to those situations which will be convincing demonstrations of their competence. Some students decide, for example, to ask questions in areas with which they are already familiar, to cultivate an impression of competence.

The general strategy that the students adopt is to mask their uncertainty and anxiety with an image of self-confidence. Image making becomes recognized as being as important as technical competence. As one student remarks: "We have to be good actors, put across the image of self-confidence, that you know it all." Referring to the importance of creating the right impression, another student said:

> Dr. Jones, who was my adviser or boss for medicine, he always came and did rounds on Wednesday mornings. Well, he didn't have very many patients on the service, but we always knew that his interest was in endocrinology, and . . . if he had an endocrine patient . . . we knew . . . that he was going to pick that endocrine patient to talk about. And so, of course, . . . any dummy can read up Tuesday night like hell on the new American Diabetic Association standards for diabetes or hyperglycemia . . . and you can handle general medicine. So the next day you seem fairly knowledgeable. . . . That afternoon you forget about it because you figure Thursday morning hematology people

make their rounds and, of course, you have to read up on hematology.

Students realize that to be a good student-physician is either to be or appear to be competent. They observe that others react to their role-playing. A student describes the self-fulfilling nature of this process when he says:

> To be a good GP, you've got to be a good actor, you've got to respond to a situation. You have to be quick, pick up the dynamics of what is going on at the time and try to make the person leave the office thinking that you know something. And a lot of people, the way they handle that is by letting the patient know that they know it all, and only letting out a little bit at a time, and as little as possible. I think that they eventually reach a plateau where they start thinking themselves they are really great and they know it all, because they have these people who are worshipping at their feet.

The process of adopting the cloak of competence is justified by students as helpful to the patient. A student summarizes the relationship between acting competently and patients responding to such a performance by getting well when he says:

> You know the patients put pressure on you to act as if you are in the know. If you know anything about the placebo effect, you know that a lot of the healing and curing of patients does not involve doing anything that will really help them, but rather creating confidence in the patient that things are being done and will be done. We know that the placebo effect for example has even cured cancer patients. If they have the confidence in the doctor . . . and what treatment they are undergoing, they are much more likely to get well, irrespective of the objective effects of the treatment.

SOURCE: Jack Haas and William Shaffir, "The Professionalization of Medical Students: Developing Competence and a Cloak of Competence," *Symbolic Interaction* 1, no. 1 (November 1977), pp. 71–88. Published by the University of California Press. Reprinted with permission.

RESOCIALIZATION

A significant change in how we live, in the kinds of people with whom we interact, or in the ways we understand others or ourselves often requires a process of **resocialization.** As part of a transformation in life, resocialization is an attempt to correct or instill particular values and behaviours. Sociologists, however, generally restrict the idea of resocialization to those contexts in which *deliberate* efforts are made to change the individual or group.

The classic example is Erving Goffman's (1961) research on total institutions. Goffman examined how people may be socialized against their will. This is the special world of **total institutions,** settings, such as the military, convents, prisons, boarding schools, and mental hospitals, within which people are isolated from the rest of society for a set period and where all aspects of a person's life are regulated under one authority. According to Goffman, total institutions impose regimented routines with the goal of resocialization into a new identity. The total institution attempts to achieve this objective by completely controlling and manipulating the environment, thus depriving its inmates of contradictory forms of social experience. Total institutions, in Goffman's words, are "the forcing houses for changing persons; each is a natural experiment in what can be done to the self" (1961: 11–12).

The above examples of settings in which resocialization unfolds suggest that individuals are typically subjected to this process against their will. On the other hand, they may, at least initially, submit to it willingly. An apparently good example of willing or voluntary resocialization occurs in religious groups where individuals are seemingly free to sever their relationships when they choose. However, studies of religious cults reveal that cult leaders exercise a powerful hold in the everyday lives of their followers. Notable examples include the leaders of the Branch Davidians and Heaven's Gate. Followers of these cults developed a blind obedience to their leaders, which resulted in a tragic ending for many of them. Interestingly, while religious cults are not in a position to apply initial physical coercion, the mental transformation demanded of the followers parallels the experiences of people confined to institutions where individuals become committed to a regimented life as they are isolated from the rest of society.

Resocialization in total institutions is a two-part process. First, the staff attempts to strip away the new inmate's established identity. This is accompanied by a

Private Lynndie England became infamous when photographs were made public showing her and other American soldiers abusing Iraqi prisoners at Abu Ghraib prison in Iraq in obvious contravention of international law. "She's never been in trouble. She's not the person that the photographs point her out to be," said her childhood friend, Destiny Gloin. Ms. Gloin was undoubtedly right. Private England at Abu Ghraib was not the Lynndie England from high school. She was transformed by a total institution, a structure of power, and a culture of intimidation that made the prisoners seem subhuman.

SOURCE: © Exclusive to *The Washington Post*/epa/Corbis.

series of experiences that include humiliations, degradations, and "mortification rituals," which may include physical pain. Second, efforts are made to reconstitute the inmate's sense of self by imposing a new identity and a new way of life on him or her. In a childlike condition of heightened ambiguity and stress created by degradation and humiliation, the person is ripe for conversion to the expectations of the more powerful group. The desire for security and acceptance often leads to imitation or adoption of the behaviour of authority figures (Light, 1980). The resocialized person often undergoes a symbolic ritual death and rebirth, shedding the old identity and taking on a new one.

An example of resocialization is basic training in the military. Here the primary goal is to modify the recruit's civilian self-image and replace it with a military identity. Recruits are removed from their civilian environment and confined to a military base, where they are required to submit to a vast range of stresses, disciplinary measures, and indoctrination to a new set of role expectations. The well-known example in which the new recruit is issued a uniform that does not fit is often presented on television or in the movies as a comic moment, but it has a symbolic significance as well. New recruits are expected to understand that the military is not concerned about them as individuals, only as soldiers. Soldiers follow commands and adapt to the needs of the military, not the other way around.

Identity change in total institutions is often dramatic. Yet even in total institutions, Goffman showed, people interact with, adapt to, and resist others with whom they are in personal contact. Much less dramatic but often anxiety-provoking resocialization occurs outside total institutions when newcomers are inducted into prestigious professions, such as law, the ministry, and medicine. The transformative experience of medical students en route to becoming professional is a case in point. Professionalization involves the moral and symbolic transformation of a layperson into an individual who can assume the special role and status claimed by a professional (Davis, 1961; Haas and Shaffir, 1987). The would-be professional must undergo public initiations involving testing and ritual ordeal before being elevated to the special status and role afforded by the profession.

The image of society Goffman presents in his research on total institutions is one in which large, impersonal institutions are gaining more and more control over people—over their actions, experience of the world, and sense of self. Resistance is possible in Goffman's view, and it is often successful, but only in the small events of everyday life, such as forming personal relationships with others or exchanging gifts and services. Yet today, with the advent of new forms of communication and technology, we find that new forms of autonomy and new sources of freedom and creativity have also emerged. Active, malleable, and innovative, human beings are not content to accept the world as they find it. They look for ways to transform the world and adapt it to their social needs and personal desires. Nothing better exemplifies this creative aspect of social life than the process of socialization.

SUMMARY

1. Socialization is an active process through which human beings become members of society, develop a sense of self, and learn to participate in social relationships with others. Through socialization we acquire knowledge, skills, and motivations for participation in society.

2. Each of us is born with a set of human potentials. Nature and nurture interact in contributing to human development.

3. Socialization is lifelong, typically involving relationships with family, school, peer groups, mass media, and occupational groups. Ours is an age-graded society as well, and early childhood, adolescence, adulthood, and old age or retirement are significant stages; different roles and responsibilities are associated with each stage.

4. Because of its importance, many scholars have focused on examining socialization as an active, interactional process. Charles Horton Cooley was noteworthy for his concept of the "looking-glass self," which stressed that we view ourselves as we think others view us. George Herbert Mead emphasized how people assume roles by imagining themselves in the roles of others. Paul Willis, looking at the ways in which young people do not merely accept the world around them but transform into a symbolic expression of their particular identity and their meaningful culture, has shown the intimate links connecting the acting individual and the broader social context.

5. Gender socialization is the learning of masculine and feminine behaviour and roles. From birth, and in every area of social life, the socialization of the sexes in terms of content and expectations makes the socially constructed gender role more significant than the biological role of male or

female. Assumptions about appropriate male and female attributes limit the range of acceptable behaviour and options for both sexes.

6. The most important agent of socialization is the family. As the examples of orphanages and child neglect demonstrate, initial warmth and nurturing are essential to healthy development. The self-concept formed during childhood has lasting consequences.

7. The central function of schools in industrial society is the teaching of skills and knowledge, but they also transmit society's central cultural values and ideologies. Schools expose children to situations in which the same rules, regulations, and authority patterns apply to everyone.

8. Peer groups provide young people with a looking glass unclouded by love or duty, and an opportunity to learn roles and values that adults do not teach.

9. The traditional mass media are impersonal and large-scale socializers. New forms of media are more interactive and allow people to play with and try out different identities.

10. During adulthood, individuals are socialized as they get jobs, marry, divorce, raise children, retire, and prepare for death. These many roles involve new and different relationships with others and guidelines for behaviour.

11. Sometimes there are abrupt changes in our self-concept, and we must learn new role identities and negotiate a new self-image. Resocialization occurs when we abandon or are forced to abandon our way of life and self-concept for a radically different one. This is most efficiently done in total institutions—for example, jails, psychiatric hospitals, and boot camps—or in religious or political conversions.

QUESTIONS TO CONSIDER

1. Consider the significant others in your life. Have they always been important to you? How have they shaped and influenced your sense of self?

2. Goffman's dramaturgical approach implies that "all the world's a stage" and all of us are merely "players." Do you agree with Goffman? Cite examples of impression management that you rely on and encounter in your life.

3. Prisons and psychiatric hospitals are socialization institutions organized to change, test, or "correct" people. How effective are these institutions and why are they not more successful in meeting their goals?

4. Think of any job you have had and consider the socialization that was required. Distinguish the formal and informal components of the socialization process.

5. What, if any, are the possible effects on personal identity of the use of the Internet? Could the consequences be greater separation and alienation from reality, others, and ourselves, or might the outcome for the user be a heightened sense of belonging, integration, and shared understanding? Are both extremes possible?

GLOSSARY

Adult socialization is the process by which adults take on new statuses and acquire new and different social identities.

Agents of socialization are the individuals, groups, and institutions that impart, and from which we acquire, the range of information required to interact effectively and participate in society.

Anticipatory socialization involves beginning to take on the norms and behaviours of a role you aspire to but do not yet occupy.

In the **game stage** of development, children have developed a generalized impression of the behaviour people expect as well as awareness of their own importance to the group and vice-versa. This is the third and final developmental stage described by Mead.

The generalized other is a conception of how people in general will respond in a situation. It is internalized.

The I is the subjective or active part of the self, according to Mead.

In the **imitative stage** of development, children two years old and under do not interact effectively with others because they cannot take the role of the other. They merely imitate the behaviour of others. This is the first developmental stage described by Mead.

Instincts are inborn patterns of behaviour that are often responses to specific stimuli.

The idea of the **looking-glass self** suggests that the gestures and reactions of others are a mirror in which we see ourselves.

The **me** is the objective element of the self, according to Mead.

A **peer group** comprises individuals who are usually of the same age and enjoy approximately equal status.

In the **play stage**, children begin to adopt the roles of significant others—a parent, a sports celebrity, a storybook hero—and their play shifts from imitative to imaginative. This is the second developmental stage described by Mead.

A **primary group** is a small group (especially the family) that is characterized by intimate, face-to-face association and cooperation.

Primary socialization is the crucial learning process that occurs in childhood and makes us members of society.

Resocialization is the deliberate attempt to correct or instill particular values and behaviours in an individual or group.

Secondary socialization is learning that occurs after people have undergone primary socialization.

The **self,** a sense of individual identity, allows us to understand ourselves and differentiate ourselves from others.

Significant others are people, such as parents, who are of central importance in the development of the self.

Socialization is the social process whereby people undergo development by interacting with the people around them.

Status refers to the culturally and socially defined position a person occupies in an interaction.

Taking the role of the other involves anticipating in advance how others will see and react to you. It is an essential skill that children must develop to be effective members of society.

Total institutions are settings in which people are isolated from the rest of society for a set period and where all aspects of a person's life are regulated under one authority.

SUGGESTED READING

Adler, Patricia A., and Peter Adler. (1998). *Peer Power: Preadolescent Culture and Identity.* New Brunswick, NJ: Rutgers University Press. Based on eight years of observation research, this is a first-rate sociological study of the role of peer groups in preadolescent socialization.

Becker, Howard S., Blanche Geer, Everett C. Hughes, and Anselm L. Strauss. (1961). *Boys in White: Student Culture in Medical School.* Chicago: University of Chicago Press. This is arguably the classic study of professional socialization. It examines how medical students negotiate their transition into the medical profession and are transformed into physicians.

Ebaugh, Helen Rose Fuchs. (1988). *Becoming an Ex: The Process of Role Exit.* Chicago: University of Chicago Press. This excellent study examines the process whereby people learn to disengage themselves from previous roles and claims to identity.

Goffman, Erving. (1961). *Asylums: Essays on the Social Situation of Mental Patients and Other Inmates.* Garden City, NY: Anchor Books. This account analyzes life in total institutions and describes what such institutions make of inmates and how the latter organize their life inside them.

WEB RESOURCES

Companion Website for This Book

http://www.newsociety6e.nelson.com
Begin by clicking on the Student Resources section of the website. Next, select the chapter you are studying from the pull-down menu. From the Student Resources page, you have easy access to InfoTrac College Edition® and other resources, such as the

Glossary, Test Yourself questions, and additional readings. The website also has many useful tips to aid you in your study of sociology.

InfoTrac College Edition Search Terms

Visit http://www.infotrac-college.com for access to more than 20 million articles from nearly 6000 sources when doing your online research.

CHAPTER FOUR

Gender and Sexuality

Rhonda L. Lenton
YORK UNIVERSITY

In this chapter you will learn that

- Sex refers to biological differences between males and females, while *gender* refers to the attitudes, beliefs, and behaviours we associate with masculinity and femininity.

- Individuals form a "gender identity" or a sense of biological, psychological, and social belonging to a particular sex. Individuals also learn to play a "gender role," that is, to act in accordance with expectations about how members of their gender are supposed to behave.

- *Sexuality* refers to activities intended to lead to erotic arousal and produce a genital response. Sexuality is guided by a set of social "scripts" that tell us whom we should find attractive, when and where it is appropriate to be aroused, when it is permissible to have sex, and so forth.

- There are two major perspectives on the relationship among sex, gender, and sexuality. One ("essentialism") holds that gender roles and sexual scripts develop naturally from biological differences between the sexes. The other ("social constructionism") holds that gender roles and sexual scripts emerge in response to the different social positions women and men occupy.

- Because of the way gender and sexuality are structured in our society, intolerance for sexual minorities is widespread and male sexual aggression against women is common.

- A substantial decrease in gender inequality is now possible. The redefinition of sexuality is an important step in that process.

INTRODUCTION

GENDER, SEX, AND THE CASE OF DAVID/BRENDA

In April 1966, identical eight-month-old twin boys were brought to St. Boniface hospital in Winnipeg to be circumcised. They had developed a condition called phimosis, or closing of the foreskin. However, because of mechanical malfunction or doctor error, the electric cauterizing needle used for the procedure released a surge of heat. It burnt off the entire penis of one baby.

The parents sought expert medical advice but were given little hope. One psychiatrist summarized the baby's future as follows: "[H]e will be unable to consummate marriage or have normal heterosexual relations . . . he will have to recognize that he is incomplete, physically defective, and that he must live apart" (quoted in Colapinto, 2001: 16). The baby's name was David Reimer.

Seven months later, now deeply depressed, David Reimer's parents happened to be watching a CBC television program featuring Dr. John Money of Johns Hopkins University in Baltimore. He was discussing how he had successfully assigned a male or female identity to children whose external sex organs and internal reproductive system were not clearly male or female. The main criterion he used for deciding the child's sex was expected "erotic functioning" as an adult. He recommended boys born with a penis shorter than 2.5 centimetres and girls born with a clitoris longer than 1 centimetre for sex reassignment, preferably within weeks of birth. According to Money, it was imperative, once the child's sex was decided, that doctors and parents never waver in their decision and never tell the child about his or her condition at birth.

Until David Reimer, Dr. Money had never had the opportunity to test his idea on a child born unequivocally a boy or girl. Therefore, when David's mother wrote to Dr. Money shortly after the television show, he urged her to bring the baby to his office in Baltimore. He considered it a bonus that David was a twin. This would allow him to compare the development of the two siblings. Dr. Money was eager to proceed. He believed that the "gender identity gate"—the time after which a child is "locked" into an identity as a male or a female—closes at two years of age. The parents nevertheless took several months to deliberate and consult with family and friends before giving the go-ahead. On July 3, 1967, David, now 22 months old, underwent surgical castration and reconstructive surgery. He became Brenda Reimer.

As the years passed, the parents tried their best to follow Dr. Money's instructions. Brenda was given dresses to wear, skipping ropes and dolls for presents, and regular doses of the female hormone estrogen at puberty.

In 1972, at a meeting of the American Association for the Advancement of Science in Washington, DC, Dr. Money unveiled the story of David/Brenda Reimer. He claimed that the experiment was an unqualified success. In *Sexual Signatures*, a co-authored book intended for the general public, he described David's sex reassignment as "dramatic proof that the gender-identity option is open at birth for normal infants." Money was equally optimistic in a 1978 journal article, where he reported that "[n]ow prepubertal in age, [Brenda Reimer] has . . . a feminine gender identity and role, distinctly different from that of her brother" (quoted in Colapinto, 1997: 72).

Then, in March 1997, a bombshell: Dr. Money, it emerged, had doctored his reports. A biologist from the University of Hawaii and a psychiatrist from the Canadian Ministry of Health started a scientific scandal when they published an article in the *Archives of Adolescent and Pediatric Medicine* showing that David/Brenda had, in fact, struggled against his/her imposed girlhood from the start. In December, a long and moving exposé of the case in *Rolling Stone* magazine gave further details.

The authors documented Brenda's resistance to being a girl, including everything from tearing off her first dress to insisting on standing to urinate. According to her brother, Kevin, there was "nothing feminine about Brenda. . . . She walked like a guy. Sat with her legs apart. She talked about guy things, didn't give a crap about cleaning house, getting married, wearing makeup. We both wanted to play with guys, build forts and have snowball fights and play army" (quoted in Colapinto, 2001: 57).

David Reimer, February 2001
SOURCE: © Reuters New Media Inc./Corbis.

By the age of seven, Brenda announced she wanted to be a boy, and she refused to have further vaginal surgery because it would make her look more like a girl. She took estrogen only after being told that failure to do so would result in her limbs being disproportionate to her body. She refused to see Dr. Money after 1978. In 1979, Brenda made the decision to stop living as a girl.

In 1980, her father finally told Brenda what had happened to her. Brenda's first reaction was relief. She then resolved to become David again. By the age of 16, she started taking male hormone treatments and had her breasts removed and a penis surgically constructed. Subsequent surgeries allowed David to have sex with a woman at the age of 23. He married the woman two years later, in 1990, and adopted her three children. That did not, however, end his ordeal. In May 2004, at the age of 38, David Reimer committed suicide.

The story of David/Brenda introduces many of the issues raised in this chapter. How do we define *female* and *male*? What is the relationship between biological sex and the attitudes and behaviours that we associate with being male or female? What are the implications of this relationship for our sexual identity and sexual relations? I will touch on all these questions here. The answers, it will emerge, are not as obvious as they may at first appear.

DEFINING MALE AND FEMALE: SEX AND GENDER

While preparing to write this chapter, I asked my then six-year-old the difference between boys and girls.

She answered: "Boys have a penis, girls have a vagina." Like most people, she distinguished men and women on the basis of biological **sex.** Your sex depends on whether you were born with distinct male or female genitalia and a genetic program that released either male or female hormones to stimulate the development of your reproductive system. Table 4.1 gives a more complete version of this common view by summarizing four key sex differences.

At the point of conception, a newly formed zygote has 46 chromosomes. If the last chromosome has an XX pattern, the zygote becomes a female. If it has an XY pattern, it becomes a male. About 1 in 400 children is born with an unusual 46th chromosome pattern caused by the failure of the sperm to divide properly (Berch and Bender, 1987). Most of these combinations are never diagnosed.

Around the sixth or seventh week of gestation, the gonads or sex glands begin to develop—testes in the case of a male, ovaries in the case of a female. The testes and ovaries subsequently produce various hormones in varying amounts. These hormones contribute to the development of the sex organs. Differences between the sex organs are noticeable by the 14th week after conception. The scientific community appears to agree about only one sex difference in the brain (Blum, 1997): The part of the brain known as the hypothalamus makes the female brain sensitive to estrogen and is responsible for creating menstrual cycles in women.

Being male or female is more than just biological sex differences, however, as the case of David/Brenda shows. Recalling his life as Brenda, David said, "[E]veryone is telling you that you're a girl. But you

TABLE 4.1 SUMMARY OF BIOLOGICAL SEX DIFFERENCES DURING TYPICAL FETAL DEVELOPMENT

VARIABLE	FEMALE	MALE
Chromosomal pattern	XX	XY
Gonadal	ovaries	testes
Hormonal	more estrogens than androgens	more androgens than estrogens + MIH
Sex organs	uterus, fallopian tubes, vagina, clitoris, labia	epididymis, vas deferens, seminal vesicles, prostate, penis, scrotum

SOURCE: Adapted from E. D. Nelson and Barrie W. Robinson, *Gender in Canada* (Scarborough, ON: Prentice Hall Allyn and Bacon, 1999), p. 48. Reprinted with permission of Pearson Education Canada.

say to yourself, 'I don't *feel* like a girl.' You think girls are supposed to be delicate and *like* girl things—tea parties, things like that. But I like to *do* guy stuff. It doesn't match" (quoted in Colapinto, 1997: 66; my emphasis). As this quotation shows, being male or female involves not just biology but also certain "masculine" and "feminine" feelings, attitudes, and behaviours. Accordingly, biological sex must be distinguished from sociological **gender.** Gender comprises the feelings, attitudes, and behaviours associated with being male or female. Furthermore, identification with, or sense of belonging to, a particular sex—biologically, psychologically, and socially—is known as **gender identity.** When people behave according to widely shared expectations about how males or females are supposed to act, they adopt a **gender role.**

Research shows that North Americans' expectations about how men and women are supposed to act have changed only somewhat since the 1960s (Bergen and Williams, 1991; Broverman, Vogel, Broverman, Clarkson, and Rosenkratz, 1972; Rosenkrantz, Vogel, Bee, Broverman, and Broverman, 1968; Williams and Bennett, 1975; Williams and Best, 1982). This is true despite significant changes in women's lives in particular. For example, in the 1960s and 1970s, males were generally expected to act tough and hide their emotions. This is still true today, albeit to a lesser extent. Boys still tend to learn at a young age that crying or displaying their feelings in public is likely to result in taunts and accusations of being a "sissy." As a result, they curb their nurturing abilities, thus fulfilling gender expectations.

Great pressure can be brought to bear on individuals who do not conform to gender expectations. Brenda is a case in point. She was ostracized and tormented by her peers for not acting feminine. **Transgendered people** report similar experiences of rejection (see Box 4.1). People are **transgendered** when their gender identity does not exactly match the sex assigned to them at birth. They blur widely accepted gender roles by, for example, cross-dressing. According to Dr. Diane Watson, a psychiatrist who heads the gender-identity clinic at Vancouver Hospital, 1 in every 5000 to 10 000 Canadians is transgendered (quoted in Nolen, 1999: D1). Moreover, says Dr. Watson, 1 in 30000 Canadians is fully **transsexual. Transsexuals** identify with the opposite sex from that assigned to them at birth,

Being male or female involves not just biology but also certain "masculine" or "feminine" feelings, attitudes, and behaviours.
SOURCE: Susan G. Scott, *The Princess.* Courtesy Susan G. Scott.

causing them to change their appearance or resort to a sex-change operation. The apparent contradiction between biological sex and gender experienced by these individuals brings us back to the question of how we define males and females.

We typically accept "masculine men" and "feminine women" as normal. That is, we expect individuals to possess unambiguous sex organs and to adopt the gender role that is consistent with their biological sex. In fact, the World Health Organization classifies transgendered individuals as suffering from a psychiatric disorder. As Canadian sociologist Margrit Eichler points out, however, if our notions of masculinity and femininity were less rigid, sex-change operations would be unnecessary since someone with a "gender identity problem" would not be defined as "sick." From Eichler's point of view, transgendered individuals represent a "problem" for most people only because our society does not recognize the validity of intermediate sexes (Eichler, 1980: 31).

In the case of David/Brenda, the rigidity of gender roles probably contributed to the failure of the sex-change operation. David had, after all, been raised as a boy for nearly two years. He had seen boys treated differently from girls on television and in storybooks. He had played only with stereotypical boys' toys. After the sex reassignment, however, he got new clothes and new toys. He was also expected to behave differently. The contrast must have been all the more evident because the constant presence of his twin brother reinforced David's early understanding of how boys ought to behave. Evidence suggests that if gender reassignment takes place before the age of 18 months, it tends to be "successful" (Creighton and Minto, 2001; Lightfoot-Klein, Chase, Hammond, and Goldman, 2000).

The rigidity just described fosters the view that gender roles are entirely natural and spring fully formed from human physiology. But no one-to-one relationship exists between sex and gender. The two may be in discord, as transgendered individuals and transsexuals demonstrate. The picture becomes still more complicated when we consider sexual behaviour. Expectations about sexual behaviour are arguably among the most rigid of our gender norms, yet sexual behaviour often departs widely from biological sex and sociological gender.

BOX 4.1 THE THIRD WAY: REFUSING TO GENDER IDENTIFY

It's not that Matt Lundie wants to be a man, particularly. He just doesn't want to be a woman.

"Just enough so people won't pick me out as being a freak"—that's his goal for the next year.

He has done two years of engineering at Carleton University in Ottawa, and he is taking the next year off to start another project. Next week, he moves to Winnipeg. In six months, he will begin to take male hormones and, a few months after that, he will have a mastectomy: both of his 38C breasts will be removed and his chest reshaped in a male contour. That will be it for the scalpel, though: "I don't have any need to modify my genitals."

He's having just enough surgery to get him what he wants: not a facsimile of a male body, just a less female one.

Matt was born Fiona, in a small southwestern Ontario town. For 21 years, he lived confused. "Even as a child I knew the expectations placed on me weren't realistic," he says, calm and resolute. "Until puberty, I thought I was a boy. The social messages of my whole childhood, of being told the boy's washroom was down the hall, was that I didn't fit, not in either mould."

Then he arrived at university and began to encounter variations on gender identity in the gay community. Last year, he tried something new: "I didn't gender identify."

He was still Fiona, but offered no other clues. That felt better, better than being a woman, anyway, but it wasn't great. When people couldn't figure him out, they reacted with confusion, awkwardness and often hostility. He got sick of dealing with that every day. So now, at 23, he's starting a new life as Matt.

"I don't believe gender is concrete, and people shouldn't be limited by their biological sex. But I can't really live in between."

Yet if he feels neither concretely male nor female, then why Matt over Fiona? "I like male clothes," he says with a small chuckle, then turns serious. "And the box you put men into has a bit more room."

He tried life in the other box. "Around Grade 11, I made an honest effort to be a traditionally gendered girl. I grew my hair; if you saw my prom picture, you'd think I was my sister or something." It didn't work. "I knew I didn't fit the mould of a woman, but I didn't know I had options. Now I know that neither of those two options fit who I am, so I'm going to stake out a third."

SOURCE: Excerpted from Stephanie Nolen, "The Third Way," *The Globe and Mail,* September 25, 1999, p. D1. Reprinted with permission of *The Globe and Mail.*

SEXUALITY

Sexuality refers to activities that are intended "to lead to erotic arousal and produce genital response" (Reiss, 1986: 20). Some people think such activities are idiosyncratic. In fact, sexual behaviour is guided by a set of **sexual scripts** that tell us whom we should find attractive, when and where it is appropriate to be aroused, what is permissible, and how to behave sexually. These scripts are linked to gender roles. Men are usually expected to be the sexual aggressors, typically more experienced and promiscuous than women are. Women are expected to desire love before intimacy. They are assumed to be sexually passive, giving only subtle cues to indicate their interest in male overtures. Lacking the urgent sex drive that preoccupies males, women are therefore often held accountable for moral standards and contraception (Jensen, 1984).

For a long time, sexuality was assumed to be heterosexuality. The term *heterosexuality* was coined about 30 years after the term *homosexuality* made its appearance in the 1860s. Homosexuality was considered a serious psychiatric disorder until 1974, when it was finally dropped from the *Diagnostic and Statistical Manual of Mental Disorders*, the standard diagnostic tool used by North American psychiatrists (Shorter, 1997: 304). Even today, many people assume that individuals should desire only members of the opposite sex. Sociologists call this assumption **compulsory heterosexuality**.

The assumption of heterosexuality has negative implications for both lesbians and gays. They face discrimination, are denied basic civil rights (such as access to spousal benefits) in most countries, and risk abuse, including "gay-bashing." In addition, some feminists say that heterosexuality puts *all* women at a disadvantage, because heterosexuality is based on unequal economic, political, legal, and social relations between women and men. Adrienne Rich (1996: 132–33) thus defines compulsory heterosexuality as "the ideologically and materially enforced insistence that women see themselves entirely as the complements of men and live under male control or risk severe sanctions ranging from social stigma to death." Rich says that the institutionalization of heterosexuality in marriage and the family is a way of ensuring males' rights to physical, economic, and emotional access to women. Some feminists even take the extreme position that women should reject heterosexuality altogether since all such relationships are based on inequality. Below, I present an opposing view—that it is not individual women's heterosexual practices and identities that need to be criticized but rather the institution of heterosexuality *insofar as it is as a system of male domination*. First, however, let us examine some research on sexual behaviour.

SEXUAL ATTITUDES AND BEHAVIOUR

Traditional sexual scripts expect each of us to meet a member of the opposite sex, fall in love, get married, and then have intercourse with our spouse. However, surveys reveal some departure from tradition and considerable diversity in sexual attitudes and behaviour. For example, premarital sex is widely accepted by the Canadian public. In 1975, 32 percent of Canadians disapproved of premarital sex, and the figure is expected to fall to half that percentage by 2010. The great majority of Canadians also approve of an unmarried couple living together (Bibby, 1995: 65–66).

Acceptance of premarital sex extends even to young people. Ninety-four percent of Canadians agree that "birth control information should be available to teenagers who want it" (Bibby, 1995: 65). Some 43 percent of 15- to 19-year-olds say they have had sexual intercourse at least once, as do about three-quarters of those of university age (Hobart, 1996: 150; Rotermann, 2008). However, according to one study, men are more willing than women to participate in unconventional sexual activities (Hatfield, 1995).

A 2006 survey of more than 26 000 people provides recent data on sexual behaviour in 26 countries, including Canada (Durex, 2008; see Figure 4.1). Two-thirds of the respondents said they had sexual intercourse at least once a week. At one extreme were the Greeks (87 percent). At the other extreme were the Japanese (37 percent). Canadians ranked 23rd at 59 percent. The survey also measured people's satisfaction with sex. With the exception of Nigerians, a considerably smaller percentage of respondents expressed satisfaction than said they had sex at least once a week. Nigerians were the most satisfied (67 percent), Japanese the least satisfied (15 percent), with Canadians ranking 10th (48 percent).

Table 4.2 shows the frequency of sexual activity by gender and age in Canada. Not surprisingly, sexual activity declines with age. However, a considerable number of people over the age of 70 say they engage

FIGURE 4.1   ANNUAL FREQUENCY OF SEXUAL INTERCOURSE AND SATISFACTION WITH SEX IN 26 COUNTRIES, 2006

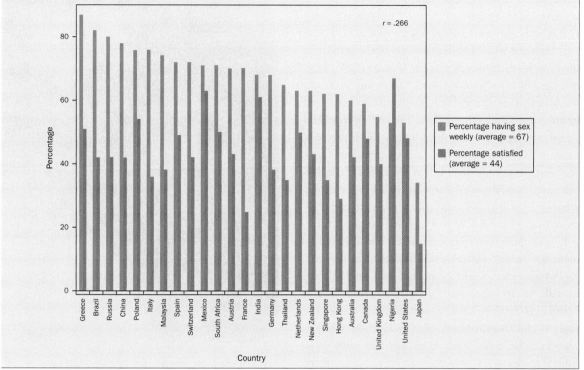

SOURCE: Durex, 2008, "Frequency of Sex versus Satisfaction Levels," http://www.durex.com/en-CA/SexualWellbeingSurvey/Fequency%20of%20Sex/pages/default.aspx (6 December 2008). Durex Wellbeing Survey, 2006. Used courtesy of SSL International Plc.

in sexual activity at least once a week. This finding challenges the myth that the elderly are asexual.

Also of interest are male–female differences. For nearly all age groups, men report more frequent intercourse than women, while women more often report abstention than men. For instance, in the 50–59 age group, 13 percent of women say they never have sex compared with only 1 percent of men.

TABLE 4.2   FREQUENCY OF SEXUAL INTERCOURSE AMONG CANADIANS BY AGE AND SEX

AGE		NEVER	SOMETIMES, BUT LESS OFTEN THAN ONCE A WEEK	ONCE A WEEK OR MORE	TOTAL
18–29	men	26	35	39	100
	women	26	27	47	100
30–39	men	2	37	61	100
	women	4	29	67	100
40–49	men	1	38	61	100
	women	5	34	61	100
50–59	men	4	37	59	100
	women	16	45	39	100
60–69	men	9	52	39	100
	women	50	29	21	100
70+	men	28	59	13	100
	women	68	26	6	100

SOURCE: Adapted from Reginald W. Bibby, *Project Canada 2005 National Survey Data*. Reprinted with permission of the author.

And in the 70+ age group, 22 percent of men say they have sex once a week or more, compared with only 7 percent of women. These figures probably reflect a tendency on the part of men to exaggerate their virility to conform to gender stereotypes.

Men and women differ in terms of the standards they use to justify sexual activity. Hobart (1996: 148) distinguishes the "love standard," according to which sexual activity is acceptable as long as the partners are in love, from the "fun standard," according to which sexual activity is acceptable as long as both partners want it. He shows that, in Canada, men and francophones are more likely than women and anglophones to endorse the fun standard. For example, almost 52 percent of Canadian francophone men and more than 37 percent of francophone women believe it is appropriate to engage in heterosexual involvement for casual, recreational reasons. The comparable figures for anglophone men and anglophone women are 36 percent and 20 percent, respectively. Hatfield (1995) similarly reports that men are somewhat more concerned than women with sex. Women are somewhat more concerned than men with love. American research shows that women are more likely to cite "affection for partner" as the major reason for their first intercourse experience (48 percent) followed by "curiosity/readiness for sex" (24 percent). Men most often mention "curiosity" (51 percent), followed by "affection" (25 percent). A small percentage of women (3 percent) report having their first sexual experience for physical pleasure. In contrast, 12 percent of men cite this reason (Michael, Gagnon, Laumann, and Kolata, 1994: 93–94). One study of 1479 Canadians over the age of 18 found that men have sexual thoughts more often than women, are more likely to have oral sex, have first intercourse at a younger age, have more sexual partners, and are more in favour of casual sex (Fischtein, Herold, and Desmarais, 2007).

Canadians are also becoming more tolerant of homosexuality and same-sex marriage (see Box 4.2). For example, in 1975 fewer than three in ten Canadians agreed that sexual relations between two adults of the same sex were "not wrong at all" or only "sometimes wrong." By 2005, that figure grew to more than six out of ten Canadians. Acceptance of homosexuality is strongly correlated with age, gender, and region; young adults, women, and residents of Quebec and, to a lesser degree, British Columbians are more accepting of homosexuality than other Canadians are (Bibby, 2006: 21–22).

Research shows that while men are somewhat more concerned with sex than women, women are somewhat more concerned with love. SOURCE: Shutterstock.

It is sometimes asserted that one in ten North Americans is homosexual. Research shows that this view is an oversimplification. Based on a sample of nearly 8000 university students in Canada and the United States, researchers found that different measures of sexual orientation produced widely different results (see Table 4.4 on p. 82). Some 3.4 percent of men and 2.4 percent of women did not define themselves as heterosexual, but 12.0 percent of men and 13.4 percent of women expressed at least occasional attraction to members of their own sex, 21 percent of men and 25.8 percent of women said they had sexual fantasies about members of their own sex at least sometimes, and 12.5 percent of men and 8.0 percent of women said they had at least one intimate sexual experience with a member of the same sex (compare "Homosexuality and Bisexuality," 2000; Laumann, Gagnon, Michael, and Michaels, 1994: 299).

These findings suggest that estimates of the prevalence of homosexuality depend on how homosexuality is measured. An estimate based on sexual identity results in a lower percentage than does an estimate focusing on **sexual orientation.** (Sexual orientation refers to the way a person derives sexual pleasure,

BOX 4.2   **SAME-SEX MARRIAGE AND CIVIL UNION**

In July 2005, Canada became the third country (after the Netherlands and Belgium) to legalize same-sex marriage. Spain, South Africa, Norway, and Sweden subsequently passed such a law. The major world religions officially disapprove of homosexuality for the most part (see Table 4.3), so it is not surprising that several Canadian church leaders spoke out strongly against the new law. Canadian public opinion remains divided, although by 2006, 59 percent of Canadians agreed that "same-sex couples should have the same right to civil marriage as opposite-sex couples" and 62 percent considered same-sex marriage to be "a settled matter" that should not be reopened and debated again in Parliament." Younger Canadians, women, and people living outside Alberta and Ontario are more likely to support same-sex marriage than are older Canadians, men, and people living in Alberta and Ontario ("Same-Sex Marriage," 2005, 2008).

Many governments have dealt with such splits in public opinion by distinguishing between marriage and "civil union." A civil union grants some of the rights and privileges of marriage to a same-sex couple. At least some jurisdictions in more than a dozen countries (including Argentina, Australia, Brazil, Denmark, Finland, France, Germany, Greenland, Hungary, Iceland, Liechtenstein, New Zealand, Switzerland, the United Kingdom, and the United States) allow homosexual couples to enter civil unions. Canadian law goes one step further by making no distinction between heterosexual and same-sex marriage. At the same time, Canadian law respects the right of religious organizations to discriminate against homosexuals who want to marry. No religious organization is required by law to marry a homosexual couple.

Canadians are becoming more tolerant of homosexuality.
SOURCE: © 2009 Jupiterimages Corporation.

TABLE 4.3   THE OFFICIAL POSITION OF THE MAJOR WORLD RELIGIONS ON SEXUAL ISSUES

RELIGION	MASTURBATION	PREMARITAL SEX	EXTRAMARITAL SEX	HOMOSEXUAL SEX
Buddhism	Acceptable	Mostly acceptable	Unacceptable	Mostly acceptable
Christianity	Generally unacceptable (but no clear position for some Protestant denominations)	Unacceptable	Unacceptable	Unacceptable (but generally tolerated in the United Church of Canada)
Hinduism	Mostly acceptable	Unacceptable	Unacceptable	Unacceptable
Islam	Unacceptable	Unacceptable	Unacceptable	Unacceptable
Judaism	No clear position	Mostly acceptable	Unacceptable	Generally unacceptable (but generally tolerated in the Reform and Reconstructionist denominations)

SOURCE: Mackay (2000: 73).

TABLE 4.4   MEASURES OF SEXUAL ORIENTATION AMONG CANADIAN AND AMERICAN UNIVERSITY STUDENTS

	MEN	WOMEN
Self-reported sexual orientation		
Heterosexual	96.6	97.6
Homosexual, bisexual, other	3.4	2.4
Total	100.0	100.0
Attraction		
Only to one's own sex	88.0	86.6
At least partly to other sex	12.0	13.4
Total	100.0	100.0
Sexual fantasies		
Always involving only the other sex	79.0	74.2
Sometimes involving the same sex	21.0	25.8
Total	100.0	100.0
Same-sex intimate sexual experiences (for those with intimate experiences)		
Only with other sex	87.5	92.0
At least once with same sex	12.5	8.0
Total	100.0	100.0

SOURCE: Ellis, Lee, Brian Robb and Donald Burke, "Sexual orientation in United States and Canadian College Students," *Archives of Sexual Behavior* 34, 2005, pp. 569–81. Reprinted with kind permission from Springer Science and Business Media.

including whether desirable partners are of the same or a different sex.) I conclude that it is inaccurate to think about sexuality in terms of a strict dichotomy between heterosexuality and homosexuality. It is more appropriate to conceptualize sexuality as comprising four continua: sexual attraction, sexual desire, sexual behaviour, and sexual identity (Michael et al., 1994: 174–79).

Attitudes about extramarital affairs are more conservative than those about homosexuality, and they are becoming more so. In 1975, 28 percent of Canadian adults felt that sex with someone other than the marriage partner was "almost always wrong" and 50 percent felt it was "always wrong." By 1995, those figures were 25 percent and 60 percent, respectively, suggesting movement in a more conservative direction (Bibby, 1995: 75). As far as actual behaviour is concerned, in a 1998 survey of 13 countries, 30–39 percent of Canadians between the ages of 16 and 45 admitted to sexual infidelity. This puts Canadians in the same league as South Africans, Australians, French, Italians, and Thais. By comparison, 40 percent or more of Americans, Russians, British, and Germans between the ages of 16 and 45 admitted to sexual infidelity. For Spaniards, Poles, and residents of Hong Kong, the comparable figure was in the 20–29 percent range (Mackay, 2000: 36–37).

Changing attitudes toward extramarital affairs are part of a more general tendency for people to have fewer sexual partners. Although there are undoubtedly several reasons for this tendency, one of the most important is the spread of sexually transmitted diseases, HIV/AIDS in particular, since about 1980. Sexual attitudes were relatively liberal in the 1960s and 1970s. During those decades, contraception and abortion were legalized. The youth counterculture successfully promoted the idea of "free love." Thus, the culture of the times encouraged people to have multiple sexual partners, while changes in the law minimized the reproductive consequences of doing so. In contrast, once the dangers of HIV/AIDS and other sexually transmitted diseases became widely known in the early 1980s, many people became more cautious in their sexual relations. Of those Canadians who took precautions against sexually transmitted infections in 2003, the most common method was to use a condom with a new partner. Still, 49 percent of Canadians had unprotected sex without knowing their partner's sexual history in 2005 (Durex, 2005; see Figure 4.2).

As the foregoing discussion shows, surveys provide evidence of wide variation in attitudes toward sex and sexual conduct over time and place. Therefore, they help to dispel myths about sexuality as natural

FIGURE 4.2   PREVENTATIVE MEASURES TAKEN BY CANADIANS AGAINST SEXUALLY TRANSMITTED INFECTIONS (IN PERCENTAGE)

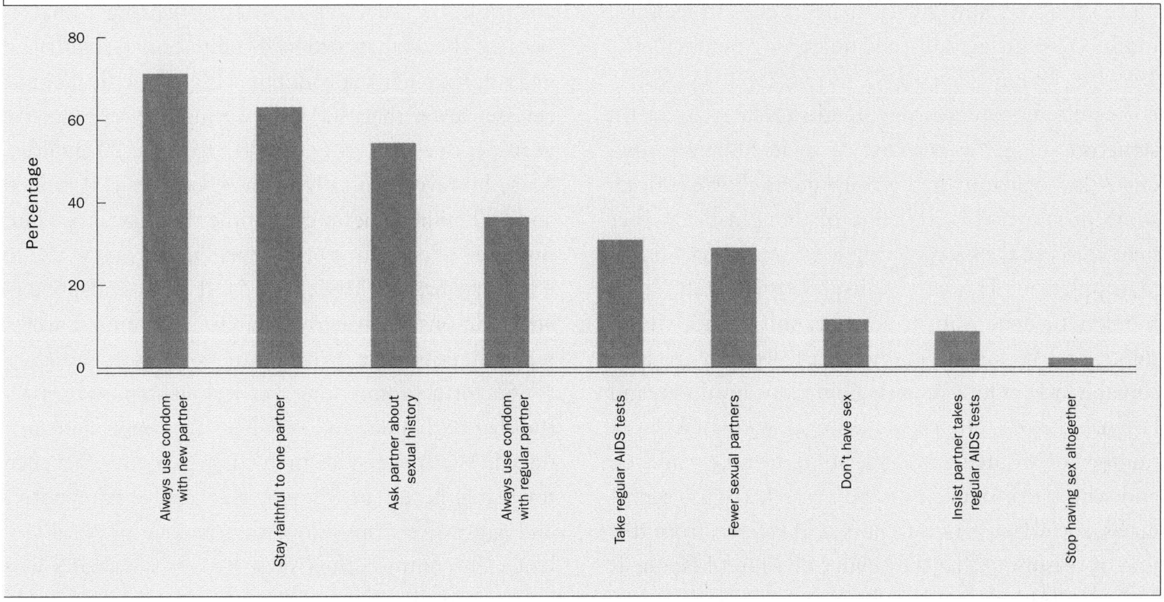

SOURCE: Durex, 2005, "Give and Receive: 2005 Global Sex Survey Results." On the World Wide Web at http://www.durex.com/cm/gss2005result.pdf (10 December 2005). Durex Global Sex Survey, 2003. Used courtesy of SSL International Plc.

or "fixed." However, they do not answer questions about the *origins* of sexual scripts or why inconsistencies exist between norms and behaviour. The next section addresses these issues by looking at the relationships among sex, gender, and sexuality.

DOES SEX DETERMINE DESTINY?

ESSENTIALISM

Most arguments about the origins of gender differences in human behaviour adopt one of two perspectives. Some analysts see gender as a reflection of naturally evolved dispositions. Others see gender as a reflection of the different social positions occupied by women and men. Sociologists call these two perspectives, respectively, essentialism and social constructionism. I now summarize and criticize essentialism. I then turn to social constructionism.

Essentialists first observe male–female differences in sexual scripts, the division of labour at home and in the workplace, mate selection, sexual aggression, jealousy, promiscuity, fidelity, and so forth. They then interpret these differences as natural and universal. According to essentialists, child rearing may exaggerate differences between men and women but nature is the ultimate force at work in shaping them.

Essentialism has many variants, most of which originate in biology and psychology. Here we briefly consider three of the most popular variants: brain studies, sociobiology, and Freudian theory.

Brain Studies

Male–female differences in brain structure are sometimes said to account for male–female differences in behaviour and achievement. The brain comprises two hemispheres of about equal size, connected by a bundle of fibres. The left hemisphere is generally associated with language abilities, the right with nonverbal perception and visual and spatial skills. About this little controversy exists in the scientific community. However, some brain researchers argue that the two hemispheres develop differently in boys and girls, as do the fibres connecting the hemispheres. Specifically, they claim that when the male fetus starts to secrete testosterone (the hormone responsible for furthering the sexual development of the male), it washes over the brain and briefly inhibits the growth of the left hemisphere. As a result, use of the *right* hemisphere becomes dominant in men. This supposedly allows men to excel in mathematical, artistic, musical, and visual-spatial abilities. Meanwhile (the theory continues), the bundle of fibres connecting the left and right hemispheres is bigger in women. This supposedly allows women to use the hemispheres more symmetrically, giving them an edge in feelings, intuition, language skills, and quick judgments (Bleier, 1984: 92; Blum, 1997: 36–63; Tavris, 1992: 45–46).

Such presumably innate differences in brain structure allegedly give rise to male–female differences in behaviour and achievement. For example, some proponents of this line of thought claim that men are best at jobs requiring logic and visual-spatial manipulation. Hence the disproportionately large number of men who work as scientists, mechanics, pilots, and so forth. For their part, women are presumably best at jobs requiring empathy, intuition, and language skills. Hence the disproportionately large number of women who stay home to raise children and who work outside the home as teachers, secretaries, social workers, and nurses. It follows from this line of reasoning that the gender division of labour is perfectly natural, structured by our brains rather than by society.

Sociobiology

Sociobiology is a second variant of essentialism, and E. O. Wilson (1975) is its leading exponent. Wilson argues that all human beings instinctually want to ensure that their genes get passed on to future generations. However, the different reproductive status of men and women means they have had to overcome different adaptive problems and develop different adaptive strategies. This gave rise to patterns of behaviour we now call "masculine" and "feminine." Individuals who possessed the characteristics that best resolved these problems—the most feminine women and the most masculine men—had a better chance of surviving and passing their genes to their offspring. Thus, over time, masculine and feminine behaviours became genetically encoded. According to sociobiology, genetic factors also trigger biochemical processes that further enhance sex differences through varying levels of hormone production in women and men.

David Buss, a well-known evolutionary psychologist, argues that four adaptive strategies or "universal features of our evolved selves" govern the relations between the sexes and contribute to the preservation of the human species (Buss, 1994: 211; see also Buss, 1995a, 1995b, 1998; Dawkins, 1976; Wilson, 1978). First, men want casual sex with women. Second, men treat women's bodies as men's property. Third, men beat or kill women who incite male sexual jealousy. And fourth, women are greedy for money.

Buss bases his argument on the claim that a woman has a bigger investment than a man in ensuring the survival of their offspring. That is because the woman produces only a small number of eggs during her reproductive life. Specifically, she releases fewer than 400 eggs during her reproductive years. At most, she can give birth to about 20 children. Men, however, typically release between 200 million and 500 million sperm every time they ejaculate. This number of sperm can be produced every 24 to 48 hours (Saxton, 1990: 94–95). It is thus adaptive in an evolutionary sense for a man to be promiscuous yet jealously possessive of his partners (Wilson and Daly, 1998), for a promiscuous yet jealous man maximizes the chance that his, and only his, offspring will be produced. Moreover, since men compete with other men for sexual access to women, men evolve competitive and aggressive dispositions that include physical violence. In contrast, Buss says, it is in a woman's best interest to maintain primary responsibility for her genetic child and to look around for the best mate with whom to intermix her genes. He is the man who can best help support the child after birth. Hence women's alleged greed for money in contemporary society.

Research certainly supports the view that men and women emphasize different characteristics in selecting a mate. Simon Davis, for example, conducted a content analysis of personal advertisements in the *Vancouver Sun*. He discovered that attractive physical features were the most frequently mentioned desirable characteristic in a partner for both men and women. However, women were more likely than men to list professional status, employment status, financial considerations, intelligence, commitment, and emotion. Men, conversely, were more likely to list attractiveness, physique, and sexiness, and to require a picture (Davis, 1990: 43–50). These results do not, however, establish that sex-typed mating preferences are *genetically* determined. As we will see, the results are also consistent with differences in how we assign status to masculine and feminine gender roles.

Freud

Freud (1977 [1905]) offered a third influential essentialist explanation of male–female differences. He believed that sexuality is the main human instinct. In his view, it motivates human behaviour and accounts for the development of distinct masculine and feminine gender roles.

According to Freud, children around the age of three to five begin to pay attention to their genitals.

As a young boy becomes preoccupied with his penis, he unconsciously develops a fantasy of sexually possessing his mother. He begins to resent his father because only his father is allowed to sexually possess the mother. But because he has seen his mother or another girl naked, the boy also develops anxiety that he will be castrated by his father for desiring his mother.[1] To resolve this fear, the boy represses his feelings for his mother. That is, he stores them in the unconscious part of his personality. In due course, this repression allows him to begin identifying with his father. This leads to the development of a strong, masculine personality.

In contrast, the young girl begins to develop a feminine personality when she realizes she lacks a penis. According to Freud:

> [girls] notice the penis of a brother or playmate, strikingly visible and of large proportions, at once recognize it as the superior counterpart of their own small and inconspicuous organ, and from that time forward fall a victim to envy for the penis. . . . She has seen it and knows that she is without it and wants to have it. (Quoted in Steinem, 1994: 50)

Because of her "penis envy," the young girl soon develops a sense of inferiority, according to Freud. She also grows angry with her mother, who, she naively thinks, is responsible for cutting off the penis the girl must have once had. She rejects her mother and develops an unconscious sexual desire for her father. Eventually, however, realizing she will never have a penis, the girl comes to identify with her mother. This is a way of vicariously acquiring her father's penis in Freud's view. In the "normal" development of a mature woman, the girl's wish to have a penis is transformed into a desire to have children. However, says Freud, since women are never able to completely resolve their penis envy, the feminine gender identity is normally immature and dependent on men. This dependence is evident from the "fact" that women can be fully sexually satisfied only by vaginally induced orgasm. Thus, a host of gender differences in personality and behaviour follow from the anatomical sex differences that children first observe around the age of three.[2]

A Critique of Essentialism

Essentialist arguments, such as those described above, have six main problems:

1. *Essentialists ignore the historical and cultural variability of gender and sexuality.* In some cultures, men are socialized to be nurturing and sensitive. Rape is incomprehensible. For example, anthropologist Margaret Mead reports that the Arapesh, a preliterate people in New Guinea, "know nothing of rape beyond the fact that it is the unpleasant custom of the Nugum people to the southeast of them" (Mead, 1935: 110). More generally, rates of rape vary widely across cultures (Sanday, 1981). This variability deflates the idea that biological constants account for innate behavioural differences between women and men, such as male aggressiveness and violence. Moreover, societies and cultures often change rapidly without any apparent genetic change taking place. Essentialist arguments have a difficult time explaining, for example, recent changes in child-care arrangements, women's participation in the labour force, and other aspects of women's lives, given the absence of any documented shift in male or female genetic structure that might account for this change.

2. *Essentialists ignore the fact that gender differences are declining rapidly and in some cases have already disappeared* (Caplan and Caplan, 1999). Hundreds of studies have shown that women are developing traits that were traditionally considered masculine. For example, psychological research shows that women have become more assertive, competitive, independent, and analytical since the early 1970s. They play more aggressive sports, choose more mathematics and science courses, perform better in standardized tests, take more non-traditional jobs, and earn more money than they used to (Twenge, 1997). In what must be considered a serious blow to brain research on alleged male–female differences, a review of 165 studies of verbal ability representing tests of more than 1.4 million people found no gender differences in verbal skills. A review of 100 studies of mathematics performance representing tests of nearly 4 million students showed small differences favouring *females* in the general population. (Larger differences favouring males were, however, found in samples of precocious individuals.) A review of dozens of studies on spatial ability reported that some studies found no gender differences, while other studies found only small differences in favour of men (Tavris, 1992: 52). Taken as a whole, this body of research suggests that few gender differences in ability remain to be explained, the few remaining differences

are small, and those few small differences are disappearing.

3. *The research evidence employed by essentialists is often deeply flawed.* Consider the sociobiologists' observation that men are more independent than women. Research shows that, in fact, girls are more dependent than boys *only at certain ages.* Thus, although infant girls seem to behave in a more dependent fashion than infant boys, girls at the age of two are more independent than boys (Feiring and Lewis, 1979; Goldberg and Lewis, 1969). Evidence from studies purporting to find a genetic cause of homosexuality is also problematic. Hamer and Copeland (1996), for example, claim to have found a possible genetic marker for homosexuality in 33 of 40 brothers who were both gay. As Peele and De Grandpre (1995) point out, however, the study did not check for the frequency of the supposed marker in *heterosexual* brothers. Nor has anyone been able to replicate the findings. More generally, sociobiologists and evolutionary psychologists have not been able to identify *any* of the genes that, they claim, cause male jealousy, female nurturance, or the unequal division of labour between men and women. Meanwhile, brain researchers have had great difficulty showing how observed physical differences between male and female brains might be related to (nonexistent, small, and shrinking) differences in male and female abilities. That is one reason several brain theories make contradictory arguments. For example, the theory reviewed previously says that men have greater right hemisphere specialization. However, a second theory holds that men have greater *left* hemisphere specialization, which gives them an intellectual advantage over women. Meanwhile, a third theory agrees that men have greater right brain specialization but insists that this gives men superior artistic and musical abilities; yet this contradicts the first theory, which says that women have the edge in musical and artistic skills, which rely on intuition and empathy (Tavris, 1992: 45–49). Lack of hard evidence encourages such unsubstantiated speculation.

4. *Essentialists tend to generalize from the average, ignoring variations within gender groups.* On average, women and men do, of course, differ in some respects. For example, one of the best-documented average differences between women and men concerns aggressiveness. Men are on average more verbally and physically aggressive than women are. However, when sociobiologists say men are *inherently* more aggressive than women are, they make it seem as if this is true of all men and all women. As Figure 4.3 shows, however, it is not. When verbal or physical aggressiveness is measured by trained researchers, scores vary widely within gender groups. Aggressiveness is distributed so that considerable overlap occurs between men and women. Thus, many women are more aggressive than the average man, and many men are less aggressive than the average woman.

5. *Essentialists exaggerate the degree to which gender differences are unchangeable.* For example, evolutionary psychologist David Buss and colleagues (1990) used data from 37 cultures to show that women consistently prefer older men with high earning capacity as partners. In contrast, men prefer women with good domestic capabilities. Buss claims that this demonstrates a genetic basis for mate selection. But Eagley and Wood (1999) re-examined Buss's data. They show that women's tendency to stress the "good provider" role in selecting male partners and men's tendency to stress women's domestic skills decrease in societies that have more gender equality. Similarly, women express less preference for older men, and men less preference for younger women, in more gender-egalitarian societies. As this example shows, gender differences vary with social conditions, a fact that essentialists ignore. Another example of how social conditions affect gender differences: The "male" hormone testosterone is associated with greater aggressiveness.

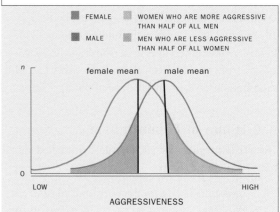

FIGURE 4.3   THE DISTRIBUTION OF MALE AND FEMALE AGGRESSIVENESS

FEMALE   WOMEN WHO ARE MORE AGGRESSIVE THAN HALF OF ALL MEN

MALE   MEN WHO ARE LESS AGGRESSIVE THAN HALF OF ALL WOMEN

female mean   male mean

LOW   HIGH

AGGRESSIVENESS

However, Pulitzer-prize-winning science writer Deborah Blum (1997: 158–88) notes that social situations involving competition and threat stimulate production of testosterone in *women* and cause them to act more aggressively (compare Caplan and Caplan, 1999). For example, when women take jobs that maximize competition and threat—when they become, say, corporate lawyers or police officers—they undergo hormonal and behavioural changes, thus decreasing behavioural differences between men and women.

6. *Essentialists offer explanations for gender differences that ignore the role of power.* Sociobiologists assume that existing behaviour patterns help ensure the survival of the species because they are the patterns that endured as humans evolved. However, their assumption overlooks the fact that some groups (such as men) are in a position of greater power and authority than are other groups (such as women). Behavioural differences between men and women may, therefore, result not from any biological imperative but from men's ability to establish their preferences over the interests of women. Indeed, from this point of view, sociobiology may be seen as an example of the exercise of male power, that is, a rationalization for male domination and sexual aggression. The same may be said of Freud's interpretation. *Must* young girls define themselves in relation to young boys by focusing on their lack of a penis? *Do* they define themselves that way? Freud offers no evidence to support his case. There is no reason why young girls' sexual self-definitions cannot focus positively on their own reproductive organs, including their unique ability to bear children. Freud simply assumes that men are superior to women and then creates a speculative theory that justifies gender differences.

SOCIAL CONSTRUCTIONISM

Social constructionism is the main alternative to essentialism. Social constructionists argue that gender differences are not the product of biological properties, whether chromosomal, gonadal, or hormonal. Instead, gender and sexuality are products of social structure and culture. *Culture* is composed of shared systems of meaning. It incorporates people's values and beliefs. Although many systems of meaning coexist and compete at any one time, patriarchy, or male domination and belief in its validity, is widely accepted in nearly all societies today. *Social structure* refers to the way major institutions, such as families, the economy, and the political system, are organized. Social structures in most societies today are patriarchal in that they reinforce inequalities between women and men.

Social constructionists stress three main sociohistorical changes that led to the development of gender inequality:

1. *Long-distance warfare and conquest.* Anthropologists have shown that a high level of gender equality existed in foraging or hunting-and-gathering societies, the dominant form of society for 90 percent of human history. Rough equality between women and men was based on the fact that women produced a substantial amount of the band's food, up to 80 percent in some cases (see Chapter 10, Families). Archaeological evidence from "Old Europe" tells a similar story. Old Europe is a region stretching roughly from Poland in the north to the Mediterranean island of Crete in the south, and from Switzerland in the west to Bulgaria in the east (see Figure 4.4, p. 88). Between 7000 and 3500 B.C.E., men and women enjoyed rough equality throughout the region. The religions of the region gave primacy to fertility and creator goddesses. Kinship was traced through the mother's side of the family. Then, sometime between 4300 and 4200 B.C.E., all this began to change. Old Europe was invaded by successive waves of warring peoples from the Asiatic and European northeast (the Kurgans) and the deserts to the south (the Semites). Both the Kurgan and Semitic civilizations were based on a steeply hierarchical and patriarchal social structure. Their religions gave primacy to male warrior gods. They acquired property and slaves by conquering other peoples and imposed their religions on the vanquished. They eliminated, or at least downgraded, goddesses as divine powers. God became a male who willed that women should be ruled by men. Laws reinforced women's sexual, economic, and political subjugation to men. Traditional Judaism, Christianity, and Islam all embody ideas of male dominance and they all derive from the tribes who conquered Old Europe in the fifth millennium B.C.E. (Eisler, 1987).

2. *Plow agriculture.* Long-distance warfare and conquest catered to men's strengths and so greatly

FIGURE 4.4   APPROXIMATE AREA FOR EARLY CIVILIZATION OF OLD EUROPE

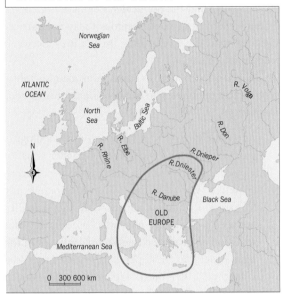

FIGURE 4.4   APPROXIMATE AREA FOR EARLY CIVILIZATION OF OLD EUROPE

SOURCE: Adapted from Marija Gimbutas, *Goddesses and Gods of Old Europe: 6500–3500 B.C.: Myths and Cult Images* (Berkeley and Los Angeles: University of California Press, 1982), p. 16. *Goddesses and Gods of Old Europe: 6500–3500 B.C., Myths and Cult Images*, by Marija Gimbutas, © 1971, 1982 by Thames and Hudson Ltd. Published by the University of California Press. Reprinted with permission.

enhanced male power and authority. Large-scale farming with plows harnessed to animals had much the same effect. Plow agriculture originated in the Middle East around 5000 years ago. It required that strong adults remain in the fields all day for much of the year. It also reinforced the principle of private ownership of land. Since men were on average stronger than women, and since women were restricted in their activities by pregnancy, nursing, and childbirth, plow agriculture made men more powerful socially. Thus, land was owned by men and ownership was typically passed from father to son (Coontz and Henderson, 1986).

3. *The separation of public and private spheres.* In the agricultural era, economic production was organized around the household. Men may have worked apart from women in the fields, but the fields were still part of the *family* farm. In contrast, during the early phase of industrialization, men's work was moved out of the household and into the factory and the office. Most men became wage or salary workers. Some assumed decision-making roles in economic and political institutions. But while men went public, most women remained in the domestic or private sphere.

The idea soon developed that this was a "natural" division of labour. This idea persisted until the second half of the twentieth century, when a variety of social circumstances, ranging from the introduction of the birth control pill to women's demands for entry into university, finally allowed women to enter the public sphere in large numbers.

So we see that, according to social constructionists, gender inequality derives historically from three main circumstances: the advent of long-distance warfare and conquest, the development of plow agriculture, and the assignment of women to the domestic sphere and men to the public sphere during the early industrial era.

Although gender inequality is decreasing somewhat in many societies today, it still persists. It is supported by a variety of economic and political arrangements discussed elsewhere in this book (see especially Chapter 7). In what follows, I fill out the social constructionist perspective by outlining just two dimensions of contemporary gender inequality. First, I show how socialization still pushes girls to act in stereotypically feminine ways and boys to act in stereotypically masculine ways. I then discuss eating disorders and male violence against women to show that the social construction of gender has far-reaching implications for women, men, and the relations between them.

CONSTRUCTING GENDER THROUGH SOCIALIZATION

PRIMARY SOCIALIZATION

Research shows that, from the moment of birth, infant boys and girls are treated differently by parents, particularly fathers. Girls are more likely to be characterized as delicate, weak, beautiful, and cute; boys as strong, alert, and well coordinated (Rubin, Provenzano, and Lurra, 1974). Interpretations of behaviour vary by sex. For example, when viewing a videotape of a nine-month-old infant, experimental subjects tend to label startled reactions to a stimulus as "anger" if the baby has been previously identified as a boy, and as "fear" if the baby is identified as a girl, *regardless of the baby's actual sex* (Condry and Condry, 1976). Parents also tend to encourage their sons to engage in boisterous behaviour and competitive play. They tend to encourage their daughters to engage in cooperative play (MacDonald and Parke, 1986). Boys are more likely than girls are to be praised for assertiveness, and girls are more likely than boys are to be rewarded for compliance (Kerig, Cowan, and Cowan, 1993). Parents reinforce gender-specific behaviour by the design of the child's room, the clothes they buy, and the toys they provide. Boys' toys, for example, are more likely to emphasize aggressive competition and spatial manipulation. Girls' toys tend to be more passive and oriented toward the home (e.g., dolls, kitchen sets, washers and dryers; Hughes, 1995). Most parents encourage their children to play with gender-stereotyped toys. Preschool boys are just as likely to play with a dish set as a tool set if given a choice—unless they are told that the dish set is a girl's toy and they think their fathers will view playing with it as "bad" (Raag and Rackliff, 1998).

SECONDARY SOCIALIZATION

The process of channelling girls into roles culturally defined as appropriately feminine and boys into roles culturally defined as appropriately masculine continues in school. In most schools, teachers still tend to assume that boys will do better in the sciences and mathematics, girls in languages. Parents reinforce these expectations at home (Eccles, Jacobs, and Harold, 1990). Teachers also praise boys more than they praise girls and give boys more help. They are more likely to agree with boys' comments during class and give boys instructions on how to complete a task rather than do the task for them. This reinforces gender stereotypes and results in a less effective learning experience for girls.

By the age of about 14, interaction with peers becomes an important factor in reinforcing gender-typed attitudes and behaviours. That is because the subcultures of male and female peer groups emphasize gender-stereotypical values. Boys tend to establish less intimate friendships than girls do. Moreover, boys' friendships tend to be based on such activities as team sports, which focus on independence, emotional control, and conquest. Girls tend to form less extensive friendship networks than boys do and focus on sociability, popularity, and attractiveness (Elkin and Handel, 1989; Udry, 1971: 76, 82).

THE MASS MEDIA

The symbolic representation of gender in the mass media also creates and reinforces gender stereotypes. The social construction of gender in the mass media begins when small children learn that only a kiss from Snow White's Prince Charming will save her from

eternal sleep. It continues in magazines, romance novels, advertisements, and music, and on television and the Internet. It is big business. For example, Harlequin Enterprises of Toronto dominates the production and sale of romance novels worldwide. The company sells more than 175 million books a year in 23 languages in more than 100 national markets. The average romance reader spends $1200 a year on the genre. Most readers of Harlequin romances consume between 3 and 20 books a month. A central theme in these romances is the transformation of women's bodies into objects for men's pleasure (Grescoe, 1996). As such, romance novels may be seen as a less extreme form of the pornography industry for men.

GENDER SOCIALIZATION AND SEXUALITY

In our society, we receive little formal socialization—that is, systematic instruction—regarding sexuality. That is probably because of our rather prudish history and the popular assumption that sexuality is a natural instinct that does not have to be taught. By default, therefore, as adults we tend to express our sexuality in

Murray Warren, a teacher in Port Coquitlam, B.C., displays two of three children's books featuring children with same-gender parents at the Supreme Court of Canada in Ottawa, June 2002. The books were banned by the Surrey School Board in which Warren teaches. What gender stereotypes do these kinds of books seek to offset?
SOURCE: The Canadian Press (Fred Chartrand).

a framework defined by our early, informal gender socialization.

Boys and girls do not always accept informal gender socialization passively; they sometimes resist it. For the most part, however, boys and girls try to develop the skills that will help them perform conventional gender roles (Eagley and Wood, 1999: 412–13). Of course, conventions change. It is important to note in this regard that what children learn about femininity and masculinity today is less sexist than what they learned just a few generations ago. For example, comparing *Cinderella* and *Snow White* with *Mulan*, we see that girls going to Disney movies today are sometimes presented with assertive and heroic female role models rather than the passive and, by today's standards, quite pathetic heroines of the 1930s and 1940s. However, the amount of change in gender socialization should not be exaggerated, nor its effects on sexuality. *Cinderella* and *Snow White* are still popular movies for girls. Moreover, for every *Mulan* there is a *Little Mermaid*, a movie that simply modernizes old themes about female passivity and male conquest. As we saw in our discussion of sexual behaviour, survey research shows that men are still more likely than women are to adhere to sexual scripts emphasizing fun, conquest, and orgasm rather than love, tenderness, and emotionality. The fact that girls learn that sexuality is something they must fear—think of unwanted pregnancy and sexual assault—also serves to perpetuate passive sexual scripts for women today (Nelson and Robinson, 1999: 351).

The social construction of gender and sexuality has far-reaching implications for men and women. As we have just seen, the social construction of gender during childhood socialization influences the way men and women express their sexuality. You will learn in detail later in this book how the social construction of gender also helps determine the kind of formal education men and women pursue, the kinds of jobs they get, and the way domestic work is divided between men and women. As you will now see, the standards of physical attractiveness that are internalized through gender socialization and sexual scripts have contributed to dieting and eating disorders.

BODY IMAGE AND EATING DISORDERS

The social construction of gender involves defining standards of physical attractiveness for women and men. These standards are reinforced by the mass media.

Physical attractiveness is especially important for women. That is because they are judged on the basis of appearance more often than men are. Moreover, unattractive women are described in more negative terms than equally unattractive men are (Wolf, 1991). Masculinity is more likely to be assessed in terms of status and power than in terms of physical attractiveness.

Weight has become an increasingly important dimension of body image since the 1960s. Research shows that *Playboy* centrefold models and Miss America contestants have grown substantially thinner since 1959. A 1997 survey shows that 89 percent of North American women want to lose weight (Garner, 1997). Canadian women list "being overweight" as one of their major health problems (Walters, 1992). Many men are concerned about their body image, too, but among women the emphasis on being thin is especially common. The "cult of thinness" has spawned major industries, including diet and self-help, cosmetic surgery, diet foods, and fitness (Hesse-Biber, 1996).

Standards of breast size pose a special problem for women. Although thin is in, large breasts have

Canadian women list "being overweight" as one of their major health problems.
SOURCE: Shutterstock.

been popular since the 1960s (Koff and Benavage, 1998). Breasts, however, are composed mainly of fat; and the amount of breast fat is associated with total body fat. Thus, it is virtually impossible for most women to achieve the ideal standard of beauty.

Many women and men resent the thin models they see in the mass media. Nonetheless, dieting to lose weight and fear of being fat are common in girls as young as nine. One study found that half of all teenage girls are on diets (Pipher, 1994: 184–85).

Body image is associated with self-esteem and behaviour. People who are dissatisfied with their bodies are less likely to desire and engage in sexual activity. Conversely, bad sexual experiences contribute to a poor body image. For example, sexual abuse is an important cause of body dissatisfaction. In the 1997 survey cited previously, 23 percent of women and 10 percent of men viewed sexual abuse as having been moderately to very important in shaping their body image in childhood or adolescence (Garner, 1997).

At the extreme, concern with body image may result in anorexia nervosa (refusal to eat enough to remain healthy) or bulimia (regular, self-induced vomiting). Estimates of the percentage of young women with such eating disorders range from 2 percent to 20 percent. For young men, estimates are in the 1 percent to 3 percent range (Averett and Korenman, 1996: 305; Garner, 1997; Lips, 1993: 254; Pipher, 1994: 184–85). Some women and men have changed their body shape by means of surgical procedures, such as liposuction and cosmetic surgery. More than 90 percent of cosmetic surgery patients are women (Hesse-Biber, 1996: 51, 53).

There are cultural variations in standards of beauty. For instance, in the United States, black women are more likely to be above the recommended body weight than are non-black women. At the same time, they are less likely to see themselves as overweight. Obesity also results in fewer social penalties in the case of black women. Thus, obese white women have smaller family incomes than non-obese white women because they are less likely to be married and more likely to face job discrimination. This is not the case for obese black women compared with non-obese black women (Averett and Korenman, 1996).

MALE VIOLENCE AGAINST WOMEN

The way in which gender and sexual scripts are socially constructed also affects the frequency with which men sexually assault and harass women. Let us now consider this issue in detail.

SEXUAL ASSAULT

The sexual assault of women is common. Surveys suggest that one in eight girls growing up in Canada today will be a victim of serious sexual abuse before the age of 16 (Bagley and King, 1990; Gadd, 1997). Perpetrators of child sexual assault are typically male, known to the victim, and in a position of authority over the child. Research demonstrates that, in general, victims of sexual assault are selected less because of sexual desirability than because of their availability and powerlessness (Duffy, 1998). One survey found that 60 percent of high school boys approve of forcing sexual activities on a girl, at least in some circumstances (Davis, Peck, and Stormant, 1993).

A survey of Canadian college and university students asked a series of questions about male violence against women during elementary school, during high school, since high school, and in the year preceding the survey (DeKeseredy and Schwartz, 1998). The researchers found that psychological or emotional abuse of women is most common, followed by sexual and then physical abuse. Males consistently reported lower levels of sexual, psychological, and physical violence against women than women reported. However, even the percentages reported by males are disturbingly high. Moreover, the percentages grow as boys turn into men and advance from high school to postsecondary education. For example, 1.5 percent of boys said they forced girls to engage in sexual activities with them in elementary school and 2.3 percent said they forced girls to engage in sexual activities with them in high school. For the year preceding the survey, the percentage was 11 percent. Fully 19.5 percent of men in Canadian colleges and universities said they had forced a woman to engage in sexual activities with them at least once since high school (see also Table 4.5, p. 92).

Of course, men are the victims of violence too. Like women, they are far more likely to be assaulted by men than by women. Some studies show that female partners are as likely as male partners to participate in abusive acts—with the exception of sexual assault, which is almost exclusively a male domain (Straus, 1995). Note, however, that women are more likely to use violence as a response to their own powerlessness, attacking partners out of self-defence or lashing out at their children following abuse by their

TABLE 4.5   INTIMATE VIOLENCE IN CANADA, 1993–2004

	1993	1999	2004
Prevalence of self-reported spousal assault, preceding five years (percentage)			
Male victims	n.a.	7	6
Female victims	12	8	7
Spousal homicide (per 100 000 men and women)			
Male victims	0.3	0.1	0.1
Female victims	0.8	0.7	0.7
Sexual assaults reported to police (per 100 000 pop.)	120	78	70
Prevalence of criminal harassment (stalking) reported to police			
By current or ex-husband or boyfriend	n.a.	1300	2125
By current or ex-wife or girlfriend	n.a.	100	200

SOURCE: Statistics Canada (2006).

Note: Figures are approximate because they were read from graphs.

husbands. Men, conversely, are more likely to use force to retain control and power over their partners and children. Moreover, abusive men are far more likely to cause serious physical injuries than are abusive women, and abused men are therefore far less likely than abused women are to report their partners' violent acts to the police (Fitzgerald, 1993; Koss et al., 1994; see Figure 4.5).

The most severe form of sexual assault involves rape. Research shows that some rapists are men who were physically or sexually abused in their youth. They develop a deep-seated need to feel powerful as psychological compensation for their early powerlessness. Other rapists are men who, as children, saw their mothers as potentially hostile figures who needed to be controlled, or as mere objects available for male gratification, and saw their fathers as emotionally cold and distant. Raised in such a family atmosphere, rapists learn not to empathize with women. Instead, they learn to want to dominate them

FIGURE 4.5   SEVERITY OF SPOUSAL VIOLENCE BY SEX OF VICTIM, CANADA, 2004

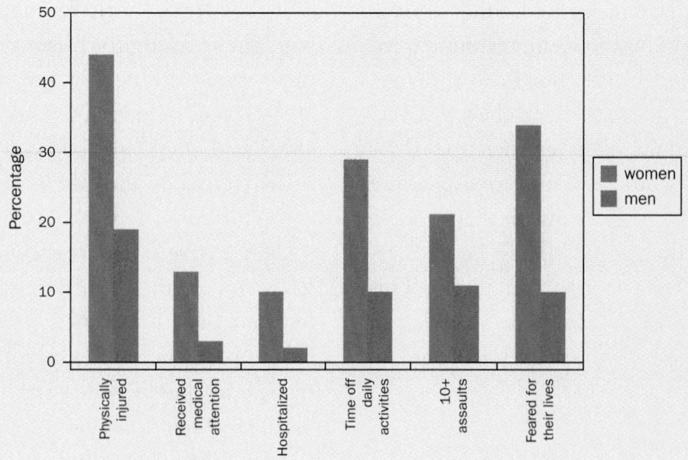

SOURCE: Statistics Canada, 2006, "Prevalence and Severity of Violence against Women." On the World Wide Web at http://www.statcan.gc.ca/pub/85-570-x/2006001/findings-resultats/4144393-eng.htm (retrieved 6 December 2008).

(Lisak, 1992). Significantly, rates of rape are highest in war situations, when many conquering male soldiers feel justified in wanting to humiliate the vanquished, who are powerless to stop them (Human Rights Watch, 1995). This suggests that, in general, rape involves using sex to establish dominance. The incidence of rape is highest in situations where early socialization experiences predispose men to want to control women, where norms justify the domination of women, and where a large power imbalance between men and women exists.

SEXUAL HARASSMENT

Two types of sexual harassment occur in the workplace. **Quid pro quo sexual harassment** takes place when sexual threats or bribery are made a condition of employment decisions. **Hostile environment sexual harassment** involves sexual jokes, comments, and touching that interferes with work or creates an unfriendly work setting. Surveys show that between 23 percent and 51 percent of women have been sexually harassed in the workplace (Gruber, 1997; Welsh and Nierobisz, 1997). When semi-public and public settings are included, up to 87 percent of women report being sexually harassed (see Table 4.5; Lenton Smith, Fox, and Morra, 1999). On the basis of available research, it seems clear that relatively powerless women are the most likely to be sexually harassed. Moreover, sexual harassment is most common in work settings that exhibit high levels of gender inequality and a culture justifying male domination of women. Specifically, women who are young, unmarried, and employed in non-professional jobs are most likely to become objects of sexual harassment. They are particularly likely to be sexually harassed if they are temporary workers, the ratio of women to men in the workplace is low, and the organizational culture of the workplace tolerates sexual harassment (Welsh, 1999).

As the foregoing discussion makes clear, large power imbalances between men and women and a culture that supports patriarchy are associated with high rates of sexual assault and harassment. Where men are much more powerful than women, and where gender inequality is justified culturally, gender is socially constructed to permit and even encourage violence against women. The research literature is clear on this point. It shows, for example, that men who most enjoy sexist jokes are most likely to report engaging in acts of sexual aggression against women (Ryan and Kanjorski, 1998). Men who link sexuality with social dominance are more likely to sexually harass women (Pryor, Giedd, and Williams, 1995). And both men and women who abuse their intimate partners value control and dominance more than harmony in interpersonal relationships (Thompson, 1991).

LOOKING AHEAD: TOWARD A NEW SEXUAL ETHIC

For the past 40 years, most sociologists of gender have criticized the essentialist view that sexual scripts are part of "human nature." Rather than seeing sexuality as natural, they have examined how it is socially constructed. They do not deny the biological basis of sexuality. They simply appreciate that the form sexual expression takes is not inevitable and immutable. In the preceding pages, I illustrated the social constructionist case by examining the historical factors that shaped the emergence of sexual scripts, the relationship between gender socialization and sexuality, the ways in which sexual relations reflect and reinforce power differentials, the privileging of heterosexuality, the marginalization of other sexual identities, and the implications of gender roles for the sexual assault and harassment of women by men.

SEXUAL PLURALISM

Social constructionism has overturned many ideas about sexuality. As a result, more and more people accept that sexuality does not have to be expressed in traditionally feminine or masculine ways. An attitude of **sexual pluralism** is growing (Weeks, 1986). For most people, sexual pluralism does *not* mean "anything goes." Most sexual pluralists recognize that there will always be a need to regulate sexual behaviour. For example, they oppose the abuse of power in sexual relations and see the need for the state to punish, and help prevent, incest, rape, and other forms of sexual abuse. Sexual pluralism *does* mean judging sexual acts only by their meaning for the participants. Are power relations at play? If so, are they harmful to the participants? These are the sorts of questions that sexual pluralists use in evaluating the validity of sexual acts. They do not automatically condemn a sexual practice because it is, say, "homosexual" or "heterosexual."

Some feminists are not sexual pluralists. They reject all forms of heterosexuality because, they say, it perpetuates male dominance (Dworkin, 1981; Jeffreys, 1990; Kitzinger and Wilkinson, 1994).

From a sexual-pluralist perspective, however, heterosexuality is not inherently about men dominating women any more than it is inherently about strict adherence to traditional masculine and feminine sexual scripts. The sexual expression of heterosexuality may involve the perpetuation of harmful relations of domination or it may not. Sexual pluralists would judge only the former negatively.

Sexual pluralism, then, fosters a view of sexuality as something more than a form of victimization because of unequal power relations. It also encourages people to see sexuality positively, as a means of achieving greater pleasure, freedom of expression, and self-realization. Consider pornography. From the 1960s to the 1980s, some feminists fought to ban pornography on the grounds that it presents women as powerless sex objects and encourages men to sexually assault women (Dworkin, 1981; MacKinnon, 1987). Most pornography does indeed have that effect. However, must it? Recently, sexual pluralists have argued that pornography does not have to reinforce the domination and degradation of women by men. For example, pornography can be a means for women to create and disseminate their own sexual scripts based on female sexual fantasies, both heterosexual and lesbian. Pornographic art, literature, and movies of this type are now being produced (Matrix, 1996). From the sexual-pluralist point of view, seeing pornography as necessarily harmful to women is little more than a new form of essentialism.

Riane Eisler (1987) convincingly argues that, for the first time in 7000 years, social conditions now make it possible for humanity to return to the state of rough gender equality that existed before the invasion of Old Europe by conquering hordes from the north, east, and south. At least in the world's rich countries, nothing prevents us from adopting social policies that would create gender equality in the workplace, the home, and other spheres of life (see Chapter 7). As this chapter demonstrates, the examination and redefinition of sexuality is an important step in the process of achieving gender equality.

SUMMARY

1. Sex refers to biological differences between males and females while *gender* refers to the attitudes, beliefs, and behaviours that we commonly associate with each sex.

2. Although it is popular to trace the origins of masculine and feminine gender roles to biological differences between the sexes, most sociologists focus on the ways in which gender is socially constructed.

3. Three major sociohistorical changes have led to the development of gender inequality: long-distance warfare and conquest, plow agriculture, and the separation of public and private spheres during early industrialization.

4. Conscious sexual learning begins around adolescence in the context of firmly established gender identities.

5. Although we receive little formal socialization regarding sexuality, sexual relationships tend to be male-dominated as a result of the character of gender socialization and men's continuing dominant position in society.

6. The social construction of gender and sexual scripts has defined standards of beauty that are nearly impossible for most women to achieve. This contributes to widespread anxiety about body image, leading in some cases to eating disorders.

7. Gender inequality and a sociocultural context that justifies and eroticizes male sexual aggression contribute to the widespread problem of male sexual aggression.

8. The mass media reflect and reinforce the relationship between heterosexuality and male domination.

9. Social constructionism encourages sexual pluralism, which assesses the validity of sexual activities in terms of the meanings of the acts to the participants.

QUESTIONS TO CONSIDER

1. Do you think sexual orientation is genetically programmed or a function of social and psychological experience? On what do you base your opinion? What type of evidence would persuade you one way or the other?

2. Design a study to test whether gender roles are inherent or socially constructed.

3. What policy recommendations would you make to lower the level of sexual assault and sexual harassment? Why do you think these policies would be effective?

GLOSSARY

Compulsory heterosexuality is the assumption that individuals should desire only members of the "opposite" sex.

Essentialists observe male–female differences in sexual scripts, the division of labour at home and in the workplace, mate selection, sexual aggression, jealousy, promiscuity, fidelity, and so forth. They then interpret these differences as natural and universal.

Gender encompasses the feelings, attitudes, and behaviours that are associated with being male or female as conventionally understood.

Gender identity refers to identification with, or a sense of belonging to, a particular sex, biologically, psychologically, and socially.

Gender roles comprise the repertoire of behaviours that match widely shared expectations about how males and females are supposed to act.

Hostile environment sexual harassment involves sexual jokes, comments, and touching that interfere with work or create an unfriendly work setting.

Quid pro quo sexual harassment involves sexual threats or bribery used to extract sexual favours as a condition of employment decisions.

Sex refers to being born with distinct male or female genitalia and a genetic program that releases either male or female hormones to stimulate the development of one's reproductive system.

Sexual orientation refers to the way a person derives sexual pleasure, including whether desirable partners are of the same or a different sex.

Sexual pluralism assesses sexual acts only by their meaning for the participants.

Sexual scripts are assumptions that guide sexual behaviour by telling us whom we should find attractive, when and where it is appropriate to be aroused, what is sexually permissible, and so on.

Sexuality involves actions that are intended to produce erotic arousal and genital response.

Social constructionism is the main alternative to essentialism. Social constructionists argue that gender differences are not the product of biological properties, whether chromosomal, gonadal, or hormonal. Instead, gender and sexuality are products of social structure and culture.

Sociobiology is the best-known variant of essentialism. It holds that all human beings instinctually want to ensure that their genes get passed on to future generations. However, the different reproductive status of men and women means that they have had to develop different adaptive strategies. This gave rise to "masculine" and "feminine" patterns of behaviour that presumably became genetically encoded because of their adaptive value.

People are **transgendered** when their gender identity does not exactly match the sex assigned to them at birth. They blur widely accepted gender roles by, for example, cross-dressing.

Transsexuals identify with the opposite sex from that assigned to them at birth, causing them to change their appearance or resort to a sex-change operation.

SUGGESTED READING

Nelson, Adie. (2006). *Gender in Canada*, 3rd ed. (Toronto: Prentice-Hall Canada). The definitive Canadian work on the subject.

Kimmel, Michael. (2008). *Guyland: The Perilous World Where Boys Become Men*. (New York: Harper Collins). Based on interviews with more than 400 boys and men between the ages of 16 and 26, this book analyzes the rules, restrictions, peer pressures, and gender policing involved in learning male identity today—and the disappointment and anger that often accompany male gender socialization.

Weeks, Jeffrey. (2003). *Sexuality*, rev. 2nd ed. (London: Routledge). A concise and authoritative introduction to the field.

NOTES

1. Freud called this set of emotions the "Oedipus complex" after the ancient Greek legend of Oedipus. Oedipus was abandoned as a child. When he became an adult he accidentally killed his father and unwittingly married his mother. Discovering his true relationship to his mother, he blinded himself and died in exile.

2. Freud called this set of emotions the "Electra complex" after the ancient Greek legend of Electra. Electra persuaded her brother to kill their mother and their mother's lover in order to avenge their father's murder. Incidentally, some sexologists call into question the existence of vaginal orgasm and stress the importance of clitoral stimulation (Masters and Johnson, 1966). This viewpoint emerged around the same time as the modern feminist movement and as more and more people came to view sexuality not just as a means of reproduction but also as a means of erotic enjoyment, including orgasm.

WEB RESOURCES

Companion Website for This Book

http://www.newsociety6e.nelson.com
Begin by clicking on the Student Resources section of
the website. Next, select the chapter you are studying
from the pull-down menu. From the Student
Resources page, you have easy access to InfoTrac
College Edition® and other resources, such as the

Glossary, Test Yourself questions, and additional readings. The website also has many useful tips to aid
you in your study of sociology.

InfoTrac College Edition Search Terms

Visit http://www.infotrac-college.com for access to
more than 20 million articles from nearly 6000
sources when doing your online research.

CHAPTER FIVE

The Mass Media

Josh Greenberg
CARLETON UNIVERSITY

Graham Knight
MCMASTER UNIVERSITY

In this chapter you will learn that

- The mass media may be examined in terms of their economic and political organization, their representation of ideas, and their effects on people.

- Newspapers ownership is highly concentrated, and dependence on advertising limits the range of views available in the press.

- English-speaking Canadians watch mostly American television programming, especially prime-time drama and comedies. Nationalists view this as a "sellout" of Canadian culture, but others regard it as an effect of globalization that does not undermine the institutional structure of society.

- Some analysts claim that news coverage has a left-liberal political bias, while other analysts argue that news coverage is conservative.

- Many analysts believe that a causal link exists between media violence and violent behaviour, but studies that demonstrate this alleged connection have been criticized on the grounds of flawed methodology. Even those who believe that media violence causes aggressive behaviour disagree about how it does so.

- Studies reveal that men tend to use TV in a more planned way than women do and watch more intently, whereas women are more likely to use TV as a focus for social interaction.

- Access to, and use of, the Internet reflects broader patterns of social inequality, although unequal access appears to be declining as the technology becomes less costly and more widely available. Use of the Internet for social interaction creates online communities that act as sources of identity and social support but that also poses new risks to personal privacy and safety.

INTRODUCTION

In 2007, the average Canadian spent 18.3 hours a week listening to radio, and 29 percent of Canadian adults aged 20 and over reported watching television 15 hours a week or more (Statistics Canada, 2008a; Statistics Canada, 2008b). Hours vary by region, employment level, and age. Quebeckers and Maritimers watch more TV than other Canadians do. Full-time workers watch less television than the unemployed. Seniors watch more TV than others do (Statistics Canada, 2008b; Statistics Canada, 2008c). Hours spent watching television have been declining, while hours spent listening to the radio have remained stable. These facts point to several changes in media technology and use. Since the early 1990s, Internet use has grown rapidly, especially in the home. By 2007, 68 percent of Canadians aged 16 and over connected to the Internet from their homes daily (Statistics Canada, 2008d). To some extent, television viewing has suffered because of the Internet, although with the emergence of streaming and torrent software more people are watching television on the Internet. Despite the apparent decline in television viewing, the overall picture of media use remains quite stable. Add movie viewing and newspaper and magazine reading to radio, television, and the Internet, and it becomes clear that we spend more time interacting with the media than doing anything else, including working.

Media is the plural of *medium*, or "middle"—hence the idea of media as the means for connecting two or more points. Media are commonly associated with communication. **Communication** means bringing together or unifying by establishing shared meanings and understandings between groups and individuals. Such unification occurs through the transmission of information, knowledge, or beliefs by means of language, visual images, and other sign systems, such as music. People once commonly distinguished **mass media** from **interactive media.** With mass media, communication flows are unidirectional, going from a transmission point, such as a television or radio station, to an audience whose members remain anonymous and isolated from one another. With interactive media, like the telephone or social networking websites, communications flow back and forth; people interact in the transmission and reception of communication.

In this chapter, we focus primarily on three mass media: newspapers, television, and the Internet. We address two main questions. First, how do the media

Between 2000 and 2007, regular home-based use of the Internet grew from 40 percent to 68 percent of Canadian households.
SOURCE: © Szefei/Shutterstock.

affect us—how do they influence individuals, groups, and institutions? Second, how do we affect the media—how does society influence and shape mass communications? To address these questions, we have organized the chapter into four main sections that deal with political economy, representation and ideology, media effects and audiences, and computer-mediated communication.

We begin by considering two theoretical approaches in media studies: technological and critical perspectives. Technological theories hold that different media technologies determine social perceptions, interactions, and institutional arrangements. Critical theorists argue that social values, interests, and conflicts shape the technological development, use, and impact of the media.

THE TECHNOLOGICAL PERSPECTIVE

The technological perspective derives primarily from the work of two seminal Canadian scholars: Harold Innis and Marshall McLuhan. From his survey of the history of human communication, Innis (1951) distinguished time-biased from space-biased media. **Time-biased media** are modes of communication that endure over time but are relatively immobile across space, such as writing on stone or clay tablets. **Space-biased media** can cover much greater space but are less durable over time—for example, writing on paper or transmitting sounds over the airwaves.

The two types of media foster different arrangements of institutions and cultural values. Time-biased media are conducive to a strong sense of tradition and custom, which promote religious forms of power and belief. Space-biased media assist territorial expansion, empire building, and secular forms of power and culture, such as the dominance of military institutions and the growth of the state. These different forms of power, in turn, create different types of social division and conflict. The elite that controls the means of communication tries to use it to preserve its own privilege and interests. Those excluded from power struggle against elite control and in the process stimulate the development of new, alternative forms of communication. Historically, such a struggle over the means of communication resulted in the shift from time- to space-biased media.

Innis's ideas influenced McLuhan (1964). However, McLuhan argued that the relationship between communication, on the one hand, and institutions and culture, on the other, was mediated by the way that forms of communication change our sense perceptions and cognitive processes. The invention of printing, for example, undermined oral communication and its emphasis on hearing, and ushered in a more visually oriented culture. Because print consists of visually separated words strung together in a linear sequence, it encourages us to see the world as comprising separate objects and to interpret that world in a linear, cause-and-effect way. Print removes communication from face-to-face interaction and so makes information more abstract. The abstracting effect of print, in turn, fosters individualism, privacy, rationality, and social differentiation. Historically, these effects of print coincided with the rise of nationalism and the weakening of social ties. Print, then, served to standardize national languages and became a principal mechanism of social identity.

For McLuhan, the spread of electronic media, particularly television, marked the end of the era of print dominance. The impact of TV is crucial for two reasons. First, unlike print, TV does not rely exclusively on one sense (sight). It integrates sight and sound and achieves a better sensory balance. For McLuhan the effect of this balance is to make TV a kind of tactile medium in the sense that it "touches" its audience more easily than print does. Second, TV allows communication to be almost instantaneous; there is no significant delay between transmission and reception of the message. These differences make TV more socially inclusive than print is and shrink social distances and time, creating a "global village" in which the expanded capacity for information gathering and transmission help make us

The invention of the printing press reduced the influence of oral communication as it lessened face-to-face interaction and made information more abstract.
SOURCE: © Kevin Foy/Alamy.

more aware of, and familiar with, life in other parts of the world. It is remarkable that McLuhan's argument that electronic media would create a "global village" predated the arrival of the Internet and other new communications technologies by two decades.

McLuhan's views, however, have proven controversial because he tended to see media technologies as an autonomous force that operates outside social and human control. Although he famously stated that "we shape our tools, thereafter our tools shape us," McLuhan has been dismissed as a technological determinist for encouraging us to think that social change is not shaped by conscious human action, but by the nature and function of technology. Those who subscribe to the critical perspective have developed this criticism most forcefully.

THE CRITICAL PERSPECTIVE

According to the **critical perspective,** institutions, such as the news media, and processes, such as socialization and social control, cannot be understood from the viewpoint of society as a whole, but only from that of unequal and conflicting groups and classes. In fact, the critical perspective has two variants, one emphasizing the relationship between media and inequality, the other emphasizing the relationship between media and social conflict.

The first variant of the critical perspective derives from orthodox Marxism. In this perspective, the role of the media is defined in terms of how the media serve the economic interests and political power of those who own and control the means of material production (i.e., the dominant class). To maintain and consolidate its power and interests, the dominant class also exercises control over the production of ideas, beliefs, values, and norms that constitute a society's **dominant ideology.** The media, by disseminating this dominant ideology, create acceptance and legitimization of the status quo.

Max Horkheimer and Theodor Adorno (1972 [1947]) first developed this argument. They saw the mass media as part of a broader "culture industry" that functions to create "mass deception" about the exploitative and oppressive character of capitalist society. In their view, the role of the mass media is to distract and pacify people by feeding them standardized images and messages that stifle the capacity for independent, critical thought. A contemporary example of this perspective, the "propaganda model," argues that the media serve the interests of the leading political and economic class by "filtering" information to reduce or eliminate radical or subversive views (Herman and Chomsky, 1988). Herman and Chomsky identify five main filters: (1) the media's orientation to profit making, (2) their dependence on advertising for revenue and profit, (3) their reliance on powerful institutions and individuals as sources of information, (4) negative reaction—what they call flak—if the media deviate from promoting elite interests and values, and (5) their adherence to anti-communism as an overarching belief system. With the decline of communism, the fifth filter has morphed into the "war on terrorism."

The second variant of the critical perspective also acknowledges that the capitalist class and other powerful groups use dominant ideology to reinforce their position and maintain the status quo. They do so through the establishment of **hegemony**—the use of the media and other cultural institutions (e.g., the school system) to represent their interests, values, and understandings as natural and universal. However, proponents of the second approach note that inequality can also spawn resistance and struggle, which create critical perspectives that allow one to interpret and criticize social reality and the dominant ideology. Although the media usually promote understandings that conform to the dominant ideology, their messages are always at least partially open to the challenge of competing interpretations. To be successful, hegemony has to be flexible enough to accommodate and incorporate a range of different viewpoints (Knight, 1998).

POLITICAL ECONOMY OF THE MEDIA

The critical perspective draws attention to how the social and cultural roles of the media depend on their role as agents of political and economic interests. The principal approach that sociologists take to analyzing this relationship empirically is that of *political economy*. Political economy focuses on the ownership and control of economic resources, and the effect of technology and economic power on cultural values, social structure, and political decision making. Media are organizations that are usually owned and controlled by large corporations or the state and that function like other bureaucracies. They have to sustain themselves economically through commercial revenue, government funding, subscriber fees and donations, or some mixture of these. What, then, are the primary goals of media organizations? Are they to inform and entertain or to capture market share and make money? In whose interests do they operate—owners, advertisers, or audiences? These questions are especially pertinent in democratic societies where such values as freedom, diversity of opinion, and the promotion of minority and national identities are strong.

Ownership and control of the mass media are generally becoming more concentrated in a smaller number of giant corporate hands. This trend is part of the wider process of economic globalization, and it is leading to the creation of large **multimedia chains**—corporations that own a diversified array of media operations and outlets in different fields, such as radio, TV, and publishing, and operate worldwide. One of the world's best-known multimedia corporations is the Walt Disney Company (see Figure 5.1), whose total revenues in 2007 stood at US$35.5 billion. The world's dominant media corporations are primarily U.S.-based. Only two of the top six media giants are headquartered outside the United States—Bertelsmann and Vivendi—and these are located in Western Europe (Rupert Murdoch's News Corporation is a joint American–Australian company). Four Canadian companies made it into the global top 50 in 2007: Rogers, Quebecor, CanWest Global, and Shaw. See Table 5.1 (p. 102).

To secure and enhance their market position, multimedia chains practise horizontal and vertical integration. **Horizontal integration** refers to the sharing of facilities and resources between different plants and outlets. **Vertical integration** involves the control of resources and assets at different stages of

FIGURE 5.1   THE WALT DISNEY COMPANY

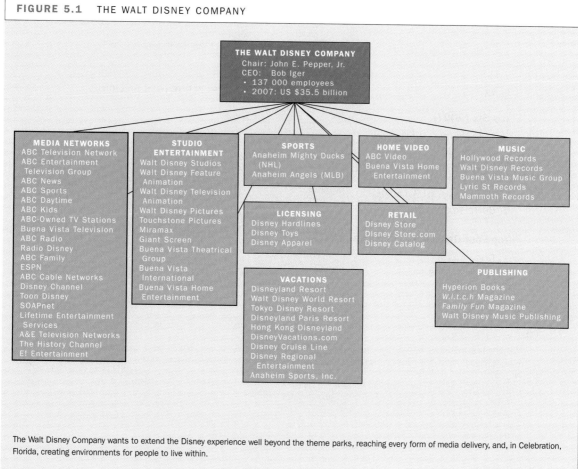

The Walt Disney Company wants to extend the Disney experience well beyond the theme parks, reaching every form of media delivery, and, in Celebration, Florida, creating environments for people to live within.

production, such as ownership of a major league sports team along with the stations and cable channels that televise the team's games. The recent development of digital technology has enhanced both horizontal and vertical integration, and has led to a series of corporate mergers, such as Time Warner, that have strengthened the position of multimedia chains as the dominant form of organization. These mergers comprise the union of delivery conduits (cable, satellite, telephony) and content (news, information, and entertainment).

Critics argue that consolidation of media properties and convergence of media platforms reduce the range of voices and perspectives that the mass media represent, leading to greater homogenization of ideas and cultural products. Although the names of the top owners may change from year to year, "the domination of the media by entertainment conglomerates exerts a consistently corrosive effect . . . undermining debate when we need it most" (*The Nation*, 2002). Moreover, the focus of mainstream corporate media on profits impedes progressive social change by

favouring the interests of the powerful (Parenti, 2004). Finally, mergers demonstrate that the traditional distinctions between print and electronic media are disappearing, at least at the level of corporate organization. However, closer inspection reveals that consolidation of media properties and convergence of media platforms do not affect all mass media the same way. This fact becomes evident if compare newspapers and television.

NEWSPAPERS: CONCENTRATION, MONOPOLY, AND ADVERTISING

In Canada, corporate ownership and control of daily newspapers has undergone rapid change since the 1970s and has become highly concentrated. CanWest Global, Quebecor Media Inc., and Torstar dominate the field today. CanWest Global owns daily newspapers in Vancouver, Calgary, Edmonton, Saskatoon, Ottawa, Montreal, and Halifax, and has control of the Toronto-based *National Post*, one of only two national newspapers. Quebecor Media Inc. controls the *Sun*

TABLE 5.1　GLOBAL ENTERTAINMENT MEDIA CORPORATIONS

"About six players now own virtually everything, all aspects of the media experience."

— Drew Marcus, Deutsche Bank media sector analyst

RANK	REVENUE (US$ BILLION)
Top Six (2007)	
1. Time Warner (U.S.)	46.5
2. Disney (U.S.)	35.5
3. Comcast (U.S).	30.9
4. Vivendi Universal (France)	29.6*
5. News Corp. (U.S./Australia)	28.7†
6. Bertelsmann (Germany)	25.7‡
Top Four Canadian Companies (2007§)	
1. Rogers	8.2
2. Quebecor Media	7.6
3. CanWest	2.3
4. Shaw	2.2

SOURCES: Bertelsmann (2008); CanWest Global (2007); Comcast (2008); Disney (2007); News Corporation (2008); Quebecor (2007); Shaw Communications (2007); Time Warner (2008); Vivendi (2008); Winseck (2008).

NOTES

* Estimated US$ equivalent; original financial data given in euros

† Estimated US$ equivalent; original financial data given in AUD$

‡ Estimated US$ equivalent; original financial data given in euros

§ Canadian rankings reflect 2006–2007 data reported in Winseck (2008). Values reported are converted from Canadian to U.S. dollars by using exchange rates (1 CAD = 0.809553 USD) at time of writing.

chain of English-language tabloids in Toronto, Ottawa, Calgary, and Edmonton, as well as French-language tabloids in Quebec City and Montreal. Torstar controls the *Toronto Star*, the largest circulation newspaper in Canada, dailies in Hamilton, Kitchener-Waterloo, and Guelph, and a minority interest (20 percent) in Bell Globemedia, the parent company of *The Globe and Mail*. CanWest Global, Quebecor Media, and now Torstar also have significant interests in other media, such as radio, television, the Internet, and cable, which, in the case of CanWest Global, reach as far as Australia, New Zealand, and Ireland.

The concentration of ownership in the hands of a few multimedia chains has raised serious questions about freedom of the press and the diversity of opinion, which are widely regarded as necessary for a democratic society. These concerns came to a head in June 2002 when CanWest Global fired Russell Mills, the long-time publisher of *The Ottawa Citizen*, for running an editorial calling for the resignation of then Prime Minister Jean Chrétien, without first gaining the approval of corporate head office. Mills's firing came on the heels of a number of changes made by

CanWest Global that tightened corporate control over the editorial content of its Southam newspapers.

Although an outcry was raised over CanWest Global's actions, the ability of newspaper proprietors to dictate news content continues to depend on the need to make a profit and the ability to attract advertisers. In 2006, daily newspapers earned $2.85 billion in advertising revenue, 75 percent of their total operating revenue (Statistics Canada, 2008e). But to attract advertisers, newspapers must also appeal to readers and subscribers that advertisers are trying to reach and persuade.

As newspapers have become more advertising dependent, the scale and costs of operation have also grown, reducing competition and creating local newspaper monopolies in all but large urban areas. Even in big cities, like Toronto, where several daily newspapers exist, papers have to specialize and appeal to particular market segments to survive.

The critical perspective sees multimedia chain ownership, local monopolies, and advertising dependence as resulting in the decline of diversity in news topics and viewpoints. However, evidence supporting the link is inconclusive. Some studies have found that monopolization leads to a decline in the volume and length of news stories, especially national and international coverage (Candussi and Winters, 1988; Trim, with Pizante and Yaraskavitch, 1983). Other research finds that monopolization brings about no significant change and may even lead to small improvements (McCombs, 1988).

A major challenge facing conventional newspapers is the Internet. All major Canadian dailies are available over the Internet, though some charge for access. While this situation does not increase the diversity of local news sources, it does make it easier for people to gain access to different newspapers from different regions and countries. In addition, the Internet has spawned a host of Net-only news and information media, ranging from the general, such as Salon.com, to outlets that have a particular political or ideological perspective, such as the web portal Rabble.ca. Net-only news media are also facing the challenge of how to raise revenue by attracting subscribers, donors, advertisers, or some mixture of these. In general, however, Net media lack the factual information capacity of conventional newspapers, which means their role is still primarily one of interpretation and commentary.

TELEVISION: ECONOMY, CULTURE, AND IDENTITY

For television as for newspapers, commercialization and advertising dependence have had the greatest impact on the content and role of the medium. Rather than being driven by cultural goals, such as promoting Canadian national identity, private television companies are motivated essentially by profit. Income and profits come largely from advertising, and this means having to cater to large audiences with programming that will be pleasurable and entertaining. To attract audiences and advertisers, private Canadian television, particularly English-language television, relies heavily on imported, mainly American, programming. Although the cost of licensing American programming has been increasing, it is still far less expensive to purchase than it is to produce comparable Canadian programming.

The issue of Canadian content pertains largely to entertainment programming, particularly English-Canadian drama. Audiences have long shown a strong preference for American dramatic programming and, as a result, the audience for domestic programs is not large enough to make Canadian drama attractive in

economic terms. Indeed, roughly 70 percent of all English-language viewing in Canada is devoted to American television, and this number climbs to 90 percent during prime time (Attallah and Foster, 2006). Reaction to this situation is split. Cultural nationalists argue that broadcasting should be an instrument of Canadian culture and identity, actively promoting Canadian content (Collins, 1990). They single out drama because of its popularity and capacity to promote and reinforce cultural myths and values that solidify a distinct national identity. Strong support for the argument that TV drama enforces cultural identity can be found in Quebec, with its commitment to francophone drama and other entertainment programming on the part of both public and private TV. Strong national and cultural identity on the part of francophone Quebeckers matches this commitment. Francophones not only watch more Canadian programming but also watch proportionately more television drama than anglophones do (see Table 5.2).

TABLE 5.2 PERCENTAGE VIEWING TELEVISION 15 OR MORE HOURS PER WEEK, CANADA, 2007

AGE COHORT	PERCENTAGE
20–24	20.0
25–34	22.4
35–44	21.5
45–54	26.1
55–64	36.1
65–74	46.9
75+	52.1
GENDER	
Male	29.5
Female	28.9
PROVINCE AND TERRITORY	
Newfoundland and Labrador	31.6
Prince Edward Island	29.0
Nova Scotia	31.3
New Brunswick	32.4
Quebec	31.1
Ontario	29.1
Manitoba	30.7
Saskatchewan	29.8
Alberta	25.7
British Columbia	26.7
Yukon	35.4
Northwest Territories	33.2
Nunavut	43.8
Canada	29.2

SOURCE: Adapted from Statistics Canada (2008e).

The federal government has addressed the issue of television drama production by establishing content requirements, offering financial inducements, such as production subsidies, sheltering the national broadcaster (CBC/Radio-Canada) from market pressures and priorities, and erecting regulatory barriers preventing foreign companies from owning too large a slice of the Canadian media pie. Although production has been increasing, economic pressure means creating the kind of programming that will attract advertisers and foreign buyers, and this often means programs lacking a distinct Canadian character. Canadian television production is increasingly part of a global market dominated by the American television industry. For critical theorists in particular, the dominance of American entertainment programming amounts to **cultural imperialism,** in which one society's media exert an overwhelming and unilateral influence over another society's culture (Tomlinson, 1997). As evidence of cultural imperialism, critical theorists point to the uneven flow of television and other cultural products between countries. Canada is one of the world's largest importers of cultural products—in 2007, Canada's cultural trade deficit was $2 billion (Statistics Canada, 2008f; see Table 5.3). The bulk of our cultural imports come from the United States.

On the other side of the debate, critics of the cultural nationalist position argue that although dramatic television is important, Canadians also develop a sense of collective national identity through their overwhelming preferences for domestic news and public affairs programming. *Grey's Anatomy* and *American Idol* may attract a larger Canadian audience than *The Rick Mercer Report* or *Little Mosque on the Prairie* do, but Canadians also overwhelmingly prefer to get their news and public affairs information from the CBC and CTV than they do from Fox or CBS. This situation contributes to Canadian national identity.

The concern that Canadian culture is under siege by American-style programming also overlooks the fact that many of the high-profile faces in American mass media are originally Canadian. Think of TV news anchors (*CNN's* John Roberts and the late Peter Jennings from *ABC News*), movie stars (Jim Carrey, Kiefer Sutherland, Michael J. Fox, Keanu Reeves), producers (*Saturday Night Live's* Lorne Roberts, Ivan Reitman of *Meatballs*, *Ghostbusters*, and *Old School* fame), directors and screenwriters like Paul Haggis (*Crash*, *Million Dollar Baby*, *Casino Royale*), David Cronenberg (*The Fly*, *A History of Violence*), and James Cameron (*The Terminator*, *True Lies*, *Titanic*), and even major studio heads such as Louis B. Mayer, a co-founder of MGM Studios. Arguably, Canadians have strongly influenced American media culture! Along with Collins (1990), we might also question the supposed Americanization of Canadian identity through the mass media by noting that Canada is quickly becoming a "postnational" society. Because of economic and cultural globalization, a strong, unified, and permanent sense of national identity may be a thing of the past. Canadians' sharing of institutions and practices seems undiminished by the fact that English Canadians can't get enough of *CSI* or *The Hills.*

TABLE 5.3   VALUE OF INTERNATIONAL TRADE IN CULTURAL GOODS, CANADA, 2007 (THOUSANDS OF DOLLARS)

IMPORTS		EXPORTS	
Written and published works	2 835 173	Written and published works	694 272
Film and video	297 338	Film and video	549 968
Sound recording/music publishing	148 660	Sound recording/music publishing	126 284
Visual art	304 220	Visual art	121 390
Architecture	1 899	Architecture	1 077
Advertising	174 190	Advertising	274 578
Heritage	58 207	Heritage	33 388
Photography	141 109	Photography	154 721
TOTAL	3 960 795	TOTAL	1 955 677

SOURCE: Adapted from Statistics Canada, 2008, "Culture Goods Trade 2007; Culture Trade-Goods: Data Tables, 2000 to 2007," Catalogue no. 87-007.

Collins's argument is similar to the postmodernist view that, in affluent societies, identities and experiences are becoming increasingly fragmented, disconnected from one another, and amenable to individual reconstruction and reinterpretation, especially on the basis of ideas and images that people consume via the mass media (Fiske, 1987). Fragmentation is also occurring at the level of political economy with the proliferation of new TV services, such as specialty channels, superstations, pay-per-view channels, and home-shopping channels, in addition to more conventional broadcast TV stations and networks (Ellis, 1992). As television becomes more differentiated, audiences become more fragmented, a process that is captured by the term *narrowcasting*. With this development, the role of TV as an agent of common culture is open to question.

REPRESENTATION AND IDEOLOGY: THE MEANING OF THE MESSAGE

Analysis of the mass media from the perspective of political economy alone is limited, because it takes for granted the nature of the messages that the mass media communicate. We emphasize the plural—*messages*. The media communicate on different levels—the pleasurable as well as the meaningful, the entertaining as well as the informative. Such communication involves the process of **representation**—that is, the use of language, visual images, and other symbolic tools to create messages people can understand and find relevant, satisfying, or enjoyable. Representation, however, is a selective process. It involves countless decisions about what is to be included and what is to be left out, what is to be emphasized and what is to be downplayed, and about the sequence in which the elements are to be connected into a coherent message. Sociologists use the term **framing** to denote the selective, organized nature of representation (Gitlin, 1980; Goffman, 1974). To frame is to set up boundaries that define where the representation begins and ends, and to organize the contents in a way that distinguishes what is being emphasized (the foreground) from what is treated as secondary (the context or background). The framing of any media product or object—a news report, an advertisement, a political cartoon or a TV drama—has ideological effects inasmuch as it entails a particular inflection or bias. Every frame is only one of several different ways of seeing and interpreting something.

NEWS AND IDEOLOGY

Outside our immediate experience, the news media are one of our principal sources of information about social reality. Conservative and critical writers disagree on how news is framed and the ideological effects of news framing. Conservatives argue that the news media have a "left-liberal" bias that runs counter to the views and interests of society's mainstream (Miljan and Cooper, 2003). According to conservative observers, bias operates in three related ways. First, the media have an anti-corporate bias and are critical of market-oriented solutions to social problems (see Box 5.1, p. 106). Second, journalists give greater or more favourable attention to the views of interest groups and constituencies that share their personal liberal or left-wing political views—for example, unions, environmentalists, social welfare organizations, and, in the case of foreign news, left-wing regimes and political movements (Miljan and Cooper, 2003). Third, the mass media concentrate on negative events, issues, and news angles, ignoring the positive aspects of social life (National Media Archive, 1993b).

In contrast to the conservative perspective, those who employ a critical perspective believe that the news media function chiefly to reproduce the values, interests, and perspectives of dominant social groups. Critical media scholars maintain that the news is ideological because corporate media organizations must make money, and therefore they depend heavily on elite sources (such as politicians, police, and corporations) for the news. This is seen not as a conscious conspiracy but as the unconscious effect of the values and practices that journalists employ when they define and gather news. Let us consider the critical perspective in greater detail.

Defining the News

How is news framed? To answer this question we must begin by asking what are the criteria, or **news values,** that the media use to determine what is newsworthy. They have three major criteria: immediacy, personalization, and extraordinariness.

Immediacy   By definition, news is about what is new or immediate. Although the media are often unable to capture events as they actually happen, the aim is to report them as quickly as possible after they occur. Immediacy has always been a major element in the competition among different mass media, and the goal of making communication faster dominates the history of media technology. Whenever possible,

BOX 5.1   **THE CONSERVATIVE CRITIQUE OF NEWS BIAS**

CANADIAN MEDIA UNCRITICALLY ACCEPT ADVOCACY GROUPS' ASSERTION THAT 1.5 MILLION CANADIAN CHILDREN LIVE IN POVERTY

During the last week in November 1993, Campaign 2000, a 45-group coalition, reported an increase in the number of children living in poverty in Canada. This finding was widely reported in most major Canadian daily newspapers as well as on the national newscasts of the networks.

Each of the reports faithfully conveyed the coalition's findings. All had given the following information as was reported by CTV's Ken Ernhofer: "The child poverty numbers are staggering. A watchdog group, Campaign 2000, says that between 1989 and 1991, an additional 250 000 Canadian children joined the ranks of the impoverished, an increase of 30 percent. In all, 1.2 million children lived in poverty, one child in every five."

Most troubling about the way in which the media reported these stories was that there was no incredulity or question that that many Canadian children were poor. The reporters covered the story in almost exactly the same way, all repeating the information provided to them by the coalition. Despite the unanimity among the reporters, a number of facts presented could have been challenged.

All reporters covering the child poverty story mentioned the statement that Canadian children were poor or were living under the poverty line. Adrienne Tanner of the *Edmonton Journal,* Alison Bray of the *Winnipeg Free Press,* the Canadian Press report in the Regina *Leader-Post,* Rosemary Spiers of the *Toronto Star,* and Carol Goar of the St. John's *Telegram* all provided the definition of the poverty line as being Statistics Canada's low-income cutoff (LICO). However, none of the reporters indicated that Statistics Canada does not endorse this as a meas-

urement of poverty: "although LICO are commonly referred to as official poverty lines, they have no officially recognized status nor does Statistics Canada promote their use as poverty lines."*

Only one reporter questioned the measurement in a story: Canadian Press journalist Helen Branswell. In an article printed in the *Winnipeg Free Press,* Branswell writes, "Some contend the low-income cutoffs aren't a good measure of poverty, because they don't assess whether people who live below them can meet their basic needs. Instead the cutoffs assess how those people fared in comparison to those who are better off." While most of the story was also printed in the Regina *Leader-Post,* that section was excluded.

The Globe and Mail also noted the LICO figures but referred to them as "the poverty threshold." And while *The Globe and Mail* indicated that former Progressive Conservative MP Barbara Greene had tried to examine a real measure of poverty, her efforts were dismissed by the man who came up with the numbers for Campaign 2000, Clarence Lougheed: "When we talk about poor families there are very few poor families who live at the cutoff, or even close to that level." Contrast this attention to that given to Barbara Greene when she chaired the parliamentary committee on poverty and actually argued that the way in which we count the poor may inflate their numbers. She was vilified in the press and her motives were impugned. For example, Debra O'Connor from the National Anti-poverty Organization said on CTV News on 8 June 1993, "And when Barbara Greene gets up and says 40 to 60 percent of the poor aren't really poor, that just reinforces people's idea that life on welfare is easy and it's too soft, and that couldn't be further from the truth. There's real suffering out there, and Barbara Greene is doing her bit to make that suffering worse."

*Statistics Canada Low Income Cut-offs, 1986, Technical Paper, 1987, p. 1.
SOURCE: National Media Archive, 1993a, "Canadian Media Uncritically Accept Advocacy Groups' Assertion That 1.5 Million Canadian Children Live in Poverty," *On Balance,* 6 (10), p. 2. Reprinted by permission of the Fraser Institute.

reporters write news in the present tense to convey the sense that events are ongoing.

The emphasis on immediacy goes beyond the present to the future. To generate interest and curiosity on the part of the audience, news stories often create a sense of uncertainty about what will happen next. The effect of this approach is that news tends to be concerned with the consequences of events and issues at the expense of their causes and development (Knight, 1982). Causes belong in the

past, and news generally lacks a sense of historical perspective and context.

Personalization   When news does deal with causes and explanations, it often reduces them to the level of individual motives and psychology. This is an effect of personalization. To communicate with an anonymous audience, news has to enable the reader or viewer to identify with news events that are often remote from everyday experience by making them more concrete and familiar. The emphasis on personalities has been intensified by the growth of TV news, where the need to be visual makes it more difficult to deal in abstract issues, such as unemployment, and easier to deal with people, such as the unemployed. Personalization is especially strong in political news coverage, as the mass media focus on party leaders and other prominent politicians and their popularity in the opinion polls. Critics often charge that this focus detracts from a fuller understanding of the political system and the more substantive aspects of political policy (Taras, 1990).

Extraordinariness Above all, news concerns events and issues that are out of the ordinary and that entail conflict, confrontation, deviance, or disorder (Knight, 1982). As conservative critics point out, this means that news is normally about the negative. For critical theorists, however, the negative emphasis of news does not undermine mainstream values and beliefs but in fact reinforces dominant ideology in at least two ways. First, by dwelling on the negative, news invokes and reproduces dominant definitions of what is normal. It identifies certain events and actors as dangerous, bizarre, or disruptive, and represents them as a threat to what is socially desirable (Knight, 1982; see Figure 5.2). Second, news coverage of deviance and conflict tends to focus on the actions of the appropriate social control authorities—the government, the police, the experts—to restore order. The threat of bad news is offset by reassurance that someone with authority is responding to the problem.

Gathering the News

Initially, newsworthy events come to the attention of the media via news releases, tips, and the routine monitoring of institutional communications, like emergency services radio. Further information is then gathered from key sources, usually by means of interviewing. In choosing their sources, news media also take account of a fourth news value: objectivity or fairness (Knight, 1982). In practice, objectivity translates into an attempt to achieve a balance of sources representing the different, often antagonistic, viewpoints that are involved in the event or issue being reported. These sources include authority figures (such as police, politicians, and experts) but also eyewitnesses, victims, and the representatives of groups and organizations ranging from big business to social activist groups that may have a stake in the event or issue.

However, just as news framing tends to focus on the activities of certain social actors, so too does it tend to rely on certain sources of information. A hierarchy of access exists to and for the media, and this has important ideological implications, as it reflects the general distribution of power in society. For example, elected politicians have a much greater obligation to speak to the media than do private sector officials, such as corporate executives, who can invoke the values of private property as a way to justify their own and their organization's privacy. At the same time, because of their power and status, corporate officials can easily gain access to the news media when they choose to do so.

FIGURE 5.2 TORONTO'S "DAYS OF ACTION" HEADLINES: DISRUPTION-RELATED THEMES IN A LOCAL NEWSPAPER, 1996

These headlines illustrate the way the media emphasize the disruptive or confrontational effects of new events rather than their causes or effects on social solidarity. They also highlight the way labour and other social movements are often portrayed as the source of social disruption and conflict.

October 24:	"Brace yourself for tough tomorrow"
October 25:	"Don't be intimidated by protesters: Harris"
	"Ambulances, police go on high alert" (continuation of previous report)
	"No mail, trash but beer's on. TTC in doubt as protest affects many services"
	"Days of action hits many services" (continuation of previous report)
	"Parade, rallies expected to jam city tomorrow"
October 26:	"Days of Disruption"
	"Day of frustration, frayed nerves" (continuation of previous report)
	"Shut out: pickets block mayor from city hall"
	"Protest a pain for many StarPhone callers"
	"TTC workers didn't ask for help: police chief says heavy police presence kept trouble to a minimum"
	"Barely a blip. The labour protest pretty much failed to disrupt Bay Street. The TSE hummed along nicely."
	"Protestors failed to tarnish Metro's image"
	"Employers cope with disruptions"

This hierarchy of access is reflected in the division of labour among three broad types of news source—official, ordinary, and alternative (Knight, 1998). **Official news sources** are representatives of dominant institutions—for example, politicians, police officers, professionals, experts, and corporate spokespeople. They appear more frequently and prominently than other sources and are usually treated by the media as authoritative and credible. Official sources are offset by **ordinary news sources.** These sources play a double role in the news as eyewitnesses or, more important, victims of newsworthy events or problems. As victims, ordinary sources personalize the harmful effects (actual and potential) of bad news. They are the ones adversely affected by deviance, conflict, and disruption. They speak more subjectively of personal experiences, feelings, and emotions—anger at what has happened to them and fear of what may happen next. **Alternative news sources** are the representatives of social movements and of social advocacy and activism groups. They stand between official and ordinary voices. Alternative sources address the social problems that underlie the harm that ordinary victims suffer. In this respect, they compete with official sources over the definition of victimhood: who is a victim, who is responsible, who should act, and what should be done. Alternative sources attempt to reframe the experiences and emotions of victims into a critical, normative, and political perspective of injustice and inequity (Carroll and Ratner, 1999).

The three types of source appear in the media to varying degrees. Although official sources represent the interests and values of particular institutions or organizations, they are often used to speak on behalf of society as a whole. This gives them an advantage in defining the news frame and establishing what the terms of the event or problem are. Deviance and disorder thus tend to be framed from a police perspective as a series of discrete events that are explained in terms of individual motives, rather than as social phenomena caused by social forces. Conversely, ordinary and particularly alternative sources are used to represent specific points of view. These may often contradict what official sources are saying, but they normally do so on grounds that have already been determined by the news frame. In the case of news about mental illness, for example, the media tend to rely on representatives from the legal and medical establishments (such as criminal prosecutors and psychiatrists) rather than on mental health advocacy groups, case workers, or people with mental illness as their *primary* source of information and interpretation. When the latter groups are included in the coverage, their views are usually framed in response to the claims of those in positions of authority (e.g., police, courts, medical professionals). This typically helps to construct a dominant interpretation of mental illness as a threatening condition associated with violence and other forms of unpredictable or dangerous behaviour. Media coverage tends to emphasize the risks and threats people with mental illnesses pose to themselves, their families, and their communities by constructing a boundary between "us" (normal and at risk) and "them" (sick and risky; Greenberg, 2006).

Alternative sources often face a dilemma in their relationship with the media. On the one hand, they are used simply as a reaction to official sources. In this case, their voice is a negative one of grievances and complaints, rather than a constructive one of analysis and proposals. On the other hand, they can attempt to draw the media's attention to their own framing of an issue or a problem. However, to do so, they may have to engage in public protests or other media stunts, events that associate their views with disruptive behaviour and can undermine their legitimacy (Hackett, 1991).

Although critical theorists see the media as generally representative of dominant ideology, they also recognize that relations between journalists and their sources involve an ongoing struggle for control (Ericson, Baranek, and Chan, 1989). The outcome depends chiefly on the status of the sources and the power they can exercise over the flow of information. In the case of crime news, the police enjoy an effective monopoly over the supply of information because there is no competing source on which the media can rely for credible, timely information. With politics, however, journalists have more leverage over sources by virtue of the adversarial structure of the political process, at least in democratic societies. This does not alter the fact that the government exercises the greatest control over the flow of information because of its political authority and control over policy. What the government does or says is intrinsically newsworthy, and governments attempt to use this fact to manage the media and mobilize popular consent and support for their actions. Governments employ various tactics to maximize favourable news coverage and minimize unfavourable coverage, such as providing news releases, freezing out hostile media by limiting access to information, staging events to attract media attention, timing the release of information to improve positive and limit negative coverage, and leaking information as a way of testing the waters or manipulating public expectations (Taras, 1990).

MEDIA EFFECTS AND AUDIENCES

What is most striking about research on media effects is its focus on socially problematic aspects of the media's relationship with its audiences. There has been little research on the "prosocial" effects of the media. Even in the area of child socialization, research has tended to focus on the way the media reproduce and disseminate negative stereotypes of, for example, gender roles, the elderly, or racial and ethnic minority groups (Buckingham, 1998: 135–36). Research shows nonetheless that the impact of the media is usually shaped by social context, as well as the psychological predispositions that children bring to their use of the media.

For example, many politicians, activists, teachers, and parents have argued that television advertising is to blame for the growing problem of childhood obesity in North America. The food industry is a major advertiser, dominating television airtime with promotions for everything from breakfast cereals to soft drinks, fast-food restaurants, and other "fun" foods. According to the Center for Science in the Public Interest, food marketers more than doubled their marketing spending between 1995 and 2004 to US$15 billion. Every day, children see about 58 commercial messages on television alone, and about half are for food products (Mayer, 2005). Children's food knowledge, preferences, and behaviours are also influenced by their class, gender, age, race, and viewing strategies (Livingstone, 2005).

We next examine two approaches to the study of media effects. The first is the study of *media violence*, and it deals most directly with the negative aspects of the media's influence. The second focuses on *audience interpretation*, the way viewers make sense of what they see and hear on television.

MEDIA VIOLENCE

The effects of portrayals of crime and violence in the media have been a longstanding topic of public policy and debate. Concerns about the effects of media violence overshadow concerns about its causes. Focusing on effects suggests the need for social

control to resolve the problem by limiting or eliminating the supply of violent imagery and overlooks the need to understand what creates demand for it.

Early research on the psychological and behavioural effects of the media swung between two poles of opinion. In the 1930s and 1940s, the effects of the media were generally thought to be harmful, direct, and strong. By the early 1960s, however, the prevailing view had been revised and media influence came to be seen as more innocuous. Media effects were thought to be minimal, mediated by a diversity of intervening social and psychological factors, and confined largely to reinforcing existing beliefs and habits (Klapper, 1960). This shift in views suggests that the issue of media effects is complex, and this is especially true in the case of media violence. Recent research on the effects of media violence, particularly on TV and in films but, increasingly, in video games marketed to youth, has generated much controversy. There has been extensive debate about what constitutes violence, how to measure its extent and intensity, and how to account for possible intervening factors, such as personality differences and social environment.

Most researchers believe that media violence has some real-life effects. Current research can be broken down into two main approaches. The first examines the effect of media violence on attitudes. The principal perspective here is known as **cultivation analysis.** It stems from research by George Gerbner and his associates. Gerbner argues that long-term exposure to television tends to cultivate perceptions that are often at odds with reality (Gerbner, Gross, Morgan, and Signorielli, 1994). One of the main arguments of the cultivation perspective is that people who watch a lot of television (or play a lot of video games) will be more exposed to violent imagery and more likely to perceive society as more violent and dangerous than it really is. This tendency is what Gerbner and his colleagues call the "mean world syndrome."

This argument has stimulated considerable research. Some of it disputes the view that a causal relationship exists between the amount of time people spend watching television or playing video games and their beliefs and emotions. Other research provides qualified support but argues that the relationship is affected by intervening factors, such as the type of programming people watch (Wober, 1998). A Canadian study suggests that what may be the central issue in cultivation analysis is the fundamental relationship between perceptions of violence, danger, and fear. The researchers found evidence to support the view that people who watch TV a lot believe the world is more dangerous than other viewers do, regardless of age and sex. However, although they found that women who thought the world was dangerous were also more likely to be fearful, they did not find this to be true for men. Moreover, for women, they could not explain the relationship between perception and fear of danger by the influence of television (Gosselin, DeGuise, Pacquette, and Benoit, 1997).

The second approach focuses on television's effects on behaviour. The predominant view is that television does play a limited role in generating real-life violence (Friedrich-Cofer and Huston, 1986; Geen and Thomas, 1986; Huesmann and Malamuth, 1986; Perse, 2001). Those who advance this view claim that the evidence is consistent with a link between TV and real-life aggressiveness, though the strength of the evidence varies according to the methodology used. The strongest support for a causal link comes from laboratory experiments (Friedrich-Coffer and Huston, 1986).

Most researchers believe that media violence has some real-life effects.

SOURCE: © John Garrett/CORBIS.

Various measures of aggressiveness have been used, among them physical and verbal aggressiveness, aggressiveness toward people and objects, actual and fantasized aggressiveness, and reduced self-discipline (lack of patience and perseverance in trying to accomplish tasks or dealing with others). The lab experiments have shown that television violence has an effect on real-life violence *independent* of the intervening factors that have been shown to affect overall levels of aggressiveness (such as personality, age, gender, and social background).

Studies of the effects of television on behaviour have been subject to a variety of criticisms, the most significant of which have been methodological. Laboratory experiments have been strongly criticized for their inability to replicate the normal social conditions under which people, particularly children, watch TV (McCormack, 1994). Children, like adults, normally watch a mixture of violent and nonviolent programming that blend together in an ongoing flow (Freedman, 2002). Younger children watch more television than older children do and they also watch it more intermittently because of their shorter attention span and because the social setting provides an easy distraction. As a result, although the TV set may be on for long periods, the children are not paying attention to it much of the time. The question of what exactly counts as an "act of violence" is also poorly defined and could include a host of examples, from shooting police officers in *Grand Theft Auto* to repeated broadcasts of the terrorist attacks on the World Trade Center in 2001. It is questionable that the effects of video game violence will be as hard-hitting and forceful as the effects of watching real acts of terrorism repeatedly play out on the evening news. Lastly, laboratory experiments have been criticized for providing research subjects with an artificial social environment. At home, if children act aggressively their parents may punish them, or their siblings or friends may retaliate; in most cases, the possibility of such a response is eliminated in the laboratory.

Despite these criticisms, the belief that a link exists between media images and aggressive behaviour has generated several theories about how the relationship functions. The most sociological of these is social learning theory, according to which violence must be learned like any other behaviour, and media violence provides scripts that teach children how and when to act aggressively. Social learning, however, does not occur in isolation from psychological factors. One of the most important findings of studies examining TV viewing in natural social settings is that the relationship between TV and real violence is bidirectional (Friedrich-Cofer and Huston, 1986). In other words, watching violent TV fosters aggressiveness, but those who prefer to watch violent TV already have more aggressive tendencies.

AUDIENCE RESEARCH: INTERPRETATION AND MEDIA USE

The effects of TV and other mass media on attitudes and emotions depend on how these media are used, and on how they are related to other activities and interests. Audiences filter, interpret, and often challenge what they see and hear according to their social context, experiences, and beliefs. But these contexts, experiences, and beliefs are themselves influenced by media use.

In the 1980s, many researchers began studying television use in its "natural" social settings, especially the home. For instance, research in the U.K. found that men and women differed in the way they watched television and what they preferred to watch. Men were more likely to use TV in a planned way, selecting programs beforehand and watching attentively, whereas women had a more "take-it-or-leave-it attitude" to program choice and a generally less attentive way of viewing (Morley, 1986: 153). Men enjoyed sports and information programming, whereas women found little they liked except soap operas. Women were also much less reluctant than men to admit that they talked about TV with their friends and co-workers, which suggests that television plays a greater role in women's patterns of sociability than men's. Morley (1986: 155) attributed this to the fact that women felt guilty about watching TV while "surrounded by their domestic obligations." Making it a topic of conversation gave it greater legitimacy.

Television has been the primary focus of audience research because it has played a central role in the definition of the private sphere in modern society—family, domesticity, gender relations, consumption, and suburban living—since World War II. During the 1950s and 1960s, the TV set became the central point of the household around which family members gathered to share a common experience, delivering images from the outside world into the heart of the primary social group (Morley, 2000). This symbolic role has since declined (see Box 5.2, p. 112). TV has spread to other social settings, such as bars, malls, classrooms, and sports stadiums. TV has also become more dispersed within the household (in the kitchen, bedroom, and even bathroom), allowing more autonomy and privacy in viewing habits. Personalized watching has also been encouraged by the proliferation of specialty channels and services catering to particular tastes and interests. And new interactive technologies, such as mobile phones, personal computers, and so-called third screens (iPods and other portable media devices), have become more accessible, creating a more complex communications environment that mediates the role and tempers the impact that any single medium can have at home, work, or school.

These changes have shifted the focus of audience research toward the ways television fits into the broader media culture. A study of media use by adolescents of Punjabi background in England illustrates the change (Gillespie, 1995). The study demonstrates how television is used to preserve a distinct sense of religious and ethnic customs, identity, and community, and to negotiate individual difference and autonomy in the face of pressures to conform to family expectations. For example, viewing Hindi films on video was a common family practice and was seen as an important way of reinforcing linguistic and cultural identification with India, especially for females, who took on the role of preserving and transmitting cultural traditions more than males did. At the same time, television also exposed these adolescents to the pressures of the wider culture with its emphasis on individualism and consumption. The marketing of products aimed at young consumers, particularly products associated with an American lifestyle, such as fast food, is becoming increasingly globalized. Thus, TV ads for McDonald's and Coca-Cola, as well as the products themselves, were consumed as a way of negotiating and accommodating the various identity demands—Punjabi, English, Asian, European, even Anglo-American—that these adolescents faced.

THE INTERNET: COMPUTER-MEDIATED COMMUNICATION

The shift in audience research toward an interest in the wider media culture is partly due to the rapid growth and use of the Internet. The Internet is a term that is now used generically to refer to a variety of different forms of **computer-mediated communication (CMC),** such as e-mail, instant messaging (IM), blogs and chat rooms, video-sharing sites, such as YouTube, and social networking applications, such as Facebook and MySpace. The fact that these media have given rise

BOX 5.2   NEW TECHNOLOGY CHANGES HOW WE WATCH TV

While cable and satellite TV companies have been trumpeting the latest specialty stations and high-definition offerings, broadcasters including Canwest Global, CTV and CBC are responding. They're making many of their most popular shows available on-demand to any viewer with a digital cable or satellite subscription. And, for those who would rather watch online, they're creating Internet libraries of prime-time TV content, as are technology companies such as Joost and Hulu. . . .

In many cases, programs offered online are supported by interactive features. Heroes viewers can chat with other fans. *Gossip Girl* fans can put questions to the actors, and fans of *The Office* can read blogs by the characters. Fans of *90210* can buy merchandise, such as the clothing being worn by the actors, and go behind the scenes to learn how the program is put together, while shows such as *Smallville* offer extra content, called webisodes, that can only be viewed online. . . .

The CBC, the National Hockey League and TV carriers such as Bell are hustling to put content online. The CBC broadcasts *Hockey Night in Canada* live on its website. The NHL has a video-based website that broadcasts games and sports highlights shows. Bell recently opened an online store that rents or sells movies and TV shows that consumers can download and watch at home. . . .

Websites like Hulu.com, created by Fox Interactive and NBC Universal to be an online library of new and old TV shows, Sling Media's Sling.com and Joost have popped up, offering hundreds of TV shows and movies at the click of a mouse. Hulu shows content from Fox and NBC, while Sling and Joost license content from production companies. . . .

In less than a year, Hulu (which is accessible only in the U.S.) has become one of the top 10 most popular places to watch video online. Even the No. 1 site, the ubiquitous YouTube, is taking notice, and recently announced that it will offer full-length TV shows to meet the new competition. Nonetheless, some analysts believe Hulu will surpass Youtube in advertising sales next year.

Advertisers are noticing as people's concept of watching television begins to change. For now, many TV programs available online are commercial-free, or have 15-second ads. As with much online content, precisely how ads will fit in remains a matter of trial and error. . . .

Bobby Tulsiani, an analyst with Forrester Research, said the biggest hurdles facing the industry are a lack of consumer awareness about what is available online, and how to access that content . . .

"The average consumer doesn't know Hulu off the tip of their tongue the way they know Facebook or Google," said Tulsiani. "It's not a replacement (for TV) right now. For some people it is, but not a mainstream replacement. As it gets easier to connect to the TV, as libraries get bigger, as the competition gets better it will raise the bar for everybody and you will see some of that substitution."

SOURCE: Pilieci, Vito, "Television's New Frontier; Online Viewing Presents Big Challenges for Traditional Broadcasters," *Ottawa Citizen*, 13 December 2008. Material printed with the express permission of: "Ottawa Citizen Group Inc.", a CanWest Partnership.

to a host of new terms, like *cyberspace*, *online communities*, *virtual reality*, *digital culture*, *Web 2.0*, and so on, suggests that the primary definition of CMC is uncertain and under continuous development. The fact that the Internet continues to change technologically and socially, and that research on its structure, use, and effects have produced divergent findings and interpretations, compounds the uncertainty.

Early research and commentary on the Internet polarized optimists and critics. Optimists understood CMC as a vehicle for greater democracy, globalism, and identity experimentation. They believed that the growth of the Internet in the 1990s promised to revive civic culture by providing broad, diverse forums for discussions. The Internet, they argued, was going to revolutionize civil society by enabling citizen-to-citizen interaction through online debate, deliberation, consultation, decision making, administration,

and scrutiny, as well as facilitating online mobilizing, organizing, petitioning, and protesting.

Critics focused on such negative effects as disengagement from "real" social relations and the detrimental effects of online communication on attention, learning, and productivity. They understood the Internet as a site of danger for both youth who made themselves vulnerable to online predators, and consumers who input home addresses and credit card numbers into databases accessed by third-party marketers and hackers.

As the Internet has developed, research has tended to paint a more complex picture of its role and how it is changing. Macrolevel research has focused not only on inequalities in terms of Internet access, usage, and scope but also on the ways in which new media technologies challenge our understanding of what CMC *means*. Microlevel research has been concerned with the reciprocal effects between offline and online interaction. These studies have addressed issues of individual and collective identity, surveillance, and social action in situations where individuals bring their offline information and interaction into their online activities.

THE DIGITAL DIVIDE: CMC AND SOCIAL INEQUALITY

Digital divide is a term that is commonly used to explain how access to and use of CMC reproduces structural inequities. While access to the Internet has grown rapidly, not only in developed nations but also in developing countries, disparities persist in terms of race, class, gender, and technology. **Web 2.0**, a term commonly used to refer to interactive web technologies, such as photo sharing and social networking embedded in websites, such as Flickr and Twitter, creates new imbalances between those who create content and share information, and those who profit from it.

Inequality of Access

In 2000, about 420 million people were estimated to be online; by 2008, the number of people online across the world surpassed 1.463 billion (or 21.8 percent of the world's population) (Internet World Stats, 2008; World Population Clock, 2008). The vast majority of people online are located in the affluent, developed nations of the world, such as Canada, the United States, and Japan, where more than 70 percent of the total population has access to the Internet (Internet World Stats, 2008). By contrast, in more populous but less economically developed countries, such as India and China, Internet users number in the range of 5 to 20 percent of the total population (Internet World Stats, 2008). Statistics on broadband access also suggest a digital divide. While rates of access are high for such countries as Canada (27.6 percent), the Netherlands (33.5 percent), the United States (23.9 percent), and Sweden (33.5 percent), this figure is significantly lower for such countries as Pakistan (0.2 percent), Algeria (0.9 percent), Sudan (0.1 percent), and Zimbabwe (0.1 percent)—indeed, much of Africa, the Middle East, and Asia (International Telecommunication Union [ITU], 2008).

The development of online access and use mirrors that of earlier media, such as television—originating in developed countries and then spreading to the developing world as the technology becomes more readily available. In this process a software gap also tends to develop. Just as global television content

continues to be dominated by programming produced in the developed world, so the Internet is dominated by content produced in the developed world. In 2007, five countries—the United States, Japan, Germany, the United Kingdom, and Canada—owned 63.3 percent of all Internet hosts worldwide (Network Wizards, 2008).

Social class also tends to be a strong predictor of who is online. Between 2005 and 2007, Internet access grew fastest for the poorest 25 percent of Canadians, increasing from 58.7 percent to 68.8 percent of people in this income category. Nevertheless, the top 25 percent of income earners still dominated usage, increasing from 83.2 to 87.9 of people in this income category (Statistics Canada, 2008g). Unequal access reflects several factors, particularly cost, occupation, and education. High-income households are likely to contain adult members who are familiar with CMC because of their work, and this makes home use easier in terms of operating skill. People with higher levels of education are more likely to be online, a pattern that holds independently of income and occupation (Dickinson and Ellison, 2000). In 2007, the percentage of Canadian Internet users with university degrees increased to 92.5 percent. For those users with less than high school education, Internet access stood at 43.2 percent (Statistics Canada, 2008h).

Big gender differences marked early access to the Internet, with males outnumbering females by a wide margin. This difference has declined over time. In Canada in 2007, men over the age of 15 only slightly outnumbered women over the age of 15 online, while women between the ages of 35 and 54 outnumbered men (Statistics Canada, 2008i). Similarly, racial and ethnic differences have become less marked

In Canadian universities, students use the latest electronic technologies in classrooms, dorms, and campus pubs.
SOURCE: © Michaeljung/Shutterstock.

(Jacobs and Albert, 2008). In the United States in 2008, Internet use was highest among English-speaking Hispanics (79 percent), followed closely by non-Hispanic whites (75 percent) and African Americans (70 percent; Pew Internet and American Life Project, 2008).

Differences of Use

E-mail is still the most commonly used form of CMC among Canadians, but overall use of the Internet is becoming more varied and it is increasing for educational, financial, and consumption purposes (see Table 5.4). Like access, use varies by social status and identity. Some research finds that women are more likely than men to have accounts on social networking sites, like MySpace and Facebook, although they are less likely than men are to participate in business-networking sites, such as LinkedIn (Rapleaf, 2007). Research on racial and ethnic differences in Internet use in the United States shows that Asian and Latino populations are less likely to do online banking and contribute to blogs than Caucasians are, while African Americans are more likely to access the Internet from their cell phones (Rainie, 2006).

Unlike differences in access, which reflect material inequalities, differences in usage indicate the different desires and needs of audience segments and their need for culturally specific content (Jacobs and Albert, 2008). Differences become inequalities to the degree that they translate into uneven advantages in terms of their offline consequences.

Web 2.0: The New Digital Divide?

Web 1.0 involved uploading and downloading text and images that users simply consumed. Web 2.0 encourages users to be digital collaborators, building web pages and blogs, creating content by uploading and mixing videos on YouTube, and editing, deleting, and adding to encyclopedic information on Wikipedia. Web 2.0 facilitates participation and creativity through RSS feeds, Comet and Ajax applications, and open platforms that enable users to produce and consume media in a user-friendly way (O'Reilly, 2005; Zimmer, 2008). Critics are skeptical of this new technology, believing that Web 2.0 is a way for media corporations to exploit users by replacing skilled labour, such as web design, with the "free" labour of audiences who spend time and energy building content for others to

---

TABLE 5.4   CANADIAN* INTERNET USE AT HOME BY INTERNET ACTIVITY, 2007

	PERCENTAGE OF CANADIAN INTERNET USERS
E-mail	92.0
General browsing	76.0
Researching other matters (family history, parenting)	69.5
Obtaining weather reports or road conditions	69.8
Looking for travel information and making arrangements	66.1
Viewing the news or sports	63.7
Banking or paying bills	62.5
Obtaining medical or health information	58.6
Searching for information on Canadian government	51.4
Searching for employment	32.3
Researching investments	25.5
Using an instant messenger	49.9
Obtaining and saving music	44.5
Playing games	38.7
Obtaining or saving software	32.5
Listening to the radio	28.1
Contributing content (blogs, photos, discussion groups)	20.3
Downloading or watching television	15.7
Downloading or watching a movie	12.5
Selling goods or services (through auction site)	8.9
Making telephone calls	8.7

SOURCE: Adapted from Statistics Canada (2008g).

*The target population for the Canadian Internet Use Survey includes individuals 16 years of age and older in 2007.

consume (Banks and Humphreys, 2008). They suggest that Web 2.0 thereby creates a new digital divide.

VIRTUAL COMMUNITY: THE INTERNET'S IMPACT

As was the case with radio and TV, the rapid growth of the Internet has prompted concern about its supposedly negative effects. For example, some studies link television watching and Internet surfing with obesity, inactive leisure time, poor diet, and declining reading rates, while others see the Internet as addictive (Hilts, 2008; National Endowment for the Arts, 2007; Statistics Canada, 2008b).

Other studies, however, point out that the Internet can be a source of valuable information that can inform and promote active and healthy lifestyles to at-risk populations and that new media opens possibilities for civic engagement and activism (Kann, Berry, Grant, and Zager, 2007; Lewis, 2007). Instead of being seen as an isolating activity, the growing number of people online and the widespread use of e-mail, instant messaging, and blogging by Canadians suggest that people are using the Internet to connect with others, thus enhancing social interaction and identity expression. Boyd (2007) notes the importance of social networking sites as spaces for youth to perform "identity work" at a time when the availability of physical social spaces, such as community centres, is declining. As such, online social networking communities can be as socially and emotionally supportive for their members as communities that are based on face-to-face interaction. Even online forums, such as newsgroups (e.g., reddit and digg), designed primarily to provide factual information, can have socially supportive side effects, as news stories permit participants to comment on and share information with others. Although virtual communities lack the kind of interpersonal cues available in face-to-face relationships, new technologies, such as webcams and Voice over Internet Protocol (VoIP) software, such as Skype, can *promote* interaction by removing risks and status or identity barriers that might normally inhibit the development of real world ties.

Surveillance and Privacy 2.0

With the implementation of social networking sites, such as Facebook and MySpace (where users tend to know each other offline), online interaction is becoming increasingly less anonymous, raising concerns about privacy and surveillance. As one commentator notes, we inhabit a paradoxical world of privacy where youth broadcast personal information and actions online while government agencies and third-party marketers collect the personal data that we input every time we log in or make a purchase (Barnes, 2006). Others understand social networking sites as spaces of digital voyeurism for individuals to spy on each other and havens for predators to prey on unsuspecting youth (Albrechtslund, 2008; Marwick, 2008). Such anxieties have led to proposals for more Internet regulation, legislation, such as the Deleting Online Predators Act (DOPA) in the United States, intervention, and education about the invisible risks and dangers associated with CMC.

Others understand privacy and surveillance differently. Some researchers cite a lack of empirical evidence that links social networking to youth abduction and note that this "technopanic" obscures the more pressing issue of the sexual exploitation of youth that occurred long before Internet use became prevalent (Boyd and Jenkins, 2006; Marwick, 2008). Accounts vary of how much personal information users disclose on their profiles in terms of real name, address, and phone number. Some research show that adolescents frequently display risky personal behaviour (e.g., sexual exploits, drug use) on their MySpace profiles (Moreno et al., 2009; see Box 5.3, p. 116). Other research shows that 40 percent of young MySpace users set their profile settings to Private, meaning that only a selected audience has access to their personal information (Hindujal and Patchin, 2008: 125). Furthermore, surveillance is not always dangerous or repressive. The great majority of youth use social networking sites to keep in touch with friends they infrequently see offline, so "participatory surveillance" becomes a way of maintaining relationships by mediating and reading about peers' activities and whereabouts (Albrechtslund, 2008; Lenhart and Madden, 2007). Moreover, police and other criminal investigations have used social networking sites to track down the locations of offenders (Zimmer, 2008). In sum, research shows unanticipated risks and rewards of participating in Web 2.0 technologies.

The Blogosphere: Social Activism 2.0

The blogosphere, a virtual community of blogs and bloggers, is another Web 2.0 technology that has social implications offline. Blogs are now easy to launch, thanks to sites like Blogspot, where users can upload images, hyperlink other articles, and syndicate their blogs to an audience through RSS feeds ("Real

Simple Syndication"—a web format used to publish frequently updated content). In 2007, there were 94.1 million U.S. blog readers (50 percent of Internet users) and 22.6 million U.S. bloggers (eMarketer, 2008). The blogosphere resembles a physical community inasmuch as it facilitates shared values, a sense of belonging, and a common purpose (Baym, 2000). People bring their offline interests to the blogosphere, just as they do to other communications media, writing about their lifestyles and political interests. The exchanges that occur between the real and virtual worlds are mediated by structures of social relevance, that is, how well experiences in one sphere relate to interests and concerns in the other (Schutz, 1970).

The prominence of the blogosphere in media coverage illustrates the power and potential of the Internet to invigorate democratic debate. While it is difficult to measure the effect blogs have on political participation or social change, they certainly have given rise to new forms of civic discourse and have made use of Web 2.0 technologies to disseminate information quickly and efficiently (Kluver, 2005). In May 2004, both television and the Internet circulated images of U.S. soldiers abusing Iraqi prisoners in an attempt to hold U.S. military and political administration accountable. While these images were rapidly transmitted on television and other traditional broadcast media, it was the "manner in which they were proliferated and archived on blogs that may make them stand as some of the most influential images of all time" (Kahn and Kellner, 2005). In this case, the blogosphere helped inspire and amplify outrage. The blogosphere also represents a space for individuals to point out errors and inaccuracies in mainstream news media. During the Israel–Hezbollah War of 2006, for example, blogs revealed that the news agency Reuters was publishing doctored images from Lebanon (Usher, 2008). Reuters had to issue a public apology, fire employees, and launch a six-month internal investigation into its coverage of conflict zones. This example illustrates the ways in which ordinary citizens have the capacity to hold mainstream mass media accountable for reporting.

Despite the potential of the Internet and other CMC technologies to enhance democracy, we would do well to heed U.S. media critic Robert McChesney's reminder that, historically, the development of new communications technologies was always met with an enthusiasm that was later tempered by processes of commodification: "Once the technologies proved profitable . . . they were turned over to private interests" (McChesney, 1996: 8). However, despite the attempts of corporate powers to control the Internet and other new avenues of communication, struggles by oppositional groups to elude or puncture the dominant informational infrastructure will always remain.

SUMMARY

1. Technological theory emphasizes the role played by media technologies on both individual psychology and social organization, and originates largely with the writings of two Canadian theorists, Harold Innis and Marshal McLuhan. Technology theory is also useful for understanding new forms of social interaction, networking, and surveillance that have resulted from the development of computer-mediated forms of communication.

2. Critical theory focuses on the impact of different interests and social inequalities on the organization (political economy) and content (ideology) of communications media. Some critical theorists emphasize the role of the media in reinforcing and sustaining dominant relations of power, wealth and other valuable resources, whereas others see the media as an arena where conflict occurs over the meaning of social reality. The two variants of critical theory are particularly evident in research on the representation of social reality found in the news media.

3. Canadian newspapers exhibit high levels of ownership concentration, are usually part of large multimedia chains, and function largely as local monopolies. The factor that has the greatest impact on news content, however, is dependency on advertising.

4. In the case of television, advertising dependency, the high costs of production, and audience preferences mean that much of the programming Canadians watch is American. This is especially so for drama and sitcoms, and particularly among anglophones. Nationalists view the situation as a sellout of Canadian culture, whereas postmodernists see it as part of the general effect of globalization and do not believe that it undermines the institutional structure of Canadian society.

5. Conservatives claim that news coverage has a left-liberal political bias that is unrepresentative of society's mainstream. Critical theorists argue that news coverage is ideologically conservative, in that it defines reality from the perspective of dominant ideology and views events and issues through the lens of social control. At the same time, some critical theorists argue that the media are not completely closed to alternative voices and viewpoints, and that these can challenge, to some extent, the hegemony of dominant social groups and interests.

6. Many observers believe that a causal link exists between television and violent behaviour, but the studies that support this view have been criticized on the grounds of flawed methodology. Moreover, the majority view is split on the issue of how television causes aggression. Some argue that watching TV counteracts the effects of socialization by weakening self-control; others believe that it socializes children in the use of violence.

7. Studies of audiences indicate that TV viewing and the responses to it vary according to gender. Men and women tend to prefer different types of programming. Men are more likely to watch attentively and privately, whereas women watch in a more interactive, social way. Women also tend to be more open about their TV viewing and use TV as a topic of casual social interaction and conversation.

8. Although early views about the development of computer-mediated communication and the Internet tended to polarize optimists and pessimists, recent research has yielded a more complex, balanced view. Inequalities of access (especially globally) and differences of use persist; however, the former show signs of declining as the technology becomes less costly. Research on the impact of the Internet shows that virtual communities develop normative structures like real communities and function as sources of identity and social solidarity. For the most part, however, life online supplements and complements real-world social interaction and involvement rather than replacing it.

QUESTIONS TO CONSIDER

1. Despite the lack of strong, consistent, and unequivocal evidence to confirm a direct link between violence in the media and in real life, why are many people convinced that such a link exists?

2. Critics of media imperialism often point to Canada as an example of a country overwhelmed by American popular culture—movies, magazines, music, and television. What is so appealing about American popular culture, not only in Canada but in other countries as well? Are Canadians vulnerable to becoming Americanized by the gross imbalance between the amount of domestic and U.S. dramatic programming we watch?

3. As more young people tune out the mainstream media and plug in to Web 2.0, what are the challenges this poses to democracy and issues of personal privacy, and what are the potential benefits to community development and the development of individual identity?

GLOSSARY

Alternative news sources are representatives of social movements and of social advocacy groups whose viewpoints often diverge from those of dominant social groups and their representatives.

Communication denotes the transmission of knowledge, ideas, meanings, and understandings.

Computer-mediated communication (CMC) refers to social interaction or information gathering through the use of computer technology.

The **critical perspective** takes the view that the media reinforce dominant ideology and the position of the dominant class and other powerful groups. The theory has two variants. One sees dominance as more open to challenge and resistance than does the other.

Cultivation analysis examines the long-term effects of television viewing on beliefs about social reality. People who watch TV a lot tend to see the world as more violent and dangerous than it really is, and tend to be more fearful.

Cultural imperialism is a situation in which one society's media exert an overwhelming and unilateral influence over another society's culture.

The **dominant ideology** comprises the interests, perspectives, viewpoints, and understandings of the dominant class and other powerful groups.

Framing is the process of defining the boundaries of a representation and the organization of its contents. Framing pertains to the selection of what is included and excluded, what is accentuated, and what is played down.

Hegemony is the exercise by the dominant class of cultural leadership by using the media to naturalize and universalize dominant ideology and to absorb the challenge of alternative and oppositional points of view.

Horizontal integration is the ownership of different outlets in a media chain for purposes of sharing resources.

Interactive media are technologically mediated means of communication in which the flow of messages is two way—between actors who transmit and receive messages (e.g., the telephone).

Mass media are technologically mediated means of communication in which the flow of messages is largely one way, from a single point of transmission to a large, anonymous, dispersed audience of receivers (e.g., television).

Multimedia chains are corporations that own and control a string of media operations or outlets in different fields of mass communication, such as television, radio, and magazines.

News values include such criteria as immediacy, personalization, and extraordinariness, in terms of which news media define and represent events and issues.

Official news sources are authoritative voices—for example, politicians, police officers, and professional experts—that the media use to define the meaning of an event or issue.

Ordinary news sources are news sources that do not derive from organizations or groups, such as eyewitnesses or victims of news events and issues.

Representation is the use of language, visual images, or other means of communication to portray something in a coherent and meaningful way that others can understand.

Space-biased media, such as print, radio, and television, enable communication over extended distances. The messages, however, are not long lasting. Space-biased media promote territorial expansion together with secular beliefs and military-political forms of power.

Time-biased media, such as stone carvings or inscriptions on clay tablets, convey durable messages but are relatively immobile.

Vertical integration refers to a media corporation's ownership and control of the means of production at all stages of the production process—for example, from producing newsprint to delivering newspapers.

Web 2.0 refers to new media technologies, such as Facebook, MySpace, Wikipedia, and YouTube, that feature user-generated content, information-sharing, collaboration, and interactive texts.

SUGGESTED READING

Atton, C. (2004). *An Alternative Internet: Radical Media, Politics and Creativity.* Edinburgh: Edinburgh University Press. Explores how new communications technology provides alternative ways of organizing social and political change.

Collins, R. (1990). *Culture, Communication and National Identity: The Case of Canadian Television.* Toronto: University of Toronto Press. Examines the effect of the Americanization of Canadian television (especially drama), from the perspective of increasing globalization, and argues that the effects are not as harmful to national identity as nationalists assume.

Miljan, L., and B. Cooper. (2003). *Hidden Agendas: How Journalists Influence the News.* Vancouver: UBC Press. The authors challenge the argument that structures of media ownership and a conservative bias lead to news coverage that is favourable to the dominant ideology. Drawing on interview data with more than 250 journalists, general population surveys, and content analyses of news, the authors argue that, "coverage of public policy issues in the Canadian media reflects journalists' opinions to a far greater extent than the views that cultural critics presume to be held by managers or owners" (p. 167).

Taras, D. (1999). *Power and Betrayal in the Canadian Media*. Peterborough, ON: Broadview Press. Presents an analysis of the Canadian media in light of the impact of such factors as corporate concentration, audience fragmentation, and technological convergence. The author sounds a critical note, warning that these changes, together with "the growing international commercial culture," are making the media "less open and diverse" despite their continuing expansion (pp. 219, 221).

WEB RESOURCES

Companion Website for This Book

http://www.newsociety6e.nelson.com
Begin by clicking on the Student Resources section of the website. Next, select the chapter you are studying from the pull-down menu. From the Student Resources page, you have easy access to InfoTrac College Edition® and other resources, such as the

Glossary, Test Yourself questions, and additional readings. The website also has many useful tips to aid you in your study of sociology.

InfoTrac College Edition Search Terms

Visit http://www.infotrac-college.com for access to more than 20 million articles from nearly 6000 sources when doing your online research.

SOURCE: © Jack Picone / Alamy

PART THREE

Inequality

SOURCE: © robcocquyt/Shutterstock

CHAPTER SIX

Social Stratification

Harvey Krahn
UNIVERSITY OF ALBERTA

In this chapter you will learn that

· Persistent patterns of social inequality are based on statuses assigned to individuals at birth and on how well individuals perform certain roles. Societies vary in the degree to which mobility up and down the stratification system occurs.

· Explanations of the origins and impact of social stratification include the theory of Karl Marx, which emphasizes the exploitation of the working class by owners of land and industry as the main source of inequality and change; the theory of Max Weber, which emphasizes the power that derives from property ownership, prestige, and politics; structural-functionalist theory, which holds that stratification is both inevitable and necessary; and several revisions of Marx's and Weber's ideas that render them more relevant to today's society.

· Although there has been considerable opportunity for upward occupational mobility in Canada, wealth and property are concentrated in relatively few hands, and one in seven Canadians is a low-income earner. Because of labour-market changes, income and wealth inequality have been increasing. Thus, the stratification structure of the future will probably not resemble the pattern that emerged in the affluent middle of the twentieth century.

· A person's position in society's stratification system has important consequences, both for lifestyle and for the quality of life. Those who are situated higher in the economic hierarchy tend to live better and live longer.

INTRODUCTION

While bundling up old newspapers for recycling, I flip through them quickly. Although the news writers don't use the term, I find myself reading about **social stratification**—that is, persistent patterns of social inequality within society.

A photograph of a 24-year-old Edmonton man and his 19-year-old pregnant girlfriend in their "home" catches my attention. They look cold, as you and I would be if our home (in late November) was an abandoned mattress in an inner-city back alley, and our possessions were limited to the clothes on our back and several old blankets. The article reports that about 3100 Edmonton residents are homeless, an increase of 18 percent from 2006 (Gerein, 2008) but notes optimistically that more than 1800 of these individuals can at least sleep in a shelter or some other building. In contrast to these "shelter homeless," the more than 1200 "street homeless," including 125 children, are even more disadvantaged. A second article describes the life and death of a 47-year-old Vancouver woman we would have to call "street homeless," using this new vocabulary. This unfortunate woman had been sleeping in her "home"—a shopping cart covered by flammable plastic covers and heated by a candle—when it caught fire and she burned to death a week before Christmas (Keevil-Fairburn, 2008).

The business section of one of the newspapers offers the headline "Job Losses Accelerating Alarmingly" (Scoffield and Koring, 2008). The lengthy news article describes how, in one month, half a million Americans and 71 000 Canadians lost their jobs as the troubled economic times that began with the collapse of the U.S. housing market, then spread to the financial sector before beginning to create havoc in the manufacturing sector, turned into a deep recession. Recognizing that these recently unemployed North Americans may still be more advantaged than the absolutely destitute homeless, I also realize that, in time, some of these jobless individuals will, in fact, join the homeless. Another lengthy cover story describes how the crisis in the North American and European

Canadian fishers have a history of making do on low incomes. Quotas on certain stocks of fish have made the situation worse.

SOURCE: Lois Dierlam OSA(L) CSPWC "Newfoundland Fishermen" Courtesy, Collection Will Andrew.

economies is making poor people in Bangladesh even poorer (Saunders, 2008). Hard-working villagers who used to earn $2 a day making bricks in northeastern Bangladesh have lost their jobs because the local brick factory has closed down. Why? Businesses owned by Bangladeshi families in the U.K. have taken a beating in the recession and their owners can no longer send money to invest in Bangladesh businesses. In addition, the sudden collapse of the international financial sector has meant that even rural Bangladeshi families cannot borrow money to buy bricks to build new homes.

Although the very poor, whether homeless or unemployed, catch our attention, so do the very rich. A news item from early in January reminds me of just how rich some people are. Within an hour of their second working day in 2007, the 100 most highly paid chief executive officers (CEOs) of companies operating in Canada had already earned as much as the typical Canadian worker earns in the whole year (Beauchesne, 2009). Imagine working for one day to earn an average $40 237 and then going on vacation for the rest of the year! But these 100 very rich individuals worked all year and reported average incomes of more than $10 million in 2007. This meant that, at the end of the year, they had earned 259 times as much as the average Canadian worker. The article goes on to observe that the gap between the earnings of the average Canadian worker and the earnings of the top Canadian CEOs was more than four times as high in 2007 as it was in 1995.

I stop to look at a photograph of a young Aboriginal man in a baseball cap. The caption explains that "Neil Stonechild, 17, disappeared in 1990. His frozen body was found outside Saskatoon." The accompanying news item explains that two Saskatoon police officers and their city police association had appealed to the Supreme Court of Canada to have the findings of a 2004 public inquiry into their involvement in the death of Mr. Stonechild overturned (Makin, 2008). The 2004 inquiry did not conclude that these police officers had actually left Mr. Stonechild to freeze to death but concluded that he had been in their custody earlier in the evening and that they had denied this fact. I am relieved to read that the Supreme Court of Canada has overturned this appeal. But I also wonder why it has taken 19 years to reach this decision. Would it take this long for (partial) justice to be realized if Mr. Stonechild had been the son of an affluent white middle-class family, not an Aboriginal Canadian?

I also wonder whether the situation would be similar, or better or worse, for recent immigrants to Canada who are also disadvantaged. A news item from my local newspaper reminds me that immigrants, particularly refugees who have been allowed into Canada for humanitarian reasons, are not only typically poor but also isolated (White, 2009). A 21-year-old woman from Myanmar (formerly Burma) who spent the last 14 years of her life in a refugee camp in Bangladesh after she and her family (and a quarter million others) were driven from their home country by ethnic and religious persecution, describes how it feels to arrive in Canada in winter after leaving 14 members of her family behind in the refugee camp. She hopes, desperately, that some or maybe even all of her immediate family members will someday be able to join her in Canada. Female, young, non-white, and a refugee, this young woman is facing multiple and severe disadvantages.

The common theme in these quite different stories is the existence of groups—the unemployed, the homeless, women, youth, refugees and other immigrants, Aboriginal Canadians—that rank lower than others in the social stratification system. A low position in this ranking typically means having little power, little wealth, and little prestige, whereas a higher position generally implies the opposite. In this chapter, I begin by discussing some of the ways in which sociologists study social stratification. I then examine a variety of theories of social stratification that attempt to explain its origins and impacts. The last section of the chapter focuses on occupational and class structures and material inequality in Canada, and concludes by asking whether inequality has been increasing.

STRATIFICATION: A CORNERSTONE OF SOCIOLOGY

Standing back and looking at the whole discipline of sociology, we see four basic areas of inquiry. Sociologists study social structure, or the way in which society is organized, both formally and informally. We also ask questions about social order. What is it that holds together a society comprising individuals with different interests, and when and why does social order break down? Inquiries about social change form a third key area within the discipline. How and why do societies, the institutions and power structures within them, and the values and beliefs held by individual members change? Finally, sociologists spend a lot of time studying social stratification, the manner in which valued resources—that is, wealth, power, and prestige—are distributed, and the way in which advantages of wealth, power, and prestige are passed from generation to generation.

It could easily be argued that social stratification is the cornerstone of sociology. Descriptions of social structure that ignore the stratification system are clearly inadequate. For example, imagine describing Canadian society to someone from another country without referring to some features of stratification. Would the listener really have an adequate understanding of our society if she or he did not know that most large corporations are run by men, that the working poor continue to struggle to make ends meet even though the majority of employed Canadians earn a decent living, that Aboriginal Canadians are much more likely than most others to be living in poverty, and that immigrants are doing less well today than they were several decades ago, even though they are better educated?

Furthermore, inequalities in wealth can threaten social stability (the poor resenting the wealthy, for example, and demanding more equality), and inequalities in power can be used to maintain social order. For example, powerful corporations might lobby provincial or territorial governments for changes in the labour laws that would make it more difficult for unions to organize company employees. In less democratic countries, direct control of the police and military by a powerful minority can lead to the quick and violent suppression of unrest among the masses.

An understanding of social stratification is also essential for studying social change, since, frequently, it is the stratification system that is undergoing change. For example, changing gender roles and the slow movement of women into positions of power and authority in North America in the past few decades are really features of a changing stratification system. The massive social, economic, and political changes that began in the former Soviet Union in the late 1980s and in China a decade earlier are, among other things, changes in stratification systems, as the main sources of power come to include both the political system and the emerging capitalist economy.

SOCIAL HIERARCHIES IN STRATIFIED SOCIETIES

Imagine a society in which stratification did not exist, in which all things of value were distributed equally. Even if you picture a very small group, perhaps a preindustrial society with only a few hundred members,

living on some isolated island where the necessities of life are easily obtained, it is still difficult to imagine a non-stratified society. A social hierarchy might emerge as a result of skill differences in fishing, in nursing the ill back to health, or in communicating with the spirits, for example. Inequalities in wealth might develop simply because some families were fortunate enough to have a larger number of children, providing more of the labour needed to accumulate valued possessions. And once accumulations of wealth began to be passed from generation to generation, a structured and relatively permanent pattern of inequality would emerge.

Perhaps you imagined some contemporary society comprising adults who, believing strongly in equality, decided to live and work together in some kind of urban or rural commune, sharing all their possessions. Again, it is easy to imagine how a social hierarchy could emerge, as those with more useful skills found themselves playing a more central role in this small-scale society. No doubt, when important decisions needed to be made, these individuals would be more likely to influence the outcome.

We do not need to repeat this mental exercise too many times before we see that social stratification in one form or another exists in all societies. But our hypothetical examples are far from typical. In most societies, stratification is much more pronounced, and basic skills are seldom the foundation of primary social hierarchies. Nevertheless, cross-cultural variations exist in the criteria by which individuals and groups are ranked, the degree to which they can move from one position to another within the hierarchy, and the extent of inequality in wealth and power that exists within the hierarchy.

ASCRIBED AND ACHIEVED STATUS

Let's begin by defining the rank or position that a person has within a social hierarchy as that person's **status.** We can further distinguish between an **ascribed status** and an **achieved status.** The former is assigned to individuals, typically at birth. An ascribed status can be a function of race, gender, age, and other factors that are not chosen or earned and that cannot be changed (a few people do choose their gender status, but they are rare exceptions). In contrast, an achieved status is precisely that—a position in a hierarchy that has been achieved by virtue of how well someone performs in some role. The most obvious example is that of occupational status—for instance, individuals who have performed well in law school are entitled to become lawyers, and high-performance athletes strive to achieve the status of "professional athlete." By the same logic, someone could achieve the status of "bum" by performing poorly in educational, employment, family, and other social roles.

Although we may accept that a completely non-stratified society is impossible, most of us would probably agree that a stratification system in which higher positions were achieved, not ascribed, would be preferable. In a **meritocracy,** everyone would have equal chances to compete for higher status positions and, presumably, those most capable would be awarded the highest rank. Such a society would exhibit a considerable degree of **social mobility,** as those who were more qualified moved up the social hierarchy to replace those who were less competent and who were consequently compelled to move down.

OPEN AND CLOSED STRATIFICATION SYSTEMS

When we compare Canada with other societies, or look back at our history, we find that this country has had what appears to be a fairly **open stratification system,** in which merit, rather than inheritance (or ascribed characteristics), determines social rank and in which social change is therefore possible. For example, dramatic changes in the status of various groups have occurred in this country over time. Although the practice was not nearly as widespread in Canada as in the United States, slaves (most of them black people from Africa but also some Aboriginal people) were bought and sold in Canada from the 1630s till the 1830s (Derreck, 2003). Chinese labourers, brought into the country to help build the railways, were kept out of most "white" jobs by law until well into the twentieth century (Li, 1982). Similarly, it was not until the 1960s that black Canadians were allowed to compete for much more than the lowest level positions in the Canadian railway industry (Calliste, 1987). However, by the 1830s, slavery had disappeared in Canada, and we now have laws against racial discrimination.

Comparing ourselves with other contemporary societies, we note that Canada does not have an aristocracy, such as the one that exists in Britain, where children of wealthy and powerful families of long standing inherit positions and titles. The degree to which Canadians compete for higher status occupations (in the education system and, later, within the workplace) stands in clear contrast to the situation in India, for example, where the caste into which an individual is born largely determines the type of work that he or she will be allowed to do. Although discrimination on the basis of caste membership has been illegal in India for many decades, the **caste system** continues to underpin a relatively **closed stratification system.** Compared with India, Canada offers many more chances for upward social mobility, an indication of a more open stratification system.

It is all too easy, however, to overlook the extent to which ascribed statuses continue to limit opportunities for many Canadians as well. Discrimination against members of Aboriginal and visible-minority groups continues to occur in Canada today. So too does discrimination against members of the gay community, against people with disabilities and seniors, and against women. These people are in lower status positions not because they competed poorly for some higher ranking in the social hierarchy, but because they are gay, have disabilities, are old, or are female.

These are fairly obvious examples of the ways in which ascribed statuses continue to play a prominent role in Canada's social stratification system. But what about the child from a wealthy family who graduates from an excellent high school in a wealthy neighbourhood, completes a degree or two in a prestigious and costly university, and then begins a career in a high-status, well-paying profession? Is this simply an example of someone achieving a deserved high status position, or did the advantages of birth (ascribed status) play some part in this success story? Similarly, when we hear of large companies laying off hundreds or thousands of workers, does their sudden downward mobility reflect their failure to compete in an open, merit-based stratification system, or were they simply unfortunate enough to be employed in a corporation that was being downsized?

As these examples illustrate, the social stratification system consists of a number of different hierarchies, some based on ascribed characteristics, others on achievement. As you make your way through this book, you will read chapters devoted to dimensions of stratification and inequality, such as gender, race, and ethnicity. Other chapters address activities (e.g., work) and institutions (e.g., education) in which stratification processes are extremely important, and still others focus on inequalities between regions and countries. Once you have read all these chapters, you will, I expect, be convinced of the central importance of social stratification in the discipline of sociology.

CLASS AND STRUCTURE

You will also notice that, even though studies of gender, race, ethnicity, and work take you in quite different directions, all frequently share an emphasis on inequalities in income, wealth, or property, and on resulting inequalities in power. On average, women earn about 75 percent of what men earn. Older women are much more likely than older men to be living in poverty. Members of visible minority groups and, particularly, Aboriginal Canadians are more likely to be unemployed and if they are employed, to be in low-paying jobs. Owners of large workplaces (employers, in other words) are wealthier than most other members of society, and employees in professional and managerial occupations typically earn a great deal more than lower-level employees. Owners, self-employed professionals, and managers typically have more job security than do non-managerial employees who either are paid by the hour or are salaried. Recognizing, then, the extent to which such material inequality (i.e., differences in income and

Employees in professional and managerial occupations typically earn a great deal more than lower-level employees do.
SOURCE: © iStockphoto.com/james steidl.

wealth or property) parallels and overlaps other social hierarchies, the rest of this chapter will focus primarily on material inequality or, after we define the terms, on social class and class structure.

Although the concept of **class** is seldom absent from discussions of social stratification, the definitions attached to it vary considerably. I will examine some of these definitions in the next section, which outlines several different theories of stratification. My own preference is to use the term in a fairly general sense, to indicate the position of an individual or a family within an economic hierarchy, along with others who have roughly the same amount of control over or access to economic or material resources. Thus, an individual can be said to be a member of a particular class, whether this is a class of large landowners, a class of wage-labourers and salaried workers (i.e., the "working class"), or a "professional/managerial class." It is their similar economic situation and opportunities, a result of their shared position within a society's system of economic production, that makes these individuals members of the same class. In turn, we can use the term **class structure** to refer to the overall economic hierarchy comprising all such classes, choosing the word *structure* deliberately to indicate the relative stability and prominence of this social ranking.

Do you think of yourself as a member of a specific social class? Probably not very often, if at all. Like most North Americans, you probably have a reasonably good idea of how well off you are compared with others in your community. You probably have some sense of where your education, occupation, and income, or the education, occupation, and income of your parents, fit in some general hierarchy of **socioeconomic status,** or position in an economic hierarchy, based on income, education, and occupation. "Class," however, is unlikely to be part of your everyday vocabulary. Nor is it typically part of the media's vocabulary. The newspaper stories I examined earlier, for example, identified a number of different dimensions of stratification, but social class was not among them.

Does this make "class" a useless concept? I argue the opposite. As I have already suggested, and as you will see in this and other chapters, pronounced patterns of material inequality exist in our society and overlap with most other dimensions of social stratification. The economic hierarchy is obviously not completely closed, but it is relatively stable and permanent, and it comprises some fairly distinct categories of individuals with similar amounts of control over material resources. Hence, it is useful to try to identify the "classes" that make up the stratification system (or class structure), to seek to understand their origin, and to examine the effects of membership in them on individuals and families. Rather than discarding the concept of "class" because few people think in these terms, we can ask why few people think about classes despite their prominence. In fact, you will see that some of the major theories of social stratification address this issue directly, inquiring about the conditions under which members of an economic class begin to recognize their shared interests and, perhaps, begin to act accordingly as a group.

In the following section, I begin with a detailed look at the ideas of the nineteenth-century social and political philosopher Karl Marx, who put social class at the very centre of his discussions of social structure and his theory of social change. In turn, some of the theories of social stratification developed in the twentieth century downplay the role of class or even ignore it completely, because the theorists believe that material inequalities are decreasing. Summing up this line of reasoning, Terry Nichols Clark and Seymour Martin Lipset (1991: 397) wrote that

> class is an increasingly outmoded concept, although it is sometimes appropriate to earlier historical periods. . . . Class analysis has grown increasingly inadequate in recent decades as traditional hierarchies have declined and new social differences have emerged. The cumulative impact of these changes is fundamentally altering the nature of social stratification—placing past theories in need of substantial modification.

As you read about the various theories of social stratification in the next section, and as you examine the data on material inequalities in Canada in the section after that, keep in mind Clark and Lipset's question: "Are social classes dying?"

EXPLANATIONS OF SOCIAL STRATIFICATION

So far, you have considered some examples of social stratification and its effects, and you have added to your vocabulary a number of useful concepts that allow you to discuss the phenomenon and to compare this society with others. But I have not really tried to explain social stratification, to account for its origins

and its impacts. In this section, I will briefly examine the theories (or explanations) of social stratification elaborated by a number of important social theorists, including some who were analyzing society many decades ago and others who have written about it more recently. As you will see, it is important to take into account the time and place in which a social theory was developed, since theorists construct their social explanations on the basis of what they see around them and expect to see in the future.

KARL MARX: CAPITALISM, EXPLOITATION, AND CLASS CONFLICT

Karl Marx had an immense impact on how we think about social stratification. He was born in Germany in 1818 but lived in England from 1849 until he died in 1883. His writings about the social and economic forces that brought about economic change look back over history but focus particularly on the rapidly changing European world that he observed during his lifetime. This was a time when industrial capitalism was transforming the economy and society. Large, mechanized, factory-based systems of production were emerging; cities were growing rapidly as rural peasants were being forced off the land or attracted to the city by the possibility of jobs in factories; and material inequality was extreme, as factory owners and merchants made huge profits while labourers lived in poverty. Trade unions, labour laws, and other arrangements that offer some protection to workers did not yet exist. Thus, as Marx observed, the Industrial Revolution was a time when both the level of economic production and the degree of inequality in society increased tremendously.

Modes of Production and Social Classes

Marx called the overall system of economic activity in a society its **mode of production.** In turn, its major components were the **means of production** (technology, capital investments, and raw materials) and the **social relations of production** (the relationships between the main classes involved in production). Slavery had been the primary mode of production in some societies in earlier times, and feudalism, an economic system in which peasants worked for landowners, not for a wage but for some share of the produce, was the mode of production that gave way to industrial capitalism in Europe.

Within industrial capitalism, Marx identified two major classes: the capitalist class, or **bourgeoisie,** which owned the means of production; and the **proletariat,** or working class, which exchanged its labour for wages. He also described a middle class—the **petite bourgeoisie**—comprising independent owners/producers (farmers, for example) and small-business owners. Marx expected this middle class largely to disappear as capitalism matured and drew some of its members up into the bourgeoisie but pushed most down into the proletariat. Of much greater importance in his theory of class inequality and social change was the relationship between workers and owners.

Marx reasoned that the value of a product sold was directly proportional to the average amount of labour needed to produce it. Thus, for example, an elegant piece of furniture was more valuable than its component pieces mainly because of the labour invested in it by the worker(s) who built it. Marx argued that the value of goods produced by wage-labourers far exceeded the amount needed to pay their wages and the cost of raw materials, technology, and other factors of production. Marx referred to this excess as **surplus value.** According to Marx, when commodities were sold, their surplus value was turned into profits for the owner. Marx viewed this as an exploitive relationship, but one that differed from the exploitive relationships that characterized slavery or feudalism. After all, factory workers were paid a wage for their labour and were not legally forced to stay with the job. However, because most workers had few other options for making a living, and because owners controlled all aspects of the work, the legal freedom of wage-labourers to change jobs was, in practical terms, an illusion.

Class Conflict and Class Consciousness

The idea of **class conflict** between the major classes in a society was the driving force behind Marx's theory of social change. Marx noted that previous modes of production had collapsed and been replaced because of class conflict. Feudalism in Europe, for example, had given way to capitalism as a result of the growing power of the merchant class relative to the traditional alliance of landowners and the aristocracy, and the deteriorating relationship between landowners and peasants. Furthermore, Marx argued, capitalism would eventually be replaced by a socialist mode of production, in which private ownership of property would disappear, along with the exploitation

and inequality it produced. The impetus for this massive change would again be widespread class conflict, this time between wage-labourers and the owners of the means of production, as inequality between these two classes became more pronounced.

Marx held that this revolution would take place only when members of the working class began to recognize that they were being exploited. In other words, Marx did not take it for granted that members of a class would see how their interests were similar. Whereas capitalists might be conscious of their group interests, wage-labourers needed to become aware of their common enemy. They needed to be transformed from a "class in itself" to a "class for itself." Thus, **class consciousness** was an important social-psychological component of Marx's theory of social inequality and social change. His vision of the future was that of a revolutionary upheaval in which the oppressed working class would recognize its enemy, destroy the institutions of capitalism, and replace them with a classless socialist society based on collective ownership of the means of production.

Responses to Marx

Over the years, many critics of Marx's ideas pointed to the communist countries, with their apparently socialist system of government and absence of private property, and noted that inequality had not disappeared there. Instead, a new hierarchy had emerged, in which control of the political and bureaucratic apparatus was the main basis of power. These observations were largely correct. As a Russian joke from the 1970s noted, under capitalism man exploits man, but under communism it is the other way around.

In fact, I expect that Marx himself would have been highly critical of the Soviet communist system, given the degree to which individual citizens were exploited and harshly treated by a powerful minority. However, it is slowly becoming apparent that the emergence of a capitalist economy in Eastern Europe over the past two decades is increasing material inequalities as it is changing their source. Today, individuals with control over some form of production or access to some marketing system are accumulating wealth while the majority of citizens appear to be no better off than before—indeed, many are worse off. The same pattern of growing social inequality has been observed in China where, despite the continued control of the economy by the Communist Party, some forms of free enterprise have been encouraged (Wu and Xie, 2002). In other words, while Marx's predictions about the inevitable emergence of a class-less society have not been borne out, his type of class analysis still has considerable relevance for understanding the changing stratification system in North America, Eastern Europe, and even communist China.

Most theories of social stratification developed after Marx's were essentially a "debate with Marx's ghost" (Zeitlin with Brym, 1991: 117). Some social philosophers and sociologists elaborated on Marx's ideas, while others attempted to refute them. Among the critics, some focused on the absence of widespread class conflict, the growth of the middle class, and the relative decline in material inequality in Western Europe and North America in the twentieth century. I will examine some of these theories below, along with others that tried to develop more complex models of the contemporary class structure while basically following Marx's form of class-based analysis.

MAX WEBER: CLASS AND OTHER DIMENSIONS OF INEQUALITY

Max Weber was born in Germany half a century after Marx—in 1864. Like Marx, he built his analysis of social stratification on a careful reading of history as well as a thorough analysis of the economic and political events of his day. But because he was only beginning his university studies about the time Marx died, Weber had the advantage of seeing the direction in which a more mature industrial capitalism was taking European society. He continued to write about many aspects of social stratification and social change until his death in 1920.

Class, Status, and Party

Weber shared with Marx a belief that economic inequalities were central to the social stratification system and that the ownership of property was a primary determinant of **power,** or the ability to impose your wishes on others, to get them to do what you want them to do. However, he argued that power could lie in controlling other types of resources as well (Weber, 1948 [1922]). Specifically, he proposed that structures of social stratification could be better understood by looking at economic inequalities, hierarchies of prestige (or social honour), and political inequalities (control of power blocs, such as political parties or other organizations)—or, in his words, at "class, status, and party." Although these different hierarchies often overlap, they need not. For example, suddenly wealthy individuals might not receive the

prestige they desire, being rejected in "high society" by those with "old money." Similarly, a politician might have considerable power through control of government resources but might not be very wealthy or, for that matter, have much prestige.

Since Weber lived to see the emergence of white-collar workers, the growth of large private- and public-sector bureaucracies, and the growing power of trade unions, he was able to write about these alternative sources of power in a stratified capitalist society. He provided an insightful analysis of how power resided in the control of top positions in large bureaucratic organizations, even if the officeholder was not an owner of the organization. He recognized that well-educated wage-labourers might not be as powerless as were the factory workers of an earlier era. He also saw that a new class of middle-level, educated workers might not necessarily align themselves with blue-collar workers, and he was less inclined to conclude, as had Marx, that the middle class would disappear (Zeitlin with Brym, 1991: 118–19). In fact, he expected that the number of educated technical and professional workers in bureaucratic capitalist society would increase.

What Weber saw, compared with what Marx saw, was considerably more complexity in the social stratification system because of the growing diversity of the occupational structure and of capitalist enterprises. And although Weber was sometimes pessimistic in his writings about the future of democracy in a bureaucratic capitalist society, he did not link inequality and class conflict to the ultimate demise of capitalism itself, as did Marx. Similarly, although Weber, like Marx, commented on how members of a class might or might not recognize their shared interests, he did not conclude that it was the inevitable destiny of the working class to become a "class for itself."

Social Class and Life-Chances

Despite these divergences in their thinking, Weber, like Marx, placed primary emphasis on the economic underpinnings of social stratification. However, he defined "class" more broadly. Rather than insisting that a limited number of class positions were based on an individual's relationship to the means of production, Weber saw a larger variety of class positions based both on ownership of property and on other labour-market statuses, such as occupation and education. Furthermore, he tended to emphasize the **life-chances** that class position offered. In other words, a higher position in the economic hierarchy, however obtained, provided more power and allowed an individual and his or her family to enjoy more of the good things in life.

It should be apparent, then, that the general approach to studying stratification that I outlined earlier, one that recognizes the central importance of class while acknowledging that gender, race, and other dimensions of social inequality can also be very important, is in the Weberian tradition. Similarly, my general definition of "class" as a relatively stable position within an economic hierarchy held by an individual or family, along with others with roughly the same amount of control over or access to material resources, follows Weber's use of the term.

DAVIS AND MOORE: A FUNCTIONAL THEORY OF STRATIFICATION

Twentieth-Century Affluence and Structural-Functionalist Theory

Although a number of other social theorists in Europe and North America wrote about social stratification in the early decades of the twentieth century, I will skip ahead to 1945, when Kingsley Davis and Wilbert Moore published their short but much-debated "principles of social stratification." In other chapters in this text, you will read about the **structural-functionalist theory** in sociology, an approach that emphasizes consensus over conflict and that seeks to explain the function, for society as a whole, of social institutions and various aspects of social structure. Davis and Moore were part of this intellectual tradition, which arose in reaction to the conflict-oriented and socially radical theories of Marx (and, to a lesser extent, of Weber).

The emergence of structural-functionalism as an alternative theoretical approach can be better understood if we view it as reflecting the optimistic view in postwar North America that affluence was increasing, social conflict was decreasing, and a harmonious future for society was dawning. For example, Arthur Schlesinger, Jr., an American historian writing in 1956, suggested that Americans should start thinking about the "miseries of an age of abundance." Rather than worrying about economic growth, employment, and improving the standard of living, it was time to concentrate on "the bettering of our mass media and the elevation of our popular culture, in short, with the quality of civilization to which our nation aspires in an age of ever-increasing abundance and leisure" (as quoted in Longman, 1985: 75). Thus, during the several decades following World War II, many social scientists were attracted to theories that downplayed conflict and emphasized the benefits, to all, of an apparently ever-expanding economy.

The Functional Necessity of Stratification

Davis and Moore (1945) argued that, because inequality exists in all societies, it must be a necessary part of society. All societies, they noted, have a variety of occupational roles that need to be filled, some requiring more training than others, some having more functional importance, and some being less pleasant and more difficult to perform. To get people to fill important roles and to perform these critical tasks well, and to spend time training for high-skill occupations, societies must ensure that the rewards for performance (money, prestige, and other intangibles) are greater. Thus, for example, doctors and schoolteachers need to be paid more than factory workers and truck drivers, and also must rank higher than the latter in terms of social honour and prestige.

In short, according to Davis and Moore, social inequality is both inevitable and functionally necessary for society. But theirs was not a class-based and conflict-prone stratification system. Rather, Davis and Moore described a much more fluid socioeconomic hierarchy, with many different occupational statuses into which individuals are slotted on the basis of their effort and ability. The system is held together by consensus and shared values (not torn apart by conflict, as Marx theorized), because members of society generally agree that the hierarchy is fair and just. It follows from this line of reasoning that efforts to reduce social inequality will be ineffective and might even be harmful to society.

Criticisms of Davis and Moore

Various criticisms have been levelled against Davis and Moore's theory. For example, although some differences in pay might be justified to reimburse those who spend more years in school preparing for an occupation, are the huge income and wealth inequalities we see in our society really necessary? Why do women often earn less than men, even if they are doing the same type of work? Are movie stars, professional athletes, and chief executive officers with million-dollar-plus annual incomes really so much more important to society than nurses, daycare workers, prison guards, and most other low-paid workers? And how does a theory like this account for inherited wealth, for the fact that wealth leads to power and the ability to accumulate more wealth?

Given these criticisms, what accounts for the appeal of this theory? Perhaps it is the kernel of truth at its core that is so attractive—namely, the recognition that, to some extent, differences in income and prestige are based on different amounts of effort and ability. After all, we can easily think of examples of better-paying occupations that require long years of education and training. Nevertheless, this is far from the complete story about inequality in our society, which is much more pronounced than what such differences in effort and ability might lead us to expect. In fact, the theory's appeal probably lies more in its apparent justification of these large inequalities. You might test this hypothesis by explaining the theory, first to someone with a high income or inherited wealth, and then to someone who is unemployed or earning very little. The odds are that the functionalist explanation of stratification would sound much more plausible to the wealthier person.

GERHARD LENSKI: TECHNOLOGY AND STRATIFICATION SYSTEMS

Writing in the 1960s, a time of economic expansion and growing prosperity in North America, Gerhard Lenski (1966) developed a theory of "power and privilege" that attempted to explain the extent of material inequality in both contemporary and past societies. Lenski's explanation recognized power and conflict much more explicitly than had the Davis and Moore functionalist explanation of stratification. And, like Weber, he identified a number of different dimensions of social stratification, such as education and ethnicity, while emphasizing the centrality of economic inequalities. Although he used the term *class*, Lenski did not define it precisely, choosing instead to talk about the ruling elites in society in general terms and about how they managed to maintain their wealth and power at the expense of the masses.

Lenski reasoned that a society's technological base largely determines the degree of inequality within it. In simple hunting-and-gathering societies, he argued, the few resources of the society were distributed primarily on the basis of need. But as societies became more technologically complex, resources in excess of those required to fulfill basic needs were produced. Control of those surplus resources, or privilege, came to be based on power, allowing ruling elites to take a much larger share of these resources for themselves. Thus, the more complex agricultural societies, such as that of pre-colonial India, developed highly structured governing and tax-collecting systems, through which the privileged ruling elites accumulated immense amounts of wealth, while the masses lived in poverty.

As a result of industrialization and the complexity of modern technology, this "age-old evolutionary trend toward ever-increasing inequality" (Lenski, 1966: 308) was reversed. Owners of the means of production could no longer control the production process directly and had to rely instead on well-educated managerial and technical workers to keep the complex system operating. Education broadened the horizons of these middle-level employees, introducing them to ideas of democracy, encouraging them to demand a larger share of the profits they were helping to produce, and making them more articulate in their demands for equality.

Thus, Lenski's theory proposed a causal link between complex industrial technology, the higher education of workers, and workers' insistence on sharing the growing wealth of an industrial society. But why would employers give in to such demands? Because, argued Lenski, the industrial elite needed educated workers—they could not produce wealth without them. Equally important, the much greater productivity of industrial societies compared with preindustrial societies meant that the elite could "make economic concessions in relative terms without necessarily suffering any loss in absolute terms" (Lenski, 1966: 314). Because the economic pie was so much bigger, everyone could have a larger slice.

In one obvious sense, Lenski's theory resembled the functionalist theory of stratification—both noted that better-educated and more highly skilled workers are paid more. However, unlike the functionalist approach, Lenski's theory clearly took power differences into account, emphasizing how the extent of accumulation of wealth by elites, or the degree of material inequality, depends on the power and bargaining ability of middle-level workers. In fact, Lenski placed material inequality at the centre of his theory of stratification. But in contrast to Marx's nineteenth-century predictions of growing inequality as industrial capitalism matured, Lenski, writing in the middle of the twentieth century, saw a movement toward a more equal distribution of society's wealth.

Although high technology has created many new jobs, it has also eliminated many. For the chronically unemployed, the closest they may get to high technology is a computer at the local unemployment office.
SOURCE: © Erik S. Lesser/Getty Images.

ERIK OLIN WRIGHT: A NEO-MARXIST APPROACH

In reaction against functionalism, Lenski brought power and conflict back into his explanation of social inequality. He placed material inequalities resulting from one group's domination of another at the centre of his model, thus coming closer to the approach taken by Marx and Weber. But he did not carry through with a traditional Marxist analysis built around the relationships of different classes to the means of production. In contrast, a number of neo-Marxist scholars, writing in the 1970s and 1980s, attempted to update the original Marxist model so that it could be applied to the late twentieth century. We will discuss only one theorist from the neo-Marxist camp, Erik Olin Wright.

Although Marx acknowledged the existence of a middle class comprising several distinct groups, including independent producers and small-business owners, he predicted that this middle class would disappear and so spent much more time writing about the relationship between the two primary classes (capitalists and workers). Wright's contribution lies in recognizing that as industrial capitalism matured, the middle class had grown and become more diverse, and in trying to understand the class dynamics of our more complex capitalist system of production. Of particular importance in Wright's theory is the emphasis on **contradictory class locations**—that is, on occupational groupings that have divided loyalties within a class structure. For example, although managers work for capitalists, supervising lower-level employees and

trying to get them to produce as much as possible, managers are themselves employees, potentially exploited by owners. Considering the substantial numbers of people in such contradictory locations, you can begin to understand why the widespread class conflict envisioned by Marx has seldom emerged.

In a later reformulation of his ideas, Wright (1985) argued that exploitation of one class by another can occur through control of property or the means of production (as Marx had insisted), as well as through ownership of skill or credential assets and control of high positions within organizations. Thus, he identified three classes of owners (the bourgeoisie, small employers, and the petite bourgeoisie with no employees), and nine classes of wage-labourers (non-owners), differentiated on two dimensions, the possession of organizational assets and of skill/credential assets (Wright, 1985: 88). For example, "expert managers" (e.g., engineers or lawyers in senior management positions within large companies) fill a class location characterized by extensive organizational assets and high skill/credential assets, in contrast to basic "proletarians," who have no specific skill/credential assets and no management or supervisory responsibilities (see Figure 6.1, p. 134).

Despite his intention of developing a neo-Marxist theoretical model updated to the late twentieth century, Wright's theory is similar to Weber's view of class structure in some ways (Grabb, 2002). Specifically, the different class locations created by the intersection of organizational and skill/credential assets remind us of the different classes Weber described as he commented on how similar educational and occupational statuses resulted in similar control over and access to material resources. Even so, Wright's theory of class structure and his observations about contradictory locations within it are useful, because he deliberately attempts to incorporate the complexities of modern capitalist society into his explanation of social inequality.

FRANK PARKIN: A NEO-WEBERIAN APPROACH

Wright attempted to bring Marx's class analysis back into the discussion of contemporary forms of social stratification. Frank Parkin (1972, 1979) was equally explicit in stating his intellectual debts to Max Weber's discussions of power, class, and social stratification (Grabb, 2002). In fact, Parkin went so far as to argue that neo-Marxist scholars, espousing what

FIGURE 6.1   ERIC OLIN WRIGHT'S TYPOLOGY OF CLASS LOCATION IN CAPITALIST SOCIETY

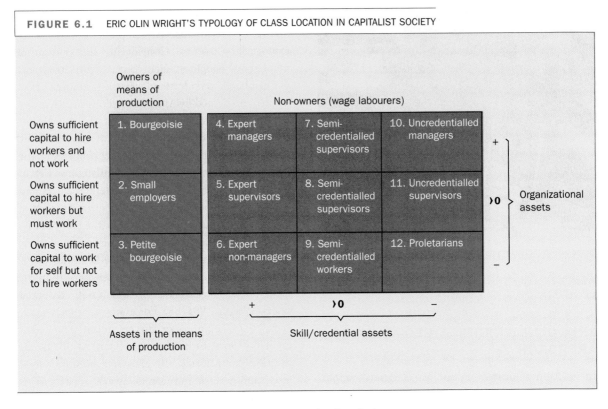

SOURCE: From Erik Olin Wright, *Classes*. 1985, p. 88. Reprinted with permission from Verso Books.

he calls "professorial Marxism" (1979: x), were merely putting forth dressed-up Weberian arguments. As a neo-Weberian, Parkin criticized traditional Marxist and contemporary neo-Marxist analyses for failing to take into account gender, race, religious, and other forms of social stratification that do not grow out of the relations of production in capitalist society but clearly have an origin and a permanency all of their own (1979: 4–5). Nevertheless, like both Weber and Marx before him, Parkin continued to emphasize the importance of property relations in contemporary stratification systems (Grabb, 2002).

Among Parkin's most useful contributions to stratification theory is his explanation of how patterns of structured inequality, whether based on class, gender, race, or some other ascribed or achieved status, are maintained or changed. To do so, Parkin returned to a concept introduced by Weber, that of **social closure.** Parkin defines this term as "the process by which social collectivities seek to maximize rewards by restricting access to resources and opportunities to a limited circle of eligibles" (1979: 44). He then goes on to elaborate two types of closure strategies that help us understand how patterns of social inequality are maintained but also sometimes altered.

Exclusion refers to the organized efforts of privileged, more powerful groups to maintain their advantaged position. Processes of exclusion can range from centuries-old caste systems in closed societies to the use, in contemporary open societies, of educational credentials to maintain power and privilege. For example, lawyers and other professional groups have managed to ensure, via legal restrictions, that only they can perform certain types of work in our society. By excluding others from engaging in such work, it is possible to maintain high incomes, enjoy a high standard of living, and exercise a great deal of power. Similarly, members of trade unions can also use legal sanctions to keep non-members, who might have the same skills, from taking on some well-paying jobs.

In contrast, **usurpation** refers to the efforts of excluded groups within a stratification system to gain advantages and power. As Parkin put it, all usurpation actions have as their goal "biting into the resources and benefits accruing to dominant groups in society" (1979: 74). As with exclusionary practices, usurpation efforts range across a continuum, from lobbying and voting for social change to outright revolt against groups in power. Thus, over the past several decades, we have seen successful efforts by women's groups,

Aboriginal groups, and other disadvantaged groups to change the balance of power and privilege in Canada. Going back further, labour unions took even stronger, sometimes illegal, actions to gain new powers and a more equitable distribution of resources for their members.

Thus, like Lenski, Parkin took a keen interest in the power struggles within society between groups with more and less power (Grabb, 2002). However, Parkin's neo-Weberian theory does not contain a premise of inevitability, either one of increased inequality and eventual social revolution as Marx predicted, or one of reduced inequality resulting from technological change and economic growth, as Lenski predicted. But Parkin did see a clear trend with respect to processes of social closure. With the growing emphasis on education in modern society, the use of educational credentials to maintain power and privilege has become more widespread. As a result, well-educated professionals have become a powerful class grouping, sometimes almost as powerful as wealthy capitalists who control the means of production (Grabb, 2002). Beneath these two powerful groups are a range of other groups with varying amounts of power, trying, when possible, to usurp more power from those above.

EXPLANATION OF SOCIAL STRATIFICATION: SUMMING UP

There are other theories of social inequality in addition to those reviewed previously (Grabb, 2002). However, having been introduced to Marx and Weber, the functionalist theory of stratification, and a number of more recent approaches, you will now have some sense of the range of existing explanations. Davis and Moore's functionalist approach stressed that inequality was inevitable and useful, and it downplayed social conflict resulting from inequality. In contrast to this consensus approach to stratification, a variety of conflict approaches highlighted differences in power resulting from and contributing to material inequality, the exploitation of some groups by others, and the social conflict that could result. Marx was the most explicit in this regard, arguing that class conflict would eventually transform capitalist society.

The theories we have reviewed differ in the assumptions they make and the conclusions they draw about the future of material inequality. Marx clearly saw inequality and exploitation of the working class

increasing, and he predicted that class conflict would lead to the death of capitalism. Although Weber was not convinced that a socialist society would eventually emerge, neither did he argue that inequalities would gradually decrease (Grabb, 2002). As a neo-Weberian, Parkin takes a similar stance. Wright's emphasis on the growing number of middle-class locations also does not suggest an increasing level of material inequality, but neither does it imply the opposite. However, the functionalists and Lenski, writing in an era of economic growth and widespread optimism about the ability of capitalism to raise the overall standard of living, clearly felt that material inequalities were shrinking in Western industrial societies.

The various explanations also differ in the degree to which they emphasize class differences in access to and control of material resources. For Marx, class was the primary determining factor in this regard. Weber, using the term *class* somewhat more broadly, emphasized its central role but recognized other important dimensions of social stratification. So, too, did Parkin, who explicitly discussed the independent effects of gender, race, and religion. Davis and Moore basically ignored the concept of class. Although Lenski again focused more directly on economic inequality, he did not really describe society in terms of distinct classes, as Wright, in his neo-Marxist approach, did. Thus, if you view these theories in temporal order, it appears that class, at least as defined in the Weberian sense, has made a comeback as an explanatory concept.

Furthermore, those who felt that the level of material inequality was remaining high or increasing viewed society from a class-based perspective. In other words, they focused on the distinctly different life-chances of individuals and families with similar amounts of access to and control over material resources. In contrast, theorists who thought economic inequalities were declining preferred a model of society composed of many different overlapping strata that reflected a variety of equally important dimensions of social stratification.

Clark and Lipset, whose question "Are social classes dying?" introduced this section, make the latter point explicitly when they state that "one simple, powerful change has affected the economy: growth. And economic growth undermines hierarchical class stratification" (1991: 405). As you turn to the next section of the chapter—an overview of statistics on occupational and class structures and material inequality in Canada today—keep this argument in mind, because the statistics allow you to assess its validity.

OCCUPATIONS, SOCIAL CLASS, AND INEQUALITY IN CANADA

OCCUPATIONAL SHIFTS OVER TIME

As noted above, explanations of social stratification differ in the extent to which they emphasize social class compared with other bases of social inequality. Some theories focus more on how occupational patterns have changed as industrial capitalism matured. But even such theorists as Erik Olin Wright, who place social class at the centre of their explanations, rely to a considerable extent on occupational data. So it would be useful to begin this section by examining occupational shifts in Canada over the past century.

Table 6.1 displays the types of occupations most common at the beginning (1911) and in the middle (1951) of the last century, and at the beginning of the twenty-first century (2006). The most prominent occupational shift over the course of the century is the

---

TABLE 6.1 OCCUPATIONAL DISTRIBUTION OF LABOUR FORCE PARTICIPANTS,* CANADA, 1911, 1951, 2006

OCCUPATION TYPE	1911	1951	2006
Managerial/administrative	5%	8%	13%
Professional/technical	4	7	23
Clerical	4	11	12
Sales	5	7	11
Service	8	10	14
Manufacturing	14	17	7
Transportation	6	8	9
Construction	5	6	6
Agriculture	34	16	2
Forestry/fishing/mining	5	4	2
Other occupations	10	6	1
Total	**100**	**100**	**100**

SOURCE: 1911 and 1951 data: adapted from 1911 and 1951 Census results, presented by Jeff O'Neill, "Changing Occupational Structure," Canadian Social Trends, Winter 1991, p. 10; 2006 data: adapted from 2006 Census results, Table 97-559-XWE2006012, http://www12.statcan.ca/census-recensement/2006/dp-pd/hlt/index-eng.cfm.
*Labour force participants include both the employed (paid employees and the self-employed) and the unemployed (those who want a paid job but who are unable to find one); based on the population aged 15 and older.

---

decline in agricultural occupations, from 34 percent of all labour force participants in 1911 to only 2 percent in 2006. We also observe a decline, albeit not as steep, in other natural resource–based occupations (forestry, fishing, mining). Manufacturing occupations increased in relative terms (from 14 percent to 17 percent) between the beginning and middle of the last century, but by 2006 had dropped to only 7 percent of the total labour force. The decline in manufacturing jobs has continued since then (Lin, 2008), intensifying further in 2009 as the Canadian economy shrank as a result of global financial and economic instability.

Manufacturing, construction, transportation, and resource-based occupations are typically called blue-collar occupations, in contrast to white-collar occupations in the managerial, professional, clerical (office jobs), sales, and service categories. It is apparent from Table 6.1 that white-collar occupations have come to greatly outnumber blue-collar occupations as industrial capitalism has matured. In 2006, 13 percent of Canadian labour force participants were identified as having managerial/administrative occupations, up from only 5 percent in 1911. Professional/technical occupations had multiplied by almost six times in relative terms, from 4 percent to 23 percent. Clerical, sales, and service occupations also had become much more common, from a total of only 17 percent in 1911 to 37 percent of all occupations in 2006.

What do these occupational changes tell you, with respect to my previous discussions of the bases of social stratification? First, as various theories have indicated, the proportion of occupations requiring higher education has increased, while the proportion of traditional blue-collar, "working-class" occupations has declined. With the expansion in white-collar occupations, average incomes rose, at least until the early 1980s. Thus, to the extent that occupational data can inform about class structure in the Weberian sense, occupational shifts over the past century suggest greater class diversity, rather than a polarization of classes, as a strict reading of Marx's theory would predict, and a rising standard of living for Canadian workers, rather than increasing poverty and exploitation.

And what do the numbers in Table 6.1 fail to tell you? First, they do not distinguish between the occupations typically held by women and those typically held by men. Since the middle of the last century, a rising proportion of women have been entering the labour force. But, as we will see (Chapter 7, Gender Inequality), women have been more likely to find employment in the clerical, sales, and service occupations (what might be called a "pink-collar sector") than in blue-collar occupations or in higher-status and better-paying managerial and professional occupations, even though there has been some movement by women into higher-level white-collar occupations in the past decades (Krahn, Lowe, and Hughes, 2006: ch. 2). Thus, gender-based labour market stratification continues to exist, intersecting with class-based stratification.

Second, even though you might draw some conclusions about social class from the occupational data in Table 6.1, the data do not directly describe workers' relationships to the means of production, in Marx's terms. Statistics Canada has never collected and categorized national data along these lines, but a series of Ontario-wide surveys have, by using Erik Olin Wright's approach to class analysis to profile the class composition of that province since the early 1980s (Livingstone, 1999: 158). In 1996, the Ontario employed labour force was described as comprising corporate capitalists (1 percent), small employers (8 percent), the own-account self-employed or petite bourgeoisie (14 percent), managers (8 percent), supervisors (4 percent), professional/semi-professional employees (19 percent), and service and industrial workers (46 percent). The small sample size in this study (about 600 respondents) means that these estimates are not precise, and the single-province focus does not allow for generalizations to all of Canada. Even so, this study clearly shows that the large class of paid workers contains several distinct types with varying amounts of decision-making authority and substantial differences in income, status, and occupational power.

Third, neither Table 6.1 (which displays occupational change over time) nor the 1996 Ontario study (which uses class data from only one point in time) can give a sense of how the Canadian class structure might be changing. But you can get one indication of change from other data on self-employment. Over the course of the century, particularly with the decline in the number of people employed in agriculture, the proportion of self-employed Canadians dropped dramatically. By 1971, only 11 percent of the Canadian labour force was self-employed. However, beginning in the 1980s, a slow reversal of the trend began in Canada, the United States, and other Western industrialized countries. By 2004, 10 percent of employed Canadians were own-account self-employed (without any employees) and 5 percent employed others

(Krahn, Lowe, and Hughes, 2006: ch. 2). Researchers still have not determined whether more Canadians are voluntarily choosing self-employment or are being pushed into it as a result of higher levels of unemployment and growing corporate and public-sector downsizing. Nevertheless, the reversal of the decline in self-employment—the increase in the size of the petite bourgeoisie—is something that theorists are trying to explain as they attempt to further update Marx's ideas of class-based stratification (Breen and Rottman, 1995: 87–88; Myles and Turegun, 1994).

Finally, the data in Table 6.1 do not reflect some of the dramatic changes in employment opportunities and outcomes that have been occurring in the past four decades. I will return to this topic later, but for now I will simply note that unemployment rates have risen and fallen and are now rising again, part-time and temporary work have become much more common, and income growth appears to have stopped, while income and wealth inequality have increased. Consequently, the higher standard of living that accompanied occupational changes in the second

Many women were able to make important inroads into the labour force during World War II, as this painting illustrates. To this day, women are more likely to find work in the pink-collar sector than in higher-status, better-paying occupations.
SOURCE: Paraskeva Clark, *Parachute Riggers*. Courtesy Canadian War Museum. Reproduced with permission of Clive and Ben Clark, Toronto.

half of the twentieth century is no longer guaranteed for all those in middle-status occupations. Thus, it is essential that we look carefully at the distributional side of the occupation and class structures, at "who gets what" in return for their employment, as well as at the occupational and class positions that people hold (Westergaard, 1995). But before beginning to examine changing patterns of material inequality in Canada, I will first discuss another important feature of stratification systems in modern societies—opportunities for occupational mobility and status attainment.

OCCUPATIONAL MOBILITY AND STATUS ATTAINMENT

Many people move up the occupational and income ladders during their careers, frequently after investing in higher education of some kind. And some move down, often because of economic circumstances beyond their control. Sociologists have conducted a great deal of research on such **intragenerational occupational mobility** (mobility within an individual's lifetime) and on **intergenerational occupational mobility,** the process of reaching an occupational location higher or lower than the location your parents held. Research of this type is interesting in itself, since we all like to compare how well we have done relative to others. However, such research is also theoretically important, since it tests hypotheses derived from theories of inequality (the functionalist perspective, for example) that propose that higher positions in society are generally filled by those most qualified, not by those who inherit them.

If the only intergenerational occupational mobility we observed was a result of better-qualified people moving up to replace those who were less qualified, we should also see an equivalent amount of downward mobility. Such a scenario of "musical jobs" or, to use the technical term, **circulatory mobility,** does not really describe the Canadian situation over the past half-century, however, because of the pronounced parallel process of **structural mobility** resulting from a significant change in the shape of Canada's overall occupational structure. As noted earlier, over the past half-century, industrial societies, including Canada, experienced a great deal of growth in white-collar occupations (clerical, managerial, and professional positions) as traditional agricultural and blue-collar industrial jobs declined in relative importance. Hence, with an increase in the number

of higher-status jobs, each generation had more chances than the preceding one to improve the status of their jobs.

Even so, Canadian studies conducted over the past several decades indicate that Canada, like the United States, has a relatively open stratification system, more so than countries like Sweden, the United Kingdom, France, the Netherlands, and Australia (Wanner, 2004). In other words, in Canada relatively more people have been able to move up the occupational ladder relative to their parents. During the second half of the last century, the Canadian occupational structure opened up for women and men in different ways. The steep decline in agricultural employment meant that many men moved out of the agricultural occupations held by their fathers. For women, the major shift was away from the housework that had been the main female occupation for their mothers' generation. For both sexes, expansion of postsecondary educational opportunities, leading to higher status occupations, played an important role (Wanner, 2004). However, most of this opening of the stratification system occurred between 1973 and 1986. Little changed in terms of mobility opportunities in the following decade.

Thus, overall, Canadian mobility studies find only a limited amount of direct occupational inheritance across generations and conclude that the occupational stratification system became somewhat more open during the 1970s and 1980s. Yet those at or near the top of the occupational hierarchy are still more likely to pass their advantages on to their children. As Richard Wanner (2004: 144) concludes, "Canada is still a stratified society characterized by a considerable amount of inheritance of privilege" (Wanner, 2004: 144). This intergenerational transfer of advantage takes place primarily through different levels of access to the postsecondary education system.

Research in Canada and other Western countries examining the process of **occupational status attainment** has shown, not surprisingly, that the most important influence on the status of an individual's current job is the status of that person's first job. Individuals who enter the labour market as articling lawyers, for example, typically make their way higher up the occupational ladder than do those who began as unskilled labourers. In turn, the status of that first job is heavily influenced by the amount of education completed. Such findings obviously lend some support to theories that suggest that more qualified people, as indicated by higher education, end up in higher-status and better-paying occupations.

However, many studies have also traced education–job linkages back to the previous generation, showing that those who obtain more education and hence better jobs are more likely to come from families with better-educated parents. For example, a 14-year longitudinal study of high-school graduates in Edmonton, Alberta, showed that young people from families in which one or both parents had completed university were almost three times as likely to complete university themselves (Krahn, 2004). For a variety of reasons (e.g., more money for higher education, more well-educated role models), children from more advantaged backgrounds can build on their initial advantages.

THE DISTRIBUTION OF WEALTH

Evidence from various sources demonstrates that a limited number of people continue to own or control a very large portion of the wealth in Canada. For example, in 2008, 50-year-old David Thomson and his family (three children) were estimated to be worth 18.9 billion dollars. While this put them all the way down at number 31 on the 2008 *Forbes Magazine* list of "The World's Billionaires" (Kroll, 2008), it nevertheless still made them Canada's wealthiest family. In contrast, in 2005, the median wealth (the difference between the total assets owned by a family, including a home, and its debt) for Canadian families with adult children was $259 500, compared with $120 200 for couples with children under age 18 (Morissette and Zhang, 2007). Such statistics highlight the immense wealth gap between average Canadians and rich families, such as the Thomsons, the Westons, and the Irvings, with business holdings spread around the globe as well as in Canada. Together with highly paid chief executive officers and corporate directors, these wealthy families clearly form a distinct upper class, the haute (or high) bourgeoisie in Marx's terms.

By way of example, in 2006, the CEOs of the top 100 companies listed on the Toronto Stock Exchange received a median compensation package (earnings, bonuses, and stock options) of $11.7 million (Pratt, 2007). It would take the average Canadian worker (employed full-time and year-round), with annual earnings of about $41 000 in 2005, about 283 years to accumulate as much money as any of these 100 CEOs receive in one year. Ironically, some of the highest paid CEOs were those who left their jobs when their company

was doing poorly. Included in this group would be John Lederer, former Loblaws CEO, who received a $12 million payout for leaving before his contract ended, on top of his $10 million in normal compensation. However, he did not survive his job loss as well as did Robert Nardelli, former CEO of Home Depot in the United States. He received a $210 million severance package, on top of the $225 million he had earned over the previous six years, a period when the value of Home Depot stock fell by 7.9 percent (McFarland, 2007).

At the other end of the wealth scale are the 14 percent of Canadian families who reported no net worth in 2005, net worth being defined as the difference between total assets (shares, bonds, savings, property, businesses, and possessions, but excluding future pension income) and total debt (Morissette and Zhang, 2007). Almost one in four families (24 percent) reported no net wealth, defined as net worth minus the value of property that could not be disposed of quickly if necessary (i.e., a home and furnishings or a business). In fact, the median "wealth" of the poorest 10 percent of Canadian families in 2005 was –$9600, indicating that, on average, their debts outstripped the value of all their assets. In contrast, the wealthiest 10 percent of families reported median family wealth of $1 194 000. This meant that the top 10 percent of Canadian families held 58 percent of all family wealth in Canada.

Over the long term, the economic growth experienced in Western industrialized countries, along with some income redistribution efforts by governments, has had an equalizing effect on the distribution of household wealth. Wolff (1991), for example, showed that inequality in household wealth decreased between 1920 and the 1970s in Sweden, Britain, and the United States. Although comparable data are not available for Canada for the same period, it is likely that a similar decline occurred here as well. However, Wolff also noted that, in the mid-1970s, wealth inequality began to increase again in the United States and Sweden (it remained constant in Britain). What about in Canada?

A recent study reveals that, on average, Canadian families were considerably wealthier in 2005 than they were in 1970 (Morissette and Zhang, 2007). However, there is more to this story of median family wealth more than doubling in 35 years. Wealth inequality declined between 1970 and 1977, stayed steady until 1984, and then increased considerably in the next 20 years. Thus, back in 1984, the top 10 percent of Canadian families held 51.8 percent of total family wealth. By 2005, this figure had increased to 58.2 percent (Morissette and Zhang, 2007). In other words, the wealth gap between rich and poor families has been growing over the past two decades in Canada.

INCOME DISTRIBUTION

High-Paying and Low-Paying Occupations

Although most people have virtually no contact with the wealthiest families in Canada, we are much more aware of, or perhaps are even members of, a larger, not quite as wealthy but still very affluent group of households containing one or more individuals in high-paying occupations. By way of example, 2006 census data for individuals working full-time year round revealed Canadian dentists earning an average of $142 100 (in 2005), while medical specialists earned even more ($201 847). Judges earned almost as much ($192 448) while lawyers had to be content with average yearly earnings of $142 345 (Statistics Canada, 2006a). In contrast, cashiers working full-time year-round earned only a fraction of this ($20 140), as did hotel clerks ($23 790), hair stylists and barbers ($19 746), and pet groomers and other animal care workers ($20 898).

Using the term *class* in the Weberian sense, you would be justified in labelling individuals in well-paid managerial and professional occupations as members of an upper-middle class, given their high incomes and their access to and control of material resources through their employment positions. In contrast, retail workers and those employed in some service occupations (e.g., food and beverage services, child-care and home support services) work in the low-paying, insecure occupations that we might describe as the lower working class.

These occupational earning patterns hide large gender differences. Thus, among people working full-time and full-year, women's earnings were 71 percent of men's in 2005, a figure that had not changed since 2000 (Statistics Canada, 2006a). Female dentists earned, on average, 63 percent of what their male counterparts earned ($100 047 and $158 094, respectively). Among senior managers, women earned 60 percent of what men earned. Female university professors, however, reported 2005 earnings of $78 798, 82 percent of the earnings of male professors ($96 281). Among the lower-paid

According to 2006 Canadian census data, cashiers earned about $20 000 per year.
SOURCE: © Jupiter Photos, 2009.

| BOX 6.1 | WILL THE GENDER WAGE GAP DISAPPEAR? |

Census data from 2006 show that, for full-time, full-year employed Canadians, women earn 71 percent of what men earn. This statistic is based on earnings comparisons for workers of all ages and with a wide range of formal education. We see a smaller gender wage gap when we look only at 25- to 29-year-old (full-time, full-year) employed Canadians. In 2005, women in this age group earned 85 percent of what men of the same age group earned. The same female–male earnings ratio was observed five years earlier in 2000. However, 20 years earlier, in 1980, 25- to 29-year-old women, working full-time year-round, earned only 75 percent of what their male counterparts did (Statistics Canada, 2008a).

Returning to the 2006 census data, when we focus on only 15- to 24-year-old, full-time full-year workers with a university degree or certificate, we generally see a much higher female–male earnings ratio or, in other words, a much smaller gender

wage gap (Statistics Canada, 2006b). For example, among elementary school teachers (a commonly held job among 15- to 24-year-olds with university training), in 2005 the female–male earnings ratio was 97 percent (Figure 6.2). In this occupation, women earned almost the same amount as men. Among auditors and accountants, university-trained young women actually earned more, on average, than their male counterparts.

Does the much smaller gender wage gap among young, university-educated Canadians signify that gender-based stratification in the workplace has almost disappeared, at least for well-educated workers? Or, as these young women and men move further into their careers in a labour market where women are still disadvantaged, and for some, into parenthood where women still carry a larger share of child-care responsibilities, will we see a gender wage gap similar to that observed for their parents?

occupations, male janitors reported annual 2005 earnings of $35 439, considerably higher than the earnings of their female counterparts ($26 980). Similar gender differences are observed in all occupational groupings but, as these examples demonstrate, the female–male earnings ratio does vary considerably by occupation (see Box 6.1 and Chapter 7, Gender Inequality).

Income Inequality

The census data discussed above give some indication of the distribution of employment earnings, the largest component of total income. If you were to look back to the middle of the last century, you would see that the distribution of total income (from employment, investments, government assistance, and all other sources) across households (families and individuals living

FIGURE 6.2 AVERAGE EARNINGS IN SIX OCCUPATIONS MOST COMMONLY HELD BY 15- TO 24-YEAR-OLDS WITH A UNIVERSITY DEGREE/DIPLOMA AND WORKING FULL-TIME, FULL YEAR BY SEX, CANADA, 2005

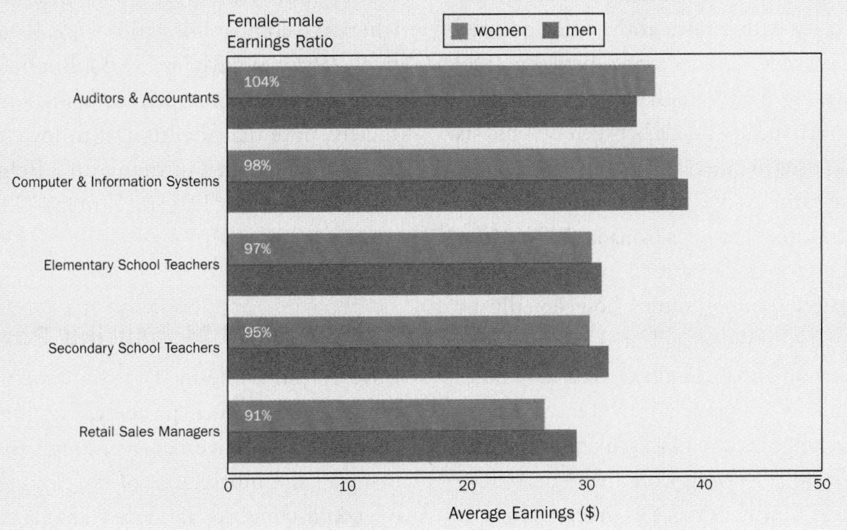

SOURCE: Compiled from statistics Canada (2006b).

alone) in Canada has changed relatively little. In 1951, the most advantaged 20 percent of households (the top quintile) received 43 percent of total Canadian income, whereas the bottom quintile (the 20 percent with the lowest incomes) received only 4 percent of all income (Statistics Canada, 1984: 6). In 2006, the distribution looked similar, at least at the bottom, where the poorest 20 percent were still taking home only 4 percent of all income (Statistics Canada, 2008b, Table 8-3).

However, a closer examination reveals that income inequality has increased—in 2006 the top quintile was receiving 47 percent of all income, up from 46 percent ten years earlier. Thus, the share of total income received by the three middle quintiles has declined, and income inequality has been slowly increasing. The three middle quintiles largely comprise working Canadians (in other words, not the unemployed or seniors) who would be most affected by a changing labour market in which some well-paying jobs have slowly been replaced by others that pay less and are less secure (Fuller and Vosko, 2008).

In addition, the lowest income quintiles have increasingly come to be filled by recent immigrants, despite the fact that most immigrants to Canada today are typically young, well educated, and well trained (see Chapter 8, Race and Ethnic Relations). As Picot and Myles (2005: 19) observe, "Low income trends among the population as a whole tend to mask an underlying divide that has opened up between the Canadian-born and immigrants to Canada." In short, over the past several decades, immigrants have come to be significantly overrepresented among Canada's working poor (Wallis and Kwok, 2008), and they are finding it increasingly difficult to catch up with equivalently well-educated Canadian-born workers. To be specific, between 1980 and 2005, the earnings (in 2005 dollars) of recent immigrants (those who arrived in Canada between two and six years before the census in question) have declined by 21 percent, while the earnings of Canadians in general have stayed roughly the same (Statistics Canada, 2008a: 40).

Although the proportion of total income received by each population quintile shows how equally or unequally income is being distributed, it tells little about the standard of living of individuals and families within each quintile. For example, if total income doubled but the percentage received by each quintile stayed the same, the bottom 20 percent with their 4 percent of total income would now have twice as much income as before (of course, the same would apply to the top quintile, who would also have twice as much). In fact, when looking back over the past six decades, you find that

average family income has increased by more than 150 percent, after taking inflation into account. In other words, the Canadian standard of living increased substantially in the decades following World War II. But most of this increase took place in the 1950s, 1960s, and 1970s. By the 1980s, inflation was typically as high as, or higher than, the income gains of Canadian families (Love and Poulin, 1991). In the 1990s, inflation declined but incomes did not increase. Unemployment rates remained high, and deficit-cutting efforts by the provincial, territorial, and federal governments led to reductions in income-support payments to both the poorly paid employed and the unemployed.

During the first decade of the twenty-first century, unemployment rates have been relatively low (at least until the recession near end of the decade), and government transfer payments have generally not been cut back further, but incomes have stagnated. In fact, a recent report by the Vanier Institute observed that, in constant dollars (in other words, taking inflation into account), average Canadian family incomes were no higher in 2005 than in 2000 and only about 1 percent higher than in 1990 (Sauvé, 2006). At the same time, average family debt had increased by 40 percent since 1990. In other words, despite Canada's strong economy in the early 2000s, Canadian families are less well off than they were 15 years ago.

Finally, how does income inequality in Canada compare with the situation in other countries? At the end of the last century, the highest earning 10 percent of Canadian families had incomes four times as high as the lowest earning 10 percent. Inequality was higher in the United Kingdom and the United States, where the comparable ratios were 4.5 and 5.4, respectively (Picot and Myles, 2005). But before we compliment ourselves too much for being a more egalitarian society, note that the highest to lowest income ratios were only 3.2 in Germany and Belgium and even lower in Sweden (3.0) and Finland (2.9).

THE POOR

Defining and Measuring Poverty

Poverty can be defined in different ways. We could talk about **absolute poverty,** arguing that the poor are those who have barely enough to stay alive, like many of the inhabitants of developing countries. Or we could concede, as most Canadians do, that **relative poverty** is really what matters. If your neighbours own their homes, drive cars, eat out at nice restaurants, put money into pension plans, and take vacations outside the country, while you rent a small apartment, ride the bus, look forward to a meal at McDonald's, have no savings, and read about foreign countries in the public library, you probably consider yourself poor. According to this definition, Canada does have a considerable number of poor people.

Most discussions of poverty in Canada rely on the **low-income cutoff** or **LICO** (commonly, though unofficially, known as the "poverty line"), estimated by Statistics Canada on the basis of data obtained from its ongoing Survey of Labour and Income Dynamics. According to this survey, the average Canadian spends about 43 percent of (pretax) income on the basic necessities (food, shelter, and clothing); to establish the LICO, Statistics Canada adds 20 percent to this figure (Statistics Canada, 2006–2007). Hence, anyone spending more than 63 percent of gross income on the basic necessities is considered a low-income earner (see Box 6.2). Obviously, some people budget better than others, so these are average cost estimates. However, there is no denying that the cost of living is higher in larger urban centres and that it takes more money to feed and clothe additional people, so different LICOs are calculated for communities of various sizes and for families of various sizes within those communities (National Council of Welfare, 2008a). For example, based on 2007 income data, Statistics Canada set the (pretax) LICO for a single person living in a city with more than half a million residents at $21 666, compared with $14 914 for a single person living in a rural area. The low-income line for a family of three in a large city was $33 159, substantially higher than that for a similar-sized family in a rural area ($22 826).

Who Are the Poor?

Rising unemployment causes the number and proportion of people living below the poverty line to increase. In 1980, for example, 16 percent of all Canadians were below the (pretax) poverty line but, with the recession of the early 1980s, that figure climbed to 18.7 percent by 1984. As the economy recovered, the proportion of poor Canadians dropped

---

| BOX 6.2 | **HOW DO WE MEASURE POVERTY?** |

Whenever a Canadian news outlet uses Statistics Canada numbers to say a certain percentage of Canadians are "below the poverty line," Statistics Canada makes it clear that its numbers say no such thing. The agency sends off letters stating that its low-income cutoff (LICO) figures are not a measure of poverty, but of income inequality. Despite this, many media companies and poverty activists use Statistics Canada's LICO as Canada's "unofficial" poverty line. The LICO counts the number of Canadians who spend 20 percent more of their gross income on food, shelter and clothing than the average Canadian. . . .

Critics of the use of the LICO as a benchmark for poverty say . . . [it] doesn't translate to a state of destitute poverty. . . . [A] feature of the LICO that causes controversy is that it's a relative measure of poverty. That is, as the economy grows and people make more money on average, the LICO moves up with it. "Using the LICO to measure the poor means poverty can never be eliminated since there will always be a range of incomes in Canada—unless we adopt a Soviet-style command economy," the *National Post* said in 2000.

Poverty activists argue that it's possible to reduce relative poverty without moving to a completely communist system. "In reality, relative poverty will not be reduced by economic growth unless there is redistribution to the poor," [Richard] Shillington wrote.

Another way to measure poverty is in absolute terms: how many people make less than what is needed to survive or lead a decent life? Human Resources and Development Canada [has developed] such a measurement, called the Market Basket Measure, based on the costs of goods and services needed for people to eat a nutritious diet, buy clothing for work and social occasions, house themselves in their community and pay for necessary expenditures, such as furniture, public transportation and entertainment. By that measure, most of the country's poverty is in Ontario and British Columbia, where the living costs are highest.

Nipissing University economics professor Christopher Sarlo developed another absolute measure of poverty for the 1992 study "Poverty in Canada." Sarlo defines poverty as lacking the means for the basic necessities of life, such as food, shelter and clothing. The first version of his Basic Needs Index put the poverty rate at just four percent. It was criticized for its frugality, though: Sarlo's weekly food budget for an elderly woman was $25. A revised version of the index was released in 2001, including such things as out-of-pocket medical expenses. That study put the poverty rate at eight percent.

SOURCE: O'Malley and Bowman (2002). Reprinted with permission from www.cbc.com.

to 14.0 percent in 1989 but then rose steeply to 20.6 percent in 1996. Eight years later, with an economic recovery in most parts of the country, the proportion of poor Canadians had again declined. Thus, in 2004, 15.5 percent of all Canadians were living below the (pretax) LICO (National Council of Welfare, 2008b). With a substantial economic downturn underway in 2009, however, we can expect to see the number and proportion of poor Canadians rise again.

Although poverty rates tend to follow unemployment rates, only a minority of Canada's poor are unemployed or out of the labour force. In 2004, for example, among low-income families whose major earners were under 65 years old, 50 percent relied solely on earnings for their livelihood. Another 14 percent combined earnings and employment insurance, while the same proportion relied on earnings and social assistance. Only 22 percent did not work at all during the year, and many of these people were seniors or individuals with disabilities that kept them from finding jobs (National Council of Welfare 2008a). In short, the **working poor,** those employed in low-wage jobs, make up a very large proportion of the poor in Canada. Hence, not only rising unemployment but also any decline in real wages will lead to an increase in the number of people below the poverty line.

Aboriginal Canadians are among the poorest citizens of our country (see Box 6.3). The most recent census data (Statistics Canada, 2008c) show unemployment rates among 25- to 54-year-old Aboriginal Canadians that are more than twice as high as among non-Aboriginals in the same age category (13 percent versus 5 percent, respectively, in 2006). Aboriginal Canadians living on reservations have the highest unemployment rates (23 percent in 2006). Consequently, the poverty rate for Aboriginal Canadians living in families (31 percent) is two and one-half times as high as for non-Aboriginal Canadian families (National Council of Welfare, 2007).

Single-parent families headed by a female are almost five times as likely as two-adult families with children to be living below the poverty line. In 2004, the poverty rates for these two groups were 47 percent and 10 percent, respectively (see Figure 6.3). The incidence of low income has not changed much since 1980 for two-adult families with children, while it has dropped somewhat for female single parents. Even so, many of the latter remain completely dependent on social assistance, since it is almost impossible for a single young mother to look after children and hold down a job.

In 2004, 38 percent of senior Canadians (65 and older) living alone had incomes below the LICO, compared with only 5 percent of senior couples. It is clear that shared incomes among seniors (or anyone else, for that matter) typically keep people above the

---

BOX 6.3   **LIVING CONDITIONS FOR FIRST NATIONS "UNACCEPTABLE"**

First Nations people in Canada live in "Third World" conditions, with a lack of access to clean water and decent housing, the national chief of the Assembly of First Nations said Tuesday [6 February 2007]. "We rank no better than a Third World country, and that is simply unacceptable. There is no good reason why our people should be as poor as they are," Phil Fontaine said in Toronto. . . .

Fontaine said problems include unsafe drinking water, crowded homes, high unemployment, high suicide rates, limited access to quality health care, and thousands of children being looked after by provincial child-welfare authorities. . . .

"When we start talking about the many crisis situations that exist in our communities, the response is usually: more money is not the answer," he said. "We all know more money is needed." Fontaine said the government has made millions available to upgrade military equipment for the

Armed Forces and to correct a perceived fiscal imbalance among some provinces. If the federal government wants to make money the answer to problems, it clearly can, he said. "The health of our people relies on clean water, clean air and healthy homes," he said.

Fontaine acknowledged, however, that First Nations people must help to find the solutions to existing problems by working with government officials and business leaders. "It is all up to us. We must do it. We must create the solutions ourselves. Our community must decide on our future. We must work together to fix the system that has produced the results that we are living today," he said. "We want to be real contributors to Canada's prosperity. We never ever wanted to be dependent on someone else. Any suggestion that we are happy with our current situation is so completely wrong."

SOURCE: Reprinted with permission from "Living conditions for First Nations 'unacceptable': Fontaine." http://www.cbc.ca/canada/north/story/ 2007/02/06/fontaine-speech.html.

FIGURE 6.3   INCIDENCE OF LOW INCOME FOR SELECTED FAMILY UNIT TYPES, CANADA, 1980, 1990, 2004

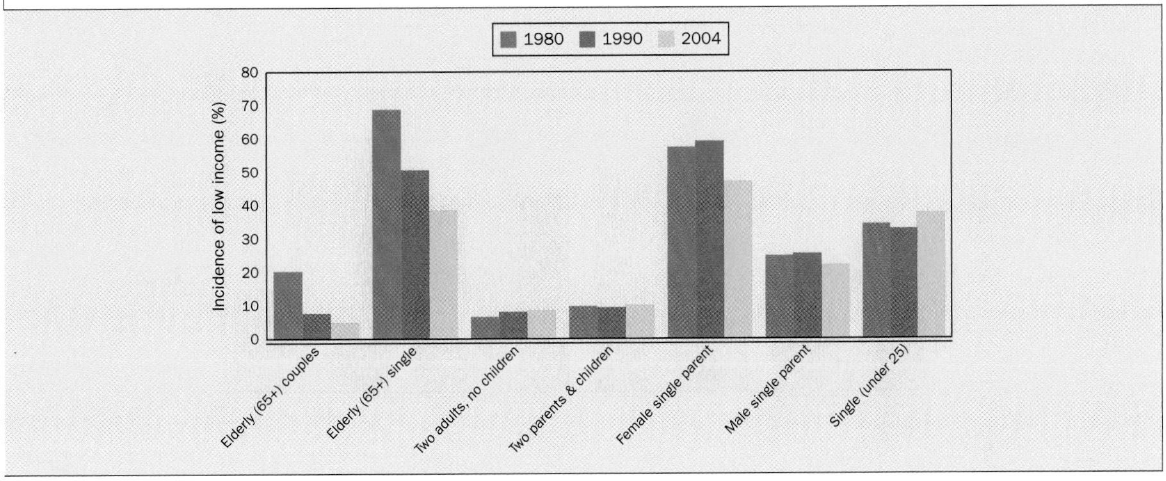

SOURCES: Compiled from National Council of Welfare (2004, 2008b).

poverty line, whereas losing a spouse and her or his income can push many seniors below the poverty line. Also, because women are less likely to be employed outside the home, and since women typically earn less than men do, older women living alone are less likely to have the pensions and savings that men in a similar position might have. Hence, in 2004, 38 percent of single older women were in the low-income category, compared with only 29 percent of single older men (National Council of Welfare, 2008b).

Figure 6.3 demonstrates that relative poverty among seniors has declined since 1980, particularly for elderly couples. Increased government transfer payments to older Canadians and an increase in the number of people retiring with pension plans and RRSPs form a large part of the explanation. In contrast, the poverty rate has not changed much for childless couples (under age 65), two-parent families with children, and non-senior (under 65) single individuals, although for the past 25 years the latter group has had a much higher poverty rate than non-seniors living as couples. In short, as labour market conditions have deteriorated and as governments have cut back on transfer payments, the working poor and the unemployed have come to make up a larger proportion of Canada's poor (Sauvé, 2006).

Although the low-income cutoff is a useful measurement tool, it can create an oversimplified picture of poverty in Canada, one that separates those who are poor and needy from those who are well off, without recognizing the large variations within each group. For example, in 2004, the depth of poverty for single women and men under age 65 who were living

below the poverty line was much greater than for single men and women over age 65 (National Council of Welfare, 2008b). Specifically, the average income for poor non-senior singles was 52 percent of the poverty line, compared with an average income of 83 percent of the poverty line for poor senior singles. Why the difference? Because many non-senior poor rely on social assistance (welfare) for at least some of their income, which, as you will see below, is far from generous in all Canadian provinces and territories. Even though government pensions paid to seniors are small, they are still considerably larger than the typical social-assistance allowances received by Canada's non-senior poor, assuming they are eligible.

Social Assistance for the Poor

A fairly common belief exists in our society that "welfare" (social assistance) and employment insurance are too easy to obtain and that the amount of money received is enough to encourage people to avoid seeking work (Swanson, 2001). Is this true? Because welfare regulations vary across provinces and territories, we will examine data from Ontario, the largest province and among the provinces with the highest welfare incomes in 2007.

Figure 6.4 shows that a single "employable" adult (i.e., an adult who did not have a disability, was not a senior, and was not considered unable to seek work because of family responsibilities) who was eligible for Ontario social assistance received $7204 in 2007, an amount only 33 percent of the poverty line and 31 percent of the median income for single adults in the province

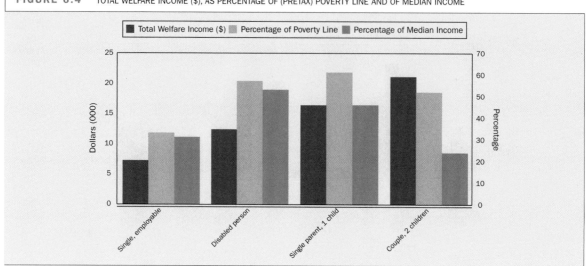

FIGURE 6.4   TOTAL WELFARE INCOME ($), AS PERCENTAGE OF (PRETAX) POVERTY LINE AND OF MEDIAN INCOME

SOURCES: Compiled from National Council of Welfare (2008d).

(National Council of Welfare, 2008a). Welfare recipients who had disabilities received a larger total annual transfer payment ($12 382), putting them at 57 percent of the LICO and at 53 percent of the median income for single adults with disabilities. Welfare rates for single parents with one child were somewhat higher ($16 439), an income level that placed them at 61 percent of the poverty line and at only 46 percent of the median income for all single parents in the province in 2007. As for couples with two children, their welfare rates were the highest ($21 058), since four or more people were being supported on this amount. But even when receiving the maximum amount of social assistance, the income of these Ontario families would only have been just over half of the amount required to get above the poverty line (52 percent), and only one-quarter (24 percent) of the median income for all couples with children in Ontario in 2007.

In short, in Ontario and across Canada, the amount of welfare assistance is very low. In fact, welfare rates have been cut, often significantly, in every province and territory over the past several decades (National Council of Welfare, 2008b). In Alberta, for example, taking inflation into account, between 1986 and 2007 welfare rates declined by 51 percent for single employable adults, by 18 percent for single parents, and by 22 percent for couples with children. In Ontario, the highest welfare rates (taking inflation into account) were recorded in 1992. By 2007 they had declined by 35 percent for single employable adults, by 25 percent for single parents, and by 28 percent for couples with

children. Consequently, it is difficult to accept the argument that overly generous welfare systems discourage people from looking for work. Many of those who receive assistance cannot work outside the home, and the money provided seldom pushes the poor who receive it anywhere even close to the poverty line.

Moving Into and Out of Poverty

Discussions of poverty can leave the impression that the poor and the non-poor are basically separate groups and that there is little mobility from one status to the other. While the proportion of Canadians living below the LICO has varied between 14 and 20 percent over the past two decades, Statistics Canada data show that, over a six-year period between 1993 and 1998, one in four Canadians (24 percent) lived in a low-income family for at least one year (Morissette and Zhang, 2001). A similar but more recent analysis shows that, even with a strong economy, this picture had not changed: Between 1996 and 2001, 25 percent of all Canadians were living below the poverty line for at least one year (Statistics Canada, 2005: 122).

The earlier study provided a more detailed multi-year analysis, showing that 8 percent of the total population experienced poverty (were in the low-income group) for four or more years out of a possible six. However, among Canadians living in lone-parent families, 38 percent had experienced poverty for at least four years between 1993 and 1998. More recent data show that, for a single year (2003–2004), about 4 percent of all Canadians slide below the poverty line while a similar proportion move above it (National Council of Welfare, 2008b). Thus, poverty is not a static status. Individuals and families do move into and out of poverty each year. Nevertheless, a sizable minority remain stuck in poverty year after year. As we noted above, losing a job, having to take a lower-paying job, becoming a single parent, or being widowed can drastically increase the chance of falling into, and remaining stuck, in poverty. In addition, welfare regulations in many provinces "claw back" social assistance benefits as soon as welfare recipients start earning even a small income (National Council of Welfare, 2008a). This predicament creates a "welfare trap" that further increases the chances of poor Canadians, particularly single-parent families, remaining poor (see Box 6.4)

MATERIAL INEQUALITY IN CANADA: SUMMING UP

Is Inequality Increasing in Canada?

Compared with some other countries, and compared with the situation in Canada a century ago, the level of material inequality in this country today is relatively low. Even so, you have seen evidence of a great deal of inequality in wealth and income. Furthermore, there are indications that, for at least several decades, the level of inequality has been slowly rising. Corporate concentration has been increasing as a small number of huge business enterprises, many of them family owned or family run, have gained control over a larger share of the assets of Canada's biggest corporations. Wealth inequality in general appears to be increasing, income inequality has risen, and the number of working poor in Canada has increased.

Looking more closely at the labour market, we see that unemployment rates have been rising slowly but steadily for several decades. Although these rates have gone up and down a number of times, and are lower now than they were a decade ago, the long-term trend since the mid-twentieth century has been upward. Hence, in 2008, the average annual unemployment rate was 6.1 percent, representing 1.12 million unemployed Canadians (Statistics Canada, 2009), a number almost equal to the populations of Saskatchewan and Prince Edward Island combined. With increasing global financial and economic uncertainty, we can expect the national unemployment rate to again rise over the next several years. Comparisons across provinces in 2008 reveal the extent of regional inequality in Canada, with unemployment rates of 13.2 percent in Newfoundland and Labrador, 8.6 percent in New Brunswick, 6.5 percent in Ontario, and only 3.6 percent in Alberta.

Part-time employment rates have also been rising over the past few decades. Forty years ago, fewer than 4 percent of employed Canadians worked part-time. In 2008, 18.4 percent had a part-time job. Since the 1980s, the number of temporary jobs has significantly increased, as employers have begun to cut long-term wage costs by offering more limited-term contract positions. By 2004, one in eight (13 percent) working Canadians had a job with a specific end date (Fuller and Vosco, 2008). Real wages are no longer increasing, and inequality in earnings has been rising as a result of these part-time and temporary employment trends as well as declines in employment in traditionally higher-paying industries and occupations (Statistics Canada, 2008b).

A More Polarized Society?

It is difficult to avoid the conclusion that, in Canada, the gap between the advantaged (those with full-time, permanent jobs) and the disadvantaged (those with

---

BOX 6.4   ONE STEP FORWARD, ONE STEP BACK: WELFARE "CLAWBACKS"

A single mother with two children aged 15 and 19 living in subsidized housing gets $13 873 annually from welfare, GST credit, and federal child benefits. The mother takes a part-time job that pays $14 000 a year and her 19-year-old enrolls in university part-time and gets a part-time job that pays $2400. Both must now take public transit. The son has a $1000 bursary. On paper, the family's income per year is $31 273. The mother's and student's earnings reduce their welfare by $8200 (half of her pay and half of his). Their earnings also cause their subsidized rent to rise by $2268 per year. Payroll taxes eat up another $815. TTC and GO Transit passes for both cost $4728 and work-related clothing another $1000. The family is now left with $14 262 ($31 273 minus $17 011) or just $389 more before taxes than they had at the start.

SOURCE: "Case Study: Why A Job Doesn't Pay." *Toronto Star* 6 December 2007: A1. Reprinted with permission from the Toronto Star.

part-time, temporary, or no jobs) is slowly increasing (Fuller and Vosko, 2008; Statistics Canada, 2008b). A similar pattern has been observed in Britain (Dorling et al., 2007) and in the United States (Cavanagh and Collins, 2008). This is not to suggest that a new era of massive inequalities is dawning. However, the evidence is clear enough that material inequalities are rising, not declining, and that society is becoming more polarized in terms of access to and control over economic resources (Picot and Myles, 2005). Using Weber's definition of class, I conclude that class differences in Canada and the United States (and in other countries, like Britain) are becoming more pronounced.

Obviously, many interrelated factors have contributed to the growth in material inequality (Krahn, Lowe, and Hughes, 2006). Although some new high-skill and well-paying jobs emerged over the past several decades in Canada, the overall outcome was still been a net reduction in employment opportunities. Globalization, the process whereby goods and services are produced by business enterprises operating in many different countries, led to a much more competitive economic environment. Business enterprises responded by shifting many of their activities to countries in which lower wages and less rigorous environmental and labour laws allowed higher profits to be made. In North America, layoffs and downsizing were a frequent response, along with the replacement of full-time permanent jobs with part-time and temporary positions. Labour unions, which traditionally resisted attempts to cut wages and jobs, lost some of their power. At the political level, an ideology emphasizing that "the market knows best," and that people need less rather than more government intervention in the economy and the labour market, led to fewer government efforts to reduce material inequalities and efforts to reduce transfer payments to the poor (National Council of Welfare, 2008a). It remains to be seen how the global financial and economic uncertainties that arose in late 2008 will affect inequality in Canada. My prediction is that the gap between the rich and the poor will increase further.

I will leave it to other authors in this text to examine associated economic, labour-market, political, and ideological trends in more detail, since this is a chapter on social stratification. Early in this chapter, I invited you to examine the evidence on changing patterns of social stratification in Canada and, while doing so, to keep in mind Clark and Lipset's (1991) question: "Are social classes dying?" Clark and Lipset answered yes, but given the evidence reviewed in this chapter, it would appear that they were wrong.

CONSEQUENCES OF MATERIAL INEQUALITY

Other chapters in this textbook will go into more detail about the many consequences of material inequality for individuals and families. You will see that position in the class structure has an effect on belief systems, behaviours, and lifestyles, and that the poor, the middle classes, and the very wealthy frequently hold different opinions on various subjects, may vote differently, and certainly enjoy different lifestyles. But, much more important, people in different positions in society's economic hierarchy experience different life-chances, to use the term introduced by Weber.

Consequences for Individuals and Families

Children from poorer families typically do not do as well as more affluent children do in school (Davies and Guppy, 2006), are more likely to be enrolled in non-university academic streams (Taylor and Krahn, 2009) and to drop out before completing high school (Tanner, Krahn, and Hartnagel, 1995), and are less likely to go on to postsecondary education (Krahn, 2004). As noted above in the discussion of occupational mobility, such effects of poverty are largely responsible for the perpetuation of class inequalities from one generation to the next.

For a variety of reasons, including better nutrition, access to better health care, and less hazardous working conditions, those who are situated higher in the economic hierarchy are typically healthier than the poor are (Raphael, 2007). On average, the poor do not live as long as those who are better off (Wilkinson, 1992). Similarly, when dealing with the criminal justice system, those with greater access to and control over economic resources tend to fare better (National Council of Welfare, 2001–2002). The poor are consequently overrepresented in jails. Aboriginal and visible minority Canadians with low incomes are particularly disadvantaged when dealing with the criminal justice system (Fitzgerald and Carrington, 2008; Wortley and Tanner, 2008). I could go on, but these examples are probably sufficient to make the point that life-chances are a function of position in the class structure and that those higher up in the economic hierarchy enjoy a better quality of life.

Consequences for Society

In addition to these substantial consequences of material inequality for individuals and families, can material inequality have other social outcomes? Specifically, given the relatively high and increasing level of inequality in Canada, can we expect more social unrest? Will conflict between the "haves" and the "have-nots" increase? Those committed to a classical Marxist theory of social change might welcome such conflict; for them, it would indicate that capitalism was finally beginning to give way to a socialist society. Others might view such conflict much more negatively. Whatever the response to such a possibility, it is clear that values and beliefs directly influence the way the people respond to evidence of inequality and its consequences.

But returning to the question, can we expect an increase in social unrest and conflict as a result of higher levels of inequality? During the early 1980s, for example, the solidarity movement in British Columbia brought together members of trade unions, social-welfare organizations, and various community-based groups in opposition to the Social Credit government's cutbacks in government programs and attempts to change labour legislation. Bryan Palmer (1986) described the protests and rallies that took place as evidence of growing class conflict. However, these events were exceptional. Much more often, the poor and the near-poor put up with their less advantaged position because they have few of the resources (e.g., money, education, organizations) that make it possible to fight for social change (Brym, 1979). In fact, in the past few years, we have seen more opposition from a better-organized middle class, in response to government cutbacks in health and education, than from the poor in response to welfare cutbacks. And we have seen intensified negative stereotyping of the poor and those on welfare, a process that Jean Swanson (2001) calls "poor-bashing."

Thus, it is by no means clear that a higher level of inequality and fewer opportunities for upward mobility will translate into greater social unrest in Canada. Nevertheless, greater inequality means greater hardship and more limited life-chances for more Canadians. Although this chapter has documented growing social inequality in Canada, other chapters in this text describe similar processes globally. The long-term consequences

for global peace and security as a result of a growing gap between rich and poor countries are difficult to predict. Even so, as Paul Krugman, the influential American economist, has noted, "The ultimate effects of growing economic disparities on our social and political health may be hard to predict, but they are unlikely to be pleasant" (Krugman, 1994: F9).

RESPONDING TO INEQUALITY

Some people believe that more equal distribution of society's resources would be preferable to the current level of inequality. They believe that existing differences in life-chances are unjust and look for ways in which social institutions, laws, and tax systems might be changed to reduce material inequality. Others, equally offended by inequality and its consequences, reject this reformist approach in favour of a more radical position, advocating the replacement of capitalist society by some kind of socialist alternative. Still others respond to evidence of extensive inequality with little ambition to change it, believing, simply, that this is "the way things are." Although perhaps bothered by its consequences, members of this group might still conclude that the existing level of inequality is inevitable and that well-intentioned efforts to reduce it will, in the long run, have little effect. They might even conclude that inequality is functional, as Davis and Moore (1945) argued more than half a century ago, and that efforts to reduce it will be counterproductive. In short, reactions to the fact of inequality, and recommendations about what, if anything, should be done about it, directly reflect personal values and political orientation.

Assuming that a lower level of inequality is a goal worth striving for, it is clear that the government has a role to play in trying to reach that goal. The Canadian state has an impact on the distribution of wealth and income through tax systems that redistribute wealth from the rich to the poor; through minimum-wage and other types of legislation; and through transfer payments, such as pensions for seniors and those with disabilities, social assistance for low-income individuals and families, and employment insurance. Even so, compared with a number of other industrialized countries, Canada spends considerably less on attempts to reduce poverty (Raphael, 2007).

Canada's "liberal" welfare policies place more faith in the power of a free market, unregulated by government legislation and policies, to produce wealth and jobs that should, it is expected, trickle down to the poor (Esping-Andersen, 1990). Unfortunately, as my review of labour-market trends indicates, there is little evidence that the free market has performed successfully in this regard. Instead, unemployment rates have risen, precarious employment has become more common, and social inequality has increased. Furthermore, during the past several decades, the political mood has changed, and concerns about reducing government deficits, streamlining government, and making Canada more competitive in the global marketplace appear to have been influencing government policy more than concerns about reducing inequality. In fact, some deficit-reducing initiatives (e.g., reductions in social-assistance payments) have led to increases in material inequality in Canada.

But other approaches to government spending do not necessarily involve this tradeoff. For example, job-creation strategies may be as useful in the long run, and tax alternatives that would raise corporate income taxes or eliminate some of the tax write-offs enjoyed by the upper and middle classes (such as tax deductions for pension plans and RRSPs) might also be appropriate.

A large part of the problem lies, of course, in the fact that any serious effort to redistribute the wealth and income from the well-off to the poor would probably be opposed by the former. If we really want to do something about material inequality in Canada, and globally, if we want a different kind of society and a different kind of world, many of us have to be willing to accept less so that others can have more.

SUMMARY

1. Persistent patterns of social inequality within a society are referred to as a structure of social stratification. Some social hierarchies within a society are based on ascribed statuses, such as gender, race, or age, which are typically assigned to an individual at birth. Other social hierarchies are based on achieved statuses, which index how well an individual has performed in some role. A society in which considerable social mobility between statuses is possible is said to have an open stratification system.

2. Social theorists have proposed a variety of different explanations of the origins and effects of social-stratification systems. In his class-based theory of social stratification, Karl Marx emphasized the exploitation of the working class by the owners of the means of production and the capacity of class conflict to generate social change. Max Weber also put considerable emphasis on the power that resides in ownership of property but argued that hierarchies of prestige and political power are influential as well.

3. The structural-functionalist theory of social stratification suggests that inequality is both inevitable and functionally necessary for a society, ensuring that the most qualified individuals are selected to fill the most important (and most rewarding) roles. Power differences are downplayed in this theory, as is conflict between different social classes. A number of more recent theories of social stratification, including those put forward by Gerhard Lenski, Frank Parkin, and Erik Olin Wright, have placed more emphasis on power and conflict. Although Wright developed a class-based theory of stratification that adapts

many of Marx's ideas to contemporary circumstances, Parkin's approach follows in the footsteps of Weber.

4. Examination of occupational shifts in Canada over the past century reveals some of the changing features of Canada's stratification system. Studies of occupational mobility show that Canada is a relatively open society. Even so, considerable evidence suggests that class-based advantages are often passed from one generation to the next.

5. A detailed analysis of material inequality in Canada reveals that ownership of wealth and property is highly concentrated and that income inequality is relatively high. By using a relative measure of poverty, we observe that about one in seven Canadians is living below the "poverty line." Considerable evidence shows that the poor and others near the bottom of the social hierarchies in our society enjoy fewer life-chances than do the well-off. For example, they are less likely to do well in school and to continue on to higher education, they are less healthy and have a shorter life expectancy, and they do not fare as well when dealing with the criminal justice system. Because of their limited access to social and material resources, the poor have seldom become an active force for social change.

6. Some theories of social stratification developed in the middle of the twentieth century suggested that material inequality was declining as the North American economy expanded. However, the period of rapid economic growth and relative affluence that characterized the middle decades

of the century appears to have ended. And, as unemployment rates rise, as part-time and temporary work becomes more common, and as

governments cut back on social-assistance programs, evidence accumulates that material inequality is also slowly increasing in Canada.

QUESTIONS TO CONSIDER

1. Does social class play a more or less significant role than do ascribed statuses (such as race and gender) in determining patterns of inequality within Canadian society?
2. How are social and material advantages passed from one generation to the next, resulting in persistent patterns of social inequality?
3. What role, if any, should governments play in addressing persistent patterns of social inequality? How successful have such attempts been in the past?

4. What does "poverty" really mean, and how should we measure it? Does Christopher Sarlo's "absolute poverty" approach (see Box 6.2 on page 143) make more sense than the "relative poverty" approach underlying Statistics Canada's low-income cutoffs?
5. As Canada becomes a more culturally diverse country, what are the implications of high levels of poverty among immigrants and Aboriginal peoples?

GLOSSARY

Absolute poverty is the state of existence of those who have so little income that they can barely stay alive.

Achieved status is a changeable status that is acquired on the basis of how well an individual performs a particular role.

Ascribed status is a status, such as age, gender, or race, that is assigned to an individual, typically at birth, not chosen by the individual.

The **bourgeoisie**, according to Marx, is one of the two main classes in the capitalist mode of production. It comprises the owners of the means of production.

A **caste system** is a closed stratification system, most common in India, with strict rules regarding the type of work that members of different castes (the strata of society into which people are born) can do.

Circulatory mobility is the occupational mobility that occurs within a society when better-qualified individuals move upward to replace those who are less qualified and who must consequently move downward.

Class is a position in an economic hierarchy occupied by individuals or families with similar access to, or control over, material resources.

Class conflict, according to Marx, is conflict between major classes within a mode of production. It eventually leads to the evolution of a new mode of production.

Class consciousness, according to Marx, is the recognition by members of a class of their shared interests in opposition to members of another class.

Class structure is the relatively permanent economic hierarchy comprising different social classes.

A **closed stratification system** is a stratification system in which little or no social mobility occurs, because most or all statuses are ascribed.

Contradictory class locations, according to Erik Olin Wright, are the locations within a class structure populated by occupational groupings with divided

loyalties (e.g., managers who supervise others and report to owners).

Exclusion, according to Frank Parkin, is the organized effort of privileged, more powerful groups to maintain their advantaged position.

Intergenerational occupational mobility refers to an individual's occupational mobility, either upward or downward, in relation to her or his parents' occupational status.

Intragenerational occupational mobility refers to an individual's occupational mobility, either upward or downward, within his or her own lifetime.

Life-chances, according to Weber, are the opportunities (or lack thereof) for a higher standard of living and a better quality of life that are available to members of a given class.

The **low-income cutoff (LICO)**, also known unofficially as the "poverty line," is an estimate of the income level below which one might be considered to be living in relative poverty. It is defined by Statistics Canada as the level of income at which more than 63 percent of income is spent on basic necessities.

The **means of production**, according to Marx, is one of the main components of a mode of production, consisting of the technology, capital investments, and raw materials used in production.

A **meritocracy** is a society in which most or all statuses are achieved on the basis of merit (how well a person performs in a given role).

The **mode of production**, according to Marx, is the overall system of economic activity within a society, comprising the means of production and the social relations of production.

Occupational status attainment refers to the process whereby an individual obtains a particular occupational status, and the factors that influence that process.

An **open stratification system** is a stratification system in which merit, rather than inheritance (or ascribed characteristics), determines social rank.

The **petite bourgeoisie,** according to Marx, is a secondary class within the capitalist mode of production, including independent owners/producers (e.g., farmers) and small-business owners.

Power is the ability to impose one's will on others.

The **proletariat**, according to Marx, is one of the two main classes in the a capitalist mode of production, comprising workers who exchange their labour for a wage.

Relative poverty is a state of existence in which individuals have significantly less income than do most others in their society, causing their lifestyle to be more restricted and their life-chances substantially curtailed.

Social closure, according to Max Weber and Frank Parkin, refers to the methods used by more powerful groups to maintain their unequal access to status and resources and to exclude others from such access.

Social mobility is the process whereby individuals, families, or other groups move up or down a status hierarchy.

Social relations of production, according to Marx, are one of the main components of a given mode of production—specifically, the relationships between the main classes involved in production.

Social stratification refers to persistent patterns of social inequality perpetuated by the way wealth, power, and prestige are distributed and passed on from one generation to the next.

Socioeconomic status refers to a person's general status within an economic hierarchy, based on income, education, and occupation.

Status is a culturally and socially defined position that a person occupies in a group.

Structural-functionalist theory is a school of thought that views social organization as analogous to a biological organism or system, in which the parts (or organs) exist because of the functions they perform in maintaining the whole. Thus, stratification exists because of vital functions it performs in maintaining social equilibrium.

Structural mobility refers to the occupational mobility in a society resulting from changes in the occupational structure (e.g., the upward mobility of many individuals resulting from the creation of more middle- and upper-level jobs in the economy).

Surplus value, according to Marx, is the value of goods in excess of the cost of production, which takes the form of profit when the product is sold.

Usurpation, according to Frank Parkin, is the effort of excluded groups within a stratification system to gain advantages and power at the expense of more powerful groups.

The **working poor** are individuals who work but whose income leaves them below a designated low-income, or poverty, line.

SUGGESTED READING

Curtis, James E., Edward Grabb, and Neil Guppy, eds. (2004). *Social Inequality in Canada: Patterns, Problems, and Policies,* 4th ed. Toronto: Pearson/Prentice Hall. A comprehensive collection of readings on the various dimensions of stratification in Canada.

McMullin, Julie. (2004). *Understanding Social Inequality: Intersections of Class, Age, Gender, Ethnicity, and Race in Canada.* Toronto: Oxford University Press. An insightful advanced undergraduate discussion of the bases of social stratification in Canada.

Raphael, Dennis. (2007). *Poverty and Policy in Canada: Implications for Health and Quality of Life.* Toronto: Canadian Scholars' Press. This book's title clearly outlines its important content.

Swanson, Jean. (2001). *Poor-Bashing: The Politics of Exclusion.* Toronto: Between the Lines. A social activist takes a critical look at how the poor and welfare recipients in Canada are stereotyped and mistreated by the media and government, and offers some useful suggestions for social change.

Wallis, Maria A., and Siu-ming Kwok, eds. (2008). *Daily Struggles: the Deepening Racialization and Feminization of Poverty in Canada.* Toronto: Canadian Scholars' Press. An inclusive collection of research papers examining the impacts of race, gender, and immigrant status on poverty and social exclusion in Canada.

WEB RESOURCES

Companion Website for This Book

http://www.newsociety6e.nelson.com
Begin by clicking on the Student Resources section of the website. Next, select the chapter you are studying from the pull-down menu. From the Student Resources page, you have easy access to InfoTrac College Edition® and other resources, such as the

Glossary, Test Yourself questions, and additional readings. The website also has many useful tips to aid you in your study of sociology.

InfoTrac College Edition Search Terms

Visit http://www.infotrac-college.com for access to more than 20 million articles from nearly 6000 sources when doing your online research.

CHAPTER SEVEN

SOURCE: © Andrew Taylor/Shutterstock

Gender Inequality: Economic and Political Aspects

Monica Boyd
UNIVERSITY OF TORONTO

In this chapter you will learn that

· A major source of inequality between women and men is the greater exclusion of women from public economic and political activity. The persistent tendency of many women to be relegated to domestic affairs leads to less income, prestige, and power.

· Although women have entered politics and the paid labour force in increasing numbers over the past century, they still tend to be chiefly responsible for meal preparation, cleaning, laundry, and child care.

· In the paid labour force, women and men still tend to be segregated in different kinds of jobs; "women's jobs" typically pay less, carry less prestige, offer less security, and bestow less authority.

· Although women make up more than half the Canadian population, only one in five members of Parliament is a woman.

· In recent years, employment equity policies and policies requiring equal pay for work of equal value have been implemented to help lessen gender inequalities, but much research and political action are still required before gender equality is achieved.

INTRODUCTION

As we look back on the twentieth century, we see enormous change in the attitudes, expectations, and behaviours of women and men. Compare the lifestyle of typical men and women born in 1925, 1950, and 1975. The pair born in 1925 would have been 25 years old in 1950. During the 1950s, they would almost certainly have married and had children. In the 1950s, most women were expected to work exclusively in the home and take complete responsibility for domestic affairs. **Social roles** are the behaviours that are expected of people occupying particular social positions. In the 1950s, women's roles were those of wives and mothers. In contrast, men were expected to have paying jobs, and their responsibilities were to meet their family's needs for food, clothing, and shelter. Their roles were those captured by the terms "provider" and "head of household."

In contrast, by the time the pair born in 1950 turned 25, the belief that women should marry and work exclusively in the home was rapidly eroding. The average age at marriage had increased, indicating that many women and men were postponing marriage. After divorce laws were revised in 1968, divorce rates rose, signalling that fewer women and men would have a single spouse for the duration of their adult lives. Other changes were blurring the line between work in the home and work in the labour force. Men were starting to become more involved in household maintenance and child rearing, and more women were joining the paid labour force.

The scenario for the pair born in 1975 and turning 25 in 2000 is different again. Most people born during the mid-1970s still see themselves as eventually having spouses or partners and raising children. Unlike the generation born in the 1920s, however, they probably also see themselves as sharing domestic responsibilities with their spouse or partner and as both holding paid jobs.

A changed world does not, however, mean an equal world. Although we often hear about the "revolution" in gender equality that has taken place in recent decades, the revolution is not finished. As I show in this chapter, gender inequality still exists: In your lifetime, you have probably seen and are likely yet to see at least some of the gender inequalities discussed here. At the same time, you are also likely to witness a variety of interventions aimed at reducing those inequalities.

I begin with a definition of gender inequality and then explore its major aspects and the three main arenas in Canadian society in which gender inequality is evident: the home, the labour force, and politics. I end with a review of the actions, policies, and laws that could reduce gender inequality in the future.

UNDERSTANDING GENDER INEQUALITY

GENDER INEQUALITY DEFINED

Social scientists usually refer to inequalities between men and women as "gender inequalities" rather than "sex inequalities." They favour *gender* because it refers to the *social* meanings associated with being a man or a woman, whereas *sex* refers to the *biological* characteristics of men and women. Gender is found in social roles, in daily interactions, and in institutions (Andersen, 2005; Martin, 2003; Wharton, 2000).

Gender Stereotypes

To better understand the gendered nature of roles, think about such words as "provider" and "caregiver." They do more than describe the expected behaviour associated with being a partner in a marriage; they also cause people to evaluate types of behaviour as "masculine" or "feminine." Once in place, these images of masculinity and femininity influence how people see themselves and how they experience the world. The observation that "it's a boy" often causes Canadian parents to decorate the child's room in bold colours, or at least in pale blue as opposed to pink.

Through parental behaviour and the media, children learn to define certain social behaviours as inherently male or female. A male child is likely to receive stuffed animals, trucks, and play toolkits, while a girl more often receives dolls, play dishes, and play makeup.
SOURCE: © Jupiter Photos, 2009.

A male child is likely to receive stuffed animals, trucks, and play toolkits rather than the dolls, play dishes, and play makeup that are likely to be given a girl. Through parental behaviour, television, movies, and print media (including schoolbooks), children learn to define certain social behaviours as inherent in being chromosomally male or female, even when such traits are largely learned. By the time children have grown into adults, they have adopted and identified with many "masculine" or "feminine" personality traits and behaviours. In turn, they are likely to treat others around them through the lenses of their own identities and understandings of masculinity and femininity. In many instances, these conceptualizations are **gender stereotypes**—that is, oversimplified beliefs about how men and women, by virtue of their physical sex, possess different personality traits and, as a result, may behave differently and experience the world in different ways.

Gender-related identities and behaviours are largely socially constructed. They are outcomes of the way we interact with others and encounter taken-for-granted rules and ways of doing things in families, schools, the legal system, politics, and the paid workplace (West and Fenstermaker, 1993).

The fact that gender is largely learned and that its content is continually renewed and altered through social interaction has three implications:

1. Gender identities and behaviours are not stable and fixed (see Chapter 4). What people take to be masculine or feminine varies from one society to the next and, within any given society, over time.

2. Gender identities—the internalized sense of being a man or a woman—and gender-specific behaviours need not be congruent with the sex assigned to individuals at birth.

3. Just like sexuality and sex, gender identities and behaviours are not polar opposites (Gagne and Tewksbury, 1998; Segal, 1998). Images of masculinity and femininity often emphasize opposites but there are in fact *degrees* of masculinity and femininity.

A fixation on the allegedly opposed characteristics of men and women is evident in such phrases as the "opposite sex" and *"vive la différence."* Psychological studies of gender stereotypes also lead us to conclude that most people think of men and women as opposites. In one famous study, psychologists asked respondents to indicate which traits, from a checklist of 122 adjectives, characterized average men and women.

They found that men were described as very aggressive, very independent, very active, very competitive, very logical, able to make decisions easily, and almost always acting as leaders. Women were described as not at all aggressive, not at all independent, very emotional, very passive, not at all competitive, very illogical, able to make decisions only with difficulty, and almost never acting as leaders (Broverman, Vogel, Broverman, Clarkson, and Rosenkranz, 1972).

These results were obtained from respondents in the late 1960s; a study today would almost certainly have some different results. But contemporary studies show that people often still view women and men as having different, and opposite, personality traits (Kite, Deaux and Haines, 2008). The persistence of stereotypical thinking about feminine and masculine characteristics as polar opposites should sensitize you to two things. First, the idea of difference is apparently a powerful one and hard to dispel even when it is contradicted by research. Second, in these polarized depictions, feminine traits are viewed as less desirable than masculine ones.

Dimensions of Inequality

Gender stereotypes shape our attitudes about girls and boys, men and women, and they are often important factors in determining the ideologies that perpetuate gender inequalities. Sociologists usually define **gender inequalities** as hierarchical asymmetries between men and women with respect to the distribution of power, material well-being, and prestige (as recognized through deference or honour). This definition does not imply that men as individuals always have greater prestige, wealth, and power than do individual women. It does imply that, *on average*, compared with women, men have more wealth, greater power, and positions that are accorded higher prestige.

Power is the capacity to impose your will on others, regardless of any resistance they might offer. It thus refers to the capacity to influence, manipulate, and control others. Power is exercised not only in the overt imposition of the will of one individual on others but also in the control or support by groups or organizations of agendas that either uphold or challenge existing conditions (Duffy, 1986). For example, professorial power over students not only reflects professors' capacity to assign grades but also the authority that the university gives them in the classroom.

Material well-being involves access to the economic resources necessary to pay for food, clothing, housing, and other possessions and advantages. Two important sources of material well-being are work-related earnings and accumulated wealth.

Prestige is the average evaluation of occupational activities and positions that are arranged in a hierarchy. It reflects the degree of respect, honour, or deference generally accorded to a person occupying a given position. Commonly, two or more differently evaluated positions are described as having higher or lower prestige. How would you rank someone who works as a physician and someone who works as a cashier at a fast-food outlet? In general, people rank the former above the latter.

The three dimensions of inequality just defined—power, material well-being, and prestige—are found in discussions of social stratification, the unequal ranking of groups in society in terms of prestige, material possessions, and power (see Chapter 6). Stratification is the result, achieved over time, of routine and frequently recurring practices and often unstated rules. Gender inequality is social stratification based on gender.

What explains gender inequalities in prestige, material well-being, and power? What form do these inequalities take? I will now examine these issues in turn.

EXPLAINING GENDER INEQUALITY

As sociology developed during the twentieth century, the earlier neglect of gender by the fathers of sociology ceased. New theories emerged that explained gender inequality and its persistence. It was mainly women who developed these theories, and they frequently included insights taken not just from sociology but also from other disciplines (Chafetz, 1999; Lengermann and Niebrugge-Brantley, 1996; Lorber, 1998). **Feminism** refers to the body of thought on the cause and nature of women's disadvantages and subordinate position in society and to efforts to minimize or eliminate that subordination. Because many different perspectives exist on the sources of gender inequality, we can discuss a variety of feminist theories.

Of the many feminist theories that exist, liberal, Marxist, and socialist feminism are three popular explanations for gender inequalities in Canada's economy and polity. Liberal feminism is rooted in the liberalism of the 1700s. It assumes that human beings are rational and will correct inequalities when they know about them. Liberalism assumes that a good society is one in which men and women enjoy equal rights and opportunities. According to liberal feminism, gender inequalities are caused and perpetuated by gender stereotyping and the division of work into "women's" and "men's" jobs. Accordingly, the two main ways to achieve gender equality are by (1) removing gender stereotyping and discrimination in education and paid work and (2) changing laws so that men and women have equal opportunities in the labour force and in politics (Lorber, 1998).

A different perspective on gender inequality derives from the writings of Karl Marx. According to Marxist feminists, women's unpaid work in the home maintains and reproduces the labour force. Capitalists benefit because they obtain refreshed workers at the beginning of each day and mothers raise children who will become future labourers. They also benefit from women's paid work because women in the paid labour force, like men, help capitalists earn profit and because they act as a "reserve army of labour" that can be hired and fired as labour demands change. Marxist feminists believe that gender equality is possible once socialism replaces capitalism.

Socialist feminists build on Marxist feminism. They agree that gender inequality is caused by the gendered division of labour and its exploitation by capitalism. However, they argue that classes constitute only one set of social relations that oppress women. The second set of social relations that performs this function is that of patriarchy, the system of male domination over women. Patriarchy predates capitalism. The forms it takes vary across time and within societies. But generally, childbearing and the sexual activities of women are the foundation of gender inequality. Moreover, because domestic and public spheres intersect, inequalities in one sphere can create disadvantages for women in the other sphere. (The "public sphere" refers to government and the world of paid work.) For socialist feminists, the steps required to decrease gender inequality include government-subsidized maternal benefits and child care, and the payment of equal wages and salaries to people who do equally valued work. Removing inequality altogether requires the eradication of male dominance as expressed in the legal system, the educational system, the family, and the economy (Chafetz, 1999; Jaggar, 1983; Lorber, 1998).

Many other feminist theories also exist. Multiracial feminism emphasizes the importance of race in understanding gender inequality. This approach modifies the socialist feminist perspective by observing that hierarchical systems of domination incorporate race. For sociologist Patricia Hill Collins

(1990), race, class, and gender combine to form a "matrix of domination." All three intersect, so the way that people experience gender inequality depends on their location within class and racially defined structures (Chafetz, 1999; Lorber, 1998; Zinn with Dill, 1997). Multiracial feminism contributes to our understanding of gender inequality in three ways. First, it highlights differences among women in terms of gender inequality. Second, it points out that women of specific races and in certain class locations are in positions of power and domination over other groups of women. Third, it emphasizes that solutions to gender inequality vary according to the location of groups of women in the matrix of domination.

EXERCISING POWER

Since the ability to control and influence others—to use power—indicates the twin processes of domination and subordination, most sociologists describe the power relations between men and women as those of male domination and female subordination.

Male influence and control over women is broadly defined. It does not, for example, refer just to the predominance of men rather than women in political positions or in the military. Instead, power pervades all social relations, routine behaviours, and commonly accepted practices. For example, denying women the right to vote clearly denied them a voice in choosing who would govern them and, equally important, denied them direct input into the formulation of laws that affect them, bestowing that right on men instead. Similarly, a workplace regulation that encouraged or compelled women to quit work upon marriage, such as the one that existed in the federal civil service until 1955, made it difficult for married women to earn income and forced many of them to depend on their husbands for money. Power is also evident in day-to-day situations, such as when a young woman becomes the object of sexual innuendo or leering by her male classmates, co-workers, or strangers. In our society, such behaviour on the part of males is often considered "normal"; it draws on conceptualizations of femininity and masculinity that define women as "sexy" or "available" and men as sexual aggressors. If she protests such attention, a woman may discover that she is the object of further derision and that no rules or formal appeal mechanisms exist to stop or penalize the offenders. In short, she cannot prevent or protest unwanted attention that arises from the social meanings attached to her biological sex.

Sexual harassment is essentially a display of power in which one person attempts to control, and often succeeds in controlling, another through sexual overtures. Although isolated cases of women harassing men have received attention from the press, in most cases of sexual harassment, it is the man who makes the sexual overtures. When the capacity or incapacity to control and influence becomes routine and patterned, we can speak of power as a *system* of dominance and exploitation.

Sexual harassment is the result of the general belief that men are superior to women and may impose their will on them. It is also the outcome of patterned ways of behaving that are based on this belief and that serve to reinforce it. For example, because of our society's higher evaluation of men (and its corresponding devaluation of women), men are more likely to be employed in positions in which they are the bosses and women are supervised by them. The harassment potential that is associated with this imbalance of power is evident in such situations as a female secretary working for a senior-level male manager or a female assembly worker supervised by a male foreman.

Gender inequalities in power also combine with racial inequalities. As a result, minority women experience the most harassment because they are both women and members of a minority group (Berdahl and Moore, 2006). For these women, the experience of harassment is doubly problematic since it includes not only sexual harassment but racial harassment as well. It also is problematic for immigrant women who, as recent arrivals, are uncertain of their rights and may have had different understandings in their home country as to what constitutes sexual harassment (Welsh, Carr, MacQuarrie, and Huntley, 2006).

SEPARATE SPHERES

Power relations are important for understanding inequality because power, prestige, and material well-being are often interrelated. For example, although the ability to control others does not necessarily depend on having a higher income or being wealthy, wealth and high income normally bestow power, just as power normally enhances the capacity to be wealthy and earn high income. In seeking to understand gender inequalities, researchers point out that, historically, women have been excluded from certain types of activities that create opportunities for acquiring power, prestige, and wealth. During the late 1800s and for much of the 1900s, the "proper place" of Canadian women was thought to be in the home, where they would be responsible for producing and raising the next generation (Ursel, 1992). They were not expected to participate in politics, to enact legislation, or to be employed. The denial of voting rights for women until the end of World War I and the existence of legislation that limited the hours and times when women could be employed limited their participation in the public sphere. The public sphere was viewed as the domain of men, who were expected to be the breadwinners and heads of households.

What have been the consequences of the separation of the public sphere for men and the private sphere for women? To answer this question, consider what is implied by work in the home. For family members, work in the home, including child care, is unpaid, and, all too frequently, the amount of skill, effort, and energy expended is not widely noticed because most housework is not done in the presence of husbands. Adding to the devaluation of work in the home is the tendency to view nurturing and caregiving activities as biologically determined traits rather than acquired skills.

Restricting women to the home reduces their access to power, prestige, and material well-being. Although a woman who works only in the home may receive part of the income of another household member, she is dependent on the person who hands over the money. Economic dependency, in turn, is likely to produce asymmetries in power between the woman and the income earner, who, after all, can withhold money for the purposes of control or influence. Similarly, if all her activities are limited to the private sphere, a woman cannot obtain direct access to power through political representation, political office, or favourable laws.

Finally, because material well-being and power are so closely connected to deference and respect, the societal evaluation of work done in the home is not high. One classic indication of the devaluation of housework is the phrase "just a housewife." Sociological research shows that many activities done in the home, such as cooking, cleaning, and babysitting, are not high in prestige (Armstrong and Armstrong, 1994: Table 16). The low regard for housework is also evident from interviews conducted with 1200 17-year-olds in Hamilton, Halifax, and rural Nova Scotia. Sociologists Dianne Looker and Victor Thiessen found that young people view

housework as women's work. They consider it tiring since it involves long hours, high pressure, and much boredom. It generates few financial rewards. It is unimportant for the community. And young men consider housework—especially if it is full-time—to be a job at the bottom of the occupational hierarchy (Looker and Thiessen, 1999).

In short, the belief that a woman's place is in the home disadvantages women relative to men in the distribution of prestige, power, and economic resources. Recognition of these disadvantages has elicited two main responses. First, some people have tried to eliminate the devaluation of domestic labour by having women's unpaid work recognized officially and having a dollar value assigned to it. In Canada, women's unpaid work was recognized officially in the 1996 census. After intense lobbying, questions on unpaid child care, unpaid home maintenance, and unpaid eldercare were included in the census (Luxton and Vosko, 1998). Assigning a dollar value to women's unpaid work was raised in feminist discussions in the 1970s and there is still interest in measuring the value of unpaid work today. One Statistics Canada economist estimated that unpaid domestic work, if done in the market for wages, would be worth about one-third of the gross national product (the total value of market-produced goods and services produced in the country over a year). He also found that women do about two-thirds of all unpaid domestic work (Jackson, 1996).

The second response to the recognition of women's disadvantages emphasizes the entry of women into the public sphere. Women's growing labour-force participation and their political activities are often viewed optimistically because many people think these developments generate more money and power for women. Liberal feminists are especially likely to hold this view. Yet the fact that women are now part of the public sphere of paid work and politics does not mean that gender equality exists. Women's **labour-force participation rate** is still lower than men's. (The labour-force participation rate is the proportion of women of working age who work full-time for money, expressed as a percentage.) Women are still less likely to become elected politicians than men. Paid work does not mean liberation from unpaid work, as you have seen. And substantial gender inequality remains in the labour force and in the political sphere. In the remainder of this chapter, I examine the movement of women into the public sphere, their continuing disproportionate involvement in unpaid work in the home, and the inequalities that still exist today in the public sphere.

SITES OF WORK

FEMALE LABOUR-FORCE PARTICIPATION

In the past, most work done by women was unpaid domestic labour. In the early days of Canadian settlement by Europeans, women processed food, wove fabric, sewed clothing, tended the sick, and produced the next generation of labourers. Women also took in boarders, did laundry, and prepared meals for others in their homes (Phillips and Phillips, 1983).

Canadian women continue to work in the home, but in the past 50 years, they have increasingly done work that is paid and usually performed outside the home. At the beginning of the twentieth century, only 14 percent of women were economically active in the paid labour force compared with 78 percent of men (Leacy, 1983). By 2008, 68 percent of women were in the paid labour force, compared with 73 percent of men (Statistics Canada, 2009).

The marital status of the female labour force participants also changed dramatically during the twentieth century. Until the 1960s, the typical female worker in the paid labour force was a never-married woman, but today married women constitute the majority. The labour-force participation rate of women with young children has also increased substantially. By 2004, almost two-thirds of women with a youngest child under the age of three were employed in the paid labour force, more than double the proportion in the mid-1970s (Statistics Canada, 2006b).

Explaining the Increase

Three factors caused these changes in the women's labour-force participation rate: changes in Canada's economy that increased the demand for workers in service jobs, decreases in the number of children born, and increases in the financial pressures on families. These factors altered attitudes toward the paid employment of women and helped remove barriers to such employment. I'll review each of them in turn.

Canada's Changing Economy In the early 1900s, most Canadian jobs were in agriculture or manufacturing. Starting in the 1920s, more and more jobs became available in firms that provided services: telephone communication, financial assistance, medical care, educational instruction, and so forth.

Women were often considered suitable employees for the newly emerging service jobs. By the early twentieth century, women—albeit mainly young and single women, in accordance with the prevailing belief that married women belonged in the home—had already supplanted men as office workers (Lowe, 1987) and teachers (Prentice, 1977). With respect to office work, this development was made possible by the introduction of the typewriter, which was thought to lower the skill requirements of secretarial work. Hiring women as teachers and secretaries was also appealing because they could be paid lower wages than men on the strength of the belief that women were economically supported by the men in their household anyway.

Fertility Decline and Labour Supply Declining fertility also facilitated women's entry into the paid labour force, since it created an imbalance between the labour demands of the expanding service economy after World War II and the available labour supply. Canada's fertility rates dropped substantially during the 1930s and early 1940s as a result of the Depression and World War II. Consequently, the supply of new workers was relatively small when the postwar Canadian economy boomed. There were too few men and young single women—the traditionally preferred source of labour—to meet the growing demands for labour in Canada's new service-based economy. In response to labour scarcity and the desire to minimize wage costs (Connelly, 1978), employers began loosening restrictions against the hiring of married women. The fact that married women were not averse to working for wages—indeed, that they were eager to do so—had been proved by the experience of their employment during World War II (Pierson, 1977). As a result, female labour-force participation rates increased rapidly in the postwar years.

Family Finances Family finances also influenced the rise in female labour-force participation. Despite the idea that a woman's proper place was in the home, women's employment had always been an important source of income for low-income families. To meet economic needs, many working-class women were employed as domestics and in factories during the late 1800s and early 1900s. After World War II, women's paid employment became an important source of family income for single-parent and two-adult families alike. Today, one in five families is headed by women who are single parents, most of whom work in the paid labour force (Statistics Canada, 2006a: Table 2.6 and

Chart 5.3). Census data show that when single-parent mothers are employed, average family income is more than 2.5 times as high as that reported by families without earnings from the mother. In husband-wife families, wives' earnings not only increase family incomes but also help to keep many families out of poverty, particularly when the husbands earn little or nothing (Statistics Canada, 1998: 15).

DOMESTIC LABOUR

"Though she may toil from sun to sun, a woman's work is never done." The exclusion of women from the public sphere was part of a more general predicament in which women were almost solely responsible for unpaid domestic production and for work associated with reproduction (bearing and rearing children). Canadian women cooked, cleaned, and took care of children, and men provided the money necessary to sustain the family. Has this structure changed with the rising labour-force participation of women?

If you think that the answer is "no," you are correct. My analysis of 2006 census data shows that women are still more likely than men to do unpaid work involving home maintenance and child care. Women also spend more hours than men do on these

activities. Both women and men are less likely to be caring for seniors than to be doing home maintenance or child care, although women are more often caregivers for seniors than men are.

Even when they are in the paid labour force, women continue to spend more time than men do on housework and child care. Figure 7.1 shows that, compared with married men, higher percentages of married women spend 15 hours or more on housework and on child care among those who have at least one child under age 15 in the household (see Chapter 10 for more on housework). Lone-parent women also spend more time on housework and child care than do lone-parent men.

Not surprisingly, women report spending less time than men do watching television, pursuing hobbies, and playing sports and games (Devereaux, 1993). Also, women are more likely than men are to report feeling stressed because of lack of time. This is especially true for women who are working full-time and who have young children (Statistics Canada, 1999: 2).

Women normally shoulder the burden of dual responsibility—for child care as well as for wage earning. Women also spend more time than their male counterparts on housework and child care.
SOURCE: © iStockphoto.com/Fertnig Photography.

FIGURE 7.1 PERCENTAGE SPENDING 15 HOURS OR MORE A WEEK ON UNPAID HOUSEWORK AND ON CHILD CARE, WOMEN AND MEN IN THE LABOUR FORCE WITH AT LEAST ONE CHILD UNDER AGE 15 IN THE HOUSEHOLD, CANADA, 2006

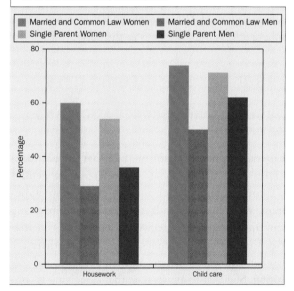

Source: Adapted from Statistics Canada, n.d., "Unpaid Work (20), Sex (3), Age Groups (9), Labour Force Activity (5), Census Family Status (6) and Presence and Age of Youngest Child (6) for the Population 15 Years and Over Living in Private Households of Canada, Provinces, Territories, Census Metropolitan Areas and Census Agglomerations, 2001 to 2006 Censuses - 20% Sample Data," *Labour, 2006 Census*. Catalogue no. 97-559-X2006007. On the World Wide Web at www12.statcan.ca/english/census06/data/topics/ListProducts.cfm?Temporal=2006&APATH=3&THEME=74&FREE=0&SUB=741&GRP=1 (8 February 2009).

The greater amount of time spent by women on unpaid work illustrates the phrase "the double day." Entering the labour force may mean fewer hours spent on work in the home, but it increases the hours of total work, paid and unpaid, performed by women. In fact, the demands on women to provide unpaid care likely will increase, because the number of senior Canadians in need of care will increase substantially. Past caregiving patterns suggest future providers of care are most likely to be women (Frederick and Fast, 1999).

In addition to increasing hours of unpaid work, caregiving responsibilities alter the way women and men lead their lives. Consider Grace, who is in her early 50s, has teenage children, and also has an 80-year-old ailing parent living nearby. She represents what is called the "sandwich" generation—individuals caught between the demands of caring for children and older relatives. As she cares for her children and parent, Grace is likely to cut back on her social activities, move closer to her parent, report that her own health is affected, and experience altered sleep patterns. The strongest impact, however, is on paid work. Grace is likely to find that caregiving activities cause her to arrive late at work, leave work early, or miss work occasionally (Cranswick, 1997; Williams, 2004). Clearly, the domestic sphere and the public spheres intersect. What people do (or don't do) in one sphere affects their activities in the other.

LABOUR-FORCE INEQUALITIES

OCCUPATIONAL SEGREGATION AND SEX TYPING

Liberal feminists explain the fact that unpaid caregivers tend to be women by referring to gender stereotypes and gender roles. Gender stereotypes imply women are generally thought to be more caring and therefore better caregivers. Gender roles emphasize that "good" daughters, wives, and mothers are women who care for their parents, partners, and offspring. Socialist feminists note that caregiving is consistent with other activities that maintain male wage workers and benefit men.

The equation of women and caregiving is also found in paid work. Although more and more Canadian women are now paid workers, they are frequently in jobs that involve caregiving, nurturing, and the sort of management functions typically found in the home. Women tend to be secretaries (the "office wife"), nurses, social workers, teachers, seamstresses, and wait staff. In contrast, men tend to be managers, doctors, professors, and factory and construction workers. This concentration of men in some occupations and women in others is often called the **sex segregation of occupations,** and the notion that a given occupation is appropriate for one sex versus the other is referred to as the **sex typing (or sex labelling) of occupations.**

Occupational Segregation

Men and women can be compared across occupations in a given place (a firm, a city, or a country). If men and women are concentrated in different occupations, the occupational structure is considered sex segregated. Figures 7.2 and 7.3 show that, according to the 2006 census, sex segregation does exist in Canada. For women, the 10 most frequent jobs include secretary, registered nurse, elementary schoolteacher, babysitter, and receptionist. For men, the 10 most frequent jobs include truck driver, janitor, retail trade manager, farmer, carpenter, and so on. The only occupation that both men and women occupy in large numbers is retail salesperson.

The figures show only the top 10 occupations. The census collects information on more than 500 different occupational titles. These longer lists confirm that women and men often are concentrated in different occupations. The degree of occupational segregation by gender has, however, declined somewhat since the 1960s. This decline is attributable mainly to the movement of women into previously male-dominated occupations rather than that of men into female-dominated occupations.

Sex labelling of occupations usually accompanies occupational segregation. Certain occupations are seen as jobs that are more appropriate for women. Other occupations are seen as jobs that are more appropriate for men. Often these views are so ingrained in our thinking that we recognize sex typing only when unstated expectations are contradicted. Consider the terms *woman doctor* and *male babysitter.* We frequently use these terms to indicate a departure from the implied norm—that men are physicians and women are babysitters. We rarely say "female babysitter" Or "male doctor." Or consider the list of the 10 most frequent occupations for men and women. What gender comes to mind for secretary, nurse, or receptionist or for truck driver, farmer, or carpenter? These occupations are strongly sex-typed both in imagery and in reality.

FIGURE 7.2   TEN MOST COMMON JOBS FOR WOMEN, CANADA, 2006

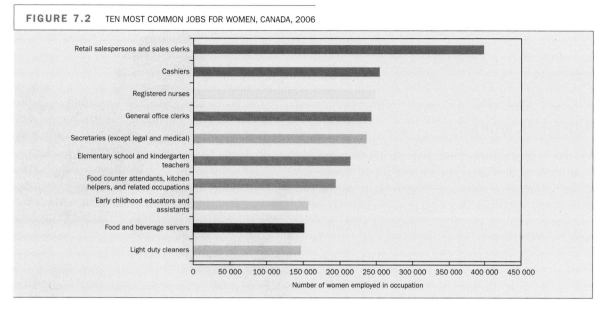

SOURCE: Adapted from Statistics Canada, 2008, "Canada's Changing Labour Force, 2006 Census." Catalogue no. 97-559-XWE2006001.

The fact that women now compose about 47 percent of the labour force is a yardstick by which occupations are female sex-typed or male sex-typed. In such occupations as actor, cook, dispatcher and radio operator, journalist, optometrist, financial and investment analyst, and veterinarian, 45 percent to 50 percent of workers are women. These occupations are not sex-typed (Statistics Canada, 2006c).

Why Care?

Why should you be concerned about sex typing and sex segregation? Because the occupations in which women are concentrated are often lower than those held predominantly by men in terms of authority, responsibility, skill requirements, mobility opportunities, and earnings. I will discuss many of these inequalities later. The important point for now is that

FIGURE 7.3   TEN MOST COMMON JOBS FOR MEN, CANADA, 2006

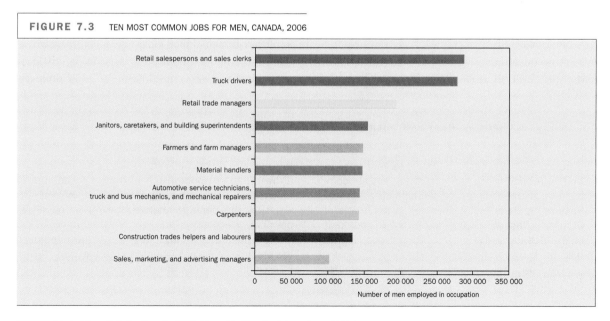

SOURCE: Adapted from Statistics Canada, 2008, "Canada's Changing Labour Force, 2006 Census." Catalogue no. 97-559-XWE2006001.

these inequalities indicate male advantages in the labour force. Furthermore, the nature of sex typing in our society implies that the work traditionally performed by women in the home has created sex stereotypes about the work that women should do in the paid labour force.

POWER AT WORK

You have seen that substantial occupational segregation exists, but to document gender asymmetry in the ability to influence and control others you need to know whether men are indeed able to make more decisions and exercise authority over women. In analyzing the 1994 Statistics Canada General Social Survey, my colleagues and I found that men were more likely than women to describe their jobs as managerial or as supervising others. Specifically, 25 percent of women and 40 percent of men described themselves as supervisors. Male supervisors managed more employees than did female supervisors. Male managers were more likely than female managers to hold top positions and plan the activities of all parts of the business (Boyd, Hughes, and Miller, 1997). This pattern illustrates the **glass ceiling** effect: Women face invisible barriers that prevent them from penetrating the highest levels of organizations where power is concentrated and exercised (see Box 7.1). Finally, men often supervise women; when women supervise, they usually exercise authority over other women. Only rarely do men have a female superior (Boyd, Mulvihill, and Myles, 1991: 424).

GENDER AND SKILL

Jobs typically held by women have lower skill requirements than do jobs typically held by men (Boyd, 1990; Myles and Fawcett, 1990). Since higher-skilled jobs

When women supervise, they usually exercise authority over other women; only rarely do men have a female superior.
SOURCE: © Monkey Business Images/Shutterstock.

usually pay more and offer more security, employment in lower-skilled jobs implies economic and quality-of-work inequalities between men and women.

Why are women less likely than men to be employed in high-skilled jobs? One possible answer is that gender bias exists in the definition of **skill**. Sex typing and a general devaluation of work done by

---

BOX 7.1	A CRACK IN THE GLASS CEILING?

"There was a 24 per cent increase last year in women occupying the top jobs at the biggest companies in the country," declares the Annual Rosenzweig Report on Women at the Top Levels of Corporate Canada. "Women now hold 7.2 per cent of the positions and men 92.8; last year it was 5.8 per cent and 94.2 respectively."

The bad news though "is that the number remains inexcusably low and corporate Canada's 'old boys' network' continues to disregard such a diverse talent pool in the workforce for leadership roles." And alas, tough economic times will slow the pace of change, the report glumly predicts.

On the other hand, it says, "We are hopeful the election of Barack Obama to the top job in the free world will boost diversity in North American boardrooms."

SOURCE: "Business," *Toronto Star,* 1 February 2009. On the World Wide Web at http://www.thestar.com/News/Ideas/article/580457 (16 July 2009). Reprinted with permission from the *Toronto Star.*

women influence commonsense evaluations of what is or is not "skilled" work. For example, nursing occupations may require high levels of interpersonal skill in dealing with relatives of dying patients but because the ability to handle distraught people is considered "natural" in a woman, it is not recognized as a professional skill in a nursing occupation. In contrast, plumbing jobs, usually performed by men, require knowledge of toilets and sinks, soldering, and pipe fitting—so-called technical skills. Bias in the evaluation of skills occurs when such technical knowledge is considered more valuable than knowledge about personal interactions and caregiving.

This example indicates that our definitions of skill are socially constructed. What we define as skill reflects other social evaluations and hierarchies—in this case, hierarchies based on gender (Gaskell, 1986; Steinberg, 1990). If people think of women as being worth less than men, they are inclined to let their attitude influence how they define the skill requirements of jobs held primarily by women or primarily by men. Jane Gaskell (1986) suggests that women are disadvantaged in the skill definitions assigned to jobs sex-typed as female because, historically, women have not been represented by strong unions that have lobbied in their interest. Furthermore, women are less likely to

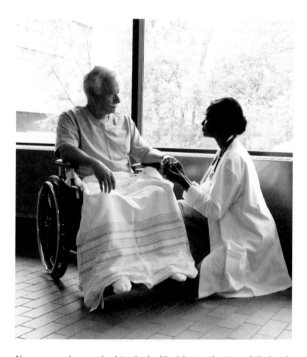

Nurses may be required to deal with dying patients and their relatives, but because the ability to handle distraught people is considered "natural" in a woman, this high level of interpersonal skill is not recognized as a professional skill in a nursing occupation. SOURCE: © Jupiter Photos, 2009.

be trained on the shop floor as apprentices. Instead, the training required for "female" jobs is often incorporated into high-school curricula, with the result that the skill-training component is less visible than it is in occupations in which training is provided on the job.

Skill undervaluation of female sex-typed occupations is a concern for two reasons. First, wage levels are associated with skill requirements. Thus, if the skill requirements of jobs in which women predominate are undervalued, the pay rates in those jobs are likely to be lower. Second, current pay equity policies often ask whether men and women are receiving equal pay for performing jobs of comparable worth. The "worth" of a job, however, includes its skill requirements. If the skill requirements of jobs employing predominantly women are already devalued, then fair comparisons between appropriate sets of jobs may not be made (Gaskell, 1991; Steinberg, 1990).

NONSTANDARD WORK

Another example of gender inequality may be seen in **standard** and **nonstandard work.** If asked to describe a typical job in the labour market, you would probably mention full-time, full-year employment with job-related benefits. This is usually what we mean by standard work. In contrast, nonstandard work includes **part-time work,** part-year employment, limited-term contract employment, employment through temporary-help agencies, self-employment, and multiple job-holding (Economic Council of Canada, 1991: 71; Krahn, 1995). Nonstandard work, also called precarious employment, is more common for women than for men (Cooke-Reynolds and Zukewich, 2004; Cranford, Vosko, and Zukewich, 2004).

Women and Part-Time Work

Compared with men at every age, women in the labour force are much more likely to be part-time workers—nearly two and a half times as likely as men in 2006 (Statistics Canada, 2007). This is significant because part-time work has been increasing as a share of all employment. Many workers now take part-time employment because they cannot find full-time employment; many women also take part-time employment so they can take care of their children.

Women and Nonstandard Work

Since 1980, women have made up around 70 percent of the part-time labour force. Part-time work can thus be seen as an employment ghetto for women. Women are also overrepresented in nonstandard work defined more broadly. Using a definition of nonstandard employment that includes self-employment, temporary work, part-time work, part-year work, and multiple job-holding, a 1994 Canadian study found that 40 percent of all currently employed women, compared with 27 percent of men, were working in nonstandard employment (Krahn, 1995). These levels of nonstandard work remained stable through the 1990s and early 2000s (Vosko, Zukewich, and Cranford, 2003: Chart A).

Concerns about Nonstandard Work

Employment in nonstandard work is of concern for two reasons. First, it is becoming more common, especially among young people. Second, compared with full-year, full-time jobs, nonstandard jobs generally provide less job security, lower pay, and fewer fringe benefits, such as pension plans (Duffy and Pupo, 1992; Fuller and Vosko, 2008). Thus, nonstandard employment in general and part-time work in particular imply a marginal work force—marginal in terms of earnings, benefits, and job security.

EARNINGS

In addition to gender inequalities in occupations, power, skill, and type of work, women in Canada earn less than men on average—less than 75 cents for every dollar earned by men in 2006. As we can see from Figure 7.4, this ratio represents gradual improvement from earlier times.

EXPLANATIONS OF WOMEN'S LOWER PAY

Observers have explained the pay gap between women and men by focusing on four factors:

1. Gender differences in the characteristics that influence pay rates
2. Gender differences in the type of work performed
3. Discrimination
4. Societal devaluation of women's work

Explanations that focus on gender differences in the characteristics that influence pay rates usually assume that earnings reflect the productivity of workers and that productivity is increased by more education, labour-force experience, and length of time on the job. Advocates of this explanation argue that the lower wages of women are caused by lower productivity resulting from women's lower educational achievements and labour-force interruptions because of women's family responsibilities.

Explanations that focus on gender differences in the type of work performed assume that the gender

---

FIGURE 7.4   RATIO OF WOMEN'S TO MEN'S EARNINGS, CANADA, 1976–2006

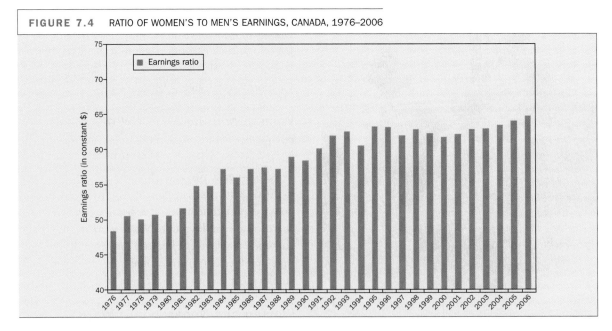

SOURCE: Statistics Canada, 2008, "Average Female and Male Earnings, and Female-to-Male Earnings Ratio, by Work Activity, 2006 Constant Dollars, Canada, Provinces and select CMAs," 2006 Census of Population, Table 2020102. On the World Wide Web at http://www.statcan.gc.ca/pub/13f0022x/2006000/5213044-eng.htm (8 February 2009).

gap in pay reflects the concentration of women in certain occupations and industries characterized by low wages, including nonstandard (particularly part-time) work.

Explanations that focus on discrimination argue that women are paid less than men because of their gender. Such discrimination can be personal and deliberate, but it is often impersonal, produced by standard, unquestioned practices, such as assigning women to certain jobs and men to other jobs, and paying men and women different wages even when they hold the same job. Much of this impersonal discrimination is called **statistical discrimination,** the process whereby employers make decisions about whether to hire and how much to pay any given woman on the basis of the employers' perceptions of the average characteristics of *all* women. For example, if an employer believes that women typically leave the labour force for long periods to raise children, or will not travel extensively or work overtime because of family responsibilities, the employer may impose those generalized beliefs on particular women. Thus, a single woman with no children might find herself being paid less than a man because of the employer's belief that women in general are less productive than men are. Alternatively, she might find herself denied opportunities for job training or advancement because of her employer's belief that women in general will leave their jobs to have families or will not perform certain tasks, such as long-distance travelling, because of family obligations.

Finally, explanations of the gender earnings gap that focus on the societal devaluation of women's work hold that the lower earnings of women reflect a general devaluation of "women's work"—that is, of tasks initially performed in the home—and the incorporation of that devaluation into pay practices. As we have seen, the work women perform in the home can be invisible and often is not viewed as work. Accordingly, people who do domestic work for money receive low wages. The devaluation of women's labour is rooted in the historical image of every woman having a male breadwinner to provide for her and not "needing" to be paid the same wage as a man who, after all, has a family to support! Once in place, pay practices persist and fuel a faulty logic that not only sustains pay differences between men and women in the same jobs but also provides a rationale for the lower wage rates paid in sex-typed occupations and jobs. Wages in occupations fall as the percentage of women in those occupations rises (England, 1993: ch. 3).

Assessing the Explanations

Most sociologists emphasize discrimination and the devaluation of work performed by women (explanations 3 and 4) as the main reasons for gender inequality in earnings. They point to the absence of proof that women are less productive than men or that they expend less effort (England, 1993: 27). They also observe that earnings gaps persist even when women and men have comparable levels of education, are in full-time, full-year jobs, and are in the same occupations (Best, 1995; see Box 7.2, p. 168).

BIRTHPLACE AND COLOUR MATTER

So far, my discussion of gender inequality in work has proceeded as if all women were alike and all men were alike. This is of course not the case. Some women and men are young and others are older. Some are married or living with a partner; others are not. Some women are born in Canada; others are born elsewhere. In addition, women differ in their colour and ancestral origins, as do men.

The intersection of gender inequality with inequalities stemming from birthplace and colour is of interest to many Canadians. That interest is fuelled by the changing ethnic and colour composition of Canada's population, initiated by changes in Canada's immigration policies starting in 1962. It has become evident since then that foreign-born women and women of colour experience not only gender inequality but also the inequalities that arise in a society that allocates privileges to certain groups and not to others on the basis of colour, ethnicity, birthplace, and class.

In popular and official usage, members of a **visible minority** are Canadian residents who are not of white European or U.S. origin and who may consequently experience discrimination. However, the term is an umbrella label for diverse groups.

Government statistics lead us to four conclusions about the earnings of women who are members of visible minorities:

1. Women who are members of Aboriginal or visible-minority groups are more likely than white women to be employed in low-skill occupations. Such occupations include cleaning hotel rooms and offices and working in manufacturing jobs in food-processing plants and the textile industry. Many workers in Canada's garment firms are immigrant women of colour, and their jobs are often characterized by irregular employment,

Is the paycheque in your purse missing a few zeros? You're not imagining it.

Young women in the workforce still earn less than their male counterparts—about 18 per cent less as of 2001—despite women's advances in education over the past 20 years.

A new Statistics Canada study found women aged 25 to 29 earned on average less than $30,000 in 2001, compared to men in the same age and education bracket who earned $36,500.

The study was titled *Has Higher Education Among Young Women Substantially Reduced the Gender Gap in Employment and Earnings?*

The answer to that question appears to be an emphatic no. Women's level of higher education has risen dramatically. . . . [but] the overall earnings gap only declined moderately over the 1990s despite rapidly rising educational attainment among young women.

What is to blame for the disparity? It may not be outright gender discrimination between employees in the same job, but rather "occupational segregation" that poorly compensates those in female-dominated fields.

"Men are more likely to take math, engineering, computer science, physical science," said Marc Frenette, a Statistics Canada research economist and co-author of the report. "Those disciplines are highly related to the high-tech sector," which boomed in the late 1990s.

"For women, we know they are more likely to take education, health, social sciences, arts, humanities," he said. "Those disciplines are more related to the public sector [that saw clawbacks and wage freezes in the 1990s]. Those events appear to have counterbalanced the fact we are seeing more women in university." Some of the wage difference couldn't be explained by measurable data, he added.

Simon Fraser University economist Marjorie Griffin Cohen agreed structural bias in the workforce accounts for some of the wage inequality. "It has to do with undervaluing the kind of work that women do, which is largely carework . . . whether it's in health or education," said Cohen, who specializes in labour-force issues.

In future, developments in those same traditional fields could help even out the gender wage gap, said Frenette, noting that public-sector unions have won wage settlements while the tech sector faltered. And women now make up 58 per cent of undergraduate students.

Preliminary studies have found weekly earnings for young men fell flat between 2000 and 2005 while young women's earnings increased by 4.5 per cent, Frenette added.

"It seems like the gender-pay gap [in the 2000s] is actually declining," he said.

Source: Elaine O'Connor, *The Province* (Vancouver, BC), 13 June 2007: A.35. Reprinted with permission from the Province.

deadlines, bad lighting, poor ventilation, and low pay (Das Gupta, 1996; Yanz, Ladd, Atlin, and Maquila Solidarity Network, 1999).

2. Foreign-born women who are permanent residents of Canada and who are members of visible minorities earn less on average than their Canadian-born counterparts. My research shows that the earnings gap increases between Canadian-born and foreign-born women when foreign-born women of colour have no knowledge of English or French (Boyd, 1999).

3. Overall, women who are members of Aboriginal or visible-minority groups earn less per week than women who are not members of visible-minority groups. My research and that of others show that earnings differentials persist between women who are and women who are not members of visible-minority groups, even when we account for the fact that differences between groups can exist with respect to age, education, and other factors that influence the levels of earnings (Pendakur and Pendakur, 1998). This means we cannot rule out discrimination as a factor and that at least part of the lower earnings of women who are members of visible-minority groups and Aboriginal women may be caused by employers not hiring these women for certain jobs, promoting them slowly, or paying them less.

4. Considerable diversity exists among women in their labour-force characteristics. Thus, we should not think of women as a homogeneous group.

These findings reaffirm the criticisms voiced by women who are members of minority groups and by foreign-born women—namely, that, for them, inequality issues are not restricted to gender but also include race and immigrant status, and that each group is unique in the kinds of disadvantages and subordinations it experiences. These criticisms are consistent with multiracial feminism.

WOMEN'S GROUPS: ORGANIZING FOR CHANGE

So far, I have discussed the increasing movement of women out of the home and into the labour force. The economy, however, is only one of several arenas in the public sphere from which women have historically been excluded and in which their participation remains very limited. Politics is another important arena that initially excluded women and that women have now begun to penetrate. The political arena includes more than voting or running for political office. It can be broadly defined to include any activity that mobilizes people to make their views known, to press for change, and to achieve objectives.

Collective actions aimed at such change are called **social movements.** The **women's movement** is a social movement that takes action to improve the status of women. Feminism is an important part of the women's movement. However, as I observed earlier, many different forms of feminism exist, each with a different understanding of the causes of gender inequality and subordination and of the actions required to improve the situation.

Over time, changes have occurred in feminist thought and in the nature of the women's movement. Both before and immediately after women were granted the right to vote, early efforts focused on improving the quality of life in the home for women and their families (Brodie, 1996). The large-scale entry of women into the paid labour force during the 1960s and 1970s elicited a different set of concerns. Based on a model of equal rights between women and men, women pressed for gender equality in employment opportunities and earnings.

Beginning in the 1960s, advocacy groups, some closely affiliated with the federal government, such as the Advisory Council for the Status of Women, and others receiving substantial government funding, presented agendas for change to parliamentarians, ministers, and key civil servants in government departments. Such direct interaction with the formal agencies and members of the state achieved some successes, depending on the party in power and how robust the economy was. For example, through the lobbying efforts of various groups, women's rights are now enshrined in the 1982 Canadian Charter of Rights and Freedoms, and legislative changes ensure

a fairer division of assets in divorce cases. However, the efforts of women's groups have been limited by at least three factors (Burt, 1993). First, because many women's groups rely on governments for funding, their roles as critics of government policy can be easily compromised. They may change their agendas or adopt a conciliatory style. The consensus-building approach found in many women's organizations constitutes a second constraint on their effectiveness. This decision-making style can be time-consuming and it can place groups at a disadvantage given that political interventions often require quick reactions. The heterogeneity of women's groups is a third factor limiting their impact. There are many different women's groups, and not all of them agree on what should be done for women. For example, diverse opinions exist among women's associations on childcare issues and on access to abortion; it is often impossible to create a coalition to lobby for one clear policy.

Women's groups still lobby governments for change, but from the 1980s on three factors changed the interaction between women's groups and governments: the electoral success of more conservative parties; the federal government's calls for economic restraint and increased provincial/territorial and private-sector responsibility; and the dissatisfaction within women's advocacy groups on agendas reflecting the concerns of white, largely middle-class women (Tremblay and Andrew, 1998). By the mid-1990s, political representatives and departments of federal and provincial governments (which in the case of Quebec and Ontario had also taken leadership on certain issues, such as pay equity) were no longer as responsive to lobby efforts by women's groups. They reduced funding. In 1995 the federal government reorganized their units dealing with women's issues and disbanded the Canadian Advisory Council on the Status of Women, which had been mandated to inform the public and the Canadian federal government on issues of concern to women. In 2006 the federal government reduced the annual budget of the federal department of the Status of Women Canada, removed the word "equality" from the mandate of the Status of Women Canada, and closed 12 of the organization's 16 offices. Alongside these changes, a different model of advocacy emerged in which women's groups operated in coalition with other social-movement-based groups, often rejecting networking and direct contact with political parties (Erickson, 1998; Young, 1998).

Recently, associations that represent the interests of women of colour, immigrant women, and lesbians have added much to the landscape of women's associations in Canada. The attention they have directed to issues of racism, sexual identity, and class inequality has forced mainstream groups representing primarily white, heterosexual, and often middle-class women to become more inclusive in their membership base and their agendas. Women of colour have argued that these groups fail to acknowledge concerns other than those of white middle-class women. The mainstream argument that gender subordination reflects the restriction of women to the private sphere fails to recognize that many women of colour have long engaged in paid work and that issues of racism in employment are of equal importance for them. Furthermore, to the extent that women of colour work as domestics, it is white women who have power over them as their employers; women of colour tend to see both gender oppression and racial oppression as important issues. Immigrant women have their own concerns, including language training, job-skill training, culturally sensitive child care, and culturally sensitive assistance in situations of domestic violence. For lesbians, areas of interest include gay rights and related issues, such as the inclusion of sexual orientation in human rights codes and the prohibition of employment discrimination on the basis of sexual orientation.

GENDER IN POLITICS

> The voice of government, as the [1971] Royal Commission on the Status of Women observed . . ., is still a man's voice. Women remain governed rather than governors, legislated rather than legislators. (Brodie, 1991: 9)

Formal politics is an important area of gender inequality because that is where laws determining rights and entitlements are formulated and public policies set. Politics and political representation are the mechanisms that translate the interests of groups into political demands and actions (Brodie, 1991: 9). If some groups are politically disenfranchised or face barriers to the representation of their interests, their needs may not be met and the premise that democratic governments represent all the people is falsified. For the first 50 years after Confederation, the notion that the private sphere was the appropriate place for women went hand in hand with the exclusion of women from politics. During the twentieth century, however, women moved into the political arena. They obtained and exercised the right to vote. They participated in political parties and were elected to political office. And they created associations to represent the interests of women, including access to abortion and child care; equality in the labour force and pensions; the prevention of family violence (including spousal violence and child abuse), prostitution, and rape; and participation in politics.

VOTING RIGHTS

Before 1915, Canadian women did not have the right to vote. Without that right, they could not elect candidates to represent their interests in government. Between 1916 and 1925, however, all provinces and territories except Quebec and the Northwest Territories enfranchised women. Quebec granted women the vote in 1940, and the Northwest Territories did in 1951. The federal government granted voting rights in 1917 to women who were British subjects and who had served with the military or had a close relative in the military. It extended those rights to women not connected to the military in 1918. But voting rights were not given to women or men of Chinese, East Indian, or Japanese ancestry until the late 1940s, to male and female Inuit until 1950, or to registered Indians living on reserves until 1960 (Maille, 1990: 1).

The suffrage movement in English Canada was a factor in winning the vote for women (Bashevkin, 1993: ch. 1). However, the vote was granted on the premise that women would use it only to improve the quality of home life and that enfranchisement would not divert women from their "natural and sacred" duties in the domestic sphere (Burt, 1993: 216).

Such sex stereotyping of women also led to the expectation that women would not be interested in politics. Men believed that women would not vote at the same rate as men. Men also believed that women would vote in a politically naive and parochial way as a result of being isolated at home. These stereotypes proved false. In Canada today, the percentage of eligible voters who cast a ballot is about the same for women and men. The political agendas of men and women differ but not because women's views are parochial. Research shows that women are more likely than men to oppose free markets and military spending and to be more concerned with social-welfare policies (Bashevkin, 1993: ch. 2). Gender differences in voting interests may be due to the fact that women and men operate in different political cultures (which have been moulded by gender differences in political socialization) and have different opportunities to participate in politics. Again and again, women hear that "politics is a man's world." Excluded from political life, women are more likely to be concerned with moral and community-based political issues than with issues pertaining to the acquisition and exercise of power (McCormack, 1975: 25–26). However, women do not act as a cohesive voting bloc on any issue (Brodie, 1991).

PARTICIPATING IN THE WORLD OF POLITICS

In the mid-1970s, women composed fewer than 4 percent of Canada's members of Parliament (MPs). After the October 2008 federal election, 22 percent of MPs were women, as were 33 percent of senators (Table 7.1). However, enthusiasm over such progress should be tempered by the recognition that women represent more than half of Canada's electorate. Table 7.1 shows variations by party in the percentages of federal MPs who are women, with the highest percentages in the New Democratic Party (NDP) and Bloc Québécois. These differences reflect such factors as the recruiting strategies of parties and barriers to women in politics, both of which are discussed later in this chapter. Other variations exist. My analysis of women who were sitting in the House of Commons in late 2002 shows that 9 of the 63 women were foreign-born, which is below the percentage in the female Canadian population as a whole. Also, visible

TABLE 7.1 NUMBERS AND PERCENTAGES OF FEDERAL POLITICAL REPRESENTATIVES WHO ARE WOMEN, CANADA, FEBRUARY 2008

	TOTAL	WOMEN	PERCENTAGE WOMEN
House of Commons			
Progressive Conservative	143	23	16
Liberal	77	19	25
Bloc Québécois	49	15	31
NDP	37	12	32
Independent	2	0	0
Total	308	69	22
Senate			
Liberal Party	59	21	36
Conservative Party	38	11	29
Progressive Conservative	3	1	33
Independent	4	1	25
Non-aligned	1	1	100
Total	105	35	33

SOURCE: Compiled from Parliament of Canada (2008).

minorities in general, and visible-minority women in particular, are underrepresented in politics (Black, 2000; Ship, 1998; Trimble and Arscott, 2003).

When elected, women are seldom found in the upper ranks of political parties (but see Box 7.3). Kim Campbell served briefly as prime minister of

---

BOX 7.3	PM PUTS FEMININE FACE ON CABINET

The federal cabinet got a more feminine touch after a higher proportion of women than ever before joined the upper ranks of government yesterday. The shuffle put 11 women into the 38-member cabinet—eight as full ministers and three as junior ministers—including three rookie members of Parliament given senior portfolios.

"It's a tremendous turnaround from seven women in 2006," said Françoise Gagnon, national director for Equal Voice, a non-profit group that promotes boosting the number of women in public office.

The numbers mean Prime Minister Stephen Harper has appointed the largest proportion—29 per

cent—of women to cabinet in Canadian history. Paul Martin held the previous record, appointing 11 women to his 39-member cabinet, or 28 per cent, in 2003.

Gagnon pointed out there is work to be done.

"We still fall short of (Quebec Premier) Jean Charest's 50 per cent provincial record for the swearing-in of women," she said.

She also said while Canada elected a record 69 women MPs on Oct. 14, they represent only 22.4 per cent of members in the House of Commons, short of the "critical mass," or one-third, the United Nations defines as adequate representation of any particular group.

SOURCE: Joanna Smith, 2008, *Toronto Star* 31 October: A.23. Reprinted with permission from the Toronto Star.

Prime Minister Stephen Harper appointed the largest proportion of women (29 percent) to cabinet in Canadian history. Some of the ministers from left, after swearing-in at Rideau Hall: Bev Oda, Leona Aglukkaq, Rona Ambrose, Lisa Raitt, and Gail Shea.
SOURCE: Bill Grimshaw.

Canada in 1993. However, the presence of women in the upper echelons of power is rare enough to be newsworthy. If gender made no difference, why would the cover of *Maclean's* run a photo of Kim Campbell over the caption "When the Boss Is a Woman" (October 4, 1993) and why would newspaper articles describe what MP Belinda Stronach was wearing? Governor General Michaëlle Jean and former U.S. Secretary of State Condoleezza Rice are also exceptions who demonstrate the scarcity of women, particularly women who are members of visible minorities, in the top echelons of power.

Table 7.1 illustrates the truth of the saying "the higher, the fewer" with respect to the participation of women in Canadian political parties. Sylvia Bashevkin (1993: ch. 3) found that women are more likely to be local riding secretaries (as opposed to presidents) and that they do the necessary clerical work, paralleling the "pink ghetto" of female-typed clerical work found in the labour force. In the 90 years since most women gained the vote federally, only three women have been elected as party leaders of Canada's major parties, all within the last two decades (in addition, Elizabeth May was elected leader of the Green Party in 2006, but that party has not yet elected any MPs). Audrey McLaughlin served as leader of the NDP between 1989 and 1995; Kim Campbell was leader of the Progressive Conservatives (PCs) between June and December 1993; and Alexa McDonough was leader of the NDP from 1995 to 2003 (Young, 1997: 82).

EXPLAINING THE POLITICAL PARTICIPATION OF WOMEN

Five major explanations exist for the underrepresentation of women in Canadian politics. The first focuses on sex-role stereotypes. It argues that certain characteristics of women keep them from participating in politics. According to this argument, women are less assertive than men, more oriented to family than to politics, and conditioned through childhood socialization to view politics as an inappropriate activity (Brodie, 1991). This explanation is less popular than it once was because it stereotypes all women, failing to acknowledge that the traits of men and women often overlap and that women have diverse traits. Moreover, this explanation invokes the behaviour of men as the standard, implying that women are "deficient," and that the problem is to be found in women rather than in the characteristics of political life.

The second explanation for the underrepresentation of women in Canadian politics reverses the emphasis by arguing that the culture of politics is "male" and therefore hostile to the participation of women. Descriptions of political life as "gladiatorial" create the image of a blood sport in which the stakes are the acquisition and display of power (Bashevkin, 1991). Such an environment creates a chilly climate for women, who may have interests beyond domination and who may prefer to resolve conflicts in nonconfrontational ways. Thus, in their research on the media coverage of women politicians, Gertrude Robinson, Armande Saint-Jean, and Christine Rioux (1991) found that, before the 1970s, the portrayal of women MPs emphasized such themes as that of the spinster or the club woman, or focused on the politician's relationship to significant family members, including her husband, as the reason for her political success. All these themes emphasized a woman's gender and looks or affiliation rather than her competence. Between the 1970s and 1990s, new labels and stereotypes came to be used, but they still failed to evaluate women's political competence. Robinson, Saint-Jean, and Rioux (1991: 142–46) describe these new labels and stereotypes as follows:

- *Superwoman:* A young, intelligent, active, and ambitious woman who succeeds on all levels and has it all
- *Champion:* Similar to "superwoman" but tends to be used in reference to older women politicians who have led a more traditional life

- *One of the boys:* A female politician who "adopts a masculine stance, which means either that she does not resort to what are called feminine wiles to achieve her goals (charm, coquetry, wheedling) or that she accepts and operates by the conventional rules of the game"
- *Wife of . . . :* Invoked whenever the interests and activities of the female politician are linked by the media to those of her spouse

Robinson and her co-authors conclude that the media continue to emphasize the personal characteristics (e.g., looks, hair, and dress) of female politicians. Writing some 10 years later, political scientists Linda Trimble and Jane Arscott (2003) report similar findings. Robinson and co-authors also note three additional characteristics of media descriptions of female politicians: (1) they fail to recognize the prior political activities of female politicians, with the result that the women's histories of acquiring competency remain unknown; (2) they suggest that female politicians are responsible for women's issues, when, in fact, gender interests may not be on the agenda of any politician, male or female; and (3) they use the term *feminism* or *feminist* to denote negative personal characteristics.

The third reason for women's underrepresentation in politics is gatekeeping. By controlling the nomination of candidates for elected office, political parties influence the gender composition of their electoral slate and the ridings that nominees represent. In the past, women candidates were often "sacrificial lambs," allowed to run mainly in ridings in which the chances of winning were small. In today's climate of striving for gender equality, few parties can afford to provide a slate of candidates with few or no women. But parties can and still do assign women to ridings in which their chances of winning are poor. Many of the representational gains that women have made are attributable to a volatile electorate and last-minute voter shifts that carry ridings in which female candidates were not expected to win (Brodie, 1991: 6).

Insufficient resources are the fourth reason for the lack of gender parity in Canadian politics. Money is an important resource for winning nominations and mounting publicity campaigns. Even 20 years ago, it cost $50 000 to contest a nomination in a winnable urban riding (Brodie, 1991: 40). Women may be at a disadvantage to the extent that they earn less than male candidates and consequently have less to put into a campaign. Whereas men who enter politics tend to come from law and business, women candidates tend to come from social work, journalism, and education, where earnings are lower (Bashevkin, 1991). Social networks are also an important resource needed for contesting nominations and elections. They are useful for obtaining financial contributions and recruiting volunteers to lobby voters. Yet, to the extent that politics is "an old boys' club," women may not have access to insider or "old boy" networks.

Finally, the clash between political and family life influences the participation of some women in politics. The culture that emphasizes politics as a man's world fails to recognize that politicians also have personal lives and family responsibilities. Indeed, the lifestyle that is part of this culture is almost anti-family. Ignoring the family needs and responsibilities of politicians affects both men and women. However, because women more than men are designated as the primary child-care providers, their participation in politics can require greater personal and child-care costs.

REPRESENTATION BY WOMEN, REPRESENTATION FOR WOMEN

Until recently, most research on women in politics focused on the question of how many women held party positions or were elected legislators. However, representation *by* women is not the same as representation *for* women. Although both men and women may use their legislative roles to place women's issues on the political agenda and to support party policies and legislation that reflect women's situations and concerns, they may not.

Jane Arscott and Linda Trimble (1997) summarize the views of numerous social scientists and women's groups when they call for "representation by women as if women mattered"—that is, the election of women who will act in the interests of women. They raise a second issue too: How are differences of class and race among women to be represented? Specifically, can women legislators and party officers understand and speak for women who are different from them and who may have different experiences and concerns? The great majority of Canadian female legislators are white, middle-class, publicly heterosexual, and well educated.

Do they understand, stand for, and speak for other women, including Aboriginal women, women of colour, immigrant women, senior women, poor women, homeless women, lesbians, and women who are victims of spousal abuse (Vickers, 1997: 28)? Furthermore, if mainstream women cannot speak for all women, then should targets or quotas be set for women of colour, poor women, lesbians, and so on? These questions are now being debated but Canadian governments at all levels appear unwilling to exercise the political will, spend the money, and change the electoral laws and party practices that would accommodate such differences.

ELIMINATING GENDER INEQUALITY

In this section, I consider the mechanisms that can be used to lessen the degree of gender inequality, starting with a review of general approaches and then looking at specific interventions designed to reduce inequality in the labour force and political representation.

MODELS OF CHANGE

One's choice of mechanism for bringing about change depends on how one explains gender inequality. If we see gender inequality as arising out of personality differences between men and women, we are likely to prefer a mechanism that influences personality traits—for example, we may seek ways of altering the messages that people receive about masculinity and femininity in schools and through the mass media. If we see inequalities as resulting from organizational rules and practices governing recruitment and promotion, we are likely to emphasize the need to change those rules and practices.

Starting in the 1970s, North American research on inequality began to shift away from perspectives that attributed unequal outcomes to individual differences in talent, educational achievement, and opportunity. That viewpoint resulted in social programs and public policies oriented to individuals, such as efforts to increase access to education and training for members of less privileged groups (Agocs and Boyd, 1993).

By the 1980s, people were becoming more aware of power relations and the influence of workplace cultures and practices as sources of gender inequality. This awareness was partly fuelled by feminism, with its twin emphases on the undervaluation of women and men's domination of women in diverse areas of social life. Accompanying such changing perspectives was growing impatience with organizations slow to change their practices voluntarily. Increased pressure was put on governments to develop public policies that lessened or eliminated gender inequalities.

Public policy refers to the statements made and the actions taken—or not taken—by governments with respect to a given problem or set of problems (Pal, 1989: 4). State intervention influences the magnitude of gender inequality and sustains or minimizes male domination of women in reproduction, family, and the labour force. In the category of reproduction are government actions pertaining to medical care, new reproductive technologies (such as in vitro fertilization), contraception, and abortion. In the category of the family are government policies regarding family law (including regulations governing divorce and property division) and child care. Government intervention in the labour force affects gender inequality through employment insurance policies, maternity- and parental-leave policies, job-training programs, employment policies, and pay policies. So far, no government policy targets gender inequality in politics.

PUBLIC POLICY AND GENDER INEQUALITY IN THE LABOUR FORCE

Two areas of policy development that bear on gender inequality in the labour force are **employment equity,** including **affirmative action,** and pay equity, as expressed in the principle of **equal pay for work of equal value** (or "work of comparable worth"). Policies in both areas seek to correct inequalities in paid work by removing barriers that handicap certain groups, including women. Many of these barriers are seen as systemic. Rather than reflecting deliberate and conscious decisions to discriminate, systemic barriers refer to organizational practices, such as informal methods of recruitment or weight and height requirements for designated jobs. These practices often privilege members of one group while handicapping others. They differ in the populations they cover, the mechanisms they employ to determine and eliminate inequalities, and the aspects of labour-force inequality that they address.

Assessing the Impact

Many publications outline the specifics of Canadian employment-equity and equal-pay policies (Agocs, Burr, and Somerset, 1992; Weiner and Gunderson, 1990). Do such policies work? Have related programs succeeded in moving women into jobs from which they were previously excluded? Is the real monetary worth of women's work in female job ghettos being acknowledged?

In answering these questions, there is good news and bad news. The good news is that legal action has been taken against some cases of inequality. In the mid-1980s, for example, litigation forced CN Rail to hire women in the St. Lawrence region. At the time of the complaint, women held less than 1 percent of blue-collar jobs in the company, and a pattern of discriminatory hiring practices was revealed (Agocs, Burr, and Somerset, 1992: 104). The company was ordered to discontinue a number of these practices and to adopt new recruiting and hiring practices. Similarly, equal-pay-for-work-of-equal-value legislation has resulted in pay adjustments in a number of cases. For example, nurses' pay has been raised to match that of orderlies and the federal court upheld the right of pay equity for federally employed women in selected female-dominated occupations. In the fall of 2005, Canada Post was ordered to pay an estimated $150 million in back wages to clerical workers who were in a mostly female bargaining unit and who were paid substantially less than workers, most of them men, performing equivalent tasks sorting mail.

A few isolated victories do not, however, amount to winning the war. Critics of employment-equity policies note three types of "bad news." First, the legislation is limited in its jurisdiction and does not apply to a large part of the population. For example, the federal Employment Equity Act of 1995, which replaced the Employment Equity Act of 1986, covers only the public service, federally regulated employers, and portions of the public sector specified by orders in council, such as contractors who have 100 or more employees and who are doing business with the government. Second, failure to comply with the legislation is penalized only lightly. Although the federal Employment Equity Act of 1995 imposes fines on employers who do not report the required data or who knowingly provide false or misleading information, the amount cannot exceed $10 000 for a single violation and $50 000 for repeated or continued violations (Canada, 1995: s. 36[2]).

Numerous criticisms have been voiced about equal-pay-for-work-of-equal-value policies. First, many of the policies exclude small firms. Second, they compare men and women within the same firms, so they do not apply to women employed in firms in which the labour force is all female. Third, the method of establishing the comparable worth of two jobs is based on existing job descriptions. Jobs that are considered similar by virtue of pay or classification are evaluated on the basis of knowledge and skills, effort, responsibility, and working conditions (England, 1993; Steinberg, 1990). But such evaluation does not correct for the *a priori* undervaluation of certain skills, as discussed earlier.

For many feminists, these and other criticisms suggest that limited change can be expected from employment-equity and pay-equity policies in their current forms. Supporters are likely to press for stronger policies and broader coverage in the decades to come. However, government and business support for such changes is not assured. Business owners may argue that such equity is unaffordable in times of economic downturn.

CORRECTING THE BALANCE: WOMEN IN POLITICS

No federal policy is aimed at reducing gender inequality among elected politicians. But numerous actions could increase the percentage of women in Canadian politics in the future. All have to do with reducing barriers erected by social roles and changing organizational aspects of political recruitment and elections:

- *Displaying good intentions.* Commonly taking the form of party statements indicating commitment to the principle of gender parity, such displays have little impact.
- *Reducing the economic barriers to winning nominations and running for office.* Reducing the financial burden facing women and some men can be achieved by introducing legislation that would allow candidates the right to take unpaid leave from employment to contest party nominations and elections; setting spending limits for nomination contests and party leadership campaigns; making contributions for nomination contests tax-deductible; reimbursing money spent on nomination contests if the candidate gets a minimum level of support (say, 15 percent of the vote); using centralized party funds for nomination battles; and treating child-care and housekeeping costs as part of the campaign costs, thereby making them subject to reimbursement (Brodie, 1991: 49–50; Erickson, 1991).
- *Recognizing family needs and responsibilities and the social roles of women.* Lynda Erickson (1991) suggests that a fixed term for governments would increase the predictability of politicians' lives rather than leaving them at the mercy of a vote of nonconfidence or a leader's prerogative to call an election. Changing the rules of elections might indirectly help politicians to anticipate their futures, taking into account the needs of their families.

- *Weakening or eliminating the gatekeeping tradition.* This reform could be accomplished by basing the amount of the government subsidy paid to political parties for their campaign expenses on an upward sliding scale according to the proportion of their elected candidates who are women (Brodie, 1991: 50). Under this system, the amount of the subsidy would vary with the number of women elected.
- *Engaging in affirmative action.* Affirmative action measures include setting quotas to ensure that a certain percentage of women are on riding nomination lists and establishing guarantees that a certain percentage of women are nominated for and are present in the party organization.
- *Centralizing decision making in political parties.* Research suggests that affirmative action measures can be difficult to implement in a single-member electoral system. Under the single-member system in Canada, a person running for office in a riding

wins by getting the most votes. This approach is conducive to the control of nominations by local party organizations. However, attempts to increase the number of women holding office are most effective in electoral systems that place decision making about nominations and party representation at levels higher than the local riding. A more centralized decision-making structure gives party elites more control over the representation of women and other minority groups. Modifying Canada's single-member system is another area in which action could be taken to increase the percentage of women politicians (Erickson, 1991).

Which, if any, of these reforms will be adopted remains to be seen. It is highly likely, however, that debate over gender inequalities in politics and the economy will remain an important issue in Canadian social life for a long time.

SUMMARY

1. Many sociologists view the segregation of women and men in the private and public spheres as an important source of gender inequality. Exclusion from the economic and political arenas of Canadian life can mean disadvantages in access to income, prestige, and power. Restricted in the past to the domestic sphere, women have been economically disadvantaged and have had little or no opportunity to influence legislation directly. In addition, their unpaid work in the home has been considered low in prestige, or at least lower in value than their spouses' paid work.

2. During the twentieth century, women entered the labour force and the political arena in ever-increasing numbers. Today, more than half of all women are in the labour force. Politically enfranchised, women have also entered the political arena, either as politicians or in connection with groups associated with the women's movement. Many of these changes have occurred—or, at least, have accelerated—in recent decades. Between the 1970s and the early 1990s, the labour-force participation rate of women more than doubled, and the number of elected women MPs quadrupled.

3. Although they do paid work, many women are still responsible for most of the meal preparation, cleaning, and laundry needs of their families. Women still tend to be considered the primary caregivers of children and of seniors. In short, women are more likely than men to work a double "shift" every day.

4. In the labour force, women and men are occupationally segregated, with women concentrated in jobs stereotyped as "women's jobs." Women are more likely than men to be employed in jobs that are part-time or otherwise nonstandard. They earn less than men do, on average, and their skills tend not to be fully recognized or fairly evaluated. These issues affect women to varying degrees, depending on their birthplace, race, and ethnicity. Nevertheless, the overall picture is one of gender inequality in the labour force, with women disadvantaged relative to men.

5. There is evidence of a gender gap in politics as well. Women represent more than half of Canada's adult population, but only 22 percent of federally elected legislators. This imbalance notwithstanding, substantial gains have been made in recent elections. And, as agents pressing for improvements in their own status, Canadian women have left a considerable legacy of influence and change.

6. Future generations will have to combat not only gender-role stereotypes, but also ideologies and structures that privilege men and handicap women. In recent years, employment-equity and equal-pay-for-work-of-equal-value policies have been developed to remedy some of the inequalities in the paid labour force. Analysts have also documented the various ways in which women's participation and influence in the political arena can be enhanced.

QUESTIONS TO CONSIDER

1. If you grew up in a two-parent household, describe the types of activities that each parent did around the house. Were they different? Did the amount of time each spent on activities in the home vary? Why?

2. Think back to jobs you have held in the past three years that involved working with other people. Reflecting on the type of work you did compared with the work of others, would you say that sex segregation or sex typing existed? Why or why not?

3. In some of the occupational skill assessments that have been conducted in recent years, the job of dogcatcher was deemed more skilled than the job of child-care worker. Why do you think such an evaluation was made? Do you agree with the ranking? Why or why not?

4. This chapter discussed the principles of political "representation by women," "representation for women," and "representation of difference." Should women legislators be elected only if they champion women's causes? Should electoral rules be changed to allow for the proportionate or even disproportionate election of women of colour and other disadvantaged women in order to represent their interests and experiences?

GLOSSARY

Affirmative action comprises the policies and programs designed to create opportunities for, and to further the achievements of, historically disadvantaged groups in the labour force. One form of action to correct past inequalities involves setting targets and quotas for the hiring and promotion of members of groups that have faced barriers and discrimination in the past. The term is often used interchangeably with employment equity; strictly speaking, it is one aspect of employment equity.

Employment equity is the principle of equal treatment of all groups in the paid labour force. Employment-equity policies and programs seek to dismantle barriers and alter workplace cultures to create opportunities for and further the advancement of historically disadvantaged groups.

Equal pay for work of equal value, also known as "equal pay for work of comparable worth," is a principle supported by policies and programs that seek to equalize the wage rates offered for different jobs that are of comparable worth or value in terms of such factors as knowledge, complexity, responsibility, and skill.

Feminism refers both to the body of knowledge about the causes and nature of women's subordination to men in society, and the various agendas, often involving political action, for removing that subordination.

Gender inequalities are inequalities between men and women in the distribution of prestige, material well-being, and power. They are also inequalities in relations of male domination and female subordination.

Gender stereotypes are a set of prejudicial generalizations about men and women based on the oversimplified belief that sex determines distinct personality traits and, as a result, causes men and women to experience the world and behave in different ways.

The **glass ceiling** is the level in an organization above which women and members of minorities are seldom found.

The **labour-force participation rate** is the percentage of the population, age 15 and older, that is in the paid labour force.

Material well-being refers to having access to the economic resources necessary to pay for adequate food, clothing, housing, and possessions.

Nonstandard work refers to one or a combination of the following types of employment: part-week employment (reduced hours per week), part-year employment, limited-term contract employment, employment through temporary-help agencies, self-employment, and multiple job-holding.

Part-time work refers to jobs involving fewer hours of work than is the norm for full-time work.

Power is the capacity to influence and control others, regardless of any resistance they might offer.

Prestige is the social evaluation or ranking, by general consensus, of occupational activities and positions in a hierarchical order that reflects the degree of respect, honour, or deference the person engaged in the activity or occupying the position is to be accorded.

Public policy refers to the government's stance on issues and problems, as expressed through its statements and actions, or its inaction.

Sex segregation of occupations refers to the concentration of women and men in different occupations.

Sex typing (or sex labelling) of occupations is the designation of an occupation as "female" or "male," depending on the sex for whom it is considered appropriate.

Skill is ability or expertise in performing a given technique or task. Researchers describe tasks as requiring more or less skill on the basis of their complexity and the degree of autonomy required to perform them. Existing rankings, incomes, and levels of education associated with various occupations are often accepted by researchers as indicators of skill.

A **social movement** is an enduring collective attempt to change part or all of society by means of rioting, petitioning, striking, demonstrating, or establishing pressure groups, unions, and political parties.

Social roles are the expectations and behaviours associated with particular positions in society.

Standard work is full-time, full-year employment, usually accompanied by job-related benefits, such as vacation leave, sick leave, and parental leave, as well as by health and pension benefits.

Statistical discrimination is the discrimination that occurs when negative decisions concerning the hiring or promotion of an individual are made on the basis of the average characteristics of the group to which the individual belongs.

A **visible minority** is a category of people (other than Aboriginal people) who are non-white and who, because of their race, may face discrimination in hiring and promotion.

The **women's movement** is a social movement that takes action to improve the conditions of women.

SUGGESTED READING

Das Gupta, Tania. (1996). *Racism and Paid Work.* Toronto: Garamond Press. Examines discrimination in paid employment as it affects immigrant women and women of colour.

Statistics Canada. (2006). *Women in Canada: A Gender Based Statistical Report,* 5th ed. Ottawa: Minister of Industry (Catalogue No. 89-503-XPE). This report contains textual overviews and data on women, covering such topics as their family status, health, educational patterns, paid and unpaid work characteristics, and treatment by the criminal justice system. Separate chapters deal with Aboriginal, visible minority, and immigrant women.

Tremblay, Manon, and Caroline Andrew. (1998). *Women and Political Representation in Canada.* Women's Studies Series. Ottawa: University of Ottawa Press. An excellent collection of essays on various aspects of the women's movement in Canada and women's involvement in politics. A chapter by Julia O'Connor looks at women in paid employment.

Trimble, Linda, and Jane Arscott. (2003). *Still Counting: Women in Politics across Canada.* Peterborough, ON: Broadview Press. This highly readable book reviews the absence of women among elected politicians, provides reasons and suggests remedies.

WEB RESOURCES

Companion Website for This Book

http://www.newsociety6e.nelson.com
Begin by clicking on the Student Resources section of the website. Next, select the chapter you are studying from the pull-down menu. From the Student Resources page, you have easy access to InfoTrac College Edition® and other resources, such as the

Glossary, Test Yourself questions, and additional readings. The website also has many useful tips to aid you in your study of sociology.

InfoTrac College Edition Search Terms

Visit http://www.infotrac-college.com for access to more than 20 million articles from nearly 6000 sources when doing your online research.

SOURCE: © Photofusion Picture Library/Alamy

CHAPTER EIGHT

Race and Ethnic Relations

Vic Satzewich
McMASTER UNIVERSITY

In this chapter you will learn that

- The study of race and ethnic relations involves the analysis of the unequal distribution of power and resources, and it involves a number of sociological approaches. Among the most important are the frustration-aggression, sociobiology, socialization, and power-conflict approaches.

- *Ethnicity* and *race* are terms used to categorize groups on the basis of cultural and physical criteria. Although the concept of race has little basis in biology, and although ethnic identities and boundaries are situational, variable, and flexible, race and ethnicity are important parts of social reality.

- Aboriginal people in Canada are Indians, Métis, and Inuit. There are two main sociological interpretations of Aboriginal people's socioeconomic status in Canada: the culture of poverty thesis and the internal colonial model.

- The nationalist movement in Quebec has deep historical roots. The contemporary nationalist movement is united around the goal of maintaining the French character of Quebec. One of the main problems facing the nationalist movement in Quebec is exactly how to define the boundaries of the nation.

- Immigration played a central role in both the early and later phases of Canadian capitalist development. Canada accepts refugee, family class, and independent immigrants. Each category is subject to different selection criteria.

- John Porter's description of Canadian society as a vertical mosaic is not as accurate as it once was.

INTRODUCTION

It started as a peaceful protest aimed at grabbing the government's attention over a dispute about an old burial ground. It ended with what journalist Peter Edwards (2001) referred to as "one dead Indian." On September 5, 1995, just after the Labour Day long-weekend campers had gone home, about 30 Kettle Point and Stoney Point band members from the Kettle Point Reserve near Sarnia occupied Ipperwash Provincial Park. Some band members believed that an ancient burial ground in the park was being desecrated and they wanted to protect their ancestors' resting place. A few weeks earlier, a group of reserve members had reclaimed land that was part of a nearby military base. That land had been lent temporarily to the federal government during World War II for military training purposes. Various provincial and federal governments had dragged their feet over the return of the land that was part of the military base for nearly 50 years, and the occupants of Ipperwash did not feel like waiting another 50 years for their concerns about the graves in the park to be dealt with.

Native protester Dudley George was shot and killed by an Ontario Provincial Police officer during the occupation of Ipperwash Provincial Park (near Sarnia) in 1995.

SOURCE: The Canadian Press (Fred Chartrand).

Dudley George was shot and killed by an Ontario Provincial Police officer in a chaotic altercation the day after the occupation of Ipperwash started. The officer who shot George was eventually convicted of criminal negligence causing death, and the larger circumstances surrounding the incident were investigated at a public inquiry in late 2005 and early 2006. Both the trial of the OPP officer and the public inquiry turned up unpleasant facts about racism within the OPP and within the provincial Conservative government of the day. For instance, the day before George was shot, two OPP officers were posing as a television crew. The lens of their camera was covered, but the audio was turned on. One officer, responding to his colleague's question about whether any members of the media were in the area, said, "No, there's no one down there. Just a big fat-fuck Indian." After a few minutes, another voice is heard: "We had this plan, you know. We thought if we could get five or six cases of Labatt's 50, we could bait them. And we would have this big net and a pit." People are heard laughing in the background. The officer calls the plan "creative thinking" and adds that it "works in the South with watermelons" (Gray, 2004: A7).

According to Murray Klippenstein, the lawyer for the George family, "the reference to baiting Indians with alcohol and the reference to the South and the watermelon are the kind of poisonous, racist talk I thought we had put behind us in Ontario. . . . The reference to blacks in the South is the kind of talk you would hear when people are dehumanizing someone, and that attitude makes it easy to lynch or shoot them" (Gray, 2004).

In November 2005, the Ipperwash inquiry into the death of Dudley George turned up some equally ugly racist views expressed by provincial government officials. Former provincial Attorney General Charles Harnick told the inquiry that at a top-level meeting to discuss how the provincial government ought to handle the occupation of the park, then Premier Mike Harris, in a moment of anger, shouted, "I want those fucking Indians out of the park" (Harries, 2005: A1). Although Mr. Harris has denied saying this, Mr. Harnick insists that "I heard what I heard" (Appleby, 2006: A7).

We may never know with certainty whether racism played a central role in why Dudley George died. Some say that although the expression of racism by some OPP officers was regrettable, it was incidental to the way the events surrounding George's death unfolded. Others say that the police do not take their marching orders from politicians, so whatever the premier might have said at the meeting was irrelevant to how the police eventually dealt with the situation.

Ethnic and racial tensions in Canada do not often end in physical violence or violent death. And, in comparison to many other countries, ethnic and racial relations seem peaceful here. But other kinds of ethnic and racial problems exist. In Ontario, the 2001 Safe Schools Act, which mandates a policy of "zero tolerance" for violent and disruptive behaviour in schools, is alleged by some to work to the disadvantage of black students (Henry and Tator, 2006: 211). In 2008, Toronto school trustees voted to establish a black-focused school in the city. Critics argued that this was a step backwards to racial segregation (Brown and Popplewell, 2008). In 2001, 1071 land claims had been filed against the federal government by First Nations; only 251 had been successfully resolved (Frideres and Gadacz, 2005: 220). Former Toronto Mayor Mel Lastman's 2001 racist jest that he was reluctant to travel to Kenya because he feared being put in a pot of boiling water by "dancing natives" probably did not help Toronto's unsuccessful bid to host the 2008 Summer Olympic Games (Walcott, 2003). Arab Canadians complain that they have faced increased stereotyping and discrimination in Canada and at the Canada–U.S. border since September 11, 2001 (Li, 2003). In 1995, the country was on the verge of collapse after nearly half the voters in Quebec voted in favour of separation. And some observers claim that the federal government's policy of multiculturalism undermines the unity of our country (Bissondath, 1994), causing "more overt hostility in Canada to those of European ancestry . . . than to the non-white minority" (Stoffman, 2002: 126).

These examples all touch in some way on the issue of what different ethnic and racial groups are allowed, and able, to do in our society, and how they are treated. In other words, they all say something about the distribution of power and resources in Canada. The sociology of ethnic and racial relations concerns primarily the study of how power and resources are unequally distributed among ethnic and racial groups. Sociologists who are interested in race and ethnic relations ask a number of interrelated questions: What are the conditions under which ethnic and racial groups come into contact? Which ethnic and racial groups hold power in a society? How do they exercise power? Are there social and economic advantages associated with having a particular ethnic or racial background? What are the social consequences of the unequal distribution of power

and resources? How have ethnic and racial groups challenged inequality and power imbalances? How have governments tried to manage and contain ethnic and racial conflict?

My aim in this chapter is to provide some sociological answers to these questions. I begin by examining what sociologists mean by the terms *ethnicity*, *race*, and *racism*, and then discuss various theoretical approaches to the study of ethnic and racial relations. Next, I examine the three main forms of ethnic and racial relations in Canada: Aboriginal and non-Aboriginal relations, French and English relations, and immigrant and non-immigrant relations. In each case, you will see how power and resource imbalances play important roles in structuring relationships among groups.

ETHNICITY AND RACE: THE SOCIAL CONSTRUCTION OF DIFFERENCE

We use the terms *race*, *racial*, *ethnic*, and *ethnicity* in a variety of ways in our everyday lives. Some students in my classes talk about how they are under pressure from their parents to marry someone of the same "race" or "ethnicity." Others are concerned that "race relations" in Canada seem to be getting worse. Yet others describe the joys of living in a "multiethnic" country, of eating meals in a variety of "ethnic" restaurants, and of observing and participating in the rituals and festivals of "ethnic" groups from around the world.

The assumption underlying our commonsense understandings of these terms is that race and ethnicity are *ascribed* characteristics. That is, we assume that we are born with a certain race or ethnicity that cannot be changed. Sociologists, however, recognize that, although we cannot change our birth parents, and generally cannot change our skin colour, we do not necessarily have fixed and unalterable ethnic and racial characteristics or identities. Instead, sociologists believe it is more useful to see race and ethnicity as certain kinds of *achieved* statuses—statuses that are acquired by virtue of social definition. In contrast, Box 8.1 (p. 182) shows how Statistics Canada used ascribed characteristics for its measurement of ethnicity and race in the 2006 census.

ETHNICITY AND RACE

Ethnicity

Sociologists do not agree on how to define and measure ethnicity. *Objective definitions of ethnicity* assume that

The census has collected information on the ancestral origins of the population for over 100 years to capture the composition of Canada's diverse population, as in these questions from the 2006 census.

ETHNIC ORIGIN

17. What were the ethnic or cultural origins of this person's **ancestors**?

An ancestor is usually more distant than a grandparent.

For example, Canadian, English, French, Chinese, Italian, German, Scottish, East Indian, Irish, Cree, Mi'kmaq (Micmac), Metis, Inuit (Eskimo), Ukrainian, Dutch, Filipino, Polish, Portuguese, Jewish, Greek, Jamaican, Vietnamese, Lebanese, Chilean, Salvadorean, Somali, etc.

RACIAL ORIGIN

19. Is this person:

Mark "x" more than one or specify, if applicable

White
Chinese
South Asian (e.g., East Indian, Pakistani, Sri Lankan, etc.)
Black
Filipino
Latin American
Southeast Asian (e.g., Vietnamese, Cambodian, Malaysian, Laotian, etc.)
Arab
West Asian (e.g., Afghan, Irainian, etc.)
Japanese
Korean
Other—specify

This information is collected to support programs that promote equal opportunity for everyone to share in the social, cultural, and economic life of Canada.

SOURCE: Adapted from Statistics Canada, 2008, "2006 Questionnaires and Guides," on the World Wide Web at http://www12.statcan.ca/ english/census06/reference/questons/index.cfm (15 July 2009).

ethnic groups exist because of people's social attachments (Isajiw, 1999). From this point of view, ethnicity is something that people possess because of differences in language, culture, customs, national origin, and ancestry. *Subjective approaches to ethnicity* focus on the process of ethnic identification. Sociologists who emphasize the socially constructed nature of perceived reality insist that ethnicity is a "transactional" process. Ethnic groups are made up of people who identify themselves, or who are identified by others, as belonging to the same ancestral or cultural group. Whether they display any of the cultural characteristics of the group with which they identify, or whether they are merely born into that group, is largely irrelevant. When subjective definitions are used, then, "ethnicity" is self-defined and reflects "a shared 'we-feeling' within a collectivity (groupness) whose symbolic components can vary [over] time and place" (Fleras and Elliot, 1996). From this perspective, ethnic identities and boundaries are situational, variable, and flexible.

Most of the ethnic categories that we take for granted are actually recent historical creations. The ethnic category "English" would have been unthinkable to the person who lived in the British Isles 800 years ago. People defined themselves, and were defined by others, as Celts, Saxons, Normans, and so on. Only some of those people came to be known as "the English" (Lieberson, 1991). Similarly, the people

whom we now think of as "Germans" did not exist 150 years ago. As these examples suggest, the way in which people define themselves, and are defined by others, is in constant flux (Lieberson, 1991: 444). If we take a long view, it is common for ethnic categories and identities to be recast and created anew.

This is what seems to be happening in Canada now. A feeling of commonality has crystallized that is the basis for a common ethnic identification. In preparing for the 1991 census, Statistics Canada held meetings, organized focus groups, and tested different ways of posing questions that tried to measure the ethnicity of our population. One thing that Statistics Canada found "was a strong tendency [for respondents] to report Canadian as their ethnic origin and as their ethnic identity" (White, 1992: 166). Largely because of political pressure, "Canadian" was included as a response category in the ethnicity question for the next census. "Canadians" are now the numerically largest ethnic group in Canada (see Table 8.1).

Why do some of us define our ethnic roots or ethnic identity as "Canadian"? Some of us may simply be unaware of or uninterested in our so-called roots and, hence, by default define ourselves as Canadian. For others, defining ourselves as Canadian is a political act used to express our dissatisfaction with the government's policy of multiculturalism (White, 1992: 168–69). At the same time, though, many of us

TABLE 8.1 TOP 25 ETHNIC ORIGINS IN CANADA, 2006

ETHNIC ORIGIN	SINGLE AND MULTIPLE REPONSES	SINGLE RESPONSES	MULTIPLE RESPONSES	INDEX OF ASSIMILATION[1]
Canadian	10 066 290	5 748 725	4 317 570	NA
English	6 570 015	1 367 125	5 202 890	79.2
French	4 941 210	1 230 535	3 710 675	75.1
Scottish	4 719 850	568 515	4 151 340	88.0
Irish	4 354 155	491 030	3 863 125	88.7
German	3 179 425	670 640	2 508 785	78.9
Italian	1 445 335	741 045	704 285	48.7
Chinese	1 346 510	1 135 365	211 145	15.7
North American Indian	1 253 615	512 150	741 470	59.1
Ukrainian	1 209 085	300 590	908 495	75.1
Dutch (Netherlands)	1 035 965	303 400	732 560	70.7
Polish	984 565	269 375	715 190	72.6
East Indian	962 665	780 175	182 495	18.9
Russian	500 600	98 245	402 355	80.4
Welsh	440 965	27 115	413 855	93.9
Filipino	436 190	321 390	114 800	26.1
Norwegian	432 515	44 790	387 725	89.6
Portuguese	410 850	262 230	148 625	36.1
Métis	409 065	77 295	331 770	80.9
British Isles, n.i.e.[2]	403 915	94 145	309 770	76.7
Swedish	334 765	28 445	306 325	91.6
Spanish	325 730	67 475	258 255	79.3
American	316 350	28 785	287 565	90.8
Hungarian (Magyar)	315 510	88 685	226 820	27.6
Jewish	315 120	134 045	181 070	57.5

SOURCE: Adapted from the Statistics Canada, 2009, "Ethnocultural Portrait of Canada Highlight Tables, 2006 Census." On the World Wide Web at http://www12.statcan.ca/english/census06/data/highlights/ethnic/index.cfm?Lang=E. (16 July 2009).
[1]Multiple responses expressed as a percentage of single plus multiple responses.
[2]Not included elsewhere.

insist that we are Canadian because that is simply the group with whom we identify and with whom we share a sense of belonging (Angus Reid Group, 1991; Howard, 1998). According to Rhoda Howard-Hassmann (1999: 528), the emergence of this sense of community means that "the ethnic English-Canadian is a new social creation."

Race

For much of the twentieth century, there was little difference between commonsense understandings of **race** and the way that race was analyzed in the social and natural sciences. Most scientists believed that races were real and objective subdivisions of *Homo sapiens*. These divisions were supposedly based on a combination of unalterable physical and genetic characteristics. Features, such as skin colour, hair texture, body and facial shape, genetic diseases, metabolic rates, and distribution of blood groups, were used to construct various racial typologies. The most common typology was the division of humanity into "Caucasoid," "mongoloid," and "negroid" races (Montagu, 1972).

During the 1930s, scientists began to raise doubts about the scientific validity of the concept of race (Barkan, 1992). Since the 1950s, the scientific consensus is that racial classifications of humanity are arbitrary, that genetic differences between groups are small, and that genetic differences are behaviourally insignificant (Montagu, 1972). Racial classifications based on a characteristic, such as skin colour, are as illogical as racial classifications based on the length of index fingers (Miles, 1982). Moreover, only a fraction of 1 percent of all human genes are necessarily shared by members of the same race, genetically defined. Thus, from a strictly genetic point of view, Stephen

Harper may have more in common with Chris Bosh than with Jack Layton.

In sum, genetic differences between races are arbitrary, extremely small, and without behavioural consequences. Ethnic boundaries and identities are flexible, negotiated, and historically variable. We should not conclude, however, that race and ethnicity are unimportant aspects of modern society. According to W. I. Thomas's famous sociological dictum, if people define situations as real, they are real in their consequences (Thomas and Znaniecki, 1918: 79). Even though race is a hollow biological concept, and even though ethnic identities and boundaries are neither fixed nor unchanging, many people believe in the existence of ethnicity and race and organize their relationships with others on the basis of those beliefs. Therefore, race and ethnicity are important parts of our social reality.

Racism

If race is a biological myth, what is racism? Is a school racist if it puts on hot dog days but not chow mein days? Are black people in Toronto subject to racist policing? Is Don Cherry a racist because he denigrates European hockey players who compete in the National Hockey League? Is Professor Philippe Rushton of the University of Western Ontario a racist because he believes that black people have smaller brains than whites and Asians? Is a black woman racist if she wants to marry only a black man? Is a white man racist if he wants to marry only a white woman? Was the Bush administration in the United States racist for the way that it managed the aftermath of Hurricane Katrina in New Orleans in September 2005?

Before we can begin to answer these kinds of questions, we need to define racism. Sociologists define racism as both a certain kind of idea and a certain kind of institutional practice. I will consider each of these definitions in turn.

Traditionally, sociologists defined racism as "the belief that humans are subdivided into distinct hereditary groups that are innately different in their social behaviour and mental capacities and that can therefore be ranked as superior or inferior" (Marger, 1997: 27). Some scholars have suggested that because ideas about the inherent superiority and inferiority of groups have been so thoroughly discredited, racism has taken new forms (Omi and Winant, 1986). Biological versions of racism may be dead, but researchers have developed the concept of **new racism** as a way of analyzing its changing manifestations.

The concept of new racism was developed by Martin Barker (1981) to analyze the way that racist ideas were being expressed in the 1970s by British members of Parliament (MPs) when they were speaking out against British immigration policy. That policy permitted people from former British colonies in Asia, Africa, and the Caribbean unrestricted entry to the country. In their speeches, the MPs did not make references to British *biological* superiority or to Indian, African, or Caribbean *biological* inferiority. Instead, they regarded immigrants from these areas as *culturally* different from British people and alleged that the ability of British people to advance the moral level of humanity was being undermined by immigration policy. The MPs' statements could not be considered "racist" by the traditional definition of racism. However, the statements had the real consequence of helping to stop almost all non-white immigration from those countries.

These events suggested that the definition of racism had to be broadened. Accordingly, Barker (1981: 21) argued that the new racism involves the beliefs that, although races of people cannot be ranked biologically, they are different from each other and that social problems are created when different groups try to live together. These beliefs should be considered racist because of their underlying intent: to socially exclude, marginalize, and denigrate certain groups of people, but to do so without reference to unalterable biology. People may even believe in abstract virtues, such as equality, justice, and fairness, yet still hold negative attitudes, and engage in discriminatory behaviour, toward minority group members (Henry and Tator, 2006: 19).

How widespread is racism? A 2006–2007 survey conducted by Léger Marketing and Sun Media found that

- 9 percent of Canadians considered themselves strongly or moderately racist.
- men are more likely to describe themselves as moderately racist (10 percent versus 6 percent of women).
- 21 percent of Canadians believed that some races are more gifted than others.
- 9 percent of Canadians would react negatively if their child married someone of a different race.
- 92 percent of Canadians have witnessed racist comments or behaviours.
- 17 percent of respondents believe that their city is more racist than it was 10 years ago (Léger Marketing, 2007).

However, Canada fares well in international comparisons. For example, although 18 percent of Canadians who were polled in a 2002 international survey felt that immigrants have a bad influence on the country, 43 percent of Americans and 50 percent of respondents in the United Kingdom said that immigrants had a bad influence on their countries (Parkin and Mendelsohn, 2003: 5).

A different indicator of the scope of racism in Canada is given in Table 8.2, which focuses on *perceived* discrimination. Table 8.2 shows the results of the Ethnic Diversity Survey conducted by Statistics Canada in 2002. Among other things, the survey asked Canadians whether they had experienced discrimination or unfair treatment during the past five years. The survey found that 64 percent of visible-minority Canadians reported that they "did not" experience discrimination or unfair treatment because of their ethnocultural characteristics in the past five years. Another 15 percent reported that they "rarely" experienced discrimination and 20 percent of respondents reported that they had "sometimes" or "often" experienced discrimination. In contrast, just 5 percent of non-visible minorities reported experiencing discrimination or unfair treatment because of their ethnocultural characteristics during the past five years.

Institutional racism refers to "discriminatory racial practices built into such prominent structures as the political, economic and education systems"

(Doob, 1996: 6). Institutional racism can take three forms. First, some institutional practices are based on explicitly racist ideas. Canadian history has plenty of examples of this form of institutional racism (Bolaria and Li, 1988). Chinese people were excluded from certain jobs and were denied the right to vote in federal elections until 1947. Japanese Canadians were denied their basic civil rights, were forcibly expelled from the west coast of British Columbia, and had their property confiscated during World War II (Bolaria and Li, 1988). Status Indians were denied the right to vote in federal elections until 1960. Residential segregation was widespread for black people living in Canada. Restrictive covenants in wills, deeds, and leases were used to ensure that property could not be sold or leased to blacks and Jews. Blacks were frequently refused service in restaurants, theatres, and recreational facilities (Henry and Tator, 2006: 69). Canada had the worst record of all Allied countries in allowing Jewish immigration during World War II, when millions of Jews were being gassed in Europe (Abella and Troper, 1982). In each case, ideas about the alleged inferiority of certain groups underpinned institutional practices.

Second, some institutional practices arose from, but are no longer sustained by, racist ideas (Miles and Brown, 2003). For example, in 1966, the federal government admitted a small number of black workers from the Caribbean to work on Canadian farms.

TABLE 8.2 PERCEPTIONS OF DISCRIMINATION BY GENERATION AND VISIBLE MINORITY STATUS, CANADA, 2002

DISCRIMINATION	TOTAL POPULATION	FREQUENCY OF DISCRIMINATION		
		SOMETIMES OR OFTEN	RARELY	DID NOT EXPERIENCE
	000s	%	%	%
Total Population	22 444	7	6	86
Not a Visible Minority	19 252	5	5	90
Visible Minority	3 000	20	15	64
First Generation	5 272	13	10	77
Not a Visible Minority	2 674	5	6	89
Visible Minority	2 516	21	14	65
Second Generation or More	16 929	6	5	89
Not a Visible Minority	16 349	5	5	90
Visible Minority	480	18	23	59

Source: Adapted Statistics Canada, 2003, "*Ethnic Diversity Survey: Portrait of a Multicultural Society,*" Catalogue no. 89-593-XIE.

Now, more than 16 000 migrant workers from the Caribbean and Mexico enter Canada each year to harvest fruits, vegetables, and tobacco in southern Ontario and other agricultural areas in Canada during the summer months. Canadian government officials originally justified this practice partly by arguing that black workers are racially suited to back-breaking labour under the hot sun but racially unsuited to the cold Canadian winters (Satzewich, 1991). The present migrant-labour policy had its origins in racist thinking, but racist ideas are no longer used to justify this migration stream.

Third, institutions sometimes unintentionally restrict the life-chances of certain groups through a variety of seemingly neutral rules, regulations, and procedures. This is sometimes referred to as *systemic discrimination.* For example, height and weight requirements for jobs with police forces and fire departments did not necessarily originate in racist ideas, but these requirements meant that for many years certain Asian groups could not get jobs as police officers or firefighters. Word-of-mouth recruiting in organizations and inflated educational requirements for nontechnical jobs are also forms of systemic discrimination because they unintentionally put minority groups at a disadvantage in the distribution of scarce resources like jobs (Special Committee on the Participation of Visible Minorities in Canadian Society [Special Committee], 1984).

The debate about racial profiling in policing is also about this kind of institutional racism. According to a study conducted by University of Toronto criminologist Scott Wortley (2005), black people in Kingston, Ontario, are nearly four times more likely to be pulled over by police than white people are. Aboriginal people are 1.4 times as likely to be pulled over as white people are. When the study results were announced, the chief of the Kingston Police Force tearfully apologized, saying "especially to the black community and the aboriginal community where there are disparities, we apologize. I apologize. I'm not asking any police officer to apologize. . . . My police officers have the right to . . . walk tall with pride. What we're doing wrong, if we're doing anything wrong, is systemic and that's my problem. So I apologize to the black community, the aboriginal community and we'll do better" (Farmer, 2005).

THEORIES OF RACE AND ETHNIC RELATIONS

There are a number of sociological approaches to the interpretation of race and ethnic relations (Rex and Mason, 1986). In this section, I discuss four approaches that seek to explain various forms of ethnic and racial hostility. Such hostility is multifaceted and, depending on the circumstances, is described as racism, prejudice, ethnocentrism, or xenophobia.

Social Psychology

Social-psychological approaches to the interpretation of race and ethnic relations focus on how **prejudice**—an unfavourable, generalized, and rigid belief applied to all members of a group—and racism satisfy the psychic needs of certain people. *Frustration-aggression* is a popular variant of social-psychological theory. It explains prejudice and racism as forms of hostility that arise from frustration. The theory suggests that people who are frustrated in their efforts to achieve a desired goal—a better-paying job, for example, or entry to a university—respond with aggression (Marger, 1997). Since the real source of frustration is usually too powerful to confront directly, or may not be known, people take out their frustrations on the less powerful. From this perspective, minority ethnic and racial groups are convenient and safe targets of displaced aggression. This displacement is also referred to as scapegoating. The concept of scapegoating is sometimes used to explain anti-Semitism—negative attitudes and everyday discrimination directed against Jews (Brym and Lenton, 1993).

Originally, racist thinking was used to justify allowing Caribbean and Mexican agricultural workers into Canada during the hot summer months but not the cold Canadian winters.
SOURCE: Shutterstock.

This kind of explanation has a seductive, almost commonsense, appeal. We all have bad days at work or at school, and when we get home, we sometimes lash out at the people close to us. However, the theory has limitations. First, people respond to frustrating circumstances in a variety of ways. Displaced aggression does not always follow frustration. We sometimes internalize our frustrations and end up giving ourselves an ulcer, or we may direct our frustrations at the real source of our problems. The theory does not say why we respond to frustrating circumstances in different ways. Second, the theory does not explain why some groups, and not others, are chosen as scapegoats.

Primordialism

The **primordialist thesis** suggests that ethnic and racial attachments reflect an innate tendency for people to seek out, and associate with, others who are similar in terms of language, culture, beliefs, ancestry, and appearance (Scott, 1990). From this point of view, ethnic prejudice and racism are ways of maintaining social boundaries. Sociobiologists offer a popular form of primordial theory. They suggest that prejudice and **discrimination**—practices that deny members of particular groups equal access to societal rewards—stem from our supposedly biologically grounded tendency to be nepotistic. Sociobiologists argue that the process of natural selection does not operate at the level of individuals, but rather at the level of kin-related groups. Clusters of genes are assumed to be passed on through kin selection (Wilson, 1978). Ethnic and racial groups are seen to be nothing more than large extended families. Since people have a "natural" tendency to want to pass on their genes, they favour their own "families." Thus, people are inherently both altruistic (prepared to sacrifice their own individual interests for the sake of the group) and ethnocentric because they want to pass on their genes to their own group. Humans, therefore, naturally favour members of their own ethnic or racial group—their "relatives"—and have a natural distrust and dislike of "nonfamily" members (van den Berghe, 1986: 255).

Are racism, prejudice, and discrimination programmed by our genes? It seems unlikely. The first problem with sociobiology is that shared ethnicity or race does not prevent conflict from erupting. In the history of the United States, white workers have struck against white-owned factories, and Americans

have killed members of their own ethnic or racial group without concern for common ethnicity or race (Bonacich, 1980). Second, sociobiology is not able to explain how and why we frequently break out of our supposed genetically programmed nepotism. For example, Canadians of diverse ethnic and racial origins participate together in various kinds of anti-racist social movements (Henry and Tator, 2006). Ethnic and racial relations, therefore, are not necessarily zero-sum games in which one group wins at the expense of another.

Normative Theories

Normative theories of ethnic and racial prejudices concentrate on the way in which prejudices are transmitted through socialization and the social circumstances that compel discriminatory behaviour (Marger, 1997). For example, the *socialization approach* focuses on how we are taught ethnic and racial stereotypes, prejudices, and attitudes by our families, peer groups, and the mass media. For instance, as a teenager in Saskatchewan in the 1970s, I remember watching the TV show *All in the Family*. People in Saskatchewan at the time held many prejudicial attitudes, particularly toward Aboriginal people. However, the television program *All in the Family* exposed my generation to a repertoire of ethnic and racial slang and stereotypes that we had not heard before. Archie Bunker, the show's central character, was supposed to be a caricature of an American "bigot," but he also taught us terms like "wop," "dago," "spic," and "nigger," and the corresponding stereotypes. Similarly, as Box 8.2 (p. 188) shows, the English language places different values on the colours black and white in subtle ways. Our language, in turn, shapes how we perceive and socially evaluate different racial groups.

Socialization theories are superior to social-psychological and primordialist approaches because they emphasize the way in which ethnic and racial prejudices and attitudes are learned through social interaction. The limitation of socialization theories is that they are unable to explain how prejudicial ideas, attitudes, and practices arise in the first place. This is where power-conflict theories come into play.

Power-Conflict Theories

Karl Marx (1967 [1867]: 751) wrote that "the turning of Africa into a warren for the commercial hunting of black-skins signaled the rosy dawn of the era of capitalist production." Marx did not take his analysis of slavery and racism much farther than that. Later

BOX 8.2   LANGUAGE, COLOUR OF RACE

Language is an integral part of our culture. Language not only expresses ideas but shapes our thought. Our childhood socialization involves, in part, the ability to use language. In the following "Short Play on 'Black' and 'White' Words," Robert Moore shows how aspects of our language help unwittingly to reproduce both negative and positive racial imagery:

"Some may blackly (angrily) accuse me of trying to blacken (defame) the English language . . . I may become a black sheep (one who causes shame or embarrassment because of deviation from the accepted standards), who will be blackballed (ostracized) by being placed on a blacklist (list of undesirables) in an attempt to blackmail (to force or coerce into a particular action) me to retract my words. But attempts to blackjack (to compel by threat) me will have a Chinaman's chance of success, for I am not

a yellow-bellied Indian-giver of words, who will whitewash (cover up or gloss over vices or crimes) a black lie (harmful, inexcusable). I challenge the purity and innocence (white) of the English language. I don't see things in black and white (entirely bad or entirely good) terms, for I am a white man (marked by upright firmness) if there ever was one. . . . While many may be niggardly (grudging, scanty) in their support, others will be honest and decent—and to them I say, that's very white of you (honest, decent).

"The preceding is of course a white lie (not intended to cause harm), meant only to illustrate some examples of racist terminology in the English language."

SOURCE: "Racist Stereotyping in the English Language" by Robert B. Moore (pp. 269–297). Reprinted from *Racism in the English Language* by Robert B. Moore, Council on Interracial Books for Children, 1976.

generations of Marxist scholars, however, have sought to link racism to the structure of capitalist societies.

Orthodox Marxists argue that racism is an *ideology*—a set of statements shaped by economic interests about the way the social world "really works." Racism is ideological insofar as it is used by capitalists to mystify social reality and justify the exploitation and the unequal treatment of groups of people.

This justification can take many forms. For example, in the seventeenth century, American and Caribbean plantation owners justified the use of Africans as slaves by denying the humanity of Africans (Williams, 1964). In Marxist terms, the existence of racist ideas did not cause slavery; rather, slavery was a particular system of labour control that was justified by racist ideology.

In the case of advanced capitalism, racism is viewed by Marxists as an ideology that justifies the especially intense exploitation of racial minority and immigrant workers (Bolaria and Li, 1988; Castles and Kosack, 1984). From this point of view, racist ideas are used by employers as a means of creating artificial divisions in the working class so as to prevent the formation of a class consciousness that would threaten the social and economic order (Bolaria and Li, 1988; Castles and Kosack, 1984; Nikolinakos, 1973). Also, racist ideas help to justify the allocation of certain groups to low-wage, socially marginal jobs.

Race and the Split Labour Market   Split labour-market theory was developed by Edna Bonacich

(1972, 1979) because of the limitations of orthodox Marxism in analyzing racism. She argues that orthodox Marxism tends to assume that the capitalist class is all-powerful and that other classes play no role in the development of racist thinking. This is inaccurate; racism is found in all classes to varying degrees. Second, orthodox Marxism portrays racism in overly conspiratorial terms. Little evidence demonstrates that capitalists sit around plotting new and devious ways of using racism to stop workers from developing class consciousness. Third, orthodox Marxism has trouble explaining why racialized conflict so often results in *exclusionary practices*—practices that deny employers access to cheaper, more exploitable labour. In 1885, for example, the Canadian government instituted a "head tax" on new immigrants from China. Chinese immigrants had to pay $50 to the federal government. In 1900, the tax was raised to $100, and in 1903 to $500. The Chinese Immigration Act of 1923 completely barred Chinese immigration until 1947 (Li, 1988: 30). If racism is developed by capitalists to justify exploitation, then why does it so often result in efforts to block the entry of new immigrants and limit the job opportunities of those already in the country? Bonacich feels that more attention has to be paid to the way in which the competition for jobs and other scarce resources among the working class creates and sustains racism.

Split labour-market theory suggests that racial and ethnic conflict is rooted in differences in the price of labour. For historical reasons—mainly involving military conquest—non-white workers have often received low wages and white workers high wages. Employers try to replace high-paid white workers with low-paid non-white workers. Meanwhile, high-paid workers, faced with displacement or the threat of displacement, try to protect their own interests by limiting capitalists' access to cheaper non-white workers. Thus, cheaper non-white workers are the victims of a complicated process of class struggle between expensive labour, cheap labour, and capitalists.

The theory applies well to Canada. During the late nineteenth and early twentieth centuries, the presence of Chinese workers and merchants in British Columbia provoked a negative response on the part of various segments of the white working class and white shop owners. As split labour-market theory predicts, the hostility of whites was rooted in differences in the price of labour. According to evidence presented at the Royal Commission on Chinese and Japanese Immigration in 1903, Chinese workers earned about one-half of the wages that white workers earned in the same jobs (Li, 1988: 44). A number of racist organizations emerged whose aim was to limit the number of places where Chinese people could work, which helped stop additional Chinese immigration (Roy, 1989).

Split labour-market theory makes three other points that are relevant to the analysis of ethnic and race relations in general. First, it argues that individual racism, ethnic prejudice, and institutional racism emerge from intergroup conflict. Second, the theory maintains that prejudicial ideas and discriminatory behaviour are ways of socially marginalizing minority groups that the dominant group sees as threats to their position of power and privilege. Third, the theory suggests that to understand ethnic and racial relations, we need to look beyond individual personalities and sociobiological processes and analyze processes of economic, social, and political competition among groups (Marger, 1997: 98).

Keeping these three observations in mind will help you understand the three main patterns of ethnic and racial relations in Canada: Aboriginal–non-Aboriginal relations, French–English relations, and immigrant–non-immigrant relations. These are the topics that we turn to next.

ABORIGINAL PEOPLES

Have you ever fumbled trying to find the right way to refer to someone who is ethnically or racially different from you? Are we supposed to say that a person is a "Native," an "Indian," an "Aboriginal," or a member of the "First Nations"? Are you sensitive about how you want others to refer to your own ethnic or racial origins? You may think that this sensitivity is an indication that political correctness has run amok. In either case, you should not dismiss the issue of labels and names easily.

Ethnic and racial labels are about power. Take the term *Indian*. A hopelessly lost Christopher Columbus thought he had found a sea route to India when he was discovered in 1492 by people indigenous to this part of the world. He mislabelled the people he met as "Indians." Britain's military, political, and economic domination of North America in the 1700s meant that it had the power to ignore the linguistic and cultural differences among indigenous groups and define them in any way they saw fit. They chose the term *Indian*.

As indigenous people have acquired more power, they have begun to challenge externally imposed labels. In the 1980s, for example, the National Indian Brotherhood renamed itself the Assembly of First Nations, and people in Alberta who were called Sarcee Indians by Europeans for most of the twentieth century now refer to themselves as Tsuu T'ina, which means "Earth People" in English (Steckley, 2003: 7). Groups have rejected externally imposed labels as part of a search for forms of consciousness, identity, and culture that are untainted by the colonizing power's definition of the situation (Jenson, 1993).

One, albeit imperfect, way to navigate through the complex issue of naming is to use the definition of "Aboriginal peoples" in the 1982 Canadian Charter of Rights and Freedoms. In the Charter, the "Aboriginal peoples" of Canada include Indians, Inuit, and Métis. In 2005, there were 748 400 Indians, and in 2006 there were 389 780 Métis, and 50 480 Inuit in Canada, who together made up nearly 4 percent of the total population.

At its simplest level, the term *Indian* (or *status* or *registered Indian*) refers to people who are recognized as "Indians" by virtue of the federal government's Indian Act. Many people now use the term "First Nations" to refer to Indians. But deciding who is an Indian under the Indian Act is a much more complicated question. Until 1985, Indian women who married non-Indian men, along with their children, lost their federally recognized Indian status; they became *non-status Indians*. In 1985, Bill C-31 was passed. It allowed these women and their dependent children to regain their Indian status. Indian bands, however, now have the power to develop their own membership codes. This means that not all individuals who have had their Indian status reinstated are members of an Indian band (Frideres and Gadacz, 2005: 35).

There are two definitions of *Métis*. Métis organizations in Western Canada tend to focus on a person's objective "roots" as the condition for being considered Métis. Thus, the Métis National Council defines the Métis as "descendants of the historic Métis who evolved in what is now Western Canada as a people with a common political will" (Métis National Council, 1983). The Congress of Aboriginal Peoples uses a broader definition suggesting that the Métis should include descendants of the historic Métis in Western Canada *and* anyone of mixed European-Indian ancestry who defines himself or herself as Métis (Congress of Aboriginal Peoples, 2008). Thus, subjective definitions of ethnic group membership are more important for groups like the Congress of Aboriginal Peoples.

Finally, *Inuit* are part of a diverse group of people who have lived for many centuries north of the tree line. In Canada, the name *Inuit* has replaced the earlier name *Eskimo*. The language of the Inuit is Inuktitut (McMillan, 1988: 240).

EXPLANATIONS OF ABORIGINAL CONDITIONS

The socioeconomic conditions of Canada's Aboriginal people are a national tragedy (Royal Commission on Aboriginal Peoples, 1996). Canada has made admirable efforts to condemn social inequality and the denial of human rights in other countries, such as South Africa when apartheid—the policy of legalized ethnic separation and inequality—was still in force. Ironically, though, the commitment to social justice for Aboriginal peoples in our own country has not been as strong. In the 1980s, the South African government routinely defended itself against our criticisms of apartheid by saying that we should first clean up our own backyard (Bourgeault, 1988; York, 1989). Statistical evidence shows that Aboriginal peoples are the most socially and economically disadvantaged groups in the country. In 2002–2003, 46.8 percent of housing units on reserves in Canada needed to be replaced or were in need of major or minor repairs (Department of Indian Affairs and Northern Development [DIAND], 2004: 62). Though DIAND statistics indicate that 98 percent of houses on reserves have adequate water supplies (DIAND, 2004: 63), the October 2005 mass evacuation of the Kashechewan

reserve in northern Ontario because of water supply problems shows that decent water supplies are not available to all reserve communities; indeed, 98 other reserve communities were also under boil water advisories at the same time (Curry, 2005).

On average, Aboriginal people have much lower family incomes, lower rates of labour-force participation, and higher rates of unemployment than non-Aboriginal Canadians do (Frideres and Gadacz, 2005: 98–107). The crude death rate for Aboriginal people in Canada was 8.0 per 1000 in 2001, compared with a rate of 5.3 per 1000 for Canada as a whole (Frideres and Gadacz, 2005: 72). In 2005, the life expectancy of status Indian men was 71.1 years, 6 years lower than the Canadian average. Life expectancy for status Indian women was higher than that for Indian men but still below life expectancy for other Canadian women: 76.3 compared with 82.4 years. In 2000, the infant mortality rate (the number of deaths of children under one year old per 1000 people) for status Indians was 6.4, which was 14 percent higher than the national rate of 5.5 (DIAND, 2004: 28).

For many years, Canadian politicians, bureaucrats, and social scientists have puzzled over where these differences and inequalities come from, how and why they persist, and what can be done about them. Indeed, when the federal government announced in 1991 the establishment of the Royal Commission on Aboriginal Peoples, Ovide Mercredi, then chief of the Assembly of First Nations, caustically commented that "Indians have been studied to death." I want first to consider the federal government's historical explanation of these conditions and then examine two sociological accounts of them: the culture of poverty thesis and the conflict theory.

The Government's View

Throughout the first half of the twentieth century, government Indian policy was premised on the belief that Aboriginal culture was both different from and inferior to European culture. Armed with this ethnocentric attitude, the federal government sought to assimilate Aboriginal people into mainstream Canadian society (Gibbins and Ponting, 1986). In 1920, this approach was summed up in the following terms by Duncan Campbell Scott, the deputy minister of the federal government's Department of Indian Affairs: "[O]ur object is to continue until there is not a single Indian . . . that has not been absorbed into the body politic and there is no [longer an] Indian question" (quoted in Titley, 1986).

The government, therefore, forcibly tried to Europeanize Aboriginal people and culture. Traditional cultural practices like the potlatch, a winter exchange of gifts and property on the British Columbia coast, and the sun dance, a summer solstice religious ceremony on the Prairies, were outlawed. Such practices were regarded as pagan, anti-capitalist rituals that inhibited the development of both Christianity and a capitalistic work ethic (Cole and Chaikin, 1990; Pettipas, 1995). The federal government also tried to assimilate and Christianize Aboriginal children by establishing a series of residential schools. These boarding schools were located far from the children's families and home communities. While in school, the children were forbidden to speak in their mother tongue and to speak with siblings of the opposite sex and had their hair shorn. Boys were given extensive training in manual labour and girls were taught domestic labour skills. The goal of this schooling was to resocialize Aboriginal children and to instill in them a new European identity (Titley, 1986). The government's legislative, regulatory, and educational approach to Aboriginal people reflected the view that inequality, poverty, and poor social conditions were rooted in Aboriginal cultural and racial inferiority.

The Culture of Poverty Thesis

In the 1960s and 1970s, many sociologists also saw Aboriginal culture as the source of the "Indian problem." To account for the origins and persistence of the problem, some sociologists proposed a variant of the **culture of poverty thesis.** The concept of a culture of poverty was first developed by Oscar Lewis (1961), an American anthropologist interested in explaining the slow pace at which Mexican Americans and Puerto Ricans were being assimilated into U.S. society. He suggested that some ethnic groups do not readily assimilate, and hence are poor, because their culture does not value economic success, hard work, and achievement.

Kazemipur and Halli (2000) have applied Lewis's framework to the issue of ethnic poverty in Canada, and Nagler (1972) has applied it to the conditions of Aboriginal people. In his view, Indian culture displayed the following characteristics: a present rather than a future time-orientation, a high value on mutual aid without the expectation of return, a lack of emphasis on the possession of material goods, a lack of appreciation for the monetary value of time, and the absence of a capitalist work ethic. These cultural characteristics meant that "a large segment of the Indian

population refuse or find themselves unable to partake in full time economic pursuits" (Nagler, 1972: 131).

Sociologists like Steven Steinberg (1981) criticize culture of poverty explanations by arguing that groups generally do not get ahead or lag behind because of their cultural values. Instead, they are born into certain stations in life and adopt the values and attitudes that are consistent with their life-chances. If Aboriginal people have low aspirations, it is likely the result of a realistic assessment of their dismal job prospects and a resignation born out of bitter personal experience. For Steinberg, the *culture* of poverty is the consequence, not the cause, of poverty.

Conflict Theory

Since the 1970s, sociologists have focused on blocked opportunities rather than culture as the explanation for inequalities between Aboriginal and non-Aboriginal people. The *internal colonial model* is the most popular variant of the conflict approach (Frideres and Gadacz, 2005). The internal colonial model analyzes the problem of inequality in terms of power imbalances and the exploitation of Aboriginal people and lands by white society.

Theorists of internal colonialism argue that the Indian Act, which outlines the federal government's policies and procedures for dealing with Indian issues, is a paternalistic document that disempowers Indian people (Frideres and Gadacz, 2005). It places real limits on the actions of both individual Indians and their band councils. When Indians from Brantford, Ontario, wanted to sue the federal government over unfulfilled treaty promises in the 1920s, the government passed a law making it illegal for them to use band funds to hire lawyers to pursue their claims (Titley, 1986). Indians did not get much help from federal or provincial/territorial politicians either. Since Indians could not vote in either federal or provincial/territorial elections until the 1960s, politicians had no need to stand up for the interests of Indians who lived in their constituency. Chiefs who failed to cooperate with the government's designs were routinely removed from their positions (Satzewich and Mahood, 1994). Band councils are still required to have their decisions approved by the federal minister of Indian Affairs. Thus, rather than helping to create the social conditions that would afford Indian people greater autonomy over their lives, government policy has fostered social marginality and dependence. This is why many Indian leaders have called for the abolition of the Indian Act.

Furthermore, most of the present-day conflicts between Aboriginal people and various levels of government originated in the past misuse of power by government officials. Present-day land-claim disputes sometimes go back 100 years, when government officials could arbitrarily lop off chunks of Indian reserve land and sell it to whites (Frideres and Gadacz, 2005). The Canadian government and private business have derived tremendous economic benefits from the exploitation of land appropriated from Aboriginal communities. According to many observers, the time has come for Canadians to pay the rent. In Alberta, Aboriginal people are suing the federal government for $1.5 billion over the nonpayment of royalties on the extraction of resources from their land. As Frideres and Gadacz (2005: 5) note, with long-term profits estimated at $1 billion to $2 billion, the government and private enterprise "are not about to give up easily."

CLASS AND GENDER DIVERSITY

Criticisms of the internal colonial model have focused on its tendency to overgeneralize about the conditions of Aboriginal people in Canada. As significant as inequalities between Aboriginal and non-Aboriginal people are, conflict and feminist sociologists argue that it is worth remembering that socioeconomic diversity also exists within Aboriginal communities. These sociologists analyze class and gender differentiation within Aboriginal communities and the implications of such differences for both individual life-chances and wider community life (Satzewich and Wotherspoon, 2001).

Feminist sociologists have been interested in the role of gender in recent debates about the inclusion of the right to self-government in the Canadian Constitution. During the debate over the Charlottetown Accord in 1992, many Aboriginal women were concerned that the proposal for self-government, which was advanced by the predominantly male leadership of Aboriginal organizations, did not contain any guarantees of gender equality (Fiske, 1996; Krosenbrink-Gelissen, 1994: 357–60). The Native Women's Association of Canada, therefore, fought against the accord in the months leading up to the referendum.

Other conflict theorists are interested in the political and economic implications of socioeconomic differentiation within Aboriginal communities. Researchers challenge the stereotype that all Aboriginal

A significant proportion of Aboriginal men and women are owners and managers of both small and large businesses. John Kim Bell, for example, put his musical career on hold to set up the Canadian Native Arts Foundation.
SOURCE: The Canadian Press (Colin McConnell).

people are either poor, unemployed, living on welfare, or working in low-skill, dead-end jobs. In fact, a small but significant proportion of Aboriginal men and women work in skilled professional and technical occupations, and others are owners or managers of small and large businesses (Gerber, 1990). Menno Boldt (1993: 124) argues that most Indian reserves are characterized by a two-class social order (see also Alfred, 1999). The first class consists of "a small, virtually closed élite class comprising influential landowners, politicians, bureaucrats, and a few entrepreneurs," while the second consists of "a large lower class comprising destitute, dependent, powerless [and wage-earning] people" (Boldt, 1993: 124). Boldt argues (1993: 125) that this two-class structure has important consequences for community life and politics:

With the élite class controlling the political agenda, lower-class interests get neglected.

Elite class interests tend to be primarily "power" not "problem" oriented; that is, such interests are related to expanding their jurisdiction and control over band/tribal political and administrative structures. . . . [These] are given preference over the problems that afflict the Indian lower class: high unemployment; excessive rates of family disintegration; alcohol and substance abuse; extraordinary levels of violence, suicide, incarceration, and so on.

Researchers are also studying the formation of a capitalist class within Aboriginal communities. Land-claim settlements, although ostensibly earmarked for the benefit of all community members, are frequently controlled by small ruling elites. In the case of the Inuit, Marybelle Mitchell (1996: 449) argues,

The state's acknowledgment in 1973 of its responsibility to negotiate land settlements with Native people led to the formation of an Inuit ruling class. Created by the state to facilitate access by the multinationals to the Arctic's natural resources, these leaders, a wholly new kind of talking chief, are signing away the land and aboriginal rights of their fellow Inuit in return for limited entitlement to land, some managerial powers and varying amounts of cash channeled through development corporations.

The members of this new capitalist class are different from other Canadian capitalists, in that they do not personally own all the wealth and capital that is at their disposal. They do, however, control the compensation that communities receive from land-claims settlements. They establish development corporations, hire and fire employees, make capital-planning and investment decisions, and decide what and how much to produce. The unanswered sociological question is whether this capitalist class will make decisions about the future that are in their own material interests or in the interests of the community as a whole.

QUEBEC: NATIONALISM AND IDENTITY

On the evening of October 30, 1995, many adult Canadians were tuned to TV or radio coverage of the Quebec referendum on separation. I followed the results that night with mixed emotions. On the one

hand, as a second-generation Canadian with no ethnic roots in the old British Empire, I could empathize with people in Quebec. On the other hand, as a child of the Trudeau years, I was socialized to believe in a vision of Canadian unity. Many on the "no" side believed that a lot of Quebeckers were just bluffing in the pre-referendum rhetoric; when it came to the crunch, they would vote in favour of staying in Canada. Then the results came in. In some parts of Quebec, 90 percent of voters were in favour of separation. As the results from around Montreal were tabulated, the "no" side gained ground. When the final count was tallied, 49.6 percent of Quebeckers voted for separation. Across Canada, people were both exhilarated and downcast because Canada had "won."

Will the issue of separation go away? Despite the ebb and flow in support for separation, the answer is clearly "no." As with other areas of ethnic relations in Canada, an understanding of the contemporary scene must begin with an appreciation of history and of power relations. In this section, I examine three main sociological questions: (1) What is the historical basis for the emergence of Québécois nationalism? (2) Who is a Québécois? (3) What does the close 1995 vote mean for ethnic relations in Quebec and the country?

THE SOCIAL BASIS OF QUÉBÉCOIS NATIONALISM

Even though the 1867 British North America Act asserted that there were two founding peoples of Canada, the English and the French, and that they had equal places in Canadian Confederation, *les Québécois* are one of the oldest colonized peoples in the world (Milner and Milner, 1973). The French government controlled the colony of New France from the early 1600s to 1763. The inhabitants of New France were expected to serve the interests of France. The colony was established in part to pursue the fur trade and to transfer economic resources to the mother country. Much of the French commercial and political elite left the colony following the British victory over France in 1763. When New France was transferred to British control—what the Québécois refer to as "The Conquest"—a new colonizing power came to dominate the society.

An anglophone—unilingual, English-speaking— elite gradually took over the economic and political affairs of the province. Most French-Canadian peasants *(habitants)* remained subsistence farmers. During the nineteenth century, some of them immigrated to the northeastern United States to work in the expanding cotton and linen mills; others moved to other provinces in Canada; and still others became part of the urban industrial working class in the province (Ramirez, 1991). By the late nineteenth century, Quebec was a province where "capital speaks English and labour speaks French" (Whitaker, 1993: 22)—a telling description of the way in which linguistic and class structures overlapped. The French Canadians in Quebec, who formed a numerical majority, were worse off than the anglophone minority in virtually every material way (Whitaker, 1993: 22).

The Catholic Church occupied a unique position as a social, political, and religious intermediary between the two groups. In addition to attending to the religious needs of its French-speaking parishioners, the Catholic Church acted as an agent of social control over French-Canadian workers and farmers. The church promoted ideologies that were conservative and anti-modern. It devalued the importance of formal education for the masses, dis-couraged workers from forming and joining secular trade unions, encouraged married couples to have large families, and vigorously discouraged French Canadians from taking up professions or establishing businesses of their own. These ideas were not in the best material interests of French-Canadian workers and farmers, but they helped ensure the survival of French-Canadian culture (Latouche, 1993).

This social structure began to change significantly during the rapid industrialization stimulated by World War I, as the industrial working class became a significant player on the political scene. One of the biggest changes in the 1940s and 1950s was the rise of a new francophone middle class of technical workers and professionals. The upper echelons of the corporate world, still under the control of anglophones, remained hostile to the advancement of francophones, even if they were bilingual. The new francophone middle class, therefore, faced a situation of blocked social mobility, which was partly responsible for the Quiet Revolution in Quebec.

The term **Quiet Revolution** describes the social, political, and cultural changes that occurred in Quebec in the 1960s, in part because of the initiatives of this new middle class. These changes included the secularization of the educational system, reform of the civil service, growth in the provincially controlled public sector, greater involvement of the Quebec provincial government in the economic affairs of the province, and questioning of the Catholic Church's authority in all areas of life. Facing blocked mobility in the corporate world, francophones created their own economic opportunities by expanding the power of the provincial government.

Social scientists and political pundits have pored over referendum and federal and provincial election results over the past 30 years in an effort to determine which social forces are responsible for sustaining the push for sovereignty. Some see the present-day sovereignty movement as an expression of *middle-class nationalism* that is a continuation of the Quiet Revolution. From this perspective, separation is being promoted by middle-class professionals as a way of furthering their own material interests. Emboldened by the success at expanding the activities of the provincial government during the Quiet Revolution, they desire even more control over their affairs (Whitaker, 1993).

However, likening the sovereignty movement to a massive job-creation project is too simplistic. First, francophone professionals are no longer shut out of the corporate sector in Quebec. Over the past 30 years, middle-class francophones have achieved upward mobility in both the private and the public sectors. Second, a diversity of class interests exists within the sovereignty movement. Many francophone professionals support sovereignty, but there is also a social democratic tradition within the movement that is trying to mobilize working people against foreign (anglophone and U.S.) capitalist domination. Their vision of a sovereign Quebec involves a reorganization of power relations between francophones and non-francophones, and between workers and capitalists. Some francophone capitalists also support the sovereignty movement (Whitaker, 1993).

Clearly, the contemporary sovereignty movement is not based on the support of only one social class. According to Fleras and Elliot (1996), the nationalist movement is sustained by a broadly based desire among most francophone Quebeckers to achieve a common goal—to create the conditions that will allow them to preserve their French language and culture and to "*voler de ses propres ailes* (fly on their own wings) by acquiring the freedom to make their own decisions on everything from cultural policy to social development" (Turp, 2005: A25). Fleras and Elliot argue that, rather than defining support for the sovereignty movement in class terms, it is more useful to conceptualize the movement as made up of groups who have differing views about how best to maintain their language and culture. Thus, the present-day sovereignty movement consists in part of moderates who want to strengthen Quebec's position within the federal system. This involves a new constitutional division of powers that has yet to be settled. Radical supporters, however, argue that the best way for the French language and culture to survive is for the people of Quebec to have their own state. They argue that they will always be a minority if they stay in Canada and that they will always be subject to the tyranny of the majority. As Louise Beaudoin of the Parti Québécois put it, "I want to be a majority in my own country" (Fleras and Elliot, 1996: 270).

WHO IS QUÉBÉCOIS?

The population of Quebec is ethnically heterogeneous—19.4 percent of the population of Quebec is made up of people whose mother tongue is not French: Jews, anglophones, allophones (people whose mother tongue is neither French nor English), visible-minority immigrants, and Aboriginal people (Fournier, Rosenberg, and White, 1997: 282). One of the central issues facing the nationalist movement in Quebec is the definition of a Québécois. This question cuts to the heart of ethnic relations in the province.

Benedict Anderson (1983) regards nations as "imagined communities." They are imagined in the sense that, even though members of the smallest nation can never know everyone in the community, there is still a common feeling of fellowship with others in the nation. People in Shawinigan do not personally know all other Quebeckers. Nevertheless, they have a comradeship that extends beyond personal relationships. Nations also possess physical and symbolic boundaries that define who is a member and who is not. Sociologists interested in nationalism want to identify the symbolic boundaries of the nation. In the case of the nationalist movement in Quebec, this issue is translated into the question of who is "in" and who is "outside" the imagined community. And if some groups are "out," will they ever be accepted as Québécois?

A majority of nationalists define the imagined community as all people who now live in the province of Quebec. For them, the social and symbolic boundaries of the nation correspond to present-day provincial boundaries. Sociologists call this a form of **civic nationalism** (Balthazar, 1993).

A minority of nationalists reject civic nationalism in favour of cultural and linguistic criteria for

With 19.4 percent of Quebec's population made up of people whose mother tongue is not French, one of the central issues facing the nationalist movement in Quebec is the definition of a Québécois.
SOURCE: Megapress/Alamy.

membership in the nation. *Ethnic nationalists* define the Québécois as people who share a common history, culture, ancestry, or language. This is where the concept of *pure laine* ("pure wool") Québécois becomes important. Some nationalists regard the true Québécois as only those who are the direct descendants of the French people who settled in the colony of New France before the conquest of 1763. Other groups in the province are regarded as "cultural communities" (Groupe de recherche ethnicité et societé [GRES], 1997: 107). According to the province's policy of interculturalism, these cultural communities must learn to accommodate themselves to the dominant francophone culture and language.

The debate about how to define a nation is not academic hairsplitting. Then Premier Jacques Parizeau commented on referendum night in 1995 that the pro-sovereignty forces were defeated by "money and the ethnic vote." After his resignation, Parizeau commented further that it was the first time in Canadian history that the majority (60 percent) of francophone Quebeckers voted in favour of sovereignty. These statements implied that ethnic minorities were not really part of the nation and that *pure laine* votes should be worth more than the votes of others. At the time, Parizeau's remarks also confirmed the worst fears of ethnic minorities—namely, that sovereigntists are not civic nationalists but rather ethnic nationalists at heart and that ethnic minorities will never be considered full and equal citizens in a sovereign Quebec (Ha, 1995).

Many people in the sovereignty movement distanced themselves from Parizeau's comments, and the movement has sought to repair the damage that they caused to ethnic relations. Yet polls conducted in 2005 indicated that just more than half of Quebeckers would vote in favour of sovereignty in a new referendum ("A Dream," 2005: 8). A possible reason for the resurgence in support for sovereignty is that the "children of Bill 101" are coming of age. Bill 101 was enacted in 1977 and requires that the children of immigrants attend francophone schools. Immigrant children educated in francophone schools are now entering the political arena and many believe that their interests would be better served in an independent Quebec (Laforest, 2005: A25; Turp, 2005: A25).

Even though some of the children of immigrants may be buying into the sovereignty movement, the nature of Quebec identity continues to be hotly debated. In 2007, the government of Quebec established the Consultation Commission on Accommodation Practices Related to Cultural Differences to investigate public discontent over the nature of change in Quebec society occurring as a result of immigration and increasing cultural and religious diversity. The "Reasonable Accommodation Commission," as it came to be known, held public forums around the province. Quebeckers from all walks of life participated in these forums. Some embraced the new diversity and called for renewed effort to welcome newcomers and ethno-religious communities. Others expressed anxiety over the future of Quebec's core, secular values and the status of the French language and French culture in North America (Bouchard and Taylor, 2008: 37). As Commissioners Gerard Bouchard and Charles Taylor suggested:

> The main danger we are facing is that the groups that make up our society combine their mistrust and (largely unfounded) reciprocal fears and thus jeopardize the *rapprochment* process now under way. In other words, there is a risk that our imaginary fears will engender a genuine danger. We are thinking, in particular, of the still fragile Quebec identity that has taken shape in recent decades and continues to grow despite our differences, or more precisely, from our differences. Moreover, and quite rightly, it is abundantly but freely sustained by the French-Canadian heritage, a very rich heritage that is thus enjoying a new life not by closing in on itself but by opening up the

> creative, fruitful contribution of the Other. This is precisely what it has done repeatedly in the past. In short, it is the future of the Quebec nation that is at stake here. (Bouchard and Taylor, 2008: 242)

Quebeckers, and Canadians more generally, intently followed the work of the Reasonable Accommodation Commission. Clearly, the larger issues it raised about the nature of Quebec identity resonate within Canada more generally.

IMMIGRATION: STATE FORMATION AND ECONOMIC DEVELOPMENT

The third aspect of ethnic and racial relations in Canada that I consider is immigrant–non-immigrant relations. In 2006, 6.2 million immigrants were living in Canada, representing 19.8 percent of our population. In large cities, the impact of immigration is even greater. In 2006, immigrants made up 20.6 percent of the population of Montreal, 24.3 percent of the population of Hamilton, 39.6 percent of the population of Vancouver, and 45.7 percent of the population of Toronto (Statistics Canada, 2008). Canada accepts more immigrants and refugees in proportion to our population than virtually any other country in the world (Li, 2003).

Migration has been a feature of our history for more than 300 years. However, the nature, sources, determinants, and consequences of immigration have varied through history. In the nineteenth century, immigrants contributed to the processes of capitalist state formation—the process of creating a capitalist system of production and governance. They did this in a number of ways. The early working class in Canada was made up largely of immigrants (Avery, 1995; Pentland, 1981). Immigrant workers helped build the canals, railways, and roads that became part of our economic infrastructure. Many nineteenth-century immigrants were farmers. Their crops were used to feed Canadian workers and, as productivity increased, were exported to feed people in other countries. Those same farmers, in turn, helped stimulate capitalist industry through their roles as consumers of goods. A significant proportion of the corporate elite in nineteenth-century Canada were made up of immigrants (Clement, 1975; Macmillan, 1985), as was a large segment of the early political elite. Canada's first prime minister, Sir John A. Macdonald, was an immigrant from Glasgow, Scotland.

Immigrants continue to make important contributions to the social reproduction of Canadian society. Demographers predict that, in the absence of new immigrants, the population of Canada would begin to decline by 2015. Without new immigrants to replenish our population, the next generation of taxpayers would have to pay far more in taxes and Canada Pension Plan contributions. Retiring at the age of 55, or even 65, would become a pipe dream for many older workers, as employers and governments would need to take steps to retain enough workers. Employers would face serious shortages of workers, and manufacturers would face a much smaller consumer market in which to sell their goods (Economic Council of Canada, 1991).

FACTORS THAT SHAPE CANADIAN IMMIGRATION

No single variable can explain the complex pattern of immigration to Canada. Over the past 100 years, six main variables have influenced which groups of people have been let into the country as immigrants.

The first variable is social class. Most immigrants are admitted to Canada because they fill jobs in the Canadian economy, have certain skills that are in demand, or because they create jobs for other Canadians. As such, the flow of immigrants to Canada has been very closely linked to the overall structure of the Canadian economy. Between 1947 and the early 1960s, for example, immigrants were regarded by the Canadian government as what Australian economist Jock Collins (1988) calls "factory fodder." Immigrants were recruited to fill unskilled and semiskilled manual jobs in agriculture, construction, mining, logging, the garment industry, and heavy manufacturing. During this time, it was common for individual employers to demand that the government recruit as many as 300 immigrant workers at a time to fill job openings (Avery, 1995).

In the early 1960s, immigration policy began to place more emphasis on the recruitment of highly skilled professional and technical workers, and on immigrants with large amounts of investment capital. As a result, by 2001, immigrants made up 18.4 percent of the population and 19.9 percent of the total Canadian labour force, but 21.7 percent of people in managerial occupations and 21.4 percent of people in professional and technical occupations (Statistics Canada, 2001).

The second determinant of immigration is ethnic and racial **stereotypes**—exaggerated, oversimplified images of the characteristics of social groups. Before 1962, Canadian immigration policy had a racialized hierarchy of desirability. Immigration policy was based on the assumption that European immigrants were racially and culturally superior to all other potential immigrants. Non-Europeans were stereotyped as racially and culturally inferior and, therefore, were not welcome. In the 1950s, for example, immigration officials could bar groups from entering Canada on the grounds that the groups were "unsuited to climatic and economic conditions" or that they were "unable to assimilate" (Bolaria and Li, 1988). These phrases were thinly veiled masks for racial preferences in the selection of immigrants.

Since 1962, ethnic and racial stereotyping in selecting new immigrants has become less important. Canadian immigration policy is now more open in terms of the ethnic and racial origins of immigrants (see Table 8.3, p. 198). Before 1961, Europeans made up more than 90 percent of total immigrants to Canada. Now, immigrants from Europe make up about 17 percent of the yearly flow of immigrants to Canada.

The third variable that shapes immigrant selection consists of a variety of geopolitical considerations stemming from Canada's relationships with other countries. Racist selection criteria were taken out of immigration regulations in the 1960s, in part because they interfered with Canadian international diplomacy. In the early 1960s, Canada began to assert itself as a middle power in world politics that could mediate social conflicts in and between other countries. Outside of Europe, though, our diplomats did not have much credibility because our immigration policy implied that certain groups were inferior and therefore not suited to life in Canada (Hawkins, 1989).

In the 1980s, the Cold War also played a role in shaping who was let in. According to Whitaker (1987), a double standard was at work in the admittance of refugees. People who managed to escape from the Soviet Union or other Eastern Bloc countries were routinely granted refugee status in Canada. In 1985, for example, it took a day for the brother of a Czech hockey star who played for the Toronto Maple Leafs to be granted refugee status in Canada. Canadian immigration bureaucrats were much more cautious, however, about admitting "socialist" refugees who were fleeing right-wing dictatorships in various Central American countries.

The fourth variable affecting immigrant selection is humanitarianism. Canada accepts immigrants and refugees partly on humanitarian and compassionate

TABLE 8.3 TOP 10 SOURCE COUNTRIES OF IMMIGRANTS (PRINCIPAL APPLICANTS AND DEPENDENTS) TO CANADA, 1968, 2007

1968		2007	
COUNTRY OF ORIGIN	NUMBER	COUNTRY OF ORIGIN	NUMBER
United Kingdom	63 291	China	27 014
Italy	31 625	India	26 054
United States	17 514	Philippines	19 064
Germany	9 263	United States	10 450
Portugal	7 930	Pakistan	9 547
France	7 872	United Kingdom	8 128
Greece	7 174	Iran	6 663
The Netherlands	3 749	Korea, Republic of	5 864
Australia	3 329	France	5 526
Switzerland	2 982	Columbia	4 833

SOURCE: Manpower and Immigration, 1967, *Immigration Statistics, 1966,* Ottawa: Queen's Printer, p. 5; Citizenship and Immigration Canada, 2008; Facts and Figures 2007; Immigration Overview—Permanent and Temporary Residents 2007; www.cic.gc.ca/english/pdf/pub/facts2007. Adapted and reproduced with permission of the Minister of Public Works and Government Services Canada, 2009.

grounds. In 1986, Canada was the first country ever to be awarded the Nansen Medal by the United Nations for its generosity and commitment to international refugee programs (Fleras and Elliot, 1996).

The influence of the fifth variable, public opinion, is more difficult to determine, in part because Canadians do not speak with one voice regarding immigration (Wilkes, Guppy, and Farris, 2008). A 1991 poll found five distinct segments of opinion regarding immigration. Twenty-three percent were "protagonists" who supported increased levels of immigration and believed that immigrants made important contributions to the betterment of Canadian society; 22 percent were "concerned supporters" who approved of current levels of immigration but who were concerned that immigration had certain negative effects on Canadian institutions; 21 percent were "indifferent" in their attitudes toward immigration and ambivalent about the contributions that immigrants make; 19 percent were "reactionaries" who felt that the government has lost control over immigration and that immigration was largely negative for Canada. The size of this segment seems to rise when cases of people who appear to be abusing the immigration system come to light. This happened during the summer of 1999, when four boatloads of what appeared to be economic migrants from China were dumped on the Vancouver Island coastline. The remaining 15 percent of Canadians in the poll had no opinion on immigration (Holton and Lanphier, 1994). Holton and Lanphier (1994; see also

Zong, 1994) suggest that these findings point to a hardening of Canadian attitudes toward immigration.

The sixth variable, security considerations, has become more important since the terrorist attacks on the United States on September 11, 2001. In the aftermath of the attacks, Canada introduced a new Permanent Resident Card and a number of new measures to increase security at Canadian borders. In addition, Canada and the United States are increasingly discussing the harmonization of immigration policies, particularly in the area of security screening of immigrants and refugees. Some commentators refer to this harmonization as a move toward a "Fortress North America" (Satzewich and Wong, 2003).

After the terrorist attack on the United States of September 11, 2001, Canada introduced a new Permanent Resident Card and a number of new measures to increase security at Canadian borders.
SOURCE: Shutterstock.

CONTEMPORARY IMMIGRATION CATEGORIES

Immigrants in Canada fit one of three main categories: refugees, family class, and independent immigrants. Altogether, 236 758 immigrants entered Canada in 2007.

Refugees

Nearly 28 000 refugees and their dependents were admitted to Canada in 2007. There are three categories of refugees that Canada accepts through its immigration program. *Convention refugees* are people who are defined as refugees by the 1951 Geneva Convention Relating to the Status of Refugees and its 1967 protocol. They are people who, by reason of their race, religion, nationality, membership in a particular social group, or political opinion, live outside of their country of nationality or their country of habitual residence and who are unable or unwilling, because of fear of persecution, to return to their country of origin (Citizenship and Immigration Canada, 1996: 28).

Country of asylum class refugees are people who are outside their country of citizenship or residence who are seriously and personally affected by civil war, armed conflict, or massive violations of human rights. Finally, *source country class* refugees include people who would meet the definition of a Convention refugee but who are still in their country of citizenship or residence. This category also includes people who have been detained or imprisoned and are suffering serious deprivations of the right of freedom of expression, the right of dissent, or the right to engage in trade union activity.

Family Class Immigrants

About 66 000 *family class immigrants* arrived in Canada in 2007. Family class immigrants have close family members already living in Canada who are willing and able to support them. A sponsor must be a Canadian citizen or a permanent resident who is over 18 years of age and who is living in Canada. Depending on the circumstances, a sponsor must be able to provide for the lodging, care, maintenance, and normal settlement needs of the family member(s) for between three and ten years (Citizenship and Immigration Canada, 2002).

Economic/Independent Immigrants

Economic immigrants numbered about 131 000 in 2007. The federal government has increased the size of this category in total immigration flows and has decreased

the number of family class immigrants, because it believes that the former are of greater economic benefit to Canada. There are five subcategories of independent immigrants. *Skilled workers and professionals* are selected by the federal government on the basis of their ability to meet certain minimum work experience requirements, to prove that they have enough funds to support themselves and their family members in Canada, and merit as measured by the **points system.** As Table 8.4 shows, applicants are awarded points for various attributes that the Canadian government deems important in determining an immigrant's economic and settlement prospects. An applicant has to earn a minimum of 67 out of 100 points to "pass" and potentially gain admission to Canada as a skilled worker. The amount of money immigrants need to have when they arrive in Canada depends on the number of family members they have. For example, an immigrant who brings three family members to Canada needs to have $16 225.

Immigrant entrepreneurs are people who will own and actively manage a business that will contribute to the economy and create jobs. They must have business experience and a minimum net worth of $300 000. *Immigrant investors* are capitalists who have a personal net worth of at least $800 000 and who plan to invest at least $400 000 in a business in Canada. *Self-employed immigrants* must have the intention and ability to create their own employment. They are expected to contribute to the cultural or artistic life

TABLE 8.4 THE POINTS SYSTEM FOR THE SELECTION OF INDEPENDENT IMMIGRANTS, CANADA, 2008

CRITERIA	UNITS OF ASSESSMENT (MAXIMUM)
Education	25 points
Ability in English and/ or French	24 points
Work experience	21 points
Age	10 points
Arranged employment in Canada	10 points
Adaptability	10 points
Pass Mark	**67 points**

SOURCE: Workpermit.com, 2008, "Canadian Immigration Points Calculator," On the World Wide Web at http://www.workpermit.com/canada/points_calculator.htm (retrieved 16 July 2009). Application for permanent residence: Federal skilled worker class. www.cic.gc.ca/English/information/application/guides/EG72.asp. Adapted and reproduced with permission of the Minister of Public Works and Government Service Canada, 2009.

of the country. They can also qualify under this program if they purchase and manage a farm in Canada. The 890 immigrant entrepreneurs admitted to Canada in 2002 invested more than $122 000 000 and created 1100 jobs after just one year in Canada (Citizenship and Immigration Canada, 2004).

Provincial nominees are a relatively recent fifth category. Provinces may fast track individuals for admission to Canada based on specific provincial labour shortages.

ETHNIC INEQUALITY AND THE CANADIAN LABOUR MARKET

JOHN PORTER AND THE VERTICAL MOSAIC

What happens to immigrants after they come to Canada? How are they sorted and placed in the socioeconomic structure? John Porter's answers to these questions in *The Vertical Mosaic* have had a profound impact on Canadian sociology. Since its publication in 1965, Canadian sociologists have been interested in whether ethnicity and race affect the operation of the labour market, social mobility, and the composition of elites.

Porter argued that Canada is a **vertical mosaic,** a society in which ethnic groups tend to occupy different and unequal positions in the stratification system. He called the first ethnic group to take control of a previously unoccupied or newly conquered territory the *charter group* of that society. One prerogative that goes to a charter group is the ability to decide "what other groups are to be let in and what they will be permitted to do" (Porter, 1965: 62). Canada has two charter groups, the English and the French. Although their power was, and is, unequal, Porter argued that the two charter groups have been able to set the terms by which other immigrants are admitted to Canada. These charter groups reserved for themselves the top positions in the occupational hierarchy. They also made up the upper ranks of the labour, political, bureaucratic, religious, and media elites.

Immigrants who arrived after these charter groups were assigned to less preferred positions. Non-English and non-French immigrants were assigned an *entrance status* that was linked in part to the social evaluation of their cultural and racial capacities. Groups from Northern and Western Europe were considered more racially and culturally like the English and French, and were accorded a higher entrance status than Southern and Eastern European immigrants. The latter were regarded as culturally, if not racially, inferior to the charter groups and were therefore placed in lower levels of the occupational hierarchy and excluded from elite positions. Non-Europeans were defined as unassimilable and were virtually barred from entry (Woodsworth, 1972).

Porter argued that once the vertical mosaic was established, it took on a life of its own. Immigrants and their descendants who were initially allocated a subordinate entrance status faced limited prospects for upward social mobility. He thought two factors accounted for the rigidity of the vertical mosaic. One was blatant prejudice and discrimination by charter groups. The other was the retention by ethnic groups of cultural practices that were incompatible with economic success in modern, industrialized societies. In other words, certain immigrants and their descendants were caught in an *ethnic mobility trap* because of their continued identification with a subordinated and marginalized ethnic group (Wiley, 1967).

In the context of its time, Porter's analysis was powerful and insightful. As we have seen, before 1962, the selection of new immigrants was based on ethnic and racial stereotypes. These stereotypes also shaped charter group perceptions of what kinds of jobs immigrants were fit to do. In the 1950s, for example, Italian immigrant men were regarded by immigration bureaucrats and members of the economic elite as culturally willing and able to "tolerate irregular employment, low wages and physically demanding work." They were recruited specifically for work in agriculture, mining, domestic service, the metal trades, and logging (Iacovetta, 1992: 28). Black women from the Caribbean were recruited specifically as housekeepers and nannies for middle-class families in the 1950s and 1960s, in part because they were believed to be nurturing and passive (Daenzer, 1993).

THE DECLINING SIGNIFICANCE OF THE VERTICAL MOSAIC

Does the vertical mosaic still exist? Is the distribution of economic rewards still based on ethnicity? Over the past two decades, debates have raged among Canadian sociologists about whether race and ethnicity continue to shape our stratification system (Brym with Fox, 1989). Gordon Darroch (1979) and Edward Herberg (1990) argue that the vertical mosaic is no longer a useful way of describing our society. Later in his life, John Porter also had doubts about its continued existence (Pineo and Porter, 1985). Other

The storefront of a downtown Toronto street reflects the ethnic diversity of most large Canadian cities.
SOURCE: Dick Hemingway.

scholars argue that, although we may be moving in the direction of greater equality, the vertical mosaic is still a useful metaphor for describing our society. Some analysts suggest that the vertical mosaic has been recast along racial lines (Fleras and Elliot, 1996); others argue that immigration status is the key to understanding patterns of inequality within the "new vertical mosaic" (Nakhaie, 2006).

What is the evidence for the view that "race" (visible minority status) and/or immigration status constitute fundamental dividing lines in Canadian society? One way to answer this question is to compare the earnings of visible minorities with the earnings of non-visible minorities; and the earnings of the Canadian-born with the earnings of the foreign-born. Table 8.5 (p. 202) provides information on the earnings of people between the ages of 25 and 65 who were working full time in Canada in 1986, 1991, and 2001. It shows that native-born visible minorities and native-born non-visible minorities earned about the same amount over the three census periods. For example, in 2001, Canadian-born non-visible minorities earned on average $40 030 and Canadian-born visible minorities earned $40 060—an earnings ratio of 0.999:1. However, larger earnings differences can be found when comparing the Canadian-born with the foreign-born. Thus, Canadian-born visible minorities earn substantially more than foreign-born visible minorities, with an earnings ratio of 1.22:1. On the other hand, non-visible minority immigrants do better than Canadian-born non-visible minorities; the non-visible minority Canadian-born earned $40 030

in 2001 compared with $43 163 for non-visible foreign-born Canadians, a ratio of 1.08:1. These findings suggest that the most economically disadvantaged category in Canada are visible-minority immigrants (Nakhaie, 2006).

These findings should lead us to be cautious about concluding that "race" constitutes a fundamental socioeconomic dividing line in Canadian society. Canada does not have a single, clear-cut pattern of ethnic or racial economic disadvantage, and significant differences exist in the relative positions of visible minority men and women.

Note that the categories "visible minority" and "white" are made up of diverse groups of people. "Visible minority" Canadians have different immigration histories, histories of settlement, and times of arrival in Canada, so some do better economically in Canada than others do. Similarly, "white" individuals of Portuguese background tend to do significantly less well in Canada than individuals of other European origins and visible minorities do. Table 8.6 (p. 202) shows, for example, that in 2001, Portuguese men had the lowest socioeconomic status for all men (tied with Aboriginal men) and that Chinese men had the second-highest occupational skill level.

Notwithstanding these cautions, at the very least the vertical mosaic metaphor seems to describe accurately the position of immigrants in Canada. Differences between immigrants who are members of visible minorities and white immigrants have been explained by the devaluation of immigrant credentials. Some suggest that education credentials

TABLE 8.5   EARNINGS* OF VISIBLE AND NON-VISIBLE ETHNO-RACIAL GROUPS, 1986–2001

	1986	1991	2001
Visible			
Native-born	$36 928	$36 892	$40 065
Foreign-born	$32 310	$31 654	$32 952
Non-visible			
Native-born	$36 439	$36 541	$40 030
Foreign-born	$36 850	$39 947	$43 163
Non-visible/Visible Ratio			
Native-born	0.987:1	0.990:1	0.999:1
Foreign-born	1.14:1	1.26:1	1.31:1
Native-born/Foreign-born Ratio			
Non-visible	0.989:1	0.915:1	0.927:1
Visible	1.14:1	1.17:1	1.22:1

SOURCE: Adapted from M. Reza Nakhaie, "Earnings of Visible and Non-visible Ethno-racial Groups 1986–2001," *Canadian Ethnic Studies, 38* (2), June 2006, pp. 19–46. Reprinted with permission.
*Adjusted to 2001 Consumer Price Index. All are age 25–64 and working full time.

TABLE 8.6   NET DIFFERENCE* IN OCCUPATIONAL STATUS (1971) AND OCCUPATIONAL SKILL GROUP (2001) BETWEEN SELECTED ETHNIC GROUPS AND THE REST OF THE LABOUR FORCE, BY SEX, CANADA

Ethnic Group	MALE		FEMALE	
	1971	2001	1971	2001
British	0.13	0.06	0.14	0.05
French	−0.06	0.04	−0.02	0.06
German	−0.08	0.04	−0.09	0.01
Dutch	−0.09	0.05	−0.10	0.04
Scandinavian	−0.08	0.07	−0.01	0.05
Ukrainian	−0.09	0.06	−0.13	0.03
Polish	−0.08	0.03	−0.12	−0.02
Hungarian	−0.06	0.07	−0.13	0.02
Italian	−0.22	0.01	−0.35	0.00
Portuguese	−0.38	−0.15	−0.62	−0.16
Greek	−0.27	0.02	−0.48	−0.04
Yugoslav	−0.12	0.03	−0.29	−0.03
Jewish	0.36	0.34	0.24	0.24
Chinese	−0.04	0.19	−0.20	0.00
South Asian	0.26	−0.05	0.19	−0.12
Aboriginal	−0.35**	−0.15	−0.23**	−0.08
Black	NI	−0.10	NI	−0.09
Mean	0.17	0.09	0.21	0.06
Number of Occupational Ranks/ Skill Groups	(498)	(4)	(464)	(4)

SOURCE: From *Society in Question* 5/E by Brym. © 2008. Reprinted with permission of Nelson, a division of Thomson Learning: www.thomsonrights.com. Fax: 800-730-2215.
*A negative figure indicates a relatively low occupational status/skill group; a positive figure indicates a relatively high status/skill group. Zero indicates equality of occupational status/skill group. The greater the absolute size of the index, the greater the inequality.
**Does not include Inuit.
NI: Not included.

of immigrants from visible minorities are devalued in the labour market and by certification authorities. In one celebrated case, an evaluation officer of the Ontario Ministry of Education wrote to a Jamaican immigrant that his honours degree from Harvard University and his Ph.D. from Stanford were equivalent to "at least Grade Thirteen in the Ontario school system" (Special Committee, 1984). Although this may have been a bureaucratic error, evidence shows that many immigrant teachers, doctors, nurses, and engineers find that their non-Western university degrees and diplomas are of little value in Canada (Basran and Zong, 1998; Henry and Tator, 2006). Some say that this devaluation of credentials is a reflection of racism in Canadian society.

Other research on employers' hiring practices has documented the influence of racial discrimination in employment. Henry and Ginsberg (1985) conducted a study in Toronto in which they sent two groups of actors with virtually identical résumés to apply for various jobs. The only difference between members of the two groups was the colour of their skin or their accent: One group consisted of actors who were white

and who had Anglo-Canadian accents, and the other group consisted of visible-minority group members, some of whom had non-Anglo-Canadian accents. The researchers found that, in both face-to-face interviews and approaches over the telephone, whites received three job offers for every job offered to applicants from visible minority groups. Applicants from visible-minority groups were five times more likely to be told that the job had been filled when a subsequent white applicant was invited for an interview (Henry and Ginsberg, 1985).

A follow-up study conducted in 1989 showed no racial discrimination in job offers following face-to-face contacts between applicants and employers. Blacks and whites received equal numbers of job offers. When it came to approaches over the telephone, however, callers with foreign accents were less likely to be invited for an interview and more likely to be told that the job was filled when in fact it was not (Henry, 1989). Without more recent research, it is difficult to know whether outright discrimination helps explain patterns of earnings inequality today.

SUMMARY

1. Ethnic categories and identities are not fixed and unchanging; they evolve socially and historically. Canadians may now be considered an ethnic group, as many of them display a strong desire to define their ethnicity as "Canadian."

2. Racism refers to ideas and institutional practices that discriminate against members of groups that are perceived as racially distinct. Institutional racism refers to circumstances in which social institutions operate, or once operated, on the basis of racist ideas.

3. Racism, prejudice, and discrimination have been analyzed from different sociological perspectives. Social-psychological theories, primordialism, normative theories, and power-conflict theories each offer different interpretations of ethnic and racial hostility.

4. The term "Aboriginal people" includes people who are defined in the Constitution as "Indian," "Métis," and "Inuit." The terms used to describe Aboriginal people are socially negotiated and change because of shifts in power relations among groups.

5. The culture of poverty thesis was used in the 1970s as a way of explaining the poor socioeconomic conditions of Aboriginal people. Problems with the culture of poverty thesis led to

the development of the internal colonial model, a variant of conflict theory. Conflict and feminist sociologists are beginning to be more interested in class and gender diversity within the Aboriginal population.

6. Material inequalities between French and English in Quebec provided the historical basis for the emergence of nationalism in Quebec. The contemporary nationalist movement has a diverse class base.

7. Debates exist in the nationalist movement about who is Québécois. Tensions exist between ethnic and civic nationalists.

8. Immigration has played different roles in Canadian history. During the nineteenth century, immigrants contributed to capitalist state formation. Now, immigrants contribute to the social and economic reproduction of Canadian society.

9. There are six main variables that have shaped immigrant selection in Canada: social class, ethnic and racial stereotypes, geopolitical considerations, humanitarianism, public opinion, and security considerations. Immigrants are categorized as refugees, family class, or independents. Independent immigrants are selected on the basis of the points system.

10. John Porter argued that Canada was a vertical mosaic, a social structure in which ethnic groups occupy different and unequal positions within the stratification system. Evidence suggests that the vertical mosaic is declining in importance, at least for European immigrants and people born in Canada. Discrimination against immigrants from visible-minority groups is still a problem.

QUESTIONS TO CONSIDER

1. What are the strengths and weaknesses of different sociological approaches to the study of the social significance of race and ethnicity?

2. To what extent do racist attitudes and behaviour affect the life-chances of people in Canada?

3. What obligations do societies have to accommodate themselves to the presence of ethno-religious diversity?

4. Do you think that the importance of class and gender diversity within Aboriginal communities will increase or decrease in the future?

5. Are Canadians an ethnic group? Why or why not?

GLOSSARY

Civic nationalism is a form of nationalism in which the social boundaries of the nation are defined in territorial and geographic terms.

The **culture of poverty thesis** is the theory that some ethnic groups do not readily assimilate, and hence are poor, because their culture does not value economic success, hard work, and achievement.

Discrimination refers to practices that deny members of particular groups equal access to societal rewards.

Institutional racism refers to discriminatory racial practices built into such prominent structures as the political, economic, and education systems.

New racism is a theory that suggests that it is natural for groups to form bounded communities. One group is neither better nor worse than another, but feelings of antagonism will be aroused if outsiders are admitted.

The **points system** is used by the Canadian government to select independent immigrants. Applicants are awarded points for various attributes that the Canadian government deems important in determining an immigrant's economic contribution to Canada.

Prejudice is an unfavourable, generalized, and rigid belief applied to all members of a group.

The **primordialist thesis** is the theory that ethnic attachments reflect a basic tendency of people to seek out, and associate with, their "own kind."

The **Quiet Revolution** refers to the social, political, and cultural changes that occurred in Quebec in the 1960s, in part because of the emergence of a large francophone middle class.

Race is a socially constructed label that has been used to describe certain kinds of physical differences between people.

The **split labour-market theory** holds that racial and ethnic conflicts are rooted in differences in the price of labour.

Stereotypes are exaggerated, oversimplified images of the characteristics of social categories.

The **vertical mosaic** is a social structure in which ethnic groups occupy different, and unequal, positions within the stratification system.

SUGGESTED READING

Frideres, James, and René Gadacz. (2005). *Aboriginal People in Canada: Contemporary Conflicts,* 7th ed. Toronto: Pearson Prentice-Hall. Presents a thorough historical and contemporary overview of Aboriginal and non-Aboriginal relations in Canada.

Hier, Sean, and B. Singh Bolaria. (2006). *Identity and Belonging: Rethinking Race and Ethnicity in Canadian Society.* Toronto: Canadian Scholars Press. Addresses tough questions about how and why ethnic and racial markers matter.

Li, Peter. (2003). *Destination Canada: Immigration Debates and Issues.* Toronto: Oxford University Press. A well-argued and critical analysis of a number of contemporary immigration issues.

Miles, Robert, and Malcolm Brown. (2003). *Racism,* 2nd ed. London: Routledge. One of the best theoretical discussions of the meaning of race and racism in modern Western societies. The authors argue for a critical, social-constructionist approach to race and racism.

Satzewich, Vic, and Nikolaos Liodakis. 2007. *"Race" and Ethnicity in Canada: A Critical Introduction.* Toronto: Oxford University Press. A critical

examination of various theoretical and empirical questions about patterns of race and ethnicity in Canada.

WEB RESOURCES

Companion Website for This Book

http://www.newsociety6e.nelson.com
Begin by clicking on the Student Resources section of the website. Next, select the chapter you are studying from the pull-down menu. From the Student Resources page, you have easy access to InfoTrac College Edition® and other resources, such as the

Glossary, Test Yourself questions, and additional readings. The website also has many useful tips to aid you in your study of sociology.

InfoTrac College Edition Search Terms

Visit http://www.infotrac-college.com for access to more than 20 million articles from nearly 6000 sources when doing your online research.

CHAPTER NINE

Development and Underdevelopment

Anthony Winson

UNIVERSITY OF GUELPH

In this chapter, you will learn that

· Global inequality is one of the most pressing issues of our times.

· A historical approach to global inequality helps us understand divergent development in different parts of the world.

· Some development theorists argue that the pursuit of economic growth by the International Monetary Fund and the World Bank has led to the *under*development of much of the world, undermining rural livelihoods, for example.

· While identifiable factors have allowed the rapid development of a few formerly poor countries, the associated social and environmental costs have been high.

· War and military aggression sponsored by developed countries have negatively influenced development in many poor countries.

· Global inequalities are staggering, and new evidence indicates that the gap between rich and poor countries is wider than earlier believed.

MY MOTHER'S PET THEORY

Many people entertain pet theories or working hypotheses about why some parts of the world are poor and others are rich. My mother lived for several years in countries that were poor by Canadian standards, and she held a theory that was popular at the time. She told me about living in a small South American mining camp in what was then British Guiana and commented that "if you had lived in that heat and humidity you would know why they are so poor." It was perhaps not surprising that a young woman who had lived through 20 Saskatchewan winters would find the tropics an obstacle to productive activity. It was just common sense to her that the climate explained why British Guiana was underdeveloped.

Decades later, my experiences and observations in Mexico and Central America challenged my mother's views. I confronted the architectural evidence of a wealthy colonial past and the archaeological wealth of complex indigenous civilizations that predated the invasion of Europeans. Excavations in Mexico City had just unearthed evidence of the rich city-state of Tenotitchlán that existed when Hernán Cortés and his Spanish soldier adventurers arrived on horseback from the Atlantic Coast in 1519. Just to the north lay the pyramids of Teotihuacán, structures that dwarf the fabled pyramids of Egypt. This city-state reached its peak between 500 and 600 C.E., encompassed 21 square kilometres, and had a population 10 times as big as that of contemporary London (Waldman, 2005). To the south, I encountered the imposing ancient hilltop city of Monte Alban near present day Oaxaca City, and evidence of several other precolonial settlements of considerable size and development along the highway leading further south into the mountains of the mist-shrouded Lacandon forest in the Mexican state of Chiapas that borders Guatemala. In the lowland regions of this zone, I came across some of the most impressive archaeological finds in the Western Hemisphere, relics of the extensive Mayan civilizations that existed from approximately 50 B.C.E. to 1000 C.E. Over time, the Mayans constructed a series of cities that boasted ornate architecture, elaborate irrigation infrastructure and palatial structures for their nobility, and massive platforms to accommodate elaborate religious rituals. Between 600 and 800 C.E. this civilization reached the highest development of its arts and sciences. By then, the Mayans had invented an elaborate system of hieroglyphic writing, a complex

calendar for predicting the seasons, accurate computations of time, and detailed astronomical observations. All of this 1500 years ago in the midst of a part of the world notable for its heat and humidity. So much for my mother's climate theory of development.

Climate is not completely insignificant in understanding the origins and development of human civilizations. Regions with year-round permafrost or great deserts do not allow dense human settlement and the agriculture it depends on, let alone the accumulation of wealth. Or at least they did not in the past. Today, as the example of the desert kingdom of Dubai shows, oil wealth can help spur impressive development in formerly inhospitable places. The key word here is *can*; other oil-rich countries, such as Nigeria, have failed to mobilize their wealth to realize development goals. They remain mired in poverty. Why? With this question we enter ongoing debates that animate the study of development and the explanations for global inequalities that flow from these debates. One of the goals of this chapter is to introduce you to key explanations or theories of development and the controversies they have engendered.

But why study development at all, you might ask? What relevance does it have for my life? What *is* development anyway? It makes sense to address these questions before we examine key debates in the field.

WHAT IS DEVELOPMENT?

The idea of development dates from the eighteenth century, when scholars in Scotland and France formulated the idea of progress. They promoted the industrialization and democratization of society based on the equal rights and freedoms of its citizens.

At first, development was just an idea. It was not until the period after World War II that the idea crystallized into a full-blown project or, more accurately, a series of projects that became part of state policy and the policy of some non-state organizations (Parpart and Veltmeyer, 2003). After World War II, development came increasingly to mean a process that generated economic growth, industrialization, and modernization in regions and countries perceived to be poor, traditional, and undeveloped. More recently, development has had a broader, more complex meaning, incorporating such notions as progress for women, empowerment of the underprivileged, and environmental sustainability.

Two main factors motivated interest in development after World War II. First, the Cold War broke out between the developed capitalist countries led by the United States and the communist countries led by the Soviet Union. Among other things, the Cold War involved intense competition between the two rival blocs to amass power by gaining influence and control over less developed countries. Second, businesses in the developed West, particularly the United States, were interested in new markets outside their traditional spheres of operation. Latin America, Africa, and Asia were thus of great interest to the Western powers for geopolitical and economic reasons.

Given the context just described, it may not surprise you to learn that some analysts have argued that development, and the study of development, have served to support world **capitalism,** an economic system based on competitive enterprises seeking to maximize profits using wage labour. However, as we shall see, other analysts deny that that genuine development can occur within the confines of capitalism. They have promoted a non-capitalist road to development.

THE RELEVANCE OF DEVELOPMENT AND GLOBAL INEQUALITIES: SOCIAL JUSTICE AND SECURITY

Earlier I asked why you should care about development. We can look at this question from two perspectives, one involving morality and social justice, the other involving self-interest and the need for security.

Development is an important issue for many people because they find it morally repugnant that more than a billion people earn a dollar or less a day (see Figure 9.1). They consider it a matter of social justice that the world's desperately poor be lifted out of a life of illiteracy, disease, and hopelessness. They regard it as unacceptable that a Canadian student buys a coffee at Starbucks for three times the average daily wage of more than a billion people or spends more on a laptop computer than the per capita gross domestic product of the world's 51 poorest countries (below US$1000; Milanovic, 2009; United Nations, 2009).

Other people are more concerned with the practical implications of having so many people in the world with so little to sustain them. Few of us would feel comfortable living in a luxurious house with expensive furnishings and two luxury cars in the driveway if several of our immediate neighbours lived in a one-room shanty with a tin roof, owned virtually nothing, lacked regular employment, and spent much of their time staring enviously at our lifestyle and property. Sooner or later, our neighbours' poverty would have unpleasant implications for us.

The higher levels of violence and unrest that accompany poverty would likely wash over to our side

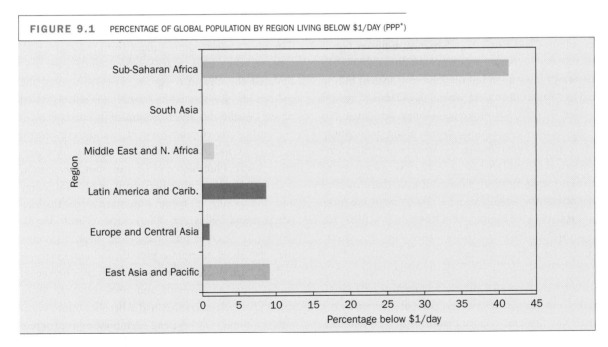

FIGURE 9.1   PERCENTAGE OF GLOBAL POPULATION BY REGION LIVING BELOW $1/DAY (PPP*)

*PPP = purchasing power parity (see Glossary).

of the street. We would have to pay higher taxes to bolster police forces to maintain order and deal with those who decide that it's not fair for us alone to have all the nice things in life. We would soon come to realize that our personal security cannot be divorced from the living conditions of our neighbours, and our failure to help raise their living standard must inevitably have serious, negative implications for us.

Life today is like the scenario painted above, but with added complications. Our poor neighbours might, for example, be living on land we own or land we took from them by using to our advantage property laws and the fact that our neighbours didn't have formal title to the land they had been living on for generations. We might allow our poor neighbours to grow crops, but they would have to give us most of their harvest for the privilege of living on our land. We might select a few of the poor neighbours to supervise the land and reward them with a disproportionate amount of the crop and some extra money under the table. We might also provide the chosen few with firearms and training so they could protect the property and especially the production of fruits and vegetables, dealing appropriately with anyone who might want to challenge existing property rights.

Challenges would likely arise because most households enjoy only a bare subsistence and grow rapidly, making less food per person available over time. Unrest would mount. We would therefore be forced to send some of our family members to help our managers keep order, and some of them would come back with injuries from the skirmishes. Before long, it would be necessary to lock up and occasionally kill people in the poorer households to maintain the status quo, and some of our own family members would undoubtedly get killed trying to police the growing violence.

When we add these complications to our fictitious neighbourhood economy, we have a model that better mirrors the world as it has existed for some time. It is a model that not only describes huge differences in income between our neighbours and us, but points out the inequality that exists *within* poor neighbourhoods. Importantly, the model also establishes that the neighbourhood economy is maintained by a system of power relations backed up by disproportionate wealth and, ultimately, our willingness to exercise violence when all else fails.

Social scientists who study development have proposed radically different theories to explain development and lack of development. It is now time to outline some of the most important of them. I begin with a brief discussion of approaches that dominated the social sciences in the 1960s.

EARLY THEORIES OF DEVELOPMENT

DEVELOPMENT IN STAGES

The social sciences emerged in the nineteenth century in the context of lively debate in the biological sciences around theories of evolution propounded by Charles Darwin and others. Debates in the natural sciences, especially concerning evolution, deeply influenced social thinkers. Human societies were like biological organisms, they reasoned. Just as animals and plants pass through stages of development, so do societies; and like animals and plants, societies are susceptible to pathologies or diseases.

Such ideas were still influential in the 1960s, when W. W. Rostow argued that societal development follows several necessary **stages of development** (Rostow, 1960). According to Rostow, in the beginning, a society might be traditional, undifferentiated, and undeveloped. When it comes into contact with a developed society, however, science and technology spread, and the traditional society enters a stage of possible "takeoff." Takeoff occurs when and if an increase in market transactions, manufacturing, and trade takes place. The society moves along the path to development the more quickly barriers to the spread of market relations are removed and the more efficiently scientific and technological diffusion occurs.

DEVELOPMENT AS A STATE OF MIND

Another popular approach in the 1960s was **modernization theory,** which emphasizes the importance of values and norms as drivers of development. David McClelland (1961), for example, argued for the importance of entrepreneurship and what he called the "need for achievement," the desire for feelings of accomplishment and personal satisfaction. People who enjoy a high need for achievement are more likely to become successful entrepreneurs, McClelland argued, and societies that encourage entrepreneurial behaviour and competitiveness are the most likely to develop economically and socially. Other writers in this tradition emphasized the importance of other values in the development process—the need for savings, investment, innovation, education, high achievement, self-control in having children, and so on. Still others recognized that poor societies also lack capital, stable governments, and business techniques (Inkeles and Smith, 1976). But what all modernization theories had in common was their assumption that most of the responsibility for economic backwardness lies with the societies of the "third world" or "global south" themselves. According to modernization theorists, development happens when the citizens of the poor countries adopt the virtues of the developed North. If they fail to do so, they remain in a pathological, undeveloped state.

DEVELOPMENT AS DEPENDENCY

Dependency theory sharply challenged the notion that lack of development is due to the deficiencies of less developed countries. It did so by taking a holistic view—recognizing that each part of the world is shaped by, and helps to shape, a wider, global reality—and attending to the history and structure of relations between countries.

Dependency theorists produced abundant evidence of strong and enduring economic and social relationships between "metropolitan powers," such as Spain, Portugal, Britain, and France, and "satellite regions" of the global south. First focusing on Latin America and the Caribbean (Frank, 1966; Cardoso and Faletto, 1979), they established that is was precisely the nature of the relationship between metropolitan powers and satellite regions that blocked economic progress in the global south. Let us consider the implications of this argument in detail.

FROM CONTACT TO CONQUEST

Evidence contradicts the notion that the societies of the global south existed in an undeveloped state, as stage and modernization theories suggest. From China through the Middle East and the Mediterranean to Central and South America, great civilizations rose and fell. For example, between 1200 and 200 B.C.E., Carthage flourished on the northern shores of Africa, while the later naval, military, commercial, and cultural advances of the Muslim people of the Maghreb region of northwestern Africa allowed them to invade and dominate Spain and Portugal until the twelfth century. In the area of east Africa now known as Zimbabwe, we find great stone constructions and evidence of extensive metallurgical development and trade across vast distances. Africans had developed a great deal on their own before

Europe began asserting its dominance over the continent (Rodney, 1972).

Initial contact between Europe and the societies of the global south took place around 1500. For the next several hundred years, the Europeans engaged in wholesale pillage and plunder, causing massive death, migration, and economic upheaval—unpleasant facts that stage and modernization theories ignore. Before Europeans could exploit the global south for its riches, they had to conquer existing civilizations. Superior technology in the form of gunpowder and firearms helped to secure the conquest, as did disease borne by the Europeans. Europeans had evolved resistance to smallpox, influenza, and other diseases that they introduced into the global south. In Mexico alone, the population was reduced from 20 million to 2 million in the first century of contact with Europe. A population collapse of similar magnitude occurred in North America, and among the Inca of Peru. Overall, some 95 percent of the New World's population was wiped out in a fairly short period after European contact (Diamond, 1999: 210–11).

Following their conquest of the New World, the Spanish established a feudalistic landholding system based on hierarchical relationships imported from Europe and subordinated to the power of the Spanish Crown. Its purpose was to support a local European landed elite and funnel valuable minerals, principally gold and silver, and agricultural commodities to the mother country. The Spanish monarchy appropriated much of the profit.

THE SLAVE TRADE

Another disruptive aspect of the relationship between Europe and the global south involved the West African slave trade. It undermined traditional state structures and forms of governance in West Africa and created deep-seated ethnic animosities.

Forced labour had existed for centuries in Europe. Muslim pirates from North Africa had undertaken raids as far afield as southern England to enslave captives. However, the trans-Atlantic slave trade initiated by Europeans after 1500 established slave economies of unprecedented size, with dire consequences for West Africa in particular.

The Portuguese initiated the trans-Atlantic slave trade near the mouth of the Congo River around 1500. Taking advantage of the custom of local African chiefs to buy household slaves, the Portuguese began trading European merchandise for human lives and

African slaves taken on board HMS *Daphne,* November 1, 1868.
SOURCE: The National Archives of the UK, ref. 84/1310.

shipping enslaved Africans across the Atlantic to work in the vibrant Portuguese colony of Brazil, where they produced first sugar, then coffee. By 1530, 5000 slaves a year were being removed from their homelands for shipment to Brazil (Hochschild, 1999: 12).

Slavery soon became a major disruptive force in West Africa. The ruler of the Kingdom of the Congo, Nzinga Mbemba Alfonso, a convert to Christianity who learned Portuguese, wrote to the King of Portugal to protest what was happening to his people:

> Each day the traders are capturing our people—children of this country, sons of our nobles and vassals, even people of our own family. . . Corruption and depravity are so widespread that our land is entirely depopulated. . . . We need in this kingdom only priests and schoolteachers, and no merchandise, unless it is wine and flour for Mass. . . . It is our wish that this kingdom not be a place for the trade or transport of slaves. (quoted in Hochschild, 1999: 13)

The King of Portugal king was unmoved. Slave trading accelerated, and before long, Dutch merchant traders began introducing slavery to the English Caribbean, initially on the island of Barbados. Later, the English established a major Caribbean sugar colony in Jamaica and the Spanish followed suit in Cuba. Later still, American rice and cotton plantations stimulated demand for still more slave labour. By the early nineteenth century, some 12 million Africans and their descendants worked on the plantations of the Caribbean and the United States.

The societies of entire regions of Africa were thus ruined, and the foundation was set for the deep, enduring impoverishment of Africa. Matters worsened when, in the nineteenth century, England, Belgium, France, and Germany carved up much of Africa for its resource wealth. They established artificial boundaries that ignored traditional ethnic spheres of influence, thereby increasing ethnic antagonism and warfare. In some areas, such as the territory that the British named Rhodesia, the colonizers imposed heavy taxes on peasant farmers, forcing them off the best agricultural lands and into wage labour for white farmers (Arrighi, 1970). Later, some dispossessed Africans began a mass migration to South Africa for work in the expanding gold and diamond mines.

Meanwhile, across the Atlantic, the slave economies of the Caribbean and the United States flourished, generating unheard of wealth for slave traders, slave owners, and the European aristocracy and royalty. Slavery enabled capital to accumulate—capital that industrialists would later use to spur European development.

THE STRUCTURAL ROOTS OF UNDERDEVELOPMENT

Dependency theory shows how social and economic structures established by European colonizing powers since about 1500 distorted local societies for the benefit of European traders and merchants, and later blocked the emergence of industrial capitalism in the global south. In the words of Andre Gundar Frank, a leading dependency theorist, "the historical development of the capitalist system generated **underdevelopment** in the peripheral satellites" (Frank, 1966: 3). At the same time, the extraction of resources from the global south propelled the rapid development of industry in Western Europe and, later, North America. What remains unclear is whether European *countries* or *classes* were responsible for underdevelopment in the global south.

Slave labour on a Caribbean sugar plantation in the 1830s.
SOURCE: HIP/Art Resource NY.

COUNTRIES VERSUS CLASSES AS CAUSES OF UNDERDEVELOPMENT

During the 1970s, debates on development and underdevelopment focused on the *mechanisms* through which metropolitan powers exploited the global south. Originally, dependency theorists conceived of underdevelopment as a process involving one area—Western Europe—extracting surplus from other areas—Latin America, Africa, and Asia. Some scholars argued that, in recent times, it was primarily through unfavourable **terms of trade** that exploitation took place. They held that prices of agricultural exports primarily from the underdeveloped south declined over time relative to prices of industrial goods made in the developed countries and imported by the poor countries. However, they still imagined that one area was exploiting another.

Robert Brenner (1977) challenged the geographical version of dependency theory and revived interest in a Marxist approach that emphasized class relationships. He argued that dependency theory ought to focus on exploitation occurring at the level of *class relationships*. In his view, by analyzing the nature of the class interests that shape underdevelopment and the types of class conflict that underdevelopment engenders, one

can gain a fuller and more precise understanding of the process of underdevelopment. Following Marx, Brenner argued that the struggle among classes to achieve dominance is the prime mover of social change. Accordingly, identifiable classes in the metropolitan countries—merchants, traders, shippers, and the aristocracies and monarchies of Spain, Portugal, Holland, Belgium, France, and England—orchestrated the plunder of the global south. Moreover, these social actors counted on elites in the global south to establish mechanisms for extracting valuable commodities using the forced labour of indigenous peoples and imported slaves. Brenner further argues that, in more recent times, the mechanisms of underdevelopment changed as England and then the rest of Western Europe began to industrialize under the direction of a new class of industrial capitalists. As industrialization occurred, so too did the nature of demands on the global south (for example, see Box 9.1).

NOT ALL COUNTRIES ARE ALIKE: CLASS ALLIANCES AND STATE CONTROL

The global south is not homogeneous. Each country has a unique history. In particular, different class

---

BOX 9.1   **THE DESTRUCTION OF THIRD WORLD DOMINANCE IN MANUFACTURING**

Before the Industrial Revolution of the late nineteenth century, many goods other than foodstuffs were produced in both Europe and the global south by traditional industry. Small workshops produced a huge variety of metal goods and wooden implements, and all manner of luxury goods made from glass, silver, gold, and so on. Grain was ground in stone grinding mills powered by water or animals. People wove textiles at home on looms from yarn or thread spun on hand-operated spinning wheels. While productivity was low, many people worked in these ways, so output was considerable. Paul Bairoch (1982) estimates that in 1830, the global south (including Japan) accounted for 63 percent of world manufacturing, compared with just 37 percent for Europe and North America. Levels of productivity differed little by region. This would soon change, however.

In England, the rising influence of modern industrialists challenged the longstanding dominance of old merchant families whose fortunes relied on trade.

The old "mercantilist" system relied on protected markets and trade monopolies within them. For example, the British East India Company was allowed to block the import of European manufactured goods into India, which was good for traders but bad for industrialists. In 1813, however, the monopoly of the British East India Company was ended by the British Parliament. Now, Birmingham textile manufacturers could export cheap textiles produced by modern machinery to India. This devastated millions of Indian domestic textile producers. Similar events took place elsewhere. As Bairoch argued, it was "in the years 1830 to 1860 that this division between the future developed world and the Third World . . . began to take shape. The industrialization of the former led to the **deindustrialization** of the latter, and the proportional contribution of each region to the total [world] output of manufacturing production was almost exactly reversed" (Bairoch, 1982: 274).

---

alliances came to control the states of the global south, with widely different consequences for the pattern of underdevelopment that ensued (Cardoso and Faletto, 1979). For example, in Argentina and Brazil, the large export-oriented economy that developed under the control of foreign capitalists allowed local elites and a sizable middle- and industrial working class to emerge by the late nineteenth century (Murmis and Portantiero, 1969). Especially in periods when foreign influence was weakest (during global recessions, for instance), internal elites and their allies were able to establish local industrial enterprises and internal markets that deepened the process of development and strengthened local economies. In contrast, foreign capital was so dominant in small countries, like Honduras, Costa Rica, and Guatemala, that middle- and industrial working classes of much political significance failed to develop, and the economy was based almost exclusively on exports of just a few commodities like bananas and coffee (Ellis, 1983; Handy, 1985; Stone, 1975; Winson, 1983, 1989).

BEYOND DEPENDENCY: AGRARIAN CLASS STRUCTURE AND UNDERDEVELOPMENT

In the 1980s and 1990s, researchers focused increasingly on the role of class structures, class alliances, and state policies to understand the processes of development and underdevelopment better. Consider, for example, research on estates—large, privately owned agricultural enterprises employing many agricultural workers to produce export crops, such as coffee, wheat, and cotton, in societies as diverse as Chile, Brazil, and Egypt. Analysts found that, for three reasons, estate agriculture was more of an impediment to development than were agrarian structures dominated by small family farms (the North American model in the nineteenth and early twentieth centuries). First, estate owners tended to compensate their workers with small plots of land rather than substantial money wages. This greatly restricted the purchasing power of rural workers, and therefore the demand for goods that small manufacturers could have produced locally. Second, with a ready supply of cheap labour at hand, estate owners had little incentive to employ advanced agricultural machinery on their estates. This limited the local market for manufacturers of agricultural machinery, who in North America were central to early industrialization. Third, estate owners exercised enormous political power. They influenced governments to maintain free trade policies so they could export agricultural products and import whatever machinery they needed, unhindered by tariffs. This made it difficult for local industry to develop. In contrast, in Canada and the United States, tariffs protected local manufacturing in the early stage of industrialization (Dean, 1969; Richards, 1976; Winson, 1989).

GEOGRAPHY AND BIOLOGICAL RESOURCES

A recent, provocative contribution to the study of development and underdevelopment is Jared Diamond's examination of the early history of human civilization. Diamond set out to understand why wealth and power are distributed as they now are rather than in some other way. For Diamond, the answer is complex but boils down to the following idea: "History followed different courses for different peoples because of differences among peoples' environments" (Diamond, 1999: 25).

To make his case, Diamond distinguished between proximate (or immediate) and ultimate (or fundamental) causes of development. He found that the development of firearms and modern metallurgy by Europeans, along with lack of resistance to deadly diseases in the peoples of the Americas, were the *proximate* causes of the defeat of established, complex civilizations by the marauding Spanish army in Latin America in 1520. The conquest set the stage for the emergence of commercial, administrative, military, and industrial structures over the next several hundred years—structures that helped to enrich Europe while retarding progress in the Americas, Australia, Africa, and much of Asia.

Why did the Europeans alone enjoy such early advantages as firearms, modern metallurgy, and resistance to diseases that proved deadly to the peoples they subjugated? What, in other words, were the *ultimate* causes of European development? Diamond argues that the geographical features of different continents and the biological resources available to early peoples were fundamentally important. Europe (and the adjacent Middle East) were especially rich in plants and animals that could be domesticated. Moreover, their east–west axis facilitated the intermingling and dissemination of a wide variety of species because geographical barriers were few and climate was roughly similar across the region. In contrast, relatively few animals were available for domestication in the Americas. Moreover, the Americas, Africa, and most of Asia ran along a north–south axis with physical barriers and climatic differences that made the dissemination of species difficult. Australia was isolated and had no animal species that could be domesticated. The wealth of species available for domestication in Europe and the Middle East allowed for the accumulation and storage of large food surpluses, which in turn enabled the growth of large, complex, hierarchical societies.

The first cities emerged in the Middle East, and so did technological advances beyond the stone tools of the pre-agricultural period, including the refinement of metal, the manufacture of implements and arms, and the construction of oceangoing vessels. These advances spread to Europe relatively easily. Dense population centres and proximity to domesticated animals also allowed germs to spread and cause the first mass epidemics. However, the survivors developed resistance to these germs. For Diamond, then, the early domestication of plants and animals made agriculture possible and was a prerequisite for the development of the guns, germs, and steel that eventually ensured the dominance of European colonizers in the Americas and later in Asia and Africa.

CRITICISMS OF DIAMOND'S THESIS

Diamond's thesis has sparked much debate. Some critics argue that he ignores the mountain ranges and deserts that surely impeded the diffusion of domesticated plants and animals across Europe. Others point out that corn, a major staple, *was* disseminated from Central to South America (Blaut, 2000). Still others note that Diamond ignores crucial political factors. For example, the Ottoman Empire cut off Europe's trade with Asia in the fifteenth century, so European merchants were encouraged to develop marine transportation technology and navigational and cartographic knowledge to reach the East by travelling around the southern African coast. Their technological advantage later allowed them to dominate the seas, exploring and exploiting much of the rest of the globe (Pickover, 2008). Despite the criticisms of Diamond's work, the broad scope of his argument and the eloquence with which he makes it has proven attractive to a wide audience.

THE NEOLIBERAL ERA: DEBT, STRUCTURAL ADJUSTMENT, AND UPHEAVAL IN THE SOUTH

THE RISE OF NEOLIBERALISM

In recent years, the **neoliberal theory** of economic development has become influential in the highest policy circles. It is worth analyzing because the most important institutions affecting development policies in the global south adopted it and still apply it today.

A central idea of neoliberal theory is that only in societies where markets are free of government interference can competitive entrepreneurs maximize economic growth for the benefit of themselves and the rest of society. This idea was not always popular. A "hands off" approach by governments contributed to the severity of the Great Depression of the 1930s, when the North American unemployment rate reached 30 percent. Thereafter, desperation brought a strong desire for a new approach to economic thinking. In the United States, the Democratic Party under Franklin Delano Roosevelt, inspired by the economic thinking of the British economist John Maynard Keynes, took the view that government *should* intervene in the market. Its policies, and those of likeminded governments in Canada, Britain, and elsewhere, favoured massive government spending to stimulate the economy and the establishment of public enterprises where the market had failed to provide viable alternatives.

The "Keynesian" approach to economic development worked well for four decades. Then, in the 1970s, it too began to run into difficulties—specifically, high inflation coupled with low or stagnant economic growth. This situation provided the context for American economist Milton Friedman and his allies to advocate a return to policies that would drastically restrict the role of government in the economy in favour of private market solutions.

What implications did the spread of Freidman's ideas have for the global south? In the 1970s, international banks and lending institutions had gone on a lending spree. Many governments in the global south were eager to accept low-interest loans to assist in the industrialization of their nations. The election of Republican president Ronald Reagan in 1981 brought a dramatic change in monetary policy along the lines advocated by Friedman. Among other things, the change entailed a drastic increase in interest rates to deal with inflationary tendencies in the economy. Interest payments on loans made by the countries of the global south soared, and a debt crisis, especially acute in South America, ensued. As governments faced defaulting on their loans, international lending agencies put in place a new set of policies poor debtor countries would have to follow in order to be bailed out of their dilemma. These policies reflected Friedman's neoliberalism.

The new policy, often called the **Washington consensus,** united the International Monetary Fund (IMF), the World Bank, and the U.S. Treasury around Freidman's neoliberalism. The chief economist at the World Bank, Joseph Stiglitz, wrote that the three pillars of this consensus are austerity, privatization, and market liberalization (Stiglitz, 2003: 53).

In practice, **structural adjustment programs (SAPs)** became the basis of the bailout of the countries of the global south facing a debt crisis. The IMF and the World Bank offered to help the debtor countries financially if they met a set of harsh conditions: Privatize state-owned enterprises, such as telephone and oil companies and national banks; let in international corporations and goods produced in the developed countries; end tariff protection of local industry and agriculture; radically curtail social welfare programs; encourage new lines of agricultural exports— these were key aspects of SAPs. Proponents of SAPs claimed they were necessary to provide needed economic discipline and achieve economic growth. Critics argued that SAPs would cause social upheaval and misery. As we shall see, the critics were right.

Neoliberals assumed that markets work perfectly if left free to do so. Demand for labour, capital, and commodities will equal supply. There will be no unemployment. The only thing that can prevent this ideal outcome is market interference. If greedy unions constrain the workings of free markets by demanding and receiving excessively high wages, or if meddling politicians encourage the growth of social policies (employment insurance, welfare, universal health insurance, and so on), then the market will not be able to work its magic. By implication, if economic problems exist, markets must be unleashed. By this logic, the solution to unemployment, for example, is a reduction in wages.

NEOLIBERALISM AND SAPs AS SOLUTIONS TO POVERTY

Proponents of neoliberal reforms in developing countries argue that they have raised incomes in poor countries and lifted millions of people out of the poverty (Neilsen, 2007). Critics have argued that neoliberalism has produced a dramatic increase in global **income inequality,** widespread misery and social dislocation. Who is right? Let us consider the conflicting evidence.

Clearly, there have been winners in the neoliberal global economy. For example, after Mexico opened its economy to foreign capital and free trade, and privatized publically owned companies, a new class of billionaires emerged. Some benefited from the sale of public sector enterprises at low prices. Others managed to monopolize lucrative new markets. Notably, Carlos Slim Helu became the richest man in the world in 2007—richer than Bill Gates. (He dropped to second place in 2008.) Large commercial agricultural producers also benefited from the development of new agro-export industries oriented to the U.S. market.

India and China also opened their economies to foreign corporations and trade, helping them realize exceptional rates of economic growth. New industries have rapidly expanded to serve oversees and domestic markets. New entrepreneurial and professional middle classes have arisen in these countries, while masses of rural poor flood into cities to take up work in new factories that provide incomes considerably higher than those available in rural areas.

Do these examples not prove the success of the neoliberal economic model? The answer depends partly on how one defines success. In narrow economic terms, policies associated with neoliberalism have succeeded in some places. The wealth of some countries has increased, as has the standard of living. New infrastructure, including hydroelectric stations, rail networks, highway systems, and air transportation facilities have been built. These facts suggest development is indeed taking place.

Nevertheless, even among the success stories, glaring problems have emerged. And then there are the many countries that have benefited little or not at all from neoliberalism or have suffered because of it. Let us consider these issues in detail.

Level of Consumption versus Quality of Life and the Environment

An increase in monetary income in India and China does not mean that the average quality of life has necessarily improved in those countries. Life in rural areas often provided non-monetary benefits—personal security, tranquility, better air quality, the benefits of having family close, and so on—that are not captured by economic indicators of well-being. Life in the city for new immigrants often brings increased personal insecurity with dramatic increases in crime and violence, negative health outcomes associated with polluted air and water, dangerous work environments, and deterioration in diet associated with the consumption of fast food and low-quality street foods.

The kind of unregulated development seen in India and China in recent years has also brought with it massive environmental destruction. For example, to power its expansion, China constructed the massive Three Gorges electric dam project on the Yangtze River. The lake it will create has displaced more than a million people and destroyed 13 cities and 140 towns, including historical sites and valuable agricultural land. Lack of regulation means that dangerous and environmentally destructive industries, such as the scavenging of waste from electronic devices and the breaking up of ships in vulnerable marine environments, are commonplace.

Agricultural expansion has denuded vast territories and resulted in the rapid spread of deserts. China is rapidly exceeding the carrying capacity of its ecosystem. Winds carry soil from highly eroded land in the northwest as far away as South Korea and Japan, while air and water pollution affect the health of hundreds of millions of families. At the same time, industrial development has claimed tremendous water resources previously devoted to agriculture. The Yellow River no longer

Workers stretch as far as the eye can see in the Cankun Factory, Xiamin City, China.
SOURCE: © Edward Burtynsky, Courtesy Nicholas Metivier Gallery, Toronto.

Environmental Destruction in China: Before the Flood, Wan Zhou, Three Gorges Dam Project, Yangtze River, China.

SOURCE: © Edward Burtynsky, Courtesy Nicholas Metivier Gallery, Toronto

reaches the sea for part of the year, or even the downstream agricultural province of Shandong. This situation has imperilled agriculture in an important food-producing region. As renowned environmentalist Lester Brown concludes, "China is on the verge of a massive ecological meltdown" (2003: 11, 37).

Absolute Poverty and Global Income Inequality

Many parts of the world have not witnessed the kind of income growth that China and India have enjoyed. In fact, as Stiglitz notes, in the last decade of the twentieth century, "the number of people living in poverty has actually increased by almost 100 million. This occurred at the same time that the total world

income increased by an average of 2.5 percent annually" (Stiglitz, 2003: 5).

Measuring the gap at the global level between people with high and low income is difficult. Various experts use different methods and come up with different results. Nevertheless, as a leading researcher states, "the most basic fact about world inequality is that it is monstrously large; that result is inescapable, whatever the method or definition" (Sutcliffe, 2005; see Box 9.2). Branko Milanovic, a leading economist with the World Bank, notes that the top 5 percent of individuals in the world receive about one-third of total world income, while the top 10 percent get one-half. On the other hand, the bottom 5 and 10 percent of people in the world get just 0.2 and 0.7 percent of world income, respectively. Looked at another way, the ratio of the richest 5 percent compared to the poorest 5 percent of world citizens is 165 to 1. The richest 5 percent earn in 48 hours about what the poorest 5 percent earn in an entire year (Milanovic, 2005: 15).

A recent international project to measure the direction of change in global inequalities provides us with a more accurate estimate of global inequalities than we have had up to now. The International Comparison Project includes data from 146 national statistical agencies and major financial and development organizations including the United Nations, the World Bank, and the International Monetary Fund. The data resulting from this international effort have recently been released. A key finding of the project is that price levels in most Asian countries, notably China, India, Indonesia, and the Philippines—countries with about 38 percent of the world's population—are much higher than was formerly assumed. This means that they have many more poor

BOX 9.2	IF 100 PEOPLE LIVED ON EARTH

If the earth's population was shrunk to exactly 100 people, and all proportions were kept the same, there would be:

58 Asians,

10 East and West Europeans,

14 North and South Americans, and

12 Africans.

About one-third would have access to clean, safe drinking water.

One-third of the population would be children, only half of which would be vaccinated against preventable infectious diseases such as measles and polio.

Of the 67 adults, one-third would be illiterate

20 people would receive 75 percent of the entire world's available income.

Only 7 people would own an automobile.

One person would have control over nuclear weapons.

One-third of the available land would be desert, tundra, pavement, and other wasteland; about one-eighth would be suitable for crops.

SOURCE: Reprinted with permission from the Sustainability Institute.

people than previously thought, with new estimates bringing incomes down some 40 percent in China and India, 17 percent in Indonesia, 41 percent in the Philippines, 32 percent in South Africa, and 24 percent in Argentina. Average incomes did not decline in all of the poorer economies, but increases in Russia, Egypt, Nigeria, and Lebanon were more modest than declines in the Asian countries. Milanovic (2008) concludes that global inequality is much greater than even the most pessimistic analysts thought.

Trends in Inequality within and between Countries

What is the *trend* in global income inequality? Is it decreasing or increasing, and if so for what time period? Scholars have marshalled evidence that gives us a good idea of inequality trends since the 1930s. The data are better for the developed countries, but trends are apparent for the global south too.

Considering inequality within developed countries, the gap between the rich and poor decreased from the 1930s to the 1960s. This was the period when the welfare state was being constructed and Keynesian economic policies were being implemented (Bornschier, 2002: 102). For the global south, the same trend is apparent for only some countries. Brazil and Mexico saw increased gaps between rich and poor between 1950 and 1970. The gap between rich and poor countries was quite stable during these decades.

After the 1970s, when neoliberal policies were implemented, the picture becomes less rosy. Inequalities within countries substantially increased. Between countries, the gap also increased, especially during the 1980s (Bornschier, 2002: 108–10; Braun, 1997). Neoliberal policies were probably not the only factor contributing to this outcome. Other causes of the growing gap between rich and poor include the increasing penetration and integration of national economies by transnational corporations and the ongoing massive technological shift away from industrial production to the digital information economy, especially in the developed countries. Nevertheless, neoliberalism helped to widen the gap between rich and poor.

Growth Needs Strong States

Neoliberal policies have not stimulated growth in the global south. To the contrary, growth rates were higher in the decade before the introduction of SAPs (an average of 2.5 percent between 1960 and 1979) than in the era when SAPs were imposed by international lending agencies (0.0 percent between 1980 and 1998; Brym et al., 2005: 1). But what does history teach us about the policies the *rich* countries followed to encourage industrialization? Did they follow the tenets of neoliberalism? Aside from Britain, the first industrializing country, they did not. As French political economist François Chesnais (2004) notes, "the United States, France, Germany and the other industrialised countries [including Japan] benefited from selective *protection* of their home market for over a century or more" (my emphasis). This gave them time to grow until they could compete with Britain in world markets. Only the countries of the global south that fell under the sway of neoliberalism have lacked the opportunity to nurture their industrial and technological base. "Time has been denied to them," writes Chesnais.

Contrary to neoliberal theory, minimal state involvement is about the last thing industrializing countries need. In recent decades, the rapid industrialization of the "Asian tigers"—South Korea, Taiwan, Singapore, and, later, China and India—depended on strong states and considerable state involvement in the economy. For example, governments in South Korea and Taiwan after World War II were highly centralized and authoritarian. They succeeded in carrying out sweeping land reforms that eliminated the class of powerful landowners—the same class that protectionist policies in Latin America. The governments of these two countries opted for a strong industrial policy that marshalled the resources of the state to develop infrastructure and use state credit to fund investment in key industrial sectors. They kept control of industrial development by preventing foreign corporations from taking over their expanding industries. They also used their power to repress labour movements, which kept wages down and made emerging industry highly competitive in the world market.

China followed suit. The all-powerful Communist Party organized a top-down transformation of the economy to encourage foreign investment—but on their terms rather than terms dictated by neoliberal institutions. The Communist Party organized massive infrastructure projects that encouraged industrial investment. It kept wages low and used violence to prevent the formation of independent labour organizations.[1]

Women under Neoliberalism

Other signs exist that neoliberalism has failed to produce the results claimed by its advocates. The dismantling of many national banks by IMF policy prescription undermined cheap credit to small farmers and imperilled rural incomes in many poor countries (Rodriguez Gomez and Torres, 1996: 157–58). Trade liberalization encouraged the import of heavily subsidized agricultural commodities from the developed countries. They undermined rural incomes, as prices for food produced by small farmers plummeted in the face of an incoming tide of low-cost food. Because of such policies, millions of rural poor have been forced off the land and into already overcrowded towns and cities. Millions more migrated to the developed world, some illegally and at great danger to themselves. Such migrants have become the source of a huge global economy in recent years. They typically do menial work and send money back to family members in Mexico, the Philippines, and elsewhere.

In some parts of the global south, such as India and Thailand, neoliberal policies have been especially hard on women, partly because women form the bulk of the agricultural work force (Shiva, 1993: 232). Elsewhere, in countries as diverse as Nicaragua and Nigeria, women have had to raise families on their own as their husbands are forced to migrate to the cities or to the developed world in search of cash income. Evidence suggests that these circumstances are breaking down long-standing patriarchal structures and forging new ties of solidarity among women as they strive to cope with the new realities, but the change involves much suffering.

Since 1999, the World Bank and the IMF have implemented policies that they believe promote gender equity. However, critics point out that these new policies have been weakly implemented and have done little to eliminate gender barriers for women wishing to access the paid workforce or engage in production for export markets. Nor do they tackle the substantial gender inequality that exists in the households of the global south (Brym et al., 2005).

STATE VIOLENCE, WAR, AND THE PRODUCTION OF POVERTY

Military aggression and war have helped to undermine development in much of the post–World War II era, and they therefore deserve to be discussed at some length. During the Cold War, mutually assured destruction by nuclear weapons made military confrontation between the Soviet Union and the United States out of the question. Nevertheless, both countries used their economic and military might to reshape the world during this period.

Under the guise of making the world "safe for democracy" and "fighting communism," the United States was directly or indirectly involved in a series of military *coups d'état* in Latin America and elsewhere from the 1950s to the late 1970s, beginning with the CIA-organized invasion of Guatemala in 1954. The government it had installed at that time prepared the ground for a series of pro-American regimes that have carried on continuous campaigns of **state terrorism** that have killed many tens of thousands of Guatemalans, often with unspeakable brutality (Falla, 1994). Over a million citizens have been forced to flee the violence in their country. For most of the decades that followed, Washington provided military aid, training, and diplomatic support for these regimes (Gareau, 2004: 63). When it became politically impossible for Washington to provide such assistance because of the Guatemalan military's gross human rights abuses, the Israeli government stepped in to provide military aid and training (Marshall, Scott, and Hunter, 1987).

The "domino theory" held that if one country fell under communist influence, its neighbours would soon follow suit. Operating with the domino theory in mind, the United States began a decade-long military intervention in Vietnam in the 1960s. This intervention followed years of French colonial domination. America's undeclared war killed more than a million North Vietnamese military personnel, between 500 000 and 2 million civilians, and more than 58 000 American military personnel. The war destroyed Vietnam's economic infrastructure; the country has only recently shown signs of recovery and economic expansion.

The main American rival on the world stage at this time was the Soviet Union, which also sought to extend its influence and promote the economic model it favoured. In so doing it used military force to block efforts to democratize and liberalize authoritarian communist regimes within its sphere of influence (Hungary in 1956, Czechoslovakia in 1968) while lending its support to pro-Soviet governments elsewhere in Eastern Europe with strong authoritarian tendencies. Throughout the Cold War, the Soviet Union provided military equipment, training, and in-country advisers to various authoritarian regimes in the Middle East, notably Syria, Algeria, and Iraq under Saddam Hussein, as it competed with the United States for influence in the region. It refrained from supplying the most advanced weaponry to these states, however, for fear that doing so would drag it into direct military confrontation with the Americans (Antonenko, 2001).

Soviet economic and military aid also assisted the struggles of different movements around the globe to remove colonial and neocolonial domination. It bolstered the Vietnamese war effort against the United States, helped the Cubans resist the American economic blockade of that country, and provided arms and materiel to Angola, Mozambique, and Nicaragua in their war against "contra" mercenary armies and the apartheid South African government. Such countries as Cuba and Nicaragua turned to the Soviet Union for military aid only after the United States had fostered economic destabilization and engaged in covert military operations with the intention of bringing down these governments.

In the 1970s the United States, with the help of allies, such as France, provided military equipment, extensive training, and expertise to help install military governments in Brazil, Uruguay, Chile, Argentina, and the Dominican Republic. When these oppressive military regimes came to power, they typically forged strong ties with multinational corporations while suppressing trade unions and popular organizations and groups that opposed them. The oppression they unleashed was brutal. In Argentina, the number of citizens killed by the pro-American dictatorships exceeded 30 000 people, with members of the younger generation the principal victims (Marchak, 1999). Increasingly, the tactics of repression developed by these dictatorships in Latin America are being used in other part of the world to stamp out dissent.

In the 1970s, popular struggles against a staunchly pro-American dictatorship in Nicaragua, and European colonial regimes in Angola and Mozambique, were successful in establishing governments that sought to redistribute land and wealth, and establish more democratic forms of popular participation. Indeed, in their first years in power they made dramatic strides in combating illiteracy and expanding health care (Vilas, 1986).

In the 1980s, the U.S. government sponsored illegal arms deals to covert armies to fight the revolutionary government in Nicaragua and support the South African government in its campaign to destabilize Mozambique and Angola (Gareau, 2004; Marshall, Scott, and Hunter, 1987). In Mozambique, the South African strategy of destabilization was responsible for destroying 718 health facilities and schools accommodating 300 000 students between 1981 and 1986 (Gareau, 2004: 139–40). In Nicaragua, more than 50 000 people were killed or wounded in what was called the "contra war." In southern Africa,

a task force appointed by the Secretary General of the United Nations estimated that damage to Mozambique, Angola, and Zimbabwe from South Africa's destabilization campaign amounted to $60 billion (1988 prices) between 1981 and 1988, an immense sum for such desperately poor countries. Moreover, 1.5 million people died from violence or violence-related disease and famine, and half the population of Mozambique and Angola was displaced (Gareau, 2004: 141).

In the twenty-first century, war has continued to plague parts of the global south, particularly sub-Saharan Africa and the Middle East, and undermined the benefits that might come from development assistance. Postcommunist Russia has become a major arms vendor. The Russian defence industry now depends on arms exports for its survival, and private interests in Russia increasingly act without government support to penetrate the lucrative Middle East arms market (Antonenko, 2001). New actors have also emerged to pursue self-serving policies that fuel war, economic turmoil, and social disruption and dislocation, China chief among them. For example, China's pursuit of oil in Sudan has led it to support the Sudanese regime, which is responsible for the ongoing genocide in Darfur.

RESISTANCE TO THE NEOLIBERAL NEW WORLD ORDER

GOVERNMENT RESISTANCE

We end our discussion by considering how governments and people in the global south have resisted neoliberal policies.

Such resistance has been particularly acute in Latin America. Since 2000, Argentina, Brazil, Bolivia, Ecuador, and Venezuela have elected governments that oppose neoliberalism. These governments have been deeply concerned with the increasing concentration of land ownership, the concomitant spread of landlessness, and skyrocketing urban poverty in recent decades. They have sought to aid the landless and the urban poor, and in some cases to nationalize key resource industries in order to capture the profits that for decades went largely to transnational companies with little local benefit. The Chavez government in Venezuela has used its oil wealth to provide substantial aid to other poor countries in Latin America. In fact, it has provided more aid than has the United States, which has an economy 90 times as large as that of Venezuela ("Chavez," 2007).

Women members of the MST *(Movimento Sem Terra)*, Brazil's Landless Workers Movement, protest against George W. Bush's visit to Brazil. The march also marked support of International Women's Day. Thousands of protesters gathered to march against the visit of then United States President George W. Bush to Brazil.
SOURCE: © Carlos Cazalis/Corbis.

POPULAR RESISTANCE

In civil society as well, broad-based organizations have challenged the neoliberal development model. Most prominent among these is the World Social Forum, which first brought together representatives from around the world in Porto Alegre, Brazil, in 2001. Their statement of principles set out their aims as follows:

> The alternatives proposed at the World Social Forum stand in opposition to a process of globalisation commanded by the large multinational corporations and by the governments and international institutions at the service of those corporations' interests, with the complicity of national governments. They are designed to ensure that globalisation in solidarity will prevail as a new stage in world history. This will respect universal human rights, and those of all citizens—men and women—of all nations and the environment and will rest on democratic international systems and institutions at the service of social justice, equality and the sovereignty of peoples. (World Social Forum, 2009)

Another notable example of popular resistance to neoliberalism is *Via Campesina*, an international organization of peasant farmers, rural women, and landless workers that seeks to achieve social justice and gender parity in the context of sustainable agricultural production (Borras, 2008). In 2007, hundreds of delegates from 86 countries met in the small village of Nyéléni in the African nation of Mali and set out their principles (see Box 9.3, p. 222).

Popular resistance to neoliberalism in both the global south and the global north often takes the form of sit-ins, demonstrations, and strikes on the part of students, non-governmental organizations, unions, peasant associations, and trade unions. Increasingly, however, resistance to neoliberalism has entered formal politics. For example, the 2008 American presidential race sparked debate over the damage done to people and the environment by the North American Free Trade Agreement. It is impossible to know where such debate will lead, or what it will eventually achieve. However, the 2008–2009 global financial meltdown suggests that the neoliberal model may have run its course and that new opportunities for constructing a sounder and more just global economic system are at hand.

BOX 9.3   EXCERPT FROM THE *DECLARATION OF NYÉLÉNI*, MALI, 2007

What are we fighting for?

A world where . . .

. . . all peoples, nations and states are able to determine their own food producing systems and policies that provide every one of us with good quality, adequate, affordable, healthy, and culturally appropriate food;

. . . recognition and respect of women's roles and rights in food production, and representation of women in all decision making bodies;

. . . all peoples in each of our countries are able to live with dignity, earn a living wage for their labour and have the opportunity to remain in their homes;

. . . where food sovereignty is considered a basic human right, recognised and implemented by communities, peoples, states and international bodies;

. . . we are able to conserve and rehabilitate rural environments, fish stocks, landscapes and food traditions based on ecologically sustainable management of land, soils, water, seas, seeds, livestock and other biodiversity;

. . . we value, recognize and respect our diversity of traditional knowledge, food, language and culture, and the way we organise and express ourselves;

. . . there is genuine and integral agrarian reform that guarantees peasants full rights to land, defends and recovers the territories of indigenous peoples, ensures fishing communities' access and control over their fishing areas and eco-systems, honours access and control over pastoral lands and migratory routes, assures decent jobs with fair remuneration and labour rights for all, and a future for young people in the countryside;

. . . where agrarian reform revitalises interdependence between producers and consumers, ensures community survival, social and economic justice and ecological sustainability, and respect for local autonomy and governance with equal rights for women and men...where it guarantees the right to territory and self-determination for our peoples;

. . . where we share our lands and territories peacefully and fairly among our peoples, be we peasants, indigenous peoples, artisanal fishers, pastoralists, or others;

. . . in the case of natural and human-created disasters and conflict-recovery situations, food sovereignty acts as a kind of "insurance" that strengthens local recovery efforts and mitigates negative impacts . . . where we remember that affected communities are not helpless, and where strong local organization for self-help is the key to recovery;

. . . where peoples' power to make decisions about their material, natural and spiritual heritage are defended;

. . . where all peoples have the right to defend their territories from the actions of transnational corporations;

What are we fighting against?

Imperialism, neoliberalism, neo-colonialism and patriarchy, and all systems that impoverish life, resources and eco-systems, and the agents that promote the above such as international financial institutions, the World Trade Organisation, free trade agreements, transnational corporations, and governments that are antagonistic to their peoples;

- The dumping of food at prices below the cost of production in the global economy;

The domination of our food and food producing systems by corporations that place profits before people, health and the environment;

Technologies and practices that undercut our future food producing capacities, damage the environment and put our health at risk. Those include transgenic crops and animals, terminator technology, industrial aquaculture and destructive fishing practices, the so-called white revolution of industrial dairy practices, the so-called 'old' and 'new' Green Revolutions, and the "Green Deserts" of industrial bio-fuel monocultures and other plantations;

The privatisation and commodification of food, basic and public services, knowledge, land, water, seeds, livestock and our natural heritage;

Development projects/models and extractive industry that displace people and destroy our environments and natural heritage;

Wars, conflicts, occupations, economic blockades, famines, forced displacement of people and confiscation of their land, and all forces and governments that cause and support them; post disaster and conflict reconstruction programmes that destroy our environments and capacities;

The criminalization of all those who struggle to protect and defend our rights;

Food aid that disguises dumping, introduces GMOs into local environments and food systems and creates new colonialism patterns;

The internationalisation and globalisation of paternalistic and patriarchal values that marginalise women, diverse agricultural, indigenous, pastoral and fisher communities around the world.

SOURCE: *La Via Campesina*, 2007

SUMMARY

1. Global inequality is perhaps the most pressing issue of our times.

2. Stages of economic growth theory posits that societies proceed through various stages of development much as biological organisms do. Contemporary American market society is considered the ultimate stage.

3. Modernization theory argues that value orientations determine the success of development in a particular country. Countries where people have a high need for achievement and value competitive behaviour are said to have a higher likelihood of success in the development process.

4. Dependency theory stresses the role of structural relationships of exploitation between rich and poor regions of the globe as important in blocking the development of the latter.

5. Bio-environmental theory, proposed by Jared Diamond, argues that environmental factors, including the geographical features of different continents and the biological resources available to early peoples, were fundamentally important in determining which part of the globe came to dominate other parts of the globe.

6. Marxist development theory places particular weight on class structure and conflict between fundamental classes within each historical epoch as central to determining development outcomes.

7. A historical and holistic approach helps us understand the divergent development of different parts of the globe.

8. Significant structural barriers have blocked or retarded the economic development of many countries.

9. Not all countries in the global south are the same; different class structures and political arrangements have produced different development outcomes.

10. Policies promoted by the International Monetary Fund and the World Bank have helped to undermine rural livelihoods in some parts of the world and have not effectively addressed the severe disadvantages women face in several regions of the global south.

11. Certain factors have allowed for the rapid development of a few formerly poor countries, but the associated costs for society and the environment have often been high.

12. War and military aggression, often sponsored by developed countries, have had a major negative impact on development in the global south.

13. Today there is general agreement that global inequalities are staggering, and new evidence indicates that the gap between rich and poor countries is wider than earlier believed.

14. Resistance to the dominant development model is growing and is particularly strong in Latin America.

QUESTIONS TO CONSIDER

1. Do you think global inequality will change over the next 25 years? In what ways? Why do you think these changes will occur? If you think global inequality will remain the same, explain why.

2. Should Canadians do anything to help alleviate global poverty? Why or why not? If you think

Canadians should help end global poverty, then what should we do?

3. What circumstances allowed some countries to escape underdevelopment in the late twentieth and early twenty-first centuries?

GLOSSARY

Capitalism is an economic system based on profit seeking in competitive markets. It is associated with dynamic technological development, the development of class inequality, and accelerating environmental destruction.

Deindustrialization is a process, linked to neoliberal policies, that facilitates businesses moving to the lowest wage jurisdictions nationally or abroad, resulting in social dislocation and economic decline in older industrial regions.

Dependency theory is an explanation of uneven global development that stresses the exploitative relationships

that have existed between Europe and the global south, to the detriment of the latter (see underdevelopment).

Income inequality is the difference in income earned by high and low income earners, whether within a country or among countries.

Modernization theory argues that economic growth and development can best be achieved if the values underlying market capitalism are aggressively fostered.

Neoliberalism calls for the elimination of government involvement in the economy, which presumably allows free markets to achieve economic growth and development.

Purchasing power parity is the number of units of a country's currency needed to buy the same amount of goods and services in the domestic market as a U.S. dollar would buy in the United States.

Stages of development in W. W. Rostow's theory are the developmental phases through which societies supposedly pass. Rostow believed that modern American capitalism represents a final developmental stage characterized by sustained economic growth.

State terrorism is a deliberate act of physical or psychological violence perpetrated by state organizations (the army, secret police, etc.) to intimidate and coerce certain groups by causing fear, anxiety, panic, and horror.

Structural adjustment programs (SAPs) are policies imposed on debtor countries by the World Bank that entail privatization of state enterprises, opening of debtor economies to imports and capital from developed countries, eliminating social poverty reduction programs, and meeting debt obligations to the financial institutions of the rich countries.

Terms of trade refers to the ratio of the price of exports to the price of imports.

Underdevelopment is the idea that the development of Europe required the exploitation of the global south and undermined its economic development.

The **Washington consensus** is the shared view of the International Monetary Fund, the World Bank, and the U.S. Treasury Department that emerged in the late 1970s promoting a neoliberal approach to economic development and stabilization in the global south.

SUGGESTED READING

Collier, Paul. (2008). *The Bottom Billion: Why the Poorest Countries Are Failing and What Can Be Done about It.* Toronto: Oxford University Press. Argues that the challenge of lifting the world's poorest billion people out of poverty is akin to rebuilding Europe after World War II, requiring not only immediate aid but also trade and security effectively promoted by multilateral institutions.

Griesgraber, Jo Marie, and Bernard Gunter, eds. (1996). *Development: New Paradigms and Principles for the Twenty-First Century (Rethinking Bretton Woods).* London, UK: Pluto Press. A critique of the Washington consensus approach to development and a detailed proposal for equitable, sustainable, and participatory development.

Veltmeyer, Henry, ed. (2008). *New Perspectives on Globalization and Antiglobalization: Prospects for a New World Order.* Aldershot, UK: Ashgate. Eleven specialists in the political economy of international relations and globalization analyze the diverse dimensions of the globalization process.

NOTE

1. As transnational manufacturing firms shifted investment to low-cost labour markets, the **deindustrialization** of many developed countries took place, devastating communities in the north of England and the north-central United States (Bluestone and Harrison, 1982, 1988). Canadian workers and communities in Ontario and Quebec have not been immune to these forces (Winson and Leach, 2002). Investment has not shifted to all low-wage countries, however, because few can offer the massive infrastructure, disciplined low-cost labour force, and political stability that China can.

WEB RESOURCES

Companion Website for This Book

http://www.newsociety6e.nelson.com
Begin by clicking on the Student Resources section of the website. Next, select the chapter you are studying from the pull-down menu. From the Student Resources page, you have easy access to InfoTrac College Edition® and other resources, such as the Glossary, Test Yourself questions, and additional readings. The website also has many useful tips to aid you in your study of sociology.

InfoTrac College Edition Search Terms

Visit http://www.infotrac-college.com for access to more than 20 million articles from nearly 6000 sources when doing your online research.

Institutions

CHAPTER TEN

SOURCE: © Baloncici/Shutterstock

Families

Bonnie Fox

UNIVERSITY OF TORONTO

In this chapter you will learn that

- Although common sense suggests that current dilemmas in family life are private problems, sociology helps uncover their public sources and solutions.

- The family does not have a universal form and its structure is therefore not a product of some biological imperative: Families vary widely in the way they are organized across different cultures and through history, and family organization is loosely related to the way material production is organized.

- Our society is organized around a gendered division of labour and the heterosexual nuclear family. This is the main reason that families that assume a different form—especially lone-parent families—have a particularly hard time meeting the needs of their members.

- Although women have increasingly assumed part of the financial support of their families, men do not share equally the work that must be done in the home, nor has society changed in ways that sufficiently accommodate this changed reality for families.

- The gendered division of labour that makes it possible for nuclear families to care for young children involves sizable liabilities for women and children. The social isolation of full-time mothers and the stress attached to their high-demand, low-control situation reduces the quality of child care.

- The chief negative effect of divorce for women and children is the loss of income that follows. The most effective solution to this problem—government support of all children—has not been adopted by the Canadian government, although most advanced industrial societies do have such a policy objective.

INTRODUCTION

Contemporary life presents difficult choices for those of us who live in or plan to live in families. The constraints on these choices affect our lives profoundly. I begin this chapter by reviewing dilemmas in family life in the light of popular myths. Because family life is so familiar to us, we all too easily accept commonsense understandings that portray family problems as personal, private, and attributable to "human nature." Commonsense solutions prescribe individual change and ignore the social context. In contrast, sociology uncovers the social origins of family patterns and the problems they entail.

As a way of challenging the commonsense perspective, the second section of this chapter examines two patterns of family life that are different from our own. In these cases, it is clear that the family patterns people have created are a response to the problems posed by the needs of daily survival. Next, I review the history that produced our own family arrangements.

In the chapter's fourth section, I explore some of the main features of family life today: sexuality, marriage, parenthood, housework, and the **gendered division of labour** (i.e., the difference in the work that men and women do). My aim is to analyze how these activities are organized so as to give you an idea of the sources of problems that often plague modern families. I then discuss divorce and its aftermath and lone-parent and reconstituted families. I finish with a brief discussion of government policies to support families.

EXPLORING THE FAMILIAR: FAMILIES IN WESTERN SOCIETY TODAY

DILEMMAS OF CONTEMPORARY FAMILY LIFE

When you imagine yourself at age 39, you probably think of yourself as married, with a child or two. You probably also assume—or at least hope—that your children will enjoy full-time mothering for their early years. You are not unusual if you envision your adulthood in family terms. Moreover, when you think of family, you likely think of the conventional **nuclear family,** in which the man is the main breadwinner and the woman has primary responsibility for the children. Alternatively, your dream may be to have occupational success and a loving, committed relationship

without children. And the relationship you imagine may be with a same-sex partner. Or perhaps you hope to raise a child without any long-term partner. Whether or not you anticipate parenthood, and whatever the gender of the partner you dream of, you likely envision a relationship in which the work and the responsibility, as well as the intimacy and joy, are shared.

Along with your dreams, you probably also have nagging concerns about your future. Full-time mothering seems a luxury few women can afford these days. Most married women—even those with young children—now have to assume some of the responsibility of breadwinning. Indeed, most women attending university anticipate building a career, which involves far more commitment and time than does simply holding a job. Building a career makes it difficult to take time out for children, because the necessary time commitment is at odds with the demands of motherhood. These realities lead to obvious questions: Women wonder when they will have time to have children and how they will care for them once they arrive.

Whereas women's concerns about family tend to focus on the difficulties of combining employment and child care, men's concerns probably centre on the growing elusiveness of occupational success in this uncertain economy. At the same time, men are increasingly pressured by the women they live with to change in ways for which they are unprepared. Manhood was once equated with occupational success, but such success is now harder to achieve and insufficient for a happy marriage. Today, many women expect men to be emotionally open in ways that women tend to find easy, in addition to aggressively pursuing occupational success *and* sharing the housework.

Lesbians and gays face even greater challenges creating families in a society organized around heterosexuality and gender divisions. Parenthood without a partner is also particularly difficult: while two-earner couples find juggling income earning and child care stressful, the task increases exponentially for a lone parent. Most obviously, the threat of poverty is far greater for a lone mother than for a couple (see Figure 10.1, p. 228). Indeed, inequalities based on social class and the disadvantages women and racial minorities face in the labour force provide the inhospitable context in which all Canadians build their families.

Full-time mothering is a luxury most women cannot afford. Combining employment and child care is an act that requires women to wear two faces.

SOURCE: Mimi Matte, *Family Outing*. Photo Courtesy Ingram Gallery.

Although conventional family patterns are in decline, our society still seems to be organized around nuclear families and the assumption that children are a private responsibility. Houses are designed for nuclear families, not extended families; social policies often assume family membership and men sharing their earnings with their wives; and, except in Quebec, governments refuse to provide adequate child-care facilities for the families needing them. The limitations of nuclear-family living and private responsibility for children are, however, clear when couples become parents. Parents (usually mothers) with infants typically face round-the-clock demands and anxieties about their new responsibilities on their own. Whatever support grandparents want to offer is inhibited by the fact that they may live in another house, if not another city, as well as by the demands of their employment. Aside from the gift giving and visiting that occurs when a baby is born, friends are unlikely to help a mother with her child-care responsibilities. Meanwhile, when mothers return to paid work, their earnings will likely be insufficient to support them and their children—so parenthood also reinforces nuclear families.

Conventional gender roles also seem central to the organization of our society. It is difficult to keep a

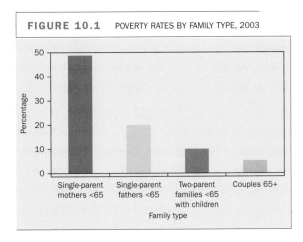

FIGURE 10.1   POVERTY RATES BY FAMILY TYPE, 2003

SOURCE: National Council of Welfare, 2006, *Poverty Profile 2002 and 2003*. Reproduced with the permission of the Minister of Public Works and Government Services Canada.

family going with no one at home to buy groceries, plan and make meals, organize doctors' appointments, and meet repair people. In English-speaking Canada, the dearth of good, affordable daycare means that having children is difficult unless the mother becomes a full-time homemaker. And men have depended on the emotional support and caring work provided by their wives to keep them happy and productive. Thus, a gendered division of labour has sustained families in an economy in which employers bear no direct responsibility for the welfare of their employees' families.

Clearly, the future poses dilemmas. How will we earn enough money to support a family and raise our children? How will we sustain loving relationships with our partners while coping with the problems outlined above? Indeed, are our ideals about family sustainable? And if the conventional nuclear family is an unlikely prospect for most of us, how will we live in a society that assumes it is an essential part of life?

MYTHS ABOUT FAMILY

Thinking through these dilemmas is especially difficult because myths about family pervade our culture. Measured against the idealized image of family life that emerged during the 1950s and was beamed into homes across the country by television, the problems in family life today assume crisis proportions. "The family" seems to be disintegrating. Actually, real families in the 1950s bore little resemblance to those depicted in *Leave It to Beaver* and *Father Knows Best*. Nevertheless, the 1950s was an unusually "familistic" decade: People married earlier, had more children, and were less likely to divorce than the generations that preceded and followed them (E. May, 1988). The 1950s are thus an odd benchmark. Moreover, researchers find that women who combine motherhood with labour-force involvement are mentally and physically healthier than those who stay home (Coontz, 1992); women who are home full-time with young children often find the situation stressful and isolating. And there is little scientific evidence to support the belief that babies and toddlers need full-time mothers at home.

Also mythical is the popular view that the traditional European family consisted of three generations of family living harmoniously under one roof, caring for all its members. In fact, **extended-family households**—consisting of three generations—were rare in preindustrial Europe. Moreover, children spent much of their childhood in the care of people other than their parents; and the elderly did not expect to be cared for lovingly by their children. Where large extended families were common—for instance, among the wealthy in ancient China—the lives of all were wholly circumscribed by the authority of the male patriarch.

Myths about family easily play into the hands of politicians who aim to reinforce individual responsibility for the welfare of children and other dependants and to avoid providing the social services necessary to support the adults who carry out those responsibilities. Calls for a return to "family values" evoke an undefined past, free of today's social problems, a time when the values we associate with family—community, decency, and morality—were dominant. Such political rhetoric uses "the family" to symbolize all that is good and decent—the bedrock on which society rests. Of course, the family in question is the heterosexual breadwinner/homemaker family, and deviations from this ideal are held responsible for myriad social problems. Moreover, the assumption is that this kind of family is "natural," and not the product of the daily efforts of women and men living in particular circumstances.

THE MYTH OF THE NATURAL FAMILY

One reason for the popular fixation on the heterosexual nuclear family is that it seems to derive from the biology of reproduction. Common sense suggests that biology produces the family. Heralded by the news media, arguments based on **biological determinism** are immensely popular these days. One common variant of this approach, known as **evolutionary psychology,** or

The decline of the nuclear family has been accompanied by the rise of other family forms.

SOURCE: (c) iStockphoto.com/Elena Korenbaum.

sociobiology, attempts to apply the laws of biological evolution to social behaviour. Sociobiologists hold that, as with physical traits, social behaviour is inherited biologically—in other words, that behaviour can be linked to specific genetic configurations. Typically, sociobiologists construct a story about the history of human evolution that assumes genetic encoding of behaviour—a problematic assumption since there is no evidence to support it (Lewontin, Rose, and Kamin, 1984).

The sociobiological argument about family is that, over the course of human history, certain behaviours were adaptive because they contributed to "reproductive success." Specifically, males who were more aggressive and females who were more nurturant had more offspring. Thus, these behaviours were "naturally selected," and turned up in more and more individuals over the generations. According to this perspective, today's behaviour is the product of human evolution—and thus inevitable. Yet research by psychologists shows that women are no more empathic or sensitive to others than men are. Nor is there a natural maternal instinct that tells mothers how to care for their newborn baby.

The family, consisting of the biological mother and father and their offspring, is also a product of evolution, according to sociobiologists. Because children represent people's genetic investment, they argue, evolutionary forces have selected a pattern that is most likely to ensure the survival of offspring—namely, the union of two biological parents in a lasting relationship.

Although sociobiology accords with common sense, its claims do not accord with observable evidence. Evidence on family patterns across various cultures indicates that, although the nuclear family is common in many cultures, it is often embedded in a larger household that constitutes the unit of production, consumption, and child care. For example, in Europe in the Middle Ages, the wealthier a married couple was, the larger the household. Spouses and their children lived amid an array of additional, unrelated people—children, teens, and adults who provided necessary labour to the household (Mitterauer and Sieder, 1982). Preindustrial European households also provide evidence that mothers do not always raise, or even live with, their biological children. In many parts of Europe until the twentieth century, the babies of women who could afford it were given to "wet nurses," who were paid to nurse and care for them, and young teens were sent into service or apprenticeship in other households.

According to ethnographic evidence, in many non-Western cultures, mothers are the primary caregivers for babies but not for older children. Siblings often take on the bulk of the care of children, although in some cultures (like Tahiti or parts of the Caribbean) the children of a young woman are given to her parents or close kin to be raised, and in others (throughout Melanesia and Polynesia) they are adopted after weaning (Edholm, 1982). Moreover, because the biology of reproduction—which we take as "given"—is interpreted in different ways across different cultures, the role of the father in conception is not always recognized. Often the social father is different from the biological father. Finally, incest rules, which we take to reflect a kind of natural avoidance of inbreeding, have sometimes allowed brother–sister marriage to ensure the "purity" of the royal line (e.g., in Egypt and Hawaii). Many of the things we often assume to be natural and universal are neither. There is a diversity of family patterns across history and cultures.

CONCEPTUALIZING AND DEFINING FAMILY

Structural Functionalism

It is widely believed that the best unit in which to raise children is the nuclear family. This commonsense notion was promoted by Talcott Parsons (Parsons and Bales, 1955), whose writings on family constituted the dominant perspective in post–World War II sociology. In arguing that an institution (in this case, the heterosexual nuclear family) exists because of the useful functions it performs for the larger society, Parsons was making an argument reflecting the school of thought called structural functionalism.

Although structural functionalism dominated the study of families until recently, this perspective has obvious problems. First, just because an institution performs a social function, there is no reason to assume that some other institution might not perform that function equally well. Whether exclusive care by the biological mother and father is best for children is an empirical question.

Another problem with the functionalist perspective is its focus on how institutions create social *order*, and its consequent failure to analyze the tensions in family life that can generate social *change*. Moreover, the functions that are emphasized allegedly meet the needs of society, not necessarily of the individuals in it. So, for instance, although Parsons recognized the problems faced by full-time homemakers, it was not until feminists analyzed family life that the power dynamics and conflicts common to heterosexual nuclear families were highlighted.

Definitions

How *family* is defined has practical, as well as methodological, consequences. Rights and responsibilities follow from definitions. For instance, state-regulated institutions, such as schools and hospitals, often use legal definitions of marriage and family to determine which people will be informed and consulted about the status of someone in the institution. Accordingly, critically ill patients may find that family members with whom they have had little recent contact are admitted to their rooms and entitled to make important medical decisions on their behalf, whereas the friends who have been constant companions and who know them best are excluded. Government entitlements, such as widows' pensions and tax deductions for the support of dependants, apply only to family relations as defined by the government. A wife of a few years may be entitled to a widow's pension, whereas a same-sex lover of 20 years is not. A woman supporting a friend who is a senior and has disabilities cannot take the same tax deduction as a father supporting a child.

Similarly, when social scientists define *family*, some of them still assume the nuclear unit. This tendency has often resulted in a focus on the frequency with which nuclear-family patterns appear across history and cultures. Conceptualizing family in a way that focuses on common properties does not serve the interests of good empirical inquiry, however. Focusing on diversity in social patterns can, in contrast, help us acquire a better understanding of the nature of families. By studying diversity and noting the social circumstances that vary with family patterns, we can derive some idea of the social forces and factors that influence those patterns.

Accordingly, I define **family** as the sets of relationships people create to share resources daily in order to ensure their own and any dependants' welfare. What this definition offers is a focus on what is of critical importance to both individual survival and generational reproduction across many cultures. At the same time, it does not exclude groupings of people who are in essence functioning as family, though they may lack formal recognition as such (e.g., female relatives who live in separate households but cooperate daily to care for their children).

This definition holds family to be the unit of **social reproduction.** As opposed to biological reproduction, social reproduction refers to a wide range of activities that "maintain existing life and . . . [in most cases] reproduce the next generation" (Laslett and Brenner, 1989: 381–403). In other words, social reproduction refers to feeding, clothing, and otherwise looking after people's subsistence needs, as well as emotionally supporting adults and usually nurturing and socializing children. A "family" is thus a set of social relationships that work to reproduce life on a daily and a generational basis.

A LOOK AT OTHER FAMILY PATTERNS

To gain some perspective on family life, it is useful to examine family patterns that are significantly different from our own. When we do, one of the things we notice is that family patterns vary with the way people organize themselves to acquire their subsistence. To illustrate this point, I describe the communal households that are characteristic of many foraging (or hunting-and-gathering) societies, and the household economies typical of agricultural societies in preindustrial Europe.

FORAGING SOCIETIES: THE COMMUNAL HOUSEHOLD

In **foraging societies,** people acquire subsistence by gathering edibles and hunting live game. Foragers live in fairly small camps, or bands, comprising people who are compatible and not necessarily related by marriage or blood. Because they live off the resources available to them in the local area, foragers are nomadic. Their ability to move when necessary is critical to survival, so they cannot accumulate many possessions and must keep the ratio of dependants (children and seniors) to productive foragers low (Lee, 1979).

Although foragers meet their subsistence needs by doing relatively little work, their inability to accumulate any surplus means that survival depends on reciprocity and cooperation among the people living together. For example, successful hunters distribute game to all members of the camp. Doing so is economically rational for an individual living in an economy based on reciprocity because giving establishes reciprocal obligations. Hunting is an especially uncertain occupation, so sharing the product is a sort of personal insurance. For the group, sharing ensures that a valuable source of protein is distributed widely.

In addition to sharing, a division of labour by gender and age organizes the acquisition of subsistence in foraging societies. Women typically gather and men typically hunt, although men also gather after an unsuccessful day of hunting and women hunt in some societies. Among the !Kung San of the Kalahari Desert in Botswana, as among many foragers, the food that women gather provides the bulk of subsistence—about 60 percent to 80 percent (Lee, 1979). In foraging societies, children and older adults typically do not forage for food.

The reciprocity that is the basis of foragers' daily subsistence no doubt generally influences the organization of their societies. Living has a communal character. Responsibilities that are assumed by families in our society—that is, responsibilities that are private— are held collectively in foraging societies. Thus, although marriage establishes the mother/father/ child (i.e., nuclear) unit, the group of cooperating adults that is crucial for survival—the unit of social reproduction—is the camp. That is, all the members of the camp decide together when and where to move, and they share food and the responsibility for children. Moreover, perhaps because individual cooperation is central to daily living, and because these societies are without authority figures who might enforce such cooperation, individuals are allowed considerable freedom.

Although women do most of the child care— which is considerable, when children are carried constantly, as they are among the !Kung San—they do not bear the burden alone. Women care for one another's children; they even breastfeed one another's babies. Men also often tend babies and children.

Life in foraging societies seems to produce an absence of possessiveness toward children and spouses. This attitude is clear in the comment of a seventeenth-century Montagnais-Naskapi (Innu) man in response to a Jesuit missionary's attempt to shame him for not practising monogamy: "Thou hast no sense. You French people love only your own children; but we all love all the children of our tribe" (Leacock, 1981: 50). With respect to spouses, anthropologist Colin Turnbull (1961: 125) writes of the Pygmies of Congo:

They think of responsibility as communal. If you ask a father, or a husband, why he allows his son to flirt with a married girl, or his wife to flirt with other men, he will answer, "It is not my affair," and he is right. It is their affair and the affair of the other men and women, and of their brothers and sisters. He will try to settle it himself . . . but if this fails he brings everyone else into the dispute.

In addition to a minimized sense of personal life as private, another consequence of communal living is that quarrelling and especially violence between spouses are seen, and treated, as community problems rather than private problems. Whatever disrupts the peace of the community is likely to be stopped— whether it is a beating or an extramarital relationship that takes an adult away from his or her responsibilities.

At the same time, the members of these communal societies have considerable autonomy. On consideration, the reasons are clear: Every adult has access to what is necessary for subsistence, so no person is in a position of dependency on another person. Moreover, because individual cooperation is essential for the survival of the collective, every person's happiness matters. For these and other reasons, relations between women and men are egalitarian: men have no more power or privilege than women do (Leacock, 1981).

Individual autonomy is evident in many aspects of family life. Although a girl's first marriage may be arranged by her parents, a divorce is fairly easy to obtain (Lee, 1979). Similarly, although women typically have babies only about every four years (largely because they breastfeed each infant for several years and because they have low body fat), they can also decide not to keep every child. Women can choose infanticide if a child is born before other children are past the need for constant attention (thereby overburdening the mother), or if a child is born who requires too much special care (thereby jeopardizing the lives of others). Sexuality is also quite unconstrained. Although monogamy is usually expected in marriage, women and men are typically able to enter into extramarital sexual relations as long as they do not interfere with the performance of their duties.

As this brief sketch demonstrates, the unit of social reproduction among foragers is larger than the nuclear family. Because foragers' survival depends on cooperation and reciprocity, the larger community assumes responsibilities that belong to nuclear families in our society. In turn, the communal basis of life and the absence of private households in foraging societies have far-reaching implications, including collective responsibility for people's welfare, individual autonomy, and gender egalitarianism.

PREINDUSTRIAL AGRICULTURAL SOCIETIES: HOUSEHOLD ECONOMIES

Our family patterns developed out of the patterns that were typical of precapitalist agricultural societies. In those societies, the household itself was the productive unit; producing subsistence was its main objective. This was true of craftsmen's households as well as those of the peasants and nobility who lived directly off the land. Thus, the social relations of family life in precapitalist households—that is, relations between spouses, between parents and children, and among residents of the same household—were also the relations of production. The chief economic relationship was that between husband and wife. Wives did necessary work that was complementary to that of their husbands, so an able-bodied wife was indispensable to the survival of the household (Tilly and Scott, 1978).

Land, which was the key means of production, was privately owned in preindustrial Europe. That meant that marriage—and thus adulthood—was predicated on acquiring land or some other means of livelihood. Consequently, people often married late—and chose their mates according to practical considerations as well as feelings (Mitterauer and Sieder, 1982). Typically, one son waited to inherit the land, his brothers were apprenticed to learn a skilled trade, and his sisters were given dowries. In the interim, children's dependence on their father to set them up for adulthood gave him considerable authority over them (Greven, 1973).

Land scarcity, and the fact that landlords extracted a substantial portion of the year's produce from the peasantry, meant that the struggle to survive was the chief household dynamic in these societies. It was constantly necessary to balance the number of productive adults against the number of dependants and the available economic resources (Tilly and Scott, 1978). Accordingly, household composition varied with changing economic requirements, especially labour requirements. In fact, much of the nature of household and family life was governed by economic considerations. So, in contrast to foragers, the interests of individuals in precapitalist agricultural societies were subordinated to those of the larger kin group and the land from which they derived subsistence.

Labour requirements dictated household membership. Various types of labourers were taken into households as they were needed. Wives who died were quickly replaced. In peasant households, children were kept home only if their labour was needed. Otherwise, they were sent to wealthier households to be raised or into neighbouring households that could use extra labour. For this reason, and because of extra adult workers, wealthy households were often huge, consisting of 15 to 30 people (Flandrin, 1979).

It was not only poor children who were sent away, however; few children from any economic background were raised exclusively at home by their mothers. Raising a child usually involved several households. Babies were often sent to "wet nurses," peasant women who were paid to care for them. About one in two children survived and returned home after several years, to be looked after, in most cases, by an older sibling. In their early teens, children were then sent off to be trained for adulthood in yet another household. They were either apprenticed to learn a skilled trade or simply sent to another household to work and thereby learn basic skills essential to adulthood (Mitterauer and Sieder, 1982). Women's critical economic role precluded their spending much time on child care or being distracted by the needs of loved ones.

Although parents no doubt loved their children and missed those who were living in other households, in many marriages sentiment and emotional connection probably took a distant back seat to practical imperatives (Mitterauer and Sieder, 1982). Similarly, the privacy that we take for granted at home was absent in preindustrial households. Because the household was a place of work, business and family life were not distinguished. Moreover, rooms were not reserved for special purposes, like sleeping. In peasant hovels, entire families often slept in the same bed (Flandrin, 1979). In wealthier households, servants often slept with members of the family. Even sexuality was not entirely a private matter. This is clear from evidence of the community's intervention to regulate behaviour—whether to humiliate newlyweds it deemed inappropriate matches, to punish women suspected of adultery, or to force men to stop beating their wives. The interests of the collective—whether the household or the peasant community—seems to have taken precedence over individual autonomy.

These were truly patriarchal households: Married women owed their husbands absolute obedience and, according to British common law, could not hold property, enter into contractual arrangements, or, in the rare event of divorce, get custody of the children. Many historians conclude that most married women were entirely subordinate to their husbands.

Nevertheless, women's work was vital to the ongoing survival of the household. The married couple was the chief labour force in every household. Whereas men did the heavy farm work (or supervised those who did), women were typically in charge of the dairy, the poultry, and the garden, as well as household management—mostly supervising the full range of household chores (Tilly and Scott, 1978).

Women's and children's interests were generally subordinated to the needs of the household far more than were men's. For example, women had little control over their sexual and reproductive lives; at a time when childbirth was life threatening, they were subject to pressure to have children, given the value of child labour in an agricultural context.

It is a myth that preindustrial agricultural households involved extended families, with three generations living under the same roof (Gottlieb, 1993). Short life spans tended to preclude the co-residence of three generations of family. Equally, however, the establishment of the next generation's family was often delayed because male property owners avoided turning the land over to their sons—on whom they would then become dependent—for as long as possible (Mitterauer and Sieder, 1982). In fact, older men typically retired only after carefully specifying in writing how they were to be provided for by their heirs; feelings between the generations were ambivalent enough that seniors had to protect themselves against possible neglect by their children.

In sum, the nuclear unit was embedded in a larger household in preindustrial Europe. Unlike today, families were not sustained by sentimental or romantic feelings. Family and household relations were primarily relations of work, and individual needs were subordinated to those of the household in order to ensure its survival. Whereas the absence of private family life empowered all adults in foraging societies, private ownership of the land and a considerable struggle to survive meant that all individuals in agricultural societies were subordinated to the household enterprise, and women were subordinated to men.

THE ORIGINS OF CONTEMPORARY FAMILY PATTERNS IN WESTERN SOCIETIES

Given how different family life today is from what I have just described, how did contemporary family patterns develop? It is only recently in Western history that the family characteristics we take for granted coalesced—namely, the gendered division of labour in which women are primarily responsible for child care and housework and men for financial provision, motherhood as women's primary vocation, and emotional intensity as the foundation of family relations. Before the nineteenth century, "family" generally referred to all the people who lived under the same roof, many of whom, as we have just seen, were not related by blood or marriage (Flandrin, 1979). Only when household economies eroded and an economy developed outside the household did our concept of family develop. As you will see, the concept of family and many of its defining features are products of the separation of public and private spheres that accompanied industrialization. As people grappled with the problems of survival in a new social order, patterns of family life changed.

THE MIDDLE CLASS

Modern ideas about family developed largely out of changes brought about by the development of an industrial capitalist economy. In both England and North America, a "cult of domesticity" developed in reaction to, and as a critique of, an unfolding capitalist economy that people experienced as cruel, immoral, and beyond human control (Cott, 1977). It was an economy in which impersonal forces of supply and demand were replacing face-to-face negotiations and customs, such as those reflected in the phrases "an honest price" and "a fair wage." It was an economy in which a person could be rich one day and penniless the next. In contrast, the domestic sphere came to be defined as a moral abode characterized by peace, virtuous behaviour, and the selfless care of loved ones— a "haven in a heartless world" (Lasch, 1977).

Domesticity as an ideology and, for those who could afford it, a practice was a way of coping with a rapidly changing social order. For the business and professional class, men's work was increasingly moving out of the household. Home and business were separating as the scale of business increased. The middle-class home became a retreat, where the concerns and evils of the world of business were banished.

Mirroring the separation of men's and women's work, a new conception of gender emerged in the nineteenth century. Probably in an attempt to make sense of the new social order, people came to believe that men and women had fundamentally different natures. Women were assumed to belong naturally in the domestic sphere, as its guardian, and to be naturally nurturing. Men were believed to be suited to the competitive world of business, although their objective there was to provide for their families. Thus, an ideology of gender difference made sense of the unfolding social order, and in the middle class an evolving gendered division of labour developed with the physical separation of public and private spheres.

More than reflecting changes in social organization, these domestic and gender ideologies were developed by the large middle class that emerged in the nineteenth century. In England, the middle class struggled to assert its social identity and establish its right to political power by claiming a moral superiority over the aristocracy and the labouring masses. Borrowing religious imagery common in the Evangelical movements to which they were drawn, members of the middle class on both sides of the Atlantic shaped a domestic ideology that juxtaposed the home and the economy just as religious imagery juxtaposed Heaven and Earth. Dissociating themselves from a world seen as devoid of morality, the middle class wore their ideology of domesticity as a social badge—a symbol of their moral distance from the business world they inhabited (Davidoff and Hall, 1987).

By the late nineteenth century, mothers and children were idealized. This image depicts a well-to-do mother (Ethel Sturgess Drummer) and her children in 1894.
SOURCE: The Schlesinger Library, Radcliffe Institute, Harvard University.

In practice, these ideas provided more than an identity for the middle class. They also reflected the strategy this class was devising to deal with the fact that in the new capitalist economy, fathers could no longer ensure their children's futures by passing on skills or property. That strategy involved educating children in ways that would equip them to adapt to the changing demands of the new economy. It involved instilling proper work habits and attitudes, and keeping them home through their teens so they might attend school rather than go to work. Central to this strategy was a role for mothers. And women themselves seem to have had a hand in fashioning the role of mother as socializer of her children, as they responded to the withdrawal of productive work from the household and the demise of their role as husbands' economic partners (Ryan, 1981). Of course, full-time motherhood—which was equated with womanhood for the middle class in the nineteenth century—entailed women's economic dependence on men.

Finally, the turn toward domesticity brought about a change in the emotional texture of family relations. When the need to produce subsistence was no longer the driving dynamic in daily household life, time and space became available for attending to emotional needs. By the end of the nineteenth century, children were the sentimental focus of middle-class family life (Davidoff and Hall, 1987).

Ironically, although nineteenth-century marriage entailed an ideal of love and companionship, the separation of men's and women's daily work undermined emotional closeness between them. In the increasingly gender-segregated world, women's emotional energy seems, in many cases, to have been directed largely toward other women—family and friends—in addition to children, rather than toward their husbands (Smith-Rosenberg, 1975).

THE WORKING CLASS

Although family life was becoming a sentimental focus for the middle class, it was nearly endangered for the working class. Men's wages were so low in the nineteenth century that their children were often forced to work for pay—at long shifts, in horrible factory conditions, for cruel bosses, and at risk of illness and early death. Although working-class wives attempted to feed and clothe their families in the tradition of peasant or farm wives, they lacked the necessities to do so, especially land. In turn, women's dependency on men—who had access to higher wages in the labour market—resulted in strained relations between men and women, marital tensions that focused on money, and probably frequent violence against women (Stansell, 1987). The ability of families to cope was so fragile that many working-class families were forced to place their children in orphanages when unemployment, illness, or death occurred (Bradbury, 1982).

As they had in preindustrial times, families developed collective survival strategies to cope with the ravages of developing capitalism. Accordingly, individual needs were often sacrificed to the imperatives of family survival. Teenagers in the labour force gave their parents most of their earnings, and young adults postponed marriage until their parents could withstand the withdrawal of their earnings (Hareven, 1982). Married women did whatever they could, over and above child care and homemaking, to contribute to household provisions—from doing mending and laundering for neighbours to hawking goods on the street and taking in boarders (Stansell, 1987). Moreover, families doubled up to save on rent; in

England, there were more extended-family households during the Industrial Revolution than before or after it (Anderson, 1971). Neighbours also helped each other out in urban environments where housing afforded few amenities and little privacy.

Meanwhile, the trade-union movement responded to the straits of working-class life with a campaign for a **family wage**—that is, a wage paid to a man sufficient to support a wife and children (M. May, 1985). Social historians continue to debate the reasons that the goal of the labour movement was a family wage rather than simply decent wages for all. Whatever the reasons, defining the struggle in these terms undoubtedly had the effect of reinforcing a working-class conception of family that was not unlike the middle-class ideal—with women defined as mothers and homemakers, dependent on men as breadwinners.

SOCIAL RELATIONS IN FAMILIES TODAY
MAIN FEATURES

We have seen how the development of an economy characterized by competition among people led to a mistrust of the public sphere and a turn toward domesticity. The family became the location identified with caring relationships. It was some time, however, before romance became a core characteristic of marriages. Only in the twentieth century did people begin to assume that romantic love, sex for the sake of pleasure, and marriage should be intimately bound together (Rapp and Ross, 1986).

An emotionally intense relationship between a man and a woman became key to marriage in the twentieth century. In the 1950s, amid a booming postwar economy, and no doubt in reaction to years of insecurity caused by the Depression and World War II and sustained by the Cold War, adults plunged into marriage and family as never before. Social historian Stephanie Coontz (1992) argues that the 1950s represented an unusual era in which adults expected that marriage and family would meet all of their needs. Women's and men's responsibilities in marriage were, of course, different: Women assumed responsibility for household and children, while men assumed responsibility for earning money. Unfortunately, although some people who married in the 1950s found family life and gender roles to be fulfilling, many women felt constrained ("trapped" according to some writers at the time) and stressed by being home all day.

Forty years after the idealized mother and children photo on p. 235, we have this harrowing photo of a migrant mother and children. This striking juxtaposition illustrates the difference between middle-class and working-class lives.

SOURCE: Dorothea Lange, *Migrant Mother, Nipomo, California* (1936). The Museum of Modern Art, New York.

Although their husbands fared better, men too often felt less than fulfilled (Coontz, 1992; E. May, 1988).

Research indicated that men benefited more from marriage than women did: Married men's mental and physical health was better than that of single men, while married women fared worse than single women (Bernard, 1972). In the worst cases, conventional gender roles—which place women in the position of meeting husbands' needs—contributed to men's violence against women, as they do today. Women are still more likely to be seriously hurt by husbands, lovers, and especially ex-partners than by anyone else (Gartner, Dawson, and Crawford, 1998–99).

An intense mother–child relationship is also typical of modern families. As we have seen, raising children has not always been a private parental responsibility. Although capitalist employers bear no responsibility for the next generation of employees, feudal master craftsmen housed and fed their young apprentices as they trained them and used their labour. In precapitalist times, several households usually contributed to the rearing of a child. Community responsibility for children extended to more recent centuries as well: In the British colonies in North America, community leaders sometimes exercised the power to order households to take in orphans and raise them to adulthood.

In recent years, the state has avoided the assumption of responsibility for the welfare of children, except for their schooling, and instead has enforced fathers' responsibility for the financial support of their children and mothers' responsibility for child care. When "mothers' allowances" were introduced in early twentieth century Canada, they were paid only to widows even though other types of lone mothers were equally in need of assistance (Baker, 1995). Newer forms of social assistance have involved "man-in-the-house" rules, which disqualify any woman who appears to have a man in her life. Moreover, one of the key government responses to growing concerns about child poverty is to strengthen attempts to force fathers who are separated from their wives to meet their child-support obligations. This strategy turns attention away from governmental and community responsibility for children's welfare. Similarly, aside from wartime emergencies, governments have failed to provide affordable daycare sufficient to meet the need for it. Child abuse sometimes results from the heavy responsibilities carried by parents, especially mothers.

In the 1950s, 1960s, and 1970s, when many men earned a "family wage," a majority of married women stayed home and assumed full-time domestic responsibilities. A gendered division of responsibility and labour was the way most families met the daily needs of adults and children. Because wages and salaries have eroded since the 1970s and most women (even those with preschool children) must work outside the home, the issue of who cares for the children is now a social problem (see Figure 10.2). Compounding it are government cuts to

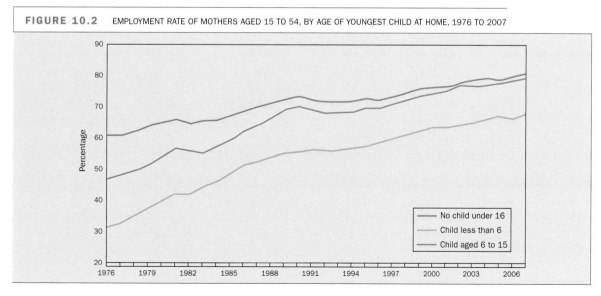

FIGURE 10.2   EMPLOYMENT RATE OF MOTHERS AGED 15 TO 54, BY AGE OF YOUNGEST CHILD AT HOME, 1976 TO 2007

SOURCE: Statistics Canada, 2008, "Employment Rates of Mothers, by Age of Youngest Child." On the World Wide Web at http://www.statcan.gc.ca/pub/71-222-x/2008001/sectionb/b-mothers-meres-eng.htm (1 March 2009).

care arrangements than heterosexual married and cohabiting couples are (Dunne, 2000; Nelson, 1996). Moreover, given the obstacles they face, the families of same-sex couples can be seen to be the products of choice to a greater degree than other families (Weston, 1991). Certainly, although women married to men often allow "fate" to decide whether or not they have children, lesbians must choose to get pregnant. In turn, the children they raise, despite the stigma they may face, show levels of well-being similar to children who grow up in other families (Stacey and Biblarz, 2001).

Still more family diversity is indicated by the growing incidence of lone-parent families. In 2006, 15.9 percent of families consisted of one parent—usually a mother—and her dependent children (see Table 10.1). Early in the twentieth century, when they were

This poster was produced by the Queer Parenting Initiative (Toronto) to "celebrate the diversity of family structures within which children live and thrive." It reflects how concepts of social relations in families have changed from just a few decades ago. SOURCE: The Queer Parenting Initiative is a joint project of the LGBTQ Parenting Network, Sherbourne Health Centre, Toronto, Ontario; Centre for Addiction and Mental Health; Gay Fathers of Toronto; Chinese Family Services, TGStation.com, and community members. For more information: parentingnetwork@sherbourne.on.ca.

as common as today, such families typically involved a widow and her children. Since the early 1990s more than half of them have involved separated or divorced women, and in 1991 about 20 percent involved never-married women (Statistics Canada, 1992: 5). More than half of these families were poor in the late 1990s (National Council of Welfare, 1998). The changes many governments are making to social assistance ("welfare") programs, which tie assistance to employment ("workfare") and thus require that one adult support the household financially and take care of children, increases the problems faced by lone-parent families.

Other trends indicate the increasing diversity of families. Decades of high rates of divorce have produced large numbers of "reconstituted" families. It is estimated that in 2001 almost 12 percent of couples with children involved a stepparent, compared with 10 percent in 1995 (Statistics Canada, 2002). Children whose parents have remarried after divorce have a fairly complicated network of family relations. In addition, more young adults are continuing to live with their parents or returning to their parents' home after leaving it. In 2001, 41 percent of adults 20 to 29 years of age lived with their parents, compared with 27.5 percent in 1981 (Statistics Canada, 2002).

Family patterns in Canada show racial, ethnic, and class differences as well, although our knowledge of them is limited. Approximately 18 percent of black women and 15 percent of Aboriginal women in Canada were lone parents in 1991, compared with 7 percent of non-Aboriginal women (Statistics Canada, 1992: 14, 19). The fact that black families in Canada are less likely to contain a married or common-law couple is related to the lower likelihood that black men can earn a stable, sizable income. Rates of marriage increase significantly with income among black Canadians (Calliste, 2001). We do not know if black lone mothers regularly compensate for low incomes and absence of a partner by relying on personal support networks of relatives and friends. In the early 1970s, poor African Americans were found to create women-centred networks whose members shared scarce resources and cooperated in child care (Stack, 1974). Certainly, a pattern of cooperation among kin, across nuclear families—including living together in extended-family households—has been typical of many working-class and immigrant Canadians and Americans (Iacovetta, 1992; Kibria, 1993).

I next discuss the practices and social relationships that are central to family life. Emotional intimacy and

Although their husbands fared better, men too often felt less than fulfilled (Coontz, 1992; E. May, 1988).

Research indicated that men benefited more from marriage than women did: Married men's mental and physical health was better than that of single men, while married women fared worse than single women (Bernard, 1972). In the worst cases, conventional gender roles—which place women in the position of meeting husbands' needs—contributed to men's violence against women, as they do today. Women are still more likely to be seriously hurt by husbands, lovers, and especially ex-partners than by anyone else (Gartner, Dawson, and Crawford, 1998–99).

An intense mother–child relationship is also typical of modern families. As we have seen, raising children has not always been a private parental responsibility. Although capitalist employers bear no responsibility for the next generation of employees, feudal master craftsmen housed and fed their young apprentices as they trained them and used their labour. In precapitalist times, several households usually contributed to the rearing of a child. Community responsibility for children extended to more recent centuries as well: In the British colonies in North America, community leaders sometimes exercised the power to order households to take in orphans and raise them to adulthood.

In recent years, the state has avoided the assumption of responsibility for the welfare of children, except for their schooling, and instead has enforced fathers' responsibility for the financial support of their children and mothers' responsibility for child care. When "mothers' allowances" were introduced in early twentieth century Canada, they were paid only to widows even though other types of lone mothers were equally in need of assistance (Baker, 1995). Newer forms of social assistance have involved "man-in-the-house" rules, which disqualify any woman who appears to have a man in her life. Moreover, one of the key government responses to growing concerns about child poverty is to strengthen attempts to force fathers who are separated from their wives to meet their child-support obligations. This strategy turns attention away from governmental and community responsibility for children's welfare. Similarly, aside from wartime emergencies, governments have failed to provide affordable daycare sufficient to meet the need for it. Child abuse sometimes results from the heavy responsibilities carried by parents, especially mothers.

In the 1950s, 1960s, and 1970s, when many men earned a "family wage," a majority of married women stayed home and assumed full-time domestic responsibilities. A gendered division of responsibility and labour was the way most families met the daily needs of adults and children. Because wages and salaries have eroded since the 1970s and most women (even those with preschool children) must work outside the home, the issue of who cares for the children is now a social problem (see Figure 10.2). Compounding it are government cuts to

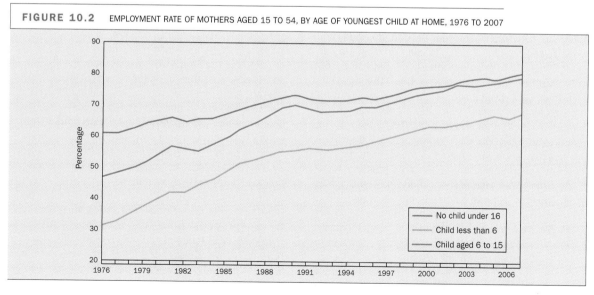

FIGURE 10.2   EMPLOYMENT RATE OF MOTHERS AGED 15 TO 54, BY AGE OF YOUNGEST CHILD AT HOME, 1976 TO 2007

SOURCE: Statistics Canada, 2008, "Employment Rates of Mothers, by Age of Youngest Child." On the World Wide Web at http://www.statcan.gc.ca/pub/71-222-x/2008001/sectionb/b-mothers-meres-eng.htm (1 March 2009).

education, health care, and other social services, which increase the work that must be done in the home. The assumption that child care is a private responsibility is increasingly problematic.

Most Canadian women face the need to juggle the fundamentally incompatible demands of employment and family every day. The stress of their "double day" of work generates considerable tension between women and their male partners, as women retain primary responsibility for child care and housework (Daly, 2004). In some cases, that tension contributes to divorce (Kurz, 1995). Nevertheless, men are doing more housework and child care now than they did decades ago. And although women who are employed full-time juggle a heavy load, and lose sleep in the process, they also are significantly healthier (mentally and physically) than other women are (Barnett and Rivers, 1996; Sayer, 2005). The change in women's lives, coupled with the lack of significant accommodating change in many areas of society, has prompted increased diversity in household patterns. More people live alone—and only partly because of population aging. People are marrying at a later age and postponing having children. The percentage of people under 45 who have never married has increased, as has the percentage of people who are neither married nor cohabiting (Fox with Yiu, 2009; see Box 10.1).

BOX 10.1   A NATION LIVING IN SIN

When Christel Kleitsch and Avrum Jacobson moved in together, they decided they never wanted to get married. They were children of the '60s, after all, from an era when free love ruled the land. Nearly 30 years later, they're both well-established Toronto writers with two grown children, and they're still not married. In the eyes of the law and among their friends, they are a couple, they say, so where's the need for a piece of paper to prove it? "There is certainly no stigma in it," Kleitsch says of their common-law arrangement. In fact, the only time she ever uses the word "husband," Kleitsch says, is for convenience, "like when the furnace repairman shows up."

South of the border, they would be aghast. While in Canada long-term common-law partnerships abound, marriage still rules in the States. Americans have almost twice as many marriages per 1,000 unmarried women each year as Canada does, and far fewer couples "living in sin." In Canada, an amazing 18.4 per cent of all couples are now "cohabiters," whereas in the U.S., the figure is 7.6 per cent. Even when we do marry, we put it off for as long as we can. Here, the average age of first marriage is 28.5 for women and 30.6 for men. In the U.S., the ages are much younger, 25.1 and 26.7 respectively. So why are we so reluctant to get that little piece of paper? There are three reasons: we're less traditional, less religious, and we have Quebec.

Quebec, it turns out, leads not just Canada but the world in common-law couplings. There, a whopping 35 per cent of couples cohabit rather than marry. Family experts say that after the Quiet Revolution in the 1960s when the Church lost much of its influence in the province, religion—and marriage—simply ceased to matter. Montrealer Benoit Laplante, the director of demography programs at the Institut national de la recherche scientifique, says Quebecers don't marry because "there is no practical reason to do it. When people decided to leave religion out, they began to disregard it in anything they did."

In the U.S., religion is still a powerful force, and marriage remains at the centre of life, especially in the southern and so-called red states. David Popenoe, a co-director of the National Marriage Project, a non-sectarian research group at Rutgers University in New Jersey, offers a historical perspective. In America before 1970, he recently wrote, cohabitation was not only uncommon, it was "a deviant and unlawful practice found only among people at the margins of society." He adds that "in the 1950s and '60s, if you showed up at a motel and you wanted a room and you had two different last names, they wouldn't give you one." More telling, he says, "It's still that way in the more religious areas of the country."

Popenoe cites a 2007 survey from the Culture and Media Institute in Virginia, which found that nearly 33 per cent of the U.S. population is religiously orthodox. Within this segment, nearly 70 per cent condemns sex between unmarried adults. The survey also found that nearly half of Americans—a group it called "independents"—don't fully accept all orthodox values, but still tend to side with that group on matters of sexual morality.

Céline Le Bourdais, a professor and Canada Research Chair in Social Statistics and Family Change at McGill University, says Canadians, in their new acceptance of common-law arrangements, have come full circle. "For a long time my friends in the U.S. thought we were more socially conservative," she says. "Now we are the open ones."

SOURCE: "A Nation Living in Sin," by Barbara Righton, *Maclean's*, July 7, 2008. Reprinted with permission from *Maclean's* Magazine.

In terms of family diversity, cohabiting men and women constitute the fastest growing type of family in Canada. They more than doubled in number between 1981 and 1991; and by 2006 over 14 percent of families involved a common-law couple (see Table 10.1). The popularity of this kind of relationship probably reflects peoples' assessment of the personal costs involved in marriage. The sacrifices that women make after they marry, and especially when they become mothers, are emotionally and financially risky, given current rates of divorce. The interdependence that is characteristic of marriage may be less attractive to younger generations than to older ones who married when women were less able to support themselves without a man and sexual activity outside marriage was less acceptable. Research on how couples handle their money indicates that independence may be an objective of people who cohabit: Common-law couples are more likely to keep their money separate than are married couples, who often create joint accounts (Singh and Lindsay, 1996). These relations are also more unstable than those involving marriage; that is, people feel freer to leave them (Marcil-Gratton, 1993).

The growing number of gay and lesbian families reflects some of the same social changes that produce common-law unions—increased social acceptance of sexual expression and women's decreased economic dependence on men. The 2001 census produced our first estimate of families headed by same-sex

common-law couples: 34 200 Canadians declared themselves to be living in same-sex relationships, representing 0.5 percent of all couples (Statistics Canada, 2002). About 15 percent of lesbian couples are raising children, and about 3 percent of gay male couples are living with children.

Same-sex couples have faced an uphill battle for acceptance as families. For decades, the courts denied child custody to lesbian mothers leaving their husbands. Same-sex partners were also denied spousal benefits and the right to adopt non-biological children they were raising. After years of protracted court battles, gays and lesbians won the right to marry in Ontario, Quebec, and British Columbia. In December 2004, the Supreme Court of Canada ruled that a definition of marriage that includes same-sex partners was not unconstitutional. After much debate, the House of Commons voted in June 2005 to approve gay marriage in Canada.

In fact, same-sex couples' relationships display characteristics that approximate family ideals. Lesbian and gay relationships are as stable as those of cohabiting heterosexual couples (Stacey and Biblarz, 2001). Their stability is impressive given the higher standards of emotional intimacy they typically involve relative to heterosexual couples, the weaker institutional pressures to stay together, and the fewer social supports (Stacey and Biblarz, 2001). Same-sex couples are also more likely to have egalitarian housework and child-

TABLE 10.1 FAMILY STRUCTURE, CANADA, 2006

	PERCENTAGE OF FAMILIES	PERCENTAGE OF CHILDREN 14 YEARS AND UNDER
Married Couples	68.6	65.7
Without children under 25 at home	34.0	
With children under 25 at home	34.6	
Common-Law Couples	15.5	14.6
Without children under 25 at home	8.7	
With children under 25 at home	6.8	
Lone-Parent	15.9	18.3
With children under 25 at home	12.4	
All children 25 and under	3.5	
Other	0	1.4*
Total	100.0	100.00

SOURCE: Statistics Canada (2007), Figures 1 and 13.
*Mostly children living with grandparents.

care arrangements than heterosexual married and cohabiting couples are (Dunne, 2000; Nelson, 1996). Moreover, given the obstacles they face, the families of same-sex couples can be seen to be the products of choice to a greater degree than other families (Weston, 1991). Certainly, although women married to men often allow "fate" to decide whether or not they have children, lesbians must choose to get pregnant. In turn, the children they raise, despite the stigma they may face, show levels of well-being similar to children who grow up in other families (Stacey and Biblarz, 2001).

Still more family diversity is indicated by the growing incidence of lone-parent families. In 2006, 15.9 percent of families consisted of one parent—usually a mother—and her dependent children (see Table 10.1). Early in the twentieth century, when they were

This poster was produced by the Queer Parenting Initiative (Toronto) to "celebrate the diversity of family structures within which children live and thrive." It reflects how concepts of social relations in families have changed from just a few decades ago.
SOURCE: The Queer Parenting Initiative is a joint project of the LGBTQ Parenting Network, Sherbourne Health Centre, Toronto, Ontario; Centre for Addiction and Mental Health; Gay Fathers of Toronto; Chinese Family Services, TGStation.com, and community members. For more information: parentingnetwork@sherbourne.on.ca.

as common as today, such families typically involved a widow and her children. Since the early 1990s more than half of them have involved separated or divorced women, and in 1991 about 20 percent involved never-married women (Statistics Canada, 1992: 5). More than half of these families were poor in the late 1990s (National Council of Welfare, 1998). The changes many governments are making to social assistance ("welfare") programs, which tie assistance to employment ("workfare") and thus require that one adult support the household financially and take care of children, increases the problems faced by lone-parent families.

Other trends indicate the increasing diversity of families. Decades of high rates of divorce have produced large numbers of "reconstituted" families. It is estimated that in 2001 almost 12 percent of couples with children involved a stepparent, compared with 10 percent in 1995 (Statistics Canada, 2002). Children whose parents have remarried after divorce have a fairly complicated network of family relations. In addition, more young adults are continuing to live with their parents or returning to their parents' home after leaving it. In 2001, 41 percent of adults 20 to 29 years of age lived with their parents, compared with 27.5 percent in 1981 (Statistics Canada, 2002).

Family patterns in Canada show racial, ethnic, and class differences as well, although our knowledge of them is limited. Approximately 18 percent of black women and 15 percent of Aboriginal women in Canada were lone parents in 1991, compared with 7 percent of non-Aboriginal women (Statistics Canada, 1992: 14, 19). The fact that black families in Canada are less likely to contain a married or common-law couple is related to the lower likelihood that black men can earn a stable, sizable income. Rates of marriage increase significantly with income among black Canadians (Calliste, 2001). We do not know if black lone mothers regularly compensate for low incomes and absence of a partner by relying on personal support networks of relatives and friends. In the early 1970s, poor African Americans were found to create women-centred networks whose members shared scarce resources and cooperated in child care (Stack, 1974). Certainly, a pattern of cooperation among kin, across nuclear families—including living together in extended-family households—has been typical of many working-class and immigrant Canadians and Americans (Iacovetta, 1992; Kibria, 1993).

I next discuss the practices and social relationships that are central to family life. Emotional intimacy and sexual expression are so important to the creation of committed relations that I examine them first. Because family life is typically organized around a gendered division of labour, I next discuss the sources of gender differences. Then I review changes in marriage. Parenthood, child care, and housework "make family," and I discuss them before considering both divorce and social policies.

SEXUALITY AND FAMILIES

Although historically families were largely arrangements for perpetuating wealth or ensuring economic survival, now it is love and the promise of ongoing intimacy and caring that propel people into long-term commitment. Increasingly, we have come to expect lasting sexual, emotional, and social happiness in a relationship. This is an ambitious expectation in a society where we also expect to grow and change as we mature, and where, for many job categories, hours of paid work have risen since the mid-twentieth century.

We also live in a society where images of sexuality surround us, and specifically where noncommitted, or recreational, sex is eroticized. Although we think of sexuality as a personal matter, our desires are clearly subject to the influence of film, TV, and advertising. Even governments attempt to exert control over their citizens' sexuality. The most obvious reason sexuality has been the object of state control is that the family is the unit of social reproduction. Society depends on families to produce and care for the next generation. Accordingly, with the aim of tying sexuality to reproduction, most Western governments in the nineteenth century passed laws banning the use of all forms of contraception. In Canada, section 179c of the 1892 Criminal Code made the selling or advertising of any contraceptive or device for performing abortion an indictable offence. This legislation was not only a form of **pronatalism** (a policy aimed at increasing the population) but also the product of the fear that white, middle-class Canadians of northern European descent were not reproducing in large enough numbers, while other immigrants were doing just that. Not until 1969 was the Criminal Code amended to make contraceptives legal. Abortion remained a criminal offence until 1988, after Dr. Henry Morgentaler's repeated challenges of the law.

Since the "sexual revolution" of the 1960s, women and men typically have become sexually active before they marry or begin to cohabit (see Chapter 4). In other words, people enter committed relationships with more knowledge of each other and a better sense of their compatibility on a number of important dimensions. At the same time, sexuality is affected by the social context in which it occurs—and the fact that it occurs between people who are products of gender socialization. Consequently, certain social patterns are common over the course of relationships, which presents couples with challenges for ensuring the vitality and endurance of long-term relationships.

The first challenge to couples who love each other and commit to a lasting relationship has to do with the fact that social context, or situation, strongly affects people's sexual behaviour. Because opportunity is a major determinant of the frequency of intercourse, people who live together are on average more active sexually (despite TV images of the singles lifestyle). Married and cohabiting men and women have sex more often than men and women who are single (Schwartz and Rutter, 1998). However, people who are married are significantly less active sexually than people who are cohabiting (comparing people of the same age, who are together the same length of time; Schwartz and Rutter, 1998). Moreover, for all types of relationship—married, common-law, gay, and lesbian—sexual activity decreases considerably over the course of a relationship, dropping especially after the first two years or so (Schwartz and Rutter, 1998). The decline over time is due not only to the reduced excitement attached to familiarity but also to the effects of having children and growing responsibilities. With an infant or a toddler in the house, sleep often becomes more valuable than sexuality. Long hours of employment, worries over money, anxieties about children, and other issues common to long-term relationships also inhibit sexual desire.

Gender differences also affect sexuality, as well as intimacy. The "sexual revolution" was limited in a number of ways. For instance, there remain different norms for men and women with respect to sexuality. Men are still expected to initiate sexual activity. Women can still cross a line—they can be too aggressive. Couples have to continually negotiate around this set of expectations.

Aside from sexuality, intimacy must also be negotiated amidst gender differences. While men typically experience sex as the route to intimacy, women typically need intimacy—and expressions of it—before sex (Rubin 1990). Intimacy is also made more difficult by gender differences in the expression of love and caring. Women typically seem to be better at discussing their feelings (as well as accessing them)—something central to our culture's definition of intimacy—while men may be more likely to express intimacy through caring activities, which may not be recognized as such. These gender differences are probably due to gendered experiences and family responsibilities; most obviously, women need to learn to nurture, given the responsibilities for children's well-being that they take on with motherhood (Tavris, 1992).

Sexual behaviour in same-sex couples also reflects gender differences. Typically, gay male couples have more frequent sex, and lesbian couples have less sex, than heterosexual couples (Schwartz and Rutter, 1998). That men find recreational sex appealing, and that women are socialized not to initiate sex, presents a variety of issues for same-sex couples. Ongoing social stigma attached to these relationships compounds the obstacles to lasting relationships—making their durability all the more impressive.

Certainly, there are obstacles to long-term heterosexual and homosexual relationships. Yet the majority of Canadians who marry stay together, so we can only assume that they find their relationships satisfying in a number of respects.

GENDER AND FAMILIES

Most nuclear families built around a heterosexual couple are organized around a division of work and responsibility between men and women. It is not surprising, then, that surveys of Canadian high-school students consistently find that girls plan to take time out of their adult employment to devote to family while boys do not. There is evidence that girls and boys are socialized differently as they are growing up, probably in part because of a pervasive conviction that boys and girls are naturally different. Yet, research that examines the choices that adults make in their lives about whether to prioritize work or family shows that childhood socialization has less effect on such choices than adult experiences in paid work and intimate relations (Gerson, 1985). Thus, a better explanation of girls' tendency to focus on domesticity emphasizes that they make decisions in light of the opportunities and constraints they face. American sociologist Arlie Hochschild (1989) has argued that an adult faces life with a gender strategy that involves, for example, a prioritization of either career/job or family relationships. That prioritization then guides their life decisions. According to Hochschild, people's gender strategies result from a combination of ideas about gender in the culture, emotionally charged reactions to childhood (especially parents' gender roles), and the opportunities and constraints that they face as they become adults.

A good illustration of gender strategy can be found in Jane Gaskell's study of the expectations of young people graduating from three high schools in working-class areas of Vancouver (1983). Most of the girls judged paid work to be more satisfying than the domestic roles of mother, wife, and homemaker. Their socialization had not produced a desire for domestic roles. At the same time, they overwhelmingly agreed that they would eventually assume primary responsibility for housework and child care. They saw their futures as bound up with domesticity for a number of reasons. First, they assumed that they would have a male partner and that he would be unwilling and unable to share the household work. Second, they predicted that their future earnings, relative to their spouse's, would be low and that it would therefore make economic sense for them to assume household responsibility rather than paid employment. Third, they felt that babies were better off at home with their mothers. The boys in the study concurred with the girls about who should take on housework and child-care duties (Gaskell, 1983). Gaskell's findings indicate that girls prioritize domestic responsibilities largely because of the lack of opportunities facing them, from good jobs to good daycare to egalitarian men.

Similarly, an American study of the decisions that women make about whether to prioritize family or paid work found that women who ended up prioritizing family and the care of loved ones often did so as a result of either a negative experience with paid work or a fulfilling intimate relationship, coupled with a dawning realization that the responsibilities of family life and paid work were incompatible (Gerson, 1985). Thus, gender inequality in the labour force promotes the gendered division of labour in the home. It also pushes women toward marriage. Women's relatively weaker market position and the growing need for two incomes when there are dependants to support means that if women want children and a decent standard of living, marriage is still a wise choice.

Labour-market inequality forces women to make difficult choices. Employers still define jobs, especially professional jobs, in terms of employees who are unencumbered by family responsibilities and are able to work after 5 p.m., at night, on weekends, and so on. Job sharing, part-time work with good benefits, workplace daycare facilities, and paid leave for tending sick children are still uncommon in Canadian workplaces. Careers and family responsibilities are still incompatible for women. Thus, many successful career women are single. In the face of little change in the workplace, dual-earner couples with children are left to design their own ways to balance conflicting responsibilities. One person—usually the woman—cuts back on paid work, works nonstandard hours, and so forth.

MARRIAGE AND DIVORCE

Today, because relatively few men earn enough on their own to support a family, and women need to do paid work, the conventional gendered division of work and responsibility is no longer viable. Old patterns die hard, however. And the contradictory nature of old family patterns existing in new circumstances has generated an increase in divorce, pressures on men to assume new family roles, and a need for new social policies.

Family law has changed to reflect the new circumstances. Before the late 1970s, the marriage contract stipulated a simple but unequal exchange between a woman and a man: He was responsible for his and her maintenance, and she owed him domestic and sexual services. Meg Luxton (1980) explored the personal consequences of the conventional gendered division of labour in her study of working-class, breadwinner/homemaker families living in Flin Flon, Manitoba, in the late 1970s. Her clearest finding was that breadwinning translated into privilege. Because men's families depended on them, their needs assumed priority—meals prepared according to their taste, children kept quiet for the sake of their need for peace, and so on. Conversely, homemakers' economic dependence typically meant an inability to get their own needs met in the relationship.

That these inequalities were typical in a conventional marriage is suggested by statistics on physical and mental health. Comparisons of men's and women's physical and mental health in the 1960s and 1970s show that men benefited from the care they received in marriage, while the work of personal care took a toll on women. Married men were significantly better off physically and mentally than single men, whereas the opposite was true for women (Bernard, 1972).

Divorce became more common over the last century and especially since 1968, when federal law was liberalized. Recently, the divorce rate has levelled off. According to popular opinion (and some sociologists), the rise in the divorce rate testifies to increased selfishness, unwillingness to make the compromises required by a relationship, and laziness when it comes to "working out" interpersonal problems. This explanation denies the rights of individuals to happiness and emphasizes instead the importance of maintaining the institution of marriage. It ignores the fact that there have tended to be two experiences of marriage—"his" and "hers"—and that women are typically the ones called on to overcome selfishness, make compromises, and work to create happy homes. In the worst marriages, women are the ones subject to severe violence (Gartner et al., 1998–99). Thus, women are more likely than men are to initiate separation and divorce—and do so for reasons often having to do with gender inequities in their marriage (Kurz, 1995).

In view of the fact that women have entered the labour market in increasing numbers—and thus gained the possibility of self-support—and have been exposed to the climate of change brought about by the women's liberation movement, it is not surprising that divorce rates have risen. It is estimated that about 40 percent of marriages in Canada will end in divorce, which is considerably below rates in the United States and Sweden but high when the consequences for children are considered. (The aftermath of divorce is considered below.) Although most adults who divorce later remarry, marriage is now no longer the only basis of family formation. Already by the late 1980s, 20 percent of Canadian babies were born out of wedlock; and by 1990, 38 percent of parents of newborns in Quebec were not married, though most were cohabiting (Marcil-Gratton, 1993).

Meanwhile, marriage as an institution has changed. In the late 1970s, with the aim of recognizing the work that women do in the home, provinces and territories across Canada reformed their family laws to omit any mention of gender-specific obligations and exchanges. Replacing the old model of a "community" of interdependent men and women was one assuming the spousal relationship to be a partnership of equal individuals, both of whom contribute to the marriage and are responsible for themselves. Under the old laws, a woman had no right to "family assets," including property that resulted from her own work over the years (because she owed her husband her labour). Now, "family assets," which include some of the fruits of advanced degrees and pensions, are to be divided equally on divorce (Morton, 1988). The new laws encourage people leaving a marriage to become independent as quickly as possible. Women are not entitled to long-term support, as they were under the old laws.

Ironically, because the new laws treat women and men equally, the results are inequitable. The assumption that women can support themselves as men do is incorrect given the gender inequality that continues to characterize the labour market. For many working-class women, there is the additional problem that sharing "family assets" means sharing the poverty. Not surprisingly, the chief result of divorce is a significantly lowered standard of living for women and the children who usually live with them (Finnie, 1993).

HOUSEWORK AND MOTHERWORK

Although the new family laws assume equality, a gendered division of labour still organizes households. Women may have assumed part of the responsibility of breadwinning but they remain largely responsible for housework and child care (Daly, 2004; Marshall, 2006).

A comparison of the work done by men and women who are (1) living alone, (2) married and childless, and (3) married with children indicates differences in men and women's family responsibilities (see Figure 10.3). Men's hours of paid work increase with marriage and especially with children while women's decrease with these changes in status. In contrast, the time men spend on housework increases a bit with marriage and children but women's increases substantially. As Chapter 7 argues, this gender difference is both a manifestation and a cause of the inequality between women and men in Canada today.

Why does this gender inequity persist? Some men translate higher earnings into privilege at home. Marriage involves negotiation—if not daily, then at least periodically and especially early in the relationship. Women's bargaining power in those negotiations is undermined by the following factors: women's disadvantage in the labour market; women's perceived disadvantage on the remarriage market (which weakens their courage to push for change in the relationship); a cultural devaluation of caring work; and cultural definitions of gender, especially masculinity (Hochschild, 1989).

Meanwhile, surveys show that couples who share housework are significantly happier than others. Among couples who do not share housework, the resulting tension in the relationship affects the men and the children as well as the women (Hochschild, 1989). Research also shows that equality in the labour market and at home goes hand in hand: Couples who do similar work, especially dual-career couples, seem to be more likely to share household work (Hertz, 1986). Given that gender inequality exists in the labour market, the unequal division of housework is likely to persist for some time.

Having children also contributes to the division of labour between women and men: When heterosexual couples become parents, their lives typically become more conventional. With motherhood, women tend to take on the bulk of the caring for their babies and a greater proportion of the housework than before they were mothers; with fatherhood, men tend to concentrate more on financial providing and also become their babies' playmates and their wives' helpers (Fox, 2001). The added financial responsibility that parenthood entails, coupled with the absence of change in employment practices to accommodate family obligations, binds men

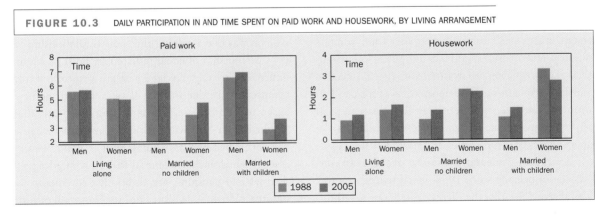

FIGURE 10.3   DAILY PARTICIPATION IN AND TIME SPENT ON PAID WORK AND HOUSEWORK, BY LIVING ARRANGEMENT

SOURCE: Katherine Marshall, 2006, "Converging Gender Roles." *Perspectives* (July). Statistics Canada Catalogue No. 75-001-XIE. On the World Wide Web at http://www.statcan.gc.ca/pub/75-001-x/10706/9268-eng.pdf (1 March 2009).

to long workdays, inhibits their sharing of baby care and housework, and thus promotes the development of a pattern of gender divisions. More than the organization of paid work induces gender divisions with parenthood, however. Gender is also at issue: Same-sex parents do not feel driven to adopt specialized roles (Dunne, 2000; Nelson, 1996).

The conviction is growing that full-time mothering is bad for women and, consequently, for their children and that men's physical absence from the home also can be detrimental to the social development of children. For women, the private nature of parenting causes problems. Because full-time mothers are home alone much of the day, many suffer from social isolation. Alone with the responsibility, most women find the full-time care of young children stressful because it combines high demands and low control over time (Rosenberg, 1987). A Canadian study likened the work of full-time mothers with young children to that of "front-line" workers servicing people with pressing needs, workers among whom "burnout" is a common problem. At work and on call 24 hours a day, full-time mothers have no "downtime" and often only minimal sleep (Rosenberg, 1987). For single mothers, of course, these problems are intensified.

These problems are the result of the way child care is organized in our society. The responsibility for child care is private, which means that it rests with the parents alone. Neither the health-care system nor the educational system provide many services for the early years of children's lives. Neighbourhood drop-in facilities, support services for full-time mothers, and good-quality daycare have yet to be considered a basic part of our social infrastructure.

At the same time, most of us are certain it is best for babies and toddlers to be at home with their mothers. On dispassionate and careful consideration, however, the more logical conclusion is that toddlers and even infants fare better when they are cared for by several adults and when they spend at least part of the time outside the home. A single, isolated caregiver inevitably loses some inspiration, enthusiasm, and even warmth over the course of a 24-hour-a-day, seven-day-a-week schedule. Moreover, the home is not designed for toddlers; it is typically more dangerous and less stimulating than it should be. Indeed, adult needs for order compete with toddler needs to explore and manipulate their environment: Housework and child care conflict. Moreover, evidence shows that children who are in good-quality daycare from an early age are significantly advantaged

in terms of cognitive and social development over those who stay at home (Clarke-Stewart, 1982).

Most mothers of young children today work outside the home, unable to afford full-time motherhood even if they prefer it. The problem they confront is in having to handle a stressful balancing act (juggling responsibilities at home and the workplace) every weekday. Although attention to this problem has typically focused on increasing men's contribution, perhaps there is just not enough time in the day to do the work that many couples face. Solutions require a collective response. But even though 68 percent of mothers of children under the age of six are employed, there are enough spaces in regulated child-care facilities for only about 17 percent of children younger than 14 (Friendly et al., 2007: 6; Statistics Canada, 2008). The Canadian government's main response to the problem has been to recruit foreign domestic workers, obliging them to provide domestic service for several years before they can obtain permanent-resident status. The use of nannies to solve the child-care problem involves the continued **privatization** of domestic labour, which, in effect, allows the community to avoid solving the problem. It allows wealthy professionals, who might otherwise combine forces to put political pressure on the government for a solution that would help everyone, to solve the problem privately. This solution also means having child care and housework done by workers who are highly vulnerable to exploitation, given their long hours of work, low pay, social isolation, lack of citizenship rights, and the private nature of their relationship with the employer (Arat-Koc, 2009).

BECOMING PARENTS

Aside from the work it entails, parenthood changes people's lives profoundly. We have already discussed the difficulties that the private responsibilities of motherhood pose for women. Even medicalized childbirth offers women limited assistance—aimed at relieving pain, minimizing physical danger, and delivering the baby.

In the past, women giving birth were assisted by other women, who continued to care for them and instruct them about mothering in the weeks following the birth. Because women giving birth in hospital today are usually without this kind of support, most experience at least one bout of postpartum depression and many begin motherhood upset or angry because of their experience of childbirth (Fox and Worts, 1999). Many new mothers are also overwhelmed by the responsibility they have taken on; most find themselves totally unprepared to care for a new baby. The licensing and public funding of midwives in Ontario, Quebec, British Columbia, and Manitoba may provide women with a good alternative to medically managed birth. Midwives provide assistance and support from before the birth to months afterward, for births in hospital as well as at home.[1]

Following a baby's birth, parents go through a challenging time of adjustment, which leads to significant changes in their lives. As we saw, the division of work and responsibility usually becomes more conventional for heterosexual couples, though usually not for same-sex couples (Fox, 2001; Patterson, 1995). Women with male partners often feel much more dependent on the men, unless they have generous amounts of support and help from other close family or friends. And this sense of dependence can push women to prioritize their partners' needs over their own, even as they struggle with the new demands they face (Fox, forthcoming). These changes obviously are not inevitable. Couples negotiate them, and some resist the various forces moving them in this direction.

Having children entails other changes in most parents' lives. Women typically feel that motherhood completely changes their lives. One study suggested that becoming a mother was not only to "fall in love" with a child but also to experience a transformation in the sense of self. Women tend to feel more loving and caring, and thus more closely identified with femininity, when they care for their children (McMahon, 1995).

DIVORCE AND ITS AFTERMATH

When people live together as a couple and a family, the dissolution of that unit brings turmoil for some time. People divorce largely because at least one spouse feels that something central to the marriage no longer exists—such as a sharing of responsibility or mutual caring. One of the chief reasons women initiate divorce is men's violence against them. Women are more likely than men to initiate divorce (Kurz, 1995).

Research indicates that serious violence committed against a woman is likely to involve a pattern of control by a man (Gartner et al., 1998–99). That some men need to be in control is a product of social forces as well as of psychological characteristics. In this culture, ideals of masculinity hold men to an expectation of some kind of dominance over women—an ideal often achieved through superior earnings. Poverty and

unemployment can, then, be factors in men's violence against women, since they pose threats to men's identity. Moreover, conventional gender roles place women living with men in the position of meeting their needs—whether that involves meeting emotional needs or ensuring that meals are prepared. A woman's failure to do so may trigger violence from a man who feels entitled to her services. Given how central men's control is to violence against women, the process of separating from a man makes a woman especially vulnerable to violence (Gartner et al., 1998–99).

When intimate relationships break up, people face considerable adjustment. Probably the most important consequence of divorce for women and the children who live with them is a significant decline in family income. This decline is often so great that many fall out of the middle class, lose their family home, move, and change schools (Finnie, 1993). Most single-parent mothers with dependent children live in poverty (National Council of Welfare, 1998: 18). Low income is especially significant because it reduces the mother's ability to provide what researchers find to be most important for children's adjustment after divorce—additional emotional support and a predictable daily schedule (Furstenberg and Cherlin, 1991).

The conflict between spouses that precedes and accompanies divorce (and persists for some couples who do not divorce) is certainly damaging for children. Yet, in the vast majority of cases, children return to normal development about two years after divorce. Nevertheless, some research indicates that women whose parents divorced are more likely to marry and have children early, give birth before marriage, and have their own marriages break up (McLanahan and Bumpass, 1988: 147). The reasons are not clear, but it is possible that the children of divorce carry emotional baggage from their childhood. As for the adults who divorce, the vast majority feel after a while that their divorce improved their lives. Even women struggling with poverty can feel relieved to be in control of the money (Graham, 1987).

Lone Parents

In the last two decades, in addition to an increase in the divorce rate, there has been an increase in the proportion of mothers who are unmarried. In 2006, 15.9 percent of all Canadian families were lone-parent families, and 18.3 percent of children lived in one-parent families (refer back to Table 10.1, p. 239). There are also racial and ethnic differences in the likelihood that children will be raised by one parent. For example, nearly one-quarter of Aboriginal families living off reserves are headed by one parent, almost twice the rate for all Canadians (McKie, 1993: 59).

The chief problem facing lone-parent families is poverty. The reasons for the poverty are clear. A woman—someone already disadvantaged in the labour market—is expected both to earn money and to care for children, since support from the former spouse (if there is one) and the state is generally meagre. Thus, the tension between employment and family is acute in these families. Evidence shows that children who grow up in female-headed families are less likely to complete high school than those living in two-parent families because of the financial stress that lone parents face, not because of the absence of a father figure (McLanahan, 1985).

Reconstituted Families

Adults who divorce usually remarry, so they and their children establish new families. Although reconstituted families find themselves in a better financial situation than lone-parent families, they face their own problems. Stepparents are in a difficult position with respect to their spouses' children; stepmothers especially face considerable challenges. According to the research, the outcomes of these new situations are uncertain. In many reconstituted families, both stepparents and stepchildren establish close relationships. In a sizable number of such families, though, tensions continue (Furstenberg and Cherlin, 1991). Many reconstituted families do not survive the early years of adjustment. Divorce rates are higher for second marriages, especially if children are present. Children in reconstituted families—like those in lone-parent families—face a heightened risk of experiencing developmental and social problems.

POLICIES TO SUPPORT FAMILIES

The chief problem for families today seems to be the difficulty of caring for children while earning enough money to support a family. The problem assumes crisis proportions for many lone-parent families, but is also of major importance in dual-earner families.

A homeless mother holds her sleeping baby.
SOURCE: © iStockphoto.com/absolut_100.

The policies that most industrial countries have developed to address this problem include direct family subsidies, significant paid parental leave following birth, and high-quality, subsidized child-care facilities—especially preschool for children over two-and-a-half years of age (Eyer, 1996). Such policies are predicated both on the assumption of the community's responsibility for all its children and on state actions to support women as mothers *and* wage earners. In some cases, they are based on goals of universality and equity. In Canada, in contrast, children are assumed to be a private responsibility, as is the problem women face in juggling family and employment (see Box 10.2).

Although most European countries provide more generous state support of families than Canada does, Sweden has especially good policies. There, it is assumed that children are a collective responsibility, and it is an official policy objective to promote gender equality in the home and the labour force. The state in Sweden acts to control the effects of market forces in order to pursue the goals of social equity and meeting human needs.

The Swedish government redistributes income from families with high incomes and without children to those with lower incomes and children. Its universal family allowances were four-and-a-half times the amount paid in Canada in 1991. Lone parents receive supplemental child support. Consequently, fewer than 5 percent of lone-parent families in Sweden were poor in the 1990s (Baker, 1995: 72, 126–27).

In Sweden, all new parents can take 18 months of parental leave (i.e., for either a mother or father)—12 months at 80 percent of their previous wage or salary, the next 3 months at a low flat rate, and the last 3 months without pay (Eyer, 1996). Most families take 12 months of maternity leave. In addition to

BOX 10.2   CHILDCARE—CANADA CAN'T WORK WITHOUT IT

Canada has begun to make a habit of garnering international criticism and low rankings on women's rights and the "gender gap," poverty and inequality, treatment of indigenous people, the environment and—most recently—provision for young children. In December, a UNICEF report card on early childhood education and childcare ranked Canada last among 25 developed nations; we shockingly met only one of 10 minimum benchmarks assessing quality and access. Canada's dismal ranking motivated the UN agency to call for swift ameliorative action. The economic downturn makes well-designed public investment in children and families more important than ever.

UNICEF observed that early childhood education and childcare has huge potential to enhance children's well-being and development with significant long-term social and economic returns. Most people—certainly most parents—would agree that participation in high quality early childhood education is an opportunity that shouldn't be missed by children once they've turned about 2 1/2 years of age. UNICEF notes that in Canada "underinvestment limits the potential to ensure that the childcare transition is good for our children."

As child development research points out, there is little value in services that fall below recognized quality thresholds. Indeed, poor quality may be harmful, especially for babies and children at risk.

Research in economics and social policy shows that public investment in childcare is also a key strategy for responding to immediate economic challenges and ensuring long-term societal prosperity. Childcare

promotes economic stimulus through job creation, parents' labour-force participation, higher government tax revenues, enhanced local economic activity, poverty reduction and lower social program costs. As families experience job and resource loss in a deepening recession, access to childcare is even more imperative.

A robust anti-poverty strategy is about much more than childcare but cannot be effective without access to early childhood education and child care programs. Good childcare allows female single parents—many poor and unlikely to have the cash for user fees for child care of any kind—to seek further education, train for work, get decent jobs, and accept job promotions.

The incidence of single mothers living below the poverty line in Quebec dropped substantially as universal access to regulated childcare spread. Childcare also helps families with two working parents to improve their economic stability and income at a time of insecure employment and stagnating wages.

Smart 21st-century governments know that investing in early childhood education and childcare is one of the best economic decisions they can make and that not doing so is bad economics. Short, medium and long-term—Canada can't work without childcare.

SOURCE: Martha Friendly and Laurel Rothman, 2009, "Childcare—Canada Can't Work Without It." *Toronto Star* 8 January. On the World Wide Web at http://www.thestar.com/printArticle/563403 (1 March 2009). Reprinted with permission from the authors.

parental leave, new parents can reduce their working hours to 30 per week and retain their job until their child is eight years old. All employees are entitled to leave from employment to care for a sick child at 90 percent of their wage or salary (Eyer, 1996).

Although Swedish babies are cared for at home by their parents, from age six months to seven years (when they enter school) they are eligible for daycare services. Since 1988, more than 70 percent of children under six years of age have been enrolled in daycare, usually in a daycare centre, but also in family daycare (where a woman takes up to four children in her home and is regularly supervised; Baker, 1995). Before-school and after-school care is also available for children up to the age of 12. Because of such support, about 90 percent of Swedish women are employed.

English Canada stands in sharp contrast to the situation in Sweden. In a political climate that prioritizes fiscal restraint, both Conservative and Liberal governments have avoided commitment to universal child care, focusing instead on assistance targeted at low-income families and social-assistance recipients. The Canada Child Tax Benefit applies only to families with incomes up to just slightly above the low-income cutoff. Although the federal government under Paul Martin was pressed by the NDP to commit substantial funding for new daycare spaces across Canada, the Conservative Party came into office promising instead to provide a small subsidy to women who stay home with their children. So, Canadians will likely continue to scramble to find care for their children, often without the resources to pay for good child care when both parents are in the labour force. About half of Canadian children under the age of 12 and with parents in paid work or full-time studies are in some form of nonparental care, and most are in unregulated care, provided by unlicensed caregivers outside the home, or nannies (Beach, Bertrand, and Cleveland, 1998). Spaces for babies and toddlers in daycare centres are limited and usually expensive. The legacy of the Liberal government is parents' right to 52 weeks of parental leave following childbirth (with considerable limits on earnings and eligibility). This policy reinforces parents' responsibility to care for their children full time and reduces demand for child-care services.

Since the late 1990s, Quebec has moved in the opposite direction—toward creating a broad set of family policies that feature universal, affordable child care (Jenson, 2002). After eliminating a long-standing tax deduction for child care of all kinds, the Parti Québécois used the savings to support and create child-care facilities featuring programs with an educational emphasis, run by professionals (Jenson, 2002). Parents pay $7 a day for child care, which is expected to be available to every child who needs it in the near future. Additionally, the Quebec government pays family allowances that are targeted to low-income parents, with additional money going to lone-parent families. So, at present, two very different policy approaches coexist in Canada.

CONCLUSION

Nuclear families centred on the emotional fulfillment of adults and the nurturing of children are relatively new in human history. Fundamental to their existence is women's assumption of domestic responsibilities and men's assumption of financial responsibilities. The fact that most men no longer earn enough to support their families and that most women are essential breadwinners has created strains in nuclear families. The stress is greatest for women, who must daily juggle the conflicting demands of family and paid work. In turn, divorce rates are high, and the number of lone-parent families is increasing.

Because the Canadian government provides little support to people raising children, families without two adult income earners are especially likely to struggle financially. Thus, family diversity exacerbates income inequality. In recent years, government cutbacks of social services have placed a bigger burden on most Canadian families, however they are organized.

Because women deal with the strain between family and employment every day, pressure on governments to provide family support, such as good-quality, affordable daycare, is likely to grow. There is also likely to be increasing pressure on employers to build flexibility into the workweek and career structures. Thus, just as recent economic developments have promoted change in family patterns, we may expect people's family concerns to cause a variety of other social changes.

SUMMARY

1. Commonsense arguments hold that current dilemmas in family life, such as how women can balance the responsibilities of family and paid work and how men can succeed at breadwinning and also do their share of the housework, are private, individual problems. Similarly, family-values advocates argue that change by individuals is the solution to family problems. In the absence of a sociological analysis, the public sources of these problems—and of their potential solutions—remain unclear.

2. Biology does not produce the family, which varies in its organization considerably across different cultures and through history. Although the nuclear family unit is common, it is not always responsible for child care. Often, the family is embedded in a larger household or community that collectively assumes responsibility for all the children of the group.

3. Family organization can be seen as loosely related to the organization of production, especially if family is defined as the set of relationships that people create to meet the daily needs of adults and children.

4. In foraging societies, the nuclear family is embedded in a larger group that cooperates with respect to subsistence, consumption, and child care. Paradoxically, the communal nature of these societies grants considerable autonomy to the individuals living in them.

5. In the agricultural societies of preindustrial Europe, households were primarily units of production in which economic need took precedence over all else. Household composition, even the texture of emotional life, reflected economic pressures.

6. Contemporary family patterns are the product of a particular history. Our history is marked by the development of an economy outside the household, in which the relations of paid employment are separated from the relations that provide for daily personal needs and the needs of children. A gendered division of labour corresponds to this separation.

7. As women have increasingly come to share the burden of family financial support, men have not proportionally increased the work they do in the home. That jobs are usually geared to people who lack family responsibilities is partly what prevents men from taking on more housework—their time is too limited. However, ideas about gender also make men reluctant to do "women's work."

8. The gendered division of labour that makes it possible for nuclear families to care for young children involves significant liabilities for women and even for children. The social isolation that full-time mothers experience, combined with the stress attached to their high-demand, low-control situation, reduces the quality of child care they are able to provide. Now that so many mothers are working outside the home, however, the problems associated with privatized responsibility for child care may prove too burdensome, and government support is likely to provide the only viable solution.

9. Because of high rates of divorce and an increasing incidence of births to unmarried women, many Canadian children will spend some part of their lives in lone-parent families. The most problematic thing about this type of family is its typically low income and the attendant stress on the parent.

10. The policies of the Canadian state pertaining to families are premised on the assumption that the welfare of family members—even children—is not the responsibility of the government or of the community. Accordingly, family law in Canada now views marriage as the union of two individuals who are responsible for their own support, even in the case of a divorcing woman who was a full-time homemaker.

QUESTIONS TO CONSIDER

1. Common sense holds that, if everyone embraced "family values," problems in family life today would disappear. Explain why this perspective is naïve, and describe some of the barriers to solving problems, such as child care, the difficult balance between the responsibilities of family and paid employment, and the unequal allocation of housework.

2. Explain how family patterns are related to the ways that people acquire their subsistence in foraging societies. Do the same for our society.

3. Explain how the development of capitalism influenced family ideals in the nineteenth century. Then sketch how the marketplace today influences family life—even aspects of it as basic as conceiving and having children.

4. Describe some of the "crises" typical of family life today, and speculate on possible solutions.

GLOSSARY

Biological determinism is the argument that individual behaviour or social organization is directly caused by biology or biological processes.

Evolutionary psychology, or sociobiology, is a type of biological determinism that views human behaviour as the product of human evolution.

Extended-family households are residential units of people who are blood relatives but consist of more than the members of a nuclear family (e.g., an extended family may consist of children, their parents, and a set of grandparents living together).

The **family** is the set of relationships people create to share resources daily in order to ensure their own and any dependants' welfare.

A **family wage** is an ideal of the trade-union movement in the nineteenth century; it refers to a wage that is paid to a man and is sufficient to support him, his wife, and his children.

Foraging societies, also known as hunting-and-gathering societies, are societies in which people acquire their subsistence from the resources around them, without cultivating the earth.

A **gendered division of labour** refers to the separation of the tasks men and women regularly do.

The **nuclear family** comprises a man who is the main breadwinner, a woman who is the main caregiver, and one or more children.

Privatization is the assumption of responsibility by the individual, the household, or the family; it is the opposite of collectivization.

Pronatalism refers to inducements by government to encourage women to have children.

Social reproduction, as opposed to biological reproduction, refers to all that is necessary to meet the needs of adults and children, from feeding them and clothing them to meeting their emotional needs and socializing them. It is "the activities and attitudes, behaviors and emotions, responsibilities and relations directly involved in the maintenance of life on a daily basis, and intergenerationally" (Laslett and Brenner, 1989: 382).

SUGGESTED READING

Carrington, Christopher. (1999). *No Place Like Home: Relationships and Family Life among Lesbians and Gay Men.* Chicago: The University of Chicago Press. With great attention to detail, Carrington documents the extensive work gay and lesbian couples undertake when they "make family." Many of his findings apply to heterosexual couples as well.

Coontz, Stephanie. (1992). *The Way We Never Were: American Families and the Nostalgia Trap.* New York: Basic Books. Fascinating, provocative, and well researched, this book reviews and criticizes "family-values" arguments by analyzing family life, past and present.

Hansen, Karen H. (2005). *Not-So-Nuclear Families: Class, Gender, and Networks of Care.* New Jersey: Rutgers University Press. A study of the networks that provide care for children whose parents are juggling paid work and household responsibilities, this book explores the impact of social class and challenges our assumptions about the independence of nuclear families.

Hochschild, Arlie. (1989). *The Second Shift: Working Parents and the Revolution at Home.* New York: Viking. This unsettling study addresses the question of why men are so slow to take on household responsibilities as their wives take over some of the responsibilities of breadwinning.

Luxton, Meg. (1980). *More Than a Labour of Love: Three Generations of Women's Work in the Home.* Toronto: Women's Press. Now a Canadian classic, this study of three generations of homemakers in Flin Flon, Manitoba, shows the changes that have occurred in women's household work over time and also how the capitalist economy shapes women's work and gender relations.

McMahon, Martha. (1995). *Engendering Motherhood: Identity and Self-Transformation in Women's Lives.* Toronto: Guilford Press. This award-winning book by a Canadian sociologist is an insightful look at the transformation many women experience when they become mothers.

NOTE

1. Based on personal communication with Ivy Bourgeault, one of Canada's leading experts on midwifery.

WEB RESOURCES

Companion Website for This Book

http://www.newsociety6e.nelson.com
Begin by clicking on the Student Resources section of the website. Next, select the chapter you are studying from the pull-down menu. From the Student Resources page, you have easy access to InfoTrac College Edition® and other resources, such as the

Glossary, Test Yourself questions, and additional readings. The website also has many useful tips to aid you in your study of sociology.

InfoTrac College Edition Search Terms

Visit http://www.infotrac-college.com for access to more than 20 million articles from nearly 6000 sources when doing your online research.

CHAPTER ELEVEN

SOURCE: © Kiselev Andrey Valerevich/Shutterstock

Work and Occupations

Sandy Welsh
UNIVERSITY OF TORONTO

In this chapter you will learn that

- The service sector dominates work in Canada.

- Employment is becoming more polarized into good and bad jobs.

- Part-time work, temporary and contract jobs, and self-employment are becoming more prevalent. Working evenings, weekends, and irregular hours is also more common.

- Job ghettos trap certain categories of workers, such as women and members of visible minorities, in bad jobs; labour-market shelters help some workers protect access to good jobs.

- The degree to which technology enhances or degrades jobs depends on management goals, the type of technology used, and the way workers react to the technology.

- Management uses a variety of strategies to organize work. These strategies attempt to help management reduce costs and increase productivity.

- The characteristics of organizations and jobs are the primary determinants of job satisfaction. If employers provide workers with challenging jobs, opportunities for advancement, and adequate pay, workers are more likely to be satisfied.

- Alienation reflects workers' lack of power over their work and lives. Several types of workplace behaviour, such as sabotage, game playing, and strikes, are reactions to alienating conditions.

- Social networks play an important role in helping people find jobs. People who are acquaintances, or friends of friends, are the best sources of useful information about job openings.

AN INTRODUCTION TO WORK IN CANADA

WORKING IN RETAIL

Zainab Taiyeb worked for several months selling electricity and gas plans door-to-door in Toronto. Every day, her supervisor picked her up at a subway station and drove her to her assigned neighbourhood. One day, however, her supervisor took her to an office of Rogers Communications, Inc. Although Zainab had been hired by a subcontractor, she received an ID card imprinted with the Rogers logo and was told she would now be selling high-speed Internet and cable services. Zainab, a recent immigrant from Pakistan, received no contract for her work at Rogers. She was also told she'd have to wait for three weeks until she was paid. After working her first month, her employer owed her $1500.

Zainab worked in good faith and expected to see a paycheque. When she and her co-workers confronted their employer, he said he was a subcontractor and that he couldn't pay them because Rogers hadn't paid him. "When I demanded to be paid, along with

How can workers have a job that pays a decent wage, treats them with respect, and offers some satisfaction?
SOURCE: © iStockphoto.com/Jaimie Duplass.

the other workers, I was given $20. Can you imagine? I had worked for one month and was given $20. It was so insulting. I cried that day" (Berinstein, 2004).

Most of us assume we will be paid for our work. However, Zainab Taiyeb's experience shows that even today this is not always a safe assumption. What would you do if this happened to you? Would you chalk it up as a lesson learned about contract work and move on? Would you push back and fight? As a contract worker, Zainab did not have access to traditional unions that cover permanent employees. So in order to overcome their situation, she and her co-workers turned to the Toronto Organizing for Fair Employment (TOFFE) and Workers Information Centre to learn about their rights. They filed a complaint with the Ontario Labour Relations Board and launched a corporate campaign to pressure Rogers to "take responsibility and force the subcontractor to pay us" (Berinstein, 2004). It took two years, but eventually Zainab was able to recoup the $1500 owed her. She also drew attention to a widespread practice: the unfair treatment of contract workers.

Zainab Taiyeb's work experience mirrors many of the issues facing all people who are current and potential employees. She is part of the rising legion of service workers employed in **nonstandard jobs,** which involve part-time, contractual, and seasonal work; multiple job holding; work secured through a temporary worker agency; and self-employment. As a woman and an immigrant, Zainab also personifies some of the key shifts in the Canadian workforce since the 1970s. Her concerns are ours: How can we have a job that pays a decent wage, treats us with respect, and offers some satisfaction? This chapter will take you through many of the key issues facing workers today. I'll discuss what the service economy and nonstandard work mean for our working lives, how employees and employers battle to gain the upper hand in determining what jobs will be like, what factors lead to "good jobs" and "bad jobs," and what influences workers satisfaction in different kinds of jobs. Whether we look at an immigrant contract worker asking for her wages or doctors fighting provincial governments for the right to choose where they practise, the study of work and occupations is a study of the constraints and the struggles that occur daily in Canadian workplaces.

THE FIRST AND SECOND INDUSTRIAL REVOLUTIONS

Zainab Taiyeb working as a contract worker for Rogers represents the most recent phase in our economic development. To understand how we reached this phase, we need to review the development of the Canadian economy.

Most researchers think of changes in the economy and the world of work as "revolutions." The Industrial Revolution started in England in the late eighteenth century, completing the transition from feudalism to capitalism. Under feudalism, most people worked as peasant farmers, and a few skilled artisans made tools and variety of goods. As a result of the growth of the textile industry and non-local markets for wool, landowners started to use their land for sheep grazing and other cash crops. Displaced by this shift in land use, and in need of work, peasant farmers migrated to urban areas, looking for jobs in the emerging factories and artisan shops.

The organization of work dramatically shifted during the Industrial Revolution. Under feudalism, most farmers produced enough to meet their own needs. There existed no clear separation between work and leisure. Agricultural labour had its own work rhythm, connected to the rising and the setting of the sun and the passage of the seasons. However, the transition to capitalism transformed peasant farmers into wage-earning factory workers. Now, workers' schedules were standardized and set by their bosses. The **division of labour** expanded, which is to say that work previously done by skilled craftspeople was broken down into smaller components, so semi-skilled workers, who were paid less than the skilled craftspeople, could perform factory jobs. An urban capitalist class and a "blue-collar" working class emerged from these processes (Polanyi, 1957).

Canada went through its own industrial revolution, though it occurred later here than in Europe or the United States (Laxer, 1989). As late as the early twentieth century, 40 percent of the Canadian population worked in agricultural pursuits (Campbell, 1996). When industrialization began, activity centred on Canada's vast natural resources, such as lumber and minerals.

In the early twentieth century, the Second Industrial Revolution started. Large corporations bought smaller companies engaged in similar lines of production. Henry Ford's assembly line and other mass-production technologies contributed to this expansion. Company owners increased their ability to dominate the market and control the activities of workers. Simultaneously, an "administrative revolution" transformed office work (Lowe, 1987). Because of the vast amounts of information produced by companies, such as personnel and transaction records, management needed efficient systems to organize their offices. This need led to the expansion of the "white-collar" job sector and the growth of bureaucratic organizations. All of these changes amounted to an increased division of labour. Now, managers managed, clerical workers handled paperwork, and production workers accomplished smaller and smaller parts of the production process.

We thus see that work as we know it in Canada and other capitalist economies is a new phenomenon. A hundred and fifty years ago, most Canadians did not live in cities and work for an employer in a large bureaucratic organization. Although we still see vestiges of the first and second industrial revolutions in our working lives, many things have changed. Most prominent is the movement from a manufacturing-based economy toward a service economy.

Contextualizing the Canadian Labour Market

Before discussing the shift to a service economy, it's useful to have some background information about the Canadian labour market. Since 1970, the labour force has changed dramatically. Some of the changes reflect demographic trends, such as the aging of the population. Some changes are due to a combination of economic and political factors, such as the increasing participation of women in the labour force. And some changes are the result of government policy to deal with predicted labour shortages, such as the increasing prominence of immigrants in the labour market.

So how exactly has the labour force changed? Compared with 30 years ago, Canada's labour force is now older (Morissette and Hou, 2006). According to Statistics Canada (2006), the proportion of workers nearing retirement grew by almost 6 percent between 1997 and 2005. In 2005, about 22 percent of the Canadian workforce was within 10 years of retirement.

Canada's population is also more educated than it was 30 years ago (Morissette and Hou, 2006). In 1971, about 16 percent of Canadian-born workers between the age of 25 and 34 had less than a high school diploma. Almost 9 percent of this age cohort had some postsecondary education. Three decades later, just 3.5 percent of workers in this age cohort had less than a high school diploma, while nearly 18 percent had some postsecondary education. The trend toward higher levels of education holds across age groups. The increased emphasis on education has made it

The Second Industrial Revolution started in the early twentieth century. Henry Ford's assembly line and other mass-production technologies transformed the workplace.

SOURCE: Ellen Griesedieck, *Rouge Assembly Line*. Courtesy Gallery Henoch.

more difficult for workers with high school education or less to do well in the labour market. For example, young workers who have not completed high school are more likely to be unemployed compared with 30 years ago (Morissette and Hou, 2006). Thus, while the increased importance of education is a good news story for those who are well educated, it is a bad news story for those who are less well educated.

A third key change in the Canadian labour market is the growing reliance on immigration to meet the demand for skilled workers (Statistics Canada, 2003). In the 1980s, approximately 125 000 immigrants arrived in Canada annually. By the 1990s, this figure soared to about 220 000. Immigrant workers today, like Canadian-born workers, are more highly educated than those who arrived earlier. In 2001, about 46 percent of immigrants in the 25–64 age cohort who arrived between 1996 and 2000 had completed at least

a bachelor's degree. The comparable figure for immigrants arriving between 1986 and 1990 was 24 percent (Statistics Canada, 2006b). The rise in the educational status of immigrants is partly explained by the federal government's immigration policy in the 1990s. This policy emphasized bringing skilled immigrants to Canada to "foster a strong and viable economy in all regions of Canada" (Statistics Canada 2006: 87). Recent immigrants are also more likely to be members of a "visible minority" compared with those arriving earlier. Recent arrivals face increasing difficulty in the labour market from discrimination and a lack of recognition of their educational credentials (see Chapter 8, Race and Ethnic Relations).

Women's participation in the labour force is the final important labour market change since the 1970s. Women now make up just under half of the paid workforce, compared with only 37 percent in 1976

(Statistics Canada, 2006b; see Chapter 7, Gender Inequality: Economic and Political Aspects, for details).

The Canadian economy has experienced four big recessions since the 1970s—one in the mid-1970s, one in the early 1980s, one in the early 1990s, and one beginning in 2008. During each of these periods, the economy shrank and unemployment rose, particularly in the manufacturing sector. Young workers were particularly susceptible to layoffs because the last hired are usually the first fired when a company struggles in a difficult economy. Recovery from the 1991–92 recession was particularly sluggish. It was not until the end of the decade that the Canadian labour market began to fire on all cylinders. By 2008, the unemployment rates had dropped below 6 percent—a level not seen since the 1960s. Then, all hell broke loose. The housing and credit markets collapsed in the United States, and the shock was soon felt globally.

Manufacturers started shutting down factories. In Canada, the auto sector was particularly hard hit. Many analysts agree that we probably won't bounce back to pre-recessionary levels of growth and employment until after 2013.

To see what the world of work will look like then, I return to my discussion of the rise of the service economy and what it means for where Canadians work as well as the quality of the jobs they hold.

WORK IN THE SERVICE ECONOMY

Many researchers argue that, in the years since World War II, Canadians have experienced a third industrial revolution (Toffler, 1980). Our economy has shifted from its early industrial base of primary production (mining, fishing, and logging) and secondary production (manufacturing) to tertiary production (service industries).

Figure 11.1 shows the shift away from goods-producing industries from 1976 to 2007 and the rapid growth of service industries. Employment in services more than doubled while employment in manufacturing increased less than 20 percent. Economic downturns affected employment in goods-producing industries more strongly than employment in services; you can plainly see the big drops in manufacturing employment in the early 1980s and the early 1990s, the two recessions covered by Figure 11.1 (Statistics Canada, 2009). The effect of the recessions on service employment was much less pronounced. From 1976 to 2007, the percentage of Canadians employed in service industries grew from 65 to 76 percent.

There are many reasons that Canada, like many industrialized countries, experienced massive growth in the service industry. Chief among them is that increased global competitiveness facilitated the movement of much manufacturing to low-wage, less-developed countries. Free-trade agreements with the United States and Mexico facilitated the migration of manufacturing jobs out of Canada (Canadian Labour Congress, 1993). Proportionately fewer manufacturing jobs means proportionately more service jobs.

In 2007, retail and wholesale trade was the largest segment of the economy; retail trade accounted for

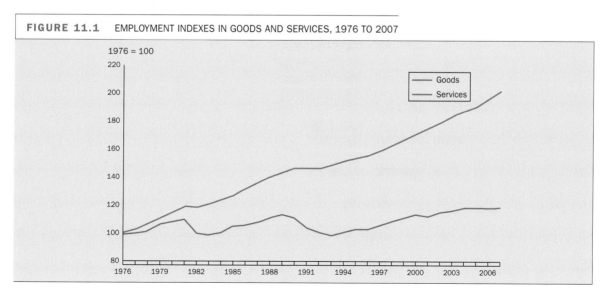

FIGURE 11.1 EMPLOYMENT INDEXES IN GOODS AND SERVICES, 1976 TO 2007

SOURCE: Statistics Canada, 2009, "The Canadian Labour Market at a Glance, 2007." Ottawa: Industry Canada (Catalogue no. 71-222-XIE), p. 38.

three-quarters of all trade. By far the largest category of retail trade is food and beverage stores, including grocery stores; specialty food stores; and beer, wine, and liquor stores (Statistics Canada, 2009). Lower-tier service jobs in such stores are characterized by low pay and nonstandard work hours: features of bad jobs (Presser, 2003).

From the early twentieth century until 1990, manufacturing industries employed more Canadians than any other segment of the labour force. By 2007, manufacturing industries ranked second. Health-care and social service industries ranked third. Considered part of the upper tier of the service industry, health-care and social services employed nearly 11 percent of the paid labour force in 2007 (Statistics Canada, 2009). Much of this growth is due to the increased health care needed by an aging population.

Given that manufacturing is the second largest employer of Canadian workers, you may wonder why there is so much concern about the decline of manufacturing. While manufacturing, along with retail and wholesale trade, and health and social services represent the largest categories of employment, they are not necessarily the industries experiencing the highest rate of growth. Business, building, and other support-service industries, along with professional, scientific, and technical services, experienced the highest rate of growth from 1987 to 2007 (Figure 11.2). Manufacturing is far

down the list in terms of growth, surpassing only the resource-based industries of forestry, fishing, mining, oil and gas, and agriculture.

Sociologists are concerned about the decline of jobs in manufacturing industries because these jobs have long represented good jobs in terms of wages, benefits, and security. These jobs also represented the best opportunities for young workers, especially young men, with high school education or less. In 2007, wages were significantly higher in manufacturing industries (on average, $21.11 an hour) compared to those in retail trade (on average, $15.39 per hour; Statistics Canada, 2009: 39).

Sociologists often refer to the shift from a goods- to a service-based economy as **deindustrialization.** Deindustrialization began in Canada and the United States in the 1970s and continues today. It reduced the number of unionized, well-paying, full-time manufacturing jobs and increased the number of "bad" jobs located in the lower-tier service industries. The process of deindustrialization also caused a host of long-term economic and labour market difficulties, such as a rise in unemployment and increasing income inequality.

GOOD JOBS OR BAD JOBS?

At the centre of our discussion of what the service economy means for Canadian workers is the question

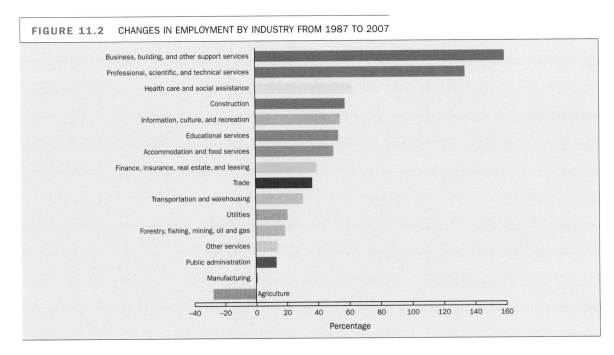

FIGURE 11.2   CHANGES IN EMPLOYMENT BY INDUSTRY FROM 1987 TO 2007

SOURCE: Statistics Canada, 2009, "The Canadian Labour Market at a Glance, 2007." Ottawa: Industry Canada (Catalogue no. 71-222-XIE), p. 40.

of whether more good or bad jobs are available for workers. At minimum, good jobs provide **extrinsic rewards,** such as high wages, good benefits, employment security, and opportunities for advancement. Good jobs can also provide **intrinsic rewards,** such as decision-making opportunities; challenging, non-repetitive work; and autonomy that allows for self-direction and responsibility over tasks.

Debate revolves around changes in the skill level of jobs in the service economy. Conventional wisdom suggests that skill requirements are increasing because of technology (Spenner, 1983). As Daniel Bell (1973) and other postindustrialists propose, we should experience an upgrading of jobs in the economy as skill requirements increase. Postindustrialists also predict that job growth will occur in the higher-skilled occupations. In contrast, Harry Braverman (1974) and other postindustrial critics believe that skill levels are being downgraded. In this view, although some highly skilled professional and technical jobs will be created, most jobs will be lower-skilled industrial and service jobs.

So which is it? Are we moving to the postindustrial world of Bell or the downgraded world of Braverman? One way to answer this question is to look at which occupations are held by Canadians. About one in four men is employed in the construction trades and as transport and equipment operators. Another one in five men is employed in sales and service occupations. Just under one-third of all women work in sales and services. About one in four women work in business, finance, and administrative occupations. Hidden within these broad categories are important distinctions. For example, sales and service occupations include cashiers, food and beverage servers, police officers, and child-care workers. Business, finance, and administrative occupations include accountants, insurance agents, and clerical workers. As discussed in Chapter 7 (Gender Inequality: Economic and Political Aspects), significant gender segregation exists within these categories.

When we examine shifts in the Canadian occupational structure, we see a more complex picture than those sketched by Bell and Braverman. Blue-collar jobs in the middle are declining. Job growth is occurring at the top and the bottom of the occupational structure (Economic Council of Canada, 1991; Myles, 1988). There is some evidence of a shift toward what Statistics Canada calls "knowledge occupations" in the Canadian labour market. Knowledge occupations are defined as those where a high proportion of workers have a university education. Some of the main knowledge occupations are in the health professions, science and engineering, and management. The percentage of Canadians in knowledge occupations increased from 14 to 25 percent between 1971 and 2001 (Baldwin and Beckstead, 2003). Whether this is indicative of a shift to a larger knowledge-based economy is something still debated by sociologists.

A service-based economy does not necessarily involve bad jobs for everyone. A misconception about the service economy is that the service sector creates only bad jobs and that the goods sector is the source of good jobs. This scenario assumes that all service jobs are alike. Instead, we should think of the service sector as having a lower tier made up of traditional services, such as retail trade, food, and personal services, and an upper tier consisting of other services, such as finance and business, utilities, health, education, and public administration. Whether you find yourself in a lower- or upper-tier service job has implications for your wages, job security, and the skill content of your work (Economic Council of Canada, 1991; Krahn, 1992).

However, these statistics are partly misleading. Statistics Canada points out that driving the growth in service occupations is an increase in part-time work and self-employment. So although business and other services have the potential to create good jobs, some of those jobs may not be full-time. The movement to a service economy has affected the types of jobs available in Canada. Some good jobs are created in financial services and health services, while bad jobs with nonstandard hours are also created, primarily in sales and service. I now explore the issue of nonstandard work more fully.

NONSTANDARD JOBS

Twenty years ago, sociologists of work did not spend much time researching nonstandard jobs. That has changed with increasing numbers of temporary, part-time, contract, and self-employed workers. Nonstandard work is now a central part of the economy. Most of us know people who work in a nonstandard job. You may have a part-time job at a local retail store that helps you pay your tuition and other bills, while giving you (almost) enough time to study. One of your parents may have been laid off because of company restructuring, only to be hired back later as an independent contractor. One of your friends may have used a "temp" agency to find work when her other attempts didn't work out.

Part-time jobs, temporary jobs where one is hired through a temporary agency, self-employment, contract work, outsourcing, and seasonal work are all considered nonstandard jobs. Some sociologists call them "precarious" jobs because they do not provide stable, long-term employment or adequate pay (Cranford, Vosko, and Zukewich, 2003). In most industrial countries, including Canada, one-quarter to one-third of all jobs are now nonstandard (Chaykowski, 2005; Cranford et al., 2003; Economic Council of Canada, 1991; Krahn, 1991, 1995).

It is not always clear what defines a job as nonstandard. Often, nonstandard jobs are defined in terms of what they are not: They are not jobs in which workers have a full-time, year-round job with one employer, located at the employers' premises, and under the supervision of that employer. In a standard job, workers also have a reasonable expectation that employment will continue indefinitely (Cranford et al., 2003: 459; Kalleberg, Reskin, and Hudson, 2000).

Nonstandard jobs, on the other hand, may lack some or all of the characteristics of a standard employment relationship. First, some nonstandard jobs lack an employer; self-employed workers do nonstandard work. They take on all the risk of their employment, including ensuring they make money, withhold taxes, and save for retirement. Second, in many nonstandard jobs, like contract and temporary work and some kinds of self-employment, workers are hired on short-term contracts and cannot assume their employment will

continue indefinitely (Cranford et al., 2003; Kalleberg et al., 2000). Third, many nonstandard jobs offer fewer than full-time hours. Fourth, in many nonstandard jobs, the legal employer, who is responsible for hiring and paying the employee, is not the employer who oversees daily work. This is the case for temporary help agency and contract jobs. For example, a worker hired by a temporary agency is legally employed by the agency but does not work for the agency (Vosko, 2000; Kalleberg et al., 2000). Rather, the temporary employee works for a client organization. When the job for which she is hired is completed, she must wait to receive payment and a new assignment from the temporary agency, not the company where she was working. This is similar to the experience of Zainab Taiyeb, whom we learned about at the beginning of this chapter. Although she was selling products for Rogers Cable, a Rogers subcontractor hired her and was responsible for paying her.

To understand nonstandard work, it is useful to look at part-time and temporary employment, two of the more common and widely discussed forms of nonstandard work. In 2007, just under 20 percent of Canadians worked in part-time jobs. Figure 11.3 shows that part-time employment is highest for workers between the age of 15 and 24. Since 1976, the part-time rate has grown for workers over the age of 55. This may be due to older workers opting for part-time work as a steppingstone to retirement (Pold, 2004). Alternatively, it could signal that older workers

---

FIGURE 11.3 PART-TIME EMPLOYMENT RATES, BY SEX AND AGE, 1976 AND 2007

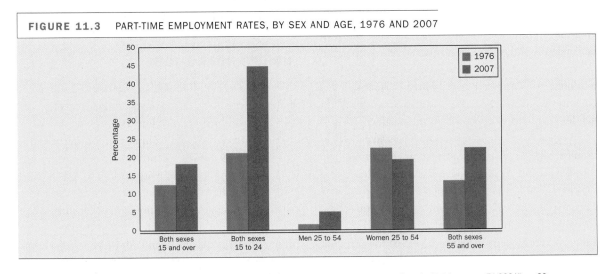

SOURCE: Statistics Canada, 2009, "The Canadian Labour Market at a Glance, 2007." Ottawa: Industry Canada (Catalogue no. 71-222-X), p. 60.

are unable to find full-time work to replace a full-time job they lost because of downsizing or corporate restructuring. Some employees, particularly women and young workers between the ages of 15 and 24, prefer the flexibility of part-time work. They voluntarily choose part-time work because it allows time for school attendance and family responsibilities or because they do not want to work full-time. In 2007, one in four part-time workers in Canada stated they would prefer to be working full-time (Statistics Canada, 2009). They are *involuntary* part-time workers. Involuntary part-time jobs are especially common in the Atlantic provinces where the unemployment rate is higher than the national average (Statistics Canada, 2009). Since 1997, the number of involuntary part-timers declined as the Canadian economy improved and the unemployment rate fell, but it is likely that the proportion of involuntary part-timers will rise because of the 2008–2009 economic downturn.

To respond to changing demand for products and services, employers increasingly rely on temporary workers, ranging from clerical help to computer programmers, hired through temporary-employment agencies. In 2007, almost 13 percent of Canadian workers were employed in temporary or contract positions (Statistics Canada, 2009). Temporary workers, who often work alongside full-time permanent workers, earn substantially less per hour than their full-time counterparts. The average hourly wage for a full-time permanent worker was $21.07 in 2007, compared with $15.99 for temporary workers. Like part-time workers, temporaries tend to be young and female (Economic Council of Canada, 1991).

Figure 11.4 shows that people between the ages of 15 and 24 are more than twice as likely as others to be temporary workers. We've also seen a sharp increase in the number of newly hired workers holding temporary jobs. In 1989, 11 percent of newly hired employees were in temporary jobs. By 2004, this increased to 21 percent (Morissette and Johnson, 2005).

WHY THE RISE OF NONSTANDARD WORK?

Scholars link the increase in nonstandard work to the rise of the service economy, instability in the global economy, privatization of government services, and organizational restructuring that occurred in the late twentieth century (Vosko, 2000). While some analysts mention the 1990s as the starting point for the rapid rise of nonstandard work, Leah Vosko discusses how we can see movement to nonstandard work as early as the 1960s (2000: p. 27; Kalleberg, 2000). During the 1960s, globalization increased competition and uncertainty for corporations. Over concern for profit, they began to rethink standard employment and its virtual guarantee of full-time, well-paying jobs. This rethinking was coupled with growing economic hardship in North America and Europe as the oil crisis of the 1970s and economic slowdowns began to affect national economies. The rise in unemployment during this period also led to concern over the ability of national economies to generate enough full-time jobs for all workers (Kalleberg, 2000). Labour laws that protected the rights of full-time employees were also called into question. As employers looked for ways to

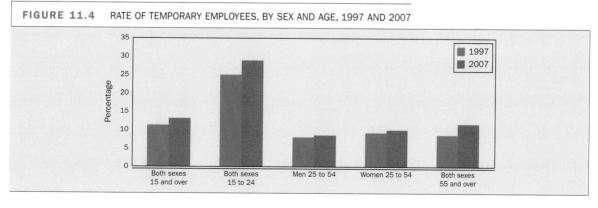

FIGURE 11.4   RATE OF TEMPORARY EMPLOYEES, BY SEX AND AGE, 1997 AND 2007

SOURCE: Statistics Canada, 2009, "The Canadian Labour Market at a Glance, 2007." Ottawa: Industry Canada (Catalogue no. 71-222-X), p. 69.

increase their "flexibility" and their ability to adjust to consumer demand, they turned increasingly to non-standard work (Kalleberg, 2000: 342).

From an employer perspective, nonstandard work is attractive since it allows for the creation of more flexible organizations. One can think about flexibility in two ways. First, there is **functional or internal flexibility** that allows employers to move workers from one job to another within an organization. However, it is a second type of flexibility—**numerical or external flexibility**—that drove employers to create nonstandard jobs. Numerical flexibility enables employers to adjust the size of their workforce by easily hiring and firing workers in response to fluctuations in labour demand (Kalleberg, 2003).

The downsizing of the 1980s and 1990s also drove the rise of nonstandard work—and not just in the private sector. In the 1990s, governments saddled with large deficits slashed jobs and privatized work previously carried out by government employees. Advances in telecommunications and information technology made it easier for private and public organizations to rely on outside suppliers and to quickly assemble (and disassemble) temporary workforces (Kalleberg, 2000). As well, some of the movement to nonstandard work is associated with the increased participation of women in the labour force. Some women, especially those with young children, prefer part-time and other nonstandard work arrangements. Nonstandard work allows some women to balance their need to earn income with their child-care responsibilities.

People commonly assume that because standard jobs predominate now, they have been the most common form of work for centuries. In reality, the standard employment relationship as we know it arose after World War II (Fudge and Vosko, 2001). Insecure jobs, such as seasonal and casual labour, have always been a big part of the Canadian economy (Smith, 1999). In addition, linking the increase in nonstandard work only to the rise of the service economy overlooks the historic use of nonstandard work by manufacturing and other goods-producing industries. Automobile manufacturers have a long history of contracting out the production of auto parts. Agriculture has long relied on day labourers and seasonal employees. Immigration policy allows Mexican men to work as temporary farm labourers in Ontario. They are expected to return to Mexico when harvesting ends. Thus, when discussing the rise of nonstandard work, one should remember that, historically, standard employment is unique.

Most employers view the recent increase in non-standard jobs positively. Employers reduce costs associated with full-time employees and they gain flexibility in competitive markets. For employees, there are more downsides. Research documents increased job insecurity, loss of benefits, and wages that are too low to allow a decent standard of living.

ARE NONSTANDARD JOBS BAD JOBS?

Much of the early literature on nonstandard jobs referred to them as bad jobs. Evidence shows that nonstandard workers are worse off than workers in standard employment relationships (Cranford et al., 2003; Kalleberg et al., 2000). However, just how bad they are varies by type of nonstandard employment. Some nonstandard jobs are low-paid (e.g., jobs secured through a temporary worker agency) while others are not (e.g., independent technical contractors; Houseman, Kalleberg, and Erickcek, 2003; Kunda, Barley, and Evans, 2002). The experience of nonstandard work is complicated and variable.

When we compare how nonstandard workers are treated by full-time employees, we find evidence for the negative evaluation of nonstandard jobs. Temporary workers placed by an agency in an organization for a short time often feel like "nonpersons" who are isolated from full-time employees (Rogers, 1995). As one temporary worker said,

> There was no Christmas present under the tree like the rest of the company would get [at the office party] . . . There were some places where it was just blatant, just terribly blatant. Whenever there was going to be a company party or something the temps had to stay and work. You know, cover the phones so the regular people got to go. You could tell where the second-class citizenship started. (quoted in Rogers, 1995: 150)

Compared with standard workers, nonstandard workers are at greater risk of experiencing alienation, isolation, and abuse.

In some European countries, strict regulations control the use of nonstandard workers. For example, in Norway, the use of fixed-term contracts and temporary help agencies is severely restricted (Olsen and Kalleberg, 2004). Some European Union countries have implemented the European Union's Framework Directive on equality of treatment for part-time and fixed-term workers. This means that companies in these countries must provide access to the same sick pay, pensions, and other benefits as full-time workers receive. Although some countries have tried to limit how the EU Directive is implemented (in Britain only 10 percent of part-time workers are covered), there is some hope that it will result in an increase in quality and stability for some forms of nonstandard work (McGovern, Smeaton, and Hill, 2004).

WORK HOURS AND WORK ARRANGEMENTS

At the same time as nonstandard jobs are becoming more numerous, many workers are increasingly concerned with the number of hours they are working. Most of the focus is on overwork, with references to a "24-hour work day," needing to be available "24/7" and an "escalation in expectations" in terms of how many hours employees should be working (Epstein and Kalleberg, 2001: 6). The mass media, corporate executives, and students in my sociology of work course often discuss work–life balance and time for life outside of work. Are we really working more than people did in previous generations, or has work changed in other ways?

To answer these questions, we first need to know how many hours per week Canadians are working. In 2006, Canadians worked approximately 36.5 hours per week on average. In 1976, Canadians worked approximately 38.6 hours (Usalcas, 2008). Contrary to the hype, Canadians are not working longer hours.

Canada is not alone in the decline in average hours worked per week. Most rich countries have experienced a decline in average work hours in recent decades. The rise of part-time work and reduction in the proportion of people working more than 50 hours per week account for most of the decline.

However, while on average Canadians today are no more overworked than their predecessors were, we are seeing another trend in work hours. As Figure 11.5 shows, a higher percentage of workers now work either longer or shorter hours compared with 30 years ago. While the 40-hour workweek was still the most common in 2005, the proportion of Canadians working a 40-hour week declined since 1976 (Statistics Canada, 2006a). Proportionately more Canadians work fewer than 40 or more than 40 hours a week. Some analysts refer to this trend as the **polarization of working hours;** some workers are experiencing overwork while others have the opposite problem.

Many explanations exist for this polarization. Some have to do with choice. Certain groups of workers, such as students and those with young children, may choose to work fewer hours to balance competing demands. In addition, the rise of service industries has increased the number of people working nonstandard schedules and hours (Presser, 2003). Other explanations for the polarization of working hours point to the effect of economic restructuring and the increase in part-time, temporary, and other forms of nonstandard work.

Polarization of work hours may not be a permanent, however. Between 1997 and 2007, there was a

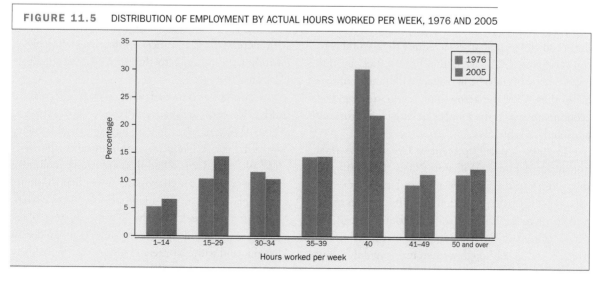

FIGURE 11.5   DISTRIBUTION OF EMPLOYMENT BY ACTUAL HOURS WORKED PER WEEK, 1976 AND 2005

SOURCE: Statistics Canada, 2006, "The Canadian Labour Market at a Glance, 2005." Ottawa: Industry Canada (Catalogue no. 71-222-XIE).

decline in the number of people working 1–14 hours and over 50 hours per week (Statistics Canada, 2009). This is a trend to keep an eye on. We may experience a shift back toward polarization of work hours during the current recession with its higher unemployment rates.

According to sociologist Harriet Presser (1999, 2003, 2004), all the attention paid to changes in work hours has ignored the other way that work schedules have shifted. Presser says the issue is not just how many hours are worked, but *which* hours of the day and days of the week are worked. She focuses on **nonstandard work schedules,** defined as either working nonstandard hours that fall outside the 9-to-5 workday (shift work) or working nonstandard days, such as Saturday and Sunday. Her research shows that nonstandard work schedules have increased because of three interrelated factors. First, the service sector demands nonstandard schedules to a much higher degree than manufacturing industries do. Linked to this is the increasing participation of women in the labour market. With more and more women working during the day, there is an increased demand for stores, restaurants, and other businesses to stay open later and on weekends. Second, demographic changes such as the postponement of marriage and the rise in family income, because of the increase in dual-earner couples, have increased the demand for recreation and leisure activities during the evenings and on weekends. The aging of the population has also increased demand for 24-hour services, especially in terms of the need for round-the-clock medical services. Third, technological changes and globalization processes have created a "24-hour economy" where workers are on call at all hours. E-mail, fax machines, and cellphones enable workers to be connected at all times and allow companies to require their workers to stay connected. As well, the head office in one country may need to be in contact with branch offices in another. Working across time zones in the global economy increases the number of employees working nonstandard schedules.

In 2005, about 28 percent of Canadians worked nonstandard hours (Williams, 2008). For example, shift work can consist of evening or late-night work, rotating shifts (where the time of shifts changes daily, weekly, or monthly), split shifts (working part of the day in the morning and part later in the day), and irregular shifts. Although women make up only about 37 percent of full-time shift workers, almost 70 percent of part-time shift workers are women (Williams, 2008). Women are also more likely than men are to work rotating shifts, evenings and weekends, while men are more likely to work in irregular shifts. Overall, evidence suggests that nonstandard schedules have increased since 1991 (Shields, 2002).

Why do employees work nonstandard schedules? The great majority of Canadians working evening shifts—65 percent of men and 53 percent of women—say they do so because they have no choice or the hours are mandated by their employers (Shields, 2002: 17). Sixteen percent of men and 20 percent of women state they work evenings because of demands from school. Caring for family is cited by 3 percent of men and 11 percent of women (Shields, 2002), with women more than men using nonstandard schedules to balance work and family needs (Presser, 2004). Thirteen percent of men and women state they work evenings because they like it. I conclude that most employees working nonstandard schedules are doing so because of the nature of their job, not by choice.

Why should we be concerned about people working nonstandard schedules? First, a variety of health and social issues are linked to shift work. Shift workers, especially those on night and rotating shifts, are more likely to experience a disruption of the natural circadian rhythm of their bodies as sleep is disrupted (Shields, 2002). Shift workers engage in more unhealthy behaviours, such as smoking, compared with other workers. Levels of psychosocial problems, such as stress and depression, are also higher among shift workers than other workers (Shields, 2002). Shift workers can also become isolated from friends and family as their life is on a different schedule. The World Health Organization has conducted research showing that working the night shift is associated with increased risk of cancer—a finding that gives an entirely new meaning to the term "graveyard shift" (MSNBC, 2007).

Second, nonstandard work schedules create a hidden form of inequality (Presser, 2003; Shields, 2003). Workers who do not have a postsecondary degree are more likely to work nonstandard schedules. Nonstandard schedules are more common among women and men working fewer than 30 hours per week and among men working more than 40 hours per week. In the United States, black workers are more likely to work shifts compared with Hispanic and white workers. The workers most likely to work shifts are those that are already disadvantaged in the workplace—workers of colour, workers lacking higher education, and those working part-time or fewer than 40 hours per week. In Canada, shift work is more common among blue-collar and sales and service occupations than professional and clerical jobs. Those most likely to work nonstandard schedules have some of the lowest-paying jobs, working as cashiers and salespeople.

We are also seeing other changes in work arrangements. Multiple-job holding, or "moonlighting," more than quadrupled between 1976 and 2007 (Statistics Canada, 2009: 85). In 1976, more than three-quarters of multiple-job holders were men. By 2007, more than half of multiple-job holders were women. It seems that to make ends meet, an increasing number of women have to cobble together more than one part-time job. While the growth in multiple-job holders may seem alarming, it's useful to keep in mind that moonlighters represented just 5.5 percent of the paid labour force in 2007. The vast majority of Canadians continue to work at one job.

Some changes to work schedules and arrangements are more positive. Evidence suggests that many employers are providing workers with more choice and flexibility, usually under the guise of creating more "family-friendly" workplaces. In 2005, just over 34 percent of Canadians worked flexible hours. Flexible hours are most common in large firms and in the information and culture industries, business services, and retail trade and consumer industries. Flexible hours are less common in manufacturing, where individualized start and stop times are not possible. Men are more likely to report working flexible hours than women are. Some 43.5 percent of university-educated workers work flexible hours (Statistics Canada, 2009). Thus, who works how many hours and when they work those hours are part of the way that inequality is structured in the Canadian labour market.

LABOUR-MARKET SEGMENTATION

You know from your study of social stratification that people with higher education and people from upper-class families are more likely than less-advantaged people to end up in good jobs. Another factor that affects your life-chances is the structure of the labour market. Although some economists think of the labour market as a single, open competition in which people are rewarded in proportion to their education and skills (Becker, 1975), **labour-market segmentation** theory offers a different perspective. Instead of assuming that we all have an equal chance of getting good jobs, labour-market segmentation theory shows that *where*

you enter the labour market may limit your chances of getting a different, better job.

Labour-market segmentation theory emphasizes that jobs are divided according to their location in the "core" or "periphery" of the economy. A core industry is a group of companies in a relatively noncompetitive market, such as the automobile industry. Core industries tend to be capital-intensive, large, and unionized, and they tend to exert control over their environment—for example, by influencing governments to limit foreign competition. For a variety of reasons, such as the need to maintain skilled workers who can operate expensive equipment, and in response to the presence of unions, jobs in core industries tend to be stable and to offer good wages and access to benefits (Morissette, 1991).

The periphery, in contrast, is characterized by lower-tier service jobs and jobs in highly competitive markets. Firms in this sector tend to be smaller, labour-intensive, and nonunionized, and the employment they offer lacks security and pays low wages. Work is also characterized by high turnover rates, owing to product-demand fluctuations and seasonal work cycles, such as in the fisheries on the east and west coasts.

Your chance of finding a good job is determined not only by the sector of the economy you enter but also by the existence of **primary labour markets,** both external and internal to firms. Internal primary labour markets provide opportunities for advancement by providing the chance to climb up the job ladder as you gain skills and knowledge (Althauser, 1989). Secondary labour-market jobs do not offer much of a job ladder. These jobs are sometimes referred to as "dead-end jobs" because of the lack of upward mobility associated with them. Workers at McDonald's may be able to move from being on the crew to assistant manager, but unless they buy their own franchise (which is rare), that is the extent of their mobility.

Employers often create primary labour markets for some employees but not for others. In a single firm, managers can have access to mobility through an internal labour market while their clerical, production, and maintenance staff may have little room to move up. In today's service economy, employers' increasing use of temporary and part-time workers is another way in which secondary labour markets are created within companies. Increasingly, these types of secondary markets are found outside the lower-tier service industries. At Canadian universities, departments have full-time professors to do research and teach. In addition, "sessional" instructors are hired to teach one or two classes. Substantial differences exist between these two groups in terms of pay, job security, and mobility opportunities. As a full-time professor, I have a multiyear contract and may be promoted if I fulfill my job duties. My colleague, who is a part-time instructor, has no access to promotions or job security. Instead, she receives year-to-year contracts only if the department needs her to teach a specific course. Although having secondary labour-market positions gives organizations the "flexibility" to unload employees when they are not needed, it increases the insecurity of these employees and decreases their chances of getting ahead, both in their jobs and in life.

Geography also plays a role in the chances of ending up in the primary or secondary labour market. Alberta, thanks to the oil and gas industry boom, has experienced lower than average unemployment rates in recent years. The Atlantic provinces have a high proportion of seasonal jobs, such as fishing and logging, and have a higher unemployment rate than the rest of Canada does (see Figure 11.6). Even if you are a highly skilled and motivated worker, you will have more trouble finding a good job in Newfoundland and Labrador than you would in Saskatchewan because there are fewer jobs to go around. Those of us who live in urban and industrial areas are more likely to end up in a better job simply because there are more such jobs in the regional labour market (Statistics Canada, 2009).

I conclude that whether you end up in a good job or a bad job is the result of more than your individual characteristics or the occupation you choose. Your chances of landing a rewarding job depend on what sector of the economy your job is in and whether your job has an internal labour market associated with it. In the next section, I develop this idea by showing how some groups of workers find themselves stuck in job ghettos.

JOB GHETTOS AND DISADVANTAGED GROUPS

Job ghettos are parts of the labour market that prevent certain groups of workers from experiencing upward mobility. Structural barriers based on stereotypes work to keep some individuals from entering the primary labour market and the best jobs. The labelling of occupations as "female" or "male" jobs is one such example. In the health-care industry, women are still more likely to become nurses than doctors, and, as doctors, women are more likely to be found in pediatric and family medicine than the higher-paying specialties of neurology and cardiology. Chapter 7 (Gender Inequality) discusses how female job ghettos are formed through occupational sex segregation, sex typing, and other forms of discrimination.

Ethnic job ghettos exist throughout the world. For example, in Canada, between 1860 and 1960, black railway workers were restricted to sleeping-car porter jobs and were not allowed to compete for the

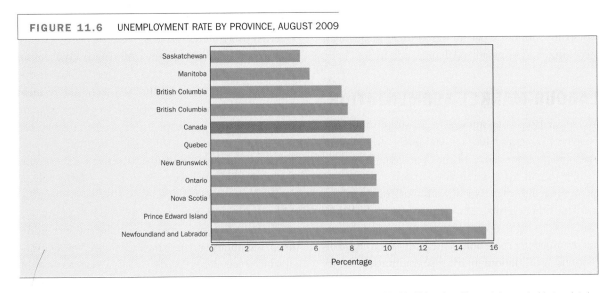

FIGURE 11.6   UNEMPLOYMENT RATE BY PROVINCE, AUGUST 2009

SOURCE: Statistics Canada, 2009, "The Latest Release from the Labour Force Survey." On the World Wide Web at http://www.statcan.ca/subjects-sujets/labour-travail/fs-epa/fs/epa-eng.htm (September 21, 2009).

Geography affects a person's chance of finding work. For example, it is more difficult to find a good job in Atlantic Canada than in Saskatchewan.
SOURCE: David Blackwood, *For Edgar Glover: The Splitting Table Etching*, 1999. Courtesy The Edward Day Gallery.

higher-paid jobs of sleeping-car conductor and dining-car steward (Calliste, 1993). Today, employer prejudice can keep qualified minorities from being hired. Since many visible minorities are also recent

Although most Canadian women in the paid labour force are seg-regated in jobs traditionally dominated by women, they are making advances in traditionally male-dominated jobs.
SOURCE: © iStockphoto.com/Lisa F. Young.

immigrants, their ability to move into better jobs is constrained by this dual status, unless they are entre-preneurs. Often, employers will request "Canadian work experience" before hiring white-collar workers. Some professional occupations, like doctor and vet-erinarian, require additional training for professionals emigrating from certain countries. Highly educated members of visible minorities in these situations may find themselves forced to take low-level service jobs, such as taxi driver or restaurant worker. (For more on this topic, see Chapter 8, Race and Ethnic Relations).

People with disabilities face barriers to good jobs because of the inaccessibility of education and work-places. In 2000, only 45 percent of men and 39 per-cent of women with disabilities were employed, compared with 79 percent of men and 69 percent of women without disabilities (Statistics Canada, 2004b). Lack of financial resources to attend school, inflexible workplace schedules, and lack of employers' commitment to hiring workers with disabilities are some of the reasons people with disabilities have trouble getting good jobs. Jamie Hunter, a 29-year-old with minimal control over his limbs because of a diving accident, experiences these barriers first-hand. Speaking about looking for work, he states,

I recall one fellow, from the personnel depart-ment of a major corporation, who was so uncomfortable he couldn't even bring himself to take me to his office. So we sat in the lobby and he read me back my resume. "You're Jamie Hunter? You graduated from York University? You worked for a summer at Ontario Hydro?" Then he said thanks and left. That was it. The interview was over and I never heard from him again. (quoted in McKay, 1993: 170)

Hiring workers who have disabilities is not as costly as some employers believe. Only a fifth of people with disabilities require changes to the physical accommodations of workplaces (Shain, 1995). Until more employers make the effort to hire people with disabilities, these workers will continue to face barriers to good jobs.

Aboriginal people face formidable barriers in their search for employment. Living in remote areas limits both their job opportunities and their access to education and work training. Even when Aboriginals move to areas where jobs are more readily available, they often lack crucial work experience. Aboriginal workers are especially vulnerable to the "bad-work syndrome" (Krahn and Lowe, 1998). Having access only to low-skill and part-time work gives individuals a spotty work history. They are then caught in a cycle where one low-skill job leads to another. For many, the "bad-work syndrome" makes it impossible to get better jobs.

Finally, the *youngest and oldest workers* may find themselves trapped in job ghettos based on age. Some employers view young workers as less serious and less interested in full-time jobs than more mature workers. Because of downsizing and early retirement incentives, older workers may find themselves out of a job before they are ready to stop working. Access to better jobs is also limited by the prejudices of employers, who tend to view older workers as less productive and more resistant to new work methods. As the population of older Canadians grows, it is increasingly difficult to ignore the effects of age discrimination.

Labour-market segmentation creates areas of better and worse jobs in the labour market. Although we would like to think that we all have an equal chance of getting good jobs, research shows that some groups of workers may be trapped in bad jobs. Moreover, as I show next, some workers are able to protect their good jobs through the labour-market shelters of professional occupations and unions.

PROFESSIONS

The occupations of doctor, lawyer, and other professions are some of the most desirable jobs in the labour

market. High pay, autonomy, and respect from the outside community are some of the advantages bestowed on members of professional occupations. Many of us consider these occupations to be different from other occupations. This special status has caught the attention of sociologists.

Early studies of professions attempted to delineate their general characteristics. First, all professional occupations control a unique body of knowledge. Second, professional occupations are autonomous. Third, professionals generally have authority over their clients and subordinates because of the special knowledge they possess. Finally, professional occupations are supposed to be altruistic because of their focus on helping clients.

Many sociologists believe that this description of professionals is an "idealized model that imperfectly describes reality" (Hodson and Sullivan, 1990: 266) and that it provides only a checklist for determining which occupations are more or less professional. Overlooked by this approach is how certain occupations became professions in the first place. To address this issue, we need to consider power and the contested nature of professions. Doing so will uncover how professions act as **labour-market shelters,** protecting their members' access to good jobs.

Doctors, dentists, and lawyers were not always considered professionals. Which occupations are viewed as legitimate professions changes historically. For example, few dentists as we know them today lived in Ontario in the nineteenth century. Many different occupations provided dental services. Itinerant "tramp dentists" travelled from town to town servicing most Ontarians. If citizens needed teeth pulled or false teeth constructed, they could go to their local blacksmith or gunsmith. When a patient came to visit, the blacksmith would "leave the forge, wipe his hands on his apron, get the old turnkey wrench, and his brawny arm would soon draw not only the sufferer's tooth, but often the screaming patient himself from the old kitchen chair" (Wood, 1989: 266, quoted in Adams, 2000: 22).

To get to where they are today, dentists, like people in other occupations, engaged in a *process* of professionalization, which involved establishing professional dominance and securing legitimacy from the public (Friedson, 1970; Pescosolido, Tuch, and Martin, 2001: 3). Professional dominance occurs when the government acknowledges an occupation's knowledge claims and expertise, and then grants an occupation the right to be the only (or one of a few) types of practitioners allowed to apply this body of knowledge. Professions also require public approval. If the public refuses to follow the instructions of members of the profession or views them as illegitimate or just one among many types of experts, then the profession will have difficulty establishing its authority.

Sometimes, battles between different professions erupt, with each profession claiming expertise over the same "turf" (Friedson, 1970). For example, until recently, only doctors had the authority to deliver babies in Canada. Doctors maintained their authority because of their monopoly over relevant knowledge. They used their national association to lobby provincial and federal governments to deny others the right to deliver babies. However, the public and other health-care practitioners questioned whether doctors ought to be the only legitimate deliverers of babies. In recent decades, because of public demand for access to midwives and the development of professional midwifery schools, doctors have lost some control over the birthing process and have lost their monopoly over this body of professional knowledge.

Some occupations are continually striving for professional status. "Semi-professions" are occupations that have only some characteristics of a profession (Hodson and Sullivan, 1990). Examples include nurses, engineers, accountants, pharmacists, and teachers. Although we may call these occupations "professions" in our everyday use of the term, the sociological definition of professions requires us to view them as semi-professions. Often, semi-professions do not have full control over their body of knowledge, or their autonomy may be constrained by a more powerful profession, as is the case with nurses. Furthermore, female-dominated semi-professions, such as teachers and librarians, face additional barriers to professionalization because of occupational sex segregation.

Third parties, such as the government, can threaten professional power by intervening in the decisions of professional organizations. We become most aware of such threats when the government pays for part or all of the services received by clients, as is the case for the Canadian health-care system. During the summer and fall of 1996, doctors in Ontario fought the provincial government over who had the right to decide where doctors work. Doctors wanted to maintain their professional autonomy to work and live where they choose, while the Ministry of Health believed it had the right to force doctors to work in underserviced areas. Some doctors did not accept new patients to protest what they saw as government interference with their autonomy. They made some gains in terms of their salaries and partly satisfied the government's demand for more doctors to work in northern areas of the province. How this battle continues to play out will determine who is the legitimate authority over doctors—their own profession or the provincial government of Ontario.

UNIONS

Like professions and their associations, unions also attempt to attain or maintain good jobs for their members. Workers have organized unions to gain respect, increase wages, reduce working hours, and gain more control over their working day. In fact, the presence of unions has helped all of us. Without union efforts, we would not have such things as the eight-hour workday, child-labour laws, and occupational health and safety standards. I return to the state of unions in Canada and the role they play in the Canadian labour market when I discuss alienation later in this chapter.

Unions and professional associations are alike in a number of respects. They both shelter members from loss of jobs, pay cuts, and other employment-related risks. Legislation that mandates the hiring of union workers, such as exists on some construction sites, protects the jobs of union members. Likewise, when the professional association of lawyers restricts access to law school and the number of new lawyers, they too are protecting the jobs and incomes of existing members. Groups of workers who organize—whether it is a local union of flight attendants or a national association of doctors—increase their ability to maintain their good jobs.

TECHNOLOGY

The use of technology has long been a part of the employer–employee relationship. One of the most famous technologies, the assembly line, was used to control the pace of work (Edwards, 1979). In today's service economy, managers are more likely to invest in computers and information technology than other forms of work reorganization to improve their firms' productivity and efficiency (Osterman, 1995). Computerized office systems can reduce the time-consuming work of filing. Robots can do heavy and dangerous work. Advanced telecommunications systems make the globalization of work possible.

No longer does geography limit the search for inexpensive labour or market expansion. Today, many companies have factories in Asia and product-development labs in the United States.

When employers introduce new technology in the workplace, skills are upgraded *and* downgraded. People must be trained to repair robots and maintain computer networks, but technology also simplifies some jobs, replaces workers, and allows work to be shifted to regions where labour is inexpensive. In recent decades, work in call centres grew quickly in bilingual, low-wage Moncton, New Brunswick, but growth slowed when call centres in even lower-wage India came online.

At Dofasco in Hamilton, computers helped to reduce the workforce from 12 500 to 7000 in the 1990s (Campbell, 1996). Automated banking machines have sharply reduced the number of tellers in banks while creating a small number of jobs for those who repair and maintain these machines (Burman, 1997). Air Canada used computer and telecommunications technology to contract out the work of full-time Air Canada sales and service workers to private travel agency employees. This strategy had the effect of changing the "good" jobs at Air Canada into insecure "bad" jobs (Shalla, 2002). These examples show the variety of ways that computer and telecommunications technology can affect employment. New technologies often create a small number of skilled jobs but degrade or eliminate a larger number of jobs.

Although technology is changing the face of work, it does not mean that we have no control over what happens. Various social and technological factors affect the way new technologies are implemented (Wallace, 1989). For example, much depends on the outcomes management wants, the type of technology that companies can afford, and whether unions and workers have a say in technological change (Shalla, 2002). According to Shoshana Zuboff (1988), management can design computer-based jobs either to increase or decrease the need for workers to use knowledge and judgment on the job. In her analysis of health insurance workers, she provides examples of job enhancement, where managers gave workers the opportunity to use computers in complex ways. However, she also found that if management was interested only in productivity and efficiency, technology had detrimental effects on the quality of work. For example, one office she studied used computers to automate and speed up the work of clerks. Any decisions that clerks formerly made about their work were programmed into the computer. (See Box 11.1.) Yet management did not go as far as they could in terms of automating work. As one manager acknowledged, the company realized it couldn't remove all variety from tasks because "there's a limit to how boring you can make a job if you want even reasonably capable people" (Zuboff, 1988: 134). This example shows that management can choose to implement technology in a way that either enhances work or downgrades it.

BUREAUCRACIES AND WORK ORGANIZATIONS

We live and work in a bureaucratic society. According to Max Weber, bureaucracies are the most efficient and rational type of organization that people have created. In bureaucracies, written rules provide guidelines for handling routine situations. A complex division of labour ensures that workers know what is required of them and helps to identify who is responsible when something goes wrong. Weber also saw bureaucracies as a mechanism for overcoming arbitrary decisions and corruption. For example, by having written rules about how decisions should be made and having a hierarchy of authority that clarifies who makes decisions, it is less likely that decision makers can decide to hire someone out of loyalty or obligation. Yet Weber was the first to admit that bureaucracies are not without their problems. Referring to bureaucracies as "the iron cage of the future," Weber was concerned about the potential for

New technologies require job retraining, even for middle-aged and older workers.

SOURCE: © iStockphoto.com/Chris Schmidt.

BOX 11.1   HOW TECHNOLOGY CAN CHANGE THE WORKPLACE

What can computer technology do to the quality of work life? In her study of technological change, Shoshana Zuboff (1988) asked office workers to draw pictures that "represented their 'felt sense' about their job experience before and after the conversion to the new computer system" that automated and standardized work. Below are two workers' views of how their work experience changed. Note the shifts in facial expressions and the loss of mobility. Even the flower on the benefit analyst's desk has wilted. As one office manager said about work after the conversion, "The system controls the transfer assistants in some ways because it ties them to the desk. It forces them to do the input and to really be tied to the machine. It forces control in terms of physically having to just be there."

TRANSFER ASSISTANT

Before

BENEFIT ANALYST

Before

After

After

"Before, I was able to get up and hand things to people without having someone say, what are you doing? Now, I feel like I am with my head down, doing my work."

"My supervisor is frowning because we shouldn't be talking. I have on the stripes of a convict. It's all true. It feels like a prison in here."

SOURCE: Adapted from *In the Age of the Smart Machine: The Future of Work and Power* by Shoshana Zuboff. Copyright © 1988 by Basic Books, Inc. Reprinted by permission of Basic Books, a member of Perseus Books, L.L.C.

bureaucracies to limit creativity and initiative (Hodson and Sullivan, 1990: 184). Bureaucracies also can be rigid, tied down by "red tape," and lead to communication problems between managers and workers (Jones, 1996).

Weber believed that increased bureaucratization was the fate of modern society. Building on Weber, sociologist George Ritzer (1993) argues that society is now undergoing a new kind of rationalization process that he calls "McDonaldization." Today, writes Ritzer, the fast-food restaurant has surpassed bureaucracy as the organizational ideal. This means that our workplace, schools, leisure activities, and culture are taking on the characteristics of the fast-food restaurant.

There are four components to McDonaldization:

1. Creating the most *efficient* way to accomplish a task.
2. Emphasizing things that can be *calculated*.

3. Creating a *predictable* product and experience.
4. Setting up systems of *control* to standardize the work of employees (Ritzer, 1993: 9–12).

Consider how one might apply Ritzer's ideas to universities. Ritzer would criticize the textbook that you are reading as part of the drive for increased efficiency, predictability, and standardization. Chapters are written by experts in each area. Instead of one author taking years to learn all of sociology, the book can be produced quicker because, presumably, each expert knows his or her area inside-out (Ritzer, 1993: 57). On the other side, you could also argue that chapters are actually better because they are written by experts. If you are like my students at the University of Toronto, your introductory sociology class is probably a large class that uses multiple-choice exams. Gone are the days of inefficient and unpredictable one-on-one examinations of students and, in many places, essay exams (Ritzer, 1993: 55). Multiple-choice exams take less time to mark compared with other ways of testing student's knowledge. I would be doing my colleagues who are teaching you a disservice if I said that the only value of multiple-choice exams is their efficiency over other testing methods; evidence shows that a well-written multiple-choice exam does a good job of capturing student's knowledge. Still, Ritzer's thesis is correct in that as universities have increased in size, faculty have been pushed to look for ways to increase the efficiency and the predictability of what they produce. This mimics some of the trends in the fast-food industry. Standardizing textbooks and exams are just two examples. If you look at other aspects of society, you will see other examples, such as vacationers who travel to other countries and stay at places like Sandals and Club Med, which offer a standard resort experience with little regard for the local culture.

If you look around at the organizations that touch your life, you will see evidence that Weber and Ritzer are correct. However, bureaucratic structure is not enough to ensure that organizations achieve their goals. As I discuss in the following section, management has also been developing strategies to organize how work is done by their employees.

MANAGERIAL STRATEGIES FOR ORGANIZING WORK

Over the past century, several approaches to organizing work in bureaucracies have come and gone.

Some have endured (Braverman, 1974). Although early strategies were geared toward removing the need for workers to think on the job, more recent strategies have paid more attention to the ability and desire of workers to participate in workplace decisions. Whether these strategies offer real participation is a question to keep in mind as you read the following sections.

Taylorism

Frederick Taylor, an American industrial engineer, was the founder of scientific management or **Taylorism**. Originating in the 1890s, scientific management was an attempt by management to regain direct control of the labour process. Based on his own experience in factories, Taylor discovered that workers knew more than their managers about the work processes. As long as that was the case, workers could control how fast they worked and how much they produced. To shift control back to management, Taylor recommended a detailed division of labour that broke complex tasks into several subtasks. To do this, management needed to learn how workers did their jobs and then convert this knowledge into formal procedures. Using time and motion studies, managers documented the exact movements of workers and the length of time required to complete the task. Taylor also believed that conceptual work should be separated from the execution of tasks. It was management's job to design work procedures and the workers' job to follow those procedures. By breaking jobs into their smallest components and removing the need for workers to think, Taylorism opened the door for management to reduce its reliance on skilled labour. Cheaper, unskilled workers could now be hired to perform simplified tasks. Managers and intellectuals worldwide, including the Russian communist leader Lenin, hailed Taylor as a pioneer in the rationalization of work.

Fordism is often discussed in relation to Taylorism. **Fordism** refers to the bureaucratically organized mass production of standardized goods by assembly-line methods. Although Henry Ford was not the first to use assembly-line technology, he was one of the most successful at using it to change the way things were made. Ford used assembly-line technology to implement many of the principles of Taylorism. This allowed him to create a division of labour in which workers stood in one place on the assembly line to do their assigned job and produce large numbers of standardized products.

Taylorism is not limited to factory work. Lowe (1987) shows how Taylorist principles rationalized office work in early twentieth-century Canada. And Taylorism is still around in many service industry jobs. Making hamburgers in a fast-food restaurant is broken down into minute tasks, and telephone reservation agents for airlines are given scripts to follow when dealing with clients. But today, as in the past, workers complain about the limited opportunities for creativity and self-fulfilment when working under scientific management.

Human Relations

One shortcoming of Taylorism is its assumption that workers are motivated only by desire for their paycheques (Bendix, 1974; Jones, 1996). In reaction to this simplistic view, the **human relations school of management** pushed management to rethink the Taylorist image of workers by showing the importance of the social aspects of work. Based on a series of experiments at the Western Electric Company's Hawthorne plant in Chicago, Elton Mayo and others found that friendly supervision and attention to the social environment increased workers' cooperation and productivity. The "Hawthorne studies" started the movement to consider how employers can fulfill employees' social needs, increase their satisfaction, and make them feel better about their jobs.

Although the validity of the Hawthorne studies has been called into question (Carey, 1967), most researchers agree that management strategies today still incorporate and build on elements of the human relations school. From suggestion boxes to workplace participation programs, organizations are trying to find the right "human touch" to decrease worker resistance and increase productivity.

Recent "Humanization" of Work and Worker Participation

During the 1970s, management efforts to "humanize" workplaces gave rise to quality-control circles, quality-of-work-life programs, and other forms of workplace participation. Management introduced some of these strategies to diminish worker resistance and boost profits (Rinehart, 1996). Unlike worker cooperatives and worker ownership, though, participation schemes implemented by management are not true examples of workplace democracy.

As their name implies, quality-control (QC) circles emphasize the need to improve production quality.

QC circles involve a small number of employees working with a team leader or supervisor. Together, these labour-management teams brainstorm about how to solve production problems. Quality-of-work-life (QWL) programs are broader in scope than QC circles. Management promotes QWL programs as democratizing the workplace, by giving workers more responsibility and control over their work through self-regulating work teams and by providing more complex jobs for workers. Although both QC circles and QWL programs make reference to worker participation, the decision-making authority of workers is usually limited to improving individual work tasks or improving the atmosphere at work. Workers are left out of decisions about "what is to be produced, investments, distribution of profits, technology, size of the work force or plant closings" (Rinehart, 1996: 169).

In the 1990s, such concepts as total quality management (TQM), Japanese management, lean production, and "just-in-time" production were promoted as the panacea for the productivity and quality problems of management. These programs emphasize quality control through communication and teamwork between management and workers. The rhetoric surrounding these programs continues to promote the potential for democratizing workplaces and increasing worker participation.

Many North American manufacturing companies, like Saturn in Tennessee, CAMI in Ingersoll, Ontario, and Subaru-Isuzu in Lafeyette, Indiana, were part of the movement to **Japanese production techniques (JPT)**. Initial reactions to these Japanese transplants and joint operations were positive. "Just-in-time" production cut costs as companies reduced their parts inventories and the need for warehouses. The use of participatory work teams led some academics and industry experts to consider JPT a valuable new way of organizing work (Womack, Jones, and Roos, 1990). They saw Japanese production as a better alternative than Taylorism and Fordism, enhancing workers' skills and participation, and promoting the use of workers' mental capacities in conjunction with their physical labour. Many observers believe that companies using JPT represent a new era in labour-management relations.

However, a growing body of research from both the United States and Canada suggests that JPT is actually an extension of Taylorism and assembly-line production (Dassbach, 1996; Robertson et al., 1993). Even though work is subdivided into teams, scientific management is apparent insofar as jobs are still broken down into small tasks. For example, instructions for the first few tasks of a welding shop job at the CAMI plant read as follows: "A) Press the cycle stop button to release the locking pin from the tray; B) Remove empty parts tray and roll over to parts bin; C) Load parts from bin into tray, using 2 hands, lifting approximately 10 parts at a time" (Robertson et al., 1993). This is followed by six or seven more detailed instructions. When the list is completed, another car has moved in front of the worker and the cycle starts all over again. Although JPT does involve some job rotation, it is usually between two similar jobs or it is instituted simply to reduce repetitive strain injuries. Also, as in traditional plants, managers and the computerized assembly-line technology, not the workers, set the speed of the line and the pace of work.

Just as the service industry incorporated Taylorism, we now see the use of JPT and total quality management in service industries. Hotel chains, grocery stores, and airlines now utilize JPT strategies. Often these programs come with names like "service excellence." Most of these programs focus on improving customer service and may allow employees some discretion in dealing with customer complaints. For example, as part of a program to increase sensitivity to individual customers, one grocery store in England encourages staff to accompany customers to products rather than just give directions and to send flowers to customers in the event of a service lapse (Rosenthal, Hill, and Peccei, 1997). Employees are given greater discretion in the hope that this will lead to improved service. How successful these programs are for improving service and increasing employee empowerment remains to be seen.

Workers are beginning to question whether these new management techniques represent increased worker participation. A statement by a local union official at the Ingersoll, Ontario, CAMI plant sums things up nicely: "This empowerment, when it's cost saving or quality problem, okay, but when it's human problems, a comfort issue, whatever, there's no empowerment. It's one sided. That's the bottom line" (quoted in Rinehart, Robertson, Huxley, and Wareham, 1994: 166).

Results from the service industry are mixed. Some evidence shows that employee empowerment schemes can increase the development of workers' interpersonal and problem-solving skills because employees have to deal with customers' problems and requests (Smith, 2001). As one employee of a copier service states, "[before the employee involvement program] I used to say [to customers] 'Here's your copies, now get out of here.' Now I have to make sure I'm communicating, *to understand their needs*. . . . I'm trying to have more sensitivity to their needs" (Smith, 2001: 44). Whether or not these strategies will lead to increased empowerment on the part of workers depends on management's attitude. As we saw in the section on technology, how management implements changes affects their outcomes. As long as these programs continue to be linked solely to management's desire for productivity increases and "the bottom line," their participatory potential will be limited. Alternatives, such as worker-owned companies, may bring us closer to real worker participation (Livingstone, 1993).

"WILL I LIKE MY JOB?" JOB SATISFACTION AND ALIENATION

The service revolution has changed the structure of work in Canada and across the world. There are more part-time jobs and increased use of computer surveillance, as well as some increases in knowledge-based jobs. Given these changes, how do Canadians feel about their jobs? According to a 2001 survey, 93 percent of Canadians reported they were satisfied with their jobs (McKenzie, 2001). Surveys show that getting respect from their bosses and feeling in control of their job mattered most to Canadian workers. Less important was the amount of money they made (see Figure 11.7). This reflects much of what we know about job satisfaction. To be satisfied at work, intrinsic rewards, such as autonomy and challenging work, are at least as important as extrinsic or material rewards (see Box 11.2).

Are 93 percent of Canadians *really* satisfied with their jobs? What do sociologists mean by **job satisfaction**? These are important questions. Job satisfaction is usually determined by a survey question, such as "How satisfied are you with your job?" In many ways the responses to job satisfaction questions are similar to replies to the question "How are you today?" (Krahn and Lowe, 1998: 408). Most of us would answer "fine" to such a general question. Similarly, many workers respond that they like their jobs when asked how satisfied they are. Some analysts believe, however, that most workers do not want to admit that they do not like their jobs.

One solution to this problem is to use more specific job satisfaction measures, especially measures that refer to behaviours or behavioural intentions (e.g., Hodson, 1991; Rinehart, 1978). For example, the 2001 survey found that 22 percent of Canadians

FIGURE 11.7   WHAT CANADIANS SAY IS VERY IMPORTANT IN A JOB

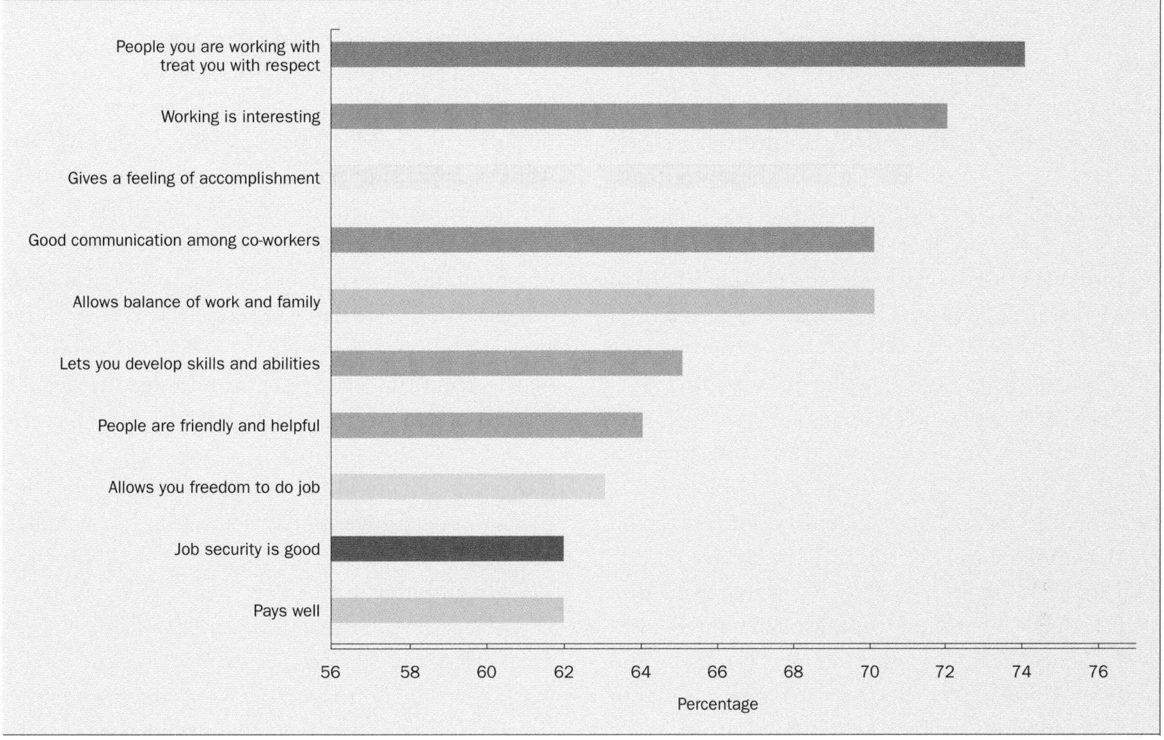

SOURCE: Canadian Policy Research Networks, 2006, "It's More than the Money—What Canadians Want in a Job." On the World Wide Web at http://www.jobquality.ca/indicator_e/rew001.stm (March 9, 2006). Reprinted by permission of Canadian Policy Research Network.

BOX 11.2   WHY EXECUTIVES QUIT: CHALLENGE, NOT MONEY

Executives are much more likely to leave a job for a greater challenge than for a bigger salary, an international survey . . . found. Lack of challenges or career growth was the reason that 33 percent of respondents changed jobs, according to the study by recruiter Korn/Ferry International, which included answers from 2000 people in 80 countries.

Ineffective leadership drove another 20 percent from their jobs, and 17 percent moved to a better job in the same field. Just 5 percent said the reason for leaving was inadequate or inconsistent compensation. Of the rest, 15 percent left involuntarily, 7 percent moved to a completely different field and 4 percent cited lack of recognition for their contributions.

The findings show that companies looking to retain top talent can get the biggest results from placing more emphasis on identifying and developing top performers, said Jack MacPhail, managing director for leadership development solutions at Korn/Ferry.

SOURCE: Wallace Immen, 2006, "Why Executives Quit: Challenge, Not Money." *The Globe and Mail* 3 March. Reprinted with permission of the Globe and Mail.

interviewed said they planned to change their job in the near future (Canadian Press/Leger Marketing, 2001). When we discuss alienation, we will look more closely at workers' behaviours to understand workers' negative reactions to their job. For now, we'll spend a bit more time on job satisfaction. Even though it is a problematic measure, it is still used by management to gauge how happy and productive their workers are.

WHAT DETERMINES JOB SATISFACTION?

A multitude of factors affect how we feel about our jobs, ranging from our individual characteristics to the size of the firm we work in. To give you an idea of this range, I'll discuss some of the major predictors of job satisfaction.

Individual Characteristics

Based on what we know about job ghettos, it might be a safe bet to predict that women, older workers, and younger workers will be some of the least satisfied groups of workers. Although it is true that younger workers are some of the most dissatisfied workers (see Table 11.1), older workers—at least those who have stable jobs—are actually a relatively happy group (Krahn, 1992). The higher job satisfaction reported by older employed workers may be the result of reduced expectations about work, more meaningful lives outside of work, or past advancement in jobs (Krahn and Lowe, 1998).

When you consider occupational sex segregation and the differences in jobs held by women and men, you might expect women to be less satisfied than men. In most studies, though, women and men report similar levels of job satisfaction (see Table 11.1 and Krahn, 1992). However, when evaluating their feelings about their work, women tend to compare themselves with other women (Hodson and Sullivan, 1990). If women compared themselves with men, their reported level of satisfaction might be lower.

Job and Organizational Characteristics

Opportunities for autonomous and complex work are important predictors of job satisfaction: Satisfaction increases with autonomy and decreases with repetitive or automated work. For example, fast-food workers who repeat the same phrases every day and autoworkers who must do the same task repeatedly are less likely to be satisfied than people who do more creative work. Opportunities for participation and decision making can increase satisfaction. Workers at the CAMI plant in Ingersoll, Ontario, were initially excited about Japanese management. But when the promise of participation faded, workers' negative feelings increased (Robertson et al., 1993). What occupation we are in also affects job satisfaction. Figure 11.8 shows that people employed in social science, government, education, and religion occupations are the most satisfied.

Organizational structure, such as technology and firm size, affect how happy we are at work. Blauner's (1964) classic study *Alienation and Freedom* shows how workers' alienation increased as technology shifted from craftwork to machine tending and assembly-line work. In contrast, technology that requires the use of conceptual skills increases job satisfaction.

Employees in small companies experience a relatively high level of satisfaction. In 2000, 30 percent of Canadians who worked in very small companies were very satisfied, compared with 23 percent who worked in small companies and 18 percent who worked in medium-sized companies (see Table 11.1). As company size increases, so do workers' feelings of isolation and powerlessness. However, large companies offer benefits and opportunities that boost job satisfaction almost to the level found in very small companies.

When I consider all the individual, job, and organizational factors that influence job satisfaction, I am struck by the realization that much of our satisfaction at work is determined by things over which we have little or no control. Our employers determine how much we are paid and how challenging and autonomous our jobs will be. And the chance to work in a small, locally owned company or a large national or multinational corporation has much to do with the employment opportunities where we live.

ALIENATION

If job satisfaction focuses on the individual worker's feelings about his or her job, alienation is linked to

TABLE 11.1 JOB SATISFACTION OF CANADIANS, 2000

EMPLOYEE CHARACTERISTICS	PERCENTAGE WHO ARE "VERY SATISFIED" WITH THEIR JOB
All Canadians	28
Size of company	
Very small	30
Small	23
Medium	18
Large	26
Age	
18–25	22
26–45	26
45+	33
Gender	
Women	29
Men	27
Employment status	
Full-time	25
Self-employed	43

SOURCE: Canadian Policy Research Networks, 2006, "Job Satisfaction." On the World Wide Web at http://www.jobquality.ca/indicator_e/rew002.stm (March 9, 2006). Reprinted by permission of Canadian Policy Network.

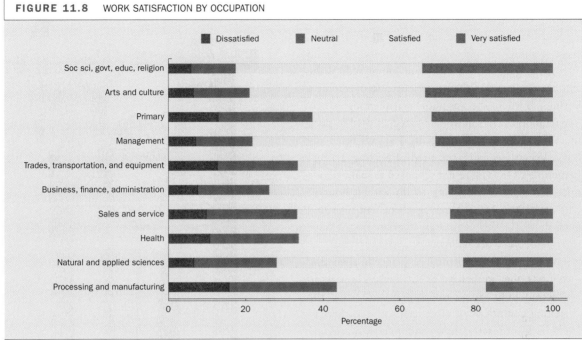

FIGURE 11.8   WORK SATISFACTION BY OCCUPATION

SOURCE: Canadian Policy Research Networks, 2006, "Satisfaction Most Common in Social Sciences, Arts/Culture and Management Occupations." On the World Wide Web at http://www.jobquality.ca/indicator_e/rew002_1.stm#2 (9 March 2006). Reprinted with permission.

the lack of control or powerlessness an individual experiences in relation to his or her job. Originating in the work of Karl Marx, the concept of **alienation** examines how the structural conditions of work lead to workers' lack of power over their work and lives (Rinehart, 1996). For Marx, alienation is an "objective condition" that stems from capitalism. Marx argued that capitalism robs workers of control over the means of production and the products of their labour and puts control in the hands of owners.

According to Marx, alienation of workers under capitalism has four sources:

1. Workers are alienated from the products they produce. They do not own them, and they have no say over how they will be used. Rather, under capitalism, work is a means to an end—work provides a paycheque so workers can buy things they need, but workers no longer directly produce what they need.

2. Workers do not control the process of production. The advanced division of labour is indicative of this condition. Decisions about how fast to work, the order in which to complete tasks, and the use of equipment are made by someone other than workers. Workers lose control over their daily work activity.

3. Workers are alienated from engaging in creative activity and thus from themselves.

4. Workers are alienated from others as they have fewer opportunities to talk and connect with co-workers. Also, work is not a collective process that can help the whole community. Overall, the division of labour under capitalism physically and emotionally isolates workers from one another.

Recently, some sociologists have conceptualized alienation as a way to think about how workers' psychological and emotional states are linked to the organization of work (Rogers, 1995). For example, when work is repetitive and does not allow for interaction between co-workers, workers may experience a high level of alienation. Some sociologists conceptualize alienation as a subjective state that arises from the reality of capitalist working conditions. Here the emphasis is on workers' feelings of powerlessness and lack of control or connection to their work and fellow employees.

Fighting Alienation: Individual and Collective Responses to Work

To understand alienation, we also need to look at how workers resist it (Schmitt and Moody, 1994). This can shed light on their negative feelings toward work.

When a worker engages in sabotage or repeatedly skips work, management may define the worker as destructive or lazy. Yet, in the minds of workers, these seemingly insubordinate behaviours may be an attempt to gain control over their job or reduce the amount of alienation they experience. To overcome a boring job where she was not assigned enough work, one temporary clerical worker stated, "I used to sleep there. Yes there's nothing to do. I always bring my book. When I get sick and tired of reading, I sleep. Sometimes, OK, you're not supposed to make phone calls, but what am I going to do with 8 hours?" (Rogers, 1995: 157). If management had provided enough work, this temporary worker might have exhibited good work habits.

When viewed as potential resistance to alienating conditions, the "misbehaviour" of workers appears in a different light. Some researchers argue that the alienating conditions of work lead some workers to "fight back" or react to these conditions (Edwards and Scullion, 1982; Rinehart, 1996). You may have had similar reactions to work, such as slacking off if you believed your supervisor required you to work too hard, or turning your work into a game to make the time go faster. Engaging in these behaviours does not mean you are lazy or incompetent. Rather, they are typical reactions to alienating work.

To cope with poor working conditions, some workers quit their jobs. Those who cannot quit may respond passively by socializing with co-workers, playing games, or reducing their productivity (Burawoy, 1979). Management often devises strategies to prevent these types of behaviours. For example, Taylorism was motivated in part by management's desire to reduce opportunities for workers to restrict their output.

For management, theft and destruction of company property is a particularly bothersome behaviour. But these criminal acts may be motivated by poor working conditions. A few years ago, an undergraduate student in my class confessed that, while working in a small T-shirt design factory, she purposely poked holes in some shirts. Because management had a policy of giving damaged T-shirts to employees, you might think she did this only to take advantage of her situation. As it turns out, though, employees were paid low wages and worked under conditions of extreme heat. This student saw her behaviour as a protest against the inadequate pay and difficult working conditions. Other workers engage in sabotage to gain concessions from management or to gain control over

Workers often resist alienating work conditions. Forms of resistance include striking, being absent, quitting, slacking off, and committing industrial sabotage.
SOURCE: Juan Manuel Sanchez. Courtesy of Nora Patrich and Joan Sanchez.

the work process. Factory workers may damage the assembly line to slow down the pace of work, or clerical workers may hide files to reduce their workload (Hodson and Sullivan, 1990; Rinehart, 1996).

Do these individual acts of resistance change the amount of alienation workers experience? The answer to this question is complex. Many sociologists, beginning with Marx, illustrate how alienation is a condition of objective powerlessness that exists regardless of whether workers themselves consciously recognize it. Some workers become aware or conscious of the alienating conditions they experience at work. As predicted by Marx, these workers may respond to these conditions by forming unions, going on strike, or engaging in revolutionary behaviour focused on overthrowing capitalism. However, most workers do not develop "class-consciousness." Sociologists Harvey Krahn and Graham Lowe state, "In the absence of a well-defined alternative to the current economic system, we would not expect most workers to be able to clearly articulate their alienation and act on it. Apathy, or an attempt to forget about work as soon as one leaves it behind, are the common responses of many workers to a situation in which there is no viable alternative" (1998: 419).

This means that hiding files or poking holes in a shirt may make the worker feel better and thus make it possible to get through the day. These types of activities may reduce the subjective feeling of alienation: Workers may feel less powerless or may feel they have more control over their working conditions. But these types of individual strategies do not change the structural conditions of work. Collective responses to workplace conditions are more likely to lead to lasting changes in how work is organized. These collective responses, such as forming a union, may not "overthrow" the economic system, but they can improve working conditions. Although playing games and stealing may momentarily increase workers' feelings of control over their jobs, most researchers agree that, for lasting change to occur, collective responses are needed. Chapter 18 provides more details about the role of strikes in the Canadian labour movement's struggle for economic and social rights.

Unions play an important role in facilitating collective action by workers. Today, 30 percent of the non-agricultural paid labour force are in unions. Compared with the experience in some other countries, such as the United States and Australia, **union density,** or the percentage of non-agricultural paid workers who are unionized, has not significantly declined in Canada over the past 30 years (Adams and Welsh, 2008). Over the past 150 years, the characteristics of unionized workers have shifted, however. During the late nineteenth century, craft workers organized; during the 1930s and 1940s, workers in the goods-producing sectors followed suit. Public-sector workers began to organize in the 1960s and 1970s. In 2003, public-sector industries had the highest rates of unionization (Statistics Canada, 2004a). Some union

supporters warn that union density will stagnate if union organizing does not expand to cover new groups of workers, particularly young workers in service industries (White, 1993). From McDonald's workers in Newfoundland and Labrador to Starbucks employees in British Columbia, we should expect to see more union drives in the service industries.

Service workers are not the only area of potential growth for unions. Over the past 30 years, the number of women in unions has increased. In 1977, women accounted for 12 percent of all union membership. In 2003, women made up 48 percent of union membership (Statistics Canada, 2004b). Part of this increase is due to the movement of women into the increasingly unionized public-service sector and some unionized male-dominated work, such as construction. Unions also have worked hard to show that they are relevant to women's working issues, including daycare, family leave, and sexual harassment.

Whether the number of unionized workers in Canada will grow or decline depends on how unions deal with changes in the labour market and the economy. The rise of nonstandard work and the ease with which companies can move their businesses to other countries raise serious challenges to unions.

FINDING WORK

One of the buzzwords of twenty-first-century job seekers is "networking." Networking is sometimes referred to as the "art of talking to as many people as you can without directly asking them for a job" (*New York Times*, quoted in Flap and Boxman, 2001: 159). Potential job applicants are often advised to "network, network, network" (Ehrenreich, 2005; see Box 11.3).

BOX 11.3 **LOOKING FOR WORK IN THE INFORMATION AGE**

Workopolis, Monster.com, Canjobs.com: these are all examples of internet job search sites available to all those looking for work. But does the proliferation of internet job search sites (and all the advice they provide) really make a difference? Or are they merely the old newspaper classified job ads wrapped up in a new technological package? In her book on the experiences of the white collar unemployed, Barbara Ehrenreich finds that job searching, thanks to the internet, has become "if not a science, a technology so complex that no mere job seeker can expect to

master it alone" (Ehrenreich, 2005, p. 16). She posted her résumé on Monster.com and Hotjobs.com only to find that after two months she had yet to receive a legitimate inquiry, even from the health and biomedical companies she electronically "pelted." She concluded that the internet alone will not get you a job.

So why use the internet for job searches? First, using the internet gives employers and job applicants cheap access to information. Job applicants can find out about job openings more easily, compared to the

(continued)

BOX 11.3   *(continued)*

past in which they had to go door-to-door to companies to look at job posting boards. Second, employers can easily obtain a pool of résumés and potential workers. Also, sending a résumé to an employer over the internet may be a signal that the job applicant is computer and internet-savvy. On the other hand, employers report that they are overloaded with résumés, especially from people who are not qualified and who they have no intention of hiring (Fountain, 2005: 1243).

Does the internet help people find jobs? Using data from two American surveys, Fountain (2005) found that, in 1998, using the internet increased searchers' chance of finding a job by 164 percent. By 2000, searchers using the internet were 28 percent *less* likely to find a job than other non-internet searchers, even after controlling for age, race, education, gender, length of unemployment, local unemployment rate and income. Fountain offers two explanations for this dramatic shift. First, if only a small number of people are using the internet, as was the case in 1998, then this group has access to information about job openings that others, who are probably equally qualified, do not have. Second,

when only a small number of workers apply through the internet, employers may use this as a marker of the skill of workers, such as being more technologically savvy resourceful than others: useful information that may affect their hiring decision. By 2000, when the number of people using the internet for job searches doubled, these advantages disappeared. Fountain concludes that even though the internet has changed the way people search for jobs, the change has been more about form than substance. The internet may provide a new way for workers to find information about employers and vice versa, it is unclear whether the information on the internet is better than information obtained elsewhere. It may simply be that there is just more of it. This finding shows the tension between information quality and quantity. The absolute quantity of information on the internet may not necessarily be better than the information found through other mean of job searching. What seemed to work for the job searchers in Fountain's study was finding a job the old-fashioned way. Placing or answering a job ad more than doubled the chances a searcher would find a job.

SOURCE: Christine Fountain, 2005, "Finding a Job in the Internet Age." From SOCIAL FORCES, Volume 27, no. 4, Copyright (c) 1949 by the University of North Carolina Press. Used by permission of the publisher. www.uncpress.unc.edu

This advice derives from the common belief that networking matters and is useful for finding a job, a belief with which sociologists concur.

Sociologists define a **social network** as a bounded set of individuals linked by the exchange of material or emotional resources, everything from money to information to friendship. The patterns of exchange determine the boundaries of the network. Network members exchange resources more frequently with each other than with non-members. Individuals in a network think of themselves as network members. The people you know personally form the boundaries of your personal network.

One measure of the quality of a personal network is the number of ties or connections in the network. Someone with many ties has a "dense" network; he or she is connected to many people. Moreover, ties may be strong or weak. Frequency of interaction, emotional intensity, and reciprocity between individuals defines the strength of ties (Yakubovich, 2005). Strong ties exist between you and family members and close friends. You see such people regularly, care deeply about them, and would help them if they needed it. Weak ties exist between you and others in your personal network—say, the friend of a friend,

someone you met via Facebook, or one of your parents' co-workers. You would not see such people often, nor would you count on them to help you in times of trouble.

In his study of professional, technical, and managerial workers in a Boston suburb, sociologist Mark Granovetter (1995 [1974]) found that 57 percent of his respondents found their job through personal contacts. Some 83 percent of these people said the contact who helped them get their job was someone they saw infrequently; they represented a weak tie. At the time his study was first published, Granovetter's finding was surprising and provocative. Common sense suggests that people to whom you are strongly tied would be most useful in helping you find a job because they are most motivated to help you. But it turns out what matters most in finding a job is good and unique information about jobs. Acquaintances who are one step removed from you are in a position to provide new (or non-redundant) information about jobs. These weak ties serve as "bridges" to "new parts of a social universe" or new parts of the labour market (Yakubovich, 2005: 410). In other words, the people you see frequently, such as your friends, probably have the same information about job openings that you do. But someone who is a weak tie in your network, such as your mom's best friend or your cousin's boss, may have information about job openings that your strong ties do not have. Because this informatiion comes through personal contacts, it may not be readily available to the public, which decreases the amount of competition for the job opening. Thus, information from acquaintances or weak ties is most likely to lead to a new job. Granovetter calls this phenomenon "the strength of weak ties."

Since Granovetter's study, sociologists have continued to examine how personal contacts or networks help people find jobs. Recent studies emphasize the role of social capital or resources in your personal network (Flap and Boxman, 2001). Having contacts in your network with good or high-status resources improves your chances of finding a better job (Marsden and Hurlbert, 1988); "good networks help to get people good jobs" (Erickson, 2001: 156).

THE FUTURE OF WORK

At the end of any discussion of work, one question remains for most students: "Where will the jobs be when I graduate?" While I do not have a crystal ball, it is possible to make some projections about future jobs.

Education and retirement play key roles in determining which job openings are growing and which are not. Almost three-quarters of the new jobs that will be created in the near future are expected to require some form of postsecondary education. They are in the fields of health, natural and applied sciences, education, social science, government service, and business and professional services. About two-thirds of the jobs opened up by retirements will also require higher education and training (JobFutures, 2002). Thus, by finishing your postsecondary degree, you will put yourself in the best position for the job market of the future.

The labour market will continue to generate a combination of good and bad jobs. Different forms of nonstandard work will continue to proliferate. One form of nonstandard work of particular interest to many undergraduates is self-employment, which will represent an ever-growing percentage of the labour force, partly because companies find outsourcing a good way to reduce labour costs. Although only 15.5 percent of Canadian workers were self-employed in 2007, the growth rate of self-employment since the 1970s has outpaced that for workers in the public and private sector (Statistics Canada, 2009). Even during economic downturns, self-employment grows. Some workers who lose jobs because of corporate restruc-

turing are pushed into self-employment as their only employment option. Other workers are drawn to self-employment because of a desire to have more control over their work. Regardless of why people become self-employed, the future appears to involve an increase in self-employment.

In the immediate future, we can expect employers to continue looking for ways to reduce operating costs. As in the past, one focus will be on reducing the cost of labour. Employers continue to move factories to countries with the lowest labour costs. Along with labour-reducing uses of technology, this tendency may further the trend toward the use of temporary and contract employees. What the head of production for the PowerPC microchip said in 1994 still rings true for many current workers: "I'm here for the duration, five years or so" (quoted in Osterman, 1995: 72).

Some analysts debate what jobs will look like in the future. The debate divides pessimists from optimists. Optimists emphasize the "end of the job" as we know it and the rise of self-employed, autonomous entrepreneurs (Bridges, 1994). Part of the optimistic scenario is based on the hope that service industry will continue to create good jobs in finance, medicine, and the like. Pessimists predict the "end of work." Based on an analysis of jobs in the United States, Jeremy Rifkin (1995) believes that as many as three-quarters of white- and blue-collar jobs could be automated, with no jobs to replace the ones lost to automation. In Rifkin's view, the unemployment level will rise and more of us will scramble for the few remaining jobs. By the middle of the twenty-first century, millions of workers could be left permanently idle, he says. These optimistic and pessimistic scenarios are linked to trends we've discussed in this chapter: Will technology increase or decrease productivity? Will the service industry create more good jobs than bad jobs? Will the polarization of work hours decline or grow? Both optimists and pessimists agree, however, that the days of most of us working in large corporations for our whole work life may be coming to an end.

As you've learned in this chapter, employers and employees have some control over whether technology creates good or bad jobs, reducing or increasing alienation. An important issue for the future of work is whether employers or employees will set the terms by which such changes will be judged. One thing is certain. The battle between workers and management will probably continue, as employees like Zainab Taiyeb try to organize their co-workers so they can improve their chances of having a say in what work looks like in the years to come.

SUMMARY

1. In the first industrial revolution, large segments of the population moved from being peasant farmers to being wage-earning factory workers living in urban areas. During the Second Industrial Revolution, companies increased in size and developed administrative offices with a complex division of labour.

2. The rise of the service economy is changing the types of jobs available in the labour market. The types of jobs available in the service economy are being polarized into good jobs in upper-tier industries and bad jobs in lower-tier industries.

3. The proportion of Canadians employed in nonstandard jobs is growing. Nonstandard jobs capture a variety of forms of work including part-time, temporary jobs, contract work, and self-employment. Young workers and older workers are overrepresented in some kinds of nonstandard jobs.

4. Contrary to media hype, Canadians are not working longer hours than they were 30 years ago. The proportion of Canadians working a 40-hour work week has declined over the past 30 years. There is some polarization of work hours, with some Canadians working too few hours and some working too many.

5. With the rise of the "24-hour economy," increase in demand for consumer services, and the aging of the population, an increase in those working nonstandard work schedules, has occurred since the 1970s.

6. The labour market comprises different segments. Good jobs are located in core industries and firms with primary labour markets, while bad jobs may be found in peripheral industries and firms with secondary labour markets. Job ghettos are areas of the labour market that trap disadvantaged groups of workers. Labour-market shelters, such as professional associations and unions, help their members maintain access to good jobs.

7. From Taylorism to Japanese production techniques, various management strategies are used to control workers and increase their productivity. Most strategies fall short on their claim to be participatory.

8. Work and organizational characteristics are the primary predictors of job satisfaction.

9. Alienation is a structural condition of powerlessness that arises from the organization of work in the capitalist economy. Workers respond to alienating conditions in various ways, such as engaging in sabotage and quitting their jobs. Strikes and other forms of collective resistance may have some success in changing the conditions of work.

QUESTIONS TO CONSIDER

1. Thinking about your own work experience, do you see evidence of the service economy creating good jobs or bad jobs? Do you see evidence of an increase in nonstandard work schedules?

2. Do Japanese production techniques (JPT) represent a different way of organizing work from Taylorism? If yes, how is JPT different? Does JPT offer new forms of participation for workers?

3. What is the difference between job satisfaction and alienation? Is Marx's concept of alienation relevant for understanding work today? Why or why not? Have you ever engaged in workplace behaviour that could be interpreted as a reaction to alienating conditions? Did this behaviour change the alienating conditions? Why or why not?

4. Think about how you or your friends have found jobs. What role have personal contacts played in your search for a job? What other ways have you (or your friends) found work?

GLOSSARY

In Marxist theory, **alienation** is a structural condition of "objective powerlessness." Workers do not have power or control over their work situation and are separated from the means of production. This situation is indicative of work in a capitalist economy.

Deindustrialization refers to the shift from a goods- to a service-based economy.

The **division of labour** refers to the specialized tasks performed by different categories of workers. The division of labour increases when work is broken down into smaller components,

Extrinsic rewards are the material benefits of working. Adequate pay, benefits, and opportunities for advancement are examples.

Fordism refers to the bureaucratically organized mass production of standardized goods by assembly-line methods.

Functional or internal flexibility in nonstandard employment allows employers to move workers from one job to another within an organization.

The **human relations school of management** emphasizes the importance of the social aspects of work. Proponents argue that more satisfied workers are more productive workers.

Intrinsic rewards are the social-psychological benefits of working. They are derived from challenging work, non-repetitive work, autonomy, and decision-making opportunities.

Japanese production techniques (JPT) form a management strategy that combines teamwork with assembly-line work to improve the productivity of workers.

Job ghettos are parts of the labour market that prevent groups of workers from experiencing upward mobility.

Job satisfaction is determined by asking workers in a survey, "How satisfied are you with your job as a whole?"

Labour-market segmentation involves the separation of the labour market into sectors of good and bad jobs.

Labour-market shelters are organizations that protect the jobs of certain groups of workers. Professional associations and unions are examples.

Nonstandard jobs include part-week employment, part-year employment, limited-term contract employment, employment through temporary-help agencies, self-employment, and multiple-job holding.

Nonstandard work schedules are characterized by either working nonstandard hours, which fall outside the 9-to-5 workday (shift work), or working nonstandard days, such as Saturday and Sunday.

Numerical or external flexibility in nonstandard employment enables employers to adjust the size of their workforce by easily hiring and firing workers in response to fluctuations in labour demand.

Polarization of working hours occurs when many workers in the labour market are working either too many hours (overwork) or too few hours (underwork).

Primary labour markets are where most good jobs may be found. They have an internal labour market that provides a job ladder and the opportunity for upward mobility.

A **social network** is a bounded set of individuals linked by the exchange of material or emotional resources, everything from money to information to friendship. The patterns of exchange determine the boundaries of the network. Network members exchange resources more frequently with each other than with non-members. Individuals in a network think of themselves as network members. The people you know personally form the boundaries of your personal network.

Taylorism, also known as scientific management, is named after its developer, Frederick Taylor. This style of management breaks job tasks into their smallest components. Work is also separated into conceptual and manual tasks, removing the need for workers to make decisions about their work.

Union density is the percentage of paid workers in a country who are unionized.

SUGGESTED READING

Adams, Tracey, and Sandy Welsh. (2008). *The Organization and Experience of Work*. Toronto: Nelson. A thorough, up-to-date overview focusing on the Canadian experience.

Ehrenreich, Barbara. (2005). *Bait and Switch: The (Futile) Pursuit of the American Dream*. New York: Metropolitan Books. Provides a provocative and humorous look at networking.

Rinehart, James W. (2006). *The Tyranny of Work: Alienation and the Labour Process,* 5th ed. Toronto: Thomson Nelson. A Canadian classic.

WEB RESOURCES

Companion Website for This Book

http://www.newsociety6e.nelson.com
Begin by clicking on the Student Resources section of the website. Next, select the chapter you are studying from the pull-down menu. From the Student Resources page, you have easy access to InfoTrac College Edition® and other resources, such as the Glossary, Test Yourself questions, and additional readings. The website also has many useful tips to aid you in your study of sociology.

InfoTrac College Edition Search Terms

Visit http://www.infotrac-college.com for access to more than 20 million articles from nearly 6000 sources when doing your online research.

CHAPTER TWELVE

SOURCE: © Nadejda Ivanova/ Shutterstock

Education

Scott Davies

MᴄMASTER UNIVERSITY

In this chapter you will learn that

- Sociologists study links between schools and society, focusing on inequality, socialization, and social organization. Theoretical approaches include structural functionalism, Marxism, human capital theory, feminism, credentialism, and institutional theory.

- Canadian schooling has been marked by three broad trends. First, to fulfill a mandate to retain the vast bulk of students in secondary levels, schools have *expanded.* Second, this expansion has necessitated a greater variety of *accommodations,* as educators attempt to address a range of student abilities and exceptionalities. Third, demands for postsecondary credentials are generating a simultaneous trend toward more intense forms of *competition.*

- Canadian school-level attainment shows a pattern of inequality, in that it varies by class, gender, and race.

- Socialization through education has become less religious and now lacks the hard-edged prescriptive tone it had in the past. Reflecting trends in pedagogical philosophy, today's schools have a more indulgent quality, with teachers using less punitive tactics to elicit compliance from students.

- Canadian schools have changed from wielding traditional authority to wielding legal-rational authority and in the process have become more bureaucratic. Today, schools are being pressured to become more "accountable" and "market-like."

INTRODUCTION

Go to the education section in any bookstore and what do you see? Dozens of titles declare schools to be in some sort of crisis. *The Catastrophe in Public Education, Public Education: An Autopsy, Failing Our Kids: How We Are Ruining Our Public Schools, The University in Ruins,* and so on. Newspapers decry the quality of schooling with headlines like "Johnny Can't Read and He's in University." Such drama! Is it really that bad?

Not if you consider several facts about schools. Until quite recently higher education was deemed to be a waste for common people. Early in the twentieth century, most people did not complete high school. But the past half-century has brought a change in ideologies. In Canada and elsewhere, advanced levels of education are seen to be not only suitable but also necessary for many people. Over 50 years, high-school attendance has become almost universal, and attaining a secondary-school diploma the norm. University enrollments have never been higher. Further, public opinion surveys show that most Canadians rate our public schools favourably and believe they are effective teachers of our youth (Canadian Council on Learning, 2007).

This highlights a key paradox. Modern schooling has been a success story in many respects, having grown immensely, reshaped the lives of most Canadians, and received billions in government funds. Yet, as schools become more central to society, they attract more and more criticism. This chapter will illuminate this paradox by exploring the transformation and changing connections between schools and Canadian society over the past century.

HOW SCHOOLS CONNECT TO SOCIETY: CLASSICAL AND CONTEMPORARY APPROACHES

Sociologists examine three major ways that schools connect to society. First, schools shape society by **selection.** Education systems have long channelled students into different types of schools and programs. This process creates stratification when programs are designated as "higher level" or "lower level" and link to better or worse job opportunities. The endless grading, judging, marking, and testing in schools sorts and certifies students with different "badges of ability." This may seem self-evident, since we have all

Schools socialize students by fostering the development of attitudes, knowledge, and skills that are necessary in adult society.
SOURCE: © Monkey Business Images/Shutterstock.

written hundreds of tests in our lives. But a sociological approach sets this process within a bigger picture: Schooling connects to societal-level inequality. In a society marked by disparities in wealth and income, and where more people go to school for longer periods, never before has the pursuit of educational credentials been as consequential for income, occupational success, and other life-chances. Sociologists ask *who* is selected for *what*, and *why?*

These kinds of questions can be traced back to the ideas of Karl Marx and the structural functionalists. Although Marx wrote little on schooling, his twentieth-century followers have examined the role of schooling in maintaining patterns of economic inequality. They have argued that schools are stratified in ways that reflect workplace hierarchies, with basic forms of schooling teaching youth to be punctual and compliant, and with higher levels encouraging students to internalize orders and the expectations of authority figures. In contrast, structural functionalists see school selection as an increasingly meritorious process in which the brightest and hardest working are identified, rewarded, and selected for training in professional work and high-level management.

Second, schools shape society as they *socialize* people. They help prepare new adults for the next generation, passing along values and knowledge. This too may seem glaringly obvious, but decisions on *which* values and knowledge are passed on can be contentious. When Émile Durkheim (1961 [1925]) was writing, industrialization and the rise of democracy were promoting individualism, and people felt freer to develop their talents to their fullest extent. As individualism flourished, Durkheim sought to understand how modern societies could replace the binding and authoritative voice of religion, which had traditionally prescribed norms to guide people's thoughts and actions. What would now keep individuals from being self-centred and acting only in their own interest? Durkheim cared deeply about "moral education," the normative element of schooling that he hoped would become society's prime tool to combat the rising culture of individualism.

When Canada was more religious, schools imparted old-fashioned virtues and moral codes. But society has changed, so contemporary sociologists now ask these questions: Do schools still impart a clear set of values? Is socialization better understood as a series of unintended consequences that are beyond anyone's control? Just how successful are schools at socializing students? Do they treat everyone the same, or does school socialization differ by class, gender, and race?

Third, education shapes society through *social organization*. Schools affect how we learn and help define different types of occupations. This was a core interest of another classical theorist, Max Weber, who was fascinated by "rationalization," supposedly the main "logic" of modern societies, embodied in bureaucratic organizations. For him, modern schooling was changing society by teaching knowledge in a systematic fashion and creating credentials to forge more formal pathways to labour markets.

Why do employers seek and hire employees with school credentials? The conventional wisdom is that schools teach skills, employers hire the most skilled, and school credentials are signals of skills. But Weber's contemporary followers have questioned whether the school–labour market connection is so simple. They contend that most school content is only loosely connected to what is demanded in most jobs. They see schools as largely serving to distribute legitimate access to jobs.

Let us now examine in depth each of the three roles of education: selection, socialization, and social organization.

SELECTION

When Canada was an agricultural society, land was a prime economic resource, and affluent families strove to pass their property to their children. When manufacturing and commerce become the key economic activities, upper-middle-class children could inherit business fortunes. But today, most youth earn their living through employment and need credentials. "Class reproduction," the passing of advantage from one generation to the next, does not operate through direct inheritance in education. No one can legally inherit his or her parents' law degree, medical licence, MBA, or teaching certificate. These things must be earned. Now that most positions of power and status require some sort of school credentials, how do the affluent pass on their advantages?

School selection occurs in two ways. First, schooling itself is structured in a stratified manner, though this structuring takes different forms across countries and over time. Second, within that structure students from different backgrounds have unequal rates of success. Families navigate their way through this structure, searching for ways to boost their children's educational success for the

FIGURE 12.1 PERCENTAGE OF CANADIAN PARENTS EXPECTING THEIR CHILDREN TO ATTEND POSTSECONDARY INSTITUTIONS, 2002

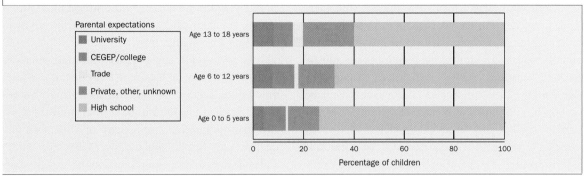

SOURCE: Statistics Canada (2002).

most prized credentials. Most parents expect their children to receive a postsecondary education (see Figure 12.1).

CHANGING SCHOOL STRUCTURE

In Canada, the traditional form of educational selection is known as "streaming." Streaming consists of splitting students into curricular groupings, one typically bound for postsecondary schooling, one headed for general training. Students in the upper tier are

exposed to advanced mathematics and works of literature, while those in the lower tiers focus on the rudiments of literacy, numeracy, and practical workplace skills. Although Canada ranks near the top of the world in reading literacy (see Figure 12.2), Canadian sociologists have long condemned streaming for limiting educational opportunity, particularly for students from working-class backgrounds. Streaming is seen to dampen their aspirations, manage their ambitions, and discourage them from moving on (Krahn and Taylor, 2007). To understand Canada's form of

FIGURE 12.2 RESULTS FROM PISA INTERNATIONAL LITERACY TEST, 2006

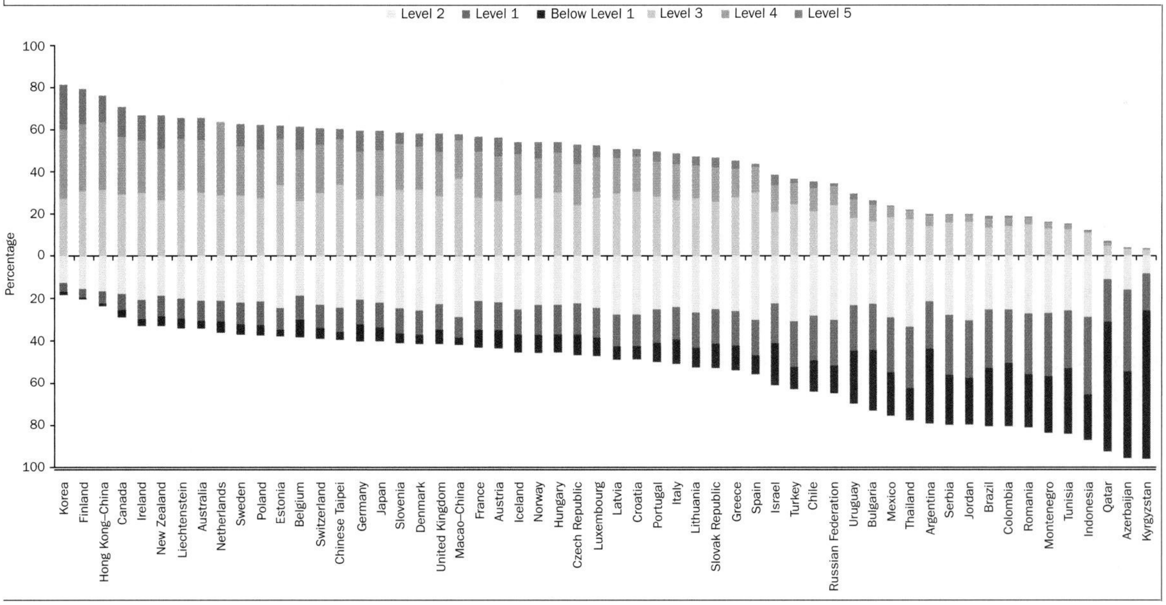

SOURCE: OECD (2007), PISA 2006: Science Competencies for Tomorrow's World: Volume 1: Analysis, pp. 286, http://dx.doi.org/10.1787/142046885031.

educational stratification, we need to set streaming in an international context.

Compared with many European countries, Canadian education has actually been relatively open and flexible. For decades, schools in Britain, France, and Germany sorted students into entirely academic or entirely vocational schools at relatively young ages (Kerckhoff, 2002). European academic secondary schools were oriented to prepare elites and preserve a heritage of classic literature, philosophy, and rigorous exams. "Excellence" was equated with high culture. Until recently it was inconceivable for French secondary-school students to study "practical" electives, such as business or accounting, for instance. Stratification was rigid; once students entered a type of school, few moved out. If a student failed an examination at age 15 or 16, they were effectively eliminated from further higher education.

To understand national differences, sociologists distinguish **sponsored mobility,** which takes place in educational systems that select relatively few youth early in their lives to enter elite universities, from **contest mobility,** which takes place in educational systems that group the bulk of youth into the same school, expose them to the same curriculum, and send larger numbers to higher education (Turner, 1960). Sponsored mobility uses highly structured streaming to restrict access to higher education, while contest mobility promotes more competition within a unitary structure. Canada is an example of a contest system, while many European countries have had sponsored systems. For most of the twentieth century, Canadian schooling did not sharply separate a "gifted" minority from the rest by creating separate schools. Academic curricula were instead given to almost everyone. From the 1960s until recently, proportionately more Canadian youth flowed into Canadian universities than European youth flowed into European universities, and even lower streams were not strongly vocational; little high-school content has been directly job-related in any stream. As a result, the high-school diploma lacks vocational meaning, and it does not guarantee any particular skill for any specific occupation. Canadian high schools channel many students to postsecondary levels and prepare few for any particular job.

This distinction may be changing, however, as nations expand their universities and colleges to take in more students (Wolf, 2002). As in Canada, European policymakers want more youth to study in university, claiming that more graduates will generate wealth and improve their nation's economic competitiveness. Most European nations are removing barriers, creating more alternative channels for youth, and moving toward an ever-more streamlined contest model. As such, the form that inequality takes in education is changing.

As more youth enter higher education, competition shifts to higher levels, and stratification *within* universities and colleges becomes increasingly important. Higher education can be seen as stratified along two main dimensions: selectivity of institution and field of study (Davies and Guppy, 1997). Universities and colleges with the best reputations offer their graduates access to elite jobs, higher wages, contacts, and other advantages. In some countries, higher education institutions differ greatly in prestige. In Europe, ancient universities, such as Oxford, Cambridge, and the Sorbonne, have much more exclusive student bodies, and they more readily provide their students with access to elite positions. In Canada, universities are generally more selective and academically intensive than are community colleges, whose vocational mandates give them a subordinate position within higher education (Dennison, 1995).

Fields of study also differ in their prestige, selectivity, access to resources, and payoffs for their graduates. High prestige was once attached to humanistic fields (such as philosophy and English) that enjoyed elite patrons, but in recent decades this has changed. Fields linked to powerful professions or commercial markets, such as medicine, law, engineering, and business, have now gained the upper hand. These fields offer students pathways to lucrative job markets (Walters, 2004).

As colleges and universities are flooded with an unprecedented number of applicants, school selection moves upward to higher education. Students in different institutions and fields face unequal prospects. Universities and colleges sort these larger masses for vastly different occupational and social opportunities. Since there are simply not enough high-paying jobs for all graduates, entry into the most advantageous slots in higher education is becoming increasingly valuable. Required high-school grades—the prime currency for entrance to universities—have steadily risen over the past decade. Many universities are boosting their entrance standards and tuition fees, gaining repute not only by admitting top students but also by rejecting large numbers of qualified students. Institutions that were already highly exclusive are increasingly selective, while the less discriminating are expanding their enrollments.

Fields linked to powerful professions or commercial markets, such as medicine, law, engineering, and business, offer students pathways to lucrative job markets.
SOURCE: © Andres/Shutterstock.

The degree of stratification in higher education differs across nations. For instance, the American system is a mix of private-sector and public institutions that are arrayed on a steep prestige hierarchy. American higher education has famous Ivy League universities, elite liberal arts colleges, and flagship public universities that greatly overshadow less-renowned entities. This steep, entrenched system makes the name of elite institutions important to employers. Canadian higher education, in comparison, not only lacks a private sector but also lacks a steep institutional hierarchy (Davies and Hammack, 2005). Until recently, Canadian governments have allowed only publicly funded universities. The resources allocated to these institutions have been fairly equal, while their American counterparts are much more unequal. Although the top American colleges and universities select from a national and international pool of applicants, only small numbers of Canadian undergraduates cross provincial or territorial borders, and most commute to their local institution. Canada has a relatively small national market for undergraduate credentials. Although degrees from top-ranked colleges in the United States can offer great opportunities there, few employers in Canada value the name of any one Canadian university over others.

Accordingly, Americans have long ranked their universities, but the practice is relatively new in Canada. The best-known Canadian rankings are compiled by *Maclean's* magazine. The magazine gives high scores to institutions with such attributes as large libraries, incoming students with top high-school grades and from other provinces and territories, faculty with research awards, and small classes. Although popular, this practice has been criticized for using questionable measures and for creating an artificial image of hierarchy and competition among our universities. But university administrators take them seriously and strive to improve their relative position. Table 12.1 (p. 290) shows the results from 2008.

Canada may be developing a more pronounced hierarchy in higher education. As our universities and colleges increasingly generate more of their own revenue, whether via large external research grants, corporate funds, alumni donations, or steeper tuition, some universities and colleges will likely enjoy advantages. If wealthier institutions are perceived by students and employers to offer a superior education, it may bring an intensified pecking order to Canadian higher education.

INEQUALITY AMONG STUDENTS

Within sociology, a debate has raged for 50 years over whether schools create equal opportunity for all. Functionalists believed that schools were increasingly rewarding the best, allowing any bright students, regardless of their social backgrounds, to enter high-paying professional and managerial positions. In contrast, Neo-Marxists contended that the very design of mass public schooling ensures that people who are born disadvantaged remain disadvantaged. In recent years, this claim has been extended to race and gender, with many analysts arguing that female students and those who are members of minority groups are treated poorly in school and are given little choice but to enter low-paying jobs in female and minority-group "job ghettos." The claim here is that schools worsen existing inequalities by stereotyping disadvantaged youth, devaluing their cultures and skills, and steering them into lower streams. Sociologists have conducted research on this topic for several decades. The early research focused mostly on social class, but it has since broadened to include gender and race. This research has consistently uncovered the following patterns.

First, educational attainment for youth from all class backgrounds has steadily risen over the past half century. As Table 12.2 (p. 291) shows, more Canadians from all walks of life attend school for more years than did their fathers. Second, despite this expansion, student success has been found to be consistently related to

TABLE 12.1   THE 2008 *MACLEAN'S* UNIVERSITY RANKINGS

RANK	PRIMARILY UNDERGRADUATE	COMPREHENSIVE	MEDICAL/DOCTORAL
1.	Mount Allison	Simon Fraser (tied for 1st)	McGill
2.	UNBC	Victoria (tied for 1st)	University of Toronto (tied for 2nd)
3.	Acadia	Waterloo	Queen's (tied for 2nd)
4.	St. Francis Xavier	Guelph	UBC
5.	Wilfrid Laurier	Memorial (tied for 5th)	Alberta
6.	Trent	New Brunswick (tied for 5th)	McMaster
7.	Lethbridge (tied for 7th)	Carleton	Calgary
8.	UPEI (tied for 7th)	Windsor	Dalhousie
9.	Winnipeg	Regina (tied for 9th)	Saskatchewan
10.	St. Mary's	York (tied for 9th)	Ottawa
11.	Brandon (tied for 11th)	Concordia	Western
12.	Lakehead (tied for 11th)		Laval
13.	Ryerson		Montreal
14.	Brock		Sherbrooke
15.	Moncton (tied for 15th)		Manitoba
16.	Mount Saint Vincent (tied for 15th)		
17.	Bishops (tied for 17th)		
18.	Laurentian (tied for 17th)		
19.	St. Thomas		
20.	Nipissing		
21.	Cape Breton		

SOURCE: *Maclean's* (2008). Reprinted by permission of *Maclean's*.

socioeconomic background. This has been true not only across time but also across the world, and, indeed, it is one of the "iron laws" in the sociology of education. Youth from less advantaged backgrounds are repeatedly overrepresented in lower streams, get lower grades, drop out of school at higher rates, and are underrepresented in higher education. Inequalities along socioeconomic lines were evident when such data were first collected and they have persisted ever since, not only in Canada but also in other Western nations (Anisef, 1974; Blossfeld and Shavit, 1993; De Broucker and Lavallée, 1998; Gamoran, 2001; Guppy and Arai, 1994; Knighton, 2002; Krahn, 2004; Porter, Porter, and Blishen, 1982; Ryan and Adams, 1999; Wanner, 2000).

To illustrate these inequalities, we can examine data from Canada's Youth in Transition Survey (Shaienks and Gluszynski, 2007; see Table 12.2). They reveal the proportion of Canadians who were aged 24–26 in December 2005 who had ever attended a postsecondary institution. The top row of Table 12.2 shows that 79 percent of Canadians in that age group had attended either a university, community college, CEGEP, or some other type of postsecondary institution. However, this percentage differs for different

levels of parental schooling. For example, the likelihood of a someone attaining a university degree was 32 percent if neither parent had graduated from high school, but it rose to 60 percent if at least one parent had earned a postsecondary degree. We see a clear socioeconomic effect in Table 12.2; the likelihood of attaining a university degree almost doubles across levels of parental education. These findings are typical of dozens of studies on this topic.

However, a different picture emerges when we compare the school success of males and females. Males once had a virtual monopoly on higher education, but this imbalance began to change in the late 1950s. By the 1980s, more women than men were attending university. Females now drop out of high school in fewer numbers, graduate more often, enter universities in greater numbers, and score higher on many standardized tests (Frenette and Zeman, 2008). Today, women have surpassed men on most measures of education attainment.

What explains this reversal? It partly reflects the success of the women's movement; partly the entry of women into traditionally male-dominated professions, such as law and medicine; and partly how some

TABLE 12.2 POSTSECONDARY PARTICIPATION OF CANADIANS AGED 24–26 IN DECEMBER 2005 (IN PERCENTAGE)

	ATTENDED A POSTSECONDARY INSTITUTION	ATTENDED COMMUNITY COLLEGE/ CEGEP	ATTENDED UNIVERSITY	ATTENDED OTHER POSTSECONDARY
All Canadians	79	33	50	17
Men	74	33	49	18
Women	85	33	52	15
Visible Minority	87	27	62	11
Non-Visible Minority	78	34	49	17
Highest Educational Attainment of Parents				
Less Than High School	63	43	32	24
High School Diploma	69	40	37	22
Some Postsecondary Education	82	35	43	21
Postsecondary Certificate/Diploma	90	28	60	12

SOURCE: Adapted from Statistics Canada data in Shaienks and Gluszynski, Participation in Postsecondary Education: Graduates, Continuers, and Dropouts, Results from YITS Cycle 4, Table 1 Page 9 and Table 2, Page 1. Reproduced with permission.

"female-dominated" occupations like teaching, nursing, and social work, not only grew but also demanded higher-level educational certificates. Men's attainment has not kept pace, partly because substantial numbers of men continue to work in blue-collar jobs, such as mining and construction, which rarely require postsecondary schooling (Guppy and Arai, 1994).

Although higher numbers of women are going to university, they often enter different fields from their male counterparts. Figure 12.3 (p. 292) shows the distribution of university graduates among selected fields of study in 2005. While the majority of all students in Canadian universities are female, women do not form the majority fields that are related to math, computer science, architecture, or engineering. Of course, these numbers are *very* different from those of previous eras. For instance, in the early 1960s, about 25 percent of university graduates were women; in some fields, such as forestry, *no* women graduated, and several others, such as law, had only a handful of female graduates (Statistics Canada, 2001). But while this pattern has certainly changed, and while such fields as business, law, and medicine have seen dramatic change, women continue to be underrepresented in several dynamic and well-paying fields (see also Buchmann, DiPrete, and McDaniel, 2008).

Racial and ethnic patterns of educational attainment reveal a more mixed picture. Table 12.2 shows that on average, young members of visible minorities exceed young whites in postsecondary participation, particularly in attending university. But what needs

emphasis is the *variation* in the attainment in the visible-minority group. Other data (see Davies and Guppy, 2006) show that Aboriginals, black, and Hispanic Canadians have lower-than-average participation rates. What accounts for these variations? An explanation must take three legacies into account: differences in socioeconomic status, colonization, and immigration policy.

The large variation among minority groups is partly a product of Canada's changed immigration policy. Whereas recruitment in previous eras targeted Europeans with relatively low levels of schooling, since the late 1960s Canada has targeted Asians with advanced educational credentials. As a result, living conditions for immigrants vary widely. Some of them enter the country with profiles that typically promote educational success—high levels of parental education, comfortable incomes, urban residence—while others do not. Thus, Canada's educational rankings partly reflect the "inputs" from the immigration system as well as its own internal processes. Meanwhile, Aboriginal Canadians are products of colonialism, segregation, and discrimination, which render them the most impoverished ethnic group in Canada.

Given these patterns of attainment, a question arises: Do schools ameliorate inequalities in society, maintain them, or make them worse? This question is difficult to settle empirically because almost everyone goes to school. If there were some groups or regions where youth didn't go to school, then researchers could see whether the presence of education worsens or improves rates of inequality. For something that

FIGURE 12.3   PERCENTAGE OF MALE AND FEMALE UNDERGRADUATE STUDENTS WITHIN EACH PROGRAM, 2005

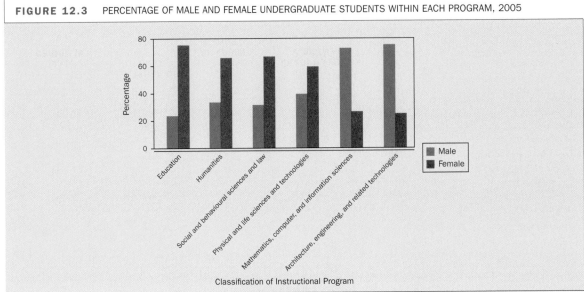

SOURCE: Statistics Canada, 2008, "University Degrees, Diplomas and Certificates Granted, by Program Level, Classification of Instructional Programs, Primary Grouping (CIP_PG) and Sex, Annual (Number), CANSIM (Database)," Table 477-0014.

resembles these conditions, sociologists have looked to the time of the year in which few students are in school: summer. Although such research is scant in Canada, a large American literature is available (Alexander, Entwistle, and Steffen-Olsen, 2007; Burkam, Ready, Lee, and LoGerfo, 2004; Downey, von Hippel, and Broh, 2004). Its basic logic runs like this: If schools gave superior treatment to middle-class children, then student learning gaps (as measured by standardized test scores) would grow over the school year and would either stagnate or shrink during the summer months. Alternatively, if such gaps grow in the summer and narrow during the school year, then schools probably do not disadvantage youth of lower socioeconomic standing and may even mitigate the effects of home and neighbourhood. This research is almost unanimous in its basic conclusion: Schooling *reduces* learning gaps along socioeconomic lines, while these gaps widen in the summer when students are not in school. Researchers conclude that schools indeed function as equalizers, at least in terms of measured learning.

The near-mountain of empirical research on school inequalities thus lends support to a more nuanced position. Schools can be seen as progressive institutions that offer opportunities for all youth but are limited in their power to eliminate inequalities. Contemporary schools have enjoyed some success in reducing inequality, but they have not come close to

totally eliminating such disparities. Affluent children have many more advantages and fare better in school because of their advantaged home environments.

SOCIALIZATION

Contemporary sociologists offer different depictions of how schools socialize their students. According to structural-functionalist theory (Dreeben, 1967), schools teach modern values. As societies industrialize, urbanize, and become more cosmopolitan, schools provide a common culture to compensate for the declining influence of religion. Schools are said to transmit values like universalism (which involves treating everyone as equal, rights-bearing individuals) and meritocracy (a system in which social rewards go to people with talent who exert effort in open competitions). But rather than teaching these new values overtly, the functionalists contend that schools teach them in a **hidden curriculum.** Teachers do not repeatedly lecture students on universalism and meritocracy but instead teach these values by running schools in a universalistic and meritocratic fashion—students learn by doing. By treating all students equally before common rules, schools are seen to embody the values of universalism, and by rewarding deserving students, they are seen to teach the value of meritocracy. Thus, modern schools teach core values by virtue of their very structure.

Marxists claim that schools impose a hidden curriculum that promotes obedience to authority.

SOURCE: PhotoDisc.

Other sociologists see a darker side to school socialization. For instance, Marxists also claim that schools impose a hidden curriculum that promotes obedience to authority, not cheery modern values (e.g., Bowles and Gintis, 1976; see Box 12.1). They contend that public education is structured to support capitalism by creating a disciplined labour force. By organizing student learning in a competitive manner and having students vie for grades and rewards, schools are said to mirror capitalist competition and individualism. Likewise, feminists and many students of race claim that schools impose subordinate identities on their students (this argument is elaborated further below).

To assess these theories, it is useful to think of school socialization as a continuum. At one extreme are boarding schools, where the institution regulates virtually all facets of life—not only lessons but also how and when students sleep, eat, dress, and play. The school becomes the student's entire social universe, resembling what sociologists call a *total institution*, an all-controlling organization that remakes people's entire identities, where people are isolated from the larger society and are strictly controlled by a specialized staff. In boarding schools, teachers become powerful socializing agents, forging identities and having an almost singular impact on how pupils speak, look, and act. At the other extreme of the continuum is online education. If a person's education consists solely of online courses taken at home, the school's position in that person's life can be marginal, something that merely appears on a computer screen, to be ignored at will. School becomes just one socializing force among many, like a television program that can be turned on or off. Most Canadian students

---

BOX 12.1   WILLIS'S LEARNING TO LABOUR

One of the most famous books in sociology is Paul Willis's *Learning to Labour* (1977). Willis observed a working-class school in England's industrial north in the mid-1970s, when many working-class boys dropped out of school at age 16 and took jobs in factories. He set out to explain why they would enthusiastically accept factory jobs that other youth would reject as inferior, degrading, and low-paying. Willis reasoned that it was too easy to say that these boys simply had no choice, since they experienced no physical coercion and actually exercised a degree of self-direction. To get his answer, Willis probed the cultural life of the school.

In his study, Willis found two male peer groups. One, nicknamed "the lads," was antagonistic toward teachers, lessons, school rules, and students who were diligent, deferent, and obedient. The second subculture, the "ear'oles," accepted school authority and strove to be upwardly mobile. The lads called them "ear'oles" because they saw these boys as overly passive, like a human ear, never *doing* anything, and always on the receiving side of orders. Crucially, the lads felt *superior* to the

ear'oles because the lads made their own fun and excitement in school.

Although *Learning to Labour*'s description of classroom antics is rich and entertaining, the book became famous as an account of how school "resistance" helps "reproduce" the class structure. That is, when youth reject what schools have to offer, their only remaining options are bottom-level jobs. The book was also controversial for its contention that the lads embodied the culture of the working class. Since most school rebels were from working-class backgrounds, Willis saw their conflict with school as a form of *class* conflict, full of unarticulated ideological meanings. For Willis, the lads' belief that school activities were useless in the workplace was an insight into the deskilled nature of work in capitalism. Their constant denigrating of teachers' advice, he felt, signalled a recognition of the capitalist hidden curriculum. Subsequent research has questioned whether Willis's ideas can be generalized to contemporary Canada, but many remain fascinated by his depiction of male peer groups' bravado and aggression.

experience school socialization somewhere between these extremes. Few attend boarding schools or take only online courses from home. Most attend public schools full-time, Monday to Friday. Bearing this reality in mind, we next explore how schools socialize students, contrasting the ways socialization in schools has changed over the past 150 years. We then consider the ways in which schools treat different groups of students differently.

CHANGING FORMS OF MORAL EDUCATION

The history of Canadian schools is one of declining religious influence and altered moral content. Canadian public schools were originally organized by churches, with Roman Catholics being granted separate schools in Ontario, and Protestants being granted separate schools in Quebec. Similar denomination-based arrangements were made in all provinces. In the mid-nineteenth century, few people questioned the proclaimed need for public schools to provide Christian teaching. The earliest schools were nominally secular, but their religious character was overt.

Egerton Ryerson, the father of public schooling in what is now Ontario, wanted schools to create literate, religious, and devoted citizens. He and other school promoters believed that religious schooling could curb an array of perceived problems, such as the rising incidence of youth crime and general ignorance (Prentice, 1977: 128). Christianity occupied a central place in public school missions for a century. Even in the 1950s, public authorities still called for strong religious influence in public schooling, with some calling for public schools to teach "cardinal virtues" and "Christian ideals" (Government of Ontario, 1950: 36–37). By the late 1960s, educators had very different ideas. Fewer educators saw their role as passing on religiously inspired wisdom, time-honoured truths, and a sense of moral duty. Instead, school socialization was to become much more individualistic. Educators increasingly sought new ways of teaching for a new age. Consider this quotation from a 1968 provincial committee report:

> Learning by its very nature is a personal matter. There is virtually a metabolism of learning which is as unique to the individual as the metabolism of digestion. Parents and teachers may create conditions with learning in mind, but the actual learning experience is intimate and subjective, for each human being reaches out to the world in his own idiosyncratic way. (Ontario Department of Education, 1968: 49)

After the late 1960s, schools saw their role less as providing moral guidance and more as creating forums for thinking about moral issues. This created a different type of moral education, at least in emerging theories of pedagogy. Students were to be exposed to a fuller range of contemporary controversies, beliefs, and ideals than before. Teachers aimed to enable students to make informed choices, rather than have them accept moral edicts. Ideals from Christianity were replaced by ideals of critical thinking, science, and multiculturalism. Educators wanted less to tell students what was unambiguously true or false and more to nurture a deeper understanding of various subject matters, based on discovery rather than repetition. More educators saw their mission as taking a critical stance toward society, exposing injustices, and questioning established interpretations of history (Hurn, 1993: 191).

What has been the impact of these changing ideals? Although both functionalist and Marxist theories can be compelling, what do empirical studies tell us about *actual* socialization in current schools?

In partial support of functionalist theory, schooling does appear to make people more "progressive," in the sense of supporting civil liberties, tolerating minorities, appreciating social justice and ethnic diversity, and embracing non-traditional roles for women (Kingston, Hubbard, Lapp, Schroeder, and Wilson, 2003; Pallas, 2000). However, schools do so in a relatively neutral and individualized manner, and they offer rather ambiguous moral messages. That is, although students are encouraged to identify with various progressive causes, such as protecting the environment, helping the homeless, fighting racism, and fundraising for overseas children, schools do this by having students relate their own experience and venture their own opinions. Classrooms increasingly have "feel-good" posters that exhort children to read and stay in school, a form of "bumper-sticker morality" containing catch-phrases for quick consumption rather than deep discussion and reflection. Yet, in support of Marxist theory, schools spend most of their time on mundane matters of personal conduct, striving to get students to be orderly and task-oriented. Much of teachers' time is spent on urging students to be respectful of one another, to participate in class, and to be cooperative (e.g., Brint, Contreras, and Matthews, 2001; Jackson, Boostrom, and Hansen, 1998).

Although studies tend to support elements of both functionalist and Marxist theory, they also suggest that modes of shaping students are changing. Teachers now treat students in a more indulgent fashion than in previous eras. They see self-esteem as essential for learning and control their classes with a lighter touch than in the past. They increasingly rely on "token economies," giving small rewards to get children to comply, rather than using overt authority. They use group projects, not just individual assignments, and especially in elementary schools, students work in rotating activity centres, freely moving around the classroom and choosing their tasks. Today's schools are making less use of classic styles of enforcing obedience. Further, teachers try to inspire *all* students. Whereas schools in the past would give up on those students deemed hopeless, whether too poor, too troubled, or too slow, today's schools work hard to engage the entire student body, even the least able performers. Indeed, the law demands that schools do so.

In some respects, the socializing power of Canadian education weakens as students progress from elementary and secondary to postsecondary levels. As Mullen (forthcoming) notes, research comparing commuters to students who reside on campus concludes that university life has a far greater impact on the values, attitudes, and psychological growth of the latter. This is especially the case for students at elite universities in the United States. However, in Canada, most college and university students are

The diversification of Canadian society has influenced the way morality is taught in school.
SOURCE: Nelson Collection.

commuters. They attend classes for 10 to 15 hours per week, so are not immersed in an intensive, all-encompassing educational environment. Further, Canadian higher education institutions are not arrayed on a steep prestige hierarchy, and so are less likely to breed social elites that are relatively homogeneous and cohesive, as American Ivy League colleges and England's Oxbridge do. Nevertheless, Canadian higher education influences students in more subtle forms by reshaping their social networks (Stevens, Armstrong, and Arum, 2008). Higher education can greatly alter the number, quality, and type of social ties students enjoy, and thereby shape their subsequent job, marriage partners, and lifestyle opportunities.

To summarize, the morality taught in public schools has shifted from religious indoctrination to a more individualized and indulgent approach that encourages students to learn by reflecting, not reciting. This change reflects the diversification of Canadian society, where moral reference points are numerous, not singular, and where there is a sentiment that schools should address social problems but should not preach a monolithic doctrine. Within this secular and individualized form of education, do schools treat everyone the same? That is the question to which we now turn.

CREATING IDENTITIES? GENDER AND RACE

Historically, Canadian education prepared girls and boys for different roles in adult society. Traditional school systems were premised on the notion that most young women should be homemakers or schooled for a narrow range of "nurturing" occupations like nursing and elementary-school teaching. Though boys and girls were mostly grouped together at lower ages, they were often segregated at older ages, with the expectation that a select few boys would move to advanced studies (Prentice, 1977: 111–12). Although both sexes attended school, their experiences were dissimilar. Few people challenged gender traditionalism until the 1960s.

Women's educational attainment has changed since then, matching and even outpacing male attainment in many areas. But despite this apparent change, critics continue to accuse schools of continuing to reinforce traditional gender roles (American Association of University Women Educational Foundation, 1998; Bennett DeMarrais and LeCompte, 1995; Kelly and Nihlen, 1982). They detect a hidden curriculum that quietly subordinates women, prepares them for a gendered division of labour, and sends messages about their inferiority. The explicit gender stereotyping of the late nineteenth century has only been masked, they argue, and they support their argument by pointing to several indicators beyond standard measures of school attainment.

First, feminist critics examine school staffing, noting that despite some change, most positions of power remain in the hands of men. Some observers have even called schools "academic harems." For instance, an elementary school can be staffed almost entirely by women, save for the most powerful position—the principal—who is often a man. While teaching positions in lower grades are held almost entirely by women, higher-level teaching and administrative positions are held by men. A second indicator of gender bias pertains to curriculum. For several decades, feminists have charged school textbooks with being loaded with sexist language, illustrations that depict most active characters as male, and stories that depict women in nurturing occupations and as stay-at-home moms. They also contend that high-school literature courses ignore female authors and that history textbooks disregard the contributions of women. Here there has been change, especially as most provincial governments have curriculum guidelines that monitor gender representation in most course material.

A third indicator of gender inequity is the fact that schools tolerate the conduct of male students that, in the adult world, would be considered sexual harassment. Feminist critics decry schools' "hostile hallways" in which sexual comments, touching, jokes, and leers are deemed "normal" and "natural" and are therefore tacitly permitted. Schools are said to accept such behaviour when they rationalize such acts as "boys being boys." Such rationalizations are linked to inequities in extracurricular programs. Schools continue to be accused of considering it natural that men's sports teams should receive higher priority and more funding than women's teams, an imbalance said to send a message of female inferiority. Finally, teachers stand accused of treating female students unfairly, directing girls toward stereotypical nurturing fields, like teaching, nursing, and administrative studies. Others claim that girls' self-esteem is damaged in the classroom when teachers ignore them in favour of boys (this particular accusation has been controversial, since research suggests teachers only give males more attention for disciplinary reasons).

The sum total of these inequities, it is argued, is a gendered "hidden curriculum" that alienates females from course material, dampens their aspirations, and ultimately reinforces gender inequality.

Similarly, some analysts argue that Canadian schools sometimes socialize minority students into racial identities. The historical episode of residential schools for Aboriginal children is the most blatant. In the nineteenth and twentieth centuries, the Canadian government set out to mould Aboriginal identities by sending up to half of all Aboriginal children to these schools with the intent of making them "modern Indians" who would speak English or French, convert to Christianity, and learn skills for menial jobs. The residential school was a total institution that separated Aboriginal children from their families and communities, interrupted the rhythms of their home lives, and implanted more regimented cultural norms. The legacy of this racism is felt in Aboriginal communities to this day. Likewise, young black children in some cases were singled for discriminatory treatment in the nineteenth and early twentieth century, labelled as "coloured," and segregated in black-only schools (Axelrod, 1997: 79).

Over the past 20 years, Canadian schools have responded to such problems in two ways. First, they have reworked curricula to make them more multicultural and inclusive of minority groups. Since the 1980s, policymakers have overseen the rewriting of history and literature to better reflect the experiences of immigrants and racial minorities, and have introduced anti-racist measures to encourage students to be more accepting of diversity. For multiculturalists, schools should also cultivate cosmopolitan world citizens who identify more deeply with the global community and its attendant concerns with peace, ecological health, and Third World development, and see themselves not only as national citizens but also as members of the human race, with obligations to all people everywhere.

Although overt segregation laws have been long removed, and although multicultural curricula have been adopted in a variety of forms, some sociologists continue to charge Canadian schools with being insensitive to the needs of youth from minority groups (Dei, 2005). Schools, they contend, "racialize" children from minority groups by making them assume racial identities and experience themselves as "different" (Lewis, 2003). In this view, schools actively reinforce racial identities and inequalities. Students who are members of minority groups are seen to be ill-treated by school practices, particularly "colour-blind" policies that ignore the disadvantages of children from these groups. School multiculturalism, it is held, only superficially addresses historical legacies of racism, while white teachers are seen to be blind to experiences that are actually colour-coded and unwilling to challenge dominant understandings of race. For instance, a commissioned report recently accused the Ontario government's Safe Schools Act and "zero tolerance" policy of being culturally insensitive and of singling out black males for punishment (Ontario Human Rights Commission, 2003).

Partly in response to these changes, Canadian schools have attempted to accommodate minorities in a second and more controversial fashion: through greater school choice. "School choice" refers to the use of public funds that give parents more discretion in their children's education. It usually entails making available to parents a wider variety of educational options beyond a standard, local public school.

Each province has developed its own mix of support for religious and linguistic minority schools, and some sociologists support the move, reasoning that public schools have failed to meet the needs of minority youth (Dei, 2005). On these grounds, the Toronto District School Board narrowly approved the opening of a black-focus school in 2007. It will undoubtedly receive much attention in the coming years from educators and the public, not only because race is a hot-button issue in Canadian education, but also because it signals a key debate about school socialization. Underlying choice reform is a more pluralist and less individualistic vision of nation building than currently exists. Reformers see the nation as a community of communities, with schools playing a vital role in its construction. From their point of view, students' ethnicity, race, religion, and gender mediate their relationships to the national community, creating "unity through diversity." Accordingly, separate schools are needed to socialize minority groups into their own culture, defined by race, language, or religion. For opponents, however, pluralist schooling segregates students. Opponents favour multicultural education as a means of integrating all groups into society. At present, insufficient evidence exists to settle the debate.

THE LIMITS OF SCHOOL SOCIALIZATION

Although claims that schools mould gender and racial identities are very popular, one difficulty is that they assume that schools have a great deal of socializing power, rather than provide convincing evidence of their effects. It is conceivable that some educational institutions, such as residential boarding schools, may wield great socializing power, but the average public school today is far more limited in its reach. We need to recognize other socializing influences. Students clearly are influenced by forces well beyond the school—their families, neighbourhoods, workplaces, and, of course, peer groups (Looker and Thiessen, 1999).

Sociologists have long examined high-school peer groups, believing they set limits on schools' socializing sway, and how varying degrees of student autonomy may *hinder* school goals. Sociologists in the 1950s and 1960s became interested in peer cultures when they found that student populations were less deferential than in previous decades. Although most school deviance was mild, consisting of minor rule-breaking, irreverence, apathy, or truancy, it still subverted educational goals by disrupting classrooms and interrupting learning. James Coleman (1961) argued that, among adolescent peers, learning and achievement mattered less than popularity and looking good. Moreover, in the peer group, being a top student did little for a person's reputation. Coleman's ideas have since spawned a large body of research on the formation of student subcultures. This research has examined how the very structure of schooling encourages youth to respond in ways that can frustrate the socializing efforts of educators (Coleman, 1961; Tanner, 2001).

Specifically, over the decades, sociologists have interpreted youth's obsession with physical appearance, hairstyles, clothing brands, and cliques as no mere byproduct of their relative immaturity. Instead, sociologists see them as responses to particular social conditions. Schools segregate youth by age, give youth little power, and require their attendance by law. Yet students do have some degree of autonomy. High school is not overly challenging for most youth. Most students have some disposable income. These conditions, sociologists argue, encourage youth to be status-conscious. Status groups emerge when social structures offer few alternative avenues for social mobility. Students become a status group because they lack power and authority but have enough autonomy to invent their own social realm within schools. By this logic, Murray Milner (2004) has likened high-school cliques to Indian castes. Castes emerged in traditional India when there was little democracy or economic mobility for people of low social rank. Upper castes obsessed about appearance, social ranking, and maintaining social distance from inferiors. They created elaborate rituals and pressures for conformity, especially for intimacies such as eating and romantic relationships.

So how are high-school cliques like castes? According to Milner, teens risk social demotion if they are seen eating or dating someone with low status. They use small cruelties and put-downs to uphold their dominance. A jock pesters a nerd to maintain his own status at the nerd's expense. Status also explains why some teens are so concerned with conforming to brand-name clothing fashions. The isolated world of high school creates pressures for cliques to display their status through consumer commodities. Since teens are largely excluded from "producer" roles in prestigious workplaces but are freely granted "consumer" roles, the latter become their main source of reputation.

Sociologists have also traced a second, more antagonistic element of student subcultures to schools' very own selection function (Cohen, 1955; Stinchcombe, 1964). In this view, since schools reward only some students and deem others to be academically unfit, they create disincentives for unsuccessful students. Low-ranked students suffer an inglorious status and get labelled as "underachievers" and channelled into streams that lead neither to postsecondary education nor to useful job-training programs. These students suffer emotional injury in schools and hunger for a more positive self-image. Accordingly, low-achieving students form anti-school subcultures as an alternative source of social recognition. These subcultures invert the values that schools try to promote, rejecting students who are rule-abiding, obedient, and hardworking, and celebrating the rule-breaker, the insolent, and the hedonist. Among males, this rebellion is epitomized by confrontations with teachers, fighting, smoking, drinking, and sexual bravado. Among females, it is marked by a flaunting of their sexuality and a preoccupation with dating. In both cases, subcultures are seen to be a youthful expression of frustration with school selection processes that thwart upward mobility.

Since the 1980s, sociologists have argued that oppositional subcultures can also take racialized forms. Fordham and Ogbu (1986) claim that African Americans denigrate their high-achieving peers for "acting white," that is, for adopting the culture and language of white America and being disloyal to their own community. Such pressures are said to discourage black students from identifying with schooling. The "acting white" thesis has become very influential, but

is it true? Several American sociologists have put it to the test, but most cast doubt on it. Some suggest that only a small portion of black students take oppositional stances to schools (Downey and Ainsworth-Darnell, 2002). Others argue that generic peer pressures are felt by *all* high-achieving students, regardless of race, and those who earn top grades are similarly labelled *geeks*, *nerds*, or *brainiacs*. Only in schools where student achievement is starkly unequal by race, they speculate, will this pressure take a racialized form (Tyson, Darity, and Castellino, 2005).

Does the "acting white" phenomenon exist in Canadian schools? Far less systematic research on the topic exists here, but some researchers claim that black Canadians sometimes form oppositional subcultures. In a field study of a Toronto high school, Patrick Solomon (1992) claimed that black males were increasingly drawn toward sports, and saw academics as a "white activity." Other sociologists, such as George Dei (2005), similarly contend that black youth are increasingly alienated from the mainstream curriculum and require alternative "black-focus" schools to nurture a more positive cultural identity, as mentioned earlier.

Studies of peer groups suggest that school selection provokes at least a mild form of antagonism from lower-achieving students and that this can frustrate the efforts of educators. But the very existence of oppositional subcultures similarly suggests that some theories may exaggerate the extent to which schools mould gender and race identities. Students learn roles in their neighbourhoods, families, media, and places of employment (which can be highly segregated), and these are competing sources of socialization that may be partly counteracted by schools.

For instance, some feminists (Holland and Eisenhart, 1990; Weis, 1990) contend that peer groups, not school officials, divert female students toward established gender roles and discourage educational advancement. Some suggest that embracing a student role may actually erode gender traditionalism. In a field study of an English secondary school, Lynn Davies (1984) found that youth in university-bound streams were relatively more "androgynous" and less conforming to gender stereotypes. In contrast, girls who were about to drop out looked forward to motherhood rather than to careers, and would-be male dropouts were more traditionally masculine. A similar pattern was found in a Canadian study that employed survey research. In a large sample of Ontario high-school students and dropouts, I found that both girls and boys in academic streams were less traditional than those in non-academic streams, and those differences widened in later grades (Davies, 1992). Since new career opportunities for academically oriented males and females may weaken traditional conceptions of gender, it is not clear that schools continue to actively enforce gendered and racial identities. Though schools certainly treated females and minority students differently in the past, contemporary research shows that public schools promote more liberal and progressive views about gender and race and that schools have long been among the few places in society where boys and girls are grouped together to perform the same role.

These findings force us to think more about the *limits* of schools' socializing role. Paradoxically, as more people go to school for more years, the socializing impact of schooling may become *weaker*. More than in any previous era, schools now compete with other socializing agents. More youth are employed part-time, popular culture is everywhere, and today's parents are spending more time on developmental activities, hiring more tutors, and purchasing more extracurricular lessons for their children (Adler and Adler, 1994; Aurini, 2004; Daly, 2004; Davies, 2004; Quirke, 2006; Sayer, Bianchi, and Robinson, 2004). Schools are losing their monopoly on structured lessons and developmental activities, at least among the middle class. The upshot is that their unique impact on students may be on the wane. Rather than being a total institution, schools are moving toward the weaker end of the socializing continuum, no longer imparting a cohesive ideology and now competing with more socializing agents than before.

SOCIAL ORGANIZATION

For Weber, modern schooling reflected the emergence of a rationalized worldview in the organizational form of bureaucracy. With schools now being one of Canada's largest expenditures, costing at least $60 billion per year, they need to be seen as legitimate organizations that generate useful skills in a relatively efficient manner. Contemporary theorists offer widely differing accounts of whether schools are indeed efficiency-seeking organizations. Some see schools as converging with Weber's ideal type of bureaucracy, others do not.

THEORIES OF SCHOOL ORGANIZATION

The most straightforward account is offered by economists. **Human capital theory** asserts that the

school's role is primarily economic: to generate needed job skills. The theory assumes that both individuals and governments "invest" their time and dollars in schools because they believe it will lead to financial prosperity. The costs of schooling—books, buildings, teacher salaries—are "inputs," and student learning is the "output" or product. Human capital theorists see schools as organized to maximize student skills. If the value of the output exceeds its cost, schooling becomes a worthwhile investment, such as when individuals' expenditures in schooling early in their life eventually raise their earnings or improve their health. Schooling is thus seen as a form of capital—*human* capital—since people cannot be separated from their knowledge and skills in the same way that they can be distinguished from their financial and physical assets (Becker, 1964).

Indeed, research consistently shows that education *does* pay. On average, people with more years of schooling earn higher wages and have better employment rates (Walters, 2004). School pays, but why? Although some analysts point directly to the skills that are generated through education, many sociologists question the extent to which schooling improves useful job-related skills and whether jobs utilize what school teach.

"Credentialists" like Randall Collins (1979) are generally skeptical of human capital theory for at least two reasons. First, usually far fewer high-skilled jobs are available than there are graduates from high schools, colleges, and universities. Employees are often overqualified; available jobs often do not require their learned skills (Livingstone, 1998). Second, Collins sees weak connections between school content and the workplace. Much schooling—hours of essay writing, studying quadratic equations and periodic tables, practising the tuba—has little to do with most job realities. School curricula develop according to their own dynamics, he argues, and seldom in response to employers' demands. Further, employers rarely bother to look at student grades when hiring. With the exception of a few professions, merely possessing a diploma, certificate, or degree will suffice. If school content were really connected tightly to the job market, Collins reasons, employers would surely use grades as vital indicators of a candidate's suitability. So why do employers seek graduates with credentials if little of their learning actually connects to job demands? Collins offers several answers.

One is **credential inflation.** Just as monetary inflation devalues money, modern education devalues credentials. Just as a dollar cannot purchase the same goods it could 30 years ago, a high-school diploma does not lead to the same job it did 30 years ago. Inflation results from intense competition in the labour market. When hiring, managers in large corporations and in government are often flooded with job applicants. The sheer number of candidates makes careful and personal consideration of each one impossible. Hence, managers need a bureaucratic screening device, a procedure to reduce the applicant pool that is seen to be fair and efficient. Over the past few decades, employers have increasingly used credentials for this purpose, even for jobs that are not complex or demanding. Hiring someone with credentials may not reflect a need for specific skills. Seeking a leg up on competitors, people comply by obtaining an educational credential. This inflation creates a growing gap between the competencies required in jobs and the level of education possessed by job occupants.

Another reason that employers seek graduates with credentials concerns **professionalization.** Professional associations, such as the Canadian Medical Association, control occupational standards by setting the educational requirements for their profession. By demanding higher levels of education, these occupations can limit the number of eligible competitors. Over the decades, many occupations have raised entry requirements—school teachers, nurses, accountants, and social workers, to name a few. Sociologists see this as part of a process of professionalization in which an occupation tries to raise its standing and command higher wages. Think of all the requirements that didn't exist 40 years ago: M.S.W., M.B.A., B.N., and so on. What fascinates Collins is that teaching, nursing, social work, and business easily survived in past generations without demanding these credentials, and little evidence suggests that these occupations have become so much more complex as to necessitate these higher levels of schooling.

Collins also contends that some employers prefer to hire employees with advanced credentials just because they are prestigious. According to Collins, many employers hire university graduates for jobs to gain trust from clients and customers. Firms want to appear serious, businesslike, and trustworthy and not "fly-by-night." For Collins, well-educated employees are the human equivalent of a nice piece of office furniture: They signal that the firm is indeed honourable. Advertising a work force with many letters trailing their names (B.A., B.Sc., L.L.B., M.B.A, M.A., Ph.D., etc.) can be a mark of status in a world where business transactions can be highly uncertain and in which clients seek signals of high repute.

SCHOOL AUTHORITY: FROM TRADITION TO RATIONALITY TO MARKETS?

Premodern schools were typically small and informal, and educational authority was decentralized. Canada had thousands of school boards, most of which controlled only a few small schools. Each teacher had little formal training and enjoyed wide discretion over his or her classroom. Lessons were taught without many formal guidelines. There was little large-scale planning and there were few educational laws. Teachers had parental-like authority over students. They could discipline largely as they pleased, often resorting to corporal punishment, with little fear of reprisal. Curricula were justified in terms of passing on time-honoured doctrine and cultural traditions. Teachers were proclaimed to be moral trustees of society.

All this changed during the twentieth century. In Weber's terms, modern institutions like schools were *rationalized.* Public education was justified less in moral terms and more by its social utility. Canadian schools cut "irrelevant" subjects like ancient languages and adopted new ones, usually justified in terms of their necessity for daily living. Teachers were seen less as trustees of the common good and more as semi-professionals with skills and responsibilities.

Rationalization was accompanied by a change in organizational form. Schools grew and looked less like little red houses and more like office buildings. They were increasingly governed by general rules. Lines of control were formalized from top to bottom, with hierarchical chains of command and clearly defined responsibilities. Regulations delegated authority to credentialled officials in a more specialized division of labour, particularly at upper grade levels. Personnel were selected for their advanced training rather than for personal ties to highly ranked officials. Public schools hired certified teachers with university diplomas. Curricula were standardized, approved by higher-ranking bodies, and arranged in uniform age-graded levels. Modern schools thus became bureaucracies.

After World War II, governments across Canada saw education as increasingly necessary for economic prosperity and the development of individual citizens. Consequently, they gave public high schools a new mandate: to retain as many youth for as many years as possible. Seeing only a few students as suitable for advanced education became passé. A new norm emerged: Virtually everyone ought to complete high school. Those who did not were to be deemed either deviant or proof of a failing system. The big challenge for schools, then, was how to translate these new ideals into new realities.

The expanded mission for schooling transformed secondary schools within a generation. School officials interpreted their mandate as delivering a broadly comparable education to all students. They further standardized schooling, from physical plant, to teacher training, to curricula. Authority and power were increasingly wielded in distant hierarchies rather than in local communities, an approach that has been dubbed, somewhat derisively, as the "one best system" (Tyack, 1974), faulted for being indifferent to the needs of individual pupils. Critics commonly portrayed schools as resembling nineteenth-century industrial factories, a "one-size-fits-all" institution.

But with a new mandate, schools needed to devise ways to motivate an increasingly wide range of students. That was not easy. In earlier times, high schools could steer students who were disinterested in academic work into jobs. But now schools were expected to retain the vast bulk of youth, including those with learning disabilities or little academic ambition. Since teachers encountered many youths who found academic work neither appealing nor absorbing, the big challenge for modern secondary schools was to accommodate a wide range of student aptitude, preparedness, abilities, and motivation than any high school had ever faced before. Again, that was not easy. Unlike the monetary incentives that some organizations offer their employees, the incentives that schools offer their students can be weak. Their most obvious reward is a grade—the prime currency for higher-education admissions. But for the "forgotten half"—youth who do not seek studies beyond high school—grades can be nearly useless. Schools have other organizational constraints too. Teachers would love to have students who enroll on a fully voluntary basis, but with truancy laws, many students attend school only through compulsion. Many teachers want to deal individually with students, but current funding levels force most classes to consist of 20 to 30 students. As it stands, teachers face large classes of captive students with greatly varying abilities and levels of motivation.

This has been the core challenge for reformers. **Progressive pedagogy,** rooted in the ideas of John Dewey in the early twentieth century, has been a force in Canadian schools since the 1960s. Progressives do not want students to be merely instrumental toward their schooling but aim instead to nurture intrinsic forms of motivation, to engage students and have them work voluntarily. Modern teachers want to entice students to do their work not just for grades or to evade sanction, but out of true curiosity. Dewey called for schools that catered to the interests of the learner. By having students direct their own learning, schools could unleash students' intrinsic motivation, he reasoned. Over the decades, many reforms have attempted to engage students within the parameters of schools' organizational constraints (Tyack and Cuban, 1995).

Progressives reformed schools by destructuring classrooms, creating curricula with fewer rote and memory-based exercises, and relaxing discipline. Traditional classrooms strictly regulated student talk and movement by arraying student desks in straight rows. But in the 1970s, progressives saw such regimentation as stifling student imaginations. They encouraged more interaction and tolerated some chatting and freer movement in the classroom. They also decorated classrooms, adorning walls with student art work and colourful posters, often next to traditional emblems like the flag. Corporal punishment was largely abandoned in favour of notions of student rights. The binding idea was that departures from traditional schooling were needed to motivate students (see Box 12.2, p. 302).

After witnessing these changes, sociologists in the 1980s offered a different take on bureaucratic schools (Powell, Farrar, and Cohen, 1985). In their eyes, decades of reform had made schools more like "shopping malls" than factories. They were struck by the transformation of schools into human service organizations that strove to accommodate their students. Schools became mall-like, they argued, by differentiating courses by degree of difficulty and creating electives to cater to student choice. They created "specialty shops" for students with different abilities, whether "gifted," ESL, or specially able. Schools bolstered extracurricular activities and devised services to address a wide variety of social, physical, and emotional problems. Educators became sensitized to different kinds of learning styles, as proclaimed by theories of "multiple intelligences," which claim that student ability in, say, dance, should be valued as much as student ability in math (Gardner, 1999; see Table 12.3, p. 303).

BOX 12.2   FREE SCHOOLS

"Free schools" took the experimental attitude of the progressives much further by de-structuring all aspects of schooling. Inspired by Summerhill, an English private school founded in the 1920s, free schools rocketed to prominence in the 1960s and early 1970s, when hundreds of them were opened across North America. These schools were founded on the belief that only self-motivated, self-regulated, and self-evaluated education could nurture true learning. In many free schools, daily activities were chosen by students. There was no mandatory attendance. Most school exercises were optional. Standard methods of evaluating students with grades or report cards were condemned, since true learning was thought to be too personal to be measured, and since grading could create power inequities between staff and students.

Free schools were to be pressure-free places for students to develop their own interests and talents, without any compulsion to compete with others or to comply with some external standard. Yet despite generating an incredible amount of excitement, most free schools closed in a few short years. Without the benefit of clear and enforceable rules for student conduct, many became unmanageable, and teachers quickly became disillusioned and fatigued. Lacking the bureaucratic trappings of education, such as standardized

curricula, certified teachers, timetables, and formal courses, the public grew skeptical of whether they were schools at all, and therefore free schools appeared to be illegitimate in the eyes of politicians. Some survived in the form of "alternative schools." Operated by public boards of education, these schools are less structured than regular schools but still use mandatory rules of attendance and approved curricula.

"Free schools," popular in the 1960s and 1970s, were so unstructured that many people questioned whether they were schools at all.
SOURCE: © Alamy.

The theory of multiple intelligence was developed by Dr. Howard Gardner, who contends that the traditional notion of intelligence based on IQ testing is an overly narrow model of human potential. Gardner instead proposes that there are eight different kinds of intelligence. Some Canadian schools have embraced this theory and are designing curricula to match each type of intelligence. By doing so they illustrate how schools are attempting to accommodate a wide range of student needs.

Although secondary schools in the past had openly promoted academic achievement, the shopping-mall high school eased expectations. Mastery of core subjects was no longer expected from all students. Students who desired a more enriched curriculum could still find it, and lower-achieving students could pass from grade to grade in return for little more than orderly attendance. High schools had evolved unwritten rules about how tough certain courses should be. These informal rules unofficially designated elective courses to be easier than required math and science courses. Teachers in the latter subjects could

legitimately demand much effort and time, but other teachers could face rebellion from students, parents, and even administrators if they dared to expect anything comparable.

The idea of the shopping-mall high school was introduced in the mid-1980s and it accurately depicted how schools were then striving to accommodate students. This effort has since sparked controversy, however. Over the past decade, educators have been stung by emerging demands to raise standards and become "accountable." Canadian policymakers are promoting higher standards as they understand them, usually in the guise of standardized performance indicators.

Today, critics are claiming that public schools are too bureaucratic. For instance, Chubb and Moe (1990) see public bureaucracies as aloof and slow to change, and requiring a mechanism to inject quality-orienting dynamics. These reformers condemn public education as an inefficient monopoly that is unresponsive to its clients, and they hail "market" reforms for their potential to create competitive pressures, similar to those

TABLE 12.3 THE THEORY OF MULTIPLE INTELLIGENCES

INTELLIGENCE	END-STATES	CORE COMPONENTS
Logical mathematical	Scientist, mathematician	Sensitivity to, and capacity to discern, logical or numerical patterns; ability to handle long chains of reasoning
Linguistic	Poet, journalist	Sensitivity to sounds, rhythms, and meanings of words; sensitivity to the different functions of language
Musical	Composer, violinist	Abilities to produce and appreciate rhythm, pitch, and timbre; appreciation of the forms of musical expressiveness
Spatial	Navigator, sculptor	Capacities to perceive the visual-spatial world accurately and to perform transformations on one's initial perceptions
Bodily kinesthetic	Dancer, athlete	Abilities to control one's body movements and to handle objects skillfully
Interpersonal	Therapist, salesperson	Capacities to discern and respond appropriately to the moods, temperaments, motivations, and desires of other people
Intrapersonal	Person with detailed, accurate self-knowledge	Access to one's own feelings and the ability to discriminate among them and draw upon them to guide behaviour, knowledge of one's own strengths, weaknesses, desires, and intelligences
Naturalist	Biologist, naturalist	Abilities to recognize and categorize objects and processes in nature

SOURCE: Adapted from Gardner, H. and Hatch, T., 1989, "Multiple Intelligences Go to School: Educational Implications of the Theory of Multiple Intelligences," *Educational Researcher, 18,* (8), 4–10, American Educational Research Association.

faced by for-profit businesses. Under the banner of "school choice," these reformers want to force schools to survive only by collecting funds directly from fee-paying clients. The imperative to attract clients, they contend, has many advantages. It can match the tastes of parents and educators. It can encourage new providers to enter the educational field, bringing innovation to schooling, and devising customized programs for their clients. And it can boost school performance in the form of standardized test scores, since market-based schools will be presumably motivated to raise their quality to attract customers (Ouchi, 2003).

School choice is indeed growing in Canada in at least two forms. One creates more choice within the public school system, expanding the menu of programs beyond standard school offerings. For instance, the City of Edmonton has largely reinvented its school system by offering a smorgasbord of pedagogical choice and offering a variety of special-theme schools, including those that specialize in sports, science, language, arts, intensive academics, alternative pedagogy, and multiple intelligences (Taylor and Woollard, 2003). Another Alberta initiative has been to create "charter schools," independently run but government funded, each pursuing a special theme, whether ESL, traditional academics, Suzuki music and philosophy, science and math, or programs aimed at gifted, Aboriginal, female, or at-risk students (Bosetti, 2001).

The second type of choice is private schooling. The proportion of Canadian students enrolled in private schools is growing, particularly in affluent locales. For instance, in Toronto, 10 percent of students are enrolled in private schools, higher than the 7 percent national average (Davies and Quirke, 2005). More than 60 non-religious private schools have opened in the city in the past 15 years. These schools attempt to appeal to their customers by developing specialty programs and small classes. Almost all offer some sort of specialty, creating an astonishing array of programs and philosophies of teaching, each seeking a niche in a competitive marketplace. Similarly, homeschooling is growing in Canada, as more parents are turning to themselves to provide educational options for their children (Arai, 2000; Aurini and Davies, 2005).

Are Canadian families embracing more competitive educational strategies? Traditionally, private education has been reserved either for elites or for members of religious minorities. But various forms of private education are now expanding. The proportion of Canadian students enrolled in private schools grew from 5 percent to 7 percent over the past decade. The number of Montessori schools is growing (Aurini, 2002). The tutoring industry has also undergone a staggering transformation over the past 30 years, with the number of tutoring businesses growing between 200 percent and 500 percent in major Canadian cities (Aurini and Davies, 2004). In 2007, a third of Canadian parents reported that they had hired tutors for their children (Canadian Council on Learning, 2007; Box 12.3).

Although these private alternatives certainly create more variety in education, there is still no evidence that they offer higher-quality schooling than regular public schools do, taking into account the socio-economic advantages of their students. Indeed, rather than being more academically intensive, many of these schools have strong "shopping-mall" and "progressive" elements, like those that have inspired public educators for decades. Proud of their customized offerings, they prize pedagogical freedom and intimate relations above all. Yet, as tuition-charging schools, they lack any mandate to ensure equal access. Despite good intentions, only wealthier families can afford them. These schools illustrate the tension between satisfying yearnings for choice and providing equity.

Indeed, a flip side of market reasoning is that the customer should pay. Such thinking has permitted Canadian universities to deregulate tuition fees for their professional schools, such as dentistry, law, medicine, and M.B.A. programs. Administrators of these professional programs believe student demand will

---

BOX 12.3 THE GROWING NICHE FOR TUTORING CHAINS: PREKINDERGARTENERS' ACADEMIC PREP

Merrick is 5. On this crisp October afternoon, he'd just finished a flashcard drill of simple words, and the children next to him were following suit. "Cap. Lap. Map. Trap," they recited. "Cat. Fat. Rat." Academic tutoring has dropped down to the sandbox-and-nap-time set. In recent years, early-childhood education experts and industry analysts say, more parents have started sending their 3- to 5-year-old children to for-profit tutoring centers to give them an academic edge in elementary school.

Tutoring for tots, some say, has been spurred by increased academic accountability in schools, heightened competition to get into top-ranked colleges, and new research that links early exposure to books, music, and language to better academic performance in later years. And the convenience and recognizable brand names of some established tutoring companies seem to attract parents, some industry-watchers say. While pre-K tutoring is now just a tiny segment of the $2.5 billion K–12 tutoring industry—about 1 percent—that share is likely to grow as more parents and policymakers emphasize early-childhood education. There is an annual growth rate of roughly 15 percent in the K–12 tutoring industry overall in the past few years.

Yet while some companies wax enthusiastic about pre-K tutoring, many early-childhood experts

decry the trend. Tutoring 3- to 5-year-olds in a classroom setting with flashcards and workbooks can be overly prescriptive, dampen enthusiasm for learning, and even spur developmental problems, some scholars say.

"Parents have the idea that education is a race, but it is not," said David Elkind, the author of the 1981 book *The Hurried Child* and a child-development professor at Tufts University in Medford, Mass. "However well-intentioned, [pre-K tutoring] is a moneymaking thing that builds on parental anxieties, with no research or support."

"Are [parents] damaging their kids for life? Hardly," said Barbara A. Willer, a deputy executive director of the Washington-based NAEYC. "But there's a larger issue. As a society, do we make sure that tutoring is available just to those who can afford it, or do we ensure that there are high-quality pre-K programs for all?"

Merrick's mother, Mary Jansen, would agree. She says the program encourages her son to achieve beyond his grade level. And that, she says, is necessary for Merrick to succeed in school. "Kids can't only be little kids anymore," she said, after her son finished his half-hour tutoring session here. "I want him to go to the college he wants. As long as it's Ivy League."

SOURCE: Rhea R. Borja, 2005, "Growing Niche for Tutoring Chains: Prekindergartners' Academic Prep," *Education Week, 25* (8), 10. Reprinted with permission from Education Week. Vol. 25, October 19, 2005.

not be deterred by soaring costs, since professional degrees often lead to high incomes, so they have raised fees well above the Canadian average of approximately $4000, sometimes charging in excess of $20 000 for a year's tuition. Although these fee hikes may not have discouraged student demand, they do appear to be influencing the composition of student bodies in these programs. A recent study suggests that when programs deregulate their fees, they become more likely to accept students who have highly educated parents and to have students from poorer backgrounds who are eligible for bursaries and scholarships. The losers in the process appear to be middle-class students, who lack advantageous family backgrounds, yet are often ineligible for income-contingent loans and bursaries (Frenette, 2005).

These tuition trends reflect broad changes in the organizational form and governance of postsecondary schooling. One hundred and fifty years ago, Canadian higher education consisted of a scattering of small and mostly religious institutions. Between 1850 and 1990, the system was expanded, secularized, socialized, rationalized, coordinated and "massified." Since 1990, most provinces have significantly reduced per-student funding, while at the same time raising performance expectations. In response, universities and colleges have become more attuned to market and government forces. In finding ways to secure new revenue sources, they have transformed themselves. For instance, to attract and accommodate new kinds of students, colleges and universities have moved far beyond their conventional weekday timetables on their main campuses, and are offering courses in evenings, on weekends, at branch campuses, or with online technologies—much as a business enterprise would change to pursue new customers. To engage in large-scale fundraising, most universities and colleges now have large public relations offices that court would-be donors and corporate sponsors. To compete with rivals, some are even engaging in "image makeovers," using consultants to "rebrand" themselves, sometimes by replacing traditional coats of arms with corporate logos and slogans (Kirp, 2004). These activities signal the encroachment of traditional missions of teaching and research by new competitive pressures, a trend decried by some as "academic capitalism" (Slaughter and Rhoades, 2004; Box 12.4).

At the same time, provinces are expecting colleges and universities to demonstrate their effective and efficient use of tax monies by participating in quality assurance programs. Politicians increasingly want closer

BOX 12.4   IS CANADA SINGING THE "IVORY TOWER BLUES"?

In *Ivory Tower Blues,* sociologists James Côté and Anton Allahar (2006) warn of a crisis in Canadian higher education. They describe how universities enroll unmotivated students and inflate their grades, with some students attaining B's with minimal levels of effort and skill. Much of their discussion draws on their own experiences at the University of Western Ontario, but they also cite findings from the National Survey of Student Engagement. The NSSE suggests that even though only 10 percent of all undergraduates are highly engaged with their studies, and 40 percent are largely disengaged, the vast majority report regularly earning A's and B's. The loss of academic integrity is tolerated by administrators who, Côté and Allahar argue, regard students as "consumers" who pay much-needed tuition, and accept the situation as the inevitable byproduct of university expansion. These ideas have sparked controversy. Supporters have championed *Ivory Tower Blues* for fearlessly exposing one of higher education's dirty secrets. Critics accuse Côté and Allahar of exaggerating problems, romanticizing the students of yesteryear, and failing to acknowledge the need for new instructional methods to inspire today's youth (for a warehouse of these debates, see http://www.ivorytowerblues.com).

Which side in the debate is correct? *Ivory Tower Blues* acknowledges that many students in past generations opted to coast toward a "Gentleman's C" rather than exert themselves for a higher grade. But Côté and Allahar contend that today's disengaged students, unlike those of yesteryear, now receive inflated grades, and on this point they are supported by other researchers (e.g., Anglin and Meng, 2000). Moreover, the authors and their critics agree that universities need new strategies to involve students. But does this combination of disengagement and grade inflation amount to a full-blown crisis? At this time, there is little evidence that Canada's universities are suffering from a loss of legitimacy, but Côté and Allahar are referring to another kind of "crisis": a longstanding erosion of liberal ideals of higher education. For them, universities should strive to transform students' hearts and minds, broaden their intellectual horizons, and create exemplary citizens. In many ways, *Ivory Tower Blues* laments the declining authority of those ideals, along with the tendency for many to champion higher education only for its economic utility. Côté and Allahar are at work on a second edition in which they respond to their critics and suggest practices to halt further decline in standards.

links between these institutions and local industries and labour markets, and to justify their receipt of public funds by meeting "key performance indicators" that signal compliance with standards of hiring, course content, and graduate placement. Importantly, however, these "KPIs" do not include any measures of student learning, but instead consist of bureaucratic formalisms that are easily counted, such as ensuring that faculty have Ph.D.s or that courses fulfill required numbers of hours. British Columbia, Alberta, Ontario, and New Brunswick have also passed legislation allowing the opening of private degree-granting bodies, reasoning that the marketplace has a role to play in helping meet new demands for higher education. These pressures are spawning greater organizational variety in higher education, one marked by private and for-profit universities, international branch campuses, transnational enrollments, corporate involvement, and online technologies. Venerable ideals of exclusive elites retreating in quiet contemplation are giving way to a new image of bustling "learning organizations" that can teach the masses by responding to ever-shifting market and political winds.

CONCLUSION

The enterprise of Canadian schooling has grown immensely. Almost all Canadians attend high school, most graduate, half now go on to postsecondary school, and many will return to some sort of educational institution later in life, as ideologies of "lifelong education" become reality. But what has been the impact of this monumental expansion? Schools partially compensate for pre-existing inequalities in student preparedness, but their selection role ensures that expansion does not bring greater equity, at least along socioeconomic lines. Further, the singular

socializing impact of school in our lives actually shrinks. School becomes a weaker socializing agent as it integrates into our lives, competing with many other agents. Some forms of schooling have become more competitive. Prestigious programs that offer the most recognition and best rewards are increasingly exclusive. Other programs are more accommodating, treating students in more progressive ways and offering more choice than ever before.

These trends remind us of the paradox discussed at the outset of this chapter. Canadian schools now serve unprecedented numbers of students for longer periods of their lives, yet they are a lightning rod for more and more criticism. This is a prime instance of "disenchantment" in Max Weber's definition: As schooling becomes ever more central to society in the modern era, it loses its "magical" quality to command deference. As all citizens attend school for most of their youth, more are familiar with schooling and have higher expectations for what schools should do for them. Education has become a "motherhood" issue that everyone supports in the abstract, yet in the process it loses its overtones of elite rituals, aristocratic cultures, and time-honoured pageantry. The caps and gowns, the great halls, and Latin-inscribed coats of arms have largely disappeared, replaced by rationalized bureaucracies that merely promise access to labour markets.

This disenchantment shouldn't cloud a sunnier accomplishment: School systems now offer unparalleled opportunities for individuals. Schooling helps extend human rights and literacy to even the poorest segments of society. Who today reminisces for bygone eras in which schooling was a privilege for the few? Such ideas now provoke a sense of outrage and are rightfully seen to deny basic rights. Schooling may be demystified, yet we cannot manage without it.

SUMMARY

1. The selection function of school systems is being transferred from secondary to postsecondary levels. In past decades, secondary-level streaming played an important gate-keeping role, so an adolescent's life-chances were shaped largely by his or her performance in high school. However, as higher education expands, life-chances are determined increasingly by where a person graduates in a stratified structure of higher education.

2. As more Canadians attain advanced levels of education, formerly valuable credentials like the

high-school diploma have become devalued. Devaluation generates demand for more schooling, leading to a spiral of educational expansion as groups jockey for advantages in the labour market.

3. A pattern of inequality exists in Canadian school attainment. Along social class lines, students from more affluent backgrounds continue to enjoy considerable advantages. In terms of gender, women now outpace men on many indicators, though considerable gender segregation remains in certain fields of study. The legacy of conquest for Aboriginals and their history of discrimination

and segregation continue to be evident in schools, while changing immigration selection policies have created a partial reversal in patterns of attainment for other racial groups.

4. Today's moral education is less religious and explicit than before. Schools now mostly aim to have students understand key issues, rather than having a hard-edged prescriptive tone. The hidden curriculum continues to emphasize the orderly completion of tasks, punctuality, and neatness. But today's schools have a more indulgent quality than they did in the past, trying to shore up students' self-esteem and capture rather than command their interests.

5. Canadian schools have changed from informal institutions that wielded traditional authority to legal-rational bureaucracies. In the latter form, progressive educators have pursued strategies to spark intrinsic learning and cater to students in ever-more accommodating ways. In the 1970s, this involved lessening teacher power in favour of students. Today, it sometimes involves the use of market-like mechanisms to treat students as if they are "customers."

QUESTIONS TO CONSIDER

1. Compare your schooling experience so far with that of one your grandparents by using the themes of selection, accommodation, competition, and sponsored and contest mobility.

2. From what you've experienced in school, how would you motivate students to be effective learners? What organizational reforms might best inspire students? Be honest and give examples.

3. Observe a classroom. Do you see socializing messages in operation? Cite examples. Sort out the socializing influences of schools from those of families, neighbourhoods, labour markets, and peer groups.

GLOSSARY

Contest mobility is a form of educational competition in which most youths are grouped into the same school and exposed to the same curriculum, and in which relatively large numbers are directed to higher education.

Credential inflation takes place when labour-market competition encourages individuals to acquire schooling and employers raise required credential levels for reasons that are not connected to their needs for skilled employees.

The **hidden curriculum** comprises elements of school content, such as rules, procedures, structures and norms, that can shape students in covert ways.

Human capital theory emphasizes how schooling can enhance productive skills and thereby generate wealth for both individuals and society.

Professionalization is the process by which an occupation attempts to raise its social standing, often including the creation of formal educational credentials.

Progressive pedagogy is an educational movement that emphasizes student-directed learning, less structured curricula, and an emphasis on inspiring students to be intrinsically motivated in their studies.

Selection is the process by which the structure of schooling feeds into broader patterns of social stratification.

Sponsored mobility is a form of educational competition in which relatively few youths are selected early in life to enter elite universities.

SUGGESTED READING

Baker, David, and Gerald LeTendre. (2005). *National Differences, Global Similarities: World Culture and the Future of Schooling.* Stanford: Stanford University Press. An international examination of schooling trends, focusing on the curriculum and student achievement.

Grubb, W. Norton, and Marvin Lazerson. (2004). *The Education Gospel: The Economic Power of Schooling.* Cambridge, MA: Harvard University Press. This book reveals the allure of Americans' longstanding faith in schooling as a remedy for all sorts of economic and social problems.

Levine-Rasky, Cynthia. (2009). *Canadian Perspectives on the Sociology of Education.* Toronto: Oxford University Press. This collection of original essays examines the complex relationship between schooling and Canadian society.

WEB RESOURCES

Companion Website for This Book

http://www.newsociety6e.nelson.com
Begin by clicking on the Student Resources section
of the website. Next, select the chapter you are
studying from the pull-down menu. From the Student
Resources page, you have easy access to InfoTrac
College Edition® and other resources, such as the

Glossary, Test Yourself questions, and additional
readings. The website also has many useful tips to
aid you in your study of sociology.

InfoTrac College Edition Search Terms

Visit http://www.infotrac-college.com for access to
more than 20 million articles from nearly 6000
sources when doing your online research.

CHAPTER
THIRTEEN

SOURCE: © Bianda Ahmad Hisham/Shutterstock

Religion

Reginald W. Bibby
UNIVERSITY OF LETHBRIDGE

In this chapter you will learn that

- Religion has been studied by sociologists since the beginnings of sociology.

- Religion has both individual and social components—people display a wide range of levels of commitment, but groups play a major role in instilling and sustaining personal religiosity.

- Since religious groups are organizations, they can best be understood by using organizational concepts and frameworks.

- For the vast majority of people, religious commitment and involvement are rooted in social institutions, particularly the family.

- Religion's influence on individuals tends to be noteworthy but not unique, while its broader role in most societies is to support social structure and culture.

- Despite the problems of some groups, religion's future in Canada and elsewhere is secure, grounded in ongoing spiritual interests and needs.

INTRODUCTION

Religion is very much alive today. In recent years, religion has received worldwide attention in such varied developments as the death of Pope John Paul II, the phenomenal sales of Dan Brown's *The Da Vinci Code*, and the exposure given to the so-called atheist books of authors like Richard Dawkins and Christopher Hitchens. Religion's presence and importance is blatant in the conflict, terrorism, and peacemaking efforts in the Middle East. In 2006 it was centre stage in the clash of values and perhaps even civilizations as European countries and their leaders experienced the protests and threats of Muslims for allowing their newspapers to publish cartoon depictions of Muhammad (Ghafour, 2006). Even more daunting in the light of September 11, 2001, has been the 1998 directive of "fundamentalist"/"extremist" Osama bin Laden that "in compliance with God's order . . . every Muslim who believes in God and wishes to be rewarded" is to "kill the Americans and plunder their money wherever and whenever they find it"—thinking that in turn has been widely condemned by most Muslim leaders.

In North America, religion's presence is also readily evident in the God-laced responses to such militancy on the part of U.S. political leaders, whose supporters frequently include large numbers of the so-called Christian Right. Apart from its links to global issues, religion in the U.S. is pervasive. Attendance at services is extremely high and the majority of people say that religion is very important to them. The organizational health of American religion can be seen in the emergence of a growing number of very large and influential "megachurches," such as Joel Osteen's much-publicized Lakewood Church that occupies a 16 000-seat former basketball arena in Houston. Far from having only a local focus, many function as religious multinational corporations—spreading the message of "how to do ministry" to other parts of the world, including Canada. Spirituality has joined religion in going public and become part of so-called pop culture, read about in books like Rhonda Byrne's *The Secret* and Eckhart Tolle's *A New Earth*, talked about on *Oprah*, and brought to life in recent years in television programs, such as *Touched by an Angel*, and films ranging from John Travolta's *Michael* to Mel Gibson's *The Passion of the Christ*.

In Canada, beyond such media offerings, the reality of religion is readily apparent in the tendency of the vast majority of people to continue to identify with a religious tradition; in the growing numbers of

Contrary to the opinion of some people, religious belief is not disappearing in Canada. In fact, in urban areas most people have many options for worship.
SOURCE: Dick Hemingway.

individuals identifying with faiths that include Islam, Hinduism, Sikhism, and Buddhism; in the widespread interest in spirituality; in debates about same-sex marriage and polygamy; in the efforts of Catholics and mainline Protestants to resolve problems relating to the legacy of residential schools; and in the imminent prime minister of the day ending his 2006 election victory speech with the words "God bless Canada."

Many early social scientists were convinced that religion's days were numbered, that it would be just a short time before it was discarded in favour of science. Through the 1990s, the widespread consensus was that religion's influence was declining and that Canadians and people in most other technologically advanced countries were leaving religion behind—although the United States stood out as a puzzling anomaly.

We now know that such observers were wrong. In the early decades of the twenty-first century, religion lives on, embraced by large numbers of people in virtually all cultures, however "advanced" or "nonadvanced." Moreover, interest in religion and spirituality is actually on the upswing in many parts of the world, including North America, Russia, and Asia. In many Islamic countries, it is not clear that the importance of religion has ever been in doubt. Today, religion is frequently associated with conflict and division. But it also continues to bring meaning, sustenance, and hope to billions of people.

I begin the chapter by taking a brief look at what some of the early and influential social scientists had to say about religion, and then discuss how sociologists go about studying religion in both its individual and group forms. After clarifying what sociologists mean by religion, I look at "how much of it" we have in Canada and proceed to examine its sources and consequences—what kinds of factors contribute to people being religious and the influence that religion has on both individuals and societies. In concluding the chapter, I reflect on the kinds of religious developments we can expect in the foreseeable future.

I'll be giving particular attention to Canada, in large part because I have spent much of my life examining religious developments here and have some fairly unique research findings I can tell you about. However, while focusing on Canada, I will keep my eyes on the rest of the world, starting with the United States.

SOCIOLOGY AND RELIGION

A number of years ago, an American evangelist who was holding services in Edmonton was asked by a fairly strident television interviewer, "How do you know there is a God?" The evangelist immediately responded, "Because I talked to Him five minutes ago." It was an interesting claim but one that a sociologist is not in a position to verify. A basic rule of science is that "what counts" as real is what we can detect through our senses—what we refer to as "empirical" knowledge. In contrast, proponents of religion have traditionally asserted that the world we know through the senses is only part of a greater reality that, because of the limitations of sense perception, can only be known through faith.

In principle, science and religion are compatible. Science limits itself to what is perceivable, and religion maintains that reality includes the non-perceivable. Conflict between the two should only arise when one oversteps its boundaries and invades the other's territory.

Still, for the most part, science is in the driver's seat. As Émile Durkheim (1965 [1912]: 479) pointed out many years ago, religion "can affirm nothing that [science] denies, deny nothing that it affirms." Try

though it might, religion cannot overrule science in refuting basic evolutionary claims or dismissing sound medical diagnoses. At the same time, since science is limited to conclusions about the observable, it too can only go so far. Sociologists cannot address the evangelist's claim that he had actually spoken to God, any more than it can evaluate the claim that a person whose cancer has gone into remission was healed by God.

Sociology consequently suffers from one serious methodological limitation in studying religion: It cannot probe the supernatural claims that religion so often is about. Sociologists nonetheless can offer considerable insight into "the observable part" of religion. For example, they can examine

- Who tends to think they have experienced God
- Who believes in life after death and what individuals think will happen when they die
- The extent to which people have spiritual needs, and what they mean by "spirituality"
- How many and what kinds of people are involved in religious groups
- The impact that religious involvement has on individuals and societies

In short, sociologists cannot address everything when it comes to religion; but they can address much, without getting caught up in the issue of religion's ultimate truth or falsity. Max Weber summed up the focus of sociological explorations into religion this way: "The essence of religion," he wrote, is not the concern of sociologists, since "we make it our task to study the conditions and effects of a particular type of social behaviour" (1963 [1922]: 1). For our purposes, whether or not religious ideas are true is not as important as the fact they are *believed* to be true. As W. I. Thomas and Dorothy Swaine Thomas noted in their classic theorem, if we define things as real, they are real in their consequences (Thomas and Znaniecki, 1918: 79). The very fact that religious ideas are held means they potentially can have an important impact on individuals and social life.

THEORETICAL TRADITIONS

Three early theorists have had a strong influence on the sociology of religion: Karl Marx, Émile Durkheim, and Max Weber.

MARX AND CONFLICT

Karl Marx grew up in a Jewish environment but came to believe that religion is a human creation. Using the language of the day, Marx (1970 [1843]: 131) wrote, "Man makes religion; religion does not make man." He argued that man has "found only his own reflection in the fantastic reality of heaven, where he sought a supernatural being," and that being religious characterized "the self-consciousness and self-esteem of a man who has either not yet gained himself or has lost himself again."

It has been argued that we can resolve undesirable conditions by either changing them or reinterpreting them. Peasants, slaves, and the marginalized in our day theoretically can rise up and revolt; they also can minimize the importance of "this world" by looking heavenward, singing spirituals, and dreaming of walking streets of gold after they die. According to Marx, religion constitutes the latter response, resulting in people who are economically and politically deprived redefining reality, rather than changing their oppressive conditions. Religion, Marx wrote, soothes the disadvantaged like a narcotic—functioning as "the opium of the people" (Marx, 1970 [1843]: 131), in the process blinding them to the inequalities at hand and bottling up their creative energies. So it is that some observers today would argue that many socially and financially deprived individuals who are unable or unwilling to play an active role in altering social conditions or even their own lives substitute religious status for social status. A taxi driver by day is the head of a temple committee by night; the housekeeper in the hotel during the week is the star soloist in the church choir on the weekend. Religious status supplants social status; the next world supplants this world.

But Marx did not see such a redefining of reality as a chance happening. On the contrary, he maintained that those who hold power encourage religious belief among the masses as a subtle tool in the process of exploiting and subjugating them. Aligned with the interests of the dominant few, religion serves to hold in check the potentially explosive tensions of a society. Consistent with his thinking, respected social historian H. Richard Niebuhr (1957 [1929]: 51) has been among those who have claimed, for example, that a widely held belief among nineteenth-century American slave owners was that religion helped African Americans to become "better" slaves. He cites one advocate of "negro missions" who asserted that "slaves well-instructed in the Christian faith were less likely to develop revolutionary inclinations than the half-educated, such as [revolt leader] Nat Turner."

Historically, said Marx, society and religion were so intertwined that attacks on feudalism, for example,

were attacks on the church, while revolutionary social and political doctrines were simultaneously viewed as theological heresies (Marx and Engels, 1963: 132). We might argue that we see similar fusion between politics and religion today, not only in theocracies such as Iran but also in such a country as the United States, where the dominant religion, according to some observers, is "the American Way of Life," supported by the country's primary religious groups. We'll return to this issue shortly.

For Marx (1970 [1843]: 131), religion was an inadequate salve for a sick society—"the sigh of the oppressed creature, the heart of a heartless world and the soul of soulless conditions." When the sickness was remedied, there would be no need for the salve. Using another metaphor, Marx (1970 [1843]: 132) wrote that his criticism of religion was an attempt to remove "the imaginary flowers from the chain, not so that man shall bear the chain without fantasy or consultation, but so that he shall cast off the chain and gather the living flowers." Freed from the panacea of religion, individuals would be able "to think, act, and fashion their reality with illusions lost and reason regained" (Marx, 1970 [1843]: 132).

If you are someone who is personally religious, you understandably are not particularly excited to have Marx suggest that you may well be disadvantaged in some way and need to open your eyes and give your energies to changing your current situation. But before you reject his thinking altogether, it is worth noting that, at minimum, Marx seems to offer considerable insight, even today, into why some people join extreme religious groups that downplay the importance of this life—encouraging them to give up what possessions they have and, in some instances, give up their lives as well.

DURKHEIM AND COLLECTIVITY

Émile Durkheim was the son of a rabbi but was raised in a Catholic educational tradition. He himself was an atheist and an anti-cleric, who believed that a scientific understanding of society has the potential to raise the quality of social life.

In his classic work *The Elementary Forms of the Religious Life* (1965 [1912]), Durkheim argued that religion's origin is social. People who live in a community come to share common sentiments, and as a result a **collective conscience** is formed. When they gather together, they have a feeling of being in the presence of something beyond themselves that is experienced by each member, yet is greater than the sum of their individual consciences. The feeling is not unlike "the electricity in the air" we experience at an exciting playoff hockey game or a big rock concert, where that feeling "out there" seems to transcend the sum of individual emotions. Durkheim maintained that the experience is so vivid that people have felt the need to label it. In reality, Durkheim asserted, "God" is the group experiencing itself. The experience *is* real, he argues; it's just that it isn't what those involved think it is.

Once people experience such an alleged supernatural reality, they proceed to designate some related objects as **sacred** and others as **profane.** Christians have accorded special status to the cross, the Bible, and holy water, in contrast to almost everything else. Symbols of the sacred are many and diverse: Jews have accorded sacred status to the Torah and Star of David, Muslims to the Qur'an and the Saudi Arabian city of Mecca, Hindus to the Vedas and the sacred syllable "Aum"(or "Om"). In Durkheim's view, religious beliefs articulate the nature of the sacred and its symbols, and religious rites provide guidelines as to how people should act in the presence of the sacred. So it is that Muslims, for example, are expected to pray at specific times five times a day, facing Mecca, and to make a pilgrimage to Mecca at least once in their lifetime; Hindus offer daily devotional prayers in the morning and evening, sometimes accompanied by ritual bathing. Sikhs, when they enter their temples, must cover their heads and remove their shoes, and,

In Durkheim's view, religious rites provide guidelines as to how people should act in the presence of the sacred. Muslims, for example, are expected to pray at specific times five times a day, facing Mecca, and to make a pilgrimage to Mecca at least once in their lifetime.
SOURCE: Shutterstock.

where the opportunity is provided, wash their hands and feet.

Because all groups feel the need to uphold and reaffirm their collective sentiments, people come together as what he refers to as a "church." According to Durkheim (1965 [1912]: 62–63), "the idea of religion is inseparable from that of the Church," since it is "an eminently collective thing." Even when religion seems to be entirely a matter of individual conscience, it still is nourished by social sources. Besides meeting needs at the individual level, he claimed, religion creates and reinforces social solidarity. Collective life is consequently both *the source* and *the product* of religion. Accordingly, Durkheim (1965 [1912]: 62) defined religion as "a unified system of beliefs and practices relative to sacred things . . . which unite into one single moral community called a Church, all those who adhere to them."

Durkheim (1965 [1912]: 475–76) observed that "we are going through a stage of transition and moral mediocrity. The great things of the past which filled our fathers with enthusiasm do not excite the same ardour in us." He added poetically, "The gods are growing old or are already dead, and others are not yet born." But despite the problems of traditional Catholicism in particular, Durkheim didn't believe that religion would disappear: "There are no gospels which are immortal, but neither is there any reason for believing that humanity is incapable of inventing new ones." The dominant groups and forms of expression might change, but the social sources that give rise to religion obviously will remain and, with them, religion. Durkheim also contended that there will always be a place for religious explanations. The reason? Science is fragmentary and incomplete, advancing too slowly—life cannot wait. Religion will therefore continue to have an important "gap-filling" role.

Durkheim's legacy has been important. You don't have to agree with his assertion that the gods are socially created to realize that God and ethical conceptions, for example, frequently reflect social and individual characteristics. In fact, an age-old concern among people valuing faith has been the inclination of humans to create the gods in their own images. What's more, Durkheim's acknowledgment that science moves too slowly for many of us anticipated the ongoing "market" for alternative explanations on the part of religious leaders and just about anyone else, including—to use just one illustration—psychics. The vast market for explanations of the unknown is suggested by the fact that, as of 2009, Yahoo was listing some 21 million entries for "Psychics"!

WEBER AND IDEAS

Max Weber was born in Germany. His grandparents were Protestants who had been refugees from Catholic persecution and eventually became successful in business. He was interested in religion from an early age but never shared the deep commitment of his Calvinist mother. His background was reflected in one of his most important works.

Weber's interest in the origin and nature of modern capitalism led him into extensive debate with Marx's ideas and stimulated much of his work in the sociology of religion. Unlike Marx and Durkheim, Weber had little interest in the question of whether religion is ultimately true or false. Rather, he maintained that religion, in addition to having a supernatural component, is largely oriented toward this world. As a result, religious ideas and behaviour should frequently be evident in everyday conduct. In *The Protestant Ethic and the Spirit of Capitalism* (1958 [1904–05]), for example, Weber examined the possibility that the moral tone that characterizes capitalism in the Western world—the *Protestant ethic*—can be traced back to the influence of the Protestant Reformation. His hope was that his work would contribute "to the understanding of the manner in which ideas become effective forces in history" (Weber, 1958 [1904–05]: 90).

Weber took the position that ideas, regardless of whether they are objectively true or false, represent a person's definition of reality and therefore have the potential to influence behaviour. Accordingly, he emphasized the need to interpret action by understanding the motives of the actor (a method he called *Verstehen*, or understanding). To achieve such awareness, he said, researchers should place themselves in the roles of those being studied.

Weber understood the need to study diverse societies, present and past, in order to examine culture's influence on religion. He therefore embarked on comparative and historical studies of religion and its relationship to social and economic life in China, India, and ancient Israel. A compilation of his writings, *Sociology of Religion* (1963 [1922]), illustrates the way that Weber approached religion. He noted that god-conceptions are strongly related to the economic, social, and political conditions in which people live. The gods of light and warmth and of rain and Earth have been closely related to practical economic needs; heavenly gods that rule the celestial order have been related to the more abstract problems of death and fate. In political conquest, the gods of the conquered are fused with the gods of the conqueror and reappear with revised characteristics. Furthermore, the growth of **monotheism** (belief in one god) is related to goals of political unification.

Beyond the social sources of the gods, Weber dealt with such major themes as the relationship between religion and social class and the nature of religious organizations. He reflected on religious leadership and the important process whereby a personal following is transformed into a permanent congregation, which he referred to as "routinization." He noted that different groups in society vary in their inclination to be religious: Peasants are religious when they are threatened; the nobility find religion beneath their honour; the middle class sees religion largely in ethical terms; the working class supplants religion with other ideologies.

Over the years I have found that students, whether religious or otherwise, appreciate the way in which Weber attempted to take religion seriously and not become embroiled in attacking it or dismissing it. His approach has become fairly typical in the contemporary study of religion. Still, along with Weber, some of the insights of Marx and Durkheim have remained appealing.

THE NATURE OF RELIGION

Are you religious? If you are like many Canadians, you may promptly say, "Yes" or "No, I'm not," perhaps adding, "I'm not religious but I am spiritual." The term "religion" is widely used, but obviously people have different ideas in mind when they use it. Up to now, I have been assuming that we have a consensual understanding of what we mean by "religion." But before we go much further, and particularly before we look at research into religion, we need to clarify what we actually mean by the term.

"Religion" can be a blurry concept. Many people use it in a functional sense: What people value most becomes their religion—money, career, family, sports. A lame story has a young boy telling a religious doorknocker, "My mother is RC; my dad is NHL." The problem with such functional definitions of religion, sociologist Peter Berger (1974: 129) once observed, is that they become like grey cats on a dark night. If religion is everything, then it is nothing.

In a pioneering work published almost five decades ago, Charles Glock and Rodney Stark (1965) offered some thoughts that continue to be helpful. They pointed out that, in defining religion for social scientific purposes, we should begin by recognizing that humans develop systems of meaning to interpret the world. Some systems—commonly referred to as "religions," including Christianity, Judaism, and Islam—have a supernatural referent. Others, such as a science-based system (scientism) or political "isms" (communism, fascism), do not. The latter systems, they suggested, might be viewed as human-centred or **humanist perspectives,** in contrast to *religious perspectives,* which are succinctly referred to here as **religions.**

The two types of perspectives differ on one critical point: Religion is concerned with discovering life's meaning, and humanist perspectives are concerned with making life meaningful. Humanist Bertrand Russell stated the difference well: "I do not think that life in general has any purpose. It just happened. But individual human beings have purposes" (in Cogley, 1968: 171). Religious perspectives suggest that our existence has meaning, preceding that which we, as humans, decide to give it. In contrast, humanist perspectives assume that life has no "ultimate meaning" and therefore focus on giving it meaning.

The dichotomy is not perfect; some would say that such criteria might lead us to see Buddhism, for example, as a humanist perspective. Here I would simply defer to commonly understood thinking and place Buddhism in its familiar religion category for the sake of communication. However, for the most part, I think the religious perspectives/humanist perspectives approach is helpful.

PERSONAL RELIGIOSITY

Now that I've clarified things a bit, let's go back to the pointed question: How religious are you? And to be less pointed, how religious are Canadians as a whole? Sociologists have not believed that the answers are arbitrary or simply subjective. They have given much effort to finding ways of defining and measuring what they have called **personal religiosity.**

Much of the early research used one of three basic indicators to determine the religiosity of a person. All three assumed group involvement: identification, membership, and attendance. In surveys, people were asked questions, such as "What is your religious preference?" "Do you belong to a congregation?" and "How often do you attend religious services?" People who indicated that they had a religious preference, belonged to a local group, or attended services with regularity were viewed as religious.

However, as you know well, simply knowing that someone is "Protestant" or "Hindu," "Jewish" or "Mennonite," tells us very little about a person's actual commitment to his or her faith. Similarly, people might be group members, but members may be may be active or inactive, committed or uncommitted. And service attendance, although measuring participation in a group, excludes people who could be very committed yet, for such reasons as age, health, work schedule, and geographical location, are not overly active in a religious organization.

Since the 1960s, social scientists have responded to the limitations of these three measures by viewing religious commitment as having a variety of dimensions. In one of the more helpful frameworks devised, Stark and Glock (1968) suggested that the religions of the world typically expect their most devoted followers to hold key beliefs, engage in certain practices, have supernatural experiences, and be aware of the central tenets of their faiths. Stark and Glock refer to these belief, practice, experience, and knowledge components of commitment as **dimensions of religiosity.** It is not enough to believe *or* practise *or* experience *or* know; all four traits are expected of the committed.

My ongoing Project Canada national surveys, which were launched in 1975 and have been carried out every five years since then, provide comprehensive data on personal religiosity in this country. The surveys have found that Canadians exhibit relatively high levels of religious belief, practice, experience, and knowledge (see Table 13.1, p. 316). Indeed, some eight in ten Canadians say they believe in God, close to seven in ten maintain there is life after death, six in ten acknowledge that they pray privately at least once a month, and about five in ten think they have experienced the presence of God. Almost half also exhibit some basic knowledge of Islam, Judaism, and Christianity. On the surface, then, early twenty-first century Canadians seem to be a fairly religious people.

However, the surveys have also found that although around 50 percent claim to be committed to Christianity or another religion, less than half of the committed demonstrate the belief, practice, experience, and knowledge characteristics that Stark and Glock (1968) saw as central to commitment. Among the other 50 percent of Canadians, about three in ten indicate that they are interested in but not committed to any religion, and the remaining two in ten simply say that they are not religious (Bibby, 2004a). According to the 2005 Project Canada survey, 25 percent of Canadians say that religion is "very important" to them, with most having fairly conventional ideas of religion in mind. Regional variations are striking, with the levels ranging from a high of about

TABLE 13.1   RELIGIOUS COMMITMENT ALONG FOUR DIMENSIONS, CANADA, 2005 (IN PERCENTAGE)

DIMENSION	RESPONSE	PERCENTAGE
Believe in God	Yes, I definitely do	49
	Yes, I think so	33
	No, I don't think so	11
	No, I definitely do not	7
Believe in life after death	Yes, I definitely do	36
	Yes, I think so	31
	No, I don't think so	21
	No, I definitely do not	12
Practise private prayer	Daily	27
	Several times a week	11
	About once a week	7
	Once or more times a month	8
	Hardly ever/never	47
Experience God	Yes, I definitely have	26
	Yes, I think so	23
	No, I don't think I have	30
	No, I definitely have not	21
Knowledge	The name of the sacred book of Islam (Qur'an)	53
	The first book in the Old Testament (Genesis)	47
	Who denied Jesus three times? (Peter)	41

SOURCE: Derived from Reginald W. Bibby, *Project Canada 2005 National Survey.*

40 percent in the Atlantic region, through around 30 percent to 35 percent in Ontario and the three Prairie provinces, to lows of 15 percent in British Columbia and 10 percent in Quebec.

An interesting footnote is worth pondering: Pollsters are continually reminding us that Americans are more religious than Canadians (Kiefer, 2004; Ray, 2003; Winseman, 2004). But New Brunswick sociologist Samuel Reimer (1995, 2003) has been arguing for some time now that we must not overlook an important qualitative difference in religious belief and commitment in the two countries. Reimer maintains that it is easier to be highly committed in the American religious environment than it is in Canada since, in his words, higher levels of religiosity in the United States have "more to do with cultural supports for religiosity than with deeper religious conviction." Since it is more difficult to be religiously committed in Canada, religious devotion, among Canadians, he argues, "is more likely to be based on conviction."

COLLECTIVE RELIGIOSITY

How many times have you heard people say, "I don't have to go to church to be religious"? Increasingly the generalization has been expanded to include temples and synagogues as well. It may be a common argument, but it doesn't have much sociological support.

Most social scientists, beginning officially with Durkheim, have maintained that personal religiosity is highly dependent on **collective religiosity,** or group support of some kind. Such dependence is not unique to religion. It stems from a basic fact of life: The ideas we hold tend to come from our interaction with other people. However creative we might like to think we are, the fact is that most of the ideas we have in our heads right now can be traced back to the people with whom we have been in contact—family, friends, teachers, authors, journalists, and any number of other so-called experts. Moreover, if we are to retain those ideas, they have to be continuously endorsed by at least a few other people whose opinions we value. Ideas are sustained by relationships.

It consequently is not surprising that researchers find that evangelicals, for example, one of the most numerically vibrant "religious families" in the country, have learned that they need to "grow their own and keep their own." They have more children than members of most other groups do, provide them with positive church-life experiences from the time they hit the church nursery, make sure they have youth-friendly programs when they are teens, and encourage them to marry each other—or if worst comes to worst, marry an outsider and bring the partner into the group—and then continue to be part of young adult and adult activities. To fail at any of those three crucial points in the biography of their daughters and sons is to run the risk of seeing them abandon evangelical faith. People cannot hold ideas or commitment for long without a measure of social support.

Seem like a strong claim? Try it on your own biography.

The Church–Sect Typology

Those who have examined religious groups in predominantly Christian settings have recognized two major kinds of organizations. First, there are numerically dominant groupings—the Roman Catholic Church in medieval Europe, the Church of England, the so-called mainline denominations in Canada and the United States (Anglican, United, Presbyterian, Lutheran), and so on. Second, smaller groups have broken away from the dominant bodies. For example, in the sixteenth century, Protestant groups, including the Church of England, broke away from the Roman Catholic Church; but Methodists in turn broke away from the Church of England, and the Salvation Army emerged as a breakaway group from the Methodists. Today, additional emerging groups include an array of Baptist and Pentecostal denominations and nondenominational, "grassroots" congregations that are found in virtually every North American city.

From this pattern of dominant groups and breakaway groups, sociologists who try to make sense of religious groups developed an analytical scheme known as the **church–sect typology.** This framework attempted to describe the central characteristics of these two types of organizations, as well as account for the origin and development of sects.

In perhaps its earliest formulation, Max Weber distinguished between church and sect primarily on the basis of theology (churches emphasize works, sects stress faith) and relationship to society (for churches, accommodation; for sects, separation). Weber noted the irony in the sect's development: Initially a spinoff from an established church, the sect gradually evolves into a church itself (Gerth and Mills, 1958). The sect at first is characterized by spontaneity and enthusiasm. In time, however, these traits give way to routinization and institutionalization.

Although the church–sect typology has been used extensively, alternative ways of understanding religious groups have become increasingly popular.

Organizational Approaches

In sociological terms, religious organizations are no different from other social organizations. Therefore, there has been a growing tendency to analyze religious groups by making use of the same frameworks we use in studying social organizations in general.

Led by the work of respected American sociologist Rodney Stark and his associates (Finke and Stark, 1992; Stark and Bainbridge, 1985; Stark and Finke, 2000), a market model for understanding religion has become prominent in recent years. Religious groups are seen as "firms" or "companies" competing for "market share."

- Seen through such eyes, the Roman Catholic, Anglican, and Eastern Orthodox churches are part of multinational corporations; so is the Salvation Army.
- A number of groups, including the United Church and the Pentecostal Assemblies of Canada, are companies that are "Canadian-owned and operated."
- Many smaller evangelical Protestant denominations have been "branch plant" operations of American groups—not unlike "Ford Canada" or "Wal-Mart Canada"—that, over the years, have become increasingly autonomous. Some other groups, including Presbyterians and some Lutherans and Baptists, have similarly evolved from overseas operations.
- Despite the fact that Jews, Muslims, Hindus, Sikhs, and Buddhists all have worldwide roots and ongoing ties with those roots, none have developed official international or national structures that oversee their Canadian businesses. They have lobby groups and other organizations that address some common interests. But their "business outlets" are typically highly autonomous, with their synagogues, mosques, and temples owned and operated by their local congregations.
- Similarly, large numbers of other religious firms operate as privately owned companies. They are started by religious entrepreneurs who are convinced that a market exists for their particular product. The early days are often modest, with operations launched in homes, schools, and warehouses. Some are successful; many are not.

Apart from provocative marketing language and corporate analogies, a general organizational approach to religious groups sheds new light on basic features of religious groups, including (1) the nature and the sources of their members, (2) their formal and informal goals, (3) the norms and roles that are established to accomplish their purposes, (4) the sanctions that are used to ensure that norms are followed and roles are played, and (5) the degree of success that groups experience in pursuing their goals. Let me briefly illustrate.

Membership When studying the membership of religious groups, it readily becomes apparent that the vast majority of those involved are following in parental footsteps. Canadian census data show that when two parents have the same faith, 95 percent of their children are also raised in that faith. As a result, new additions to almost any given congregation are primarily active members who are on the move geographically. These include people coming to Canada from other countries. For example, during the 1980s and 1990s immigrants contributed most of the growth to Hindu, Sikh, Muslim, and Buddhist groups.

Congregations frequently compete with one another for members and staff, especially in urban areas where some "outlets" are larger and more affluent than others. The more attractive congregations typically have the resources to search farther for their leaders and hold them longer.

They also have better physical facilities. It's not just a Protestant or Catholic phenomenon: Muslims, Hindus, Sikhs, Buddhists, and Jews typically define

During the 1980s and 1990s immigrants contributed most of the growth to Hindu, Sikh, Muslim, and Buddhist groups in Canada.
SOURCE: © iStockphoto.com/David P. Lewis.

their meeting places as important centres for social activity. Consequently groups tend to build structures as lavish as their resources will permit. In recent years, a number of Protestant "megachurches" have come into being in both Canada and the United States. They typically have seating for 1000 to 4000 people, are serviced by many full-time staff members, and have annual budgets in the millions of dollars. They are found in major cities, such as Toronto, Montreal, Winnipeg, Edmonton, Calgary, and Vancouver. But they also are appearing in smaller communities, such as Abbotsford, Red Deer, and St. Catharines. These megachurches make it difficult for other congregations to compete. Catholics are showing signs of following suit, recognizing that one way of dealing with the priest shortage is to have larger, regional parishes.

Congregations, like secular businesses, also expand their services and personnel in keeping with their economic means. Some of the megachurches, for example, offer many of the typical worship and educational opportunities of more traditional, older groups. But they also have extensive programs aimed at children, teenagers, young adults, and seniors. The programs range from small but sophisticated groups studying in homes ("cell groups"), through well-developed music and drama programs, to multimedia education, entertainment, and elaborate Internet sites. A room in one well-known British Columbia megachurch resembles a 1950s diner—complete with a car front, jukeboxes, booths, and stools. As the church's head youth minister told me, "The young people love this room; but, I have to admit, the seniors love it too."

An obvious point of tension involves maintaining integrity while providing products that attract customers.

Goals The conscious and unconscious goals of local religious groups vary by congregation and members. Like the goals of other social groupings, these conscious and unconscious goals commonly appear to be in conflict. For years observers have noted that the formal goals derived from religious doctrine, such as spiritual growth, frequently exist in tension with "survival goals" relating to numerical growth that translate into necessary human and financial resources (Metz, 1967).

Similarly, congregations frequently have difficulty in reconciling their pastoral or "comfort" function with their prophetical or "challenge" function (Glock, Ringer, and Babbie, 1967). For example, the national leadership of the United Church of Canada viewed itself as prophetic in its call during the mid-1980s to allow homosexuals to be eligible for ordination as ministers. In taking such a controversial position the denomination lost a sizable number of dissenting members and, in some cases, entire congregations (O'Toole, Campbell, Hannigan, Beyer, and Simpson, 1993). Prophecy has its organizational price.

There is an additional point of tension: how to satisfy the needs of the existing clientele while reaching out to new people who are not involved, yet have important needs themselves. It is a dilemma that congregations of virtually all religious stripes are not particularly adept at resolving (Bibby, 2004b), with obvious negative implications for growth.

Norms, Roles, and Sanctions If groups, like companies, are to achieve their official and unofficial goals, they have to be able to establish norms for what has to be done and assign roles for their members to play. An examination of congregational roles reveals that most groups in Canada—led by Catholics, evangelicals, Muslims, Hindus, and Sikhs—often have a human resource problem for two main reasons. The first is that they are top-heavy with men and often inadequately tap the resources of women, a reality that has been variously met with acquiescence, resistance, and a measure of change (Nason-Clark, 1993; Nesbitt, 1997; Speaker-Yuan, 2005; Stackhouse, 2005). The second problem is that groups typically rely on volunteers to carry out key roles. These are the same people who congregational leaders have to work hard to recruit and retain—people on whom they depend for involvement and financial support. They are not hired and they can't exactly be fired. It adds up to a situation in which religious groups are frequently fragile and inefficient companies (Bibby, 1993; Brannon, 1971; Monahan, 1999).

Success In their studies of religion in Canada, researchers have tended to emphasize "the numerical bottom lines" of religious groups and to focus on such indicators of success as attendance, membership, and finances.

Through the early 1990s, the research news was not particularly good for organized religion. Overall, attendance and membership were down, with some groups feeling great hardship as a result of inadequate finances. The mainline Protestant groups—the United, Anglican, Presbyterian, and Lutheran churches—were the most severely hit, along with Roman Catholics in Quebec. Despite some attendance and membership losses, the Roman Catholic

Church outside of Quebec appeared to be relatively healthy. And although their numbers were not as large as many people think, conservative Protestant groups were at least able to hold their own and grow modestly—a significant accomplishment, given that they have represented only about 8 percent of the population since 1871 and could have readily been absorbed by larger competitors. Other faith groups, such as Hindus, Muslims, Sikhs, Jews, and Buddhists, were having a difficult time growing, primarily because they were having considerable difficulty holding on to their offspring, who all too frequently were marrying Catholics and Protestants.

The size of a group is largely a function of birth and mortality factors. What was disconcerting for religious leaders in Canada through the early 1990s was that most groups were top-heavy with older people, and many did not seem able to replace them with comparable numbers of younger people. As a result, it was estimated that, by 2015, weekly attendance would drop dramatically for mainline Protestants and Quebec Catholics, decline slightly for "Other World Faith" groups, and remain fairly stable for conservative Protestants and Roman Catholics elsewhere in Canada. The result? There was a very real possibility that the dominant players on the Canadian religious scene would soon be Roman Catholics and evangelical Protestants.

However, as we will see shortly, there is good reason to believe that this "old story" is being replaced by a "new story." There are signs that Canada's well-established religious groups are beginning to make something of a comeback. This embryonic renaissance has not taken place by chance but appears to reflect the explicit efforts of groups to be more effective in addressing the needs and interests of children, teenagers, and young adults.

The Canadian Situation

Affiliation with religious groups has been widespread in Canada since the founding of this country. Close ties have always been apparent between Canadians of British descent and the Church of England, Methodism, and Presbyterianism; between the French and the Roman Catholic Church; and between other ethnic groups and the churches of their homelands. As noted earlier, Islam, Hindu, Sikh, and Buddhist growth in recent years has been directly related to immigration from Asia.

In the 2001 census, 84 percent of Canadians indicated that they have a religious preference.

Nationally, Catholics compose 45 percent of the population; Protestants, 29 percent; and unspecified Christians 3 percent. Seven percent consist of those with other religious preferences, and 16 percent have no specified religion (Table 13.2).

Such data suggest that it is an exaggeration to think of Canada as a highly diversified religious mosaic. As Statistics Canada (2003: 5) noted in releasing the census findings, Canada is "still predominantly Roman Catholic and Protestant." It's true that Muslims, Hindus, Sikhs, and Buddhists all doubled in size between 1991 and 2001, and they have added diversity and vitality to the Canadian religious scene. Yet, measured against the Canadian population, their numbers are still relatively small. It is also premature to assume that their numbers will continue to grow, given the tendency of many of their offspring to socialize with and marry people outside their groups—a reality and challenge well known, for example, to Canada's Jewish community. Christian groups not only continue to hold a large monopoly; they frequently are the primary beneficiaries of such intermarital "religious defection." Time will fill out the story.

The Christian faith also continues to be pervasive in the United States, where surveys show that close to nine in ten Americans identify with Christian groups (Gallup, 2006). However, the numerically dominant groups in the United States are not the same as those in Canada. Whereas one in two Canadians is Catholic, the same is true of only one in four Americans. Furthermore, just one in ten Canadians identifies with conservative Protestant (evangelical) groups, in contrast to more than three in ten Americans. A tipoff on the difference is that slightly more than 40 percent of Americans claim that they are "born again" (Winseman, 2005); the term itself is not even particularly common in Canadian religious group circles, even among many of today's evangelicals. In fact, 31 percent of Canadians in our 2005 survey told us that if they were in the presence of someone they didn't know who was "born again," their immediate reaction would be to feel uncomfortable. They'd better not wander too far into the United States.

When Canadians are asked about actual *membership* in religious groups, as opposed to mere affiliation or identification, more people—about 30 percent—claim to belong to churches than to any other single voluntary

TABLE 13.2   RELIGIOUS IDENTIFICATION, CANADA AND THE PROVINCES AND TERRITORIES, 2001 (IN PERCENTAGE)

	CANADA	BC	AB	SK	MB	ON	QC	NB	NS	PE	NL	YT	NT	NU
Catholic	**45**	**19**	**28**	**33**	**29**	**37**	**84**	**54**	**37**	**48**	**37**	**22**	**46**	**24**
Roman	43	18	26	31	27	34	83	54	37	47	37	22	46	23
Eastern Orthodox	2	1	2	2	2	2	1	<1	<1	<1	<1	<1	<1	<1
Protestant	**29**	**32**	**39**	**48**	**45**	**35**	**5**	**37**	**49**	**43**	**60**	**34**	**31**	**67**
United	10	9	14	20	16	12	<1	10	16	20	17	9	6	1
Anglican	7	8	6	7	8	9	1	8	13	5	26	15	15	58
Presbyterian	1	1	1	<1	<1	3	<1	1	3	6	<1	1	1	<1
Lutheran	2	3	5	8	5	2	<1	<1	1	<1	<1	2	1	<1
Baptist	3	3	3	2	2	3	<1	11	11	5	<1	4	2	<1
Pentecostal	1	1	1	2	2	1	<1	3	1	1	7	2	3	4
Other	8	7	9	9	12	5	3	4	4	6	10	1	3	4
Christian: Other	**3**	**5**	**4**	**3**	**4**	**3**	**1**	**1**	**1**	**2**	**1**	**4**	**3**	**3**
Other faiths	**7**	**8**	**6**	**<1**	**3**	**9**	**4**	**<1**	**<1**	**<1**	**<1**	**1**	**2**	**<1**
Jewish	1	<1	<1	<1	1	2	1	<1	<1	<1	<1	<1	<1	<1
Muslim	2	2	2	<1	<1	3	2	<1	<1	<1	<1	<1	<1	<1
Hindu	1	<1	<1	<1	<1	2	<1	<1	<1	<1	<1	<1	<1	<1
Buddhist	1	2	1	<1	<1	1	1	<1	<1	<1	<1	<1	<1	<1
Sikh	<1	4	<1	<1	<1	<1	<1	<1	<1	<1	<1	<1	<1	<1
Other	<1	<1	<1	<1	<1	<1	<1	<1	<1	<1	<1	<1	<1	<1
No religion	**16**	**36**	**23**	**16**	**19**	**16**	**6**	**8**	**12**	**6**	**2**	**39**	**18**	**6**

SOURCE: Adapted from Statistics Canada, 2003, "Religions in Canada," Analysis Series, 2001 Census, Catalogue no. 96F0030XIE2002015.

group. About one in four attends services approximately once a week, and roughly the same proportion of parents with school-age children expose their children to Sunday schools or similar kinds of religious instruction on a fairly frequent basis.

However, between approximately the 1940s and 2000, church attendance in Canada declined sharply, documented by Gallup poll findings summarized in Figure 13.1. Gallup had been asking Canadians if they attended a service "in the last seven days"—the phrasing of the inquiry adds sporadic attenders to those who claim they attend every week. Using such a measure, Gallup found that Protestant attendance dropped from around 60 percent to about 30 percent between the 1940s and mid-1970s, rebounding to around 40 percent by the mid-1990s. The decline in Roman Catholic attendance appears to have started around 1965, dropping from roughly 85 percent to 40 percent by the mid-1990s—led by low church-going in Quebec. No such dramatic decline in attendance has taken place in the United States: Weekly attendance has remained remarkably steady at just more than 40 percent dating back to the late 1930s when polling began.

To the surprise of almost everyone, evidence suggests that an attendance reversal may have started to take place in Canada. In 1984, 23 percent of the country's 15- to 19-year-olds were attending services weekly; by 1992 the figure had dropped to 18 percent. It was assumed

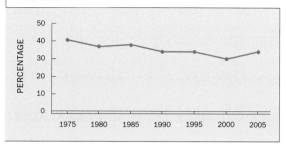

FIGURE 13.2 MONTHLY-PLUS ATTENDANCE IN CANADA, 1975–2005

SOURCE: Reginald W. Bibby, *Project Canada Survey* Series.

that the level would drop to around 13 percent by 2000. However, that year the weekly figure for this age group rebounded to 21 percent, where it remains today (Bibby, 2009). A major contributing factor appears to be the accelerated emphases on youth ministry by a wide array of Protestant, Catholic, and other faith groups. In addition, for the first time in decades, the 1990s saw the proportion of weekly attending 18- to 34-year-olds level off and in some group instances increase, rather than decline—a situation that has continued through the present time. The only notable exception? Quebec. There, regular attendance has continued to decline among people young and old.

Nonetheless, overall, there are signs of a possible renaissance of religion in Canada (Bibby, 2004a, 2006, 2009). After declining steadily for four decades, national weekly service attendance increased from 21 percent to 25 percent between 2000 and 2005. Monthly-plus attendance, probably a more reasonable measure of involvement, has returned to levels of the late 1980s and early 1990s (Figure 13.2). What we are seeing may turn out to be just a temporary blip. But maybe not.

THE SOURCES OF RELIGION

More than a few religious leaders over the years who have seen their best efforts to involve people come up empty have murmured, "There is only so much we can do." It's an insightful lament. The best programs and ministries in the world will not hit a responsive chord with everybody. Personal and societal factors also play critically important roles in determining who embraces religion and religious groups and who does not.

Much of the early work in the scientific study of religion by people like Durkheim focused on preliterate cultures in which religion was highly pervasive. Everyone was religious, or so it seemed. Consequently, it's not surprising that observers gave considerable

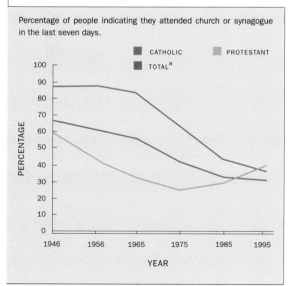

FIGURE 13.1 ATTENDANCE AT RELIGIOUS SERVICES, CANADA, 1946–2000

Percentage of people indicating they attended church or synagogue in the last seven days.

aTotal refers to all Canadians, regardless of faith.
SOURCE: Gallup Canada, Inc., surveys, 1946–1995.

attention to the origin of religion itself, rather than examining variations in religious commitment.

However, individual differences in religion's importance in contemporary societies have called for explanations as to why some people are religious and others are not. The explanations tend to focus either on individuals or on social structure.

INDIVIDUAL-CENTRED EXPLANATIONS

At least three dominant "person-centred" explanations of religious commitment have emerged. See to what extent you see yourself and others in what the experts have had to say.

Reflection

The desire to comprehend reality is widespread among humans. In the course of reflecting on the meaning of existence, people have commonly concluded that life has a supernatural, "transempirical" dimension. As Weber (1963 [1922]: 117) put it, religion is the product of an "inner compulsion to understand the world as a meaningful cosmos and take up a position toward it."

There is little doubt that Canadians, like people elsewhere, reflect on life's so-called big questions. Some 80 percent say they think about such issues as the origin and purpose of life, the meaning of suffering, and what happens after we die. Such questions take on particular urgency when people have to come to grips with such events as the attacks on September 11 or a devastating tsunami—or have to deal with the suicide of a friend or the loss of a parent. Still, although such times of reflection may provide religious groups with an opportunity to respond, reflection in itself does not usually lead to religious commitment and involvement. Fewer than one in three Canadians who often raise these meaning questions give evidence of being religiously committed.

Socialization

A second person-centred explanation sees religious commitment as the product of learning—socialization factors that were the focus of Chapter 3. Freud (1962 [1928]) went so far as to say that religion is learned pretty much like the multiplication table. He may not have been exaggerating. I have never forgotten a high-school teacher who had played for the Edmonton Eskimos telling us that if we had grown up in India, we would all be Hindus. As Durkheim emphasized, personal religiosity has social origins and, consequently,

will strongly reflect the social environments from which we come, beginning with our family.

Why is an Iraqi a Muslim, a Londoner Church of England, a Ute (as in Utah) a Mormon, a Quebecker a Catholic? The answers are obvious. What is less clear is why some of those four people take their religion more seriously than the others. To address the question, we probably would start by looking at the commitment level of their parents. Beyond family, we would expect that individuals who are devout have been exposed to additional social sources that are positive toward religion—friends, an ethnic group, an institution, a community or region, perhaps an entire society. Religion is very much a learned phenomenon.

Accommodation to social pressures, notably those of primary groups, seems to be a related source of religious group involvement. For example, one marriage partner may become more active in response to the hopes and expectations of the other, friends in response to friends, parents in response to having young children, children in response to their parents. As John McEnroe of tennis fame once put it, "I can go to church once in a while, just for Mom." In small communities where religion is pervasive and normative, accommodation would be expected to be an important source of religious involvement.

It's important to keep in mind that socialization appears to be a *necessary* but not a *sufficient* cause of religiosity. That is to say, to the extent that Canadians are currently involved in religious groups, most had parents who also were involved. However, the fact that Canadians had parents who were involved does not ensure that their sons and daughters will follow suit. Although about eight in ten of today's weekly attenders had parents who attended weekly, only about three in ten Canadians whose fathers or mothers attended weekly have followed their example.

With a decreasing number of parents actively involved in religious groups in recent decades, fewer have been passing the experience of organized religion on to their children. For example, in 1975, some 35 percent of Canadians with school-age children claimed that they and their children were attending services on a regular basis. By 2000, that figure had dropped to around 20 percent. Such a pattern, if it had continued, obviously would have had devastating numerical consequences for organized religion. But as of 2005, it had increased to 23 percent. The fact that the decline appears to have been halted provides another signal that a shift in participation patterns could be taking place.

One of the strongest predictors of adult religiosity is childhood religious practice. When parents participate in religious observance with their children, the early socialization experience is often imprinted for life.
SOURCE: © iStockphoto.com/Sean Locke.

If religious involvement and commitment are to last a lifetime, they need to receive ongoing social support. Our surveys have found that the commitment level of a partner is strongly related both to personal involvement and to the importance placed on religion. In more than seven in ten cases, if one partner is a weekly attender, so is the other. In fewer than three in ten cases does a person attend weekly or view religion as "very important" if the partner does not.

Deprivation

A third person-centred explanation of religious commitment is that the devout are drawn primarily from the ranks of society's deprived or disadvantaged. Religion provides them with compensation, sometimes now, sometimes later. The roots of such thinking, of course, are found in the work of Marx and Freud.

The deprivation argument was developed more fully by Glock and Stark (1965), whose work was disseminated widely and consequently has been very influential. They maintained that five types of deprivation are predominant in the rise and development of religious and secular movements: economic, social, organismic (that is, physical or mental), psychic, and ethical. The first three types of deprivation are self-explanatory. Psychic deprivation refers to the lack of a meaningful system of values, and ethical deprivation refers to having values that are in conflict with those dominant in a society.

Some research attempts to evaluate the deprivation thesis in the 1970s and 1980s by using objective indicators, such as income, health, and social relationships, did not find deprivation to be a particularly good predictor of broad religious participation in either the United States (Roof and Hoge, 1980) or Canada (Hobart, 1974). The learning perspective has far more applicability.

The world's attention has been fixed on suicide bombing since 2001. Because such attacks are often religiously inspired, and because they are so violent, you might expect the attackers to be driven by extreme deprivation. And, in fact, some observers initially hypothesized that suicide bombers must be poor, unemployed, uneducated, unmarried, socially marginal young adults with little to lose. Analysts assumed that people with such characteristics could be relatively easily convinced to exchange their lives of suffering in the here-and-now for promises of glory and martyrdom in the hereafter.

Research has demonstrated, however, that the deprivation argument does not hold in the case of suicide bombers. As Canadian sociologists Robert Brym and Bader Araj note in their study of suicide bombings in Israel, the West Bank, and Gaza from 2000 to 2005, suicide bombers typically come from working-class and middle-class backgrounds and they are generally better educated than the populations from which they are drawn. For example, the suicide bombers who were responsible for the attacks of September 11, 2001, were all well-educated, middle-class men (Brym and Araj, 2006). Studies of extreme forms of religious participation thus lead us to the same conclusion as studies of general populations: Deprivation does not appear to be systematically associated with religious commitment. This leads us to additional explanations of religious commitment.

STRUCTURE-CENTRED EXPLANATIONS

Suicide bombers hardly exist in isolation. On the contrary, they typically are members of political and military groups found in the Middle East and, in the case of the Tamil Tigers, Sri Lanka. The groups to which they belong in turn are committed to getting rid of occupying forces, overthrowing existing regimes in their own countries or, in the case of a group like Hamas—the largest Palestinian resistance movement—obliterating Israel and creating an Islamic theocracy. Structural conditions clearly play an important role in such "religio-political" organizations coming into being and in individuals being recruited as members.

Such realities remind us that, in addition to personal characteristics of the reflection, socialization, and deprivation variety, religious commitment is strongly influenced by the broader national, regional, and group contexts in which people find themselves. You might immediately think of a theocracy, such as Iran, where the president and legislature are subject to clerical supervision. But in virtually every society, Canada included, history and culture combine to create milieux that, to varying degrees, do or do not support religion.

Those proclivities often vary not only along national lines but also by the region in which people live and the groups of which they are a part. Historically, Canada's "Bible Belt" has been viewed as Alberta, when by every conceivable measure it probably has actually been the Atlantic region. Regardless, to grow up in either of these two regions results in being exposed to environments that are far more "pro-religious" than people experience in a province like British Columbia. Social environments are important determinants of religious commitment and involvement.

Two early prominent Canadian sociologists, S. D. Clark (1948) and W. E. Mann (1962) argued that, historically, the emergence of sect-like groups, such as indigenous Baptists and Pentecostals, in Canada was tied to the existence of unstable conditions, which were produced by such factors as immigration and economic depression. With industrialization and increased prosperity and stability, some of these smaller, independent evangelical groups evolved into denominations—a process referred to as **denominationalism.** A further example of the impact of societal factors on religion can be found in Quebec. Much of the drop-off in Roman Catholic attendance between 1965 and 1980 was related to the accelerated modernization of Quebec, including the Church's relinquishing of much of its important role in education and social services to the provincial government (Beyer, 1993, 1997; Rouleau, 1977).

The climate that present-day societies provide for religion is the subject of considerable debate. Some observers maintain that increasing industrialization and postindustrialization contribute to a decline in the pervasiveness and importance of religion. This widely held **secularization thesis** has

been prominent in the social sciences, largely because of the influence of Durkheim, Marx, and Freud. It's a framework that seems particularly appropriate to developments in much of Protestant Europe. It also is the dominant explanatory framework the media and Statistics Canada use in making sense of religious developments in Canada (Catto, 2003; Shackleton, 2005; Statistics Canada, 2004a, 2004b; Valpy, 2006).

But there is also another take on religious developments—what we might call the **persistence thesis.** Proponents of this position, among them Daniel Bell (1977) and Rodney Stark and William Bainbridge (1985), claim that religion—traditional or otherwise—persists in industrial and postindustrial or postmodern societies, continuing to address questions of meaning and purpose, and responding to widespread interest in spirituality. Stark maintains that some religious groups or companies will fail, but because of ongoing market demand, new ones will emerge to pick up the slack. What is in doubt is not the persistence of religion, only the identity of the key players.

In Canada, we can readily explore the relationship between religious involvement and commitment and some of the correlates of social and cultural change—such as age, urbanization, education, and employment status. If the secularization thesis is correct, we would expect religiosity to be pretty low for everyone by this point in our history, particularly so for Canadians who are younger, are living in larger communities, are well educated, and are part of the paid work force. Conversely, if the persistence thesis is correct, we would expect some variations in these anticipated patterns.

Here are the main findings:

- Differences in religious participation and commitment exist for older Canadians versus those 35 to 54. But younger adults (18 to 34) break with the pattern, attending services more often and placing more importance on religion than 35- to 54-year-olds do (Table 13.3).
- There are no significant differences by community size. Regionally, there is some support for the idea that secularization is most advanced in those parts of Canada that were first to experience extensive economic development—central Canada and the west coast.
- Obtaining a university education is not related to a drop in religiosity.

Full-time employment, however, is associated with a noticeable decline in both attendance and the importance given to religion. In large measure, the key issue

TABLE 13.3 SERVICE ATTENDANCE, COMMITMENT, AND SPIRITUAL NEEDS BY SOCIAL CHANGE CORRELATES, CANADA, 2005 (IN PERCENTAGE)

	WEEKLY ATTENDERS	RELIGION "VERY IMPORTANT"	SEE SELF AS HAVING SPIRITUAL NEEDS
Nationally	**25**	**25**	**72**
Age			
55 and over	32	30	72
35–54	17	18	70
18–34	27	31	74
Community Size			
Under 30 000	25	26	72
30 000–400 000	25	27	73
Over 400 000	25	25	72
Region			
Atlantic	39	41	82
Prairies	31	34	77
Ontario	28	31	71
British Columbia	17	16	67
Quebec	15	9	69
Education			
High school or less	25	29	68
Some postsecondary	19	21	72
Degree or more	28	25	75
Paid Labour-Force Participation (65 & under)			
Not employed outside the home	29	31	74
Employed outside the home	17	18	70
Women	*14*	*18*	*77*
Men	*19*	*18*	*66*

SOURCE: Derived from Reginald W. Bibby, *Project Canada 2005 National Survey*.

here seems to be time pressures experienced by parents with young children and particularly by women. In my mind, this is an extremely important finding. The post-1950s rise of families with two parents in the paid labour force and the implications of the rise of this family form for the highly selective use of time may be largely responsible for the decline in mainline Protestant and Catholic attendance in Canada after the 1950s. Religious groups needed to adapt by providing "ministries" that responded to changing family life. Few did (Bibby, 2005; Brown, 2001).

Of considerable importance, despite the variations in their inclination to be involved in religious groups and to place a high value on religion, Canadians of every social and demographic stripe tend to acknowledge that they have spiritual needs. Such an admission is consistent with what observers from Durkheim to Stark have expected. It also points to the fact that an extensive market for religion and spirituality persists in Canada.

THE CONSEQUENCES OF RELIGION

In today's increasingly pragmatic world, Canadians face what seem like unlimited choices and limited resources. We need to sort out what is worth our time and what is not. Religion gets no exemption from such selective consumption.

Gone is the day when religious leaders could expect people to become involved in their groups because it's "their duty." Our 2005 national survey found that 61 percent of Canadians believed that their parents "felt they were supposed to go to church." Eighty-seven percent of respondents maintain that, today, "people who attend religious services should

Canadians of every social and demographic stripe tend to acknowledge that they have spiritual needs.
SOURCE: Shutterstock.

not go because they feel they have to but because they find it to be worthwhile."

Is religion "worthwhile"? On balance, does it enhance personal and social life?

PERSONAL CONSEQUENCES

Research findings on religion and what we might refer to generally as "mental health" are contradictory. Important early work carried out by highly respected social psychologist Milton Rokeach (1965: 2) led him to conclude, "We have found that people with formal religious affiliation are more anxious [than others]. Believers, compared with non-believers, complain more often of working under great tension, sleeping fitfully, and similar symptoms." Yet research dating back to the 1970s has consistently found a negative relationship between religious commitment and *anomie*—valuelessness and rootlessness (Lee and Clyde, 1974). Over the years a number of researchers have argued that involvement in groups, such as sects and cults, has contributed to upward mobility, providing an improved self-image and hope in the face of economic and social deprivation (e.g., Johnson, 1961; Whyte, 1966), During the 1970s and 1980s, considerable literature emerged warning against the psychological and emotional damage that could be inflicted by the alleged "brainwashing" of cults (Dawson, 2006: 95ff).

Gale Frankel and W. E. Hewitt (1994) of the University of Western Ontario have been among the researchers who have found a positive relationship between religious group involvement and good mental health. Research into the "Toronto Blessing" congregation has even maintained that physical

healing sometimes occurs (Poloma, 1997; Poloma and Hoelter, 1998). National denominational surveys that I have carried out for the United Church of Canada and the evangelical Christian and Missionary Alliance document a fairly predictable conclusion: People who are highly involved in established religious groups claim that their involvement significantly enriches their lives (Bibby, 1994, 1999).

What seems apparent from all this is that some forms of religiosity are connected with well-being, while others are not.

My own analyses of our survey data dating back to 2000 suggest that, overall, Canadians who exhibit religious commitment are slightly more inclined than others to claim a high level of happiness; to find life exciting; to express a high level of satisfaction with family, friends, and leisure activities; and to view death with hope rather than with mystery or even fear (Bibby, 2004a: 128–29; Figure 13.3). However, when the impact of other factors, such as age, education, community size, and region, is taken into account, the apparent modest influence of commitment typically disappears or at least has to be qualified. For example, Gee and Veevers (1990) found that religious involvement and life satisfaction were positively related nationally, but not in British Columbia.

In short, religious commitment by itself appears to have a fairly limited influence on valued personal characteristics. Moreover, it is often less important than such variables as age, education, or employment in predicting personal well-being.

An important word of caution: this "no difference" finding does not mean that faith is not adding

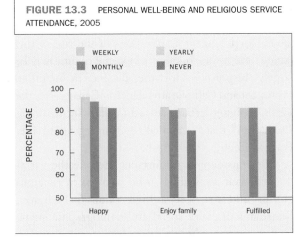

FIGURE 13.3   PERSONAL WELL-BEING AND RELIGIOUS SERVICE ATTENDANCE, 2005

SOURCE: Reginald W. Bibby, *Project Canada 2005.*

something to the lives of people who value faith. Rather, in light of the high levels of happiness and contentment reported by Canadians generally, it suggests that large numbers of other people are finding alternative pathways to personal well-being. Religion is having an impact but not necessarily a unique impact.

INTERPERSONAL CONSEQUENCES

One of the first attempts to examine the relationship between religious commitment and compassion was carried out by Clifford Kirkpatrick in Minnesota in 1949. He found that religiously committed people were somewhat less humanitarian in their outlook than others.

Some 20 years later, Rokeach (1969), drawing on U.S. national data, observed that religious commitment was *negatively* related to social compassion; in the case of Roman Catholics, no relationship—positive or negative—existed. Rokeach concluded that "the results seem compatible with the hypothesis that religious values serve more as standards for condemning others . . . than as standards to judge oneself by or to guide one's own conduct" (Rokeach, 1969: 35).

These findings, however, have not gone unchallenged. Research conducted on specific religious groups and in certain locales has found a positive relationship between commitment and compassion. In a more immediate relational sense, Wilcox (1998) has found that, although conservative Protestant parents are more likely than others to use corporal punishment in disciplining their children, they also are more likely than other parents to praise and hug their children. Extensive research on religion and racial prejudice, such as Smith's (1999) look at anti-Semitism and "the Religious Right," has yielded contradictory results.

However, some three decades ago, Richard Gorsuch and Daniel Aleshire claimed to have found the key reason for the discrepancies. Church members often appear to be more prejudiced than those who have never joined a church. But, they say, it is not because of religious involvement. On the contrary, when involvement level is taken into account, the people who turn out to be the most prejudiced are the "marginally involved" members. Gorsuch and Aleshire concluded, "The highly committed religious person is—along with the nonreligious person—one of the least prejudiced members of our society" (Gorsuch and Aleshire, 1974: 287). If this is the case, then, as with personal characteristics, religion may be

making a difference interpersonally—but it is not a unique difference.

Ongoing analyses of Project Canada data have found that religiously committed people in this country do not differ significantly from others with respect to their interpersonal relationship attitudes (Bibby, 1987, 1995, 2004a). They hold a similar view of people, claim a comparable level of compassion, and appear to be no more or less tolerant of deviants, members of minority groups, and people of other religious faiths than are other Canadians. Furthermore, in contrast to the findings of Rokeach and Stark and Glock, no noteworthy differences appear in the interpersonal attitudes held by Roman Catholics and Protestants.

There is, however, one area where religion still appears to speak with a fairly loud if not unique voice—the area of personal morality, notably sexuality. With few exceptions and with varying degrees of explicitness, religious groups tend to oppose "moral innovation." Examples include opposition to changing sexual standards, legal abortion, and distribution of pornographic materials (see Table 13.4, p. 328).

That said, there is considerable variation in the position that religious groups take on many sex-related issues, as well as in the inclination of average people who identify with those groups to "follow the party line." Generally speaking, evangelical Protestants are the most likely to be opposed to changes in the sexual realm, Quebec Catholics—despite the official position of their Church—the most receptive, with their openness exceeded only by Canadians with no religion.

But this just in. Two recent analyses that I have carried out on adults and teens show that there is a consistent, positive relationship between holding clear-cut belief in God and endorsing interpersonal values that make for civility—traits like honesty, concern for others, politeness, and the like. Canadians who "definitely believe in God" consistently differ from atheists (Bibby, 2009; see Table 13.5, p. 328). That's not to say that theists necessarily come through behaviourally, or that there is no social compassion, for example, among atheists. The findings do suggest, however, that belief in God is one, if only one, potential source of civility. To the extent that's the case, there could be some significant social value in people believing in God. Recent atheist media in blitzes in Canada and elsewhere—using such catch lines as, "There's probably no god. Now stop worrying and enjoy your life"—may, in the end, have limited interpersonal payoffs.

TABLE 13.4   PERCENTAGE OF CANADIANS OPPOSED TO SELECTED ISSUES BY SERVICE ATTENDANCE AND GROUP IDENTIFICATION, 2005

	PRE-MARITAL SEX	EXTRA-MARITAL SEX	HOMO-SEXUALITY	SAME-SEX MARRIAGE	ABORTION: RAPE	ABORTION: CHILD UNWANTED	DISTRIBUTION OF PORNOGRAPHY
Attendance							
Weekly	60	96	75	62	45	79	69
Less than weekly	7	82	25	20	4	36	31
Religious Group Identification							
Conservative Protestants	64	98	74	64	41	82	69
Christian Unspecified	30	92	45	44	28	65	44
RC: Outside Quebec	25	91	47	37	25	62	47
Other World Faiths	21	86	38	33	12	46	39
Mainline Protestants	13	89	35	28	6	40	43
RC: Quebec	10	78	33	22	6	40	35
No Religion	3	73	10	7	1	19	17

SOURCE: Derived from Reginald W. Bibby, *Project Canada 2005 National Survey.*

SOCIETAL CONSEQUENCES

I've looked at some personal and interpersonal consequences of religious involvement and commitment. But what about the net consequences for societies more generally? On balance, is religion a plus or a minus—or simply irrelevant?

A cursory look at the historical evidence in Canada provides mixed reviews. Many would argue that religion has played and continues to play an important role in helping immigrants adjust to life in Canada, providing resources in the form of both personal faith and social support. Others would quickly add that many religious groups, notably the United, Anglican, and Roman Catholic churches, along with the Jewish community, have played important roles in helping to establish a just society, where diversity and inclusiveness today are valued on a level matched by

few countries anywhere in the world. In addition, the claim can be made that religious groups are among the few organizations in Canada that explicitly attempt to instill morality, ethics, and compassion, thereby making an important contribution to civility.

Those things said, you hardly need me to remind you that other views of religious groups are not so charitable. For example:

- In the course of taking their place in the country, a number of Christian groups were anything but just and compassionate in their treatment of Aboriginal peoples.
- The "Quiet Revolution" in Quebec in the 1960s that saw the province take over many services from the Catholic Church was not accompanied by an overt revolt. But, covertly, large numbers of Catholics had found the Church to be highly oppressive and began to stay away (Graham, 1990: 114ff).
- A variety of highly publicized sexual abuse cases that spanned the country—from the Mount Cashel orphanage in Newfoundland and Labrador, through the "Orphans of Duplessis" in Quebec and the Christian Brothers in Ontario, to the Catholic Diocese in Prince Rupert, B.C.—left many Canadians stunned and disenchanted with organized religion (see Bibby, 1993: 68ff).
- Catholics, Jews, and Muslims, along with smaller religious bodies, including Mennonites, Hutterites, Jehovah's Witnesses, Scientologists, and Doukhobors, have been on the receiving end of hostility and discrimination at various points in our nation's history.

TABLE 13.5   VALUES OF THEIST AND ATHEIST TEENS, PERCENTAGE INDICATING "VERY IMPORTANT"

	NATIONALLY	THEISTS	ATHEISTS
Trust	84	88	78
Honesty	81	86	89
Concern for others	65	73	54
Politeness	64	71	56
Forgiveness	60	72	45
Working hard	54	61	49
Patience	44	54	35

SOURCE: SOURCE: Bibby (2009).

Clearly the evidence to date is mixed. Religion adds to the quality of life in the country and sometimes subtracts. What does seem to contribute to a fairly unique religious situation in Canada is the entrenchment of pluralism. Religious groups here have to play by the rules of diversity, being respectful of one another—not making excessive claims of uniqueness, not being overly aggressive in raiding each other's ranks, not being exploitive of vulnerable categories, such as immigrants, children, and seniors. And they have to respect individual rights, in keeping with the Charter of Rights.

So contained, religious organizations that might otherwise have a detrimental effect on collective life in Canada are kept in check. We have no effective "Moral Majority," like the United States does. The same-sex marriage issue was not allowed to become an unrestrained and uncivil debate, and if someone tested the boundaries—as one Alberta bishop was tempted to do on occasion—public opinion tended to result in public relations retreats. This is not a country where Christians can call other people "heathen," but they also cannot be ridiculed as "bigoted Bible-thumpers." This is not a country where Muslims can call for the heads and hands of artists who draw caricatures of Mohammed, but it also is not a place where artists can insult and incite Muslims. Some groups don't always like the rules, but that's the way the religion game is played in Canada. So contained and so retrained, religion—it seems to me—is positioned to contribute positively to our individual and collective life (Box 13.1).

BOX 13.1   WHY THE GLOBAL RAGE HASN'T ENGULFED CANADA: MULTICULTURALISM AND MEDIA LIKELY MUTED PROTESTS

Why haven't Muslims in Canada taken to the streets in large numbers to protest against cartoons of the Prophet Mohammed? It's not because everyone in Canada is so nice to each other, say Canadian Muslim leaders and Islamic scholars. It's because Canada's multiculturalism is complex.

They say Muslim immigration into Canada has been different. So has Muslim integration into Canadian society. And so has the political action of Canadian Muslim organizations around the highly sensitive issue of Islamic religious fundamentalism.

The difference is illustrated by events in France in 2004 and Canada in 2005, said Tarek Fatah, a leader of the Muslim Canadian Congress.

In France, few if any representative voices within the French Muslim community were heard in the news media speaking in favour of a law banning conspicuous religious symbols, such as the traditional Muslim head scarf, in public schools.

This was the case even though a significant percentage of French Muslims had no problem accepting the law within the cultural context of French secular society.

The powerful Muslim opposition that was heard, Mr. Fatah said, came from "the mosque structure" but "the mobilization of moderate Muslim voices never happened."

In contrast, in Canada in 2005, the news media pointedly reported that the most vociferous opposition to an Ontario law permitting Islamic religious tribunals to arbitrate family and marital disputes came from Muslim organizations themselves.

In Mr. Fatah's view, the mainstream Muslim community in Canada has recognized the need to take what he calls "ownership of the word Muslim." It has become actively involved in Canadian political life and not marginalized as is the case in many Western countries.

"It's a shift, for Canadian Muslims, that has not happened anywhere else."

Mohamed Elmasry, president of the Canadian Islamic Congress, said violent demonstrations simply aren't a fit with the Canadian Muslim community—which, because of Canada's immigration requirements, he said, is the most highly educated Muslim community in the world.

"They would find legal and peaceful means of protest far more productive," said the imam and professor at the University of Waterloo. "With demonstrations, you cannot have full control over who does what."

His organization, the largest Muslim umbrella group in Canada, has actively discouraged demonstrations over the cartoons and has spoken publicly against the violent protests—as has the Muslim Canadian Congress.

Earle Waugh, a University of Alberta Islamic scholar, said most Muslim immigrants to Canada do not feel sidelined, a factor significantly fuelling the protests in European countries.

"There is no sympathy within the Canadian Muslim community for a radical approach," he said. "No sympathy for the fundamentalists."

Canada has had no legacy of Muslim colonies like that of the British and French, and no history of migrant Muslim guest workers like that of Germany.

SOURCE: Michael Valpy, 2006, "Why the Global Rage Hasn't Engulfed Canada: Multiculturalism and Media Likely Muted Protests," *The Globe and Mail* 8 February, p. A14. Reprinted with permission from The Globe and Mail.

Peter Berger (1961) has observed that Durkheim's assertion that religion functions primarily to integrate societies seems to offer a good description of religion in the United States. Religion, or at least the mainline segment of organized Christianity that historically has embraced the largest number of members, has tended to endorse American culture rather than to challenge it, to endorse the status quo rather than call for social transformation. So intense has been the bond between religion and American life that a number of years ago Robert Bellah (1967) and others described the phenomenon as American **civil religion.** In his influential book *Protestant, Catholic, Jew,* Will Herberg (1960: 75) put it this way:

> Americans, by and large, do have their "common religion" and that "religion" is the system familiarly known as the American Way of Life. . . . By every realistic criterion the American Way of Life is the operative faith of the American people. . . . To be a Protestant, a Catholic, or a Jew are today the alternative ways of being an American.

Canada, committed as it is to diversity and a downplaying of overt nationalism—except for the occasional international hockey championship—has no such civil religion. As Stahl (1986: 16) colourfully puts it, "Other than a few bands and firecrackers, Confederation was not attended by much emotional outpouring." And religious groups have done little to add fervour to our rather lifeless expressions of nationalism. Still, Harold Fallding (1978) reminds us that, historically, "Canadian Protestant churches have reflected the British position of legitimizing authority through supporting government, offering prayers, for example, for its success in securing order and justice." The fusion of Catholicism with life in Quebec, Anglicanism with the status quo in southern Ontario, and conservative Protestantism with political and social life in Alberta are obvious examples.

On occasion, of course, religion has challenged North American culture. The civil rights movement in the United States received much of its leadership and impetus from African-American evangelical churches. American Catholic bishops and the National Council of Churches have frequently spoken out against perceived injustices, including poverty, racism, and war. Jerry Falwell's "Moral Majority," which peaked in the 1980s, contributed to a very vocal "Christian Right," committed to altering the nature of American life by influencing the country's major institutions.

In Canada, religious groups have had and continue to have the freedom to address governments. To varying degrees they have availed themselves of the opportunity—and responsibility. Protestant churches, for example, have received mixed reviews for their concern about the plight of Jews during World War II; some churches and individuals were silent, while others were not (Davies and Nefsky, 1997). In the 1940s, a radical effort was made by the Roman Catholic Church to support striking workers, a preview of the ongoing inclination of the Canadian Conference of Catholic Bishops to support average Canadians and to be vocal in criticizing the profit orientation of the nation's economy. Protestant groups, often led by the United Church, along with a growing number of ecumenical consortia and initiatives, and, more recently, evangelical churches, have been making concerted efforts to bring about social change (Crysdale, 1961; Lewis, 1993; Stiller, 1997) In recent years, religious coalitions—such as the national Citizens for Public Justice and, in Ontario, the broad-based Interfaith Social Assistance Reform Coalition (ISARC)—have been among those calling for greater and more effective attention being directed toward such issues as social programs, the environment, and Aboriginal issues.

It is important to note that locally, nationally, and globally religion clearly has the potential both to bring people together and to tear them apart. Religion's role in contributing to conflict, past and present, is well known. Globally, what seems like never-ending conflict in the Middle East and elsewhere provides further contemporary examples of religion playing a role in contributing to divisiveness. At times I wonder about the long-term outcome of what seems to be a deepening chasm between the West and the Muslim world.

Yet, in the aftermath of both the September 11, 2001, attacks and the fury over the publishing of the Mohammed caricatures in 2006, significant numbers of Muslim leaders were among the first to decry violence and bloodshed, and to call on people worldwide to find peaceful means of resolving their differences. Therein lies the paradox of religion: It can both enrich and destroy social life.

THE FUTURE OF RELIGION

One thing is certain: Religion is not going to disappear. Proponents of the secularization thesis expected religion to be replaced by science and reason as societies evolved. Opponents of the secularization thesis countered that humans have needs, notably the need to come to grips with death, that only religion can satisfy. Consequently, even if secularization leads to the demise of some religious groups, new providers are bound to appear. Ironically, rather than signalling the death of religion, secularization stimulates innovation (Stark and Bainbridge, 1985).

Emerging religious forms will include sects—groups that break away from established religions, and new religious movements **(cults)** with origins outside of older religions. From this point of view, shifts in the overall "religious economy" over time involve "the rising and falling fortunes of religious firms, not the rise and fall of religion per se" (Finke and Stark, 1992: 275).

As we glance around the globe, there is no need to spend time debating religion's future with the wise social scientists of old. Religion is simply everywhere.

In Canada, there are signs that a modest rise in religious involvement is taking place that will continue in the immediate future. However, it is due not so much to the arrival of new religions as it is to the rejuvenation of the older, well-established ones.

Census and survey data reveal that fairly small numbers of Canadians have opted for new religious groups in recent decades. The proportion of Canadians who identified with such groups as Jehovah's Witnesses and Mormons has never been more than one-half of 1 percent. In a country of more than 32 million people, newer, sect-like groups remain on the margins of the Canadian religious scene.

Further, we now know that relatively few people have been switching from one group to another—apart from a fair amount of movement *within* conservative Protestantism, where people who are Pentecostal move to a Baptist church, for example. The amount of "inter-family" switching—such as Roman Catholics becoming Protestants, or Jews or Muslims opting for Catholicism—has been grossly exaggerated.

A big surprise? Despite the fact that the proportion of Canadians who say they have "no religion" increased from 4 percent in 1971 to 16 percent in 2001, most people haven't really been dropping out permanently. The majority of people in this category are young and single. About one-third have come from mainline Protestant homes, another one-third from Catholic homes; only about one in three have parents who also have no religion. As they get a bit older, marry, have children, and want religious weddings, baptisms, and the like, lo and behold, many proceed to tell pollsters that they are "Catholic" or

"United" or "Jewish"—again. Using the panel component of our national surveys, we have found that, within five years, one in three people who said he or she had "no religion" proceeds to have one; within ten years that figure jumps to two in three. The "no religion" category is a temporary residence for most people—sort of like living in an apartment before moving into a house (Bibby, 2004b: 29–51).

We consequently have a situation in which Canada's established religious groups find themselves with lots of "affiliates" who identify with the group and aren't about to turn elsewhere. I'm not talking only about adults. Our national surveys of teenagers between the ages of 15 and 19 have found that the country's "emerging generation" closely resembles adults when it comes to current service attendance levels. About 90 percent of teens claim the same group affiliation as their parents, and only about 2 percent indicate any strong interest in new religions. Their belief, practice, experience, and knowledge levels, while typically lower than those of adults, are appreciable and, in at least some instances, can be expected to rise as teens move into their 20s and beyond. Some three in ten say religious involvement is important to them and their level of

TABLE 13.6 A PROFILE OF RELIGION AND SPIRITUALITY IN CANADA: TEENAGERS AND ADULTS (IN PERCENTAGE)

	ADULTS	TEENAGERS
Beliefs		
God	82	67
Atheism	7	16
Life after death	67	75
Spirit world contact	46	46
Practice (weekly)		
Pray privately	45	30
Attend religious services	25	21
Read the Bible/other scriptures	19	9
Experience		
Have experienced God	49	39
Knowledge		
Denier of Jesus	41	23
Sacred book of Islam	53	30
Religious Involvement		
Is important	53	30
Is enjoyed	25	26
Spirituality		
Have spiritual needs	72	54

SOURCES: Bibby, 2006, 2009.

enjoyment of religious groups is on par with that of adults. In addition, more than half acknowledge that they have spiritual needs (see Table 13.6).

So let's add all this up: Canadians are not doing much switching or dropping out. The overwhelming majority continue to hold beliefs, engage in practices, experience the gods, and express spiritual needs. But maybe they just aren't interested in organized religion. Not so. Our surveys over the past couple of decades have been documenting a consistent finding: More than one in two people who attend services less than once a month says they are receptive to greater involvement if it is worthwhile for themselves or their families (Figure 13.4). And what do these people see as "worthwhile"? Such things as having their spiritual needs met, getting some insight into how they might have better relationships with partners and children and friends, and maybe finding some emotional resources to help them cope with the needs they face in living everyday life. Likewise, about 40% of seldom-attending teens say they are open to greater involvement — "if I found it to be worthwhile" (Bibby, 2009).

In short, many people in Canada haven't given up on religion—and haven't even given up on religious groups. But in the midst of living lives that are full, where time and other resources are often being severely stretched, they have to find significance in religious participation. Otherwise, why bother?

The research suggests that, to the extent that groups literally find "their affiliates" and succeed in touching their lives in significant ways, many will

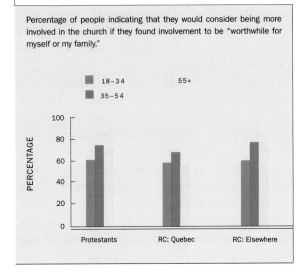

FIGURE 13.4 RECEPTIVITY TO GREATER INVOLVEMENT IN THE CHURCH BY AGE COHORT, PROTESTANTS AND CATHOLICS ATTENDING LESS THAN ONCE A MONTH, 2005

SOURCE: Bibby, 2006, 202.

become involved. As I have been noting throughout, there are signs that something of a participation shift may be occurring, as groups attempt to be more responsive, starting with improved ministries to children, teenagers, and young adults. To the extent such efforts continue, particularly on the part of the biggest player—the Roman Catholic Church—we may well continue to see something of a renaissance of religion in Canada.

SUMMARY

1. Sociology uses the scientific method to study religion. Religion explores reality beyond what can be known empirically.

2. The sociology of religion has been strongly influenced by the theoretical contributions of Marx, who stressed the compensatory role of religion in the face of economic deprivation; Durkheim, who emphasized both the social origin of religion and its important social cohesive function; and Weber, who gave considerable attention to the relationship between ideas and behaviour.

3. Religion can be defined as a system of meaning with a supernatural referent used to interpret the world. Humanist perspectives make no such use of the supernatural realm, attempting instead to make life meaningful.

4. Personal religious commitment increasingly has come to be seen as having many facets or

dimensions. Four such dimensions are commonly noted: belief, practice, experience, and knowledge. Personal commitment is created and sustained by collective religiosity. In Canada, organized religion has experienced a considerable decline in participation in recent years, a trend that has had critical implications for commitment at the individual level.

5. Variations in the levels of individual commitment that characterize complex societies have led to explanations that emphasize individual and structural factors. Reflection, socialization, and deprivation have been prominent among the individual explanations, while the dominant structural assertion has been the secularization thesis.

6. At the individual level, religion appears to be, at best, one of many paths leading to valued

characteristics, such as personal happiness and compassion. Although religion can be socially disruptive, Canada's emphasis on social and cultural diversity functions to put limits on how religion can be expressed, thereby optimizing the possibility of religions contributing positively to social and collective life.

7. Although proponents of secularization saw religion as being replaced by science and reason, it is now apparent that religion continues to be important throughout the world, including Canada. Its future is not in doubt.

8. The search for alleged religious switchers and dropouts in Canada reveals that few have turned elsewhere or permanently opted for "no religion." Most still identify with the country's established groups.

9. Canadians young and old, in very large numbers, continue to hold religious beliefs, claim religious experiences, and express spiritual needs. Many also say they are receptive to greater involvement with religious groups.

10. To the extent that groups can locate and respond to their "affiliates"—as it appears they have been doing in recent years—there is good reason to believe that the embryonic "renaissance of religion" in Canada will continue.

QUESTIONS TO CONSIDER

1. Which of the three key theorists do you find to be the most helpful in understanding religion: Durkheim, Marx, or Freud?

2. What does it mean to be religious?

3. To what extent are people in Canada today interested in (a) spirituality and (b) organized religion? What do you mean by the term *spirituality*?

4. What kinds of people do you find are interested in (a) spirituality and (b) organized religion? Do you see any signs of increased interest on the part of young people?

5. Does religion make any difference in the lives of the people you know? Would Canadian society be any different if organized religion disappeared?

6. Are Canadians interested in the supernatural? What is the evidence?

7. Do you think it is true that secularization stimulates religious innovation—that the decline of old groups provides the opportunity for new groups to surface and prosper?

8. Imagine that you are serving as a consultant to a major Canadian religious group. What might you suggest it consider doing in order to (a) keep the young people it has and (b) gain the interest of Canadians who are not actively involved?

GLOSSARY

The **church–sect typology** is a framework, originating with Weber, in which religious organizations are studied in terms of ideal-type characteristics.

Civil religion refers to the tendency for nationalistic emphases to be nurtured by a society's religions, so that a culture takes on many religious-like characteristics. The term is most often used with respect to the United States.

Collective conscience is Durkheim's term referring to awareness that a group is more than the sum of its individual members and the belief that what is being experienced is the supernatural.

Collective religiosity is religious commitment as manifested in and through religious groups; it is key to the creation and sustenance of personal religiosity.

Cults are religious groups that have their origins outside older religions. Sects, in contrast, are groups that have broken away from established religions.

Denominationalism refers to the tendency for a wide variety of Protestant religious groups to come into being, seemingly reflecting variations not only in

theology but also—and perhaps primarily—in social characteristics.

Dimensions of religiosity are the various facets of religious commitment; Glock and Stark (1965), for example, identify four: belief, experience, practice, and knowledge.

Humanist perspectives are systems of meaning used to interpret the world that do not have a supernatural referent (e.g., communism, scientism).

Monotheism refers to belief in one god.

The **persistence thesis** is the assertion that religion will continue to have a significant place in the modern world, because it has never actually declined or because people continue to have interests and needs that only religion can satisfy.

Personal religiosity refers to the level of religious commitment characterizing an individual.

Profane See *sacred and profane*.

Religions are systems of meaning for interpreting the world that have a supernatural referent (e.g., Christianity, Hinduism).

Sacred and **profane** are the two categories by which Durkheim claimed all things are classified; the sacred represents those things that are deemed to warrant profound respect, and the profane encompasses essentially everything else.

The **secularization thesis** holds that religion as it has been traditionally known is continually declining, resulting in a loss of religious authority, societally and individually, as well as changes in religious organizations themselves.

SUGGESTED READING

Bramadat, Paul, and David Seljak, eds. (2008). *Christianity and Ethnicity in Canada.* Toronto: University of Toronto Press. A superb reader by leading Canadian scholars examining the relationships between religious and ethnic identity in nine major religious traditions. Complements their earlier reader (2004), *Religion and Ethnicity in Canada,* Toronto: University of Toronto Press.

Bibby, Reginald W. (2004). *Restless Gods: The Renaissance of Religion in Canada.* Ottawa: Novalis. Draws on the extensive national adult and youth surveys of the author and the work of others in examining religious trends in Canada since the mid-twentieth century, giving attention to developments both inside and outside religious groups that suggest a religious renaissance may be taking place in Canada.

Christiano, Kevin J., William H. Swatos, Jr., and Peter Kivisto. (2008). *Sociology of Religion: Contemporary Developments.* Walnut Creek, CA: AltaMira Press. An excellent overview of theory,

methods, and up-to-date findings on religion and society.

Clark, S. D. (1948). *Church and Sect in Canada.* Toronto: University of Toronto Press. This Canadian classic examines the social factors contributing to the rise of different types of religious groups in this country.

Dawson, Lorne L. (2006). *Comprehending Cults: The Sociology of New Religious Movements,* 2nd ed. Toronto: Oxford University Press. A succinct overview of cults that have emerged from the 1970s onward, dealing with such issues as why cults emerge, who joins, and their social significance.

Noll, Mark. (2007). *What Happened to Christian Canada?* Vancouver: Regent College Publishing. This is a short but detailed and invaluable essay in which a renowned American historian examines religious change in Canada since the 1950s, and contrasts the religious histories of Canada and the United States.

WEB RESOURCES

Companion Website for This Book

http://www.newsociety6e.nelson.com
Begin by clicking on the Student Resources section of the website. Next, select the chapter you are studying from the pull-down menu. From the Student Resources page, you have easy access to InfoTrac College Edition® and other resources, such as the Glossary, Test Yourself questions, and additional

readings. The website also has many useful tips to aid you in your study of sociology.

InfoTrac College Edition Search Terms

Visit http://www.infotrac-college.com for access to more than 20 million articles from nearly 6000 sources when doing your online research.

PART FIVE

Change and Conflict

CHAPTER FOURTEEN

SOURCE: © Willie eCole/ Shutterstock

Deviance and Crime

Julian Tanner
UNIVERSITY OF TORONTO

Is this chapter you will learn that

- People are worried about, and fascinated by, crime and deviance.

- The study of crime and deviance is about the behaviour itself and societal reaction to that behaviour.

- Many deviant and criminal incidents never become known to the police.

- Official crime statistics are not just a record of criminal behaviour; many other factors influence their composition.

- The crime rate in Canada is not increasing.

- The more serious the crime, the less likely it is to occur.

- The correlates of crime and deviance include age and gender.

- Numerous, often competing, explanations of criminal behaviour exist.

- Society responds to crime and deviance in different ways.

- Much of the public concern with crime centres on young people. Extreme and disproportionate reactions to crime and deviance have been conceptualized as moral panics.

INTRODUCTION

For much of our everyday lives, we take for granted that our routine activities will follow an orderly and predictable pattern. When we drive on the highway, we can rely on the fact that others will also be driving on the right-hand side of the road and will stop their vehicles at a red light. If they did not, the result would be chaos—or worse. Likewise, when we want our morning cup of coffee, we expect to join the line-up at Tim Hortons—and we don't like other patrons pushing in front of us. Everyday life depends on people following, however unconsciously, agreed-upon rules.

A good part of the sociological enterprise is concerned with explaining the orderliness of human behaviour (Giddens, 1991; Robertson, 1989). And yet just a moment's reflection will tell you that human behaviour is not always predictable, that the rules are not always obeyed, and that we don't always live up to other people's expectations. People do jump the queue and break the speed limit on the highway. They also do much worse things; they steal, cheat, rape, and murder. How and why people break rules—why they deviate from the expectations of other people—is an

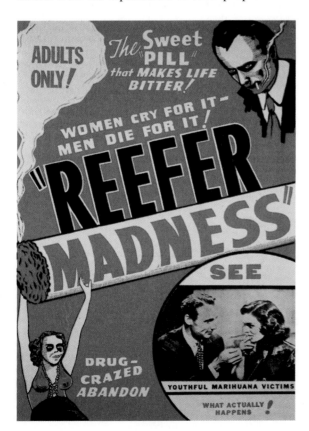

This 1936 movie poster illustrates how relative deviance is. The movie suggests that people go insane after smoking marijuana.
SOURCE: *Reefer Madness*, 1936. Directed by Louis Gasnier.

important part of the subject matter of the sociology of crime and deviance.

We have a complicated relationship with crime and deviance. On the one hand, survey after survey confirms that deviance—particularly violent interpersonal crime—is one of the major discontents of our society. Many people, especially the elderly, live in fear of crime. On the other hand, crime and deviance fascinate us. Crime stories constitute an important part of our entertainment culture. No new TV season would be complete without its roster of programs like *Law and Order, CSI,* and *The Sopranos.* Movies, books, and newspapers also rely on crime and deviance for much of their content. In fact, this dependency seems to be increasing—crime coverage in the mass media has expanded substantially over the past decade or so (Sacco, 2005: 80). The very ambiguity of our feelings about crime and deviance makes it fertile ground for exercising the sociological imagination.

CONCEPTIONS OF CRIME AND DEVIANCE

CRIME AND DEVIANCE AS NORM-VIOLATING BEHAVIOUR

If I were to ask you what you consider examples of crime or deviance, you would probably include such acts as murder, rape, bank robbery, and theft. You might also mention drug use, some types of sexual behaviour, drunk driving, as well as a host of other acts of seemingly lesser importance: speeding on the highway, talking in theatres, jaywalking, and—increasingly—cigarette smoking.

These acts are all examples of rule-breaking behaviour. One way of conceptualizing crime or deviance is to emphasize its rule-breaking qualities, focusing in particular on its behavioural dimensions. Sociologists refer to the rules in question as **norms,** or generally accepted ways of doings things. The most important norms are written *laws,* or norms that the state enforces. **Deviance** involves breaking a norm. **Crime** involves breaking a law.

All known human societies have norms about appropriate behaviour. Some norms have wide scope, applying to more or less everybody in the community—prescriptions against murder and armed robbery, for instance. Other norms may only apply to particular subgroups of society. For example, there are prohibitions on the behaviours of adolescents that do not apply to adults. They involve some types of sexual behaviour, for example, and alcohol use. In the United States, some jurisdictions have laws prohibiting young people from being in a public place after a certain time in the evening. Such curfew regulations (which some people would like to see introduced into Canada) do not apply to adults. Normative behaviour can be gendered too. When I first visited Canada from the U.K. in 1970, I was surprised to find that women had to have a male escort if they wanted to enter a bar in Ontario.

Norms are enforced in many ways. The most important of them are laws, which are regulated by a **criminal justice system** that includes police, courts, prisons, and so on. The criminal justice system responds to law violators in legally prescribed ways, with the most grievous offences evoking the most severe sanctions. In Canada and all of Western Europe, life imprisonment is the most severe sanction afforded by the criminal code. In other parts of the world—the United States and China, for instance—capital punishment (the death penalty) remains the ultimate sanction.

Many of the norms that control everyday life do not require legal intervention. They are more likely to be enforced informally. People who insist on talking in a theatre are liable to be admonished by the people around them. Communal pressure is enough to regulate such behaviour.

How might we distinguish between diverse kinds of rule-breaking behaviour? One answer has been provided by John Hagan (1991), who suggests that norm violations can be differentiated by how serious they are, as gauged by three different measures of seriousness: (1) how harmful the act in question is deemed to be; (2) how much agreement there is that the behaviour in question is wrong; and (3) the

severity of the sanction, or punishment, imposed on that behaviour (see Figure 14.1).

We have the sense that more harm is inflicted by, say, physical violence than soft drug use. The brutal murder of a small child grievously affects not just the victim but also her family, friends, and neighbours. In some high-profile cases—the decapitation of a passenger on a Greyhound bus in Manitoba in August 2008, for instance—the broader society shares a communal sense of horror and outrage. Contrast that example with the case of the person who occasionally uses marijuana. Many (though not all) people would say that marijuana has little or no harmful effects; and even if there are harmful effects, the only victims are the users themselves. Similarly, whereas most of us would agree that deliberately hurting somebody by physically assaulting him or her with a weapon is morally wrong, there is significant disagreement about how inherently wrong using marijuana is. Finally, we punish acts that we regard as very harmful and wrong more severely than those deemed less harmful and wrong. These days, convicted marijuana users are unlikely to receive a prison sentence (they are more likely to receive a fine or a probation order). By contrast, those convicted of physical assault with a weapon are likely to receive a lengthy prison term.

Hagan employs his conception of "seriousness" to identify different kinds of deviance. He designates a small group of offences as **consensus crime**—acts that are felt to be very harmful and wrong, and for which the harshest criminal sanctions are reserved. What he calls consensus crimes are referred to in legal philosophy as crimes *mala in se*—crimes that are evil in themselves. Homicide, attempted homicide, violent assault with a weapon, violent sexual assault,

---

FIGURE 14.1   TYPES OF DEVIANCE AND CRIME

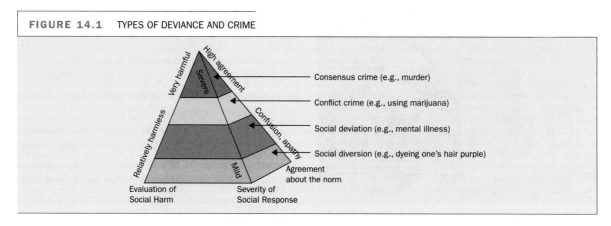

SOURCE: Hagan, 1991. Reprinted with permission from John Hagan.

armed robbery, kidnapping, and theft are all examples of crimes *mala in se*.

A second group of illegal behaviours is what Hagan calls **conflict crime.** Here, "conflict" means not that they involve acts of interpersonal violence or aggression, but that members of the community disagree over whether the behaviours in question are harmful, wrong, or deserving of severe criminal sanction. In legal terminology, these acts are referred to as crimes *mala prohibita*—crimes wrong by definition. In the conflict crime category, we find such offences as euthanasia, gambling, prostitution, drug use, and public drunkenness—all examples of what are sometimes referred to as morality offences.

The important point about conflict crime is that its presence in the criminal code is loaded with controversy. A decade ago, much public debate surrounded the appropriateness of a lengthy prison term for Saskatchewan farmer, Robert Latimer, who killed his severely handicapped daughter in what he regarded as an act of mercy. Some people regularly call for the decriminalization of marijuana use, or even prostitution, much to the horror of other people. The public is divided about how wrong, harmful, and deserving of strict punishment these offences are. With marijuana use, for example, we have a situation in which large numbers of people, particularly young people, have used it and believe that they, as well as other people, should be allowed to use it.

Not all norm-violating behaviour is illegal. While we may condemn the person who refuses to come to the assistance of somebody involved in a road accident, there is no law requiring that person to be a good Samaritan (Siegel and McCormick, 2006: 6–7). Nor is it illegal to be mentally ill, gay, or addicted to drugs, or to attempt suicide. Nonetheless, people who are mentally ill, homosexual, or alcohol- or drug-dependent are still subject to varying degrees of **social stigma**; they may be condemned, ostracized, and medicalized because of a marker that sets them off from others (Conrad and Schneider, 1992; Goffman, 1963). Research indicates that finding a job, somewhere to live, a circle of friends, or a marital partner is significantly more difficult for a person who is recognized as a "former mental patient" than it is for others (Link, 1982). The experience of former mental patients in this regard is not much different from that of ex-convicts. Historically, Roman Catholics and Jews who commit suicide cannot be buried on consecrated ground. Such stigmatized acts are not illegal, and Hagan categorizes them as "social deviations."

Same-sex marriage became legal in Canada in 2005, but only after decades of political and legal battles.
SOURCE: The Canadian Press (Fred Thornhill).

Hagan reserves the term "social diversion" for minority heterosexual and homosexual activities as well as forms of symbolic or expressive deviance involving adolescents. About the latter, the important point to remember is that young people often find themselves condemned as antisocial, threatening, or dangerous not because of what they do or don't do, but because of how they appear to others by virtue of the clothes they wear, the music that they listen to, and their hairstyle. It is not illegal to shave your head, colour your hair purple, cover your body in tattoos, have a stud in your nose, wear saggy pants, or listen to gangsta rap, but doing so often invites a censorious response from adults. Particular clothing or hairstyles or musical choices are interpreted as signs of putative deviant or criminal behaviour.

Generally speaking, the more serious the form of deviance, the less likely it is to occur. The most serious criminal acts—homicide and other violent interpersonal assaults—do not happen often. In 2007, violent crime accounted for 13 percent of all crime committed in Canada, and homicide for less than 0.2 percent of all violent crime (Dauvergne, 2008; Li, 2008) Conversely, other deviant acts occur routinely—so much so, in fact, that some commentators ponder whether the behaviours in question (speeding on the highway, for instance) actually warrant characterization as deviant.

I must make one more point about Hagan's typology: it is subject to change. The acts, behaviours, and conditions that constitute his various categories vary over time. For instance, there was a time when drunk driving was not regarded as a serious offence, when it was inconsistently enforced and rarely punished with a prison sentence. Nowadays, we regard it as a more serious offence—indeed, it has become a consensus crime. Offenders are more likely to be charged, receive a prison term upon conviction, and face condemnation from the broader community. The same may be said about violence against women, which is now treated more seriously than it was in the past in Canada.

One of the biggest changes in societal definitions of acceptable behaviour involves cigarettes. While it has long been known that smoking is addictive and dangerous to health, it is only relatively recently that legal restrictions have been placed on the practice. In the recent past, smoking was normative—socially acceptable behaviour—and in some quarters seen as a sign of adult sophistication and maturity. Change also works in the opposite direction. For example, abortion is no longer illegal in Canada. The law prohibiting abortion was repealed in 1988. In July 2008, the decision was made to award the Order of Canada to Dr. Henry Morgentaler, who started performing abortions in Canada in 1969, before it was legal. Likewise, while the use of marijuana has not been decriminalized, it is not the serious crime that it once was, and mental illness has become a medical problem rather than a criminal problem, with those affected by it treated, not punished.

CRIME AND DEVIANCE AS LABELS AND SOCIAL CONSTRUCTS

Labelling Theory

Because what was once illegal is now illegal, and vice versa, you should understand that while the study of crime and deviance is about rule-breaking behaviour, it is not *just* about rule-breaking behaviour. It is also about how members of society react to some behaviours. This understanding is the starting point for a second approach to the study of deviance and crime, one that sees deviance and crime as a matter of definitions or labels that have been applied to some behaviours but not others. **Labelling theorists** believe that publicly recognizing somebody as criminal or deviant is an important cause of criminal or deviant behaviour.

From a definitional perspective, crime and deviance are not distinctive types of human behaviour. We cannot divide human activity into its

criminal and noncriminal variants based on behaviour alone (Becker, 1963). Few if any acts are viewed as wrong under all circumstances. On the one hand, all known human societies identify some activities as morally reprehensible and worthy of condemnation and punishment. In this sense, crime and deviance are universal. On the other hand, different human societies pronounce different acts and behaviours criminal or deviant. In other words, crime and deviance may be universal, but there are no universal forms of crime and deviance (Conrad and Schneider, 1992: 5–6).

That what counts as deviant or criminal behaviour varies by time and place is well illustrated by cases where the argument about the universality of crime and deviance appears weakest. Take, for instance, the intentional killing of one person by another. You might think that murder would be universally acknowledged as a serious offence. However, intentional killing is not defined as murder in the context of war, when those doing the killing are our own soldiers, acting in the line of duty. Similarly, the fatal shooting of suspects by police officers rarely results in criminal charges. When the state (or government) kills on our behalf (in those nations that still have the death penalty, for instance), those doing the killing are not called murderers; they are public executioners.

Incest is another interesting example. While most societies have legal prohibitions against incest, significant variation exists regarding what counts as incest. Some jurisdictions forbid only sexual relationships between brothers and sisters, while others extend the ban to include third cousins (Conrad and Schneider, 1992: 5–6). Note too that while prostitution is legal in the state of Nevada in the United States and the city of Amsterdam, Holland, it is illegal in Canada. Similarly, while adult alcohol use is a legal and normal feature of Canadian lifestyles, in parts of the Middle East it is treated as a serious offence requiring a severe penalty—in some cases, corporal punishment.

Turning to drug use, we find that opiates have been illegal in Canada only since 1908. Before then, no legal prohibitions on their use existed. Opiate-based cough syrups and tonics were routinely prescribed by doctors and sold in pharmacies in a variety of forms. People who were dependent on opiate-based drugs were not stigmatized as criminal or deviant, nor was opiate dependency seen as a sign of mental illness.

Opiate drugs were also used for recreational purposes in smoking dens on Canada's West Coast. Their main users were Chinese immigrants who were brought to Canada to build the transcontinental railroad and received much lower wages than their European counterparts did. Public concern about the morality of recreational drug use served as a conduit for anti-Asian sentiment rooted in stiff competition for jobs after the Canadian Pacific Railroad was completed. The first Canadian antinarcotics legislation introduced in 1908 targeted the opium dens, making the recreational usage of opiates a criminal offence for which there were heavy penalties. No such penalties accompanied the medicinal use of opiates (Cook, 1969).

Sociologists who study the social reaction to drug use conclude that the legality of a drug is determined as much by the status of its users as by the amount of harm done by the drug. The lower the status of the user, the more likely the drug will be criminalized (Becker, 1963). Consider that cocaine in its powdered form has been a drug of choice of sport stars and entertainment celebrities since the early 1970s. However, it became a significant social problem only when it became associated with poor, unemployed racial minorities in U.S. inner cities, who ingested it in small, precooked units as crack cocaine. Once cocaine travelled down from the Hollywood Hills to the inner city, it became a major crime problem, one measure of which is that penalties for crack cocaine convictions have been more severe in the United States than for other forms of cocaine use (Reinarman and Levine, 1989).

Social Constructionism

Social constructionism is similar to the labelling approach. In fact, in some accounts they are indistinguishable. They differ, if at all, in that social constructionism is broadly concerned with all kinds of social problems, whereas labelling theory applies specifically to crime and deviance. Both theories stand in contrast to the norm-violation approach that we began with—what constructionists like to call an objectivist approach to crime and deviance.

In contrast to labelling and social-constructionist explanations, objectivist accounts of crime and deviance focus on the behaviour itself. It is assumed that we know what crime and deviance is, how much damage and harm it causes, and what needs to be done about it (Sacco, 2005). Researchers working in this tradition are likely to pose the following kinds of questions: Are rates of crime and deviance increasing? What kinds of people become bank robbers, prostitutes, or murderers? What factors predict rampage school shootings, corporate

Whether certain subcultures are deviant is a source of much debate.
© Jupiter Images, 2009.

crime, youth gang activity, and so on? Do people who break one kind of rule also break other kinds?

Labelling and social-constructionist theorists argue that crime and deviance become problematic because some people—usually the most powerful—define them as such. Sociologists working in this tradition focus on activities and claims that result in new crimes being defined. They are more likely to ask, "Why do we care more about youth crime than corporate crime?" than "What causes youth crime and corporate crime?"

More generally, social constructionism advises that so-called objective facts are not always responsible for the criminal or deviance status of a particular condition. They like to remind us that alcohol—a legal drug—is more damaging and harmful to individuals and society than some illegal drugs. They point out that the number of deaths associated with tobacco and alcohol is much larger than the number stemming from the use of illegal drugs. They sometimes use such evidence to support the decriminalization of illegal drugs. (Note, however, that their argument has been challenged by other analysts who say that because illegal drugs are not widely available, we do not yet know enough about their risks to reach valid conclusions; South, 2007: 811).

In some extreme cases, people have defined and reacted to social problems without showing that they exist. In the United States, satanic crime has received considerable media attention, even though not a shred of evidence supports repeated claims that it is a serious problem. Special crime units have even been set up to tackle the problem, and parental advisory groups formed to prevent the spread of satanic imagery and, presumably, satanic values and lifestyles in popular music (Sacco, 2005). Based on such cases, constructionists argue that while objective conditions and agreed-upon facts play a role in the designation of deviance, they are rarely the decisive determinants of whether a particular behaviour is defined as such.

Thankfully, we do not have to choose between objectivist and constructionist perspectives. It is quite possible to study the same phenomenon and ask different but complimentary questions about them. We could ask how and why hate crime has become a new crime problem (a constructionist question) and, at the same time, inquire about the characteristics of those who perpetrate hate crimes (an objectivist question). From an objectivist vantage point, you might ask, Does listening to rap music cause crime and deviance? From the constructionist perspective, the crucial question is, Why are we so concerned about the violent content of rap music but pay so little attention to the violent content of country music? Both are perfectly good research questions, and a full understanding of crime and deviance requires both the norm-violation and labelling/constructionist approaches (Thio, 2001).

CRIME IN THE NEWS

How are crime and deviance represented in the news media and popular culture and why does it matter? You may have heard the expression "If it bleeds, it leads." It's a good summary of the importance of crime to news organizations. The public has a big appetite for crime stories that the news media are happy to accommodate.

However, the media do not report all criminal incident. Violent crime is reported more regularly than property or **white-collar crime,** which may be defined as crime conducted by high-status individuals in the course of their occupation or profession. Research consistently shows that crimes of violence appear in news reports in numbers disproportionate to their incidence in official crime statistics (Reiner, 2007; Sacco, 2005).

The commonsense view about the relationship between the mass media and crime and deviance is that journalists simply record events as they happen. In this view, media accounts provide a more or less faithful reflection of objectively verifiable crime problems. However, news organizations do more than just record the facts. Whether they realize it or not, journalists shape how readers, viewers, and listeners feel and think

about crime and deviance. Research on media institutions indicates that the news we consume is a result of a selection process (see Chapter 5, The Mass Media). News items compete for time and space. Crime stories have an advantage in this competition because they are deemed highly newsworthy.

In his study of law and order reporting, British sociologist Steve Chibnall (1997) identified a number of informal criteria that are regularly used by journalists to select stories. Visible and spectacular incidents with political and sexual connotations rank highest. Similar rules determine how crime stories are presented—how many and which photographs will accompany a story, what headlines will be used, and so forth.

I am not suggesting that news organizations make up stories about crime or that crime problems would disappear if journalists chose to ignore them. My argument is that what we read in the newspapers and watch on the TV is a result of a predictable selection process. The mass media typically exaggerate the nature and scope of crime, presenting rare cases as if they are typical or the start of a new and worrying trend.

How news organizations construct crime stories is of more than academic interest because it influences how citizens think about crime. For example, research shows that Canadians overestimate crime and **recidivism** (repeat offending) rates and underestimate the severity of criminal sanctions for crimes. Crucially, the same research also tells us that most people rely mainly on the mass media for their knowledge of crime (Roberts, 2004).

COUNTING CRIME AND DEVIANCE: NUMBERS AND MEANING

OFFICIAL STATISTICS

People naturally want to know about the amount of criminal and deviant activity in Canada, and whether or not it is increasing. One answer to these questions is provided by official statistics compiled by the government. Most accounts of crime and deviance are made persuasive by the use of data collected by the police, the courts, and other governmental agencies. Moreover, virtually every important theory of deviant behaviour, and especially criminal behaviour, relies on information about offences and offenders collected by or on behalf of the government. It is therefore important to know how these data are collected. For starters, note that the more serious the norm violation, the more comprehensive the data collection. Thus, we have considerably more information about crime and delinquency, and alcohol and drug use, than we do about the expressive or symbolic deviancy of adolescents (Tanner, 2010).

Since 1962, a system of uniform crime reports has provided the basic count of criminal infractions in Canada. According to an arrangement originally pioneered in United States, police departments across the country file information on "crimes known to the police" (in official parlance). The system is designed to produce consistent, comparable, nationwide crime statistics. For crime to become known to the police, one of two things must happen. Either members of the public experience or observe a criminal incident and pass that information on to the police, or the police themselves detect the incident.

One of the few incontrovertible facts about the official count of crime is that it underestimates the actual amount of crime occurring in any jurisdiction at any given time. This is not a comforting thought for people already concerned about the level of crime in society. There are well-documented reasons that citizens choose not to share their knowledge of some criminal events with the police. They may fear reprisals from offenders, particularly if they know them. They may feel that the incident is too trivial to bother the police. They may be too embarrassed to report the incident. They may mistakenly believe that stolen items were lost. Some crimes are never reported to the police because the crime in question is a commercial transaction between, say, a prostitute and her client or a drug dealer and a drug buyer. In each of these cases, neither party has an interest in reporting details of the deal to the police.

The public reports most of the crime that the police know about. No more than 10 percent of crime is discovered by the police in the course of their own patrols or investigations (Sacco and Kennedy, 2002). One of the difficulties that the police face is that many crimes are committed so as to avoid detection. Most burglars, for instance, do not break into houses when they know that the police are in the area or when residents are likely to be at home.

The number of criminal incidents that remain unknown to the police is often referred to as the **dark figure of crime.** It is a large figure. How large? In one of my studies, I found that just 33 percent of robberies, 23 percent of rapes, and 21 percent of assaults with a weapon were reported by young victims to the police (Tanner and Wortley, 2002). A more recent survey of

Toronto high-school students found that less than half of all self-reported deviant acts had been discovered by parents, teachers, or the police (Savoie, 2006).

What happens if, for any reason, members of the public become more inclined to report crime to the police—if, say, it becomes easier for them to report crime because of the widespread use of cellphones or because the organizations they work for require them to report incidents that were previously dealt with informally? What happens if police departments are allowed to hire more police officers and acquire improved information technology? The answer, of course, is that we would start to see an increase in recorded crime, regardless of whether or not there had been any real change in criminal behaviour in the population. The important lesson here is that official statistics are affected by more than just the deviant motivations and behaviour of perpetrators (Liska and Messner, 1999).

In Canada in 2007, 2.3 million crimes were known to the police (Dauvergne, 2008). Roughly 48 percent were classified as property crimes; another large category (39 percent) comprised "other offences," including "mischief" and bail violations. The smallest category, at 13 percent, was violent crime. Because there can be year-to-year fluctuations in the crime rate, experts agree that authoritative statements about trends in crime require comparison over long periods—several decades rather than a few years.

Figure 14.2 (p. 344) reveals that the overall crime rate in 2007 was lower than at any time since 1977. People who worry about crime tend to be most worried about violent crime. It, too, was down in 2007. In fact, violent crime was at its lowest level in nearly two decades. Note too that "violent crime" includes everything from homicide, attempted homicide, and sexual assault to minor pushing and shoving ("common assault"). While common assault is, well, common, homicide and attempted homicide are not.

REGIONAL VARIATIONS IN CRIME RATES

Official crime figures reveal intriguing regional variations. Generally speaking, provinces and cities in the western part of the country have higher crime rates than those in the east. This pattern has existed for a long time, and applies to both the overall crime rate and specific types of crime.

FIGURE 14.2   CRIME RATES IN CANADA, 1962 TO 2007

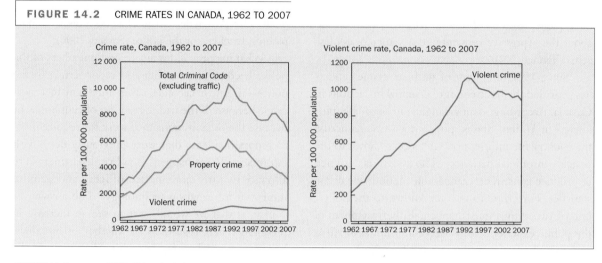

Crime rate, Canada, 1962 to 2007

Total *Criminal Code* (excluding traffic)

Property crime

Violent crime

Rate per 100 000 population

Violent crime rate, Canada, 1962 to 2007

Violent crime

Rate per 100 000 population

SOURCE: M. Dauvergne, 2008, "Crime Statistics in Canada, 2007," *Juristat, 28* (7). Statistics Canada, Catalogue no. 85-002-X.

Why is the West more crime-prone? Tim Hartnagel (2004) offers a persuasive answer. He suggests that, like its American counterpart, Western Canada encourages a "frontier mentality" favouring individualism, independence, and risk-taking. On occasion, risky behaviours lead to criminal ones. The Western provinces have more migrants from the rest of Canada than almost any other part of the country does (see Chapter 15, Population and Urbanization). Migration loosens the social controls that prevent law-violating behaviour. It is easier to break rules as a stranger in town than in the community where you grew up, where everybody knows your name and where informal social control is stronger. In addition, the populations of the Western provinces are relatively young, and crime is associated with youth. Finally, Aboriginal Canadians are proportionately more numerous in Western Canada than in the rest of the country, and Aboriginal Canadians have especially high crime rates (Brym, 2009), for reasons I will discuss later.

HOMICIDE RATES

Homicide rates are the most valid and reliable crime indicator, partly because it is hard to hide bodies. Homicide is less susceptible to the reporting and detection problems described earlier. Consensus about the gravity of the offence means that it is a crime with exceptionally high report rates. The police are also more successful at detecting homicides than most other kinds of criminal offences. What, then, do official statistics tell us about the pattern of homicide in Canada?

In 2007, there were 594 homicides in Canada—1.8 homicides per 100 000 Canadians. These figures represent both a short-term decrease—12 fewer homicides than 2006—and the continuance of a long-term decline. The Canadian homicide rate more than doubled between the early 1960s and the mid-1970s, from 1.3 in 1966 to 3.2 in 1975, but has been decreasing ever since (Li, 2008), a trend profiled in Figure 14.3.

As has always been the case, males are more likely than females to be both victims and perpetrators of homicide. In 2007, three-quarters of all homicide victims were men, as were 90 percent of the accused. Homicide rates are higher in the West than in the East. Winnipeg is the murder capital of Canada, with a homicide rate of 3.5.

And Toronto, Canada's largest city? While Toronto had a larger *number* of homicides than any other Canadian city in 2007, its homicide *rate* ranked fifth among Canada's nine largest metropolitan urban areas. Recent research suggests that while Toronto does not have an especially high homicide rate, the nature of homicide in the city is changing. Gartner and Thompson (2004) have shown that homicide victims in Toronto have become younger over time. In the 1970s, victims were on average 37 years old, and only 25 percent were under the age of 25. Since 1998, the average age of victims has dropped to 33, with 40 percent of victims below the age of 25. Second, while males have always had higher rates of homicide victimization than females have, the gender gap has widened. There are more males and fewer female

FIGURE 14.3   HOMICIDES IN CANADA, 1961–2007

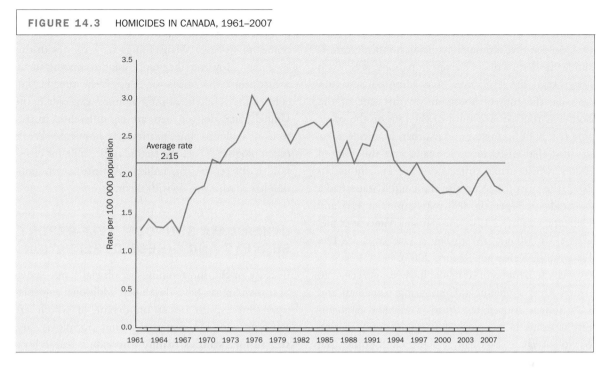

SOURCE: G. Li, 2008, "Homicide in Canada, 2007," *Juristat, 28* (9). Statistics Canada, Catalogue no. 85-002-X.

victims. Finally, the risk of homicide is not the same among different racial and ethnic groups. Black people are five times more likely than white people to become homicide victims, and they are also more likely to be perpetrators.

Homicide in Toronto has increasingly become a crime committed in public places, such as bars, city streets, and parks, rather than in private. For many people, the increasingly public nature of homicide is what makes it especially frightening; it suggests growing victimization of innocent bystanders in seemingly random acts of violence. Exemplifying these fears is the case of Jane Creba, a 15-year-old high-school student who was shot and killed outside Toronto's Eaton's Centre on December 20, 2005. She was caught in the crossfire of a gun battle involving male youth.

The Creba case also illustrates that death by handgun is a largely urban phenomenon. In Canada's nine largest metropolitan areas, 81 percent of "firearm homicides" were attributable to handguns, compared with 29 percent for the rest of the country. The larger urban areas are also sites of most gang-related homicides, which account for about one in five of all homicides in Canada. Gang-related homicides are also most likely to involve the use of firearms.

Sociologists of homicide are interested in the relationship between murderers and their victims.

The frequent crime-story image of this relationship is one of a predatory killer dispatching victims otherwise unknown to him (it usually is a him). Reality is different. Most victims know their killer. In 2007, strangers perpetrated only 16 percent of solved homicides. This figure has changed little over the past three decades. Most stranger homicide occurs during the course of another criminal incident— during a robbery or as the culmination of a sexual assault, for instance. People we know as family members or acquaintances are a greater threat to our safety than strangers are. Acquaintances kill about one-third of homicide victims, family members another one-third.

A familial relationship of particular interest involves husbands and wives, and common-law spouses. Women are four times as likely to be victims of intimate partner homicide as men are. Likewise, women are at greater risk from the violent attentions of former spouses than men are. The rate of spousal homicide has, however, been decreasing over the past three decades; the current rate is at its lowest level since the mid-1960s.

Child victims of homicide are rare. They are killed primarily by women. Women who kill are, in fact, likely to kill children. Female killers tend to be under the age of 21, single, and mentally ill (Li, 2008).

We can also compare Canada's homicide rate with those of other countries. Looking at Figure 14.4, you can see that although Canada's homicide rate is similar to that of many European nations, it is much lower than the U.S. rate. According to Statistics Canada, the rate of homicide on this side of the border is roughly one-third of the rate on the other side (Li, 2008). However, non-urban homicide rates are not that different in Canada and the United States, while urban differences are enormous. In 2007, the city of Baltimore in the United States had a homicide rate (per 100 000 population) of 43.5 and Detroit a rate of 42.1. By comparison, Vancouver had a rate of 3.0 and Montreal a rate of 1.5 (The Geographic Reference Report, 2007).

Many people in Canada have easy access to American TV channels. Comparing Canadian and U.S. violent crime rates affords a splendid opportunity to examine one particularly popular explanation of violent crime, especially violent youth crime: that exposure to violent media contributes to real-life violence.

This is an argument with a long history. Beginning with dime store comics and continuing with movies, TV, and popular music—first, rock 'n' roll, now rap—popular culture has often been held responsible for crimes of violence. Many things are wrong with this argument. However, the point I want to concentrate on is that people in Canada watch much the same kind of entertainment and news programming as people in the United States do, yet there are big differences in patterns of violent crime, particularly homicide. While criminologists debate the factors responsible for cross-border differences, it is unlikely that media consumption has anything to do with them.

OTHER DATA SOURCES: SELF-REPORT SURVEYS AND DIRECT OBSERVATION

Because of the shortcomings of official crime statistics, sociologists have developed additional information sources, the most important of which are self-report and observational studies. Sociologists use **self-report studies** mainly to conduct research on deviance among young people, particularly those in high school. They ask students about their deviant behaviour and, less often, their experiences of victimization. Respondents complete a questionnaire that

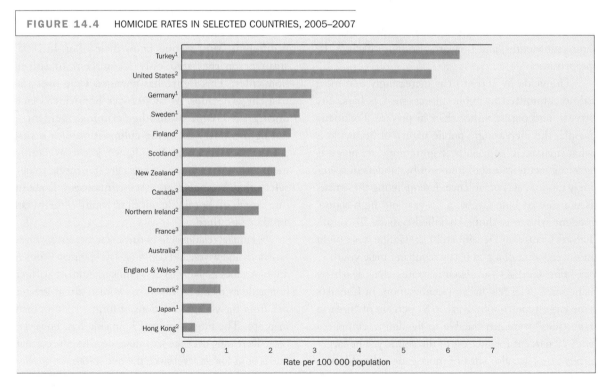

FIGURE 14.4   HOMICIDE RATES IN SELECTED COUNTRIES, 2005–2007

[1]Figures reflect 2005 data.
[2]Figures reflect 2007 data.
[3]Figures reflect 2006 data.
SOURCE: G. Li, 2008, "Homicide in Canada, 2007," *Juristat, 28* (9). Statistics Canada, Catalogue no. 85-002-X.

asks them to report on their own deviant activities or experiences of victimization. Statistics Canada also conducts surveys of adult victimization periodically. Self-report studies have their drawbacks. As with any survey on a sensitive subject, researchers must be careful to ensure that respondents give truthful answers to questions about criminal activity, drug use, and sexual assault. However, self-report studies have served sociologists well. First, they give a sense of the amount and type of crime and deviance that does not find its way into the official record. Second, their findings force us to abandon the idea that we can neatly divide the adolescent population into deviants and non-deviants; self-report studies show that many more adolescents are involved in activities that could get them into trouble with the law than are known to the police. Third, they show that young people who are charged by the police and prosecuted by the courts differ from "hidden" delinquents insofar as they are more likely to be repeat offenders and to commit serious crimes.

Researchers use **observational studies** to collect information about crime and deviance by watching it happen, either as outside observers or as participant observers. Many gang researchers have engaged in observational studies. A good example is Daniel Wolf's (1991) study of adult bike gangs in Edmonton. While observational studies provide texture and detail to our understanding of deviance, they too have their downside. Observing people can sometimes change their behaviour. Researchers studying prostitution might station themselves on a street corner to watch the action, but prostitutes, seeing the researchers, might conclude that they are police officers or investigative journalists and discontinue negotiations with potential customers (Liska and Messner, 1999: 24).

Police and court data, self-report surveys, and observational studies are different ways of collecting information about crime and deviance but they are not necessarily alternative methods. Some investigations of crime and deviance combine different methods, gathering some information from surveys and official statistics, and additional information from observational or self-report research.

The overall profile of crime and deviance documented by the different sources is similar in many crucial respects. Students of crime and deviance are often interested in the characteristics of populations and individuals most involved with rule-breaking behaviour. Official police and court statistics and

self-report studies often paint a roughly similar picture of these characteristics, as we will now see.

CORRELATES OF CRIME

A correlate is a phenomenon that is associated with another phenomenon. Factors associated with criminal and deviant activity are correlates of crime. When we ask about the characteristics of people most likely to engage in crime—are they old or young, male or female, rich or poor?—we are posing questions about the correlates of crime.

Age is an important correlate of crime. Irrespective of whether crime rates are high or low in a particular time or place, people in their teens and early 20s will be disproportionately represented. Arrests typically begin in early adolescence, increase steadily throughout the teenage years, and then taper off when individuals reach their 20s. Some criminologists have argued that the age basis of crime is universal and the single most important fact about crime requiring explanation (Gottfredson and Hirschi, 1990).

Crime also correlates with gender. Crime is not simply a young person's game; it is a young man's game. Again, this is a universal and enduring characteristic of all modern societies, and it is especially evident with respect to violent crime. Debate exists, however, over the degree to which the gender gap in criminality may be narrowing.

Two other correlates of crime are mired in controversy. Official police, court, and prison data often indicate an inverse relationship between social class and criminality—that is, the lower people's social and economic standing, the more likely they are to be involved in crime. However, this relationship is considerably less likely to manifest itself in self-report studies, leading some experts to conclude that the relationship between class and crime is a myth and to recommend that class not be considered an explanation of crime.

This argument does not persuade everybody in the criminology community. Detractors suggest that self-report studies fail to find a connection between class and crime because they neglect to ask questions about serious crime—murder, armed robbery, and rape, for example. Instead, they pose questions about relatively minor offences. Moreover, self-report studies often focus on students, but the most disadvantaged and marginal people are the least likely to attend school. Crucially, they are also the people most likely to be involved in criminal behaviour. When surveys include both school and street populations, and contain measures of serious crime, class re-emerges as a significant correlate of crime.

Significantly, which class is most involved with crime depends about what type of crime we are talking about. **Street crime**—robbery, burglary, and the like—involves mainly people from low-status backgrounds. White-collar or business crime is more likely to involve people from more privileged backgrounds. This observation stands as a corrective to the suggestion that only the poor and disadvantaged are criminals.

The second controversial correlate of crime is race. Unlike the United States, Canada does not officially record details about the racial characteristics of offenders or their victims. People who oppose the collection of race-related crime statistics argue that any evidence showing the overrepresentation of particular racial or ethnic groups in crime might result in increased public hostility toward those groups. People who support collecting race-based crime statistics argue that if racial and ethnic minorities are treated differently by the criminal justice system—if they are more likely to be stopped, searched, arrested, and charged by the police, and more harshly punished by the courts—then the only way such bias can be exposed and changed is by gathering racial data.

Aboriginals and blacks are overrepresented in Canada's prison population. Does this mean that members of those groups are actually committing more crime or that they are more likely to come to the attention of the police and the courts? Research on Aboriginals in Western Canada suggests both racial bias in the treatment of Aboriginal offenders and greater criminal activity by Aboriginal people. Sociologists typically explain high crime rates among Aboriginal Canadians by the fact that Aboriginals were a subjugated, colonized people who suffered enforced cultural assimilation and abuse in residential schools. As a result, they now experience relatively low levels of educational achievement, dysfunctional families, high rates of substance abuse, severe estrangement from Canadian society—and high crime rates (Grekul and LaBoucane-Benson, 2008).

Research with ethnically and racially diverse high-school students in Toronto indicates that their encounters with police officers are predicted by their own self-reported criminal activity. That is, youth who report offending most often are the most likely to be stopped, searched, and charged by the police, regardless of racial background. However, researchers have also discovered racial disparities in police apprehension among students who report little or no deviant activity.

Black youth uninvolved in crime were at significantly greater risk of arrest than their equally innocent white counterparts. The researchers conclude that these findings are consistent with what has become known as **racial profiling,** or targeting by police officers of members of particular racial or ethnic groups (Wortley and Tanner, 2005).

THEORIES OF CRIME AND DEVIANCE

When we hear about a criminal incident, especially a violent, dramatic one (a school rampage, for instance) the first question usually asked is, Why did he do it? Sociological theories of crime and deviance drawn from the objectivist (norm violations) tradition are designed to answer these kinds of causal questions.

Sociologists are not alone in asking causal questions. Nor are they alone in answering them. Sociological explanations of crime compete with media accounts and biological and psychological explanations as well. A major difference between biological and psychological explanations of crime and deviance, on the one hand, and sociological explanations, on the other, is that sociologists are more interested in group-based variations in deviant and criminal activity. The psychologist will try to explain why particular individuals decided to end their lives, but sociologists, beginning with Émile Durkheim, will want to know why, for instance, Protestants are more inclined to suicide than Roman Catholics are or why men are more likely to commit suicide than women are.

Different theories may explain the same deviant act. Do people steal because they have few other legitimate means of acquiring possessions or money? Because they have failed to develop strong social bonds to society? Because they pursue everyday routines that provide them with plentiful opportunities to do so with impunity? One of the tasks of sociological research is to determine which theory best explains the agreed-upon facts.

Many theories of crime and deviance exist, and I will now introduce you to the most important ones.

STRAIN THEORY

Strain theory holds that crime and deviance are the result of societal pressures to break rules. We may trace the theory back to Durkheim's concept of anomie. (Recall from Chapter 1 that, according to Durkheim, anomie exists when norms governing behaviour are vaguely defined.) Robert Merton (1938) modified the concept to explain patterns of crime and deviance in the twentieth-century United States.

All societies, wrote Merton, establish culturally approved goals for their members and socially approved means of achieving those goals. However, some societies, such as the United States, pay more attention to such goals as wealth, power, and prestige than to appropriate ways of achieving them. The imbalance between goals and means creates stress for lower-class people. They want what all Americans want—a nice house, a big car, a steady job—but lack legitimate means of achieving them, notably school and work opportunities. Rebuffed, they respond in a variety of deviant ways to the resulting stress. One modes of adaptation (Merton called it "innovation") involves using criminal means to achieve economic success goals.

People involved in money-making criminal enterprises exemplify Merton's innovators. Gangsters like the fictional Tony Soprano or the real life Al Capone subscribed to the American dream. They believed in, and aspired to, power, wealth, and status. Where they differed from non-criminals is in their chosen means of achieving those goals. Instead of pursuing educational qualifications and legitimate careers, they opt for illegal strategies.

Several studies add weight to strain theory by examining the relationship between income inequality and rates of homicide. They find that people in the lowest income group were most inclined to homicidal activity. This finding is consistent with the view that pressure to deviate is strongest among people with the fewest conventional opportunities. Moreover, the relationship is strongest in societies that most strongly emphasize success goals and where material inequalities are greatest (Krahn, Hartnagel, and Gartrell, 1986).

Other strain theories of crime and deviance focus on thwarted ambition and its criminal consequences among lower-class male youth. Albert Cohen (1955) saw delinquency among working-class boys as resulting from school experiences. Encouraged to strive for universal success goals, they find their ambitions blocked because the sort of socialization they have received at home prepares them poorly for success in school. Frustrated because of their inability to measure up to what Cohen calls the school's "middle-class measuring rod," they react against the school system by engaging in activities that directly counter those valued and sponsored by the school. Hence, they commit delinquent behaviour that appears to be without purpose, such as vandalism. According to

Though white-collar criminals (like Conrad Black, pictured here) often express contempt for the law, share an organizational or business culture that rewards rule breaking, and associate with others from whom they can learn both the skills and the rationalizations needed to carry out their crimes, sociologists have continued to focus on street crime more than "suite" crime.
SOURCE: Joshua Lott/Bloomberg News/LANDOV.

Cohen, destructive behaviour is its own reward, a way of subverting the middle-class measuring rod.

A third variant of strain theory combines elements from both Merton and Cohen. According to Cloward and Ohlin (1960), deviant motivation, in the form of limited opportunity, is not enough to explain criminal behaviour. Frustrated adolescents also need access to deviant opportunities in order to become delinquent. Not all would-be delinquents have the opportunity to become criminal innovators, as Merton supposes. Low-status people become involved in different types of deviant subculture depending on the opportunities available to them. Those who have the opportunity to learn from adult thieves gravitate to criminal gangs. Those without those networks but in possession of the necessary physical attributes and combat skills may join fighting gangs. Those without conventional or criminal opportunities may end up in drug-based subcultures.

Some contemporary applications of strain theory document the social pressures that result in higher rates of deviance among socially disadvantaged groups. Other extensions of classic strain theory seek to explain the frustrations that drive some individuals to crime and deviance. An important and influential example of the latter is Robert Agnew's (1992) general strain theory, which focuses on the stresses that ensue from different social relationships, not just those that result from chasing inaccessible success goals. Agnew argues that negative relationships generate negative emotions, such as anxiety, fear, and anger, that, in turn, generate deviant responses. First, relationships with others may hinder the achievement of a valued goal. Adolescents might see parents or teachers as barriers to desired outcomes, such as spending leisure time with friends. Second, adolescents may lose or be threatened with losing something or someone of value to them—a job, say, or a parent through divorce. The third type of toxic relationship involves situations from which adolescents find it difficult or impossible to extricate themselves, such as the clutches of bullies at school or an abusive father at home. Agnew suggests that these myriad strains sour relationships with others and can lead to deviant and disreputable behaviour of various kinds. Much research supports Agnew's claims. Among young people who are experiencing the sorts of strains listed above, delinquency provides more relief than do non-deviant solutions (Vold, Bernard, and Snipes, 2002).

Schissel and Fedec's (1999) study of young prostitutes in Regina is a good example of the application of strain theory in Canada. Using information gleaned from social service agencies, they examined the factors that encouraged the involvement of 400 young women in the sex trade. Stressful family circumstances were prominent. The women often came from backgrounds where neglect and abuse, including sexual abuse, were common. Wanting to escape stressful relationships at home, they took to the streets, turning to prostitution to make a living. Other Canadian research has also found links between early sexual abuse and later deviant behaviour (O'Grady and Gaetz, 2004).

SOCIAL LEARNING THEORIES: EDWIN SUTHERLAND AND DIFFERENTIAL ASSOCIATION

The basic proposition of learning theories is that willingness to break rules is a consequence of the sorts of socialization experience to which individuals have been exposed. Some people are motivated to engage in crime because they have acquired favourable opinions about what others regard as deviant behaviour. The learning of antisocial conduct and practices takes place in a variety of settings, beginning with the family and continuing with the peer group and the neighbourhood setting. Within each of these contexts, people see as normal what others regard as wrong, dangerous, harmful, and shameful.

The best-known proponent of the learning perspective is Edwin Sutherland (1947), who insisted that a process of **differential association** is primarily responsible for deviant or non-deviant behaviour. Specifically, if people experience more non-deviant than deviant associations as they grow up, they are likely to follow the straight and narrow. Otherwise, they are likely to become deviants. According to Sutherland, criminals need to learn the skills of the trade—how to steal a car or rob a bank, for instance. No less importantly, they must also learn rationalizations that tell them that stealing other people's money or property is justifiable. More association with deviant than non-deviant lifestyles teaches people these two important sets of lessons. Moreover, learning continues later in life. For example, research that I conducted with Scot Wortley showed that ex-inmates often believe that their time in prison has been a learning experience. The ex-inmates we interviewed described how prison enabled them to become more immersed in gang culture, learn new skills, and develop additional reasons for hating the police (Wortley and Tanner, 2006).

CONTROL THEORY

Travis Hirschi (1969) pioneered **control theory.** Its basic argument is that a set of ties bind young people to the conventional world, and when those ties are weak, deviance and crime occur. No special motivation is required. According to Hirschi, we all have within us a natural inclination for rule breaking that is only kept in check because we have developed *attachments* to family and friends, *commitments* to conventional ambitions and activities in school and at work, prosocial *values and beliefs* that we share with people who are important to us, and conventional *activities* at school and at work. Individuals not constrained by such ties are likely to become involved in crime and deviance.

Control theory has a solid reputation as a predictor of relatively minor and occasional deviance involving adolescents. However, when more serious crime and delinquency is involved, and when the deviant behaviour in question appears more motivated or has a political underpinning, it is less plausible. In the fall of 2005, visible minority youth, mainly of Arab background, took to the streets of major French cities in protest against poor educational opportunities, inadequate housing, racial discrimination in the labour market, and heavy-handed policing. In Montreal in the summer of 2008, minority youth publicly rioted when one of their numbers was shot and killed by a police officer. Reference to weak ties alone cannot explain this sort of politically inspired collective action. Control theory fails to explain why members of disadvantaged groups fail to develop conventional attachments to society in the first place.

A more recent variant of control theory is the so-called General Theory of Crime, which argues that all deviance has a common cause in low self-control. Gottfredson and Hirschi (1990) propose that rule breaking of all sorts shares common features. It is easy to execute, immediately satisfying, risky, exciting, produces few long-lasting rewards, and is harmful to others. The personality characteristics of individuals with low self-control include impulsivity, a taste for risk, an action orientation, and short-term thinking. Low self-control presumably originates in early socialization when parents are too busy or unconcerned to police their children's behaviour and unable or unwilling to teach them the difference between right and wrong. Canadian research finds that low self-control predicts driving under the influence of alcohol and school-related behavioural problems among high-school students (Keane, Maxim, and Teevan, 1993; Nakhaie, Silverman, and Lagrange, 2000).

ROUTINE ACTIVITIES THEORY

Routine activities theory, by locating the source of crime in the structuring of everyday life, also downplays the significance of criminal motivation. It argues that much criminal behaviour is not dependent on complex causation. The presence of a suitable target and the absence of capable guardians suffice. From this point of view, the convergence in space and time of motivated offenders, suitable targets, and lack of capable guardians brings about deviance and crime.

Cohen and Felson (1979; Felson, 2002) suggest that the development of expensive and highly valued consumer goods has encouraged property crime because items like iPods, computers, and cellphones are easy to steal and transport. They also reason that residential property is less easy to protect because increased labour force participation means that fewer homeowners are around during the day to deter burglars, and that, compared with earlier eras, the amount of leisure time that teenagers have at their disposal provides them with the opportunity and motivation for delinquent episodes.

Routine activities theorists argue that crime rates vary not just because of the number of individuals in the population willing and prepared to commit crime, but also because of the presence or absence of capable guardians, and because of the daily routines that people follow. Research shows that some routines are more closely linked to criminal offending and criminal victimization than others are. People who spend large stretches of time away from home each day at work and out on the town in the evening and on weekends report higher levels of victimization than those who live more home-centred lives. Teenagers who spend large stretches of time in unsupervised leisure activities with other teenagers are at particular risk of criminal victimization and offending.

A useful illustration of how daily routines structure deviant behaviour is Hagan and McCarthy's (1997) study of street youth and crime in Toronto. They demonstrate that a substantial amount of criminal activity by street youth is motivated by situational exigencies. Nothing very surprising about this observation, you might say—except for the fact that most theories of crime have looked to the past to explain the criminal present. Strain and learning theories identify the roots of crime in lack of opportunity and differential association; control theories explain deviance by the failure to develop prosocial bonds early on at home or in school. Hagan and McCarthy argue that while these theories do a good job of explaining why some young people leave home and are on the street in the first place, they are less useful for explaining patterns of crime that occur afterward. Crime on the streets has more immediate causes. Street life thus becomes a relatively independent influence on such activities as theft and prostitution.

TYPES OF CRIME AND DEVIANCE

So far, I have looked at conceptions of deviance and crime, ways of measuring their incidence, and prominent theories of criminal deviance. I now turn to several subfields of the sociological study of crime and deviance.

GENDER AND CRIME

Sociological studies of female crime and deviance are a comparatively recent development. In the past, sociologists ignored female wrongdoers because they thought their numbers were small or assumed that all female deviants were prostitutes. They judged male deviance a law-and-order problem and female deviance a sexual problem. This sexualized view of female deviance derives from the criminal records of known offenders. Historically, most girls and women were arrested and incarcerated for prostitution or because they were suspected carriers of venereal disease.

Self-report studies have done much to dispel the notion of female offenders as sexual deviants. They show that girls and women are no strangers to deviant behaviour of all types. Official and unofficial measures of crime and deviance indicate that the major difference between males and females is largely one of volume. Males are more inclined than females to crime and deviance (especially violent crime), start their deviant activities earlier, and end them later.

Increasingly, however, sociologists see female crime as a growing problem. Women and girls are becoming more violent, more involved in gang activity, and so on. High-profile cases, such as the murder in 1997 of 14-year-old Reena Virk in Victoria and the subsequent trials of one of the young females accused of the crime, have done much to consolidate this kind of argument.

The belief that we are witnessing shifting patterns of female crime and deviance has led to the development theories that link these changes to the effects of changing gender roles in society. In the 1970s, sociologists proposed the "liberation hypothesis," suggesting that as women less frequently perform traditional domestic roles as wives and mothers, and begin entering the paid labour force in larger numbers, their patterns of crime and deviance are bound to resemble those of males (Adler, 1975; Simon, 1975). However, available evidence offers little support for the liberation hypothesis. Differences in male and female crime rates, particularly violent crime, are quite stable over time.

Recently, some sociologists have asserted that while young women may be less physically violent and aggressive than their male counterparts are, they are more likely to take part in psychological aggression directed against other girls, such as name calling, spreading harmful gossip, and rumour mongering. This argument, too, has been challenged by research showing that psychological aggression is not the exclusive prerogative of "mean girls," and that girls who are victims of relational aggression are targeted by boys too (Chesney-Lind, Morash, and Irwin, 2007).

Currently, two schools of thought exist about how to account for similarities and differences between the deviant activities of males and females. Some analysts think that female wrongdoing can be best explained by the same concepts and theories used to explain male wrongdoing. Accordingly, an important task for generic theories is to explain the lower level of deviance and criminality among females than males. As we have seen, control and opportunity have been key concepts in sociological theories of crime and deviance. Canadian research shows how these concepts can explain the relatively low level of female deviance and crime.

With information supplied by Toronto high-school students, John Hagan and his colleagues set out to explain gender differences in involvement in minor forms of deviance (Hagan, Gillis, and Simpson, 1987). They argue that the gender of the deviant and the class background of parents shape how much control over teenage activity is exercised in the family home. Generally speaking, they note, parents attend to, and control, teenage girls' leisure activity more than they do teenage boys' leisure activity. Contrary to what you might expect, however, parents who have most power and authority in the workplace are most likely to tolerate the mildly deviant activities of their children—particularly their boys. Boys are freer to deviate than girls, and the freest are upper-class boys. They find that the gap between male and female delinquency rates was largest in families headed by parents (primarily fathers) who exert most control at work. Later research found that the delinquent profiles of girls and boys are most similar in egalitarian families, where both parents exert control in their jobs. The gender gap is widest in patriarchal families where the male head exerts control in the workplace while his wife takes chief responsibility for monitoring and controlling the behaviour of their children.

Sociologists influenced by feminist ideas are more likely to argue for gender-specific theories of crime and deviance. They argue that it is unreasonable to suppose that theories devised with male behaviour in mind, and tested exclusively with information supplied by males, will prove equally applicable to female deviants. The idea that we might need different theories to explain male and female deviance receives partial support from a recent U.S. study. Researchers found that depression was a cause of female delinquency but not male delinquency. They also reported that playing sports increases male violence but not female violence (Daigle, Cullen, and Wright, 2007).

Should squeegee kids' actions be considered criminal, a nuisance, or a form of subsistence work?
SOURCE: CP Picture Archive/Fred Thornhill.

YOUTH, CRIME, AND DEVIANCE

Young people are at the heart of most people's concerns about crime and deviance (Tanner, 2010). It has been this way for a long time, with successive adult generations believing that the behaviour of young people has never been worse than it is now. Media coverage encourages such views, preferring bad news stories to more uplifting ones, and focusing on high-profile and unrepresentative crimes of violence, rather than more typical shoplifting incidents, for example.

Moral panics are extreme reactions to deviance and crime, and social constructionists have extensively examined them. Episodes of moral panic are characterized by the conviction that the deviance or crime in question is sufficiently dangerous that it constitutes a threat to the core values and well-being of society. Politicians, newspaper editors, and prominent personages clamour for immediate action. They typically say that something has to be done right away or the situation will only get worse. Some examples of moral panic in Canada have focused on raves (Hier, 2002) and squeegee youth (Parnaby, 2003).

Most moral panics involve young people for two main reasons. First, many adults view them as vulnerable to corrupting influences from "satanic" adults to violent movies, video games, and rap music. Second, young people represent the future. If bad influences corrupt them now, what will become of the nation when they reach adulthood?

How can we spot moral panics? Moral panics exist when the public reaction to deviance or crime is out of proportion to the nature and scope of the problem—when, for instance, there is little or no

factual basis to claims about increased levels of drug use among young people or incidents of lethal violence in schools (Ben-Yehuda, 1986; Lawrence and Mueller, 2003; see Box 14.1, p. 354).

School Shootings

While sociologists have studied school shootings and youth gangs as moral panics, they have also studied them as cases of objectively problematic, norm-violating behaviour. It is instructive to review this research to see how we can distinguish moral panic from reasonable fear.

Although they don't happen often, and there is no indication of any upward trend in their incidence, school shootings are extremely worrisome. They are particularly frightening because they don't fit the normal profile of youth crime. Those who do the shooting, mainly white males, have no long history of violent or aggressive behaviour; they are not the angry and frustrated adolescents who populate the gang delinquency literature. Moreover, school shootings take place mainly in rural or suburban areas blessed with good schools, not blighted inner-city neighbourhoods with rundown schools. Finally, most of them have occurred in the United States during a time when overall rates of violent youth crime have been declining.

Katherine Newman and her colleagues provide the most thorough examination of rampage school shootings (Newman et al., 2004). Focusing on two incidents, she and her research team collected a large volume of information from students, teachers, parents, and community members. Popular explanations of school shootings focus on exposure to violent media, mental illness, availability of guns, and bullying. Newman argues that no single factor accounts for their occurrence. While each of these factors contributes something to the fatal outcome, each provides only a partial explanation. For example, while school shooters have been found to have psychological problems, so too do many high-school students who do not go on to become school shooters. Likewise, school shooters are not alone in liking violent movies. Newman argues that what best explains rampage school shootings is an interaction between vulnerable offenders (whose vulnerability is not always self-evident in advance of the event) and school and community factors.

Teachers do not often receive details of students' academic and behavioural history when students enter high school. They therefore don't know which

BOX 14.1   IS IT A CRIME TO BE A TEENAGER?

A "teen repellant" anti-loitering device that has sparked controversy in some European countries is catching on fast in Canada.

The Mosquito emits an irritating high-frequency sound that can only be heard by those between the ages of 13 and 25, raising concerns in some European countries that the device is discriminatory toward young people.

Due to presbycusis—age-related hearing loss—people over 25 cannot detect the sound of the Mosquito. Although only 85 decibels, young people find the sound extremely annoying and disperse within minutes of hearing it.

This has made the Mosquito increasingly popular with school boards, malls, convenience stores and municipalities seeking to deter rowdy gangs of teens from getting up to no good late at night.

At the Maple Ridge/Pitt Meadows school district in British Columbia's Lower Mainland, the device has been credited with lowering exterior vandalism at one school by about 40 per cent says Kathie Ward, board of education vice-chair and chair of the district's anti-vandalism committee.

> "We weren't finding the broken bottles, party paraphernalia, the broken windows. . . . To see the significant drop of vandalism at that school we thought we were being successful with the Mosquito."

Now the board is planning to use the device at another school in the district where youth have been lighting small fires and causing other damage.

Mike Gibson, president of the Mosquito Group, the company that markets the device in North America, says about 200 have sold so far in Canada, mostly in British Columbia.

But thousands are in use in the United Kingdom, where a row is brewing over whether the device infringes on kids' civil liberties. A human rights group has started a campaign to have the Mosquito banned, calling it a "sonic weapon directed against children and young people." Ian Kerr, Canada research chair in Ethics, Law and Technology at the University of Ottawa, says the Mosquito raises issues such as equality, privacy and the invasion of peoples' personal space without consent.

Because it has the power to control certain groups by moving them along, he says such technology could have a broader—and more sinister—application in the future.

"These technologies are rapidly developing and rapidly emerging. If you had a host of these technologies working in concert what we'd really be getting at would be a different way of controlling society rather than the social negotiation of having a rule and talking with people. . . . It removes people from the equation which is one of the things I've been concerned about."

Simon Davies, director of Privacy International, in a *National Post* article called such devices "an assault on human dignity." Davies even went so far as to say that "ultrasonic technology used in this way should be regarded as criminal assault."

Gibson says the Mosquito is simply a harmless, non-confrontational way to get teenagers to move away from areas at times when they're not supposed to be there. Businesses such as convenience stores use remote controls to activate it.

> "If kids are standing outside the door drinking pop they don't deploy it at that point. But if you get teenagers deterring customers from coming into the store, making customers feel uncomfortable, that's when they activate it, and it only stays on for 20 minutes."

Gibson adds that his company employs standards to ensure that the Mosquito isn't abused.

> "This is meant for private property—you can't be mounting this on your car. We get a lot of calls from people who own homes and we do not sell to residents. This is for commercial use only."

Welsh inventor Howard Stapleton, creator of the Mosquito, has asked European governments to legislate guidelines governing its use.

Cell phone ring-tones are now available that use a similar high-frequency sound and has become popular with teens who want to hide their incoming calls from teachers or parents.

Ward says that in the 2007/08 school year, the cost of vandalism at the Maple Ridge/Pitt Meadows school district came to $600,000, an amount she believes would be much higher if not for the Mosquito and other anti-vandalism deterrents employed by the school.

> "I don't believe [the Mosquito] is infringing on their rights. We have the right to protect our buildings. We clearly have them marked that after 10 pm you're trespassing. So those who are hanging around our school after that time: what are you doing there, shouldn't you be at home in bed?"

SOURCE: Joan Delaney, 2008, "'Mosquito' Prompts Teens to Buzz Off," *Epoch Times* (Victoria) 6 August. Reprinted with permission.

students require special attention. Peer culture at school and in the community enforces a code of silence that discourages teenagers from reporting suspicions about peers to parents. Similarly, concerns parents might have about teenagers in the community are not shared with the parents of those teenagers. Newman admits that it is nearly impossible to predict where and when the next rampage shooting incident will occur. She suggests, however, that schools with students experiencing a broad range of risk factors and nested in suburban or rural community settings are most likely to experience this rare event (see Box 14.2).

Youth Gangs

Youth gangs have emerged as a major crime problem in Canada over the past decade because of an apparent increase in gang activity in large cities. However, gang activity has attracted more media attention than academic research. Much of the research is several decades old and based on small samples of already-identified groups of young people in specific geographic locations—for instance, immigrant gangs in British Columbia (Gordon, 2000).

I recently conducted an investigation of youth gang activity in Toronto with Scot Wortley (Wortley and Tanner, 2004). We interviewed a sample of high-school students and street youth. We learned that many of our respondents who reported past or present gang membership were not involved in criminal activities at all. Their gang membership had more to do with the pursuit of legitimate leisure activities than deviant ones. Membership in organizations involved with crime and deviance, such as drug trafficking and violent conflict with other gangs, was more common among street youth than among high-school students.

We also found that poverty, race and ethnicity, family structure, and living arrangements influence gang membership. These factors reflect the patterns of inequality, disadvantage, and discrimination to which strain theorists draw our attention. Other recent Canadian research tells a similar story. For example, disadvantaged Aboriginal youth in the West are recruited into gangs who provide them with the status and the income (largely from the drug trade, where they work as low-level dealers) otherwise denied them in cities like Winnipeg and Regina or on the reserve. The larger American research literature documents the same pattern.

Serious and repetitive gang activity can result in incarceration for gang members. Evidence suggests that the prison system also functions as a recruiting ground for gang members. On occasion, gangs formed

---

BOX 14.2   **PROFILE OF A SCHOOL SHOOTER**

Tim Kretschmer killed nine students and three teachers at the Albertville secondary school after stealing a 9mm Beretta automatic pistol legally owned by his father, Jörg.

Almost all of Kretschmer's victims in the attack in Winnenden, near Stuttgart, were girls. Friends confirmed that he was a misogynist with a particular grudge against one of his former female teachers, who had told him he would "end up on the rubbish heap."

He had also become infatuated with a local girl who had snubbed his advances.

Kretschmer killed nine students and three teachers at the Albertville secondary school. . . . Armed with more than 200 rounds of ammunition, he also randomly killed three passers-by after fleeing the school and hijacking a car. He shot himself after having been cornered by police in a town 25 miles away.

Asked if the authorities might have missed an opportunity to spot the danger, Konrad Jelden, Stuttgart's police chief, said: "It is a problem for the whole of society. We know so little about his psychology; his teachers and his parents described him as a shy young man without special problems."

Friends and neighbours, however, said Kretschmer had been deeply troubled.

One neighbour said: "He always complained about one of his teachers.

"He said that she bullied him and threatened him that if he continued as he was he would end up on the rubbish heap. He completely hated her, as he did all women in general."

Michael Veit, 19, a neighbour and childhood friend of Kretschmer, said he had fallen out with him two years ago because he had "changed."

"Tim was never interested in anything but he was fascinated by guns," he said. "He showed me the Beretta from his father's collection . . ."

Fabienne Böhm, another former friend, said: "He wrote to his parents saying he was suffering and couldn't go on. He was teased by others, felt bullied. He stored it all up."

SOURCE: Rayner and Bingham (2009). © Telegraph Media Group Limited, 2009.

in prison extend their activities onto the street once members are released (Grekul and LaBoucane-Benson, 2008). American research has found a similar pattern with bike gangs and white supremacist groups.

RESPONDING TO CRIME AND DEVIANCE

When sociologists study reactions to deviant behaviour, they are examining the ways in which societies try to prevent or control that behaviour.

INCARCERATION

The prison is the chief means by which we seek to control crime. Prisons are, however, a relatively recent invention. Canada's first prison was Kingston penitentiary, opened in 1835. Before then, convicted offenders received other forms of punishment, including hanging and deportation. Canada introduced prisons to incapacitate and punish offenders and discourage them (as well as other potential offenders) from committing additional crimes. Prisons were also expected to reform offenders, encouraging them to live law-abiding lives by teaching them work skills while serving time.

Canada's prison population has been decreasing in recent years. However, while the staggeringly high rate of incarceration in the United States and Russia is the main story told in Figure 14.5, it is worth noting that Canada is more likely to imprison offenders than several Western European nations, as well as Japan and India.

Prisons do a poor job of rehabilitating prisoners. Many studies show that the recidivism rate among ex-prisoners is high, with a large proportion of the prison population at any one time made up of people who have been there before—sometimes, several times before (Morgan and Liebling, 2007).

Prison inmates suffer numerous deprivations. They are denied their freedom, required to abide by other peoples' rules and schedules, not allowed to wear their own clothing, have limited contact with friends and family from the outside, and required to live in an overcrowded, dirty, smelly, and violent environment. The unpleasantness of prison life is not a problem for people who believe that prison's main purpose is to punish, deter, and incapacitate offenders. It is a problem for people who adhere to rehabilitative ideals.

Prisons fail to rehabilitate for three reasons. First, commitment to the rehabilitative ideal has never been

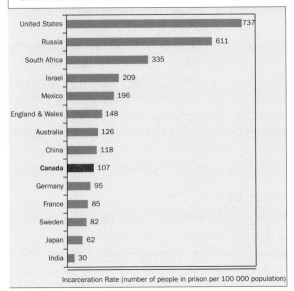

FIGURE 14.5 RATE OF INCARCERATION IN SELECTED NATIONS

Nation	Rate
United States	737
Russia	611
South Africa	335
Israel	209
Mexico	196
England & Wales	148
Australia	126
China	118
Canada	107
Germany	95
France	85
Sweden	82
Japan	62
India	30

Incarceration Rate (number of people in prison per 100 000 population)

SOURCE: The Sentencing Project, 2006, "New Incarceration Figures: Thirty-Three Consecutive Years of Growth." Reprinted with permission from The Sentencing Project.

strong to begin with, with relatively few resources allocated to that goal. Second, in response to the harsh conditions that they encounter, prisoners have developed an inmate subculture with its own code of conduct that often challenges the regime imposed upon them. Third, prisoners learn new criminal skills from other prisoners and learn how to justify the use of violence (Sykes, 1958). Given immersion in the prison subculture, prison time is more likely to lead to more prison time than rehabilitation.

Prisons are the centrepiece of approaches to crime control that emphasize suppression. Calls for tougher law enforcement—more proactive policing, longer prison sentences for habitual criminals, mandatory minimum sentences for violent, gun, and gang-related crime—are all examples of suppressive strategies.

Deterrence theory holds that getting tough on crime will lead to its eradication or at least reduce the probability of offending. Deterrence can take one of two main forms. *General deterrence* is the process by which the punishment of some law violators discourages other potential law violators from breaking the law. *Specific deterrence* is the process by which an individual who has been caught and punished for an offence will find the experience sufficiently costly that he or she will not repeat the wrongdoing again.

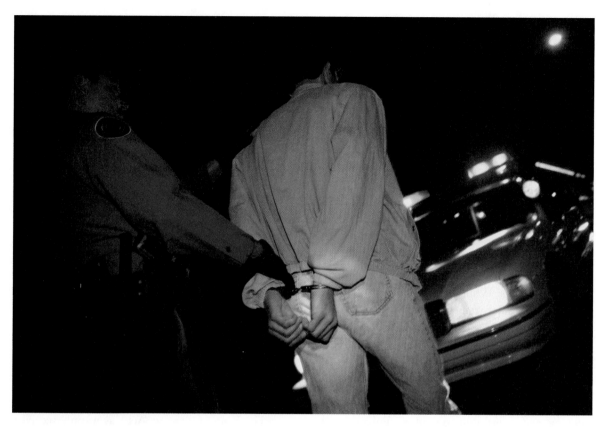

Contrary to the belief of many people, crime rates in Canada are declining. Nonetheless, Canada has a higher incarceration rate than most Western European Countries.
SOURCE: Photodisc.

Deterrence, whether specific or general, has three elements. The first involves the severity of the penalty. Are offenders given jail time or just a fine? The second involves the certainty of punishment. When drivers consider the chance of getting caught speeding, they are considering the certainty of punishment. The final element is the speed of punishment. How long after law violators have been apprehended do they have to wait for punishment? Deterrence theory holds that law-violating behaviour will be low when severity, certainty, and speed of punishment are high.

Most practical applications of deterrence theory concentrate on the severity or harshness of legal sanctions. Hence the advocacy of capital punishment, long prison terms, and boot camp. However, most research does not support the proposition that harsh punishment deters. Where it exists, the death penalty has not reduced homicide rates (Fuller and Wozniak, 2006: 266). Boot camp has been less effective than other means of dealing with young offenders (Doob and Cesaroni, 2004). Longer prison terms are no more effective in reducing recidivism than are shorter terms (Doob and Webster, 2003).

The problem with deterrence theory is its assumption that criminals are rational calculators, carefully calibrating the costs of crime against its rewards. However, most criminals have only an imprecise understanding of the punishment they might receive for a given offence. Moreover, many violent crimes are prefigured by anger, which works against rational calculation. More evidence supports the **certainty principle,** which holds that potential offenders are more often deterred by the thought of certain but moderate punishment than by the guarantee of severe punishment for an act they believe they can get away with (Von Hirsch, Bottoms, Burney, and Wikstrom, 1999).

In addition to not necessarily producing lower crime rates, get-tough policies come with a high price tag. Keeping people in prison costs a lot. Mandatory minimum sentences mean that there will be more people in prison. More people in prison means that more people coming out of prison and trying to find a job and accommodation will be burdened with the stigma of being an ex-convict. In the United States, the "war on drugs" has resulted in the incarceration of bit players in the drug trade: addicted users and minor suppliers. The sheer expense of locking up minor criminals means that fewer tax dollars are available for other kinds of law enforcement and anti-crime policies that focus on prevention and intervention.

INTERVENTION

Many sociologists view community intervention on behalf of young offenders as an effective strategy for reducing crime. Interventionist policies assume that we can most effectively tackle crime by weakening motivations, and minimizing opportunities, for law-breaking. Interventions include recreational programs for neighbourhood youth, counselling sessions, and the assignment of youth workers to neighbourhood street gangs. While programs of this sort have always commanded tremendous loyalty from their practitioners, they are expensive and have rarely been properly evaluated for their effectiveness.

PREVENTING CRIME

Too much of our thinking about crime focuses on catching and controlling offenders. Public policy debates about crime rarely discuss non-legal solutions. Yet given what we know about the risk factors associated with serious and repetitive criminality among youth, one may reasonably suggest that expanded daycare, for example, might be a less costly and more effective investment of taxpayers' dollars than imprisonments.

Evidence that some criminal justice policies do not work, or do not work as well as we would like them to, does not mean that they are going to be abandoned. Criminal justice policies are driven by political ideology, not criminological research. This is particularly true for juvenile justice policy.

Much if not most of the controversy surrounding criminal justice policy in Canada centres on young people. Over the past century, young people in trouble with the law have fallen under the provisions of the Juvenile Delinquents Act of 1908, the Young Offenders Act of 1984, and the Youth Criminal Justice Act of 2003.

The Juvenile Delinquents Act of 1908 was based on a **welfare model of juvenile justice**. It stipulated that juvenile offenders were to be viewed and treated differently from adult offenders. They were not to be treated as hardened criminals but as youth with the capacity for rehabilitation. Hence, Canada developed a separate juvenile justice system to rehabilitate them. It also developed a probation service, and the police and courts were advised to handle juvenile offenders

informally. When custodial sentences were handed out, emphasis was on treatment rather than punishment.

Fast-forward half a century. The Juvenile Delinquents Act fell into disrepute in the 1960s and 1970s, when it became apparent that the rate of juvenile crime was skyrocketing. Dissatisfaction with the act eventually led to the passage of the Young Offenders Act in 1984. The Young Offenders Act, while not abandoning all the principles of the welfare model, drew on two other models of juvenile justice for its philosophical intent: the due process model and the crime control model.

The **due process model** assumes that criminals are rational actors who find crime more rewarding than conformity. To make crime less attractive, wrongdoers are punished in proportion to the severity of their crimes. Young offenders are held accountable for their actions and accorded the same legal considerations as adult offenders are. The **crime control model** is more attentive to the safety and well-being of law-abiding citizens than the treatment and civil rights of young offenders. It encourages suppressive policies, such as custodial sentences, that incapacitate and presumably deter future offending.

The Young Offenders Act was warmly received when first introduced. However, it quickly wore out its welcome. Ironically, many of the criticisms directed against it were identical to the earlier complaints against the Juvenile Delinquents Act. Once again, the legislation was deemed too soft on youth crime and, accordingly, held responsible for increased rates of offending. While the evidence supporting these contentions was not compelling (youth crime neither increased in volume nor became worse in kind during its tenure) the Young Offenders Act was replaced in 2003 by the Youth Criminal Justice Act.

The new legislation emphasizes getting tough on serious, repeat young offenders while adopting less punitive strategies for the far more numerous minor offenders, including warnings and community-based diversionary programs. The most recent youth crime statistics suggest that, as intended, occasional and non-serious young offenders are being diverted.

Figure 14.6 shows how in recent times, and particularly since the introduction of the Youth Criminal Justice Act in 2003, the number of youths charged by the police has declined significantly, while the numbers dealt with by extrajudicial measures has increased. However, it is important to note that the offences most likely to result in a charge under the Youth Criminal Justice Act are the same offences that brought criminal charges under its predecessor, the

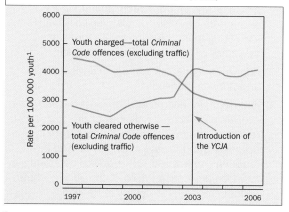

FIGURE 14.6   RATES OF YOUTH FORMALLY CHARGED WITH A CRIME SINCE INCEPTION OF THE YOUTH CRIMINAL JUSTICE ACT (YCJA)

[1]Youth aged 12 to 17.

SOURCE: Andrea Taylor-Butts and Angela Bressan, 2006, "Youth Crime in Canada," *Juristat, 28* (3). Statistics Canada, Catalogue no. 85-002-XIE.

Young Offenders Act. In other words, the judicial leniency represented by alternative measures is not extended to more serious offences.

At the same time, significant portions of the public would prefer still more punitive measures for serious young offenders (see Box 14.3). Prime Minister Harper is attentive to this constituency. He has accordingly proposed amendments to the Youth Criminal Justice Act that would allow for the easier transference of serious young offenders to the adult court, where they would be eligible for adult sentences, that is, lengthy prison terms. While the wisdom of sentencing a 14-year-old murderer to life imprisonment is not immediately apparent to sociologists, lawyers, and judges, the government remains firm in its resolve to deliver stricter juvenile justice policy. As Doob and Sprott (2004: 214) remark, "It is easier to be tough on crime than to be smart about crime."

BOX 14.3   15-YEAR-OLD GIRL CHARGED AS ADULT IN MURDER OF 14-YEAR-OLD STEPHANIE RENGEL

Sentencing a 15-year-old girl to an adult penalty, even for first-degree murder, is a major step for Canadian justice. The adult penalty is a mandatory life term. But it is the right step in the case of the Toronto girl known as M.T., convicted last week and awaiting sentence for her role in the stabbing death of 14-year-old Stephanie Rengel.

Canada's courts tend to look assiduously, as they should, for any hope of rehabilitation in the young. But the adult penalty for those 17 and under has a special parole clause. At age 15, M.T. would be eligible for parole after five to seven years, at the trial judge's discretion. This is a built-in form of leniency, a promise that those who deserve a chance at rehabilitation can get that chance while they are still young. It is not really an adult penalty, but a hybrid of the adult and youth penalties. And it fits these circumstances.

The killing of Stephanie Rengel was not a crime of passion, a "mistake" in judgment which might be blamed on youthful immaturity. Its cold-

bloodedness chills the spine. For months, over countless e-mails, text messages and cellphone conversations, M.T. urged her 17-year-old boyfriend to kill Ms. Rengel, a girl she had never even met, on the apparent basis of a grudge she had developed against her. (The boyfriend is about to be tried for first-degree murder.) When he said he might be recognized, she told him to cut leotards and put them over his face. When the boy missed an earlier deadline for the killing, she withdrew sexual favours. When it was done, she re-enacted the killing with the boyfriend. Later, she protested to police that she and the boyfriend had talked of mundane things, in addition to the killing, as if that made her less of a killer.

None of this takes the onus off the boy who allegedly stabbed Ms. Rengel six times on New Year's Day, 2008, leaving her to bleed to death in agony, with only a kind passerby to comfort her. But it does mean that M.T., who was nearly 16, is a serious threat to public safety.

SOURCE: *Globe and Mail*, "Cold Blood and Adult Penalties" (editorial), 24 March 2009. Reprinted with permission from the Globe and Mail.

SUMMARY

1. While crime and deviance are universal phenomena, there are no universal forms of crime and deviance. What counts as crime and deviance varies by time and place. Crime and deviance also vary by how serious they are judged to be. The more serious the offence, the more severe the punishment.

2. Crime and deviance can be studied as objective behaviours and social constructs. Objectivist and constructionist perspectives tend to ask different, though not necessarily alternative, questions about crime and deviance.

3. Official counts of crime and deviance underestimate the amount of crime and deviance occurring in society. There is an inverse relationship between the seriousness of crime and deviance and the frequency of its occurrence. The homicide rate is generally regarded as the most valid and reliable measure of criminal activity in the community.

4. Canada's crime rate has been declining over the past several decades. There are significant variations in rates of crime across the country.

5. The shortcomings of official crime statistics are well known. To reduce reliance on them, self-report and observational studies have been developed as additional data sources.

6. There are a number of important correlates of crime, including age and gender. However, correlation does not necessarily imply causation.

Sociological theories of crime and deviance are designed to answer questions about causation.

7. Historically, the deviant and criminal activities of girls and women have been ignored or sexualized. Increasingly, however, sociologists are paying more attention to the forms and frequency of female crime and deviance.

8. Concern about youth crime and deviance has always been prominent.

9. Imprisonment and other deterrence-based policies have been a mainstay of the societal response to criminal behaviour. Research suggests that they are not very effective in reducing crime levels. Other anti-crime strategies focus on prevention. Much of the public debate about criminal justice policy in Canada concentrates on young offenders.

QUESTIONS TO CONSIDER

1. What are moral panics? Why do they often involve young people?

2. Why is studying reaction to crime and deviance often as important as studying criminal and deviant behaviour itself?

3. Choose a particular form of criminal or deviant activity (for instance, youth gangs, drug use, serial killers) and consider how it might be

studied from both objectivist and social constructionist perspectives.

4. How do the mass media influence criminal and deviant behaviour?

5. What are the most important causes of crime?

6. Are girls and women become becoming more violent and aggressive?

GLOSSARY

The **certainty principle** is a component of deterrence theory that argues that it is the probability of punishment, rather than its severity, that dissuades potential offenders from breaking the law.

Conflict crime involves criminal acts that are subject to disagreement about their wrongfulness, the amount of harm they cause, how wrong they are, and how severely they should be punished.

Consensus crime involves criminal acts that are generally agreed to be seriously harmful, wrong, and deserving of severe penalty.

Control theories argue that crime and deviance are likely to occur when internal and external controls are weak or absent.

Crime is a breach of the criminal law that is liable to prosecution and punishment.

The **crime control model of criminal justice** advocates custodial sentences and other harsh punishments as the best means of reducing crime and increasing public safety.

The **criminal justice system** comprises the social institutions charged with the task of apprehending, prosecuting, and punishing known offenders.

The **dark figure of crime** is the number of criminal incidents that take place unknown to the police.

Deterrence theory argues that the threat of punishment discourages criminal violation.

Deviance is the breaking of a norm.

Differential association theory proposes that criminal behaviour is learned through contact with other individuals and groups.

The **due process model of criminal justice** emphasizes that wrongdoers should be punished in proportion to the severity of their crime.

Labelling theory argues that public identification of individuals as criminal or deviant leads to more crime or deviance by those individuals.

Moral panics are extreme reactions to crime and deviance.

Norms are rules that prescribe standards of everyday behaviour.

In **observational studies,** information about crime and deviance is collected by observing it.

Racial profiling is a selective enforcement of the law based upon racial (or ethnic) characteristics of those apprehended by police officers.

Recidivism is repeat offending, particularly following punishment or rehabilitation.

Routine activities theory argues that in addition to a motivated offender, criminal events require a suitable target and the absence of a capable guardian.

In **self-report studies**, respondents report about their involvements with crime and deviance as offenders and victims.

Social constructionism is a broad theoretical perspective concerned with the subjective meanings of social problems.

Social stigma is a damaged reputation or status.

Strain theory argues that people are pressured into breaking the rules because they have few opportunities to achieve dominant success goals by legitimate means.

Street crime refers to conventional violent and property crime. It is often contrasted with white-collar crime.

The **welfare model of juvenile justice** argues that young offenders should be treated differently from adult offenders.

White-collar crime is crime committed by high-status people in the course of their occupational careers.

SUGGESTED READING

Cohen, Stanley. (2002). *Folk Devils and Moral Panics,* 3rd ed. New York: Taylor and Francis. A sociological classic. The story of how societal reaction ("moral panic") turned mildly deviant youth groups (the mods and the rockers) into "folk devils" in mid-1960s Britain.

Sacco, Vince. (2005). *When Crime Waves.* Thousand Oaks, CA: Sage. A stimulating examination of a wide range of crime and deviance issues, including media representations of crime, the use and abuse of statistics, and fear of crime, from a social constructionist perspective.

Tanner, Julian. (2010). *Teenage Troubles: Youth and Deviance in Canada,* 3rd ed. Toronto; Oxford University Press. A comprehensive overview of what is known about juvenile crime and deviance in Canada. It examines a number of themes—schools and delinquency, deviant subcultures, youth gangs—from both objectivist and constructionist perspectives.

Venkatesh, Sudhir. (2008). *Gang Leader for a Day: A Rogue Sociologist Takes to the Streets.* New York: Penguin. A fascinating account of how a young researcher came to study gang activity in a notoriously tough Chicago community. Important for what it tells us about gang activity and the challenges and rewards of doing observational research.

WEB RESOURCES

Companion Website for This Book

http://www.newsociety6e.nelson.com
Begin by clicking on the Student Resources section of the website. Next, select the chapter you are studying from the pull-down menu. From the Student Resources page, you have easy access to InfoTrac College Edition® and other resources, such as the Glossary, Test Yourself questions, and additional readings. The website also has many useful tips to aid you in your study of sociology.

InfoTrac College Edition Search Terms

Visit http://www.infotrac-college.com for access to more than 20 million articles from nearly 6000 sources when doing your online research.

CHAPTER FIFTEEN

Population and Urbanization

John Hannigan
UNIVERSITY OF TORONTO

In this chapter you will learn that

- Especially rapid population growth occurs when breakthroughs in hygiene, public health, nutrition, and medical knowledge cause the death rate to fall, while lack of industrialization, urbanization, and modernization prevent the birth rate from falling.

- The choice of opportunities, experiences, and lifestyles available to urban residents is shaped and constrained by three sets of factors: those related to the physical environment; those associated with population size, distribution, and composition; and those dictated by the changing structure of the wider economy.

- Contrary to the theory that the core of Canadian cities is hollowing out, recent evidence suggests that city centres are remaining relatively stable economically and demographically. In contrast, the rings of older suburbs around city cores are stagnating, losing jobs and population to constellations of edge cities in the surrounding regions.

- The fastest-growing middle-class neighbourhoods are private communities, where control over local government, public services, and security rests in the hands of nonelected professional managers. One popular form of such neighbourhoods is the gated community, where nonresidents are considered intruders and are monitored and kept out by guards, alarm systems, and surveillance cameras.

- Cities are becoming multiethnic, with many neighbourhoods in the largest cities becoming home to members of visible minorities. This is generating racial and ethnic residential and commercial patterns that stand in marked contrast to the ecology of the older, industrial city.

INTRODUCTION

A dozen years ago, *The Globe and Mail* published an opinion piece by Elinor Florence, a British Columbia woman who, with her husband and three teenage children, had moved from Richmond, a rapidly developing suburb on the southern boundary of Vancouver, to Invermere, an alpine town of 3000 near the Alberta border. Leaving behind a mushrooming population, the stresses of urban driving, and "a junk culture that undeniably rears its head everywhere but snarls louder in cities" (Florence, 1997), the Florence family appears to have found happiness in the shadow of the Rockies. Among the benefits that she cites are a slower pace of life, more leisure time, a greater sense of personal security, no fast-food restaurants, and the ability to walk everywhere.

Elinor Florence's profile of small-town life highlights a theme that has resounded through the discipline of sociology since its founding in the nineteenth century. Urban life, it is said, is qualitatively different from a rural or small-town existence: meaner, more stressful, more alienating. Obsessed as they are with efficiency and making money, urbanites are said to have no time for relating to others in a more holistic and humane way. Increasing population size and density, such as that beginning to plague Richmond, bring with them a host of urban problems, from traffic gridlock and pollution to family breakdown and crime.

The tale of the Florences illustrates one of the most influential ways of looking at residential settings. Termed **environmental-opportunity theory** (Michelson, 1973), it posits that people actively choose where they want to live depending on the extent to which a particular place either meshes with or constrains their preferred lifestyle. Not all of us, of course, get to choose our community freely, but people will always strive to match their choices with their needs. This is well illustrated in the case of "Prairie Edge," a small Alberta municipality where residents perceived the "rural advantage" as being directly linked to the reduced parental anxiety that comes from a "safe" everyday environment (see Box 15.1, p. 364).

A second lens through which urban life can be viewed is that of *demography*—the study of populations: their size, distribution, and composition. As you will learn later in this chapter, in the preindustrial city significant growth was constrained by a high birth rate and a high death rate. Only when the death rate began to fall because of advances in hygiene, nutrition, medical knowledge, and public health did the

Is urban life meaner, more stressful, more alienating than small-town life? Richmond, B.C., proved too stressful for one family.
SOURCE: Al Harvey/The Slide Farm.

industrial city thrive, bringing with it a distinctive spatial organization and way of life. Today, the social organization and character of cities are being powerfully influenced by flows of highly diverse groups of immigrants between countries. This has resulted in the re-urbanization of the central city, the growth of the multiethnic city, and other urban changes.

A third approach asserts that the urban experience is constrained not just by the nature of the physical environment or by demographic forces but also by the changing configuration of international, national, and local economic arrangements. In recent years, the emergence of a globalized economy has had profound implications for North American cities, changing both their physical form and their social-class patterns. In particular, it has resulted in an increasing polarization between rich and poor, affecting the homeless person sleeping in the park, the highly paid professional eating in the chic urban restaurant, and the suburban homeowner shopping in a "big-box" megastore on the fringes of the city (Kleniewski, 1997: 135).

Similarly, resource towns and farming communities have been hard hit by international trade agreements and a harsher rural–urban division of labour in the global economy. In this changing climate, the countryside comes to serve two new and very different purposes: vacation playground and toxic dumping ground. Thus, while towns in the British Columbia interior and the Alberta foothills are transformed into ski and golfing resorts linked to global tourism, other communities are forced to "grasp at environmentally dubious schemes like hazardous waste treatment,

BOX 15.1   PRAIRIE EDGE: A "RURBAN" COMMUNITY

"Prairie Edge" is a pseudonym for Camrose, Alberta, a community of 14 000 about 100 kilometres from Edmonton. In the early 1990s, a survey research firm, John Yerxa Research Inc., asked residents of Prairie Edge (and three other "rural communities") to compare their place of residence with that of Edmonton. Just more than 80 percent reported that they believed a rural setting was a better place to raise a family. Residents particularly appreciated a quieter and smaller setting for its easy social interaction and perceived high level of personal safety. However, they recognized that their community lacked the wide choice of shopping and entertainment opportunities that were more readily available in Edmonton.

Sociologist Kieran Bonner resided in Prairie Edge around the time of the survey and independently carried out his own study among the middle-class parents who were his neighbours. Bonner found that they stressed three interrelated themes—safety, convenience, and reduced parental anxiety as the key benefits of the "life world" of a smaller centre. Each of these, in turn, flowed out of the high visibility and familiarity that resulted from smallness. However, some of his informants, especially those who had moved from a larger city, indicated that the familiarity resulting from high visibility (it was difficult to be a "stranger" in Prairie Edge) led to an ethic of helping and politeness but not to sociability and friendliness. In other words, people trusted their local environment more, especially with regard to potential dangers to children, but they did not necessarily share a strong sense of "community." Prairie Edge, Bonner concluded, possessed both rural and urban characteristics and thus could be described as being "rurban."

SOURCE: Adapted from Kieran Bonner, *A Great Place to Raise Kids: Interpretation, Science, and the Urban-Rural Debate*, Montreal and Kingston: McGill-Queen's University Press, 1997.

strawboard manufacture, tire incineration and mega-hog barns" (Epp and Whitson, 2001: xv).

In this chapter, I will look at this three-pronged influence of environment and structure on city life over the past century. In the course of the discussion, you will encounter three main types of cities: the industrial city, the corporate city, and the **postmodern city**. The industrial city originated in the nineteenth century and reached its zenith in the 1920s and 1930s, the corporate city arose after World War II and dominated during the 1950s and 1960s, and the postmodern city dates from the 1970s up to the present.

EARLY CITIES

Cities are "relatively large, dense, permanent settlements in which the majority of the residents do not produce their own food" (McGahan, 1995: 1). By most accounts, the city as a distinct form dates back five or six thousand years to 3000–4000 B.C.E, when it first appeared in Mesopotamia (now southern Iraq) and Egypt. Initially, ancient cities were established largely as centres of religious worship and were not much larger than most single-industry towns in Canada today. For example, Memphis, at the head of the Nile River delta, had an estimated population of 40 000 in 3000 B.C.E. Cities later swelled: Babylon had a population of 200 000 during the reign of Nebuchadnezzar in the seventh century B.C.E.;

Alexandria, Egypt, surpassed 300 000 three centuries later; and Rome reached 800 000 at its peak in the second century C.E. (Chandler and Fox, 1974).

Three elements of prime importance characterized these preindustrial cities: the existence of a food surplus in fertile valleys, which permitted the specialization of labour in zones of dense settlement; the achievement of literacy among scribes, priests, and other elite members of society, which allowed for the keeping of financial and other records; and technological innovations, notably metallurgy, agricultural irrigation, and the harnessing of wind and water power for sailing and grain milling.

After the fall of Rome to Germanic tribes in the fifth century C.E., cities stagnated and declined over large parts of Europe. They continued to flourish, though, in the rising Islamic empire, which, at its zenith, stretched from Spain to India. More decentralized than the Roman world, the Islamic empire contained a number of cities that reached impressive levels of size and sophistication. For example, more than 500 000 people lived in Cairo in the fourteenth century, when Egypt held a trade monopoly on the east–west spice route (Abu-Lughod, 1991: 38).

From the eleventh century on, a number of city-states along the Mediterranean—Florence, Genoa, Venice, Pisa—succeeded in re-establishing trade routes to Asia and the Middle East by means of the

Crusades. The commercial revival that followed was felt even in the merchant towns of the North Sea and the Baltic, which themselves had begun to develop a brisk trade in wool and cloth. From this renaissance developed a distinct class of professional merchants who established their own municipal laws and institutions distinct from those in the surrounding feudal society, and there also emerged a market for housing and a variety of other goods and services, which generated further urban growth (Golden, 1981: 120–22).

Although preindustrial cities were important as centres of commerce, knowledge, and art, they never contained much more than a small fraction of the overall population. Even at their height, ancient and medieval cities were incapable of supporting urban populations of more than 5 or 10 percent of society, primarily because they could not generate a sufficiently large agricultural surplus to feed a huge urban populace. When the cities did begin to swell, periodic outbreaks of the bubonic plague (the notorious "Black Death"), spread by fleas from infected rats, killed as many as half the people in Europe's cities. Thus, by 1800, of the roughly 900 million people in the world, only about 3 percent lived in urban places of 5000 or more inhabitants (Hauser, 1965: 7). And, despite significant changes in architectural styles and building materials, the physical layout of the communities in which they lived had not changed all that much from antiquity to the eighteenth century—they were still built up within protective walls and organized around a central market square and places of worship, such as cathedrals, temples, or mosques (Abu-Lughod, 1991: 49–50).

POPULATION ISSUES AND URBAN GROWTH

Urban growth is a product not only of technological progress and social invention but also of the broader patterns of population growth that shape a society. These demographic forces operate in conjunction with other social and economic factors to create a slow-moving but powerful current that relentlessly moves us in certain directions (McQuillan, 1994: 229).

THE DEMOGRAPHIC TRANSITION

For much of human history, societies hovered in a steady state in which both birth rates and death rates were high. As a result, the overall size of the population remained more or less uniform from decade to decade.

In the absence of any effective form of birth control, women in preindustrial societies were destined to bear a large number of children. This was deemed necessary for several reasons. Infant and childhood mortality rates were high; routinely, only about half of the children born survived to adulthood. Thus, it was necessary to have large families in the hope that some would escape the grim reaper. Furthermore, in traditional societies offspring were viewed as having considerable economic value, especially in the poorer classes where children were expected to help with the farm work or were sent off to work as servants in the homes of the rich. In the absence of pension plans or retirement funds, parents fortunate enough to reach old age depended on their children to care for them.

The human life span was much shorter than it is today. For example, in 1867, the year Canada officially became a country, the average life expectancy was 42 years as compared with 77.4 years (for men) and 82.4 years (for women) in 2003 (Beaujot, 2004: 446; Statistics Canada, 2005: 27). Even the most learned medical authorities did not understand the causes of and proper treatments for illnesses, attributing them to intangibles, such as "vapours" and the like. Those who fell ill were "bled" by leeches and subjected to other such treatments.

Beginning in the eighteenth century, this pattern began to change dramatically with breakthroughs in hygiene, public health, nutrition, and medical knowledge. Once it was understood that often-fatal maladies, such as cholera, were preventable by establishing a pure water supply, the death rate declined significantly. Now the causes of death were more likely to be degenerative diseases, such as cancer and heart disease. Especially important strides were made in reducing infant mortality. Note, for example, the declining infant mortality rate in Canada: in 1831, 1 in 6 children did not survive his or her first year; in 1931 it was 1 in 14, and by 1999 this dropped to 1 in 190 (Beaujot, 2004: 446).

While death rates plunged, birth rates, at first, remained relatively high. Deeply ingrained cultural traditions and beliefs remained stubbornly embedded. Large families remained the norm and the use of birth control was outlawed. The result was a period of rapid population growth, especially in urban areas.

Eventually, however, birth rates also began to fall. Contributing to this was a series of changes associated with increasing modernization, industrialization, and urbanization. One crucial factor was the offloading of responsibilities formerly attached to the family onto the state. Children now were required to remain in school until they were adolescents; consequently, childrearing became more costly. Primary care for seniors began to shift from adult children to government-operated programs and institutions. This change from high to low birth and death rates is known as the **demographic transition** (see Figure 15.1). Initially, this change was most characteristic of cities in Western Europe and North America, but ultimately it spread to rural districts as new health technologies and medical treatments expanded beyond the city limits.

From the mid-1960s onward, wealthier nations in the developed world entered a new demographic era that differs in several ways from that associated with the demographic processes outlined above. First, fertility plunged below 2.1 births per woman—the **replacement level** at which births and deaths balance and the population level remains stationary, ignoring population inflows from other countries (immigration) and population outflows to other countries (emigration). This reflects a fundamental shift in contemporary values, especially among the middle class. Whereas previously the pressure to raise a family was paramount, now the emphasis shifted to equality of opportunity and freedom of choice. Increasingly, women entered the paid labour force on a full-time basis, not just out of economic necessity but in pursuit of self-fulfillment. With declining fertility rates, the population as a whole is becoming older, especially in countries where immigration has concurrently slowed down. Some analysts have described this as the "second demographic transition" (Champion, 1993; Van de Kaa, 1987).

Malthus versus Marx

As the initial demographic transition loomed, fears arose over the possibility of overpopulation. Alarm was first sounded by the British clergyman and political economist Thomas Malthus.

With declining fertility rates, the population as a whole is becoming older.
SOURCE: © Jupiter Images, 2009.

Under normal conditions, Malthus (1798) believed, there exists a natural "urge to reproduce" that flows from the attraction between the sexes. The resulting population growth is potentially limited by two checks. "Positive checks" are related to mortality: famine, epidemics, wars, and plagues, such as the Black Death. Positive checks are generally beyond human control. In contrast, "preventive checks" are related to fertility. Since Malthus condemned the use of contraception as immoral, the only remaining remedy was for couples to exercise "moral constraint." For all practical purposes, this meant postponing marriages as long as possible.

Of greater interest today are Malthus's comments about the relationship between population growth and resource (especially food) depletion. Malthus argued that population, if left unchecked, would increase geometrically or exponentially (as in the series 2, 4, 8, 16). Meanwhile, food supply would increase only arithmetically (as in the series 2, 4, 6, 8). Eventually, population would outstrip the food supply, resulting in widespread poverty, hunger, and misery. Malthus concluded that only grinding poverty would ultimately succeed in discouraging people from marrying early and raising large, healthy families.

Karl Marx was one of Malthus's most outspoken critics. According to Marx, Malthus was blind to the real cause of excess population: the capitalist economic system. Capitalism, Marx insisted, is organized to keep the working class in a perpetual state of poverty and unemployment. That is because it is to the financial advantage of capitalists to have more workers than jobs. The excess supply of workers allowed factory and mill owners to keep wages low and easily replace workers

FIGURE 15.1   THE DEMOGRAPHIC TRANSITION

STAGE 1   STAGE 2   STAGE 3

BIRTH AND DEATH RATES
(PER 1000 POPULATION)

40

30   Birth rate

20

10   Death rate

TIME

who created trouble. Furthermore, it facilitated the maintenance of a "reserve army of labour" that could be expanded or shrunk depending on whether the economy was expanding or in recession. Rapid population growth, then, was less a result of a mismatch between population and resources and more a case of deeply flawed social and economic arrangements.

The contrasting views of Malthus and Marx have reappeared in today's environmental debate. In the 1960s, several authors became widely known for their doomsday scenarios concerning overpopulation and dwindling resources. In the spirit of Malthus, conservation biologist Paul Ehrlich warns in his provocatively titled *The Population Bomb* (1968) that world population is expanding out of control, especially in Asia and Africa. At the same time, he holds, the unchecked consumption habits of people in the world's rich countries are depleting supplies of food, oil, and water. The result will be catastrophic, Ehrlich predicts. One notable critic of this viewpoint is economist Julian Simon, who argues that Ehrlich is wrong in identifying a pending population crisis. Simon notes that the price of most resources has been dropping, cities are becoming less polluted, and humans can be counted on to cope with population pressures through their technological ingenuity (Simon and Kahn, 1984).

THE INDUSTRIAL CITY

By the end of the eighteenth century, a new type of city had begun to emerge, first in England and later in continental Europe and America. This *industrial city* was larger, more complex, and more dynamic than any urban settlement that had preceded it. At century's end, more than 50 percent of the population of England and Wales lived in places with 20 000 or more people, compared with only 17 percent a century earlier (Weber, 1963 [1899]: 47). Global urbanization trends from 1800 to 2000 are shown in Figure 15.2.

What contributed to the growth of industrial cities? One popular theory emphasizes advances in transportation and agricultural technology, inasmuch as these factors contributed to the production and movement of agricultural surpluses from farm to city. Among the innovations were better methods of land drainage, the use of fertilizers, methods of seed selection, techniques of animal breeding, toll-road building, and the application of steam power to farm machinery and rail transport. Other scholars emphasize a boom in trade and commerce, which provided a powerful inducement to greater investment, techno-

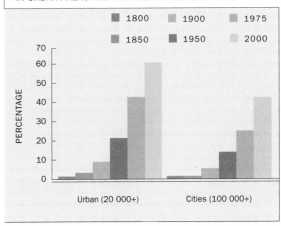

FIGURE 15.2 PERCENTAGE OF WORLD POPULATION LIVING IN URBAN AREAS AND IN LARGE CITIES 1800–2000

SOURCE: Adapted from Kingsley Davis, 1995, "The Origin and Growth of Urbanization in the World," *American Journal of Sociology*, 60, p. 430. Reprinted with permission from the estate of Jefferson Davis.

logical improvements, and, ultimately, increased agricultural productivity.

Another key factor appears to have been a shift in the sources of capital accumulation—that is, how factory owners raised the investment money needed to build and improve their manufacturing facilities. In England after 1850, capital investment was facilitated by the creation of the joint stock company, a business structure that pooled the capital of many investors and that had limited liability (i.e., the shareholders could not be held personally responsible for enterprises that failed).

Finally, urban growth has been linked to the invention of the factory. Previously, under the "putting-out" system, piecework was done in village or rural cottages and collected at regular intervals by the agents of merchant entrepreneurs. With the advent of the factory system, workers were required to work in a central location. Initially, factories had to be located next to rivers, in order to run directly on water power. Then, as steam-powered machines became the standard, factories concentrated in cities because steam power could not be distributed economically over a wide grid, as electrical systems can be today.

THE DEVELOPMENT OF AN URBAN-INDUSTRIAL ECONOMY IN CANADA

At the time of Confederation in 1867, Canada lagged significantly behind both Britain and the United States in the development of an urban-industrial economy. The British North American colonies, both inside and outside the new political union, traded very little with one another, looking instead to the United States or

Great Britain. According to the first manufacturing census in 1870, such localized activities as sawmilling, flour milling, shoemaking, and clothing manufacture accounted for almost half the value of the manufactured goods produced in Canada (Nader, 1975: 207). At the same time, only a tiny minority of Canadians lived in urban areas. In 1871, fewer than 1 in 5 (18 percent) lived in a town or a city (Stone, 1967: 29).

As the twentieth century dawned, Canada had a population of just more than 5 million, with two-thirds of these people living in rural areas and dependent for their livelihood on farming and the farm economy (Kremarik, 2000: 19). Soon however, industrial cities finally began to emerge. Although Toronto and Montreal were the largest industrial centres, factory towns also grew up elsewhere in Ontario, chief among them Windsor, because of its proximity to industry and markets in Detroit, and Hamilton, because of its port and strategic location on the Great Lakes. In addition to strategic location, the availability of investment capital played a significant role in directing where industry was established. The Canada Bank Act of 1871 was instrumental in concentrating economic power in a few national metropolitan centres, notably Toronto and Montreal. The act adopted the British model of a branch-banking system wherein a handful of major banks each established a network of branches. In contrast, under the U.S. unit-banking system, many more banks are independent. Investment capital was thus concentrated in a handful of urban centres rather than being widely dispersed across the country (Nader, 1975: 215).

Through various interventions by the federal government—the building of the transcontinental railroad, the imposition of a protective tariff system to encourage domestic manufacturing, a vigorous immigration policy that encouraged agriculture on the Prairies—a system of national economic markets was eventually established. In particular, at the turn of the twentieth century, these interventions found form in the expansion of wheat production for export. With cash from wheat sales jingling in their pockets, Prairie grain farmers were able to purchase manufactured goods from the factories of Ontario and Quebec, thus stimulating a marked upsurge in Canadian urbanization from 1891 to 1911 (Stone, 1967: 20–21). By 1911, four cities had populations exceeding 100 000: Montreal (470 480), Toronto (376 538), Winnipeg (136 035), and Vancouver (100 401). However, the formation of a national market led to the deindustrialization of the Maritime provinces (Brym, 1986).

As the twentieth century progressed, the proportion of the Canadian population classified as "urban" increased dramatically, crossing the 50 percent mark before 1931 and reaching 70 percent in 1951. By 2001, 77 percent of the Canadian population was living in towns and cities (see Table 15.1).

Most increases in urbanization in recent decades are accounted for by a handful of large urban regions. As of 2006, 45 percent of the Canadian population lived in one of the six largest CMAs (census metropolitan areas)—Toronto, Montreal, Vancouver, Ottawa-Gatineau, Calgary, and Edmonton—and these areas were growing at a faster rate (8 percent between 2001 and 2006) than were Canada's other 27 CMAs over the same period (Statistics Canada, 2008a: 11).

While Toronto and Montreal continue to hold the largest number of Canadians, the fastest growth rates since 1951 have been in Western Canada. Between 1991 and 1998, Calgary's population grew by 18.4 percent and that of Vancouver by 21.2 percent. This compares with 8.1 percent for the nation as a whole (Little, 1999). By the beginning of the millennium, Western Canada's growth rate had started to slow down. Nevertheless, between 2001 and 2006 Calgary's population grew by 13 percent, Vancouver's by 7 percent, and that of Edmonton by 10 percent. According to the 2006 census, the population of Toronto's CMA now stands at 5 million, while 3.6 million people reside in Montreal, over 2 million in Vancouver, and just over 1 million in each of Ottawa-Gatineau, Calgary, and Edmonton (Statistics Canada, 2008a).

A historical analysis of census data reveals some interesting differences in the way that Canada's largest cities grew at the end of the twentieth century. Net international migration (immigrants minus emigrants) has been the single biggest source of

TABLE 15.1 URBAN–RURAL POPULATION, CANADA, 1931–2001

	1931	1951	1991	2001
Rural farm	31%	11%	3%	2%
Rural nonfarm	15	19	20	18
Urban	54	70	77	80
Total	100	100	100	100

SOURCES: Adapted from Statistics Canada, "Urban vs. Rural Population," http://www.statcan.ca (September 20, 1996). Used by authority of the Minister of Industry, 2000; Lance W. Roberts, Rodney A. Clifton, Barry Ferguson, Karen Kampen and Simon Langlois, 2005, *Recent Social Trends in Canada*, Montreal and Kingston: McGill-Queen's University Press, p. 33.

population increase in Toronto (85 percent of the total between 1991 and 1997) versus 68 percent in Vancouver. By contrast, migrants from the rest of Canada accounted for 29 percent of Vancouver's growth, whereas Toronto actually lost people to other provinces (2 percent of the city's population). Calgary fired on all cylinders, with natural increase (births minus deaths) accounting for 43 percent, net international immigration for 31 percent, and interprovincial migration for 22 percent of growth (Little, 1999). The latter figures reflected the strong growth of Alberta's natural resources sector, coupled with a continuing decline in manufacturing in central Canada.

RESEARCHING THE INDUSTRIAL CITY: THE CHICAGO SCHOOL

By the final quarter of the nineteenth century, U.S. cities were seeing jumps in population that rivalled and even surpassed those in Britain. Nowhere was this more dramatic than in Chicago, which mushroomed from 122 000 people in 1860 to 1.7 million in 1900 and 3.4 million in 1930. Such rapid growth left in its wake social dislocation and human misery. Among those who sought to address these problems was the chairman of the sociology department of the University of Chicago, Robert E. Park.

Park and his colleagues believed that they could improve conditions for the disadvantaged by discovering what made the city "tick" and then using this knowledge to help solve its "social pathologies": crime, juvenile delinquency, family breakdown, and mental illness. To carry out this task, they employed an assortment of methods and models. On the one hand, Park argued that researchers should consider themselves urban anthropologists who would venture out into the field and study the natives, and their customs, beliefs, and practices. This inspired a rich ethnographic tradition of urban research in which Park's colleagues and students rendered richly detailed, first-hand accounts of such things as homeless men, gangs, and "taxi-dance" halls. At the same time, Park also urged his students to consider the city of Chicago as a kind of social laboratory in which various natural processes took place. One way of documenting these processes was through the development of urban-growth models (discussed in the next section) by which the changing social and spatial structure of the city could be depicted visually. Another was to use "ecological spot maps" in which differences in the rate of various deviant behaviours,

such as juvenile delinquency and schizophrenia, could be plotted geographically in order to discover underlying patterns. Some of the most memorable work to come out of the Chicago School tradition drew upon personal documents and other biographical materials (Zorbaugh, 1929).

To put this mountain of data into some kind of theoretical order, Park and his colleagues used several approaches. First, they tapped into a long tradition of exploring the contrast between rural and urban life. In the latter part of the nineteenth century, the German social philosopher Ferdinand Tönnies (1957 [1887]) had attempted to depict the difference between traditional and modern societies by introducing a distinction between a *Gemeinschaft*—the "community of feeling" that exists in villages, tribes, and small communities—and *Gesellschaft*—the characteristic feature of social relations in the city. Tönnies favoured *Gemeinschaft* and saw its decline as a loss of all that is natural and satisfying about small-town life. In contrast, he wrote, *Gesellschaft* denotes a lifestyle based on money, commercial contracts, individual interest, and class antagonism. Although he was more positive about the possibilities for individual freedom in modern urban life, the German sociologist Georg Simmel (1950) used the same rural–urban contrast as a central method of dealing with the meaning of the shift to an urban society.

This rural–urban dichotomy runs through much of Chicago School theorizing. Thomas and Znaniecki (1918–20), for example, depict the city as being responsible for destroying the traditional institutions of Polish peasant life—family, neighbourhood, church—and substituting nothing but an empty well of social disorganization. Freed from the ties that

German philosopher Ferdinand Tönnies contrasted the community of feeling that exists in villages and small communities with the commercialism and individualism of the city.
SOURCE: Sheila Maloney, *Zephyr Ontario*. Courtesy Nancy Poole's Studio.

formerly bound the community together, marriages dissolve, teenagers run wild, and even murder is not uncommon. In his modification of Simmel's social-psychological profile of urban life, Louis Wirth (1938) proposed that the city is characterized by the concurrent trends of increasing size, density, and heterogeneity. In his view, the city creates a distinct way of life—**urbanism**—that is economically efficient but socially destructive. Wirth's list of urban characteristics includes the decline of the family, the disappearance of the neighbourhood, and the undermining of traditional bases of social solidarity. Urbanites are said to be superficial, unable to step outside their narrow occupational roles to relate to people in a holistic and meaningful way, and guided by an all-consuming drive for success and money.

A century later, the rural–urban typology is still pervasive in the popular imagination. In the final weeks of December 2008, the Canadian media featured several stories from the British Columbia interior that accented small-town altruism and solidarity. One of these stories cast the people of McBride, a village hard-hit by mill closings and job losses, as heroes for fighting freezing cold to dig a kilometre-long passageway through massive snowfalls to rescue two trapped and starving horses. In a second, more tragic case, residents of Sparwood, a coal-mining town 300 kilometres southwest of Calgary, came together at a candlelight vigil to remember seven local men who perished in an avalanche during a snowmobile ride in the backcountry. "Each and every one of us know them," Sparwood's mayor told the hundreds of mourners at the vigil (Montgomery, 2008). By contrast, a 28-year-old man who was found dead on Christmas morning in the east-Toronto district of Scarborough was depicted by the press as a virtual stranger. According to one report, no one seemed acquainted with the victim, although a couple of people had heard loud arguments coming from his apartment. The 11-storey block of community housing units where he resided was described as "not a place where tenants know their neighbours" ("Slain Man Mystery to Tenants," 2008).

ECOLOGY OF THE INDUSTRIAL CITY

Industrial cities were also unique in their ecology—that is, their spatial layout, physical structure, and distribution of population. To depict the spatial or ecological patterns of the city, a group of sociologists and geographers from the University of Chicago

devised a set of urban-growth models in the 1920s and 1930s.

Burgess's **concentric-zone model** conceptualized the expansion of cities as a succession of concentric rings, each of which contained a distinct resident population and type of land use (Burgess, 1961). This concentric model of urban growth identified five zones (see Figure 15.3).

Zone 1, the central business district (CBD), is the commercial pulse of the city. It is the site of the major department stores, live theatres, hotels, banks, and office space. The land is the most valuable in the city, which means that residential and low-rent commercial uses are inevitably displaced in favour of big-money commercial enterprises.

Zone 2 is called the zone in transition. In the 1920s, large parcels of land in Chicago's transitional zone were being held by speculators who fully expected that the CBD would push outward, making them millionaires. In the meantime, Zone 2 stood as an area of cheap housing that became the initial resting point for each new wave of immigrants who took jobs in the nearby factories. Also located here were a variety of marginal businesses—pawn shops,

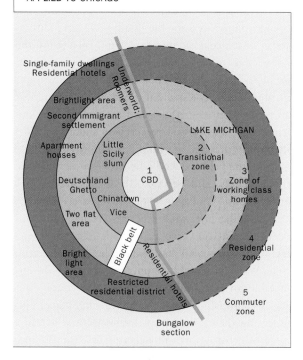

FIGURE 15.3   BURGESS'S CONCENTRIC ZONE MODEL APPLIED TO CHICAGO

SOURCE: Redrawn from Ernest W. Burgess, 1961, "The Growth of the City: An Introduction to a Research Project," in George A. Theodorson, ed., *Studies in Human Ecology*, Evanston, IL: Row, Peterson, p. 41.

tattoo parlours, second-hand stores—that could not afford the high rents of the city centre. The transitional zone also attracted a raft of illegal commercial activities—gambling, prostitution, drug dealing—that needed to be accessible to clientele in the CBD but that were considered socially unacceptable in the high-profile heart of the downtown area.

Zone 3, the zone of working-class homes, denotes the area settled by second-generation immigrants and rural migrants. In Burgess's time, Zone 3 was a neighbourhood of semidetached, two-family homes where fathers still worked in inner-city factories but from which the upwardly mobile children aspired to escape, into the middle-class suburban zones.

Zone 4, the zone of better residences, was where the bulk of the middle class could be found: small-business people, professionals, sales personnel, and office employees. Initially, it was an area of single-family detached houses, but by the mid-1920s, it was increasingly characterized by apartment buildings and residential hotels.

Finally, Zone 5, the commuter zone, was an area beyond the political boundaries of the city composed of satellite towns and suburbs. With the growth of commuter railroads and automobile travel, Zone 5 was a precursor of the suburbs that boomed after World War II.

Burgess's concentric-zone model made three interrelated assumptions. First, all commercial growth was said to emanate from the dominant city-centre nucleus and proceed outward in an orderly and predictable manner. Second, residential growth took place at the periphery, where it was easier and cheaper to obtain open land for development purchases. New housing was added here, but it was intended primarily for the middle and upper classes, who were increasingly able to take advantage of newly constructed commuter rail lines and, later, expressways. Third, the model was dynamic in that it assumed a sort of filtering-down process. As housing aged, it deteriorated, became less desirable, and was abandoned by better-off citizens, who moved into newer housing farther away from the city centre. The homes they left behind, some of them mansions, were subdivided into rooming houses, flats, and dormitories for artists and students. In recent years, many of these have been restored to a measure of their former glory, either by residential "gentrifiers" or by commercial users, such as restaurateurs or hair stylists. Furthermore, Burgess assumed that, as immigrant newcomers to the industrial city found their balance and began to prosper, they would want to upgrade their housing. For example, the second generation of "white ethnics"—the acculturated sons and daughters of those who had come as part of the Polish, Italian, German, and other European immigration around the turn of the twentieth century—could be expected to settle in the zone of working-class homes, which possessed superior housing to that occupied by their parents in the transitional zone.

Burgess's urban-growth model appears to have fitted Chicago in the 1920s reasonably well, but, as a scheme for understanding all cities in different places and times, it does not do as well. First, the notion of a single growth nucleus has not held up very firmly. Such cities as Calgary and Edmonton, which developed later in the century and which were shaped largely by the automobile, are more likely to possess more than one nucleus or growth centre. Similarly, Los Angeles is widely known as "the city without a downtown." This was first recognized in the 1940s by geographers Chauncey Harris and Edward Ullman (1945), who proposed a **multiple-nuclei model** of urban growth in which were located a series of growth centres—retail, wholesale, residential—each representing the concentration of a specific function or activity within the urban economy.

Second, Burgess seems to have underestimated the importance of transportation corridors as magnets for urban growth. Geographer Homer Hoyt (1939) developed a **sector model** of urban growth after studying 142 U.S. cities during the Depression years. He argued that cities grew not in concentric circles but in sectors or wedges along major transportation arteries, extending like the tentacles of an octopus from the CBD. Within each sector, the social character of the residential housing would remain constant. For example, upper-income groups would follow a northward progression, and working-class groups a southward path, thereby producing a distinct sectoral pattern to the developing city. Montreal and Vancouver seem to fit this sector model, because their populations tended to spread out along the natural shorelines of the bodies of water on which they are located (Driedger, 1991: 90).

Third, Burgess failed to appreciate that some resident groups would develop strong residential attachments to their neighbourhoods and refuse to move on, even in the face of an aging housing stock. This was first pointed out by Walter Firey (1947) in his study of Boston. Firey gives several examples that span the socioeconomic spectrum, from Beacon Hill, an elite area near the city centre, to the North End, a blue-collar Italian area where the residents chose to remain in their old neighbourhoods because the places were cherished as symbols of the residents' family connections, traditions, and culture.

URBANIZATION OF THE DEVELOPING WORLD

A century ago, most urban growth was concentrated in the rapidly industrializing countries of Europe and North America. Today, nearly two-thirds of the world's urban population resides in the less developed regions of Asia, Oceania, Africa, Latin America, and the Caribbean (Gugler, 1996: vii). In the Southern hemisphere, the demographic transition is moving faster and with far greater numbers than those experienced in the past (Ness and Law, 2000). Over the next three decades, cities in the global south are expected to double in size to about 4 billion people, with 19 cities reaching a population of more than 10 million by 2015 (see Figure 15.4).

Although urbanization in the Southern hemisphere has followed sundry paths, it has displayed some common features. To a greater extent than with Northern cities, cities of the South are characterized by a high degree of **urban primacy.** This describes a situation in which one metropolitan centre, usually the capital city, is considerably larger and more dominant than any of the others. In Mexico, for example, this primacy is indicated by roadside markers throughout the country that indicate the distance to Mexico City, which is six times the size of its nearest rival, Guadalajara (Flanagan, 1995: 154). Primacy is most evident on the African continent, where 11 out of the 20 most extreme examples of primacy systems occur (Clark, 1996: 27). In many cases, they are located along the sea coast, a legacy of colonial times when they operated as shipping points for raw materials on their way to Spain, France, England, and other imperial powers. Much the same pattern exists in present times; resource-producing regions funnel export commodities to big coastal cities, where the goods are subsequently shipped overseas. This is said to contribute to the underdevelopment of the interior, where provincial towns and cities tend to stagnate, unable to sustain a robust local industrial and commercial base.

In recent years, however, cities with populations between 100 000 and 500 000 have experienced remarkable growth, especially in some Latin American countries. In Argentina, for example, intermediate cities have grown faster than Buenos Aires, while in Mexico, interior cities that have plugged into the international economy have outstripped the growth rate of Mexico City (De Oliveira and Roberts, 1996).

Cities of the South are often described as victims of **overurbanization.** This means that the population of urban areas is growing faster than the urban

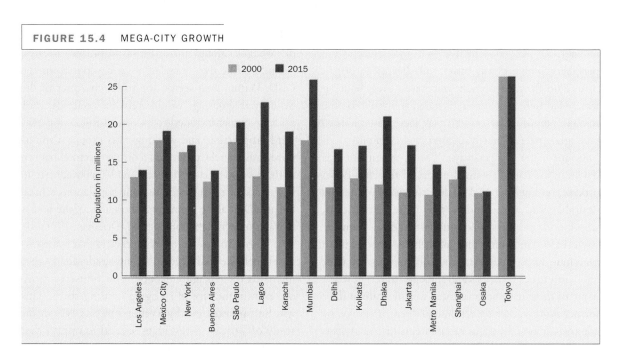

FIGURE 15.4 MEGA-CITY GROWTH

SOURCE: Reprinted by kind permission of the New Internationalist. Copyright New Internationalist, www.newint.org.

economy, services, and resources can absorb it. This creates an underclass of residents who live in illegal squatter settlements and employ themselves in marginal trades, such as selling food and lottery tickets on street corners (Flanagan, 1995: 153). Canadian cities have recently had a taste of this in the form of growing numbers of panhandlers, "squeegee kids," and other homeless urban people, but the numbers in Southern cities are much larger. With public housing scarce, "squatter settlements" are common. In such settlements, people occupy urban land without legal title, frequently organizing "invasions" at set times and places. Once they have staked out their plots, the squatters put up makeshift shelters and establish basic public services, such as water supply and sewage disposal. Some squatter settlements remain poor, but others significantly upgrade their housing and eventually persuade municipal governments to extend utilities and health and sanitation services into the area.

The concept of overurbanization has provoked debate among social scientists. Some claim that overurbanization is the single most important factor leading to the generation and intensification of serious social problems in Southern cities: grinding poverty, mass unemployment, inadequate services, social unrest, increasing crime, and political instability (D. Smith, 1996: 148). Others claim that it is misleading to isolate the mismatch between demographic growth and employment opportunities, arguing that it makes more sense to look to larger structural factors, such as undue reliance on foreign multinational corporations and continued deep inequality between an urban-based elite and the urban and rural masses.

Some countries in Asia, Africa, and Latin America have exhibited distinctive patterns of **peri-urbanization** whereby the rural and the urban have become blurred in unplanned settlements on the outskirts of large cities. The motivation for this is mostly economic: Land in these peri-urban zones is cheaper and more easily obtained; shelter can be constructed economically by using locally available materials; and families can keep farm animals and cultivate subsistence crops without violating any of the restrictions of the formal planning system (Stren and Halfani, 2001: 478). In contemporary Asian cities, for example, urbanization is increasingly characterized by the *desakota* (from the Indonesian words for "village" and "city"). Here, most people continue to live in village settings and almost all the land is under cultivation, but most family income comes from non-agricultural sources. Some family members may even commute to work in the

city, or live in the city and remit portions of their salaries to their families (Ginsburg, Koppel, and McGee, 1991). The linked processes of peri-urbanization and *desakota* challenge the conventional paradigm of the urban transition derived from the case of Western Europe and North America in the nineteenth and early twentieth centuries. Rather than remain strictly separated, the rural and the urban coexist in densely populated areas on the fringe of large mega-urban regions (McGee, 1991: 4–5).

Finally, sociologists who study urbanization in the South have been much concerned with urban bias, that is, uneven investment and development that favour urban over rural areas. Despite the problems generated by overurbanization, landless migrants continue to flow into cities, which they see as their best chance to improve their lot in life. Economic growth strategies focus primarily on these rapidly growing cities, while the rural hinterland is overlooked. Thus, for the two decades following independence (the 1960s and 1970s) many of Africa's first-generation political leaders penalized agriculture through their monetary and tax policies in order to obtain resources to finance industrial development in the cities. In addition, public services were concentrated in the large cities, especially national capitals (Lofchie, 1997: 24–25). Although poverty statistics are not always reliable, recent figures from the United Nations and the World Bank suggest that absolute poverty in rural areas continues to overshadow that found in the cities. For example, in Brazil, where there are notoriously poor slums in Rio de Janeiro and São Paulo, 65.9 percent of the population in rural areas continues to live below the poverty line versus 37.7 percent in the cities. In Mexico, the figures follow the same pattern. Much the same holds for most African nations. India, by contrast, shows more or less comparable levels of poverty in urban and rural areas (Drakakis-Smith, 1988).

THE CORPORATE CITY

Although the industrial city continued to exist in North America into the 1970s, it began to lose ground after 1945 to a new urban form. Simply defined, the **corporate city** denotes the perception and organization of the city as a vehicle for capital accumulation—that is, as a money-making machine.

The corporate city comprises five major elements (Lorimer, 1978; Reid, 1991): (1) the corporate suburb, (2) the shopping centre, (3) the suburban industrial park, (4) the downtown office tower, and (5) the high-rise apartment building.

Each of these five elements of the corporate city has evolved over the years. Some of their central features have recently changed. Facing the spectre of shopper boredom and increased competition from both revitalized downtown retail districts and exurban big-box stores (e.g., Home Depot, Costco, Wal-Mart), shopping centres have been undergoing a redesign that includes a more diverse mix of retail tenants. In the face of changing demographics, suburban developments have also been forced to include a greater variety of housing types, including more townhouses and row houses and such innovations as "granny flats" (separate quarters for aged parents). After years of being half-empty, some downtown office buildings have begun to convert to condominiums. Nevertheless, the process by which the corporate city has been assembled and maintained remains much the same and stands in marked contrast to that which undergirds the building of the industrial city. Nowhere has this been more evident than in the case of the corporate suburb.

THE CORPORATE SUBURB

Before World War II, North American cities, such as Toronto, were configured in a grid system, with residential avenues crossing long commercial streets at right angles. Since most urban residents lived within a few blocks of neighbourhood stores and services, pedestrian traffic constantly moved up and down the streets. This spawned a lively "front-yard culture" in which passers-by regularly interacted with porch sitters, since front yards and families faced the street rather than the house itself (Fowler, 1992: 205).

When cities expanded, they did so incrementally, often a dozen houses at a time. The cost of extending sewers, water lines, and other city services was assumed by the municipality and paid for over 20 or 30 years through tax increases or special bonds. Lots were narrow and houses two or three storeys high. Parking space was mostly on the street and, as auto ownership spread rapidly, increasingly scarce.

In the early 1950s, all this changed with the building of Don Mills, Canada's first mass suburb, on the northern fringe of Toronto. Don Mills emphasized a system of short curving roads in the form of circles and crescents. Initially, this layout was probably meant to convey a sense of privileged exclusivity, although over time it also came to reflect a desire to shield children from the perceived danger of through-traffic.

In any case, it made public transit difficult, consigning buses to main arterial roads on the perimeter of the housing subdivision. Don Mills houses were placed on wider lots with larger setbacks from the streets. With no sidewalks, small front porches, and minimal pedestrian traffic (most residents drove to the nearby Don Mills Plaza to shop), the social action shifted to the fenced-in backyards, which were, in any case, favoured by parents, who appreciated being able to keep an eye on their toddlers from the kitchen window. Don Mills was one of the first residential areas in Canada to be planned completely from scratch and built all at once. In contrast to the development pattern in the central city, almost all the servicing costs, including that of a sewage treatment plant along the Don River, were assumed by the developer, E. P. Taylor. By doing so, Taylor changed the rules of urban development, relegating the municipality to a more passive role and introducing corporate success as a major planning consideration (Sewell, 1993: 95).

With the triumph of Don Mills, the corporate suburb spread rapidly across Canada and the United States. (The United States had already introduced its own early prototype of a planned, mass-produced suburb in Levittown, Long Island, 32 kilometres, or 20 miles, from New York City.) Although there were local differences, these first-generation postwar suburbs shared five main characteristics: a peripheral location, relatively low population densities, architectural similarity, a relatively low purchase price for houses, and a fairly high degree of economic and racial homogeneity (Jackson, 1985: 238–43).

Suburbanism as a Way of Life

In the 1950s, the suburbs were routinely disparaged as being sterile social and cultural wastelands where conformity ruled and individual taste and thought were stifled. This notion was given wide exposure in the 1956 best-seller *The Organization Man*, a study of Park Forest, Illinois, 48 kilometres (30 miles) south of Chicago, by *Fortune* magazine writer William H. Whyte (1956). Suburban dwellers were invariably depicted as living in mass-produced housing that was uniform in design and decoration. This image is bitingly evoked in folk singer Malvina Reynolds's 1950s ditty "Little Boxes" (Reynolds, 1964: 28):

Little Boxes on the hillside
Little Boxes made of ticky tacky,
Little Boxes on the hillside,
Little Boxes all the same.

Not only was the physical appearance of suburban areas said to be homogeneous, but life there was also said to revolve around a "dry-martini culture." During the workweek, fathers commuted in car pools or by rail to jobs at IBM, General Motors, and other corporate giants, while mothers ferried the children around in the family station wagon and socialized at coffee parties. On the weekend, the husbands washed the cars and tended well-manicured lawns, while the wives shopped for groceries at nearby plazas. At night, couples socialized in one another's homes, around the pool or the barbecue.

For sociological researchers, **suburbanism** represented an important trend. In a much-quoted 1956 article, "Suburbanism as a Way of Life," Sylvia Fava did a take on Louis Wirth's classic 1938 essay. Fava claimed that suburbanites were far more likely than their counterparts in the central city to be both sociable and socially active. Similarly, in a much-cited before-and-after study of middle-class couples in Toronto who chose to relocate during the early 1970s, Michelson (1973) found that suburban movers increased their involvement with neighbours, while city relocators increased interactions with friends and relatives.

Another key feature of the suburban lifestyle was its emphasis on children and the family. Perhaps the most influential study with regard to the importance of children in suburban communities was that by Seeley and Loosley (1956) in *Crestwood Heights*, a profile of the affluent community of Forest Hill Village in 1950s Toronto. Although Crestwood Heights was more a neighbourhood on the northern edge of the city, its organization around the needs of its children (schools, camps, counselling) was said to be typical of the developing suburbs of the time.

Suburbanism was further depicted as a lifestyle choice rather than a strictly economic decision. City dwellers who packed up and left the central city were said to be embracing a new, family-oriented way of life, seduced by advertisements in the real estate section of the Saturday newspaper promising "bourgeois utopias" (Fishman, 1987). Not all residents, however, embraced this lifestyle with equal enthusiasm. Women in the suburbs frequently felt cut off from the social and cultural stimulation of the central city with its theatres, art galleries, restaurants, and shopping streets. Sociability in the corporate suburb was restricted to private gatherings in the home or the backyard with neighbours. Not surprisingly, a number of researchers found that women were less satisfied than their husbands with their choice of

residence, often having a sense of stagnation and isolation despite relatively frequent visiting and entertaining (Michelson, 1973).

Significantly, this lifestyle did not appear to be replicated in working-class suburbs, where people's values and social behaviours remained firmly anchored in blue-collar culture. Berger (1960) refers to the myth of suburbia, by which he means a standardized and stereotyped view of the suburbs as uniformly middle-class, homogeneous, conformist, child-centred, female-dominated, and hotbeds of sociability.

It is possible to discern three alternative interpretations of the relationship between suburban residence and lifestyle patterns (McGahan, 1995: 232–36). According to the *structural* interpretation, the environmental and demographic characteristics of the suburb encourage a distinct style of life. For example, by excluding stores and services, such as restaurants, bars, and movie theatres, from residential neighbourhoods and by discouraging public transit, the Don Mills model promoted a greater reliance on private sociability, as evidenced by the weekday morning coffee klatches and weekend pool parties that came to be identified with suburban life in the 1950s and 1960s.

In contrast, the *selective migration* interpretation denies that the suburban environment exercises any independent effect on behaviour patterns. Rather, it is suggested that those who chose to move to the corporate suburbs after World War II were already primed to embrace **familism**—a lifestyle that places a high value on family living, marriage at a young age, a brief period of childlessness after marriage, and child-centredness of the type that Seeley and his colleagues observed in Crestwood Heights (Bell, 1968: 147).

Finally, the *class and life-cycle* interpretation proposes that what Berger had branded the "suburban myth" was nothing more than a snapshot of middle-class life at mid-century. Today, many of the same characteristics—child-centredness, commuting, backyard culture—can be observed in the second wave of gentrification in the central city. As the corporate suburb matured, it changed appreciably, with a new set of social activities replacing those that had prevailed at an earlier stage in the life cycle of both the suburb and the families who settled there.

Whether it was the Don Mills–style suburb or downtown office towers, the corporate city did not just happen: It was the deliberate product of an alliance between government and business interests.

Logan and Molotch (1987) have termed this alliance an **urban-growth machine,** a loosely structured coalition of local economic and political interest groups with a commitment to sustained growth and development. Urban-growth machines can include an extensive cast of players: businesses, property owners, investors and developers, politicians and planners, the media, utilities, cultural institutions (museums, theatres), professional sports teams, labour unions, and even universities. Growth machines pursue a narrow band of interests, sacrificing the sentimental and symbolic value of places—which is associated with jobs, neighbourhood, home town, and community—in favour of a strict emphasis on land use as an investment and commodity to be bought and sold (Palen, 1995: 20). Although government and business may honestly believe that local communities thrive only if they continue to expand economically, it could also be said that the structure that growth machines impose on urban living gives people a minimum of freedom to live their lives in the corporate city as they choose (Lorimer, 1978: 220).

THE POSTMODERN CITY

In recent years, a new kind of urban form has appeared on the global landscape: the postmodern city. Although there is some debate over what exactly is meant by this term, several aspects do seem clear.

First, the postmodern city is the product of the simultaneous operation of the forces of re-urbanization and counter-urbanization.

Counter-urbanization occurs when people move from central cities and inner suburbs into the surrounding rural hinterland (Berry and Gillard, 1987). Writing a quarter century ago, respected Canadian urban planner Hans Blumenfeld (1982, 1983) ventured that, if sustained, counter-urbanization might well result in a new urban form—the exurb. A decade later, exurbs in Canada and the United States were already home to nearly 60 million people, making them the fastest growing component of the continental landscape (Davis, Nelson, and Dueher, 1994). Initially entirely residential, exurbs today are increasingly likely to take the form of edge cities that include significant commercial, leisure, and entertainment components.

At the same time, the central city has been staging a comeback from the dismal days of the 1960s and 1970s, an era in which it was effectively abandoned by middle-class families who moved in large

numbers to the corporate suburbs. In part this re-urbanization of inner city districts reflects the continuing gentrification of older neighbourhoods. Additionally, however, it has been powered by the global migration of immigrants from around the world, a process that Fishman (2005) has called the "fifth great migration" to North America.

Second, cities are becoming multiethnic, with many ethnic neighbourhoods in the largest cities becoming home to visible minority groups. This is generating racial and ethnic residential and commercial patterns that stand in marked contrast to the ecology of the industrial city that I discussed in an earlier section of this chapter. These new urban settlers can be found both in suburban subdivisions and inner-city precincts. In Toronto, most of the recent growth in the foreign-born population has occurred in the "905" area—the ring of satellite towns and cities, named after the area code, that surrounds the urban core. For example, Brampton to the northwest of Toronto, once a symbol of small-town Ontario conservatism, attracted 42 900 immigrants between 2001 and 2006, roughly a tenth of all newcomers to the Toronto metropolitan area. Two-thirds of the new residents came from three countries: India, Pakistan, and the Philippines. In Vancouver, many recent immigrants headed for the suburban

The postmodern city is characterized by the privatization of public space, as shown in this mall scene.
SOURCE: © Norman Chan/Shutterstock.

municipalities of Richmond, Burnaby, and Surrey. In Richmond, foreign-born people, about half from the People's Republic of China, made up 57.4 percent of the population in 2006, the highest proportion of those born elsewhere in all of Canada's municipalities (Statistics Canada, 2008b).

Third, the postmodern city is characteristically fragmented, even chaotic. Elizabeth Wilson (1991: 136) describes it as resembling "a split screen flickering with competing beliefs, cultures and 'stories.'" Geographically and socially split, the postmodern city does not have a single "way of life" of the sort identified by Wirth for the industrial city and Fava for the corporate suburb.

Finally, the postmodern city is characterized by the privatization of public space. Privatization occurs across a wide spectrum of settings, from downtown malls and festival marketplaces to private, "gated" communities on the fringes of the city. Although suburban dwellers have always put a premium on private space, from the enclosed backyard to the drive-in theatre, this value is now washing over the city as a whole and, in the process, drastically reducing the number of public places where people can come together to shop or socialize (Goldberger, 1996: 139).

While some urban observers have applauded the changing contours of the postmodern city, especially those associated with re-urbanization, others have expressed serious reservations. In particular, they have displayed considerable unease over the escalating "suburbanization" of the inner city.

I next examine three overlapping components of the postmodern city: the edge city, the multiethnic city, and the dual city. Although each component has real-life spatial and demographic components, none exists in pure form. Instead, they are constructs, formulated by academic researchers or journalists, that help us visualize an important dimension of the globalized, privatized, and fragmented postmodern city.

THE EDGE CITY

Although they differed significantly in their patterns of housing, transportation, and shopping, the industrial city and the corporate city displayed more or less the same spatial configuration: an urban core containing the bulk of the office space, cultural institutions, factories, and a ring of suburbs where much of the more affluent middle class resided. Even with the growth of shopping centres and industrial parks in the 1950s and 1960s, the lion's share of jobs and services

remained within the city itself, and suburbanites were daily commuters.

During the past quarter-century, however, this traditional pattern has been turned inside out with the rapid growth of **edge cities** (Garreau, 1991). Situated in exurbia—the rural residential area around the suburbs within commuting range of the city—edge cities have no dominant single core or definable set of boundaries; they are typically "clusters of malls, office developments and entertainment complexes that rise where major highways cross or converge" (Fishman, 1990: 18). Some edge cities are expansions of existing satellite cities, but others sprout up in unincorporated townships, lacking clearly definable borders and legal status as places (Palen, 1995: 187).

What has led to the growth of edge cities? Leinberger and Lockwood (1986) offer five reasons for edge cities' recent emergence. First, there has been a major shift in North American economies from manufacturing to a service and knowledge base. One result of this shift is that middle-class employees are now more willing to live near where they work than they used to be when jobs were located in factories that were dirty, noisy, and unattractive. An example of the older pattern can be found in Ontario's steel industry, where the managers and executives at Stelco and Dofasco traditionally settled on the other side of the Skyway Bridge in Burlington, while the mill workers remained in Hamilton. In contrast, Kanata, the outer suburban location of Ottawa's microchip computer industry, is solidly middle class.

The tremendous growth of technology, such as fax machines, cellular phones, and e-mail, has geographically freed many employees whose linkages to the workplace are now activated on the road or from home offices.

SOURCE: © Jupiter Images, 2009.

Second, there have been significant changes in transportation patterns that favour trucks and cars over subways, streetcars, and trains. As a result, urban facilities have scattered over the exurban landscape, unfettered by the requirement of locating along established transportation corridors.

Third, recent advances in telecommunications technology have reduced the necessity for offices to locate downtown in close physical proximity. Some types of businesses—stock brokerages, banks—still prefer to be close to one another and to central city services. But the tremendous growth of technology, such as fax machines, cellular phones, and e-mail, has geographically freed many employees whose linkages to the workplace are now activated on the road or from home offices.

Fourth, as it has become increasingly expensive to operate in the city, offices, industries, and professional practitioners (lawyers, accountants, etc.) have pulled up their roots and moved to cheaper locations in exurbia. Among other things, parking is more plentiful and less expensive out of the city.

Fifth, the coming of age of dual-income, baby-boom families with one or two children has meant that people's lives are increasingly governed by considerations of time, convenience, and efficiency. The clustering of offices, shopping centres, and recreational facilities at the juncture of exurban highways meets the needs of this subpopulation, the members of which have little time left in their lives to commute downtown to shop, eat, or be entertained.

These changes have shown up in the form of new patterns of commuting to work in large urban areas. In Canada, census data from 1996 and 2001 point to several significant trends (Heisz and LaRochelle-Coté, 2005: 16). First, the number of workers who commute within a suburb or across the city from suburb to suburb has risen appreciably. Second, the growth of "reverse commuters" (those who travel from the city centre to the suburbs) has uniformly outstripped that of traditional commuters (those who travel from outside to inside the city centre).

Edge cities have been of particular interest to urban sociologists because they are neither suburbs nor centralized cities but a hybrid that incorporates elements of each. Unlike the typical suburb, which is primarily residential, edge cities contain many of the functions of the traditional city: shopping, office space, housing, entertainment facilities. Also, in contrast to suburbanites, who commute to work in the central city by rail or car, edge-city residents are inclined to live and work in the same geographic area. Commuting now means driving to an adjoining suburb or exurb, rather than heading downtown. This can be seen in the "905 belt" surrounding Metro Toronto, where a number of areas now function as "magnets." That is, more people travel to jobs there each day than journey out of the community to jobs elsewhere in the Greater Toronto Area. Finally, in contrast to the typical suburb, which lacks a well-developed infrastructure of sports, entertainment, and cultural facilities, the edge city is increasingly the site of a burgeoning number of performing arts centres, sports palaces, and entertainment complexes.

Nevertheless, it would be wrong to think that there are no real differences between edge cities and the older cities. Unlike the industrial city, the edge city lacks a single centre. In the former, it was always possible to start downtown and eventually reach the outer boundaries of the city. In contrast, the spatial logic of the edge city dictates that centres and boundaries are not needed. Instead, the edge city is made up of three overlapping types of socioeconomic networks: household networks, networks of consumption, and networks of production. Each of these runs on the guiding principle of convenience. Two-income families with children, who make up the largest demographic segment of the edge-city population, are increasingly pressed for time and, as a result, frequently create their own "personal cities" out of the destinations they can reach within a manageable time (Fishman, 1990).

THE MULTIETHNIC CITY

According to Statistics Canada's most recent population projections, by the year 2017 nearly one Canadian in five (21 percent) is likely to be a member of a visible minority group. This contrasts with 13 percent in 2001 and less than 5 percent in 1981. (Bélanger and Malenfant, 2005). Nearly 75 percent of members of visible minorities are expected to reside in the census metropolitan areas (CMAs) of Montreal, Toronto, and Vancouver; about half the population of the latter two cities will comprise members of visible minority groups (see Table 15.2). This new demographic makeup has important implications for our understanding of contemporary urban structures and processes (Fong and Shibuya, 2005).

In particular, we are likely to witness the growth of a new generation of residentially segregated neighbourhoods (Fong, 1996; Fong and Wilkes, 1999).

TABLE 15.2 VISIBLE MINORITY PERSONS IN SELECTED CANADIAN CMAS, 2001–2017 (PROJECTED)

	NUMBER OF VISIBLE MINORITY PERSONS (000S)		PERCENTAGE OF TOTAL POPULATION	
	2001	2017	2001	2017
Canada	4038	7121	13	21
Census metropolitan area				
Toronto	1753	3194	37	51
Vancouver	741	1261	36	49
Montreal	454	749	13	19
Ottawa–Gatineau	139	316	17	28
Calgary	166	295	17	24
Edmonton	136	211	14	18
Hamilton	64	125	9	15
Winnipeg	84	115	12	16
Windsor	40	97	13	23
Kitchener	45	79	10	15
Rest of Canada	418	679	3	4

SOURCE: Adapted from Bélanger and Malenfont (2005, p. 21).

Whereas newcomers from Northern and Western European nations tended to blend in residentially with Canadians from the charter groups (British and French), members of most Asian ethnic groups are likely to cluster together, apart from other groups. The evidence so far indicates that these visible minority neighbourhoods are formed when nonvisible minority residents move out as large numbers of a visible minority group move into the neighbourhood (Hou and Picot, 2004).

Contrary to the classic urban-growth model proposed by the Chicago School's human ecologists, the postmodern city doesn't exhibit a simple pattern of first-generation immigrant settlement (i.e., in the zone of transition adjacent to the commercial core). Using data from New York and Los Angeles, Logan, Alba, and Zhang (2002) distinguish between two very different types of ethnic communities: the traditional immigrant enclave with dense concentrations of immigrants and high levels of poverty and other urban problems, and the more desirable ethnic neighbourhood whose residents are much better endowed both financially and socially. This dual pattern is especially evident in suburban neighbourhoods in major Canadian cities. Whereas some groups, notably the Chinese, settle here to take advantage of a more plentiful supply of new owner-occupied housing, others with fewer resources come for affordable subsidized social housing (Bourne, 1996).

What is less well understood is the nature of social relations among multiple minority groups in a multiethnic context and how these relationships shape urban structures and processes between minority groups and members of charter groups (Fong and Shibuya, 2005). One thing that we do know is that relatively little overlap exists in the minority neighbourhoods of different groups. In 2001, for example, among the 135 visible minority neighbourhoods in Toronto, only in three did both Chinese and South Asians combined represent at least 30 percent of the neighbourhood population (Hou and Picot, 2004: 11).

THE DUAL CITY

With the edge city increasingly becoming the occupational, residential, and commercial centre for the middle classes, what has become of urban downtowns? The central city, some analysts suggest, has become polarized between two starkly different realities that are spatially discrete and that have only the name of the city and some public places in common. Situated just blocks or streets away from one another, the "city of despair and squalor" and the "city of hope and splendour" are light years apart. This split reality has been called the "dual city."

The term **dual city** has come to refer to the urban expression of two increasingly divergent streams in the global economy. On the one hand, there is an information-based, formal economy rooted in financial services, telecommunications, and the microchip. Typically, those who are part of this upper-tier informational city live in a world of computer software, fax machines, cellphones, and Internet surfing. Residentially, they can be found in "gentrified" niches of the inner city (gentrification is discussed below) or in exclusive suburbs, where they isolate themselves both socially and geographically from the rest of the city. In Castells's (1989) description, these spaces constitute a microsociety with their own separate circuit of leisure, lifestyle, and services.

On the other hand, juxtaposed to the informational city is an "informal economy" that has been excluded from the main loop. Residents here rely not on high-technology communications, but on face-to-face social networks, usually established on the basis of shared race and ethnicity. People are engaged in a wide range of activities, from labouring in immigrant sweatshops in the clothing trade to offering such services as furniture making, home renovation, and auto repairs (Gordon and Sassen, 1992). Although this informal economy cannot be equated with urban poverty per se, its participants stand relatively little chance of ever penetrating the upper-tier information economy.

Gentrification

In the 1970s and 1980s, considerable attention was paid by urban researchers to the phenomenon of **gentrification** in the dual city. By gentrification, I mean the transformation of working-class housing into fashionable downtown neighbourhoods by middle- and upper-income newcomers. Gentrification is neither anticipated nor accounted for by the ecological growth

models discussed above. Similarly, it runs counter to predictions about the mass flight to the suburbs that dominated urban sociology in the 1950s and 1960s. A comparison of the suburban lifestyle and the postmodern urban lifestyle as typified by gentrification is set out in Table 15.3.

Four primary explanations for gentrification have been advanced (Ley, 1991: 182–85). First, demographic changes led to gentrification in the 1970s and 1980s. At this time, the baby boomers who were born and raised in the suburbs began to look for housing of their own. Facing high demand levels and a shortage of supply, they turned to inner-city housing, which was cheap but in dire need of rehabilitation. They opposed demolition, favoured by urban-renewal advocates. Unlike suburban settlers in the previous period, many of these urban migrants were childless and career-oriented. This meant that schools, playgrounds, and parks were not their major concerns and they were happy with smaller housing units without the big backyards and basement recreation rooms that were characteristic of Don Mills–type housing. Since many of these young professionals worked downtown, they were willing to trade space for proximity to their places of employment and to downtown cultural and entertainment facilities.

Second, gentrification may be accounted for by economic changes related to the flow of capital in and out of the housing market. In this view, gentrification functions as a "back to the city movement by capital, not people" (N. Smith, 1979). As you have seen, in the 1950s and 1960s, financial capital flowed into the building of the suburbs under the guidance of governments that viewed the construction of large-scale projects by development companies as the fastest, most efficient way of coping with the pressures

TABLE 15.3 COMPARISON OF SUBURBAN AND POSTMODERN URBAN LIFESTYLES

	SUBURBAN	POSTMODERN GENTRIFIED URBAN
Neighbourhood social involvement	Deliberate and sustained	Incidental
Lifestyle focus	Family	Consumerism
Typical activities	Home activities (gardening, entertaining)	Dining out, shopping
Typical occupation of resident	Middle manager	Architect, corporate lawyer, etc.
Housing type	Split-level, detached	Victorian, semidetached
Social composition	Class-exclusive	Socially and culturally diverse
Ideology	Anti-urban	Pro-urban

SOURCE: John A. Hannigan, 1995, "The Postmodern City: A New Urbanization?" *Current Sociology,* 43(1), p. 180.

created by the baby boom. Developers were encouraged by an array of incentives: tax breaks, government-backed mortgages, guarantees, and insurance with low premiums. By the 1970s, the profit levels in suburban building had begun to shrink, and capital flow switched back to the urban centre to take advantage of the rent gap—that is, the difference between the current value of land in its "depressed" state and the value that could be charged given a higher or better land use (Smith and LeFaivre, 1984).

Third, middle-class newcomers to the central city arrived in search of a lifestyle that was more distinctive and cosmopolitan than that available within the constraints of suburban conformity. In the central city, they could express a distinctive aesthetic and style of consumption, characterized by a dislike of mass-produced goods and a penchant for objects and buildings from a bygone era, notably the Victorian age (Filion, 1991: 554). This new lifestyle also extended to the surrounding neighbourhood, which filled up with wine bars, California-style restaurants, franchise coffee outlets, and trendy boutiques.

A fourth explanation of gentrification looks to the kinds of changes in the urban economy that were described at the beginning of the section on the dual city. With the tremendous boom in jobs in advanced service industries, such as those connected to the "globalized information economy," there has been a dramatic increase in the number of well-paying occupations located downtown. This growth has, in turn, produced a pool of middle-class workers interested in trying the experience of inner-city living.

It should be emphasized that the image of gentrifiers as returning from the suburbs is false; gentrification is, in fact, a "stay in the city" rather than a "back to the city" movement (Wittberg, 1992: 27). Ley (1991: 186) cites data from Canadian cities that indicate that only 2 percent to 3 percent of a sample of households moving into Toronto's Don Vale neighbourhood between 1966 and 1976 originated in the suburbs. Similarly, a high percentage of those in Ottawa's Centretown (55 percent); Vancouver's False Creek (78 percent); and Montreal's Milton-Parc, Plateau Mont-Royal, and Papineau (79 percent) neighbourhoods had previous addresses in the central city. This research suggests that gentrifiers are devoted to an inner-city lifestyle, even when they have reached a stage in the life cycle where they might have predictably moved to the suburbs.

Among those most likely to settle in gentrified areas of the inner city are women. Summarizing the empirical evidence available from these studies, Warde (1991: 228) lists the following as typical of gentrified enclaves:

> a female population increasing faster than the male population; an unusually high proportion of young and single women; very high proportions of women in professional and technical occupations; high levels of academic credentials; a high proportion of dual-earner households, but few families; presence of young professional women; and the postponement of marriage and childbearing.

Why do gentrified neighbourhoods appeal to the women described by Warde? One explanation is that inner-city communities help relieve some of the pressures of women's dual roles as both members of the paid labour force and mothers of young children. The advantages include relatively cheap housing, public transit, and readily available child-care and social-support systems. Travel time is an especially important consideration. Female gentrifiers tend to have jobs in downtown office buildings, so inner-city housing allows them to lead their lives on a tight schedule, with such services as shopping, schools, daycare, and medical clinics located nearby. In contrast, suburban residence requires long daily commutes, especially when the weather is bad, as well as the devotion of a good share of leisure time to travelling to widely scattered stores and services. Gentrification thus represents an environmental solution to a potential set of social problems (Rose, 1984: 66).

Private Communities

In recent years, another phenomenon—the rise of private communities—has been embraced by an even greater number of middle-class homeowners than has gentrification. Located in the newer suburbs and in edge cities, private communities compete with central cities for residents, offering as incentives a homogeneous middle-class population, physical security, stable housing values, local control, and freedom from exposure to the social problems of the inner city.

In the United States, nearly 4 million residents are estimated to live in access-controlled developments (Sanchez, Lang, and Dhavale, 2005) and another 28 million in areas governed by private community associations. In Canada, although there are some gated communities around Toronto and cities in British Columbia's Okanagan Valley, the majority can be found in rural areas, usually in vacation, resort, or retirement sites. As can be seen in Table 15.4, only a small percentage of these are equipped with the guards and video surveillance that are more standard in gated projects in the United States.

In her detailed case studies of ten gated communities in British Columbia, Ontario, and Nova Scotia, Grant (2005) found that the residents were less likely than their equivalents in other countries, such as the United States and Brazil, to cite security concerns as the major reason for moving there. Rather, they were in search of a privileged enclave where they could separate themselves from younger generations (many were seniors and empty nesters) and those who are less well off. The gates, Grant concludes, "function to secure homogeneity within a wider context of urban diversity" (p. 309).

The Fortress City

At the same time as middle-class homeowners are barricading themselves in private gated communities, the public–private partnerships that increasingly dictate what happens to postmodern cities are said to be systematically privatizing and militarizing public space in order to secure it against the homeless and the poor. Emerging from such alliances is the "fortress city" in which the urban disadvantaged are isolated socially and spatially from office workers, tourists, and suburban day trippers.

The fortress city has been described in *City of Quartz*, Mike Davis's (1990) sweeping examination of present-day Los Angeles. LA, Davis notes, is a city obsessed with urban security. What passes for a downtown, a series of billion-dollar, block-square

megastructures around Bunker Hill, has been insulated by removing almost all pedestrian linkages to the poor immigrant neighbourhoods that surround it on every side. To make public facilities and spaces as unlivable as possible for the homeless and the poor, the city is engaged in a virtual war against them. Tactics and defences include the establishment of barrel-shaped, "bum-proof" bus benches that make sleep impossible, the random deployment of outdoor overhead sprinklers in Skid Row Park to discourage overnight camping, and the removal of public toilets and washrooms in areas patronized by vagrants. To secure its garbage, one popular seafood restaurant has spent $12 000 to build a "bag-lady-proof trash cage" out of three-quarter-inch steel rods with alloy locks and vicious curved spikes. To cope with a burgeoning inmate population, law-enforcement agencies are building downtown jails and prisons designed by celebrity architects to look like hotels, convention centres, or office buildings, thus camouflaging their real purpose.

Nor is the fortress city restricted to Los Angeles. In the late 1970s, Henry Ford II persuaded the heads of 50 large corporations in Detroit to put equity capital into the Renaissance Center, a $357 million megaproject along the Detroit River opposite Windsor, Ontario. Poorly planned, the hotel-office venture resembles a castle with virtually invisible pedestrian entrances. It is cut off from downtown Detroit by a wide road and railroad tracks. It stands as a "symbol of isolation: an extreme case of a self-contained, inward-facing complex, surrounded by fortress-like two-story walls covering the heating and ventilating equipment" (Frieden and Sagalyn, 1989: 222).

TABLE 15.4 DOCUMENTED GATED PROJECTS IN CANADA, MARCH 2004

PROVINCE	TOTAL GATED PROJECTS	PROJECTS WITH 500 UNITS OR MORE	PROJECTS WITH GUARDS	VIDEO SURVEILLANCE	ADULT PROJECTS	SENIOR PROJECTS
British Columbia	228	3	5	5	44	36
Alberta	21	3	1	2	2	2
Saskatchewan	8	–	–	–	–	–
Manitoba	1	–	–	–	–	1
Ontario	49	8	9	5	10	7
Nova Scotia	7	–	–	2	1	1
Canada	314	14	15	15	57	47

SOURCE: Jill Grant, 2005, "The Function of the Gates: The Social Construction of Security in Gated Developments." *Town Planning Review*, 76, 291–313. Reprinted by permission of Town Planning Review, Liverpool University Press.

Note: Adult communities discourage children—some suggest 19+ years, other say 25+ years. Those that use the word *senior* or have age limits over 40 are classified as seniors' projects.

A homeless person carrying her cat is evicted from her dwelling in the shantytown on Toronto's waterfront on September 24, 2002. Home Depot, the company that owns the land, requested that police remove the squatters.
SOURCE: CP Picture Archive/Frank Gunn.

The clash between the guardians of the fortress city and the urban poor was recently highlighted in the "Tent City Eviction" in Toronto. Tent City was a two-hectare (five-acre) plot of polluted, abandoned industrial land near the shore of Lake Ontario. For five years, as many as 110 residents had been squatting on the waterfront property owned by big-box building supplies store Home Depot, making it Canada's largest homeless community. After a high-profile story in the *New York Times* described the site, which seemed to be increasingly hosting prostitution and drug-dealing activities, Home Depot abandoned any further pursuit of plans to erect safe, affordable housing and sent in private security guards accompanied by police to evict the squatters. Guards were posted and the former residents were given 72 hours to retrieve their belongings.

SUMMARY

1. Cities are relatively large, dense, permanent settlements in which the majority of the residents do not produce their own food.

2. Until the Industrial Revolution, cities were incapable of supporting more than about 5 percent of the total societal population, largely because of the absence of agricultural surpluses large enough to feed a big urban population. In addition, high mortality rates, especially among children under 10 years of age, dictated that, even with high birth rates, urban population growth was limited.

3. Demographic transition theory holds that the main factors underlying population dynamics are industrialization and the growth of modern cultural values. In the preindustrial era, both birth rates and death rates were high, and population growth was therefore slow. In the first stages of industrialization, death rates fell, so population growth was rapid. As industrialization progressed and people's values about having children changed, the birth rate fell, resulting in slow growth again.

4. Malthus argued that while food supplies increase slowly, populations grow quickly. Because of this presumed natural law, only war, pestilence, and famine can keep human population growth in check. In contrast, Marx argued that overpopulation is not a problem of too many people. Instead, it is a problem of too much poverty. Marx said that if the exploitation of workers under capitalism is ended, then poverty will disappear along with the overpopulation problem.

5. The best-known urban-growth model in the social sciences is Ernest Burgess's concentric-zone scheme in which the expansion of cities is conceptualized as a successive series of rings, each of which segregates a distinct resident population and type of land use. Other, more recent models favour patterns of urban growth resembling pie-shaped wedges that develop along transportation routes or multiple nodes of economic activity, each with its own nucleus.

6. In contrast to the rise of the city in Western Europe and North America, cities of the South have grown at a much faster rate than the industrial economy. The resulting "overurbanization" has accelerated problems of poverty and unemployment, which are rooted in basic structural inequalities and uneven development.

7. The corporate city of the 1950s and 1960s was the product of an urban-growth machine in which a coalition of politicians, planners, real-estate developers, business people, and other interest groups joined forces to engineer economic development and progress. The main products of this alliance were (a) the corporate suburbs, (b) shopping centres, (c) suburban industrial parks, (d) downtown office towers, and (e) high-rise apartment buildings.

8. Three theories—structural, selective migration, and class and life-cycle stage—have been proposed to explain the relationship between suburban residence and lifestyle patterns. Although all three have merit, the suburban way of life observed by many researchers in the 1950s and 1960s appears to have been a unique product of a particular time and place.

9. In recent decades, the contemporary city has mirrored and incorporated a split global economy. On the one hand, the members of the upper-tier information city work in jobs related to financial services, telecommunications, and high technology, and live either in gentrified downtown neighbourhoods or in private communities on the edge of the city. On the other hand, the members of the informal economy are excluded from the information city and live in ethnic or racial ghettos that are often, but not necessarily, located in the inner city. Together, the information city and the informal economy constitute the dual city whose residents have little in common with each other.

10. Cities are becoming multiethnic, with many ethnic neighbourhoods in the largest cities becoming home to visible minority groups. This is generating racial and ethnic residential and commercial patterns that stand in marked contrast to the ecology of the industrial city.

11. One of the defining characteristics of the postmodern city is the increasing privatization of public spaces. Privatization is manifested in the booming growth of gated communities and other private residential enclaves where outsiders are not welcome and in the construction of fortress cities where tourists and other affluent consumers are kept in while the homeless and the urban poor are kept out.

QUESTIONS TO CONSIDER

1. Map out your own "personal city" by keeping a record for a full week of all the trips you take to work, school, shopping, medical and dental appointments, friends' houses, restaurants and night clubs, and so on. What proportion of these trips occurs within your neighbourhood? Within the community in which you live? Across the wider metropolitan area?

2. To what extent does the big city in which you live or that you live closest to constitute a dual city?

3. How has suburban life been depicted in the mass media? Think, for example, of popular television series, such as *Desperate Housewives* and *The Simpsons*. To what extent do these depictions support the "myth of suburbia"?

4. Visit Statistics Canada's website (http://www. statcan.gc.ca). What kinds of questions about cities could you answer by using this data source?

GLOSSARY

A **city** is a relatively large, dense, permanent settlement in which most of the residents do not produce their own food.

The **concentric-zone model** is the classic urban-growth model proposed by Ernest Burgess in which the expansion of cities is visualized as a successive series of concentric rings, each of which contains a distinct resident population and type of land use. As social groups become more established and prosperous, they move farther away from the city centre.

The perception and organization of the city as a vehicle for capital accumulation create a **corporate city**. The corporate city contains five major elements: the corporate suburb, high-rise apartments, suburban industrial parks, downtown office towers, and shopping malls.

The **demographic transition** is the change from high to low birth and death rates that characterized modernization, industrialization, and urbanization.

The juxtaposition and mutual isolation of an upper-tier information city and a lower-tier city creates a **dual city**. Members of the upper tier work in jobs related to financial services, telecommunications, and high technology, and live in gentrified neighbourhoods and private communities on the edge of the city. A lower tier of people work in informal and low-technology jobs and live in ethnic or racial ghettos.

Edge cities include self-contained entertainment, shopping, and office areas and have emerged in formerly suburban areas or just beyond the fringe of suburbia.

The **environmental-opportunity theory** proposes that people choose where they want to live depending on the extent to which a particular place meshes with or constrains their preferred lifestyle.

Familism is a lifestyle that places a high value on family living, marriage at a young age, a brief period of childlessness after marriage, and child-centredness.

In **gentrification**, working-class houses are transformed into fashionable downtown neighbourhoods by middle- and upper-income migrants.

The **multiple-nuclei model** is a model of urban growth characterized by a series of growth centres—retail, wholesale, residential—each representing the concentration of a specific function or activity within the urban economy.

Overurbanization is the process whereby the population of urban areas is growing faster than the urban economy, services, and resources can absorb. It is especially evident in large cities in the southern hemisphere.

Peri-urbanization is a process of urbanization observed in Asia, Africa, and Latin America whereby the rural and the urban have become blurred in unplanned settlements on the outskirts of large cities. One instance of this is the *desakota* in Indonesia.

The **postmodern city** is a new urban form that is more privatized and more socially and culturally fragmented and globalized than the corporate city.

The **replacement level** is the number of children that each woman must have on average to sustain the size of a population, ignoring immigration and emigration. The replacement level is 2.1 children.

The **sector model** of urban growth proposes that the city expands outward from the centre in a series of sectors or wedges along major transportation arteries, such as highways and railroad lines.

Suburbanism is a way of life outside city centres that is organized mainly around the needs of children and involves higher levels of conformity and sociability than life in the central city.

The **urban-growth machine** is a loosely structured coalition of local economic and political interest groups that hold in common a commitment to sustained growth and development.

Urbanism is a way of life that involves increased tolerance but also emotional withdrawal and specialized, impersonal, and self-interested interaction.

Urban primacy is a situation in which one metropolitan centre in a country, usually the capital city, is considerably larger and more economically dominant than any other city in the country.

SUGGESTED READING

Bishop-Stall, Shaughnessy. (2004). *Down to This: Squalor and Splendor in a Big-City Shantytown.* Toronto: Random House. This is an engaging but disturbing first-person account by a journalist of a year spent residing in Tent City, located on a marginal property along Toronto's waterfront.

Hannigan, John. (1998). *Fantasy City: Pleasure and Profit in the Postmodern City.* London and New York: Routledge. In this thoroughly researched and comprehensive account of the rise of the city as theme park in the 1980s and 1990s, Hannigan argues that megaplex cinemas, themed restaurants, casinos, and other large-scale entertainment spaces allow leisure and conviviality without real social interaction.

Hiller, Harry H., ed. (2005). *Urban Canada: Sociological Perspectives.* Toronto: Oxford University Press. The first new text in the field published in Canada in over a decade, this collection of 14 articles explores a broad range of topics in Canadian urban sociology, historical and contemporary.

Palen, John J. (1995). *The Suburbs.* New York: McGraw Hill. A concise, information-packed, and up-to-date overview of the suburban experience. It includes a useful discussion of edge cities and private communities.

Sewell, John. (1993). *The Shape of the City: Toronto Struggles with Modern Planning.* Toronto: University of Toronto Press. A generously illustrated history of urban growth and planning in Canada's largest city, by a well-known activist, author, and former mayor of Toronto.

WEB RESOURCES

Companion Website for This Book

http://www.newsociety6e.nelson.com
Begin by clicking on the Student Resources section of the website. Next, select the chapter you are studying from the pull-down menu. From the Student Resources page, you have easy access to InfoTrac College Edition® and other resources, such as the

Glossary, Test Yourself questions, and additional readings. The website also has many useful tips to aid you in your study of sociology.

InfoTrac College Edition Search Terms

Visit http://www.infotrac-college.com for access to more than 20 million articles from nearly 6000 sources when doing your online research.

SOURCE: © Daniel Zuckerkandel/
Shutterstock

CHAPTER SIXTEEN

Sociology and the Environment

John Hannigan
UNIVERSITY OF TORONTO

In this chapter you will learn that

- A major focus of the sociology of the environment is the conflict between environmentalists and their opponents in industry and science.

- Support for environmentalism has remained constant for nearly three decades, with most people generally supportive of environmental values and a young, well-educated, urban, liberal group leading the movement for environmental change.

- To mobilize the reluctant majority, organizers of the environmental movement develop and spread interpretations of events that play up the possibility of environmental crises.

- The goals of conserving resources, reducing pollution, and restricting population increase are especially difficult to achieve in the developing world.

- At the community level, willingness to act on environmental problems rises as trust in authority figures declines.

- Environmental problems are often contested on the basis of acceptable risk: the definition of what is acceptable risk is strongly influenced by the distribution of power in society, with more powerful individuals and groups better able to determine what is and what is not risky.

INTRODUCTION

When the March break arrives, thousands of harried Canadian parents and their children will head for the airport en route to sun-soaked holidays in Florida, the Caribbean, and Mexico. For many, getting there will most certainly not be half the fun. Crowded airports, flight delays and cancellations, and border security problems will all contribute to the stress. A handful of vacationers will choose not to fly at all, on the grounds that air travel is a highly polluting activity that releases significant amounts of carbon dioxide at an altitude where its effect on global climate change is double that on the ground. In Britain, the environmental case against flying has found a voice in the launch of "Flight Pledge," a campaign whose website offers conscientious objectors a choice between a "gold" pledge—a promise to take no flights in the coming year and a "silver" pledge, representing a maximum of two short-travel or one long-haul flight per year, except in case of emergency (Robbins, 2006). Charging that "aviation is the biggest contributor to climate change in this country and nobody is doing anything against it," another eco-activist group in the U.K., Plane Stupid, scaled the roof of Parliament and launched paper airplanes made of documents that criticize the expansion of London's Heathrow airport (Milmo and Bowcott, 2008).

In this chapter, I examine how sociology has dealt with the rising global crescendo of environmental awareness, signified by the movement to limit air travel voluntarily on ecological grounds. After briefly discussing the traditional lack of concern with the environment in sociology, I outline the basic value conflict in contemporary societies between those who favour unlimited economic expansion and technological solutions to human problems and those who embrace a new "ecological" view of the world, in which nature is accorded a central place. Next, I review theory and research in the four principal areas of sociological inquiry relating to the environment (Buttel, 1987): (1) environmental attitudes, concern, and behaviour; (2) the environmental movement; (3) the political economy of the environment; and (4) environmental risk and risk assessment. I conclude by arguing that it is important to deal with the environment from a "social-constructionist" perspective in order to bring more sociology into the sociological study of the environment.

TOWARD ENVIRONMENTAL SOCIOLOGY

In contrast to some other social sciences, notably anthropology and geography, sociology's interest in the environment is of relatively recent vintage, stretching back only to the 1970s. There are several reasons for this neglect (Dunlap and Catton, 1983).

First, for the early-twentieth-century pioneers of sociology, the term *environment* came to mean something quite different from our physical surroundings. To carve out a distinctive place for sociology as a new academic discipline, Émile Durkheim and the other founders of the field downplayed the role of biological and physical factors in influencing human affairs while at the same time elevating the importance of "social facts," such as norms, groups, and institutions. In accounting for the emergence of a wide range of

One focus of environmental sociology is the conflict between environmentalist and mainstream views. According to the mainstream view, people have the unalienable right to dominate nature, even if that involves polluting the environment, as this McDonnell Douglas plant does.
SOURCE: Dick Hemingway.

behaviours, from juvenile delinquency to racism, sociologists opted for explanations that framed these behaviours in terms of "nurture" rather than "nature."

A second explanation for sociology's reluctance to embrace the study of the environment concerns sociologists' own view of technology, natural resources, and human progress. In the past, most sociologists shared the assumption of the general public that the world would see steady gains in material progress, fuelled by an apparently unlimited availability of natural resources, such as coal, lumber, and water. From this perspective, technology functioned as the linchpin of economic development, allowing humans to overcome the challenges presented by hostile habitats, such as jungles, swamps, and deserts. This **human-exceptionalism paradigm** featured the ideals of steadily evolving social progress, increasing prosperity and material comfort, and class mobility for all segments of society. This worldview had little room for sociological attention to the environmental costs of growth—pollution, health hazards in the workplace, and the loss of diversity in plant and animal species. Nor was much consideration given to the constraints that might be imposed on further economic expansion because of declining resources, the exhaustion of nutrients in the soil, and the destruction of natural ecosystems.

By the early 1970s, stimulated by increased societal attention to urban decay, pollution, overpopulation, resource shortages, and so on, a number of sociologists began at last to study environmental issues. In the first comprehensive review of the emergence of environmental sociology as a distinct area of inquiry, Dunlap and Catton (1979) distinguished between a "sociology of environmental issues" and "environmental sociology." The former, they observed, was concerned primarily with environmentally related phenomena, such as resource management problems in wildland recreation areas or the origins, membership, and beliefs of the environmental movement. The latter focused on "the physical environment as a factor that may influence (or be influenced by) social behavior" (Dunlap and Catton, 1979: 255). This suggests that the environment can function as a contextual, an independent, or a dependent variable—that is, as background, cause, or effect.

Today, "environmental sociology" has become a catchall for the study of all social aspects of the environment. This has both advantages and disadvantages. On the plus side, it has propelled sociological inquiry into a number of important new areas—for example, studying public opposition to, and mobilization

against, toxic wastes. At the same time, the very breadth of the field has made it difficult to assemble a cohesive body of work built on strong theoretical foundations. Rather than emerging from a central core, the sociological study of the environment has developed from multiple nuclei, each reflecting a different philosophical position and a corresponding research agenda. This tendency has been exacerbated by the decision of some authors, journals, and organizations to consider both the natural and the human-built environments under the same umbrella. Furthermore, some terms—notably, social ecology—have come to acquire several very different meanings, depending on the branch of environmental sociology to which the researcher claims allegiance. One unifying element, however, is the widely shared recognition of the existence of a key value conflict in contemporary society between those who hold an "environmentalist" view of the world and those who do not.

ENVIRONMENTAL VALUE CONFLICT

Values are guideposts that help us to sort out the choices we make in life. Although the vast majority of the Canadian population may be in agreement on some values (freedom, humanitarianism), other values are more controversial.

A central focus for many sociologists interested in the environment is the value cleavage between environmentalists and their opponents. At the core of this disagreement is the long-accepted notion that the environment is something to be actively used and exploited. Many of the key values that have governed North American life—activism, achievement, progress, pursuit of the good life, materialism—permit this orientation toward the environment (Turner, 1981: 87). Environmentalists, in contrast, support a different value orientation, one that advocates a more passive, less manipulative approach to nature.

How environmentalists differ from the mainstream population has been most explicitly set out by British sociologist Stephen Cotgrove (1982). Cotgrove lays out two conflicting paradigms (a *paradigm* is a type of social lens through which we view the world)—the **dominant paradigm** and the **alternative environmental paradigm** (see Table 16.1, p. 390).

The dominant paradigm is anchored by two core values: the moral imperative of material-wealth creation and the moral conviction that humans have the inalienable right to dominate nature and harness

TABLE 16.1 COUNTER-PARADIGMS OF THE ENVIRONMENT

	DOMINANT PARADIGM	ALTERNATIVE ENVIRONMENTAL PARADIGM
Core Values	Economic growth Domination over nature Natural environment valued as resource Natural environment intrinsically valued	Self-actualization Harmony with nature
Economy	Market forces Risk and reward Rewards for achievement Inequality Individual self-help	Public interest Safety Income related to need Equality Collective/social provision
Polity	Authoritative structure (experts influential) Hierarchical Law and order	Participative structure (citizen/worker involvement) Nonhierarchical Liberation
Society	Centralized Large scale Associational Ordered	Decentralized Small scale Communal Flexible
Nature	Ample reserves Nature hostile/neutral Environment controllable	Earth's resources limited Nature benign Nature delicately balanced
Knowledge	Confidence in science and technology Rationality of means Separation of fact/value, thought/feeling	Limits to science Rationality of ends Integration of fact/value, thought/feeling

SOURCE: S.F. Cotgrove, 1982, "Catastrophe or Cornucopia: The Environment, Politics, and the Future," Chichester, UK: John Wiley & Sons, 1982. Copyright John Wiley & Sons Limited. Reproduced with permission.

the environment to that end. All major institutions reflect the widespread acceptance of this paradigm. Governments at all levels operate ministries, consulates, and trade offices that have a mandate to promote commerce and attract foreign investment. University business schools run programs in entrepreneurship. The media act as cheerleaders, linking political competence and achievement with an expanding economy and job creation. Economic growth carries with it a number of supplementary values: the view that society is best organized on a large-scale, centralized basis; respect for authority; the ascendancy of law and order; and confidence in science and technology.

Allied with the moral imperative of material wealth is the conviction that humans have a right and even a responsibility to dominate nature. Progress is interpreted as the increasing encroachment of civilization on jungles, deserts, frozen tundra, and other "wild" geographic environments. History, as it has been taught in our schools, is an account of how the explorers, missionaries, traders, and industrialists rolled back the frontier, "tamed" nature, and brought prosperity to "virgin" lands. Typically, one popular Hollywood epic of the

1960s was titled *How the West Was Won*. The great achievements of the last two centuries, including the opening of the Panama Canal, the completion of the Canadian transcontinental railway, and the landing of astronauts on the moon, all represent a triumph by science and industry over natural hazards and barriers.

The alternative environmental paradigm categorically rejects both pillars of enterprise culture (Cotgrove, 1982: 28–29):

Not only do [environmentalists] challenge the importance attached to material and economic goals, they by contrast give much higher priority to the realization of non-material values—to social relationships and community, to the exercise of human skills and capacities and to increased participation in decisions that affect our daily lives. . . . They have little confidence in science and technology to come up with a technological fix to solve the problems of material and energy shortages. And this is in part rooted in a different view of nature, which stresses the

In the dominant paradigm of our society, progress is interpreted as the increasing encroachment of civilization on jungles, deserts, frozen tundra, and other "wild" geographic environments.
SOURCE: © Blaze Kure/Shutterstock.

delicate balance of ecological systems and possible irreversible damage which may result from the interventions of high technology.

Adherents of the alternative environmental paradigm value the natural environment for its own sake, thus questioning the human right to domination. Earth's resources, they claim, are limited and must therefore be conserved. Drawing on the insights of the economist E. F. Schumacher (1973), they believe that "small is beautiful." In this view, society should adopt small-scale, decentralized economic and political structures that are in harmony with nature.

The value conflict just described arches over a wide spectrum of issues and problems related to sociology and the environment. It is, for example, at the core of the dispute over commercial logging of the old-growth forests of Vancouver Island and of the Temagami region of northern Ontario. It infuses the continuing debate over world population growth as a primary factor contributing to environmental degradation. It helps account for the rise of the "Greens" in Western Europe and of other political ecology parties whose vision closely parallels the alternative environmental paradigm. Most recently, it has surfaced in connection with the debate over global warming, where two sets of people can be identified: those who hope that new technologies, such as capturing and storing carbon, will provide a viable solution, and those who seek a fundamental reconstruction of the way humans live ("Captivating Remedy," 2008).

A major attempt to bridge the differences between the dominant and alternative environmental outlooks

can be found in the idea of **sustainable development.** This concept achieved global currency in 1987 as a result of its use in the report of the United Nations World Commission on Environment and Development, more commonly known as the Brundtland report (after the chair of the commission, Norwegian Prime Minister Gro Harlem Brundtland). The Brundtland report defined sustainable development as "development that meets the needs of the present without compromising the ability of future generations to meet their own needs" (World Commission on Environment and Development, 1987: 43). It foresaw a new form of economic growth, especially for developing nations, that would be both environmentally aware and egalitarian, integrating objectives for social development with the demands of science. In short, the Brundtland report suggested that it is possible to have the best of both worlds: continued economic growth but not at the expense of the environment.

However, many environmentalists have been critical of the concept of sustainable development. They argue that, in real life, it is difficult to balance economic growth and natural-resource use with environmental protection. For example, they would argue that situating a jetport in the middle of an environmentally sensitive natural area would be ecologically destructive no matter what measures were taken to reduce noise pollution or catch the run-off of aviation fuel. In fact, environmentalists, such as David Suzuki, insist that the environmental dangers we face today are so extensive that we can survive as a species only by totally dismantling the "buzz saw of progress" in the industrial nations of the North and by halting its advance in the less-developed countries.

Furthermore, critics of the Brundtland report point out that sustainable development requires an extraordinary degree of cooperation and a deep commitment to reform. This is difficult to achieve, especially in the nations of the Southern Hemisphere, where rural economies are often still controlled by wealthy landowners, and the poor are forced to engage in ecologically damaging practices, such as stripping the rapidly dwindling forests for cooking fuel, in order to survive.

ENVIRONMENTAL ATTITUDES, CONCERNS, AND BEHAVIOURS

The existence of a distinct set of environmental attitudes and concerns in our society has been documented by a large number of polls conducted since the 1970s. One of the first and most important efforts to develop a research tool with which to measure an environmental view of the world was Dunlap and Van Liere's (1978) new environmental paradigm (NEP) scale. Using survey data from two samples of Washington state residents and from the membership of a statewide environmental organization, Dunlap and Van Liere developed a 12-item scale that measures the extent of agreement with such statements as "the balance of nature is very delicate and easily upset" and "humans need not adapt to the natural environment, because they can remake it to suit their own needs" (see Table 16.2). The researchers found that the general public moderately accepted the content of the emerging environmental paradigm, whereas environmentalists strongly endorsed it.

Two other techniques have been used to measure environmental concern. One simple and straightforward approach is to ask people how worried or upset they are about a series of environmental problems. A second strategy, which strives for greater concreteness, is to ask respondents to weigh tradeoffs between, for example, environmental protection and jobs (Freudenburg, 1991).

Has public concern with environmental quality changed since the first survey results were carried out in the early 1970s? Two complementary hypotheses address this question (Jones and Dunlap, 1992). Grossman and Potter (1977) formulated the **broadening-base hypothesis,** which predicts that environmental concern will eventually diffuse throughout all groups. Buttel (1975) promoted the **economic-contingency hypothesis,** which suggests that the broadening of the social bases of environmental concern depends on prevailing economic conditions. Buttel argued that when economic conditions worsen or are perceived to be getting worse, those who are least well off will be the first to shift their focus from the environment to the economy. However, other researchers, using U.S. data for the years 1973–90, found little support for either hypothesis (Jones and Dunlap, 1992); they found instead that the level and social location of support for environmental protection have remained remarkably stable for nearly 20 years.

What are the social bases of environmental concern? It was originally thought that support for environmentalism was limited to the affluent. However, most surveys in the 1970s and 1980s found that income and occupational prestige were only weakly related to environmental concern (Buttel, 1987; Van Liere and Dunlap, 1980). Instead, higher levels of education, youth, political liberalism, and urban residence were found to be the best predictors of concern with environmental quality (Dunlap and Catton, 1979).

TABLE 16.2   AVERAGE SCORES ON THE NEW ENVIRONMENTAL PARADIGM (NEP) SCALE BY THE GENERAL PUBLIC SAMPLE (GPS) AND THE ENVIRONMENTAL ORGANIZATION SAMPLE (EOS)[a]

		GPS	EOS
1.	We are approaching the limit of the number of people the earth can support.	3.00	3.63
2.	The balance of nature is very delicate and easily upset.	3.18	3.68
3.	Humans have the right to modify the natural environment to suit their needs.	3.30	2.76
4.	Humankind was created to rule over the rest of nature.	2.63	3.67
5.	When humans interfere with nature, it often produces disastrous consequences.	3.03	3.49
6.	Plants and animals exist primarily to be used by humans.	3.61	2.81
7.	To maintain a healthy economy, we will have to develop a "steady-state" economy in which industrial growth is controlled.	2.85	3.48
8.	Humans must live in harmony with nature in order to survive.	3.52	3.86
9.	The earth is like a spaceship with only limited room and resources.	3.21	3.85
10.	Humans need not adapt to the natural environment, because they can remake it to suit their own needs.	3.74	3.25
11.	There are limits to growth beyond which our industrialized society cannot expand.	2.94	3.64
12.	Humankind is severely abusing the environment.	3.11	3.81

SOURCE: Adapted from Riley E. Dunlap and Kenneth D. Van Liere, 1978, "The New Environmental Paradigm: A Proposed Measuring Instrument and Preliminary Results," *Journal of Environmental Education*, 9, 10–19, 1978. Reprinted with permission of the Helen Dwight Educational Foundation. Published by Heldref Publications, M319 Eighteenth St., NW, Washington, DC, 20036-1802. Copyright © 1978.
[a]High scores indicate strong agreement with the pro-NEP position. Range = 1.0–4.0. Eight of the items are worded such that agreement reflects acceptance of the NEP, while for the other four (3, 4, 6, 10) disagreement reflects acceptance of the NEP. Respondents were assigned scores of 4 for "strongly agree," 3 for "mildly agree," 2 for "mildly disagree," and 1 for "strongly disagree" for the eight non-NEP items; scoring for the four anti-NEP items was reversed.

The social bases of environmental concern remained more or less the same from 1973 to 1990, as did levels of support (Jones and Dunlap, 1992). Greenbaum (1995) has characterized the social bases of environmental concern as "complex and subtle." That is because environmental concern spans a wide variety of subject matters, from species extinction and the thinning of the ozone layer to the contamination of local drinking waters by toxic chemicals. Although it may be possible to isolate general clusters of environmental concern, as have Dunlap and Van Liere (1978) in their NEP scale (see Table 16.2), people may not be very consistent across various issues. Part of the reason for inconsistency is that individual environmental problems may affect us in very different ways. How concerned we will be about a particular environmental problem, or whether we even perceive it as a problem, will depend on how the activity in question affects our interests—that is, how we will be affected by its benefits, costs, and risks (Greenbaum, 1995: 127; and see Box 16.1).

Do pro-environmental attitudes convert directly into environmentally friendly behaviour? Most studies have failed to confirm such a linkage. As Maloney and Ward (1973: 585) have noted, "most people say they are willing to do a great deal to help curb pollution problems and are fairly emotional about it, but in fact they actually do very little and know even less." In a study carried out in Pennsylvania in the 1990s, Theodori and Luloff (2002) found that those who indicated in a survey that they were "proactive" in their

---

BOX 16.1   ADVICE FROM FOUR "ECO-PATHFINDERS"

COLLEEN McCRORY: NEVER GIVE UP

Colleen McCrory, executive director of the Valhalla Wilderness Society, can claim numerous victories. Her tenacity helped bring a stop to clear-cutting on British Columbia's South Moresby Island and establish the Valhalla Wilderness Park. "Not everyone has to join an organization," she says. "It's more important that the environment is an important part of your everyday life. If you're working on an issue, never give up and never let go. Even if you lose, what you've done will help the next person continue the battle."

BRUCE WALKER: DON'T SACRIFICE CREDIBILITY

In the fall of 1972, Bruce Walker was a 20-year-old college dropout living in Montreal. Now, 27 years later, Walker is research director for the Society to Overcome Pollution. The organization has played a large role in introducing curbside blue box recycling to the Montreal region, getting an island-wide sewage-treatment system installed, and establishing air-quality monitoring, as well as educating the public. . . .

If you want to make an impact, [Walker] advises, don't wait for an issue to hit you over the head. . . . [And] never assume every issue is being taken care of by other organizations. "You'll need loads of patience, persistence, and a sense of humour," he says. "Be vigilant, and use your five senses, plus a sixth—common sense—to detect environmental threats. And lastly, never sacrifice credibility for visibility; state the facts without exaggeration."

LINDA MANZER: FOCUS YOUR ANGER

For Linda Manzer, Toronto-based guitar maker for the stars, the journey down the activist road began with a chance television viewing of an elephant hunt. She was among the first guitar artisans to stop using ivory, and soon others followed suit. "I started asking questions about where products came from," she says. "Some suppliers had good answers, others squirmed." She then focused her attention on the old-growth spruce required to make top-grade instruments. She now ensures that only trees downed by the wind serve as her medium. . . .

Manzer urges people to volunteer. "It's easier than you think," she says. "Jump in where your heart tells you. Focus your anger; use it as a tailwind and a positive force."

SHEILA WATT CLOUTIER: RESPECT THE CIRCLE

A head of the Inuit Circumpolar Conference, Sheila Watt Cloutier spends much of her time convincing southern Canadians of the importance of traditional foods. Caribou, whale, and seal have sustained her people for thousands of years, and the suggestion that Inuit should switch to imported beef, pork, and chicken angers her.

Cloutier advises those who want to make the world a better place to remember the connectedness of all living things. "I can't imagine, with all the challenges we face as a people, that we now have to worry about breast-feeding our children," she says, referring to the presence of persistent organic pollutants in arctic wildlife. "People must realize that a poisoned Inuk child is a poisoned Arctic is a poisoned planet."

SOURCE: Martin Silverstone and Kendra Toby, 1998, "Pathfinder Talk," *Equinox*, August/September, p. 90. Reprinted with permission from the authors.

positions on environmental issues (5.5 percent of the total) were significantly more likely to report engaging in pro-environmental behaviours than were those who described themselves as being "sympathetic" (62.2 percent). In particular, they were more inclined to attend a public hearing and meeting about the environment and to contact a government agency to get information or complain about an environmental problem. For the most part, however, those who score positively in environmental-concern polls do not show any particular willingness to go beyond low-cost, personal actions (recycling, buying "green" products) to make deep-cutting sacrifices for the environment. Uusitalo (1990), for example, found that support for measures to help the environment declined when they required any change of personal habits.

From this evidence, it appears that most people are willing to pay lip service to protecting the environment and will behave responsibly as long as it is not appreciably more expensive or inconvenient to do so. After studying recycling behaviour across Alberta, Derksen and Gartrell (1993) concluded that the key factor accounting for participation in recycling programs was the easy availability of curbside pickups rather than positive attitudes toward the environment. In fact, those who were environmentally concerned were no more likely to recycle than those who were unconcerned. Data from Statistics Canada's *Households and the Environment Survey* (2009) indicate that, in 2006, almost half (45 percent) of Canadian households were considered to be "very active" in participating across a range of six environmental behaviours (use of reduced-volume toilets, use of low-flow showerheads, use of compact fluorescent light bulbs, recycling, composting, and lowering the thermostat). Of the six, the participation rate for recycling was the highest (97 percent), no doubt because it now has become a legal requirement in most municipalities. Least likely was composting (30 percent), which may indicate the perceived level of difficulty or possibly lack of a basic knowledge on how to compost (Babooram, 2008: 8).

Furthermore, some pro-environmental behaviours possess more "symbolic power" than do others. As an illustration, some Canadians today have enthusiastically embraced the idea of reducing their "carbon footprint"—considered by many environmentalists a measure of each person's contribution to global warming—by eating locally produced food. Thus, the concept of "food miles"—the distance a product travels from the farm to your home—is often used as a kind of shorthand to talk about climate change in general. No matter that the algebra of food miles is incredibly complex and sometimes produces a contrary result. For example, the environmental costs of importing apples from New Zealand to Northern Europe or New York can be lower than if the apples were raised 80 kilometres away (Specter, 2008: 48).

THE ENVIRONMENTAL MOVEMENT

Although environmental concern exists across a wide cross-section of the population, it has been most intensely concentrated in the environmental movement. One study from the 1990s of 733 residents of Cornwall, Ontario, found that only one in ten could be labelled an "activist" willing to invest time and energy in behaviours aimed at preserving or improving the quality of the environment. And even here, there was a big difference between easy-to-perform actions, such as voting for a government proposing environmentally conscious policies, and more demanding behaviours, such as participating in protests against current environmental conditions and writing letters to firms that manufacture harmful products (Séguin, Pelletier, and Hunsley, 1998). Movement activists have waged environmental battles with loggers, utility companies, whalers, agricultural corporations, developers, and other defenders of the dominant paradigm. Although the environmental movement has not always represented a "vanguard for a new society" (Milbrath, 1984), it does directly incorporate many of the elements of the alternative environmental paradigm in its philosophies and actions.

SOCIAL BASE AND COMPOSITION

In its early manifestations in the nineteenth century, the environmental movement was largely the creation of an elite. For example, the leadership and much of the membership of American wildlife-preservation organizations, such as the Sierra Club, the Save the Redwoods League, and the Boone and Crockett Club were drawn almost exclusively from a tightly knit network of lawyers, educators, and wealthy businessmen. Similarly, in England, preservationist causes were pursued primarily by members of the clergy and the aristocracy. Occasionally, these elite organizations would enlist the support of the general public in specific campaigns. In the fight to save Niagara Falls (1906–10), for example, a national publicity campaign waged in the pages of American popular magazines, such as *Ladies' Home Journal*, resulted in more than

6500 letters written in support of the preservation of the falls (Cylke, 1993: 22).

In Canada, the conservation movement developed in a different fashion. Environmental initiatives, such as the establishment of national parks and the protection of wildlife, were more likely to be developed by small groups of dedicated civil servants who were able to convince the federal government to take action (Foster, 1978). Two of the most significant events in early Canadian conservation history, the establishment of the first national park in Banff in 1887 and the signing of the Canada–U.S. Migratory Bird Convention in 1917, followed this pattern.

When the modern environmental movement emerged in the late 1960s and early 1970s, it was largely a creature of the upper middle classes. The dominant social groups in environmental organizations were well-educated professionals from urban and suburban backgrounds and university students from white-collar backgrounds (Gale, 1983). Mainstream environmental movement organizations (EMOs) consequently favoured issues related to "saving" nature over those relating to urban environments. For example, few EMOs in the 1970s showed much interest in pursuing problems related to high concentrations of lead in the soil of inner-city properties, despite the fact that lead levels detected in the blood of local children were far above normal. These organizations only took up the issue when it became evident that lead emissions from motor vehicles were unacceptably high.

More recently, environmentalists have been identified as members of a "new middle class" drawn primarily from social and cultural specialists—teachers, social workers, journalists, artists, and professors—who work in creative or public-service-oriented jobs. This new middle class is on the firing line in the day-to-day conflicts between the engineers and technocrats who tend to ignore the human costs of progress and the ordinary citizens who are victimized by them.

There are two kinds of explanations for why members of the new middle class tend to be more radical as a group than the population as a whole. On the one hand, they are more likely to seek out jobs in the public sector, away from the pressures of a business environment that is often hostile to their values. At the same time, they tend to become personally involved in the problems faced by their clients, even to the point of becoming advocates for

The environmental movement has grown tremendously since the 1960s. Some members of the middle class in particular are now more personally involved in the environmental movement and raise environmentally conscious children.

SOURCE: © iStockphoto.com/Carrie Bottomley.

their interests (Kriesi, 1989: 1084). For example, a doctor working in a community health centre whose patients suffer an unusually high incidence of asthma might recognize that the source of the illness is a local incinerator and may campaign to have the polluting facility closed.

Evidence for the new middle class theory of social movements comes from different countries. Cotgrove and Duff (1981) found that 43.4 percent of their sample of environmentalists in England (compared with only about 12 percent of the general public) were employed in service, welfare, and creative occupations. Kriesi (1989) found that 23 percent of those who reported having participated in the Dutch ecology movement (compared with 12 percent of the population as a whole) were social and cultural specialists. And Tindall (1994) showed that people who had higher levels of income and education or were employed in the public sector were more likely to join the Vancouver Island wilderness-preservation movement, although these factors did not affect their level of participation after joining.

ENVIRONMENTAL MOBILIZATION

In addition to researching the social composition of the environmental movement, sociologists have also been interested in learning how environmentalists mobilize people to their cause.

Much of the research on this topic has focused on community-based, grassroots environmental organizations. Formed in opposition to the pollution problems caused by local industries and utilities, these citizens' groups differ somewhat from the rest of the environmental movement insofar as they draw their members from blue-collar as well as white-collar neighbourhoods. The prototype of the grassroots, locally based environmental group is the Love Canal Homeowners Association, formed in the 1970s by some Niagara Falls, New York, homeowners whose properties had been contaminated by toxic waste buried 30 years earlier by a local chemical company.

It is by no means a simple matter to mobilize neighbours in the face of an environmental threat. In fact, most people want to avoid trouble and must be actively convinced that their present situation is both unjust and intolerable before they will consider taking action. Capek (1993: 11) describes the initial reluctance of homeowners in Carver Terrace, a contaminated residential subdivision in the U.S. South, to recognize the dangers facing them:

> Residents knew at some level about bad-smelling air, mysterious illness or deaths among people with no prior history of medical problems, plants that would not grow or grew strangely, animals becoming ill or [being] born deformed, and a variety of other experiences that lacked explanation. The amorphous and invisible nature of chemical exposure, however, and the difficulty of diagnosing its consequences either at a popular or professional level worked against the integration of this knowledge.

Caught up in the demands of everyday life, respectful of the voices of authority who downplay the problem, and blinded by the pride of home ownership, people tend to accept the status quo and must be persuaded to redefine their situation in such a way that they can see it as a violation of their basic rights. This is easier to do when citizens are ideologically primed to question the image of progress as continual economic development (Ladd and Laska, 1991), but even those who lack this attitudinal underpinning can be brought around.

Based on archival research and two and a half years of ethnographic fieldwork in Flammable (its actual name), an Argentine shantytown surrounded by one of the largest petrochemical compounds in the country, Auyero and Swistun (2008) conclude that common neighbourhood perceptions about a toxic environment do not form easily or automatically. The researchers pose three questions. How do people perceive an environmentally risky situation? When do they fail to understand what is objectively a clear and present danger? How and why are (mis)perceptions shared within a community? It is possible, they say, to isolate two reasons that shared critical understandings regarding toxic danger are slow to develop. First, risk perceptions are "relationally anchored." In the case of Flammable, this meant that the process of contamination was slow and gradual rather than suddenly imposed. Residents' perceptions of hazards were embedded in their everyday routines (building families, enjoying their friends, working). These familiar routines provided a sense of security and masked the unpleasant, even as lead and other toxic chemicals gradually accumulated in the ground and streams, and in people's bodies. Toxic uncertainty also derived from the "labour of confusion" performed by powerful actors. For example, state politicians and officials in Flammable showed minimal concern, initially promising action when the media publicized toxic leaks, but then doing nothing and averting their gaze. Local doctors wavered between expressing concern and contending that the anemia, respiratory problems, and other illnesses affecting their patients did not differ from those affecting other poor areas around Buenos Aires. While Auyero and Swistun could not directly attribute the collective quiescence and inaction that was apparent in the neighbourhood to the social production of toxic uncertainty, they strongly suggest that the two are related.

In those cases where collective action does occur, local communities pass through four stages in the process of challenging polluters (Cable and Benson, 1993). In the first phase, residents come to see themselves as "victims" of corporate environmental crime. In phase two, they make individual appeals to government regulatory agencies to take action to force an end to the toxic dumping or other problem situation. In the third phase, the complainants become disillusioned with the slow pace or absence of official action and begin to seek environmental justice. In the final phase, increased democratic pressure has either convinced government regulators to enforce environmental standards or proven insufficient, in which case the problem continues unchecked.

Like other social movements, the environmental movement aims to convince as wide a segment of the public as possible that its interpretation of the world is correct and should, therefore, be acted on. To that end, members of the movement develop **frames**—that is, interpretations of events and their meanings. Successful framing involves three elements: diagnostic, prognostic, and motivational. Diagnostic framing involves identifying a problem and assigning the blame for it. Prognostic framing offers a proposed solution to the diagnosed problem. Motivational framing is a call to arms to potential recruits to take specific corrective action. The better these three frames are integrated, the greater their capacity for mobilizing people (Gerhards and Rucht, 1992: 583).

Contemporary environmental frames are frequently constructed around the image of an impending global collapse. In the early 1970s, this approach was typified by the best-selling book *The Limits to Growth* (Meadows, Meadows, Randers, and Behrens, 1972), in which the authors forecast that Earth's **carrying capacity**—that is, the optimum population size that the planet can support under present environmental conditions—would eventually be exceeded. With the aid of a computer model, they estimated how five interrelated factors—population growth, industrial output, food production, pollution, and nonrenewable natural resources—would interact over time. They predicted that, within a century, we would face a major crisis brought on by uncontrolled population growth and rising levels of pollution.

In the 1980s, the threat shifted to that of "biosphere crisis," generated by global climatic changes resulting from increased emissions of "greenhouse" gases, such as carbon dioxide, chlorofluorocarbons, methane, and nitrous oxide, into the atmosphere. Such changes in global weather patterns have the potential to trigger major environmental changes, including rising sea levels, hotter summers, more frequent and more severe droughts, dust storms, forest fires, and the rapid extinction of thousands of species of plants and animals.

The solution, environmentalists claim, is to embrace wholeheartedly the alternative environmental paradigm. In *Beyond the Limits* (1992), the sequel to *The Limits to Growth*, Meadows, Meadows, and Randers caution that we must draw back and ease down: conserve resources, reduce pollution, and adopt deliberate social constraints on population and industrial growth. In the less-developed nations, this means both controlling family size and finding new, more sustainable avenues of economic expansion. In the industrialized world, a new value system is said to be necessary so that people will stop trying to use material growth to satisfy what are in fact non-material needs for acceptance, self-importance, and community identity (Fields, 1993: 40).

More research is needed on the relationship between grassroots mobilizations protesting toxic dumps, incinerators, nuclear power plants, and other pollution sources and these wider ecological worldviews. Although we might assume that environmentalists, in accordance with the popular slogan "think globally, act locally," first become imbued with the alternative environmental paradigm and then put it to practical use in their own neighbourhoods and communities, another possibility is that ecological values arise directly out of firsthand experience. In the latter view, it is the process of dealing with recalcitrant polluters, bureaucratic cover-ups, and overly cautious scientists that eventually causes the penny to drop for local environmentalists who previously had not given much thought to broad environmental philosophies. Members of community-based, grassroots environmental organizations thus engage in a form of social learning as they go about researching their case against polluters. This social learning is further facilitated by the assembly of a widening net of environmental contacts. Irene Paparo-Stein, a Winnipeg woman who formed a citizens' lobby group to fight chemical spraying in her city, describes the environmental networking process this way (Stein, 1988: 52):

> One thing I had discovered, there was quite a network in the U.S. And the Americans, once I explained the situation and the need for information, were ready with their help. They understood the enormity of the problem, of the laypersons up against the governments, bureaucracy, and industry, and knew what to do. They were generous with their aid. We had soon compiled a list of contacts from all over the U.S.

Inevitably, someone in the network introduces the community activist to an "ecological" perspective.

IDEOLOGICAL DIVISIONS

Although we often speak of the environmental movement as a single entity, there has, in fact, long been a basic philosophical split between "value-oriented environmentalists," whose main concern is to change the way we view the world, and "success-oriented environmentalists," whose chief goal is to stop pollution and other activities that damage the physical environment (Eyerman and Jamison, 1989). These two factions differ significantly in their perceptions of the root causes of environmental problems, their preferences among strategies for coping, and their visions of an ecologically sound society (Cylke, 1993: 69).

This division became evident at the beginning of the twentieth century in the differing ideological approaches to the environment taken by the two main wings of the U.S. conservation movement—the "resource conservationists" and the "preservationists." The former wanted to "manage" natural resources by applying modern engineering and administrative techniques, whereas the latter, guided by aesthetic and even spiritual ideals, believed it was necessary for the government to intervene in order to preserve areas of natural beauty and scientific importance. For example, in a difference of opinion that has carried over to the present day, resource conservationists wanted to "harvest" public forests in a "scientific" manner, whereas preservationists advocated setting these lands aside as natural parks in which logging would be prohibited.

On Canada's West Coast, where logging is still a major industry and source of employment, the heirs to the resource conservation wing of the early twentieth century are the 300 organizations that belong to the Forest Alliance of British Columbia. An industry-sponsored coalition of corporations, community associations, and municipalities, the Forest Alliance "aims to find ways to balance environmental, social and economic values in forest-use decisions" ("End War in Woods," 2000: 5). In recent years, much of the strategic action undertaken by this coalition has centred on efforts to counter claims of environmental opponents and establish public confidence in the industry's environmental performance through "certification" schemes. Operated through such organizations as the Canadian Standards Association and the Forest Stewardship Council, forest certification is a voluntary tool directed toward lumber retailers, homebuilders, and other big customers designed to reassure them (and their customers) that their purchases are derived from "well-managed" forests. The Forest Alliance's promotional literature especially favours the notion of "sustainable development" (the title of its newsletter is *Sustainability Update*).

Furthermore, value differences over the true meaning of environmentalism have become the basis for the emergence of various alternative ecophilosophies, the best known of which are "deep ecology" and "ecofeminism." Whereas success-oriented environmentalists are primarily concerned with the direct effects of industrial pollution on individuals and communities, value-oriented environmentalists stress the survival of all living and nonliving things as components of healthy ecosystems. In doing so, they come closest to any segment of the environmental movement to popularizing the alternative environmental paradigm.

Deep Ecology

The **deep ecology** argument was set out in the early 1970s by Norwegian philosopher Arne Naess (1973) and was elaborated by U.S. ecological thinkers Bill Devall and George Sessions (1985). In contrast to the **anthropocentrism** that characterizes much of the environmental movement, deep ecologists believe in a "biocentric" approach, which emphasizes that humans are one species among many on Earth and have no special rights or privileges. This **biocentric egalitarianism** states that all things on Earth have an equal right to live and blossom and reach their own forms of self-realization.

Although the intellectual roots of this principle are varied, it owes much to the thinking of John Muir, the leading preservationist in the early American conservation movement. A second touchstone for deep ecology is the "land ethic" of Aldo Leopold, an American naturalist. Formulated in 1949, Leopold's land ethic affirms the right of soils, waters, plants, and animals to coexist in their natural state with humans, whose role is viewed not as conqueror of the land but as member and citizen of it.

Deep ecologists believe that the relation of the individual to nature cannot be fully grasped intellectually but must ultimately be experienced directly. This sets deep ecology in opposition to mainstream environmentalism, which is primarily concerned with gathering "facts" about nature and our despoiling of it. Indeed, deep ecologists regard science and scientists with suspicion, depicting them as being a part of the problem as much as a part of its solution. An exception to this is the **Gaia hypothesis,** formulated in the late 1960s by British scientist James Lovelock

The biocentric egalitarianism of deep ecology states that all things on Earth have an equal right to live and blossom and reach their own forms of self-realization.
SOURCE: © Glen Gaffney/Shutterstock.

(1987) and American microbiologist Lynn Margulis, which holds that Earth is a living superorganism with its own internal system of regulation. From this perspective, it is possible to see ourselves as having a moral obligation not just to plants, animals, and other human beings but also to the planet itself (Yearley, 1991: 145).

Ecofeminism

A second alternative ecophilosophy is **ecofeminism.** The term was first coined in 1974 by the French writer Françoise d'Eaubonne, who believes that the oppression and exploitation of women and the domination of the natural environment are part of the same phenomenon. Ecofeminists identify a distinctly "feminine" way of thinking and being that is more nurturing, cooperative, and communal than the mainstream, paternalistic culture. *Mother Nature*, a long-accepted term in the English language, is given a new meaning and significance by ecofeminists, who celebrate the ancient pagan tradition of Goddess worship and nature cults; the Goddess is seen as the symbol of ecological wisdom.

Both deep ecologists and ecofeminists express the need for developing a new human consciousness and vision. However, a certain degree of tension exists between these two ecophilosophies, centred on differing conceptions of the main cause of the current environmental crisis: Deep ecologists point to a gender-neutral anthropocentrism, whereas ecofeminists claim that "androcentrism" (male-centredness) is the real culprit. Furthermore, deep ecologists have trouble accepting the ecofeminist claims that women are innately and more sensitively attuned to nature than men are and, therefore, have the unique capacity to construct a new, more enlightened approach to the environment (Warren, 1990).

In a recent transnational study, Perron, Vaillancourt, and Durand (2001) identified three types of "green" orientations among leaders of environmental NGOs that they surveyed in Quebec and Costa Rica: ecologists (*n* = 30), mainstream environmentalists (*n* = 107), and market environmentalists (*n* = 83). Mainstream and market environmentalists perceived science and technology more positively than did ecologists; however, market environmentalists were less likely to accept economic sacrifices for the sake of the environment than were mainstreamers. This typology, Perron and his colleagues (2001: 849) claim, is "consistent with studies using the NEP scale of Dunlap and Van Liere (1978), but, instead of differentiating

Greenpeace activists put a banner on the statue of Christ the Redeemer in Rio de Janeiro, Brazil, September 5, 2002. The protest was held to draw attention to lack of focus on renewable energy at the World Summit on Sustainable Development. The banner read, "Rio + 10 = A SECOND CHANCE, Greenpeace." SOURCE: © Reuters New Media Inc./Corbis.

between those who support the NEP and those who do not, it reveals differences within the NEP."

POLITICAL ECONOMY OF THE ENVIRONMENT

A third major area of inquiry within environmental sociology is the study of the political economy of the environment. A starting point for many studies undertaken from a political-economy perspective is Alan Schnaiberg's *The Environment: From Surplus to Scarcity* (1980). Schnaiberg distinguishes between production and consumption activities in society and blames the environmental crisis on production activities. Rather than looking to irresponsible consumers who insist on embracing an extravagant, wasteful lifestyle despite its harmful environmental effects, Schnaiberg identifies the real villain as the relentless process of economic development that is controlled by industrial capitalists and buttressed by the state.

According to Schnaiberg, the political economy of environmental problems and policies is shaped by modern industrial society's **treadmill of production.** This term refers to the inherent need of our economic system to continually yield profits by creating consumer demand for new products, even where this means expanding the ecosystem to its furthest limits. Corporate producers create demand primarily through the medium of advertising. For example, in a recent issue of a leading Canadian urban-living magazine, readers are advised that a Porsche will stir the "power of passion" in its owner, a Jenn-Air stove system is "the sign of a great cook," and a Kohler spray-and-brush attachment will "turn your shower into a personal luxury spa." Consumers are thus persuaded from early childhood to become part of a dominant materialistic culture in which personal identity depends on material possessions.

The state is said to buttress this treadmill of production by providing a variety of economic incentives to new industries, from tax breaks to worker-training programs. Traditionally, the state has also encouraged untrammelled economic growth by ensuring a continual flow of natural resources to industrial producers. For example, in the latter years of the nineteenth century, the "gospel of efficiency" (Hays, 1959) in U.S. politics dictated that the growing power of the federal government be used to regulate competition and ensure a steady supply of lumber and other resources to industry. The idea was that only government measures could ensure that resources be set aside and then be exploited in a controlled fashion, rather than squandered in the cutthroat competition of the unregulated marketplace (Koppes, 1988: 234). In Canada, the prevailing view has been that nature can be privately requisitioned virtually without limit (Williams, 1992), as evidenced by our export of oil, natural gas, minerals, lumber, and, more recently, water, to industrial centres in the United States, often despite negative environmental consequences.

One far-reaching example of this approach to natural resources is the Great Whale hydroelectric project, initiated by former Quebec Premier Robert Bourassa and Hydro Quebec. Great Whale is the second phase of the massive James Bay hydroelectric project, which calls for the diversion or alteration of 20 northern rivers through the construction of 36 dams and more than 1000 dikes. The project is now on hold because of Cree objections and expert opinion, but if it is ever completed, the development will flood "23 000 square kilometres of land the size of Newfoundland island and Labrador combined and [shatter] two cultures that have flourished there—surviving both natural disaster and foreign intrusion—for 5000 years" (Dwyer, 1992: 30).

Of course, the despoiling of the environment is not limited to countries that have functioned under a capitalist system: Soviet-style societies devastated the environment to an even greater degree. Two of the most memorable photographic images to come out of Eastern Europe in the early 1990s were of the

Romanian town of Copsa Mica totally blackened by carbon dust from the local Carbosin plant and of schoolchildren from the Czechoslovakian town of Most who had to wear face masks on "sulphur dioxide alert" days to filter the pollution-laden air. There are also indications that recent economic expansion in China has produced its own environmental nightmares. In 1988, for example, Benxi, a city covering 43 square kilometres, vanished from satellite photographs beneath a cloud of smog (Silvertown, 1989: 550). In 2005, an explosion at a PetroChina chemical plant in the northeastern province of Jilin severely damaged the Sanghua River, one of the country's largest, and the main source of drinking water for more than 3 million residents of the city of Harbin. The blast released an estimated 100 tonnes of cancer-causing benzene compounds into the river, resulting in contamination that reached levels that initially were 108 times above national safety standards (Saiget, 2005). Thus, the accusing finger should be pointed not at the capitalist system but at unbridled industrialism, with its accompanying lack of environmental responsibility.

Schnaiberg has described a pervasive conflict in advanced industrial societies between the treadmill of production and the rising public demand for protecting the environment. That is, governments are increasingly torn between a commitment to promote economic development and job creation and the goal of environmental preservation. The bitter conflict over the future of old-growth forests on Vancouver Island is a dramatic illustration of the conflict.

Environmentalists argue that the temperate rain forests of Clayoquot Sound and other parts of the province have nearly disappeared and must be declared out of bounds to further logging, particularly if it employs "clear-cutting" methods. The forestry industry replies that this solution would cripple one of British Columbia's major industries, throwing tens of thousands of loggers out of work.

In such situations, governments search for a viable compromise. In British Columbia, such a compromise was recently announced with reference to the Great Bear Rainforest, one of the world's largest remaining temperate rain forests. The proposed land-use agreement, the product of a decade of negotiations among the forestry companies, the B.C. provincial government, and a handful of major environmental organizations (Greenpeace, Sierra Club, Rainforest Action Network, ForestEthics), opens Great Bear to provincially subsidized logging for the first time. In return, portions of the cedar old-growth forests, salmon rivers, the Kermode bear, and most sensitive ecosystems will be protected from logging and mining.

One approach to resolving the contradictions noted by Schnaiberg involves the adoption of "environmental management" techniques. **Environmental management** refers to moderate government intervention that affords limited protection to the environment without seriously curtailing economic development. The agreement on the Great Bear Rainforest, for example, is the product of a much heralded new enviro-industrial concept called "environment-based management" that bases decisions on a combination of environmental factors and the social and economic needs of resource-dependent communities (Solomon, 2006). In this case, the extent of the protection provided by the rain forest agreement has been contested by some critics, notably members of the David Suzuki Foundation, who contend that the protected areas of Great Bear are unacceptably small.

Politicians and bureaucrats also engage in environmental management through co-opting and controlling dominant policy discourses (a discourse is a discussion or dialogue). This allows them to appear to be undertaking environmental reform without actually having to do so. As Davidson and MacKendrick (2004) have shown, the province of Alberta has successfully manipulated policy discourse associated with "integrated resource management," a policy that purports to manage conflicts between users across a range of natural resource sectors in a manner that is flexible, consultative, and fair. Beginning in the late 1990s, integrated resource management policy was increasingly expressed in terms that tapped into the discourse of "sustainable development" or "ecological modernization." This allowed the Alberta government to appear to be progressive and visionary in its approach to resource development, even as it was engaged in expanding oil and gas production and logging.

The treadmill of production exerts a major influence on the developing nations as well, where many people want access to the consumer culture that we enjoy. The unsustainable development that some industrializing countries have consequently espoused has led to considerable friction with environmentalists from Northern countries, who fear that it will lead to serious worldwide environmental problems (e.g., increased destruction of tropical rain forests can lead to accelerated global warming). Leaders of the developing world reply that, having

enjoyed the benefits of a century of industrial growth, environmental activists from Europe and North America cannot in fairness now deny developing countries the fruits of economic expansion on ecological grounds. (For an attempt to reconcile development with environmental integrity in the developing nations, see Adams, 1990.) At the same time, planners and politicians in developing countries have not always learned from the mistakes of their counterparts in the North.

A second source of environmental degradation in the low-income countries is that associated with "unsustainable impoverishment." In other words, the poor engage in ecologically damaging practices just to survive from day to day (Gallopin, Gutman, and Maletta, 1989). For example, rural dwellers are often forced to strip the rapidly dwindling forests to obtain fuel for cooking. As the Brundtland commission recognized, it is futile to attempt to deal with environmental problems in the developing world without addressing broader issues of poverty and inequality. These problems in turn are rooted in a variety of social arrangements, from the continuing dominance of wealthy elites in the developing nations to economic dependency on the industrialized countries, both of which are associated with massive debt.

Nevertheless, it is important to note that environmental violations in the high-income countries of the North are directly tied to potential ecological catastrophes in the poorer nations of the South. Roberts (2001) has shown how global warming, which is linked to emissions of greenhouse gases in rich nations (20 percent of the world's population is responsible for 60 percent of current emissions of greenhouse gases), threatens poor nations with devastating disasters: draughts, floods, heat waves, and so on. At the same time, global warming contributes to the "pollution of poverty," whereby the world's poor are forced to use highly polluting energy sources for their basic fuel needs. As Roberts (2001: 508) stresses, "equity and ecology must be dealt with together" through aggressive efforts to support national advancement in the South, if a healthy planet is to be maintained.

RISK AND RISK ASSESSMENT

Risk refers to the probability that a particular hazard will actually occur. Everyday life is full of risks, from slipping on the ice on our front steps to being hit by a bolt of lightning on the golf course. Normally, we base our decision on whether to take a particular course of action that carries with it a degree of risk on a series of individual factors: past experience, confidence in our own abilities, and our assessment of the apparent safety of a situation. In the present-day world, however, it is increasingly difficult to make such judgments, especially with regard to new technologies and environmental conditions. For example, a summer afternoon spent sunning on the beach may seem innocent, but it may, in fact, contribute to the onset of skin cancer unless a sun-block lotion is applied to counteract the ultraviolet rays coming through the thinned-out ozone layer. Many of today's environmental hazards are invisible to the naked eye.

To cope with such risks, we have increasingly come to rely on the judgment of medical and scientific experts, who appear to be best qualified to decide what is safe. We avoid high-fat foods, buckle our seat belts, and buy organic bananas because risk professionals tell us that it may be risky not to do so. Everyday items that were deemed safe yesterday are judged to be harmful today. For example, Teflon cookware, with its non-stick properties, was once regarded as a valuable addition to the kitchen. Now, researchers have revealed that Teflon can emit toxic fumes at high temperatures, causing flu-like symptoms in some people. The syndrome even has a name—"fume fever" ("Recent Research," 2008).

Each week seems to bring some newly discovered risk to our attention. Increasingly, such risks are environmentally related—from dioxins and heavy metals in our drinking water through radiation leaks from nuclear power plants to urban smog that can cause respiratory problems. Toxic hazards are particularly devastating because they render many of the seemingly innocuous or even beneficial things that we depend on—the air we breathe, the water we drink, the sea and soil that nourish the food we eat— dangerous (Clarke and Short, 1993).

Sociologists have taken a particular interest in three aspects of risk and risk assessment: the organizational basis of risk, the community perception of risk, and the social distribution of risk.

ORGANIZATIONAL BASIS OF RISK

One consequence of the increasing size and complexity of modern industrial systems is that the source of risk has shifted to large-scale organizations that are all but beyond individual control. When environmentally threatening accidents happen, they are attributable to more than human error; they reflect a set of structural arrangements that make breakdowns inevitable. For example, the gigantic 1989 oil spill that occurred after the supertanker *Exxon Valdez* ran aground in Prince William Sound, Alaska, was attributable to cutbacks in maritime safety standards as much as to personal lapses by the captain (Smith, 1992). Similarly, a recent report by a review group of the American Society of Civil Engineers concluded that the levee breaches that left more than 75 percent of New Orleans flooded after Hurricane Katrina did not result from construction-related flaws. Rather, they indicated a massive and catastrophic organizational failure wherein all the agencies tasked with levee upkeep—local levee boards, parish governments, state agencies, bureaucracies within the Army Corps of Engineers—operated independently and sometimes in conflict with one another (Schwartz, 2006).

Indeed, **normal accidents**—the inevitable failures in nuclear power facilities, petrochemical plants, air-traffic control nets, and other high-risk technologies—are common. Sometimes these flaws are identified during the construction process, but on other occasions, design flaws manifest themselves only years later, in the form of disasters, such as the Three Mile Island nuclear accident. Rather than being anomalies, such technological accidents are the normal consequences of profit-driven, high-risk systems (Perrow, 1984).

Organizations are not only the source of accidents but also the groups responsible for responding to them. The ways in which they do so often amplify the risk (Clarke and Short, 1993: 392). For example, in the wake of the 1984 gas leak at a Union Carbide pesticide plant in Bhopal, India, in which 8000 people were killed and an estimated 300 000 were injured, neither the company, which lacked the necessary support structure and contingency plans for dealing with major accidents, nor the immense government bureaucracy, which took a long time to mobilize, was able to move quickly enough to cope with the catastrophe (Shrivastava, 1987).

COMMUNITY PERCEPTION OF RISK

Contrary to expectations, it is not possible to predict the public perception of risk accurately on the basis of the standard set of demographic and sociological variables (age, gender, political affiliation, etc.). Instead, the best predictor of whether people are likely to perceive risk is the degree to which they trust the ability of expert institutions, including local industries themselves, to manage danger (Freudenburg, 1993; Wynne, 1992). For example, during the Windscale Inquiry into the establishment of a nuclear reprocessing facility on the east coast of England, the nuclear experts and the judge who chaired the inquiry approached the issue from a completely different vantage point from local citizens. Whereas the former restricted the scope of the inquiry to technical risk considerations, the latter wanted to deal with larger questions, such as how adequate the past performance of the nuclear plant had been and what the future of nuclear power should be. As a result, public trust in both the project and the inquiry was undermined and the perception of risk magnified (Wynne, 1992).

Frederick Street in Sydney, Nova Scotia, runs alongside the Sydney tar ponds, the worst toxic waste site in Canada and arguably the worst in North America. With a legacy of 100 years of steelmaking, the tar ponds contain 35 times as much toxic sludge as New York's infamous Love Canal. As a result, Sydney has the highest cancer rate in Canada—19 percent for men and 14 percent for women, more than double the national averages. After 12 years of trying to clean up the mess, the clean-up project was declared a failure and the residents of Frederick Street were relocated in 1999. The toxic waste remains.
SOURCE: © Warren Gordon/Frederick Street: Life and Death on Canada's Love Canal.

Trust in institutions varies among the members of a community. Those who trust institutions least are most likely to define environmental conditions as risky and therefore actionable. In the Love Canal case, the residents of the neighbourhood that was affected by toxic seepage could be divided into two types: *minimalists*, who denied that there was a problem at all or acknowledged a problem of only minor significance, and *maximalists*, who believed that the risks were substantial and that the chemical contamination might be more widespread than officially acknowledged. Minimalists were generally found to be social isolates in their neighbourhoods, without children at home, with occupational links to the chemical industry, and with strong attachments to their homes, which they viewed as their principal economic resource in old age. In contrast, the maximalists were typically young parents who shared common interests, placed greater emphasis on health than on property issues, and were active in seeking risk information, especially from non-official sources (Fowlkes and Miller, 1987). In other cases, too, researchers have confirmed that a major motivation for families to become involved in neighbourhood action against toxic wastes is concern about the quality of the community for raising children (Hallman and Wandersman, 1992). Environmental-risk perception, then, is not only a product of how much trust citizens put in the explanations and assurances offered by those in authority positions but is also linked to people's participation in family life, neighbourhood social networks, and community affairs.

It is important to note that sharing a perception of risk is no guarantee that community members will work together to respond to or mitigate an environmental problem. Flint and Luloff (2005) have recently proposed a "mid-range conceptual model of community response to risk and disaster" that contains three main elements: risk context (a combination of socioeconomic and biophysical vulnerability), community risk perception, and interactional capacity (the ability of community residents to work together on issues and problems). They see communities with high levels of interactional capacity as more likely to act in response to perceived risks. For example, in a study of six Alaska communities under serious threat from a massive invasion of spruce bark beetles, Flint (2004) found that towns with traditionally high levels of community participation and involvement were better prepared and more willing to act collectively. By contrast, in communities with low interactional capacity, responses to forest-related risks defaulted to individuals and government agencies.

SOCIAL DISTRIBUTION OF RISK

Finally, recent research in the sociology of environmental risk has documented how marginal groups in society bear a disproportionate burden of the risk associated with oil refineries, chemical plants, toxic dumps, garbage and sewage incinerators, and other sources of hazardous exposure. Racial and ethnic minorities, women, low-income urban dwellers, and residents of poor, isolated rural regions are particularly affected. After analyzing the distribution of toxic "Superfund" hazardous waste site locations in Texas and Louisiana, Denq, Constance, and Joung (2000) concluded that the three dimensions of class, status, and power are all important in explaining why toxic dumps are disproportionately located in communities with higher percentages of minorities and poor people. Rather than "environmental racism," they argue that the environmental justice issues involved here are better conceptualized as "environmental classism." Disadvantaged communities are overrepresented as risk sites because corporate polluters view them as constituting the path of least resistance, since their inhabitants are generally both economically poor and politically powerless. In many cases, existing patterns of discrimination are closely linked with inequalities in the distribution of environmental hazards.

Disadvantaged people are the primary victims of pollution (most of it generated by or on behalf of the middle and upper classes) because they live closest to the sources of pollution: power plants, industrial installations, and, in central cities, heavy vehicle traffic. Usually, they have no choice as to where they live. Discrimination created the situation, and those with wealth and influence have the political power needed to keep polluting facilities away from their homes. Living in a poor area is bad enough; high levels of pollution make it worse (Bullard, 1990).

Although the scale of environmental-risk inequality is smaller in Canada than in the United States, some striking parallels exist. For example, in July 1993, a Mi'kmaq band in Pictou Landing, Nova Scotia, was reported to have accepted a federal government package worth an estimated $35 million as compensation for the pollution of Boat Harbour, the body of water adjoining the band's reserve. At one time, Boat Harbour had clear beaches and was a source of fish and lobster for the Mi'kmaq, but in the mid-1960s, almost half the harbour was purchased for $60 000 to treat wastewater from a kraft mill operated by Scott Maritimes, a subsidiary of Scott Paper Company. The harbour subsequently became one of the most polluted spots in the province, with 87 million litres of a coffee-coloured effluent processed each day by the provincial treatment lagoon.

A similar case occurred two decades earlier in northern Ontario, when the Reed pulp-and-paper plant at Dryden was found to be responsible for dumping nine tonnes of mercury into the English Wabigoon river system between 1962 and 1970 (Macdonald, 1991: 106). The Ojibwa who lived in the area suffered serious health and economic problems. Not only were they penalized by a commercial fishing ban, but they also were found to be suffering from "Minimata disease"—mercury poisoning from fish—a toxic syndrome named after a fishing village in Japan, where victims took court action against Chisso Corporation, a large chemical firm.

Environmentally risky activities are also more likely to be located in peripheral communities, areas that are out of the mainstream by virtue of their relative geographic remoteness, their economic marginality, their political powerlessness, or their social isolation. For example, Sellafield, a town in northwest England on the Irish Sea, became a major repository for nuclear waste reprocessing. Sellafield was the archetype of a peripheral community, accessible only by twisting road and branch railway, situated in an area of high unemployment, and economically dependent on the local nuclear power plant (Blowers, Lowry, and Solomon, 1991). Such cases as these are often found in regions that Gidengil (1990) has termed the "vulnerable periphery" and the "depressed periphery," regions with chronic economic problems and dependencies and a high susceptibility to boom-and-bust industries.

Research on the social distribution of risk not only is important for humanitarian reasons but also influences how we think about power, decision making, and institutional analyses of environmental risk (Clarke and Short, 1993: 394). Among other things, it suggests that risk decisions are not based entirely on "objective" technical and scientific criteria but are influenced by sociological factors related to inequality and power. This represents an important addition to public-policy debates on the dynamics of risk, which have tended to treat risk allocation as something that takes place outside the normal workings of society.

SOCIAL CONSTRUCTION OF ENVIRONMENTAL PROBLEMS

The most promising areas of research in environmental sociology today are informed by social constructionism. According to this perspective, environmental issues rarely arise spontaneously; rather, they must be discovered, presented, promoted, and kept alive. Furthermore, environmental problems, like social problems in general, are not free-floating but are owned and managed by policy entrepreneurs in science, environmental-movement organizations, and the mass media. These "environmental claims-makers" invest considerable time and resources in attempting to elevate such problems as acid rain, global warming, and ozone depletion onto national and international agendas for action.

Consider, for example, the issue of indoor air pollution from radon gas. In the United States, policy entrepreneurs in Congress aggressively pressed the Environmental Protection Agency to take action to publicize the problem. Citizen groups were influential in making the public aware of the dangers of radon, especially when they were first discovered in the state of Pennsylvania. In contrast, a lack of comparable environmental claims-makers in Canada meant that the problem never really "caught on" here beyond a few investigative stories in *The Globe and Mail* (Harrison and Hoberg, 1991).

As I note elsewhere, there are three central tasks in the construction of environmental claims—assembling, presenting, and contesting—each of which involves its own activities, opportunities, and pitfalls (Hannigan, 1995). To secure public attention and support, prospective problems must surmount a series of hurdles. They have to be considered newsworthy, they must acquire a measure of scientific credibility, and they have to be skillfully navigated across the shoals of political interest and policy relevance. Finding a way around these roadblocks is more likely if several conditions are met. First, it helps to have onside one or more scientific "popularizers," like David Suzuki, who can bridge the gap between environmentalism and science, packaging claims so that they appeal to editors, journalists, political leaders, and other opinion-makers. Second, success is more likely if there are positive incentives for taking action. Moral appeals can effectively direct attention toward an environmental problem, but unless there are stakeholders in undertaking a concerted program of action, the issue may fizzle out. Protecting endangered species and conserving biodiversity in the tropical rain

forest, for example, are made more attractive by the possibility that failure to do so would mean losing a wealth of as-yet-undiscovered pharmaceuticals that may be hidden there. Finally, it is crucial to recruit the support of institutional sponsors, such as the Rockefeller Foundation and the United Nations, to ensure both continuity and legitimacy, as well as financial support.

Social constructionists depict environmental problems as passing through a series of stages, from initial discovery to the waning of public interest. Earlier work in political science characterized environmental concern as inevitably proceeding through the five stages of a fixed **issue-attention cycle** (Downs, 1972). In the pre-problem stage, some highly undesirable social or environmental condition exists but has not yet captured much public attention, even though experts or interest groups may have identified it. In the second stage—"alarmed discovery and euphoric enthusiasm"—the public becomes aware of, and frightened by, the problem and is convinced that it can be solved if action is taken immediately. By the third stage, the public begins to realize the cost of significant progress and to perceive that solving the problem will not be as easy as it first seemed; solutions require money, sacrifice, and loss of benefits for some. In the fourth stage, intense public interest gradually declines as the growing realization of how difficult any solutions will be sinks in. In the final, post-problem stage, the issue moves off the public-policy agenda, although it may recapture public interest in the future.

More recent research has suggested that environmental issues rise and fall in the public eye in response to a number of different factors, including the clarity and viability of scientific evidence, the ability of environmental claims-makers to sustain a sense of dramatic crisis, and the rise of competing new environmental problems (Ungar, 1992).

A basic assumption of the social-constructionist perspective is that neither the appearance of collective values, such as those described by the alternative environmental paradigm, nor the documented existence of an actual environmental threat is sufficient, by itself, to create an environmental problem that ranks on the public agenda. For example, although tropical rain forest destruction in Malaysia is every bit as serious as its counterpart in Brazil, the latter has received extensive worldwide publicity whereas the former is rarely discussed. Rather, what is significant is the process through which environmental claims-makers pressure those who hold the reins of power to recognize definitions of environmental problems, to implement them, and to accept responsibility for solving them.

It is important to note that the social construction of environmental problems does not occur in isolation. Rather, just as socioeconomic structures influence the social distribution of risk, so the powerful in society have the ability to determine what is and what is not relevant with respect to the environment. It is this synergy between social definition and power inequality that makes social constructionism a distinctively sociological route to studying environmentalism and the environment.

SUMMARY

1. Sociological interest in the natural environment first developed in the early 1970s. Sociology's reluctance to embrace the study of the environment reflects its heritage, wherein biology and nature were banished from the discipline in favour of socially based theories of behaviour.

2. A central focus for much of the sociological examination of the environment has been the deep-seated value cleavage between environmentalists and their opponents in industry and science. The latter support a dominant social paradigm that stresses materialism, economic growth, and the human right to dominate nature. In contrast, environmentalists propose an alternative environmental paradigm that emphasizes the need to adopt small-scale, decentralized economic and political structures that are in harmony with nature. This value-oriented environmentalism has found its fullest expression in a number of "ecophilosophies"—deep ecology and ecofeminism—that have recently flourished on the margins of the environmental movement.

3. Support for environmentalism has remained remarkably constant for nearly 30 years. Although the majority of the population is generally supportive of environmental values, a young, well-educated, urban, liberal core has taken the lead in working for environmental change. Most other Canadians will recycle, purchase "green" products, and act positively toward the environment, but only to the extent that such action does not require any real sacrifice in terms of time and money.

4. To mobilize the reluctant majority, environmental-movement organizers develop frames (interpretations of events) that play up the possibility of an impending global collapse as a result of uncontrolled population growth and continued industrial growth. Global warming, expanding holes in the ozone layer, and the worldwide loss of biodiversity are the most recently identified symptoms of the impending crisis. The only solution, it is claimed, is to draw back and ease down, conserving resources, reducing pollution, and restricting population increase. However, these goals are especially difficult to achieve in the expanding economies of the developing world, where the environment is threatened by both unsustainable development and unsustainable impoverishment.

5. At the level of the local community, willingness to act on environmental problems rises as trust in expert institutions declines. This loss of trust is characteristic of neighbourhood-based environmental conflicts, in which citizens typically find the explanations and assurances offered by scientists and other authority figures to be faulty. Environmental-risk perception and action are also linked to people's participation in local social networks and community affairs.

6. The role of environmental entrepreneurs or claims-makers is vital in moving environmental issues from free-floating concerns to problems that are recognized and acted on by those in power. These promoters, situated in science, environmental organizations, and the media, define such problems as acid rain, global warming, and ozone depletion; package them; and elevate them to action agendas.

7. The social construction of environmental problems does not occur in a vacuum but is shaped by political and economic factors, to the extent that the powerful in society have the ability to act as gatekeepers, determining what is relevant with respect to the environment. Environmental problems, then, are actively contested, often on the basis of acceptable or unacceptable risk. Social constructionism in the context of power inequality represents a promising sociological route to understanding the environment-society relationship.

QUESTIONS TO CONSIDER

1. What types of environmental hazards do you and members of your community routinely face? Who do you think determines what is an acceptable level of risk in these situations? Scientists? The government? The media?

2. Analyze the environmental content of your local newspapers or television news programs for several weeks. Is environmental coverage balanced or does it favour a specific point of view? What types of media frames (interpretations of events) are used to organize information relating to environmental issues?

3. Keep a diary of all your consumer activities (shopping, transportation, leisure) for a week. Which of the products you buy and services you use are most likely to contribute to the deterioration of the environment? Which show signs of a "green" attitude among manufacturers, merchants, and service providers?

4. In the 1970s, Downs (1972) estimated that concern over the environment was about midway through the issue-attention cycle. Where in the cycle do you think it is now? What factors do you think have influenced its progression over the last three decades?

5. What is meant by the term *environmental management*? Think of some specific examples from Canadian political life in which governments have sought to use this strategy to distance themselves from environmental controversies.

GLOSSARY

The **alternative environmental paradigm** comprises a set of beliefs that challenge the centrality of economic growth, technological progress, and the human domination of nature as pillars of society. This paradigm stresses the need to adopt small-scale, decentralized economic and political structures that are in harmony with nature.

Anthropocentrism means human-centredness. It is an ideology that assumes that humans are separate from and superior to all other natural things and that judges human actions in the natural environment accordingly.

Biocentric egalitarianism is the principle, held by deep ecologists, that all things on Earth have an equal right to exist. In this view, humans have no special rights or privileges that allow them to subdue and destroy their natural surroundings.

The **broadening-base hypothesis** holds that environmental concern will eventually spread beyond its present social base—that is, of young, well-educated, urban, politically liberal citizens—to all of society.

Carrying capacity refers to the optimum population size that the planet can support under present environmental conditions.

Deep ecology is an environmental ethic emphasizing that all species are of equal value. Our experience of nature, deep ecologists claim, should be the foundation for an energetic environmentalism that opposes the present domination by rational science.

The **dominant paradigm** is a widely accepted view of the world that emphasizes the moral imperative of material-wealth creation and the moral conviction that humans have the inalienable right to dominate nature and harness the environment to that end.

Ecofeminism is an environmental ethic that sees androcentrism (male-centredness) as the root of ecological destruction. Ecofeminists identify a distinctly feminine way of thinking and acting that is nurturing, cooperative, communal, and sensitive to nature.

The **economic-contingency hypothesis** says that the broadening of the social base of environmental concern is contingent on prevailing economic conditions. When economic conditions worsen or are perceived as worsening, those who are least well off will be the first to shift their focus away from the environment to the economy.

Environmental management refers to moderate government intervention in environmental conflicts that accords limited protection to the environment without seriously curtailing economic development.

Frames are interpretations of events and their meanings. Successful framing involves diagnostic, prognostic, and motivational elements.

The **Gaia hypothesis** is a controversial idea that proposes that Earth is a living organism that adjusts and regulates itself in the same manner as does the human body.

The **human-exceptionalism paradigm** is a worldview that features the ideals of steadily evolving social progress, increasing prosperity and material comfort, and class mobility for all segments of society, while ignoring the environmental costs of economic growth.

The **issue-attention cycle** is a five-stage sequence through which the "career" of most social problems is said to pass.

Normal accidents are inevitable failures in nuclear power stations, petrochemical plants, air-traffic control nets, and other high-risk technological systems. Such accidents are regarded by corporate organizations as an inevitable consequence of operating a hazardous facility.

Risk refers to the probability that a particular hazard will occur.

Sustainable development is economic development that meets the needs of the present without compromising the ability of future generations to meet their own needs.

The **treadmill of production** is the inherent need of our economic system to continually yield profits by creating consumer demand for new products, even when this means expanding the ecosystem to its furthest limits.

SUGGESTED READING

Barlow, Maude, and Elizabeth May. (2000). *Frederick Street: Life and Death on Canada's Love Canal.* Toronto: HarperCollins. This compelling dramatic account by two well-known social activists details the struggle by residents of a Cape Breton neighbourhood to force politicians and bureaucrats to clean up what could be Canada's single worst toxic site. The final chapter provides a useful survey of other toxic hot spots across the country.

Bullard, Robert D. (1990). *Dumping in Dixie: Race, Class and Environmental Quality.* Boulder, CO: Westview Press. This pioneering study looks at the environmental impact on poor black communities in the U.S. South of locating petrochemical factories, oil refineries, hazardous waste facilities, and other sources of industrial pollution in their neighbourhoods.

Hannigan, John (2006). *Environmental Sociology,* 2nd ed. London: Routledge. This book contends that the essential ingredients of environmental sociology are questions of risk, media, science, nature, emergence, and social movements. In this accessible overview of the field, students are provided with a social-constructionist model for analyzing environmental issues that can form the basis for their own research projects.

Harrison, Kathryn, and George Hoberg. (1994). *Risk, Science and Politics: Regulating Toxic Substances in Canada and the United States.* Montreal: McGill-Queen's University Press. This is a comparative study of government regulation of toxic substances in two neighbouring countries. The authors present case studies of six controversial substances suspected of causing cancer in humans: the pesticides Alar and alachlor, urea-formaldehyde foam insulation, radon gas, saccharin, and asbestos.

WEB RESOURCES

Companion Website for This Book

http://www.newsociety6e.nelson.com
Begin by clicking on the Student Resources section of the website. Next, select the chapter you are studying from the pull-down menu. From the Student Resources page, you have easy access to InfoTrac College Edition® and other resources, such as the Glossary, Test Yourself questions, and additional readings. The website also has many useful tips to aid you in your study of sociology.

InfoTrac College Edition Search Terms

Visit http://www.infotrac-college.com for access to more than 20 million articles from nearly 6000 sources when doing your online research.

CHAPTER SEVENTEEN

SOURCE: © Monkey Business Images/Shutterstock

Health and Aging

Neena L. Chappell
UNIVERSITY OF VICTORIA

Margaret J. Penning
UNIVERSITY OF VICTORIA

In this chapter you will learn that

- People are living longer and healthier lives than they did in the past. Although this is a triumph, we tend to consider the increasing size of the older population to be a social problem that has negative implications for demands on the nation's resources.

- In contrast to generally accepted beliefs, not all aspects of health decline as we age.

- In Canada, significant inequalities in health exist. Health varies with such factors as socioeconomic position, gender, ethnicity, race, and age.

- Among elderly adults, the most common forms of health care include self-care and informal care, provided primarily by family members. Most people who provide health care are women.

- Recent years have seen an upswing in privatization and profit making in Canada's health-care system, particularly for services that are most important to elderly adults. As a result, people who are most in need of care are the least likely to gain access it and the most likely to have to rely on themselves and their family members.

CHALLENGING COMMONSENSE BELIEFS ABOUT HEALTH AND AGING

We can learn much about health and aging by reading stories of people's lives. Each story has unique features, but we can find common elements in the social factors that influence them and provide the context within which they play out. For example, Jean was born in 1925 on a small rural Manitoba farm, one of seven children of a Swedish immigrant mother and a Métis father. She graduated from high school, finished a year of teacher's college, and joined the air force to see the world. After World War II, Jean returned to her community. She met John at a local dance, dated him for a time, got pregnant, and married him. He had had a hard childhood and been forced to quit school after grade 8 to work on the family farm. Together, they settled on a small farm across the road from his parents. The farm was John's passion. He dreamed of the day when he could buy more land and make a good living for himself and his family. Until then, John worked in the local steel mill, tending to the farm during the evening and on weekends. Meanwhile, Jean supported him in his work, taking care of their children and his parents, and doing various chores on the farm when she had the time.

In 1953, John developed polio and spent the next year and a half in bed. Throughout his ordeal, Jean nursed him and cared for his parents. To make ends meet, she also worked the night shift as a nurse's aide at a local nursing home. Money was tight and there were numerous mouths to feed. With five children and another on the way, they were overjoyed when, after 12 years on the farm, they were able to add indoor plumbing. No more hand-washed diapers and no more running to the outhouse in the middle of winter! Living on a farm meant that although they could not afford much beyond necessities, there was always plenty to eat. Chickens and livestock ensured a steady supply of eggs, milk, and meat. Jean also had a big garden, and each fall she spent weeks canning and preserving fruits and vegetables to keep the family fed through the winter. She sold the best of everything, but what remained was adequate to feed the family. After she fed John and the children, Jean ate the leftovers. Although often salty and high in fat, she considered hearty food important for warmth and energy.

Over the years, economic circumstances improved as the children grew older and were able to help. Yet the years of poverty, hard work, and deprivation had

At Confederation, average life expectancy in Canada was 42 years. In 2008, it was approaching 81 years. The number of people aged 65 years and older has increased because of improved hygiene, sanitation, and nutrition, as well as health care.
SOURCE: © Monkey Business Images/Shutterstock.

left their mark. In 1991, at the age of 68, John died of a malignant brain tumour. Although no one was sure, family members speculated about whether it had anything to do with the years spent in the steel foundry and breathing the chemical sprays that kept the weeds at bay on the farm. The pension that John earned at the steel mill did not provide Jean with an income so she was forced to sell the family farm and rent an old house close to one of her daughters, whose children she cared for as her daughter worked. However, helping became increasingly difficult as Jean's health declined. After years of childbirth, Jean had varicose veins that made it painful to walk. Although she had quit smoking as soon as she heard about the problems it caused, she had developed a cough that would not go away. It left her winded, and she was unable to walk very far. For several years, she had also battled weight problems and was eventually diagnosed as having diabetes. A year after moving, Jean suffered a stroke and died. She was 69— old from the point of view of someone in his or her 20s but not in terms of the life expectancy of women in Canada. (**Life expectancy** is the number of years that the average person can expect to live.)

Jean's life story points to the many complexities we encounter when thinking about aging, health, and health care. When Jean died, people wondered aloud: Why hadn't she taken better care of herself? Why did she let her weight go? Why hadn't she quit smoking before it became such a problem? Why didn't she get more exercise? Why hadn't she sought paid work when her children were grown up? Why had she opted to live in an area far from health services? After all, she was a bright and capable woman; if any woman could look after herself, it was Jean.

The assumption that Jean should have been able to make choices that would have been more beneficial to her health ignores the complex role of social-structural factors such as social class, gender, age, ethnicity, and rural–urban residence in defining the available range of choices and their implications for health and longevity. At the time that Jean and John grew up, working-class people found it difficult to get an advanced education, particularly if they lived in rural areas and their labour was needed to support the family farm. During and after the Depression and World War II, living and working conditions were often harsh, and services or benefits, such as health care, unemployment insurance, and pensions, that might soften the impact of these conditions were often limited or nonexistent. Gender also played an important role. At the time Jean and John were married, family fortunes were generally tied to men's occupations and income levels. The fact that Jean's work was largely unpaid and that she assumed responsibility for the care of other family members, continually placing their needs (including their health) above her own, was typical of the experience of women at the time. As a Métis woman, Jean may also have experienced additional barriers in her ability to gain access to employment, health care, and other resources. By the time John died, Jean was experiencing the accumulated health effects of her earlier life circumstances. However, old age and its associated low status also appear to have played a role, possibly undermining her health further by limiting access to economic resources, affordable housing, and appropriate health care.

Sociology offers a lens through which to examine the social factors linked to people's health and longevity as they age. This chapter discusses these issues. In doing so, it brings together two areas of sociology often considered separately—the sociology of health and illness (also known as medical sociology) and the sociology of aging. One may easily connect the two: Aging tends to be equated with, and defined in terms of, ill health. Health tends to be a major problem in later life, and older adults account for much of the illness, disability, and health care utilization in any society.

We begin by focusing on individual and population aging and the role of social factors in influencing how people age. Next, we address health as people age, including the relations between social inequalities, health, health care, and aging. Finally, we examine health-related issues in Canada in the context of international and global trends in health care.

INDIVIDUAL AND POPULATION AGING

Today, most Canadians can expect to live to old age, barring accidents and wars. This was not always the case, as we can see in Table 17.1 (p. 412). In 1920, at birth, Canadian men lived to their late 50s, women to around 60. People can now expect to live more than 20 years longer than if they had been born in 1920. Once they reach age 65, they can expect to live even longer. In 2005, a 65-year-old could expect to live another 19.5 years (17.9 more if a man; 21.1 more if a woman) or to age 84.5. That is 4.1 years more than could be expected at birth. It is not until their 90s that men and women can expect to have approximately the same number of years left to live.

The fact that almost everyone can expect to live to old age distinguishes our era from earlier historical periods. In the past, some individuals lived as long as people live today, but never before has the vast majority expected to live to old age. With most of us now living to old age, it will not surprise you that older adults represent an increasing proportion of the Canadian population (see Box 17.1, p. 412). In 1921, just over 5 percent of the population was age 65 and over; this cohort is projected to constitute 20 percent of the population by 2021 (Desjardins and Dumas, 1993).

The main reason for the increasing proportion of older adults in the population is not obvious. It reflects decreases in fertility. With declines in the number and proportion of children in the population, the proportion of older persons necessarily increases. Fertility was the major predictor of population aging until the population reached a life expectancy at birth of 70 years of age. At that point, almost all young

TABLE 17.1 LIFE EXPECTANCY IN CANADA, 1920–2005

YEAR	LIFE EXPECTANCY @ BIRTH FOR WOMEN	LIFE EXPECTANCY @ 65 FOR WOMEN	LIFE EXPECTANCY @ BIRTH FOR MEN	LIFE EXPECTANCY @ 65 FOR MEN	LIFE EXPECTANCY @ BIRTH FOR TOTAL POP'N	LIFE EXPECTANCY @ 65 FOR TOTAL POP'N
1920	61	77	59	76	60	76.5
1930	62	78	60	77	61	77.5
1940	66	79.7	63	77.7	64.5	78.7
1950	71	80	66	78	68.5	79
1960	74	80.5	68	78	71	79.3
1970	76	81.5	69	78	72.5	79.8
1980	79	82.5	72	78.5	75.5	80.5
1990	81	81.5	75	81.5	78	81.5
2000	82	85.6	76.9	82.2	79.3	84.1
2005	82.7	86.1	78	82.9	80.4	84.5

SOURCES: Human Resources and Skills Development Canada (2009); Munroe (2003); Organization for Economic Co-operation and Development (2009); Statistics Canada (2003, 2006b).

persons survive. Further declines in mortality are now concentrated at the older ages (Chappell, McDonald, and Stones, 2007) resulting in relatively larger older age groups and thus contributing more to population aging. Deaths in old age usually result from chronic degenerative diseases. Circulatory diseases, including heart disease and stroke, are the major causes of death, followed by cancer, respiratory diseases, and infectious diseases (Statistics Canada, 2006a).

We now live much of our lives assuming that an extended future is before us. Consequently, forward thinking has become realistic. Most of us now have multigenerational families. Unlike in the past, young people today often know their grandparents and even their great-grandparents. Increased longevity also means that illnesses and disabilities accompanying old age are more prominent and that different demands are placed on the health-care system than was the case when fewer people lived to old age. Longer life

expectancy results in more health-care and service jobs for the younger generation. It affects when people retire and what they do after they retire. Now that mandatory retirement has disappeared from virtually all Canadian provinces, more people will likely continue to be employed into their 70s and 80s (see Figure 17.1).

How the lives of elderly people are experienced is influenced by the social construction of old age—that is, how society views elderly people. In contemporary Western societies, we tend to stereotype older persons, a tendency referred to as **ageism.** We are inclined to see elderly people as poor; frail; having no interest in, or capacity for, sexual relations; being socially isolated and lonely; and lacking a full range of abilities in the workplace. Researchers have documented ageism in students' attitudes toward older people, health-care treatment, literary and dramatic portrayals, humour, and legal processes (Chappell, McDonald, and Stones, 2007).

BOX 17.1 DEFINING OLD AGE

The most common way to define old age is to refer to all those age 65 and over. This definition arose in the late nineteenth century. Otto von Bismarck, Chancellor of Germany, chose this age for his military personnel to be eligible to receive pension benefits. The decision was made because he believed offering a pension would increase the loyalty and productivity of his men. Knowing the average life expectancy at the time, he was assured that most of his men would die

before or shortly after that age, so the pensions would cost little. After Bismarck, private and government pension plans adopted the same definition of old age. The definition took into account neither the characteristics nor the needs of older people. As people live longer and healthier lives, people increasingly question whether 65 should be the age of retirement. In the United Sates and Canada, many jurisdictions have abolished mandatory retirement.

FIGURE 17.1 CANADIAN POPULATION AGE STRUCTURE 1851–2006

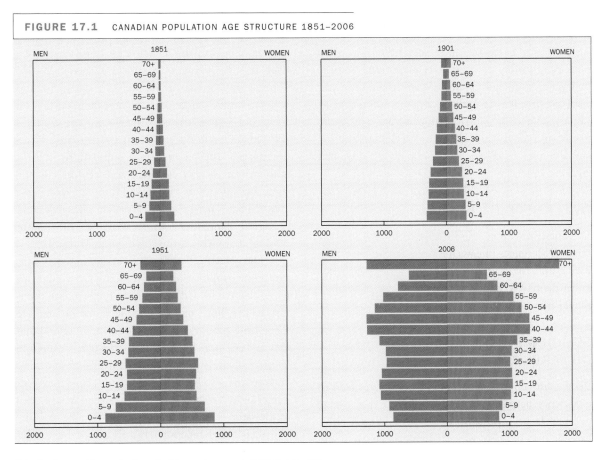

Note: Numbers are thousands of people; figure scales are constant between years.
SOURCE: Calculated from Statistics Canada data.

They have called it a "quiet epidemic" that contributes to indifference (Stones and Stones, 1997). However, ageism speaks to our treatment of older people as a social category and not necessarily to interpersonal antagonism. We may treat our grandmothers well while also referring to and treating other older adults with indifference or even contempt.

Ageism exists for several reasons. Some analysts point to the importance of structural factors, such as the segregation of young and old cohorts in society (Hagestad and Uhlenberg, 2005). However, ageist attitudes vary within cohorts. For example, students who have had positive interactions with older people and those who have learned about aging tend to have fewer negative attitudes toward elderly people as a group (Palmore, 1988; Matthews, Tindale, and Norris, 1985). This finding suggests that lack of knowledge and interaction contribute to ageism. Other researchers attribute ageism to younger people's fears of their own future (Martens, Goldenberg, and Greenberg, 2005). Old age is not only associated with death but also with declining health, both physical and, in some instances, mental. Indeed, old age has been medicalized, so aging tends to be equated with poor health or disease. **Medicalization** refers to the social and political process whereby more and more areas of life come under the authority and control of medicine (Zola, 1983). Because of the legitimacy accorded to medicine in present-day society, the appropriate response to aging (defined as disease) becomes treatment by physicians (Estes, 1979).

This outcome can be devastating. For example, there is no definitive test for dementia, but a diagnosis of Alzheimer's disease (the most common type of dementia) means that one is considered senile. There is no cure. Some elderly people suffer from depression, which often has the same symptoms as dementia and is treatable, but if doctors diagnose them with dementia, they will face stigmatization and inappropriate pharmacological treatment. Note too that not all cultures view the type of changed behaviour that tends to accompany dementia in the same manner.

The Chinese, for example, view dementia as part of normal aging and not as a signal that the individual is ineligible for participation in social life. The West places high value on cognitive functioning and the ability to reason, but Chinese culture embraces a dual concept of self that includes both mind and heart (affect). Affect is considered prior to, and more authentic than, reason. Therefore, in Chinese culture, society more readily accepts people with dementia (Ikels, 2002).

DIVERSITY IN AGING

Of course, not all people who are 65 or older are the same. Differences in class position, gender, race, ethnicity, and rural–urban living environments distinguish them. We now examine the effects of some of these differences.

SOCIOECONOMIC AND CLASS DIFFERENCES

People who enjoy socioeconomic advantages tend to experience better health and live longer than others do. This fact is especially evident in middle age but it extends into old age, when individuals generally are no longer part of the paid labour force (Mustard, Derkson, Berthelot, Wolfson, and Roos, 1997).

Economic disadvantage follows many people into old age. In 2003, 38 percent of all older (65+) unattached adults in Canada lived below the low-income cutoff (on which see Chapter 6, Social Stratification). The figure was 32 percent for unattached older males and 41 percent among unattached older females (Chappell, McDonald, and Stones, 2007). The protection of living in a family is striking—only 5.3 percent of older adults living in families were living in poverty. Having few economic resources affects one's everyday life in profound ways: everything from the type of house and neighbourhood you live in to the schools you attend, the food you eat, the people you associate with, the leisure activities and vacations you can afford, whether you have a car, a pension, investments, and much else. We carry all of these experiences into later life and, as we will see, they have important implications for our health.

GENDER

Some researchers consider aging a women's issue for good reason. There are more elderly women than there are elderly men, and the gender imbalance increases in older age cohorts. For example, in 2006, 56 percent of those aged 65 and over in Canada were women. The comparable figure for those aged 80 and over was 65 percent (Statistics Canada, 2007b). Women live longer than men do partly because women are the hardier sex, biologically speaking, but social and economic reasons are also important. Thus, the female–male difference in the **mortality rate** (deaths per 1000 people in a population) is lower among more highly educated and wealthier people than among others (Rogers, Hummer, and Nam, 2000). That is partly because working-class men often engage in dangerous jobs, such as construction and mining, that increase the risk of an early death.

The gender difference in mortality rates has other important implications. It means that women are more likely to be widowed, not to remarry, and therefore to live alone or in a nursing home in later life. They tend to be grandparents for a longer period than men and are more likely to be poor in old age, not only because of their general lower earning power when younger but also because their savings have to cover a longer time. Women are likely to have more age peers in the same situation and are therefore able to maintain their social support networks into old age. Men tend to die before their spouses do because they have shorter life expectancies and because they tend to marry women younger than they are. Men who outlive their wives are more likely to remarry than are women who outlive their husbands. That is because, late in life, there are more unmarried women than men who are available as potential partners. Because it is more socially acceptable for men to marry younger women than it is for women to marry younger men, there is an even larger pool of potential partners from which elderly men can choose. However, if they do not remarry, elderly men appear to be at greater risk of social isolation because they are less likely to maintain social support networks than women are. Women are often the "kin keepers" in society, whereas men tend to rely on their wives for social connectedness.

ETHNICITY AND RACE

Like gender, ethnicity and race represent fundamental organizing principles of society that are pervasive, socially constructed, and operate throughout the life course. Their effects are evident in the lack of social, economic, and political power of some racial and ethnic minorities. Among Canadian seniors, there are more foreign-born individuals than there are in the younger population. In 2006, 19.8 percent of Canada's total population was foreign-born compared to 28 percent of the older adult (65+) population. Most foreign-born seniors immigrated to Canada when they were younger. Thus, the ethnocultural composition of our older adult population is heavily influenced by the immigration policies that were in effect in the past. For example, half a century ago, the government granted entry mainly to English- and French-speaking people from Europe and other Western countries. Most visible minority group members came to Canada only in recent decades. Thus, in 2006, only 8.5 percent of seniors were members of visible minority groups (see Box 17.2).

Aboriginal seniors comprise fewer than 5 percent of Canada's total Aboriginal population because of high fertility rates and high mortality rates (and therefore shorter life expectancies; see Figure 17.2, p. 416). However, it is expected that the number of seniors in the Aboriginal population will more than double by 2017 and will represent about 6.5 percent of the population at that time (Statistics Canada, 2005b). These older adults are more likely to live on reserves than younger Aboriginal people are, raising questions about the availability of appropriate care to older adults. Reserves, like most other rural locations across the country, see young adults leave for educational and employment opportunities in urban settings; most do not return.

APOCALYPTIC DEMOGRAPHY

Demography is the study of the characteristics of populations and the dynamics of population change. The belief that a demographic trend, such as population aging, has drastic negative consequences for society is

sometimes called *apocalyptic demography* (Gee, 2000). Apocalyptic demography reduces the complex issue of an aging population to the notion that society cannot afford a growing percentage of elderly people. In this view, the increasing proportion of elderly adults places tremendous strain on government-financed services, especially medicare, so government debt and deficits rise to dangerous levels. At the same time, most elderly adults are supposedly well off, and can afford to pay for such services themselves. It follows that we can and should dismantle or at least cut back on social services. If we don't, the country could go bankrupt.

The problem with such apocalyptic thinking is that it draws inappropriate conclusions from nonfacts. In the first place, we *can* afford better social services for the elderly. That is partly because economic productivity is increasing—over time, each Canadian produces more goods and services—and partly because the proportion of young people is decreasing as fast as the proportion of elderly people is increasing. Apocalyptic thinkers also ignore government statistics showing that, by any reasonable definition of the term, fewer than half of Canada's elderly population is well to do. In fact, nearly half of elderly women without a spouse live in poverty. Finally, although we spend much money on pensions and health care, population aging accounts for only a small part of future health-care costs and will require little increase in public expenditures (Evans, McGrail, Morgan, Barer, and Hertzman, 2001). Costs for Canada's health-care system are increasing, but mainly because of the rising price of pharmaceuticals and biotechnology rather than aging. In short, apocalyptic demography does not withstand a careful review of the evidence.

BOX 17.2	VISIBLE MINORITY SENIORS

Canadian immigration policy defines various categories of immigrants, including independent immigrants with educational and professional skills, close relatives of citizens and permanent residents of Canada, and business immigrants with substantial investment capital. Among those younger than 65 years of age, fully 35 percent of recent immigrants were born in Asia and another 12 percent in Africa or the Caribbean (Citizenship and Immigration Canada, 1999). This means that future generations of Canadian seniors will be much more ethnically and racially diverse than is true today.

Approximately 6000 older adults (65+) immigrate to this country every year, most often as family-class immigrants. Most of them are of non-European origin. Because members of their family sponsor them, their economic resources tend to be modest and they are not eligible for Old Age Security until after they have resided in Canada for 10 years. Many of them cannot communicate in English or French. For example, in one study of urban Chinese-Canadian seniors, 83 percent chose to be interviewed in Cantonese, fewer than 25 percent spoke English well, and only 3 percent chose to be interviewed in English (Chappell, 2005).

FIGURE 17.2   ABORIGINAL AND NON-ABORIGINAL POPULATION AGE, 2006 (PERCENTAGE)

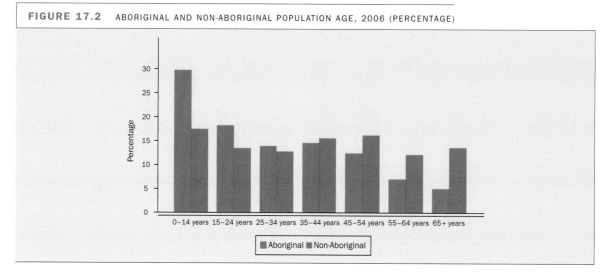

SOURCE: Statistics Canada, 2008, *Aboriginal Peoples in Canada in 2006: Inuit, Metis and First Nations, 2006 Census.* Ottawa: Ministry of Industry. Catalogue no. 97-558-XIE.

HEALTH AND OLD AGE

People often equate old age with declining health. Although the equation is valid with regard to physical health, it is less true of psychological and emotional health and of social well-being.

With advancing age, about 77 percent of men and 85 percent of women aged 65 and over suffer from at least one **chronic condition**—a persistent physical or mental health problem (Gilmour and Park, 2005). The most common chronic conditions are arthritis and rheumatism, eye problems, such as cataracts or glaucoma, back problems, heart disease, and diabetes (Gilmour and Park, 2005). Such conditions do not necessarily interfere with day-to-day functioning. Fewer older adults encounter limitations on activities than prevalence figures for chronic conditions suggest. For example, many people of all ages wear glasses because of deteriorating eyesight but function well with corrective lenses. Similarly, when people with diabetes take their medication and follow appropriate nutritional and exercise regimens, they generally cope well. Many people with high blood pressure feel no effects; often they do not know they have the disease. A **functional disability** exists when a health problem interferes with day-to-day functioning. About one-third of adults age 65+ (25 percent of men and 34 percent of women) experience restrictions in their daily activities because of health problems. This figure rises to 40 percent among those aged 75 and over.

Pain is an important area of physical health that is not captured when examining disease, chronic conditions, and functional disability. Pain is a problem for many but certainly not all elderly adults. In Canada, 25 percent of people aged 65 and over suffer from chronic pain or discomfort. This increases to 29 percent among those aged 75 and over. Some 84 percent of people suffering from chronic pain take some form of medication for their pain, either prescription or over-the-counter (Statistics Canada, 2004).

Mental or brain disorders are viewed as diseases by the medical profession. Often, they have physical causes. Dementia is an example. In Canada, 6 to 8 percent of adults 65+ have dementia (Canadian Study of Health and Aging, 1994). About three-quarters of elderly adults with dementia live in long-term care facilities. As is true of other illnesses, the "old old" (variously defined as those aged 75+, 80+, or 85+) are more likely to have this illness; about 20 percent of those aged 80 and over have some form of dementia.

A correlation exists between mental and physical health. People in better physical health tend to enjoy better mental health. Therefore, as people age and their physical health declines, one would expect their mental health to decline. Paradoxically, however, elderly adults do not have poorer mental health than members of younger age cohorts do (Statistics Canada, 2007b). Although physical health deteriorates as people age, older adults tend to rate their general health as good, very good, or excellent (73 percent overall, with little difference between men and women). For those aged

75 and over, the overall figure is 68 percent (Statistics Canada, 2007b). A similar picture is evident if we examine measures of psychological well-being. Those aged 75 and over are three times as likely as 18- and 19-year-olds to score high on a sense of coherence (that is, to view their lives as meaningful, events as comprehensible, and challenges as manageable). Self-esteem and feelings of mastery or control also seem to improve with age, peaking in middle age, followed by modest declines in later life (Statistics Canada, 2001, 2007b). According to a recent national survey, fully 90 percent of adults 65+ reported being satisfied with their lives. The figure was 84 percent among 15–24 year olds (Statistics Canada, 2005a). It is unclear why elderly adults often have such good psychological health despite having to cope with worse physical health than younger people. Perhaps they have learned to cope with the exigencies of life or they compare themselves with those who are worse off (including those who have died); or perhaps the importance of material and physical matters wanes over the course of time.

We find the same type of situation when we examine the social lives of seniors, which tend to be healthy and characterized by social integration, not social isolation. A minority of elderly adults, particularly those who are poor, very old, or physically frail, are vulnerable to social isolation. However, most are embedded in **modified extended family** networks characterized by mutual and close intergenerational ties, responsible filial behaviour, and contact between the generations (Litwak, 1960). Sociological research conducted since the 1970s has debunked the notion that families abandon their older members. Most elderly adults enjoy extensive social contacts, live close to at least one of their children, and can name friends and confidantes (Antonucci, 1990).

Although sociologists of health and aging often focus on the problems of old age, and particularly on how elderly adults can prevent, delay, and cope with declining physical health, they also study quality of life. They want to know how society can ensure that old age is a stage of life when individuals are valued and consider their lives worthwhile. This focus has led to an interest in increasing the number of years of life that are free from disability. According to the **compression of morbidity hypothesis** (Fries, 1983), Western industrialized nations are successfully postponing the age of onset of chronic disability. Many analysts think that eventually we will all be able to live relatively healthy lives until very shortly before death, when our bodies will deteriorate rapidly. Until recently, evidence on this

subject was contradictory (Hayward, Crimmins, and Saito, 1998; Roos, Havens, and Black, 1993). However, recent research suggests that although we are far from a dependency-free old age, Canadians nonetheless are experiencing a later age of onset of functional limitations. (However, the same is not necessarily true of chronic illnesses, such as diabetes.) This is good news, especially if the trend continues. To do so, it would probably need to occur in all segments of the population. Unfortunately, the vagaries of old age are not evenly distributed, as you will now learn.

INEQUALITY, HEALTH, AND AGING

Research suggests that in recent decades the declining death rate has been steeper in some segments of the population than in others (Schalick, Hadden, Pamuk, Navarro, and Pappas, 2000). In general, people with more education, income, and wealth live longer than others do. They also tend to spend a greater proportion of their lives in good health.

Education

People with more education are able to avoid or postpone disability to a greater extent than those with less education, although education may be of less benefit once disability is present (Huisman et al., 2005). People with a university degree often feel healthy and function well late into their 60s, 70s, and 80s, whereas those with less education do not (Ross and Wu, 1996). A recent Canadian study focused on changes in health over a three-year period among adults aged 50 and over, all of whom were in good health in the first year. It found that the likelihood of remaining in good health was greater among men and women in the highest educational and income groups (Buckley, Denton, Robb, and Spencer, 2005).

Income

Income is also important to health; it has been estimated that 23 percent of **premature mortality** (that is, years of potential life lost) among Canadians is linked to income differences (Raphael, 2005). One report shows that men with the lowest 5 percent of earnings before retirement are twice as likely to die between 65 and 70 years of age as men with the highest 5 percent of earnings. High-income earners (using various definitions) experience considerably more years of good health than those with lower incomes (also defined variously), with some reporting as much as a 12-year difference (Segall and Chappell, 2000). The pattern holds among elderly adults. Low-income elderly adults with disabilities tend to be more functionally disabled than their high-income counterparts are. As a result, even though people with low income are less likely to live to old age, those who do so are more likely to be institutionalized in long-term care facilities than those with higher income are (Trottier, Martel, Houle, Berthelot, and Légaré, 2000).

Gender

Although women tend to live longer than men do, they are generally found to be less healthy than men are. Thus, women report more multiple health problems associated with chronic conditions, such as arthritis and rheumatism, high blood pressure, back problems, and allergies (Chappell, McDonald, and Stones, 2007). Among elderly women, 85 percent report one or more chronic conditions, compared to 78 percent of elderly men. Although the likelihood of disability increases with age for both men and women, women are more likely to report limitations in activities of daily living or disability in later life than men are (Gilmour and Park, 2005). Women also report more severe disability than men do. That is, although men have lower life expectancy, they live a greater proportion of their lives without disabling conditions. While recent evidence suggests that men and women experience similar levels of mental health problems, they manifest them differently—for example, as depression in women and as alcohol and drug abuse and suicidal behaviour in men (Simon, 2000).

Race, Ethnicity, and Immigration Status

In Canada, big differences exist in the health and well-being of Aboriginal versus non-Aboriginal adults. Although the gap appears to have decreased somewhat in recent years, the life expectancy of Aboriginal Canadians currently remains six years shorter than that of non-Aboriginal Canadians (Cooke, Mitrou, Lawrence, Guimond, and Beavon, 2007). Differences are also evident within the Canadian Aboriginal population (see Figure 17.3). Aboriginal populations also suffer from more chronic illnesses and disabilities, including heart disease and diabetes, than non-Aboriginals do (Anand et al., 2001). In 2001, 70 percent of Aboriginal adults aged 65 and over reported one or more disabilities, including difficulties hearing, seeing, walking, climbing stairs, bending, and doing various other activities, nearly twice the rate for non-Aboriginal people of the same age (Statistics Canada, 2007b). Although most elderly Canadian adults rate their health as excellent or very good, fewer than one-half of non-reserve Aboriginal adults over the age of 64 report having excellent or very good health.

Reasons for these differences in health and life expectancy are numerous. In Aboriginal populations, death from infectious and parasitic diseases is associated with inadequate housing and unsanitary conditions. According to one government report, 75 percent of Aboriginal community water systems pose a high or medium risk to water quality (Indian and Northern Affairs Canada, 2003). Suicide rates are also high, as are death rates from drowning, fire,

---

FIGURE 17.3   ABORIGINAL AND NON-ABORIGINAL CANADIANS' LIFE EXPECTANCY AT BIRTH BY SEX, 1991 AND 2001

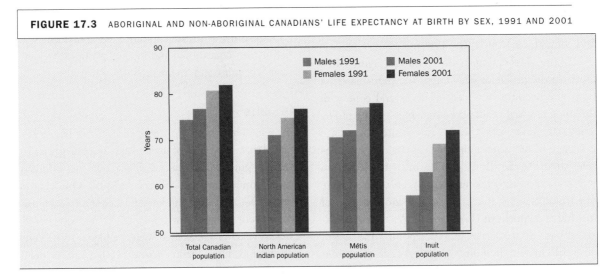

SOURCE: Statistics Canada, 2007, *A Portrait of Seniors in Canada, 2006.* Ottawa: Minister of Industry, Catalogue no. 89-519-XIE, p. 224.

The life expectancy of Aboriginal Canadians is about six years shorter than that of non-Aboriginal Canadians.
SOURCE: PhotoDisc.

homicide, and motor vehicle accidents (Allard, Wilkins, and Berthelot, 2004). Racism and discrimination increase risks of psychological distress, depression, and unemployment, and lack of access to opportunities and resources is conducive to poor health (Noh, Beiser, Kaspar, Hou and Rummens, 1999).

Health inequities are also evident when we compare other ethnic and racial groups. Health and longevity vary widely from one country to the next (see Table 17.2). Less than one-quarter of Canadians

aged 65 and over who were born in Canada or in the United States, Europe, Australia, and Asia tend to report fair or poor health. This percentage is considerably higher (about 33 percent) among those born in Central and South America and Africa (Chappell, McDonald, and Stones, 2007). Interestingly, however, immigrants, especially recent arrivals, generally enjoy better health than their Canadian-born counterparts, a pattern observed to varying degrees for such health outcomes as chronic diseases, disability, dependency, life expectancy, and disability-free life expectancy (Chen, Ng, and Wilkins, 1996). This **healthy immigrant effect** may seem surprising at first glance. However, it likely reflects the Canadian government requirement that potential immigrants meet a minimum standard of health before they are admitted to the country. Immigrants who have lived in Canada for a long period do not have a similar advantage. Does this mean that immigrants' health tends to decline after immigration? In fact, this seems to be what is taking place (Pérez, 2002). The search is on for explanations of this phenomenon. Most analysts focus on the negative health implications of changes in diet and activity levels, discrimination, declines in income and other resources, and difficulties in accessing

TABLE 17.2   LIFE EXPECTANCY AT BIRTH AND AT AGE 60 FOR SELECTED COUNTRIES WITH HIGH AND LOW LIFE EXPECTANCY, 2002–2006

COUNTRY OR AREA	YEAR	LIFE EXPECTANCY AT BIRTH		LIFE EXPECTANCY AT AGE 60	
		WOMEN	MEN	WOMEN	MEN
Japan[1]	2005–2010	86	79	28	22
China, Hong Kong[1]	2005–2010	85	79	27	22
Australia[3]	2005–2010	84	79	26	22
France[2]	2005–2010	84	77	26	21
Sweden[2]	2005–2010	83	79	25	21
Canada[4]	**2005–2010**	**83**	**78**	**25**	**22**
United Kingdom[2]	2005–2010	82	77	24	20
United States of America[4]	2005–2010	81	76	24	20
Kenya[6]	2005–2010	55	53	17	15
Rwanda[6]	2005–2010	48	45	16	14
Afghanistan[1]	2005–2010	44	44	14	13
Zimbabwe[6]	2005–2010	43	44	16	13
Mozambique[6]	2005–2010	42	42	16	13
Swaziland[6]	2005–2010	39	40	15	12

Notes: [1]Asia, [2]Europe, [3]Oceania, [4]North America, [5]South America, [6]Africa

SOURCE: United Nations, Department of Economic & Social Affairs, Population Division (2007), *World Population Prospects: 2006 Revision.* CD-Rom Edition— Comprehensive Dataset (United Nations); supplemented by official national statistics published in *Demographic Yearbook 2005,* available from the United Nations Statistics Division website, http://unstats.un.org/unsd/demographic/products/indwm/tab3a.htm (November 2008).

420   PART FIVE   •   CHANGE AND CONFLICT

health-care services in the years following immigration (Gee, Kobayashi, and Prus, 2004).

EXPLAINING SOCIAL INEQUALITIES IN HEALTH

What is it about age, gender, ethnicity, race, social class, and other inequalities that result in poorer health? Early research focused on biological explanations and on differences associated with health services use, including differences in the likelihood that people would follow doctors' orders and inequalities in access to health-care services. Indeed, the view that creating a universally equitable health-care system would eliminate or at least reduce health inequalities was a major argument for the creation of a universal health-care system in this country. More recently, evidence indicating that inequalities in health and longevity have persisted despite the introduction of a universal health-care system has led to renewed attempts to account for such differences (Crompton, 2000). Some researchers have offered explanations that are specific to one or another type of inequality. Others have focused on explanations associated with many sources of inequality. In general, the literature highlights three types of explanations— one focusing on individual health behaviours and lifestyles, one on social psychological resources, and one on material conditions and resources.

Many researchers argue that inequalities in health reflect the impact of individual lifestyle choices, including decisions about consuming tobacco, alcohol, and food, and getting exercise.

One survey asked Canadians what the major determinants of health are. The most common responses referred to factors like those just listed (Canadian Institute for Health Information, 2005).

Although research finds a link between social location and lifestyle factors, sociologists often criticize such explanations because they ignore how social inequalities typically trump individual decisions in determining health outcomes. Thus, studies comparing the importance of individual decisions against social factors, such as income adequacy, routinely find that the latter are more important (House, 2001; Williamson, 2000). Moreover, when researchers focus on individual decision making, they often neglect the fact that people rarely make choices freely from a full range of possible options. We can criticize low-income earners for failing to exercise more, but only if we ignore that they may live in neighbourhoods where an evening jog is dangerous, affordable recreational facilities don't exist,

When surveyed, Canadians identified a person's smoking, eating, weight, experience of stress, and exercise habits as the major determinants of health.
SOURCE: © Neil Roy Johnson/Shutterstock.

and lack of child-care options means they have little time for such pursuits in any event. As this example shows, social inequalities structure choices. Attending only to individual decision making often amounts to blaming victims for structured inequalities.

A second explanation for how social location generates health inequalities draws attention to the role of stress and other psychosocial factors, including depression and perceptions of relative deprivation. From this perspective, inequality and lack of access to economic and other resources generate stress, leading to poor health. In addition, some analysts argue that more than poverty is at work here. They note that if poverty were the only problem, we would expect to find substantial differences in health between the poor and the non-poor, but little or no difference between those who are only moderately well off versus those who are wealthy. Yet this is not the case. Instead, each increment in education and income brings additional health advantages. This finding suggests that it is not just poverty but the *perception* of inequality that leads to bad health. This is the **hierarchy stress perspective,** which suggests that when people compare their situation with that of others and see their situation negatively, they experience stress and their health declines (Link and Phelan, 2000). In addition to causing poor health, stress can operate indirectly by leading people to smoke tobacco, consume too much alcohol, eat too much or too little, sleep too little, and take dangerous drugs—all of which eventually have a negative impact on health in their own right (Link and Phelan, 2000).

NEL

Finally, we arrive at explanations that emphasize resources and material conditions as the mechanisms linking people's social location to health outcomes. Such arguments hold that one's social class, age, gender, race, ethnicity, and so on, contribute to differential access to a range of resources that contribute to good or poor health. These resources include enough income to buy nutritious food, enough education to be aware of health issues, such as what constitutes a nutritious diet, access to means of illness prevention, the ability to avoid risk factors, such as living in environments where dangerous chemicals are present, and so on (Link and Phelan, 2000). Some researchers operating in this tradition insist that we should focus less on the resources that contribute to good or poor health and more on the way social class, age, gender, race, and ethnicity, directly contribute to "systematic material, social, cultural, and political exclusion from mainstream society" (Raphael, 2005: 4; see Box 17.3). These structural factors are the fundamental causes of health status, influencing access to health-related resources (Link and Phelan, 2000).

Debate continues regarding whether individual behaviours and lifestyle characteristics, stress and other psychosocial factors, or material conditions and resources are important for understanding inequalities in health. The answer may well be "all of the above." As one study notes, "material conditions are intimately tied to psychological states, health behaviors, and social circumstances that also influence health," and we can see "these psychosocial states and health behaviors . . . as responses to adverse conditions imposed by broader social and economic structures" (Lynch and Kaplan, 2000: 25).

INTERSECTING INEQUALITIES AND HEALTH OVER THE LIFE COURSE

Increasingly, sociologists are interested in the effects of multiple statuses on health outcomes. For example, the **age as leveller hypothesis** argues that age effects cut across all other statuses, in effect levelling inequalities from earlier in life.

The competing **multiple jeopardy hypothesis** argues that the effects of membership in multiple low-status groups is cumulative. Thus, being female and old has more negative consequences that being either female *or* old (Markides, 1983). More recently,

---

BOX 17.3	WHICH TIPS FOR BETTER HEALTH ARE CONSISTENT WITH THE EVIDENCE?

Governments, health associations, and health workers give the public a host of messages related to health issues. Traditional health tips focus on individual decision making and assume that ordinary people are entirely free to decide what to do with their lives. A second set of health tips takes a sociological approach and is more consistent with available evidence on the determinants of health. Contrast the two sets of messages below.

Traditional, individualistic tips for better health:

1. Don't smoke. If you can, stop. If you can't, cut down.
2. Eat a balanced diet with plenty of fruit and vegetables.
3. Keep physically active.
4. Manage stress by, for example, talking things through, and making time to relax.
5. If you drink alcohol, do so in moderation.
6. Cover up in the sun, and protect children from sunburn.
7. Practice safe sex.
8. Use cancer-screening opportunities.
9. Be safe on the roads.
10. Learn the first aid ABCs: airway, breathing, circulation.

Ten sociological tips for better health:

1. Don't be poor. If you can, stop. If you can't, try not to be poor for long.
2. Don't have poor parents.
3. Don't own a car.
4. Don't work in a stressful, low-paid manual job.
5. Don't live in damp, low-quality housing.
6. Be able to afford to go on a foreign holiday.
7. Don't become unemployed.
8. Use all benefits you are entitled to if you are unemployed, retired, or sick or have a disability.
9. Don't live next to a busy road or near a polluting factory.
10. Learn how to fill in the complex housing benefit/asylum application forms before you become homeless and destitute.

By contrasting these two sets of health tips, we do not mean to suggest that people lack all choice, only that choices are socially structured.

SOURCE: D. Raphael, 2005, *Social Determinants of Health: Canadian Perspectives,* Toronto: Canadian Scholars' Press, p. 13. Reprinted by permission of Canadian Scholars' Press Inc.

researchers have argued that statuses cannot simply be added together to judge their effects. Instead, statuses intersect and interact, and we cannot fully understand them apart from one other (McMullin, 2004). For example, occupations influence health but do so differently for men and women. Living in poverty has a stronger negative effect on women's health than on men's health (Prus and Gee, 2002). As a result, the greatest differences in life expectancy between men and women occur in the poorest areas (DesMeules, Manuel, and Cho, 2004). Similarly, the gap in perceived health status of Aboriginal people and the total Canadian population widens in older age groups (Statistics Canada, 2003).

On the other hand, some factors shrink health inequalities later in life. For example, the gap in health between upper and lower income groups increases as people reach their middle years (40s, 50, and 60s) and declines thereafter (Martel, Bélanger, Berthelot, and Carrière, 2005). Does this mean that socioeconomic inequalities in health diminish with age? This seems unlikely because many poor people die before reaching old age, a fact that comparisons of the health status of survivors ignores.

Finally, we note that, as a person ages, the social and economic factors that influence health change. According to the **life course perspective,** the circumstances of later life *and* those of early life combine to influence what happens to health in later life.

HEALTH CARE

Our views concerning the causes of health problems influence how we deal with them. If we see the health problems of older adults as the result of what happens only in later life, we will target interventions to older adults. If we adopt a life course perspective and conclude that many of the health problems of elderly adults have their roots in lifelong experiences with poverty, inequality, and lack of access to social, economic, and other resources, we will want to address what happens earlier in life as well. If we attribute health problems to personal behaviours and see these as freely chosen, we will consider older adults responsible for their own health problems and will likely implement solutions aimed at educating people, hoping they will make different choices in the future; or we will demand that people deal with the problems they themselves have created. If we attribute health inequalities to perceptions of stress, we may focus our energies on altering how people view their circumstances rather than

changing the circumstances themselves. Finally, if we see the organization of society and the distribution of economic and social resources as the main determinants of health, we will likely direct attention to economic and social policies as a means of improving health (Raphael, 2005). How then do Canadians deal with health care?

SELF-CARE AND INFORMAL CARE

Before turning to this topic, note that most people care for themselves most of the time; **self-care** is the primary form of care even when health declines and we require help from others and the health-care system. We wash our hands, exercise, choose what to eat, establish any number of lifestyle practices, try to have a positive attitude toward life, and select health-care providers.

Except in emergencies, we generally turn first to family members and friends when we need help as a result of our health. This is as true in old age as it is when we are young. Indeed, throughout history,

Responsibility for the care of older adults falls to an informal network of family members in virtually all developed countries, regardless of what type of health-care system is available.
SOURCE: Shutterstock.

networks of family members and friends have been the first resource for care.

Despite what you may hear about modern, Western societies such as Canada being individualistic, youth-oriented, and dismissive of the elderly, we continue to care for older family members in need. Sociologists estimate that in nearly all developed societies about three-quarters of all care to elderly adults comes from family members and, to a lesser degree, friends (Kane, 1990). It is, first of all, the spouse who provides care when the health of the other spouse fails. Typically, the wife first provides care for her husband because men have a shorter life expectancy and women tend to marry men a few years older than them. As a result, the husband's health often begins to fail before that of his wife and his wife is usually available to care for him in his last years.

After the husband's death, the wife may enjoy a few more years of good health before she needs assistance. In this situation, it tends to be her children, typically daughters, who provide most of the care before her death. Notice that informal caring comes primarily from wives and daughters. Sons provide mainly financial assistance and advice, while daughters provide mainly emotional support and hands-on caring. However, if no daughter is available and a son is close by, then the son usually steps in and provides the necessary care (Keating, Fast, Frederick, Cranswick, and Perrier, 1999). This is possible because the great majority of elderly adults live close to at least one child.

Usually, families assume responsibility for elderly care readily. Research has put to rest the myth that families in contemporary Western societies abandon their elderly (Montgomery, Borgatta, and Borgatta, 2000). Moreover, despite what we have been hearing for many years about changing family forms, more and more women working in the paid labour force, fewer children being available to provide help, and greater geographic mobility, there is no indication that families are decreasing involvement in senior care.

FORMAL MEDICAL AND HOME CARE

Often, family members cannot provide all the care loved ones need. Sometimes care calls for specialized knowledge, skill, medicine, and equipment that only physicians and other health care personnel can provide. Sometimes, the sheer amount of time and effort required to care for loved ones exceeds the family's capabilities. At such times, people turn to the formal health-care system. Canada's publicly funded health-care system, like the health-care systems of other rich countries (the United States excepted), offers universal access to physician and acute care hospital services for its citizens based on need rather than the ability to pay. In Canada, this system is known as medicare.

A Brief History of Medicare

Prior to the establishment of medicare, people needing health care were required to pay for it or do without. This situation was especially problematic for poor people whose health needs were great—among them a disproportionately large number of the elderly, the unemployed, and the chronically disabled. In Canada, gaps in access to health care were particularly apparent in the years that followed World War I and the Depression of the 1930s. With Tommy Douglas, the leader of the CCF party and premier of Saskatchewan, leading the way, Canada gradually introduced legislation to address these needs. In 1957, the Hospital Insurance and Diagnostic Services Act was introduced, leading to hospital care coverage for the entire population. In 1966, the Medical Care Act was passed, laying the groundwork for universal health insurance for physician services. By 1972, all Canadian provinces and territories had joined the program. At that time, the federal government agreed to a 50/50 cost sharing arrangement with the provinces for both physician and hospital services.

From the outset, health care in Canada was structured as a provincial responsibility. The federal government develops policy and assists with funding services, but each province is responsible for delivering services. Through medicare, every province offers physician and acute care hospital services at no out-of-pocket cost to its residents. Services are publicly funded. This does not mean that we have "socialized medicine." Rather, a third party (the government) pays for most services on our behalf. Most physicians in Canada operate as private entrepreneurs; governments pay them for the services that they decide are necessary and that they render. In other words, we publicly finance health care but physicians provide it privately. The more services physicians provide, the more they earn. The difference between their jobs and those of other private entrepreneurs is that their incomes are virtually guaranteed. They hold this privileged position because of the importance society attaches to their specialized expertise, which makes them the gatekeepers to our health-care system. Only physicians can order medical tests, prescribe certain drugs, admit us to hospital, and certify that we are sick.

Historically, Canada structured its health-care system mainly to provide physician-dominated medical care in physicians' offices and hospitals. We defined health as the absence of disease, excluding from coverage preventative measures and those that took a broad view of health as a state of physical, social, and psychological well-being. We did not cover home care, the services of chiropractors and physiotherapists, and drugs prescribed outside hospital. In 2006, health-care expenditures in Canada totalled $151.3 billion, 70 percent of which was paid for by public sources (i.e., government). Most of these funds (69 percent) were used to cover the cost of physicians and other medical professionals, hospitals, and drugs. Another 10 percent went to other health-care institutions, such as nursing homes and psychiatric hospitals, while 21 percent covered all other health-care expenditures, including public health, home care, building costs, equipment, administration, and so on (Canadian Institute for Health Information, 2008).

The availability of many types of health care, such as home care, nursing homes, physiotherapy, home nursing, counselling, chiropractic services, podiatry, and massage therapy, varies across provinces. Some provinces provide these services as part of their health-care system at no cost to the user. Others provide them at minimal cost or on a means-tested basis. In the latter case, people's finances are assessed, and if they can afford a required service, they pay for it. Otherwise, the government subsidizes the cost. Access to such services also varies—for example, some places require a physician referral while others permit self-referral. Services also vary across regions within provinces.

Home Care Services in an Aging Society

Although different health services are important to different people at different times, one type of health service that is especially important in an aging society is home care It brings services into people's homes to help them live there rather than move to a nursing home. Most people, including older adults, prefer living in their own home as opposed to a long-term care facility. Adequate home-care services are critically important because they allow older individuals to remain independent. That is their preference, and it is also much less expensive that maintaining them in nursing homes (Chappell, Havens, Hollander, Miller, and McWilliam, 2004; Hollander and Chappell, 2001).

Typically, home care includes nursing, physiotherapy, and housekeeping services. It can also include adult daycare and respite services. Home nursing and physiotherapy services notwithstanding, home care is not primarily about providing medical care. Instead, it offers social care that a medical condition prevents us from providing for ourselves. Within home care, housekeeping is considered a health service because as people become increasingly frail, they are often unable to do housework without risking injury. For some services, such as adult daycare, the person leaves the home for a few hours one or two days a week. Adult daycare offers socialization and stimulation. It also offers necessary respite for family members. For many elderly adults, staying in their own homes requires not only home care but also the presence of an unpaid caregiver. If an unpaid caregiver is not available, their only option may be to go to a nursing home.

Despite its importance, home care receives relatively little governmental funding. Instead, we have deeply entrenched the medical focus on physicians and acute care hospitals. Home care lies outside medicare. Today, most provinces favour a system in which about half the cost of home care is borne by government-subsidized nonprofit agencies and the other half by patients who buy services from for-profit businesses.

HEALTH-CARE SYSTEM CHANGE AND REFORM

In the years following the establishment of medicare, the cost of health care rose. Federal and provincial governments responded by trying to contain costs. By the 1980s, the federal government had shifted away from its 50/50 cost sharing agreement with the provinces. The provinces began experimenting with user fees and extra billing to offset federal funding cuts. In response to these experiments, in 1984, the federal government passed the Canada Health Act. It required the provinces to maintain certain standards, including universal coverage, reasonable access to services, portability of benefits across provinces and territories, comprehensive services, and nonprofit administration by a public agency. It also banned user fees and extra billing. Fiscal concerns nevertheless remained. In the late 1980s and 1990s, the provinces, territories, and the federal government further restricted health-care spending and appointed commissions to review their health-care systems and recommend reform. During this period, public debate erupted around the viability of a publicly funded health-care system, and within government the discussion broadened from financing to whether we needed a different type of health-care system. For the first time since the introduction of medicare, Canadian citizens and governments asked whether the right providers were providing the right services to the right people.

Without denying the importance of medical care by physicians, nearly all of the reviews of the health-care system carried out in the 1980s and 1990s reached the same conclusion. We need to shift away from a system that is almost entirely biomedically focused and concerned only with the treatment and cure of disease. We must pay more attention to a broader conception of care that incorporates health promotion and disease prevention—acknowledging health as "a state of complete physical, mental, and social well-being and not merely the absence of disease or infirmity" (World Health Organization, 1948). Deinstitutionalizing health services and providing more care outside hospitals was a big part of the recommended reorientation.

Major reforms followed. Most provinces regionalized health-care services, yielding authority to subprovincial health boards. Fewer people received acute and extended care. Hospital admissions fell. Length of hospital stays dropped. Many surgical treatments moved to outpatient settings (Brownell, Roos, and Roos, 2001; Carriere, Roos, and Dover, 2000). Still, major components of the recommended reforms have yet to be adopted (Lewis, Donaldson, Mitton and Currie, 2001). For example, there is little evidence of an expanded focus on health promotion and disease prevention. While home-care budgets have increased, it appears that funds are being directed mainly to short-term post-hospital and nursing care rather than meeting the long-term chronic care needs of elderly adults (Penning, Brackley and Allan, 2006). Increased demand for intensive short-term post-hospital care is a result of the shortened length of hospital stays and the increase in outpatient surgeries. The Commission on the Future of Health Care in Canada (2002), widely known as the Romanow Commission, argued that short-term post-hospital home care should be part of Canadian medicare, but this has not yet happened.

The Romanow Commission did not discuss the needs of older adults who suffer primarily from chronic degenerative conditions. Medicine does not have cures for such conditions. Pharmaceutical and technological advances have opened up a new world of possibilities for the home care of elderly people

with chronic degenerative conditions. However, the enhancement of short-term post-hospital home care reinforces a medical focus, demonstrating Canada's weak support for a social model of health care that acknowledges the needs of those with chronic conditions. As we will now see, failure to acknowledge the need for enhanced long-term home-care services is tied to the internationalization of capital, often referred to as globalization.

GLOBALIZATION AND PROFIT MAKING

Economic globalization involves the use of a variety of technologies to boost transnational investment, finance, advertising, and consumption, thereby increasing the profitability of multinational corporations (see Chapter 19, Globalization). Proponents of globalization emphasize the need for privatization and profitization. **Privatization** involves turning publicly owned organizations into privately owned companies; private companies can include ones that are not-for-profit. **Profitization** involves turning institutions into profit-making organizations. The privatization and profitization of state services (including health-care services) expands the playing field for big business but renders low-income citizens less well protected.

Some analysts interpret recent changes in Canada's health-care system, such as shortened hospital stays, removal of beds from the system, and the decline of long-term chronic home care, as symptoms of globalization. Private funding accounts for an increasing share of Canada's health-care budget (Armstrong, Armstrong, and Coburn, 2001). Increases in outpatient surgery and post-surgical care have created profitable opportunities for private corporations with headquarters outside Canada (Williams, Deber, Baranek, and Gildiner, 2001). Of concern is that the terms of the North American Free Trade Agreement (NAFTA) can be interpreted as meaning that, once the Canadian government allows businesses to enter an area that was once in the public sector, returning it to the public sector is permissible only if the government compensates for-profit firms for lost future profits—which means, de facto, that it is practically impossible. There is currently a law suit against the Ontario government claiming precisely this. That is why the Romanow Commission devoted an entire chapter of its report to arguing that Canada must state publicly and at every opportunity that our health-care services are not to be included in NAFTA. To date, our government has failed to do so.

FIGURE 17.4   ADMINISTRATIVE COSTS AS A PERCENTAGE OF HEALTH-CARE SPENDING, SELECTED COUNTRIES

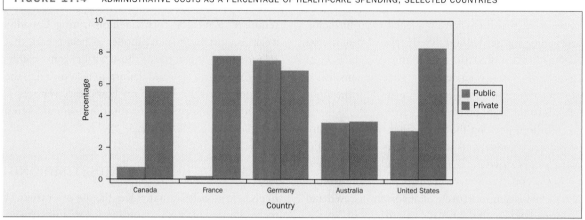

SOURCE: R. G. Evans, K. M. McGrail, S. G. Morgan, M. L. Barer, and C. Hertzman, 2001, "Apocalypse No: Population Aging and the Future of Health Care Systems." *Canadian Journal on Aging, 20* (Suppl. 1), 160–91.

For-profit health care tends to be more expensive than universal public schemes. For-profit health care costs governments less, but people who use the services pay more. Much of the increased cost comes from administrative "overhead" charges (Marmor and Sullivan, 2000; see Figure 17.4). A for-profit system also leaves many citizens without any health insurance. In the United States, one-sixth of the population lacks such insurance and another one-sixth lacks adequate coverage. Canada's medicare system provides adequate care to all people in need. People who earn low income, the elderly population, and women receive more services because their needs tend to be greater.

The risk is that as more of our health-care services are profitized, more people with health-care needs are going to be disadvantaged. Access to needed care will increasingly vary by class, gender, and racial and ethnic inequalities. With fewer health-care options available, people lacking economic resources will do without health services or will rely on self-care or care from family and friends (Arber and Ginn, 1991).

For this reason, many sociologists argue that economic globalization does not support the type of health-care system that is appropriate for an aging society—a system that combines medical care *and* a strong long-term home-care program including social services for the elderly. Instead, globalization is dismantling many existing services. It is adding new inequalities in access to health-care services to existing inequalities in health-care needs. Disadvantaged seniors and their families are feeling most of the resulting pressure. It can be otherwise, but whether Canada's citizens will demand greater equality in health care, and whether governments will choose to do so, remains to be seen.

SUMMARY

1. Many Canadians see the increasing health and longevity of the Canadian population as a social problem. In their view, elderly adults are overly dependent on health and social services, responsible for the crisis in the health-care system, and depriving others of their fair share of the nation's limited resources. They overlook the fact that elderly people are not the primary source of increases in health-care costs. Moreover, the declining percentage of young people in the population offsets the increasing percentage of elderly people who require health and social programs.

2. Health is about physical, social, and psychological well-being, not just the absence of disease, and not all aspects of health status decline as we age. Elderly adults generally assess their health in positive terms and have good mental health and social well-being.

3. Despite the overall picture of good health in old age in Canada, significant inequalities in health

exist. They are associated with such factors as socioeconomic position, gender, race, and ethnicity. Past increases in health and longevity have been concentrated in more advantaged social groups. Aboriginal and immigrant seniors, elderly women, and the poor continue to experience major health disadvantages.

4. Health-related inequalities have been attributed to individual health behaviours and lifestyle factors; psychosocial factors, such as stress; and material conditions and resources. Research findings suggest that economic circumstances, living conditions, and other material factors contribute most to health-related inequalities and that health-related lifestyles and stress levels largely reflect these conditions.

5. We tend to equate health care with medical care provided by physicians in clinics or hospitals. However, the most common forms of health care are self-care and informal care by family members. When it comes to formal health-care services, home care is particularly important to the health and well-being of elderly adults, yet it is not included in Canada's nationally insured health-care system.

6. In recent years, increased emphasis has been placed on privatization and profit-making in Canada's health-care system, particularly when it comes to services that are most important to elderly adults. As a result, people who are most in need of care have the least access to it and are the most likely to have to rely on themselves and family members for care.

QUESTIONS TO CONSIDER

1. What are the major myths about old age? How does the reality of old age in Canada compare with these myths?

2. What are the arguments against apocalyptic demography?

3. How can we best account for inequalities in health among elderly Canadians?

4. How well does Canada's health-care system currently meet the health-care needs of its elderly population?

5. What are some of the consequences of economic globalization for Canada's health-care system?

GLOSSARY

The **age as leveller hypothesis** holds that aging renders everyone disadvantaged, regardless of their other statuses.

Ageism is prejudice based on age.

A **chronic condition** is a persistent physical or mental problem.

The **compression of morbidity hypothesis** suggests that by postponing the onset of people's first chronic illness, the lifetime burden of illness may be compressed into a shorter period of time before death.

Demography is the study of the characteristics of populations and the dynamics of population change.

Functional disability is a long-term restriction or lack of ability to perform various activities of daily living (e.g., personal care, housework) because of a health condition or health problem.

The **healthy immigrant effect** refers to the tendency for recent immigrants to enjoy better health than their Canadian-born counterparts. The effect dissipates over time.

The **hierarchy stress perspective** is an approach to understanding health inequality that emphasizes the stress associated with occupying a lower position in the social hierarchy and its negative impact on health.

The **life course perspective** draws attention to the interplay between individual life course change and larger societal changes.

Life expectancy is the number of years that the average person can expect to live.

Medicalization refers to the social and political process whereby more and more areas of life come under the authority and control of medicine.

The **modified extended family** is characterized by mutual and close intergenerational ties, responsible behaviour on the part of adult children, and contact between the generations.

The **mortality rate** is the number of deaths per 1000 people in a population.

The **multiple jeopardy hypothesis** holds that the effect of occupying multiple low statuses is cumulative.

Premature mortality refers to years of potential life lost.

Privatization involves turning publicly owned organizations into privately owned companies.

Profitization involves turning institutions into profit-making organizations.

Self-care is the range of activities that individuals undertake to enhance health, prevent disease, and restore health. Individuals may engage in these activities on their own or in conjunction with health professionals.

SUGGESTED READING

Armstrong, Pat, Hugh Armstrong, and David Coburn. (2001). *Unhealthy Times: Political Economy Perspectives on Health and Care in Canada.* Toronto: Oxford University Press. This collection of papers uses a political economy perspective to explore reforms that influence our health and health care.

Bolaria, B. Singh, and Harley D. Dickinson. (2009). *Health, Illness, and Health Care in Canada,* 4th ed. Scarborough, ON: Nelson Education. This collection of critical articles examines key sociological issues in the areas of health, illness, and health care.

Chappell, Neena L., and Margaret J. Penning. (2009). *Understanding Health, Health Care and Health Policy in Canada: Sociological Perspectives.* Don Mills, ON: Oxford University Press. This book provides a comprehensive sociological examination of health and health care in the Canadian context.

Chappell, Neena L., Lynn McDonald, and Michael Stones (2007). *Aging in Contemporary Canada,* 2nd ed. Toronto: Pearson Education. This comprehensive introduction to the area of aging covers such topics as demography, theory, and social research methods; issues of health and well-being; the involvement of social institutions in the aging process; and the realities of social policy regarding aging in Canada.

Novak, Mark, and Lori Campbell. (2006). *Aging and Society: A Canadian Perspective,* 5th ed. Toronto: Thomson Nelson. This text is a highly readable introduction to aging in Canada.

WEB RESOURCES

Companion Website for This Book

http://www.newsociety6e.nelson.com
Begin by clicking on the Student Resources section of the website. Next, select the chapter you are studying from the pull-down menu. From the Student Resources page, you have easy access to InfoTrac College Edition® and other resources, such as the Glossary, Test Yourself questions, and additional readings. The website also has many useful tips to aid you in your study of sociology.

InfoTrac College Edition Search Terms

Visit http://www.infotrac-college.com for access to more than 20 million articles from nearly 6000 sources when doing your online research.

SOURCE: © Zzvet/Shutterstock

CHAPTER EIGHTEEN

Politics and Social Movements

Robert J. Brym

UNIVERSITY OF TORONTO

In this chapter you will learn that

- The level of democracy in a society depends on the capacity of citizens to influence the state through their support of political parties, social movements, and other groups. That capacity increases as power becomes more widely distributed in society.

- The degree to which power is widely distributed influences the success of particular kinds of parties and policies.

- People sometimes riot, strike, and take other forms of collective action to correct perceived injustices. When they do so, they are participating in social movements.

- People are more inclined to rebel against the status quo when they are bound by close social ties to other people who feel similarly wronged and when they have the money and other resources needed to protest.

- For social movements to grow, members must make the activities, ideas, and goals of the movement congruent with the interests, beliefs, and values of potential new recruits.

- The history of democracy is a struggle for the acquisition of constantly broadening citizenship rights.

INTRODUCTION

I almost caused a small riot once. It happened in grade 11, shortly after I learned that water combined with sulphur dioxide produces sulphurous acid. The news shocked me. To understand why, you have to know where I lived: in Saint John, New Brunswick, about 100 metres downwind of one of the larger pulp and paper mills in Canada. Acrid waves of sulphur dioxide billowed day and night from the mill's imposing smokestacks. The town's pervasive rotten-egg smell was a longstanding complaint in the area. But, for me, disgust turned to upset when I realized the fumes were toxic. Suddenly it was clear why many people I knew—especially people living near the mill—woke up in the morning with a kind of "smoker's cough." By the simple act of breathing we were causing the gas to mix with the moisture in our bodies and form an acid that our lungs tried to expunge, with only partial success.

Twenty years later, I read the results of a medical research report showing that area residents suffer from rates of lung disease, including emphysema and lung cancer, significantly above the national average. However, even in 1968 it was evident a serious problem was brewing in my hometown. I therefore hatched a plan. Our high school was about to hold its annual model parliament. The event was notoriously boring, partly because, year in, year out, virtually everyone voted for the same party, the Conservatives. But here was an issue, I thought, that could turn things around. The pulp and paper mill was owned by K.C. Irving, an industrialist so powerful that his companies were said to control 40 percent of New Brunswick's economic output. *Forbes* magazine in the United States annually ranked Irving among the wealthiest men in the world. I figured that once I told my fellow students the political implications of the fact that water combined with sulphur dioxide produces sulphurous acid, they would quickly demand the closure of the mill until Irving guaranteed a clean operation.

Was *I* naïve. As head of the tiny Liberal Party, I had to address the entire student body during assembly on election day to outline the party platform and mobilize votes. When I got to the part of my

Nineteen sixty-eight was a year of student rebellion worldwide. Here students run from police in Paris, France.
SOURCE: © Bettmann/Corbis.

speech explaining why K.C. Irving was our enemy, the murmuring in the audience, which had been growing like the sound of a hungry animal about to pounce on its prey, erupted into loud "boos." A couple of students rushed the stage. The principal suddenly appeared from the wings and commanded the student body to settle down. He then took me by the arm and informed me that, for my own safety, my speech was finished. So, I discovered on election day, was our high school's Liberal Party. And so, it emerged, was my high school political career.

This incident troubled me for many years, less because of the embarrassment it caused me than because of the puzzles it presented. Why did I almost cause a small riot? Why didn't my fellow students rebel in the way I thought they would? Why did they continue to support an arrangement that was enriching one man at the cost of a community's health? Why weren't they enraged? Couldn't they see the injustice? Other people did. Nineteen sixty-eight was not just the year of my political failure at Saint John High School. It was also the year that student riots in France nearly caused the fall of the government of Charles de Gaulle. It was the year in which the suppression of student strikes by the Mexican government left dozens of students dead. It was the year in which American students at Berkeley, Michigan, and other universities fought with unprecedented vigour for free speech on their campuses, an end to American involvement in the war in Vietnam, increased civil rights for American blacks, and an expanded role for women in public affairs.

I didn't know it at the time, but by asking why students in Paris, Mexico City, and Berkeley rebelled while my fellow students did not, I was raising the main question that animates the sociological study of politics and social movements. Why are some groups more successful than others in formulating their demands and getting them carried out? In other words, who gets what and under what social circumstances? That is the main issue addressed by this chapter.

Power is the ability of an individual or a group to impose its will on others, even if they resist (Weber, 1946 [1922]: 180). In the first section of this chapter, you will learn that the power of a group may be widely recognized as legitimate or valid under some circumstances. If it is, raw power becomes legitimate **authority** (see Box 18.1). The people who occupy the command posts of institutions are then generally seen as **authorities.** Under other circumstances, however, power flows to non-authorities. This undermines the legitimacy of authority. In this case, non-authorities form **social movements,** or collective attempts to change part or all of the social order. They may riot, petition, strike, demonstrate, and establish pressure groups, unions, and **political parties** (organizations that seek to control state power) to achieve their aims.

The terms defined above allow us to distinguish between "normal politics" and "politics beyond the rules." Normal politics is politics as it is practised when authorities are firmly in power. Politics beyond the rules is politics as it is practised when the legitimacy of authority grows weak. Sociologists have proposed various theories to explain the two types of politics. In the second and third sections of this chapter, I evaluate these theories using mainly Canadian data.

| BOX 18.1 | THREE BASES OF AUTHORITY |

Max Weber (1947) argued that authority can have one of three bases:
1. *Traditional authority:* Particularly in tribal and feudal societies, rulers inherit authority through family or clan ties. In such circumstances, people believe the right of a family or clan to monopolize leadership derives from a god's will.
2. *Legal-rational authority:* In modern societies, authority derives from respect for the law. Laws specify how one can achieve office. People generally believe these laws are rational. If someone achieves office by following these laws, their authority is respected.

3. *Charismatic authority:* Sometimes, extraordinary, charismatic individuals challenge traditional or legal-rational authority. They claim to be inspired by a god or some higher principle that transcends traditional authority, such as the principle that all people are created equal. Their claim is widely believed. Charismatic figures often emerge during a **political revolution,** a concerted attempt by many people to overthrow political institutions and establish new ones. Political revolutions take place when widespread and successful movements of opposition clash with crumbling traditional or legal-rational authority (Skocpol, 1979).

Finally, in the chapter's concluding section, I place our discussion in historical context. How has politics developed over the past 300 years? What developments can we reasonably expect in the near future? This section will help you better to understand your political options in coming years.

POWER FROM ABOVE: NORMAL POLITICS

In 1998, the RCMP used pepper spray to disperse Vancouver crowds demonstrating against visiting Indonesian President Suharto. The incident caused a scandal because it was widely seen as excessive use of force sanctioned by the prime minister. The solicitor general, who is responsible for the RCMP, was forced to resign over the incident.

This incident illustrates the use of **force** or coercive power by authorities. Paradoxically, the use of force by authorities is a sign of their weakness: If authorities are truly in a position of strength, their rule will be widely recognized as legitimate. They will not need to use force to impose their will because most people agree with their policies. Here, politics will be routine, nonviolent, or "normal." To be sure, minor outbursts of violence occur even under normal politics. However, such events are unusual in Canada

today. They rarely result in fatalities. For the most part, Canadian politics today is normal politics.

Power is exercised in all social settings, from the family to the classroom to the workplace. However, the ultimate seat of power in society is the state. The **state** is a set of institutions that formulate and carry out a country's laws, policies, and binding regulations. Why is the state's power "ultimate?" Because its authority stands above all others, and if the state needs to use force to maintain order or protect its borders, most people will regard its actions as legitimate.

In democratic countries, such as Canada, the government is formed by the elected members of the political party that wins the most seats in a general election (see Figure 18.1). It comprises the head of the party, who becomes prime minister, and the cabinet ministers whom the prime minister selects to advise him or her. It is the job of the government to initiate policies, propose laws, and see that they are enforced. That is why the government is also called the *executive* branch of the state. Proposed laws are turned into operating statutes by the *legislature*, which consists of all the people elected to Parliament. It is the responsibility of the *judiciary* or court system to interpret laws and regulations, that is, to figure out whether and how particular laws and regulations apply in disputed cases. The state's *administrative*

FIGURE 18.1   THE INSTITUTIONS OF STATE AND CIVIL SOCIETY

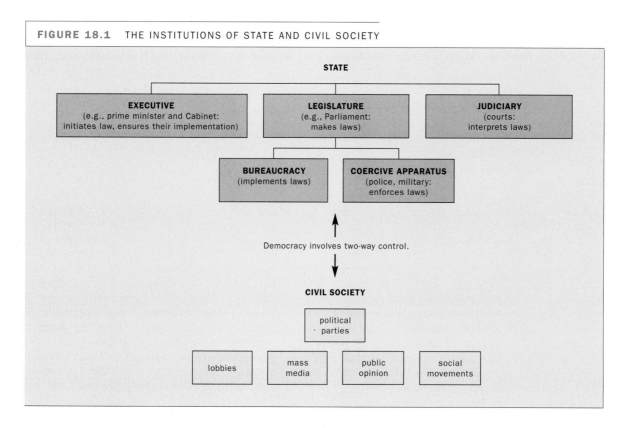

apparatus or *bureaucracy* undertakes enforcement of laws. If laws are broken or the state's security is jeopardized, it is the role of the *coercive apparatus*—the police and military—to enforce the law and protect the state.

The state, then, is a set of institutions that exercise control over society. However, individuals in **civil society,** the private sphere of life, also exercise control over the state through a variety of organizations and institutions. We have already noted how social movements may influence the state. In addition, the mass media are supposed to keep a watchful and critical eye on the state and help keep the public informed about the quality of government. Pressure groups or "lobbies" are formed by trade unions, manufacturers' associations, ethnic groups, and other organizations to advise politicians of their members' desires. Lobbies also remind politicians how much their members' votes and campaign contributions matter. Finally, political parties regularly seek to mobilize voters as they compete for control of government.

How democratic is the Canadian state? Does the interaction between state and civil society ensure that every citizen has a roughly equal say in the determination of laws and policies? Or, as George Orwell asked in *Animal Farm*, are some citizens more equal than others? Do we, as Abraham Lincoln claimed for the Americans, enjoy "government of the people, by the people, for the people?" Or is it more accurate to say, in the words of one wit, that we are subjected to "government of the people, by the lawyers, for the business owners"? These are among the chief questions asked by sociologists who study the state and its operations. It is now time to consider them in greater detail.

PLURALIST THEORY

Pluralist theory is one interpretation of the relationship between state and civil society (Dahl, 1961; Polsby, 1959). According to pluralists, we live in a heterogeneous society with many competing interests and centres of power. For example, the interests of parents with school-age children may differ from the interests of pensioners. Parents may want school budgets to grow. Pensioners may want them to shrink. Because of such heterogeneity, no one group can control politics, according to the pluralists. They argue that, over time, all voters and interest groups influence the political process almost equally. Sometimes one category of voters wins a political

battle, sometimes another. Most often, however, politics involves negotiation and compromise among competing groups. According to the pluralists, because no one group of people is always able to control the political agenda or the outcome of political conflict, democracy is guaranteed.

ELITE THEORY

Elite theorists, C. Wright Mills (1956) foremost among them, sharply disagree with the pluralist account. *Elites* are small groups that occupy the command posts of a society's institutions. In the United States, the country that Mills studied, the most powerful elites are the people who run the country's several hundred biggest corporations, the executive branch of government, and the military. Mills wrote that the men who control these institutions (they are almost all men) make the important decisions that profoundly affect members of society. Moreover, they do so without much regard for elections or public opinion.

Mills showed how the corporate, state, and military elites are interconnected. People move from one elite to another over their careers. Their children intermarry. They maintain intimate social contacts on a day-to-day basis. They tend to be recruited from the upper-middle and upper classes. However, Mills denied that these similarities and interconnections turn the three elites into a **ruling class,** that is, a self-conscious and cohesive group of people, led by corporate executives and owners of big business, who act to advance their common interests. The three elites are independent of each other, Mills insisted. They may see eye-to-eye on many issues, but each has its own jealously guarded sphere of influence, and conflict between elite groups is therefore common (Mills, 1956: 277).

The Elitist Critique of Pluralism

Most political sociologists today question the pluralist account of democratic politics because research has established the existence of large, persistent, wealth-based inequalities in political influence and political participation.

John Porter's classic, *The Vertical Mosaic* (1965), was the first in a series of Canadian studies that demonstrate the weaknesses of pluralism and corroborate some aspects of elite theory (Brym, 1989; Clement, 1975; Olsen, 1980). These studies show that a disproportionately large number of people in Canada's political and other elites come from upper- and upper-middle-class

TABLE 18.1   FEDERAL POLITICAL CONTRIBUTORS PER 10 000 TAX FILERS, BY INCOME AND REGION

ANNUAL INCOME	ATLANTIC	QUEBEC	ONTARIO	WEST	CANADA
Less than $25 000	21	17	34	80	42
$25 000–$49 999	126	73	126	253	150
$50 000–$74 999	429	242	304	467	353
$75 000+	1149	679	790	964	830

SOURCE: Based on Jeffrey Frank, 1994, "Voting and Contributing: Political Participation in Canada," *Canadian Social Trends*, Vol. 2, Toronto: Thompson Educational Publishing, Inc., p. 337.

families. For example, about 40 percent of Canadian prime ministers, premiers, and Cabinet ministers were born into the richest 10 percent of families in the country (Olsen, 1980: 129). In their youth, members of Canada's elites are likely to have attended expensive private schools. As adults, they tend to marry the offspring of other elite members and belong to exclusive private clubs. In the course of their careers, they often move from one elite to another. Arguably, people with this sort of background cannot act dispassionately on behalf of all Canadians, rich and poor.

Controversy persists over whether Canada's elites form a ruling class. Porter (1965), noting frequent conflict among elites, argued against the view that a ruling class controls Canada. His top students disagreed. They argued that the interests of large corporations dominate Canadian political life (Clement, 1975; Olsen, 1980). However, both Porter and his students did agree on one point: Contrary to pluralist claims, Canada's well-to-do consistently exercise disproportionate influence over political life in this country.

Studies of political participation in Canada add weight to the elitist view (Blais, Gidengil, Nadeau, and Nevitte, 1997; Frank, 1994; Mishler, 1979: 88–97). Many surveys show that political involvement decreases with social class. For example, the likelihood of voting falls with a person's class position. The likelihood of phoning or writing a member of Parliament, helping a candidate in an election campaign, contributing money to a political party, and running for office declines even more steeply as we move down the class hierarchy (see Table 18.1). As intensity of political participation declines, so does political influence. Consequently, although political apathy and cynicism are high among Canadians, the poorest Canadians are the most politically apathetic and cynical of any income category. They have less interest in politics than do the well-to-do, and they are more likely to think that government does not care what they think

(see Figure 18.2). As one of the world's leading political sociologists writes, "The combination of a low vote and a relative lack of organization among the lower-status groups means that they will suffer from neglect by the politicians who will be receptive to the wishes of the more privileged, participating, and organized strata" (Lipset, 1981: 226–27; see Box 18.2).

The Marxist Critique of Elite Theory

Although compelling in some respects, elite theory has its critics, Marxists foremost among them. Some Marxists, known as "instrumentalists," deny that elites enjoy more or less equal power. Actually, they say, elites form a ruling class dominated by big business. From their point of view, the state is an arm (or "instrument") of the business elite. Big business gains control of the state in three main ways. First, members of wealthy families occupy important state positions in highly disproportionate numbers. Second, government officials rely mainly on the representatives of big business for advice. Third, political parties rely mainly on big

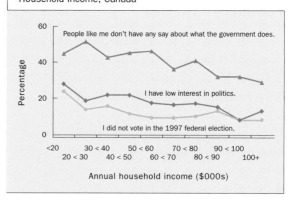

FIGURE 18.2   Political Apathy and Cynicism, by Annual Household Income, Canada

SOURCE: Canada Election Survey, 2004 (2005). Reprinted by permission of Professor Andre Blais.

DEFEATING POLITICAL CYNICISM: TECHNOLOGY, ORGANIZATION, AND THE OBAMA EFFECT

Turnout in the American presidential election of 1996 reached an all-time low. Just 48 percent of the voting-age population went to the polls. However, in subsequent elections, turnout increased, reaching 56 percent in 2008. Why the upturn? At 59 percent in the 2008 federal election, Canadian voter turnout remains higher than voter turnout in the United States, but for more than a decade, Canadian voter turnout dropped while American voter turnout increased. Why the different trends in the two countries?

The competitiveness of elections in the United States and Canada may be part of the answer to the questions just raised. Big fights tend to turn out big crowds, and the three most recent American presidential elections were intensely competitive. Over the same period, Canadians were arguably presented with less stark party alternatives than Americans were. Canadian cynicism about politics may have remained high because less seemed to be at stake in Canadian elections. The result: persistently declining voter turnout in Canada.

Another factor that has contributed to the recent American upturn in voter turnout is that technological and organizational improvements encourage more people to vote in the United States.

Party organizers now use the Internet intensively to solicit donations, recruit volunteers, and communicate with them. They employ census and survey data to identify persuadable voters. Then, they send entire armies of the party faithful out to contact persuadable voters face-to-face and encourage them to vote (McDonald 2008a, 2008b). Canadian federal elections seem to be less technologically and organizationally advanced than American presidential elections are. Persistent declines in Canadian voter turnout may result from the technological and organizational lag.

Finally, the "Obama effect" is partly responsible for the most recent uptick in American voter turnout. President Barack Obama is of course a young, attractive, inspirational leader. In the 2008 presidential election, his message of hope and change appealed strongly to the most cynical age cohort: youth. Voters between the age of 18 and 29 supported Obama over McCain by a 2-to-1 margin, and they came out to the polls in droves (MSNBC, 2008). Meanwhile, voter turnout among Canadian youth is the lowest among all age cohorts (see Figure 18.3). We await our Obama.

FIGURE 18.3 VOTER TURNOUT, CANADIAN FEDERAL ELECTIONS

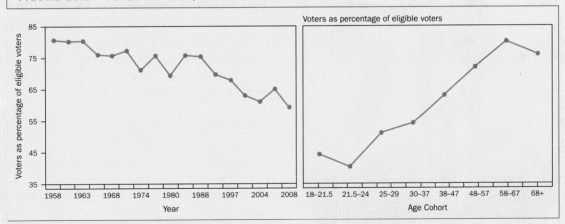

SOURCE: Created with data from the following: Elections Canada, 2005, 2006, and 2008, www.elections.ca; McDonald, Michael P. 2008a. "This May Be the Election of the Century," *Politico,* http://www.politico.com/news/stories/0908/13798.html (5 November 2008); McDonald, Michael P., 2008b, "Voter Turnout," *United States Elections Project,* http://elections.gmu.edu/voter_turnout.htm (5 November 2008); MSNBC, 2008, "United States—President." http://www.msnbc.msn.com/id/26843704 (5 November 2008).

business for financial support. According to some Marxists, members of different elites may disagree about specific issues. However, as a result of the three control mechanisms listed above, they always agree about one issue: the need to maintain the health of the capitalist system (Miliband, 1973 [1969]).

A second group of Marxists, known as "structuralists," offers a somewhat different interpretation of why the state in capitalist society is necessarily biased in favour of big business. For the structuralists, it is not so much the social origins of high government officials or the social ties linking them with big business that encourages the state to act with a pro-capitalist bias. Rather, they argue, the capitalist state acts as an arm of big business because it is constrained to do so by the nature of the capitalist system itself. For example, if the Canadian government doubled the corporate tax rate, investment would be redirected to countries with regimes that are kinder to company profits. Such a move would cost Canada jobs and prosperity. It would be highly unpopular. The government could easily fall. Fearing such outcomes, governments in capitalist societies find their field of action restricted to policies that ensure the well-being of big business. According to the structuralists, it is the very fact that the state is embedded in a capitalist system that forces it to act in this way (Poulantzas, 1975 [1968]).

It follows from both the instrumentalist and the structuralist positions that ordinary citizens, and

Karl Marx predicted that capitalism would create a large mass of impoverished workers who would eventually take over the state, eliminate private property, and forge a communist society. After the revolution of 1917, the Soviet Union became the first self-proclaimed communist society. This early May Day poster reads: "Workers of all countries unite. The 1st of May work holiday. Long live the international unity of the proletariat!"
SOURCE: © Corbis.

especially members of the working class, rarely have much influence over state policy. According to Marxists, true democracy can emerge only if members of the working class and their supporters overthrow capitalism and establish a socialist system in which economic differences between people are eliminated or at least substantially reduced.

POWER-BALANCE THEORY

Pluralists assume that all major groups in society enjoy approximately equal power. Elitists assume that members of the upper class enjoy most power. Both approaches, however, assume that the distribution of power in society does not change much over time, except in those rare instances when revolutions take place.

In contrast, **power-balance theorists** argue that the distribution of power in society changes significantly more frequently. They admit that power is usually concentrated in the hands of the wealthy. However, they also note that other classes sometimes gain power. This has big implications for political life. Among other things, the distribution of power determines how democratic a society is.

To make their case, power-balance theorists first measure variations in the social distribution of power. They then show how those variations are reflected in the successes and failures of different political parties and the rejection and adoption of different state policies. Along with the pluralists, they recognize that society is truly democratic only when power is widely distributed. Along with the elitists, they recognize that society is not very democratic when power is highly concentrated in the hands of a few wealthy citizens. However, by treating the distribution of power as a variable, they improve our understanding of the relationship between power and democracy.

We can better understand power-balance theory by examining Canadian politics in comparative perspective. We first note that a group's power is partly determined by the degree to which it forms organizations to further its interests. For example, unionized blue-collar and white-collar workers are more powerful than their nonunionized counterparts. That is because unions allow workers to speak with one voice. Unions enable workers to effectively bargain with employers and governments for improved wages, working conditions, and social policies. Moreover, if bargaining fails, they can go out on strike to force the issue.

If level of unionization increases working-class power, that should be reflected in the political behaviour

The peak year of strike activity in Canada was 1919. In that year, 17.3 strikes took place for every 100 000 non-agricultural workers in the country. This photo was taken on "Bloody Saturday," June 21, 1919, during the Winnipeg General Strike. It shows a violent confrontation between rioters and Mounties and special police.

SOURCE: David Miller Collection/National Archives of Canada/C-33392.

of citizens and the policies adopted by governments. And, in fact, it is. Compare Sweden and Canada, for example (Casper, McLanahan, and Garfinkle, 1994; Korpi, 1983; Myles, 1989; O'Connor, 1996; O'Connor and Brym, 1988; O'Connor and Olsen, 1998; Olsen, 2002; Olsen and Brym, 1996). In Sweden, more than three-quarters of blue- and white-collar workers are union members. In Canada, only three out of ten non-agricultural workers are members of unions. Several consequences follow:

- 59 percent of Canadians voted in the 2008 federal election, compared with 82 percent of Swedes in the 2006 Swedish federal election. The difference is largely due to the fact that working-class Swedes are more likely to vote than working-class Canadians are.
- The Swedish socialist party has formed the government almost continuously since World War II. In contrast, Canada's socialist party, the NDP, has never formed the federal government or even had a representative in the federal cabinet. The parties that have formed Canada's federal governments (Liberals, Progressive Conservatives, and Conservatives) are those that are most strongly supported by business (see Figure 18.4, p. 438).

- Swedish governments have acted more vigorously than Canadian governments have to eradicate poverty and equalize incomes. Thus, fewer than 4 percent of Swedes are classified as living below the poverty line (as defined by the low income cutoff; see Chapter 6, Social Stratification). The comparable figure for Canadians is about 15 percent. In Sweden, about 20 percent of all income goes to the top 10 percent of income earners. The comparable figure for Canada is about 30 percent of all income. And in Sweden, a broader range of retired people receive more generous pensions and more frequent cost-of-living adjustments than pensioners in Canada.
- Since women are disproportionately concentrated in low-income, low-status jobs (see Chapter 7, Gender Inequality), they benefit more than men do when the working class is more powerful. As a result, the ratio of women's to men's earnings is about 80 percent in Sweden and 67 percent in Canada. Moreover, in Sweden, the ratio of women to men who live below the poverty line is just above 90 percent, while in Canada the comparable figure is nearly 130 percent. Finally, parental benefits are superior in

FIGURE 18.4   CONTRIBUTIONS TO FEDERAL POLITICAL PARTIES BY SOURCE

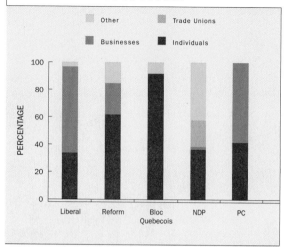

NOTE: Data are for 1997.
SOURCE: Data used to create the above chart was taken from the website of Elections Canada, www.elections.ca, 2006. It is used with the permission of the Chief Electoral Officer. Adaptation and analysis are the responsibility of the author.

Sweden and child-care facilities are more widely available and affordable.

We thus see that elections matter a great deal in the lives of ordinary people. Elections determine the types of parties that get elected. Elected parties, in turn, shape government policies. The outcome of any particular election depends on the appeal of party leaders, their effectiveness in presenting issues to the public, and myriad other short-term factors (Clarke, Jenson, LeDuc, and Pammett, 1996; see Figure 18.5). But considering the types of parties that get elected over several decades, as we did previously, we see that the distribution of power between classes and other groups shapes the character of politics in a country.

The preceding analysis also implies that Sweden is more democratic than Canada. True, citizens of both countries are legally free to vote and influence their governments. But because the working class is more powerful in Sweden, Swedes' legal right to vote and influence governments has been turned into real political influence on a wider scale. In general, only if more citizens wield more clout can society become more democratic.

STATE-CENTRED THEORY

Power-balance theory suggests that democratic politics is a contest among various classes and other groups to control the state for their own advantage. When power is substantially redistributed—when, for example, a major class gets better organized while

FIGURE 18.5   RESULTS OF 2008 CANADIAN FEDERAL ELECTION

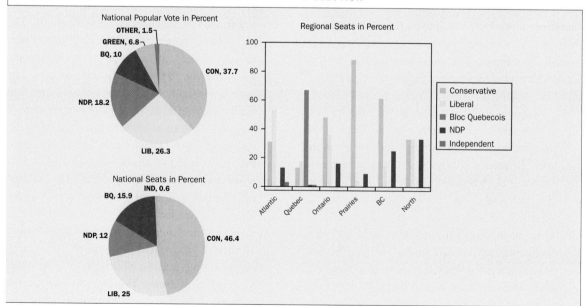

SOURCE: Data used to create the above chart was taken from the website of Elections Canada, www.elections.ca, 2008. It is used with the permission of the Chief Electoral Officer. Adaptation and analysis are the responsibility of the author.

another major class becomes less socially organized—old ruling parties usually fall and new ones take office.

Note, however, that a winner-take-all strategy would be nothing short of foolish. If winning parties monopolized the spoils of office, passing laws that benefit only their supporters, they might cause massive outrage and even violent opposition. Yet allowing opponents to become angry, organized, and resolute would be counterproductive. After all, winners want more than just a moment of glory. They want to be able to enjoy the spoils of office in a stable political environment over the long haul. To achieve such stability, it is crucial that people who *lose* elections are given a say in government. To a degree, the party in power must attend to the wants of losing minorities. That way, even determined opponents are likely to recognize the legitimacy of the government and its right to rule. Pluralists thus make a good point when they say that democratic politics is about accommodation and compromise; they only lose sight of the fact that accommodation and compromise typically give more advantages to some than others, as both elite theorists and power-balance theorists stress.

There is, however, more to the story of politics than conflict between classes and between other groups. Theda Skocpol and other **state-centred theorists** have shown how the state itself can structure political life independently of the way power is distributed among classes and other groups at a given time (Block, 1979; Evans, Rueschemeyer, and Skocpol, 1985; Skocpol, 1979). Their argument is a valuable supplement to power-balance theory.

To illustrate how state structures shape politics, consider the problem of nonvoting in the United States. In presidential elections, voter turnout fell more or less steadily between the end of World War II and 1996, when it stood at just 48 percent of the voting age population. Turnout increased in 2000 (50 percent), 2004 (55 percent), and 2008 (56 percent), but the United States still has one of the lowest voter turnouts of any rich democracy in the world (Piven and Cloward, 1989: 5). How can we explain this?

The high rate of nonvoting is largely a product of voter registration law—a feature of the American political structure, not of the current distribution of power. In every democracy, laws specify voter registration procedures. In some countries, such as France, citizens are registered to vote automatically once they receive state-issued identity cards at the age of 18. In other countries, such as Canada, a database of citizens who are eligible to vote was first created by state-employed canvassers who went door-to-door to register voters. The database is updated between elections with information supplied mainly by provincial, territorial, and federal data sources. Only in the United States do individual citizens have to take the initiative to go out and register themselves in voter registration centres. Yet many American citizens are unable or unwilling to register. As a result, the U.S. has a proportionately smaller pool of eligible voters than the other democracies do. Only about 65 percent of American citizens are registered to vote (Piven and Cloward, 1989: 256–59).

Apart from shrinking the pool of eligible voters, American voter registration law has a second important consequence. Because some *types* of people are less able and inclined than others to register, a strong bias is introduced into the political system. Specifically, the poor are less likely to register than the better-off are. People without much formal education are less likely to register than the better educated are. Members of disadvantaged racial minority groups, especially African Americans, are less likely to register than whites are. Thus, American voter registration law is a pathway to democracy for some but a barrier to democracy for others. The American political system is less responsive than other rich democracies to the needs of the disadvantaged. That is partly because, as state-centred theory suggests, the law requires citizen-initiated voter registration. As a result, many disadvantaged people are effectively disenfranchised.[1]

Big shocks sometimes rock state structures. In general, however, they are resistant to change. The foundations of state structures are anchored by constitutions, which can be altered only by large majorities of federally elected representatives and state- or provincial-level legislatures. Their upper stories are girded by laws, regulations, and policies, some of which help to keep potentially disruptive social forces at bay. American voter registration law is a case in point.[2] And then there are the many ideological reinforcements. All states create anthems, flags, ceremonies, celebrations, sporting events, and school curricula that stimulate patriotism and serve in part to justify existing political arrangements.

In sum, each school of thought reviewed above makes a useful contribution to our appreciation of normal democratic politics (see Table 18.2, p. 440). Pluralists teach us that normal democratic politics is about compromise and the accommodation of all group interests. Elite theorists teach us that, despite compromise and accommodation, power is concentrated in the hands of higher-status groups, whose

TABLE 18.2   FIVE SOCIOLOGICAL THEORIES OF DEMOCRACY COMPARED

	PLURALIST	ELITE	MARXIST	POWER BALANCE	STATE-CENTRED
How is power distributed?	dispersed	concentrated	concentrated	concentrated	concentrated
Who are the main power holders?	various groups	elites	ruling class	upper class	state officials
On what is their power based?	holding political office	controlling major institutions	owning substantial capital	owning substantial capital	holding political office
What is the main basis of public policy?	the will of all citizens	the interests of major elites	capitalist interests	the balance of power between classes, etc.	the influence of state structures
Do lower classes have much influence on politics?	yes	no	rarely	sometimes	sometimes

interests the political system therefore serves best. Power-balance theorists teach us that, despite the concentration of power in society, substantial shifts in the distribution of power often occur, and they have discernible effects on voting patterns and public policies. Marxists highlight the rare occasions when political power is rapidly redistributed by revolutionary upheavals. And state-centred theorists teach us that, despite the influence of the distribution of power on political life, state structures exert an important independent effect on politics too.

POWER FROM BELOW: POLITICS BEYOND THE RULES

RELATIVE-DEPRIVATION THEORY

All five theories of democracy reviewed above focus on normal politics. We know, however, that politics is sometimes anything but normal. Routine political processes can break down. Social movements can form. Large-scale political violence can erupt. As Vladimir Lenin, the leader of the Russian revolution of 1917, said, people sometimes "vote with their feet."

Until about 1970, many sociologists argued that social movements tend to emerge when people experience **relative deprivation.** People feel relatively deprived when they experience an intolerable gap between the social rewards they think they deserve and the social rewards they expect to receive. (Social rewards are widely valued goods, including money, education, security, prestige, and so on.) Accordingly, people are most likely to rebel against authority when rising expectations (brought on by, say, rapid economic

growth and migration) are met by a sudden decline in social rewards (because of, say, economic recession or war; Davies, 1969). In addition, until about 1970, many sociologists held that the people who lead and first join social movements are likely to be outsiders who lack strong social ties to their communities.

A large body of research has now discredited these ideas. For example, we now know that the leaders and early joiners of social movements are usually well-integrated members of their communities, not socially marginal newcomers. In the 1930s, for example, Saskatchewan farmers and workers formed the Cooperative Commonwealth Federation (CCF) to protest federal government policy toward the West in general and Western agriculture in particular. The movement's leaders and early recruits were not outsiders. The workers were mainly local trade union activists. The farmers had been involved in the establishment of community-owned retail stores, credit unions, and marketing cooperatives (Lipset, 1971).

Much research also calls into question the idea that relative deprivation leads to the formation of social movements. For example, sociologists have compared measures of relative deprivation with the frequency of demonstrations, strikes, and acts of collective violence in France, Italy, Germany, and England. They have found that, in general, outbreaks of collective unrest do not increase with mounting relative deprivation (Lodhi and Tilly, 1973; Snyder and Tilly, 1972; Tilly, 1979a; Tilly, Tilly, and Tilly, 1975).

RESOURCE MOBILIZATION THEORY

Because of the inadequacies of relative deprivation theory noted above, an alternative approach to the study of social movements has gained popularity over the past 30 years. **Resource mobilization theory** is based on the idea that social movements emerge only when disadvantaged people can marshal the means necessary to challenge authority (Jenkins, 1983; McCarthy and Zald, 1977; Oberschall, 1973; Tilly, 1978). Foremost among the resources they need to challenge authority is the capacity to forge strong social ties among themselves. Other important resources that allow disadvantaged people to challenge authority include jobs, money, arms, and access to means of spreading their ideas.

You can appreciate the significance of resource mobilization theory by considering patterns of strike activity in Canada. When blue-collar and white-collar workers go out on strike, they are withholding their labour to extract concessions from employers or governments in the form of higher wages and improved social welfare benefits. When are workers most inclined to challenge the authority of employers and governments in this way? Research shows that in Canada since World War II, strike activity has been high when (1) unemployment is low, (2) union membership is high, and (3) governments have shown themselves to be generous in their provision of social welfare benefits. Low unemployment indicates a strong economy. Workers are inclined to strike when business activity is robust because they know employers and governments can afford to make concessions. (Employers make bigger profits and governments collect more taxes during economic booms.) A high level of unionization is also conducive to more strike activity

because unions provide workers with leadership, strike funds, and coordination. Thus, as resource mobilization theory predicts, strong social ties among workers (as indicated by a high level of unionization) and access to jobs and money (as indicated by a booming economy) increase challenges to authority (as indicated by strikes).[3]

Figure 18.6 shows the pattern of strike activity in post–World War II Canada. It supports the arguments of resource mobilization theory. Until 1974, the trend in strike activity was upward. (In the 1970s, Canada was, in fact, the most strike-prone country in the world.) This was a period of growing prosperity, low unemployment, expanding state benefits, and increasing unionization. With increasing access to organizational and material resources, workers often challenged authority in the three decades after World War II. In 1973, however, economic crisis struck. Oil prices tripled, and then tripled again at the end of the decade. Inflation increased and unemployment rose. Soon, the government was strapped for funds and had to borrow heavily to maintain social welfare programs. Eventually, the debt burden was so heavy that the government felt obliged to cut various social welfare programs. Unionization reached a peak in 1978, stabilized, and then began to fall (see Figure 18.7, p. 442). Thus, in the post-1973 climate, the organizational and material resources of workers fell. As a result, strike activity plummeted. In 1974, nearly 16 strikes took place for every 100 000 Canadian workers. By 2006, that figure had fallen to just over 1 (Brym, 2008).

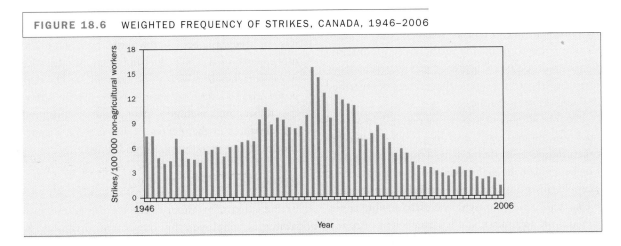

FIGURE 18.6   WEIGHTED FREQUENCY OF STRIKES, CANADA, 1946–2006

SOURCES: Human Resources and Skills Development Canada (1999, 2001); International Labour Organization (2008); Canada Department of Labour (1973: xxii–xxiii); Human Resources Development Canada (1995: xiii); Human Resources Development Canada (1998: 15); Canada Department of Labour (1970: 12–13); Canada Department of Labour (1985: 9); Workplace Information Directorate (1996).

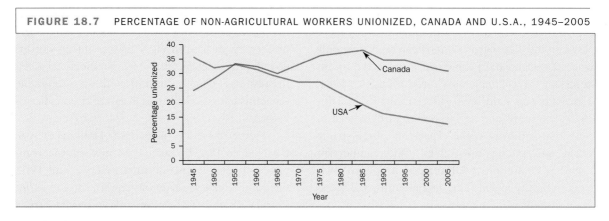

FIGURE 18.7   PERCENTAGE OF NON-AGRICULTURAL WORKERS UNIONIZED, CANADA AND U.S.A., 1945–2005

SOURCES: Human Resources and Social Development Canada (2008); Canada Department of Labour (1973: xxii–xxiii; 1995: xiii); Human Resources Development Canada (1998: 15); "Union Membership in Canada—2000" (2000).

FRAMING DISCONTENT

As you have seen, resource mobilization theory is a useful approach to the study of social movements, such as the strike movement in Canada. Even so, the emergence of a social movement sometimes takes sociologists by surprise. In addition, the failure of an aggrieved group to press its claim is sometimes equally unexpected. And movements that do emerge are successful to varying degrees. It seems, therefore, that something lies between (1) the capacity of disadvantaged people to mobilize resources for collective action and (2) the recruitment of a substantial number of movement members. Sociologists call that "something" **frame alignment** (Goffman, 1974; Snow, Rochford, Worden, and Benford, 1986). Frame alignment is the process by which individual interests, beliefs, and values either become congruent and complementary with the activities, ideas, and goals of the movement or fail to do so. Thanks to the efforts of scholars operating mainly in the symbolic interactionist tradition (see Chapters 1 and 3), frame alignment has recently become the subject of sustained sociological investigation.

Frame alignment can be encouraged in several ways. Social movement leaders can reach out to other organizations that, they believe, contain people who may be sympathetic to the social movement's cause. For example, an anti-nuclear movement may use the mass media, telephone campaigns, and direct mail to appeal to feminist, anti-racist, and environmental organizations on the assumption they are likely to have members who would agree at least in general terms with the anti-nuclear platform. In addition, social movements can idealize values that have so far not featured prominently

in the thinking of potential recruits. They can also elevate the importance of positive beliefs about the movement and what it stands for. For example, in trying to win new recruits, movement members might emphasize the seriousness of the social movement's purpose. They might analyze in a clear and convincing manner the causes of the problem the movement is trying solve. Or they might stress the likelihood of the movement's success. By doing so they might increase the movement's appeal to potential recruits and win them over to the cause. Social movements can also stretch their objectives and activities to win recruits who are not initially sympathetic to the movement's original aims. This may involve watering down the movement's ideals. Alternatively, movement leaders may decide to take action calculated to appeal to non-sympathizers on grounds that have little or nothing to do with the movement's purpose. When rock, punk, or reggae bands play at nuclear disarmament rallies or gay liberation festivals, it is not necessarily because the music is relevant to the movement's goals. Nor do bands play just because movement members want to be entertained. The purpose is also to attract non-members. Once attracted by the music, non-members may make friends and acquaintances in the movement and then be encouraged to attend a more serious-minded meeting.

REFRAIN: BACK TO 1968

Frame alignment theory stresses the interaction strategies employed by movement members to recruit non-members who are like-minded, apathetic, or even initially opposed to the movement's goals. Resource mobilization theory focuses on the broad social-structural conditions that facilitate the

The Assembly of First Nations, which represents 633 Native groups, demands that Aboriginal Canadians have the right to formulate their own laws and reject some Canadian laws. Here, Aboriginal people protest certain taxes outside a government office.

SOURCE: Dick Hemingway.

emergence of social movements. One theory usefully supplements the other.

The two theories certainly help clarify the 1968 high school incident I described at the beginning of this chapter. It now seems clear that two main factors prevented me from influencing my classmates in New Brunswick when I spoke to them about the dangers of industrial pollution:

1. Disadvantaged people in New Brunswick were relatively powerless. They had access to few resources they could mobilize on their own behalf. That is because New Brunswick's economy was underdeveloped. Both per capita income and the level of unionization were among the lowest in the country. The unemployment rate was among the highest. In contrast, K. C. Irving, who owned the pulp and paper mill against which I railed, was so powerful that most New Brunswickers could not even conceive of the need to rebel against the conditions of life that he created for them. He owned most of the industrial establishments in the province—the oil refinery and its network of gas stations, the dry docks, the pulp mills, the mines, and the logging operations. Every daily newspaper, most of the weeklies, all of the TV stations, and most of the radio stations were his too. Little wonder we rarely heard a critical word about his operations. Many people also believed that Irving could make or break provincial governments single-handedly. Should I therefore have been surprised that mere high school students refused to take him on? In their conservatism, my fellow students were only mimicking their parents, who, on the whole, were as powerless as Irving was mighty (Brym, 1979).

2. Many of my classmates did not share my sense of injustice. Most of them regarded K. C. Irving as the great provider. They thought his pulp and paper mill, as well as his myriad other industrial establishments, gave many New Brunswickers jobs. They regarded that fact as more important for their lives and the lives of their families than the pollution problem I raised. Frame-alignment theory suggests I needed to figure out ways of building bridges between their understanding and mine. I did not. I therefore received an unsympathetic hearing.

THE HISTORY AND FUTURE OF SOCIAL MOVEMENTS

I. THE RICH COUNTRIES

Three hundred years ago, social movements were typically small, localized, and violent. In Europe, poor residents of a particular city might riot against public officials in reaction to a rise in bread prices or taxes. Peasants on a particular estate might burn their landowner's barns (or their landowner) in response to his demand for a larger share of the crop. But then the reach of the state grew, soon encompassing most aspects of life. The state taxed nearly all of its citizens at higher and higher rates as government services expanded. It imposed a uniform language and a common curriculum in a compulsory education system. It drafted most young men for army service. It instilled in its citizens all the ideological trappings of modern nationalism, from anthems to flags to historical myths. And in the process, social movements changed. They became national in scope, typically directing themselves against central governments rather than local targets. They grew in size, partly because potential recruits were now literate and could communicate using the printed word, partly because big new social settings—factories, offices, densely populated urban neighbourhoods—could serve as recruitment bases. And, in most cases, social movements became less violent. Their size and organization often allowed them to stabilize, bureaucratize, and become sufficiently powerful to get their way without frequent resort to extreme measures (Tilly, 1978, 1979a, 1979b; Tilly, Tilly, and Tilly, 1975).

Social movements often used their power to expand the rights of citizens. We may identify four stages in this process. In Britain, for example, rich property owners struggled against the king in the eighteenth century for **civil citizenship:** the right to free speech, freedom of religion, and justice before the law. The male middle class and the more prosperous strata of the working class struggled against rich property owners in the nineteenth century for **political citizenship:** the right to vote and run for office. In early-twentieth-century Britain, women and poorer workers succeeded in achieving these same rights despite the opposition of well-to-do men in particular. During the remainder of the century, blue- and white-collar workers struggled against the well-to-do for **social citizenship:** the right to a certain level of economic security and full participation in the social life of the country by means of the creation of the modern welfare state (Marshall, 1965).

In the last third of the twentieth century, the struggle to broaden citizenship rights entered a new phase, which we now examine in greater detail. The broadening of the struggle for citizenship rights was signalled by the emergence of so-called **new social movements** in the 1960s and 1970s (Melucci, 1980, 1995). What is new about new social movements is the breadth of their goals, the kinds of people they attract, and their potential for going global. I will consider each of these issues in turn.

Goals

Some new social movements, such as the peace movement, the environmental movement, and the human rights movement, promote the rights not of specific groups but of humanity as a whole to peace, security,

and a clean environment. Other new social movements, such as the women's movement and the gay rights movement, promote the rights of particular groups that have been excluded from full social participation. Accordingly, gay rights groups have fought for laws that eliminate all forms of discrimination based on sexual orientation. They have also fought for the repeal of laws that discriminate on the basis of sexual orientation, such as anti-sodomy laws and laws that negatively affect parental custody of children (Adam, Duyvendak, and Krouwel, 1999).

Since the 1960s, the women's movement has succeeded in getting admission practices altered in professional schools, winning more freedom of reproductive choice for women, and opening up opportunities for women in the political, religious, military, educational, medical, and business systems (Adamson, Briskin, and McPhail, 1988; see Box 18.3).

The emergence of the peace, environmental, human rights, gay rights, and women's movements marked the beginning of a fourth stage in the history of social movements. This fourth stage involves the promotion of **universal citizenship,** or the extension of citizenship rights to all adult members of society and to society as a whole (Roche, 1995; Turner, 1986: 85–105).

Membership

New social movements are also novel in that they attract a disproportionately large number of highly educated, well-to-do people from the social, educational, and cultural fields: teachers, professors, journalists, social workers, artists, actors, writers, and student apprentices to these occupations. Such people are predisposed to participate in new social movements for several reasons. Their higher education exposes them to radical ideas and makes those ideas appealing. They tend to hold jobs outside the business community, which often opposes their values. And they often get personally involved in the problems of their clients and audiences, sometimes even becoming their advocates (Brint, 1984; Rootes, 1995).

Globalization Potential

Finally, new social movements possess more potential for globalization than old social movements did. In the 1960s, social movements were typically *national* in scope. That is why, for example, the intensity and frequency of urban race riots in the United States in the 1960s did not depend on such local conditions as the degree of black–white

BOX 18.3   THE WOMEN'S MOVEMENT

The women's movement was the first new social movement.

A century ago, women began to play a smaller role in domestic and farm work and started to enter the paid labour force in significant numbers. Owning more of their own economic resources, they became more independent-minded. They began to realize they might free themselves of oppressive authority in the home. They also started to understand there was nothing inevitable about their receiving less pay and working in worse conditions than men with comparable jobs (Strong-Boag, 1986: 179).

Formulating a program for social change requires such resources as time, money, and education. Not surprisingly, therefore, the "first wave" of the women's movement comprised highly educated professionals. A group of women with just that social profile established the Canadian Woman Suffrage Association in Toronto in 1883. By demonstrating, petitioning, and gaining the support of influential liberal-minded men, women won the right to vote federally in 1918, in all provinces and territories but Quebec and Northwest Territories by 1925, in Quebec in 1940, and in the Northwest Territories by 1951.

Along with the right to vote, women won the right to run for public office. They immediately exercised that right, running mainly on the CCF and Liberal tickets. A woman was first elected to provincial office in Alberta in 1917 and to the federal Parliament in 1921.

In provincial and territorial legislatures and the federal Parliament, women sought institutional reform through government action. Specifically, they pursued equitable pay for women, easier access to higher education, protection from domestic violence, and a fair share of family assets and child support in case of divorce or desertion. But progress was slow on all these fronts. That was partly because women's representation in the country's legislatures remained meagre. Even as late as the federal election in 2008, women composed just 21 percent of federal MPs (Bashevkin, 1986; "Women in National Parliaments," 2008). Moreover, some female MPs were hardly advocates of women's rights.

Because of slow progress, feminists developed a strategy in the 1960s and 1970s that was less oriented toward established political institutions and more oriented toward grassroots action. The new strategy sought to achieve change not just "from above," by means of party politics but also "from below," by creating a whole network of new organizations such as study groups, consciousness-raising circles, women's bookstores, rape crisis centres, abortion clinics, shelters for battered women, and opportunities to publicize the importance of feminist aims, such as International Women's Day marches.

It was not only slow progress on the established political front that led women to create this network of new organizations. Many "second-wave" feminists were deeply involved in the student movement of the 1960s and 1970s. They were appalled to discover that, despite much rhetoric about liberation and equality, men controlled the student movement and often refused to allow feminist issues to become part of their agenda. To pursue their aims they felt it was necessary to create new organizations run by women.

Today, the women's movement operates at both the grassroots level and within established political organizations to achieve its aims. It is internally differentiated. *Liberal feminists* believe that women can participate fully in society if they achieve equality of opportunity with men. They therefore advocate policies aimed at pay equity and the elimination of gender discrimination in the workplace. *Radical feminists* hold that male domination is rooted in the family. They champion free and safe contraception and abortion, an equitable division of domestic labour, and the like. *Socialist feminists* maintain that legal equality is not enough to ensure that women can participate fully in society. In addition, they argue, the state should provide affordable and accessible daycare facilities and other services. These services, they say, could alleviate the economic burdens that prevent most women, especially those from the working class, from taking full advantage of available opportunities for education and employment. *Anti-racist and postmodernist feminists* have criticized liberal, socialist, and radical feminists for generalizing from the experience of white women and failing to see how women's lives are rooted in particular historical and racial experiences. These new currents have done much to extend the relevance of feminism to previously marginalized groups. Thus, despite their different emphases, the various types of feminism share a strong desire to see members of a previously marginal group expand their citizenship rights and become full participants in society.

inequality in a given city (Spilerman, 1970, 1976). Instead, congressional and presidential action (and lack of action) on civil rights issues, national TV coverage of race issues, and growing black consciousness and solidarity helped to create the view among African Americans that racial problems are nationwide and can be solved only by the federal government.

Many new social movements that gained force in the 1970s increased the scope of protest still further. For example, members of the nuclear disarmament and environmental movements viewed federal legislation as a necessary but insufficient solution to the issues that troubled them. Once they recognized that, say, the condition of the Brazilian rain forest affects climatic conditions worldwide and that the spread of weapons of mass destruction can easily destroy all of humanity, movement activists pressed for international agreements binding all countries to stop environmental destruction and nuclear proliferation. Social movements went global.

The globalization of social movements was facilitated by the ease with which people in various national movements could travel and communicate with like-minded activists from other countries. In the age of CNN, inexpensive jet transportation, fax machines, and e-mail, it was possible not only to see the connection between apparently local problems and their global sources but also to act locally and globally. Greenpeace, for instance, is a highly successful environmental movement that originated in Vancouver in the mid-1970s and now has offices in 41 countries, with its international office in Amsterdam ("Greenpeace," 1999). Among many other initiatives, it has mounted a campaign to eliminate the international transportation and dumping of toxic wastes. Its representatives visited local environmental groups in African and other developing countries, supplied them with organizing kits to help them tie their local concerns to global political efforts, and published a newsletter to keep activists up to date about legal issues. Thus, Greenpeace coordinated a global campaign that enabled weak environmental organizations in developing countries to act more effectively, and raised the costs of continuing the international trade in toxic waste. Greenpeace is hardly alone in its efforts to go global. In 1953, there were 110 international social movement organizations. Forty years later, there were 631. About a quarter were human rights organizations and about a seventh were environmental organizations, the latter representing by far the fastest growing organizational type (Smith, 1998: 97).

The globalization of social movements can be further illustrated by coming full circle and returning to the anecdote with which I began this chapter. In 1991, I visited my hometown. I had not been back in years. As I entered the city, I vaguely sensed that something was different. I could not define the change precisely until I reached the Irving pulp and paper mill. Suddenly, it became obvious: the rotten-egg smell was virtually

gone. I subsequently discovered that in the 1970s a local woman whose son developed a serious case of asthma took legal action against the mill and eventually won. The mill owner was required by law to install a "scrubber" in the main smokestack to remove most of the sulphur dioxide emissions. Soon, the federal government was putting pressure on the mill owner to purify the polluted water that poured out of the plant and into the St. John River and the Bay of Fundy. Apparently, local citizens and the environmental movement had caused a change in the climate of opinion, influencing the government to force the mill owner to spend millions of dollars on a cleanup. It took decades, but what was political heresy in 1968 eventually became established practice because environmental concerns had been amplified by the voice of a movement that had grown to global proportions. In general, as this case illustrates, globalization helps to ensure that many new social movements transcend local and national boundaries and that many of them—but, as you will now learn, not all—promote universalistic goals.

II. THE OTHER 85 PERCENT

With variations, the pattern of social movement evolution sketched previously applies to the 20 or so rich countries of North America, Western Europe, Australia, New Zealand, and Japan. As we have seen, social movements in these rich countries typically sought to broaden democracy through the expansion of citizenship rights. In contrast, social movements in the other 85 percent of the world developed differently. They focused less on broadening the bases of democracy than on ensuring more elemental human rights, notably freedom from colonial rule and freedom to create the conditions for independent economic growth.

The "other 85 percent" of the world is weak economically, politically, and militarily because it began substantial industrialization only after World War I and in some cases after World War II. This circumstance allowed the early industrializers (Britain, France, Japan, Russia, etc.) to carve up most of Asia, Africa, and South America into colonies, protectorates, mandates, spheres of influence, and other administrative forms of subjugation. The nineteenth century was the age of imperialism. The early industrializers used the rest of the world as a captive market for their manufactured goods and a source of inexpensive raw materials and labour. They enriched themselves even as they limited economic growth and welfare in the less-developed countries.

Events in the Muslim world were in many respects typical and may therefore illustrate the problem (Hourani, 1991: 265–349). Already by the 1830s the armed forces of France had taken control of part of Algeria, those of Britain had taken control of part of the Arabian peninsula, and those of Russia had taken over the Muslim lands of the Caucasus. A century later, almost the entire Middle East and North Africa were under British and French control. Egyptian cotton fed the looms of Lancashire. Iraqi oil supplied half of France's needs. British and French ships brought European machinery and textiles to the region. British and French financiers profited handsomely from their control of local banking. Some indigenous merchants and landowners benefited from the new economic relations too. However, the growing number of peasants and urban workers remained poor and powerless.

In the world's rich countries, a strong bourgeoisie— an affluent and politically powerful class of merchants, industrialists, and financiers—did much to promote the growth of democracy in its early stages (Moore, 1967). In contrast, in the Muslim countries and the rest of the less economically developed world, the bourgeoisie was small, weak, and dependent on imperial interests. As a result, democratic ideals had little chance to sink deep roots. Instead, European and (after World War II) American domination of less-developed countries bred resentment, resistance, and revolt. Peasants, urban workers, intellectuals, and military officers were increasingly attracted to anti-imperialist independence movements based on various forms and mixes of socialism and nationalism (Brym, 1980: 50–53; Wolf, 1999 [1969]).

In the Muslim world, Islam was an additional source of anti-imperialist sentiment. In 1928, a movement known as the Society of the Muslim Brothers was formed in Egypt ("Muslim Brotherhood Movement," 2002). It served as a prototype for many similar groups. The Muslim Brothers argued against Western values and imperialist domination. They called for a return to the teaching of the Qur'an and demanded that Egypt become an Islamic state based on religious law (*shari'a*). This type of Islamic fundamentalism became popular in Egypt and throughout the Muslim world in the twentieth century, gaining impetus especially in Iran from the 1960s on and then spreading to Algeria and as far afield as Afghanistan and Sudan by the end of that

Anti-globalization street protests are now expected at meetings of international trade and finance organizations, such as the World Trade Organization. (This is a scene from 2002 protests in Quebec City.) The anti-globalization movement is a globalized movement too.
SOURCE: © Getty Images.

century. A clear line of intellectual influence and development leads from the early Muslim Brothers to the assassins of Egypt's President Anwar Sadat in 1981 after he made peace with Israel to Osama bin Laden today (Worth, 2001). Bin Laden's chief aims are to remove all Western (especially American) influence from countries and regions with Muslim majorities, create in their place societies based on a fundamentalist interpretation of Islamic law, and destroy Israel as a Jewish state.

However much al-Qaeda is influenced by ideas dating back eight decades, it is every inch a global movement that relies on modern technology for its successes. Al-Qaeda has placed operatives in as many as 60 countries. It finances itself through a complex international network of legitimate businesses, charitable and relief organizations, private donors, and opium trafficking operations (Shahar, 2001). Bin Laden communicated with his operatives via satellite telephone until U.S. law enforcement authorities inexplicably revealed they were tapping calls from his base in Afghanistan. Once he learned of these taps, he increased his use of another, more effective means of global communication: sending messages that are easily encrypted but difficult to decode via the Internet (Kelley, 2001; McCullogh, 2000). Some analysts think such

messages were used to help plan and coordinate the complex, virtually simultaneous jet hijackings that resulted in the crash of an airliner in Pennsylvania and the destruction of the World Trade Center and part of the Pentagon on September 11, 2001, killing some 3000 people.

Al-Qaeda is an extremist movement with few like it. However, it is also one in a whole range of reactions against Western power and influence that grips much of the developing world. In its extreme forms, this anti-Western reaction has little or no respect for minority rights, multiculturalism, elections, relatively open markets, and many of the other freedoms we enjoy and often take for granted in the West. Yet the anti-Western reaction is everywhere, even in its most extreme forms, based on the desire of people to restore the independence and dignity they lost when the industrialized world showed up on their doorstep uninvited. One of the great tasks the West faces in the twenty-first century is to defend itself against violence while doing its utmost to remove the ultimate source of that violence: the gap between rich and poor countries that opened up at the time of the Industrial Revolution and that has widened ever since. Whether we are up to the task is anyone's guess.

SUMMARY

1. Democracy involves a two-way process of control between the state (the set of institutions that formulate and carry out a country's law, policies, and binding regulations) and civil society (the private sphere, consisting of social movements, political parties, etc.).

2. The level of democracy in a society depends on the capacity of civil society to influence the state through citizen support of social movements, political parties, and other groups. That capacity increases as power becomes more widely distributed in society.

3. Although pluralists correctly note that democratic politics is about negotiation and compromise, they fail to appreciate how advantaged groups tend to have more political influence than others.

4. Although elite theorists are correct to note that power is concentrated in the hands of advantaged groups, they fail to appreciate how variations in the distribution of power influence political behaviour and public policy.

5. While power-balance theorists focus on the effect of changes in the distribution of power in

society, they fail to appreciate what state-centred theorists emphasize—that state institutions and laws also affect political behaviour and public policy.

6. The degree to which power is widely distributed influences the success of particular kinds of parties and policies. Widely distributed power is associated with the success of labour parties and policies that redistribute wealth.

7. Research does not support the view that social movements emerge when relative deprivation spreads.

8. Research suggests that people are more inclined to rebel against the status quo when they are bound by close social ties to many other people who feel similarly wronged and when they have the money and other resources needed to protest.

9. For social movements to grow, members must engage in frame alignment, making the activities, goals, and ideology of the movement congruent with the interests, beliefs, and values of potential new recruits.

10. The history of democracy is a struggle for the acquisition of constantly broadening citizenship

rights—first the right to free speech, freedom of religion, and justice before the law, then the right to vote and run for office, then the right to a certain level of economic security and full participation in the life of society, and finally the right of marginal groups to full citizenship and the right of humanity as a whole to peace and security.

11. In the developing world, social movements have focused less on broadening the bases of democracy than on ensuring more elemental human rights, notably freedom from colonial rule and freedom to create the conditions for independent economic growth. In some cases these movements have taken extreme, anti-democratic forms.

QUESTIONS TO CONSIDER

1. Have you ever participated in a social movement or been actively involved in a political party? If so, explain how your political choices (e.g., which party you joined, your level of participation, the timing of your recruitment) were influenced by the sociological factors discussed in this chapter. If you have never participated in a social movement or been actively involved in a political party, explain how the sociological factors discussed in this chapter influence you to remain politically inactive.

2. How would you achieve a political goal? Map out a detailed strategy for reaching a clearly defined aim, such as a reduction in income tax or an increase in university funding. Who would you try to recruit to help you achieve your goal? Why? What collective actions do you think would be most successful? Why? To whose attention would these actions be directed? Why? Write a manifesto that frames your argument in a way that is culturally appealing to potential recruits.

3. Do you think that social movements will be more or less widespread in the twenty-first century than they were in the twentieth? Why or why not? What kinds of social movements are likely to predominate?

4. Do you think that the twenty-first century will be more or less democratic than the twentieth? Why or why not?

GLOSSARY

Authorities are people who occupy the command posts of legitimized power structures.

Authority is power that is widely viewed as legitimate.

Civil citizenship recognizes the right to free speech, freedom of religion, and justice before the law.

Civil society is the private (non-state) sphere of social life.

Elite theory maintains that well-to-do people consistently have more political influence than people who are less well-to-do and that society is therefore not as democratic as it is often portrayed.

Force is coercive power.

Frame alignment is the process by which individual interests, beliefs, and values either become congruent and complementary with the activities, goals, and ideology of a social movement or fail to do so.

New social movements are post-1950s movements that attract a disproportionately large number of highly educated people in the social, educational, and cultural fields and universalize the struggle for citizenship.

Pluralist theory holds that society has many competing interests and centres of power and that no one interest or power centre predominates in the long run.

Political citizenship recognizes the right to run for office and vote.

Political parties are organizations that seek to control state power.

A **political revolution** is a concerted attempt on the part of many people to overthrow existing political institutions and establish new ones. Political revolutions take place when widespread and successful movements of opposition clash with crumbling traditional or legal-rational authority.

Power is the ability of an individual or a group to impose its will on others, even if they resist.

Power-balance theory suggests that social movement formation and success depend on how powerful authorities are compared with partisans of change. It also holds that societies with widely distributed power are more democratic and more egalitarian than societies with narrowly held power.

Relative deprivation is an intolerable gap between the social rewards people feel they deserve and the social rewards they expect to receive.

Resource mobilization theory holds that social movements crystallize and succeed in achieving their goals to the degree that they have access to scarce resources, such as money and effective communication facilities.

A **ruling class** is a self-conscious and cohesive group of people, led by corporate executives and owners of big business, who act to advance their common interests.

Social citizenship recognizes the right to a certain level of economic security and full participation in social life.

Social movements are enduring collective attempts to change part or all of the social order by means of rioting, petitioning, striking, demonstrating, and establishing pressure groups, unions, and political parties.

The **state** is a set of institutions that formulate and implement a country's laws, policies, and binding regulations. It consists of an executive branch (which initiates laws), a legislative branch (which makes laws), a judicial branch (which interprets laws), and an administrative and coercive apparatus (which enforces laws and protects state security).

State-centred theory shows how the state structures political life independently of the way power is distributed among classes and other groups at a given time.

Universal citizenship recognizes the right of marginal groups and the rights of humanity as a whole to full citizenship.

SUGGESTED READING

Baer, Doug, ed. (2002). *Political Sociology: Canadian Perspectives.* Toronto: Oxford University Press. This useful compendium of Canadian materials covers major issues and debates.

Tilly, Charles, and Sidney Tarrow. (2007). *Contentious Politics.* Boulder CO: Paradigm Publishers. An accessible, and innovative introduction to political sociology by two grand masters.

Wolf, Eric. (1999 [1969]). *Peasant Wars of the 20th Century.* Norman, OK: Oklahoma University Press. The best introduction to Third World social movements.

NOTES

1. In addition, fewer than 13 percent of the American working class are unionized, making it the least organized working class in any of the world's rich countries.

2. For example, in the 1890s, a coalition of white and black southern farmers threatened the established American political parties. It was precisely for this reason that American electoral laws were made more restrictive.

3. Some of these generalizations do not apply to countries with a long tradition of labour government. For example, since World War II, Sweden has experienced high levels of unionization and low strike rates. That is because Swedish workers and their representatives are involved in government policymaking. Decisions about wages and benefits tend to be made in negotiations between unions, employer associations, and governments rather than on the picket line.

WEB RESOURCES

Companion Website for This Book

http://www.newsociety6e.nelson.com
Begin by clicking on the Student Resources section of the website. Next, select the chapter you are studying from the pull-down menu. From the Student Resources page, you have easy access to InfoTrac College Edition® and other resources, such as the Glossary, Test Yourself questions, and additional readings. The website also has many useful tips to aid you in your study of sociology.

InfoTrac College Edition Search Terms

Visit http://www.infotrac-college.com for access to more than 20 million articles from nearly 6000 sources when doing your online research.

SOURCE: © iStockphoto.com/ Britta Kasholm

CHAPTER NINETEEN

Globalization

Josée Johnston
UNIVERSITY OF TORONTO

In this chapter you will learn that

- Globalization is a term used to describe how the world "shrinks" as capital, ideas, corporations, commodities, and workers rapidly cross vast distances. You will learn about the complexities of globalization, a term much used and abused, and acquire a working definition of it.

- Globalization is not a distant force, but a real-world phenomenon that affects you daily as you eat, drink, work, and go shopping. By the end of the chapter, you will better understand how globalization relates to you as a consumer, a worker, and a citizen.

- Globalization is dynamic because it is contested by different social forces promoting different kinds of globalization. This chapter will give you a conceptual framework that will allow you to appreciate the "top-down" forces of globalization that promote global capitalism and the "bottom-up" forces demanding greater democracy, social justice, and sustainability in the global system.

INTRODUCTION

THE BURGER AND FRIES GO GLOBAL

Think about your average fast-food meal: a burger, fries, and a pop. This is the food of North America—simple, greasy, fast, and familiar. Maybe fast food has something to do with the sociology of health or the sociology of food, but what does it have to do with the sociology of globalization?

It turns out that globalization has a lot to do with everyday events like eating fast food. The average North American meal travels over 1600 kilometres to reach your dinner table, so there is a good chance that your burger and fries have been *globalized*.

Let's start with the burger. Although Canadian ranchers pride themselves on their cattle exports, at least 30 percent of the beef eaten in Canada is imported from the United States, Australia, New Zealand, and Uruguay. Even if the beef in your burger did originate in Canada, the process of transforming a cow into your hamburger was deeply affected by globalization processes. Due to global market pressures, the meatpacking industry in Canada was restructured

SOURCE: © Dwight Cendrowski/Alamy.

in the 1980s and 1990s; the goal was to cut costs by centralizing production and finding cheaper labour supplies. Today, just two slaughterhouse plants (owned by U.S. multinational corporations) account for 80 percent of Canada's slaughtering capacity in heifers and steers (MacLachlan, 2004: 46). The small town of Brooks, Alberta, is home to one of these plants, Lakeside Packers, which is owned by American meat giant Tyson Fresh Meats, the world's largest beef and pork supplier. Brooks is now a temporary home for hundreds of immigrants from Sudan who come to work at the plant. In fact, more than 20 languages are spoken inside the factory walls, including Arabic, French, Spanish, Tagalog, Chinese, and Cambodian.

Even a vegetarian's fast-food choices are affected by globalization. In 2001, six vegetarians from British Columbia working with an American lawyer moved to sue McDonald's after it was revealed that McDonald's French fries use beef fat for "flavouring." After hearing the announcement, vegetarian activists in India held demonstrations and attacked a McDonald's in Bombay, demanding that McDonald's leave the country (CBC News, 2001). McDonald's settled the lawsuit in 2002 by agreeing to donate $10 million dollars to Hindu and other consumer groups.

If our fast food is influenced by global forces, North American fast food also influences global eating. North American markets became relatively saturated with fast-food outlets in the 1980s, so McDonald's made a push in the 1990s for international expansion. The number of countries with a McDonald's doubled from 59 in 1991 to 114 in 1998, and by the end of the 1990s an estimated 60 percent of McDonald's corporate profits come from its international division (McDonald's, 1999). McDonald's opens a new restaurant every 17 hours and is the world's largest user of beef. Ronald McDonald himself is the second most recognized figure in the world, next to Santa Claus (Brownell and Horgen, 2004: 58). In 2005, sales in the United States accounted for only 34 percent of McDonald's revenue (Workman, 2006).

It turns out, then, that everyday activities—like eating a hamburger and fries—have a lot to do with globalization. In an obvious way, the resources and labour that make up a fast-food meal originate from locations all around the globe. But even when the ingredients come from close to home, the food itself can be affected by global events like international trade agreements, European social movements, international labour migration, faraway protests against McDonald's, and global food scares, like mad cow disease.

GLOBALIZATION OR "GLOBALONEY"?

But before going any farther, let's raise perhaps our most difficult question in this chapter: What do we mean by *globalization*? It is one of the most frequently heard buzzwords in the English language, yet there is no consensus on its meaning. The term was coined in the late 1970s, and today there are thousands of globalization books, conferences, university courses, and references in newspapers and magazines, many of which contradict each other. This confusion has led some academics to dismiss the term altogether as a confused mixture of globalization and baloney—what some crankily refer to as "globaloney."

While it is hard to find agreement on a definition of globalization, you don't have to look hard to find controversy about whether globalization is good or bad. A common tendency on both the left and the right of the political spectrum is to depict globalization in simplistic terms. For right-wing free-marketers, globalization represents the welcome spread of capitalism throughout the world. For many left-wing social activists and politicians, globalization is more like a Death Star. In the words of Barry Lynn, former executive director of *Global Business* magazine,

> Globalization is many things, and much has been written about it and said. But throw all the tomes and studies and placards into a giant try-works, and you'll render two simple arguments: 1) Globalization is good because it spreads what is good in America, such as a liberal approach to business, and McDonald's. 2) Globalization is bad because it spreads what is worst about America, such as a liberal approach to business, and McDonald's. (Lynn, 2002: 34)

A primary objective of this chapter is to get beyond this kind of simplistic thinking and gain a more sophisticated sense of what exactly is meant by globalization. The objective is not to provide the ultimate definition of globalization that will ring true for all people until the end of time, but to understand how different political and economic interests struggle to promote their own brand of globalization.

DEFINING GLOBALIZATION

While figuring out exactly what we mean by globalization is a primary objective of the chapter, we need a neutral definition to get us started: **Globalization** is a social, economic, and political process that makes it easier for people, goods, ideas, and capital to travel around the world at an unprecedented pace (Waters, 1995: 3). Globalization makes the world look and feel smaller.

Of course, the world is not shrinking literally. What is instead occurring is that people, money, corporations, and ideas travel across the globe more quickly and efficiently than ever before. Distance no longer seems as relevant, and time lags that used to characterize our social relations are diminished. We no longer think it's crazy to have a romantic relationship with somebody across the country or even across the world. One can now communicate instantly through telephone, e-mail, Instant Messenger, or a web-camera connection. If we want to see our special sweetheart in person, we can take a relatively inexpensive plane trip rather than waiting for an ocean-going vessel to take us for a week-long journey across the seas. If our beloved is broke and needs money, we don't have to put a cheque in the mail. Instead we can transfer money instantly through electronic banking networks. And if you are single, you can systematically search the world for love through the thousands of online dating sites, some of which are devoted just to vegetarians, tattoo artists, and cat lovers.

One term for this shrinking world phenomenon is **time–space compression,** which suggests that we are no longer slowed down by long distances and time differences (Harvey, 1990: 284). Not only do we feel less constrained by time and distance, but some global phenomena seem to transcend the idea of physical space altogether. The Internet has facilitated the creation of **virtual communities**, in which people can meet, share ideas, and build relationships across state borders without ever meeting face-to-face. Use of the Internet has increased dramatically, although it still involve less than 15 percent of the world's population (see Table 19.1, p. 454).

There are many examples of time–space compression but there are also many instances where time still passes slowly, the limits of geography are still relevant, and people are excluded from virtual communities. Not all people and ideas have access to channels of globalization like the Internet or even the telephone. Inequality of access to means of communication is known as the **digital divide** (see Table 19.2, p. 454).

There is a lot of academic debate about how recent globalization is. We won't venture far into this hotly contested territory, but it is important to note that the world has been shrinking for a long time. Time–space compression can be traced back at least to the 1500s with the beginning of transoceanic European exploration. The world became smaller

TABLE 19.1   WORLD INTERNET USERS AND POPULATION

WORLD REGIONS	POPULATION (2008 EST.)	INTERNET USERS 31-DEC-00	INTERNET USERS, LATEST DATA	PENETRATION (% OF POPULATION)	USER INCREASE 2000–2008 (%)	USERS, % OF WORLD POPULATION
Africa	955 206 348	4 514 400	51 065 630	5.30	3.50	0.76
Asia	3 776 181 949	114 304 000	578 538 257	15.30	39.50	8.67
Europe	800 401 065	105 096 093	384 633 765	48.10	26.30	5.76
Middle East	197 090 443	3 284 800	41 939 200	21.30	2.90	0.63
North America	337 167 248	108 096 800	248 241 969	73.60	17.00	3.72
Latin America/ Caribbean	576 091 673	18 068 919	139 009 209	24.10	9.50	2.08
Oceania/Australia	33 981 562	7 620 480	20 204 331	59.50	1.40	0.30
WORLD TOTAL	6 676 120 288	360 985 492	1 463 632 361	21.90	100.00	21.92

SOURCE: Adapted from Internet World Stats, 2008, "World Internet Usage and Population Statistics." www.internetworldstats.com. (Retrieved 19 August 2009). Copyright © 2001–2008. Miniwatts Marketing Group. All rights reserved.

with the invention of the steamship and the locomotive—two technologies that connected distant populations at a rate unimagined by previous generations. Colonial relationships in the eighteenth and nineteenth centuries moved millions of people and shiploads of wealth around the world.

The current phase of time–space compression is not radically different in form, but its pace has grown especially quickly since the 1980s. A jet is much faster than a steamship. E-mail is less cumbersome than

mail travelling by truck or ship. Ships moving silver, spices, and opium across the ocean can transfer wealth globally, but not as quickly as the enormous and instantaneous flows of capital that move in and out of the stock market in seconds.

THE GLOBAL AND THE ETHICAL

Understanding globalization as a series of processes connecting people, resources, and capital across the

TABLE 19.2   GLOBALIZATION AND TIME–SPACE COMPRESSION

EXAMPLE	HOW IT COMPRESSES SPACE AND TIME	LIMITS TO GLOBALIZATION
The telephone	Person-to-person communication is made possible across oceans and most national boundaries.	Many of the world's inhabitants do not have access to a telephone. The executive deputy president of South Africa in 1996, Thabo Mbeki, made a speech at the Information Society and Development Conference, where he informed the delegates that "half of humanity has never made a telephone call."
The Internet	Ideas, images, articles, videos, music, and text forms can be transmitted instantly across vast geographic distances.	On a global scale, access to the Internet is even more limited than access to the telephone. (See Table 19.1.)
Satellite television	Television is no longer restricted to local television stations; satellites allow transmission of programming from multiple points of production around the world.	Television ownership is concentrated in wealthy countries, television production is controlled by a small number of media monopolies centred in the industrialized North, and television content globally is fairly homogenous and closely linked to consumer capitalism (McKibben, 1993).
Electronic money markets	Capital can flow across national borders almost instantly.	Most of the world's citizens do not have a bank account, let alone access to electronic financial markets.

globe gets us away from seeing it as either a blessing or an evil. Globalization is inherently neither good nor bad, but the consequences of globalization processes do affect human lives and the environment. These consequences generate strong opinions and ethical positions, particularly as they relate to economic processes and the role of the U.S. on the global stage.

Ethical debates surrounding globalization became particularly pronounced after the September 11 terrorist attacks against the United States, symbolically centred on the World Trade Center, the heart of U.S. and global capitalism, and the Pentagon, the planning and coordination centre of the U.S. military. While the Bush administration explained the attacks as part of a global war of good against evil, others used the terrorist attacks as an opportunity to raise critical questions about the inequities of global capitalism and the role of the U.S. in the global system. On the first anniversary of the attacks, then Prime Minister Jean Chrétien incited a national controversy by suggesting in a CBC television interview that the victims of global capitalism could not be expected to suffer silently, and that the wealthy, powerful countries should behave with greater humility in the international arena. In Chrétien's words, the Western world is "looked upon as being arrogant, self-satisfied, greedy and with no limits. The 11th of September is an occasion for me to realize it even more" (CBC News, 2002a). Responding to this controversy, popular Canadian radio and television personality Rex Murphy expressed public anxiety about the widening gap between rich and poor in the global economy:

> Here in the West, a ball player can sign a $100-million contract for playing a game or Britney Spears can yodel and grind for 60 seconds and Pepsi shells out a fortune. The excesses of our way of life must scream like an obscenity. To those parts of the world where children starve and die by the tens of thousands daily, the disproportion between our safety and well being, our nutrition and health compared to so many others does make us arrogant, careless and obnoxious. This is not the germ pile from which Osama and his butcheries were spawned. But it is a situation of grave conscience. It is the theme that leaders should address and it is a subject that Prime Minister Chrétien did well in thinking and talking aloud. (CBC News, 2002b)

TOP-DOWN VERSUS BOTTOM-UP GLOBALIZATION

Questions of equality, security, and social justice are critical in the ongoing debate about globalization and will be explored in the rest of this chapter. These debates can be understood as part of the tension between top-down and bottom-up globalization. **Top-down globalization** involves the actions of groups promoting globalized capitalism and free trade. The term *globalization* was first widely used by the American Express credit card company, which boasted in the 1970s that its card was accepted worldwide (Harvey, 1990: 13). The term was then taken up in financial and business circles, where it came to represent hopes for a world where capital could flow freely around the world, uninhibited by national boundaries or governments insisting on national regulations and taxation.

Top-down globalization has been dominated by **neoliberal** economic policies, which have become prevalent in both rich and poor countries since the 1980s. Neoliberal policies are associated with a retreat from state spending and regulation, a focus on individual responsibility for one's own welfare, less protection for labour and the environment, privatization of state resources, and faith in the power of the market and the profit motive to create wealth (see Chapter 9, Development and Underdevelopment). Top-down globalization is also strongly associated with the United States due to its role promoting neoliberal policies globally through institutions like the International Monetary Fund (IMF) and World Bank, headquartered in Washington D.C. For this reason, top-down globalization has also been referred to as the "Washington consensus." In addition, the United States is often perceived as an exemplar of neoliberal policy domestically, even though it seems to deviate on key matters like balanced budgets (in part because of high levels of U.S. military spending).

Globalization from below describes the actions of groups that criticize the injustices that result from globalization processes. The mass media frequently describe these groups as being opposed to globalization. That is not entirely accurate. Many groups that criticize the injustices resulting from globalization actually support particular types of globalization, such as the spread of international human rights and global labour standards. Moreover, they use technologies, like the Internet, to help them organize and communicate internationally. In general, groups that support globalization from below advocate more democracy, environmental protection, and social justice in the global system. Bottom-up globalizers are against the neoliberal forms of globalization that put capital mobility and profits before people's basic needs, and they criticize the powerful economic, political, and military influence of transnational corporations and the United States government.

Top-down globalization has been targeted by environmentalists, peasant organizations, and farmers' unions, but it has also been criticized by capitalist insiders such as world-famous economist and policy advisor Jeffrey Sachs; international financier George Soros, and Joseph Stiglitz, Nobel Prize winner and former chief economist and vice-president of the World Bank (Sachs, 2005; Soros, 1998; Stiglitz, 2003). While everyone from rock stars to prime ministers demands greater justice in the global system, how to achieve it is not clear. There is no consensus on whether moderate capitalist reforms are sufficient, whether trade liberalization will help the poor, or whether the answer lies in partial or total withdrawal from global markets. Because of these differences, globalization from below should be understood less as a cohesive movement and more as a broad framework that encompasses multiple perspectives, including moderate critiques of neoliberalism, radical anticapitalist positions, various forms of anarchism, armed peasant uprisings, and fair-trade coffee projects.

How then do the forces of globalization operate in our daily lives? People are involved with globalization processes as capitalists, consumer, workers, and citizen (Robbins, 2005: 2–4). In the remainder of this chapter, we explore the profound influence of time–space compression in each of these realms.

CAPITALISTS GO GLOBAL
THE RISE OF FINANCIAL CAPITAL

In economic terms, money used for investment, currency trading, and so forth is "financial capital." In the globalized economy, financial capital has grown much faster than production and trade. More than US$1.5 trillion flow through electronic financial channels every day, and an estimated 98 percent of these flows are purely speculative, meaning they are unrelated to the buying and selling of physical goods but involve short-term trading of things like foreign currencies. Global trade in goods and services equalled $6.5 billion in 1998. While this seems an impressive number, it is equal to only 4.3 days' worth

of trade on foreign exchange markets (Ellwood, 2001: 72). Using a fully computerized global financial system, traders can move around billions of dollars to profit from minuscule changes in currency rates.

The rise of financial capital has been labelled "casino capitalism" since financial speculators, like casino gamblers, stand to make or lose millions of dollars in short periods of time (Strange, 1986). The rise of casino capitalism has been facilitated by the financial deregulation that has occurred under neoliberal regimes since the 1980s as governments gave up regulatory powers. The danger with casino capitalism is that investor speculation (a process akin to placing a bet) makes financial systems unstable. Money floods into markets during periods of optimism, creating a financial "bubble" that drives markets up. The bubble bursts when investors realize that the market is overpriced relative to the value of real assets. This causes a period of panic involving an outflow of capital and, in due course, economic recession.

A snowball of financial panic is precisely what the world witnessed during the 1997 Asian financial crisis, which started in Thailand and went on to affect the currencies, stock markets, and asset prices of a host of Asian countries, including Indonesia, South Korea, and Hong Kong as well as the financial systems of Brazil and Russia. In 2007–2009, a similar crisis occurred when the real estate market collapsed in the United States. Initially inexpensive mortgages lured millions of Americans into the housing market. All was well while house prices rose. People felt richer, and they borrowed more and more money against the value of their homes. Then people had to renew their mortgages at higher interest rates, and many of them could not afford it. Foreclosures increased. With more houses on the market, house prices began to fall. The spiral of falling house prices and skyrocketing foreclosures soon put some large financial institutions in a position of not having enough cash on hand to continue operations. Some of them went bankrupt while others sought government assistance to stay in business. Then the problem went global because financial institutions around the world had invested heavily in U.S. debt. Some institutions, such as Iceland's three biggest private banks, went bankrupt, while governments had to lend money to keep others afloat. Among other things, the crisis demonstrated how porous global financial borders are. In the words of the chief European economist at Deutsche Bank, "In this day and age, a bank run spreads around the world, not around the block" (Landler, 2008).

OVERCAPACITY AND CENTRALIZATION

The growth of casino capitalism is also linked to declining profits and overcapacity in the economy of goods and services. Put simply, global corporations are producing more things than the world's consumers can afford to purchase. There is an estimated 40 percent excess capacity in China's manufacturing sector and 30 percent excess capacity in global automotives (Bello, 2001: 129). In 1997, the chairman of General Electric, Jack Welch, told the *Financial Times* of London that "[t]here is excess global capacity in almost every industry." In 2000, the automotive industry produced 80 million vehicles for fewer than 60 million buyers. While financial markets boomed throughout the early 2000s, and wealth appeared to be growing exponentially for some people, a number of economists worried that excess capacity in the productive economy—accompanied by growing inequality and global poverty that erodes the worldwide consumption base—meant that a global recession was in the works (Bello, 2002). The 2007–2009 U.S. financial crisis demonstrated both the overcapacity problem and the interpenetration of global financial markets. Global investors worried about the bankruptcy even of giants of the productive economy like General Motors and Chrysler, and the U.S. slowdown spread to national economies around the world. In 2008, the Indian high-tech and outsourcing industries, which rely heavily on business from the U.S. financial sector, began to freeze wages and announce layoffs for software programmers and workers in call centres (Kahn, 2008). Even China, whose rapid growth has been powered by exports, experienced a drop in exports at the end of 2008, leaving Communist Party officials worrying about employing the millions of workers in the export sector, which in turn depends on American consumers (Jacobs and Barboza, 2008).

Besides creating complex webs of interdependence between national economies, the creation of a global economy has changed the way corporations look and operate. In short, these conditions have made corporations leaner, meaner, bigger, more diverse in terms of the goods they produce, and more involved in complex financial dealings and investments throughout the world.

To survive problems of overcapacity and economic slowdown, corporations have merged to trim operating costs. Volvo and Ford have made an alliance, Renault took over Nissan, and Chrysler temporarily teamed up with Daimler-Benz. Chasing the high profits found in the financial sector, traditional corporations have gotten into the money-lending business, while banks have become involved in new kinds of businesses like trading securities. Today, transnational corporations find it hard to survive without diversifying into multiple goods in many countries, and this explains why the last decades have witnesses the greatest rate of mergers and consolidation in history (International Forum on Globalization [IFG], 2001: 6; see Figure 19.1). It also helps explain why the same handful of corporations can be found almost everywhere, offering a similar range of products in the world's shopping malls

FIGURE 19.1 FOREIGN DIRECT INVESTMENT AND CROSS-BORDER MERGERS AND ACQUISITIONS

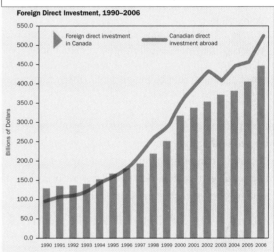

SOURCE: Treasury Board of Canada Secretariat, 2007, "Canada's Performance Report 2006–07—Annexes." On the World Wide Web at http://www.tbs-sct.gc.ca/reports-rapports/cp-rc/2006-2007/ann/ann17-eng.asp (retrieved 19 August 2009).

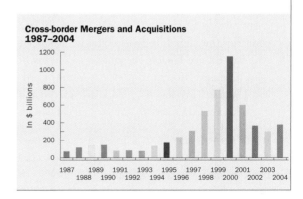

SOURCE: United Nations Conference on Trade and Development, n.d. "Table 8.2. Cross-border M&A purchases, by region/economy of purchaser, 1987–2004."
http://www.unctad.org/Templates/Download.asp?docid=6085&intItemID=3277&lang=1 (retrieved 19 August 2009).

The Kraft food brand demonstrates the complexity and expansiveness of a diversified transnational corporation. Today, it is difficult to go shopping without buying a Kraft product, even if you are a vegan and don't eat cheese. Kraft Foods is the largest food producer in the United States and the second-largest in the world, sells in 145 countries, has more than 200 production facilities, and has a global work force of more than 103 000. Even though Kraft is both large and omnipresent, it can be difficult to keep track of the many corporate structures linked to Kraft products. Kraft's story began simply enough, when it was founded as a wholesale cheese company in Chicago in 1903. Kraft's corporate genealogy quickly became very complicated as it acquired new products, took over other firms, and was in turn acquired by another corporation.

In 1988, Philip Morris—a multinational tobacco company—purchased Kraft Foods for US$12.9 billion. Some analysts speculated that Kraft's family-friendly image might offset the nega-

tive associations of Philip Morris being the world's biggest tobacco company. Philip Morris combined Kraft with General Foods a year later to form Kraft General Foods. Like other corporations in the early 1990s, Kraft General Foods experienced merger mania; Kraft gobbled up multiple companies around the world that sold coffee, candy, cheese, chocolate (including Toblerone), and cereals (including Shreddies and Shredded Wheat). In 1995, Kraft General Foods was reorganized and renamed Kraft Foods, while Kraft General Foods International became Kraft Foods International. In 2000, Philip Morris purchased Nabisco Holdings (a giant cracker and snack company), which it also merged into the Philip-Morris Kraft empire. In 2003, after negative publicity about a tobacco giant making food, as well as rising concern about the company's liability in tobacco and obesity class action suits, a company with the vague name of Altria became the parent company to the Kraft and Philip Morris family of food, cigarettes, and beer.

and airports (Box 19.1). These giant corporations trade with each other, but they also trade goods and services internally. Economists estimate that a third of all global trade involves transfers between different branches of the same corporation (Ellwood, 2001:54).

GROWTH OF THE CORPORATE GIANTS

Corporations have become bigger and more powerful than many national governments (May, 2006). Consider just these two facts (Anderson and Cavanaugh, 2000; IFG, 2001: 6):

- Of the largest 100 economies in the world, 51 are corporations (measured by sales), and 49 are countries (measured by gross domestic product).
- The world's five biggest corporations in terms of sales (General Motors, Wal-Mart, Mobil, Ford, and DaimlerChrysler) have sales that exceed the gross domestic product of 182 countries combined.

It will perhaps surprise you to learn that big corporations do not necessarily pay big taxes. In fact, corporations are paying less in taxes than they used to in percentage terms. Companies regularly play nation-states off one another, pressuring governments to lower taxes rates by threatening to move production to a more favourable location. The resulting decline in corporate taxes can be observed across all developed countries in the last two decades as mobile individuals

and corporations increasingly take advantage of global tax shelters, forcing governments to rely on taxes paid by less mobile individuals and small businesses (Figure 19.2). Between 1996 and 2000, two-thirds of corporations operating in the United States paid no taxes at all (including Microsoft, which paid no taxes in 1999 even though it reported income of $12.3 billion), while firms like Enron, Colgate-Palmolive, and Goodyear received tax refunds from the government (Burtner, 2004). In 2005, the U.S. Government Accountability Office reported that more than one-quarter of large corporations paid no taxes at all, while two-thirds of all corporations did not pay taxes every year between 1998 and 2005 (Borosage, 2008). Canadian corporations have also enjoyed big tax breaks, which they justify by their need to compete with low tax rates in the United States. Reductions in corporate taxes between 2000 and 2010 will decrease the Canadian government's federal revenues by $12.5 billion a year (Jackson, 2005).

CRITICS OF CORPORATE POWER

Bottom-up globalizers have reacted to the growth of global corporations in various ways (Bello, 2002; Starr, 1999). For example, the 1990s saw the emergence of an anti-sweatshop movement in North America after poor working conditions in the garment industry were exposed (Ross, 1997). Of particular importance was the 1996 Kathie Lee Gifford controversy, which

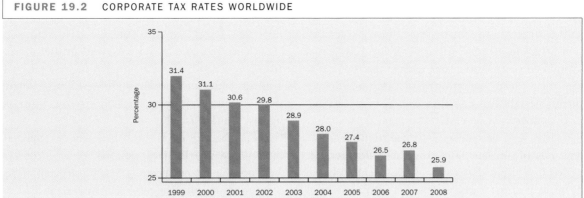

FIGURE 19.2   CORPORATE TAX RATES WORLDWIDE

SOURCE: KPMG, 2008, *KPMG's Corporate and Indirect Tax Rate Survey 2008*. http://www.kpmg.com/SiteCollectionDocuments/Corporate-and-Indirect-Tax-Rate-Survey-2008v2.pdf (retrieved 19 August 2009). Reprinted with permission from KPMG International.

revealed that her Wal-Mart clothing line was produced by child labour and involved human rights abuses. In 2000, Naomi Klein's *No Logo* became an international best-seller. She argued that large corporate brands are vulnerable to a backlash against corporate power. "Today," she wrote, "more and more campaigners are treating multinationals, and the policies that give them free reign, as the root cause of political injustices around the globe" (Klein, 2000: 338). AdBusters, a rabble-rousing media organization headquartered in Vancouver, launched multiple campaigns to "un-cool" famous brand names associated with sweatshop labour and environmental degradation (Adbusters, 2005). Corporate Accountability International (formerly Infact) launched a Kraft boycott in 1994 to expose the business practices of its parent company, Philip Morris, such as its alleged promotion of tobacco to children. More recently, the Sierra Club criticized Kraft for using genetically engineered ingredients in its food products. Other corporations have been criticized on issues ranging from labour practices (particularly in coffee production), environmental sustainability, animal welfare, and relationships with the military-industrial complex operating in Iraq.

Corporations have responded to anti-corporate criticism in various ways. For example, some have changed their name, diverting attention from their infamous brand. Philip Morris became Altria, much to the dismay of anti-smoking groups who argued this was an underhanded public relations move to obscure the company's roots in the tobacco industry. After receiving bad publicity about its genetic engineering, Monsanto became Pharmacia for most of its communications after merging with pharmaceutical giants Pharmacia and UpJohn.

Another way that global corporations are attempting to stem the tide of bad press is through a growing movement for corporate social responsibility, in which corporations voluntarily try to introduce best practices for labour and the environment. The Gap, for example, released a report in 2004 that openly admitted a host of wage, health, and safety violations by its production subcontractors and promised to do better. There is continued controversy over what is certified as responsible corporate behaviour and who is in control of the certification process. Philip Knight, CEO of Nike, withdrew a $30 million donation to the University of Oregon in May 2000 after the university endorsed a student-run regulatory organization (Workers' Right Consortium) instead of the Fair Labor Association, a labour-rights group backed by the White House with corporate executives on its board of directors.

The growing power of corporations has not emerged in a political vacuum. As corporations have grown in strength, some governments have lost ground, both to corporate power and to international institutions like the World Trade Organization. This has lead many analysts to wonder if the age of globalization means the end of the state system.

ARE STATES RELEVANT IN THE GLOBAL WORLD?

Critics of neoliberal policies have wondered about the extent to which states continue to be the main instrument of democratic governance. Has the state been replaced by a kind of "global governance?" Does real power rests in the hands of unelected officials in the world's three biggest international financial institutions, the International Monetary Fund (IMF), the World Bank, and World Trade Organization (WTO), sometimes called "the three sisters"? Because of pressure to meet the demands of these three very powerful international financial institutions, some critics argue that states have become less oriented to meeting the demands of citizens. The result is a **democratic deficit** in which ordinary citizens are disenfranchised from the process of governance. Let's look briefly at how the three sisters challenge the capacity of states to make democratic decisions for average citizens.

THE THREE SISTERS

The IMF was established after World War II. Its official role was to maintain the stability of the international monetary system. Since the 1980s, the IMF has come to serve a different, yet important role as the gatekeeper of the institutional financial system. IMF loans are conditional on the lending government following a package of reforms of known as "structural adjustment programmes" (renamed "poverty reduction strategies" in 1999; Brym et al., 2005; Woodroffe and Ellis-Jones, 2000). IMF reforms typically require

countries to deregulate capital markets, remove price subsidies, decrease social spending, orient the economy toward exports, and privatize state-run industries. If a country refuses to adopt the reform package, it can find itself shut out of international lending circles and unable to service its debt. Many poor countries have witnessed massive protests against the IMF (see Figure 19.3).

Like the IMF, the World Bank was also established after World War II, and its job was to make loans to help postwar reconstruction. Most World Bank loans were made to poor countries and were often tied to large development projects such as hydroelectric dams. As a condition of receiving loans, the World Bank required that certain structural adjustment criteria be met. Like the IMF, the World Bank has had its share of critics, both external and internal (Chapter 9, Development and Underdevelopment). In response, the World Bank increased its collaboration with local non-governmental organizations (NGOs). While some observers applaud these efforts as part of the Bank's self-help approach to social problems, others argue that the Bank's NGO collaborations do not change its fundamentally undemocratic nature or the severity of its structural adjustment reforms.

The WTO emerged in 1995 out of the postwar trade treaty, the Global Agreement on Tariffs and

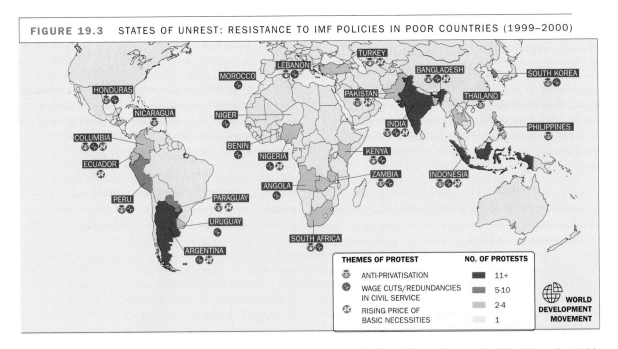

FIGURE 19.3   STATES OF UNREST: RESISTANCE TO IMF POLICIES IN POOR COUNTRIES (1999–2000)

SOURCE: World Development Movement, 2003, "States of Unrest III: Resistance to IMF and World Bank Policies in Poor Countries." http://www.wdm.org.uk/resources/maps/statesofunrestmap01122002.pdf (retrieved 10 August 2009). Reprinted with permission from the World Development Movement.

Trade (GATT). The WTO's job is to lower trade barriers, thereby increasing international trade and, presumably, prosperity. The WTO became known to many North Americans with the famous "Battle of Seattle" in 1999. WTO meetings in that city were met by huge, disruptive street protests. Every major meeting of the WTO since then has elicited protests, often from citizens of poor countries who charge that international trade works only to the benefit of the rich and ignores the unfair protection of corporate agribusiness at the expense of farmers. While some globalization-from-below organizations argue that trade liberalization will help the poor (e.g., Oxfam and Live 8 organizers), others argue that it will not, and that entry to the WTO forces countries to comply to a set of trade rules written by wealthy countries for their own benefit (Bivens and Hirch, 2003).

A U.S. EMPIRE?

While the IMF, World Bank, and WTO influence state policies throughout the world, not all states are equally affected by these institutions. Some observers note that the age of globalization is also an age of more power for some states, notably the United States, and powerlessness for states at the bottom of the global hierarchy. Critics of the United States

accuse it of acting like an empire. Neoconservative thinkers in Washington acknowledge that the United States acts like an empire, although they argue that it uses its power benevolently to promote peace and democracy throughout the world.

Analysts debate whether the United States is a modern empire or a fading superpower (Ferguson, 2004; Wallerstein, 2002). The United States still enjoys enough political, economic, and military power to make unilateral foreign policy decisions (such as invading Iraq, which it did without United Nations endorsement), adopt unorthodox economic policies (like running huge fiscal deficits), and maintain a substantial global military presence (see Figure 19.4). On the other hand, the United States is also the world's biggest debtor. Accordingly, especially after the 2007–2009 financial crisis hit, some analysts argued that the power of the United States was waning relative to that of the countries that lend it money, notably China, with its $2 trillion in debt holdings (Fallows, 2008).

GLOBAL INEQUALITY AND THE "FOURTH WORLD"

Another feature of the global state system is a widening power gap between and within states. In the 1970s, analysts often divided the world into three

---

FIGURE 19.4 U.S. MILITARY BASES WORLDWIDE

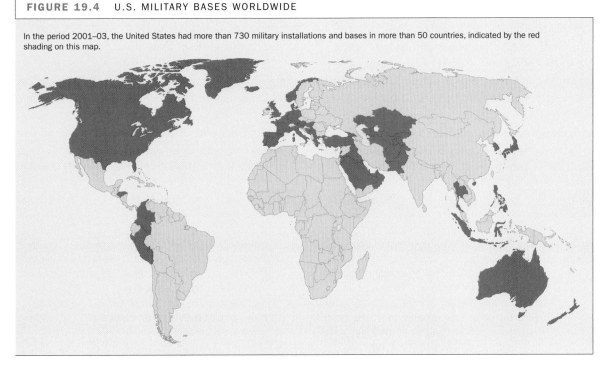

In the period 2001–03, the United States had more than 730 military installations and bases in more than 50 countries, indicated by the red shading on this map.

SOURCE: Global Policy Forum, (n.d.), "U.S. Military Expansion and Intervention." Reprinted with permission.

parts. The "first world" comprised the wealthy capitalist countries. The "second world" comprised the countries of the communist bloc. The "third world" comprised all the rest. This division is now inaccurate. The old third world now comprises a disparate assortment of nations that don't necessarily share common traits, the communist second world has for the most part collapsed, and it has become evident that widespread poverty exists even in the rich first world.

To meaningfully capture asymmetries among the world's countries today, analysts sometimes refer to the division between the "global north" and the "global south" or between developed and developing countries. Another useful terminological distinction is between the "majority world," which is generally poor and lacks basic social goods like housing, food, employment, and education, and the "minority world," which is generally well-educated and has access to good jobs and public goods like health care.

People from the privileged minority world may live in wealthy countries like Canada, but they can also live in Mexico City or Hong Kong. Similarly, people from the majority world can be homeless and searching for adequate food and shelter in downtown Toronto. The majority world–minority world distinction serves as a valuable reminder that state borders do not always indicate who benefits and suffers in a globalized economic system, and that the high living standard of the Canadian middle class is a global anomaly (Milanovic, 2005; see Box 19.2).

While the global economy has made a portion of the world's population wealthy, a large proportion of the world's people (at least 50 percent) are considered poor (live on less than US$2 a day). The global economy operates independently of large populations and geographical areas, which are seen as irrelevant for its functioning. These marginalized populations and

regions are sometimes called the **fourth world** (Cardoso, 1993; Castells, 1998; Hoogvelt, 1997: 66, 162). The fourth world exists as a result of the new economic and technological paradigm of global competitiveness, where only a portion of the world's states and inhabitants are competitive in the global economy.

Recognizing that time–space compression and the global economy affect people differently allows our understanding of globalization to become more nuanced. Globalization does involve a number of intense connections within the core of the global system, as people in the minority world travel more, hold global investments, and integrate the Internet into their daily lives. At the same time, globalization also involves a process of *peripheralization* that marginalizes certain groups. Some people in rich countries like Canada—Aboriginal peoples, the homeless—are subject to exclusionary processes like those that affect people in parts of Africa, Asia, and Latin America (Hoogvelt, 1997: 129).

THE GLOBAL CONSUMER

Maybe you have yet to be convinced that globalization has anything to do with you. But have you gone shopping lately? If you consume commodities—meaning goods purchased in the marketplace rather than made from your own labour—then you are inevitably part of globalization. The tags on your clothing are more likely to read, "Made in China" or "Made in Bangladesh" than "Made in Canada."

A **global commodity chain** is "a [worldwide] network of labor and production processes, whose end result is a finished commodity" (Hopkins and Wallerstein, 1986: 159). Global commodity chains are not transparent to the casual consumer. When you eat a tomato on a fast-food hamburger, you usually don't

---

BOX 19.2   GLOBAL EXTREMES

The following facts illustrate the extent of economic inequality in the world.
- The wealth of the world's three biggest billionaires in 1999—Bill Gates (US$90 billion), Warren Buffett (US$36 billion), and Paul Allen (US$30 billion)—was greater than the combined income of 600 million people living in 48 of the world's least developed countries.
- In 2004 one family—the Waltons, heirs to the Wal-Mart fortune founded by Sam Walton—con-

trolled US$100 billion. The Waltons are worth more than the GDP of New Zealand and more than the GDP of 123 of the world's nations.
- In 2004 the collective worth of the 100 wealthiest people on the *Forbes* list of the world's elite jumped half a trillion dollars from 2003 to reach US$1.9 trillion.
- About 1.2 billion people lived on less than US$1 per day in 2004.

know whether it has been shipped from Mexico or a local greenhouse. When you buy a pair of running shoes, the price tag doesn't tell you much about the workers who made the shoes or the company's environmental track record. In this section we will learn about the critical role consumption plays in the global economy, as well as some of the social and environmental critiques of globalized consumerism.

A GLOBAL GLUT

While consumers don't always understand the complexity of global commodity chains, consumption plays a critical role in driving growth in the global economy. High consumer spending increases economic growth, while a lack of consumer confidence is associated with economic slowdown and recession. Because North American and European markets are relatively saturated consumer markets, many corporations see expansion into global markets as essential for growth. **Consumerism**—a way of life in which one's identity and purpose is oriented primarily to the purchase and consumption of material goods—is currently being exported to the world's middle and working classes.

As noted above, the global economy suffers from a problem of overcapacity that makes finding new consumer markets essential. In particular, many corporations are looking to expand sales to China, the world's most populous country, to solve the problem of overcapacity. So far, Chinese production has been focused mainly on export markets, thereby worsening the problem of global overproduction (Bello, 2002). This situation is beginning to change. China is now the largest single market for cellphones, and consumer spending accounts for a growing percentage of the country's economic growth (Chien, 2008).

CULTURE AS COMMODITY?

Another characteristic of globalized consumerism is the tendency to treat culture like any other commodity. The United States has been instrumental in advancing this viewpoint—not surprisingly, given the tremendous size and power of the culture/entertainment industry in the United States. The biggest U.S. export consists of mass-produced products of popular culture (Barlow, 2001).

While many countries have a tradition of protecting cultural products, like films and magazines, the United States has used the WTO to prohibit states from using subsidies and quotas to protect domestic cultural products like films, music, magazines, books, and music. For

example, in 1997 the WTO supported a U.S. complaint and ruled that the Canadian government's usage of preferential tax and postal rates to protect domestic magazine industry was unlawful. (U.S. magazines make up 85 percent of the magazines found on Canadian newsstands, even with these trade disadvantages.)

A growing movement to resist this interpretation of culture as a commodity is centred around a 2005 UN treaty: the United Nations Educational, Scientific, and Cultural Organization's (UNESCO) Convention on Cultural Diversity (CCD). The UNESCO Convention was vehemently opposed by the United States, since the treaty will allow states to exclude cultural policies from free trade deals. As with most treaties, the devil will ultimately lie in the legal details, yet the CCD opens up the possibility for states legally to protect domestic cultural industries from the rules of trade.

CULTURAL IMPERIALISM?

The global spread of consumerism has been criticized as form of **cultural imperialism** (Barlow, 2001). From this viewpoint, global corporations, bolstered by sophisticated advertising tools, media monopolies, and declining trade barriers, are exporting a Western way of life throughout the world (Tomlinson, 1991). Cultural imperialism is often associated with liberal values around sexuality, feminism, and secularism.

Of course, people are not passive recipients of Western cultural products, which can be taken up in unique ways. A Japanese game show like *The Iron Chef*, for instance, represents a unique cultural hybrid that combines an American game-show format with Japanese cultural and culinary mores. The result is unlike any show made by American television producers, yet it was a huge hit on the American-based cooking network, and spawned *Iron Chef America*, an English-language version of the show.

Western cultural products are transformed as they are consumed by different global cultures. However, this does not mean that the world's cultural products compete as equals. Free trade favours large economies and big economic actors. Canadians are more likely to eat in a McDonald's than they are to eat in a Jollibee, the leading fast-food restaurant in the Philippines. Because of the tremendous economic power of Hollywood, filmgoers in Canada are more likely to watch a movie made in Hollywood than we are to watch a film made in Denmark or even a film made in Canada (see Table 19.3, p. 464). French political figures, such as former President Jacques Chirac, have been particularly

TABLE 19.3   U.S. MARKET SHARE OF FILM
INDUSTRY FOR SELECTED COUNTRIES, 2001

COUNTRY OR REGION	PERCENTAGE OF FILM INDUSTRY BELONGING TO U.S. MOVIES
United States	93.1
Canada	85.0
United Kingdom	81.4
Australia	80.6
Spain	67.0
European Union	65.4
Italy	59.7
France	51.0

SOURCES: Global Policy Forum, 2003; Canadian statistic from Copps, 1997.

The Church of Stop Shopping, led by "Reverend Billy," promotes "retail interventions" into corporations like Starbucks. To see material on the Reverend's anti-consumer campaign and its intervention scripts see http://www.revbilly.com.
SOURCE: Reprinted by permission of Reverend Billy.

vocal in criticizing the cultural power of Hollywood. He used the French state to protect and promote the French film industry. Chirac warned of a "catastrophe" for global diversity if U.S. cultural dominance goes unchallenged (Agence France-Presse, 2004).

Although tremendous economic and cultural power is centred in the corporate culture of the United States and Europe, there are important exceptions. Arab-language television network al-Jazeera counters the global prevalence of CNN, offering an Arab alternative to U.S.-produced news. An English-language channel of al-Jazeera, featuring such Western journalists as famed British interviewer David Frost, went on air in 2006, making al-Jazeera's presence felt even more widely. The largest producer of movies in the world is not Hollywood, but Bollywood—the film industry based in Mumbai (formerly Bombay), India, which produces over 1000 films a year and attracts more than 10 million Indians to the cinema every single day. Bollywood films are seen in Russia, the Middle East, Africa, and Indian immigrant communities around the world. The cultural pervasiveness of Bollywood films is so great that smaller Asian countries, like Bangladesh, have reacted against the perceived domination of Indian movies, which crowd out Bangladeshi films. In addition to Bollywood, a film industry arising out of Nigeria, called Nollywood, produces films with actors and themes that are wildly popular with African viewers, and which some Nigerians believe have "eliminated the cultural stranglehold of Hollywood" (Kennedy, 2004).

GLOBAL BRAND BACKLASH

While the term *cultural imperialism* may drown out the subtlety of global cultural exchange, visible signs of antagonism toward Western-style consumerism remain. One way that global consumerism is being contested is through a backlash against corporate brand names. Branded goods, like Coke, Barbie, and Nike, have a particular political, social, and cultural importance because of their connections to global corporations (Klein, 2000: 5). Just as transnational corporations have spread globally, so have their brands, and now McDonald's, the Gap, and Starbucks are all frequent targets of street protests around the world.

McDonald's has been the target of protests in more than 50 countries, and Hindu activists have demanded that the prime minister shut down all McDonald's because it offends traditional Indian vegetarian food culture (Brownell and Horgen, 2004: 61). Tens of thousands of Indians protested the opening of the first Kentucky Fried Chicken outlet in 1995, bringing together environmentalists, farmers, health officials, and anti-globalization activists. Eventually, KFC abandoned business in that country (Brownell and Horgen, 2004: 61; Schlosser, 2001: 244; Wall, 2000). Anti-American sentiment also affected Coke throughout the world. Consumption has dropped off in favour of domestic soft drinks, leading Coke to retool its sales strategy by focusing on specialized local drinks (Hays, 2000).

The idea that corporate globalization can be effectively fought by protesting against branded products is controversial. Many people argue that global corporations are geniuses at using social dissent to sell new consumer products (Frank, 1997; Heath and Potter, 2004). Just as 1960s radicals wore tie-dyed T-shirts and drove around in Boogie Vans, today it is also possible to purchase consumer products that express one's disgust with the global capitalist system. You can wear a Che Guevara T-shirt while reading *Adbusters* and listening to

Public Enemy on your iPod. The extent to which counter-cultural consumption disrupts global flows of wealth is unclear. Marketing gurus are well aware of such consumer tendencies and advise global corporations to advance their brand by using anti-establishment messages to sell products to young people around the world (Lindstrom, 2003: 132).

CONSUMER ALTERNATIVES: FAIR TRADE

Subverting corporate logos is not the only tactic used to disrupt global commodity chains. Bottom-up globalizers also focus on developing consumer products that are environmentally sustainable and produced by well-paid workers. The fair-trade movement is one of the main proponents of this approach, arguing that producers should be paid a fair price rather than the free market price (Figure 19.5).

The fair-trade movement has paid special attention to coffee. Around the turn of the twenty-first century, the market for coffee plummeted to a 30-year low, leaving coffee prices below the cost of production for many farmers and causing heightened levels of poverty and debt for 25 million coffee-producing families throughout the world (Oxfam, 2002). According to its proponents, fair-trade coffee is an important solution to the "sweat-shops in the field" that characterize contemporary coffee production. Fair-trade coffee allows producers to earn a living wage while protecting the environment since most fair-trade coffee is "shade-grown" (grown alongside trees that support wildlife and biodiversity).

While the market for fair-trade coffee is growing steadily, it represents only a small fraction of the total coffee market. Although big brands have increasingly agreed to sell certified fair-trade coffee in their retail outlets, it represents a minuscule percentage of their total sales (an estimated 3.7 percent of the coffee sold at Starbucks is fair-trade, and 3.3 percent of all the coffee sold in the United States is fair-trade certified; Downie, 2007; Organic Consumers Association, 2007). Fair-trade coffee organizations must also convince consumers to pay more for their coffee—a choice that goes against the socialization of most consumers to shop around for the best deal.

ECOLOGICAL CONSEQUENCES OF CONSUMERISM

Global consumerism has also been criticized for being based on a Western high-consumption lifestyle that is

FIGURE 19.5   FAIR TRADE AND FREE TRADE COFFEE PRICES, 1989–2006

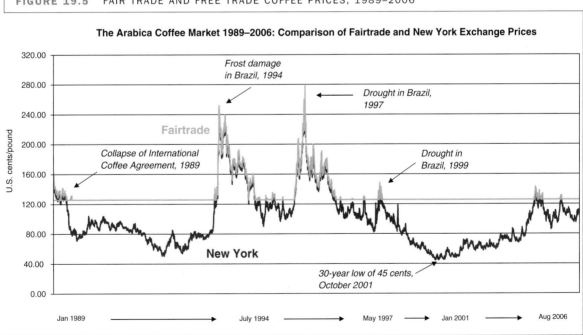

This graph shows a comparison of minimum Fairtrade price and the world market price for coffee, as measured on the New York Stock Exchange.
NOTES: Fairtrade minimum price = 121 cents/lb + 5 cents/lb premium. When the New York price is 121 cents or above, the Fairtrade price = New York price + 5 cents.
SOURCE: Fairtrade Foundation , 2006, *The Arabica Coffee Market: 1989–2006: Comparison of Fairtrade and New York Exchange Prices* (London, UK: Author). Reprinted with permission from the UK Fair Trade Foundation.

ecologically unsustainable, particularly if it is adopted by more people around the world. Twenty percent of the world's population (1.2 billion people) living in the industrialized developed world currently consume two-thirds of the world's resources and create 75 percent of all waste and pollution (Speidel, 2003: 5). What would be the implications if even a quarter of the remaining 80 percent of the world's people began to consume at the rate of wealthy Europeans and North Americans?

The size of China's economy has increased dramatically since it introduced free-market reforms in 1978, and it currently consumes more grain, meat, fertilizer, steel, and coal than the United States does (Speidel, 2003: 5). If China consumed as much oil per capita as the United States, China's total oil demand would be 80 million barrels a day—and currently the world only produces 60 million barrels a day (Speidel, 2003: 5). While some analysts say the solution to this problem is to find more oil, most experts believe that the world does not have enough reserves to sustain this level of consumption for long. Moreover, current levels of fossil fuel consumption are linked to atmospheric ozone depletion and global climate change. Sustainable consumption probably lies somewhere between the world's two extremes of overconsumers and underconsumers—at levels maintained by the roughly 3.3 billion people who eat moderate amounts of food (especially meat), rely primarily on sustainable modes of transportation

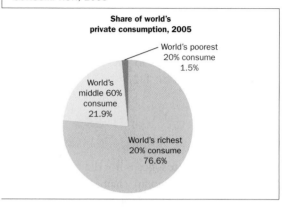

FIGURE 19.6   SHARE OF WORLD'S PRIVATE CONSUMPTION, 2005

Share of world's private consumption, 2005

- World's poorest 20% consume 1.5%
- World's middle 60% consume 21.9%
- World's richest 20% consume 76.6%

Source: World Bank, 2008, "World Bank Development Indicators." http://www.rrojasdatabank.info/wdi2008toc.htm (retrieved 19 August 2009). Copyright 2008 by World Bank. Reproduced with permission of World Bank in the format Textbook via Copyright Clearance Center. Online material reproduced with the permission of World Bank.

Some observers think that a Western, high-consumption lifestyle is ecologically unsustainable if it is adopted by people around the world. For example, each passenger taking a round trip from Toronto to Vancouver on Air Canada (economy class) is responsible for putting nearly 533 kg of carbon dioxide into the atmosphere (see the Carbon Footprint Calculator at http://www.terrapassaviation.com/carbon-footprint-calculator/). What happens when hundreds of millions of additional people take to the skies?

SOURCE: © iStockphoto.com/EGDigital.

like walking and public transportation, and consume minimal amounts of raw materials in their daily lives (Durning, 1992; see Figure 19.6).

While proponents of top-down globalization hope to turn the global middle-income stratum into overconsumers, the ecological challenge is to extend middle-income consumption habits to the world's poor underconsumers and the world's elite overconsumers. This will not be an easy political feat given the push to expand global consumption to address the problem of overcapacity in global production. The global economic system is currently organized around, and requires, high levels of consumption. In addition, it seems that the world's consumer class is often more interested in maximizing their individual consumption possibilities than they are in voluntarily curbing their consumption habits. Surveys shows that totally committed ethical shoppers constitute only a small percentage of the shopping population (Bird and Hughes, 1997: 160) and two-thirds of Americans in the US$75 000+ income bracket believe they need 50 percent to 100 percent more income to satisfy their consumption desires (Schor, 1998). It is unclear how to build a more sustainable economy that also provides economic opportunities and good jobs—a topic to which I now turn.

GLOBAL WORKERS

Karl Marx and Friedrich Engels (1972 [1848]) ended the *Manifesto of the Communist Party* with the now famous phrase, "Proletarians [workers] of all countries, unite." The political unification of working people across national borders is, however, relatively rare. Capitalists, in contrast, have proven adept at global planning and organization. Global capitalists have used numerous organizations and venues to formulate economic policy and interact with government policy makers, like the World Economic Forum held annually in Davos, Switzerland.

Global workers are relatively immobile and politically fragmented. Some of them cross international borders, but working abroad is constrained by international travel restrictions, work permits, and the limitations of passports. When workers do move abroad to work, they are not always able to take their families with them and may be separated from loved ones for years at a time. Labour unions are struggling to protect workers in the competitive, footloose business environment of neoliberalism. While capital can move across borders with relative ease, unions are primarily organized within rather than across states. There have been attempts to increase the level of transnational union organization and solidarity, but most unions are primarily oriented to protecting domestic workers and wages against competition from foreign workers. In addition, many workers who travel abroad work in sectors that are relatively nonunionized and under-regulated (e.g., nannying, the sex trade, agricultural workers), leaving them vulnerable to exploitation. While serious obstacles to organizing global workers remain, globalization processes have increased public awareness of sweatshop exploitation in factories around the world, leading some companies to ban the use of sweatshop labour. This section details some of the opportunities and challenges that globalization presents for global workers.

WAGE LABOUR AND WAGE INEQUALITY

The world of global labour might seem relatively mundane compared with the branded world of transnational corporations and global consumer goods. Yet without a global labour force there would be no goods for consumers to consume and no profits for capitalists. For most of human history, people acquired daily necessities through their own work—baking their own bread, making their own clothes, and trading minimally and locally for other daily staples. Today, people in industrialized countries understand the concept of wage labour as both normal and "natural." Most people

exchange their labour for a wage, which they then use to pay their rent, buy groceries, and so forth.

Throughout the world, however, there is still a sizable section of the population for which the concept of wage labour is new. These people gain access to food, water, and shelter directly through their own work rather than receiving a wage and purchasing needed commodities. Half the world's people still make a living off the land and subsist mainly on what they produce themselves. In South Asia and sub-Saharan Africa, a full 70 percent of the population makes its living off the land, and 80 percent of the Chinese population are peasants (Ainger, 2003; Ross, 2004:124).

As the use of wage labour spreads across the globe, so does the *segmentation* of labour markets. Women, people of colour, rural workers, and the people from the developing world in general are over-represented at the bottom of the wage hierarchy. There is a tremendous disparity in global wages, particularly when we compare lower level employees' salaries to CEO earnings (see Figure 19.7, p. 468).

While income inequality in the United States is the most extreme among the world's rich countries, income and wealth inequality is also a problem in Canada, and one that worsened in the late 1990s (Picot and Myles, 2005). A 2007 study found the income gap between the richest 10 percent and poorest 10 percent of the population to be at a 30-year high (Yalnizyan, 2007). The average Canadian worker earned around $36 200 in 2003, while the average CEO earned $3.2 million (McFarland, 2005). Disparities in the Canadian labour market are based on class, as well as on race and country of birth. While many Canadians try to avoid minimum-wage work, thousands of migrants from Mexico and the Caribbean travel to Canada each year to work at agricultural jobs for minimum wages seven days a week with no overtime pay or statutory holidays (Basok, 2002).

While Mexicans working in Canada are denied labour rights granted Canadian citizens, minimum-wage jobs in Mexico are worse in terms of remuneration. Wages in Mexico remain stubbornly low despite the 1994 North American Free Trade Agreement (NAFTA) that Mexico signed with Canada and the United States. NAFTA was sold as a "rising tide" that would "lift the boats" of workers in the three countries. Yet the Mexican Labour Ministry reported that in 2003 workers earned an average of $360 a month, 16 percent less than they earned a decade earlier (Dussell Peters, 2004:4; Jordan, 2003). Because 87 percent of Mexicans

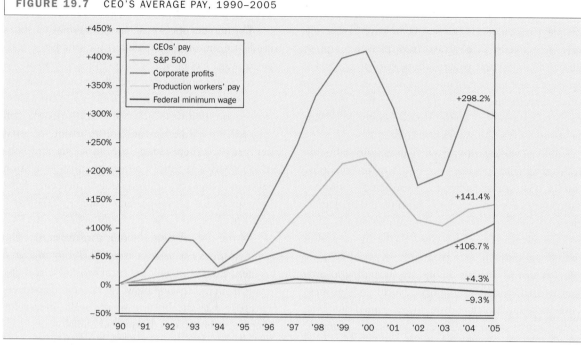

FIGURE 19.7 CEO'S AVERAGE PAY, 1990-2005

SOURCE: Institute for Policy Studies and United for a Fair Economy, 2006, "Executive Excess 2006," www.ips-dc.org/getfile.php?id=155 (retrieved 19 August 2009). Reprinted with permission.

earn less than half of the minimum wage in the United States, the incentive to migrate (legally or illegally) remains higher than ever before, and cross-border migration remains a serious economic and political issue in both Mexico and the United States (Pickard, 2005).

Are low wages an age-old problem, or are they a unique result of globalization? The historical record shows that the search for cheap labour has been going on for hundreds of years. Indentured workers were brought from China to construct the North American railway system, while impoverished Irish immigrants competed with freed African-American slaves for unskilled work in nineteenth-century North America. Globalization has heightened corporate competition for cheap labour, however. Firms use the threat of relocation as a way of keeping wages low. In effect, workers from different parts of the world compete against one another to attract foreign investment, driving wages down.

Given growing corporate competitiveness to find cheap labour, employment in a solid blue-collar job can no longer be taken for granted. Millions of North American workers in the manufacturing sector were laid off in the 1980s and 1990s (Beder, 2000: 132) and organized labour suffered serious setbacks, especially in the United States (Nissen, 2000: 3). Not only have

North American manufacturing jobs declined since the 1980s, but corporations have thinned out their management tiers, eliminating white-collar positions, **outsourcing** service jobs (e.g., call-centre jobs and computer programmers) to South Asia, and making it unclear whether a university degree guarantees middle-class economic status (Anderson, Cavanagh, Lee, and the Institute for Policy Studies, 2005: 33; Ehrenreich, 2005). The solid blue-collar manufacturing job or white-collar office job that allowed men to support a stay-at-home wife and two children in a middle-class lifestyle is now relatively rare, and about two-thirds of Canadian mothers work outside the home. Economists report that a third of Canada's economic growth between 1997 and 2005 was due to the proliferation of two-income households (CBC News, 2005).

Although manufacturing jobs were lost to lower-wage settings in the globalization period, service sectors jobs have mushroomed in the world's rich countries. Certain well-paying job sectors have expanded their ranks (e.g., teachers and nurses), but most new jobs are created in low-wage, temporary sectors of the service sector with median wages that fall near or below the poverty line (e.g., retail salespersons, cashiers, food preparation and serving, janitors, home care workers, and waiters; Anderson et al., 2005: 43–44). Economic analysts have identified the problem of "sub-employment" and the "working poor," terms that describe a situation in which workers have work but it is poorly paid, unstable, nonunionized, and fails to lift workers above the poverty line (CBC Radio One, 2004; Ehrenreich, 2001; Sheak and Morris, 2002; Shipler, 2004). The number of such workers increased substantially in the 2007–2009 recession, which drove the unemployment rate up to 9.7 percent in the United States and 8.6 percent in Canada by July 2009 (Statistics Canada, 2009; U.S. Bureau of Labor Statistics, 2009).

The growth in service jobs has been partially met by a rising number of migrant labourers who moved from developing countries to Europe and North America. Labour migration has increased the ethnic diversity of the labour force in the world's rich countries and, in turn, fuelled a racist, anti-immigrant backlash in some countries, raising questions about the meaning and practice of multicultural ideals. Despite these political conflicts, international migration is likely to continue to Europe and North America given that the baby-boom generation of workers is aging, birth rates are low, and a potential shortage of skilled workers looms in the future for most advanced industrialized countries. Together, these trends have increased competition between Canadian provinces and between highly industrialized countries to attract highly educated immigrants (Howlett, 2005: A7). The trend of south-to-north labour migration has raised questions in countries like Canada about how to recognize foreign credentials and integrate new immigrants into the economy, particularly since new immigrants experience a disproportionate degree of poverty and lower levels of unionization (Milkman, 2000; Picot and Myles, 2005: 20). Meanwhile, voices from less developed countries speak of a "global brain drain" in which skilled professionals leave their homeland to seek better opportunities in developed countries, a trend thought to cost India US$2 billion a year (United Nations, 2001).

SEARCHING FOR CHEAP LABOUR: "THE RACE TO THE BOTTOM"

Governments have reacted in different ways to the global competition to create jobs and attract corporate investment. In the less developed countries, some states have set up **export processing zones (EPZs)** where special financial deals—tax holidays, preferential rates for electricity and telecommunications,

special exemptions from national labour laws, and the like—are used to lure corporations to set up shop and provide jobs. The most famous EPZ in North America is the *maquiladora* region in northern Mexico. *Maquiladoras* are factories that allow companies to assemble goods for export using low-cost Mexican labour and imported high-tech machinery and parts.

Maquiladoras employ low-cost labour compared with the United States and Canada, but since 2001 hundreds of thousands of *maquiladora* workers have been laid off, threatened with layoffs, paid lower wages, and compelled to work in worse conditions. Why? Mexican labour is cheap, but not cheap enough in a global marketplace where transnational firms try to find the world's least expensive, least regulated, and least unionized labour supply. Although Mexican wages are a bargain by Canadian standards, low-cost manufacturing has increasingly moved to Indonesia, Vietnam, and China, where labour is even cheaper (the Chinese legal minimum wage is 31 cents per hour; Bacon, 2003; Ross, 2004: 8). Wage competition pits workers against one another in a "race to the bottom." Globalization has placed Mexico in a difficult position: wages are too low to alleviate poverty rates yet too high to continue to attract low-cost manufacturing.

Although working conditions in the factories of the developing countries are often wretched, some members of the world's labour force suffer in conditions that resemble slavery in the literal sense of the word. An estimated 27 million people worldwide are enslaved in economic relationships generating $13 billion of goods and services each year (Bales, 1999). We are connected to this extreme form of labour exploitation through global commodity chains. In the words of Kevin Bales, a sociologist and expert in global slavery,

> Slaves in Pakistan may have made the shoes you are wearing and the carpet you stand on. Slaves in the Caribbean may have put sugar in your kitchen and toys in the hands of your children. In India they may have sewn the shirt on your back and polished the ring on your finger. They are paid nothing. . . . Your investment portfolio and your mutual fund pension own stock in companies using labor in the developing world. Slaves keep your costs low and returns on your investments high. (1999: 3–4).

The injustices of the global labour system have not gone unnoticed or uncontested, even though serious obstacles lie ahead for unions and workers. In Canada, unionized workers as a percent of non-agricultural workers fell from a high point of 38 percent in 1981 to 32 percent in 2003, while the American unionization rate fell to just 12.5 percent in 2004. Historically, unionism arose in large capitalist factories, yet globalized firms often decentralize and subcontract work to small, independent firms, making unionization and labour regulation more difficult. Unions have responded to these conditions by developing new strategies that include cross-border organization, transnational solidarity campaigns, emphasizing the importance of good wages for all working people (not just union members), and drives to organize service-sector workers, such as janitors, hotel workers, and security guards (Babson, 2000; Frundt, 2000; Milkman, 2000; Nissen, 2000).

The anti-sweatshop movement of the 1990s also raised awareness of labour exploitation by transnational firms (Ross, 1997, 2004). Today, prominent retail corporations, like Nike and the Gap, must at least appear to take global labour issues seriously (recent reports suggest that working conditions are still abysmal in Nike's subcontracted operations; Ross, 2004: 42). Although it was unimaginable to promote a "sweatshop-free" clothing line in the early 1990s, the popular label American Apparel has proven that it is possible to run a successful business without the use of sweatshop labour. Although American Apparel rejects unions, it pays its Los Angeles workers rates that fall above the state's minimum wage and houses all of its workers in one building in Los Angeles (Ross, 2004: 1). Other clothing lines like "No Sweat" use unionized labour in North America *and* developing countries. According to the "No Sweat" website, "We believe that the only viable response to globalization is a global labor movement" (No Sweat, 2005).

GLOBAL ECOLOGY

Consumers, workers, citizens, and nations all play critical roles in the globalization processes we have outlined. In turn, all of these actors fit together in a larger global ecology that connects people, resources, and commodities. To better understand these ecological connections, I now examine the globalized food system.

GLOBAL FOOD

Global trade in agriculture allows relatively prosperous consumers to consume a wide variety of exotic fruits, imported bottled water, and distant marine life like shrimp and fresh tuna. Although the global trade in food products is a boon for discriminating eaters, critics of industrialized global agriculture question its environmental costs. Trade experts and environmental groups warn that agriculture is the largest contributor of greenhouse gas when food production and distribution chains are taken into account, and suggest that the global food system represents the biggest environmental challenge facing humanity (Clay, 2004; Shrybman, 2000).

One of the major environmental problems with the world's agricultural system is the immense amount of fossil fuel required to produce, package, and transport food. Fossil fuel consumption generates greenhouse gases such as carbon dioxide, which is linked to the eroding ozone layer and global climate change. But why is food so closely linked with carbon dioxide emissions? The first and simplest answer is transportation. Today, most Europeans and North Americans eat foods that have travelled a long distance to get to their plate. Food's travel time is captured in the concept of "food kilometres," a measure of the distance food travels from production to consumption, and an indicator of the amount of fossil fuels burned in the process. A Toronto study compared the food kilometres of conventional agricultural products purchased at a discount supermarket with the same basket of goods purchased at a nearby farmers' market (Bentley, 2004). While the supermarket food travelled 5734 kilometres on average, the same farmers' market produce travelled an average of only 101 kilometres to get to the consumer (Bentley, 2004: 7).

Food transported from far away might add variety to our diet, but it frequently involves an unsustainable and irrational energy tradeoff. For a head of iceberg lettuce transported from California to the United Kingdom, 127 calories of non-renewable fossil fuel energy are required to produce 1 calorie of food energy (Sustain/Elm Farm Research Centre, 2001: 1). The way that most of our foods are produced and packaged also relies heavily on fossil fuels. The food processing industry uses 10 calories of fossil fuel energy to produce 1 calorie of food energy. Intensive livestock operations are even more wasteful: 1 calorie of beef requires 35 calories of fossil fuel, and 1 calorie of pork requires 68 calories of fossil fuel. Because of these energy-intensive production techniques, food scholars estimate that if the entire world adopted North American food habits, fossil fuel reserves would be gone in just seven years (Manning, 2004: 42, 44).

Just as consumers in India and China move toward a meat-intensive diet, increasing demand for both animal feed and oil calls into question the stability of global food supplies. Despite short-term fluctuations, demand for oil is increasing while supply is just about stagnant. As a result, the price of oil increases, and agricultural crops, such as corn, are increasingly turned into biofuel to offset oil supply problems. However, the diversion of food crops into biofuel production causes food prices to rise. In 2007–2008, news headlines reported food riots by poor people in many developing countries, ignited by sharply rising food prices (Walt, 2008).

Soil, Water, and Genetic Engineering

Besides relying heavily on fossil fuel, industrial methods of food production are associated with global environmental problems like deforestation, soil erosion, and declining water tables. In the past 40 years, soil degradation has caused farmers around the world to abandon about 430 million hectares of arable land. This area amounts to one-third of all cropland (Kindall and Pimentel, 1991; see Figure 19.8). Every year, 130 000 square kilometres of forest, an area four times the size of Switzerland, are destroyed to make way for agriculture. By 2020, an estimated 22 million hectares of savannah and forest, an area as large as the United Kingdom, will be cut down in South America to meet global demand for soya, a crop that is used largely for livestock feed and vegetable oil (World Wildlife Fund, 2004).

Even when adequate land can be found to grow crops, water is also needed. Seventy percent of world water usage is for irrigation, and food analysts worry about an emerging "world water deficit" (Brown, 2005: 10). Underground aquifers refill slowly and are currently being pumped at rates that are unsustainable. In Northern China, for instance, groundwater levels are falling by at least one metre a year, while aquifers in the United States are being pumped at a pace that vastly exceeds replacement rates (Pimentel and Wilson, 2004).

Some scientists believe that global agriculture problems can be addressed by switching to genetically engineered (GE) crops that have been designed to be drought- and pest-resistant by reengineering the plant's genetic structure. This technological solution is opposed by many environmentalists who worry about the long-term health and ecological impact of GE cropping, particularly the negative impact on biodiversity, since GE crops tend to outcompete and contaminate related species. GE canola

---

FIGURE 19.8 GLOBAL SOIL DEGRADATION

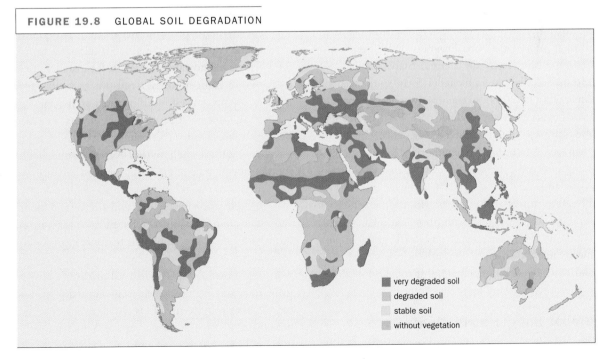

very degraded soil
degraded soil
stable soil
without vegetation

SOURCE: UNEP, International Soil Reference and Information Centere (ISRIC), World Atlas of Desertification, 1997. Philippe Rekacewicz. Degraded Soils (2002). In UNEP/GRID-Arendal Maps and Graphics Library. Retrieved May 17, 2009. http://maps.grida.no/go/graphic/degraded.soils

has already infected organic canola in Western Canada to such an extent that it is impossible for organic farmers to grow and market uncontaminated (GE-free) organic canola. Saskatchewan farmer Percy Schmeiser launched a lawsuit against seed giant Monsanto, suing for damages, and was awarded an out-of-court settlement. Activists in less developed countries are concerned that GE crops will permit large corporations to consolidate their control over agriculture and erode traditions of seed saving and innovation by farmers.

Because of these controversies over GE technology, most of the world's genetically modified crops are grown in just a handful of countries; 99 percent are from Canada, the United States, Argentina, China, and Brazil. Because of the huge capital investment in these technologies, multinational bioscience companies would like to increase adoption rates globally. One way this is occurring is through food aid, which contains genetically engineered crops. This issue made headlines in 2001–2002, when southern Africa experienced a famine and was given genetically modified maize by the United States. African leaders protested, not only for health and safety reasons but for fear that the GE corn would contaminate their own supplies (assuming that people would save some of the corn to plant in future harvests), and endanger export markets in Europe, where GE foods are banned (African Centre for Biosafety, 2005).

In 2005, scientists discovered that food delivered through the World Food Program (WFP), especially grain supplies from the United States Agency for International Development (USAID), to Central American and Caribbean countries was heavily contaminated with genetically modified corn. Eighty percent of the samples tested included GE corn, including "StarLink," corn that is not authorized for human consumption in the United States (Organic Consumers Association, 2005). The UN Cartagena Protocol on Biosafety stipulates that genetically engineered crops can enter countries only with prior informed consent, but the WFP's heavy reliance on USAID grain supplies means that this right is currently not being enforced and that genetic contamination of the world's global grain supplies seems likely to continue.

Global Hunger amid Plenty

The world grows enough grain to provide nearly 3000 calories per person (Lappe, 2005: 13) yet the number of undernourished people in the world has risen since the early 1980s, totalling at least 842 million people today (Wheeler and Thompson, 2004: 212). World grain production is a general measure of global food security. Per capita grain production has been falling since 1984, while overall grain production was flat between 1996 and 2003 (Brown, 2005: 4).

It is especially troubling to consider these numbers in the context of widespread soil erosion, loss of crop land to urbanization, rising global temperatures, and shrinking water supplies—all of which will have a negative impact on the capacity of global grain production (Brown, 2005: 7). With population rising to an estimated 9 billion people by 2050, and the low likelihood of expanding global grain supplies much further, grain prices will likely rise in the future. For affluent consumers, this would make food supplies, particularly meat, more expensive. For the world's malnourished people—half the global population by some estimates—this situation will make it increasingly difficult to access the basic food staples needed for survival.

Think Globally, Eat Locally

Is there an alternative to the current system of global agriculture? In Europe and North America there is a growing movement to eat foods that are locally grown and produced with organic farming techniques. Researchers in the U.K. have estimated that if all farms in the U.K. became organic, an estimated $1.1 billion in environmental costs would be saved (Lang and Pretty, 2005; Lappé and Lappé, 2002).

The move to promote organic, locally grown food is not confined to the affluent minority world. The Nadvanya movement in India, for instance, aims to promote indigenous agricultural techniques to counter the presence of multinational agribusiness in ways that improve the environment and increase people's food security (Navdanya, 2005). A growing number of Africans believe that organic farming techniques, not genetic engineering or food aid, are the answer to famines and food shortages (Hall, 2005).

The tension between local and global food represents the challenge and the paradox of bottom-up globalization. It is a challenge because most small-scale activists and food producers, like most of the world's workers, are rooted in local places where they grow food and are not nearly as globalized as corporate agribusiness and its CEOs. It is a paradox because peasant and small farmer movements want to encourage *local* food consumption, defend *local* agricultural ecosystems, and, at the same time, use *global* networks to fight these battles. Their motto could be "think globally, eat locally."

Cuba: An Island's Isolation and Innovation

What would happen if globalization processes were reversed, and a country suddenly found itself isolated, without the ability to trade for food in global markets? Cuba provides a real-life answer to that question. It is literally an island, but is also a metaphorical island in that it is largely isolated from the major ebbs and flows of global food trade. The United States has refused to trade with Cuba since 1960, a year after the Cuban revolution in 1959. After the collapse of the Soviet Union, Cuba lost access to an extremely important source of the food supplies and fossil fuels it received from the Soviet Union. Suddenly, the nation was hungry. Calorie consumption per person fell from 3000 calories in 1989 (the year the Soviet Union collapsed) to 1600 calories four years later.

Without fossil fuels or cheap grain supplies, Cuba's agriculture had to change, and change it did. Cuban agronomists began experimenting with more sustainable, low-input agriculture that used crop rotation to provide natural fertilization. They developed large urban gardens to feed and employ thousands of Cubans. Farmers began using oxen instead of tractors, saving fossil fuel. Today, almost completely cut off from global agricultural trade, Havana feeds itself from gardens within city limits. There are still problems ensuring adequate supplies of milk and meat, yet Cuban agriculture is remarkably successful, leading some analysts to suggest that the Cuban model is a possible future scenario for what agriculture could look like when fossil fuel supplies become scarce and the environmental consequences of globalized industrial agriculture become too onerous to ignore (McKibben, 2005: 69).

In an article profiling the costs and benefits of the Cuban agricultural experiment, environmental journalist Bill McKibben concludes with a provocative and difficult question that we would do well to ponder—a question that applies not only to Cuban agriculture, but to globalization more generally:

Is it also possible . . . that there's something inherently destructive about a globalized free-market society—that the eternal race for efficiency, when raised to a planetary scale, damages the environment, and perhaps the community, and perhaps even the taste of a carrot? Is it possible that markets, at least for food, may work better when they're smaller and more isolated? The next few decades may be about answering that question. (McKibben, 2005: 69)

SUMMARY

1. Globalization effectively shrinks the world; workers, commodities, ideas, and capital cross distances more quickly. Sociologists use the term "time–space compression" to describe this process.

2. Globalization processes have generated contradictory outcomes that benefit some groups but have also been linked to poverty, economic marginalization, democratic deficits, and the digital divide.

3. Developments in information technology have facilitated the economic integration of financial markets. Consequently, global flows of financial capital are much bigger than global flows of tangible goods and productive capital.

4. Corporations in the global era have become much bigger and are under pressure to become more competitive in the global marketplace. Local or even national competitiveness is no longer seen as sufficient for economic survival.

5. Politically, the globalization era has witnessed the creation of new international institutions of governance like the IMF, World Bank, and WTO, which have diminished the power and sovereignty of some states.

6. Globalization processes have allowed communities around the world to gain knowledge of the injustice and suffering inflicted by the global economy. Such awareness has inspired efforts to increase social justice in the global system. These efforts are known as "globalization from below."

7. Most of the goods Canadians consume connect them to workers and production processes thousands of kilometres away. The globalization process is almost impossible to escape given the extent of global commodity chains.

8. The period of globalization is associated with a shift in manufacturing employment out of the more developed countries. Competitive pressure is driving corporations to seek the lowest wages possible in the less developed countries (the so-called race to the bottom).

9. Global ecology is not something that exists separately from globalization processes. It is connected to the actions of citizens, consumers, workers, and states.

QUESTIONS TO CONSIDER

1. How do you benefit from globalization processes? What is the negative impact of these processes? Consider your role as a worker, consumer, and citizen.

2. Do you think globalization has caused the Canadian state to lose sovereignty? Do you think Canadians suffer from a democratic deficit?

3. Do you think that consumer activism and social movement campaigns like the anti-sweatshop campaign are an effective way of making global commodity chains more equitable? Do you think that the corporate movement for social responsibility offers a more promising avenue for change? Is voluntary corporate action sufficient or are governments needed to make legislation and enforce corporate responsibility?

GLOSSARY

Consumerism is a way of life devoted primarily to the purchase and acquisition of commodities. While traditionally thought of as a problem for North America and Europe, consumerism is increasingly recognized as a cultural and ecological issue among affluent populations in the less developed countries.

Cultural imperialism is a controversial theory of cultural domination according to which powerful economic and political actors (primarily Euro-American) are thought to impose their values, norms, and lifestyles on other populations. Cultural imperialism often refers to the export of certain Euro-American cultural practices, such as materialism, consumerism, and sexual liberalism through the media of television, music, and film.

A **democratic deficit** involves the disenfranchisement of ordinary citizens from the decisions and process of governments. Democratic deficits are often attributed to the influence of corporate actors and international financial institutions on governments and the transfer of governance to institutions like the International Monetary Fund (IMF) and World Trade Organization (WTO), which do not permit average citizens to vote or influence decisions.

The **digital divide** is the gap between people who are easily able to access communication technologies like the Internet and cellular phones, and people who lack the material resources, education, or infrastructure to access these technologies.

Export processing zones (EPZs) are manufacturing areas in which government programs provide special incentives to help promote export-oriented manufacturing. Sometimes EPZs are actual territorial zones demarcated by fences and borders, while in other cases they indicate programs that apply to all industries within a nation. For instance in 1991, Sri Lanka declared the entire nation an EPZ.

The **fourth world** comprises marginalized populations and regions that are not competitive in the global economy.

A **global commodity chain** is a worldwide network of labour and production processes, the end result of which is a finished commodity.

Globalization is a social, economic, and political process that facilitates the movement of people, goods, ideas, and capital around the globe. With globalization processes, the world appears to shrink, although the ability to cross borders varies tremendously depending on your position in the global economy (e.g., whether you are a corporate executive or a factory worker).

Globalization from below is a short-hand way of describing a diverse range of projects seeking greater democracy, equality, and sustainability in globalization processes. These projects are generally opposed to neoliberal policies and U.S. hegemony in the global system and are also referred to as alternative globalization, the global social justice movement, and anti-globalization.

Neoliberalism refers to economic policies that became prominent from the late 1970s onward in both developed and developing countries. Neoliberalism draws from the classical free market economic theory of Adam Smith but is considered new or "neo" because it followed a historical period of vigorous state economic regulation known as Keynesianism (1930s–70s). Neoliberalism is associated with a retreat from state intervention and regulation, greater focus on individual responsibility, less protection for labour and the environment, privatization of state resources, and faith in the power of the market and the profit motive to provide the greatest good for the greatest number.

Outsourcing occurs when firms contract production and services to smaller, independent firms. When outsourcing occurs on a global level, multinational corporations contract production and services to firms in less developed countries.

Time–space compression refers to the diminished importance of geography and time lags because of globalization, especially since the late 1970s.

Top-down globalization refers to the extension of capitalism globally, particularly as a result of the neoliberal policies and programs authorized by international financial authorities, such as the IMF and World Bank, and implemented by national governments. Top-down globalization is organized by elites in governments, corporations, and international institutions with little democratic input.

A **virtual community** is a group whose members share interests and meet primarily on the Internet.

SUGGESTED READING

Ehrenreich, Barbara, and Arlie Russell Hoschschild, eds. (2002). *Global Woman: Nannies, Maids, and Sex Workers in the New Economy*. New York: Metropolitan Books. This captivating account offers personal and insightful analyses of how globalization affects women around the world. The economics of globalization come to life through the stories told in these chapters.

Sachs, Jeffrey. (2005). *The End of Poverty. Economic Possibilities for Our Time*. New York: Penguin. You may not agree with Sachs's hopeful analysis, but this is an undeniably influential account written by one of the world's most important economists (and endorsed by none other than Bono, who writes the Foreword). The book is highly readable and combines economic analysis with personal stories from the author's travels in the world's poverty-stricken areas.

Smith J., ed. (2007). *Global Democracy and the World Social Forums*. Boulder, CO: Paradigm Publishers. This book provides a non-specialist's account of the World Social Forum (WSF), one of the most exciting and important global activist events of the globalization period. Each chapter is written by a scholar who has participated in the WSF, and together they show how the WSF is a critical part of the transnational movement for global peace, justice, and democracy.

WEB RESOURCES

Companion Website for This Book

http://www.newsociety6e.nelson.com
Begin by clicking on the Student Resources section of the website. Next, select the chapter you are studying from the pull-down menu. From the Student Resources page, you have easy access to InfoTrac College Edition® and other resources, such as the Glossary, Test Yourself questions, and additional readings. The website also has many useful tips to aid you in your study of sociology.

InfoTrac College Edition Search Terms

Visit http://www.infotrac-college.com for access to more than 20 million articles from nearly 6000 sources when doing your online research.

PART SIX

Methods

SOURCE: © Luis Francisco Cordero/Shutterstock

CHAPTER TWENTY

Research Methods

Neil Guppy

UNIVERSITY OF BRITISH
COLUMBIA

In this chapter you will learn that

- Science is one of several sources of knowledge. Like other sources of knowledge, it can be wrong. However, unlike other ways of knowing, science uses methods of gathering theoretically relevant evidence that are designed to minimize error.

- Research methods are used by sociologists to gather evidence in order to test theories about recurring patterns of human activity. Underlying these techniques is a variety of assumptions about the nature of facts, objectivity, and truth.

- In comparison with the evidence available to natural scientists, an added complexity confronts social scientists: Humans assign meaning to their actions, and interpreting meaningful action is complicated.

- Sociologists have devised many useful methods of obtaining evidence about the social world, including experiments, interviews, observational techniques, and surveys.

- Good sociological research adds to our knowledge of the social world, expanding opportunities and options by helping to solve social problems.

INTRODUCTION

Social research involves systematic, purposeful study. The systematic nature of sociological research comes, in part, from the methods sociologists use. Fundamental to methods is the careful collection of evidence. However, only evidence relevant to theoretical ideas is useful in social research. The purposeful structuring of sociological inquiry comes from asking theoretically informed questions. Systematic sociological study integrates sound theory with careful methods.

This chapter introduces you to the principles of research methods. I begin by outlining some basic assumptions involved in social science research, including assumptions about personal values or bias, the nature of facts, and the sources of knowledge. Next I explain how the subject matter of the social sciences—people—differs from the objects of inquiry in the natural sciences (e.g., molecules, plants). People studying people adds a level of complexity to social research. This added complexity comes from people interpreting their own behaviour, and the behaviour of others, by trying to understand meanings. Various methods of social research have been designed to deal with this complexity, and I review these techniques in the final section of the chapter. Methods of observation and questioning lie at the heart of research, and I review the strengths and weaknesses of each of these approaches.

PERSPECTIVE

Guy Paul Morin and David Milgaard were convicted of murder. In January 1995, three years after his conviction, but subsequent to new DNA tests, Guy Paul Morin was formally exonerated of all charges against him. David Milgaard had to endure prison longer but in July 1997, after 23 years in prison, he too was exonerated. Again DNA testing was instrumental. Judges, juries, and prosecutors had weighed evidence that they believed demonstrated the guilt of these men. Circumstantial evidence, filtered by personal expectations and values, had led justice astray. Subjective judgments had seriously compromised these men's lives.

An inquiry into Guy Paul Morin's conviction claimed that science helped both to convict and to exonerate him (Kaufman, 1998). In sharp contrast, Gold (1998) claimed that "good science" exonerated Morin, but it was "not science that helped convict him." But what makes for "good science"?

Wrongful convictions are rare. The criminal justice system minimizes such error through rules of evidence and presumptions of innocence. Likewise, science is organized to minimize error. Science is not perfect, however, and it is important not to put scientific practice on a pedestal, somehow immune to human foibles. Like all human activities, the social practice of science is influenced by subjectivity.

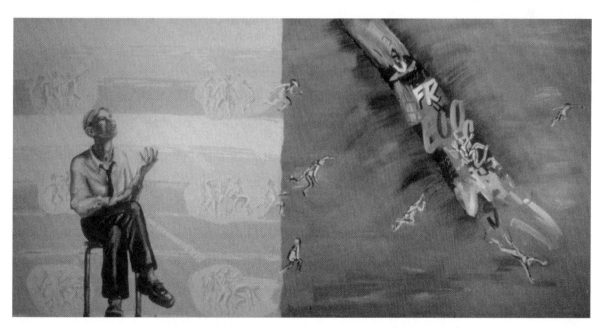

Sociological theories were first proposed in the nineteenth century as secular accounts of rapid social change. By the early twentieth century, systematic methods for empirically testing hypotheses were being introduced.

SOURCE: Carol Wainio, *Untitled* (1985). Acrylic on canvas, 330" × 500". Photograph courtesy of the S. L. Simpson Gallery, Toronto. Reproduced with permission of the artist.

SCIENCE AS A SOCIAL PRACTICE

Science needs subjectivity but it cannot be overwhelmed by subjectivity. Subjectivity is important to certain phases in the practice of science while detrimental to other phases. Understanding the complexities of scientific methods requires distinguishing between times when subjectivity is beneficial and times when it is not. But just what is subjectivity? Most people would agree that our personal values and expectations are a core part of subjectivity. Frequently people separate the world into facts and values; the real and objective versus the personal and subjective.

But what appears to us as reality is filtered or screened. Reality exists, certainly—it is no figment of the imagination. However, our values and expectations filter reality. While the saying "what you see is what you get" has an intuitive appeal, we know the claim is false. It exaggerates. Other things, especially our expectations and values, affect what we see.

Here is an example of filtering. The sun is real. It is no figment of our imagination. We commonly speak about "sunsets" and "sunrises." But these terms deceive. Although we have all watched a "sunset," the sun does not set. Our language conditions us to think of a moving sun, but Earth rotates around the sun. Earth's spin creates the *illusion* of a moving sun.

Being skeptical of my claim about a filtered reality is important. Values and expectations influence our perceptions of reality, but they do not completely determine what we see. This is a critical point. The *extent* to which values and expectations influence what we see is debatable, but that is a secondary point. The key point is that *if* our perceptions of reality can be affected by our values, *then* how can scientists ever know for certain that what they "see" is true? Put another way, if observation cannot be a rock-solid foundation of scientific knowledge, then how is the practice of science to be understood?

An important claim of this chapter is that reality does not exist as some neutral scientific judge. Pure observation does not rule supreme. To think of an individual scientist as a detached, arm's-length observer of the physical or social world, making observations to test ideas, is to profoundly misunderstand science. The scientific method is not a mechanical process of collecting facts to prove things. Science is a much more complex social activity, and the methods of scientists are designed in the face of such complexity. Here is an illustration of how values and expectations may creep into scientific work.

Recall from your high-school biology classes the work of Gregor Mendel. Mendel was the father of genetics. He cross-fertilized varieties of pea plants and noted that inherited traits followed consistent numerical ratios (i.e., the expression of dominant and recessive genes over successive generations). These experiments, demonstrating landmark principles of heredity, remain controversial (see Orel, 1996). R. A. Fisher, while a Cambridge University undergraduate, demonstrated that Mendel's results seemed fabricated. The likelihood that Mendel produced results conforming so closely to his hunches about heredity was, Fisher showed, in the order of 1 in 30 000.

Mendel may have been lucky, producing possible but very unlikely results. Alternatively, Mendel, or his assistant, may have unconsciously misclassified some pea plants. Classifications made by Mendel were not clear-cut, and so his experimental results may have been interpreted as favouring his preconceived ideas. Mendel may not have rigorously checked the experimental results because they proved what he expected. In this vein, Fisher (1966 [1936]: 123) claimed that Mendel's results were a "carefully planned demonstration of his conclusion."

"Observer bias" (making unconscious mistakes in classifying or selecting observations) is now commonly discussed as a danger to good methodological procedure. Mendel did not clearly and publicly describe his procedures. His data are no longer available for re-examination. Although it is impossible to know exactly why his results came out as they did, his ideas about genetics have proven invaluable.

Good research methods are designed to minimize the types of errors that have been attributed to Mendel's experimental evidence. These methods do not eliminate the biasing effect that values and expectations have on scientific research. They do, however, seek to minimize their impact.

MINIMIZING BIAS IN SOCIAL SCIENCE

Sociologists apply scientific practices to the study of human society. These practices incorporate several ways of reducing bias, especially the twin pillars of public (open) scrutiny and skeptical reasoning. Scientific ideas become provisionally accepted only after scrutiny by the scientific community. It is not enough for an individual scientist to proclaim a link between family background and children's school success or between HIV and AIDS; these links must be demonstrated by presenting research findings at scientific conferences, subjecting findings to peer review, and ensuring that research results can be replicated. The scientific community is organized to promote critical scrutiny.

Scrutiny is not enough, however. If the scrutiny is not rigorous and probing, then it is of little value. Scientific practice also encourages skeptical reasoning. New ideas are accepted only after others have critically examined them, only after they have withstood a barrage of questions from doubters. Examples of this doubting come from questions like this: Could something other than HIV cause AIDS? If HIV does cause AIDS, exactly how does the causal process work? Does HIV cause AIDS among all people? This process of doubting is built into the way science is conducted.

Scientists are also trained in methods of research designed to minimize the influence of their personal values and expectations on the results of their research work. They work to root out error in reasoning and observation. So, for example, scientists learn to collect and analyze information according to rules that reduce the risk that results will be affected by bias. Much of the latter part of this chapter focuses on these specific research techniques.

Science has prospered because of this healthy skepticism and public scrutiny. Both natural and social sciences have played a pivotal role in making our world a better place in which to live, by helping to curtail malaria, improving the life chances of children with disabilities, and reducing gender inequity. Scientists are not infallible saints, however. The scientific community is not some sacred haven where only truth and enlightenment reign. Fraud and deceit are also part of science (Park, 2000).

It is also important to correct a possible misinterpretation about the role of values and expectations. I have portrayed these as "problems." This is too one-sided. Science would be substantially weaker, if not impotent, without values and expectations. Science is soaked through with individual judgments. Mendel's brilliance came from his expectation that passive and recessive genes played a fundamental role in explaining inheritance. Mendel provided a new way of seeing the world, a new conceptual map for understanding.

Expectations and values are in tension within the scientific enterprise. Without them the spark of creativity and passion would be low, but with them we can be led to false conclusions (as judges and juries are occasionally misled). Put differently, objectivity and subjectivity each play an important role in science, including sociology. **Objectivity,** which is what courtroom judges and jurors strive for, stresses that observations should be free of the distorting effects

of a person's values and expectations. Conversely, subjectivity is essential to change and innovation. Without people championing their own visions, we would have little creativity. A hallmark of science is its creativity. Mendel's was a beautiful solution to the mystery of inheritance, even if he may have been too exuberant in his experimental claims.

Science depends on both the creativity of new explanations about how things work and the assessment of whether these explanations are plausible. In sociology this dual character resides in a division between theory (explanations of how the world works) and methods (ways of assessing the veracity of explanations).

Most of this chapter is about assessing evidence. It explores how sociologists work within the rules of scientific method. First, however, I contrast scientific knowledge with other forms of knowledge. The discussion moves next to the steps involved in the sociological research process. I then describe the main methods of gathering sociological data and the decisions that have to be made during the research process. Finally, I return in the conclusion to the role of subjectivity in research.

SCIENTIFIC VERSUS NONSCIENTIFIC THINKING

To differentiate good and bad science, consider what characterizes scientific thinking. Before the 1700s and the rise of science, our ancestors knew many things about the world. Much of this was custom or common sense—when to plant, what to plant, where to plant. Religious knowledge held centre stage in community life. Stories of creation, of how we came to be on Earth, were powerful tales that gave coherence to peoples' lives. Religious doctrine and common sense remain powerful in many societies, but scientific ways of knowing have increasing authority in industrial nations.

What characterizes this scientific way of knowing? A key contribution came from the Scottish philosopher David Hume (1711–76). He disputed the popular argument of his day that science begins with observation. Hume argued that no matter how many observations you make, you cannot infer your next observation. This is known as the *problem of induction*. Put more graphically, no matter how many white swans you see, you cannot logically infer that all swans are white. However, observing one black swan is sufficient to refute the claim that all swans are white.[1] Hume was railing against Francis Bacon's claim that observation was the bedrock of science. For Hume the collection of "facts" is useless unless you understand how to interpret them.

In Charles Dickens's *Hard Times*, Mr. Gradgrind demands facts: "What I want is Facts. . . . Facts alone are wanted in life." Contrary to the popular saying, though, facts do not speak for themselves. Blue mould growing on spoiling food is a fact of life that many people have observed. It was only in 1928, however, that Alexander Fleming recognized this blue mould as a potent medical tool. Many people had seen blue mould, but only Fleming understood it as penicillin. Mr. Gradgrind could have collected blue mould for a lifetime, but to little effect. Science is not a collection of facts. However, among other things, it is a method of collecting facts.

Facts are bits of evidence, information that you or I can verify by using our senses. Because trillions of bits of human activity might be taken as facts, how do we select what should count as evidence? How do sociologists avoid idiosyncratic fact gathering? Sociological theory provides guidance for the hunting and gathering of facts. Evidence is gathered to test ideas, hunches, or theories. Only selected bits of human activity are used as evidence. Those selected bits are chosen because they relate to a sociologist's theory about how the world works.

In the twentieth century, Sir Karl Popper (1977 [1934]) improved this thinking with his provocative notion of falsification. As he claimed, observations refuting a well-conceived idea are always more important than evidence supporting or proving a theory (e.g., observing one black swan was more important than observing yet another white swan). For Popper, science does not start by gathering raw facts. It starts with a question or hunch, or in his words, a well-conceived conjecture.

Two core ideas about distinguishing scientific thinking from other ways of thinking have been presented earlier: public scrutiny and skeptical reasoning. Popper added the principles of testability and uncertainty. Testability is easy to understand. For an idea to be scientific it must have testable implications; it must be falsifiable (i.e., *if* an assertion is false, this can be demonstrated by evidence).

The concept of uncertainty may be more difficult to accept. Many people misunderstand science as a doctrine of certainty. As Park (2000: 39) puts it, "many people are uneasy standing on . . . loose soil; they seek a certainty that science cannot offer." As Hume argued centuries before, observations cannot be the bedrock of science because of the problem of induction. Equally, however, science cannot proceed, as Popper correctly argued, without the possibility of observations that could refute a scientific claim. Observations based on well-reasoned methods can ferret out error and misunderstanding, although these same observations cannot guarantee universal truth or perfect certainty (see Box 20.1).

NATURAL VERSUS SOCIAL SCIENCE

The scientific practices of chemists and sociologists share many elements. The research methods of both disciplines help in understanding and explaining why certain patterns emerge. Furthermore, values are important in this process because these values underlie the creative imagination so central to scientific puzzle solving. Values also have the potential to bias or distort observations, and both the natural and the social sciences guard against distortion. If the scientific method is defined as a set of practices or procedures for testing knowledge claims, then both chemists and sociologists are doing science.

There is, however, a profound difference between the subject matter of the natural and the social sciences: Bacteria don't blush. This phrase neatly captures the key distinction. Human beings are conscious and creative; we can think, act, reason, and decide. We are, as Anthony Giddens (1984) phrases it, "knowledgeable actors." As sociologists, we study "ourselves"—that is, our contemporaries and our ancestors. Bacteria, having no knowledge of social norms, do not blush when exposed to the beam of an electron microscope. Bacteria cannot think, act, reason, and decide; they cannot consciously control their surroundings or reactions in the same way human beings can.[2]

Perhaps the single most important difference is that, unlike chemists, sociologists study **meaningful action**—that is, activities that are meaningful to the people involved. For example, bacteria may not blush when studied, but people often react self-consciously when they know they are being observed. To study love, friendship, or charisma depends on learning something about the meanings people ascribe to actions. This has advantages and disadvantages for sociologists. Unlike chemists, we can ask questions of the people whom we study (bacteria don't talk either). But this advantage can also be a disadvantage. Interpreting people's answers is not easy.

Because of this difference in subject matter, sociologists have developed an array of methods to help in understanding and explaining human

One of the most influential academic books of the twentieth century was Thomas Kuhn's (1962) *The Structure of Scientific Revolutions.* Before Kuhn, many people held a "brick-building" conception of scientific progress. They thought that individual scientists contributed to building a structure called scientific knowledge, one brick at a time. As scientific knowledge accumulated, the structure became taller and sturdier.

Kuhn challenged this view on several fronts. First, he held that science developed through contributions from a community of scholars who use "paradigms" as guiding tools about how the world is organized (Mendelian genetics is such a paradigm). Paradigms guide questions and answers. Evidence not fitting a paradigm is ignored. However, if anomalous evidence persists, a "scientific revolution" results. Scholars opt for a new guiding paradigm. The transition from Newton's mechanics to Einstein's relativity illustrates a paradigm shift, or a scientific revolution (Kleppner and Jackiw, 2000).

Second, Kuhn proposed a discontinuous view of scientific progress. The community of scholars did not keep building the Newtonian structure but shifted to a new structure defined by the Einsteinian paradigm. This discontinuous view of scientific progress also influenced debates about truth. Earth as the "third rock from the sun" we now hold as a fundamental truth. But our ancestor's were equally convinced that Earth was the universe's central rock. In the future, will our "third rock" conception seem equally odd? Kuhn's view suggests that truth is contextual. A new paradigm establishes a new context, showing us that beliefs we once held to be true were naive or misleading (like a setting sun).

Finally, the argument about community was sociologically compelling. In Kuhn's hands the practice of science was not understood as individual scientists ruthlessly questioning all ideas. To the contrary, paradigms provided a set of convictions about how the world was ordered. With faith in a paradigm, a community of scholars searched for what they were convinced existed. Paradigms had a disciplining effect, focusing attention on a delimited set of questions and answers. Notice also that Kuhn's view emphasized that scientific change was not gradual, but sudden (revolutionary) and that the change was organized or predictable (structured).

activity. Since asking questions has advantages and disadvantages, good sociological research either employs a variety of ways to ask questions or relies on observational techniques to aid understanding and explanation.

METHODS OF SOCIAL RESEARCH

EXPLANATION

Sociologists have shown repeatedly that the years of schooling people receive is strongly influenced by family background. Children raised in poverty tend not to go as far in school as do children from upper-class families. Although this research demonstrates a link between family background and educational attainment, this link is, as I have reported it, descriptive, not explanatory. I have offered no reason *why* this relationship between family origin and educational destination exists. It is true that I have noted a potential cause (family background) and an effect (years of schooling), but I have failed to provide any mechanisms through which this implied causal process might operate. An **explanation** would be judged adequate only if it could show how family background actually influences educational outcomes.

The mere association or correlation between social origin and educational destination does not prove causality. The relationship between smoking and lung cancer is a good example of the rule that *correlation does not prove* **causation.** Smoking has long been linked to lung cancer, but only in the past three decades have we learned more about the causal mechanisms underlying this correlation. Cigarette companies, especially, have argued that the presumed connection was **spurious,** meaning that something other than smoking caused lung cancer (see Box 20.2, p. 484). Accumulated evidence and a more precise notion of the underlying modes of transmission have established that the original correlation is causal.

We might try to explain the link between family and schooling in several ways (Davies and Guppy, 2006). An obvious factor is money. Although public schooling is free, costs are incurred for field trips, tutoring, international tours, postsecondary education, and a host of other events. Children living in poverty may remain in school for fewer years than their upper-class peers because of these costs (and they may seek employment sooner to help with family income).

Money seems to be a partial explanation for the link, but other factors may be at work as well. Many skills and values taught in school may be more readily

BOX 20.2   CORRELATION AND CAUSATION

Where fires cause much damage, many fire trucks gather. This is a correlation; a lot of damage tends to go along with many trucks, while minimal damage tends to draw only a few trucks. But this "truck and damage" correlation does not prove causation. Consider Figure 20.1. The curved, double-headed arrow depicts the correlation between the amount of damage and the number of fire trucks. The single-headed, straight arrows show the direction of causation. The size of the fire is a common prior cause of both other variables (number of trucks and amount of damage).

Causality is controversial because it often involves something we cannot observe directly. For example, no one can see lung cancer being caused by smoking. We infer that conclusion from assembled evidence that fits with theoretical conjecture.

Here is another example. Women living in poverty typically eat less nutritious meals and consequently are more likely than better-off women to have premature babies. But not all women living in poverty have premature babies. There is a correlation between poverty levels and the incidence of premature births, and nutrition level has been identified as a key causal mechanism. Notice, however, that living in poverty does not guarantee premature births. Living in poverty only raises the probability that a mother will have a premature baby.

In a causal relationship, a change or variation in one thing produces a change or variation in another. If four basic conditions are met, causality may be established. First, two variables must be associated or correlated. Consider two variables—the likelihood of premature births and poverty. Premature births must be more likely to occur among poor women than among women who are not poor if a causal relationship exists. Second, the cause, or independent variable, (poverty level) must precede the effect, or dependent variable, (premature births) in time. (For more on independent and dependent variables, see p. 487.) Establishing that a woman is poor (or not) while she is pregnant confirms the

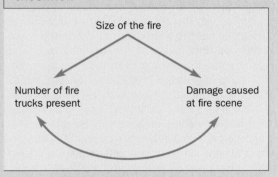

FIGURE 20.1   AN EXAMPLE TO ILLUSTRATE THAT CORRELATION DOES NOT PROVE CAUSATION

causal ordering or temporal sequencing of the variables.

Third, the original association must not disappear once the effects of other variables on the dependent variable are examined. We need to verify that we have not made a false inference. Does the causal process really go from poverty to poor diet to premature babies?

Could it be that stress, and not poverty, is the causal agent? It may be that poor women are under more stress and that stress, not poverty, increases the likelihood of premature births. The initial causal relation between poverty and premature births would be spurious if stress was determined to be the operative factor (poverty may be correlated with stress, of course, but stress may still be the real causal agent).

Finally, we must offer a theoretical account of how one variable causes another. We must illustrate the social mechanism(s) through which causation operates. This theoretical reasoning also enables us to establish which variables are important to examine when we test to see whether a causal relation might be spurious. In the example, we theorize that poverty affects nutrition, which in turn affects the likelihood of premature birth.

grasped by children from upper-class families, not because these children are smarter than are children living in poverty, but because the home environments of the children may expose them to different skills and values. The classroom culture may be more like the culture in upper-class homes (e.g., abstract word games are valued, reading and music are prized) and these children may therefore be advantaged.

The first explanation is largely about money and material resources. The policy implications of this

explanation point to eliminating or reducing the costs of schooling. This has been accomplished in large measure in Canada. However, even when the costs of postsecondary education have also been reduced (e.g., in Quebec), social-class disparities in educational attainment have remained. The second explanation points to cultural factors in the home (e.g., reading) as a reason for the family–school link. This explanation has influenced policies related to compensatory education, such as Head Start and After Four, educational programs designed to help disadvantaged children by giving them educational enrichment (see also Guppy and Davies, 2009).

The mechanisms by which causes have effects are essential for adequate explanation (Gross, 2009). You might think of these mechanisms as the social "cogs and levers" greasing the wheels that link causes with effects. Furthermore, multiple causes are involved in social-scientific explanations; a single, unitary cause rarely provides a sufficient explanation. Sociologists search for the multiple factors that can help explain some particular state of affairs. So, in the family–school example, although only two explanations for the link are mentioned here, other explanations may also be tested and refined as sociologists attempt to see how equality of educational opportunity might be attained.

UNDERSTANDING

Sociologists must not be content merely to offer explanations for why a particular relationship exists. These explanations are often sterile unless they also address the meaningfulness of human activity. People make the social world happen, and in doing so they give meaning to their actions and to the actions of others. A failure to address these meanings would leave sociology underdeveloped.

It is no simple matter, however, to understand what someone or some group means by their actions or utterances. One way to think about **understanding** is as follows. The first time I saw a traditional Greek dance, I was unable to follow the patterns of movement or appreciate the symbolism of certain motions. Similarly, the first time I watched a cricket match, I could not fathom what was happening. To the extent that I have come to understand these complex social activities, I have learned *how to proceed with the activity*. To understand a Greek dance or a cricket match means being able to participate fully in the activity, knowing what others mean by their actions and utterances, and knowing how others will interpret our actions and utterances.

A fundamental social process, called "taking the role of the other," nicely captures this idea of understanding. By imagining yourself in another person's role, you come to appreciate someone else's point of view. You come to understand, to reflect on, his or her ideas and issues. I do not mean that you must become Caesar to understand him; that would be impossible. Instead, sociologists focus on the web of relations in which people interact, paying attention to how people

understand and interpret the views of others. They pay attention to "the definition of the situation," to the meanings of the people involved.

Erving Goffman's work in an insane asylum (as it was called then) is a good illustration of sociological understanding (Goffman, 1961). Goffman was not interested in getting inside the heads of the patients to learn what and how they thought about things. Rather, he was interested in how the patterns of social activity in the asylum were organized. He came to see the mental hospital from the patients' point of view. By dispensing with the medical categories and scientific labels assigned to individual patients, Goffman began to understand the ways in which patients worked cooperatively to produce a coherent social structure. He learned to appreciate how the patients defined the routine activities of the asylum and how they coped with institutional procedures that denied them privacy and stripped them of their personal identities (e.g., by issuing institutional clothing and removing personal objects).

Goffman (1961: 129) also learned about what he calls the "careers" of patients with mental illnesses: "Persons who become mental-hospital patients vary widely in the kind and degree of illness that a psychiatrist would impute to them. . . . But once [in treatment] they are confronted by some importantly similar circumstances and respond to these in some importantly similar ways. Since these similarities do not come from mental illness, they would seem to occur in spite of it." Although social life on the "inside" might seem unique or even bizarre at first, Goffman argues that anyone, patient or researcher, would, in time, come to find it much like many other communities in which he or she has participated, possessing an identifiable social organization and rhythm of activity.

Returning to the education example, explanations of high-school dropout rates that ignore the attitudes and values of the people who drop out are one-sided. An appreciation of the experiences of people who drop out is essential to a more complete account of the schooling process. Especially important here is the resistance of students to authority, often expressed through music and clothing. This resistance is not some idiosyncratic expression of random individuals, but represents part of a youth subculture that must be understood by anyone who wants to alter the schooling process to make it a better environment. How young school resisters define the situation of schooling is important to a full appreciation of dropping out.

Explanations of high-school dropout rates that ignore the attitudes and values of those who drop out are one-sided. An appreciation of the experiences of students who drop out is essential
to a more complete account of the schooling process.
SOURCE: © iStockphoto.com/Rosmarie Gearhart.

Understanding and explanation work together.
Although explanations of dropping out that ignore
student values are deficient, merely reporting the
stories of young resisters would be equally vacuous.
A full appreciation of dropping out, or of any other
social activity, requires both understanding and
explanation. Often these activities are pursued by
different researchers and their combined results
contribute to fruitful research programs leading to
social change.

TECHNIQUES OF SOCIAL RESEARCH

Sociologists have developed a variety of techniques for
gathering evidence. I will review three of the most
important: experiments, survey research, and observational studies. As you read my accounts of research
procedures, keep asking yourself, How do sociologists

go about developing insights about, or knowledge of,
the social world? How do they come to know what they
claim to know? What methods do they use and how
believable are the results generated by these methods?

EXPERIMENTS

Experiments are the hallmark of scientific research
and are commonly, though inaccurately, equated with
science itself. Experiments are useful because they
enable researchers to isolate causes and measure their
effects. By no other method can researchers determine causation so precisely. An example is the best
way to illustrate the point.

In exploring how ethnicity influences social
interaction, Martha Foschi and Shari Buchan (1990)
assigned people to one of two experimental conditions. Each person was told that he or she would be
working with a partner in making judgments about
the relative size of images. After seeing two contrasting images, but before finally selecting the larger,
people were told of their partner's choice. People
often change their mind when they hear what others
think. Foschi and Buchan wanted to know whether
the ethnicity of a partner would affect people's likelihood of changing their minds.

In one case ("condition one") the partner was
described as East Indian, while in the second case
("condition two") the partner was described as
English Canadian.[3] Because the experimenters
wanted to examine the effects of ethnicity on personal
judgments, they had to ensure that the only difference
between conditions one and two was the partner's
ethnicity. They could not, for example, let the participants meet their partners because that would expose
them to more than just the partner's ethnicity (e.g.,
the partner's demeanour, clothing, height). All of the
participants in the experiment were of European
ancestry, but their "partners" were either East Indian
or English Canadian. How could the experimenters
subtly inform people of their partner's ethnicity,
without arousing suspicion?

Foschi and Buchan developed a clever solution.
First, they asked everyone to complete a questionnaire. Then, under the guise of wanting to let the participants know something about their partners, the
experimenters gave everyone their partner's completed questionnaire. In fact, each participant
received a questionnaire that Foschi and Buchan had
previously completed. By design, only two fictitious
partners existed and they differed only by surname

(Sidhu or Edwards), country of birth (India or Canada), and language (English/Punjabi or English). Apart from those three attributes (i.e., the difference between conditions one and two), participants in the experiment received identical descriptions of their partner (e.g., same sex, age, level of schooling).

The experimental results showed that men were less likely to be influenced by East-Indian than by English-Canadian partners. Women did not systematically change their judgments according to their partner's ethnicity. The experimenters were confident that ethnicity was the only factor influencing the men since it was the only factor on which their partner's differed—an English-Canadian or an East-Indian partner.

Random assignment or **randomization** lies at the heart of experimental design. Using a random procedure (e.g., flipping a coin, rolling a die), people in an experiment are assigned to an experimental condition on the basis of chance. If the flipped coin comes up heads, a person is automatically placed in experimental condition one; if the coin comes up tails, the person is assigned to condition two. Although individual participants will differ with respect to sex, age, abilities, and so on, the two experimental groups will contain an approximately equal number of women and men; the average age of the two groups will be similar; and so on. This group similarity is accomplished by random assignment. Foschi and Buchan (1990) used random assignment to ensure that the only difference between conditions one and two was the partner's ethnicity.

For women, the partner's ethnicity made no difference. The treatment condition—East-Indian or English-Canadian partner—had no effect on the judgments women made. Exactly why men were influenced by ethnic cues and women were not remains open to debate. Foschi and Buchan (1990) suggest that women might be less prejudiced than men, perhaps because women have more frequently themselves been the victims of discrimination. More recently Foschi, Lai, and Sigerson (1994) have shown men are more likely to use gender as another "cue to competence," a finding that resonates with the results of the experiment just described.

By dissecting the Foschi and Buchan experiment, we can examine more carefully several key design features. The researchers began with a **hypothesis**—an unverified but testable knowledge claim. They hypothesized that ethnicity affects behaviour in social interaction. More formally, Foschi and Buchan (1990: 5) "predicted different perceptions of competence and resulting behaviour for White subjects performing a task with a partner, depending on whether the partner was White or East-Indian."

To test this hypothesis, Foschi and Buchan examined the relationship between two **variables.** A variable is a measurable concept that can have more than one value. Age is a concept we use in referring to how long someone has lived. For newborns, age is measured in weeks or months, but for everyone else it is measured in years. One variable studied by Foschi and Buchan (1990) is ethnicity. They designed the experiment so that ethnicity could have one of two values: East Indian or English Canadian. In this experiment, ethnicity is the **independent variable,** which is presumed to affect other variables. Differences in this variable are hypothesized to affect a second variable, the **dependent variable.** In the experiment by Foschi and Buchan, the dependent variable is the amount of influence a person will accept from his or her partner. It was measured by the frequency with which people changed their initial judgments after learning of their partner's choice.

Nevertheless, how do Foschi and Buchan know that only a partner's ethnicity and not another factor, such as a partner's age or social class, influence judgments? They are confident of their conclusion because, by design, they know that only the ethnicity of the fictitious partner differed between conditions one and two. By randomly assigning people to one or the other condition, the experimenters guaranteed ethnicity was the only systematic difference. Because participants cannot choose which treatment condition to enter (i.e., they cannot self-select), the groups can be made alike.

Sociology experiments of the type conducted by Foschi and Buchan are relatively rare, in large part because many social processes that interest sociologists are not amenable to laboratory testing. Ethical and practical problems limit the use of laboratory experiments (see Box 20.3, p. 488). Furthermore, we must be cautious in generalizing the results of laboratory experiments to non-laboratory situations. The latter problem is technically expressed as the issue of **external validity,** or the degree to which experimental findings remain valid in a non-laboratory situation. External validity is often low; relationships discovered in sociological experiments do not always hold in more "real-life" settings because these settings differ from the laboratory. Still, the relevance of laboratory findings is an empirical question. There is reason to be cautious about generalization, but often findings from the laboratory apply in other real-life contexts.

BOX 20.3 ETHICS IN SOCIAL RESEARCH

Three groups share an interest in the conduct of sociological research: the sociological investigator, the people being observed or questioned, and the members of the larger society who enable such research to occur. Sociologists have a self-interest in their own research but it is imperative that proper weight also be given to the interests of research participants and the public. Although primary responsibility for the rights and welfare of both participants and the public must reside with the sociologist as researcher, the self-interest of the sociologist requires that some arm's-length body review research designs and procedures to ensure the protection of all.

What are the typical risks involved in social research? These are of two broad types: risks to individuals and risks to the communities or social groups. Understanding the first type—individual harm—is fairly straightforward. Social research can cause harm by asking people threatening questions that cause individual trauma (e.g., asking Aboriginal people about their memories of residential schools). Appreciating the second type—collective harm—may be less obvious. The results of social research can harm communities or groups by, for example, reinforcing stigmas and stereotypes (e.g., people living in poverty smoke more) or supporting policies that help some groups at the expense of others. Who sponsors the research of the sociolo-

gist is an important issue, especially in this latter context. Here, too, relations between political advocacy and scientific research come to the fore.

Ethically responsible research must minimize threats or risks. Informed consent is one key strategy. Researchers must ensure that people not only consent but that they also consent knowing what the research entails. Very occasionally in sociological research, deception is involved. This occurs in cases where the research requires that people not know exactly what is being studied (on the grounds that such knowledge may lead them to change their behaviour or lead them to respond in certain ways). For example, if you tell respondents your research is about the environment and then ask them what the most important problem is facing their region, many more will respond "environment" than if you did not provide this initial cue (Urmetzer, Blake, and Guppy, 1999).

In discussing a range of research projects in the remainder of the chapter, I will comment further on issues of ethics. An insightful sociological analysis of ethics is also provided by Kevin Haggerty (2004), who discusses "ethics creep" as a form of surveillance. For more details on ethics, see the Statement of Professional Ethics of the Canadian Sociology Association at http://www.csaa.ca/structure/Code.htm.

Field experiments have been used in sociology in an attempt to avoid some of the problems of laboratory experiments, especially problems of external validity. A good example of a field experiment is one undertaken in Toronto by Effie Ginsberg and Frances Henry (1985; Henry, 1999). They investigated the extent of job discrimination faced by people of different ethnic backgrounds. In one study, they sent actors, one black and one white, to apply for advertised job vacancies. The actors had similar credentials and were trained to make their job-search behaviour as identical as possible. The researchers wanted to test the hypothesis that racial discrimination existed in the Toronto labour market. Their independent variable was the race of the job applicant and their dependent variables—their measures of discrimination—included the number of interviews granted and job offers made to each actor. They found evidence supporting a discrimination hypothesis, with whites having a 3-to-1 advantage over blacks in job offers (for discussion of a similar test of this hypothesis, see Reitz, 1993: 35).

The field experiment, conducted in a natural as opposed to a laboratory setting, reduces problems of

artificiality. However, Ginsberg and Henry could explore only a limited range of jobs and were unable to focus on other urban centres, where discrimination may be more or less of a problem.

As I mentioned earlier, when people know they are being studied, they often become self-conscious. The very fact of being studied may influence their behaviour. This was demonstrated in productivity experiments conducted by Roethlisberger and Dickson (1939) at the Western Electric Company's Hawthorne factory. They found that productivity (the dependent variable) increased when they brightened the lighting, but then also increased when they dimmed the lighting. The researchers realized that people worked harder whenever the research team was studying them. Productivity increased in response to the researchers' presence, not because of changes they introduced. Social scientists have subsequently used the term **Hawthorne effect** when referring to changes in people's behaviour caused by their awareness of being studied. Sociologists have had to develop other techniques for collecting sociological evidence to avoid some of the problems associated with experiments.

One field experiment that investigated the extent of job discrimination faced by people of different ethnic backgrounds found that whites had a 3-to-1 advantage over blacks in job offers.
© iStockphoto.com/DWlabs Inc.

SURVEY RESEARCH

The social survey is the primary means of collecting social science evidence. Researchers collect information using surveys by asking identical questions of a sample of people. Political pollsters, market researchers, labour unions, governments, and university researchers all rely heavily on survey-based knowledge. Survey research is useful because it provides a method of systematically comparing answers to identical questions from a large sample of people, and it allows researchers to generalize the results to the larger population from which the sample was chosen. Questions can be posed either on a **self-administered questionnaire** or through a personal **interview**. Increasingly the Internet is used as a way to conduct surveys (Brym and Lenton, 2001).

Rhonda Lenton (1990) used survey research to investigate parents' aggression toward their children. Because of strong taboos against child abuse, asking questions about abusive behaviour is very difficult. The privacy surrounding child discipline makes observation or experiments inappropriate. Furthermore, asking blunt questions about "smacking your child" is unacceptable. Many alcoholics deny they have a drinking problem, just like many child abusers think of themselves as "strict disciplinarians." Parents use different strategies to influence their children, and Lenton wanted to examine the full range of this behaviour. Therefore, she chose to use a survey in which parents could be questioned by experienced and trained interviewers. She included questions covering an array of child–parent interactions, from praising and positive modelling through withholding privileges and love to spanking, slapping, and hitting.

A key problem facing Lenton was whether her questions about aggression and discipline would really measure child abuse. Child abuse is a theoretical concept. You and I may use the same term to mean different things. What types of maltreatment ought to be considered as child abuse? Lenton (1990: 159) defines child abuse as "any act, excluding sexual mistreatment [which she separated as sexual abuse], carried out by a parent . . . that has the intention of, or is perceived as having the intention of, hurting a child." Lenton wanted to include as "abuse" any act that a parent understands may hurt the child. To measure abuse, she asked parents whether they had done any of the following, ever, and in the past year: yell at a child, ridicule a child, withdraw emotionally from a child, hit a child with an object, withhold food from a child, and 24 other actions. Do these items provide an indication of what Lenton defines as child abuse? That is, are these valid indicators? **Validity** refers to accuracy or relevancy. Lenton's measurement of child abuse is valid to the degree that the items she uses as measures of abuse actually measure abuse as she defines it theoretically.

Lenton interviewed each parent and child separately. Each family member was asked to complete a child-discipline questionnaire, on which each of the 29 abuse items was listed. This sheet was completed privately and handed to the interviewer in a sealed envelope. By comparing the responses of all family members, Lenton could determine the consistency with which abuse was reported by different family members. This gave her confidence in the **reliability** of her measure. **Measurements** are reliable if they are consistent or repeatable. If different measures or indicators of the same concept give similar results, the measurements are reliable or, in other words, internally consistent.

Lenton faced another problem. She needed to find families with children. No publicly available list of such families exists. Lenton selected a random sample of Toronto families from the telephone directory. After first phoning to ensure that children lived in the household, members of the research team visited each eligible address to ask for permission to interview parents and children.

Surveys always involve **sampling.** Lenton's research team could never have interviewed all Toronto families (a complete enumeration of all families would be a *census*), nor would the expenditure of time and money have been efficient. Although the entire population could not be interviewed, it is this larger population about which Lenton wanted to draw conclusions. To use a different example, in doing research on urban household waste, interviewing all city dwellers is both unnecessary and impractical, even though the intention might be to use survey results to help design city policy. Information obtained from a subset of the population, the *sample*, is used to represent the views and characteristics of everyone. Samples selected by using rules of chance or probability provide random samples. These random samples give surveys better external validity than experiments do.

Samples must represent the larger population from which they are drawn. For example, one or even a few kindergarten classes cannot be taken to represent all kindergarten classes, because not all kindergarten classes are alike. Therefore, if we want to generalize about social processes common to all kindergarten classes, we need to select a number of classes for study.

Exactly how many kindergarten classes or, more generally, how many units must be included in a sample is a complex question. How many families should Lenton have selected? The precise answer depends mainly on the amount of variation or heterogeneity in the population and the degree of accuracy required in the study's conclusions. If you need very accurate results, you need a larger sample. Likewise, if the population is very variable, you need a larger sample to reflect that heterogeneity adequately. In studies of the Canadian electorate, very accurate forecasts of voting can be achieved with a random sample of about 1200 voters. The mathematical laws of probability can be used to generate efficient sample sizes.

Selecting samples is not as easy as it might seem. How would you go about selecting a random sample of students in your faculty or program? Distributing questionnaires in classes would be one method, but many students do not attend every class. Students who attend regularly are, by definition, different from those who attend infrequently. A sample of students present in classes would therefore be biased. Using e-mail addresses might seem practical, but many students do not let schools know their working addresses or would filter surveys out as junk mail. Registration lists give an approximation of the student population, but these lists are never perfect. Students drop out as the term progresses, while others change their addresses and phone numbers. If you were studying student retention or student financial needs, the people who might be hardest to find might be the very people to whom it is most important to speak. Even with this severe limitation, however, student lists maintained by the registrar might be the best alternative available. The list from which a sample is selected is called the sampling frame. This frame must come as close as possible to including everyone in the population.

Market-research firms use telephone interviews in conducting their surveys. These firms usually rely on *random-digit-dialling* procedures to establish random samples. They select "banks" (i.e., lists) of working telephone numbers (e.g., 902-424-79xx), and let the computer randomly dial the last, or the last two, numbers. This method, used by Statistics Canada in some of its surveys, provides a random sample of households, including households with unlisted telephone numbers. Two important refinements are used. First, some households have more than one telephone number, increasing their chances of inclusion. Statistics Canada asks respondents how many working telephone numbers there are in a house so that it can correct for this small bias. Second, the person who is interviewed in the house must also be randomly selected (because, for example, women are more likely than men to answer the phone even when both are at home). One popular strategy for obtaining a random sample of household members is to interview the person who has had the most recent birthday.

Telephone surveys require that people be interviewed. An alternative to interviewing is the use of self-administered questionnaires, which can be either mailed or delivered to members of the sample. Mailing questionnaires to people and handing them out to groups (e.g., students in a classroom, patients in a clinic) are less expensive than interviewing.

Researchers collect information using surveys by asking people in a representative sample a set of identical questions. People interviewed on a downtown street corner do not constitute a representative sample of a country's adults. That is because the sample does not include people who live outside the urban core, underestimates the number of seniors and people with disabilities, does not take into account regional diversity, and so on.

SOURCE: © Janine Wiedel Photolibrary/Alamy.

However, questionnaires lack the personal touch of interviewing. In an interview, misunderstandings can be clarified and responses can be expanded on. This cannot be done with self-administered questionnaires. Questionnaires work best with what are called close-ended questions, like those on multiple-choice exams, to which there are a limited number of set answers. Interviews, especially face-to-face as opposed to telephone interviews, allow for more open-ended questions, where respondents can be encouraged to elaborate their responses to ensure that they are properly understood. Lenton, for example, chose to use personal interviews because she thought that the subject matter was best handled with face-to-face interaction. Notice, however, that she incorporated a short questionnaire on disciplinary techniques because she thought the questionnaire would be less threatening to people in that it was more anonymous.

Once Lenton had established her sample and pretested her research strategy to ensure that she would obtain usable information, she set out to gather evidence that would allow her to evaluate the merits of three different hypotheses. A "cycle of violence" hypothesis holds that practices of child abuse are handed down from generation to generation. A "social-situational" hypothesis maintains that abusive parents may be reacting to stress and that stress itself may be linked to a family's socioeconomic status. Finally, a "cultural" hypothesis suggests that it is the attitudes of the family toward corporal punishment that best differentiate between the use of aggressive and nonaggressive behaviour in child discipline. Her research was designed to yield evidence that would help her decide which hypotheses were wrong. After analyzing the data, Lenton (1990: 176) concluded that "parents are inclined to use the disciplinary repertoires they learned when they were children—but only as long as certain current structural conditions are consonant with these repertoires." In particular, she pointed to structural conditions, such as unemployment in the family and low family income. To the extent that these structural conditions can be eliminated or reduced, the "cycle of family violence" can be arrested.

I mentioned earlier that the ability of sociologists to ask questions of people has both advantages and disadvantages. Lenton's work illustrates this. The physical punishment of children in the privacy of the home represents social activity that is not easily studied by any sociological method. Yet, as Lenton argues, child abuse is a public issue, not a private matter. By asking questions of people, she was able, first, to describe the extent of physical aggression used to discipline children and, second, to explain why some families were more likely than others to use physical discipline. The disadvantage of asking questions of people, especially questions that people may find threatening, is that people may distort their responses. For example, Lenton found that in more than 75 percent of all families, children had been spanked or slapped in the previous year. Given current social norms about child abuse, this estimate of physical discipline is more likely to be an underestimate than an overestimate of such activity. If, however, different social classes subscribe to these norms to different degrees, people's responses to the 29 disciplinary measures might have altered. Lenton herself anticipated this criticism and asked people not just about their behaviour but also about their attitudes. She was therefore able to examine whether people from different social classes held different norms about child discipline.

This distinction between attitudes and behaviours, or words and deeds, is important. I always intend to give more money to charity than I do. Most people believe that littering is irresponsible, but most people still litter sometimes. When you read research focusing on people's attitudes, remember that thought is not easily translated into action. This distinction goes beyond the asking of questions to issues of policy as well. Too often, people think that changing attitudes will solve social problems—if only people knew more, they would act more responsibly. A broken New Year's resolution is but one simple reminder of how often good intentions fail to translate into good deeds, no matter how aware we might be of the consequences.

Interpreting the answers that people give to researchers' questions is complicated by more than this behaviour–attitude distinction. In asking people questions, either in interviews or on questionnaires, we must be careful about making assumptions (Guppy and Gray, 2008):

- *Do not assume that people understand what you are asking.* Language is notorious for its ambiguity. How many friends did you see yesterday? This question may look simple at first, but people will differ in their understanding of "friends" and others will take "see" in the most literal way. The same words may mean different things to different people.

- *Do not assume that people know the answer to questions.* Most people do not want to appear ignorant when asked a question. This was illustrated nicely in a study of the prestige of occupations by Peter Pineo and John Porter (1967). They asked people to rate the prestige of two fictitious jobs: archaeopotrist and biologer. Most respondents cooperated and assigned these nonexistent jobs a prestige rating. When asked about their attitude on some issue, many people feel they must respond, even if they have no opinion on the topic or only a weakly formulated view.

- *Do not assume that people will admit the answer to themselves.* Alcoholics frequently claim that they can "quit any time." They refuse to admit that they are addicted. Similarly, child abusers may define themselves as strict disciplinarians. People routinely deceive themselves, sometimes only in minor ways, but "admitting the truth to ourselves" is a problem.

- *Do not assume that people will give valid answers to others.* People feel better about themselves when they are seen in a favourable light. In asking questions of people, researchers face the potential problem of "social desirability," because respondents may only give answers that reflect well on them. "What type of work do you do?" "Oh, I'm in public relations." Such a response could come from people working as telephone receptionists, tour guides, or corporate representatives.

Sociologists use many techniques in asking questions to gather valid and reliable evidence. For example, they will ask several questions rather than relying on only a single question, use supplementary questions to expand on or clarify answers, and test questions before using them to improve any wording that is unclear or misleading (see Houtkoop, 2000).

Survey researchers do not focus only on individuals, although it is individuals who respond to survey questions. For example, it is possible to survey organizations, groups, corporations, electoral ridings, or job vacancies. Although people answer survey questions, the questions may apply to a unit or group of which someone is a member. For example, Janice Aruni (2004) studied private tutoring businesses by using a semi-structured interview survey to gather information about businesses that provide for-profit, supplementary instruction in academic subjects (e.g., K–12 school subjects).

I am making two points here. First, surveys can focus on different units of observation (individuals, businesses, workplaces, etc.). Second, individuals can act as informants to report information that pertains not to themselves but to some group or unit about which they have information. People can, for example, report on individual events (e.g., job vacancies), family composition, or corporate policy. Although each of these represents different units of observation, individuals are still answering the questions.

OBSERVATIONAL STUDIES

Another method commonly used by sociologists to gather information is observation. Sometimes sociologists act as outside observers, at other times as insiders or **participant observers.** The obvious advantage of observation is that sociologists can see what people actually do, rather than relying on reports of what people say they do. One disadvantage is that gaining access to private actions or events can be difficult. For example, Lenton might have tried to observe parents disciplining their children rather than relying on what parents told her they did. But entering people's homes to make such observations would have been difficult. Furthermore, her presence may have influenced the type of discipline parents used (the Hawthorne effect).

In observation studies, examining the intentionality of social action is especially important. Max Weber (1949 [1904]) was one of the first sociologists to address the issue of intention as a focus of social research. Weber argued that in interacting with other people, we draw on meanings. For example, the clothing we choose to wear speaks to others. We attribute meaning to bow ties, jack boots, Laura Ashley scarves, and baseball caps. None of this is done naïvely, because what we wear helps define who we are. Skateboarders, for example, dress in a particular style; they wear a uniform of sorts. Making social life intelligible is part of what Weber thought sociologists must address. To understand skateboarding, it is essential to see how skateboarders "define the situation." It is important to learn about their culture and to understand their systems of meaning. The aim of such research is not to explain the behaviour of skateboarders from an outside point of view, but to investigate their shared values and beliefs—their "worldview."

Weber maintained that causal logic can be used to accomplish some of what sociologists want to explain. He thought, however, that sociology also had to make intelligible the subjective basis of social action. Weber used the German word *Verstehen,* or understanding, to refer to this mode of sociological analysis. To understand the meaning of social action requires being able, at least in principle, to fully engage in the social activity. An example is the best way to illustrate such understanding.

Youth subculture in Canada seems less influential and less prominent than in countries like the United Kingdom or the United States. Sometimes this is expressed in the claim that youth culture in Canada is derivative of trends south of the border or across the Atlantic. However, as skateboarders and squeegee kids have risen in profile, as youth unemployment has grown, and as the plight of young criminal offenders has been debated, understanding Canadian youth subcultures has become increasingly important. For that reason, Brian Wilson (2002) undertook a study of the rave subculture in Southern Ontario.

Locking up all youth considered deviant is an all-too-frequent suggestion for social policy. Banishing squeegee kids or skateboarders to some less visible place, be it jail, another neighbourhood, or "just off the streets," is one reaction. Denouncing ravers as irrational, for amphetamine drug use and social disturbance, is another. What these suggestions mainly reflect is a misunderstanding of youth culture and its social context. Gaining an appreciation of the rave subculture was Wilson's intent. Among the issues he pursued were the reasons for people participating in this subculture—put simply, was it the lure of adventure and excitement in the rave scene or was it a push from family or school that led to involvement with the rave subculture?

To gain an understanding of this process he chose participant observation as one of his methodological strategies. He attended more than a dozen raves, hung out in rave record stores, sat in on rave radio sessions, and attended public meetings focused on the rave phenomena. He observed the rave subculture by participating in it, by being a part of the party. By participating with ravers in rave parties and in rave

In participant observation, it is often necessary to "look" the part. Brian Wilson participated in rave parties to study first-hand the rave subculture of Southern Ontario.
SOURCE: © Alexandru/Shutterstock.

settings he was able to learn, first-hand, about their lifestyles, values, and aspirations.

However, Wilson did more than just participate in the rave scene. He also interviewed 37 young people who were active participants. He used what he calls "in-depth, open-ended, semi-formal interviews" (Wilson, 2002: 301). An in-depth interview means that he explored specific topics in great detail, often pursuing nuances and tangents. They were open-ended in the sense that he allowed those he interviewed to range widely in the subject matter they discussed. Finally, they were semi-structured in that he had a set of general issues he wanted to discuss, but he did not ask every person he interviewed exactly the same questions in exactly the same order. His goal was to have a meaningful conversation with each person, guided by his interest in the subject but also by their knowledge, willingness, and interest in pursuing specific details.

He also did not interview a representative sample of rave participants. Such a sample would be difficult

to define since no one has a list of regular rave members. Instead, Wilson sought to talk with a variety of people and he was careful not to draw all of the people he interviewed from the same place. Diversity was more important to him than was representation.

Finally, Wilson also paid particular attention to written materials that form part of the rave scene. This included magazines (both hard copy and e-zines), flyers promoting specific raves, and rave recordings (complete with commentary by the DJ). These provided another window into how ravers communicated with one another, what they stressed and emphasized.

In essence, he used a cluster of methods, with observation being his primary source of data. The participant observation was critical in giving him personal access to the subculture. He supplemented this by reading material and listening to rave productions. Finally, he also interviewed people to test out his interpretations of the rave subculture. In particular, he used the interviews to assess his own impressions of the rave scene.

Ethnographers study people in their own environment or their own natural setting. Although **ethnography** includes the researcher being immersed in a group or a subculture, it also typically involves a cluster of methods, including both in-depth, unstructured interviewing and the analysis of documents. Speaking with key informants who are central to the group or the subculture is crucial (Cresswell, 1998).

In part, Wilson came to understand the rave subculture in generational terms. Youth rebellion against perceived autocratic organizations (school, family, the justice system) leads to a lifestyle of resistance—to escaping authority, flaunting convention, and disregarding conservative norms. But it is a resistance that is not about political change or efforts to alter organizational forms. It is a resistance focused mainly on creating an autonomous space where social identity can be fostered, nourished, and supported. In this sense the subculture has a "magical" quality where the reality of other worlds can be transcended or bracketed. It is a movement based more on personal identity than on political protest. Contrast this with, for example, the student-led demonstrations in many countries pushing for stronger democratic governance—China, Indonesia, Iran, Korea—or the resistance to globalization seen at World Trade Organization meetings (Tanner, 2001).

Wilson was able to gain an understanding of the rave lifestyle by participating in the life of the group. By hanging out with them, he gained an in-depth appreciation of their activity. As a participant observer, he was able to ask many questions of many different group members, gradually drawing a sociological portrait of the rave scene. In particular he was able to contrast various interpretations of the rave scene—was it about resistance, simple pleasure-seeking, or simply escapism? As his work progressed, Wilson was able to refine his understanding. He could cross-reference his observations by seeing how other group members reacted to each new insight he gained, thereby increasing both the reliability and the validity of his conclusions. In short, he came to "define the situation" as rave participants themselves define it.

As with experiments, the external validity of ethnography can be problematic. How confident can Wilson be that his conclusions are not dependent on the impressions he formed from a single group of ravers? The intensive, in-depth nature of ethnography makes generalizability problematic. The key tradeoff is between the richly textured, "thick description" of ethnography and the insularity of detailed study of one or a few settings. Unlike survey researchers, ethnographers do not select different sets of random individuals or groups. The groups or settings they investigate are purposively chosen, sometimes because of easy access. For example, Wilson did not randomly choose rave subcultures; he made arrangements to participate with some rave scenes in Southern Ontario, and even then it was only one form of youth subculture. Imagine also, the ethical issues Wilson confronted (see also Haggerty, 2004).

Wilson's research portrays a culture from its members' points of view. There are potential pitfalls of which Wilson had to be aware. First, how much did his presence influence his findings? Did people act differently when he was not around? In principle, there is no way of answering this question, although ethnographers have tried to account for the effect of their presence in various ways. Some researchers conceal their research role; in effect, they try to be known to the other participants as one of them, rather than as a researcher (the ethics of this are dicey). Other researchers report that, with time, participants' awareness of their presence fades and they are treated as a member. Notice that this problem of presence is the Hawthorne effect in another guise. Whether in survey research, experiments, or observation studies, the researcher's presence can distort the domain of investigation. Researcher presence may undermine validity.

Beyond the potential pitfall of mere presence is the second problem: the findings of researchers may be ethnocentric. That is, researchers may impose their own values—their own worldviews—on the subject matter of their study. How do we know, for example, that Wilson depicted the ravers' point of view and not his own? One method of reducing personal bias is known as the "member test of validity" (Douglas, 1970: 21). For example, if the rave participants Wilson spoke with did not recognize themselves in his account—that is, if they saw Wilson's account as inauthentic—then we would worry about bias or distortion. Wilson was careful to "test" his tentative observations and insights on his informants by asking them questions and checking for observations that would falsify his impressions. Again, this is a research problem that extends well beyond ethnography. In fact, ethnography can be seen as the method that takes most seriously the task of understanding the members of a group from the members' point of view, stressing in particular their definition of the situation.

A third problem beyond presence and ethnocentrism is this: How do researchers know that the "tools" of their inquiry (e.g., questions, instructions, requests) did not in fact "create" or "generate" the resulting "findings"? For example, did Wilson create a finding by focusing attention on the ravers' resistance to dominant culture? Alternatively, did Lenton invent a relationship between social class and child discipline by asking questions that might be interpreted in different ways by the members of different classes? Again, this involves issues of reliability and validity. Lenton can be confident that she did not construct or create a pseudo-relationship between class and discipline to the extent that she shows that the basic pattern of findings is repeated across different questions about the disciplining of children. Wilson distinguished between (1) ravers' comments made in response to his questions and (2) statements his informants volunteered or that he overheard during his fieldwork. In addition, he used information provided to him by others on the margins of the rave scene: DJs, security guards, and radio station personnel. These alternative sources of information helped him avoid the problem of "creating" meaning. If ravers volunteered information that corroborated Wilson's impressions, and if these impressions were further reinforced by other knowledgeable observers, his faith in the authenticity of his account increased.

Not all observation can involve participation. Rik Scarce (2000) was interested in nature, and especially human domination of nature. His interest was in whether we could still speak of "wild salmon" or whether, like the cow and the dog, salmon were now domesticated. He argues that the very concept of "resource management," a buzz phrase among fishery specialists for several decades, speaks to the idea of humans improving on nature, of scientists enhancing nature.

In studying the "domestication of salmon," Scarce used ethnographic methods. He could not participate as a scientist, but he could observe what scientists did, interview them, read their papers, and listen to their testimony at public inquiries. After doing all these things, he wrote an ethnographic account called *Fishy Business: Salmon, Biology, and the Social Construction of Nature.*

He was especially interested in how salmon on both the Atlantic and the Pacific coasts had been manipulated to serve human ends. In the modern fishery, phrases like fish farming, aquaculture, genetic engineering, fish stocking, and fish hatcheries are commonplace. In British Columbia, few natural river systems remain. We have engineered a new breed of salmon, mixing wild stocks and creating farmed salmon (see also Schreiber, Matthews, and Elliott, 2003).

Scarce learned about this in his ethnographic research by hanging around fish hatcheries and asking questions, by visiting fishery research centres and watching what scientists were doing in their experiments, and by talking with scientists at their conventions and at public inquiries. He learned about the controversies and the anxiety that existed among scientists, many of whom worried about how we were increasingly controlling nature, but all too often in ways that were unsophisticated and too superficial. He came to see the fish hatchery as a biological factory and to understand how salmon were increasingly "tooled" and "engineered." Observation was his staple method. He immersed himself in the science of salmon to learn about the social practices of fishery biologists.

The believability of Scarce's research is enhanced by the fact that he observed events in their natural settings. He did not create a situation to see how people reacted (e.g., laboratory experiments) nor did he rely on people reporting on their own attitudes or behaviours (as in survey research). He was not a participant in the activity and so his involvement could not have distorted events (as may occur in participant observation). His presence as an observer may have influenced people, but he often was one of many observers (e.g., at scientific conferences and public inquiries).

OTHER METHODS OF RESEARCH
Historical Sociology

Many sociologists study social change. Max Weber, for example, attempted to explain the rise of capitalism by showing how Protestantism invigorated capitalist growth. Émile Durkheim was interested in how moral education helped to socially integrate a rapidly changing society. Both writers sought to answer sociological questions by examining historical change as evidence of significant social processes. Sociologists are more likely than historians to use historical evidence to test theories of social change. Sociologists place less emphasis on history for history's sake.

Liliana Riga's (2008) work shows how sociologists make effective use of historical methods (see also Brym, 1978). Riga re-examined the nature of revolutionary Bolshevism among the leadership of the 1917–23 Russian Revolution. She wanted to understand the roots of the socialist ethic that inspired the revolution. This critical juncture in world history has often been contextualized within a framework stressing the class basis and "Russian" ethnicity of the revolutionary leadership. Riga argues that in large measure it was social inequalities made most visible by diverse ethnicities, and not so much by social class, that lay behind the radical mobilization. She arrived at this conclusion after systematically comparing the experiences of class and ethnicity among the revolutionary elite leaders.

Of course these leaders have long since died, and so Riga could not interview or observe them. What she could do, however, was reconstruct their biographies. She used autobiographies, biographies, and memories, supplemented by police arrest records where ethnic backgrounds were often noted. She used sources predominantly constructed prior to the late 1920s. This latter refinement was essential when you recall that revolutionary leaders first had to mask their true identities in Tsarist Russia but even more importantly had to maintain social identities consistent with the *soviet* revolutionary movement (especially problematic in the Stalinist era from 1922 to 1953).

The logic of Riga's analysis is not unlike that of other sociological research. Her key dependent variable is the revolutionary identity and politics of the

Bolshevik elite. She wanted to know how important social class, ethnicity, and their intersection was to formation of this radical group. She therefore needed to measure social class and did so by examining such indicators as landholding, occupation, education, and relations to capital of individual members of the elite (and their parents). She also needed to measure ethnicity, and this too is complicated. In the end she used a mixture of birthplace, religion, and nationality. She concludes by noting that "ethnocultural identities were often more salient dimensions to many of their social experiences—and therefore to identities and politics—than was class."

Sociologists like Riga sometimes rely on other researchers' historical accounts. She relied primarily on biographical materials for the 93 individuals she included in the Bolshevik elite. Other sociologists return to original sources to reconstruct a historical record pertinent to their focus. For example, Gillian Creese (1988, 1999) examined gender relations in the Vancouver labour force and labour movement early in the last century. Her aim was to improve our understanding of the historical dynamics leading to the segregated work of women and men. Included in the archival material that she used were the full proceedings of the Royal Commission on Labour Conditions in British Columbia, documents on strikes and lockouts between 1907 and 1939, the minutes of local labour unions, and press coverage from newspapers. Any single source could give only partial coverage of the events she wanted to examine. By using a variety of sources, she was able to increase the reliability of her findings. Creese also relied on published data from the Canadian censuses for the decades in which she was interested.

Documentary Analysis

Sociologists have also made useful contributions to knowledge through the examination of official documents. Scott Davies (2002) examined how education reformers consciously designed their recommendations about policy change to fit with historically current political priorities and cultural settings. He shows how three successive education commissions in Ontario (1950, 1968, and 1995) each designed messages based on "progressive education," while simultaneously making policy recommendations that were diametrically opposed (e.g., some supported and some rejected standardized testing). Most change agents want to do "progressive" things. By carefully analyzing commission reports, Davies shows how the language of progressive education was reshaped by successive commissions to sell their brand of education reform.

Renisa Mawani (2003) examined archival documents including colonial maps to demonstrate a social process whereby geographical spaces were rendered "vacant" and therefore accessible to settlement and development. By showing how Aboriginal land use was made to vanish at some points, only to have later colonial authorities redraw the maps to show their presence, Mawani demonstrates the contested nature of landscape, both then and now. She also draws on legal documents, such as cases and statutes to understand how the rule of law was also used to displace Aboriginal peoples and, again reflecting contestation, how it was used by Aboriginal peoples in resistance. As a third methodological strategy she examines the ways in which an Aboriginal presence has been commemorated (e.g., via totem poles). By a careful comparison of the evidence offered through these documented sources, she argues that Vancouver's civic identity has shifted from a settler society to a postcolonial, multicultural city.

Use of Official Statistics

Governments have a long history of collecting statistical data. Government bureaucracies first began to collect statistics to help rulers determine both the size of their taxation base and the number of men they could put on the battlefield. Since then, the scope of government or official statistics has expanded and now includes information on births and deaths, unemployment rates, imports and exports, and so on. Sociologists have made good use of official statistics (see especially Haggerty, 2001).

For example, Brym (1986) was interested in how support for social-democratic political parties was related to the resources on which different social classes could draw. His dependent variable, electoral support for leftist political parties, was measured as the percentage of voters casting ballots supporting social-democratic or communist parties in ten capitalist democracies, including Canada. He focused on three key independent variables: a measure of the inequality of income in a country, the type of electoral system in a nation, and the percentage of the labour force that was unionized. His measures of these variables (except the type of electoral system) were derived from official statistics. Brym showed that, contrary to earlier research, class-based political activity was still strong in many countries he studied, especially if there were leftist political parties with the resources necessary to run effective campaigns.

McMullan and Swan (1989) used official statistics in their investigation of arson in Nova Scotia. They relied on police-reported arson for the period 1970–85. The data showed a substantial rise in both the actual number and the rate of reported arson (number of arsons per 1000 fires) between 1973 and 1981, with a modest decline in later years. Arson, of course, is difficult to prove, and McMullan and Swan were careful to check with a second source to verify the pattern they had established. When they used fire-marshal data, as opposed to police-report data, they found similar trends. In accounting for the fluctuating arson rate (their dependent variable) they pointed to interest rates and unemployment rates as the variables affecting arson rates. On the basis of official reports, and from interviews that they conducted with enforcement and insurance officials, McMullan and Swan concluded that most arson involves the burning of a person's own property, even though the criminal definition of arson continues to emphasize vandalism.

The arson example illustrates a central problem with official statistics. These statistics are not objective facts on which everyone agrees. The very definition of arson makes it difficult to prove. Furthermore, different interest groups have a great deal at stake over whether a fire is officially reported as arson. Often arsonists are property owners themselves, and their interests are opposed by those of insurance investigators, who do not want to pay settlements for illegal fires. Again, issues of validity are at stake: Do the official definitions used to generate, say, arrest statistics, arson rates, or strike statistics correspond to sociologists' theoretical concepts? In addition, sociologists must be certain that official statistics reflect changes they are examining, rather than changes in the practices of the officials collecting the statistics.

THE ANALYSIS OF NUMERICAL DATA

Sociological evidence frequently comes in numerical form—that is, as quantifiable evidence (e.g., number of disciplinarians, arsons, or voters). Finding and interpreting patterns in numerical data is complex. To help in summarizing numerical information, social scientists routinely rely on statistical techniques. In this section I briefly illustrate some key aspects of the process. I explore the following simple question: Do women and

men earn the same income as a result of having the same levels of education? Men and women have, on average, similar levels of schooling. However, as a group, men have higher incomes than do women.

Notice the causal logic here. Education is hypothesized to affect income. However, since women and men earn different wages in the labour market, yet have similar levels of schooling, maybe the causal link between education and income differs by sex. Although I can present only an elementary analysis here, issues of a wage gap between the sexes are part of the continuing debate over pay equity, comparable worth, and employment equity, all important policy questions (Fortin, 2005).

To begin, we need to examine the link between education and income. I do this by using data from the 2003 General Social Survey (2004), a survey conducted by Statistics Canada of a nationally representative sample of Canadians (24 951 randomly chosen Canadians, to be precise). Does education have a big effect on income? Table 20.1, called a contingency table or a cross-tabulation, gives us an answer. Education, the independent variable displayed across the top of the table, has three categories (low—high school or less; medium—some postsecondary education; and high—university degree or higher). For ease of presentation, annual personal income, the dependent variable, has two categories (low—personal income below $30 000 annually; and high—annual income at or above $30 000).

Notice first the table's arrangement. The title describes the two variables being related. The independent

TABLE 20.1   THE RELATIONSHIP BETWEEN LEVEL OF EDUCATION AND INDIVIDUAL INCOME FOR PEOPLE AGED 25–34, 2003

	Level of Education			
Income	**Low**	**Medium**	**High**	**Row Totals**
Low	53% (333)	45% (783)	31% (358)	42% (1473)
High	47% (296)	55% (939)	69% (814)	58% (2049)
Column totals	100% (629)	100% (1722)	100% (1172)	100% (3522)

SOURCE: Data is adapted from Statistics Canada, "SCF Public Use Microdata File: Income of Census Family Units," Catalogue no. 13M0001XDB, 19 August 1999.

variable (education) is placed on the top of the table and its values are clearly delineated. Below each value for education is a column of numbers. The dependent variable (income) is arrayed on the side of the table, again with the value labels clearly shown. Beside each value of the dependent variable is a row of numbers. To illustrate, Table 20.1 shows that there are 333 people in the top left-hand cell, the cell defined by a low level of education and a low income. At the intersection of each column and row is a table cell (there are six cells here because row and column totals are ignored in counting the number of cells in a table).

The concept of a contingency table comes from the idea that the category into which a person falls on the dependent variable is contingent on, or depends on, the category that a person occupies on the independent variable. If the hypothesis were true in this case, we would expect that, as we move across the education categories from low to high, the number of people receiving high incomes ought to rise. Do the data reveal this pattern? For people with low education, 296 had high incomes. For people with a high level of education, 814 had high incomes. These figures seem, at first glance, to support our expectation. Notice, however, that because of how education was categorized, 629 people had what I defined as low education, while 1172 had high education. Comparing the actual number of people in each cell is therefore misleading, because there are different numbers of people in each column.

Rather than focusing on the raw numbers, a better understanding of the patterns comes when we standardize the data. We need to ask what *percentage* of people in each education category had high incomes. By expressing the numbers as percentages—that is, by standardizing the data—it is much easier to see the patterns. So, 296 of 629 people in the low-education column had high incomes, or 47 percent (296 divided by 629 and then multiplied by 100). This tells us that for every 100 people with low education, 47 had high incomes. Making the same calculation for the high education column—(814/1172) $\times$ 100—we find that 69 percent of highly educated people earned high incomes (or 69 of every 100 people).

If you examine Table 20.1, you will see that the percentages are entered in the table. The actual number of people in each cell appears in parentheses. Notice that the percentages are calculated separately for each column, summing to 100 percent at the bottom of each column.

So, do relatively more people with high education receive high income in comparison with people with low education? Yes. Of every 100 people in the high-education column, 69 receive high income (69 percent), compared with only 47 of every 100 in the low-education column (47 percent). The difference between these two percentages (22 percent) is one measure of the strength of the relationship between education and income; the higher the percentage difference, the stronger the relationship.

In studying this table, some readers may have taken exception to my definitions of high and low incomes. Why should earning more than $30 000 be considered a high income? What is defined as low and high income is arbitrary. However, when I define the lows and highs of income and education differently and produce several different tables, the basic patterns in the tables do not change. This replication gives me confidence that my decisions about how to categorize the variables do not affect the results.

The evidence in Table 20.1 corroborates the first part of the question about the relationship between education and income. But how does gender figure into the pattern? Table 20.2 (p. 500) contains two contingency tables. Here the question is how the link between education and income varies for women in comparison with men. Table 20.2 can be usefully thought of as Table 20.1 but with women and men separated into their own subtables.

For women, the basic pattern of Table 20.1 is repeated in Table 20.2: 66 percent of women with a high level of education are likely to have high income, whereas only 23 percent of women with a low level of education are likely to have a high income. The difference between these two cell percentages is 43 percent.

For men, although the pattern is similar, the percentage difference is smaller. Of men with a high level of education, 73 percent have a high income, whereas for men with a low level of education, 64 percent have a high income. The percentage difference is only 9 percent. This suggests that for men education level is not as important as it is for women in earning a high income. Contrasting the percentage differences between the two subtables in Table 20.2 gives us a way of comparing the strength of the link between income and education for women versus men. A more complex method of investigating the causal linkages between gender, education, and income relies on multiple regression—see Box 20.4. (p. 501)

So, what do we learn from this analysis? We learn first, from Table 20.1, that people with more education are likely to earn higher incomes. Second, from

TABLE 20.2   THE RELATIONSHIP BETWEEN LEVEL OF EDUCATION, INDIVIDUAL INCOME, AND GENDER FOR PEOPLE AGED 25–34, 2003

	Women Level of Education				Men Level of Education			
Income	**Low**	**Medium**	**High**	**Total**	**Low**	**Medium**	**High**	**Total**
Low	78%	60%	34%	(893)	37%	32%	27%	(580)
High	23%	40%	66%	(778)	64%	68%	73%	(1270)
Totals	100%	100%	100%			100%	100%	100%
	(252)	(822)	(599)	(1671)	(377)	(900)	(573)	(1851)

SOURCE: Data from Statistics Canada, 2003 General Social Survey.
NOTE: Column and row totals are not equal for women because of rounding.

Table 20.2 we learn that this is especially true for women, in that for men education level has less of an impact on earning high incomes than is the case for women (remember only people between 25 and 34 are included in the tables).

Why is the link between education and income different for women and men? First, men without university education may still earn high pay in resource and manufacturing jobs where education level is less important. That could account for the difference. Second, the labour force is still at least partially differentiated into "male" and "female" jobs, and education level may be more important for finding work in traditional female jobs than in certain male jobs (e.g., nursing versus oil rigging). Third, women and men could be working different numbers of hours per week, or weeks per year, and these differences could be related to both education and income. Many other possible explanations exist, and further research is essential to sort them out (Fortin, 2005; Guppy and Davies, 1998).

THE FUTURE OF SOCIAL RESEARCH

Social research involves systematically studying the social world. The aim of such research activity is to develop explanations and understandings of social patterns beneficial to improving the human condition. Today, it is becoming increasingly obvious that we need to find innovative ways of organizing and running our human affairs. Starvation, environmental degradation, terrorism, and social injustice are among the many social problems we must confront. Solutions require adequate explanations and understandings for how these problems arise and persist.

Earlier in the chapter, I outlined several sources of knowledge: common sense, religious faith, and science. Although these forms of knowledge share certain features (e.g., they are all imperfect), scientific reason encourages a set of practices, open review and critical skepticism, which together work to reduce error.

Another way of emphasizing what is distinctive about the scientific method is to compare how social research differs from the work of other professionals who concentrate on similar social issues (e.g., the environment, gender relations). For example, what differentiates the work of documentary filmmakers, novelists, or journalists from that of social researchers? I have emphasized three features of scientific research that, in combination, separate it from the work of these other professionals:

1. Research results are confronted by the critical skepticism of other scientists.
2. Social theory guides, either directly or indirectly, the evidence gathered.
3. Evidence is systematically collected and analyzed.

Although some of these features are found in the work of other professionals, such as journalists, all three features are found in good social research. Replication and reproducibility have high currency in science as ways of encouraging skepticism. Good research contributes new ideas or evidence to our common stock of social theory. Finally, good research publicly displays the careful collection and analysis of evidence.

These principles are a feature of all good research, but the methods that sociologists use to pursue their goal of explaining and understanding the social world take many forms. This diverse array of methods, including observing, questioning, and experimenting,

BOX 20.4   INTRODUCING STATISTICAL IDEAS ABOUT REGRESSION ANALYSIS

In further exploring the linkage among gender, education, and income, I would want to introduce a series of alternative explanations. Testing each of these ideas using contingency tables would be extremely difficult because, with so many possible confounding variables, the tables I would generate would quickly become huge and unwieldy. An alternative to contingency-table analysis is regression analysis. The basic idea of regression, in summarizing the linkages between variables, can be explained most easily in graphic form.

Figure 20.2 is a graph with years of schooling arrayed along the horizontal axis (x-axis) and annual income displayed along the vertical axis (y-axis). On this graph I can plot where each person in the sample falls. In other words, I can choose someone from the sample and move along the x-axis until I come to the level of education attained by the selected person. I can then proceed up from there, now using the y-axis as a guide, until I reach the level of the same person's annual income. The point that I reach is the intersection of two perpendicular lines, one drawn vertically from the x-axis (at the person's level of education) and the other drawn horizontally from the y-axis (at that person's annual income). For each person in the sample, I can locate exactly where these two lines fall in the graph and

place a mark at the appropriate spot. The result, similar to what I have depicted, is a scatterplot.

A scatterplot can be summarized statistically by using regression techniques. To summarize the relationship between education and income, a straight line can be drawn through the data points in such a way that the distance from each point to the line can be minimized. If all points lie exactly on the line, the fit of the line to the data will be perfect. The farther the points are from the best-fitting line, the poorer is the ability to use a straight line to summarize the information and the weaker is the association between the two variables. The strength of association between two variables in a scatterplot is given by the correlation coefficient (r). The value of r can vary from -1 (a perfectly inverse relationship or negative association) to 0 (no association) to $+1$ (a perfectly proportionate relationship or positive association). The farther r is from 0, the stronger the association. The correlation coefficient is, then, analogous to the percentage difference in tables.

With the education and income scatterplot, I can capture the central characteristics of the best-fitting line with two numbers. One number captures the slope of the line and tells how much vertical increase (or decrease) occurs in the line for every unit of horizontal change along the x-axis. Using my example, for every additional year of schooling, how much does annual income increase? An easy way to remember this is to think of this number as the rise (income increase) over the run (change in years of schooling). A second number tells at what point the line intersects the y-axis. If I have a perfectly fitting line, the equation for a straight line can be expressed as $y = a + bx$, where x and y are values on the two axes of the graph, a is the point at which the line crosses the y-axis, and b is the slope of the line.

What I have described here is a statistical technique known as simple linear regression, for one independent and one dependent variable. To explore the alternative interpretations for the link among gender, education, and income that I offered earlier, you would need to use multiple regression, where one dependent variable can be linked to a series of independent variables. This data analysis approach has been instrumental in shaping social policy and refining sociological knowledge.

FIGURE 20.2 HYPOTHETICAL RELATIONSHIP BETWEEN EMPLOYMENT INCOME AND YEARS OF SCHOOLING

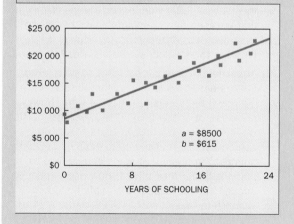

$a = \$8500$
$b = \$615$

YEARS OF SCHOOLING

---

offers sociologists many ways of inquiring responsibly and ethically about the social world. Each method has different strengths and weaknesses, which makes the choice of research strategy dependent on the sociological question.

Social science research will continue to contribute to our sense of the world around us. Research

on the environment, reproductive technology, multiculturalism, violence, and social-support networks all point to practical ways in which our human problems can be influenced by research findings. Effective policy solutions that benefit all people require sound social research.

SUMMARY

1. Research methods are ways of obtaining evidence to test suppositions about the world around us. Behind the various techniques we use to obtain evidence and expand our knowledge of the social world (e.g., experiments, interviews), we must recognize important assumptions about such things as facts, objectivity, and truth.

2. Science is one of several sources of knowledge. Like other kinds of knowledge, scientific knowledge can be wrong. However, unlike other ways of knowing, science incorporates explicit methods designed to reduce error in what is currently accepted as scientific knowledge. Evidence must be systematically collected and rigorously evaluated.

3. Good science integrates both strong theory and robust research. Theories are ideas about how the world works or claims about how to explain or understand the recurring, patterned nature of human activity.

4. Evidence is crucial to developing, revising, or discarding theoretical claims. In comparison with the evidence available in the natural sciences, the evidence available to social scientists presents added complexity because of the meaningful character of human social action. People, unlike molecules, assign meaning to their actions and to the actions of others.

5. Sociologists have devised many useful methods for obtaining evidence about the social world. Observation and questioning are the two principal techniques, although each of them is conducted by using a variety of formats, including experiments, surveys, participant observation, and interviews.

6. Good research adds to our knowledge of the world around us. Such knowledge expands our opportunities and options. Sociological knowledge helps either in solving social problems or by sensitizing us to the human condition, expanding our social horizons.

QUESTIONS TO CONSIDER

1. The teaching of faculty members in university and college departments could be evaluated in various ways. Suggest some different sociological methods of doing such an evaluation and comment on the strengths and weaknesses of each approach.

2. Lenton (1990) chose to examine issues of child abuse by focusing more broadly on child discipline and by surveying parents about their disciplinary techniques. Suggest alternative designs for her study, commenting on the strengths and weaknesses of the various approaches, including important ethical considerations.

3. Policymakers frequently debate raising or lowering age restrictions on activities, such as driving a car, drinking alcoholic beverages, or voting. Suggest how you might design a study that could provide evidence about the possible consequences of either raising or lowering one of these age restrictions.

4. Immigration levels remain a contentious issue in Canada. Construct a short series of interview questions designed to assess people's knowledge of current immigration practices. Ask these questions of your friends or family. Ask how many immigrants enter Canada and from which countries they originate. Compare your findings with official statistics that are available in government publications at your college or university or on the Internet. How might you explain the patterns you discovered?

5. Discuss the claim that "facts speak for themselves." What problems exist in making this claim? Conversely, what problems exist in claiming that facts do not "speak for themselves"? Consider especially the claim that we need firm standards against which to evaluate ideas or theoretical claims. Is it possible to establish such standards?

6. At parties, people are expected to be relaxed. Parties are times for having fun, for stepping outside the routines of school or work. However, phrases like "party pooper" suggest that parties too have rules and that violators of such rules can be ostracized. Others are glorified as "party animals," implying that some people take to partying better than others. How might you engage in a participant observation study to investigate these hunches systematically? Do such categories as "party animal" or "party pooper" exist, and, if so, how are they understood? Do "rules" exist at a party even though parties are in very important ways "escapist"? How might a sociologist seek to understand party life at your college or university?

GLOSSARY

Causation involves a relationship between two variables where change or variation in one variable produces change or variation in a second variable. Four criteria are essential to establishing a causal relation between two variables: association, time ordering, non-spuriousness, and theoretical rationale.

The **dependent variable** is a variable that is assumed to depend on or be caused by one or more other variables (independent variables); it is the variable that is the effect, or outcome, in a cause–effect relationship.

Ethnography is the detailed description of a particular culture or way of life, or the written results of a participant-observation study.

An **experiment** is a controlled test of the causal effects of a particular variable or set of variables on a dependent or outcome variable.

An **explanation** is an account of the causal logic that shows how and why variables influence one another.

External validity is the generalizability of a particular finding from the study group to a larger population; the relevance of conclusions for a larger population; or the ability to infer that the results of a study are representative of processes operating for a broader population.

In the **Hawthorne effect**, people involved in a study may be influenced by the very process of being studied; the study has an impact on the subjects of the study.

A **hypothesis** is a knowledge claim or hunch about how the world works; it is a testable statement, derived from a theory, about the relationship between two variables.

The **independent variable** is a variable that is presumed to affect or influence other variables; it is the causal variable.

An **interview** is a method of collecting information by asking people questions, either in person or over the telephone. Interviews range from highly structured (preset questions in a fixed order) to loosely structured (topic guidelines, but no prescribed question wording).

In **meaningful action**, human action, as distinct from physical behaviour, occurs with specific intentions or reasons in mind. The uncontrollable tic in a person's eye is physical behaviour, which differs from that of a person who is winking at

someone, where intention or purpose is central to understanding what is happening. Most human activity is meaningful action, or social action.

Measurement comprises procedures for assigning numbers to observations according to preset rules; it is the act of finding data or information relevant to theoretical concepts.

Objectivity is the attempt to minimize the effect of personal bias on research results or the idea of impartiality, of "fair hearings." Objectivity is an ideal enhanced by the work of any single researcher being open to the critical scrutiny of others. Objectivity as complete impartiality is a myth.

In **participant observation**, the study of social life involves the participation of the researcher, to varying degrees, in the activities of the group under investigation; it attempts to give an "insider's" account of a particular way of life or cultural system.

Randomization is a procedure used in experiments to assign test subjects to experimental conditions on the basis of chance.

Reliability is the consistency of measurements and the ability to reproduce the same measurements on repeated occasions.

Sampling is the process of selecting units from a larger population. Random sampling involves the selection of representative units (e.g., people, organizations) from a population (e.g., all Canadians, voluntary organizations in a city). Samples may be selected by probability (where every unit has a nonzero chance of selection) or nonprobability (where chance does not enter into the selection of sample units).

A **self-administered questionnaire** is a method of collecting information by having people record their own answers to preset questions.

Spuriousness is an incorrect inference about the causal relations between variables.

Understanding is the ability to provide a definition of a situation that members of a culture find authentic and valid.

Validity is the relevance or accuracy of measurement in relation to the theoretical concept that it is supposed to measure.

A **variable** is something that varies or an attribute or event that can take on more than one value (e.g., unemployment rates, age, sex).

SUGGESTED READING

Babbie, Earl, and Lucia Benaquisto. (2002). *Fundamentals of Social Research.* Toronto: Thomson Nelson. Babbie and Benaquisto provide the best general account of research methods available in sociology. This is a Canadian adaptation covering an array of methodologies with many illustrations and examples to emphasize key points.

Becker, Howard. (1998). *Tricks of the Trade: How to Think about Your Research While You're Doing It.* Chicago: University of Chicago Press. Written by one of sociology's best qualitative researchers, Becker's book discusses how to think about research and is valuable to both qualitative and quantitative researchers.

Cresswell, John. (2003). *Research Design: Qualitative, Quantitative, and Mixed Methods Approaches,* 2nd ed. Thousand Oaks, CA: Sage Publications. This text offers an excellent balanced view of the strengths and weaknesses of various research designs and is a useful guide to conducting good research by using multiple methods.

Denzin, Norman. (1997). *Interpretative Ethnography: Ethnographic Practices for the 21st Century.* Thousand Oaks, CA: Sage. Denzin provides a good general introduction to the practices and debates of qualitative research.

Guppy, Neil, and George Gray. (2008). *Successful Surveys: Research Methods and Practice,* 4th ed. Toronto: Thomson Nelson. This is a practical guidebook to developing research designs and using effective survey research techniques. The authors cover questionnaires and interviews.

NOTES

1. Black swans, native to Tasmania and Australia, were unknown to Europeans before exploration. The idea that all swans are white is thus similar to the idea that Earth is the central body in the solar system—a claim once understood to be true but now thought to be false.

2. Please do not overinterpret this claim. As a community we have frequently treated humans as exceptional. We have distanced ourselves from nature. Our theories and actions often evince a "control of nature" paradigm. Highlighting differences between the subject matter of the natural and the social sciences is extremely complicated. For example, monkeys make friends with zoologists and, when studied, may react in similar ways as humans. It is important to consider in what ways the studying of people by people may add complexity to research, and how this in turn may stimulate us to think differently about how people study non-humans. For example, issues of animal rights and environmental ethics raise questions about our traditionally human-centric view of the world. Perhaps bacteria do blush and we are just too ignorant to notice!

3. Foschi and Buchan (1990) use the term "White" rather than English Canadian.

WEB RESOURCES

Companion Website for This Book

http://www.newsociety6e.nelson.com
Begin by clicking on the Student Resources section of the website. Next, select the chapter you are studying from the pull-down menu. From the Student Resources page, you have easy access to InfoTrac College Edition® and other resources, such as the Glossary, Test Yourself questions, and additional readings. The website also has many useful tips to aid you in your study of sociology.

InfoTrac College Edition Search Terms

Visit http://www.infotrac-college.com for access to more than 20 million articles from nearly 6000 sources when doing your online research.

CHAPTER 1

Allen, Robert C. (1999). *Education and Technological Revolutions: The Role of the Social Sciences and the Humanities in the Knowledge Based Economy*. Ottawa: Social Sciences and Humanities Research Council of Canada. On the World Wide Web at http://www.sshrc.ca/english/resnews/researchresults/allen99.pdf (8 May 2001).

Babbie, Earl. (2000). *The Practice of Social Research*, 9th ed. Belmont, CA: Wadsworth Publishing.

Bell, Daniel. (1976). *The Coming of Post-industrial Society: A Venture in Social Forecasting*. New York: Basic Books.

Clark, S. D. (1968). *The Developing Canadian Community*, 2nd ed. Toronto: University of Toronto Press.

Coleman, James S. (1961). *The Adolescent Society*. New York: Free Press.

Douglas, Jack D. (1967). *The Social Meanings of Suicide*. Princeton, NJ: Princeton University Press.

Durkheim, Émile. (1951 [1897]). *Suicide: A Study in Sociology*. G. Simpson, ed.; Trans J. Spaulding and G. Simpson. New York: Free Press.

Edel, Abraham. (1965). "Social Science and Value: A Study in Interrelations." In Irving Louis Horowitz, ed., *The New Sociology: Essays in Social Science and Social Theory in Honor of C. Wright Mills* (pp. 218–38). New York: Oxford University Press.

Eichler, Margrit. (1987). *Nonsexist Research Methods*. Boston: Allen and Unwin.

Eichler, Margrit. (1988). *Families in Canada Today*, 2nd ed. Toronto: Gage.

Fukuyama, Francis. (1992). *The End of History and the Last Man*. New York: HarperCollins.

Garfinkel, Harold. (1967). *Studies in Ethnomethodology*. Englewood Cliffs, NJ: Prentice-Hall.

Giddens, Anthony. (1982). *Sociology: A Brief but Critical Introduction*. New York: Harcourt, Brace Jovanovich.

Giddens, Anthony. (1990). *The Consequences of Modernity*. Stanford, CA: Stanford University Press.

Goffman, Erving. (1959). *The Presentation of Self in Everyday Life*. Garden City, NY: Anchor.

Granovetter, Mark. (1973). "The Strength of Weak Ties." *American Sociological Review, 78* (6), 1360–80.

Guillén, Mauro F. (2001). "Is Globalization Civilizing, Destructive or Feeble? A Critique of Five Key Debates in the Social Science Literature." *Annual Review of Sociology, 27*. On the World Wide Web at http://knowledge.wharton.upenn.edu/PDFs/938.pdf (6 February 2003).

Guppy, Neil, and R. Alan Hedley. (1993). *Opportunities in Sociology*. Montreal: Canadian Sociology and Anthropology Association.

Hersch, Patricia. (1998). *A Tribe Apart: A Journey into the Heart of American Adolescence*. New York: Ballantine Books.

Hochschild, Arlie, with Anne Machung. (1989). *The Second Shift: Working Parents and the Revolution at Home*. New York: Viking.

Kuhn, Thomas. (1970). *The Structure of Scientific Revolutions*, 2nd ed. Chicago, University of Chicago Press.

Marx, Karl. (1904 [1859]). *A Contribution to the Critique of Political Economy*. Trans. N. Stone. Chicago: Charles H. Kerr.

Marx, Karl, and Friedrich Engels. (1972 [1848]). "Manifesto of the Communist Party." In R. Tucker, ed., *The Marx-Engels Reader* (pp. 331–62). New York: Norton.

Merton, Robert K. (1968 [1949]). *Social Theory and Social Structure*. New York: Free Press.

Mills, C. Wright. (1959). *The Sociological Imagination*. New York: Oxford University Press.

Ornstein, Michael D. (1983). "The Development of Class in Canada." In J. Paul Grayson, ed., *Introduction to Sociology: An Alternate Approach* (pp. 224–66). Toronto: Gage.

Parsons, T. (1951). *The Social System*. Glencoe, IL: Free Press.

Porter, John. (1965). *The Vertical Mosaic: An Analysis of Social Class and Power in Canada*. Toronto: University of Toronto Press.

Robbins, Liz. (2005). "Nash Displays Polished Look: On the Court, of Course." *New York Times* 19 January. On the World Wide Web at http://www.nytimes.com (19 January 2005).

Russett, Cynthia Eagle. (1966). *The Concept of Equilibrium in American Social Thought*. New Haven, CT: Yale University Press.

Statistics Canada. (2004). "Suicide in Canada's Immigrant Population." *The Daily* 29 March. On the World Wide Web at http://www.statcan.ca/Daily/English/040329/d040329a.htm (6 July 2006).

Statistics Canada. (2008). CANSIM, "Deaths, by cause, Chapter XX: External causes of morbidity and mortality (V01 to Y89), age group and sex, Canada, annual (number) (table)"; "Estimates of population (2001 Census and administrative data), by age group and sex. Canada, provinces, territories, health regions (June 2005 boundaries) and peer groups, annually (Number)." On the World Wide Web at http://dc1.chass.utoronto.ca.myaccess.library.utoronto.ca/cgi-bin/cansimdim (3 January 2008).

Thompson, Kenneth, ed. (1975). *Auguste Comte: The Foundation of Sociology*. New York: Wiley.

Tierney, John. (1997). "Our Oldest Computer, Upgraded." *New York Times Magazine* September 28: 46–49, 97, 100, 104–05.

Tillyard, E. M. W. (1943). *The Elizabethan World Picture*. London: Chatto and Windus.

Toffler, Alvin. (1990). *Powershift: Knowledge, Wealth, and Violence at the Edge of the 21st Century*. New York: Bantam.

United Nations. (2004). *World Development Report 2004*. On the World Wide Web at http://hdr.undp.org/reports/global/2004/ (1 February 2005).

Weber, Max. (1946). *From Max Weber: Essays in Sociology*. Eds. and trans. Hans Gerth and C. Wright Mills. New York: Oxford University Press.

Weber, Max. (1958 [1904–05]). *The Protestant Ethic and the Spirit of Capitalism*. New York: Scribner.

World Health Organization. (2002). "World Report on Violence and Health." On the World Wide Web at http://www.who.int/violence_injury_prevention/violence/world_report/en/full_en.pdf (22 April 2005).

Yates, Gayle Graham, ed. (1985). *Harriet Martineau on Women.* New Brunswick, NJ: Rutgers University Press.

CHAPTER 2

Adams, Michael. (1997). *Sex in the Snow: Canadian Social Values at the End of the Millennium.* Toronto: Penguin.

Albas, Daniel, and Cheryl Albas. (1989). "Modern Magic: The Case of Examinations." *The Sociological Quarterly, 30,* 603–13.

Baudrillard, Jean. (1988 [1986]). *America.* Trans. Chris Turner. London: Verso.

Beck, Glen. (2002). "Dan Quayle Likes Ozzy." On the World Wide Web at http://www.newsmax.com/showinsidecover. shtml?a52002/5/9/195211 (1 August 2006).

Bibby, Reginald W. (1987). *Fragmented Gods: The Poverty and Potential of Religion in Canada.* Toronto: Irwin.

Bierstedt, R. (1963). *The Social Order.* New York: McGraw-Hill.

Bissoondath, Neil. (2002). *Selling Illusions: The Cult of Multiculturalism in Canada,* rev. ed. Toronto: Penguin.

Bronowski, J. (1965). *Science and Human Values,* rev. ed. New York: Harper and Row.

Brym, Robert J. (2001). "Hip-Hop from Dissent to Commodity: A Note on Consumer Culture." In R. Brym, ed., *New Society: Sociology for the 21st Century,* 3rd ed. (pp. 78–81). Toronto: Harcourt Brace Canada.

Brym, Robert J. (2009). *Canadian Society and the 2006 Census.* Toronto: Nelson.

Brym, Robert J., with Bonnie J. Fox. (1989). *From Culture to Power: The Sociology of English Canada.* Toronto: Oxford University Press.

Carpenter, Dave. (2003). "McDonald's High-Tech with Kitchen, Kiosks." KioskCom. On the World Wide Web at http:// www.kioskcom.com/articles_detail.php?ident51856 (23 October 2003).

Citizenship and Immigration Canada. (2006). "Annual Report to Parliament on Immigration, 2006." On the World Wide Web at http://www.cic.gc.ca/english/pub/annual-report2006/ section1.html (13 April 2007).

Clarke, Harold D., Jane Jenson, Lawrence LeDuc, and Jon H. Pammett. (1996). *Absent Mandate: Canadian Electoral Politics In an Era of Restructuring,* 3rd ed. Toronto: Gage.

Delmos, Monika. (2002). "Mangled Words Divide Generations in Japan." *Globe and Mail* 24 August: A14.

Durkheim, Émile. (1976 [1915]). *The Elementary Forms of the Religious Life.* Trans. Joseph Ward Swain. New York: Free Press.

Elections Canada. (2008). "Elections Canada: Past Elections." On the World Wide Web at http://www.elections.ca/intro.asp?sec-tion=pas&document=index&lang=e (31 December 2008).

Fleras, Augie, and Jean Leonard Elliott. (2002). *Engaging Diversity: Multiculturalism in Canada.* Toronto: Nelson.

Frank, Thomas, and Matt Weiland, eds. (1997). *Commodify Your Dissent: Salvos from the Baffler.* New York: Norton.

Gap.com. (1999). On the World Wide Web at http://www.gap.com/onlinestore/gap/advertising/khakitv.asp (14 September 1999).

Gleick, James. (2000). *Faster: The Acceleration of Just About Everything.* New York: Vintage.

Gunderson, Edna, Bill Keveney, and Ann Oldenburg. (2002). "'The Osbournes' Find a Home in America's Living Rooms." *USA Today,* 19 April: 1A–2A.

Hall, Edward, (1959). *The Silent Language.* New York: Doubleday.

Hanke, Robert. (1998). "'Yo Quiero Mi MTV!' Making Music Television for Latin America." In Thomas Swiss, Andrew Herman, and John M. Sloop, eds., *Mapping the Beat: Popular Music and Contemporary Theory* (pp. 219–45). Oxford, UK: Blackwell.

Harris, Marvin. (1974). *Cows, Pigs, Wars and Witches: The Riddles of Culture.* New York, Random House.

Hobsbawm, Eric. (1994). *Age of Extremes: The Short Twentieth Century, 1914–1991.* London: Abacus.

Ignatieff, Michael. (2000). *The Rights Revolution.* Toronto: Anansi.

Kristof, Nicholas D. (1997). "With Stateside Lingo, Valley Girl Goes Japanese." *New York Times,* 19 October: section 1, 3.

Lipset, Seymour Martin. (1963). "Value Differences, Absolute or Relative: The English-Speaking Democracies." In *The First New Nation: The United States in Historical Perspective* (pp. 248–73). New York: Basic Books.

Lowe, Graham S. (2001). "Quality of Work—Quality of Life." Keynote talk at the Work/Life Balance and Employee Wellness Strategies Conference. Edmonton, Alberta, 14 May. On the World Wide Web at http://www.cprn.com/work/files/ pzqwq_e.pdf (25 August 2002).

"Mad about Hockey: Superstitions." (2002). On the World Wide Web at http://www.mcg.org/societe/hockey/pages/ aasuperstitions_2.html (20 June 2002).

McCrum, Robert, William Cran, and Robert MacNeil. (1992). *The Story of English,* new and rev. ed. London: Faber and Faber.

McLuhan, Marshall. (1964). *Understanding Media: The Extensions of Man.* New York: McGraw-Hill.

Nevitte, Neil. (1996). *The Decline of Deference: Canadian Value Change in Cross-National Perspective.* Peterborough, ON: Broadview Press.

Pinker, Steven. (1994). "Apes—Lost for Words." *New Statesman and Society,* 15 April: 30–31.

Pool, Robert. (1997). *Beyond Engineering: How Society Shapes Technology.* New York: Oxford University Press.

Postman, Neil. (1992). *Technopoly: The Surrender of Culture to Technology.* New York: Vintage.

Rifkin, Jeremy. (1998). *The Biotech Century: Harnessing the Gene and Remaking the World.* New York: Jeremy P. Tarcher/Putnam.

Ritzer, George. (1993). *The McDonaldization of Society: An Investigation into the Changing Character of Contemporary Social Life.* Thousand Oaks, CA: Pine Forge Press.

Ritzer, George. (1996). "The McDonaldization Thesis: Is Expansion Inevitable?" *International Sociology, 11,* 291–308.

Rural Advancement Foundation International. (1999). "The Gene Giants: Masters of the Universe?" On the World Wide Web at http://www.rafi.org/communique/fltxt/19992.html (29 June 1999).

Schlosser, Eric. (2002). *Fast Food Nation: The Dark Side of the All-American Meal.* New York: Perennial.

Schor, Juliet B. (1992). *The Overworked American: The Unexpected Decline of Leisure.* New York: Basic Books.

Scott, James C. (1998). *Seeing Like a State: How Certain Schemes to Improve the Human Condition Have Failed.* New Haven CT: Yale University Press.

Statistics Canada. (2005). "Population by Religion, by Provinces and Territories (2001 Census)." On the World Wide Web at http://www40.statcan.ca/l01/cst01/demo30a.htm?sdi5religion (29 October 2005).

Thompson, E. P. (1967). "Time, Work Discipline, and Industrial Capitalism." *Past and Present, 38*: 59–67.

United Nations. (1998). "Universal Declaration of Human Rights." On the World Wide Web at http://www.un.org/Overview/rights.html (29 August 2002).

U.S. Department of Commerce. (1998). "Statistical Abstract of the United States: 1998." On the World Wide Web at http://www.census.gov/prod/3/98pubs/98statab/sasec1.pdf (8 October 2000).

"Voter Turnout." (2004). Elections Almanac.com. On the World Wide Web at http://www.nodice.ca/election2004/voterturnout.html (29 October 2005).

Weber, Max. (1946 [1922]). "Bureaucracy." In H. Gerth and C. Mills, eds. and trans., *From Max Weber: Essays in Sociology* (pp. 196–264). New York: Oxford University Press.

Woodbury, Anthony. (2003). "Endangered Languages." Linguistic Society of America. On the World Wide Web at http://www.lsadc.org/web2/endangeredlgs.htm (19 July 2003).

World Values Survey, 2000. (2001). Machine readable file. Ann Arbor, MI: Inter-University Consortium for Political and Social Research.

CHAPTER 3

Adams, Natelie, and Pamela Bettis. (2003). "Commanding the Room in Short Skirts: Cheering as the Embodiment of Ideal Girlhood." *Gender & Society, 17* (1): 73–91.

Adler, P. A., and P. Adler. (1998). *Peer Power: Preadolescent Culture and Identity.* New Brunswick, NJ: Rutgers University Press.

Albas, Daniel, and Cheryl Albas. (1994). "Studying Students Studying: Perspectives, Identities, and Activities." In Mary Lorenz Dietz, Robert Prus, and William Shaffir, eds., *Doing Everyday Life: Ethnography as Human Lived Experience* (pp. 273–89). Toronto: Copp Clark Longman Ltd.

Ariès, Philippe. (1981). *The Hour of Our Death.* New York: Knopf.

Atchley, R. C. (1994). *Social Forces and Aging,* 7th ed. Belmont, CA: Wadsworth.

Baker, Maureen, ed. (1989). *Families: Changing Trends in Canada,* 2nd ed. Toronto: McGraw-Hill Ryerson.

Baker, Maureen. (1985). *What Will Tomorrow Bring? A Study of the Aspirations of Adolescent Women.* Ottawa: Canadian Advisory Council on the Status of Women.

Ballantine, Jeanne. (1997). *The Sociology of Education: A Systematic Analysis,* 4th ed. Englewood Cliffs, NJ: Prentice-Hall.

Barber, K., and K. Allen. (1992). *Women and Families: Feminist Reconstructions.* New York: Guilford Press.

Begley, S. (1995). "Gray Matters." *Newsweek* 7 November: 48–54.

Benokraitis, Nijole V. (1993). *Marriages and Families: Changes, Choices, and Constraints.* Englewood Cliffs, NJ: Prentice-Hall.

Berger, Peter L. (1970). "Identity as a Problem in the Sociology of Knowledge." In J. Curtis and J. Petras, eds., *The Sociology of Knowledge* (pp. 373–84). New York: Praeger.

Best, Raphaela. (1983). *We've All Got Scars: What Boys and Girls Learn in Elementary School.* Bloomington: Indiana University Press.

Bibby, Reginald. W. (2006). *The Boomer Factor.* Toronto: Bastian Books.

Blau, F., and M. Ferber. (1992). *The Economics of Women, Men, and Work.* Englewood Cliffs, NJ: Prentice Hall.

Bodine, A. (2003). "School Uniforms and Discourses on Childhood." *Childhood, 10* (1): 43–63.

Brim, Orville G., Jr. (1968). "Socialization through the Life Cycle." In Orville G. Brim, Jr., and Stanton Wheeler, eds., *Socialization after Childhood: Two Essays* (pp. 3–49). New York: John Wiley.

Brooks, B., J. Jarman, and Robert M. Blackburn. (2003). "Occupational Gender Segregation in Canada, 1981–1996: Overall, Vertical and Horizontal Segregation." *Canadian Review of Sociology and Anthropology, 40* (2): 197–213.

Burgess, R. L., and R. A. Richardson. (1984). "Child Abuse during Adolescence." In R. M. Lerner and N. L. Galambos, eds., *Experiencing Adolescents: A Sourcebook for Parents, Teachers and Teens* (pp. 119–52). New York: Garland.

Buysse, Jo Ann M., and Melissa Sheridan Embser-Herbert. (2004). "Constructions of Gender in Sport: An Analysis of Intercollegiate Media Guide Cover Photographs." *Gender & Society, 18* (1): 66–81.

Clausen, John A. (1986). *The Life Course.* Englewood Cliffs, NJ: Prentice Hall.

Cohen, Philip N. (2004). "The Gender Division of Labor: 'Keeping House'" and Occupational Segregation in the United States." *Gender & Society, 18* (2): 239–52.

Coleman, John C., and Leo Hendry. (1990). *The Nature of Adolescence,* 2nd ed. New York: Routledge, Chapman, and Hall.

Cooley, Charles Horton. (1902). *Human Nature and the Social Order.* New York: Scribner's.

Corsaro, William A. (1992). "Interpretive Reproduction in Children's Peer Cultures." *Social Psychology Quarterly, 55,* 160–77.

Davies, Bronwyn. (1990). *Frogs and Snails and Feminist Tales.* New York: Pandora Press.

Davis, Fred. (1961). "Professional Socialization as Subjective Experience: The Process of Doctrinal Conversion Among Student Nurses." In Howard S. Becker, David Riesman, Blanche Geer, and Robert Weiss, eds., *Institutions and the Person* (pp. 235–51). Chicago: Aldine Publishing Company.

Davis, Kingsley. (1947). "Final Note on a Case of Extreme Isolation." *American Journal of Sociology, 52* (March), 232–47.

Devine , D. (2002). "Children's Citizenship and the Structuring of Adult-Child Relations in Primary School." *Childhood, 9* (3): 303–20.

Duffy, Jim, Kelly Warren, and Margaret Walsh. (2001–2002). "Classroom Interactions: Gender of Teacher, Gender of Student, and Classroom Subject." *Sex Roles, 45,* 579.

Erikson, Erik H. (1982). *The Life Cycle Completed.* New York: Norton.

Evans, Donald, and William W. Falk. (1986). *Learning to be Deaf.* New York: Mouton de Gruyter.

Fox, Bonnie, ed. (2001). *Family Patters, Gender Relations,* 2nd ed. Toronto: Oxford University Press.

Fox, Bonnie. (1998). "Motherhood, Changing Relationships and the Reproduction of Gender Inequality." In S. Abbey and A. O'Reilly, eds., *Redefining Motherhood.* Toronto: Second Story Press.

Fussel, James. A. (2003). "Violent Video Game Has Parents, Experts Concerned." *The Hamilton Spectator* 1 March: D16.

Garbarino, J. (1999). *Lost Boys: Why Our Sons Turn Violent and How We Can Save Them.* New York: The Free Press.

Giordano, Peggy C., Stephen A. Cernkovich, and Alfred DeMaris. (1993). "The Family and Peer Relations of Black Adolescents." *Journal of Marriage and the Family, 55* (May), 277–87.

Glaser, Barney, and Anselm L. Strauss. (1967). *The Discovery of Grounded Theory: Strategies for Qualitative Research*. Chicago: Aldine.

Goffman, Erving. (1961). *Asylums*. New York: Anchor Books.

Goffman, Erving. (1979). *Gender Advertisements*. New York: Harper.

Gooden, Angela M., and Mark A. Gooden. (2001). "Gender Representation in Notable Children's Picture Books: 1995–1999." *Sex Roles, 45*, 89–101.

Gould, Stephen J. (1996). *The Mismeasure of Man*. New York: Norton.

Haas, J., and W. Shaffir. (1977). "The Cloak of Competence." *Symbolic Interaction, 1*, 1 (Fall), 71–88.

Haas, Jack, and William Shaffir. (1987). *Becoming Doctors: The Adoption of a Cloak of Competence*. Greenwich, CT: JAI Press.

Handel, Gerald. (1990). "Revising Socialization Theory." *American Sociological Review, 55*, 463–66.

Hebdige, Dick. (1979). *Subculture: The Meaning of Style*. London: Methuen.

Hendricks, Jon, and C. Davis Hendricks. (1986). *Aging in Mass Society: Myths and Realities*, 3rd ed. Boston: Little, Brown.

Herrnstein, Richard J., and Charles Murray. (1994). *The Bell Curve*. New York: Free Press.

Hogan, Dennis P., and Nan Marie Astone. (1986). "Transition to Adulthood." *Annual Review of Sociology, 12*, 109–30.

Hooyman, N. R., and H. A. Kiyak. (1993). *Social Gerontology*, 3rd ed. Boston: Allyn and Bacon.

Hopf, D., and C. H. Hatzichristou. (1999). "Teacher Gender-Related Influences in Greek Schools." *British Journal of Educational Psychology, 69*, 1–18.

Huston, A. C. (1983). "Sex-Typing." In Paul H. Mussen, ed., *Handbook of Child Psychology*. Vol. 4, 4th ed. (pp. 387–467). New York: Wiley.

Jackson, John J., and Michael Rosenberg. (2004). *Recognition and Mis-Recognition: Radio as Interlocutor—A Study of Second Generation Immigrant Use of Radio*. Final report submitted to the Multiculturalism Branch of Heritage Canada. Centre for Broadcasting Studies, Concordia University, Montreal, July.

Joanisse, Leanne. (2005). "'This Is Who I Really Am': Obese Women's Conceptions of Self Following Weight Loss Surgery." In Dorothy Pawluch, William Shaffir, and Charlene Miall, eds., *Doing Ethnography: Studying Everyday Life* (pp. 248–59). Toronto: Canadian Scholars' Press.

Kitsuse, John. (1970). "Editor's Preface." *American Behavioral Scientist, 14*, 2 (November/December).

Kohn, Melvin L., Atsushi Naoi, Carmi Schooler, and Kazimiercz M. Slomczynski. (1990). "Position in the Class Structure and Psychological Functioning in the United States, Japan, and Poland." *American Journal of Sociology, 95*, 964–1008.

Kortenhaus, C. M., and J. Demarest. (1993). "Gender Role Stereotyping in Children's Literature: An Update." *Sex Roles, 28*, 219–32.

Lareau, A. (1987). "Social Class Differences in Family-School Relationships." *Sociology of Education, 60*, 63–72.

Lawson, David. (1996). "The Brave New World of Work." *The Silhouette* 7 November.

Leming, M. R., and G. E. Dickinson. (1990). *Understanding Dying, Death, and Bereavement*, 2nd ed. New York: Holt, Rinehart and Winston.

Light, Donald L., Jr. (1980). *Becoming Psychiatrists: The Professional Transformation of Self*. New York: W.W. Norton.

Lightfoot, Cynthia. (1997). *The Culture of Adolescent Risk-Taking*. London: Guilford Press.

Luster, Tom, Kelly Rhoades, and Bruce Haas. (1989). "The Relation between Parental Values and Parenting Behavior: A Test of the Kohn Hypothesis." *Journal of Marriage and the Family, 51* (February), 139–47.

Lytton, Hugh, and David Romney. 1991. "Parents' Differential Socialization of Boys and Girls: A Meta-analysis." *Psychological Bulletin, 109*, 267–96.

Mackie, Marlene. (1991). *Gender Relations in Canada: Further Explorations*. Toronto: Butterworths Canada.

Massoni, Kelley. (2004). "Modeling Work: Occupational Messages in *Seventeen* Magazine." *Gender & Society, 18* (1): 47–65.

Mead, George H. (1934). *Mind, Self and Society*. Chicago: University of Chicago Press.

Montemurro, Beth. (2005). "Add Men, Don't Stir: Reproducing Traditional Gender Roles in Modern Wedding Showers." *Journal of Contemporary Ethnography, 34* (1), 6–35.

Piaget, Jean. (1950). *The Psychology of Intelligence*. Boston: Routledge and Kegan Paul.

Raby, Rebecca. (2005). "Polite, Well-Dressed and on Time: Secondary School Conduct Codes and the Production of Docile Citizens." *Canadian Review of Sociology and Anthropology, 42* (1): 71–91.

Richer, Stephen. (1988). "Equality to Benefit from Schooling: The Issue of Educational Opportunity." In D. Forcese and S. Richer, eds., *Social Issues: Sociological Views of Canada* (pp. 262–86). Toronto: Prentice Hall.

Rubin, J., F. Provenzano, and Z. Luria. (1974). "The Eye of the Beholder: Parents' Views on Sex of Newborns." *American Journal of Orthopsychiatry, 44*, 512–19.

Russell, Rachael, and Melissa Tyler. (2002). "Thank Heaven for Little Girls: 'Girl Haven' and the Commercial Context of Feminine Childhood." *Sociology, 36*, 619–37.

Scott, Robert A. (1969). *The Making of Blind Men: A Study of Adult Socialization*. New York: Russell Sage Foundation.

Sebald, H. (1992). *Adolescence: A Social Psychological Analysis*. Englewood Cliffs, NJ: Prentice Hall.

Shanas, Ethel, Peter Townsend, Dorothy Wedderburn, Henning Friis, Paul Milhøj, and Jan Stehouwer. (1972). *Old People in Three Industrial Societies*. New York: Atherton.

Shepard, Jon M. (1993). *Sociology*, 5th ed. New York: West.

Skolnick, Arlene. (1991). *Embattled Paradise: The American Family in an Age of Uncertainty*. New York: Basic Books.

Solomon, Yvette, Jo Warin, Charlie Lewis, and Wendy Langford. (2002). "Intimate Talk Between Parents and Their Teenage Children: Democratic Openness or Covert Control?" *Sociology, 36*, 965–83.

South, S., and S. Spitze. (1994). "Housework in Marital and Nonmarital Households." *American Sociological Review, 59*, 327–47.

Spitz, Rene A. (1945). "Hospitalism: An Inquiry into the Genesis of Psychiatric Conditions in Early Childhood." *The Psychoanalytic Study of the Child, 1*, 53–74.

Stebbins, Robert A. (1990). *Sociology: The Study of Society*, 2nd ed. New York: Harper and Row.

Stockard, Jean, and Miriam M. Johnson. (1992). *Sex and Gender in Society*, 2nd ed. Englewood Cliffs, NJ: Prentice-Hall.

Stryker, Sheldon. (1980). *Symbolic Interactionism*. Menlo Park, CA: Benjamin/Cummings.

Thorne, B. (1993). *Gender Play: Girls and Boys in School.* New Brunswick, NJ: Rutgers University Press.

Weitzman, Lenore. (1979). *Sex-Role Socialization: A Focus on Women.* Palo Alta, CA: Mayfield Publishing Co.

Williams, L. Susan. (2002). "Trying On Gender, Gender Regimes, and the Process of Becoming Women." *Gender & Society, 16* (1): 29–52.

Willis, Paul. (1990). *Common Culture: Symbolic Work at Play in the Everyday Cultures of the Young.* Milton Keynes: Open University Press.

Wolff, Michael. (1973). "Notes on the Behavior of Pedestrians." In A. Birenbaum and E. Sagarin, eds., *People in Places: The Sociology of the Familiar.* New York: Praeger.

Wuthnow, Robert. (1998). *Loose Connections.* Cambridge, MA: Harvard University Press.

CHAPTER 4

Averett, Susan, and Sanders Korenman. (1996). "The Economic Reality of the Beauty Myth." *The Journal of Human Resources, 31,* (2): 304–30.

Bagley, Christopher, and Kathleen King. (1990). *Child Sexual Abuse: The Search for Healing.* London: Tavistock/Routledge.

Berch, D. B., and B. G. Bender. (1987). "Margins of Sexuality." *Psychology Today,* December: 54–57.

Bergen, D. J., and J. E. Williams. (1991). "Sex Stereotypes in the United States Revisited: 1972–1988." *Sex Roles, 24,* 413–23.

Bibby, Reginald W. (1995). *The Bibby Report: Social Trends Canadian Style.* Toronto: Stoddart.

Bibby, Reginald W. (2006). *The Boomer Factor.* Toronto: Bastian Books

Bleier, Ruth. (1984). *Science and Gender: A Critique of Biology and Its Theories on Women.* New York: Pergamon.

Blum, Deborah. (1997). *Sex on the Brain: The Biological Differences between Men and Women.* New York: Penguin Books.

Broverman, I. K., S. R. Vogel, D. M. Broverman, F. E. Clarkson, and P. S. Rosenkratz. (1972). "Sex-Role Stereotypes: A Current Appraisal." *Journal of Social Issues, 28,* 59–78.

Buss, D. M. (1994). *The Evolution of Desire.* New York: Basic Books.

Buss, D. M. (1995a). "Evolutionary Psychology: A New Paradigm for Psychological Science." *Psychological Inquiry, 6,* 1–30.

Buss, D. M. (1995b). "Psychological Sex Differences: Origins through Sexual Selection." *American Psychologist, 50,* 164–68.

Buss, D. M. (1998). "The Psychology of Human Mate Selection: Exploring the Complexity of the Strategic Repertoire." In C. Crawford and D. L. Krebs, eds., *Handbook of Evolutionary Psychology: Ideas, Issues, and Applications* (pp. 405–29). Mahwah, NJ: Erlbaum.

Buss, D. M., M. Abbott, A. Angleitner, A. Asherian, A. Biaggio, A. Blanco-Villasenor, et al. (1990). "International Perspectives in Selecting Mates: A Study of 37 Cultures." *Journal of Cross-Cultural Psychology, 21* (1), 5–47.

Caplan, Paula J., and Jeremy B. Caplan. (1999). *Thinking Critically about Research on Sex and Gender,* 2nd ed. New York: Longman.

Colapinto, John. (1997). "The True Story of John/Joan." *Rolling Stone* 11 December: 54–73, 92–97.

Colapinto, John. (2001). *As Nature Made Him: The Boy Who Was Raised as a Girl.* New York: Perennial.

Condry, J., and S. Condry. (1976). "Sex Differences: A Study of the Eye of the Beholder." *Child Development, 47,* 812–19.

Coontz, Stephanie, and Peta Henderson, eds. (1986). *Women's Work, Men's Property: The Origins of Gender and Class.* London: Verso.

Creighton, Sarah, and Catherine Minto. (2001). "Managing Intersex." *British Medical Journal, 323* (7324), 1264–65.

Davis, Simon. (1990). "Men as Success Objects and Women as Sex Objects: A Study of Personal Advertisements." *Sex Roles, 23,* 43–50.

Davis, T., G. Peck, and J. Stormant. (1993). "Acquaintance Rape and the High School Student." *Journal of Adolescent Health, 14,* 220–24.

Dawkins, Richard. (1976). *The Selfish Gene.* London: Oxford University Press.

DeKeseredy, Walter S., and M. D. Schwartz. (1998). *Woman Abuse on Campus: Results from the Canadian National Survey.* Thousand Oaks, CA: Sage.

Duffy, Ann. (1998). "The Feminist Challenge: Knowing and Ending the Violence." In Nancy Mandell, ed., *Feminist Issues: Race, Class and Sexuality* (pp. 132–59). Scarborough, ON: Prentice Hall Allyn and Bacon Canada.

Durex. (2005). "Give and Receive: 2005 Global Sex Survey Results." On the World Wide Web at http://www.durex.com/cm/gss2005result.pdf (10 December 2005).

Durex. (2008). "Frequency of Sex versus Satisfaction Levels." On the World Wide Web at http://www.durex.com/en-CA/SexualWellbeingSurvey/Fequency%20of%20Sex/pages/default.aspx (6 December 2008).

Dworkin, Andrea. (1981). *Pornography: Men Possessing Women.* New York: Penguin.

Eagley, Alice H., and Wendy Wood. (1999). "The Origins of Sex Differences in Human Behaviour. Evolved Dispositions versus Social Roles." *American Psychologist, 54,* 408–23.

Eccles, J. S., J. E. Jacobs, and R. D. Harold. (1990). "Gender-Role Stereotypes, Expectancy Effects and Parents' Socialization of Gender Differences." *Journal of Social Issues, 46,* 183–201.

Eichler, Margrit. (1980). *The Double Standard.* London: Croom Helm.

Eisler, Riane. (1987). *The Chalice and the Blade.* New York: HarperCollins.

Elkin, F., and G. Handel. (1989). *The Child and Society: The Process of Socialization,* 5th ed. New York: Random House.

Ellis, Lee, Brian Robb, and Donald Burke. (2005). "Sexual Orientation in United States and Canadian College Students." *Archives of Sexual Behavior, 34,* 569–81.

Feiring, C., and M. Lewis. (1979). "Sex and Age Differences in Young Children's Reactions to Frustration: A Further Look at the Goldberg and Lewis Subjects." *Child Development, 50,* 848–53.

Fischtein, Dayna S., Edward S. Herold, and Serge Desmarais. (2007). "How Much Does Gender Explain in Sexual Attitudes and Behaviors? A Survey of Canadian Adults." *Archives of Sexual Behavior, 36,* 451–61.

Fitzgerald, Louise F. (1993). "Sexual Harassment against Women in the Workplace." *American Psychologist, 48,* 1070–76.

Freud, Sigmund. (1977 [1905]). *On Sexuality.* Trans. James Strachey; Angela Richards, ed., Vol. 7, Pelican Freud Library. Harmondsworth, UK: Penguin Books.

Gadd, Jane. (1997). "More Boys Physically Abused Than Girls." *The Globe and Mail* 9 July: A1, A6.

Garner, David M. (1997). "The 1997 Body Image Survey Results." *Psychology Today, 30* (January–February): 30–44, 74–80, 84.

Gimbutas, Marija. (1982). *Goddesses and Gods of Old Europe: 6500–3500 B.C. Myths and Cult Images.* Berkeley and Los Angeles: University of California Press.

Goldberg, S., and M. Lewis. (1969). "Play Behaviour in the Year-Old Infant: Early Sex Differences." *Child Development, 40,* 21–31.

Grescoe, P. (1996). *The Merchants of Venus: Inside Harlequin and the Empire of Romance.* Vancouver: Raincoast.

Gruber, J. E. (1997). "An Epidemiology of Sexual Harassment: Evidence from North America and Europe." In W. O'Donohue, ed., *Sexual Harassment: Theory, Research and Treatment* (pp. 84–98). Boston: Allyn and Bacon.

Hamer, D., and P. F. Copeland. (1996). *The Science of Desire: The Search for the Gay Gene and the Biology of Behaviour.* New York: Touchstone Books.

Hatfield, Elaine. (1995). "What Do Women and Men Want from Love and Sex?" In E. D. Nelson and B. W. Robinson, eds., *Gender in the 1990s: Images, Realities, and Issues* (pp. 257–75). Toronto: Nelson Canada.

Hesse-Biber, Sharlene. (1996). *Am I Thin Enough Yet? The Cult of Thinness and the Commercialization of Identity.* New York: Oxford University Press.

Hobart, Charles. (1996). "Intimacy and Family Life: Sexuality, Cohabitation, and Marriage." In Maureen Baker, ed., *Families: Changing Trends in Canada* (pp. 143–73). Toronto: McGraw-Hill Ryerson.

"Homosexuality and Bisexuality." (2000). Report #5 to the *Toronto Sun* in the Third Annual Sun/COMPAS Sex Survey. On the World Wide Web at http://www.compas.ca/html/archivesdocument.asp?compasSection5Sun1Media1Sex1PollandGO5GOandcompasID561 (9 August 2002).

Hughes, Fergus P. (1995). *Children, Play and Development,* 2nd ed. Boston: Allyn and Bacon.

Human Rights Watch. (1995). *The Human Rights Watch Global Report on Women's Human Rights.* New York: Human Rights Watch.

Jeffreys, Sheila. (1990). "Heterosexuality and the Desire for Gender." In Diane Richardson, ed., *Theorising Heterosexuality* (pp. 75–90). Buckingham, UK: Open University Press.

Jensen, Margaret Ann. (1984). *Love's Sweet Return: The Harlequin Story.* Toronto: Women's Press.

Kerig, Patricia K., Philip A. Cowan, and Carolyn Pape Cowan. (1993). "Marital Quality and Gender Differences in Parent–Child Interaction." *Developmental Psychology, 29,* 931–39.

Kitzinger, Celia, and Sue Wilkinson. (1994). "Problematizing Pleasure: Radical Feminist Deconstructions of Sexuality and Power." In H. L. Radtke and H. J. Stam, eds., *Power/Gender: Social Relations in Theory and Practice.* London: Sage.

Koff, Elissa, and Amy Benavage. (1998). "Breast Size Perception and Satisfaction, Body Image, and Psychological Functioning in Caucasian and Asian American College Women." *Sex Roles, 38* (7/8), 655–73.

Koss, Mary P., L. A. Goodman, A. Browne, L. F. Fitzgerald, G. P. Keita, and N. F. Russo. (1994). *No Safe Haven: Male Violence against Women at Home, at Work, and in the Community.* Washington, DC: American Psychological Association.

Laumann, Edward O., John H. Gagnon, Robert T. Michael, and Stuart Michaels. (1994). *The Social Organization of Sexuality: Sexual Practices in the United States.* Chicago: University of Chicago Press.

Lenton, Rhonda, Michael D. Smith, John Fox, and Norman Morra. (1999). "Sexual Harassment in Public Places: Experiences of Canadian Women." *Canadian Review of Sociology and Anthropology, 36,* 517–40.

Lightfoot-Klein, Hanny, Cheryl Chase, Tim Hammond, and Ronald Goldman. (2000). "Genital Surgery on Children below the Age of Consent." In Lenore T. Szuchman and Frank Muscarella, eds., *Psychological Perspectives on Human Sexuality* (pp. 440–49). New York: John Wiley and Sons.

Lips, H. M. (1993). *Sex and Gender: An Introduction,* 2nd ed. Mountain View, CA: Mayfield.

Lisak, David. (1992). "Sexual Aggression, Masculinity, and Fathers." *Signs, 16,* 238–62.

MacDonald, K., and R. D. Parke. (1986). "Parent–Child Physical Play: The Effects of Sex and Age on Children and Parents." *Sex Roles, 15,* 367–78.

Mackay, Judith. 2000. *The Penguin Atlas of Human Sexual Behaviour.* New York: Penguin.

MacKinnon, C. A. (1987). *Feminism Unmodified: Discourses on Life and Law.* Cambridge, MA: Harvard University Press.

Masters, W. H., and V. E. Johnson. (1966). *Human Sexual Response.* Boston: Little, Brown.

Matrix, C., ed. (1996). *Tales for the Clit.* Edinburgh: AK Press.

Mead, Margaret. (1935). *Sex and Temperament in Three Primitive Societies.* New York: Dell.

Michael, Robert T., John H. Gagnon, Edward O. Laumann, and Gina Kolata. (1994). *Sex in America: A Survey.* Boston: Little, Brown.

Nelson, E. D., and Barrie W. Robinson. (1999). *Gender in Canada.* Scarborough, ON: Prentice Hall Allyn and Bacon Canada.

Nolen, Stephanie. (1999). "Gender: The Third Way." *The Globe and Mail* 25 September: D1, D4.

Peele, Stanton, and Richard De Grandpre. (1995). "My Genes Made Me Do It." *Psychology Today,* 50–68.

Pipher, M. (1994). *Reviving Ophelia: Saving the Selves of Adolescent Girls.* New York: Ballantine.

Pryor, John B., J. L. Giedd, and K. B. Williams. (1995). "A Social Psychological Model for Predicting Sexual Harassment." *Journal of Social Issues, 51,* 69–84.

Raag, Tarja, and Christine L. Rackliff. (1998). "Preschoolers' Awareness of Social Expectations of Gender: Relationships to Toy Choices." *Sex Roles, 38,* 685–700.

Reiss, I. (1986). *Journey into Sexuality: An Exploratory Voyage.* Englewood Cliffs, NJ: Prentice Hall.

Rich, Adrienne. (1996). "Compulsory Heterosexuality and Lesbian Existence." In Stevi Jackson and Sue Scott, eds., *Feminism and Sexuality: A Reader* (pp. 130–43). New York: Columbia University Press.

Rosenkrantz, P., S. R. Vogel, H. Bee, I. K. Broverman, and D. M. Broverman. (1968). "Sex-Role Stereotypes and Self Concepts in College Students." *Journal of Consulting and Clinical Psychology, 32,* 287–95.

Rotermann, Michele. (2008). "Trends in Teen Sexual Behaviour and Condom Use." *Health Reports, 19* (3), 1–5

Rubin, J. Z., F. J. Provenzano, and Z. Lurra. (1974). "The Eye of the Beholder." *American Journal of Orthopsychiatry, 44,* 512–19.

Ryan, Kathryn M., and Jeanne Kanjorski. (1998). "The Enjoyment of Sexist Humor, Rape Attitudes, and Relationship Aggression in College Students." *Sex Roles, 38,* 743–56.

"Same-Sex Marriage: Canadian Public Opinion Polls: 2005-JAN-01 to the Present." (2005). On the World Wide Web at http://www.religioustolerance.org/homssmpoll05.htm (10 December 2005).

"Same-Sex Marriage in Canada: Public Opinion Polls 2006 to Now." (2008). http://www.religioustolerance.org/homssmpoll06.htm (retrieved December 6, 2008)

Sanday, Peggy. (1981). *Female Power and Male Dominance.* Cambridge, UK: Cambridge University Press.

Saxton, Lloyd. (1990). *The Individual, Marriage and the Family,* 7th ed. Belmont, CA: Wadsworth.

Shorter, Edward. (1997). *A History of Psychiatry.* New York: John Wiley and Sons.

Statistics Canada. (2006). "Prevalence and Severity of Violence against Women." On the World Wide Web at http://www.statcan.gc.ca/pub/85-570-x/2006001/findings-resultats/4144393-eng.htm (retrieved 6 December 2008).

Steinem, G. (1994). *Moving beyond Words.* New York: Simon and Schuster.

Straus, Murray. (1995). "Trends in Cultural Norms and Rates of Partner Violence." In Sandra M. Stith and Murray A. Straus, eds., *Understanding Partner Violence: Prevalence, Causes, Consequences, and Solutions* (pp. 30–33). Minneapolis, MN: National Council on Family Relations.

Tavris, Carol. (1992). *The Mismeasure of Woman: Why Women Are Not the Better Sex, the Inferior Sex, or the Opposite Sex.* New York: Touchstone.

Thompson, Linda. (1991). "Family Work: Women's Sense of Fairness." *Journal of Family Issues, 12,* 181–96.

Twenge, Jean M. (1997). "Changes in Masculine and Feminine Traits over Time: A Meta-analysis." *Sex Roles, 36,* 305–25.

Udry, J. R. (1971). *The Social Context of Marriage,* 2nd ed. Philadelphia: J.B. Lippincott.

Walters, Vivienne. (1992). "Women's Views of Their Main Health Problems." *Canadian Journal of Public Health, 83* (5), 371–74.

Weeks, Jeffrey. (1986). *Sexuality.* London: Routledge.

Welsh, Sandy. (1999). "Gender and Sexual Harassment." *Annual Review of Sociology, 25,* 169–90.

Welsh, Sandy, and A. Nierobisz. (1997). "How Prevalent Is Sexual Harassment? A Research Note on Measuring Sexual Harassment in Canada." *Canadian Journal of Sociology, 22,* 505–22.

Williams, J. E., and S. M. Bennett. (1975). "The Definition of Sex Stereotypes via the Adjective Check List." *Sex Roles, 1,* 327–37.

Williams, J. E., and D. L. Best. (1982). *Measuring Sex Stereotypes: A Thirty-Nation Study.* Beverley Hills, CA: Sage Publications.

Wilson, Edward. (1975). *Sociobiology.* Cambridge, MA: Harvard University Press.

Wilson, Edward. (1978). *On Human Nature.* Cambridge, MA: Harvard University Press.

Wilson, Margo, and Martin Daly. (1994). "Lethal and Nonlethal Violence against Wives and the Evolutionary Psychology of Male Sexual Proprietariness." In R. Emerson Dobash and Russell P. Dobash, eds., *Rethinking Violence against Women* (pp. 199–230). Thousand Oaks, CA: Sage Publications.

Wolf, Naomi. (1991). *The Beauty Myth.* Toronto: Vintage Books.

CHAPTER 5

Albrechtslund, Anders. (2008). "Online Social Networking as Participatory Surveillance." *First Monday, 13,* (3). On the World Wide Web at http://firstmonday.org/htbin/cgiwrap/bin/ojs/index.php/fm/article/view/2142/1949. (22 December 2008).

Attallah, P., and D. Foster. (2006). "Television in Canada." In P. Attallah and L. Regan Shade, eds., *Mediascapes: New Patterns in Canadian Communication,* 2nd ed. (pp. 179–95). Toronto: Thomson.

Banks, S., and J. Humphreys. (2008). "The Labour of User Co-creators: Emergent Social Network Markets?" Convergence, 14 (4), 401–18.

Barnes, Susan B. (2006). "A Privacy Paradox: Social Networking in the United States." *First Monday, 11* (9). On the World Wide Web at http://firstmonday.org/htbin/cgiwrap/bin/ojs/index.php/fm/article/view/1394/1312 (22 December 2008).

Baym, N. (2000). *Tune In, Log On: Soaps, Fandom, and Online Community.* Thousand Oaks and London: SAGE Publications.

Bertelsmann. (2008). *Annual Report 2007.* On the World Wide Web at http://www.bertelsmann.de/bertelsmann_corp/wms41//customers/bmcorp/pdf/Gesamt_PDF_GB_2007_englisch.pdf (9 July 2009).

Boyd, D. (2007). "Why Youth [Heart] Social Network Sites: The Role of Networked Publics in Teenage Social Life." In David Buckingham, ed., *MacArthur Foundation Series on Digital Learning—Youth, Identity, and Digital Media Volume* (pp. 119–42). Cambridge, MA: MIT Press. On the World Wide Web at http://www.danah.org/papers/WhyYouthHeart.pdf (22 December 2008).

Boyd, D. and H. Jenkins. (2006). "Discussion: MySpace and Deleting Online Predators Act (DOPA)." *MIT Tech Talk,* May 26. On the World Wide Web at http://www.danah.org/papers/MySpaceDOPA.html (22 December 2008).

Buckingham, D. (1998). "Children and Television: A Critical Overview of Research." In R. Dickinson, R. Harindranath, and O. Linné, eds., *Approaches to Audiences: A Reader* (pp. 131–45). London: Arnold.

Candussi, D. and J. Winters. (1988). "Monopoly and Content in Winnipeg." In R. Picard, J. P. Winter, M. McCombs, and S. Lacy, eds., *Press Concentration and Monopoly: New Perspectives on Newspaper Ownership and Operation* (pp. 139–45). Norwood, NJ: Ablex.

CanWest Global. (2007). *Annual Report 2007.* On the World Wide Web at http://www.canwest.com/investors/investor_documents/F07/CWG_Annual_Report_web.pdf (9 July 2009).

Carroll, W., and R. Ratner. (1999). "Media Strategies and Political Projects: A Comparative Study of Social Movements." *Canadian Journal of Sociology, 24* (1), 1–34.

Collins, R. (1990). *Culture, Communication and National Identity: The Case of Canadian Television.* Toronto: University of Toronto Press.

Comcast. (2008). *2007 Annual Review.* On the World Wide Web at http://www.comcast.com/2007annualreview/report.htm (9 July 2009).

Dickinson, P., and J. Ellison. (2000). *Plugging In: the Increase of Household Internet Use Continues into 1999.* Ottawa: Ministry of Industry, Connectedness Series. Catalogue No. 56F0004MIE.

Disney. (2007). "Financial Highlights." *2007 Annual Report.* On the World Wide Web at http://corporate.disney.go.com/investors/annual_reports/2007/fh/part1.html (9 July 2009).

Ellis, D. (1992). *Split Screens: Home Entertainment and the New Technologies.* Toronto: Friends of Canadian Broadcasting.

eMarketer. (2008). "The Blogosphere: A Mass Movement from Grassroots." On the World Wide Web at http://www.emarketer.com/Reports/All/Emarketer_2000494.aspx (22 December 2008).

Ericson, R., P. Baranek, and J. Chan. (1989). *Negotiating Control: A Study of News Sources.* Toronto: University of Toronto Press.

Fiske, J. (1987). *Television Culture.* London: Methuen.

Freedman, J. L. (2002). *Media Violence and Its Effect on Aggression: Assessing the Scientific Evidence.* Toronto: University of Toronto Press.

Friedrich-Cofer, L., and A. Huston. (1986). "Television Violence and Aggression: The Debate Continues." *Psychological Bulletin, 100* (3), 364–71.

Geen, R., and S. Thomas. (1986). "The Immediate Effects of Media Violence on Behaviour." *Journal of Social Issues, 42* (3), 7–27.

Gerbner, George, Larry Gross, Michael Morgan, and Nancy Signorielli. (1994). "Growing Up with Television: The Cultivation Perspective." In J. Bryant and D. Zillmann, eds., *Media Effects: Advances in Theory and Research* (pp. 17–41). Hillsdale, NJ: Lawrence Erlbaum Associates.

Gillespie, M. (1995). *Television, Ethnicity and Cultural Change.* London and New York: Routledge.

Gitlin, T. (1980). *The Whole World Is Watching.* Berkeley: University of California Press.

Goffman, E. (1974). *Frame Analysis.* Philadelphia: University of Pennsylvania Press.

Gosselin, A., J. DeGuise, G. Pacquette, and L. Benoit. (1997). "Violence on Canadian Television and Some of Its Cognitive Effects." *Canadian Journal of Communication, 22,* 143–60.

Greenberg, J. (2006). *The Media and Mental Health: An Analysis of Local News Coverage.* Ottawa: Canadian Mental Health Association.

Hackett, R. (1991). *News and Dissent: The Press and the Politics of Peace in Canada.* Norwood, NJ: Ablex.

Herman, E., and N. Chomsky. (1988). *Manufacturing Consent: The Political Economy of the Mass Media.* New York: Pantheon.

Hilts, M. (2008). "Internet Dependency, Motivations for Internet Use and Their Effect on Work Productivity: The 21st Century Addiction." ETD Thesis. On the World Wide Web at http://hdl.handle.net/1850/6920 (22 December 2008).

Hinduja, S., and J. W. Patchin. (2008). Personal Information of Adolescents on the Internet: A Quantitative Content Analysis of MySpace. *Journal of Adolescence, 31* (1), 125–46.

Horkheimer, M., and T. Adorno. (1972 [1947]). *Dialectic of Enlightenment.* Trans. John Cumming. New York: Continuum Books.

Huesmann, L., and N. Malamuth. (1986). "Media Violence and Anti-Social Behaviour: An Overview." *Journal of Social Issues, 42* (3), 1–6.

Innis, H. (1951). *The Bias of Communication.* Toronto: University of Toronto Press.

International Telecommunications Union (ITU). (2008). "Internet Indicators: Subscribers, Users and Broadband Subscribers." On the World Wide Web at http://www.itu.int/ITU-D/icteye/Reporting/ShowReportFrame.aspx?ReportName=/WTI/InformationTechnologyPublic&RP_intYear=2007&RP_intLanguageID=1 (22 December 2008).

"Internet World Stats." On the World Wide Web at http://www.Internetworldstats.com/stats.htm (22 December 2008).

Jacobs, R., and T. Albert. (2008). "Ethnicity, Internet Adoption and Use of Online Services." Paper presented at the annual meeting of the Association for Education in Journalism and Mass Communication, Chicago, IL, August 6. On the World Wide Web at http://www.allacademic.com/meta/p272850_index.html (22 December 2008).

Kahn, R., and D. Kellner. (2005). "Oppositional Politics and the Internet: A Critical/Reconstructive Approach. *Cultural Politics, 1* (1), 75–100.

Kann, M., J. Berry, C. Grant, C., and P. Zager. (2007). "The Internet and Youth Political Participation." First Monday, 12 (8). On the World Wide Web at http://firstmonday.org/htbin/cgiwrap/bin/ojs/index.php/fm/article/view/1977/1852. (22 December 2008).

Klapper, J. (1960). The Effects of Mass Communication. Glencoe: Free Press.

Kluver, R. (2005). "US and Chinese Policy Expectations of the Internet." *China Information, 19,* 299–324.

Knight, G. (1982). "News and Ideology." *Canadian Journal of Communication, 8* (4), 15–41.

Knight, G. (1998). "Hegemony, the Media, and New Right Politics: Ontario in the Late 1990s." *Critical Sociology, 24* (1/2), 105–29.

Lenhart, A., and M. Madden. (2007). "Teens, Privacy and Online Social Networks: How Teens Manage Their Online Identities and Personal Information in the Age of MySpace." Pew Internet & American Life Project. On the World Wide Web at http://www.PewInternet.org/PPF/r/211/report_display.asp (22 December 2008).

Lewis, B. (2007). "Should the Internet Be Used to Promote Healthy Living?" *The Lancet, 370* (9603): 1891–92.

Livingstone, S. (2005). "Assessing the Research Base for the Policy Debate over the Effects of Food Advertising to Children." *International Journal of Advertising, 24* (3), 273–96.

Marwick, A. (2008). "To Catch a Predator? The MySpace Moral Panic." *First Monday, 13* (6), May. On the World Wide Web at http://firstmonday.org/htbin/cgiwrap/bin/ojs/index.php/fm/article/view/2152/1966 (22 December 2008).

Mayer, C. E. (2005). "Group Takes Aim at Junk-Food Marketing." *The Washington Post* 7 January: E3.

McChesney, R. (1996). "The Global Struggle for Communication." *The Monthly Review, 48* (2), 1.

McCombs, M. (1988). "Concentration, Monopoly, and Content." In R. Picard, J. Winter, M. McCombs, and S. Lacy, eds., *Press Concentration and Monopoly: New Perspectives on Newspaper Ownership and Operation* (pp. 129–37). Norwood, NJ: Ablex.

McCormack, T. (1994). "Codes, Ratings and Rights." *Institute for Social Research Newsletter, 9* (1).

McLuhan, M. (1964). *Understanding Media: The Extensions of Man.* New York: Mentor Books.

Miljan, L., and B. Cooper. (2003). *Hidden Agendas: How Journalists Influence the News.* Vancouver: UBC Press.

Moreno, M. A., M. R. Parks, F. J. Zimmerman, T. E. Brito, D. A. Christakis. (2009). "Display of Health Risk Behaviors on MySpace by Adolescents." *Archives of Pediatrics & Adolescent Medicine, 163* (1), 27–34.

Morley, D. (1986). *Family Television: Cultural Power and Domestic Leisure.* London: Comedia.

Morley, D. (2000). *Home Territories: Media, Mobility and Identity.* London and New York: Routledge.

The Nation. (2002). "The Big Ten." 7–14 July. On the World Wide Web at http://www.thenation.com/special/bigten.html (12 August 2006).

National Endowment for the Arts. (2007). "To Read or Not to Read: A Question of National Consequence." Research report #47. November. On the World Wide Web at http://www.nea.gov/research/ToRead.pdf (22 December 2008).

National Media Archive. (1993a). "Canadian Media Uncritically Accept Advocacy Groups' Assertion That 1.5 Million Canadian Children Live in Poverty," *On Balance, 6* (10).

National Media Archive. (1993b). "Immigration I: The Human Interest Story." *On Balance, 6* (3), 1–8. Vancouver: The Fraser Institute.

Network Wizards. (2008). "Data on Internet Activity Worldwide (Hostcount)." On the World Wide Web at http://www.mclink. it/personal/MC8216/data/data1.htm (22 December 2008).

News Corporation. (2008). *Annual Report 2007*. On the World Wide Web at http://www.newscorp.com/Report2007/ AR2007.pdf (9 July 2009).

O'Reilly, T. (2005). "What Is Web 2.0?" *O'Reilly Network,* September 30. On the World Wide Web at http://www. oreillynet.com/pub/a/oreilly/tim/news/2005/09/30/what-is-web-20.html (22 December 2008).

Parenti, M. (2004). "Methods of Media Manipulation." In C. Jensen, ed., *20 Years of Censored News* (pp. 27–32). New York: Seven Stories Press.

Perse, E. M. (2001). *Media Effects and Society.* Mahwah, NJ, and London: Lawrence Erlbaum Associates, Publishers.

PEW Internet and American Life Project. (2008). "Demographics of Internet Users. PEW Tracking Survey." On the World Wide Web at http://www.PewInternet.org/trends/ User_Demo_10%2020%2008.htm (22 December 2008).

Pilieci, Vito. (2008). "Television's New Frontier; Online Viewing Presents Big Challenges for Traditional Broadcasters," *Ottawa Citizen,* 13 December 2008.

Quebecor. (2007). *Financial Review 2007*. On the World Wide Web at http://www.quebecor.com/Gallery/financial_review_2007. pdf (9 July 2009).

Rainie, L. (2006). *Life Online: The Growth and Impact of the Internet (and Related Technologies).* CTCNet Conference, Washington DC. July 28. On the World Wide Web at http://www. PewInternet.org/ppt/2006%20-%207.28.06%20CTCNet% 20—%20final.pdf (22 December 2008).

Rapleaf. (2007). "Statistics on Google's Open Social Platform End Users and Facebook Users. (press release). November 12. On the World Wide Web at http://business.rapleaf.com/ company_press_2007_11_12.html. (22 December 2008).

Rogers. (2008). "Delivering Results in 2007." *2007 Annual Report.* On the World Wide Web at https://www.rogers.com/cms/ investor_relations/annual_html/2007/html/HTML2/rogers_ communications_ar2007_0002.htm (9 July 2009).

Schutz, A. (1970). *Reflections on the Problem of Relevance.* R. M. Zaner, ed., New Haven, CN: Yale University Press.

Shaw Communications. (2007). *Annual Report.* On the World Wide Web at http://www.shaw.ca/NR/rdonlyres/0334D932-B13E-44D9-B9C9-B373F0E40318/0/SCIAR07.pdf (9 July 2009).

Statistics Canada. (2008a). "Canadian Internet Use Survey (2007)." *The Daily* 12 June. On the World Wide Web at http://www. statcan.gc.ca/daily-quotidien/080612/dq080612b-eng.htm (22 December 2008).

Statistics Canada. (2008b). "Canadian Internet Use Survey, Internet Use at Home, by Internet Activity, Urban or Rural Distribution, Every 2 Years (percent)." CANSIM Table 358-1030. On the World Wide Web at http://cansim2.statcan. gc.ca/cgi-win/cnsmcgi.exe?Lang=E&RootDir=CII/ &ResultTemplate=CII/CII___&Array_Pick=1&ArrayId= 3580126 (22 December 2008).

Statistics Canada. (2008c). "Canadian Internet Use Survey, Internet Use, by Location of Access and Income Quartile, Every 2 Years (percent)." CANSIM Table 358-0126. On the World Wide Web using E-STAT at http://estat.statcan.ca/ cgi-win/cnsmcgi.exe? Lang=E&ESTATFile=EStat\ English\CII_1_E.htm&RootDir=ESTAT/ (22 December 2008).

Statistics Canada. (2008d). "Canadian Internet Use Survey, Internet Use, by Location of Access and Level of Education, Every 2 Years (percent)." CANSIM Table 358-0125. On the World Wide Web using E-STAT at http://estat.statcan.ca/ cgi-win/cnsmcgi.exe?Lang=E&ESTATFile=EStat\English\ CII_1_E.htm&RootDir=ESTAT/ (22 December 2008).

Statistics Canada. (2008e). "Canadian Internet Use Survey, Internet Use, by Location of Access, Sex and Age Group, every 2 Years (percent)." CANSIM Table 358-0124. On the World Wide Web using E-STAT at http://estat.statcan.ca/cgi-win/ cnsmcgi.exe?Lang=E&ESTATFile=EStat\English\CII_1_ E.htm&RootDir=ESTAT/. (22 December 2008).

Statistics Canada. (2008f). "Culture Goods Trade 2007; Culture Trade-Goods: Data Tables, 2000 to 2007." Catalogue 87-007.

Statistics Canada. (2008g). "International Trade in Culture Goods." *The Daily* October 9. On the World Wide Web at http://www. statcan.gc.ca/daily-quotidien/081009/dq081009c-eng.htm (22 December 2008).

Statistics Canada. (2008h). "Newspaper Publishers." *The Daily* April 1. On the World Wide Web at http://www.statcan.gc.ca/ daily-quotidien/080401/dq080401b-eng.htm (22 December 2008).

Statistics Canada. (2008i). "Percentage Viewing Television 15 or More Hours per Week, by Province/Territory and Health Region, Household Population Aged 20 Years or Older, Canada, 2007." *2007 Canadian Community Health Survey.* On the World Wide Web at http://www.statcan.gc.ca/pub/82-003-x/ 2008002/article/10600/t/5202431-eng.htm (22 December 2008).

Statistics Canada. (2008j). "Radio Listening." *The Daily* September 18. On the World Wide Web at http://www.statcan.gc.ca/ daily-quotidien/080918/dq080918d-eng.htm (22 December 2008).

Statistics Canada. (2008k). "Screen Time among Canadian Adults: A Profile." *Health Reports, 19* (2), June. On the World Wide Web at http://www.statcan.gc.ca/pub/82-003-x/2008002/ article/10600-eng.pdf (30 January 2009).

Statistics Canada. (2008l). "Study: Screen Time among Canadian Adults." *The Daily* June 8. On the World Wide Web at http://www.statcan.gc.ca/daily-quotidien/080618/ dq080618c-eng.htm (22 December 2008).

Taras, D. (1990). *The Newsmakers: The Media's Influence on Canadian Politics.* Scarborough, ON: Nelson.

Time Warner. (2008). "Time Warner Inc. Reports Results for 2007 Full Year and Fourth Quarter." (press release). On the World Wide Web at http://files.shareholder.com/downloads/ TWX/488957236x0x166405/85024152-00de-438e-be35-a78cd1ed3ca9/q407earningsrelease.pdf (9 July 2009).

Tomlinson, J. (1997). "Cultural Globalization and Cultural Imperialism." In A. Mohammadi, ed., *International Communication and Globalization* (pp. 170–90). London: Sage Publications.

Trim, K., with G. Pizante and J. Yaraskavitch. (1983). "The Effect of Monopoly on the News: A Before and After Study of Two Canadian One Newspaper Towns." *Canadian Journal of Communication, 9* (3), 33–56.

Usher, Nikki. (2008). "Reviewing Fauxtography: A Blog-Driven Challenge to Mass Media Power without the Promises of Networked Publicity." *First Monday. 13* (2). On the World Wide Web at http://firstmonday.org/htbin/cgiwrap/bin/ojs/index.php/fm/article/view/2158/2055 (22 December 2008).

Vivendi. (2008). *2007 Annual Review.* On the World Wide Web at http://www.vivendi.com/vivendi/IMG/pdf/20080422_annual_report_2007-4.pdf (9 July 2009).

Winseck, Dwayne. (2008). "Media Merger Mania." *Canadian Dimension, 42* (1), 30–32.

Wober, J. M. (1998). "Cultural Indicators: European Reflections on a Research Paradigm." In R. Dickinson, R. Harindranath, and O. Linné, eds., *Approaches to Audiences: A Reader* (pp. 61–73). London: Arnold.

Zimmer, Michael. (2008). "Critical Perspectives on Web 2.0." (preface). *First Monday, 13* (3). On the World Wide Web at http://firstmonday.org/htbin/cgiwrap/bin/ojs/index.php/fm/article/view/2137/1943 (22 December 2008).

CHAPTER 6

Beauchesne, Eric. (2009). "CEOs Earn More on Day 1 Than Their Staff Do All Year." *Edmonton Journal* 3 January: F3.

Breen, R., and D. B. Rottman. (1995). *Class Stratification: A Comparative Perspective.* Hertfordshire, UK: Harvester Wheatsheaf.

Brym, Robert J. (1979). "Political Conservatism in Atlantic Canada." In Robert J. Brym and R. James Sacouman, eds., *Underdevelopment and Social Movements in Atlantic Canada* (pp. 59–79). Toronto: New Hogtown Press.

Calliste, Agnes. (1987). "Sleeping Car Porters in Canada: An Ethnically Submerged Split Labour Market." *Canadian Ethnic Studies, 19,* 1–20.

Cavanagh, John, and Chuck Collins. (2008). "The Rich and the Rest of Us." *The Nation* 30 June. On the World Wide Web at http://www.thenation.com/doc/20080630/cavanagh_collins (12 July 2009).

Clark, Terry Nichols, and Seymour Martin Lipset. (1991). "Are Social Classes Dying?" *International Sociology, 6,* 397–410.

Davies, Scott, and Neil Guppy. (2006). *The Schooled Society: An Introduction to the Sociology of Education.* Toronto: Oxford University Press.

Davis, Kingsley, and Wilbert E. Moore. (1945). "Some Principles of Stratification." *American Sociological Review, 10,* 242–49.

Derreck, Tom. (2003). "In Bondage." *The Beaver, 83* (1), 14–19.

Dorling, Daniel, J. Rigby, B. Wheeler, D. Ballas, B. Thomas, E. Fahmy, D. Gordon, and R. Lupton. (2007). *Poverty, Wealth and Place in Britain, 1968 to 2005.* Bristol: Policy Press.

Esping-Andersen, Gøsta. (1990). *Three Worlds of Welfare Capitalism.* Princeton, NJ: Princeton University Press.

Fitzgerald, Robin T., and Peter J. Carrington. (2008). "The Neighbourhood Context of Urban Aboriginal Crime." *Canadian Journal of Criminology and Criminal Justice, 50* (5), 523–57.

Fuller, Sylvia, and Leah F. Vosko. (2008). "Temporary Employment and Social Inequality in Canada: Exploring Intersections of Gender, Race and Immigration Status." *Social Indicators Research, 88,* 31–50.

Gerein, Keith. (2008). "Most Homeless Ever." *Edmonton Journal* 22 November: B1.

Grabb, Edward G. (2002). *Theories of Social Inequality,* 4th ed. Toronto: Harcourt Canada.

Keevil-Fairburn, Rosemary. (2008). "Homeless B.C. Woman Burns to Death While Trying to Keep Warm." *The Globe and Mail* 20 December: A4.

Krahn, Harvey. (2004). "Choose Your Parents Carefully: Social Class, Post-secondary Education, and Occupational Outcomes." In J. Curtis, E. Grabb, and N. Guppy, eds., *Social Inequality in Canada: Patterns, Problems, Policies,* 4th ed. (pp. 187–203). Toronto, ON: Pearson/Prentice Hall.

Krahn, Harvey, Graham S. Lowe, and Karen Hughes. (2006). *Work, Industry and Canadian Society,* 5th ed. Scarborough: Thomson Nelson.

Kroll, Luisa. (2008). "The World's Billionaires." Forbes Magazine. On the World Wide Web at http://www.forbes.com/lists/2008/10/billionaires08_The-Worlds-Billionaires_Rank.html (12 July 2009).

Krugman, Paul. (1994). "Long-term Riches, Short-term Pain." *The New York Times* September 25, p. F9.

Lenski, Gerhard. (1966). *Power and Privilege: A Theory of Social Stratification.* New York: McGraw-Hill.

Li, Peter. (1982). "Chinese Immigrants on the Canadian Prairie, 1919–47." *Canadian Review of Sociology and Anthropology, 19,* 527–40.

Lin, Jane. (2008). "Trends in Employment and Wages, 2002 to 2007." *Perspectives on Labour and Income* (Autumn), 5–15.

Livingstone, David. (1999). *The Education-Jobs Gap: Underemployment or Economic Democracy.* Toronto: Garamond Press.

Longman, Phillip. (1985). "Justice between Generations." *Atlantic Monthly* June, 73–81.

Love, Roger, and Susan Poulin. (1991). "Family Income Inequality in the 1980s." *Perspectives on Labour and Income, 3* (Autumn), 51–57.

Makin, Kirk. (2008). "Saskatoon Police Lose Bid to Quash Stonechild Inquiry." *The Globe and Mail* 19 December: A4.

McFarland, Janet. (2007). "'Big Leavers' Lever Bigger Pay Packages." *The Globe and Mail* 4 June: B5.

Morissette, René, and Xuelin Zhang. (2001). "Experiencing Low Income for Several Years." *Perspectives on Labour and Income* (Summer): 25–35.

Morissette, René, and Xuelin Zhang. (2007). "Revisiting Wealth Inequality." *Perspectives on Labour and Income* (Spring): 6–17.

Myles, John, and Adnan Turegun. (1994). "Comparative Studies in Class Structure." *Annual Review of Sociology, 20,* 103–24.

National Council of Welfare. (2001–2002). *The Cost of Poverty.* Ottawa: Minister of Public Works and Government Services Canada. Cat. no. H68-53/2002E.

National Council of Welfare. (2004). *Poverty Profile 2001.* Ottawa: Minister of Public Works and Government Services Canada. Catalogue no. SD25-1/2001E-PDF.

National Council of Welfare. (2007). *First Nations, Métis and Inuit Children and Youth: Time to Act.* Ottawa: Author. Catalogue no. HS54-1/2007E-PDF.

National Council of Welfare. (2008a). *Welfare Incomes, 2006 and 2007.* Ottawa. Author. Catalogue no. HS51-1/2007E.

National Council of Welfare. (2008b). *Poverty Profile 2004.* Ottawa: Author. On the World Wide Web at http://www.ncwcnbes.net/en/research/povertyprofile/webonly2004.html (12 July 2009).

O'Malley, Martin, and John Bowman. (2002). "How Do We Measure Poverty?" *CBC News Online,* 7 May. On the World Wide Web at http://cbc.ca/news/features/poverty_line.html (4 November 2002).

O'Neill, Jeff. (1991). "Changing Occupational Structure." *Canadian Social Trends* (Winter): 10.

Palmer, Bryan. (1986). *The Character of Class Struggle: Essays in Canadian Working Class History, 1850–1985*. Toronto: McClelland and Stewart.

Parkin, Frank. (1972). Class, *Inequality and Political Order*. London: Paladin.

Parkin, Frank. (1979). *Marxism and Class Theory: A Bourgeois Critique*. London: Tavistock.

Picot, Garnett, and John Myles. (2005). *Income Inequality and Low Income in Canada: An International Perspective*. Statistics Canada Analytic Studies Branch Research Paper. Catalogue no. 11F0019MIE, No. 240.

Pratt, Courtney. (2007). "'New Big Thing' Could Put Brakes on CEO Pay." *The Globe and Mail* 11 June: B2.

Raphael, Dennis. (2007). *Poverty and Policy in Canada: Implications for Health and Quality of Life*. Toronto: Canadian Scholars' Press.

Saunders, Doug. (2008). "Crisis Comes to Sylhet." *The Globe and Mail* 27 December: B1.

Sauvé, Roger. (2006). *The Current State of Canadian Family Finances: 2005 Report*. Ottawa: Vanier Institute of the Family.

Scoffield, Heather, and Paul Koring. (2008). "Job Losses 'Accelerating Alarmingly'." *The Globe and Mail* 6 December: A1.

Statistics Canada. (1984). *Charting Canadian Incomes, 1951–1981*. Catalogue no. 13-581E. Ottawa: Supply and Services Canada.

Statistics Canada. (2005). *Income in Canada*. Cat. No. 75-202-XIE. Ottawa: Minister of Industry.

Statistics Canada. (2006a). "Employment Income Statistics (4) in Constant (2005) Dollars, Work Activity in the Reference Year (3), Occupation—National Occupational Classification for Statistics 2006 (720A) and Sex (3) for the Population 15 Years and Over With Employment Income of Canada, Provinces and Territories, 2000 and 2005—20% Sample Data." *2006 Census: Data Products/Topic-based Tabulations*. Catalogue no. 97-563-XWE2006062. On the World Wide Web at http://www.statcan.gc.ca/bsolc/olc-cel/olc-cel?catno=97-563-X2006062&lang=eng (12 July 2009).

Statistics Canada. (2006b). "Wage and Salary Statistics (4) in Constant (2005) Dollars, Work Activity in the Reference Year (3), Highest Certificate, Diploma or Degree (5), Age Groups (5A), Occupation—National Occupational Classification for Statistics 2006 (720B) and Sex (3) for the Paid Workers 15 Years and Over With Wages and Salaries of Canada, Provinces, Territories, 2000 and 2005—20% Sample Data." *2006 Census: Data Products/Topic-based Tabulations*. Catalogue no. 97-563-XWE2006069. On the World Wide Web at http://www.statcan.gc.ca/bsolc/olc-cel/olc-cel?catno=97-563-X2006069&lang=eng (12 July 2009).

Statistics Canada, (2006–2007). *Low Income Cut-offs for 2007 and Low Income Measures for 2006*. Catalogue no. 75F0002M-no. 004. On the World Wide Web at http://www.statcan.gc.ca/pub/75f0002m/75f0002m2008004-eng.pdf (12 July 2009).

Statistics Canada. (2008a). *Earnings and Incomes of Canadians Over the Past Quarter Century, 2006 Census*. Catalogue no. 97-563-X. Ottawa: Author.

Statistics Canada. (2008b). *Income in Canada 2006*. Catalogue no. 75-202-X. Ottawa: Author.

Statistics Canada. (2008c). *Canada's Changing Labour Force, 2006 Census*. Catalogue no. 97-559-X. Ottawa: Author.

Statistics Canada. (2009). "Labour Force Survey Tables by Subject: Employment and Unemployment." On the World Wide Web at http://www40.statcan.gc.ca/l01/ind01/l3_2621_1803-eng.htm?hili_none (12 July 2009).

Swanson, Jean. (2001). *Poor-Bashing: The Politics of Exclusion*. Toronto: Between the Lines.

Tanner, Julian, Harvey Krahn, and Timothy F. Hartnagel. (1995). *Fractured Transitions from School to Work: Revisiting the Dropout Problem*. Toronto: Oxford University Press.

Taylor, Alison, and Harvey Krahn. (2009). "Streaming in/for the New Economy." In Cynthia Levine-Rasky, ed., *Canadian Perspectives on the Sociology of Education* (pp. 103–23). Toronto: Oxford University Press.

Wallis, Maria A., and Siu-ming Kwok (eds.). (2008). *Daily Struggles: The Deepening Racialization and Feminization of Poverty in Canada*. Toronto: Canadian Scholars' Press.

Wanner, Richard A. (2004). "Social Mobility in Canada: Concepts, Patterns, and Trends." In J. Curtis, E. Grabb, and N. Guppy, eds., *Social Inequality in Canada: Patterns, Problems, Policies*, 4th ed. (pp. 131–47). Toronto, ON: Pearson/Prentice Hall.

Weber, Max. (1948 [1922]). From *Max Weber: Essays in Sociology*. Eds. and trans. H. H. Gerth and C. W. Mills. London: Routledge and Kegan Paul.

Westergaard, John. (1995). *Who Gets What? The Hardening of Class Inequality in the Late Twentieth Century*. Cambridge, UK: Polity Press.

White, Marianne. (2009). "Refugees Happy with New Life, but Long to See Absent Relatives." *Edmonton Journal* 4 January: A8.

Wilkinson, R. G. (1992). "Income Distributions and Life Expectancy." *British Medical Journal*, 304, 165–68.

Wolff, Edward N. (1991). "The Distribution of Household Wealth: Methodological Issues, Time Trends, and Cross-sectional Comparisons." In Lars Osberg, ed., *Economic Inequality and Poverty: International Perspectives* (pp. 92–133). Armonk, NY: Sharpe.

Wortley, Scott, and Julian Tanner. (2008). "Data, Denials and Confusion: The Racial Profiling Debate in Toronto." In Maria Wallis and Siu-ming Kwok, eds., *Daily Struggles: The Deepening Racialization and Feminization of Poverty in Canada* (pp. 183–96). Toronto: Canadian Scholars' Press.

Wright, Erik Olin. (1985). *Classes*. London: Verso.

Wu, Xiaogang and Yu Xie. (2002) "Does the Market Pay Off? Earnings Returns to Education in Urban China." *American Sociological Review* 68 (June): 425–42.

Zeitlin, Irving M., with Robert J. Brym. (1991). *The Social Condition of Humanity*, Cdn. ed. Toronto: Oxford University Press.

CHAPTER 7

Agocs, Carol, and Monica Boyd. (1993). "The Canadian Ethnic Mosaic Recast for the 1990s." In James Curtis, Edward Grabb, and Neil Guppy, eds., *Social Inequality in Canada: Patterns, Problems and Policies* (pp. 330–52). Scarborough, ON: Prentice Hall.

Agocs, Carol, Catherine Burr, and Felicity Somerset. (1992). *Employment Equity: Cooperative Strategies for Organizational Change*. Toronto: Prentice Hall Canada.

Andersen, L. Margaret. (2005). "Thinking about Women: A Quarter Century's View." *Gender and Society*, 19 (4), 437–55.

Armstrong, Pat, and Hugh Armstrong. (1994). *The Double Ghetto: Canadian Women and Their Segregated Work*, 3rd ed. Toronto: McClelland and Stewart.

Arscott, Jane, and Linda Trimble. (1997). "Introduction—In the Presence of Women: Representation and Political Power." In Jane Arscott and Linda Trimble, eds., *In the Presence of Women: Representation in Canadian Governments* (pp. 1–17). Toronto: Harcourt Brace.

Bashevkin, Sylvia B. (1991). "Women's Participation in Political Parties." In Kathy Megyery, ed., *Women in Canadian Politics: Toward Equity in Representation* (pp. 61–79). Toronto: Dundurn Press.

Bashevkin, Sylvia B. (1993). *Toeing the Lines: Women and Party Politics in English Canada*, 2nd ed. Toronto: Oxford University Press.

Berdahl, Jennifer L., and Celia Moore. (2006). "Workplace Harassment: Double Jeopardy for Minority Women." *Journal of Applied Psychology, 91* (2), 426–36.

Best, Pamela. (1995). "Women, Men and Work." *Canadian Social Trends, 36* (1), 30–33.

Black, Jerome H. (2000). "Entering the Political Elite in Canada: The Case of Minority Women as Parliamentary Candidates and MPs." *Canadian Review of Sociology and Anthopology, 37* (2), 143–66.

Boyd, Monica. (1990). "Sex Differences in Occupational Skill: Canada, 1961–1986." *Canadian Review of Sociology and Anthropology, 27*, 285–315.

Boyd, Monica. (1999). "Integrating Gender, Language and Visible Minority Groups." In Shiva S. Halli and Leo Driedger, eds., *Immigrant Canada: Demographic, Economic and Social Challenges* (pp. 282–306). Toronto: University of Toronto Press.

Boyd, Monica, Brenda Hughes, and Jamie Miller. (1997). "Power at Work: Women and Men in Management, Supervision and Workplace Planning." Unpublished paper. Department of Sociology, Florida State University.

Boyd, Monica, Maryann Mulvihill, and John Myles. (1991). "Gender, Power and Postindustrialism." *Canadian Review of Sociology and Anthropology, 28*, 407–36.

Brodie, Janine. (1991). "Women and the Electoral Process in Canada." In Kathy Megyery, ed., *Women in Canadian Politics: Toward Equity in Representation* (pp. 3–59). Toronto: Dundurn Press.

Brodie, Janine, ed. (1996). *Women and Canadian Public Policy.* Toronto: Harcourt Brace.

Broverman, I., S. R. Vogel, S. M. Broverman, F. E. Clarkson, and P. S. Rosenkranz. (1972). "Sex Role Stereotypes: A Current Appraisal." *Journal of Social Issues, 28* (2), 59–78.

Burt, Sandra. (1993). "The Changing Patterns of Public Policy." In Sandra Burt, Lorraine Code, and Lindsay Dorney, eds., *Changing Patterns: Women in Canada*, 2nd ed. (pp. 212–37). Toronto: McClelland and Stewart.

"Business." (2009). *Toronto Star* 1 February. On the World Wide Web at http://www.thestar.com/News/Ideas/article/580457 (16 July 2009).

Canada. (1995). *Laws. Statutes of Canada. Employment Equity Act.* 43–44 Elizabeth II, Vol. II, Chapter 44.

Chafetz, Janet Saltzman. (1999). "The Varieties of Gender Theory in Sociology." In Janet Saltzman Chafetz, ed., *The Handbook of the Sociology of Gender* (pp. 3–23). New York: Kluwer Academic/Plenum Publishers.

Collins, Patricia Hill. (1990). *Black Feminist Thought, Knowledge, Consciousness, and the Politics of Empowerment.* Boston: Unwin Hyman.

Connelly, Patricia. (1978). *Last Hired, First Fired: Women and the Canadian Work Force.* Toronto: Women's Press.

Cooke-Reynolds, Melissa, and Nancy Zukewich. (2004). "The Feminization of Work." *Canadian Social Trends, 72* (Spring), 24–29.

Cranford, Cynthia J., Leah F. Vosko, and Nancy Zukewich. (2003). "The Gender of Precarious Employment in Canada." *Industrial Relations, 58* (3), 454–79.

Cranswick, Kelly. (1997). "Canada's Caregivers." *Canadian Social Trends, 48* (Winter), 2–6.

Das Gupta, Tania. (1996). *Racism and Paid Work.* Toronto: Garamond Press.

Devereaux, Mary Sue. (1993). "Time Use of Canadians in 1992." *Canadian Social Trends, 8* (3), 13–16.

Duffy, Ann. (1986). "Reformulating Power for Women." *Canadian Review of Sociology and Anthropology, 23*, 22–46.

Duffy, Ann, and Norene Pupo. (1992). *Part-Time Paradox: Connecting Gender, Work and Family.* Toronto: McClelland and Stewart.

Economic Council of Canada. (1991). *Employment in the Service Economy.* Ottawa: Supply and Services Canada.

England, Paula. (1993). *Comparable Worth: Theories and Evidence.* New York: Aldine de Gruyter.

Erickson, Lynda. (1991). "Women Candidates for the House of Commons." In Kathy Megyery, ed., *Women in Canadian Politics: Toward Equity in Representation* (pp. 101–25). Toronto: Dundurn Press.

Erickson, Lynda. (1998). "Entry to the Commons: Parties, Recruitment and the Election of Women in 1993." In Manon Tremblay and Caroline Andrew, eds., *Women and Political Representation in Canada* (pp. 219–58). Ottawa: University of Ottawa Press.

Frederick, Judith A., and Janet E. Fast. (1999). "Eldercare in Canada: Who Does How Much?" *Canadian Social Trends, 54* (Autumn), 26–30.

Fuller, Sylvia, and Leah F. Vosko. (2008). "Temporary Employment and Social Inequality in Canada: Exploring Intersections of Gender, Race and Immigration Status." *Social Indicator Research, 88*, 31–50.

Gagne, Patricia, and Richard Tewksbury. (1998). "Rethinking Binary Conceptions and Social Constructions: Transgender Experiences of Gender and Sexuality." In Marcia Texler Segal and Vasilikie Demos, series eds. *Advances in Gender Research*, Vol. 3 (pp. 73–102).

Gaskell, Jane. (1986). "Conceptions of Skill and the Work of Women: Some Historical and Political Issues." In Roberta Hamilton and Michele Barrett, eds., *The Politics of Diversity: Feminism, Marxism and Nationalism* (pp. 361–80). London: Verso.

Gaskell, Jane. (1991). "What Counts as Skill? Reflections on Pay Equity." In Judy Fudge and Patricia McDermott, eds., *Just Wages: A Feminist Assessment of Pay Equity* (pp. 141–59). Toronto: University of Toronto Press.

Jackson, Chris. (1996). "Measuring and Valuing Households' Unpaid Work." *Canadian Social Trends, 42* (4), 25–29.

Jaggar, Alison M. (1983). *Feminist Politics and Human Nature.* New York: Rowman and Allanheld Publishers.

Kite, Mary E., Kay Deaux, and Elizabeth L. Haines. (2008). "Gender Stereotypes." In Florence Denmark and Michele Antoinette Paludi, eds., *Psychology of Women: A Handbook of Issues and Theories* (pp. 205–36). Westport, CT: Praeger.

Krahn, Harvey. (1995). "Non-standard Work on the Rise." *Perspectives on Labour and Income*, 7 (4), 35–42.

Leacy, Frank, H. (1983). *Historical Statistics of Canada*, 2nd ed. Ottawa: Statistics Canada. Catalogue No. 11-516-XIE.

Lengermann, Patricia Madoo, and Niebrugge-Brantley, Jill. (1996). "Contemporary Feminist Theory." In George Ritzer, ed., *Modern Sociological Theory* (pp. 299–305). New York: McGraw.

Looker, E. Dianne, and Victor Thiessen. (1999). "Images of Work: Women's Work, Men's Work, Housework." *Canadian Journal of Sociology, 24*, 2 (Spring), 225–54.

Lorber, Judith. (1998). *Gender Inequality: Feminist Theories and Politics.* Los Angeles: Roxbury Publishing Company.

Lowe, Graham. (1987). *Women in the Administrative Revolution: The Feminization of Clerical Work.* Cambridge, UK: Polity Press.

Luxton, Meg, and Leah F. Vosko. (1998). "Where Women's Efforts Count: The 1996 Census Campaign and 'Family Politics' in Canada." *Studies in Political Economy, 56* (Summer), 49–81.

Maille, Chantal. (1990). *Primed for Power: Women in Canadian Politics.* Ottawa: Canadian Advisory Council on the Status of Women.

Martin, Y. Patricia. (2003). "'Said and Done' versus 'Saying and Doing': Gender Practices, Practicing Gender at Work." *Gender and Society, 17* (3), 342–66.

McCormack, Thelma. (1975). "Toward a Nonsexist Perspective on Social and Political Change." In Marcia Millman and Rosabeth Moss Kanter, eds., *Another Voice: Feminist Perspectives on Social Life and Social Science* (pp. 1–33). Garden City, NY: Anchor Books.

Myles, John, and Gail Fawcett. (1990). "Job Skills and the Service Economy." Working Paper no. 4. Ottawa: Economic Council of Canada.

Pal, Leslie. (1989). *Public Policy Analysis.* Toronto: Nelson Canada.

Parliament of Canada. (2008). *Women—Political Representation: 1867 to Date.* On the World Wide Web at http://www2.parl.gc.ca/Parlinfo/compilations/parliament/WomenRepresentation.aspx?Language=E (8 February 2009).

Pendakur, Krishna, and Ravi Pendakur. (1998). "The Colour of Money: Earnings Differentials among Ethnic Groups in Canada." *Canadian Journal of Economics, 31* (3), 518–47.

Phillips, Paul, and Erin Phillips. (1983). *Women and Work.* Toronto: Lorimer.

Pierson, Ruth. (1977). "Women's Emancipation and the Recruitment of Women into the Labour Force in World War II." In Susan Mann Trofimenkoff and Alison Prentice, eds., *The Neglected Majority* (pp. 125–45). Toronto: McClelland and Stewart.

Prentice, Alison. (1977). "The Feminization of Teaching." In Susan Mann Trofimenkoff and Alison Prentice, eds., *The Neglected Majority* (pp. 49–65). Toronto: McClelland and Stewart.

Robinson, Gertrude J., and Armande Saint-Jean, with the assistance of Christine Rioux. (1991). "Women Politicians and Their Media Coverage: A Generational Analysis." In Kathy Megyery, ed., *Women in Canadian Politics: Toward Equity in Representation* (pp. 127–69). Toronto: Dundurn Press.

Segal, Edwin S. (1998). "Male Genders: Cross Cultural Perspectives." In Marcia Texler Segal and Vasilikie Demos, series eds, *Advances in Gender Research*. Vol. 3 (pp. 37–77).

Séguin, Rhéal. (1996). "Quebec Puts Brakes on Pay Equity." *The Globe and Mail* 8 November: A7.

Ship, Susan Judith. (1998). "Problematizing Ethnicity and 'Race' in Feminist Scholarship on Women and Politics." In Manon Tremblay and Caroline Andrew, eds., *Women and Political Representation in Canada* (pp. 311–40). Ottawa: University of Ottawa Press.

Statistics Canada. (1998). "1996 Census: Sources of Income, Earnings and Total Income, and Family Income." *The Daily* 12 May. On the World Wide Web at http://www.statcan.ca/Daily/English/980512/d980512.htm (11 September 2006).

Statistics Canada. (1999). "General Social Survey: Time Use." *The Daily* 9 November, 2–5.

Statistics Canada. (2006a). "Labour Force and Participation Rates by Sex and Age group (2001–2005)." On the World Wide Web at http://www40.statcan.ca/l01/cst01/labor05.htm (11 September 2006).

Statistics Canada. (2006b). "Labour Force Activity (8), Presence of Children by Age Groups (11), Age Groups (9), Marital Status (7) and Sex (3) for the Population 15 Years and Over Living in Private Households of Canada, Provinces, Territories, Census Divisions and Census Subdivisions, 2006 Census—20% Sample Data." On the World Wide Web at www12.statcan.ca/english/census06/data/topics/RetrieveProductTable.cfm?Temporal=2006&PID=92110&GID=771240&METH=1&APATH=3&PTYPE=88971%2C97154&THEME=74&AID=&FREE=0&FOCUS=&VID=0&GC=99&GK=NA&RL=0&TPL=RETR&SUB=741&d1=2&d2=0&d3=0 (8 February 2009).

Statistics Canada. (2006c). *Women in Canada: A Gender Based Statistical Report*, 5th ed. Ottawa: Minister of Industry. Catalogue No. 89-503-XPE.

Statistics Canada. (2007). *Women in Canada: Work Chapter Updates.* Tables 7 and 8. Catalogue no. 89R0133XIE.

Statistics Canada. (2008). "Average Female and Male Earnings, and Female-to- Male Earnings Ratio, by Work Activity, 2006 Constant Dollars, Canada, Provinces and select CMAs," 2006 Census of Population, Table 2020102. On the World Wide Web at www.statcan.gc.ca/pub/13f0022x/2006000/5213044-eng.htm (8 February 2009).

Statistics Canada. (2009). "Labour Force and Participation Rates by Sex and Age Group." On the World Wide Web at www40.statcan.gc.ca/l01/cst01/labor05-eng.htm (8 February 2009).

Steinberg, Ronnie J. (1990). "Social Construction of Skill." *Work and Occupations, 17*, 449–82.

Tremblay, Manon, and Caroline Andrew, eds. (1998). *Women and Political Representation in Canada.* Women's Studies Series. Ottawa: University of Ottawa Press.

Trimble, Linda, and Jane Arscott. (2003). *Still Counting: Women in Politics Across Canada.* Peterborough, ON: Broadview Press.

Ursel, Jane. (1992). *Private Lives, Public Policy: 100 Years of State Intervention in the Family.* Toronto: Women's Press.

Vickers, Jill. (1997). "Toward a Feminist Understanding of Representation." In Jane Arscott and Linda Trimble, eds., *In the Presence of Women: Representation in Canadian Governments* (pp. 20–46). Toronto: Harcourt Brace.

Vosko, Leah, Nancy Zukewich, and Cynthia J. Cransford. (2003). "Precarious Jobs: A New Typology of Employment." *Perspectives on Labour and Income, 4* (10), 16–26.

Weiner, Nan, and Morley Gunderson. (1990). *Pay Equity: Issues, Options and Experiences.* Toronto: Butterworths.

Welsh, Sandy, Jacquie Carr, Barbara MacQuarrie, and Audrey Huntley. (2006). "'I'm Not Thinking of It as Sexual Harassment:' Understanding Harassment across Race and Citizenship." *Gender and Society,* 20 (1), 87–107.

West, Candace, and Sarah Fenstermaker. (1993). "Power, Inequality and the Accomplishment of Gender: An Ethnomethodological View." In Paula England, ed., *Theory on Gender/Feminism on Theory* (pp. 151–74). New York: Aldine de Gruyter.

Wharton, S. Amy. (2000). "Feminism at Work." *The Annals of the American Academy,* 571, 167–82.

Williams, Cara. (2004). "The Sandwich Generation." *Perspectives on Labour and Income,* 5 (9), 5–12.

Yanz, Lynda, Deena Ladd, Joan Atlin, and Maquila Solidarity Network. (1999). *Policy Options to Improve Standards for Garment Workers in Canada and Internationally.* Ottawa: Status of Women Canada.

Young, Lisa. (1997). "Fulfilling the Mandate of Difference: Women in the Canadian House of Commons." In Jane Arscott and Linda Trimble, eds., *In the Presence of Women: Representation in Canadian Governments* (pp. 82–103). Toronto: Harcourt Brace.

Young, Lisa. (1998). "The Canadian Women's Movement and Political Parties, 1970–1993." In Manon Tremblay and Caroline Andrew, eds., *Women and Political Representation in Canada* (pp. 195–218). Ottawa: University of Ottawa Press.

Zinn, Maxine Baca, with Bonnie Thornton Dill. (1997). "Theorizing Difference from Multiracial Feminism." In Maxine Baca Zinn, Pierrette Hondagneu-Sotelo, and Michael A. Messner, eds., *Through the Prism of Difference: Readings on Sex and Gender* (pp. 23–29). Boston: Allyn and Bacon.

CHAPTER 8

Abella, Irving, and Harold Troper. (1982). *None Is Too Many: Canada and the Jews of Europe, 1933–1948.* Toronto: Lester and Orpen Dennys.

Alfred, Taiaiake. 1999. *Peace, Power and Righteousness: An Indigenous Manifesto.* Toronto: Oxford University Press.

Anderson, Benedict. (1983). *Imagined Communities: Reflections on the Origin and Spread of Nationalism.* London: Verso.

Angus Reid Group. (1991). *Multiculturalism and Canadians: National Attitude Study 1991.* Ottawa: Multiculturalism and Citizenship Canada.

Appleby, Timothy. (2006). "Harnick Testimony 'Shocked' Harris." *The Globe and Mail* 17 February: A7.

Avery, Donald. (1995). *Reluctant Host: Canada's Response to Immigrant Workers.* Toronto: McClelland and Stewart.

Balthazar, Louis. (1993). "The Faces of Quebec Nationalism." In Alain-G. Gagnon, ed., *Quebec: State and Society,* 2nd ed. (pp. 2–17). Scarborough, ON: Nelson.

Barkan, Elazar. (1992). *The Retreat of Scientific Racism.* Cambridge, UK: Cambridge University Press.

Barker, Martin. (1981). *The New Racism: Conservatives and the Ideology of the Tribe.* London: Junction Books.

Basran, Gurcharn, and Li Zong. (1998). "Devaluation of Foreign Credentials as Perceived by Non-white Professional Immigrants." *Canadian Ethnic Studies,* 30, 6–23.

Bissoondath, Neil. (1994). *Selling Illusions: The Cult of Multiculturalism.* Toronto: Stoddart.

Bolaria, B. Singh, and Peter Li. (1988). *Racial Oppression in Canada.* Toronto: Garamond.

Boldt, Menno. (1993). *Surviving as Indians: The Challenge of Self-Government.* Toronto: University of Toronto Press.

Bonacich, Edna. (1972). "A Theory of Ethnic Antagonism: The Split Labor Market." *American Sociological Review,* 37, 547–59.

Bonacich, Edna. (1979). "The Past, Present and Future of Split Labor Market Theory." *Research in Race and Ethnic Relations,* 1, 17–64.

Bonacich, Edna. (1980). "Class Approaches to Ethnicity and Race." *Insurgent Sociologist,* 10, 9–23.

Bouchard, Gérard, and Charles Taylor. (2008). *Building the Future: A Time for Reconciliation.* On the World Wide Web at http://www.accommodements.qc.ca/documentation/rapports/rapport-final-integral-en.pdf (16 July 2009).

Bourgeault, Ron. (1988). "The South African Connection." *Canadian Dimension,* 21, 6–10.

Brown, Louise, and Brett Popplewell. (2008). "Board Okays Black-Focused School." *Toronto Star* 30 January. On the World Wide Web at http://www.thestar.com/News/article/298714 (15 July 2009).

Brym, Robert, with Bonnie Fox. (1989). *From Culture to Power: The Sociology of English Canada.* Toronto: Oxford University Press.

Brym, Robert, and Rhonda Lenton. (1993). "The Distribution of Anti-Semitism in Canada in 1984." In Robert Brym, William Shaffir, and Morton Weinfeld, eds., *The Jews in Canada* (pp. 112–19). Toronto: Oxford University Press.

Castles, Stephen, and Godula Kosack. (1984). *Immigrant Workers and Class Structure in Western Europe.* London: Oxford University Press.

Citizenship and Immigration Canada. (1996). *You Asked About . . . Immigration and Citizenship.* Ottawa: Supply and Services Canada.

Citizenship and Immigration Canada. (2002). "Family Class Immigration." On the World Wide Web at http://www.cis.gc.ca/english/sponsor/index.html (10 September 2003).

Citizenship and Immigration Canada. (2004). "Business Immigration Program Statistics, 2002." On the World Wide Web at http://www.cic.gc.ca/english/business/bus-stats2002.html (13 March 2005).

Citizenship and Immigration Canada. (2008). "Facts and Figures 2007—Immigration Overview: Permanent and Temporary Residents." On the World Wide Web at http://www.cic.gc.ca/english/resources/statistics/menu-fact.asp (15 July 2009).

Clement, Wallace. (1975). *The Canadian Corporate Elite.* Toronto: McClelland and Stewart.

Cole, Douglas, and Ira Chaikin. (1990). *An Iron Hand upon the People: The Law against the Potlatch on the Northwest Coast.* Vancouver: Douglas and McIntyre.

Collins, Jock. (1988). *Migrant Hands in a Distant Land: Australia's Post-war Immigration.* Sydney: Pluto Press.

Congress of Aboriginal Peoples. (2008). "The Forgotten People and the Indian Act." On the World Wide Web at http://www.abo-peoples.org/about/Indian_Act.html (15 July 2009).

Curry, Bill. (2005). "The Government Responds: Indian Affairs Minister Announces Plan to Relocate Settlement, Improve Sanitation." *The Globe and Mail* 28 October: A1.

Daenzer, Pat. (1993). *Regulating Class Privilege.* Toronto: Canadian Scholars Press.

Darroch, Gordon. (1979). "Another Look at Ethnicity, Stratification and Social Mobility in Canada." *Canadian Journal of Sociology,* 4, 1–25.

Department of Indian Affairs and Northern Development (DIAND). (2004). *Basic Departmental Data 2003*. Ottawa: Minister of Public Works and Government Services Canada.

Doob, Christopher. (1996). *Racism: An American Cauldron*. New York: HarperCollins.

"A Dream That Does Not Fade (Quebec's Sovereignty)." (2005). *The Economist* 3 December: 8.

Economic Council of Canada. (1991). *Economic and Social Impacts of Immigration*. Ottawa: Supply and Services Canada.

Edwards, Peter. (2001). *One Dead Indian: The Premier, the Police, and the Ipperwash Crisis*. Toronto: McClelland and Stewart.

Farmer, Nathan. (2005). "Kingston Police Chief Apologizes for Force's Systemic Racism." On the World Wide Web at http://friendsofgrassynarrows.com/item.php.?427F (12 November 2005).

Fiske, Jo-Anne. (1996). "The Womb Is to the Nation as the Heart Is to the Body: Ethnopolitical Discourses of the Canadian Indigenous Women's Movement." *Studies in Political Economy*, 51, 65–96.

Fleras, Augie, and Jean Elliot. (1996). *Unequal Relations: An Introduction to Race, Ethnic and Aboriginal Dynamics in Canada*. Scarborough, ON: Prentice Hall.

Fournier, Marcel, Michael Rosenberg, and Deena White. (1997). *Quebec Society: Critical Issues*. Scarborough, ON: Prentice Hall.

Frideres, James, and René Gadacz. (2005). *Aboriginal People in Canada*, 7th ed. Toronto: Pearson Prentice-Hall.

Gerber, Linda. (1990). "Multiple Jeopardy: A Socioeconomic Comparison of Men and Women among the Indian, Métis and Inuit Peoples of Canada." *Canadian Ethnic Studies*, 22, 69–84.

Gibbins, Roger, and J. Rick Ponting. (1986). "Historical Background and Overview." In J. Rick Ponting, ed., *Arduous Journey* (pp. 18–56). Toronto: McClelland and Stewart.

Gray, Jeff. "Officers Make Racist Remarks on Tape. Members of Ontario Provincial Police Slag Natives before Protester Killed in 1995." *The Globe and Mail* 21 January: A7.

Groupe de recherche ethnicité et société (GRES). (1997). "Immigration and Ethnic Relations in Quebec: Pluralism in the Making." In Marcel Fournier, Michael Rosenberg, and Deena White, eds., *Quebec Society: Critical Issues* (pp. 95–112). Scarborough, ON: Prentice Hall.

Ha, Tu Thanh. (1995). "The PQ's Narrow Ethnic Vision." *The Globe and Mail* 11 November: D1.

Harries, Kate. (2005). "Harris Uttered Slur, Ipperwash Inquiry Told." *The Globe and Mail* 29 November: A1.

Hawkins, Freda. (1989). *Critical Years in Immigration: Canada and Australia Compared*. Montreal and Kingston, ON: McGill-Queen's University Press.

Henry, Frances. (1989). "Who Gets the Work in 1989?" Background Paper. Ottawa: Economic Council of Canada.

Henry, Frances, and Effie Ginsberg. (1985). *Who Gets the Work: A Test of Racial Discrimination in Employment*. Toronto: Urban Alliance on Race Relations and the Social Planning Directorate.

Henry, Frances, and Carol Tator. (2006). *The Colour of Democracy: Racism in Canadian Society*, 3rd ed. Toronto: Thomson Nelson.

Herberg, Edward. (1990). "The Ethno-racial Socioeconomic Hierarchy in Canada: Theory and Analysis in the New Vertical Mosaic." *International Journal of Comparative Sociology*, 31, 206–21.

Holton, Robert, and Michael Lanphier. (1994). "Public Opinion, Immigration and Refugees." In Howard Adelman, Allan

Borowski, Meyer Burstein, and Lois Foster, eds., *Immigration and Refugee Policy: Australia and Canada Compared*, Vol. 1. Toronto: University of Toronto Press.

Howard, Rhoda. (1998). "Being Canadian: Citizenship in Canada." *Citizenship Studies*, 2, 133–52.

Howard-Hassmann, Rhoda. (1999). "Canadian as an Ethnic Category: Implications for Multiculturalism and National Unity." *Canadian Public Policy*, 25 (4), 523–37.

Iacovetta, Franca. (1992). *Such Hardworking People: Italian Immigrants in Postwar Toronto*. Montreal and Kingston, ON: McGill-Queen's University Press.

Isajiw, Wsevolod. (1999). *Understanding Diversity: Ethnicity and Race in the Canadian Context*. Toronto: Thompson Educational Publishing.

Jenson, Jane. (1993). "Naming Nations: Making Nationalist Claims in Canadian Public Discourse." *Canadian Review of Sociology and Anthropology*, 30, 337–58.

Kazemipur, Abdolmohammad, and Shiva Halli. (2000). *The New Poverty in Canada*. Toronto: Thompson Educational Publishers.

Krosenbrink-Gelissen, Ernestine. (1994). "The Native Women's Association of Canada." In James Frideres, ed., *Native Peoples in Canada* (pp. 335–64). Scarborough, ON: Prentice Hall.

Laforest, Guy. (2005). "Can Canada Win Back the Children of Bill 101? YES: Canada Can Woo Back Quebeckers—by Admitting Past Insults and Decentralizing, Says a Former ADQ Leader, Guy Laforest." *The Globe and Mail* 20 December: A25.

Latouche, Daniel. (1993). "'Quebec: See under Canada': Quebec Nationalism in the New Global Age." In Alain-G. Gagnon, ed., *Quebec: State and Society*, 2nd ed. (pp. 40–51). Scarborough, ON: Nelson.

Leger Marketing, 2007. *Sun Media: Racial Tolerance Report*. On the World Wide Web at www.legermarketing.com/documents/SPCLM/070119ENG.pdf (15 July 2009).

Lewis, Oscar. (1961). *The Children of Sanchez*. New York: Random House.

Li, Peter. (1988). *The Chinese in Canada*. Toronto: Oxford University Press.

Li, Peter. (2003). *Destination Canada: Immigration Debates and Issues*. Toronto: Oxford University Press.

Lieberson, Stanley. (1991). "A New Ethnic Group in the United States." In Norman Yetman, ed., *Majority and Minority* (pp. 444–56). New York: Allyn and Bacon.

Macmillan, David. (1985). "Scottish Enterprise and Influences in Canada, 1620–1900." In R.A. Cage, ed., *The Scots Abroad: Labour, Capital and Enterprise, 1750–1914* (pp. 46–79). London: Croom Helm.

Manpower and Immigration. (1967). *Immigration Statistics, 1966*. Ottawa: Queen's Printer.

Marger, Martin. (1997). *Race and Ethnic Relations: American and Global Perspectives*, 4th ed. New York: Wadsworth.

Marx, Karl. (1967 [1867]). *Capital*, Vol. 1. New York: International Publishers.

McMillan, Alan. (1988). *Native Peoples and Cultures of Canada*. Vancouver: Douglas and McIntyre.

Métis National Council. (1983). *A Brief to the Standing Committee on Legal and Constitutional Affairs*. Ottawa: Author.

Miles, Robert. (1982). *Racism and Migrant Labour*. London: Routledge.

Miles, Robert, and Malcolm Brown. (2003). *Racism*, 2nd ed. London: Routledge.

Milner, Henry, and Sheilagh Hodgins Milner. (1973). *The Decolonization of Quebec*. Toronto: McClelland and Stewart.

Mitchell, Marybelle. (1996). *From Talking Chiefs to a Native Corporate Elite*. Montreal and Kingston, ON: McGill-Queen's University Press.

Montagu, Ashley. (1972). *Statement on Race*. London: Oxford University Press.

Moore, Robert B. (1976). *Racism in the English Language*. New York: Council on Interracial Books for Children.

Nagler, Mark. (1972). "Minority Values and Economic Achievement: The Case of the North American Indian." In Mark Nagler, ed., *Perspectives on the North American Indian* (pp. 131–42). Toronto: McClelland and Stewart.

Nakhaie, M. Reza. (2006). "A Comparison of the Earnings of the Canadian Native-Born and Immigrants, 2001," *Canadian Ethnic Studies, 38* (2), 19–46.

Nikolinakos, Marios. (1973). "Notes towards an Economic Theory of Racism." *Race, 14*, 365–81.

Omi, Michael, and Howard Winant. (1986). *Racial Formation in the United States: From the 1960s to the 1980s*. New York: Routledge and Kegan Paul.

Parkin, Andrew, and Mattew Mendelsohn. (2003). *A New Canada: An Identity Shaped by Diversity*. Montreal: Centre for Research and Information on Canada.

Pentland, H. Clare. (1981). *Labour and Capital in Canada, 1650–1860*. Toronto: Lorimer.

Pettipas, Katherine. (1995). *Severing the Ties That Bind*. Winnipeg: University of Manitoba Press.

Pineo, Peter, and John Porter. (1985). "Ethnic Origin and Occupational Attainment." In Monica Boyd, John Goyder, Frank Jones, Hugh McRoberts, Peter Pineo, and John Porter, eds., *Ascription and Achievement: Studies in Mobility and Status Attainment in Canada* (pp. 357–93). Ottawa: Carleton University Press.

Porter, John. (1965). *The Vertical Mosaic*. Toronto: University of Toronto Press.

Ramirez, Bruno. (1991). *On the Move: French-Canadian and Italian Migrants in the North Atlantic Economy 1860–1914*. Toronto: McClelland and Stewart.

Rex, John, and David Mason, eds. (1986). *Theories of Race and Ethnic Relations*. Cambridge: Cambridge University Press.

Roy, Patricia. (1989). *A White Man's Province*. Vancouver: University of British Columbia Press.

Royal Commission on Aboriginal Peoples. (1996). *Report*. Ottawa: Supply and Services Canada.

Satzewich, Vic. (1991). *Racism and the Incorporation of Foreign Labour*. London: Routledge.

Satzewich, Vic, and Linda Mahood. (1994). "Indian Affairs and Band Governance: Deposing Indian Chiefs in Western Canada, 1896–1911." *Canadian Ethnic Studies, 26*, 40–58.

Satzewich, Vic, and Lloyd Wong. (2003). "Immigration, Ethnicity and Race: The Transformation of Transnationalism, Localism and Identities." In Wallace Clement and Leah Vosko, eds., *Changing Canada: Political Economy as Transformation*. Montreal and Kingston: McGill-Queen's University Press.

Satzewich, Vic, and Terry Wotherspoon. (2001). *First Nations: Race, Class and Gender Relations*. Regina: Canadian Plains Research Centre.

Scott, George. (1990). "A Resynthesis of the Primordial and Circumstantial Approaches to Ethnic Group Solidarity: Towards an Explanatory Model." *Ethnic and Racial Studies, 13*, 147–71.

Special Committee on the Participation of Visible Minorities in Canadian Society [Special Committee]. (1984). *Equality Now!* Ottawa: Supply and Services Canada.

Statistics Canada. (2001). "2001 Census." On the World Wide Web at http://www12.statcan.ca/english/census01/home/Index.cfm (13 September 2006).

Statistics Canada. (2003). *Ethnic Diversity Survey: Portrait of a Multicultural Society*. Ottawa: Minister of Industry. Catalogue No. 89-593-XIE.

Statistics Canada. (2008). "Immigration and Citizenship Highlight Tables, 2006." On the World Wide Web at http://www12.statcan.ca/english/census06/data/highlights/Immigration/index.cfm (15 July 2009).

Steckley, John. (2003). *Aboriginal Voices and the Politics of Representation in Canadian Introductory Sociology Textbooks*. Toronto: Canadian Scholars Press.

Steinberg, Stephen. (1981). *The Ethnic Myth*. New York: Knopf.

Stoffman, Daniel. (2002). *Who Gets In: What's Wrong with Canada's Immigration Program—and How to Fix It*. Toronto: Macfarlane Walter and Ross.

Thomas, W. I., and Florian Znaniecki. (1918). *The Polish Peasant in Europe and America*. New York: Knopf.

Titley, Brian. (1986). *A Narrow Vision: Duncan Campbell Scott and the Administration of Indian Affairs in Canada*. Vancouver: University of British Columbia Press.

Turp, Daniel. (2005). "Can Canada Win Back the Children of Bill 101? No: Canada Isn't First in the Hearts of Young Quebeckers, Regardless of Their First Language, says PQ MNA Daniel Turp." *The Globe and Mail* 20 December: A25.

van den Berghe, Pierre. (1986). "Ethnicity and the Sociobiology Debate." In John Rex and David Mason, eds., *Theories of Race and Ethnic Relations* (pp. 246–63). Cambridge, UK: Cambridge University Press.

Walcott, William. (2003). "The Toronto Mayor and the Mombassa Natives." *Canadian Ethnic Studies, 35* (2), 100–15.

Whitaker, Reginald. (1987). *Double Standard: The Secret History of Canadian Immigration*. Toronto: Lester and Orpen Dennys.

Whitaker, Reginald. (1993). "From the Quebec Cauldron to the Canadian Cauldron." In Alain-G. Gagnon, ed., *Quebec: State and Society*, 2nd ed. (pp. 18–39). Scarborough, ON: Nelson.

White, Pamela. (1992). "Challenges in Measuring Canada's Ethnic Diversity." In Stella Hryniuk, ed., *20 Years of Multiculturalism: Success and Failure* (pp. 163–82). Winnipeg: St. John's College Press.

Wiley, Norbert. (1967). "Ethnic Mobility and Stratification Theory." *Social Problems, 15*, 147–59.

Wilkes, Rima, Neil Guppy, and Lily Farris. (2008). "'No Thanks, We're Full': Individual Attitudes National Context and Changing Attitudes toward Immigration." *International Migration Review, 42* (2), 303–28.

Williams, Eric. (1964). *Capitalism and Slavery*. London: Andre Deutsch.

Wilson, Edward. (1978). *On Human Nature*. New York: Vintage.

Woodsworth, J. S. (1972). *Strangers within Our Gates*. Toronto: University of Toronto Press.

Workpermit.com. (2008). "Canadian Immigration Points Calculator," On the World Wide Web at http://www.workpermit.com/canada/points_calculator.htm (16 July 2009).

Wortley, Scot. (2005). *Bias Free Policing: The Kingston Data Collection Project, Preliminary Results.* Toronto: Centre of Criminology, University of Toronto and the Centre of Excellence for Research on Immigration and Settlement (CERIS).

York, Geoffrey. (1989). *The Dispossessed.* Toronto: Lester and Orpen Dennys.

Zong, Li. (1994). "Structural and Psychological Dimensions of Racism: Towards an Alternative Perspective." *Canadian Ethnic Studies, 26,* 122–34.

CHAPTER 9

Antonenko, Oksana. (2001). "Russia's Military Involvement in the Middle East." *Middle East Review of International Affairs 5,* (1). On the World Wide Web at http://meria.idc.ac.il/journal/2001/issue1/jv5n1a3.html (18 March 2009).

Arrighi, Giovanni. (1970). "Labour Supplies in Historical Perspective: A Study of the Proletarianization of the African Peasantry in Rhodesia." *Journal of Development Studies, 6* (3), 197–234.

Bairoch, Paul. (1982). "International Industrialization Levels from 1750 to 1980." *Journal of European Economic History, 11,* 269–331.

Blaut, James M. (2000). *Eight Eurocentric Historians.* New York: Guilford Press.

Bluestone, B., and B. Harrison. (1982). *The De-Industrialization of America: Plant Closings, Community Abandonment, and the Dismantling of Basic Industries.* New York: Basic Books.

Bluestone, B., and B. Harrison. (1988). *The Great U-Turn: Corporate Restructuring and the Polarizing of America.* New York: Basic Books.

Bornschier, Volker. (2002). "Changing Income Inequality in the 2nd Half of the 20th Century: Preliminary Findings and Propositions for Explanation." *Journal of World Systems Research, 8,* 100–127.

Borras, Saturnino. (2008). "Contemporary Land Policies and Land Struggles." in *Critical Development Studies: Readings for Change.* Zacatecas, Mexico: Global Capital and Alternative Development Unit, Doctorate in Development Studies, Universidad Autonoma de Zacatecas and CDS Network.

Braun, D. (1997). *The Rich Get Richer: The Rise of Income Inequality in the United States and the World.* Chicago: Nelson-Hall Publishers.

Brenner, Robert. (1977). "The Origins of Capitalist Development: A Critique of Neo-Smithian Marxism." *New Left Review, 104* (July–August), 25–92.

Brown, Lester. (2003). *Plan B: Rescuing a Planet Under Stress and a Civilization in Trouble.* New York: Norton.

Brym, Robert J., et al. (2005). "In Faint Praise of the World Bank's Gender Development Policy." *Canadian Journal of Sociology, 30,* 95–100. On the World Wide Web at http://www.cjsonline.ca/articles/brymetal05.html (7 March 2009)

Cardoso, Fernando Henrique, and Enzo Faletto. (1979). *Dependency and Development in Latin America.* Berkeley: University of California Press.

"Chavez: Venezuela Aiding Latin America." (2007). *Miami Herald* 15 March.

Chesnais, François. (2004). "Globalisation against Development: Liberalisation, Deregulation and Privatisation and the Contemporary Performance of the International Economy." On the World Wide Web at http://www.nadir.org/nadir/initiativ/agp/free/wsf/mumbai2004/0117chesnais.htm (7 March 2009).

Dean, Warren. (1976). *Rio Claro: A Brazilian Plantation System, 1820–1920.* Palo Alto, CA: Stanford University Press.

Diamond, Jared. (1999). *Guns, Germs and Steel: The Fates of Human Societies.* New York: Norton.

Ellis, Frank. (1983). *Las Transnacionales del Banano en Centroamérica [Banana Transnationals in Central America].* San Jose: EDUCA.

Falla, Ricardo. (1994). *Massacres in the Jungle: Ixcan, Guatemala 1975–1982.* Boulder, CO: Westview.

Frank, Andre Gundar. (1966). *Capitalism and Underdevelopment in Latin America: Historical Studies of Chile and Brazil.* New York: Monthly Review Press.

Gareau, Frederick H. (2004). *State Terrorism and the United States.* Atlanta: Clarity Press.

Handy, Jim. (1985). *A Gift of the Devil: A History of Guatemala.* Toronto: Between the Lines.

Hochschild, Adam. (1999). *King Leopold's Ghost: A Story of Greed, Terror, and Heroism in Colonial Africa.* New York: Mariner Books.

Inkeles, Alex, and David H. Smith. (1976). *Becoming Modern: Individual Change in Six Developing Countries.* Cambridge MA: Harvard University Press.

La Via Campesina. (2007). "Declaration of Nyéléni." On the World Wide Web at http://www.viacampesina.org/main_en/index.php?option=com_content&task=view&id=282&Itemid=38 (20 March 2009).

Marchak, Patricia. (1999). *God's Assassins: State Terrorism in Argentina in the 1970s.* Montreal-Kingston: McGill–Queen's University Press.

Marshall, Jonathan, Peter Dale Scott, and Jane Hunter. (1987). *The Iran-Contra Connection.* Montreal: Black Rose Books.

McClelland, David. (1961). *The Achieving Society.* Princeton NJ: Van Nostrand.

Milanovic, Branko. (2005). "Global Income Inequality: What It Is and Why It Matters?" DESA Working Paper No. 26. On the World Wide Web at http://129.3.20.41/eps/hew/papers/0512/0512001.pdf (7 March 2009).

Milanovic, Branko. (2008). "An Even Higher Global Inequality Than Previously Thought: A Note on Global Inequality Calculations Using the 2005 International Comparison Program Results." *International Journal of Health Services, 38,* 421–29.

Milanovic, Branko. (2009). "Developing Countries Worse Off Than Once Thought." Washington: Carnegie Endowment for International Peace. On the World Wide Web at http://www.carnegieendowment.org/publications/index.cfm?fa=view&id=19907 (12 July 2009).

Murmis, Miguel, and Juan Carlos Portantiero. (1969). *Estudios Sobre Los Orígenes del Peronismo.* Buenos Aires: Siglo XXI.

Neilsen, François. (2007). "Income Inequality in the Global Economy: The Myth of Rising World Inequality." *Harvard College Economics Review, 1* (2): 23–26.

Parpart, Jane, and Henry Veltmeyer. (2003). "The Dynamics of Development Theory and Practice: A Review of its Shifting Dynamics." *Canadian Journal of Development Studies, 25* (1: Special Issue), (CD).

Pickover, Charles. (1997). "Why Did Human History Evolve Differently on Different Continents for the Last 13,000 Years?" Edge Foundation. On the World Wide Web at http://www.edge.org/discourse/diamond_evolution.html (7 March 2009).

Richards, Alan. (1976). "The Political Economy of Gutswirtschaft: A Comparative Analysis of East Elbian Germany, Egypt, and Chile." *Comparative Studies in Society and History*, 21 (3), 483–518.

Rodney, Walter. (1972). *How Europe Underdeveloped Africa*. London: Bogle-L'Ouverture Publications.

Rodriguez Gomez, Guadalupe, and Gabriel Torres. (1996). "El Barzón y la Comagro: La Resistencia de los Agricultores a la Politica Neoliberal." In Grammont and Tejera Gaona, eds., *La Sociedad Rural Mexicana Frente al Nuevo Milenio*. Mexico City: Plaza y Valdez Editores.

Rostow, W. W. (1960). *The Stages of Economic Growth: A Non-communist Manifesto*. Cambridge UK: Cambridge University Press.

Shiva, Vandana. (1993). "GATT, Agriculture and Third World Women." In Maria Mies and Vandana Shiva, eds. *Ecofeminism* (pp. 241–5). Halifax: Fernwood Books.

Stiglitz, Joseph. (2003). *Globalization and Its Discontents*. New York: Norton.

Stone, Samuel. (1975). *La Dinastia de los Conquistadores*. San Jose, Costa Rica: EDUCA.

Sutcliffe, Robert. (2005). "Interview with Bob Sutcliffe: Measuring Global Inequality." Amherst: University of Massachusetts, Political Economy Research Institute, 23 February 23. On the World Wide Web at http://www.peri.umass.edu/ (12 July 2009).

United Nations. (2009). "Indicators on Income and Economic Activity." *Social Indicators*. On the World Wide Web at http://unstats.un.org/unsd/demographic/products/socind/inc-eco.htm (12 July 2009).

Vilas, Carlos. (1986) *The Sandinista Revolution*. New York: Monthly Review Press.

Waldman, Carl. (2005). "Teotihuacán." *Microsoft Encarta* 2006 [CD]. Redmond WA: Microsoft.

Winson, Anthony. (1983). "The Formation of Capitalist Agriculture in Latin America and Its Relationship to Political Power and the State." *Comparative Studies in Society and History*, 25, 83–104.

Winson, Anthony. (1989). *Coffee and Democracy in Modern Costa Rica*. London: Macmillan.

Winson, Anthony, and Belinda Leach. (2002). *Contingent Work, Disrupted Lives: Labour and Community in the New Rural Economy*. Toronto: University of Toronto Press.

World Social Forum. (2009). "World Social Forum Charter of Principles." On the World Wide Web at http://www.forumsocialmundial.org.br/main.php?id_menu=4&cd_language=2 (20 March 2009).

CHAPTER 10

Anderson, M. (1971). *Family Structure in NineteenthBCentury Lancashire*. Cambridge, UK: Cambridge University Press.

Arat-Koc, S. (2009). "The Politics of Family and Immigration in the Subordination of Domestic Workers in Canada." In B. Fox, ed., *Family Patterns, Gender Relations*, 3rd ed. (pp. 428–52). Toronto: Oxford University Press.

Baker, M. (1995). *Canadian Family Policies*. Toronto: University of Toronto Press.

Barnett, R., and C. Rivers. (1996). *She Works, He Works: How Two-Income Families are Happier, Healthier, and Better-Off*. San Francisco: Harper.

Beach, J., J. Bertrand, and G. Cleveland. (1998). *Our Child Care Workforce: From Recognition to Remuneration*. Main Report for the Child Care Sector Study Steering Committee. Ottawa: HRDC.

Bernard, J. (1972). *The Future of Marriage*. New Haven, CT: Yale University Press.

Bradbury, B. (1982). "The Fragmented Family: Family Strategies in the Face of Death, Illness and Poverty, Montreal, 1860–1885." In J. Parr, ed., *Childhood and Family* (pp. 109–29). Toronto: McClelland and Stewart.

Calliste, A. (2001). "Black Families in Canada: Exploring the Interconnections of Race, Class, and Gender." In B. Fox, ed., *Family Patterns, Gender Relations*, 2nd ed. Toronto: Oxford University Press.

Clarke-Stewart, A. (1982). *Daycare*. Cambridge, MA: Harvard University Press.

Coontz, Stephanie. (1992). *The Way We Never Were: American Families and the Nostalgia Trap*. New York: Basic Books.

Cott, N. (1977). *Bonds of Womanhood: "Women's Sphere" in New England, 1780–1835*. New Haven, CT: Yale University Press.

Daly, Kerry. (2004). "The Changing Culture of Parenting." Contemporary Family Trends series. Ottawa: Vanier Institute of the Family.

Davidoff, L., and C. Hall. (1987). *Family Fortunes: Men and Women in the English Middle Class, 1780–1850*. Chicago: University of Chicago Press.

Dunne, Gillian. (2000). "Opting into Motherhood: Lesbians Blurring the Boundaries and Transforming the Meaning of Parenthood and Kinship." *Gender and Society* 14 (1), 11–35.

Edholm, F. (1982). "The Unnatural Family." In E. Whitelegg, M. Arnot, E. Bartels, V. Beechey, L. Birke, S. Himmelweit, D. Leonard, S. Ruehl, and M. Speakman, eds., *The Changing Experience of Women*. London: The Open University.

Eyer, D. (1996). *Motherguilt: How Our Culture Blames Mothers for What's Wrong with Society*. New York: Random House.

Finnie, R. (1993). "Women, Men and the Economic Consequences of Divorce: Evidence from Canadian Longitudinal Data." *Canadian Review of Sociology and Anthropology*, 30 (2), 205–41.

Flandrin, J. (1979). *Families in Former Times: Kinship, Household and Sexuality*. Cambridge, UK: Cambridge University Press.

Fox, B. (2001). "The Formative Years: How Parenthood Creates Gender." *Canadian Review of Sociology and Anthropology*, 38 (4), 373–90.

Fox, B. (forthcoming). *When Couples Become Parents: The Creation of Gender in the Transition to Parenthood*. Toronto: University of Toronto Press.

Fox, B. with J. Yiu. (2009). "As Times Change: A Review of Trends in Family Life." In B. Fox, ed., *Family Patterns, Gender Relations*, 3rd ed. (pp. 180–208). Toronto: Oxford University Press.

Fox, B., and D. Worts. (1999). "Revisiting the Critique of Medicalized Childbirth." *Gender and Society*, 13 (3), 326–47.

Friendly, M., J. Beach, C. Ferns, and M. Turiano. (2007). *Trends & Analysis 2007: Early Childhood Education and Care in Canada 2006*. Toronto: Childcare Resource and Research Unit.

Friendly, Martha, and Laurel Rothman. (2009). "Child Care—Canada Can't Work Without It." *Toronto Star* 8 January. On the World Wide Web at http://www.thestar.com/printArticle/563403 (1 March 2009).

Furstenberg, F., and A. Cherlin. (1991). *Divided Families: What Happens to Children When Parents Part*. Cambridge: Harvard University Press.

Gartner, R., M. Dawson, and M. Crawford. (1998–99). "Woman Killing: Intimate Femicide in Ontario, 1974–1994." *Resources for Feminist Research, 3* (4), 151–73.

Gaskell, J. (1983). "The Reproduction of Family Life: Perspectives of Male and Female Adolescents." In J. Veevers, ed., *Continuity and Change in Marriage and Family* (pp. 219–34). Toronto: Holt, Rinehart and Winston.

Gerson, K. (1985). *Hard Choices: How Women Decide about Work, Career and Motherhood.* Berkeley, CA: University of California Press.

Gottlieb, B. (1993). *The Family in the Western World.* New York: Oxford University Press.

Graham, H. (1987). "Being Poor: Perceptions and Coping Strategies of Lone Mothers." In J. Brannen and G. Wilson, eds., *Give and Take in Families: Studies in Resource Distribution* (pp. 56–74) London: Allen and Unwin.

Greven, P. (1973). "Family Structure in Seventeenth-Century Andover, Massachusetts." In M. Gordon, ed., *The American Family in Social-Historical Perspective* (pp. 77–100). New York: St. Martin's Press.

Hareven, T. (1982). *Family Time and Industrial Time: The Relationship between Family and Work in a New England Industrial Community.* Cambridge, UK: Cambridge University Press.

Hertz, R. (1986). *More Equal than Others: Women and Men in Dual-Career Marriages.* Berkeley, CA: University of California Press.

Hochschild, A. (1989). *The Second Shift: Working Parents and the Revolution at Home.* New York: Viking.

Iacovetta, F. (1992). *Such Hardworking People: Italian Immigrants in Postwar Toronto.* Montreal and Kingston, ON: McGill-Queen's University Press.

Jenson, Jane. (2002). "Against the Current: Child Care and Family Policy in Quebec." In S. Michel and R. Mahon, eds., *Child Care Policy at the Crossroads: Gender and Welfare State Restructuring.* New York: Routledge.

Kibria, N. (1993). *Family Tightrope: The Changing Lives of Vietnamese Americans.* Princeton, NJ: Princeton University Press.

Kurz, D. (1995). *For Richer, For Poorer: Mothers Confront Divorce.* New York: Routledge.

Lasch, C. (1977). *Haven in a Heartless World: The Family Besieged.* New York: Basic Books.

Laslett, B., and J. Brenner. (1989). "Gender and Social Reproduction: Historical Perspectives." *Annual Review of Sociology, 15,* 381–404.

Leacock, E. B. (1981). *Myths of Male Dominance: Collected Articles on Women Cross-Culturally.* New York: Monthly Review Press.

Lee, R. B. (1979). *The !Kung San: Men, Women and Work in a Foraging Society.* Cambridge, UK: Cambridge University Press.

Lewontin, R. C., S. Rose, and L. Kamin. (1984). *Not in Our Genes: Biology, Ideology and Human Nature.* New York: Pantheon.

Luxton, M. (1980). *More Than a Labour of Love: Three Generations of Women's Work in the Home.* Toronto: Women's Press.

Marcil-Gratton, N. (1993). "Growing Up with a Single Parent: A Transitional Experience? Some Demographic Measurements." In J. Hudson and B. Galaway, eds., *Single-Parent Families: Perspectives on Research and Policy* (pp. 73–90). Toronto: Thompson Educational Publishing.

Marshall, K. (2006). "Converging Gender Roles." *Perspectives* (July). Statistics Canada, Catalogue No. 75-001-XIE. On the World Wide Web at http://www.statcan.gc.ca/pub/75-001-x/10706/9268-eng.pdf. (1 March 2009).

May, E. (1988). *Homeward Bound: American Families in the Cold War Era.* New York: Basic Books.

May, M. (1985). "Bread before Roses: American Workingmen, Labor Unions and the Family Wage." In R. Milkman, ed., *Women, Work and Protest: A Century of U.S. Women's Labor History* (pp. 1–22). Boston: Routledge and Kegan Paul.

McKie, C. (1993). "An Overview of Lone Parenthood in Canada." In J. Hudson and B. Galaway, eds., *Single Parent Families: Perspectives on Research and Policy* (pp. 53–72). Toronto: Thompson Educational Publishing.

McLanahan, S. (1985). "Family Structure and the Reproduction of Poverty." *American Journal of Sociology, 90* (4), 873–901.

McLanahan, S., and L. Bumpass. (1988). "Intergenerational Consequences of Family Disruption." *American Journal of Sociology, 94* (1), 130–52.

McMahon, Martha. (1995). *Engendering Motherhood: Identity and Self-Transformation in Women's Lives.* New York: Guilford Press.

Mitterauer, M., and R. Sieder. (1982). *The European Family: Patriarchy to Partnership from the Middle Ages to the Present.* Oxford: Basil Blackwell.

Morton, M. (1988). "Dividing the Wealth, Sharing the Poverty: The (Re)formation of 'Family' in Law in Ontario." *Canadian Review of Sociology and Anthropology, 25* (2), 254–76.

National Council of Welfare. (1998). *Poverty Profile 1996.* Ottawa: Supply and Services Canada.

National Council of Welfare. (2006). *Poverty Profile, 2002 and 2003.* On the World Wide Web at http://www.ncwcnbes.net/documents/researchpublications/ResearchProjects/PovertyProfile/2002-03Report_Summer2006/ReportENG.pdf (1 March 2009).

Nelson, Fiona. (1999). *Lesbian Motherhood: An Exploration of Canadian Families.* Toronto, Canada: University of Toronto Press.

Parsons, T., and R. Bales. (1955). *Family, Socialization and Interaction Process.* New York: Free Press.

Patterson, C. (1995). "Lesbian Mothers, Gay Fathers, and Their Children." In A. R. D'Augelli and C. J. Patterson, eds., *Lesbian, Gay and Bisexual Identities over the Lifespan: Psychological Perspectives.* New York: Oxford University Press.

Rapp, R., and E. Ross. (1986). "The 1920s: Feminism, Consumerism and Political Backlash in the U.S." In J. Friedlander, B. Cook, A. Kessler-Harris, and C. Smith-Rosenberg, eds., *Women in Culture and Politics* (pp. 52–62). Bloomington, IN: Indiana University Press.

Righton, Barbara. (2008). "A Nation Living in Sin." *Macleans.ca* June 25. On the World Wide Web at http://www.macleans.ca/canada/national/article.jsp?content=20080625_31050_31050&page=2 (1 March 2009).

Rosenberg, H. (1987). "Motherwork, Stress and Depression: The Costs of Privatized Social Reproduction." In H. J. Maroney and M. Luxton, eds., *Feminism and Political Economy: Women's Work, Women's Struggles* (pp. 181–97). Toronto: Methuen.

Rubin, L. (1990). *Erotic Wars: What Happened to the Sexual Revolution?* New York: Farrar, Straus & Giroux.

Ryan, M. (1981). *Cradle of the Middle Class: The Family in Oneida County, 1790–1865.* Cambridge, MA: Cambridge University Press.

Sayer, Liana C. (2005). "Gender, Time, and Inequality: Trends in Women's and Men's Paid Work, Unpaid Work, and Free Time." *Social Forces, 84* (1), 285–303.

Schwartz, P., and V. Rutter. (1998). *The Gender of Sexuality.* Thousand Oaks, CA: Pine Forge Press.

Singh, S., and J. Lindsay. (1996). "Money in Heterosexual Relationships." *Australia and New Zealand Journal of Sociology, 32* (4), 56–69.

Smith-Rosenberg, C. (1975). "The Female World of Love and Ritual: Relations between Women in Nineteenth-Century America." *Signs, 1* (1), 1–31.

Stacey, J., and T. Biblarz. (2001). " (How) Does the Sexual Orientation of Parents Matter?" *American Sociological Review, 66* (2) 159–83.

Stack, C. (1974). *All Our Kin: Strategies for Survival in a Black Community.* New York: Harper and Row.

Stansell, C. (1987). *City of Women: Sex and Class in New York, 1789–1860.* Urbana, IL: University of Illinois Press.

Statistics Canada. (1992). *Lone Parent Families in Canada.* Ottawa: Industry, Science and Technology Canada. Catalogue No. 89-522E.

Statistics Canada. (2002). "Profile of Canadian Families and Households: Diversification Continues," *The Daily* 22 October.

Statistics Canada. (2007). *Family Portrait: Continuity and Change in Canadian Families and Households in 2006.* 2006 Census Analysis. Ottawa: Statistics Canada, Catalogue no. 97-553-XIE.

Statistics Canada. (2008). "Employment Rates of Mothers, by Age of Youngest Child." On the World Wide Web at www.statcan.gc.ca/pub/71-222-x/2008001/sectionb/b-mothers-meres-eng.htm (1 March 2009).

Tavris, C. (1992). *The Mismeasure of Woman.* New York: Touchstone.

Tilly, L., and J. W. Scott. (1978). *Women, Work and Family.* New York: Holt, Rinehart and Winston.

Turnbull, C. (1961). *The Forest People.* New York: Doubleday.

Weston, K. (1991). *Families We Choose: Lesbians, Gays, Kinship.* New York: Columbia University Press.

CHAPTER 11

Adams, Tracey L. (2000). *A Gentleman and a Dentist: Gender and the Rise of Dentistry in Ontario.* Toronto: University of Toronto Press.

Adams, Tracey, and Sandy Welsh. (2008). *The Organization and Experience of Work.* Toronto: Nelson.

Althauser, Robert. (1989). "Internal Labor Markets." *Annual Review of Sociology, 15,* 143–61.

Baldwin, John R., and Desmond Beckstead. (2003). "Knowledge Workers in Canada's Economy, 1971–2001." Statistics Canada, Catalogue No. 11-624-MIE, Research Paper No. 004. Ottawa: Ministry of Industry

Becker, Gary S. (1975). *Human Capital: A Theoretical and Empirical Analysis with Special Reference to Education, 3rd ed.* Chicago: University of Chicago Press.

Bell, Daniel. (1973). *The Coming of Post-industrial Society.* New York: Basic Books.

Bendix, Reinhard. (1974). *Work and Authority in Industry.* Berkeley, CA: University of California Press.

Berinstein, Juana. (2004). "Temp Workers and Deadbeat Bosses." *Our Times* (October–November).

Blauner, Robert. (1964). *Alienation and Freedom.* Chicago: University of Chicago Press.

Braverman, Harry. (1974). *Labor and Monopoly Capital: The Degradation of Work in the Twentieth Century.* New York: Monthly Review Press.

Bridges, William. (1994). *Job Shift: How to Prosper in a Workplace without Jobs.* Don Mills, ON: Addison-Wesley.

Burawoy, Michael. (1979). *Manufacturing Consent: Changes in the Labour Process under Monopoly Capitalism.* Chicago: University of Chicago Press.

Burman, Patrick. (1997). "Changes in the Patterns of Unemployment: The New Realities of Joblessness." In Ann Duffy, Daniel Glenday, and Norene Pupo, eds., *Good Jobs, Bad Jobs, No Jobs: The Transformation of Work in the 21st Century,* (pp. 190–216). Toronto: Harcourt Brace Canada.

Calliste, Agnes. (1993). "Sleeping Car Porters in Canada: An Ethnically Submerged Split Labour Market." In Graham S. Lowe and Harvey Krahn, eds., *Work in Canada: Readings in the Sociology of Work and Industry* (pp. 139–53). Scarborough, ON: Nelson.

Campell, Andrew. (1996). "From Shop Floor to Computer Room." *The Globe and Mail* 30 December: A1, A8.

Canadian Labour Congress. (1993). "Two Years under Free Trade: An Assessment." In Graham S. Lowe and Harvey Krahn, eds., *Work in Canada: Readings in the Sociology of Work and Industry* (pp. 115–19). Scarborough, ON: Nelson.

Canadian Policy Research Networks. (2006a). "It's More Than the Money—What Canadians Want in a Job." On the World Wide Web at http://www.jobquality.ca/indicator_e/rew001.stm (9 March 2006).

Canadian Policy Research Networks. (2006b). "Satisfaction Most Common in Social Sciences, Arts/Culture and Management Occupations." On the World Wide Web at http://www.jobquality.ca/indicator_e/rew002_1.stm#2 (9 March 2006).

Canadian Press/Leger Marketing. (2001). *How Much Importance Canadian Place on Their Work.* Montreal.

Carey, Alex. (1967). "The Hawthorne Studies: A Radical Criticism." *American Sociological Review, 32,* 403–16.

Chaykowski, Richard. (2005). *Non-Standard Work and Economic Vulnerability,* Vulnerable Workers Series, No. 3. Ottawa: CPRN.

Cranford, Cynthia, Leah Vosko, and Nancy Zukewich. (2003). "The Gender of Precarious Employment in Canada." *Relations Industrielles/Industrial Relations, 58* (3), 454–79.

Dassbach, Carl H. A. (1996). "Lean Production, Labor Control, and Post-Fordism in the Japanese Automobile Industry." In William C. Green and Ernest J. Yanarella, eds., *North American Auto Unions in Crisis: Lean Production as Contested Terrain* (pp. 19–40). Albany, NY: SUNY Press.

Economic Council of Canada. (1991). *Good Jobs, Bad Jobs: Employment in the Service Economy.* Ottawa: Supply and Services Canada.

Edwards, P. K., and Hugh Scullion. (1982). *The Social Organization of Industrial Conflict.* Oxford: Blackwell.

Edwards, Richard. (1979). *Contested Terrain: The Transformation of the Workplace in the Twentieth Century.* New York: Basic Books.

Ehrenreich, Barbara. (2005). *Bait and Switch: The (Futile) Pursuit of the American Dream.* New York: Metropolitan Books.

Epstein, Cynthia Fuchs, and Arne Kalleberg. (2001). "Time and the Sociology of Work: Issues and Implications." *Work and Occupations, 28* (1):5–16.

Erickson, Bonnie. (2001). "Good Networks and Good Jobs: The Value of Social Capital to Employers and Employees." In Nan Lin, Karen Cook, and Ronald Burt (eds.), *Social Capital: Theory and Research* (pp. 127–58). New York: Aldine de Gruyter.

Flap, Henk, and Ed Boxman. (2001) "Getting Started: The Influence of Social Capital on the Start of the Occupational Career. In Nan Lin, Karen Cook, and Ronald Burt (eds.), *Social Capital: Theory and Research* (pp. 159–81). New York: Aldine de Gruyter.

Fountain, Christine M. (2005). "Finding a Job in the Internet Age." *Social Forces, 83* (3), 1235–62.

Friedson, Eliot. (1970). *The Profession of Medicine: A Study in the Sociology of Applied Knowledge.* New York: Harper and Row.

Fudge, J., and L. F. Vosko. (2001). "By Whose Standards? Re-Regulating the Canadian Labour Market." *Economic and Industrial Democracy, 22* (3), 327.

Granovetter, Mark. ([1974] 1995). *Getting a Job: A Study of Contacts and Careers,* 2nd ed. Cambridge, MA: Harvard.

Hodson, Randy. (1991). "The Active Worker: Compliance and Autonomy at the Workplace." *Contemporary Ethnography, 20* (April), 271–90.

Hodson, Randy, and Teresa Sullivan. (1985). "Totem or Tyrant? Monopoly, Regional and Local Sector Effects on Worker Commitment." *Social Forces, 63* (3), 716–31.

Hodson, Randy, and Teresa Sullivan. (1990). *The Social Organization of Work.* Belmont, CA: Wadsworth.

Houseman, Susan, Arne Kalleberg, and George Erickcek. (2003). "The Role of Temporary Agency Employment in Tight Labour Markets." *Industrial and Labor Relations Review, 57* (1), 105–27.

Immen, Wallace. (2006). "Why Executives Quit: Challenge, Not Money." *The Globe and Mail* 3 March. On the World Wide Web at http://globecareers.workopolis.com (9 March 2006).

JobFutures. (2002). "Job Futures" World of Work," national ed. On the World Wide Web at http://www.jobfutures.ca/en/brochure/JobFuture.pdf (9 March 2006).

Jones, Frank E. (1996). *Understanding Organizations: A Sociological Perspective.* Cooksville, ON: Copp Clark.

Kalleberg, Arne. (2000). "Nonstandard Employment Relations: Part-time, Temporary, and Contract Work." *Annual Review of Sociology, 26,* 341–65.

Kalleberg, Arne. (2003). "Flexible Firms and Labor Market Segmentation: Effects of Workplace Restructuring on Jobs and Workers." *Work & Occupations, 30* (2),154–75.

Kalleberg, Arne L., Barbara F. Reskin, and Ken Hudson. (2000). "Bad Jobs in America: Standard and Nonstandard Employment Relations and Job Quality in the United States." *American Sociological Review, 65,* 256–78.

Krahn, Harvey. (1991). "Non-standard Work Arrangements." *Perspectives on Labour and Income* (Winter).

Krahn, Harvey. (1995). "Non-standard Work on the Rise." *Perspectives on Labour and Income* (Winter), 35–42.

Krahn, Harvey J. (1992). *Quality of Work in the Service Economy.* General Social Survey Analysis Series 6. Ottawa: Statistics Canada. Catalogue No. 11-612E.

Krahn, Harvey J., and Graham S. Lowe. (1998). *Work, Industry and Canadian Society,* 3rd ed. Scarborough, ON: ITP Nelson.

Kunda, Gideon, Stephen R. Barley, and James Evans. (20002). "Why Do Contractors Contract? The Experience of Highly Skilled Technical Professionals in a Contingent Labor Market." *Industrial and Labor Relations Review, 55* (2), 234–61.

Laxer, Gordon. (1989). *Open for Business: The Roots of Foreign Ownership in Canada.* Don Mills, ON: Oxford University Press.

Livingstone, D. W. (1993). "Conclusion: Aging Dinosaurs or All-Round Workers?" In June Corman, Meg Luxton, D. W. Livingstone, and Wally Secombe, eds., *Recasting Steel Labour: The Stelco Story* (pp. 145–55). Halifax: Fernwood.

Lowe, Graham S. (1987). *Women in the Administrative Revolution: The Feminization of Clerical Work.* Toronto: University of Toronto Press.

Marsden, Peter, and J. Hurlbert. (1988). Social Resources and Mobility Outcomes. *Social Forces, 66,* 1038–59.

McGovern, Patrick, Deborah Smeaton, and Stephen Hill. (2004). "Bad Jobs in Britain: Nonstandard Employment and Job Quality." *Work and Occupations, 31,* (2), 225–49.

McKay, Shona. (1993). "Willing and Able." In Graham S. Lowe and Harvey Krahn, eds., *Work in Canada: Readings in the Sociology of Work and Industry* (pp. 166–71). Scarborough, ON: Nelson.

McKenzie, Donald. (2001). "90% Satisfied with Their Jobs: Poll: 70% Happy with Salary." *Financial Post* 31 December: FP3.

Morissette, René. (1991). "Are Jobs in Large Firms Better?" *Perspectives on Labour and Income* (Autumn), 40–50.

Morissette, René, and Feng Hou. (2006). "Unemployment since 1971". *Perspectives on Labour and Income* (May). Ottawa: Statistics Canada (Catalogue no. 75-001-XIE).

Morissette, René, and Anick Johnson. (2005). *Are Good Jobs Disappearing in Canada?* Statistics Canada: Ministry of Industry. Catalogue No. 11F0019MIE.

MSNBC. 2007. "Graveyard Shift Linked to Cancer Risk." On the World Wide Web at November 29. On the World Wide Web at http://www.msnbc.msn.com/id/22026660/ (retrieved 26 March 2009).

Myles, John. (1988). "The Expanding Middle: Some Canadian Evidence on the Deskilling Debate." *Canadian Review of Sociology and Anthropology, 25* (3), 335–64.

Olsen, Karen M., and Arne Kalleberg. (2004). "Non-standard Work in Two Different Employment Regimes: Norway and the United States." *Work, Employment and Society, 18* (2), 321–48.

Osterman, Paul. (1995). "The Transformation of Work in the United States: What the Evidence Shows." In Bryan Downie and Mary Lou Coates, eds., *Managing Human Resources in the 1990s and Beyond* (pp. 71–92). Kingston, ON: Industrial Relations Centre Press.

Pescocolido, Bernice, Steven Tuch, and Jack Martin. (2001). "The Profession of Medicine and the Public: Examining Americans' Changing Confidence in Physician Authority from the Beginning of the 'Health Care Crisis' to the Era of Health Care Reform." *Journal of Health and Social Behavior, 42* (March), 1–16.

Polanyi, Karl. (1957). *The Great Transformation.* Boston: Beacon Press.

Pold, Henry. (2004). "Duration of Non-standard Employment" *Perspectives on Labour and Income, 5* (12).

Presser, Harriet. (1999). "Toward a 24-Hour Economy." *Science, 284* (June 11), 1778–89.

Presser, Harriet. (2003). "Race-Ethnic and Gender Differences in Nonstandard Work Shifts." *Work & Occupations, 30* (4), 412–39.

Presser, Harriet. (2004). *Employment in a 24/7 Economy: Challenges for American Families.* New York: Russell Sage.

Rifkin, Jeremy. (1995). *The End of Work: The Decline of the Global Labor Force and the Dawn of the Post Market Era.* New York: G.P. Putnam.

Rinehart, James. (1978). "Contradictions of Work-Related Attitudes and Behaviour: An Interpretation." *Canadian Review of Sociology and Anthropology, 15*, 1–15.

Rinehart, James. (1996). *The Tyranny of Work: Alienation and the Labour Process*, 3rd ed. Toronto: Harcourt Brace.

Rinehart, James, David Robertson, Chris Huxley, and Jeff Wareham. (1994). "Reunifying Conception and Execution of Work under Japanese Production Management? A Canadian Case Study." In Tony Elger and Chris Smith, eds., *Global Japanization? The Transnational Transformation of the Labour Process* (pp. 152–74). London: Routledge.

Ritzer, George. (1993). *The McDonaldization of Society*. Newbury Park, CA: Pine Forge.

Robertson, David, James Rinehart, Christopher Huxley, Jeff Wareham, Herman Rosenfeld, Alan McGough, and Steve Benedict. (1993). *The CAMI Report: Lean Production in a Unionized Auto Plant*. North York, ON: CAW Research.

Rogers, Jackie Krasas. (1995). "Just a Temp: Experience and Structure of Alienation in Temporary Clerical Employment." *Work and Occupations, 22* (2), 137–66.

Rosenthal, Patricia, Stephen Hill, and Riccardo Peccei. (1997). "Checking out Service: Evaluating Excellence, HRM and TQM in Retailing." *Work, Employment and Society, 11* (3), 481–503.

Schmitt, R., and T.E. Moody. (1994). *Alienation and Social Criticism*. Atlantic Highlands, NJ: Humanities Press.

Shain, Alan. (1995). "Employment of People with Disabilities." *Canadian Social Trends* (Autumn), 8–13.

Shalla, Vivian. (2002). "Jettisoned by Design? The Truncated Employment Relationship of Customer Sales and Service Agents under Airline Restructuring." *Canadian Review of Sociology and Anthropology, 27* (1), 1–32.

Shields, Margot. (2002). "Shift Work and Health." *Health Reports, 13* (4), 11–33. Statistics Canada Catalogue no. 82-003.

Shields, Margot. (2003). "The Health of Canada's Shift Workers. *Canadian Social Trends* (Summer), 21–25. Statistics Canada Catalogue no. 11-008.

Smith, Michael. (1999). "Insecurity in the Labour Market: The Case of Canada since the Second World War." *Canadian Journal of Sociology, 24* (2), 193–224.

Smith, Vicki. (2001). *Crossing the Great Divide: Worker Risk and Opportunity in the New Economy*. Ithaca and Cornell: IRL Press.

Spenner, Kenneth. (1983). "Deciphering Prometheus: Temporal Change in the Skill Level of Work." *American Sociological Review, 48* (6), 824–37.

Statistics Canada. (2003). "The Changing Profile of Canada's Labour Force." *2001 Census: Analysis Series*. Ottawa: Ministry of Industry (Catalogue no. 96F0030XIE2001009).

Statistics Canada. (2004a). "Changes in Employment, by Industry." *The Canadian Labour Market at a Glance, 2003*. Ottawa: Ministry of Industry. Catalogue No. 71-222-XIE.

Statistics Canada. (2004b). *Canada E-book*. On the World Wide Web at http://142.206.72.67/r000_e.htm (22 September 2006).

Statistics Canada. (2006a). "The Canadian Labour Market at a Glance, 2005." Ottawa: Industry Canada (Catalogue no. 71-222-XIE).

Statistics Canada. (2006b). "Latest Release from the Labour Force Survey." *The Daily* 4 August. On the World Wide Web at http://www.statcan.ca/english/Subjects/Labour/LFS/lfs-en.htm (22 September 2006).

Statistics Canada. (2009). "The Canadian Labour Market at a Glance, 2007." Ottawa: Industry Canada (Catalogue no. 71-222-X).

Toffler, Alvin. (1980). *The Third Wave*. New York: Bantam.

Usalcas, Jeannine. (2008). "Hours Polarization Revisited." *Perspectives on Labour Market and Income*, (March), 5–15. (Statistics Canada Catalogue no. 75-001X).

Vosko, Leah. (2000). *Temporary Work: The Gendered Rise of a Precarious Employment Relationship*. Toronto: University of Toronto Press.

Wallace, Michael. (1989). "Brave New Workplace: Technology and Work in the New Economy." *Work and Occupations, 16* (4), 393–415.

White, Julie. (1993). "Patterns of Unionization." In Linda Briskin and Patricia McDermott, eds., *Women Challenging Unions: Feminism, Democracy and Militancy* (pp. 191–206). Toronto: University of Toronto Press.

Williams, Cara. (2008). "Work-Life Balance of Shift Workers" *Perspectives on Labour and Income, 9* (8), 5–16 (Statistics Canada Catalogue no. 75-001-X).

Womack, J., D. Jones, and D. Roos. (1990). *The Machine That Changed the World*. New York: Rawson and Associates.

Yakubovich, Valery. (2005). "Weak Ties, Information and Influence: How Workers Find Jobs in a Local Russian Labor Market." *American Sociological Review, 70* (3), 408–21.

Zuboff, Shoshana. (1988). *In the Age of the Smart Machine: The Future of Work and Power*. New York: Basic Books.

CHAPTER 12

Adler, Patricia A., and Peter Adler. (1994). "Reproduction of the Corporate Other: The Institutionalization of After-School Activities." *Sociological Quarterly, 35* (2), 309–28.

Alexander, Karl L., Doris Entwisle, and Linda Steffel Olsen. (2007). "Lasting Consequence of the Summer Learning Gap." *American Sociological Review, 72*, 167–80.

American Association of University Women Educational Foundation. (1998). *Gender Gaps: Where Schools Still Fail Our Children*. American Institutes of Research. Washington, DC: AAUW Educational Foundation.

Anglin, P. M., and R. Meng. (2000). "Evidence on grades and grade inflation at Ontario's universities." *Canadian Public Policy, 26*, 361–68.

Anisef, P. (1974). *The Critical Juncture*. Toronto: Ministry of Colleges and Universities.

Arai, A. Bruce. (2000). "Changing Motivations for Homeschooling in Canada." *Canadian Journal of Education, 25* (3), 204–17.

Aurini, Janice. (2002). "Fostering the Unique Child: New Trends in Childrearing, A Case Study." Unpublished paper, McMaster University.

Aurini, Janice. (2004). "Educational Entrepreneurialism in the Private Tutoring Industry: Balancing Profitability with the Humanistic Face of Schooling." *Canadian Review of Sociology and Anthropology, 41* (4), 475–91.

Aurini, Janice, and Scott Davies. (2004). "The Transformation of Private Tutoring: Education in a Franchise Form." *Canadian Journal of Sociology, 29* (3), 419–38.

Aurini, Janice, and Scott Davies. (2005). "Choice without Markets: Homeschooling in Context of Private Education." *British Journal of Sociology of Education, 26* (4).

Axelrod, Paul. (1997). *The Promise of Schooling: Education in Canada, 1800–1914*. Toronto: University of Toronto Press.

Becker, Gary. (1964). *Human Capital,* 2nd ed. New York: Columbia University Press.

Bennett DeMarrais, Kathleen, and Margaret D. LeCompte. (1995). *The Way Schools Work: A Sociological Analysis of Education,* 2nd ed. White Plains, NY: Longman.

Blossfeld, H.P., and Y. Shavit. (1993). "Persisting Barriers: Changes in Educational Opportunities in Thirteen Countries." In Y. Shavit and H.P. Blossfeld, eds., *Persistent Inequality: Changing Educational Attainment in Thirteen Countries.* Boulder, CO: Westview.

Borja, Rhea R. (2005). "Growing Niche for Tutoring Chains: Prekindergartners' Academic Prep." *Education Week, 25* (8), 19 October: 10.

Bosetti, Lynn. (2001). "The Alberta Charter School Experience." In Claudia R. Hepburn, ed. *Can the Market Save Our Schools?* (pp. 101–20). Vancouver: The Fraser Institute.

Bowles, Samuel, and Herbert Gintis. (1976). *Schooling in Capitalist America: Educational Reform and the Contradictions of Economic Life.* New York: Basic Books.

Brint, Steven, M.F. Contreras, and M.T. Matthews. (2001). "Socialization Messages in Primary Schools: An Organizational Analysis." *Sociology of Education, 74,* 157–80.

Buchmann, Claudia, Thomas A. DiPrete and Ann McDaniel. (2008). "Gender Inequalities in Education." *Annual Review of Sociology, 34,* 319–37.

Burkam, David, Douglas Ready, Valerie Lee, and Laura LoGerfo. (2004). "Social Class Differences in Summer Learning between Kindergarten and First Grade: Model Specification and Estimation" *Sociology of Education, 77,* 1–31.

Canadian Council on Learning. (2007). *2007 Survey of Canadians' Attitudes Towards Learning: Results for Elementary and Secondary Learning.* Ottawa: Author.

Chubb, John E., and Terry M. Moe. (1990). *Politics, Markets and America's Schools.* Washington, DC: The Brookings Institution.

Cohen, Albert. (1955). *Delinquent Boys: The Culture of the Gang.* Glencoe, IL: Free Press.

Coleman, James. (1961). *The Adolescent Society.* New York: Free Press.

Collins, R. (1979). *The Credential Society.* New York: Academic Press.

Côté, James, and Anton Allohar. (2006). *Ivory Tower Blues: A University System in Crisis.* Toronto: University of Toronto Press.

Daly, Kerry. (2004). *The Changing Culture of Parenting.* Ottawa: Vanier Institute for the Family.

Davies, Lynn. (1984). *Pupil Power: Deviance and Gender in School.* London: Falmer Press.

Davies, Scott. (1992). *In Search of the Culture Clash: Explaining Class Inequalities in Education.* Doctoral Dissertation, Department of Sociology, University of Toronto.

Davies, Scott. (2004). "Stubborn Disparities: Explaining Class Inequalities in Schooling." In James Curtis, Edward Grabb, and Neil Guppy, eds., *Social Inequality in Canada: Patterns, Problems, and Policies,* 4th ed. (pp. 138–150), Toronto: Prentice Hall.

Davies, Scott, and Neil Guppy. (1997). "Fields of Study, College Selectivity, and Student Inequalities." *Social Forces, 73* (4), 131–51.

Davies, Scott, and Neil Guppy. (2006). *The Schooled Society: An Introduction to the Sociology of Education.* Toronto: Oxford University Press.

Davies, Scott, and Floyd Hammack. (2005). "Channelling Competition in Higher Education: Comparing Canada and the US." *Journal of Higher Education, 76* (1), 89–106.

Davies, Scott, and Linda Quirke. (2005). "Providing for the Priceless Student: Ideologies of Choice in an Emerging Educational Market" *American Journal of Education 111* (4), 596–608.

De Broucker, Patrice, and Laval Lavallée. (1998). "Getting Ahead in Life: Does Your Parents' Education Count?" *Education Quarterly Review, 5* (1), 22–28.

Dei, George. (2005). "The Case for Black Schools." *Toronto Star* 4 February.

Dennison, John D., ed. (1995). *Canada's Community Colleges at the Crossroads.* Vancouver: UBC Press.

Downey, Douglas, and James Ainsworth-Darnell. (2002). "The Search for Oppositional Culture among Black Students." *American Sociological Review, 67,* 156–64.

Downey, Douglas B., Paul T. von Hippel, and Beckett A. Broh. (2004). "Are Schools the Great Equalizer? Cognitive Inequality During the Summer Months and the School Year." *American Sociological Review, 69* (5), 613–35.

Dreeben, Robert. (1967). *On What Is Learned in School.* Reading, MA: Addison-Wesley.

Durkheim, Émile. (1961 [1925]). *Moral Education: A Study in the Theory and Application of the Sociology of Education.* New York: Free Press.

Fordham, Signithia, and John Ogbu. (1986). "Black Students' School Success: Coping with the 'Burden' of 'Acting White.'" *The Urban Review, 18,* 176–206.

Frenette, Marc. (2005). "The Impact of Tuition Fees on University Access: Evidence from a Large-Scale Price Deregulation in Professional Programs." Ottawa: Statistics Canada. Catalogue No. 11F00119MIE.

Frenette, Marc, and Klarka Zeman. 2008. "Why are the Majority of University Students Women?" *Education Matters, 5*(1).

Gamoran, Adam. (2001). "American Schooling and Educational Inequality: A Forecast for the 21st Century." *Sociology of Education* (extra issue), 135–53.

Gardner, Howard. (1998). "A Multiplicity of Intelligences." [Special Issue]. *Scientific American 9* (4), 18–23.

Gardner, Howard. (1999). *Intelligence Reframed: Multiple Intelligences for the 21st Century.* New York: Basic Books.

Gardner, Howard, and T. Hatch. (1989). "Multiple Intelligences Go to School: Educational Implications of the Theory of Multiple Intelligences." *Educational Researcher, 18* (8), 4–10.

Government of Ontario. (1950). *Aims of Education: Report of the Royal Commission on Education in Ontario (The Hope Report).* Toronto: The King's Printer.

Guppy, Neil, and Bruce Arai. (1994). "Teaching Sociology: Comparing Undergraduate Curricula in the Unted States and Canada." *Teaching Sociology, 22,* 217–30.

Holland, D. C., and M. Eisenhart. (1990). *Educated in Romance: Women, Achievement, and College Culture.* Chicago: University of Chicago Press.

Hurn, C. J. (1993). *The Limits and Possibilities of Schooling: An Introduction to the Sociology of Education.* Boston: Allyn and Bacon.

Jackson, Philip W., Robert E. Boostrom, and David T. Hansen. (1998). *The Moral Life of Schools.* San Francisco: John Wiley and Sons.

Kelly, Gail, and Ann Nihlen. (1982). "Schooling and the Reproduction of Patriarchy: Unequal Workloads, Unequal Rewards." In Michael Apple, ed., *Cultural and Economic Reproduction in American Education: Essays in Class, Ideology, and the State* (pp. 162–80). London, UK: Routledge.

Kerckhoff, Alan C. (2002). "The Transition from School to Work." In Jeylan Mortimer and Reed W. Larson (eds.), *The Changing Adolescent Experience* (pp. 52–87). New York: Cambridge University Press.

Kingston, P. W., R.. Hubbard, B. Lapp, P. Schroeder, and J. Wilson. (2003). "Why Education Matters." *Sociology of Education, 76* (1), 53–70.

Kirp, David. L. (2004). *Shakespeare, Einstein and the Bottom Line: The Marketing of Higher Education.* Cambridge MA: Harvard University Press.

Knighton, T. (2002). "Postsecondary Participation: The Effects of Parents' Education and Household Income." *Education Quarterly Review, 8* (3), 25–31.

Krahn, Harvey. (2004). "Social Class, Postsecondary Education, and Occupational Outcomes: Choose Your Parents Well." In James E. Curtis, E. E. Grabb, and N. Guppy., eds., *Social Inequality in Canada: Patterns, Problems, Policies,* 4th ed. (pp. 187–203). Scarborough, ON: Pearson Prentice-Hall.

Krahn, Harvey and Alison Taylor. (2007). "Streaming in the 10th Grade in Four Canadian Provinces in 2000." *Education Matters,* 4(2).

Lewis, Amanada, ed. (2003). *Race in the Schoolyard: Negotiating the Color Line in Classrooms and Communities.* New Brunswick, NJ: Rutgers University Press.

Livingstone, David W. (1998). *The Education-Jobs Gap: Underemployment or Economic Democracy.* Boulder, CO: Westview Press

Looker, Diane, and Victor Thiessen. (1999). "Images of Work: Women's Work, Men's Work, Housework." *Canadian Journal of Sociology, 24* (2), 225–51.

Maclean's. (2005). "Guide to Canadian Universities 05: Your Complete Handbook for Choosing a University."

Milner, Murray, Jr. (2004). *Freaks, Geeks, and Cool Kids: American Teenagers, Schools, and the Culture of Consumption.* London, UK: Routledge.

Mullen, Ann. (Forthcoming). *Degrees of Inequality: Culture, Class and Gender in American Higher Education.* Baltimore: Johns Hopkins University Press.

Ontario Department of Education. (1968). *Living and Learning: The Report of the Provincial Committee on the Aims and Objectives of Education in the Schools of Ontario.* Toronto: Author.

Ontario Human Rights Commission. (2003). *The Ontario Safe Schools Act: School Discipline and Discrimination.* Ottawa: Author. On the World Wide Web at http://www.ohrc.on.ca/english /consultations/safe-schools.pdf (20 September 2005).

Ouchi, William. (2003). *Making Schools Work: A Revolutionary Plan to Get Your Children the Education They Need.* New York: Simon and Schuster.

Pallas, A. (2000). "The Effects of Schooling on Individual Lives. In M. T. Hallinan, ed., *Handbook of the Sociology of Education* (pp. 499–525). New York: Kluwer Academic/Plenum Publishers

Porter, J., M. Porter, and B. Blishen. (1982). *Stations and Callings: Making It through the School System.* Toronto: Methuen.

Powell, A. G., E. Farrar, and D. K. Cohen. (1985). T*he Shopping Mall High School: Winners and Losers in the Educational Marketplace.* Boston: Houghton Mifflin.

Prentice, A. (1977). *The School Promoters.* Toronto: McClelland and Stewart.

Quirke, Linda. (2006). "'Keeping Young Minds Sharp': Children's Cognitive Stimulation and the Rise of Parenting Magazines, 1959–2003." *Canadian Review of Sociology, 43* (4), 387–406.

Ryan, B. A., and Adams, G. R. (1999). "How do Families Affect Children's Success in School?" *Education Quarterly Review, 6* (1), 30–43.

Sayer, L. C., S. M. Bianchi, and J. P. Robinson. (2004). "Are Parents Investing Less in Children? Trends in Mothers' and Fathers' Time with Children." *American Journal of Sociology, 107,* 1–43.

Shaienks, Danielle, and Tomasz Gluszynski. (2007). "Participation in Postsecondary Education: Graduates, Continuers and Dropouts, Results from YITS Cycle 4." Ottawa: Minister of Industry.

Slaughter, Sheila, and Gary Rhoades. (2004). *Academic Capitalism and the New Economy.* Baltimore: Johns Hopkins University Press.

Solomon, R. Patrick. (1992). *Black Resistance in High School: Forging a Separatist Culture.* Albany, NY: SUNY Press.

Statistics Canada. (2001). *Education in Canada, 2000.* Ottawa: Ministry of Industry.

Stevens, Mitchell L., Elizabeth A. Armstrong, and Richard Arum. (2008). "Sieve, Incubator, Temple, Hub: Empirical and Theoretical Advances in the Sociology of Higher Education." *Annual Review of Sociology, 34,* 127–51.

Stinchcombe, Arthur. (1964). *Rebellion in a High School.* Chicago: Quadrangle Books.

Statistics Canada. (2002). *Survey of Approaches to Educational Planning.* Public Use Microdata File.

Statistics Canada. (2008). "University Degrees, Diplomas and Certificates Granted, by Program Level, Classification of Instructional Programs, Primary Grouping (CIP_PG) and Sex, Annual (Number), CANSIM (Database)," Table 477-0014.

Tanner, Julian. (2001). *Teenage Troubles: Youth and Deviance in Canada,* 2nd ed. Toronto: Nelson Thomson Learning.

Taylor, A., and L. Woollard. (2003). "The Risky Business of Choosing a High School." *Journal of Education Policy 18* (6), 617–35.

Turner, Ralph H. (1960). "Sponsored and Contest Mobility and School System." *American Sociological Review, 25,* 855–67.

Tyack, David B. (1974). *The One Best System: A History of American Urban Education.* Cambridge, MA: Harvard University Press.

Tyack, David, and Larry Cuban. (1995). *Tinkering toward Utopia: A Century of Public School Reform.* Cambridge, MA: Harvard University Press.

Tyson, Karolyn, William Darity, Jr., and Domini Castellino. (2005). "It's Not a Black Thing: Understanding the Burden of Acting White and Other Dilemmas of High Achievement." *American Sociological Review, 70* (4), 582–605.

Walters, David. (2004). "'Recycling': The Economic Implications of Obtaining Additional Postsecondary Credentials at Lower or Equivalent Levels." *Canadian Review of Sociology and Anthropology, 40* (4), 463–77.

Wanner, Richard. (2000). "Expansion and Ascription: Trends in Educational Opportunity in Canada 1920–1994." *Canadian Review of Sociology and Anthropology, 36* (3), 409–43.

Weis, L. (1990). *Working Class without Work: High School Students in a De-industrializing Economy*. New York: Routledge.

Willis, Paul. (1977). *Learning to Labour: How Working Class Kids Get Working Class Jobs*. Saxon House: Westmead.

Wolf, Alison. (2002). *Does Education Matter? Myths about Education and Economic Growth*. London: Penguin.

CHAPTER 13

Bell, Daniel. (1977). "The Return of the Sacred: The Argument on the Future of Religion." *British Journal of Sociology, 28*, 419–49.

Bellah, Robert. (1967). "Civil Religion in America." *Daedalus, 96*, 1–21.

Berger, Peter. (1961). *The Noise of Solemn Assemblies*. New York: Doubleday.

Berger, Peter L. (1974). "Some Second Thoughts on Substantive Versus Functional Definitions of Religion. *Journal for the Scientific Study of Religion, 13*, 125–33.

Beyer, Peter. (1993). "Roman Catholicism in Contemporary Quebec." In W. E. Hewitt, ed., *The Sociology of Religion: A Canadian Focus* (pp. 133–55). Toronto: Butterworths.

Beyer, Peter. (1997). "Religious Vitality in Canada: The Complementarity of Religious Market and Secularization Perspectives." *Journal for the Scientific Study of Religion, 36*, 272–88.

Bibby, Reginald W. (1987). *Fragmented Gods: The Poverty and Potential of Religion in Canada*. Toronto: Stoddart.

Bibby, Reginald W. (1993). *Unknown Gods: The Ongoing Story of Religion in Canada*. Toronto: Stoddart.

Bibby, Reginald W. (1994). *Unitrends*. Toronto: United Church of Canada, Department of Stewardship Services.

Bibby, Reginald W. (1995). *The Bibby Report: Social Trends Canadian Style*. Toronto: Stoddart.

Bibby, Reginald W. (1999). *The Alliance Future Survey*. Toronto: Christian and Missionary Alliance.

Bibby, Reginald W. (2004a). *Restless Gods: The Renaissance of Religion in Canada*. Ottawa: Novalis.

Bibby, Reginald W. (2004b). *Restless Churches. How Canada's Churches Can Contribute to the Emerging Religious Renaissance*. Ottawa: Novalis.

Bibby, Reginald W. (2005). "The Untold Story of the Role of Women in the Fall and Rise of Religion in Canada." Presented at the annual meeting of the Pacific Sociological Association, Portland, Oregon, April.

Bibby, Reginald W. (2009). *The Emerging Millennials*. Lethbridge: Project Canada Books.

Brannon, Robert. (1971). "Organizational Vulnerability in Modern Religious Organizations." *Journal for the Scientific Study of Religion, 10*, 27–32.

Brown, Callum. (2001). *The Death of Christian Britain*. London: Routledge.

Brym, Robert, and Bader Araj. (2006). "Suicide Bombing as Strategy and Interaction: The Case of the Second *Intifada*," *Social Forces, 84*, 1965–82.

Catto, Susan. (2003). "In Search of the Spiritual." *Time* 24 November: 72–80.

Clark, S. D. (1948). *Church and Sect in Canada*. Toronto: University of Toronto Press.

Cogley, John. (1968). *Religion in a Secular Age*. New York: New American Library.

Crysdale, Stewart. (1961). *The Industrial Struggle and Protestant Ethics in Canada*. Toronto: Ryerson Press.

Davies, Alan, and Marilyn F. Nefsky. (1997). *How Silent Were the Churches? Canadian Protestantism and the Jewish Plight during the Nazi Era*. Waterloo, ON: Wilfrid Laurier University Press.

Dawson, Lorne L. (2006). *Comprehending Cults: The Sociology of New Religious Movements*. Toronto: Oxford University Press.

Durkheim, Émile. (1965 [1912]). *The Elementary Forms of the Religious Life*. New York: Free Press.

Fallding, Harold. (1978). "Mainline Protestantism in Canada and the United States: An Overview." *Canadian Journal of Sociology, 2*, 141–60.

Finke, Roger, and Rodney Stark. (1992). *The Churching of America, 1776–1990*. New Brunswick, NJ: Rutgers University Press.

Frankel, B. Gail, and W. E. Hewitt. (1994). "Religion and Well-Being among Canadian University Students." *Journal for the Scientific Study of Religion, 33*, 62–73.

Freud, Sigmund. (1962 [1928]). *The Future of an Illusion*. New York: Doubleday.

Gallup. (2006). *Religion*. Poll released January 25.

Gee, Ellen M., and Jean E. Veevers. (1990). "Religious Involvement and Life Satisfaction in Canada." *Sociological Analysis, 51*, 387–94.

Gerth, H., and C. Wright Mills. (1958). *From Max Weber: Essays in Sociology*. New York: Oxford University Press.

Ghafour, Hamida. (2006). "Muslim Fury over Cartoons Hits Britain." *The Globe and Mail* 4 February.

Glock, Charles, Benjamin Ringer, and Earl Babbie. (1967). *To Comfort and to Challenge*. Berkeley, CA: University of California Press.

Glock, Charles Y., and Rodney Stark. (1965). *Religion and Society in Tension*. Chicago: Rand-McNally.

Gorsuch, Richard, and Daniel Aleshire. (1974). "Christian Faith and Ethnic Prejudice: A Review and Interpretation of Research." *Journal for the Scientific Study of Religion, 13*, 281–307.

Graham, Ron. (1990). *God's Dominion: A Sceptic's Quest*. Toronto: McClelland and Stewart.

Herberg, Will. (1960). *Protestant, Catholic, Jew*, rev. ed. New York: Doubleday.

Hobart, Charles. (1974). "Church Involvement and the Comfort Thesis." *Journal for the Scientific Study of Religion, 13*, 463–70.

Johnson, Benton. (1961). "Do Holiness Sects Socialize in Dominant Values?" *Social Forces, 39*, 309–16.

Kiefer, Heather Mason. (2004). "Divine Subjects: Canadians Believe, Britons Skeptical." Washington: The Gallup Poll.

Kirkpatrick, Clifford. (1949). "Religion and Humanitarianism: A Study of Institutional Implications." *Psychological Monographs, 63* (9).

Lee, Gary, and Robert Clyde. (1974). "Religion, Socioeconomic Status, and Anomie." *Journal for the Scientific Study of Religion, 13*, 35–47.

Lewis, David L. (1993). "Canada's Native Peoples and the Churches." In W.E. Hewitt, ed., *The Sociology of Religion: A Canadian Focus* (pp. 235–51). Toronto: Butterworths.

Mann, W. E. (1962). *Sect, Cult, and Church in Alberta*. Toronto: University of Toronto Press.

Marx, Karl. (1970 [1843]). *Critique of Hegel's "Philosophy of Right."* Trans. Annette Jolin and Joseph O'Malley. Cambridge, MA: Harvard University Press.

Marx, Karl, and Friedrich Engels. (1964). *On Religion*. New York: Schocken Books.

Metz, Donald. (1967). *New Congregations: Security and Mission in Conflict.* Philadelphia: Westminster Press.

Monahan, Susanne C. (1999). "Who Controls Church Work? Organizational Effects on Jurisdictional Boundaries and Disputes in Churches." *Journal for the Scientific Study of Religion, 38,* 370–85.

Nason-Clark, N. (1993). "Gender Relations in Contemporary Christian Organizations," in W.E. Hewitt, ed., *The Sociology of Religion* (pp. 215–34). Toronto: Butterworth.

Nesbitt, P. D. (1997). *The Feminization of the Clergy in America.* New York: Oxford University Press.

Niebuhr, H. Richard. (1957 [1929]). *The Social Sources of Denominationalism.* New York: Henry Holt and Co.

O'Toole, Roger, Douglas F. Campbell, John A. Hannigan, Peter Beyer, and John H. Simpson. (1993). "The United Church in Crisis." In W. E. Hewitt, ed., *The Sociology of Religion: A Canadian Focus* (pp. 273–87). Toronto: Butterworths.

Poloma, Margaret M. (1997). "The 'Toronto Blessing': Charisma, Institutionalization and Revival." *Journal for the Scientific Study of Religion, 36,* 257–71.

Poloma, Margaret M., and Lynette F. Hoelter. (1998). "The 'Toronto Blessing': A Holistic Model of Healing." *Journal for the Scientific Study of Religion, 37,* 257–72.

Ray, Julie. (2003). "Worlds Apart: Religion in Canada, Britain, U.S." Washington: The Gallup Poll.

Reimer, Sam. (2003). *Evangelicals and the Continental Divide.* Montreal: McGill–Queen's University Press.

Reimer, Samuel H. (1995). "A Look at Cultural Effects on Religiosity: A Comparison between the United States and Canada." *Journal for the Scientific Study of Religion, 34,* 445–57.

Rokeach, Milton. (1965). *Paradoxes of Religious Belief.* Information Service, National Council of Churches, 1–2.

Rokeach, Milton. (1969). "Religious Values and Social Compassion." *Review of Religious Research, 11,* 3–23.

Roof, Wade Clark, and Dean R. Hoge. (1980). "Church Involvement in America: Social Factors Affecting Membership and Participation." *Review of Religious Research, 21,* 405–26.

Rouleau, Jean-Paul. (1977). "Religion in Quebec: Present and Future." *Pro Mundi Vita: Dossiers, 3* (November–December).

Shackleton, Eric. (2005). "Pastors and Priests Face Ever More Empty Seats in 2006." Canadian Press Newswire, 20 December.

Smith, Tom W. (1999). "The Religious Right and Anti-Semitism." *Review of Religious Research, 99,* 244–58.

Speaker-Yuan, Margaret, ed. (2005). *Women in Islam.* Detroit: Greenhaven Press/Thomson-Gale.

Stackhouse, John G., Jr. (2005). *Finally Feminist: A Pragmatic Christian Understanding of Gender.* Grand Rapids, MI: Baker Academic.

Stahl, William. (1986). "The Land That God Gave Cain: Nature and Civil Religion in Canada." Presented at the annual meeting of the Society for the Scientific Study of Religion, Washington, DC, November.

Stark, Rodney, and William Sims Bainbridge. (1985). *The Future of Religion.* Berkeley, CA: University of California Press.

Stark, Rodney, and Roger Finke. (2000). *Acts of Faith: Explaining the Human Side of Religion.* Berkeley, CA: University of California Press.

Stark, Rodney, and Charles Y. Glock. (1968). *American Piety.* Berkeley, CA: University of California Press.

Statistics Canada. (2003). *2001 Census: Analysis Series—Religions in Canada.* Ottawa: Minister of Industry. Catalogue no. 96F0030XIE2002015.

Statistics Canada. (2004a). "General Social Survey: Social Engagement. *The Daily* 6 July.

Statistics Canada. (2004b). National Survey of Non-profit and Voluntary Organizations. *The Daily* 20 September.

Stiller, Brian. (1997). *From the Tower of Babel to Parliament Hill.* Toronto: HarperCollins.

Thomas, W.I., and Florian Znaniecki. (1918). *The Polish Peasant in Europe and America.* New York: Knopf.

Valpy, Michael. (2006). "Why the Global Rage Hasn't Engulfed Canada: Multiculturalism and Media Likely Muted Protests." *The Globe and Mail* 8 February: A14.

Weber, Max. (1958 [1904–05]). *The Protestant Ethic and the Spirit of Capitalism.* New York: Scribner's.

Weber, Max. (1963 [1922]). *The Sociology of Religion.* Trans. Ephraim Fischoff. Boston: Beacon Press.

Whyte, Donald. (1966). "Religion and the Rural Church." In M. A. Tremblay and W. J. Anderson, eds., *Rural Canada in Transition* (pp. 79–92). Ottawa: Agricultural Economics Research Council of Canada.

Wilcox, W. Bradford. (1998). "Conservative Protestant Childrearing: Authoritarian or Authoritative?" *American Sociological Review, 63,* 796–809.

Winseman, Albert L. (2004). *Britons Lack American Cousin's Piety.* Washington, DC: The Gallup Poll.

Winseman, Albert L. (2005). *Who Has Been Born Again?* Washington, DC: The Gallup Poll.

CHAPTER 14

Adler, Freda. (1975). *Sisters in Crime.* New York: McGraw-Hill.

Agnew, Robert. (1992). "Foundation for a General Theory of Crime and Delinquency," *Criminology, 30,* 47–87.

Becker, Howard. (1963). *Outsiders: Studies in the Sociology of Deviance.* New York: Free Press.

Ben-Yehuda, Nachman. (1986). "The Sociology of Moral Panics: Toward a New Synthesis," *Sociological Quarterly, 4,* 495–513.

Brym, Robert, (2009). *The 2006 Census and Canadian Society.* Toronto: Nelson

Chesney-Lind, Meda, Merry Morash, and Katherine Irwin. (2007). "Policing Girlhood? Relational Aggression and Violence Prevention." *Youth Violence and Juvenile Justice, 5* (3), 328–45.

Chibnall, Steve. (1977). *Law and Order News.* London: Tavistock.

Cloward, Richard, and Lloyd Ohlin. (1960). *Delinquency and Opportunity: A Theory of Delinquent Gangs.* New York: Free Press.

Cohen, Albert. (1955). *Delinquent Boys.* Chicago: Free Press.

Cohen, Lawrence, and Marcus Felson. (1979). "Social Change and Crime Rate Trends: A Routine Activity Approach." *American Sociological Review, 44* (August), 588–608.

Conrad, Peter, and Joseph Schneider. (1992). *Deviance and Medicalization.* Philadelphia: Temple University Press.

Cook, Shirley. (1969). "Canadian Narcotics Legislation, 1880–1923: A Conflict Model Interpretation." *Canadian Review of Sociology and Anthropology, 6,* 36–46.

Daigle, Leah, Francis Cullen, and John Paul Wright. (2007). "Gender Differences in the Predictors of Juvenile Delinquency: Assessing the Generality–Specificity Debate." *Youth Violence and Juvenile Justice, 5,* 254–86.

Dauvergne, Mia. (2008). "Crime Statistics in Canada, 2007." Juristat, volume 28, number 7. Statistics Canada Catalogue no. 85-002-X, volume 28, no.7.

Delaney, Joan. (2008). "'Mosquito' Prompts Teens to Buzz Off," *Epoch Times* (Victoria) 6 August.

Doob, Anthony, and Carla Cesaroni. (2004). *Responding to Youth Crime in Canada*. Toronto: University of Toronto Press.

Doob, Anthony, and Jane Sprott. (2004). "Changing Models of Youth Justice in Canada." In M. Tonry and A. Doob, eds., *Youth Crime and Youth Justice: Comparative and Cross-national Perspectives*. Chicago: University of Chicago Press.

Doob, Anthony, and Cheryl Webster. (2003). "Sentence Severity and Crime: Accepting the Null Hypothesis." In Michael Tonry, ed., *Crime and Justice: a Review of Research*, vol. 30 (pp. 143–95).

Felson, Marcus. (2002). *Crime and Everyday Life*, 3rd ed. Thousand Oaks, CA: Pine Forge Press.

Fuller, John, and Wozniak, John. (2006). "Peacemaking Criminology: Part, Present, and Future. In Francis Cullen, John Paul Wright and Kristie Blevins, eds., *Taking Stock* (pp. 251–73). New Brunswick, NJ: Transaction.

Gartner, Rosemary, and Sarah Thompson. (2004). "Trends in Homicide in Toronto." In Bruce Kidd and Jim Phillips, eds., *Research on Community Safety* (pp. 28–41). Toronto: The Centre of Criminology, University of Toronto.

The Geographic Reference Report. (2007). *City Crime Rates.*

Giddens, Anthony. (1991). *Introduction to Sociology*. New York: Norton.

Globe and Mail. (2009). "Cold Blood and Adult Penalties" (editorial). 24 March. On the World Wide Web at http://www.theglobeandmail.com/servlet/story/RTGAM.20090323.weStephanie24/BNStory/specialComment/home (29 March 2009).

Goffman, Erving. (1963). *Stigma: Notes on the Management of Spoiled Identity*. Englewood Cliffs, NJ: Prentice Hall.

Gordon, Robert. (2000). "Criminal Business Organizations, Street Gangs and Wanna-Be Groups: A Vancouver Perspective." *Canadian Journal of Criminology*, 42 (1), 39–60.

Gottfredson, Michael, and Travis Hirschi. (1990). *A General Theory of Crime*. Palo Alto, CA: Stanford University Press.

Grekul, Jana, and Patti LaBoucane-Benson. (2008). "Aboriginal Gangs and Their (Dis)placement: Contextualizing Recruitment, Membership, and Status." *Canadian Journal of Criminology and Criminal Justice*, 50 (1), 59–82.

Hagan, John. (1991). *The Disreputable Pleasures: Crime and Deviance in Canada*, 3rd ed. Toronto: McGraw-Hill Ryerson.

Hagan, John, Ron Gillis, and John Simpson. (1987). "Class in the Household: A Power-Control Theory of Gender and Delinquency." *American Journal of Sociology*, 92, 788–816.

Hagan, John, and Bill McCarthy (1997). *Mean Streets*. Cambridge: Cambridge University Press.

Hartnagel, Tim. (2004). "Correlates of Criminal Behavior." In *Criminology: A Canadian Perspective*, 5th ed. Toronto: Harcourt Brace.

Hier, Sean. (2002). "Raves, Risks and Ecstasy Panic: A Case Study in the Subversive Nature of Moral Regulation." *Canadian Journal of Sociology*, 27 (1), 33–57.

Hirschi, Travis. (1969). *Causes of Delinquency*. Berkeley: University of California Press.

Keane, Carl, Paul Maxim, and James Teevan. (1993). "Drinking and Driving, Self-Control and Gender: Testing the General Theory of Crime." *Journal of Research in Crime and Delinquency*, 30, 30–46.

Krahn, Harvey, Tim Hartnagel, and John Gartrell. (1986). "Income Inequality and Homicide Rates: Cross-National Data and Criminological Theories." *Criminology*, 24, 269–95.

Lawrence, Richard, and David Mueller. (2003). "School Shootings and the Man Bites Dog Criterion of Newsworthiness." *Youth Violence and Youth Justice*, 1 (4), 330–45.

Li, Geoffrey. (2008). *Homicide in Canada, 2007. Juristat, 28* (9). Statistics Canada Catalogue no. 85-002-X.

Link, Bruce. (1982). "Mental Patient Status, Work, and Income: An Examination of the Effects of a Psychiatric Label." *American Sociological Review*, 47, 202–15.

Liska, Allen, and Steven Messner. (1999). *Perspectives on Deviance*, 3rd ed. Englewood Cliffs, NJ: Prentice-Hall.

Merton, Robert. (1938). "Social Structure and Anomie." *American Sociological Review*, 3, 672–87.

Morgan, Rod, and Alison Liebling. (2007). "Imprisonment: An Expanding Scene." In Mike Maguire, Rod Morgan, and Robert Reiner, eds., *The Oxford Handbook of Criminology*, 4th ed. (pp. 1100–1138). New York: Oxford University Press.

Nakhaie, Reza, Robert Silverman, and Teresa LaGrange. (2000). "Self-Control and Resistance to School." *Canadian Review of Sociology and Anthropology*, 37 (4), 444–60.

Newman, K., Cybelle Fox, David Harding, Jal Mehta, and Wendy Roth. (2004). *Rampage: The Social Roots of School Shootings*. New York: Basic Books.

O'Grady, Bill, and Steve Gaetz. (2004). "Homelessness, Gender and Subsistence: The Case of Toronto Street Youth." *Journal of Youth Studies*, 7 (4), 397–416.

Parnaby, Patrick. (2003). "Disaster through Dirty Windshields: Law, Order and Toronto's squeegee Kids." *Canadian Journal of Sociology*, 28 (3), 281–307.

Rayner, Gordon, and John Bingham. (2009). "German Shooting: Gunman Had Failed to Turn up to Therapy." Telegraph.co.uk 13 March. On the World Wide Web at http://www.telegraph.co.uk/news/worldnews/europe/germany/4982556/German-shooting-Gunman-had-failed-to-turn-up-to-therapy.html (29 March 2009).

Reinarman, Craig, and Harry Levine. (1989). "The Crack Attack: Politics and Media in America's Latest Drug Scare." In J. Best, ed., *Images of Issues: Typifying Contemporary Social Problems* (pp. 147–90). New York: Aldine De Gruyter.

Reiner, Robert. (2007). "Media-Made Criminality: The Representation of Crime in the Mass Media." In Mike Maguire, Rod Morgan, and Robert Reiner, eds., *Oxford Handbook of Criminology* (pp. 302–37). New York: Oxford University Press.

Roberts, Julian. (2004). "Public Opinion and the Evolution of Juvenile Justice Policy in Western Nations." In Michael Tonry and Anthony Doob, eds., *Youth Crime and Youth Justice: Comparative and Cross-National Perspectives* (pp.495–542). Chicago: University of Chicago Press.

Robertson, Ian. (1989). *Society: A Brief Introduction*. New York: Worth.

Sacco, Vince. (2005). *When Crime Waves*. Thousand Oaks, CA: Sage.

Sacco, Vince, and Les Kennedy. (2002). *The Criminal Event: An Introduction to Criminology in Canada*, 3rd ed. Toronto: Nelson.

Savoie, Josée. (2006). "Youth Self-Reported Delinquency, Toronto." *Juristat*, 27 (6).

Schissel, Bernard, and Kari Fedec. (2002). "The Selling of Innocence." *Canadian Journal of Criminology*, 41 (1), 33–56.

The Sentencing Project. (2006). "New Incarceration Figures: Thirty-Three Consecutive Years of Growth." On the World Wide Web at http://www.sentencingproject.org/doc/publications/inc_newfigures.pdf (29 March 2009).

Siegel, Larry, and Chris McCormick. (2006). *Criminology in Canada*. Toronto: Nelson.

Simon, Ruth. (1975). *Women and Crime*. Lexington, MA: Lexington Books.

South, Nigel. (2007). "Drugs, Alcohol and Crime." In M. Maguire, R. Morgan, and R. Reiner, eds., *The Oxford Handbook of Criminology*, 4th ed. (pp. 810–40). New York: Oxford University Press.

Sutherland, E. H. (1947). *Principles of Criminology*, 4th ed. Chicago: Lippincott.

Sykes, Gresham. (1958). *Society of Captives: A Study of a Maximum Security Institution*. Princeton: Princeton University Press.

Tanner, J. (2010). *Teenage Troubles: Youth and Deviance in Canada (3rd edition)*. Oxford: Toronto

Tanner, Julian, and Wortley, Scot. (2002). *The Toronto Youth Crime and Victimization Survey*. Toronto: Centre of Criminology, University of Toronto.

Taylor-Butts, Andrea, and Angela Bressan. (2006). "Youth Crime in Canada." *Juristat, 28* (3). Statistics Canada Catalogue no. 85-002-XIE.

Thio, Alex. (2001). *Deviant Behavior*, 6th ed. Boston: Allyn and Bacon.

Vold, George, Thomas Bernard, and Jeffrey Snipes. (2002). *Theoretical Criminology*, 5th ed. New York: Oxford University Press.

Von Hirsch, Andrew, Anthony Bottoms, and Per-Olof Wikstrom. (1999). *Criminal Deterrence: An Analysis of Recent Research*. Oxford: Hart.

Wolf, Daniel. (1991). *The Rebels*. Toronto: University of Toronto Press.

Wortley, Scot, and Julian Tanner. (2004). "Social Groups or Criminal Organizations? The Extent and Nature of Youth Gang Activity in Toronto." in B. Kidd and J. Phillips, eds., *Research on Community Safety*. Toronto: Centre of Criminology, University of Toronto.

Wortley, Scot, and Julian Tanner. (2005). "Inflammatory Rhetoric? Baseless Accusation? A Response to Gabor's Critique of Racial Profiling Research in Canada." *Canadian Journal of Criminology and Criminal Justice, 47* (3), 581–614.

CHAPTER 15

Abu-Lughod, Janet L. (1991). *Changing Cities: Urban Sociology*. New York: HarperCollins.

Beaujot, Roderic. (2004) "Population, Aging, and Health." In Robert J. Brym, ed., *New Society: Sociology for the 21st Century*, 4th ed. (pp. 431–64). Toronto: Nelson.

Bélanger, Alain, and Éric Caron Malenfant. (2005). "Ethnocultural Diversity in Canada: Prospects for 2017." *Canadian Social Trends, 79*, 18–21.

Bell, Wendell. (1968). "The City, the Suburbs and a Theory of Social Choice." In Scott Greer, Dennis McElrath, David W. Minar, and Peter Orleans, eds., *The New Urbanization* (pp. 132–68). New York: St. Martin's Press.

Berger, Bennett. (1960). *Working Class Suburb*. Berkeley, CA: University of California Press.

Berry, Brian J. L., and Quentin Gillard. (1977). *The Changing Shape of Metropolitan America*. Cambridge, MA: Ballinger Publishing Co.

Blumenfeld, Hans. (1982). *Have the Secular Trends of Population Distribution Been Reversed?* Research paper 137. Toronto: Centre of Urban and Community Studies.

Blumenfeld, Hans. (1983). "Metropolis Extended." *Journal of the American Planning Association, 52* (3), 346–48.

Bonner, Kieran. (1997). *A Great Place to Raise Kids: Interpretation, Science, and the Urban-Rural Debate*. Montreal and Kingston: McGill-Queen's University Press.

Bourne, L. S. (1996). "Reinventing the Suburbs: Old Myths and New Realities." *Progress in Planning, 46*, 163–84.

Brym, Robert J. (1986). "An Introduction to the Regional Question in Canada." In Robert J. Brym, ed., *Regionalism in Canada* (pp. 1–45). Toronto: Irwin.

Burgess, Ernest W. (1961). "The Growth of the City: An Introduction to a Research Project." In George A. Theodorson, ed., *Studies in Human Ecology* (pp. 37–44). Evanston, IL: Row, Peterson.

Castells, Manuel. (1989). *The Informational City: Information, Technology, Economic Restructuring and the Urban–Regional Process*. Oxford and Cambridge, MA: Blackwell.

Champion, A. G. (1993) "Urban and Regional Demographic Trends: The Developed World." In Ronan Paddison, Bill Lever, and John Money, eds., *International Perspectives in Urban Studies 1* (pp. 136–59). London and Philadelphia: Jessica Kingsley.

Chandler, Tertius, and Gerald Fox. (1974). *3000 Years of Urban Growth*. New York and London: Academic Press.

Clark, David. (1996). *Urban World, Global City*. London and New York: Routledge.

Davis, Judy S., Arthur C. Nelson, and Kenneth J. Dueher. (1994). "The New 'Burbs: The Exurbs and their Implications for Planning Policy." *Journal of the American Planning Association, 60*, 45–59.

Davis, Kingsley. (1955). "The Origin and Growth of Urbanization in the World," *American Journal of Sociology, 60*, 430.

Davis, Mike. (1990). *City of Quartz: Excavating the Future in Los Angeles*. London and New York: Verso.

De Oliviera, Orlandino, and Bryan Roberts. (1996). "Urban Development and Social Inequality in Latin America." In J. Gugler, ed., *The Urban Transformation of the Developing World* (pp. 250–314). Oxford: Oxford University Press.

Drakakis-Smith, David. (1988). "Third World Cities: Sustainable Urban Development II—Population, Labour and Poverty." In R. Paddison and B. Lever, eds., *International Perspectives in Urban Studies 5* (pp. 70–101). London and Bristol, PA: Jessica Kingsley.

Driedger, Leo. (1991). *The Urban Factor: Sociology of Canadian Cities*. Toronto: Oxford University Press.

Ehrlich, Paul R. (1968). *The Population Bomb*. New York: Ballantine Books.

Epp, Roger, and Dave Whitson. (2001). "Writing Off Rural Communities." In R. Epp and D. Whitson, eds., *Writing Off the Rural West* (pp. xii–xxxv). Edmonton: The University of Alberta Press/Parkland Institute.

Fava, Sylvia Fleis. (1956). "Suburbanism as a Way of Life." *American Sociological Review, 21*, 34–37.

Filion, Pierre. (1991). "The Gentrification–Social Structure Dialectic: A Toronto Case Study." *International Journal of Urban and Regional Research, 15*, 553–74.

Firey, Walter. (1947). *Land Use in Central Boston.* Cambridge, MA: Harvard University Press.

Fishman, Robert. (1987). *Bourgeois Utopias: The Rise and Fall of Suburbia.* New York: Basic Books.

Fishman, Robert. (1990). "Megalopolis Unbound." *The Wilson Quarterly* (Winter), 25–45.

Fishman, Robert. (2005). "Longer View: The Fifth Migration." *Journal of the American Planning Association, 71,* 357–66.

Flanagan, William G. (1995). *Urban Sociology: Images and Structure.* Boston: Allyn and Bacon.

Florence, Elinor. (1997). "A Happy Hoofer Gets On with Life." *The Globe and Mail* 7 January: A18.

Fong, Eric. (1996). "A Comparative Perspective of Racial Residential Segregation: American and Canadian Experiences." *The Sociological Quarterly, 37,* 501–28.

Fong, Eric, and Kumiko Shibuya. (2005). "Multiethnic Cities in North America." *Annual Review of Sociology, 31,* 258–304.

Fong, Eric, and Rima Wilkes. (1999). "The Spatial Assimilation Model Re-examined: An Assessment By Canadian Data." *International Migration Review, 33,* 594–620.

Fowler, Edmund P. (1992). *Building Cities That Work.* Montreal and Kingston, ON: McGill-Queen's University Press.

Frieden, Bernard J., and Lynne B. Sagalyn. (1989). *Downtown, Inc.: How America Rebuilds Cities.* Cambridge, MA: MIT Press.

Garreau, Joel. (1991). *Edge City: Life on the New Frontier.* New York: Doubleday.

Ginsburg, N., B. Koppel, and T. G. McGee, eds. (1991). *The Extended Metropolis: Settlement Transition in Asia.* Honolulu: University of Hawaii Press.

Goldberger, Paul. (1996). "The Rise of the Private City." In Julia Vitullo Martin, ed., *Breaking Away: The Future of Cities* (pp. 135–47). New York: Twentieth Century Fund Press.

Golden, Hilda H. (1981). *Urbanization and Cities.* Lexington, MA: Heath.

Gordon, Ian, and Saskia Sassen. (1992). "Restructuring the Urban Labor Markets." In Susan S. Fainstein, Ian Gordon, and Michael Harloe, eds., *Divided Cities: New York and London in the Contemporary World* (pp. 105–28). Oxford and Cambridge, MA: Blackwell.

Grant, Jill. (2005). "The Function of the Gates: The Social Construction of Security in Gated Developments." *Town Planning Review, 76,* 291–313.

Gugler, Josef. (1996). "Preface." In J. Gugler, ed., *The Urban Transformation of the Developing World.* Oxford: Oxford University Press.

Hannigan, John A. (1995). "The Postmodern City: A New Urbanization?" *Current Sociology, 43* (1), 180.

Harris, Chauncey, and Edward Ullman. (1945). "The Nature of Cities." *Annals of the American Academy of Political and Social Science, 242* (November), 7–17.

Hauser, Philip M. (1965). "Urbanization: An Overview." In Philip M. Hauser and Leo F. Schnore, eds., *The Study of Urbanization.* New York: Wiley.

Heisz, Andrew, and Sébastien LaRochelle-Coté. (2005). "Getting to Work." *Canadian Social Trends, 79* (Winter), 16.

Hou, Feng, and Garnett Picot. (2004). "Visible Minority Neighbourhoods in Toronto, Montréal, and Vancouver." *Canadian Social Trends, 72,* 8–13.

Hoyt, Homer. (1939). *The Structure and Growth of Residential Neighborhoods in American Cities.* Washington, DC: Federal Housing Authority.

Jackson, Kenneth T. (1985). *Crabgrass Frontier: The Suburbanization of the United States.* New York: Oxford University Press.

Kleniewski, Nancy. (1997). *Cities, Change and Conflict: A Political Economy of Urban Life.* Belmont, CA: Wadsworth.

Kremarik, Frances. (2000). "Urban Development." *Canadian Social Trends, 59,* 18–22.

Leinberger, Christopher B., and Charles Lockwood. (1986). "How Business Is Reshaping America." *The Atlantic Monthly* October: 43–52.

Ley, David. (1991). "Gentrification." In Kent Gerecke, ed., *The Canadian City* (pp. 181–96). Montreal: Black Rose Books.

Little, Bruce. (1999). "Tale of Three Canadian Cities: What Makes Them Grow So Big." *The Globe and Mail* 20 September: A20.

Lofchie, Michael F. (1997). "The Rise and Demise of Urban-Biased Developmental Policies in Africa." In Josef Gugler, ed., *Cities in the Developing World: Issues, Theory and Policy* (pp. 23–39). Oxford: Oxford University Press.

Logan, John R., Richard D. Alba, and Wenquan Zhang. (2002). Immigrant Enclaves and Ethnic Communities in New York and Los Angeles." *American Sociological Review, 67,* 299–322.

Logan, John R., and Harvey L. Molotch. (1987). *Urban Fortunes: The Political Economy of Place.* Berkeley, CA: University of California Press.

Lorimer, James. (1978). *The Developers.* Toronto: Lorimer.

Malthus, T. R. (1798). *An Essay on the Principle of Population, as It Affects the Future Improvement of Society. With Remarks on the Speculations of Mr. Godwin, M. Condorcet and Other Writers.* London: J. Johnson.

McGahan, Peter. (1995). *Urban Sociology in Canada,* 3rd ed. Toronto: Harcourt Brace.

McGee, T. G. (1991). "The Emergence of Deschata Regions in Asia." In N. Ginsberg, B. Koppel and T. G. McGee, eds., *The Extended Metropolis* (pp. 3–25). Honolulu: University of Hawaii Press.

McQuillan, Kevin. (1994). "Population." In Robert Hagedorn, ed., *Sociology,* 5th ed. Toronto: Harcourt Brace and Company.

Michelson, William D. (1973). *Environmental Change.* Research Paper No. 60, Centre for Urban and Community Studies, University of Toronto.

Montgomery, Shannon. (2008). "Avalanche Survivors Devastated by 7 Deaths." *Toronto Star* 30 December: A1, A4.

Nader, George A. (1975). *Cities of Canada, Volume One: Theoretical, Historical and Planning Perspectives.* Toronto: Macmillan.

Ness, Gayl D., and Michael M. Low. (2000). *Modelling Asian Urban Population—Environment Dynamics.* Singapore: Oxford University Press.

Palen, J. John. (1995). *The Suburbs.* New York: McGraw-Hill.

Reid, Barton. (1991). "A Primer on the Corporate City." In Kent Gerecke, ed., *The Canadian City* (pp. 63–78). Montreal: Black Rose.

Reynolds, Malvina. (1964). *Little Boxes and Other Handmade Songs.* New York: Oak.

Roberts, Lance W., Rodney A. Clifton, Barry Ferguson, Karen Kampen, and Simon Langlois. (2005). *Recent Social Trends in Canada.* Montreal and Kingston: McGill-Queen's University Press.

Rose, D. (1984). "Rethinking Gentrification: Beyond the Uneven Development of Marxist Urban Theory." *Environment and Planning D: Society and Space, 2* (1), 47–74.

Sanchez, T. W., R. E. Lang, and D. M. Dhavale. (2005). "Security Versus Status? A First Look at the Census's Gated Community Data." *Journal of Planning Education and Research, 24,* 281–91.

Seeley, R. A. Sim, and E. W. Loosley. (1956). *Crestwood Heights: A Study of the Culture of Suburban Life.* New York: Wiley.

Sewell, John. (1993). *The Shape of the City: Toronto Struggles with Modern Planning.* Toronto: University of Toronto Press.

Simmel, Georg. (1950). "The Metropolis and Mental Life." In Kurt H. Wolff, ed. and trans., *The Sociology of Georg Simmel* (pp. 409–24). Glencoe, IL: Free Press.

Simon, Julian L., and Herman Kahn. (1984) *The Resourceful Earth: A Response to Global 2000.* Oxford: Blackwell.

"Slain Man Mystery to Tenants." (2004). *Metro* (Toronto) 29 December: 4.

Smith, David A. (1996). *Third World Cities in Global Perspective: The Political Economy of Uneven Urbanization.* Boulder, CO: Westview Press.

Smith, Neil. (1979). "Towards a Theory of Gentrification." *Journal of the American Planning Association, 45,* 538–48.

Smith, Neil, and Michael LeFaivre. (1984). "A Class Analysis of Gentrification." In John J. Palen and Brian London, eds., *Gentrification, Displacement and Neighborhood Revitalization* (pp. 43–64). Albany, NY: SUNY Press.

Statistics Canada. (2005). "Deaths." *The Daily* 21 December. On the World Wide Web at http://www.statcan.ca/Daily/English/051221/d051221b.htm (6 October 2006).

Statistics Canada. (2008a). "Census Snapshot of Canada—Urbanization." *Canadian Social Trends, 84* (Winter), 11–12. Statistics Canada Catalogue no. 11-008.

Statistics Canada (2008b). "Census Snapshot—Immigration in Canada: A Portrait of the Foreign-Born Population, 2006 Census." *Canadian Social Trends, 85* (Summer), 46–53. Statistics Canada Catalogue no. 11-008-X.

Stone, Leroy O. (1967). *Urban Development in Canada.* Ottawa: Dominion Bureau of Statistics.

Stren, R., and M. Halfari. (2001). "The Cities of Sub-Saharan Africa: From Dependency to Marginality." In Ronan Paddison, ed., *Handbook of Urban Studies* (pp. 466–85). London: Sage Publications.

Thomas, William I., and Florian Znaniecki. (1918–20). *The Polish Peasant in Europe and America,* 5 vols. Chicago: University of Chicago Press.

Tönnies, Ferdinand. (1957 [1887]). *Community and Society.* Trans. Charles Loomis. East Lansing, MI: Michigan State University Press.

Van de Kaa, Dirk. (1987). "Europe's Second Demographic Transition." *Population Bulletin, 42* (1), 1–58.

Warde, Alan. (1991). "Gentrification as Consumption: Issues of Class and Gender." *Environment and Planning D: Society and Space, 9* (2), 223–32.

Weber, A. F. (1963 [1899]). *The Growth of Cities in the Nineteenth Century.* Ithaca, NY: Cornell University Press.

Whyte, William H. (1956). *The Organization Man.* New York: Simon and Schuster.

Wilson, Elizabeth. (1991). *The Sphinx in the City: Urban Life, the Control of Disorder, and Women.* London: Virago Press.

Wirth, Louis. (1938). "Urbanism as a Way of Life." *American Journal of Sociology, 44,* 1–24.

Wittberg, Patricia. (1992). "Perspectives on Gentrification: A Comparative Review of the Literature." *Research in Urban Sociology, 2,* 17–46.

Zorbaugh, Harvey. (1929). *The Gold Coast and the Slum.* Chicago: University of Chicago Press.

CHAPTER 16

Adams, W. M. (1990). *Green Development: Environment and Sustainability in the Third World.* New York: Oxford University Press.

Auyero, Javier, and Debora Swistun. (2008). "The Social Production of Toxic Uncertainty." *American Sociological Review, 73,* 357–79.

Babooram, Avani. (2008). "Canadian Participation in an Environmentally Active Lifestyle." *EnviroStats* (Statistics Canada), *2* (4), 7–11.

Blowers, A., D. Lowry, and B. D. Solomon. (1991). *The International Politics of Nuclear Waste.* London: Macmillan.

Bullard, R. D. (1990). *Dumping in Dixie: Race, Class and Environmental Quality.* Boulder, CO: Westview Press.

Buttel, F. H. (1975). "The Environmental Movement: Consensus, Conflict and Change." *Journal of Environmental Education, 7,* 53–63.

Buttel, F. H. (1987). "New Directions in Environmental Sociology." *Annual Review of Sociology, 13,* 465–88.

Cable, S., and M. Benson. (1993). "Acting Locally: Environmental Injustice and the Emergence of Grassroots Environmental Organizations." *Social Problems, 40,* 464–77.

Capek, S. M. (1993). "The Environmental Justice Frame: A Conceptual Discussion and an Application." *Social Problems, 40,* 5–24.

"A Captivating Remedy." (2008). *The Guardian Weekly* (UK) 6 June, 20.

Clarke, L., and J.F. Short, Jr. (1993). "Social Organization and Risk: Some Current Controversies." *Annual Review of Sociology, 19,* 375–99.

Cotgrove, S. (1982). *Catastrophe or Cornucopia: The Environment, Politics, and the Future.* Chichester, UK: Wiley.

Cotgrove, S., and A. Duff. (1981). "Environmentalism, Values and Social Change." *British Journal of Sociology, 32,* 92–110.

Cylke, F. K., Jr. (1993). *The Environment.* New York: HarperCollins College.

Davidson, Debra J., and Norah A. MacKendrick. (2004). "All Dressed Up and Nowhere to Go: The Discourse of Ecological Modernization in Alberta, Canada." *Canadian Review of Sociology and Anthropology, 41* (1), 47–65.

d'Eaubonne, F. (1974). *La Feminisme ou la Mort.* Paris: P. Horay.

Denq, F., D. H. Constance, and S. Joung. (2000). "The Role of Class, Status, and Power in the Distribution of Toxic Superfund Sites in Texas and Louisiana." *Journal of Poverty, 4,* 81–100.

Derksen, L., and J. Gartrell. (1993). "The Social Context of Recycling." *American Sociological Review, 58,* 434–42.

Devall, B., and G. Sessions. (1985). *Deep Ecology: Living as if Nature Mattered.* Salt Lake City, UT: Peregrine Smith Books.

Downs, A. (1972). "Up and Down with Ecology: The 'Issue-Attention Cycle.'" *The Public Interest, 28,* 38–55.

Dunlap, R. E., and W. R. Catton, Jr. (1979). "Environmental Sociology." *Annual Review of Sociology, 5,* 243–73.

Dunlap, R. E., and W. R. Catton, Jr. (1983). "What Environmental Sociologists Have in Common (Whether Concerned with 'Built' or 'Natural' Environments)." *Sociological Inquiry, 53*, 113–35.

Dunlap, R. E., and K. D. Van Liere. (1978). "The New Environmental Paradigm: A Proposed Measuring Instrument and Preliminary Results." *Journal of Environmental Education, 9*, 10–19.

Dwyer, A. (1992). "The Trouble at Great Whale." *Equinox* (January/February): 28–41.

"End War in Woods, Poll Says." (2000). *Sustainability Update: A Quarterly Publication of the Forest Alliance of British Columbia* (Spring), 5.

Eyerman, R., and A. Jamison. (1989). "Environmental Knowledge as an Organizational Weapon: The Case of Greenpeace." *Social Science Information, 28*, 99–119.

Fields, D. M. (1993). "We Can't Grow on Like This (Review of Beyond the Limits)." *The Futurist* (January–February), 40–41.

Flint, C. G. (2004). *Community Response to Forest Disturbance in Alaska's Kenai Peninsula*. Ph.D. dissertation, Pennsylvania State University.

Flint, Courtney G., and A. E. Luloff. (2005). "Natural Resource-based Communities, Risk, and Disaster: An Intersection of Theories." *Society & Natural Resources, 18*, 399–12.

Foster, J. (1978). *Working for Wildlife.* Toronto: University of Toronto Press.

Fowlkes, M., and P. Miller. (1987). "Chemicals and Community at Love Canal." In B.B. Johnson and V.T. Covello, eds., *The Social and Cultural Construction of Risk* (pp. 55–78). Dordrecht, Holland: Reidel.

Freudenburg, W. R. (1991). "Rural–Urban Differences in Environmental Concern: A Closer Look." *Sociological Inquiry, 61*, 167–98.

Freudenburg, W. R. (1993). "Risk and Recreancy: Weber, the Division of Labour and the Rationality of Risk Perceptions." *Social Forces, 71*, 909–32.

Gale, R. P. (1983). "The Environmental Movement and the Left: Antagonists or Allies?" *Sociological Inquiry, 53*, 179–99.

Gallopin, G. C., P. Gutman, and H. Maletta. (1989). "Global Impoverishment, Sustainable Development and the Environment: A Conceptual Approach." *International Social Science Journal, 41*, 375–97.

Gerhards, J., and D. Rucht. (1992). "Mesomobilization: Organizing and Framing in Two Protest Campaigns in West Germany." *American Journal of Sociology, 98*, 555–95.

Gidengil, E. (1990). "Centres and Peripheries: The Potential Culture of Dependencies." *Canadian Review of Sociology and Anthropology, 27*, 23–48.

Greenbaum, A. (1995). "Taking Stock of Two Decades of Research on the Social Bases of Environmental Concern." In Michael D. Mehta and Eric Ouellet, eds., *Environmental Sociology: Theory and Practice* (pp. 125–52). North York, ON: Captus Press.

Grossman, G. M., and H. R. Potter. (1977). "A Trend Analysis of Competing Models of Environmental Attitudes." Working Paper no. 127. Department of Sociology and Anthropology, Purdue University, West Lafayette, IN.

Hallman, W. K., and A. Wandersman. (1992). "Attribution of Responsibility and Individual and Collective Coping with Environmental Threats." *Journal of Social Issues, 48*, 101–18.

Hannigan, J. A. (1995). *Environmental Sociology: A Social Constructionist Perspective.* London and New York: Routledge.

Harrison, K., and G. Hoberg. (1991). "Setting the Environmental Agendas in Canada and the United States: The Cases of Dioxin and Radon." *Canadian Journal of Political Science, 24*, 3–27.

Hays, S. (1959). *Conservation and the Gospel of Efficiency: The Progressive Conservation Movement.* Cambridge, MA: Harvard University Press.

Jones, R., and R. E. Dunlap. (1992). "The Social Bases of Environmental Concern: Have They Changed over Time?" *Rural Sociology, 57*, 28–47.

Koppes, C. (1988). "Efficiency, Equity, Esthetics: Shifting Themes in American Conservation." In D. Worster, ed., *The Ends of the Earth: Perspectives on Modern Environmental History* (pp. 230–51). Cambridge, UK: Cambridge University Press.

Kriesi, H. (1989). "New Social Movements and the New Class in the Netherlands." *American Journal of Sociology, 94*, 1078–16.

Ladd, A. E., and S. Laska. (1991). "Opposition to Solid Waste Incineration: Pre-Implementation Anxieties Surrounding a New Environmental Controversy." *Sociological Inquiry, 61*, 299–313.

Lovelock, J. (1987). *Gaia: A New Look at Life on Earth.* Oxford: Oxford University Press.

Macdonald, D. (1991). The Politics of Pollution: Why Canadians Are Failing Their Environment. Toronto: McClelland and Stewart.

Maloney, M., and M. Ward. (1973). "Ecology: Let's Hear from the People: An Objective Scale for the Measurement of Ecological Attitudes and Knowledge." *American Psychologist, 28*, 583–86.

Meadows, D. H., D. L. Meadows, and J. Randers. (1992). *Beyond the Limits: Confronting Global Collapse, Envisioning a Sustainable Future.* Post Mills, VT: Chelsea Green.

Meadows, D. H., D. L. Meadows, J. Randers, and W. W. Behrens. (1972). *The Limits to Growth.* New York: Universe Books.

Milbrath, L. W. (1984). *Environmentalists: Vanguard for a New Society.* Albany, NY: SUNY Press.

Milmo, Dan, and Owen Bowcott. (2008). "Next Generation of Swampies Makes a Stand." *The Guardian Weekly* (UK) 7 March, 16.

Naess, A. (1973). "The Shallow and Deep Long-Range Ecology Movement." *Inquiry, 16*, 95–100.

Perron, B., J. G. Vaillancourt, and C. Durand. (2001). "A Global Problem for a Global Movement? An Exploratory Study of Climate Change Perception by Green Groups' Leaders from Québec (Canada) and Costa Rica." *Society and Natural Resources, 14*, 837–55.

Perrow, C. (1984). *Normal Accidents.* New York: Basic Books.

Robbins, Tom. (2006). "What Is the Real Price of Cheap Air Travel?" *Observer* (UK), January 29.

Roberts, J. T. (2001). "Global Inequality and Climate Change." *Society and Natural Resources, 14*, 501–09.

Saiget, Robert J. (2005). "China Admits Chemical Blast Polluted Major River, City Without Water." *Sino Daily* 23 November.

Schnaiberg, A. (1980). *The Environment: From Surplus to Scarcity.* New York: Oxford University Press.

Schumacher, E. F. (1973). *Small Is Beautiful.* New York: Harper.

Schwartz, John. (2006). "Panel Urges Corps to Study Oversight of Levees." *New York Times* 22 January: 1–23.

Séguin, C., L. G. Pelletier, and J. Hunsley. (1998). "Toward a Model of Environmental Activism." *Environment and Behavior,* 30 (5), 628–52.

Shrivastava, P. (1987). *Bhopal: Anatomy of a Crisis.* Cambridge, MA: Ballinger.

Silverstone, Martin, and Kendra Toby. (1998). "Pathfinder Talk," *Equinox* (August/September): 90.

Silvertown, J. (1989). "A Silent Spring in China." *New Scientist* (July), 55–58.

Smith, C. (1992). *Media and Apocalypse: News Coverage of the Yellowstone Forest Fires, Exxon Valdez Oil Spill, and Loma Prieta Earthquake.* Westport, CT: Greenwood Press.

Solomon, Lawrence. (2006). "Great Bear Hug: Environmentalists Are Cheering, but Are They the Losers in an Agreement Reached Over B.C.'s Last Rain Forest Area?" *National Post* 10 February.

Specter, Michael. (2008). "Big Foot." *The New Yorker,* 25 February, 44–53.

Statistics Canada. (2009). *Households and the Environment Survey (HES).* On the World Wide Web at http://www.statcan.gc.ca/cgi-bin/imdb/p2SV.pl?Function=getSurvey&SDDS=3881&lang=en&db=imdb&adm=8&dis=2 (retrieved 13 August 2009).

Stein, I. P. (1988). *Cities under Siege.* Toronto: Atlantic Press.

Theodori, G. L., and A. E. Luloff. (2002). "Position on Environmental Issues and Engagement in Pro-Environmental Behaviors." *Society and Natural Resources, 15,* 471–82.

Tindall, D. B. (1994). "Collective Action in the Rainforest: Personal Networks, Collective Identity, and Participation in the Vancouver Island Wilderness Preservation Movement." Ph.D. thesis, Department of Sociology, University of Toronto.

Turner, J. H. (1981). *Sociology: Studying the Human System,* 2nd ed. Santa Monica, CA: Goodyear.

Ungar, S. (1992). "The Rise and (Relative) Decline of Global Warming as a Social Problem." *Sociological Quarterly, 33,* 483–501.

Uusitalo, L. (1990). "Are Environmental Attitudes and Behavior Inconsistent? Findings from a Finnish Study." *Scandinavian Political Studies, 13,* 211–26.

Van Liere, K. D., and R. E. Dunlap. (1980). "The Social Bases of Environmental Concern: A Review of Hypotheses, Explanations and Empirical Evidence." *Public Opinion Quarterly, 44,* 181–97.

Warren, K. J. (1990). "The Power and Promise of Ecological Feminism." *Environmental Ethics, 12,* 125–46.

Williams, G. (1992). "Greening the New Canadian Political Economy." *Studies in Political Economy, 37,* 5–30.

World Commission on Environment and Development [The Brundtland Commission]. (1987). *Our Common Future: Report to the United Nations General Assembly.* New York: Oxford University Press.

Wynne, B. (1992). "Risk and Social Learning: Reification to Engagement." In S. Krimsky and D. Golding, eds., *Social Theories of Risk* (pp. 275–97). Westport, CT: Praeger.

Yearley, S. (1991). T*he Green Case: A Sociology of Environmental Issues, Arguments and Politics.* London: HarperCollins Academic.

CHAPTER 17

Allard, Y. E., R. Wilkins, and J.-M. Berthelot. (2004). Premature Mortality in Health Regions with High Aboriginal Populations. *Health Reports, 15*(1), 51–60.

Anand, S. S., S. Yusuf, R. Jacobs, A. D. Davis, Q. Yi, H. Gerstein. P. A. Montague, and E. Lonn. (2001). "Risk Factors, Atherosclerosis, and Cardiovascular Disease among Aboriginal People in Canada: The Study of Health Assessment and Risk Evaluation in Aboriginal peoples (SHARE-AP)." *The Lancet, 358,* 1147–53.

Antonucci, T. C. (1990). "Social Supports and Social Relationships." In R.H. Binstock and L.K. George, eds. *Handbook of Aging and the Social Sciences,* 3rd ed (pp. 205–44). New York, NY: Academic Press.

Arber, S., and Ginn, J. (1991). *Gender and Later Life.* London: Sage Publications.

Armstrong, P., H. Armstrong, and D. Coburn. (2001). *Unhealthy Times. Political Economy Perspectives on Health and Care in Canada.* Don Mills: Oxford University Press.

Bolaria, B. S., and Dickinson, H.D. (2009). *Health, Illness, and Health Care in Canada,* 4th ed. Scarborough: Nelson Education Ltd.

Brownell M. D., N. P. Roos, and L. L. Roos. (2001). "Monitoring Health Reform: A Report Card Approach." *Social Science Medicine, 52,* 657–70.

Buckley, N. J., F. T. Denton, A. L. Robb, and B. G. Spencer. (2005). "Healthy Aging at Older Ages: Are Income and Education Important?" *Canadian Journal on Aging,* Supplement, S155–S169.

Canadian Institute for Health Information. (2005). *Select Highlights on Public Views of the Determinants of Health. Canadian Population Health Initiative.* Ottawa: Author.

Canadian Institute for Health Information. (2008). *National Health Expenditure Trends, 1975–2008.* Ottawa: Author.

Canadian Study on Health and Aging. (1994). "The Canadian Study of Health and Aging: Study Methods and Prevalence of Dementia." *Canadian Medical Association Journal, 150* (6), 899–913.

Carriere, K. C., L. L. Roos, and D. C. Dover. (2000). "Across Time and Space: Variations in Hospital Use during Canadian Health Reform." *Health Services Research, 35* (2), 467–87.

Chappell, N. L. (2005). "Perceived Change in Quality of Life among Chinese Canadian Seniors: The Role of Involvement in Chinese Culture." *Journal of Happiness Studies, 6* (1), 69–91.

Chappell, N. L., B. Havens, M. J. Hollander, J. Miller, and C. McWilliam. (2004). "Comparative Costs of Home Care and Residential Care." *The Gerontologist, 44* (3), 389–400.

Chappell, N. L. , L. McDonald, and M. Stones. (2007). *Aging in Contemporary Canada,* 2nd ed. Toronto: Pearson Educational.

Chappell, N. L., and Penning, M. J. (2009). *Understanding Health, Health Care and Health Policy in Canada: Sociological Perspectives.* Don Mills: Oxford University Press.

Chen J., E. Ng, and R. Wilkins. (1996). "The Health of Canada's Immigrants in 1994–95." *Health Reports, 7* (4), 33–45.

Citizenship and Immigration Canada. (1999). *Facts and Figures, 1998.* Ottawa: Minister of Public Works and Government Services Canada. Catalogue No. MP43-333/1999E.

Commission on the Future of Health Care in Canada (The Romanow Report). (2002). *Building on Values: The Future of Health Care in Canada, Final Report.* Ottawa: National Library of Canada. Catalogue No. CP32-85/2002E-IN.

Cooke, M., F. Mitrou, D. Lawrence, E. Guimond, and D. Beavon. (2007). "Indigenous Well-Being in Four Countries: An Application of the UNDP's Human Development Index to

Indigenous Peoples in Australia, Canada, New Zealand, and the United States." *BMC International Health and Human Rights*, 7, 9.

Crompton, S. (2000). "100 Years of Health." *Canadian Social Trends*, 59, 12–17.

Desjardins, B., and J. Dumas. (1993). *Population Aging and the Elderly: Current Demographic Analysis*. Ottawa: Minister of Industry. Catalogue no. 91-533E.

DesMeules, M., D. Manuel, and R. Cho. (2004). "Mortality: Life and Health Expectancy of Canadian Women." *BMC Women's Health*, 4 (Suppl. 1), S1–S9.

Estes, C. L. (1979). *The Aging Enterprise*. San Francisco: Jossey-Bass.

Evans, R. G., K. M. McGrail, S. G. Morgan, M. L. Barer, and C. Hertzman. (2001). "Apocalypse No: Population Aging and the Future of Health Care Systems." *Canadian Journal on Aging*, 20 (Suppl. 1), 160–191.

Fries, J. F. (1983). "Compression of Morbidity." *Milbank Memorial Fund Quarterly*, 61, 397–419.

Gee, E. M. (2000). "Living Arrangements and Quality of Life among Chinese Canadian Elders." *Social Indicators Research*, 51, 304–29.

Gee, E. M., K. M. Kobayashi, and S. G. Prus. (2004). "Examining the Healthy Immigrant Effect in Mid-to-later life: Findings from the Canadian Community Health Survey." *Canadian Journal on Aging* (Suppl.), S55–S63.

Gilmour, H., and Park, J. (2005). "Dependency, Chronic Conditions and Pain in Seniors." *Health Reports*, 16 (Suppl.), 21–31.

Hagestad, G., and P. Uhlenberg. (2005). "The Social Separation of Old and Young: A Root of Ageism." *Journal of Social Issues*, 61, 343–60.

Hayward, M. D., E. M. Crimmins, and Y. Saito. (1998). "Causes of Death and Active Life Expectancy in the Older Population of the United States." *Journal of Aging and Health*, 10, 192–213.

Hollander, M., and Chappell, N. (2001). *Synthesis Report: Final Report of the National Evaluation of the Cost-Effectiveness of Home Care*. A report prepared for the Health Transition Fund, Health Canada. Hollander Analytical Services Ltd., Victoria, B.C., Centre on Aging, University of Victoria, B.C.

House, J. S. (2001). "Understanding Social Factors and Inequalities in Health: 20th Century Progress and 21st Century Prospects." *Journal of Health and Social Behaviour, 43*, 125–42.

Huisman, M., A. Kunst, D. Deeg, F. Grigoletto, W. Nusselder, and J. Mackenbach. (2005). "Educational Inequalities in the Prevalence and Incidence of Disability in Italy and the Netherlands Were Observed." *Journal of Clinical Epidemiology, 58*, 1058–65.

Human Resources and Skills Development Canada. (2009). Indicators of Well-Being in Canada. On the World Wide Web at http://www4.hrsdc.gc.ca/indicator.jsp?lang+eng&indicatorid=3 (19 August 2009).

Ikels, C. (2002). "Constructing and Deconstructing the Self: Dementia in China." *Journal of Cross-Cultural Gerontology*, 17, 233–51.

Indian and Northern Affairs Canada. (2003). *National Assessment of Water and Wastewater Systems in First Nations Communities*. Ottawa: Author.

Kane, R. L. (1990). "Introduction." In R. L. Kane, J. G. Evans, and D. McFadyen, eds., *Improving the Health of Older People: A World View* (pp. 15–18). New York: Oxford University Press.

Keating, N., J. Fast, J. Frederick, K. Cranswick, and C. Perrier. (1999). *Eldercare in Canada: Context, Content and Consequences*. Ottawa: Statistics Canada, Housing, Family and Social Statistics Division. Catalogue No. 89-570-XPE.

Lewis, S., C. Donaldson, C. Mitton, and G. Currie. (2001). "The Future of Health Care in Canada." *British Medical Journal, 323*, 926–29.

Link, B. G., and Phelan, J. C. (2000). "Evaluating the Fundamental Cause Explanation for Social Disparities in Health." In C. E. Bird, P. Conrad and A. M. Fremont, eds., *Handbook of Medical Sociology*, 5th ed. (pp. 33–46). Upper Saddle River, NJ: Prentice-Hall.

Litwak, E. (1960). "Geographic Mobility and Extended Family Cohesion." *American Sociological Review, 25*, 385–94.

Lynch, J., and G. Kaplan. (2000). "Socioeconomic Position." In L. F. Berkman and I. Kawachi, eds., *Social Epidemiology* (pp. 13–35). New York: Oxford University Press.

Markides, K. S. (1983). "Minority Aging." In M. W. Riley, B.B. Hess and K. Bond, eds., *Aging in Society: Reviews of Recent Literature*. Hillsdale: Lawrence Erlbaum.

Marmor, T. R., and K. Sullivan. (2000). "Canada's Burning! Media Myths about Universal Health Coverage." *Washington Monthly* July/August. On the World Wide Web at http://www.washingtonmonthly.com/features/2000/0007.marmorsul.html#byline (21 November 2006).

Martel, L., A. Bélanger, J.-M. Berthelot, and Y. Carrière. (2005). *Health Aging*. Ottawa: Statistics Canada. Catalogue no. 82-618-MWE2005004.

Martens, A. J. L. Goldenberg, and J. Greenberg. (2005). "A Terror Management Perspective on Ageism." *Journal of Social Issues, 61*, 223–39.

Matthews, A. M., J. A. Tindale, and F. E. Norris. (1985). "The Facts on Aging Quiz: A Canadian Validation and Cross-cultural Comparison." *Canadian Journal on Aging, 3*, 165–74.

McMullin, J. (2004). *Understanding Social Inequality: Intersections of Class*, Age, Gender, Ethnicity and Race in Canada. Don Mills: Oxford University Press.

Munroe, S. (2003). "2003 Canadian Life and Death Statistics—Life Expectancy and Statistics on Deaths in Canada." About.com: Canada Online. On the World Wide Web at http://canadaonline.about.com/od/statistics/a/deathstats2003.htm (19 August 2009).

Montgomery, R. J. V., E. F. Borgatta, and M. L. Borgatta. (2000). "Societal and Family Change in the Burden of Care." In William T. Liu and Hal Kendig, eds., *Who Should Care for the Elderly: An East-West Value Divide* (pp. 27–54). Singapore: Singapore University Press, National University of Singapore and World Scientific Publishing.

Mustard, C. A., S. Derkson, J.-M. Berthelot, M. Wolfson, and L. L. Roos. (1997). "Age-Specific Education and Income Gradients in Morbidity and Mortality in a Canadian Province." *Social Science and Medicine, 45* (3), 383–97.

Noh, S., M. Beiser, V. Kaspar, F. Hou, and J. Rummens. (1999). "Perceived Racial Discrimination, Depression, and Coping: A Study of Southeast Asian Refugees in Canada." *Journal of Health and Social Behavior, 40* (3), 193–207.

Novak, M., and Campbell, L. (2006). *Aging and Society: A Canadian Perspective*, 5th ed. Toronto: Thomson Nelson.

Organization for Economic Co-Operation and Development (OECD). (2009). Health Data 2008: Statistics and Indicators

for 30 Countries. On the World Wide Web at http://www.
ecosante.org/OCDEENG/111000.html (19 August 2009).

Palmore, E. B. (1998). *Facts on Aging Quiz: A Handbook of Uses and
Results*. New York: Springer.

Penning, M .J., M. Brackley, and D. E. Allen. (2006). "Home Care
and Health Reform: Changes in Home Care Utilization in
One Canadian Province, 1990–2000." *The Gerontologist, 46* (6),
744–58.

Pérez, C. E. (2002). "Health Status and Health Behaviour among
Immigrants." *Health Reports, 13,* 1–12.

Prus, S. G., and Gee, E. (2002). *Gender Differences in the Influence of
Economic, Lifestyle and Psychosocial Factors on Later-life Health.*
Hamilton: Program for Research on Social and Economic
Dimensions of an Aging Population, McMaster University.

Raphael D. (2005). "Introduction to the Social Determinants of
Health." In D. Raphael, ed., *Social Determinants of Health:
Canadian Perspectives* (pp. 1–19). Toronto: Canadian Scholars
Press.

"Recent Research Reveals Teflon's Dark Side." (2008). *Metro*
(Toronto) 8 April, 13.

Rogers, R. G., R. A. Hummer, and C. Nam. (2000). *Living and
Dying in the USA.* San Diego, CA: Academic Press.

Roos, N. P., B. Havens, and C. Black. (1993). "Living Longer but
Doing Worse: Assessing Health Status in Elderly Persons at
Two Points in Time in Manitoba, Canada, 1971 and 1983."
Social Science and Medicine, 36, 273–82.

Ross, C. E., and C. Wu. (1996). "Education, Age, and the
Cumulative Advantage in Health." *Journal of Health and Social
Behavior, 37,* 104–20.

Schalick, L. M., W. C. Hadden, E. Pamuk, V. Navarro, and G.
Pappas. (2000). "The Widening Gap in Death Rates among
Income Groups in the United States from 1967 to 1986."
International Journal of Health Services, 30, 13–26.

Segall, A., and N. L. Chappell. (2000). *Health and Health Care in
Canada.* Toronto: Pearson Education Canada.

Simon, R. (2000). "The Importance of Culture in Sociological
Theory and Research on Stress and Mental Health. A Missing
Link?" In C. E. Bird, P. Conrad, and A. M. Fremont, eds.,
Handbook of Medical Sociology, 5th ed. Englewood Cliffs:
Prentice-Hall.

Statistics Canada (2001). *Self-Esteem, by Age Group and Sex,
Household Population aged 12 and over, Canada Excluding
Territories, 1994/95.* Ottawa: Minister of Industry. Catalogue
no. 82-221-XIE.

Statistics Canada. (2003). *Aboriginal Peoples Survey 2001—Initial
findings: Well-Being of the Non-reserve Aboriginal Population.*
Ottawa: Minister of Industry. Catalogue no. 89-589-XIE.

Statistics Canada (2003). *Annual Demographic Statistics* (Catalogue
no. 91-213-XIB/XPB).

Statistics Canada (2004). *Canadian Community Health Survey 2003.*
Ottawa: Ministry of Industry.

Statistics Canada. (2005a). *Canadian Community Health Survey,
2004.* Ottawa: Ministry of Industry.

Statistics Canada (2005b). *Projections of the Aboriginal Populations,
Canada, Provinces and Territories, 2001 to 2017.* Ottawa:
Minister of Industry. Catalogue No. 91-547-XIE.

Statistics Canada. (2006a). *Causes of Death, 2003.* Ottawa: Ministry
of Industry. Catalogue No. 84-208 XIE. On the World Wide
Web at http://www.statcan.ca/english/freepub/84-208-XIE/
84-208-XIE2005002.htm (10 October 2006).

Statistics Canada, (2006b). *Life Tables, Canada, Provinces and
Territories, 2000 to 2002.* http://www.statcan.gc.ca/pub/
84-537-x/4064441-eng.htm (10 October 2006).

Statistics Canada. (2007a). *Portrait of the Canadian Population in
2006, by Age and Sex, 2006 Census.* Catalogue no. 97-551-XIE.
Ottawa: Minister of Industry.

Statistics Canada. (2007b). *A Portrait of Seniors in Canada, 2006.*
Ottawa: Minister of Industry. Catalogue no. 89-519-XIE.

Statistics Canada. (2008). *Aboriginal Peoples in Canada in 2006:
Inuit, Métis and First Nations, 2006 Census.* Ottawa: Minister
of Industry. Catalogue no. 97-558-XIE.

Stones, M. J., and Stones, L. (1997). "Ageism: The Quiet
Epidemic." *Canadian Journal of Public Health, 88* (5), 293–94.

Trottier, H., L. Martel, C. Houle, J.-M. Berthelot, and J. Légaré.
(2000). "Living at Home or in an Institution: What Makes the
Differences for Seniors?" *Health Reports, 11,* 49–59.

United Nations. (2005). *Demographic Yearbook, 2005.* On the World
Wide Web at http://unstats.un.org/unsd/demographic/
products/dyb/default.htm (16 December 2008).

United Nations Department of Economic & Social Affairs,
Population Division. (2007). *World Population Prospects: 2006
Revision.* CD-ROM Edition—Comprehensive Dataset.
On the World Wide Web at http://unstats.un.org/unsd/
demographic/products/indwm/tab3a.htm (November
2008).

Williams, A. P., R. Dever, P. Baranek, and A. Gildiner. (2001).
"From Medicare to Home Care: Globalization, State
Retrenchment, and the Profitization of Canada's Health Care
System." In P. Armstrong, H. Armstrong, and D. Coburn, eds.,
*Unhealthy Times: Political Economy Perspectives on Health and
Care in Canada* (pp. 7–30). New York: Oxford University Press.

Williamson, D. J. (2000). "Health Behaviours and Health:
Evidence That the Relationship Is Not Conditional on Income
Adequacy." *Social Science and Medicine, 51* (12), 1741–54.

World Health Organization. (1948). *Official records of the World
Health Organization,* #2. New York: WHO Interim
Commission, UN.

Zola, I. K. (1983). *Socio-Medical Inquiries.* Philadelphia: Temple
University Press.

CHAPTER 18

Adam, Barry, Jan Willem Duyvendak, and Andre Krouwel. (1999).
The Global Emergence of Gay and Lesbian Politics. Philadelphia:
Temple University Press.

Adamson, Nancy, Linda Briskin, and Margaret McPhail. (1988).
*Feminist Organizing for Change: The Contemporary Women's
Movement in Canada.* Toronto: Oxford University
Press.

Bashevkin, Sylvia. (1986). "Independence versus Partisanship:
Dilemmas in the Political History of Women in English
Canada." In V. Strong-Boag and A. Fellman, eds., *Rethinking
Canada: The Promise of Women's History* (pp. 246–75). Toronto:
Copp Clark Pitman.

Blais, André, Elisabeth Gidengil, Richard Nadeau, and Neil
Nevitte. (1997). *1997 Canadian Election Survey.* On the World
Wide Web at http://prod.library.utoronto.ca/datalib/
codebooks/utm/elections/1997/ (20 June 2002).

Block, Fred. (1979). "The Ruling Class Does Not Rule." In R.
Quinney, ed. *Capitalist Society* (pp. 128–40). Homewood IL:
Dorsey Press.

Brint, Stephen. (1984). "New Class and Cumulative Tend Explanations of the Liberal Political Attitudes of Professionals." *American Journal of Sociology, 90,* 30–71.

Brym, Robert J. (1979). "Political Conservatism in Atlantic Canada." In Robert J. Brym and R. James Sacouman, eds., *Underdevelopment and Social Movements in Atlantic Canada* (pp. 59–79). Toronto: New Hogtown Press.

Brym, Robert J. (1980). *Intellectuals and Politics.* London, UK: Allen and Unwin.

Brym, Robert J. (1989). "Canada." In Tom Bottomore and Robert J. Brym, eds., *The Capitalist Class: An International Study* (pp. 177–206). New York: New York University Press.

Brym, Robert. (2009). *The 2006 Census and Canadian Society.* Toronto: Nelson.

Brym, Robert J. (2008). "Affluence, Power and Strikes in Canada, 1973–2000." In Edward Grabb and Neil Guppy, eds., *Social Inequality in Canada: Patterns, Problems, Policies,* 6th ed. (pp. 55–68) Scarborough ON: Prentice-Hall Canada.

Canada Department of Labour. (1970). *Strikes and Lockouts in Canada 1968.* Ottawa: Economic and Research Branch, Department of Labour. Catalogue no. L2-1/1968.

Canada Department of Labour. (1973.) *Labour Organizations in Canada 1972.* Ottawa: Economics and Research Branch, Canada Department of Labour. Catalogue no. L2-2-1972.

Canada Department of Labour. (1985). *Strikes and Lockouts in Canada 1985.* Ottawa: Minister of Supply and Services Canada. Catalogue no. L160-2999/85B.

Casper, L. M., S. S. McLanahan, and I. Garfinkel. (1994). "The Gender-Poverty Gap: What Can We Learn from Other Countries?" *American Sociological Review, 59,* 594–605.

Clarke, Harold D., Jane Jenson, Lawrence LeDuc, and Jon H. Pammett. (1996). *Absent Mandate: Canadian Electoral Politics In an Era of Restructuring,* 3rd ed. Toronto: Gage.

Clement, Wallace. (1975). *The Canadian Corporate Elite: An Analysis of Economic Power.* Toronto: McClelland and Stewart.

Dahl, Robert A. (1961). *Who Governs?* New Haven, CT: Yale University Press.

Davies, James C. (1969). "Toward a Theory of Revolution." In Barry McLaughlin, ed. *Studies in Social Movements: A Social Psychological Perspective* (pp. 85–108). New York: Free Press.

Evans, Peter B., Dietrich Rueschemeyer, and Theda Skocpol. (1985). *Bringing the State Back In.* Cambridge, UK: Cambridge University Press.

Frank, Jeffrey. (1994). "Voting and Contributing: Political Participation in Canada." In *Canadian Social Trends* (pp. 333–37). Toronto: Thompson Educational Publishers.

Goffman, Erving. (1974). *Frame Analysis.* Cambridge, MA: Harvard University Press.

"Greenpeace Contacts Worldwide." (1999). On the World Wide Web at http://adam.greenpeace.org/information.shtml (29 April 2004).

Hourani, Albert. (1991). *A History of the Arab Peoples.* New York: Warner Books.

Human Resources Development Canada. (1995). *1994–1995 Directory of Labour Organizations in Canada.* Ottawa: Minister of Supply and Services Canada. Catalogue no. L2-2-1995.

Human Resources Development Canada. (1998). *1998 Directory of Labour Organizations in Canada.* Ottawa: Workplace Information Directorate.

Human Resources and Skills Development Canada. (1999). "Chronological Perspective on Work Stoppages in Canada."

On the World Wide Web at http://labour.hrdcdrhc.gc.ca/doc/wid-dimt/eng/ws-at/table.cfm (30 June 2004).

Human Resources and Skills Development Canada. (2001). "Chronological Perspective on Work Stoppages in Canada (Work Stoppages Involving One or More Workers), 1976–2000." On the World Wide Web at http://labour-travail. hrdc-drhc. gc.ca/doc/wid-dimt/eng/ws-at/table.cfm (27 March 2006).

International Labour Organization. (2008). "Yearly Data." On the World Wide Web at http://laborsta.ilo.org/ (9 January 2008)}

Jenkins, J. Craig. (1983). "Resource Mobilization Theory and the Study of Social Movements." *Annual Review of Sociology, 9,* 527–53.

Kelley, Jack. (2001). "Terror Groups Hide Behind Web Encryption." *USA Today* 19 June. On the World Wide Web at http://www.usatoday.com/life/cyber/tech/2001-02-05-binladen.htm (13 September 2001).

Korpi, Walter. (1983). *The Democratic Class Struggle.* London UK: Routledge and Kegan Paul.

Lipset, Seymour Martin. (1971). *Agrarian Socialism: The Cooperative Commonwealth Federation in Saskatchewan,* rev. ed. Berkeley, CA: University of California Press.

Lipset, Seymour Martin. (1981). *Political Man: The Social Bases of Politics,* 2nd ed. Baltimore: Johns Hopkins University Press.

Lodhi, Abdul Qaiyum, and Charles Tilly. (1973). "Urbanization, Crime, and Collective Violence in 19th Century France." *American Journal of Sociology, 79,* 296–318.

Marshall, T. H. (1965). "Citizenship and Social Class." In T. H. Marshall, ed., *Class, Citizenship, and Social Development: Essays by T. H. Marshall* (pp. 71–134). Garden City, NY: Anchor.

McCarthy, John D., and Mayer N. Zald. (1977). "Resource Mobilization and Social Movements: A Partial Theory." *American Journal of Sociology, 82,* 1212–41.

McCullogh, Declan. (2000). "Bin Laden: Steganography Master?" *Wired* 7 February. On the World Wide Web at http://www.wired.com/news/print/0.1294.41658.00.html (13 September 2001).

McDonald, Michael P. (2008a). "This May Be the Election of the Century." On the World Wide Web at http://www.politico.com/news/stories/0908/13798.html (retrieved 5 November 2008).

McDonald, Michael P. (2008b). "Voter Turnout." On the World Wide Web at http://elections.gmu.edu/voter_turnout.htm (retrieved 5 November 2008).

Melucci, Alberto. (1980). "The New Social Movements: A Theoretical Approach." *Social Science Information, 19,* 199–226.

Melucci, Alberto. (1995). "The New Social Movements Revisited: Reflections on a Sociological Misunderstanding." In Louis Maheu, ed., *Social Classes and Social Movements: The Future of Collective Action* (pp. 107–19). London: Sage.

Miliband, Ralph. (1973 [1969]). *The State in Capitalist Society.* London: Fontana.

Mills, C. Wright. (1956). *The Power Elite.* New York: Oxford University Press.

Mishler, William. (1979). *Political Participation in Canada: Prospects for Democratic Citizenship.* Toronto: Macmillan.

Moore, Barrington, Jr. (1967). *Social Origins of Dictatorship and Democracy: Lord and Peasant in the Making of the Modern World.* Boston: Beacon.

MSNBC. (2008). "United States—President." On the World Wide Web at http://www.msnbc.msn.com/id/26843704 (retrieved 5 November 2008).

"Muslim Brotherhood Movement Homepage." (2002). On the World Wide Web at http://www.ummah.org.uk/ikhwan/ (7 May 2003).

Myles, John. (1989). *Old Age in the Welfare State: The Political Economy of Public Pensions*, revised ed. Lawrence, KS: University Press of Kansas.

Oberschall, Anthony. (1973). *Social Conflict and Social Movements.* Englewood Cliffs, NJ: Prentice-Hall.

O'Connor, Julia S. (1996). "From Women in the Welfare State to Gendering Welfare State Regimes." *Current Sociology, 44* (2), 1–130.

O'Connor, Julia S., and Robert J. Brym. (1988). "Public Welfare Expenditure in OECD Countries: Towards a Reconciliation of Inconsistent Findings." *British Journal of Sociology, 39*, 47–68.

O'Connor, Julia S., and Gregg M. Olsen, eds. (1998). *Power Resources Theory and the Welfare State: A Critical Approach.* Toronto: University of Toronto Press.

Olsen, Dennis. (1980). *The State Elite.* Toronto: McClelland and Stewart.

Olsen, Gregg. (2002). *The Politics of the Welfare State: Canada, Sweden, and the United States.* Toronto: Oxford University Press.

Olsen, Gregg, and Robert J. Brym. (1996). "Between American Exceptionalism and Swedish Social Democracy: Public and Private Pensions in Canada." In Michael Shalev, ed., *The Privatization of Social Policy? Occupational Welfare and the Welfare State in America, Scandinavia and Japan* (pp. 26 1–79). London: Macmillan.

Piven, Frances Fox, and Richard A. Cloward. (1989). *Why Americans Don't Vote.* New York: Pantheon.

Polsby, Nelson W. (1959). "Three Problems in the Analysis of Community Power." *American Sociological Review, 24*, 796–803.

Porter, John. (1965). *The Vertical Mosaic: An Analysis of Social Class and Power in Canada.* Toronto: University of Toronto Press.

Poulantzas, Nicos. (1975 [1968]). *Political Power and Social Classes.* Trans. T. O'Hagan. London: New Left Books.

Roche, Maurice. (1995). "Rethinking Citizenship and Social Movements: Themes in Contemporary Sociology and Neoconservative Ideology." In Louis Maheu, ed. *Social Classes and Social Movements: The Future of Collective Action* (pp. 186–219). London: Sage.

Rootes, Chris. (1995). "A New Class? The Higher Educated and the New Politics." In Louis Maheu, ed., *Social Classes and Social Movements: The Future of Collective Action* (pp. 220–35). London: Sage.

Shahar, Yael. (2001). "Tracing bin Laden's Money: Easier Said than Done." International Policy Institute for Counter-Terrorism. On the World Wide Web at http://www.ict.org.il/ articles/ articledet.cfm?articleid=387 (30 July 2002).

Skocpol, Theda. (1979). *States and Revolutions: A Comparative Analysis of France, Russia, and China.* Cambridge, UK: Cambridge University Press.

Smith, Jackie. (1998). "Global Civil Society? Transnational Social Movement Organizations and Social Capital." *American Behavioral Scientist, 42*, 93–107.

Snow, David A., E. Burke Rochford, Steven K. Worden, and Robert D. Benford. (1986). "Frame Alignment Processes, Micromobiization, and Movement Participation." *American Sociological Review, 51*, 464–81.

Snyder, David, and Charles Tilly. (1972). "Hardship and Collective Violence in France, 1830–1960." *American Sociological Review, 37*, 520–32.

Spilerman, Seymour. (1970). "The Causes of Racial Disturbances: A Comparison of Alternative Explanations." *American Sociological Review, 35*, 627–49.

Spilerman, Seymour. (1976). "Structural Characteristics of Cities and the Severity of Racial Disorders." *American Sociological Review, 41*, 771–93.

Strong-Boag, Veronica. (1986). "Ever a Crusader: Nellie McClung, First-Wave Feminist." In V. Strong-Boag and A. Fellman, eds., *Rethinking Canada: The Promise of Women's History* (pp. 178–90). Toronto: Copp Clark Pitman.

Tilly, Charles. (1978). *From Mobilization to Revolution.* Reading MA: Addison-Wesley.

Tilly, Charles. (1979a). "Collective Violence in European Perspective." In H. Graham and T. Gurr, eds., *Violence in America: Historical and Comparative Perspective*, 2nd ed. (pp. 83–118). Beverly Hills: Sage.

Tilly, Charles. (1979b). "Repertoires of Contention in America and Britain, 1750–1830." In Mayer N. Zald and John D. McCarthy, eds., *The Dynamics of Social Movements: Resource Mobilization, Social Control, and Tactics* (pp. 126–55). Cambridge, MA: Winthrop.

Tilly, Charles, Louise Tilly, and Richard Tilly. (1975). *The Rebellious Century, 1830–1930.* Cambridge, MA: Harvard University Press.

Turner, Bryan S. (1986). *Citizenship and Capitalism: The Debate over Reformism.* London, UK: Allen and Unwin.

"Union Membership in Canada—2000." (2000). *Workplace Gazette: An Industrial Relations Quarterly, 3* (3) 68–75.

Weber, Max. (1946 [1922]). "Class, Status, Party." In H. H. Gerth and C. Wright Mills, eds. and trans., *From Max Weber: Essays in Sociology* (pp. 180–95). New York: Oxford University Press.

Weber, Max. (1947). *The Theory of Social and Economic Organization.* T. Parsons, ed. Trans. A. M. Henderson and T. Parsons. New York: Free Press.

Wolf, Eric. (1999 [1969]). *Peasant Wars of the 20th Century.* Norman, OK: Oklahoma University Press.

"Women in National Parliaments." (2008). On the World Wide Web at http://www.ipu.org/wmn-e/classif.htm (retrieved 27 November 2008).

Workplace Information Directorate. (1996). *Special Tabulation of Strikes Statistics for 1986–95.* Ottawa: Human Resources Development Canada.

Worth, Robert. (2001). "The Deep Intellectual Roots of Islamic Terror." *The New York Times on the Web.* On the World Wide Web at http://www.nytimes.com (13 October 2002).

CHAPTER 19

Adbusters. (2005). Homepage. On the World Wide Web at http://www.adbusters.org/home/ (20 March 2005).

African Centre for Biosafety. (2005). Homepage. On the World Wide Web at http://www.biosafetyafrica.net/index.htm (7 March 2005).

Ainger, Katherine. (2003). "The New Peasant's Revolt." *New Internationalist Magazine, 353* (January–February). On the World Wide Web at http://www.newint.org/issue353/ keynote.htm (17 March 2005).

Anderson, Sarah, and John Cavanagh. (2000). *Top 200: The Rise of Global Corporate Power*. On the World Wide Web at http://www.corpwatch.org/article.php?id=377 (17 March 2005).

Anderson, Sarah, and John Cavanagh with Thea Lee and the Institute for Policy Studies. (2005). *Field Guide to the Global Economy*. New York: New Press.

Babson, Steve. (2000). "Cross-Boarder Trade with Mexico and the Prospect for Worker Solidarity: The Case of Mexico." *Critical Sociology*, 26 (1/2), 13–35.

Bacon, David. (2003). "Anti-China Campaign Hides Maquiladora Wage Cut." ZNET. On the World Wide Web at http://www.globalpolicy.org/socecon/inequal/labor/2003/0203maq.htm (3 February 2003).

Bales, Kevin. (1999). *Disposable People: New Slavery in the Global Economy*. Los Angeles, CA: University of California Press.

Barlow, Maude. (2001). "The Global Monoculture: 'Free Trade' Versus Culture and Democracy." *Earth Island Journal*, 16, 3. On the World Wide Web at http://www.earthisland.org/eijournal/new_articles.cfm?articleID=270&journalID=48 (22 November 2006).

Basok, Tanya. (2002). *Tortillas and Tomatoes: Transmigrant Mexican Harvesters in Canada*. Montreal: McGill–Queen's University Press.

Beder, Sharon. (2000). *Selling the Work Ethic: From Puritan Pulpit to Corporate PR*. Carlton North, Victoria, Australia: Scribe.

Bello, Walden. (2001). *The Future in the Balance. Essays on Globalization and Resistance*. Oakland, CA: Food First Books.

Bello, Walden. (2002). "Drop Till We Shop?" *The Nation Online*. On the World Wide Web at http://www.thenation.com/doc.mhtml?i520021021andc51ands5bello (3 October 2002).

Bentley, Stephen. (2004). "Fighting Global Warming at the Farmers' Market. The Role of Local Food Systems in Reducing Greenhouse Gas Emissions." *A FoodShare Research in Action Report*. On the World Wide Web at http://www.foodshare.net/resource/files/ACF230.pdf (9 January 2004).

Bird, Kate, and David Hughes. (1997). "Ethical Consumerism: The Case of 'Fairly-Trade' Coffee." *Business Ethics. A European Review*, 6, 159–67.

Bivens, Lyle J., and Adam Hersh. (2003). "A Rough Row." *Global Policy Forum*. On the World Wide Web at http://www.globalpolicy.org/socecon/bwi-wto/wto/2003/0909rough.htm (9 September 2003).

Borosage, Robert. (2008). "The Great Corporate Tax Heist." *Huffington Post* 14 August. On the World Wide Web at http://www.huffingtonpost.com/robert-l-borosage/the-great-corporate-tax-h_b_118479.html (18 August 2009).

Brown, Lester. (2005). *Outgrowing the Earth. The Food Security Challenge in an Age of Falling Water Tables and Rising Temperatures*. Washington, DC: Earth Policy Institute.

Brownell, Kelly, and Katherine Battle Horgen. (2004). *Food Fight. The Insight Story of the Food Industry, America's Obesity Crisis, and What We Can Do About It*. Toronto: Contemporary Books.

Brym, Robert J., et al. (2005). "In Faint Praise of the World Bank's Gender Development Policy." *Canadian Journal of Sociology*, 30, 95–111.

Burtner, Bruno. (2004). "Tax Me If You Can." *Canadian Centre for Policy Alternatives Monitor*. On the World Wide Web at http://www.policyalternatives.ca/index.cfm?act5newsanddo5Articlean

dcall5954andpA5BB736455andtype52,3,4,5,6,7 (1 October 2004).

Cardoso, Fernando Henrique. (1993). "The Challenges of Social Democracy in Latin America." In Menno Vellinga, ed., *Social Democracy in Latin America: Prospects for Change*. Boulder, CO: Westview Press.

Castells, Manuel. (1998). *The Information Age: Economy, Society and Culture: Vol. 3, End of the Millennium*. Malden, MA: Blackwell.

CBC News. (2001). "McDonald's Apologies for Beefy Fries." On the World Wide Web at http://www.cbc.ca/stories/2001/05/24/Consumers/beefyfries_010524 (25 May 2001).

CBC News. (2002a). "PM Says West Seen as 'Arrogant, Greedy.'" On the World Wide Web at http://www.cbc.ca/stories/2002/09/11/chretienjumbo020911 (12 September 2002).

CBC News. (2002b). "Chrétien's Comments on Sept. 11, 2002." On the World Wide Web at http://www.cbc.ca/national/rex/rex20020913.html (13 September 2002).

CBC News. (2005). "Canadians Made Little Economic Headway in Last 15 Years: TD Economists." On the World Wide Web at http://www.cbc.ca/story/business/national/2005/01/18/tdeconomy-050118.html (18 January 2005).

CBC News Online. (2002). "PM says West seen as 'arrogant, greedy'." On the World Wide Web at http://www.cbc.ca/stories/2002/09/11/chretienjumbo020911. (12 September 2002).

CBC Radio One. (2004). "Paid to be Poor." On the World Wide Web at http://www.cbc.ca/paidtobepoor/index.html (28 March 2004).

Chien, Kirby. (2008). "Chinese firms bank on domestic consumption." *Reuters.com* 6 November. On the World Wide Web at http://www.reuters.com/article/ChinaSummit08/idUSTRE4A53B120081106 (retrieved 19 August 2009).

Church of Stop Shopping. (n.d.). "Anti-Starbucks/Anti-Brand protest photo from Reverend Billy." *Retail Interventions and Actions: Starbucks Invasion Kit*. New York: Church of Stop Shopping.

Clay, Jason. (2004). *World Agriculture and the Environment: A Commodity-by-Commodity Guide to Impacts and Practices*. Washington, DC: Island Press.

Copps, Sheila. (1997). "Culture and Heritage: Making Room for Canada's Voices." Media Awareness Network. On the World Wide Web at http://www.media-awareness.ca/english/resources/articles/sovereignty_identity/culture_heritage.cfm (29 April 2004).

Downie, Mark. (2007). "Fair Trade in Bloom." *New York Times Online* 2 October. On the World Wide Web at http://www.nytimes.com/2007/10/02/business/worldbusiness/02trade.html

Durning, Alan. (1992). *How Much Is Enough? The Consumer Society and the Fate of the Earth*. New York: Norton.

Dussell Peters, Enrique. (2004). "Conditions and Evolution of Wages and Employment in Mexico." Occasional Paper published by *The Jus Semper Global Alliance*. On the World Wide Web at http://www.jussemper.org/Resources/Economic%20Data/mexicowagecondit.html (15 April 2004).

Ehrenreich, Barbara. (2001). *Nickel and Dimed. On (Not) Getting By in America*. New York: Henry Holt.

Ehrenreich, Barbara. (2005). *Bait and Switch. The (Futile) Pursuit of the American Dream*. New York: Henry Holt.

Ellwood, Wayne. (2001). *The No-Nonsense Guide to Globalization*. London: Zed Books.

Fairtrade Foundation. (2006). *The Arabica Coffee Market: 1989–2006: Comparison of Fairtrade and New York Exchange Prices*. London, UK: Author.

Fallows, James. (2008). "Be Nice to the Countries that Lend You Money," An Interview with Gao Xiqing. *Atlantic Monthly, 302* (December), 62–65.

Ferguson, Niall. (2004). *Colossus. The Rise and Fall of the American Empire*. New York: Penguin Books.

Frank, Thomas. (1997). *The Conquest of Cool.* Chicago: University of Chicago Press.

Frundt, Henry. (2000). "Models of Cross-Border Organizing in the Maquila Industry." *Critical Sociology, 26* (1/2), 36–55.

Global Policy Forum. (2003). "US Market Share of Film Industry for Select Countries." On the World Wide Web at http://www.globalpolicy.org/component/content/article/109/27533.html (29 April 2004).

Global Policy Forum. (n.d.). "U.S. Military Expansion and Intervention." *Empire.* New York: Author. On the World Wide Web at http://www.globalpolicy.org/empire/intervention/ (14 October 2006).

Hall, Sally. (2005). "Hungry for an Alternative." *The Independent* (UK) 28 June.

Harvey, David. (1990). *The Condition of Postmodernity.* Cambridge, MA: Blackwell.

Hays, Constance. (2000). "Learning to Think Smaller at Coke." *New York Times* 6 February: business section.

Heath, Andrew, and Joseph Potter. (2004). *The Rebel Sell: Why the Culture Can't Be Jammed.* Toronto: Harper Collins.

Hoogvelt, Ankie. (1997). *Globalization and the Postcolonial World.* Baltimore, ML: Johns Hopkins University Press.

Hopkins, Terrence, and Immanuel Wallerstein. (1986). "Commodity Chains in the World Economy Prior to 1800." *Review, The Journal of the Fernand Braudel Center, 10* (1), 157–70.

Howlett, Karen. (2005). "Ontario Eyes Brightest Immigrants." *The Globe and Mail* 11 October: A7.

Institute for Policy Studies and United for a Fair Economy. (2006). "Executive Excess 2006." www.ips-dc.org/getfile.php?id= 155 (retrieved 19 August 2009).

International Forum on Globalization. (2001). *Does Globalization Help the Poor? A Special Report by The International Forum on Globalization.* San Francisco: Author.

Internet World Stats. (2008). "World Internet Usage and Population Statistics." On the World Wide Web at www.internetworldstats.com. (retrieved 19 August 2009).

Jackson, Andrew. (2005). *The Case Against More Corporate Tax Cuts.* Ottawa: Canadian Institute for Policy Alternatives.

Jacobs, Andrew, and David Barboza. (2008). "Chinese Exports Decline Sharply in November." *New York Times* 10 December. On the World Wide Web at http://www.nytimes.com/2008/12/11/business/11yuan.html?em (retrieved 19 August 2009).

Jordan, Mary. (2003). "Workers Falling Behind in Mexico." *Washington Post* 15 July. On the World Wide Web (Global Policy Forum) at http://www.globalpolicy.org/globaliz/special/2003/0716mexico.htm (15 July 2003).

Kahn, Jeremy. (2008). "Recession Trickles to India." *New York Times* 3 December. On the World Wide Web at http://www.nytimes.com/2008/12/04/business/worldbusiness/04rupee.html (retrieved 19 August 2009).

Kennedy, Dawn. (2004). "Nollywood Thinks Outside the Box." *Sunday Independent.* On the World Wide Web at http://www.sundayindependent.co.za/index.php?fSectionId51083andfArticleId52324573 (28 November 2004).

Kindall, Henry, and David Pimentel. (1994). "Constraints on the Expansion of the Global Food Supply," *Ambio, 23*, 3.

Klein, Naomi. (2000). *No Logo.* Toronto: Knopf Canada.

KPMG. (2008). *KPMG's Corporate and Indirect Tax Rate Survey 2008.* On the World Wide Web at http://www.kpmg.com/SiteCollectionDocuments/Corporate-and-Indirect-Tax-Rate-Survey-2008v2.pdf (retrieved 19 August 2009).

Landler, Mark. (2008). "The US Financial Crisis Is Spreading to Europe." *New York Times* 30 September. On the World Wide Web at http://www.nytimes.com/2008/10/01/business/worldbusiness/01global.html?partner=rssnyt&emc=rss (retrieved 19 August 2009).

Lang, Tim, and Jules Pretty. (2005). "Farm Costs and Food Miles: An Assessment of the Full Cost of the UK Weekly Food Basket." *Food Policy, 30* (1).

Lappé, Frances Moore. (2005). "Diet for a Smaller Planet: Real Sources of Abundance." In Andrew Heintzman and Evan Solomon, eds., *Feeding the Future* (pp. 125–54). Toronto: Anansi Press.

Lappé, Anna, and Frances Moore Lappé. (2002). *Hope's Edge: The Next Diet for a Small Planet.* New York: Tarcher/Penguin.

Lindstrom, Martin. (2003). *Brandchild. Remarkable Insights into the Minds of Today's Global Kids and Their Relationships with Brands.* Sterling, VA: Millward Brown.

Lynn, Barry. (2002). "Unmade in America. The True Cost of the Global Assembly Line." *Harper's Magazine, 304* (1825), 34–41.

MacLachlan, Ian. (2004). "Betting the Farm: Food Safety, Risk Society, and the Canadian Cattle and Beef Commodity Chain," In Andrew Heintzman and Evan Solomon, eds., *Feeding the Future—From Fat to Famine: How to Solve the World's Food Crises* (pp. 40–69). Toronto: Anansi Press.

Manning, Richard. (2004). "The Oil We Eat: Following the Food Chain Back To Iraq." *Harper's Magazine* February. On the World Wide Web at http://www.harpers.org/TheOilWeEat.html (15 October 2006).

Marx, Karl, and Friedrich Engels. (1972 [1848])."Manifesto of the Communist Party." In R. Tucker, ed. *The Marx-Engels Reader* (pp. 331–62). New York: Norton.

May, Christopher, ed. (2006). *Global Corporate Power.* Boulder, CO: Lynne Rienner.

McDonald's. (1999). Media.McDonald's.com. On the World Wide Web at http://www.media.mcdonalds.com/secured/research/international_news.html (30 April 2004).

McFarland, Janet. (2005). "CEOs Rake It In." *The Globe and Mail* 30 April.

McKibben, Bill. (1993). *The Age of Missing Information.* New York: Plumb.

McKibben, Bill. (2005). "The Cuba Diet. What Will You Be Eating When the Revolution Comes?" *Harper's Magazine* April. On the World Wide Web at http://www.harpers.org/TheCubaDiet.html (15 October 2006).

Milkman, Ruth. (2000). "Immigrant Organizing and the New Labor Movement in Los Angeles." *Critical Sociology, 26* (1/2), 59–81.

Navdanya. (2005). Homepage. On the World Wide Web at http://www.navdanya.org/ (1 October 2006).

Nissen, Bruce. (2000). "Editor's Introduction: The Labor Movement in a New, Globalized Environment." *Critical Sociology, 26* (1/2), 3–8.

No Sweat. (2005). "Changing an Industry." On the World Wide Web at http://www.nosweatapparel.com/ (1 October 2006).

Organic Consumers Association. (2005). "Prohibited Gene-Altered Corn Found in Latin American & Caribbean Food Aid Shipments. Source: Environmental News Service <www.ens-newswire.com>." On the World Wide Web at http://www.organicconsumers.org/ge/caribbean21705.cfm (16 February 2005).

Organic Consumers Association (OCA). (2007). "OCA Declares Victory in Its Frankenbucks Campaign." On the World Wide Web at http://www.organicconsumers.org/starbucks/index.cfm (retrieved 19 August 2009).

Oxfam. (2002). "Mugged: Poverty in your Coffee Cup." Research paper. On the World Wide Web at http://www.oxfamamerica.org/newsandpublications/publications/research_reports/mugged (September 2002).

Pickard, Miguel. (2005). "In the Crossfire: MesoAmerican Migrants Journey North." *IRC Americas*. On the World Wide Web at http://www.yorku.ca/hdrnet/images/uploaded/0503migrants.pdf (18 March 2005).

Picot, Garnett, and John Myles. (2005). "Income Inequality and Low Income in Canada: An International Perspective." Statistics Canada Research Paper. On the World Wide Web at http://www.statcan.ca/english/research/11F0019MIE/11F0019MIE2005240.pdf (10 February 2005).

Pimentel, David, and Anne Wilson. (2004). "World Population, Agriculture, and Nutrition," *World Watch Magazine*, Sept/October. On the World Wide Web (Energy Bulletin Website) at http://www.energybulletin.net/3834.html (5 January 2005).

Rekacewicz, Philippe. (1997). "Overview of the State of Soil Degradation in the World." *Atlas of Desertification in the World*, 2nd ed. London, UK: Arnold Publishers. On the World Wide Web at http://www.povertymap.net/mapsgraphics/index.cfm?data_id523360andtheme5 (14 October 2006).

Robbins, Richard H. (2005). *Global Problems and the Culture of Capitalism*, 3rd ed. Boston: Pearson.

Ross, Andrew, ed. (1997). *No Sweat. Fashion, Free Trade, and the Rights of Garment Workers*. New York: Verso.

Ross, Andrew. (2004). *Low Pay, High Profile. The Global Push for Fair Labor*. New York: The New Press.

Schlosser, Eric. (2001). *Fast Food Nation. The Dark Side of the All American Meal*. Boston: Houghton Mifflin.

Schor, J. B. (1998). *The Overspent American*. New York: Basic Books.

Sheak, Bob, and Melissa Morris. (2002). "The Limits of the Job Supply in U.S. Capitalism: Subemployment Measures and Trends." *Critical Sociology*, 28 (3), 389–415.

Shipler, David. (2004). *The Working Poor*. New York: Knopf.

Shrybman, Steven. (2000). *Trade, Agriculture, and Climate Change: How Agricultural Trade Policies Fuel Climate Change*. Institute for Agriculture and Trade Policy. On the World Wide Web at http://www.iatp.org (3 November 2000).

Speidel, Joseph. (2003). "Environment and Health. Population, Consumption, and Human Health." In *Global Environmental Challenges of the 21st Century. Resources, Consumption, and Sustainable Solutions*. USA: Scholarly Resources Inc. 1–13.

Speidel, Joseph. (2003). "Environment and Health. Population, Consumption, and Human Health." In *Global Environmental Challenges of the 21st Century. Resources, Consumption, and Sustainable Solutions* (pp. 1–13). New York: Scholarly Resources Inc.

Starr, Amory. (1999). *Naming the Enemy: Anti-Corporate Movements Confront Globalization*. London: Zed Books.

Statistics Canada. (2009). "Latest Release from the Labour Force Survey." *The Daily* 7 August. On the World Wide Web at http://www.statcan.gc.ca/subjects-sujets/labour-travail/lfs-epa/lfs-epa-eng.htm (19 August 2009).

Strange, Susan. (1986). *Casino Capitalism*. London: Blackwell Books.

Sustain/Elm Farm Research Centre Report. (2001). "Eating Oil. Food in a Changing Climate." On the World Wide Web at http://www.sustainweb.org/pdf/eatoil_sumary.pdf (15 December 2001).

Tomlinson, John. (1991). *Cultural Imperialism: A Critical Introduction*. Baltimore: John Hopkins University Press.

Treasury Board of Canada Secretariat. 2007. "Canada's Performance Report 2006–07—Annexes." http://www.tbs-sct.gc.ca/reports-rapports/cp-rc/2006-2007/ann/ann17-eng.asp (retrieved 19 August 2009).

United Nations. (2001). *United Nations Human Development Report 2001*. New York: UNDP.

United Nations Conference on Trade and Development. (n.d.). "Table 8.2. Cross-border M&A purchases, by region/economy of purchaser, 1987–2004." On the World Wide Web at http://www.unctad.org/Templates/Download.asp?docid=6085?=1&intItemID=3277 (retrieved 19 August 2009).

U.S. Bureau of Labor Statistics. (2009). *Labor Force Statistics from the Current Population Survey*. On the World Wide Web at http://www.bls.gov/cps/ (19 August 2009).

Wall, Melissa. (2000). "KFC into India: A Case Study of Resistance to Globalization Discourse." In Robin Andersen and Lance Strate, eds., *Critical Studies in Media Commercialism* (pp. 291–309). Oxford: Oxford University Press.

Wallerstein, Immanuel. (2002). "The Eagle Has Crash Landed." *Foreign Policy* 131 (July/August), 60–68.

Walt, Vivienne. (2008). "The World's Growing Food-Price Crisis." *Time* 27 February. On the World Wide Web at http://www.time.com/time/world/article/0,8599,1717572-2,00.html (27 February 2008).

Waters, Malcolm. (1995). *Globalisation*. New York: Routledge.

Wheeler, David, and Jane Thompson. (2004). "The Brand Barons and the Business of Food," In A. Heintzman and E. Solomon, eds., *Feeding the Future* (pp. 191–236). Toronto, Canada: Anansi Press.

Woodroffe, Jessica, and Mark Ellis-Jones. (2000). "States of Unrest: Resistance to IMF Policies in Poor Countries," *World Development Movement Report*. On the World Wide Web (Global Policy Forum) at http://www.globalpolicy.org/socecon/bwi-wto/imf/2000/protest.htm (8 September 2000).

Workman, Daniel. (2006). "McDonalds Global Sales: Big Mac's International Revenues Sizzle in 2006." *Suite 101.com*. On the World Wide Web at http://internationaltrade.suite101.com/article.cfm/mcdonalds_global_sales (retrieved 19 August 2009).

World Bank. (2008). "World Bank Development Indicators." http://www.rrojasdatabank.info/wdi2008toc.htm (retrieved 19 August 2009).

World Development Movement. (2003). "States of Unrest III: Resistance to IMF and World Bank Policies in Poor Countries." On the World Wide Web at http://www.wdm.org.uk/resources/maps/statesofunrestmap01122002.pdf (retrieved 10 August 2009).

World Wildlife Fund (WWF). (2004). "Soy Boom: Doom or Boon for South America's Forests and Savannah." On the World Wide Web at http://www.wwf.org.uk/news/scotland/n_0000001332.asp (2 September 2004).

Yalnizyan, Armine. (2007). *The Rich and the Rest of Us: The Changing Face of Canada's Growing Gap.* Toronto: Canadian Centre for Policy Alternatives.

CHAPTER 20

Aruni, Janice. (2004). "Educational Entrepreneurialism in the Private Tutoring Industry: Balancing Profitability with the Humanistic Face of Schooling." *Canadian Review of Anthropology and Sociology, 41* (4), 475–91.

Brym, R. (1978). *The Jewish Intelligentsia and Russian Marxism: A Sociological Study of Intellectual Radicalism and Ideological Divergence.* London: MacMillan.

Brym, R. (1986). "Incorporation versus Power Models of Working Class Radicalism with Special Reference to North America." *Canadian Journal of Sociology, 11,* 227–51.

Brym, R., and Lenton, R. (2001). *Love Online: A Report on Digital Dating in Canada.* Toronto: MSN.CA

Creese, G. (1988). "The Politics of Dependence: Women, Work, and Unemployment in the Vancouver Labour Movement before World War II." *Canadian Journal of Sociology, 13,* 121–42.

Creese, G. (1999). *Contracting Masculinity: Gender, Class and Race in a White-Collar Union, 1944–1994.* Toronto: Oxford University Press.

Cresswell, J. W. (1998). *Qualitative Inquiry and Research Design: Choosing among Five Traditions.* Thousand Oaks, CA: Sage.

Davies, Scott. (2002). "The Paradox of Progressive Education: A Frame Analysis." *Sociology of Education, 75* (4), 269–86.

Davies, Scott, and Neil Guppy. (2006). *The Schooled Society: An Introduction to the Sociology of Education.* Toronto: Oxford University Press.

Douglas, J. (1970). "Understanding Everyday Life." In J. Douglas, ed., *Understanding Everyday Life* (pp. 3–44). Chicago: Aldine.

Fisher, R. A. (1966 [1936]). "Has Mendel's Work Been Rediscovered?" In C. Stern and E. Sherwood, eds., *Origin of Genetics; A Mendel Sourcebook* (pp. 139–72). San Francisco: W.H. Freeman.

Fortin, N. (2005). "Gender Role Attitudes and the Labour-Market Outcomes of Women across OECD Countries." *Oxford Review of Economic Policy, 21* (3), 416–38.

Foschi, M. and S. Buchan. (1990). "Ethnicity, Gender, and Perceptions of Task Competence." *Canadian Journal of Sociology, 15,* 1–18.

Foschi, M., L. Lai, and K. Sigerson. (1994). "Gender and Double Standards in the Assessment of Job Applicants." *Social Psychological Quarterly, 57* (4), 326–39.

Giddens, A. (1984). *The Constitution of Society.* Berkeley, CA: University of California Press.

Ginsberg, E., and F. Henry. (1985). *Who Gets the Work?* Toronto: Urban Alliance on Race Relations and the Social Planning Council of Toronto.

Goffman, E. (1961). *Asylums: Essays on the Social Situations of Mental Patients and Other Inmates.* New York: Doubleday/Anchor.

Gold, A. D. (1998). "President's Report." *Criminal Lawyers Newsletter, 19* (2). On the World Wide Web at

http://www.criminallawyers.ca/newslett/19-2/gold.html (3 November 2000).

Gross, N. (2009). "A Pragmatist Theory of Social Mechanisms" *American Sociological Review, 74,* 358–79.

Guppy, N., and S. Davies. (1998). *Education in Canada.* Ottawa: Statistics Canada.

Guppy, N., & S. Davies. (2009). "School's Out for the Summer: Should It Be?" In E. Grabb and N. Guppy (eds.), *Social Inequality in Canada: Patterns, Problems, and Policies* (pp. 429–31). Toronto: Pearson Prentice Hall.

Guppy, Neil, and George Gray. (2008). *Successful Surveys: Research Methods and Practice,* 4th ed. Toronto: Thomson Nelson.

Haggerty, K.D. (2001). *Making Crime Count.* Toronto: University of Toronto Press.

Haggerty, K. D. (2004). "Ethics Creep: Governing Social Science Research in the Name of Ethics." *Qualitative Sociology, 24* (4), 391–414.

Henry, F. (1999). *The Colour of Democracy: Racism in Canadian Society.* Toronto: Harcourt Brace.

Houtkoop, H. (2000). *Interaction and the Standardized Survey Interview: The Living Questionnaire.* Cambridge, MA: Cambridge University Press.

Kaufman, F. C. M., Q.C. (1998). *Report of the Kaufman Commission on Proceedings Involving Guy Paul Morin* (Morin Inquiry Executive Summary Report) (Conclusion 1). On the World Wide Web at http://www.attorneygeneral.jus.gov.on.ca/html/MORIN/exesumrec/morin_concl.pdf (17 July 2000).

Kleppner, D., and Jackiw, R. (2000). "One Hundred Years of Quantum Physics." *Science, 289* (August), 893–98. On the World Wide Web at http://vega.bac.pku.edu.cn/,rxxu/teach/qp100.htm (21 September 2000).

Kuhn, T. S. (1962). *The Structure of Scientific Revolutions.* Chicago: University of Chicago Press.

Laxer, G. (1989). *Open for Business: The Roots of Foreign Ownership in Canada.* Toronto: Oxford University Press.

Lenton, R. (1990). "Techniques of Child Discipline and Abuse by Parents." *Canadian Review of Sociology and Anthropology, 27,* 157–85.

Mawani, Renisa. (2003). "Imperial Legacies (Post)Colonial Identities: Law, Space, and the Making of Stanley Park, 1859–2001." *Law/Text/Culture, 7,* 98–141.

McMullan, J., and P. Swan. (1989). "Social Economy and Arson in Nova Scotia." *Canadian Journal of Criminology,* 281–308.

Orel, Vitezslav. (1996). *Gregor Mendel: The First Geneticist.* Trans. Stephen Finn. Oxford, UK: Oxford University Press.

Park, R. (2000). *Voodoo Science: The Road from Foolishness to Fraud.* New York: Oxford University Press.

Pineo, P., and J. Porter. (1967). "Occupational Prestige in Canada." *Canadian Review of Anthropology and Sociology, 4,* 24–40.

Popper, Karl. (1977 [1934]). *The Logic of Scientific Discovery,* 14th ed. New York: Harper.

Reitz, J. (1993). "Statistics on Racial Discrimination in Canada." *Policy Options, 14,* 32–36.

Riga, L. (2008). "The Ethnic Roots of Class Universalism: Rethinking the 'Russian' Revolutionary Elite." *American Journal of Sociology, 114,* 649–705.

Roethlisberger, F. J., and D. W. Dickson. (1939). *Management and the Worker.* Cambridge, MA: Harvard University Press.

Scarce, R. (2000). *Fishy Business: Salmon, Biology, and the Social Construction of Nature.* Philadelphia: Temple University Press.

Schreiber, D., R. Matthews, and B. Elliott (2003). "The Framing of Farmed Fish: Product, Efficiency, and Technology" *Canadian Journal of Sociology, 28* (2), 153–69.

Statistics Canada. (2004). *General Social Survey on Social Engagement, Cycle 17: An Overview of Findings.* Catalogue No. 89-598-XIE. Ottawa: Statistics Canada. On the World Wide Web at http://www.statcan.ca/bsolc/english/bsolc?catno589-598-XIE (14 October 2006).

Tanner, J. (2001). *Teenage Troubles: Youth and Deviance in Canada,* 2nd ed. Toronto: Nelson Thomson Learning.

Urmetzer, P., D. Blake, and N. Guppy. (1999). "Individualized Solutions to Environmental Problems: The Case of Automobile Pollution." *Canadian Public Policy, 25* (3), 345–59.

Weber, M. (1949 [1904]). *The Methodology of the Social Sciences.* Glencoe, IL: Free Press.

Wilson, B. (2002). "The Canadian Rave Scene and Five Theses on Youth Resistance." *Canadian Journal of Sociology, 27,* 373–412.

INDEX

Bold numbers indicate pages where a term is defined; numbers starting with "W-" refer to Chapter 21.

A

Aboriginal people, 34
  class diversity, 192–93
  colonialism and, 213
  criminal victimization of, 348
  culture of, 189–91
  discrimination against, 126
  education of, 296
  families, 240
  foragers among, W-20
  health of, 418
  incarceration patterns, 348
  job ghettos, 268
  land use, 497
  names given to, 189–90
  non-status, 189
  poverty of, 124, 126–27, 144, 191
  seniors, 415
  term origins, 189
Aboriginal rights, 38
Abortion, 241
Absolute poverty, **142**, **151**
Abstraction, **30**, **46**
Abu Ghraib, 69
"Academic harems," 296
Accidents, normal, **402**, **407**
Achieved status, **125–26**, **151**, 181
"Acting white" phenomenon, 298
Action, meaningful, **482**, **503**
Adolescence
  defined, 58
  education, 296
  job ghettos, 268
  justice system and, 358–59
  socialization during, 58–59
Adolescents
  friendships, 59
  sexuality, 58
  suicide, 7
Adorno, Theodor, 100
Adult socialization, **59–61**, **71**
Advertisements, 43–44
Advocacy groups, 169
Affirmative action, **174**, **177**
Affluence. *See* Wealth
Africa
  foragers in, W-20
  HIV/AIDS in, W-8
  peri-urbanization in, 373
  urban development, 372–73

African-Americans
  "acting white" phenomenon, 298
  families, 240–41
  incarceration patterns, 348
  restrictive covenants, 185
  voting and, 439
Age as leveller hypothesis, **421**, **427**
Ageism, **412**, **427**
Agents of socialization, **61**, 62
Aggression, gender differences in, 84
Aging
  commonsense beliefs about, 410–11
  crime risks, 347
  diversity within, 414–15
  gender differences, 414
  health care and, 422–24
  inequality, 417–22
  population, 411–14
  self-care and, 422–23
  suicide rates and, 7
Agricultural societies, W-**20**–W-21, W-**25**
Agriculture and globalization, 470–73
Albas, Cheryl and Daniel, 29, 60
Aleshire, Daniel, 327
Alexander the Great, 4
Alfonso, Nzinga Mbemba, 211
Alienation
  capitalism and, 277
  concept of, 276–79
  defined, **277**, **306**
  fighting, 277–79
Alienation and Freedom (Blauner), 276
Alignment, frame, **442**, **449**
Allahar, Anton, 305
Allen, Paul, 462
All in the Family, 187
al-Qaeda, 448
Alternative environmental paradigm, **389–91**, **407**
Alternative news sources, **108**, **118**
Alternative oppositional viewpoints, 100
Alternative schools, 302
Alternative viewpoints, **118**
Altruistic suicide, **6**, **24**
Alzheimer's disease, 416
American Academy of Pediatrics, 65
American Idol, 104
American Revolution, 10, 35
Amnesty International, 36
Ancestors, **182**
Anderson, Benedict, 195
"Androcentrism," 399
Animal Farm (Orwell), 433

Anomic suicide, **6**, **24**
Anomie, 326, 348
Anorexia nervosa, 91
Anthropocentrism, **398**, **407**
Anticipatory socialization, **59**, **71**
Anti-racist feminists, 445
Anti-school subculture, 298
Anti-Semitism, 186, 327, W-3
Apocalyptic demography, 415
Appearance of unanimity, W-11
Aquatic foragers, W-19
Aristotle, 11
Arscott, Jane, 173
Aruni, Janice, 493
Asch, Solomon, W-10–W-11
Ascribed characteristics, 181
Ascribed status, **125–26**, **151**
Asia. *See also specific countries*
  drug use, 341
Asian Tigers, 218
Assault, sexual, 91–93
Assembly-line technology, 272–73
Assembly of First Nations, 189, 190, 443
Association, differential, **360**
Athletic teams, 66
Attachments, 350
Attainment, occupational status, **151**
Attitudes, behaviour *versus*, 491–93
Attitudes, sexual, 78–83
Audience research, 111
Authoritarian leadership, W-**17**, W-**25**
Authority
  defined, **431**, **449**
  erosion of, 39
  respect for, 40
  structures of, W-3–W-5
  use of force by, 432
Autonomy, 232
  versus constraint, 21

B

Bacon, Francis, 481
Bacon, Kevin, W-6
Bad jobs, 254, 258–59
  technology, 270
Badges of ability, 285
Bad-work syndrome, 268
Bainbridge, William, 324
Bairoch, Paul, 213
Bales, Kevin, 469
Barker, Martin, 184
Barrymore, Drew, W-12
Bashevkin, Sylvia, 172
Baudrillard, Jean, 44

Beaudoin, Louise, 195
Behaviour
    attitudes *versus*, 491–93
    gender-specific, 88–89
    sexual, 78–83
Beliefs, 350
Bell Globemedia, 102
Bell, Daniel, 259, 324, W-21–W-22
Bell, John Kim, 192
Bellah, Robert, 330
Berger, Peter, 314, 330
Bertelsmann, 100
Betrayal, W-3
Beyond the Limits (Meadows et al.), 397
Bhopal, India, 402
Bias
    minimizing, 480–81
    observer, 480
    urban, 373
Bibby, Reginald W., 38, 78
Bible Belt, 324
Big Historical Project, 40
bin Laden, Osama, 313, 455
Biocentric egalitarianism, **398**, **407**
Biological determinism, **229**, **251**
Biosphere crisis, 397
Birth rate, 365
Black, Conrad, 349
Black Hawk Down, W-3
Black Sabbath, 44
Blair, Tony, 23
Blogosphere, 115–16
Blogs, 114
Blue-collar sector, 136
Blue-collar workers/jobs, 20, 175, 255
Blum, Deborah, 87
Blumenfeld, Hans, 376
Boat Harbour, 404
Body image, 90–91
Bohm, Fabienne, 355
Boldt, Menno, 192
Bollywood, 464
Bonacich, Edna, 188
Bonner, Kieran, 364
Bosh, Chris, 184
Bottom-up globalization, 455–56
Bouchard, Gerard, 196
Bourassa, Robert, 400
Bourgeoisie, **128**, **151**
Brain hemispheres, 83–84
Brainwashing, 326
Branch Davidians, 69
Branswell, Helen, 106
Braverman, Harry, 259
Bray, Alison, 106
Brenner, Robert, 212
Britain, 213
British East India Company, 213
British North America Act, 193
Broadening-base hypothesis, **392**, **407**

Brown, Dan, 310
Brown, Lester, 217
Brundtland, Gro Harlem, 391, 401
Brym, Robert J., 497, W-2
Buchan, Shari, 486–87
Buddhism, 81
Buffett, Warren, 462
Bulger, James, W-11
Bulimia, 91
Bumper-sticker morality, 294
Bureaucracy
    characteristics, 270–72
    defined, **432**–33, W-**5**, W-**25**
    dehumanization of, W-**15**
    dyadic relationships, W-15
    efficient, W-17–W-18
    function of, 433
    inefficiency, W-13–W-16
    inertia in, W-**15**, W-**25**
    informal side, W-16–W-17
    innovative, W-17
    leadership, W-17
    organization, W-18
    ritualism, W-**15**, W-**25**
    Weber's views of, 270–71
Burgess, Ernest W., 370–71
Bush, George W., 310
Buss, David, 84, 86–87
Byrne, Rhonda, 310
Bystander apathy, W-11

C
Calgary, 371
    growth of, 368
Calment, Jeanne, 441
Cameron, James, 104
Campbell, Kim, 171–72
Canada
    aging in, 411–14
    apocalyptic demography, 415
    ascribed status in, 126
    cities, 368
    college ranking, 289–90
    crime in, 342–47
    criminal justice trends, 356–58
    cultural diversity in, 33–36
    cultural evolution, 35
    cultural identity in, 40
    drug use in, 340–41
    environmental risk in, 404
    equality of women and men, 35
    ethnic diversity, 378–79
    ethnic identification in, 181–83
    family policy, 247–49
    family structure, 236–41
    gender inequality and, 160–70
    health care, 412, 423–25
    health inequality in, 418–19
    homicide rates, 344–46
    identity, 35

    immigration in, 196–200
    income inequality in, 141–47
    indigenous people, treatment of, 190–92
    industrial economy in, 367–69
    Industrial Revolutions in, 255
    job satisfaction in, **274**
    labour force, 258–59
    labour market, 255–56
    labour market inequality, 200–203
    LICO, 142–46
    media monopolies, 101–3
    Muslims in, 329–30
    occupational sh ifts in, 136–38
    political participation, 434
    postmodernism in, 38
    race issues in, 180–81
    racism in, 185–86
    religious commitment in, 315, 319–21, 324
    religious diversity in, 310, 315–16
    respect for authority in, 40
    retirement in, 61
    rights revolution in, 36–38
    same-sex marriage in, 80
    schools in, 286–92, 300–306
    sense of identity in, 103–4
    service economy in, 257–61
    sexual attitudes in, 78–83
    sexual violence in, 91–93
    sociological paradigms, 19
    sociology jobs in, 23
    strike patterns, 441
    suicide profile in, 6–7
    suicide rate, 5
    television and, 103–5
    unions, 279
    wage inequality in, 131–32
    wealth distribution in, 139–40
    welfare policies, 147
    women's education, 295–96
Canadian Advisory Council on the Status
    of Women, 169
Canadian Charter of Rights and
    Freedoms, 169, 189
Canadian Standards Association, 398
Candid Camera, W-10
CanWest Global, 100, 101–3, 112
Capitalism, **208**, **223**
    alienation and, 277
    casino, 456–57
    class conflict and, 128–30
    globalization and, 456, 467
    Marx's view, 366
    symbolic interactionism, 16
Capitalist class, 255
Capone, Al, 349
Carbon footprint, 394, 466
Cardoso, Fernando, 23
Careers. *See* Jobs
Carrey, Jim, 104
Carrying capacity, **397**, **407**

Cartagena Protocol on Biosafety, 472
Casino capitalism, 456–57
Castes, 297–98
Caste system, 126, **151**
Causation, **483**
    correlation *versus*, 484
    defined, **503**
CBC, 112
CCD (Convention on Cultural Diversity), 463
CCF (Cooperative Commonwealth
    Federation), 440
Centralization, 457
Certainty principle, **357, 360**
Challenger space disaster, W-13–W-14
Change, social, 349–50
Chanukah, 33
Charest, Jean, 171
Charismatic authority, 431
Charity, 8
Charlottetown Accord, 192
Charter group, 200
Charter of Rights and Freedoms, 169, 189
Chávez, Hugo, 220
Cherry, Don, 184
Chesnais, François, 218
Chibnall, Steve, 342
Chicago School, 369–70
Child abuse, 237
Child care
    gender roles, 245
    men, 238
    nonparental, 245
    policy agenda, 248
    Quebec, 249
    women, 159, 161
Child-labour laws, 269
Children
    abuse of, 491–92
    ads directed at, 43–44
    care of, 365–66
    development stages, 54–55
    extended families and, 229
    gender identities, 155–56
    gender socialization of, 57
    identity and, 55–56
    immigrant, 196
    latch-key, 63
    mass media's influence, 65
    middle-class families, 234–35
    mother's responsibility for, 236–41
    poverty, 237
    preindustrial economies, 233–34
    raised in isolation, 51
    socialization of, 49–52, 242
    working-class families, 236
Child Tax Benefit, 249
China
    development, 218
    economic development, 466
    foreign investment, 218

Chinese, prejudice against, 188
Chinese Immigration Act, 188
Chirac, Jacques, 463–64
Chomsky, Noam, 100
Chrétien, Jean, 102, 455
Christakis, Dimitri, 116
Christianity
    American culture and, 330
    Canada, in, 319–21
    gender inequality, 87
    goals, 318–19
    membership, 318
    organizational approaches, 317–18
    organization types, 315–16
    Polish, W-3
    sexual issues and, 81
Christian right, 310, 329, 330
Christmas, 33
Chronic conditions, **416, 427**
Church–sect typology, 317, **333**
Cinderella, 90
Circulatory mobility, **138, 151**
Cities
    Canadian, 368
    corporate, **373–76**
    defined, **364, 385**
    dual, 379–83
    edge, **377–78**
    industrial, 367–72
    postmodern, 376–83
    preindustrial, 364–65
Citizenship
    civil, **444, 449**
    political, **444, 449**
    social, **444, 450**
    universal, **444**
City of Quartz (Davis), 382
Civic nationalism, **195, 204**
Civil citizenship, **444, 449**
Civil religion, **330, 333**
Civil society, **433, 449**
Civil union, 80, 81
Clark, S. D., 19, 324
Clark, Terry Nichols, 128, 135
Class conflict, **129, 151**
Class consciousness, **129**, 278
Classes, 132
    Aboriginal people and, 192–93
    agrarian class structure, 213
    concept of, 127
    conflict, 15, 128–30
    consciousness, 15
    defined, **127, 151**
    division of, W-21
    gender, 347–48
    immigrants, 197
    income distribution, 140
    Internet usage, 113
    labour, 213
    life-chances and, **130**–31

    mode of production and, 128–29
    political parties and, 129
    ruling, **433**
    school selection and, 286–87
    sociological imagination, 9
    status and, 130
    structure, 126–28
    suburban environment, 375
    underdevelopment, 212
    See also Middle class; Working class
Class reproduction, 286
Class structure, **127, 151**
Clawbacks of social assistance, 147
Clayoquot Sound, 400
Clear-cutting, 400
Climate change, 20–21
Closed stratification systems, **126, 151**
Closure, social, **152**
Cloutier, Sheila Watt, 393
CMC. *See* Computer-mediated communi-
    cation (CMC)
Cohen, Albert, 349
Cohen, Marjorie Griffin, 168
Cold War, 207, 208, 219
    immigration, 197
Coleman, James S., 297–98, W-23
Collective conscience, **333**
Collective religiosity, **316**–17, **333**
Collectives, W-5, W-23
Colleges and universities. *See* Higher education
Collins, Jock, 197
Collins, Patricia Hill, 157
Collins, Randall, 299–300
Colonialism
    deindustrializing effects, 213
    handicraft industry and, 213
    impact of, 210
Colonization, 9
Columbia disaster, W-11, W-13–W-14
Columbine High School, 65
Columbus, Christopher, 189
Comfort zone and culture, 31–32
Commercialization, 55
Commitments, 350
Commodity, 462–63
Commonsense knowledge, 12–13
Communal households, 231–33
Communication, 54–55
    computer-mediated, 98
    defined, **98, 118**
    instantaneous, 98–99
    print, 99
Communism, 41
Communities
    environmental mobilization, 395–97
    private gated, 381–82
    risk perception, 402–4
    small town, 363
    virtual, 115–16, **118**
    visible minority, 379

Commuters, reverse, 378
Compassion, lack of, W-4
Compensation packages, 139
Competence, cloak of, 67–68
Compression of morbidity hypothesis, **417, 427**
Compulsory heterosexuality, **78, 95**
Computer-mediated communication (CMC), 98, **111, 118**
Computers
    job outlook and, 270
    productivity and, 270
    workplace and, 270
Comte, Auguste, 11, 13, 17
Concentric-zone model, **370**–71, **385**
Confinement institutions, popularity of, 356–58
Conflict, class, 128–30, **151**
Conflict and culture, 30
Conflict crime, **339, 360**
Conflict theories of deviance
    defined, **25**
    ethnic relations and, 191–92
    features of, 15–16
    race relations and, 191–92
    symbolic interactionism, 16
Conformity, W-2–W-3, W-10
Confucius, 11
Congress of Aboriginal Peoples, 190
Conscience, collective, **333**
Consciousness, class, **129**
Consensus-building approach, 169
Consensus crime, **338, 360**
Consequences, 15
Conservationist, resource, 398
Conservatives, 105, 106
Constitutional rights, 38
Constraint, W-23
    autonomy versus, 21
Constructionism, social
    defined, **95**
    deviance, 341–42
    environment and, 405–6
    gender differences, 87–88
Consumerism, **474**
    counterculture, 44–45
    culture and, 43–44
    defined, **46, 463**
    ecological consequences, 465–66
    fair trade and, 465
    global, 462–63
Contest mobility, **288, 307**
Contraception, 241–42
Contradictory class locations, **133**
Control, social
    crime and, 348
    defined, **30**
    deviance and, 337–38, 356–58, **360**
    Internet and, 115
    theories of, 348, 350–51

Control theories, **360**
Convention on Cultural Diversity (CCD), 463
Convention refugees, 199
Cooley, Charles Horton, 52–53
Coontz, Stephanie, 236
Cooperation, **30**
    culture and, 30
    defined, **46**
    group, W-11
Cooperative Commonwealth Federation (CCF), 440
Copernicus, 10, 11
Core values, 41
Corporate cities
    defined, **373, 385**
    description, 373–74
    suburbs of, 374–76
    way of life, 374–76
Corporations
    cultural imperialism and, 463–64
    global growth of, 458
    organizational environment, W-18
    power of, 458–59
    tax rate, 458
Correlation, 484
Cortés, Hernán, 207
Cosmetic surgery, 91
Côté, James, 305
Cotgrove, Stephen, 389–90
Counterculture
    consumerism and, 44–45
    defined, **44, 46**
    subculture and, 44–45
Counter-urbanization, 376
Country of asylum class refugees, 199
Cow worship, 32
Craftspeople, 255
Creativity, 56
Creba, Jane, 345
Credential inflation, **299**–300, **307**
Creese, Gillian, 497
Crestwood Heights (Seeley, Loosley), 375
Crick, Francis, W-22
Crime, **337, 360**
    Canadian, 342–47
    conception of, 337–42
    conflict, **339**
    consensus, **338**
    control theories, 350–51
    corporate, 349–50
    dark figure of, **343, 360**
    definitions of, 338–40
    direct observation, 346–47
    gays and lesbians, 339
    gender, 347–48
    gender stratification and, 351–52
    globalization and, 349–50
    homicide rates, 344–46
    incest, 340

    learning theories, 350–51
    measuring, 342–50
    motivational theories, 348–50
    patterns of, 342–50
    recidivism, **342**
    regional variation in, 343–44
    risk factors, 348
    self-report studies, 346–47
    social change and, 349–50
    social class, 347–48
    statistics, 342–43
    strain theories, 348–50
    street, **348**
    suicide, 339
    trends, 342–47
    white-collar, **341,** 349
    youth, 353–56
    See also Deviance
Crime control model of justice, **358, 360**
Crimes *mala in se*, 338, 339
Crimes *mala prohibita*, 339
Criminal justice
    models, 358
    system, **338,** 358–59, **360**
    trends, 358–59
Critical perspective, **99**
    defined, **118**
    media, 99–100, 108
Critical thinking, 3
Cronenberg, David, 104
Crusades, moral, 341–42
CTV, 112
Cuba, 473
Cultivation analysis, **109, 118**
Cult of domesticity, 234
Cult of thinness, 90
Cults, 69, 326, **331, 333**
Cultural diversification, 33–36, 37–40
    Canada, 34–35
Cultural hypothesis, 491–92
Cultural imperialism, **104, 463, 474**
    backlash, 464–65
    corporations and, 463–64
    media's role, 104, **118**
    spread of, 463–64
Culture
    ambivalence in, 31–32
    comfort zone, 31–32
    commercialization, 55
    commodity, as, 463
    conflict, 30
    constraining aspects of, 41–45
    constructionists' views, 87
    consumerism, **33,** 43–44
    dangerous aspects of, 41–45
    defined, **29, 46**
    differences, 31–32
    diversification, 33–36
    freedom, as, 33–41
    gender, 56–57

globalization and, 33–36
group, W-11
identifying with, 40
material, 30, **46**
origins of, 30–31
postmodernism and, 38–41
problem-solving function, 29–30
rationalization, **32**–33, 41–43
religion, 33–34, 328–30
rights revolution in, 36–38
socialization and, 49–50
youth, 493
Culture industry, 100
Culture of poverty thesis, **191**, **204**
Curriculum, hidden, 64, **292**–93,
    295–96, **307**
Cyberactivism, 116

D

Dark figure of crime, **343**, **360**
Darroch, Gordon, 200
Darwin, Charles, 209
Dasko, Donna, 23
Davies, Lynn, 298
Davies, Scott, 497
Davies, Simon, 354
Da Vinci Code, The (Brown), 310
Davis, Kingsley, 131, 135
Davis, Mike, 382
Davis, Simon, 84
Dawkins, Richard, 310
Dead-end jobs, 265–66
Death, 29
    denial of, 61–62
    old age, 412
    rates, 365, 412–13
d'Eaubonne, Françoise, 399
Debt, foreign, 214–19
Declaration of Nyeleni, 222
Deep ecology, **398**, **407**
Dehumanization, W-**15**, W-**25**
Dei, George, 297, 298
Deindustrialization, 213, **223**, 224,
    258, **282**
Democracies
    deficits in, 462, **474**
    leadership in, W-17, W-**25**
    power in, 432–33
    revolution and, 10, **25**
Democratic deficit, **474**
Democratic leadership, W-**17**
Democratic revolution, defined, **25**
Demographic transition, 365–66, **385**
Demography, 363, 415, **427**
Denominationalism, **324**, **333**
Dependency, economic, 159–60
Dependency theory, **210**, **223**
Dependent variables, **487**, **503**
"Depressed periphery," 404
Depression, 4

Deprivation, relative, **440**, **449**
Deprivation, religious, 323
Desakota, 373
Descartes, René, 10
Determinism, biological, **229**, **251**
Deterrence theory, **356**, **360**
Devall, Bill, 398
Developing countries, 9
Development
    biological resources, 214
    China, 218
    climate, 207
    debt, 214–19
    dependency theory, 210–13
    geography of, 214
    global inequality, 208–9
    history of, 207–8
    idea of, 207
    poverty, 215–19
    relevance of, 208–9
    security, 208–9
    social justice, 208–9
    stages of, **209**
    structural adjustment, 214–19
    tariffs, 213
    theories of, 209–13
    underdevelopment, 211
Development, economic
    immigration and, 196–200
    neoliberal perspective, 214–15
    preindustrial world, 210–13
    sustainable, 391, **407**
Deviance, 4, **360**
    conception of, 337–42
    defining, **337**
    measuring, 342–50
    medical model of, 356–58
    news media and, 108
    patterns of, 342–50
    social construction of, 341–42
    social control and, 342–50
    women, 352
    youth, 353–56
    See also Crime
Dewey, John, 301
*Diagnostic and Statistical Manual of Mental
    Disorders*, 78
Diamond, Jared, 214
Dickens, Charles, 482, W-21
Diddy, 45
Differential association, **350**, **360**
Digital divide, 113, **453**, **474**
    new, 114–15
Dimensions of religiosity, **315**, **333**
Direct observation and crime, 346–47
Disabilities as work barriers, 268–69
Disability, functional, **416**
Discontent, framing, 442
Discrimination, **187**, **204**
    Aboriginal people, 126

statistical, **167**, 178
systemic, 186
Disinhibition, 110
Diversification. *See* Cultural diversification
Diversity
    aging, 414–15
    class, Aboriginal, 192–93
    cultural, 33–36, 463
    ethnic, 378–79
    families, 236–41
    musical, 36
    religious, 310
    uniformity, 21, W-2
Division of labour, **255**, **282**
    communal households, in, 231–32
    gender, **227**, **251**
    natural, 88
    workplace, 272–73
Divorce
    aftermath, 246–47
    families and, 243–44
    gender inequality, 155
    patriarchy, 8
    preindustrial households, 233
    suicide, 7
    suicide rates and, 7
Diwali, 33
DNA, discovery of structure, W-22–W-23
Doctors, 268–69
Documentary analysis, 497
Domesticity, cult of, 234
Domestic labour, 161–62
Dominant ideology, **100**, **118**
Dominant paradigm, **389**–90, **407**
Domino theory, 219
Don Mills, building of, 374
"Double day," 162, 238
Douglas, Tommy, 423
Dowries, 233
Drugs, 340–41
Drummer, Ethel Sturgess, 235
Dual city, 379–83, **385**
Dual-income families, 377
Due-process model, **358**, **360**
Durkheim, Émile, 6–7, 13, 14–15, 17,
    286, 311, 312–13, 314, 321, 388, 496
Dyads, W-**8**, W-**15**, W-**25**
Dysfunctional consequences, **15**, **25**
Dyson, Freeman, W-23

E

East Asia. *See* Asia
East India Company, 213
Eating disorders, 90–91
Ecofeminism, 398–**99**, **407**
Ecological spot maps, 370
Ecology
    deep, **398**, **407**
    global, 470–73
    industrial cities, 370–71

social, 389
See also Environment
Economic-contingency hypothesis, **392,
    407**
Economic dependency, 159–60
Economic development
    immigration and, 196–200
    neoliberal perspective, 214–15
    preindustrial world, 210–13
    sustainable, 391
Economic immigrants, 199–200
Economy
    gentrification and, **380**–81
    industrial, 367–69
    manufacturing/service shift, 378
    political, 100–105, 399–401
    preindustrial households, 233–34
    service, 257–61
Economy, service
    Canadian, 257–61
    globalization and, 468–69
    job satisfaction measures, 274–81
    technology and, 269–70
Eco-pathfinders, 393
Edge cities, 377–78, **385**
Edison, Thomas, 34
Edmonton, 371
Education
    Aboriginal children, 296
    classical approaches, 285–92
    contemporary approaches, 285–92
    data analysis, 498–500
    economic necessity, 300–301
    gender identity and, 295–96
    health and, 417
    higher, 288–92, 304–5
    immigration policy and, 291–92
    Internet usage, 113
    jobs and, 299–300
    Marxist theory of, 286, 293, 294
    moral, 286, 294–95
    multiculturalism, 296
    occupational status and, 139
    preparation, 299
    progressive, 497
    race, 295–96
    racial identity and, 296
    rationalization for, 300
    reform, 301–4
    self-esteem, 296
    sexual harassment, 296
    social organization and, 286
    socioeconomic status and, 292
    voting and, 439
    See also Higher education; Schools
Edwards, Peter, 180
Efficiency, W-5
Efficiency, gospel of, 400
Egalitarianism, biocentric, **398, 407**
Egoistic suicide, **6, 25**

Egypt, social movements in, 448
Ehrenreich, Barbara, 279
Ehrlich, Paul, 367
Eichler, Margrit, 19, 77
Einstein, Albert, 483
Eisler, Riane, 94
Elderly. *See* Seniors
Electronic money markets, 453
Elementary Forms of the Religious Life, The
    (Durkheim), 312
Elites
    Aboriginal, 192–93
    defined, 433
    Mills' view of, 433
Elite theory
    defined, **449**
    Marxist critique of, 434–36
    pluralism critique by, 433–34
    theorists, **433**
Employment
    changes by industry, 259
    dead-end, 265–66
    equity, **174**, 177
    most common, 259
    networks and, W-7
    nonstandard, 259–61, 283
    opportunities, 265–66
    service, 257–61
    sociology, 23
    suicide, 7
    See also Jobs
Employment Equity Act (1986/1995), 175
Engels, Friedrich, 15, 466
England, Lynndie, 69
English, globalization of, 37
Entrance status, 200
Entrepreneurs, immigrant, 199
Environment, 5, 20–21
    attitudes toward, 391–94
    behaviour toward, 391–94
    concerns over, 391–94
    global consumerism and, 465–66
    organizational, W-18, W-**25**
    political economy and, 399–401
    pollution and, 401
    population and, 367
    population growth and, 389
    risk assessment, 401–4
    social construction and, 405–6
    sociological perspective, 388–89
    values, 389–91
    See also Ecology
Environment: From Surplus to Scarcity, The
    (Schnaiberg), 399
Environmental management, **401, 407**
Environmental movement
    composition, 394–95
    frames, **396**
    ideological divisions, 397–99
    mobilization, 395–97

organizations, 395, 396
    origins, 394
    pathfinders, 393
    social base, 394–95
Environmental movement organizations
    (EMOs), 395
Environmental-opportunity theory, **363,
    385**
EPZs. *See* Export processing zones (EPZs)
Equality, 3, 169
    men, 5, 35
    nonstandard jobs, 262–63
    women, 5, 35
Equal pay for equal work, **174**, 177
Equestrian foragers, W-19
Equity, employment, **174**, 177
Erickson, Lynda, 175
Ernhofer, Ken, 106
Eskimo, 190
Essentialism, **83**
    critique of, 85–87
    defined, **95**
    gender differences and, 83–87
Ethics
    globalization, 454–55
    research, 488
    sexual, 93–94
Ethnicity
    aging, 414–15
    ascribed characteristics, 196
    common identity, 181–83
    crime risks, 348
    definitions of, 181–83
    educational inequality and, 291–92
    gangs, 355
    health and, 418–19
    higher education, 291
    immigration and, 197–200
    job ghettos, 266
    postmodern cities, 376, 378–79
    vertical mosaic and, 200–203
Ethnic mobility trap, 200
Ethnic prejudices
    normative theories of, 186–89
    primordialist thesis, 187
    social-psychological approach, 186–87
    theories of, 186–89
Ethnocentrism, **32, 46**
Ethnography, **494**–95, **503**
Ethnomethodology, **25, 26**
Europe, 88
European Union, 36
Evil, social origins of, W-2–W-4, W-5
Evolutionary psychology, **229, 251**
Exclusion, 134, **151**
Exclusionary practices, 188
Executive branch, 432
Experiments
    defined, **486, 503**
    design features, 486–87

field, 488
Hawthorne effect, **488**
randomization, **487**
variables in, 487
Explanation, **483**, **503**
Export processing zones (EPZs), **469**, **474**
Extended-family households, **229**, **251**
External flexibility, **262**, **283**
External validity, **487**, **503**
Extramarital affairs, 82
Extraordinariness, news, 107
Extrinsic rewards, **259**, **282**
Exxon Valdez, 403

F
Factory fodder, 197
Factory laws, 17
Factory system, 367
Fair Labour Association, 459
Fair trade, 465
Fairy tales, 90
Falwell, Jerry, 330
Families, **251**
    Aboriginal, 240
    African American, 240–41
    communal, 231–33
    conceptualizing, 230–31
    contemporary, 234–41
    contemporary dilemmas, 227–29
    definitions of, **231**, **251**
    diversity of, 236–41
    division of labour in, 227
    divorce and, 243–44
    dual-income, 378
    finances, 160–61
    foraging societies, 231–33
    gangs, 355
    gay and lesbian, 227
    gender and, 242–43
    gender roles, 228–29
    housework, 242–43
    immigrant, 199
    marriage and, 243–44
    material inequality and, 148–49
    middle class, 234–35
    modified extended, **417**, **427**
    multigenerational, 411
    myths about, 229–30
    natural, 231
    nuclear, 227–29
    patterns, 231–34
    policies supporting, 247–49
    preindustrial, 233–34, 364–65
    reciprocity, 231–32
    reconstituted, 240, 247
    relations, 236–41
    sexuality and, 241–42
    social assistance to, 240
    socialization role, 62–63

    structural functionalists' view of, 230–31
    working class, 235–36, 243
Familism, **375**, **385**
Family-friendly workplaces, 265
Family values, 229
Family wage, **236**, **237**, **251**
Famines, causes of, 4
Faraday, Michael, 34
Fatah, Tarek, 329
Father Knows Best, 229
Fava, Sylvia, 375
Female, defining, 75–77
Femininity, 155–56
Feminism, **157**
    defined, **25**, 177
    features of, 17–18
    gender inequality explanations, 157–58
    women's movement and, 169, 445
Feminist theory, **17**
    defined, **17**, **25**
    patriarchy, 17, 18
    power, 18
Fertility dances, 35
Fertility rates, 160
Feudalism, 255
Filtered reality, 480
Financial crisis, U.S., 457
Firey, Walter, 371
First Nations, 189
Fleming, Alexander, 482
Flight Pledge campaign, 388
Florence, Elinor, 363
Fontaine, Phil, 144
Food
    Cuba, 473
    genetically engineered, 471
    global trade, 470
    hunger and, 472
    kilometres, 470
    locally grown, 472
    organic, 472
    production, 471–72
    transportation, 470–71
Food miles, 394
Foraging societies, 231–33, **251**, W-19–W-20, **W-25**
    social reproduction in, 232–33
Forbes Magazine, 139
Force, **432**, **449**
Ford, Henry, 255, 272–73
Ford, Henry, II, 382
Fordism, **272**–73, **282**
Foreign aid
    global inequality, 9
    global structure, 8
Foreign debt, 214–19
Forest Alliance of British Columbia, 398
Forest Stewardship Council, 398

Formal organizations, W-13, **W-25**
Fortress cities, 382–83
Fortress North America, 198
Foschi, Martha, 486–87
Fourth world, **474**
Fox, Michael J., 104
Frame alignment theory, **442**, **449**
Frames/framing, **105**, **118**, **396**, **407**, 442
France, suicide rate, 7
Frank, Andre Gundar, 211
Frankel, Gale, 326
Freedom, W-23
Free schools, 302
French Revolution, 10, 11, 35
Frenette, Marc, 168
Freud, Sigmund, 84–85, 322
Friedman, Milton, 215
Friendships, adolescence, 59
Front-yard culture, 374
Frost, David, 464
Frustration-aggression, 186
Fume fever, 402
Functional disability, **416**, **427**
Functional flexibility, **262**, **283**
Functionalism, **14**
Functionalist theory
    defined, **14**, **25**
    education, 294, 295
    families, 230–31
    features, 14–15
    symbolic interactionism, 16
Functions, latent, **25**

G
Gagnon, Françoise, 171
Gaia hypothesis, **398**, **407**
Galileo, 10, 11
Games, video, 66
Game stage, **54**, **71**
Gang-related homicide, 345
Gardner, Howard, 301–3
Gaskell, Jane, 165, 242
Gates, Bill, 216, 462
GATT (Global Agreement on Tariffs and Trade), 460–61
Gays and lesbians
    crime, 339
    rights, 38
    See also Homosexuals
Gemeinschaft, 369
Gender, 155
    biology of, 75–76, 155
    class, 347–48
    conventional roles, 228–29
    crime, 347–48
    culture, 56–57
    David/Brenda Reimer case, 74–77
    defined/defining, **75**–76, **95**
    division of labour, **227**, **251**
    families and, 242–43

inequality, 17, 18
Internet usage, 113
mortality rate, 414
occupational segregation, 162–63
reassignment, 77
scripts, 57
skill, 164–65
social class, 347–48
socialization, 50, 56–58, 65, 89–90
social stratification, 157
stereotypes, 155–56, 162–64
strategy, 242, **251**
stratification, 351–52
Gender bias, 296
Gender differences
    aging, 414
    brain studies, 83–84
    constructionists' views, 87–88
    decline in, 85
    essentialism and, 83–87
    Freud's views, 84–85
    health and, 418
    Internet use, 113
    power and, 87
    sexual attitudes, 79–80
    sexuality and, 242–43
    sociobiology, 84
    television viewing, 111
    theories, 83–88
    See also Men; Women
Gendered division of labour, **227**, 296
    contemporary family life, 234
Gender identity
    defined, **76**, **95**
    education and, 295–96
    refusing, 77
Gender identity gate, 74
Gender inequality
    Aboriginal people, 192–93
    birthplace and, 167–69
    causes of, 155
    Christianity, 87
    defined, **155**, **156**, 177
    development of, 87–88
    dimensions of, 156–57
    divorce, 155
    eliminating, 174–76
    explaining, 157–58
    history of, 87–88, 155
    hunter–gatherer societies, 87
    industrialization, 88
    Islam, 87
    Judaism, 87
    kinship, 87
    labour market and, 242–43
    mass media and, 89
    politics and, 170–74
    power and, 158
    public policy and, 174–75
    religion, 87

skin colour and, 167–69
slavery, 87
socialization and, 87–88
understanding, 155–60
wage gap, 140–41
women's movement and, 169–70
work, at, 160–70, 174–75
    See also Men; Women
Gender roles
    adopting, 76
    defined, **76**, **95**
    family, 228–29
    occupational, 162
Gender stereotypes, **156**, **177**, 296
General deterrence, 356
Generalized other, **54**, **71**
General Social Survey, 498
General Theory of Crime, 351
Generation gap, 65
Genetic engineering, 471–72
Geneva Convention Relating to the Status
    of Refugees, 199
Genocide, 38, 220
Genovese, Kitty, W-11
Gentrification
    advantages of, 381
    defined, **385**
    explanations for, 380–81
    phenomenon of, **380**
Geopolitics, 197
George, Dudley, 180–81
Gerbner, George, 109
Germany, Jewish assimilation in, W-12
Germany, Nazis in, W-2–W-5
Gesellschaft, 369
Gestation, 75
Gibson, Mel, 310
Gibson, Mike, 354
Giddens, Anthony, 23, 482–83
Gifford, Kathie Lee, 458
Ginsberg, Effie, 488
Glass ceiling, **164**, **177**
Global Agreement on Tariffs and Trade
    (GATT), 460–61
Global commodity chains, **462**, 463, 469,
    474
Global inequality
    country trends, 218
    development, 208–9
    growth, 218
    measurement of, 217–18
    neoliberal theory, 218
    poverty, 217–18
Globalization, **474**
    agriculture, 470–73
    bottom-up, 455–56
    capitalism and, 467
    centralization and, 457
    consumers, 462–63
    controversy, 453

corporations and, 458
crime and, 348
Cuban experiment, 473
culture and, 33–36
defined/defining, **25**, **453**
ecology and, 470–73
ethics of, 454–55
fair trade and, 465
financial capital, 456
governance and, 458–59
health care and, 425–26
inequality, 461–62
labour inequality and, 467–69
media and, 100–103, 453
monetary policy, 458–59
neoliberal economic policies, 455–56
news, 464
overcapacity and, 457
poverty and, 148
process, 452
roots of, 36
social movements and, 444–46
technology, 269–70
time–space compression, 453–54
top-down, **455–56**, **475**
trade policy, 460–61
unions and, 467
wage inequality and, 467–69
Globalization from below, **474**
Global north, 462
Global south, 210, 462
Global structure, **8**, **25**
    charity, 8
    colonization, 9
    developing countries, 9
    foreign aid, 8
    poverty, 9
Global village, 36, 99
Global warming, 397
Globe and Mail, The, 102, 363
Glock, Charles, 314–15
Gloin, Destiny, 69
Goar, Carol, 106
Goffman, Erving, 19, 68–69, 485
Goldfarb, Martin, 23
"Good jobs," 254, 258–59
    technology, 270
Gore, Tipper, 44
Gorsuch, Richard, 327
Gospel of efficiency, 400
Gossip Girls, 112
Governments
    Aboriginal culture and, 190–92
    administrative apparatus, 432–33
    agricultural societies, W-21
    democratic, 432–33
    media influence, 108
    professions and, 268–69
    women in, 171–74
    See also Political power

Grand Theft Auto, 110
Grand Theft Auto: Vice City, 66
Granovetter, Mark, 280–81, W-7
Great Bear Rainforest, 400–401
Great Depression, 14, 215
Great Whale hydroelectric project, 400
Greene, Barbara, 106
Greenhouse gases, 397, 401
Greenpeace, 36, 446
"Greens," rise of, in Western Europe, 391
Gretzky, Wayne, 29
Griffin Cohen, Marjorie, 168
Groups
    betrayal, W-3
    boundaries separating, W-12
    categories, W-9–W-10
    cohesiveness, W-11
    conformity, W-10–W-13
    cooperation, W-12
    experiences, W-9
    formal organizations, W-**13**
    imagination and, W-13
    in, W-**25**
    inclusion, W-11–W-12
    love and, W-9–W-10
    loyalty, W-4, W-9–W-10
    out, W-**25**
    pressure, 433
    primary, **53**, **72**, W-**9**, W-**25**
    reference, W-13
    secondary, W-**10**
    size, W-11
    status and, W-11
Groupthink, W-10, W-**11**, W-**25**
Growth
    Canadian cities, 368
    costs of, 389
    economic, 401
    edge cities, 377–78
    global inequality, 218
    industrial economy, 367–69
    limits to, 397
    population, 365–67
    senior population, 414
    urbanization and, 365–66

H

Hagan, John, 338, 352
Haggerty, Kevin, 488
Haggis, Paul, 104
Hamlet, 4
Handicraft industry, 213
Hard Times (Dickens), 482
Harlequin Enterprises of Toronto, 89
Harnick, Charles, 180
Harper, Stephen, 171, 183–84
Harris, Chauncey, 371
Harris, Mike, 180
Hawthorne effect/studies, 273, **488**, 495, **503**, W-16

Head tax, 188
Health
    commonsense beliefs, 410–11
    education and, 417
    gender and, 418
    income, 417–18
    social equalities, 420–21
Health care
    aging and, 422–24
    Canadian, 412, 423–25
    costs of, 423–24
    for-profit, 424–26
    formal, 423–25
    globalization and, 425–26
    inequality in, 421–22
    informal, 422–23
    long-term, 423
    NAFTA and, 425–26
    reform, 424–25
    self, 422–23
Health inequality
    aging and, 417–22
    explanations for, 420–21
    health care, in, 421–22
    life course link, 422–24
Healthy immigrant effect, **419**, **427**
Heaven's Gate, 69
Hegemony, **100**, **118**
Helu, Carlos Slim, 215–16
Henry, Frances, 488
Herberg, Edward, 200
Herberg, Will, 330
Herman, Edward, 100
Heterosexuality, 78, **95**
Hewitt, W. E., 326
Hidden curriculum, 64, **292**–93, 295–96, **307**
Hierarchies
    higher education, 289–90
    news access, 108
    social, 125–28
    stress perspective, **420**, **427**
Higher education
    competition for, 288–89
    ethnicity, 291
    fields of study, 288, 291
    hierarchy in, 289–90
    Maclean's ranking, 291
    men, 290, 291
    race, 291
    ranking institutions, 289–90
    satisfaction in, 289
    stratification, 288, 289
    tuition fees, 305
    women, 290, 291
    women's movement, 290
Himelfarb, Alex, 23
Hinduism, 81
Hip-hop music, 45
Hirschi, Travis, 350

Hispanic Americans, assimilation of, 191
Historical sociology, 496–97
Hitchens, Christopher, 310
Hitler, Adolf, W-12
HIV/AIDS, W-8
Hobbes, Thomas, 10
Hochschild, Arlie, 242
Hockey Night in Canada, 112
Holocaust, W-2–W-5
Home health care, 423–24
Homelessness, 382–83
Homicide, 4
    gang-related, 345
    rates, 344–46
    spousal, 345
    stranger, 345
Homosexuality, 78
Homosexuals
    couples' sexuality, 242
    families of, 227, 239
    family socialization patterns, 63
    marriage by, 80
    prevalence of, 82
Horizontal integration, **100**, **118**
Horkheimer, Max, 100
Horticultural societies, W-**20**, W-**25**
Hostile environment sexual harassment, **93**, **95**
House of Commons, 171
Households
    communal, 231–33
    extended-family, **229**
    preindustrial, 230, 233–34
Households and Environment Survey, 394
Housework, 159–60, 243–44
Housing, inner city, 380
How the West Was Won, 390
Hoyt, Homer, 371
Human behaviour, 4
Human capital theory, **299**, **307**
Human-exceptionalism paradigm, **389**, **407**
Humanist perspectives, **315**, **333**
Humanitarianism, 197–98
Humanization, 273–74
Human relations school of management, **273**, **283**
Hume, David, 481, 482
Hunger, 472
Hunter, Jamie, 267–68
Hurricane Katrina, 402
Hurried Child, The (Elkind), 304
Hussein, Saddam, 219
Hypotheses, **487**
    broadening-base, **392**, **407**
    cultural, 491–92
    defined, **487**, **503**

economic-contingency, **392**, **407**
Gaia, **398**, **407**
social-situational, 491

I

I, **55**, **71**
Ibn Khaldun, 11
Identity
Canadian sense of, 103–4
creativity and, 56
cultural, 40
ethnic, 181–83
gender, **76**, **95**, 155–56
Québécois, 193–96
social change and, 67
total institutions and, 69
Identity work, 115
Ideology
dominant, **100**, **118**
environmental movement, 397–99
media and, 105–9
news and, 105–9
Ignatieff, Michael, 31
Imagination, sociological
defined, **9**, **25**
groups and, W-12–W-13
origins of, 10
IMF. *See* International Monetary Fund
(IMF)
Imitative stage, **54**, **71**
Immediacy, news and, 105–6
Immigrant entrepreneurs, 199
Immigrant investors, 199
Immigrants
categories of, 199–200
children, 196
drug use among, 341
entrance status, 199
Immigration
benefits of, 196–97
categories of, 199–200
Chinese, 188
economic development, 196–200
education and, 291–92
geopolitics and, 197
humanitarianism and, 197–98
labour market, 256
points system, **199**
public opinion and, 198
security considerations, 198
selective, 375
seniors, 414–15
social class and, 197
state formation, 196–200
stereotypes and, 197–98
Imperialism
American, 461
cultural, **104**, **118**, 463–64
Muslims and, 447
Incarceration, 356–58

Incest
crime, 340
rules, 230
Income
dual, 378
inequality, 131–32, 141–47
social stratification and, 123–24
women's, 166–67
Income distribution by class, 140
Income inequality, **215**, **223**
Independent immigrants, 199–200
Independent variables, **487**, **503**
India
caste system in, 126
cow worship in, 32
films, 464
organic food movement in, 472
pollution in, 402
Indian Act, 189, 191
Individual motives, W-5
Induction, problem of, 481
Industrial cities
concentric-zone model, 370–71
development, 367–69
ecology of, 370–71
growth in, 367–69
researching, 369–70
urban-growth model, 370–71
Industrial economy, 367–69
Industrialization, 11, 41
gender inequality, 88
Industrial Revolution, **10**, 11, 213, 255
British, 213
Canadian, 255
characteristics of, 18–20
defined, **10**, **25**
economic development before, 210–13
first, 254–55
Marx's view of, 128–29
origins, 255
second, 254–55
sociological imagination and, 10–11
Industrial societies, W-**21**, W-**25**
Industries
employment changes, 259
environmentalist, 398
societies and, W-21, W-**25**
Inefficiency, bureaucratic, W-13–W-16
Inequality
aging, 417–22
educational, 14–15
environmental risk, 404
ethnic, 200–203
gender, 17, 18
globalization, 461–62, 467–69
health, 417–22
Internet access and, 113–14
material, 133, 140–47
nonstandard work schedule, 264
prosperity *versus*, 21

structured, patterns of, 144
trends toward, 142
wage, 467–69
wealth, 124–25
Inequality, gender, 17, 18
birthplace and, 167–69
causes of, 155
defined, **155**, **177**
dimensions of, 156–57
eliminating, 174–76
explaining, 157–58
history, 155
industrialization and, W-21
labour market and, 242–43
politics and, 170–74
power and, 158
public policy and, 174
skin colour and, 167–69
socialization and, 87–88
understanding, 155–60
women's movement and, 169–70
work, at, 160–70, 174–75
Inertia, bureaucratic, W-**15**
Inflation, credential, 299–300, **307**
Informal care, 422–23
In-groups, W-**11**, W-**25**
Innis, Harold, 98, 99
Instincts, **50**, **71**
Institutional racism, **185**
Institutions
people-processing, 66
racism in, 185–86, **204**
total, **68**–69, **72**, 293
Instrumentalists, 434
Integration, vertical, **100**, **118**
Intelligences, multiple, 301–3
Interactionism, symbolic
defined, **25**
features of, 16–17
foundation of, 53
Interactive media, **98**, **118**
Intergenerational occupational mobility,
138, **151**
Internal colonial model, 191
Internal flexibility, **262**, **283**
Internalization, 54
International Monetary Fund (IMF), 36,
215, 455
establishment of, 460
U.S. influence on, 461
International Typographical Union, W-23
Internet
access inequality, 113–14
creativity and, 56
digital divide, 113
early research, 113
effects of, 113–15
impact of, 115–16
Movie Database, W-6
social control and, 115

social movements and, 448
time–space compression, 453
usage growth, 98
use, 113–14
Interviews, **489**, **503**
Intimacy, 241
Intragenerational occupational mobility, **138**, **151**
Intrinsic rewards, **259**, 282
Inuit, 190
Investors, immigrant, 199
Ipperwash Provincial Park, 180
Iraq, invasion of, 20
Iron cage, 43
Iron Chef America, 463
Iron Chef, The, 463
Irving, K. C., 430–31, 443, 446
Islam, 329
    anti-imperialist sentiment, 447
    Canada, in, 329–30
    countries, 310
    gender inequality, 87
    sexual issues and, 81
Isolation, social, 51
Issue-attention cycle, **405**, **407**
Italian Job, The, 43
Ivory Tower Blues (Côté and Allahar), 305

J

Jacobson, Avrum, 238
James Bay hydroelectric project, 400
Jansen, Mary, 304
Japan
    corporate bureaucracy, W-18
    English impact on, 37
    management model, 273–74
Japanese, expulsion of, 185
Japanese production techniques (JPT), **273**, 283
Jean, Michaëlle, 172
Jennings, Peter, 104
Jews
    assimilation of, W-12
    Christian conversion of, W-12
    genocide, W-5
    Holocaust and, W-2–W-5
    restrictive covenants, 185
    saving of, W-2–W-4
    suicide rate, 6–7
Job ghettos, **266**–68, 283, 289
Jobs
    dead-end, 265–66
    high-paying, 140–41
    low-paying, 140–41
    manufacturing, 468
    mobility and, 138–39
    most common, 259
    nonstandard, 259–61, 283
    opportunities for, 265–66
    power and, 164

professional, 268–69
segregation, 162–70
service, 257–61, 469
sex segregation of, 177
sex typing, 177
shifts over time, 136–38
sociology, 22, 23
status attainment and, 138–39
wealth distribution and, 139–40
work satisfaction by, 276
See also Labour force
Job satisfaction
    alienation and, 276–79
    Canadian, 274
    defined, 283
    executives, 275
    individual characteristics, 276
    organizational characteristics, 275
John Paul II, 310
Joint stock company, 367
JPT. *See* Japanese production techniques (JPT)
Judaism, 81, 87
Judas Priest, 44
Judiciary, 432
Justice system. *See* Criminal justice
Juvenile Delinquents Act of 1908, 358

K

Kanter, Rosabeth Moss, W-16, W-17
Katrina, Hurricane, 402
Kerr, Ian, 354
Kettle Point Reserve, 180
Keynes, John Maynard, 215
Khakis rock (Gap), 43
Kinship and gender inequality, 87
Kirkpatrick, Clifford, 327
Kiss, 44
Klein, Naomi, 459
Kleitsch, Christel, 238
Klippenstein, Murray, 180
Knight, Philip, 459
Knowledge, commonsense, 12–13
Knowledge occupations, 259
Kraft, 458
Krahn, Harvey, 278–79
Kretschmer, Tim, 355
Krugman, Paul, 149
Kuhn, Thomas, 483
!Kung of Kalahari, W-20
Kwakiutl, W-20

L

Labelling perspective, 340–41, **360**
Labelling theorists/theory, **340**, **360**
Labour
    cheap, 469–70
    class, 213
    division of, 88
    domestic, 161–62
    global inequality in, 467–69

globalization and, 467–69
injustices in, 469–70
service sector, 468–69
Labour force
    alienation of, 276–79
    Canadian, 258–59
    criminal acts by, 278
    empowerment, 274
    female participation, 160–70
    fertility rates and, 160
    gender inequality in, 174–75
    industrial protest by, 18
    insubordination by, 278–79
    occupational segregation of, 162–70
    participation rate, **159**, 160–61, 177
    postindustrial, W-22
    skilled, 199–200
    See also Jobs
Labour markets
    Canada, 255–56
    ethnic inequality and, 200–203
    gender inequality and, 242–43
    geography, 266
    immigration, 256
    primary, 265–66, 283
    secondary, 265
    segmentation, 265–69, 283, 467
    shelters, 283
    skilled workers, 256
    women, 256
Labour-market segmentation, **265**, **283**
Labour-market shelters, **268**, **283**
Labour of confusion, 396
Labour organizations
    bureaucratization, 270–74
    division of labour, 272–73
    executives, 276
    humanization, 273
    Japanese model, 273–74
    job satisfaction and, 276
    managerial strategies, 272–74
    Taylorism, 272–73
    technology, 270
    See also Unions
Laissez-faire leadership, W-**17**, W-**25**
Language, globalization of, 37
Language, racist, 187
Language rights, 38
Language, racist, 188
Languages, as symbols, 30
Laplante, Benoit, 238
Lastman, Mel, 181
Latch-key children, 63
Latent, **15**
Latent functions, **25**
Latimer, Robert, 339
Latin America
    peri-urbanization in, 373
    urban development, 372–73
    See also specific countries

Law and Order, 337
Laws, criminal, 338, 339
Laws, voter registration, 439
Layton, Jack, 184
Leadership
    authoritarian, W-**25**
    bureaucratic, W-17
    democratic, W-**25**
    laissez-faire, W-**25**
Lean production, 273–74
Learning theories of deviance, 111
Learning to Labour (Willis), 293
Leave It to Beaver, 229
Le Bourdais, Céline, 238
Lederer, John, 139
Lefkowitz, Bernard, W-4
Legal-rational authority, 431
Legislatures, 432
Lenin, Vladimir, 272
Lenski, Gerhard, 132
Lenton, Rhonda L., 489, 491–92, 495
Leopold, Aldo, 398
Lesbians. *See* Homosexuals
Less-developed countries
    colonialism effects, 213
    foreign debt of, 214–19
    globalization and, 461–62
    preindustrial, 210–13, 214
Lewis, Oscar, 191
Liberal feminists, 157, 445
Liberalism as development perspective,
    214–15
Liberal Party, 430
Liberation theory, 352
LICO. *See* Low-income cutoff (LICO)
Life, 29
Life-chances, **130**–31, **151**
Life course, health inequality link,
    422–24
Life course, perspective, 422, **427**
Life-cycle interpretation, 375
Life expectancy, 190, **411**, **427**
Lifestyles
    health inequality and, 420–21
    men, 155
    suburban, 374–76
    suburban/urban, 380
    women, 155
Lightfoot, Cynthia, 65
Limits to Growth, The (Meadows, et al.),
    397
Lincoln, Abraham, 433
Liposuction, 91
Lipset, Seymour Martin, 128, 135, W-23
Little Mermaid, 90
Little Mosque on the Prairie, 104
Lone-parent families
    poverty, 144
    suicide, 7
    women, 161

Lone parents, 246–47
Looker, Dianne, 159
Looking-glass self, **52**, **71**
Los Angeles, 371
    fortification of, 382
Loughheed, Clarence, 106
Love Canal, 396, 403
Lovelock, James, 398
Lowe, Graham, 278
Low-income cutoff (LICO), 106, **143**–46,
    151, 249
Low-paying occupations, 140–41
Loyalty, W-4, W-9–W-10
Lundie, Matt, 77
Luxton, Meg, 243
Lynn, Barry, 453

M
Macdonald, John A., 196
MacPhail, Jack, 275
Macrostructures, **8**, **25**
Majority world, 462
Male, defining, 75–77
Malthus, Thomas, 366–67
Management
    environmental, **401**
    group conformity to, W-11
    Japanese model, 273–74
    strategies, 272–74
Mandatory prison sentences, 357
Manifest, **15**, **25**
Manifesto of the Communist Party, 466
Mann, W. E., 324
Manson, Marilyn, 44
Manufacturing, 468–69
Manzer, Linda, 393
Maquiladoras, 469
Margulis, Lynn, 399
Market Basket Measure, 143
Market research, 489–90
Markets, electronic money, 453
Marley, Bob, 36
Marriage, 4
    benefits of, 237
    definition of, 239
    extramarital affairs in, 82
    families and, 243–44
    nineteenth century, 235
    religion, 238
    same-sex, 80
    socialization and, 60
    suicide, 6
Marsden, Lorna, 23
Marshall, S. L. A., W-10
Martin, Paul, 171, 249
Martineau, Harriet, 17
Marx, Karl, 13, 14, 15–16, 17, 122,
    128–29, 135, 137, 157, 187, 212,
    277, 286, 311, 312, 314,
    366–67, 466

Marxism
    alienation, 277
    critique of elite theory by, 434–36
    education and, 286, 293, 294
    gender inequality, 157
    racism and, 188
    religion and, 188
    social stratification, 127–30
Masaryk, Tomas, 23
Masculine, 155, 156
Mass deception, 100
Mass media, 5
    advertising's effects, 109
    audiences, 109–11
    counterculture and, 45
    critical perspective, 99–100, 108
    defined, **98**, **118**
    dominant paradigm and, 389
    effects of, 109–11
    gender inequality and, 89
    gender socialization and, 57, 90–91
    global, 100–103
    globalization and, 453
    ideology and, 105–9
    interactive, **118**
    news, 105–9
    ownership of, 100–103
    political economy and, 100–103
    print, 101–3
    socialization role, 65–66
    society and, W-6
    space-biased, **98**, **118**
    technological perspective, 98–99
    theories, 98–100
    time-biased, **98**, **118**
    types of, 98
    violence, 109–11
    See also Internet; Movies; News;
        Television
Material culture, **30**, **46**
Material inequality
    consequences of, 148–49
    income distribution and, 140–47
    increases in, 148
    poverty and, 142–47
    responding to, 149–50
    social assistance and, 145–46
    societal effects and, 148–49
    wealth distribution and, 139–40
Material well-being, **156**, 177
Mathematical notations, 30
Matrix of domination, 158
Mawani, Renisa, 497
Maximalists, 403
May, Elizabeth, 172
Mayer, Louis B., 104
Mayo, Elton, 273
McChesney, Robert, 116
McClelland, David, 209
McCrory, Colleen, 393

McDonaldization, 41–43, 271–72
McDonald's, 42, 265
McDonough, Alexa, 172
McEnroe, John, 322
McKibben, Bill, 473
McLaughlin, Audrey, 172
McLuhan, Marshall, 36, 98–99
Me, **55, 71**
Mead, George Herbert, 16, 52–55
Mead, Margaret, 85
Mean girls, 352
Meaningful action, **482, 503**
Means of production, **128, 151**
Mean world syndrome, 109
Measurements, **489**–90, **503**
Media, 98
Medicalization, **413, 427**
Megachurches, 318
Membership, 55, 56
    churches, 318
Members of Parliament, 171
Member test of validity, 495
Men
    child care, 238
    education, 498–500
    equality, 5, 35
    higher education, 290–91
    homicide rates, 345
    housework, 238
    industrial societies and, W-21
    lifestyle, 155
    middle-class families, 235
    misconduct, W-4
    mortality rates, 414
    most common jobs, 259
    poverty, 145
    preindustrial households, 234
    reproductive status, 83–84
    self-care, 422–23
    sexual attitudes, 79–80
    television viewing of, 111
    violence against women by, 91–93
Mendel, Gregor, 480
Mercredi, Ovide, 190
Mercy killing debate, 339
Mergers, 100–103
Meritocracy, **126, 151**
Merton, Robert, 15, 349–50
Metallica, 44
Métis, 124, 190
Métis National Council, 190
Mexico, labour force, 469
Mi'kmaq band, 404
Michael, 310
Microstructures, **8, 25**
Middle class, 129
    environmental movement and, 395
    families, 234–35
    francophone, 194
    gentrification and, 381

new, 395
    socialization patterns, 63
Midwives, 269
Milanovic, Branko, 217
Milgaard, David, 479
Milgram, Stanley, W-3–W-5, W-6
Mills, C. Wright, 9, 433
Mills, Russell, 102
Milner, Murray, 297–98
Minimalists, 403
Minimata disease, 404
Minorities, visible, **167**, 178
Minority world, 462
Mitchell, Marybelle, 193
Mobility
    circulatory, **138, 151**
    contest, **288, 307**
    occupational, 138–39
    poverty, 147
    social, **126, 152**
    sponsored, **288**–89, **307**
    structural, **138**
Modernization theory, **209, 224**
Modes of production, **128**–29, **151**
Modified extended family, **417, 427**
Money, John, 74
Money markets, 453
Monopolies, 101–3
Monotheism, **314, 333**
Montreal, 371
Moonlighting, 265
Moore, Wilbert, 131, 135
Moral crusades, 341–42
Moral education, 286, 294–95
Moral Majority, 329
Moral panics, **353, 360**
Moreno, Megan A., 116
Morgentaler, Henry, 241, 340
Morin, Guy Paul, 479
Mortality rate, **414, 427**
Mortification rituals, 70
Mother Nature, 399
Mothers' allowances, 237
Motherwork, 244–45
Motivational theories of deviance
    learning variant, 350–51
    strain variant, 348–50
Motives, individual, W-5
Movies
    cultural impact of, 104
    gender socialization and, 90
    Indian, 464
    See also specific films
MTV, 36
Muhammad, 310
Muir, John, 398
Mulan, 90
Multiculturalism, 34–35, 182–83, 329
    education, 296
    religion, 329

Multigenerational families, 411
Multimedia chains, **100, 118**
Multiple intelligence theory, 301–3
Multiple jeopardy hypothesis, **421, 427**
Multiple-job holding, 265
Multiple-nuclei model, **371, 385**
Multiracial feminism/feminists, 157–58
Murdoch, Rupert, 100
Murphy, Rex, 455
Music, counterculture, 44–45
Music, cultural diversity, 36
Music, group membership, 56
Muslim Brotherhood, 447–48
Muslims. *See* Islam
Myles, John, 259
Myths
    families, 229–30
    suburbia, 375

N

Nadvanya movement, 472
Naess, Arne, 398
NAFTA. *See* North American Free Trade Agreement (NAFTA)
Nagging tactics, 43–44
Nardelli, Robert, 139
Nash, Steve, 23
National Aeronautics and Space Administration (NASA), W-13–W-16
National Indian Brotherhood, 190
Nationalism
    civic, **195, 204**
    Québécois, 193–96
National Post, 101, 354
Natural families, 231
Nature, 10, 50–52
Nazis, W-2–W-5
Nazism, 41
Neoliberal economic policies
    defined, **474**
    development perspective, 214–19
    globalization and, 455–56
    government resistance to, 220–22
Neoliberalism, **223**
Neoliberal theory, **214**–19
    global inequality, 218
    women, 219
NEP. *See* New environmental paradigm (NEP) scale
Networks
    analysis, W-5–W-7
    building blocks, W-8–W-9
    defined, W-6
    dense, 280
    function of, W-5–W-7
    job search and, W-7, W-8
    social, **W-6, W-25**
Never Been Kissed, W-12
Newcomb, Theodore, W-12

New Democratic Party, 171
New Earth, A (Tolle), 310
New environmental paradigm (NEP)
    scale, 392–93, 399
Newman, Katherine, 353, 355
New middle class, 395
New racism, **184**, **204**
News
    access hierarchy, 108
    conservative critique of, 105–9
    defining, 105–7
    extraordinariness of, 107
    gathering, 107–9
    globalization, 464
    government influence, 108
    ideology and, 105–9
    immediacy of, 105–6
    objectivity, 108
    personalization, 106–7
    sources, 108
    values, **105**, **118**
News Corporation, 100
New social movements, **444**, **449**
Newspapers, 101–3, 107
Newton, Sir Isaac, 10, 11, 34
Niebuhr, H. Richard, 312
Non-governmental organizations
    (NGOs), 460
Nonstandard jobs, **254**, 259–61, 283
    equality, 262–63
    rise in, 261–62
    women, 262
Nonstandard work, **165–66**, 177
Nonstandard work schedules, **264**, **283**
    inequality, 264
Non-status Indians, 189
Normal accidents, **402**, **407**
Normative theories, 187
Norms
    culture and, 30
    defined, **30**, **46**, **337**, **360**
    religious, 319
    socialization and, 49
    solidarity, W-2–W-3
North American Free Trade Agreement
    (NAFTA), 221, 425–26, 467
Novels, romance, 89
Nuclear family, **227–29**, 230, **251**
Numerical data analysis, 498–500
Numerical flexibility, **262**, **283**
Nurture, nature *versus*, 50–52

O

Obama, Barack, 164, 435
Obama effect, 435
Obedience, W-3
Obesity, 91
Objectivity, 108, **481**, **503**
Observational studies, **347**, **360**
    application, 493–96

function of, 493–96
    potential pitfalls, 494–96
Observer bias, 480
Occupational health and safety standards,
    269
Occupational segregation, 162–63
Occupational sex segregation, 269
Occupational status attainment, **138**, **151**
Occupations
    high-paying, 140–41
    See also Jobs
O'Connor, Debra, 106
O'Donnell, Rosie, 44
Office, The, 36, 112
Official news sources, **108**, **118**
Official statistics, 497
Old age, defining, 412
Old boys' network, 164, 173
Old School, 104
Oligarchy, W-**15**, W-**25**
Oliver Twist (Dickens), W-21
Ontario Labour Relations Board, 254
Open stratification systems, **126**, **152**
Oprah, 310
Ordinary news sources, **108**, **118**
Organic food, 472
Organizational environment, W-**18**
Organization Man, The (Whyte), 374
Organizations
    bureaucratic, W-18
    criminal, 383
    education and, 286, 299–300
    environmental, W-**25**
    formal, W-**25**
Organizations, religious
    approaches, 317–18
    goals, 318–19
    types, 315–16
Organizations, work
    culture of, 272
    diversity in, 272–73
    division of labour, 272–73
    environmental risks and, 401–4
    executives, 276
    formal, W-13
    humanization, 275
    human relations, 275
    Japanese model, 273–74
    job satisfaction and, 276
    managerial strategies, 272–73
    Taylorism, 272–73
    technology, 270
Orwell, George, 433
Osbourne, Ozzy and Sharon, 44–45
Osteen, Joel, 310
Other
    generalized, **54**, **72**
    significant, **53**, **72**
    taking role of, **54**, **72**, 485
Ottawa Citizen, The, 102

Ottoman Empire, 214
Out-groups, W-**11**, W-**25**
Outsourcing, **468**, **474**
Overcapacity, 457
Overurbanization, **372–73**, **385**

P

Pain, 416–17
Paparo-Stein, Irene, 397
Paradigms, 19, 483
Parents
    adolescents and, 59
    becoming, 245–46
    gender role socialization, 57
    lone, 246–47
    middle class, 235
    modern trends, 237
    preindustrial societies, 233
Parents' Music Resource Center, 44
Parizeau, Jacques, 195
Park, Robert E., 369
Parkin, Frank, 133–35
Parsons, Talcott, 15, 230–31
Participant observation, **503**
Participant observers, **493**
Part-time work, **165–66**, 177
Part-time workers, 261
Passion of the Christ, The, 310
Pastoral societies, W-**20**, W-**25**
Patriarchy, **8**, **25**
    divorce, 8
    feminist theory, 17, 18
    women, 8
Pay equity, 174
Pay gap, 166, 168
P. Diddy, 45
Pedestrian foragers, W-19
Peer abuse, 65
Peer groups
    defined, **64**, **71**
    school socialization and, 297–98
    socialization role, 64–65
Penis envy, 85
People-processing institutions, 66
People with disabilities, 268
Peripheralization, 462
Peripheral satellites, 211
Peri-urbanization, **373**, **385**
Persistence thesis, **324**, **333**
Personalization, news, 106
Personal religiosity, **315–16**, **333**
Petite bourgeoisie, **129**, 136–37, **152**
Phillip Morris, 458
Pictou Landing, Nova Scotia, 404
Pineo, Peter, 492
Pink-collar sector, 137
Pink ghetto, 172
Plato, 11
Playboy, 90
Play stage, **54**, **71**

Plow agriculture, 87–88
Pluralist theory
    defined, **433**, **449**
    elitist critique of, 433–34
    principles, 433
    sexuality, 93, **95**
Points system, **199**, **204**
Polarization of working hours, **263**, **283**
Polarized society, 147–48
Polish Christians, W-3
Political citizenship, **444**, **449**
Political economy, 100–103, 399–401
Political parties
    defined, **449**
    environmental, 391
    function of, 431
    social class and, 129
    support for, 497
Political power
    elite theory of, 433–34
    Marxist view of, 434–36
    pluralist theory of, 433
    power-balance theory of, **436**–38
    relative-deprivation theory, **440**
    resource-mobilization theory, 440–**41**
    state-centred theory, 438–40
Political revolution, **431**, **449**
Politics
    gender inequality and, 170–74
    normal, 432–40
    voting rights, 170–71
    women in, 172–74, 175–76
Pollution, 401, 402–4
    poverty, of, 401
Pool, Robert, 34
Poor
    countries (*See* Less-developed
        countries)
    social assistance for, 145–46
    working, **144**, **152**
Popenoe, David, 238
Popper, Karl, 482
Population Bomb, The (Ehrlich), 367
Populations
    aging, 411–14
    demographic transition, 365–66
    environment and, 367
    Malthus's view, 366
    Marx's view, 366–67
    urban, 368–98
Porter, John, 19, 200, 433–34, 492
Positive checks, 366–67
Postindustrial economy. *See* Service
    economy
Postindustrial Revolution
    defined, **20**, **25**
    globalization and, 20–21
    impact of, 18
Postindustrial societies, W-**21**–W-22,
    W-**25**

Postmodern cities, **364**, **385**
    characterization, 376
    components, 377–83
    dual, 379–83
    edge-city component, 377–78
    fortress cities, 382–83
    gentrification, 380–81
    multiethnicity of, 376, 378–79
    private communities, 381–82
Postmodernism
    culture and, 38–41
    defined, **46**
    feminism and, 445
Postnational society, 104
Postnatural societies, W-22–W-**23**, W-**25**
Potlatch, 191
Poverty
    Aboriginal, 124, 191
    absolute, **142**, **151**
    child, 237
    culture of, 191, **204**
    defining, 142–47
    development, 215–19
    environmental degradation and, 401
    environmental risk and, 404
    global inequality, 217–18
    globalization and, 148
    global structure, 8, 9
    health and, 420–21
    measuring, 142–47
    men, 145
    mobility of, 147
    pollution, 401
    relative, **142**, **152**
    reserves, on, 144
    single-parent families, 144
    war, 219–20
    women, 145
    youth gangs, 355
Poverty reduction strategies, 460
Power
    above, from, 432–40
    corporate, 458–59
    defined, **130**, **156**, 177, **431**, **449**
    exercising, 158
    feminist theory, 18
    gender differences and, 87
    occupational, 164
    professions, 268
    separate spheres of, 159–60
    state, 432
Power-balance theory, **436**–38, **449**
Power-conflict theories, 187–88
Prairie Edge, 363, 364
Preindustrial societies
    British, 213
    cities, 364–65
    economic development, 210–13
    family size, 364–65
    family structure, 233–34

    households, 230, 233–34
    sexuality, 233
Prejudice, **186**, 187, **204**
Premarital sex, 78
Premature mortality, **417**, **427**
Preservationists, 398
Presser, Harriet, 264
Pressure groups, 433
Prestige, 58, **157**, 177
Primary deviance, 388
Primary groups, **53**, **72**, W-**9**, W-**25**
Primary labour markets, **265**–66, 283
Primary socialization, **50**, **72**, 88
Primordialism, 187, **204**
Primordialist thesis, **187**
Print communication, 99, 101–3
Printing press, 99
Privacy 2.0, 115
Privacy International, 354
Private gated communities, 381–82
Private property, W-21
Privatization, **245**, **251**, **425**, **427**
Privilege, **152**
Production
    culture and, 30
    defined, **30**, **46**
    food, 471–72
    lean, 273–74
    means of, 128, **151**, 273–74
    modes of, 128, **151**
    social relations of, 128, **152**
    treadmill of, **399**, 401, **407**
Productivity, computers and, 270
Productivity paradox, 270
Profane, **313**, **334**
Professionalism, **300**, **307**
Professions, 268–69
Professorial Marxism, 134
Profitization, **425**, **427**
Progressive pedagogy, **301**, **307**
Project Canada surveys, 315–16
Proletariat, **129**, **152**
Pronatalism, **241**, **251**
Propaganda model, 100
Prosperity, 21
Protestant, Catholic, Jew (Herberg), 330
Protestant ethic, **16**, **25**
*Protestant Ethic and the Spirit of Capitalism,
    The* (Weber), 314
Protestant Reformation, 35
Psychic deprivation, 323
Psychology, evolutionary, **229**, **251**
Puberty ceremonies, 35
Public and private spheres, 87
Public Enemy, 45
Public opinion and immigration, 198
Public policy
    defined, **174**, 177
    family-oriented, 247–49
    gender inequality and, 174

Puff Daddy, 45
Punishments, 30
Purchasing power parity, 208, **224**
Pure laine Québécois, 195
Putting-out system, 367

Q

QC (quality-control) circles, 273
Quality circles, W-18
Quality-control (QC) circles, 273
Quality-of-work-life (QWL)
  programs, 273
Quayle, Dan, 45
Quebec and child care, 249
Québécois nationalism, 193–96
  religion, 194
Quebecor, 100, 101, 102
Quebec Referendum, 193
Questionnaires
  interpreting, 492
  self-administered, **489**, **503**
  telephone, 491
Quid pro quo sexual harassment, **93**, **95**
Quiet Revolution, **194**, **204**, 238, 328
QWL (quality-of-work-life)
  programs, 273

R

Race, 183
  aging, 414–15
  ascribed characteristics, 181
  census questions, 182
  conflicts over, 180–81
  defined, **204**
  education and, 291–92, 295–96
  gender inequality and, 167–69
  higher education, 291
  immigration and, 197–98
  indigenous people, 189
  language, 187, 188
  split labour-market theory, 188–89
  stereotypes, 197
  youth gangs, 355
Race to the bottom, 469
Racial profiling, 186, 348, **360**
Racism, 38, 184–86
  definitions of, 184–86
  institutional, **185**, **204**
  new, concept of, 186, 204
  normative theories of, 187
  power-conflict theories, 187–88
  primordialist thesis, 187
  scope of, 185–86
  social-psychological approach, 186–87
  theories of, 186–89
Radical feminists, 445
Radio, 98
Random-digit-dialing, 490
Randomization, **487**, **503**
Rape, 4, 92–93

Rationalization, **32**–33, 34, 41–43, **46**
Raves, 493–96
Reagan, Ronald, 23, 215
Reality, filtered, 480
Real Simple Syndication (RSS) feeds,
  115–16
Reasonable Accommodation Commission,
  196
Recidivism, **361**
Reciprocity in families, 231–32
Recombinant DNA, W-**22**, W-**26**
Reconstitituted families, 240, 247
Reeves, Keanu, 104
Reference group, W-**12**, W-**26**
Reflection, 322
Refugees, 199
Regression analysis, 501
Reimer, David/Brenda, 74–77
Reitman, Ivan, 104
Relative deprivation, **440**, **449**
Relative poverty, **142**, **152**
Reliability, **489**–90, **503**
Religion, 5, **315**
  Canadian identification with, 33–34,
    315, 319–21, 324
  church–sect typology, 317
  civil, **333**
  collective religiosity, 316–17
  consequences of, 325–30
  culture, 33–34
  defined, **333**
  Durkheim's view of, 312–13
  education, 294–95
  essence of, 311
  fanaticism, 41
  future of, 330–32
  gender inequality and, 87–88
  humanist view of, 315
  individual-centred explanations,
    322–23
  interpersonal consequences of, 327
  marriage, 238
  Marx's view of, 312
  modern presence, 310–11
  multiculturalism, 329
  nature of, 314–21
  norms, 319
  personal consequences of, 325–30
  personal religiosity, 315–16
  postmodernism and, 38
  problem-solving function, 29
  Québécois nationalism, 194
  resocialization, 69
  revolutions, 35–36
  roles, 319
  sanctions, 319
  sexual issues and, 81
  societal consequences of, 328–30
  sociology, 310
  sources of, 321–25

structure-centred explanations,
    323–25
  success of, 319
  suicide, 7
  symbolic interactionism, 16
  theoretical traditions, 311–14
  Weber's view of, 314
Religiosity
  collective, 316–17, **333**
  dimensions of, **315**, **333**
  personal, 315–16, **333**
Renaissance, 35
Rengel, Stephanie, 359
Rent gap, 380–81
Reparations, 38
Replacement level, **366**, **385**
Representation, **105**, **118**
Reproduction, 231, **251**
Reproductive status, 83–84
Research, 5
  bias and, 480–81
  bias minimization, 479
  causation and, 484
  correlation and, 484
  defined, **14**, **25**
  documentary analysis, 497
  ethics, 488
  experiments, 487–88
  explanation, 483–85
  future of, 500–501
  historical, 496–97
  numerical data, 498–500
  observational studies, 493–96
  official statistics, 497
  perspective, 479–83
  principles, 479
  scientific method, 11–13, 480–81
  survey, 489–93
  techniques, 486–98
  understanding, 485
Reserve army of labour, 157
Residential schools, 296
Resocialization, **68**–69, **72**
  basic training, 70
  religion, 69
Resource conservationist, 398
Resource-mobilization theory,
  440–**41**, **449**
Restrictive covenants, 185
Retirement, 61
Reverse commuters, 378
Revolutions
  American, 10
  democratic, **10**, **25**
  French, 10, 11
  industrial, **10**, 11 (*see also* Industrial
    Revolution)
  political, 35, **431**, **449**
  postindustrial, 18, 20–21, **25**
  religious, 35–36

rights, 36–38
    scientific, **10**–13
Rewards, 30, 259, 283
Reynolds, Malvina, 374
Rice, Condoleezza, 172
Rich, Adrienne, 78
Rich countries
    preindustrial (1750), 210–13
    social movements in, 443–46
Rick Mercer Report, The, 104
Rifkin, Jeremy, 281
Riga, Liliana, 496
Rights revolution, **36**–38, **46**
Rioux, Christine, 172
Risk, environmental
    assessment, 402–4
    community perception of, 402–4
    defined, **401**, **407**
    organizational basis of, 402
    social distribution of, 404
Rites of passage, **38**, **46**
Ritualism, W-**15**, W-**25**
Rituals, 35
Ritzer, George, 42, 271–72
Robber's Cave Study, The, W-12
Roberts, John, 104
Roberts, Lorne, 104
Robinson, Gertrude, 172
Robots, 269–70
Rogers, 100
Rokeach, Milton, 326, 327
Roles
    gender, **76**, **95**, 162
    religious, 319
Romance novels, 89
Romanow Commission, 425
Romeo and Juliet, W-9
Roosevelt, Franklin Delano, 215
Rostow, W. W., 209
Routine activities theory, **351**, **361**
Routinization, 314
Royal Commission on Aboriginal Peoples,
    190
Royal Commission on Chinese and Jewish
    Immigration, 189
Royalty, W-21
Ruling class, **433**, **449**
Rural advantage, 363
Rural areas
    Latin America, 373
    seniors in, 415
    urban dichotomy, 369
Rushton, Philippe, 184
Russian Revolution, 496
Ryerson, Egerton, 294

S

Sachs, Jeffrey, 456
Sacred, **313**, **334**
Sadat, Anwar, 448

Safe Schools Act, 181, 297
Safe Streets Act, 369
Saint-Jean, Armande, 172
Same-sex marriage, 80, 81, 236–41
Sample selection, 489–90
Sampling, **490**, **503**
Sanctions, **30**, **46**, 319
    negative, 30
    positive, 30
Sarlo, Christopher, 143
Sartre, Jean-Paul, W-23
Satellite regions, 210
Satellite television, 453
Scale, NEP, 392–93, 399
Scarce, Rik, 495–96
Schmeiser, Percy, 472
Schindler's List, W-2
Schlesinger, Arthur, Jr., 131
Schnaiberg, Alan, 399–400, 401
Schools
    authority, 300–306
    Canadian, 286–92, 300–306
    changing structure, 288–89
    choice in, 302–4
    free, 302
    gender inequality in, 89
    middle-class measuring rod, 349
    one-size-fits-all, 301
    organization theories, 299–300
    private, 303–4
    responsibility for, 237
    selection process, 285–86
    shootings, 353–55
    socialization, 55
    socialization role, 63, 292–99
    societal connection, 285–92
    subcultures, 297–98
    working class, 293
    zero tolerance, 181
    See also Education
Schumacher, E. F., 391
Science, rationalization of, 34
Science, sociology as, 480–83
Scientific method
    commonsense *versus,* 12–13
    defined, 11, 14
    natural methods *versus,* 482–83
    nonscience *versus,* 480–81
    process of, 480
Scientific revolution, **10**–13, **25**, 35
Scott, Duncan Campbell, 190
Seaga, Edward, 23
Seasonal festivals, 33
Secondary groups, W-**10**, W-**26**
Secondary labour markets, 265
Secondary socialization, **50**, **72**, 89
Secret, The (Byrne), 310
Sector model, **371**, **385**
Secularization thesis, **324**, **333**
Security, immigration and, 198

Segmentation
    educational, 297
    labour market, 467
    occupational, 162–70
Segregation, 296
Selection, **307**
    defined, **285**
    education and, 285, **307**
    immigration and, 375
Self
    care, **422**–23, **427**
    defined, **49**, **72**
    developmental stages, 54–55
    looking-glass, **52**, **71**
    me and the I, the, 55
    sense of, 49
    socialization and, 52
    true, 67
Self-administered questionnaires, **489**, **503**
Self-employed, 137, 199
Self-employed immigrants, 199
Self-employment, 281
Self-esteem and body image, 91
Self-report studies, **346**–47, **361**
Sellafield, England, 404
Semi-professions, 269
Seniors
    defining, 412
    demographic transition, 366
    foreign-born, 414–15
    job ghettos, 268
    job prospects, 260
    social solidarity of, 6
    socialization and, 61–62
Separatism, 193
September 11, 2001, 20, 455
Service-based economy, 259
Service economy
    Canadian, 257–61
    globalization and, 468–69
    job satisfaction measures, 274–81
    technology and, 269–70
    women in, W-22
Service excellence, 274
Sessions, George, 398
Sex
    crime risks, 348
    defined, **75**, **95**
    premarital, 78
    segregation of occupations, 177
    typing, **162**–63, 177
Sex labelling of occupations, **162**
Sex segregation of occupations, **162**–64
Sex stereotyping, 170
Sex typing, **162**, 163
Sexual
    assault, 91–93
    attitudes, 78–83
    differentiation, 75
    harassment, 93, 158

orientation, **80**, **95**

pluralism, **93**, **95**

scripts, **78**, **95**

Sexual attitudes

frequency of sexual activity, 78–79

fun standard, 80

HIV/AIDS, 82

love standard, 80

premarital sex, 78

recreational sex, 80

sexually transmitted diseases, 82

Sexual harassment, 296

Sexuality, **78**, **95**

adolescents, 58

communal households, in, 232–33

defined, **78**, **95**

families and, 241–42

gender differences in, 85

gender socialization and, 89–90

new ethic for, 93–94

preindustrial households, 233

preindustrial societies, 233

same-sex couples, 242

Sexual orientation, **80**

Sexual revolution, 241

Sexual Signatures (Money), 74

Shakespeare, William, 10

Shaw, 100

Shift workers, 264

Sierra Club, 459

Significant others, **53**, **72**

Signs, 30

Silver, Lee, W-23

Simmel, Georg, 369, W-8

Simon, Julian, 367

Single-parent families, 144

Skills

defined, **164**, 177

gender, 164–65

requirements, female, 164–65

workers, 199–200

Skocpol, Theda, 439

Slavery, 17, 187, 188, 210–11

gender inequality, 87

Slavery, global, 469

Slave trade, 210–11

Smallville, 112

Snow White, 90

Social assistance

Canadian policies, 149–50

families, to, 240

types of, 145–47

Social categories, W-**9**, W-**26**

Social causes, 4

Social change, 67, 349

Social citizenship, **444**, **450**

Social class

crime, 347–48

gender, 347–48

Internet usage, 113

Social closure, **134**, **152**

Social constructionism, **341**, **361**

defined, **95**

deviance, 341–42

environment and, 405–6

gender differences, 87–88

status conflict and, 341–42

Social context, 56

Social control

crime and, 348

defined, **30**, **46**

deviance and, 340–42, 356–58

Internet and, 115

theories of, 348, 350–51

Social ecology, 389

Social feminists, 157

Social groups, W-**9**, W-**26**

Social isolation, 51

Socialist feminists, 445

Socialization

adolescence, 58–59

adult, 59–61, **71**

agents of, 61–67, **71**

anticipatory, **59**, **71**

athletic teams' role in, 66

change and, 67

childhood and, 49–52

defined, **49**, **72**

education's role in, 286

family's role in, 62–63

gender and, 56–58, 89–90

gender inequality and, 88–89

mass media's role in, 65–66

nature and, 50–52

peer group's role in, 64–65

people-processing institutions, 67

primary, 50, **72**, 88–89

religious, 322–24

school, 55

school's role in, 63, 292–99

secondary, 50, **72**, 89

self and, 52

seniors and, 61–62

Socialization approach, 187

Socialized medicine, 423

Social justice, 208–9

Social learning, 110

Social mobility, **126**, **152**

Social movements, 169

defined, 178, **431**, **450**

frame alignment, **442**

function of, 431

globalization and, 444–46

goals of, 444

history of, 443–46

Internet and, 115

membership, 444

Muslims, 447

new, **444**

new middle class theory, 395

relative deprivation theory and, **440**

rich countries, in, 443–46

women's, 169–70, 445

See also Environmental movement

Social network/networking, 114, **280**, **283**, W-**6**, W-**26**

Social organization, 286, 299–300

Social relations, 4

Social relations of production, **128**, **152**

Social reproduction, **231**, **251**

foraging societies, 232–33

Social roles, **155**, 178

Social-situational hypothesis, 495

Social solidarity, 6–7, 14, **25**

suicide, 7

Social stigma, **339**, **361**

Social stratification

affluence and, 131

Davis and Moore's view of, 131–32

defined, **123**, **152**

descriptions of, 124–25

explanations of, 128–35

gender, 157

hierarchies and, 125–28

income and, 123–24

Lenski's view of, 132

Marx's view, 127–30

mobility and, 126

necessity of, 131

occupations and, 136–39

open and closed systems, 126

technology and, 132

Weber's view of, 130–31

Social structure, 14

authority, W-3–W-5

bureaucratic, W-16

constructionists' views, 87

defined, **8**, **25**

global, 8

macro, 8–9, **25**

micro, 8, **25**

sociological imagination and, 9–10

suicide, 14

understanding, 8–9

unemployment, 14–15

Socially transmitted ideas, 29

Societies, W-**26**

agricultural, W-**25**

civil, **433**

components of, W-18

defined, **29**, **46**, W-**18**

foraging, W-19–W-20

horticultural, W-**20**, W-**25**

industrial, W-21, W-**25**

mass media and, W-6

pastoral, W-**20**, W-**25**

postindustrial, W-21–W-22

post-national, 104

post-natural, W-22–W-23

problem-solving function, 29–30

schools' connection to, 285–92
transformation of, W-19
Sociobiology, **84**, **95**, 187
Socioeconomic status
    Aboriginal people, 190–92
    defined, **127**
    education and, 292
Sociological imagination, **9**, **25**
    origins of, 10–11
Sociological research, 5
Sociology
    careers in, 22–23
    defined, **4**, 11, **25**
    function of, 22–24
    origins of, 11–13
    science, as, 480–83
Sociology of Religion (Weber), 314
Solidarity, social
    defined, **25**
    degree of, 6–7
    norms of, W-2–W-4
Solomon, Patrick, 298
Sopranos, The, 337
Soros, George, 456
Source country class of refugees, 199
Space-biased media, **98**, **118**
Space–time compression, 453–54, **475**
Spears, Britney, 455
Specific deterrence, 356
Spiers, Rosemary, 106
Split labour-market theory, **188**–89, **204**
Sponsored mobility, **288**–89, **307**
Spuriousness, **483**, **503**
Stages of development, **209**, **224**
Standard work, **165**–66, 178
Starbucks, 465
Stark, Rodney, 314–15, 317, 324
State, defined, **432**, **450**
State-centred theory, 438–40, **450**
State terrorism, **219**, **224**
Statistics
    discrimination in, **167**, 178
    official, 497
    regression analysis, 501
Status, **58**
    achieved, **125**–26, **151**
    ascribed, **125**–26, **151**
    attainment, occupational, 138–39
    defined, **72**, **125**, **152**
    group, W-11
Status-conflict perspective, 341–42, **361**
Status-consciousness, 298
Status Indians, 189
Steinberg, Steven, 191
Stereotypes
    defined, **197**, **204**
    gender, 155–56
    gender socialization and, 57–58,
        298–99
    old age, 416

racial, 197
    video games and, 66
Stiglitz, Joseph, 215, 456
Stonechild, Neil, 124
Stouffer, Samuel, W-10
Strain theory, **348**–50, **361**
Stranger homicide, 345
Stratification, social, **152**
    affluence and, 131
    Davis and Moore's view of, 131–32
    description of, 124–25
    explanations of, 128–35
    hierarchies and, 125–28
    income and, 123–24
    Lenski's view of, 132
    Marx's view of, 127–30
    mobility and, 126
    necessity of, 131
    occupations and, 136–39
    open, 138
    open and closed systems, 126
    technology and, 132
    Weber's view of, 130–31
Streaming, 287
Street crime, **348**, **361**
Street homeless, 123
Stress, 420, 421, **427**
Strike patterns, 441
Stronach, Belinda, 172
Structural adjustment programs
    (SAPs), **215**, 216–19, **224**, 460
Structural-functionalist theory
    defined, **131**, **152**, 231
    families, 230–31
    stratification, 131–32
    suburbs, 375
Structural mobility, **138**
Structure, social
    authority, W-3–W-5
    bureaucratic, W-16
    class, **152**
    constructionists' views, 87
    defined, **25**
    global, 8
    macro, 8–9, **25**
    micro, 8, **25**
    schools, of, 287–89
    sociological imagination and, 9–10
    understanding, 8–9
Structure of Scientific Revolutions (Kuhn), 483
Students, 67–68, 291–92
Subcultures
    counterculture and, 44–45
    defined, **44**, **46**
    influence of, 50
    school, 298–99
    youth, 493–96
Subjectivity, 480
Suburbanism, **375**, **385**
Suburbs, 374–76

Success-oriented environmentalists, 397
Suffrage, 170
Suicide, 4
    adolescents, 7
    altruistic, **24**
    anomic, **24**
    bombers, 323
    Canadians, by, 6–7
    crime, 339
    divorce, 7
    egoistic, **25**
    employment, 7
    function of analysis, 5
    lone-parent families, 7
    marriage, 6
    social solidarity, 7
    social structures, 14
    sociological explanation of, 6
    symbolic interactionism, 17
    theory of, 14
    unemployment, 7
    working-age people, 7
    youth, 7
Sun newspaper chain, 101–2
Superstitions, 29
Surplus value, **129**, **152**
Surveillance, 115
Survey research
    firms, 490–91
    interviews, 489–90
    numerical data, 498–99
    questionnaires, 488–89
    random-digit-dialling, 490
    sample selection, 489–90
    telephone, 491
    use of, 488–89
Sustainability Update, 398
Sustainable development, **391**, **407**
Sutherland, Edwin, 350–51
Sutherland, Kiefer, 104
Sutton, Willy, 33
Suzuki, David, 391, 401, 405
Sweden, 248, 249
Symbolic interactionism
    capitalism, 16
    conflict theories of deviance, 16
    defined, **17**, **25**
    features of, 16–17
    foundation of, 53
    functionalist theory, 16
    religion, 16
    suicide, 17
Symbols, **30**
    culture and, 30
    defined, **46**
    sacred, 313
Systemic discrimination, 186

T

Taiyeb, Zainab, 254, 260, 281
Taking role of other, **54**, **72**

Tanner, Adrienne, 106
Tariffs, 213
Taylor, Charles, 196
Taylor, E. P., 374
Taylor, Frederick, 272–73
Taylorism, **272**–73, 283
Technology, 29
  assembly-line, 272–73
  bad jobs, 270
  globalization, 269–70
  good jobs, 270
  mass production, 255
  media, 98–99
  service economy and, 269–70
  social stratification and, 132
  television and, 110
  workplace changes and, 270
Teen repellent, 354
Telecommunications, 378
Telephones, 453, 491
Television
  audience fragmentation, 104–5
  audience research, 111
  Canadian content of, 103–5
  culture and, 45
  effects on behaviour, 109–11
  satellite, 453
  social learning and, 110
  socialization role, 65
  technology and, 110
  time spent watching, 98
  viewing-time distribution, 103
Tent City eviction, 383
Terms of trade, **212, 224**
Terrorist attacks, 110
Theories
  control, 348, 350–51
  crime, 348–51
  defined, **14, 25**
  deviance (see Conflict theories of deviance)
  environmental-opportunity, **363**
  feminist, 17–18, **25**, 157–58
  functional (see Functionalist theory)
  gender differences, 83–88
  human capital, **299, 307**
  media, 98–100
  multiple intelligence, 301–3
  neoliberalism, 214–19
  normative, 187
  opportunity, 348
  origins of, 11–13
  political power, 433–40
  power-conflict, 187–88
  socialization of self, 52–58
  split labour-market, 188–89
  strain, 348–50, **361**
  structural functional (see Structural
    functional theory)
  suicide, 14
  symbolic interactionism, 16–17

Thiessen, Victor, 159
Thinness, cult of, 90
Third world, 210
Thomas, Dorothy Swaine, 311
Thomas, William I., 184, 311, 369
Thomson, David, 139
Three Mile Island, 402
Time and motion studies, 272
Time-biased media, **98, 118**
Time–space compression, **453**,
    462, **475**
Time Warner, 101
Tolerance, male misconduct, W-4
Tolle, Eckhart, 310
Tönnies, Ferdinand, 369, W-8
Top-down globalization, **455**–56, **475**
Toronto
  905 belt, 378
  private communities in, 381
  suburban, 374
  Tent City eviction, 383
Toronto Organizing for Fair Employment
    (TOFFE), 254
Toronto Star, 102
Torstar, 101, 102
Total institutions, **68**–69, **72**, 293
Total quality management (TQM), 273
Touched by an Angel, 310
TQM (total quality management), 273
Trade liberalization, 219
Trade policy, 460–61
Traditional authority, 431
Transgendered people, **76, 95**
Transnational corporations, 36, 457
Transportation, food, 470–71
Transportation patterns, 377–78
Transsexuals, **76, 95**
Travers, Jeffrey, W-6
Travolta, John, 310
Treadmill of production, **399**,
    401, **407**
Triad, W-**8**, W-**26**
Trimble, Linda, 173
Trow, Martin A., W-23
Trudeau, Pierre, 193
Tsuu T'ina, 189
Tulsiani, Bobby, 112
Turnbull, Colin, 232
Turner, Nat, 312
Tutoring chains, 304
Two-class social order, 192

U

Unanimity, appearance of, W-11
Underachievers, 298
Underdevelopment, **211, 224**
  causes of, 212
  classes, 212
  development, 211
  peripheral satellites, 211

structural roots, 211
  tariffs, 213
Understanding
  defined, **485, 503**
  gender inequality, 155–60
  gender stereotypes, 155–60
  inequality, 155–60
  race, 183–84
  research, 485–86
Unemployment
  social structures, 14–15
  sociological imagination, 9
  suicide, 7
UNESCO (United Nations Educational,
    Scientific and Cultural
    Organization), 463
Uniformity, diversity *versus*, 21, W-2
Union density, **279, 283**
Unions
  Canadian, 279, 441
  collective action by, 279
  function, 269
  globalization and, 467
  membership levels, 436–37, 441
  strike patterns, 441
  women in, 279
  young people in, 281
United Nations Educational, Scientific
    and Cultural Organization
    (UNESCO), 463
United States
  Christians in, 320
  college ranking by, 289–90
  corporate bureaucracy, W-18
  cultural identity in, 40
  empire of, 461
  environmental risk in, 404
  financial crisis, 457
  health care policies, 423, 426
  Hispanic assimilation in, 191
  media influence of, 103–4
  military bases, 461
  religiosity of, 317
  respect for authority in, 40
United States Agency for International
    Development (USAID), 472
Universal citizenship, **444, 450**
"Unsustainable impoverishment," 401
Urban bias, 373
Urban growth machine,
    376, 385
Urban growth model, 370–71
Urbanism, **370, 385**
Urbanization, 41
  Chicago school, 369–70
  counter, 376
  developing world, in, 372–73
  growth and, 365–66
  population growth and, 368–69
  preindustrial cities, 364–65

small towns, 363–64
theories, 363–65
Urban primacy, **372**–73, **385**
USAID (United States Agency for
    International Development), 472
Usurpation, **134**, **152**

V

Validity, **489**
    external, **487**, **503**
    member test of, 495
    survey, 489
Value-oriented environmentalists, 397
Values, 350
    defined, **14**, **25**
    environmental, 389–91
    family, 229
    news, **105**, **118**
    surplus, **129**, **152**
Van Susteren, Greta, 44
Vancouver, 371
Vandalism, 354
Variables, **487**
    dependent, **487**, **503**
    independent, **487**, **503**
Veit, Michael, 355
Venezuela, 220
Versace, 45
Verstehen, 16, 314, 493
Vertical integration, **100**, **118**
Vertical mosaic, **200**–203, **204**
Vertical Mosaic, The (Porter), 200–201, 433
Via Campesina, 221
Victimization, types of, 348
Video games, 66
Viewpoints, alternative, **118**
Violence
    against women, 91–93
    cycle of, 491
    divorce and, 246
    mass media and, 65–66
    media, 109–11
    sexual, 91–93
    social learning and, 110
    television's role, 110–11
Virk, Reena, 65, 352
Virtual commodities, **474**
Virtual communities, 115–16, **453**
Visible minority, **167**, 178, 380
Vivendi, 100
von Bismarck, Otto, 412
Vosko, Leah, 261
Voter turnout, 435
Voters
    registration laws, 439
    rights of, 170–71
    shrinking pool of, 439
Voting, 17
Voting rights of women, 159
"Vulnerable periphery," 404

W

Wabigoon River, 404
Wage gap, 168
Wage inequality, 467–69
Wages, family, 235–36, **251**
Walker, Bruce, 393
Walt Disney Company, 100
Walton, Sam, 462
War, 4
    poverty, 219–20
Ward, Kathie, 354
Warren, Murray, 89
Washington consensus, **215**
Water deficit, 471
Water pollution, 401
Watson, Diane, 77
Watson, James, W-22
Waugh, Earle, 329
Wealth
    distribution of, 139–40
    horticultural societies and, W-20
    inequality of, 124–25
    pastoral societies and, W-20
    social stratification and, 131
Web 2.0, **113**, 114–15, **118**
Weber, Max, 13, 14–16, 17, 43, 122, 130,
    135, 286, 306, 311, 314, 317, 322,
    431, 493, 496, W-5, W-16, W-17
Welch, Jack, 457
Welfare model of criminal justice, **361**
Welfare model of juvenile justice, **358**
Welfare trap, 147
Well-being, material, **156**
Wellman, Barry, W-8
Werkglocken, 41–43
Wet nurse, 230, 233
White-collar crime, **342**, **361**
White-collar workers/sector, 20, 137, 255
Whyte, William H., 374
Widowhood, 61
Willer, Barbara A., 304
Willis, Paul, 55–56, 293
Wilson, Brian, 493–95
Wilson, E. O., 84
Wilson, Elizabeth, 377
Windscale Inquiry, 403
Winnipeg General Strike, 437
Winter solstice holiday, 33
Wirth, Louis, 370, 375
Women
    aggression, 87
    body image, 90–91
    child care, 159, 161
    childbearing responsibility,
        236–37, 246
    colour, of, 170
    cosmetic surgery, 91
    deviance, 352
    divorce and, 246–47
    domestic responsibilities, 161–62

earnings of, 166–67
eating disorders, 90–91
economic dependency of, 159–60
education of, 295–96, 498–500
equality, 5, 35
family life, 227
fertility rates, 160
fields of study, 291
gatekeeping, 173
government, in, 171–74
health and, 418
higher education, 290, 291
homicide rates, 345
housework, 159, 244–45
industrial societies and, W-21
job ghettos, 266
labour market, 256
labour-force participation rate, 159,
    160–61
lifestyle, 155
liposuction, 91
lone parent, 161
male violence against, 91–93
middle-class domesticity, 234
middle-class family life, 235
mortality rates, 414
jobs, most common, 259
jobs, nonstandard, 261, 262
neoliberal theory, 219
occupational shifts by, 137
part-time work by, 165–66
patriarchy, 8
politics, in, 172–74, 175–76
poverty, 126, 145
preindustrial economies, in, 234
preindustrial households, 234
reproductive status, 83–84
self-care, 422–23
service sector, in, W-22
sexual assault and, 91–93
sexual attitudes, 79–80
sexual harassment of, 93
skills gap, 164–65
skill undervaluation, 165
social solidarity of, 6
subordination of, W-4
television viewing of, 111
union membership, 279
voting, 17, 437
voting rights, 159
wage gap, 140–41
working-class domesticity, 235
Women's movement
    defined, **169**, 178
    funding, 169
    gender inequality, 169–70
    higher education, 290
    history of, 445
Women's rights, 38
Women's work, 167

Work
collective responses to, 277–79
equal pay for, 178
future of, 281
nonstandard, **165**–66, 177
part-time, **165**–66, 177
participation, 273
preindustrial economies,
233–34
quality circles, W-18
standard, **165**–66, 178
See also Organizations, work
Work arrangements, 263–265
Work clocks, 41–43
Worker participation, 274
Workers Information Centre, 254
Workers' Right Consortium, 459
Working class, 127, 129, 136
families, 235–36, 243
occupations, 137
schools, 293
socialization patterns, 63
unionization and, 436–37

Working poor, **144**, **152**
Work hours, 263–65
World Bank, 215, 455, 456
establishment of, 460
U.S. influence on, 461
World Commission on Environment and
Development, 392
World Food Program (WFP), 472
World Social Forum, 221
World Trade Center, 20, 110
World Trade Organization (WTO),
460–61
World Wide Web, 21, 65
Wortley, Scott, 186, 350
Wright, Erik Olin, 133, 137
W.R. Myers High School, 65
WTO. *See* World Trade Organization
(WTO)
Wu-Tang Clan, 45

X
XX pattern, 75
XY pattern, 75

Y
Young Offenders Act of 1984, 358,
359
Youth
crime, 353–56
deviance, 353–56
gangs, 355–56
membership in gangs, 355
suicide, 7
Youth Criminal Justice Act of 2003,
358–59
Youth culture, 493
Youth in Transition Survey, 290

Z
"Zero tolerance" policy, 181, 297
Znaniecki, Florian, 369
Zuboff, Shoshana, 270, 271